Officially Licensed

NASCAR

Record
&FACT *Book*

2007 EDITION

SportingNews BOOKS

PHOTO CREDITS

T=top T2=2nd from top B=bottom B2=2nd from bottom L=left C=center R=right

CONTRIBUTING PHOTOGRAPHERS

Jay Drowns/Sporting News – 12L; 21L; 30L; 62; 75BR; 76TR; 87; 116B; 133; 155B; 388; 391

Bob Leverone/Sporting News – 16L; 20R; 25C; 30R; 32R; 38C; 42L; 60; 120B; 125C; 351B

Michael McNamara/Sporting News Archives – 5; 41R; 42R; 58R; 85; 137B; 138; 342

Rusty Burroughs for Sporting News – 8; 55L; 59B; 102

Bill Gutweiler for Sporting News – 31; 76BL; 84; 122T; 147B; 150B; 151B; 153T,B2,B; 158T,B

Harold Hinson for Sporting News – 12R; 14; 15L,C; 16R; 17C,R; 19; 20L,C; 21C,R; 23C,R; 25R; 26L,R; 27; 29L,C; 30C; 32L,C; 33L,C; 34L,C; 36L; 38L,R,B; 39C,R; 40; 41L,C; 42C; 44; 46L,C; 47C,R; 48L,R; 49R; 50-51; 52C,R; 54C,R; 55C; 56C,R,B; 57L,C; 58L,C; 59C,R; 61; 63TC,TR,B(3); 64C,R; 66-67; 68L; 69; 71C; 73; 75BL; 76TL,BR; 77; 78-79; 83; 88; 104T; 105; 107-108; 109T2,B2,B; 110-111; 113B; 116T,C; 119; 121; 122C,B; 123-124; 125T; 126-127; 129-130; 132T; 134; 135T,C; 136; 137T,C; 139-140; 142; 144; 146; 147C; 148C; 149; 151T; 152T,B2; 153T2; 154T2,B2; 155B2; 156C,B; 157T2,B2; 158C; 159-161; 164TR,B; 165; 170; 172; 210-213; 235; 263; 331; 332; 348-349; 357; 360; 379; 392

Alan Marler for Sporting News – 1; 13BC; 16C; 17L; 22; 24; 26C; 37; 47L; 48C; 49L,C; 53; 54L; 59L; 64L; 68R; 70; 99; 135B; 136; 137TC; 141; 145; 147T; 150T; 152T2; 225

Erik Perel for Sporting News – 11; 18; 23L; 25L; 36CR; 39L; 52L; 56L; 59; 63TL; 71L; 72; 74; 75TL,TR; 104C,B; 109T; 113T; 114; 117-118; 120T; 125B; 132CB; 148T,B; 154T; 155T,T2; 156T; 157T,B; 164TL;166; 168; 334; 345; 359; 362; 375

Don Hunter – 6-7; 246; 253; 285; 301; 313; 324-326; 328-329

Jay LaPrete/AP/Wide World Photos – 154B; 376

LAT Images/B. Czobat – 13TR; 68BR

Michael L. Levitt/LAT Photographic – 57R; 71R

Ronald Martinez/Getty Images – 13TL,TR

David Allio – 299

Bill Davis Racing – 46R

Phil Cavali – 15R

Ric Feld/AP/Wide World Photos – 269

Getty Images for NASCAR – 10

Howie and Mary Hodge – 400

Rusty Jarrett/Getty Images for NASCAR – 29R

Marty Lederhandler/AP/Wide World Photos – 279

NASCAR/AP/Wide World Photos – 267(inset)

Richard Childress Racing – 33R

Alison Sidlo/The Morning News/AP/Wide World Photos – 267T

Mike Simmons/CIA Stock Photography – 34R

Wewrner Slocum/AP/Wide World Photos – 275

Stock-Car Montreal, L.P. – 152B

Morgan-McClure Motorsports – 19 (car only)

Worth Canoy/VPS Motorimages – 13BL, BC, BR;

NASCAR RECORD & FACT BOOK

Editors: Matt Crossman, Jessica Daues, Ryan Fagan, Erin Farrell, Jim Gilstrap
Cover and book design by: Chad Painter
Photo editors: Matthew Kutz, Paul Nisely
Prepress specialists: Steve Romer, Vern Kasal, Russ Carr

ISBN: 0-89204-864-6

>> 2007 RACE SCHEDULE <<

NASCAR NEXTEL Cup Series

Date	Race	Track	TV/Radio	Time (Eastern)	2006 winner
February 10	Budweiser Shootout*	Daytona International Speedway	FOX/MRN	8:30 p.m.	Denny Hamlin
February 15	Gatorade Duel No. 1*	Daytona International Speedway	SPEED/MRN	2:10 p.m.	Elliott Sadler
February 15	Gatorade Duel No. 2*	Daytona International Speedway	SPEED/MRN	3:40 p.m.	Jeff Gordon
February 18	Daytona 500	Daytona International Speedway	FOX/MRN	2:30 p.m.	Jimmie Johnson
February 25	Auto Club 500	California Speedway	FOX/MRN	4:05 p.m.	Matt Kenseth
March 11	UAW-DaimlerChrysler 400	Las Vegas Motor Speedway	FOX/PRN	4:35 p.m.	Jimmie Johnson
March 18	Golden Corral 500	Atlanta Motor Speedway	FOX/PRN	1:30 p.m.	Kasey Kahne
March 25	Food City 500	Bristol Motor Speedway	FOX/PRN	2:10 p.m.	Kurt Busch
April 1	DIRECTV 500	Martinsville Speedway	FOX/MRN	2 p.m.	Tony Stewart
April 15	Samsung/RadioShack 500	Texas Motor Speedway	FOX/PRN	2 p.m.	Kasey Kahne
April 21	Subway Fresh 500	Phoenix International Raceway	FOX/MRN	8:25 p.m.	Kevin Harvick
April 29	Aaron's 499	Talladega Superspeedway	FOX/MRN	2:10 p.m.	Jimmie Johnson
May 5	Crown Royal 400	Richmond International Raceway	FOX/MRN	7:30 p.m.	Dale Earnhardt Jr.
May 12	Dodge Charger 500	Darlington Raceway	FOX/MRN	6:55 p.m.	Greg Biffle
May 19	NEXTEL Open*	Lowe's Motor Speedway	SPEED/MRN	7:30 p.m.	Scott Riggs
May 19	NASCAR NEXTEL All-Star Challenge*	Lowe's Motor Speedway	SPEED/MRN	9 p.m.	Jimmie Johnson
May 27	Coca-Cola 600	Lowe's Motor Speedway	FOX/PRN	5:30 p.m.	Kasey Kahne
June 3	Neighborhood Excellence 400	Dover International Speedway	FOX/MRN	2:10 p.m.	Matt Kenseth
June 10	Pocono 500	Pocono Raceway	TNT/MRN	2:10 p.m.	Denny Hamlin
June 17	3M Performance 400	Michigan International Speedway	TNT/MRN	1:40 p.m.	Kasey Kahne
June 24	Dodge/Save Mart 350	Infineon Raceway	TNT/PRN	3:40 p.m.	Jeff Gordon
July 1	Lenox Industrial Tools 300	New Hampshire International Speedway	TNT/MRN	2:10 p.m.	Kyle Busch
July 7	Pepsi 400	Daytona International Speedway	TNT/MRN	7:55 p.m.	Tony Stewart
July 15	USG Sheetrock 400	Chicagoland Speedway	TNT/MRN	3:35 p.m.	Jeff Gordon
July 29	Allstate 400 at the Brickyard	Indianapolis Motor Speedway	ESPN/IMS	2:40 p.m.	Jimmie Johnson
August 5	Pennsylvania 500	Pocono Raceway	ESPN/MRN	2:10 p.m.	Denny Hamlin
August 12	AMD at the Glen	Watkins Glen International	ESPN/MRN	1:35 p.m.	Kevin Harvick
August 19	GFS Marketplace 400	Michigan International Speedway	ESPN/MRN	2:30 p.m.	Matt Kenseth
August 25	Sharpie 500	Bristol Motor Speedway	ESPN/PRN	7:40 p.m.	Matt Kenseth
September 2	Sony HD 500	California Speedway	ESPN/MRN	8 p.m.	Kasey Kahne
September 8	Chevy Rock & Roll 400	Richmond International Raceway	ABC/MRN	7:40 p.m.	Kevin Harvick
September 16	Sylvania 300	New Hampshire International Speedway	ABC/MRN	1:10 p.m.	Kevin Harvick
September 23	Dover 400	Dover International Speedway	ABC/MRN	1:10 p.m.	Jeff Burton
September 30	Banquet 400	Kansas Speedway	ABC/MRN	2:10 p.m.	Tony Stewart
October 7	UAW-Ford 500	Talladega Superspeedway	ABC/MRN	2:30 p.m.	Brian Vickers
October 13	Bank of America 500	Lowe's Motor Speedway	ABC/PRN	7:10 p.m.	Kasey Kahne
October 21	Subway 500	Martinsville Speedway	ABC/MRN	1 p.m.	Jimmie Johnson
October 28	Bass Pro Shops 500	Atlanta Motor Speedway	ABC/PRN	2:55 p.m.	Tony Stewart
November 4	Dickies 500	Texas Motor Speedway	ABC/PRN	2:55 p.m.	Tony Stewart
November 11	Checker Auto Parts 500	Phoenix International Raceway	ABC/MRN	3:25 p.m.	Kevin Harvick
November 18	Ford 400	Homestead-Miami Speedway	ABC/MRN	2:50 p.m.	Greg Biffle

NOTE: Race names and start times are from 2006 and are subject to change. *Non-points events.

CONTENTS

NASCAR NEXTEL Cup Series race schedule 3

Inside NASCAR 5
NASCAR NEXTEL Cup Series milestones 6-9
The France family 10

NASCAR NEXTEL Cup Series drivers 11
2007 lineup 12
Biographies, statistics 13-76

NASCAR competition 77
Car manufacturers 78-79
Technical elements 80
Cutaway car 81
Inside the cockpit 82
Car of Tomorrow 83
Technical inspection 84
Qualifying 85
Flags, race procedures 86-87
Chase for the NASCAR NEXTEL Cup 88
Glossary...89-96
Freezing the field 91
Drafting, HANS device..93
Tight vs. loose conditions 95
Race tire vs. street tire 97
Anatomy of a pit stop 98

NASCAR Tracks 99
Track locations 100
Track distances, facts 101
Tracks...102-158

2006 season review 159
2006 champion 160
2006 Raybestos Rookie of the Year 161
2006 points standings, miles leaders 162-163
2006 season race by race review 164-172
Race results 173
Race by race boxscores 174-209
Budweiser Shootout at Daytona 210
Gatorade Duel at Daytona 211
NASCAR NEXTEL All-Star Challenge 212

NASCAR teams 213
Team owners 214-225
Crew chiefs 226-234

NASCAR champions and notable drivers 235
Series champions 236
Champion crew chiefs 237

Inactive champions 238-243
Notable drivers 243-247
Inactive drivers with 50-plus victories 247-252

NASCAR History 253
All-time race winners 254
Speedway, short track, road course winners 255
All-time wins by car number 256
Driver records, all-time money leaders 257
All-time pole winners..258
Speedway, short track, road course pole winners 259
Qualifying records 260
All-time starts 261
Season by season review....................................262-330

NASCAR Busch Series 331
NASCAR Busch Series milestones........................332-333
2007 schedule 334
2007 drivers 335-345
2006 points standings....................................346-347
2006 race results 348
2006 champion 349
Series champions 350
Past champions 351-358
2006 Raybestos Rookie of the Year 359
Records 360
All-time race, pole winners..................................361
Season by season review....................................362-374

NASCAR Craftsman Truck Series 375
NASCAR Craftsman Truck Series milestones 376-378
2007 schedule 379
2007 drivers 380-385
2006 points standings, race results.......................386-387
2006 champion 388
Past champions 389-390
2006 Raybestos Rookie of the Year 391
Records 392
All-time race, pole winners.................................393
Season by season review....................................394-399

NASCAR ladder system 400

INSIDE NASCAR

NASCAR NEXTEL CUP SERIES
MILESTONES

Since its inception as the "Strictly Stock" division, what is now the NASCAR NEXTEL Cup Series has seen many changes take place. In the beginning, the racecars were driven off the street and onto the track, but as safety technology advanced, changes were made to cars; the racing machines of today are more complicated and technological than ever. NASCAR has grown with the series from the small organization formed on the beaches of Daytona to a thriving sport. Important milestones for NASCAR:

December 14, 1947: Bill France Sr. organizes a meeting at the Streamline Hotel in Daytona Beach, Fla., to discuss the future of stock car racing. NASCAR, the National Association for Stock Car Auto Racing, is conceived.

February 15, 1948: NASCAR runs its first race in Daytona Beach at the beach road course, which is won by Red Byron in a Ford.

February 21, 1948: NASCAR is incorporated.

June 19, 1949: The first NASCAR "Strictly Stock" (current NASCAR NEXTEL Cup Series) race is held at Charlotte (N.C.) Fairgrounds Speedway. Jim Roper wins the race, Bob Flock wins the first pole and Sara Christian, who finishes 14th, is credited as the first woman to start a race in NASCAR's premier division.

October 16, 1949: Driver Red Byron becomes the NASCAR "Strictly Stock" champion. Byron earns $5,800 in six starts and collects two wins.

1950: Bill France Sr. changes the name of NASCAR's top series from "Strictly Stock" to Grand National.

September 4, 1950: Darlington Raceway, NASCAR's first paved superspeedway, hosts the 500-mile Southern 500. This, the first 500-mile event in NASCAR history, is won by Johnny Mantz in a 1950 Plymouth. Seventy-five drivers start the event, which features only two caution periods and lasts more than six hours.

April 8, 1951: The first NASCAR Grand National race west of the Mississippi River is held at Carrell Speedway, a half-mile dirt track in Gardena, Calif.

1952: Sponsors step up in the NASCAR Grand National division. Pure Oil provides contingency monies and free gasoline during Daytona's Speedweeks, and Champion Spark Plugs contributes $5,000 to the year-end point fund.

June 13, 1954: The International 100 is held at Linden Airport in New Jersey, becoming the first road race in what now is the NASCAR NEXTEL Cup Series.

1955: Car owner Carl Kiekhaefer enters NASCAR. During the 1955 season, Kiekhaefer enters cars in 40 Grand National events and wins 22 of them. Kiekhaefer is the first car owner to introduce the concept of major sponsorship when he provides drivers with major financial and technical backing.

Carl Kiekhaefer's Chrysler 300s were big winners in 1955 and 1956. A group of the cars sits ready at Asheville-Weaverville (N.C.) Speedway.

1958: The Florida Sports Writers vote Fireball Roberts as Professional Athlete of the Year. This is the first time the honor is given to a racecar driver.

February 23, 1958: Paul Goldsmith captures the final race on Daytona's famed Beach and Road Course.

February 22, 1959: The high-banked 2.5-mile Daytona International Speedway hosts the first Daytona 500. More than 41,000 fans are in attendance for the inaugural event in which the winner isn't decided until 61 hours after the checkered flag flew, as the result of a dramatic photo finish. Lee Petty is declared the race winner by two feet after conclusive evidence from a news-reel is reviewed by Bill France Sr.

January 31, 1960: CBS Sports broadcasts its first live NASCAR Grand National events. "CBS Sports Spectacular" televises the Grand National Pole Position races from Daytona. The two-hour program is the first devoted entirely to stock car racing.

June 19, 1960: Lowe's Motor Speedway hosts its first NASCAR event. The World 600 is won by Joe Lee Johnson in a time of just over 5½ hours.

July 4, 1960: Bud Moore and driver Jack Smith communicate via two-way radio in the Firecracker 250 at Daytona International Speedway, the first time two-way radio communication is used in the sport.

July 16, 1961: ABC Sports televises the Firecracker 250 from Daytona International Speedway as a part of its Wide World of Sports.

September 13, 1962: Mamie Reynolds becomes the first female winning car owner when Fred Lorenzen takes the checkered flag at Augusta (Ga.) Speedway.

February 24, 1963: Tiny Lund subs in for an injured Marvin Panch and wins the Daytona 500.

December 1, 1963: Wendell Scott becomes the first African-American to win a race in NASCAR's premier series, beating Buck Baker at Jacksonville Speedway.

1964: Goodyear Tire & Rubber Company tests and begins use of an inner-liner for all NASCAR Grand National racing tires.

1964: Richard Petty, NASCAR's all-time victories leader, captures his first of seven driving championships.

1965: The Firestone Racesafe Fuel Cell bladder is introduced into NASCAR.

1967: Richard Petty sets three records by collecting the most wins in one season (27), most consecutive wins (10) and most victories from the pole in one season (15).

September 14, 1969: Alabama International Speedway opens in Talladega, Ala., as the largest oval (2.66 miles) on the NASCAR circuit.

March 24, 1970: Buddy Baker becomes the first driver to post a test-run speed faster than 200 mph in a stock car, doing so at Talladega.

September 30, 1970: The final NASCAR Grand National division race is run on dirt at State Fairgrounds Speedway in Raleigh, N.C.

1971: R.J. Reynolds' Winston brand becomes the title sponsor of NASCAR's top division the NASCAR Winston Cup Grand National Division.

February 14, 1971: Motor Racing Network (MRN) broadcasts its first Daytona 500. Ken Squier anchors the broadcast for the racing network.

January 10, 1972: The founder of NASCAR, Bill France Sr., hands over the reins of leadership to his son Bill France Jr., who becomes the second president in NASCAR's history.

1972: The NASCAR Winston Cup Grand National Division schedule is trimmed from 48 races to 31, marking the beginning of the "Modern Era."

February 15, 1976: David Pearson and Richard Petty battle on national television in the Daytona 500. When their cars

are involved in an accident near the finish line, Pearson wins by hobbling to the checkered flag.

February 20, 1977: Janet Guthrie becomes the first woman to qualify for the Daytona 500. She qualifies 39th and finishes 12th.

1978: President Jimmy Carter and First Lady Rosalyn Carter invite NASCAR stars as guests to the White House, the same year Cale Yarborough wins his record third straight series title.

February 18, 1979: CBS Sports presents the first live flag-to-flag coverage of a NASCAR event with the Daytona 500, a show not soon to be forgotten as Richard Petty avoids an incident between Cale Yarborough and Donnie Allison on the last lap to win the race.

Richard Petty, sharing a fun moment with his son Kyle, could drive anything with four wheels on it—and make it go fast.

April 8, 1979: The teaming of David Pearson and the Wood Brothers ends at Darlington.

September 3, 1979: David Pearson replaces rookie Dale Earnhardt in the Southern 500 at Darlington and leads the final 70 laps to claim the victory.

November 18, 1979: Richard Petty wins his record seventh series championship.

April 29, 1982: Benny Parsons becomes the first dri-

ver in NASCAR history to record an official qualifying lap over 200 mph, accomplishing the feat at Talladega.

May 6, 1984: NASCAR's most competitive race takes place at Talladega, in which 75 lead changes are spread among 13 drivers.

July 4, 1984: Richard Petty earns his 200th win in the Firecracker 400 at Daytona International Speedway, setting a mark that has yet to be challenged.

July 29, 1984: Another competitive race at Talladega where nearly 70 lead changes take place, causing officials to use photos to sort the final finishing order.

September 1, 1985: Bill Elliott claims a $1 million bonus from R.J. Reynolds for winning three of the four crown jewel races on the schedule. Elliott is victorious in the Daytona 500, the Winston 500 at Talladega and the Southern 500 at Darlington. Elliott earns the nickname "Million Dollar Bill."

1985: Darrell Waltrip trails Bill Elliott by 206 points with eight races to go, but goes on to win the NASCAR Winston Cup Series championship.

1986: NASCAR drops the "Grand National" name from its top division, renaming it the NASCAR Winston Cup Series.

April 30, 1987: Bill Elliott sets the fastest lap time in NASCAR history when he turns a blazing lap of 212.809 mph at Talladega Superspeedway.

1987: Dale Earnhardt makes his famous "pass in the grass" in The Winston, the all-star race at Charlotte Motor Speedway, shooting through the grass and back onto the track to maintain the lead and eventually win the race.

February 14, 1988: Bobby Allison and his son Davey finish first and second, respectively, in the Daytona 500.

1989: For the first time since its inception, every race in NASCAR's top series is televised.

February 18, 1990: Dale Earnhardt leads 155 of 200 laps of the Daytona 500, but loses the race with a mile to go, blowing a tire on a piece of debris.

September 1991: Harry Gant, at age 51, is tabbed "Mr. September" after winning four consecutive races in the month.

May 16, 1992: Lowe's Motor Speedway holds The Winston under the lights for the first time, ending in an incident as Davey Allison takes the checkered flag before losing control of his car.

November 15, 1992: Richard Petty retires after 35 years of racing in NASCAR. He ends his career with 200 wins and 555 top five finishes in 1,184 starts. The championship is won by Alan Kulwicki, who leads one more lap than Bill Elliott to earn a five-point bonus in the season finale at Atlanta Motor Speedway, clinching the series championship by only 10 points. At the time, it is the closest points battle in series history.

August 6, 1994: The series schedule expands to include the famed 2.5-mile Indianapolis Motor Speedway. Jeff Gordon claims the win in the first NASCAR event at the Brickyard.

1994: Dale Earnhardt joins Richard Petty as the only driver to win seven NASCAR series championships.

August 9, 1996: Dale Earnhardt, with a broken collarbone, wheels around Watkins Glen to win the pole and set a new track record.

November 24, 1996: NASCAR runs a demonstration race at Suzuka, Japan.

November 16, 1997: Jeff Gordon clinches his second series championship, making him the youngest two-time winner of the prize.

1997: Two new tracks—California Speedway and Texas Motor Speedway—appear on the schedule. The two inaugural races occur in front of sold-out crowds.

1998: NASCAR celebrates its 50th anniversary while adding Las Vegas Motor Speedway to the season schedule. Mark Martin wins the inaugural event on March 1.

February 1999: NASCAR President Bill France Jr. hands over the day-to-day operations of NASCAR to Senior Vice President and Chief Operating Officer Mike Helton, marking the first time someone from outside the France family has controlled the operations of the sport.

November 11, 1999: NASCAR announces multi-year partnerships with FOX, NBC and Turner Sports; consolidated television package begins in 2001.

January 2000: R.J. Reynolds increases the series point fund from $5 million to $10 million. Champion's share increases to $3 million.

November 28, 2000: Mike Helton becomes the third president in NASCAR history as Bill France Jr. passes the torch of leadership to a non-France family member for the first time.

February 18, 2001: FOX Sports telecasts the Daytona 500, its first telecast as part of an six-year network TV agreement along with its cable network partner FX. Michael Waltrip's victory in the Daytona 500 marked his career-first win in his 463rd start.

July 7, 2001: NBC Sports kicks off its six-year network TV agreement by telecasting the Pepsi 400. NBC's cable partner

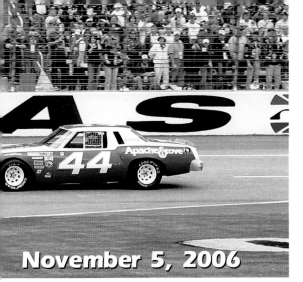

November 5, 2006

Terry Labonte was honored at Texas before his final race. He won two NASCAR NEXTEL Cup Series championships.

TNT also televises seven races in 2001.

September 25, 2001: NASCAR Radio, the first 24-hour radio station dedicated to a single sport, debuts on XM Satellite Radio, the first commercial satellite radio service in the United States.

2001: The series visits two new tracks: Chicagoland Speedway and Kansas Speedway.

January 2003: The official unveiling of the NASCAR Research and Development Center is a signal to the motorsports world of NASCAR's unprecedented level of commitment to the future and safety of its sport. It is the first research and development center owned and operated by a sanctioning body of a major motorsports series. The 61,000-square-foot NASCAR Research and Development Center in Concord, N.C., is a $10 million facility devoted to safety initiatives, enhancing competition and containing costs for its teams. It also is a portion of an investment in excess of $50 million to achieve those objectives over the next decade.

June 13, 2003: NASCAR announces California Speedway will host a second race in 2004 over Labor Day weekend. The Southern 500 at Darlington Raceway, traditionally run on that weekend, will replace North Carolina Speedway's second date in November. The move is part of NASCAR's Realignment 2003 and Beyond program.

June 19, 2003: NASCAR announces a 10-year deal for Nextel to replace longtime series sponsor R.J. Reynolds' Winston brand beginning in 2004.

August 15, 2003: NASCAR announces a 10-year deal for Sunoco to replace Unocal 76 as the Official Fuel of NASCAR beginning in 2004.

October 2003: Brian Z. France becomes the new Chairman of the Board and CEO of NASCAR, replacing his father Bill France Jr.

November 16, 2003: In the final race of the Winston era, race leader Bill Elliott cuts a tire on the last lap, allowing Bobby Labonte to win the season finale at Homestead-Miami Speedway. Roush Racing's Matt Kenseth becomes the final champion of the NASCAR Winston Cup Series era.

2004: NASCAR begins its first season under the banner of Nextel, with the series becoming known as the NASCAR NEXTEL Cup Series. A new format is implemented to determine the series champion, the Chase for the NASCAR NEXTEL Cup. After the completion of the season's first 26 races, the top 10 drivers in the championship standings, as well as any additional drivers within 400 points of the leader, are eligible to compete for the championship over the final 10 races of the season.

November 21, 2004: Kurt Busch gives his team owner, Jack Roush, back-to-back championships by winning the first NASCAR NEXTEL Cup Series championship in the tightest points battle in series history. Busch beats runner-up Jimmie Johnson by only eight points.

January 11, 2005: Richard Petty unveils Dodge's new Charger at Daytona International Speedway. The new version of the classic racer, reintroduced after 28 years, will compete in NASCAR beginning with the 2005 season.

September 4, 2005: Kyle Busch, 20, wins the Sony HD 500 at California Speedway to become the series' youngest race winner since Donald Thomas won at Atlanta's Lakewood Speedway on November 15, 1952.

November 20, 2005: Tony Stewart picks up his second NASCAR NEXTEL Cup Series championship at Homestead-Miami Speedway. Stewart sets a NASCAR record with more than $13 million in winnings for the season. The race is the last for Rusty Wallace and Ricky Rudd as full-time drivers in the NASCAR NEXTEL Cup Series.

December 7, 2005: NASCAR announces an eight-year television agreement in which NASCAR races will be broadcast on a combination of networks that includes FOX, SPEED, Turner's TNT and ABC/ESPN beginning in 2007. FOX becomes the official home for the Daytona 500.

January 23, 2006: NASCAR and Toyota announce that the manufacturer will compete in the NASCAR NEXTEL Cup Series and NASCAR Busch Series in 2007, fielding the Toyota Camry model.

January 23, 2006: NASCAR announces that the Car of Tomorrow, which offers safety and performance upgrades, will be used in 16 races in the NASCAR NEXTEL Cup Series beginning in 2007. The COT is scheduled to be used in 26 races in 2008 and all races beginning in 2009.

November 5, 2006: Terry Labonte, winner of NASCAR NEXTEL Cup Series championships in 1984 and 1996, competes in his final NASCAR NEXTEL Cup Series race, the Dickies 500 at Texas Motor Speedway, ending a career that began in 1978. He ran 848 races and posted 22 victories.

November 19, 2006: Jimmie Johnson wins his first NASCAR NEXTEL Cup Series championship, finishing ninth in the season finale at Homestead-Miami Speedway and holding off Matt Kenseth, the 2003 champion, by 56 points. Denny Hamlin finishes third in points, the highest for a rookie in the modern era and best since James Hylton finished second in 1966.

>>THE FRANCE FAMILY<<

You need look only at the France family tree to understand NASCAR's history—and its current position at the pinnacle of American motorsports.

From founder William H.G. France to his son William C. France to third-generation leader Brian Z. France—who took over the sport's leadership in October 2003—the family's expertise is obvious, evidenced by NASCAR's steady growth.

When Brian Z. France was announced as NASCAR's Chairman of the Board and Chief Executive Officer, replacing his father, William C. France, it completed a natural progression. Brian has been at the forefront of NASCAR's dramatic sponsorship growth, including the ground-breaking 2003 announcement of Nextel Communications as the new sponsor of the NASCAR NEXTEL Cup Series beginning in 2004.

Brian has led a host of marketing initiatives, including internalizing the sanctioning body's licensing efforts and developing NASCAR's consolidated television plans. Under the new eight year agreements, NASCAR races will be broadcast on a combination of networks that includes FOX, SPEED, Turner's TNT and ABC/ESPN beginning in 2007.

Brian clearly respects—and represents—the vision of his grandfather "Big Bill" France, who created the National Association for Stock Car Auto Racing (NASCAR) in 1948 to organize and promote stock car racing on tracks such as the one carved out of the sand of Daytona Beach. With tracks scattered throughout the Southeast, each with different rules and facilities, the sport needed leadership. That's exactly what Big Bill

Brian France (left) replaced Bill France as the sport's leader in October 2003, completing a natural progression.

delivered. Through dogged determination, he legitimized a sport that was, at the time, an unorganized hobby of sorts.

Big Bill also founded the International Speedway Corporation (ISC), which gave NASCAR two of its premier facilities in the form of Daytona International Speedway in 1959 and Talladega Superspeedway in 1969.

His two sons, Bill and Jim, were handed the reins to the company upon their father's retirement. Bill became president, and Jim took over the role of executive vice president and secretary, as well as president of ISC.

Other than the creation of the organization, Bill France's ascension to the leadership role of NASCAR is likely the most important event in the sanctioning body's history. As rule maker, promoter, ambassador and salesman, he set the standard by which all other

forms of motorsports are measured.

In November of 2000, Bill France announced that he would serve as chairman of a newly formed five-member board of directors for NASCAR that consisted of him, Jim France, Brian Z. France, Lesa France Kennedy and Mike Helton with responsibility for developing policy and vision for the sport. At that time, Bill stepped down as president and was replaced by Helton.

Helton became the first person outside the France family to take over day-to-day operations of NASCAR when he was promoted from his position as vice president for competition and was named senior vice president and chief operating officer in February 1999.

Brian's move into the Chairman/CEO positions resulted in Bill becoming a NASCAR vice chairman. Bill's wife Betty Jane continues to serve as NASCAR assistant secretary.

Lesa France Kennedy, Brian's sister, joined the NASCAR board and has worked her way to president of ISC, and serves on the ISC board, helping to oversee the company's 12 race tracks and the successful Daytona USA motorsports attraction.

Gary Crotty, the secretary and general counsel for NASCAR, was named to the board of directors in August 2006.

Big Bill France passed away in 1992. His induction into the International Motorsports Hall of Fame and the National Motorsports Press Association Hall of Fame are testaments not only to his accomplishments but to the efforts of his entire family.

NASCAR NEXTEL CUP SERIES DRIVERS

>>2007 LINEUP <<

NASCAR NEXTEL Cup Series

Car	Driver	Make	Sponsor	Team	Crew chief
00	David Reutimann	Toyota	Burger King/Domino's Pizza	Michael Waltrip Racing	TBA
*01	Mark Martin	Chevrolet	U.S. Army	Ginn Racing	Ryan Pemberton
*01	Regan Smith	Chevrolet	U.S. Army	Ginn Racing	Ryan Pemberton
07	Clint Bowyer	Chevrolet	Jack Daniel's	Richard Childress Racing	Gil Martin
1	Martin Truex Jr.	Chevrolet	Bass Pro Shops	Dale Earnhardt Inc.	Kevin Manion
2	Kurt Busch	Dodge	Miller Lite	Penske Racing	Roy McCauley
4	Ward Burton	Chevrolet	State Water Heaters	Morgan-McClure	Chris Carrier
5	Kyle Busch	Chevrolet	Kellogg's	Hendrick Motorsports	Alan Gustafson
6	David Ragan	Ford	AAA	Roush Racing	Jimmy Fennig
7	Robby Gordon	Ford	Harrah's/Jim Beam/Menards	Robby Gordon Motorsports	Greg Erwin
8	Dale Earnhardt Jr.	Chevrolet	Budweiser	Dale Earnhardt Inc.	Tony Eury Jr.
9	Kasey Kahne	Dodge	Dodge Dealers/UAW	Evernham Motorsports	Kenny Francis
10	Scott Riggs	Dodge	Valvoline/Stanley Tools	Valvoline Evernham Racing	Rodney Childers
11	Denny Hamlin	Chevrolet	FedEx	Joe Gibbs Racing	Mike Ford
12	Ryan Newman	Dodge	Alltell/Mobil 1	Penske Racing	Mike Nelson
13	Joe Nemechek	Chevrolet	TBA	Ginn Racing	Peter Sospenzo
14	Sterling Marlin	Chevrolet	Waste Management	Ginn Racing	Richard Labbe
15	Paul Menard	Chevrolet	Menards	Dale Earnhardt Inc.	Tony Eury Sr.
16	Greg Biffle	Ford	Ameriquest	Roush Racing	Pat Tryson
17	Matt Kenseth	Ford	DeWalt Tools	Roush Racing	Robbie Reiser
18	J.J. Yeley	Chevrolet	Interstate Batteries	Joe Gibbs Racing	Steve Addington
19	Elliott Sadler	Dodge	Dodge Dealers/UAW	Evernham Motorsports	Josh Browne
20	Tony Stewart	Chevrolet	The Home Depot	Joe Gibbs Racing	Greg Zipadelli
^21	Ken Schrader	Ford	Little Debbie/Motorcraft	Wood Brothers Racing	Ernie Cope
^21	Jon Wood	Ford	Air Force/Ore-Ida/Delimex	Wood Brothers Racing	Ernie Cope
22	Dave Blaney	Toyota	Caterpillar	Bill Davis Racing	Kevin Hamlin
24	Jeff Gordon	Chevrolet	DuPont	Hendrick Motorsports	Steve Letarte
25	Casey Mears	Chevrolet	GMAC/National Guard	Hendrick Motorsports	Lance McGrew
26	Jamie McMurray	Ford	Crown Royal/Irwin Tools	Roush Racing	TBA
28/88	Ricky Rudd	Ford	Mars	Robert Yates Racing	Butch Hylton
29	Kevin Harvick	Chevrolet	Shell/Reese's	Richard Childress Racing	Todd Berrier
31	Jeff Burton	Chevrolet	Cingular	Richard Childress Racing	Scott Miller
36	Jeremy Mayfield	Toyota	360 OTC	Bill Davis Racing	Derrick Finley
38	David Gilliland	Ford	M&M's	Robert Yates Racing	Todd Parrott
40	David Stremme	Dodge	Coors Light/Lonestar	Chip Ganassi Racing	Steve Lane
41	Reed Sorenson	Dodge	Target	Chip Ganassi Racing	Jimmy Elledge
42	Juan Pablo Montoya	Dodge	Texaco/Havoline	Chip Ganassi Racing	Donnie Wingo
43	Bobby Labonte	Dodge	Cheerios/Betty Crocker	Petty Enterprises	Paul Andrews
44	Dale Jarrett	Toyota	UPS	Michael Waltrip Racing	Matt Borland
45	Kyle Petty	Dodge	Wells Fargo/Marathon Oil	Petty Enterprises	Bill Wilburn
48	Jimmie Johnson	Chevrolet	Lowe's	Hendrick Motorsports	Chad Knaus
55	Michael Waltrip	Toyota	NAPA	Michael Waltrip Racing	David Hyder
66	Jeff Green	Chevrolet	Best Buy	Haas CNC Racing	Harold Holly
70	Johnny Sauter	Chevrolet	Yellow Transportation	Haas CNC Racing	Robert "Bootie" Barker
78	Kenny Wallace	Chevrolet	Furniture Row	Furniture Row Racing	Jay Guy
83	Brian Vickers	Toyota	Red Bull	Team Red Bull	Doug Richert
84	A.J. Allmendinger	Toyota	Red Bull	Team Red Bull	Rick Viers
96	Tony Raines	Chevrolet	DLP/Texas Instruments	Hall of Fame Racing	Brandon Thomas
99	Carl Edwards	Ford	Office Depot	Roush Racing	Bob Osborne

Note: Some information subject to change. *Martin will drive 20 races, Smith 16 in the No. 01. ^Schrader and Wood will split time in the No. 21.

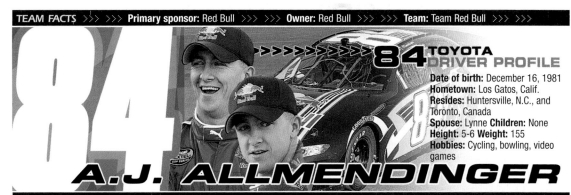

84 TOYOTA DRIVER PROFILE

Date of birth: December 16, 1981
Hometown: Los Gatos, Calif.
Resides: Huntersville, N.C., and Toronto, Canada
Spouse: Lynne **Children:** None
Height: 5-6 **Weight:** 155
Hobbies: Cycling, bowling, video games

A.J. ALLMENDINGER

Crew chief: Rick Viers >>> >>> **Engine builder:** Toyota Racing Development >>> >>> **Website:** www.teamredbull.com >>>

>> NASCAR ACHIEVEMENTS

No NASCAR NEXTEL Cup Series starts

>> CAREER HIGHLIGHTS

- Will drive the No. 84 Camry in his first full year in stock car racing. He attempted to start in the fall Atlanta race (qualifying was rained out) and the fall Texas race (he failed to qualify) in 2006.

>> FAST FACTS

- Made his NASCAR Craftsman Truck Series debut, at New Hampshire, in 2006 and finished 15th. His second start was even more impressive; he finished fifth at Talladega.
- Won his first Champ Car pole and finishing fifth in Champ Car points in 2005. In 2006, he won his first Champ Car race, at Portland, and finished the season with five victories.
- In 2004, he became the first American since 1991 to earn the rookie of the year award in Champ Car.
- Set a record in the Toyota Atlantic series with eight wins, the most ever for a rookie, on his way to the series championship and rookie of the year award in 2003.
- Earned the Barber Dodge Pro Series championship in 2002.
- Missed the Formula Dodge National Championship by two points in 2001. Allmendinger finished second to Julio Campos.
- Took part in the inaugural Champ Car Stars of Tomorrow program in Las Vegas in 2000.
- Is a two-time International Karting Federation Grand National Champion.

16 FORD DRIVER PROFILE

Date of birth: December 23, 1969
Hometown: Vancouver, Wash.
Resides: Mooresville, N.C.
Spouse: None
Children: None
Height: 5-9 **Weight:** 170
Hobbies: Flying, fishing

GREG BIFFLE

Crew chief: Pat Tryson >>> >>> **Engine builder:** Roush-Yates Engines >>> >>> **Website:** www.roushracing.com >>> >>>

>> NASCAR ACHIEVEMENTS

First NASCAR NEXTEL Cup Series start: April 28, 2002 (California; started 29th, finished 13th)
Best points finish: 2nd (2005)
Career victories: 11—2006: Darlington, Homestead; 2005: California (a), Texas (a), Darlington, Dover (a), Michigan (a), Homestead; 2004: Michigan (b), Homestead; 2003: Daytona (b)
First victory: July 5, 2003 (Daytona; career start No. 23)
Last victory: November 19, 2006 (Homestead)
Career poles: 3—2006: Las Vegas, Richmond (a); 2004: Daytona (a)
First pole: February 8, 2004 (Daytona; career start No. 43)

>> CAREER HIGHLIGHTS

- Regressed in 2006 after an excellent season in 2005. Early in the season, Biffle had great cars but nothing to show for them. Down the stretch, he had bad cars, and he failed to make the Chase for the NASCAR NEXTEL Cup. He dropped sharply in every major statistical category except for poles and average start.
- Finally, in 2005, had the breakout season expected of a

─────────── Greg Biffle continued ───────────

NASCAR Busch Series and NASCAR Craftsman Truck Series champion. Biffle was particularly strong on intermediate tracks and also won at Darlington and Dover. He showed no fear, whipping a loose car around corners and righting it down the straightaways. Rules changes that made tires softer and spoilers shorter played to his strengths.

- Had an up-and-down sophomore year in 2004. He showed that when he had a fast car, he went to the front and stayed there. His season ended on a positive note, leading the most laps and winning at Homestead. Biffle needed to work on restrictor-plate racing—his average finish was 21.5.
- His 20th-place points finish in 2003 was impressive, considering he missed a race, failing to qualify in Las Vegas. He got his first win, in the night race at Daytona in July, by holding off teammates Jeff Burton and Bobby Labonte in the closing laps. He finished second to Jamie McMurray for Raybestos Rookie of the Year honors.
- Qualified in the top five in three events he ran in 2002. He made four starts subbing for Bobby Hamilton, two starts for Petty Enterprises and one for Roush Racing.

>> FAST FACTS

- Progressed through every level in NASCAR racing before making his NASCAR NEXTEL Cup Series debut in 2002. Biffle is the only driver to win both the NASCAR Craftsman Truck Series and the NASCAR Busch Series championships.
- Was the 2002 NASCAR Busch Series champion, winning four races and five poles and posting 25 top 10 finishes. He beat Jason Keller by 264 points.
- Named 2001 NASCAR Busch Series Rookie of the Year.
- Won 2000 NASCAR Craftsman Truck Series championship, winning five races and four poles to give Roush Racing its first NASCAR championship.
- Won a season-record nine NASCAR Craftsman Truck Series races in 1999 and finished second in points.
- Named the 1998 NASCAR Craftsman Truck Series Rookie of the Year.
- Participated in the Raybestos Brakes Northwest Series in 1997, capturing one victory.
- Competed in the NASCAR Weekly Racing Series presented by Dodge from 1994-97, winning late model track championships at Tri-City Raceway in West Richland, Wash., and at Portland Speedway.

CAREER STATISTICS

Year	Car owner	Races	Champ. finish	Wins	Top 5	Top 10	DNF	Poles	Money won
2002	Andy Petrie	4	48	0	0	0	1	0	$218,700
	Petty Enterprises	2		0	0	0	0	0	$96,014
	Jack Roush	1		0	0	0	0	0	$80,059
2003	Jack Roush	35	20	1	3	6	6	0	$2,805,673
2004	Jack Roush	36	17	2	4	8	5	1	$4,092,877
2005	Jack Roush	36	2	6	15	21	1	0	$8,354,052
2006	Jack Roush	36	13	2	8	15	6	2	$5,347,623
TOTALS		**150**		**11**	**30**	**50**	**19**	**3**	**$20,994,998**

2006 RESULTS

Race	Track	Start	Finish	Laps	Led	Winnings	Status	Rank
1. Daytona 500	Daytona	16	31	203/203	1	$258,758	Running	30
2. Auto Club 500	California	2	42	229/251	168	$106,005	Engine	38
3. UAW-DaimlerChrysler 400	Las Vegas	1	8	270/270	6	$125,025	Running	25
4. Golden Corral 500	Atlanta	8	16	325/325	128	$104,175	Running	21
5. Food City 500	Bristol	2	7	500/500	52	$105,150	Running	15
6. DIRECTV 500	Martinsville	10	31	436/500	0	$86,100	Running	18
7. Samsung/RadioShack 500	Texas	5	42	81/334	49	$98,860	Accident	23
8. Subway Fresh 500	Phoenix	2	15	311/312	151	$102,350	Running	21
9. Aaron's 499	Talladega	7	38	45/188	0	$96,175	Engine	23
10. Crown Royal 400	Richmond	1	4	400/400	54	$143,300	Running	20
11. Dodge Charger 500	Darlington	9	1	367/367	170	$290,175	Running	14
12. Coca-Cola 600	Lowe's	7	7	400/400	20	$134,650	Running	13
13. Neigh. Excellence 400	Dover	20	8	400/400	2	$112,800	Running	12
14. Pocono 500	Pocono	7	6	200/200	34	$106,425	Running	12
15. 3M Performance 400	Michigan	10	4	129/129	11	$115,300	Running	10
16. Dodge/Save Mart 350	Infineon	7	4	110/110	0	$141,700	Running	9
17. Pepsi 400	Daytona	12	31	160/160	1	$102,175	Running	11
18. USG Sheetrock 400	Chicagoland	27	11	270/270	0	$113,000	Running	11
19. Lenox Industrial Tools 300	New Hamp.	26	3	308/308	25	$142,950	Running	10
20. Pennsylvania 500	Pocono	20	24	200/200	0	$83,000	Running	12
21. Allstate 400 at Brickyard	Indianapolis	7	33	160/160	0	$156,625	Running	12
22. AMD at the Glen	Watkins Glen	41	38	75/90	0	$78,075	Running	13
23. GFS Marketplace 400	Michigan	6	7	200/200	0	$99,850	Running	12
24. Sharpie 500	Bristol	35	19	499/500	0	$108,775	Running	12
25. Sony HD 500	California	21	24	249/250	0	$105,650	Running	13
26. Chevy Rock & Roll 400	Richmond	8	6	400/400	0	$107,425	Running	12
27. Sylvania 300	New Hamp.	8	14	300/300	0	$93,675	Running	12
28. Dover 400	Dover	8	5	400/400	57	$123,825	Running	12
29. Banquet 400	Kansas	29	12	267/267	2	$112,400	Running	12
30. UAW-Ford 500	Talladega	5	41	137/188	15	$88,735	Accident	13
31. Bank of America 500	Lowe's	33	37	111/334	0	$80,725	Engine	13
32. Subway 500	Martinsville	38	32	486/500	0	$85,050	Running	13
33. Bass Pro Shops 500	Atlanta	13	5	325/325	0	$135,625	Running	13
34. Dickies 500	Texas	39	35	324/339	0	$113,075	Accident	13
35. Checker Auto Parts 500	Phoenix	6	34	306/312	0	$82,350	Running	13
36. Ford 400	Homestead	22	1	268/268	47	$323,800	Running	13

Biffle

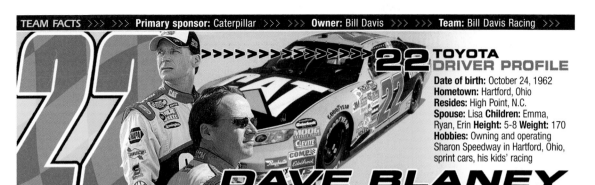

22 TOYOTA
DRIVER PROFILE

Date of birth: October 24, 1962
Hometown: Hartford, Ohio
Resides: High Point, N.C.
Spouse: Lisa **Children:** Emma,
Ryan, Erin **Height:** 5-8 **Weight:** 170
Hobbies: Owning and operating
Sharon Speedway in Hartford, Ohio,
sprint cars, his kids' racing

DAVE BLANEY

>>> **Crew chief:** Kevin Hamlin >>> >>> **Engine builder:** Terry Elledge >>> >>> **Website:** www.billdavisracing.com >>> >>>

>> NASCAR ACHIEVEMENTS

First NASCAR NEXTEL Cup Series start: October 25, 1992
(Rockingham; started 36th, finished 31st)
Best points finish: 19th (2002)
Career victories: 0
Best race finish: 3rd (March 16, 2003, Darlington)
Career poles: 1—2003: Rockingham (a)
First pole: February 21, 2003 (Rockingham, career start
No. 113)

>> CAREER HIGHLIGHTS

- Returned to Bill Davis Racing for a third stint in 2006, this time behind the wheel of the No. 22 Dodge. Blaney's season resembled the rest of his career—mediocre but serviceable. Blaney completed an impressive 98.3 percent of laps but finished on the lead lap just 11 times. He scored consecutive top 10s (Richmond, New Hampshire) for the first time since 2003. Blaney will remain with Bill Davis Racing in 2007, driving Toyota Camrys.
- Had a disappointing season in 2005 driving for Richard Childress Racing, but RCR had a down year across the board. Blaney couldn't stay out of trouble and rarely finished on the lead lap. He lost his ride to Clint Bowyer.
- Posted impressive results in 2004, considering he drove for different teams in different situations in cars manufactured by different companies. He posted top 15s in a Bill Davis Racing Dodge and in a RCR Chevy.
- Had a hot start in 2003 with his first pole (Rockingham) and three top 10 finishes in the first five races, including his first-ever top five, which vaulted him to as high as seventh in points. But he had only one more top 10 finish, dropped to the mid-20s and never made much progress from there.
- In 2002, his first season driving for Jasper Motorsports, Blaney cracked the top 20 with a 19th finish in points, the highest rank for a driver with no top five finishes that year. After the season, crew chief Ryan Pemberton left Blaney's team to work with Jerry Nadeau and MB2 Motorsports.
- In his final season with Bill Davis in 2001, had six top 10 finishes, including career bests of sixth at Texas, Michigan

and Homestead. He qualified third at Atlanta in November and led 70 laps before mechanical problems ruined his run.
- Never finished higher than 31st in points in his first two seasons with Davis. His best race finish in 1999 was 23rd, at Homestead. Blaney's 2000 season was an improvement: He finished with two tops 10s in the final three races and was third in the Raybestos Rookie of the Year standings.

>> FAST FACTS

- Finished seventh in the NASCAR Busch Series in 1999, posting five top fives, 12 top 10s and four poles in 31 starts.
- Made his first NASCAR Busch Series start in 1998. Won one pole and competed in 20 races.
- Won the 1995 World of Outlaws championship and was named the Sprint Car Driver of the Year.
- Was the runner-up in the World of Outlaws sprint car circuit in 1993, 1994, 1996 and 1997.
- Won the Syracuse Nationals at the New York State Fairgrounds in 1987 and 1993.
- Won the Pacific Coast Nationals at Ascot Speedway (Calif.) in 1990.
- Posted 76 top five finishes in 85 races in sprints and modifieds in 1989.
- Won the Easter World Sprint Car championship in 1988 in Hagerstown, Md.
- Won first career World of Outlaws series race at Tri-City in 1985.
- Won USAC Silver Crown championship in 1984, becoming the youngest driver to win that division.
- Won Rookie of the Year honors on the All-Star Circuit of Champions sprint series in 1983.
- Began professional racing career in 1981, racing sprint cars.
- Has competed in all three major sprint car associations— World of Outlaws National Challenge Series, United Sprint Association and All-Star Circuit of Champions.
- Brother, Dale, played college basketball at West Virginia, was drafted by the L.A. Lakers and played in the NBA and CBA.
- Owns Sharon Speedway in Hartford, Ohio, with his family.
- His father, Lou, also raced sprint cars. His son, Ryan, races quarter midgets.

— Dave Blaney continued —

CAREER STATISTICS

Year	Car owner	Races	Champ. finish	Wins	Top 5	Top 10	DNF	Poles	Money won
1992	Stanton Hover Jr.	1	80	0	0	0	1	0	$4,500
1999	Bill Davis	5	51	0	0	0	2	0	$212,170
2000	Bill Davis	33	31	0	0	2	7	0	$1,272,689
2001	Bill Davis	36	22	0	0	6	6	0	$1,827,896
2002	Doug Bawel	36	19	0	0	5	3	0	$2,978,593
2003	Doug Bawel	36	28	0	1	4	4	1	$2,828,692
2004	Richard Childress	8	38	0	0	0	1	0	$709,064
	Bill Davis	6		0	0	0	2	0	$608,932
	Jack Roush	1		0	0	0	1	0	$88,087
	James Smith	1		0	0	0	1	0	$55,555
2005	Richard Childress	36	26	0	0	2	2	0	$3,342,288
2006	Bill Davis	36	26	0	1	2	2	0	$3,479,643
TOTALS		235		0	2	21	32	1	$17,435,743

2006 RESULTS

Race	Track	Start	Finish	Laps	Led	Winnings	Status	Rank
1. Daytona 500	Daytona	34	22	203/203	0	$271,241	Running	22
2. Auto Club 500	California	24	30	249/251	0	$91,583	Running	26
3. UAW-DaimlerChrysler 400	Las Vegas	28	31	269/270	0	$90,833	Running	29
4. Golden Corral 500	Atlanta	30	32	323/325	0	$75,797	Running	33
5. Food City 500	Bristol	32	23	499/500	0	$96,683	Running	31
6. DIRECTV 500	Martinsville	14	17	499/500	0	$89,233	Running	29
7. Samsung/RadioShack 500	Texas	31	29	330/334	0	$92,475	Running	31
8. Subway Fresh 500	Phoenix	41	27	309/312	2	$75,172	Running	32
9. Aaron's 499	Talladega	38	24	183/188	1	$94,858	Running	30
10. Crown Royal 400	Richmond	19	20	399/400	0	$85,808	Running	28
11. Dodge Charger 500	Darlington	32	27	364/367	1	$84,158	Running	31
12. Coca-Cola 600	Lowe's	29	32	395/400	0	$82,775	Running	33
13. Neigh. Excellence 400	Dover	31	30	398/400	0	$87,047	Running	32
14. Pocono 500	Pocono	30	27	199/200	0	$77,033	Running	31
15. 3M Performance 400	Michigan	33	30	129/129	0	$72,600	Running	30
16. Dodge/Save Mart 350	Infineon	36	39	79/110	0	$67,250	Drive shaft	32
17. Pepsi 400	Daytona	41	27	160/160	0	$97,833	Running	33
18. USG Sheetrock 400	Chicagoland	15	17	270/270	0	$106,233	Running	30
19. Lenox Industrial Tools 300	New Hamp.	28	13	308/308	0	$95,783	Running	29
20. Pennsylvania 500	Pocono	24	16	200/200	0	$84,333	Running	29
21. Allstate 400 at Brickyard	Indianapolis	42	29	160/160	0	$149,797	Running	30
22. AMD at the Glen	Watkins Glen	25	40	61/90	0	$57,600	Accident	29
23. GFS Marketplace 400	Michigan	19	24	200/200	0	$87,983	Running	29
24. Sharpie 500	Bristol	22	14	500/500	0	$113,758	Running	29
25. Sony HD 500	California	41	28	249/250	0	$101,718	Running	29
26. Chevy Rock & Roll 400	Richmond	15	4	400/400	0	$130,983	Running	28
27. Sylvania 300	New Hamp.	21	9	300/300	5	$103,033	Running	28
28. Dover 400	Dover	38	12	399/400	0	$96,983	Running	26
29. Banquet 400	Kansas	17	21	266/267	0	$98,983	Running	26
30. UAW-Ford 500	Talladega	35	28	186/188	0	$82,897	Running	26
31. Bank of America 500	Lowe's	36	26	278/334	0	$65,475	Running	26
32. Subway 500	Martinsville	6	33	485/500	0	$77,722	Running	26
33. Bass Pro Shops 500	Atlanta	26	18	323/325	0	$106,858	Running	26
34. Dickies 500	Texas	30	32	330/339	0	$93,475	Running	27
35. Checker Auto Parts 500	Phoenix	31	23	312/312	0	$81,983	Running	26
36. Ford 400	Homestead	25	26	266/268	0	$78,033	Running	26

TEAM FACTS >>> >>> Primary sponsor: Jack Daniel's >>> >>> Owner: Richard Childress >>> >>> Team: Richard Childress Racing

07 CHEVROLET

DRIVER PROFILE

Date of birth: May 30, 1979
Hometown: Emporia, Kan.
Resides: Mooresville, N.C.
Spouse: None **Children:** None
Height: 6-0 **Weight:** 165
Hobbies: Boating, old cars

CLINT BOWYER

>>> >>> Crew chief: Gil Martin >>> >>> Engine builder: Jon Richardson >>> >>> Website: www.rcrracing.com >>> >>>

>> NASCAR ACHIEVEMENTS

First NASCAR NEXTEL Cup Series start: April 23, 2005 (Phoenix; started 25th, finished 22nd)
Best points finish: 17th (2006)
Career victories: 0
Best race finish: 3rd (September 3, 2006, California)
Career poles: 0
Best starting position: 2nd (August 6, 2006, Indianapolis)

>> CAREER HIGHLIGHTS

- Surfed through an up-and-down 2006 season, typical of rookies. Bowyer probably had a better car overall than his 17th-place finish in the points suggests. He had several strong runs that ended in bad luck, including a blown engine at Michigan.
- Made his first NASCAR NEXTEL Cup Series start early in 2005 at Phoenix, where he started 25th and finished 22nd. His successful season in the NASCAR Busch Series (he finished second in points) and lackluster performance by Dave Blaney's No. 07 team in 2005 convinced owner Richard Childress to promote Bowyer in 2006.

>> FAST FACTS

- Notched his first win in the NASCAR Busch Series, at Nashville, in 2005. More than doubled his top fives (12) and top 10s (22) from 2004 and was finished second to Martin Truex Jr. for the 2005 NASCAR Busch Series title.
- Joined the NASCAR Busch Series in 2004 with Richard Childress Racing, splitting time with Kevin Harvick in the No. 21 Chevrolet. Scored seven top 10s and four top fives in 17 races. Won his first NASCAR Busch Series pole at Talladega in April.
- Won two NASCAR Dodge Weekly Series track champi-

onships at Lakeside and Heartland and the NASCAR Dodge Weekly Series Midwest Region championship in 2002.
- Drove in the Pony Stock class at Thunderhill Speedway in Kansas and won the 2000 Modified division championship.
- Raced motocross for nine years, winning more than 200 races and numerous championships.

CAREER STATISTICS

Year	Car owner	Races	Champ. finish	Wins	Top 5	Top 10	DNF	Poles	Money won
2005	Richard Childress	1	69	0	0	0	0	0	$61,700
2006	Richard Childress	36	17	0	4	11	4	0	$4,550,134
TOTALS		37		0	4	11	4	0	$4,611,834

2006 RESULTS

Race	Track	Start	Finish	Laps	Led	Winnings	Status	Rank
1. Daytona 500	Daytona	37	6	203/203	0	$411,683	Running	8
2. Auto Club 500	California	32	14	251/251	0	$100,425	Running	8
3. UAW-DaimlerChrysler 400	Las Vegas	20	15	270/270	0	$105,800	Running	7
4. Golden Corral 500	Atlanta	16	27	324/325	0	$78,060	Running	10
5. Food City 500	Bristol	27	29	495/500	0	$90,800	Running	14
6. DIRECTV 500	Martinsville	42	22	496/500	0	$84,250	Running	16
7. Samsung/RadioShack 500	Texas	12	19	333/334	0	$116,075	Running	13
8. Subway Fresh 500	Phoenix	8	5	312/312	21	$122,325	Running	12
9. Aaron's 499	Talladega	15	40	16/188	0	$83,525	Accident	18
10. Crown Royal 400	Richmond	20	10	400/400	0	$91,025	Running	15
11. Dodge Charger 500	Darlington	3	23	365/367	0	$84,400	Running	16
12. Coca-Cola 600	Lowe's	15	19	399/400	0	$101,725	Running	15
13. Neigh. Excellence 400	Dover	22	17	400/400	0	$93,150	Running	16
14. Pocono 500	Pocono	42	21	200/200	8	$79,875	Running	16
15. 3M Performance 400	Michigan	9	39	86/129	0	$76,805	Running	18
16. Dodge/Save Mart 350	Infineon	28	16	110/110	0	$87,875	Running	18
17. Pepsi 400	Daytona	30	10	160/160	0	$114,875	Running	18
18. USG Sheetrock 400	Chicagoland	38	9	270/270	0	$114,425	Running	16
19. Lenox Industrial Tools 300	New Hamp.	31	27	307/308	23	$80,375	Running	16
20. Pennsylvania 500	Pocono	14	41	194/200	0	$68,035	Running	19
21. Allstate 400 at Brickyard	Indianapolis	2	4	160/160	0	$271,900	Running	17
22. AMD at the Glen	Watkins Glen	14	14	90/90	0	$85,700	Running	17
23. GFS Marketplace 400	Michigan	29	33	197/200	6	$78,000	Engine	19
24. Sharpie 500	Bristol	27	38	415/500	0	$90,070	Running	20
25. Sony HD 500	California	3	3	250/250	0	$167,950	Running	18
26. Chevy Rock & Roll 400	Richmond	16	12	400/400	0	$83,975	Running	16
27. Sylvania 300	New Hamp.	18	24	299/300	0	$81,700	Running	17
28. Dover 400	Dover	16	8	400/400	0	$90,625	Running	16
29. Banquet 400	Kansas	6	9	267/267	43	$109,425	Running	16
30. UAW-Ford 500	Talladega	32	35	171/188	5	$77,200	Accident	18
31. Bank of America 500	Lowe's	8	23	329/334	3	$75,700	Running	17
32. Subway 500	Martinsville	37	23	500/500	0	$78,800	Running	18
33. Bass Pro Shops 500	Atlanta	18	25	322/325	0	$93,375	Running	18
34. Dickies 500	Texas	14	5	339/339	3	$176,625	Running	17
35. Checker Auto Parts 500	Phoenix	20	33	306/312	0	$71,225	Oil pump	17
36. Ford 400	Homestead	10	10	268/268	0	$85,400	Running	17

TEAM FACTS >>> >>> **Primary sponsor:** TBA >>> >>> **Owner:** Richard Childress >>> >>> **Team:** Richard Childress Racing >>>

31 CHEVROLET DRIVER PROFILE

Date of birth: June 29, 1967
Hometown: South Boston, Va.
Resides: Huntersville, N.C.
Spouse: Kim **Children:** Kimberle, Harrison **Height:** 5-7 **Weight:** 155
Hobbies: Duke basketball, boating, deep sea fishing

JEFF BURTON

>>> **Crew chief:** Scott Miller >>> >>> **Engine builder:** Greg Gunnell >>> >>> **Website:** www.rcrracing.com >>> | >>>

>> NASCAR ACHIEVEMENTS

First NASCAR NEXTEL Cup Series start: July 11, 1993 (New Hampshire; started 6th, finished 37th)
Best points finish: 3rd (2000)
Career victories: 18—2006: Dover (b); 2001: Lowe's (a), Phoenix; 2000: Las Vegas, Daytona (b), New Hampshire (b), Phoenix; 1999: Las Vegas, Darlington (a,b), Lowe's (a), New Hampshire (a), Rockingham (b); 1998: New Hampshire (a), Richmond (b); 1997: Texas, New Hampshire (a), Martinsville (b)
First victory: April 6, 1997 (Texas, career start No. 96)
Last victory: September 24, 2006 (Dover)
Career poles: 6—2006: Daytona (a), Chicagoland, Indianapolis, Michigan (b); 2000: Richmond (b); 1996: Michigan (b)
First pole: August 16, 1996 (Michigan, career start No. 80)
Last pole: August 18, 2006 (Michigan)

>> CAREER HIGHLIGHTS

- Enjoyed a resurgent season, winning at Dover and qualifying for the Chase for the NASCAR NEXTEL Cup. He was in title contention until a stretch of bad finishes at Talladega, Martinsville and Texas. Throughout 2006, he struggled to finish races as well as he ran in the middle of them; he dominated Indianapolis and Bristol but didn't win either.
- Never sniffed the top 10 in points in 2005, as Richard Childress Racing suffered across the board. His car rarely was better than mid-pack and lacked horsepower and consistency. His string of winless seasons extended to four.
- Left his No. 99 team at Roush Racing for Richard Childress' No. 30 car in the middle of the 2004 season, and results for both teams greatly improved. The switch wasn't that easy, though—in his first race in the No. 30, he mistakenly approached the No. 99's pit box. It's interesting that Burton is with Childress—the late Dale Earnhardt, who drove for Childress, named Burton as a driver to replace himself.
- In 2002, finished outside of the top 10 in points and was winless for the first time since 1996. Similar

—————————— Jeff Burton continued ——————————

disappointment followed in 2003 after a promising start to the season. He was ninth in points after four races, but engine failures and inconsistent performances left Burton with his second straight 12th-place finish in points and again without a victory in the season.

- Won the Coca-Cola 600 at Lowe's in May 2001, his second victory in three seasons in the longest event in the NASCAR NEXTEL Cup Series. He also won in 1999.
- Finished a personal-best third in points in 2000. He beat out his brother, Ward, for two wins (Las Vegas and Darlington) that season. Ward finished second in both.
- Swept the Darlington races in 1999.
- Won at least one New Hampshire race for four straight seasons (1997-2000).
- Joined Roush Racing in 1996 and experienced a breakthrough year in 1997, winning his first race in April at Texas, then finding victory lane at New Hampshire and

Martinsville. He punctuated his emergence with a fourth-place finish in series points.
- Won Raybestos Rookie of the Year honors in 1994.

>>FAST FACTS

- Continues to compete part time in the NASCAR Busch Series; has run races in the series for 11 consecutive seasons.
- Won five NASCAR Busch Series races in 2002, in 13 starts.
- Won seven of 21 late model stock races at South Boston Speedway in 1988 and was voted the track's most popular driver.
- Began racing in the pure stock class at South Boston in 1984.
- Was a two-time Virginia state go-kart champion and finished second four times; began racing go-karts at age 8.
- Was an outstanding high school athlete in several sports.
- Is a huge fan of Duke basketball and has a longtime involvement with Duke Children's Hospital.

CAREER STATISTICS

Year	Car owner	Races	Champ. finish	Wins	Top 5	Top 10	DNF	Poles	Money won
1993	Filbert Martocci	1	83	0	0	0	1	0	$9,550
1994	William Stavola	30	24	0	2	3	7	0	$594,700
1995	William Stavola	29	32	0	1	2	6	0	$630,770
1996	Jack Roush	30	13	0	6	12	1	1	$884,303
1997	Jack Roush	32	4	3	13	18	1	0	$2,296,614
1998	Jack Roush	33	5	2	18	23	4	0	$2,626,987
1999	Jack Roush	34	5	6	18	23	3	0	$5,725,399
2000	Jack Roush	34	3	4	15	22	2	1	$5,959,439
2001	Jack Roush	36	10	2	8	16	1	0	$4,230,737
2002	Jack Roush	36	12	0	5	14	5	0	$4,244,856
2003	Jack Roush	36	12	0	3	11	4	0	$4,384,752
2004	Jack Roush	22	18	0	1	3	5	0	$2,746,370
	Richard Childress	14		0	1	3	1	0	$1,307,940
2005	Richard Childress	36	18	0	3	6	3	0	$4,815,924
2006	Richard Childress	36	7	1	7	20	2	4	$6,439,995
TOTALS		**439**		**18**	**101**	**176**	**46**	**6**	**$46,898,336**

2006 RESULTS

Race	Track	Start	Finish	Laps	Led	Winnings	Status	Rank
1. Daytona 500	Daytona	1	32	202/203	18	$302,603	Running	32
2. Auto Club 500	California	6	5	251/251	0	$158,970	Running	14
3. UAW-DaimlerChrysler 400	Las Vegas	8	7	270/270	0	$145,270	Running	11
4. Golden Corral 500	Atlanta	3	25	324/325	1	$97,870	Running	11
5. Food City 500	Bristol	18	34	467/500	0	$104,845	Running	18
6. DIRECTV 500	Martinsville	20	33	426/500	0	$92,845	Running	21
7. Samsung/RadioShack 500	Texas	21	6	334/334	0	$172,220	Running	16

Race	Track	Start	Finish	Laps	Led	Winnings	Status	Rank
8. Subway Fresh 500	Phoenix	37	9	312/312	0	$108,870	Running	13
9. Aaron's 499	Talladega	40	4	188/188	0	$176,745	Running	12
10. Crown Royal 400	Richmond	15	15	399/400	0	$98,270	Running	11
11. Dodge Charger 500	Darlington	20	9	367/367	0	$115,320	Running	10
12. Coca-Cola 600	Lowe's	11	6	400/400	12	$154,520	Running	8
13. Neigh. Excellence 400	Dover	17	4	400/400	48	$164,245	Running	7
14. Pocono 500	Pocono	5	9	200/200	11	$104,520	Running	7
15. 3M Performance 400	Michigan	12	11	129/129	0	$109,295	Running	7
16. Dodge/Save Mart 350	Infineon	13	7	110/110	0	$122,120	Running	6
17. Pepsi 400	Daytona	39	15	160/160	0	$122,920	Running	7
18. USG Sheetrock 400	Chicagoland	1	2	270/270	60	$250,220	Running	4
19. Lenox Industrial Tools 300	New Hamp.	2	7	308/308	37	$127,870	Running	3
20. Pennsylvania 500	Pocono	6	9	200/200	23	$105,720	Running	3
21. Allstate 400 at Brickyard	Indianapolis	1	15	160/160	87	$243,995	Running	3
22. AMD at the Glen	Watkins Glen	16	11	90/90	0	$97,645	Running	4
23. GFS Marketplace 400	Michigan	1	42	17/200	0	$100,530	Engine	9
24. Sharpie 500	Bristol	2	9	500/500	263	$145,720	Running	7
25. Sony HD 500	California	7	16	250/250	0	$120,145	Running	10
26. Chevy Rock & Roll 400	Richmond	2	9	400/400	25	$104,995	Running	8
27. Sylvania 300	New Hamp.	22	7	300/300	52	$137,570	Running	5
28. Dover 400	Dover	19	1	400/400	6	$230,370	Running	1
29. Banquet 400	Kansas	10	5	267/267	1	$155,595	Running	1
30. UAW-Ford 500	Talladega	34	27	187/188	5	$99,845	Running	1
31. Bank of America 500	Lowe's	6	3	334/334	0	$176,870	Running	1
32. Subway 500	Martinsville	28	42	217/500	0	$90,605	Engine	5
33. Bass Pro Shops 500	Atlanta	5	13	323/325	0	$122,595	Running	5
34. Dickies 500	Texas	29	38	269/339	0	$118,595	Running	7
35. Checker Auto Parts 500	Phoenix	18	10	312/312	0	$108,845	Running	7
36. Ford 400	Homestead	5	14	268/268	0	$95,895	Running	7

Jeff Burton

4 CHEVROLET
DRIVER PROFILE

Date of birth: October 25, 1961
Hometown: South Boston, Va.
Resides: Halifax, Va.
Spouse: Tabitha
Children: Sarah, Jeb, Everett
Height: 5-6 **Weight:** 150
Hobbies: Hunting,
outdoor activities

LUCAS WARD BURTON

>>> **Crew chief:** Chris Carrier >>> >>> **Engine builder:** Ron Puryear >>> >>> **Website:** www.morgan-mcclure.com >>> >>>

>> NASCAR ACHIEVEMENTS

First NASCAR NEXTEL Cup Series start: March 6, 1994
(Richmond; started 29th, finished 35th)
Best points finish: 9th (1999)
Career victories: 5—2002: Daytona (a), New Hampshire (a);
2001: Darlington (b); 2000: Darlington (a); 1995:
Rockingham (b)
First victory: October 25, 1995 (Rockingham, career start
No. 53)
Last victory: July 21, 2002 (New Hampshire)
Career poles: 7—2002: Richmond (a); 1999:
Michigan (b); 1998: Michigan (a), Pocono (b); 1997:
Martinsville (b); 1996: Darlington (a); 1994: Lowe's (b)
   First pole: October 7, 1994 (Lowe's, career start No. 23)
Last pole: May 3, 2002 (Richmond)

>> CAREER HIGHLIGHTS

- Returned to race in Larry McClure's No. 4 car in the
  NASCAR NEXTEL Cup Series after a nearly two-year
  absence in 2006. He finished on the lead lap at Martinsville
  and a season-high 25th at Texas. In the offseason, Burton
  signed a deal to drive the No. 4 full-time in 2007.
- While driving Gene Haas' No. 0 Chevrolet in 2004, Burton
  had his worst season since his first in 1994, finishing with
  only three top 10s and only eight finishes on the lead lap.
  He was replaced by Mike Bliss with two races left.
- Was booted from his Bill Davis Racing ride late in the 2003
  season after he had scored only four top 10s for Davis that
  season. It was Burton's ninth year with the organization. He
  caught on with Haas CNC Racing and ran the final four
  races in the No. 0 Chevrolet.
- Won a career-high two NASCAR NEXTEL Cup Series races
  in 2002, including a Daytona 500 victory. The other win
  came at New Hampshire. But he dug himself into a major
  points hole with a midseason string of six finishes of 30th
  or worse, which dropped him from 14th to 25th in points.
- Struggled early in the 2001 season as he and his team
  adjusted to the new Intrepid, and scored only one top 10 in
  his first 11 races.
- Had eight top 10 finishes in the 2000 season's first 13

races and was as high as second in the points standings.
Burton stumbled in the second half with four DNFs but still
managed to finish 10th in points.
- Finished second three times in 1999, and all three were
  behind his brother, Jeff. He finished a career-high ninth in
  points.
- Began the 1995 season driving for A.G. Dillard and scored
  two top 10s in 20 races. He switched to Bill Davis Racing in
  late August, and Burton showed the move was a good one
  two months later by winning his first NASCAR NEXTEL Cup
  Series race at Rockingham.
- Didn't look good early in his first NASCAR NEXTEL Cup
  Series season in 1994. While driving for A.G. Dillard, he
  missed the first two races and recorded DNFs in the third
  and fourth race of the season. The season got better,
  though: Burton came in second at Pocono and scored his
  first pole at Lowe's.

>> FAST FACTS

- Finished eighth (1992) and sixth (1993) in his only two full
  NASCAR Busch Series seasons.
- Won three races and was voted Most Popular Driver at
  South Boston Speedway in 1989.
- Raced mini-stocks and street stocks in South Boston, Va.,
  before moving to late models in 1986.
- Spent two years after college in a cabin, surviving off the land.
- Attended Hargrave Military Academy beginning in 10th
  grade and ranked first on the school's rifle team.
- Began racing go-karts at age 8 and raced on the Virginia
  Karting Association series until he was 16.
- Operates the Ward Burton Wildlife Foundation, which purchas-
  es land in an effort to conserve and protect wildlife habitats.

Ward Burton

— Ward Burton continued —

CAREER STATISTICS

Year	Car owner	Races	Champ. finish	Wins	Top 5	Top 10	DNF	Poles	Money won
2005	Richard Childress	1	69	0	0	0	0	0	$61,700
1994	Alan Dillard	26	35	0	1	2	12	1	$304,700
1995	Alan Dillard	20		0	0	2	4	0	$334,330
	Bill Davis	9	22	1	3	4	2	0	$300,325
1996	Bill Davis	27	33	0	0	4	10	1	$873,619
1997	Bill Davis	31	24	0	0	7	7	1	$1,004,944
1998	Bill Davis	33	16	0	1	5	4	2	$1,516,183
1999	Bill Davis	34	9	0	6	16	3	1	$2,405,913
2000	Bill Davis	34	10	1	4	17	4	0	$2,699,604
2001	Bill Davis	36	14	1	6	10	9	0	$3,633,692
2002	Bill Davis	36	25	2	3	8	9	1	$4,899,884
2003	Bill Davis	32		0	0	4	4	0	$3,280,950
	Gene Haas	4	21	0	0	2	2	0	$347,650
2004	Gene Haas	34	32	0	0	3	8	0	$2,471,940
2006	Larry McClure	3	53	0	0	0	0	0	$232,450
TOTALS		359		5	24	82	78	7	$24,256,185

2006 RESULTS

Race	Track	Start	Finish	Laps	Led	Winnings	Status	Rank
32. Subway 500	Martinsville	35	26	500/500	0	$68,750	Running	64
34. Dickies 500	Texas	37	25	338/339	0	$98,275	Running	58
35. Checker Auto Parts 500	Phoenix	24	28	311/312	0	$65,425	Running	53

TEAM FACTS >>> >>> Primary sponsor: Miller Lite **>>> >>> Owner:** Roger Penske **>>> >>> Team:** Penske Racing **>>>**

2 DODGE DRIVER PROFILE

Date of birth: August 4, 1978
Hometown: Las Vegas
Resides: Concord, N.C.
Spouse: Eva **Children:** None
Height: 5-11 **Weight:** 150
Hobbies: Jet skiing, water skiing, snow skiing

KURT BUSCH

>>> Crew chief: Roy McCauley **>>> >>> Engine builder:** Penske-Jasper Engines **>>> >>> Website:** www.penskeracing.com

>> NASCAR ACHIEVEMENTS

First NASCAR NEXTEL Cup Series start: September 24, 2000 (Dover; started 10th, finished 18th)
Best points finish: 1st (2004)
Career victories: 15—2006: Bristol (a) 2005: Phoenix (a), Pocono (b), Richmond (b); 2004: Bristol (a), New Hampshire (a,b); 2003: Bristol (a,b), Michigan (a), California; 2002: Bristol (a), Martinsville (b), Atlanta (b), Homestead.
First victory: March 24, 2002 (Bristol, career start No. 48)
Last victory: March 26, 2006 (Bristol)
Career poles: 9—2006: California (a,b), Infineon, Watkins Glen, Bristol (b), Martinsville (b); 2004: Homestead; 2002: Homestead; 2001: Darlington (b)
First pole: September 1, 2001 (Darlington, career start No. 32)
Last pole: October 20, 2006 (Martinsville)

>> CAREER HIGHLIGHTS

- Missed the 2006 Chase for the NASCAR NEXTEL Cup after making the first two. In his first season at Penske Racing, Busch won the spring race at Bristol but struggled overall. He needed time to adjust to the Dodge Charger, and a late-season run to make the Chase fell short. He showed surprising qualifying strength, picking up six poles.
- Was involved in nasty wrecks early in 2005 but bounced back to bring momentum into the Chase for the NASCAR NEXTEL Cup. That lasted only two laps, when he wrecked at New Hampshire. He never got going after that and was suspended by Roush Racing for the last two races because of a reckless driving incident at Phoenix. Busch also was criticized for forcing his release from Roush so he could take over Penke Racing's No. 2 car from Rusty Wallace, who retired after the 2005 season.
- Became the first champion in the NASCAR NEXTEL Cup Series era by being consistent—not his strength before the 2004 season. The aggressive Busch gave way to a Busch who showed Matt Kensethian patience. He ripped off nine top 10 finishes during the 10-race Chase for the NASCAR NEXTEL Cup. A short track ace, Busch showed improvement at restrictor-plate and intermediate tracks. He was great on flat tracks, pulling off a sweep at New Hampshire.
- Busch's four 2003 wins were second-best on the circuit but were offset by 10 finishes outside of the top 35. Three of those poor finishes came in succession in October and cost him a top 10 points finish.
- Showed his short-track prowess by sweeping the 2003 races at Bristol.
- Had a breakthrough season in 2002, with four wins (Bristol, Martinsville, Atlanta and Homestead), three in the final five weeks of the season.
- His incredible success with Roush Racing in the 2000 Craftsman Truck Series led owner Jack Roush to move Busch straight to NASCAR NEXTEL Cup Series racing in 2001, an unprecedented move. Busch quieted skeptics when he finished in the top 10 six times and finished

- second for Raybestos Rookie of the Year honors.
- Ran seven NASCAR NEXTEL Cup Series events in 2000, with a best finish of 13th in October at Lowe's.

>> FAST FACTS

- Was runner-up in the 2000 NASCAR Craftsman Truck Series and had four victories.
- Competed in the Featherlite Southwest Series from 1997 to 1999, recording seven wins.
- In 1999, won the Featherlite Southwest Series NASCAR Touring championship driving for Craig Keough. Was the youngest driver to win that series' championship at age 21.
- Named Featherlite Southwest Series Rookie of the Year in 1998.
- Won the 1996 Hobby Stock track championship at Las Vegas Speedway Park.
- Was the 1996 Legend Cars National Rookie of the Year and Legend Cars Western States champion.
- Won the Nevada Dwarf Car championship in 1995.
- Was the 1994 Nevada State Dwarf Car Rookie of the Year.
- Began racing at age 14, in Dwarf Cars at Parhump Valley Speedway near Las Vegas.
- A lifelong Cubs fan, his favorite athlete is Andre Dawson.

CAREER STATISTICS

Year	Car owner	Races	Champ. finish	Wins	Top 5	Top 10	DNF	Poles	Money won
2000	Jack Roush	7	48	0	0	0	0	0	$311,915
2001	Jack Roush	35	27	0	3	6	7	1	$2,170,629
2002	Jack Roush	36	3	4	12	20	4	1	$5,105,394
2003	Jack Roush	36	11	4	9	14	8	0	$5,587,384
2004	Jack Roush	36	1	3	10	21	3	1	$9,661,513
2005	Jack Roush	34	10	3	9	18	3	0	$7,667,861
2006	Roger Penske	36	16	1	7	12	3	6	$5,681,655
TOTALS		**220**		**15**	**50**	**91**	**28**	**9**	**$36,194,280**

2006 RESULTS

Race	Track	Start	Finish	Laps	Led	Winnings	Status	Rank
1. Daytona 500	Daytona	13	38	187/203	1	$280,366	Accident	38
2. Auto Club 500	California	1	16	251/251	7	$144,558	Running	25
3. UAW-DaimlerChrysler 400	Las Vegas	6	16	270/270	0	$126,583	Running	22
4. Golden Corral 500	Atlanta	9	37	321/325	22	$99,153	Running	27
5. Food City 500	Bristol	9	1	500/500	33	$175,858	Running	16
6. DIRECTV 500	Martinsville	9	11	500/500	0	$111,683	Running	14
7. Samsung/RadioShack 500	Texas	7	34	286/334	0	$124,633	Running	17
8. Subway Fresh 500	Phoenix	7	24	310/312	0	$103,833	Running	17
9. Aaron's 499	Talladega	5	7	188/188	9	$143,233	Running	16
10. Crown Royal 400	Richmond	13	29	397/400	0	$105,008	Running	18
11. Dodge Charger 500	Darlington	10	19	366/367	0	$115,633	Running	18
12. Coca-Cola 600	Lowe's	20	39	290/400	0	$122,858	Running	19
13. Neigh. Excellence 400	Dover	4	16	400/400	0	$122,658	Running	18
14. Pocono 500	Pocono	2	2	200/200	31	$193,258	Running	17
15. 3M Performance 400	Michigan	13	9	129/129	0	$117,583	Running	16
16. Dodge/Save Mart 350	Infineon	1	5	110/110	29	$145,433	Running	14
17. Pepsi 400	Daytona	16	3	160/160	0	$196,233	Running	13
18. USG Sheetrock 400	Chicagoland	19	8	270/270	0	$138,958	Running	13
19. Lenox Industrial Tools 300	New Hamp.	10	38	285/308	0	$108,533	Running	14
20. Pennsylvania 500	Pocono	7	2	200/200	4	$182,758	Running	13
21. Allstate 400 at Brickyard	Indianapolis	3	12	160/160	0	$211,933	Running	13
22. AMD at the Glen	Watkins Glen	1	19	90/90	38	$117,333	Running	12
23. GFS Marketplace 400	Michigan	16	40	127/200	1	$109,523	Accident	14
24. Sharpie 500	Bristol	1	37	446/500	27	$128,413	Running	14
25. Sony HD 500	California	1	27	249/250	11	$135,918	Running	14
26. Chevy Rock & Roll 400	Richmond	18	27	398/400	0	$105,808	Running	14
27. Sylvania 300	New Hamp.	3	19	300/300	0	$114,058	Running	14
28. Dover 400	Dover	10	4	400/400	0	$153,233	Running	14
29. Banquet 400	Kansas	7	25	265/267	0	$122,133	Running	14
30. UAW-Ford 500	Talladega	29	3	188/188	3	$169,108	Running	14
31. Bank of America 500	Lowe's	42	32	208/334	0	$102,258	Running	16
32. Subway 500	Martinsville	1	27	496/500	19	$112,118	Running	16
33. Bass Pro Shops 500	Atlanta	16	14	323/325	0	$131,333	Running	16
34. Dickies 500	Texas	3	8	339/339	37	$164,833	Running	15
35. Checker Auto Parts 500	Phoenix	8	8	312/312	0	$116,083	Running	14
36. Ford 400	Homestead	36	43	9/268	0	$100,506	Accident	16

5 CHEVROLET DRIVER PROFILE

KYLE BUSCH

Date of birth: May 2, 1985
Hometown: Las Vegas
Resides: Mooresville, N.C.
Spouse: None **Children:** None
Height: 6-1 **Weight:** 160
Hobbies: Video games, reading

>> NASCAR ACHIEVEMENTS

First NASCAR NEXTEL Cup Series start: March 7, 2004 (Las Vegas; started 18th, finished 41st)
Best points finish: 10th (2006)
Career victories: 3—2006: New Hampshire (a); 2005: California (b), Phoenix (b)
First victory: September 4, 2005 (California, career start No. 31)

Last victory: July 16, 2006 (New Hampshire)
Career poles: 2—2006: Phoenix (a); 2005: California (a)
First pole: February 26, 2005 (California, career start No. 8)
Last pole: April 20, 2006 (Phoenix)

>> CAREER HIGHLIGHTS

- Made the 2006 Chase for the NASCAR NEXTEL Cup and then fell apart. Busch made headlines in and out of the car:

––––––––– Kyle Busch continued –––––––––

In it, he won at New Hampshire and showed newfound patience, qualifying for the Chase; out of it, he chucked his restraint device at Casey Mears at Lowe's.

- Set marks as the youngest driver to win a pole and the youngest to win a race in 2005. Busch ran away with the Raybestos Rookie of the Year title. He drove a lot like his brother, Kurt, did early in his career: with the pedal smashed to the floorboard.
- Ran a limited schedule for Hendrick Motorsports in 2004 in preparation for his rookie season. Busch didn't wow anyone at the NASCAR NEXTEL Cup Series level—his best finish was 24th in September at California—but he was named to take over the No. 5 Chevrolet from Terry Labonte.

>> FAST FACTS

- Finished second at Lowe's during his 2003 NASCAR Busch Series debut. He ran seven races, finishing in the top 10 three times.

- Surprised many by signing with Hendrick Motorsports, rather than Roush Racing, for whom his brother, Kurt, drove full-time in the NASCAR NEXTEL Cup Series at the time.
- Won twice in seven ARCA starts for Hendrick Motorsports before he turned 18 on May 2, 2003, making him eligible for NASCAR competition.
- Spent the 2002 season driving for Roush Racing in ASA, placing third in the Rookie of the Year standings.
- Ran six NASCAR Craftsman Truck Series events for Roush Racing in 2001 as a high school junior and had two top 10 finishes. But he wasn't allowed to compete in the season finale because Marlboro was a sponsor of the weekend's events, and he was only 16. Soon after, NASCAR wrote a rule that all drivers had to be at least 18 to compete.
- Graduated, with honors, a year early from Durango (Nev.) High School in order to accelerate his racing career.
- Began racing Legends cars at his hometown track, Las Vegas Motor Speedway, at 13 and won two championships.

CAREER STATISTICS

Year	Car owner	Races	Champ. finish	Wins	Top 5	Top 10	DNF	Poles	Money won
2004	Rick Hendrick	6	52	0	0	0	4	0	$394,489
2005	Rick Hendrick	36	20	2	9	13	8	1	$4,730,471
2006	Rick Hendrick	36	10	1	10	18	2	1	$6,077,337
TOTALS		78		3	19	31	14	2	$11,202,297

2006 RESULTS

Race	Track	Start	Finish	Laps	Led	Winnings	Status	Rank
1. Daytona 500	Daytona	4	23	203/203	5	$281,833	Running	21
2. Auto Club 500	California	7	10	251/251	0	$105,225	Running	12
3. UAW-DaimlerChrysler 400	Las Vegas	4	3	270/270	0	$204,775	Running	6
4. Golden Corral 500	Atlanta	17	12	325/325	0	$88,025	Running	8
5. Food City 500	Bristol	20	8	500/500	34	$102,450	Running	5
6. DIRECTV 500	Martinsville	17	5	500/500	0	$98,400	Running	5
7. Samsung/RadioShack 500	Texas	26	15	334/334	0	$129,725	Running	7
8. Subway Fresh 500	Phoenix	1	36	259/312	7	$84,425	Running	9
9. Aaron's 499	Talladega	13	32	150/188	0	$95,025	Running	9
10. Crown Royal 400	Richmond	21	5	400/400	7	$113,600	Running	8
11. Dodge Charger 500	Darlington	29	7	367/367	0	$120,625	Running	7
12. Coca-Cola 600	Lowe's	28	38	313/400	0	$99,935	Accident	10
13. Neigh. Excellence 400	Dover	30	5	400/400	22	$132,925	Running	10

Race	Track	Start	Finish	Laps	Led	Winnings	Status	Rank
14. Pocono 500	Pocono	9	22	200/200	0	$81,175	Running	10
15. 3M Performance 400	Michigan	15	14	129/129	9	$91,725	Running	12
16. Dodge/Save Mart 350	Infineon	19	11	110/110	0	$97,575	Running	12
17. Pepsi 400	Daytona	14	2	160/160	0	$210,525	Running	8
18. USG Sheetrock 400	Chicagoland	23	3	270/270	2	$178,075	Running	8
19. Lenox Industrial Tools 300	New Hamp.	4	1	308/308	107	$242,175	Running	4
20. Pennsylvania 500	Pocono	8	12	200/200	0	$86,275	Running	4
21. Allstate 400 at Brickyard	Indianapolis	37	7	160/160	8	$209,825	Running	5
22. AMD at the Glen	Watkins Glen	9	9	90/90	0	$88,025	Running	5
23. GFS Marketplace 400	Michigan	11	39	132/200	3	$86,540	Running	7
24. Sharpie 500	Bristol	19	2	500/500	1	$202,375	Running	4
25. Sony HD 500	California	10	8	250/250	11	$114,775	Running	5
26. Chevy Rock & Roll 400	Richmond	12	2	400/400	248	$184,550	Running	4
27. Sylvania 300	New Hamp.	16	38	276/300	0	$85,500	Running	10
28. Dover 400	Dover	27	40	110/400	0	$81,800	Engine	10
29. Banquet 400	Kansas	13	7	267/267	64	$128,625	Running	9
30. UAW-Ford 500	Talladega	6	11	188/188	10	$96,475	Running	10
31. Bank of America 500	Lowe's	18	6	334/334	1	$112,050	Running	9
32. Subway 500	Martinsville	15	18	500/500	0	$85,400	Running	10
33. Bass Pro Shops 500	Atlanta	10	27	321/325	0	$98,775	Running	10
34. Dickies 500	Texas	11	4	339/339	2	$204,250	Running	8
35. Checker Auto Parts 500	Phoenix	9	38	291/312	0	$79,625	Running	10
36. Ford 400	Homestead	3	38	206/268	28	$78,600	Running	10

Kyle Busch

8 CHEVROLET DRIVER PROFILE

Date of birth: October 10, 1974
Hometown: Kannapolis, N.C.
Resides: Mooresville, N.C.
Spouse: None **Children:** None
Height: 6-0 **Weight:** 165
Hobbies: Car restoration, music, computers, video games

DALE EARNHARDT JR.

Crew chief: Tony Eury Jr. >>> >>> **Engine builder:** Dale Earnhardt Inc. >>> >>> **Website:** www.daleearnhardtinc.com

>> NASCAR ACHIEVEMENTS

First NASCAR NEXTEL Cup Series start: May 30, 1999 (Lowe's; started 8th, finished 16th)
Best points finish: 3rd (2003)
Career victories: 17—2006: Richmond (a); 2005: Chicagoland; 2004: Daytona (a), Atlanta (a), Richmond (a), Bristol (b), Talladega (b), Phoenix; 2003: Talladega (a), Phoenix; 2002: Talladega (a,b); 2001: Daytona (b), Dover (b), Talladega (b); 2000: Texas, Richmond (a)
First victory: April 2, 2000 (Texas, career start No. 12)
Last victory: May 6, 2006 (Richmond)
Career poles: 6—2002: Michigan (b), Kansas; 2001: Texas, Atlanta (b); 2000: Lowe's (a), Michigan (b)
First pole: May 24, 2000 (Lowe's, career start No. 17)
Last pole: September 27, 2002 (Kansas)

>> CAREER HIGHLIGHTS

- Rebounded in 2006 with crew chief Tony Eury Jr. after a terrible 2005. His win at Richmond signaled his return, but it was a fourth-place finish at Martinsville, in a car that looked like he got it from a junkyard, that proved he is as talented as any current driver. Earnhardt made the Chase for the NASCAR NEXTEL Cup but was not a title contender because he didn't have enough horsepower.
- The team underwent a makeover entering 2005. Pete Rondeau began the season as the new crew chief, but he was replaced after 11 races by DEI technical director Steve Hmiel. Earnhardt led just two of the first 13 races—a total of five laps at Daytona and Talladega—and won his only race, at Chicagoland, with late pit strategy. Tony Eury Jr. took over as crew chief for the last 10 races of 2005.
- Was a title contender throughout the 2004 Chase for the NASCAR NEXTEL Cup. He came back strong after suffering burns in practice for a non-NASCAR race in August. He also won two races in the Chase for the NASCAR NEXTEL Cup, but an accident late in the October Atlanta race hurt his title chances. His six wins overall were second to Jimmie Johnson's eight and a career high.
- His victory in the Daytona 500 made Dale Earnhardt/Earnhardt Jr. only the third father-son combination to win the event, along with Lee and Richard Petty and Bobby and Davey Allison.
- Resiliency was the key to Earnhardt's success in 2003; he followed four of his five finishes outside of the top 30 with a top 10. He finished third in points, a career-best, and ended a long drought on non-superspeedway tracks with a victory at Phoenix. He led 24 races, a career high, and scored 880 points on short tracks to pace all drivers.
- Led 1,068 laps in 2002, more than any other driver, and swept the races at Talladega.
- Finished second in all three nonpoints events in 2002: the Budweiser Shootout, a Twin 125 qualifying race and the All-Star race.
- First win of the 2001 season came in the July Daytona race, the first race held there since his father's death in the Daytona 500 on February 18. His next victory was at Dover, in the NASCAR NEXTEL Cup Series' first race after the September 11 terrorist attacks. He punctuated that win with a victory lap carrying an American flag. His third win was at Talladega, the site of his father's final career victory a year earlier. He went on to win four consecutive Talladega races (the second race in 2001, both races in 2002 and the first race in 2003).
- Made a splash as a rookie in 2000 with two wins (Texas, Richmond) and two poles (Lowe's, Michigan) and was only 42 points shy of winning the Raybestos Rookie of the Year title, behind Matt Kenseth. Earnhardt matched the modern-era record (two wins in first 16 races) set by Davey Allison in 1987. He also became the first rookie to win the All-Star race.

>> FAST FACTS

- Is co-owner of Chance 2 Motorsports, which won the 2004 and 2005 NASCAR Busch Series championship with Martin Truex Jr. Also owns JR Motorsports, which competed in the NASCAR Busch Series in 2006 with driver Mark McFarland.
- Says his hero is his father, seven-time NASCAR NEXTEL Cup Series champion, Dale Earnhardt.
- Voted Most Popular Driver in 2003, 2004, 2005 and 2006.
- Won his first NASCAR Busch Series race as a driver/owner

— Dale Earnhardt Jr. continued —

in September 2002 at Richmond.
- When he raced in the Pepsi 400 at Michigan in 2000 along with his late father, Dale, and brother Kerry, it was the second time a father and two sons ran in the same NASCAR NEXTEL Cup Series event. Lee Petty also raced against his sons, Richard and Maurice.
- Won back-to-back NASCAR Busch Series championships in 1998 and 1999, his only two full seasons of NASCAR Busch Series competition.
- 1998 NASCAR Busch Series title made him the first third generation NASCAR champion. Other champion Earnhardts were his father, Dale, and his grandfather, Ralph. His maternal grandfather, Robert Gee, was a NASCAR fabricator and mechanic.

- Began racing in the NASCAR Busch Series in 1996 but his career took off in 1998, winning the NASCAR Busch Series title in his first season paired with crew chief Tony Eury Sr.
- Won three feature victories in his NASCAR late model stock career from 1994-96.
- Began his professional career at age 17, competing in the street stock division at Concord Motorsport Park and later moving up to late model stock division.
- Raced against brother Kerry and sister Kelley at the beginning of his career.
- He and Kerry sold a go-kart for $500 to purchase a 1978 Chevy Monte Carlo street stock car for $200. Later they sold the car to NASCAR Busch Series competitor Hank Parker Jr.
- His favorite sports team is the Redskins.

CAREER STATISTICS

Year	Car owner	Races	Champ. finish	Wins	Top 5	Top 10	DNF	Poles	Money won
1999	Teresa Earnhardt	5	48	0	0	1	1	0	$162,095
2000	Teresa Earnhardt	34	16	2	3	5	7	2	$2,801,881
2001	Teresa Earnhardt	36	8	3	9	15	4	2	$5,827,542
2002	Teresa Earnhardt	36	11	2	11	16	3	2	$4,970,034
2003	Teresa Earnhardt	36	3	2	13	21	4	0	$6,980,807
2004	Teresa Earnhardt	36	5	6	16	21	4	0	$8,906,860
2005	Teresa Earnhardt	36	19	1	7	13	6	0	$6,284,577
2006	Teresa Earnhardt	36	5	1	10	17	3	0	$7,111,739
TOTALS		**255**		**17**	**69**	**109**	**32**	**6**	**$42,945,535**

2006 RESULTS

Race	Track	Start	Finish	Laps	Led	Winnings	Status	Rank
1. Daytona 500	Daytona	7	8	203/203	32	$377,694	Running	6
2. Auto Club 500	California	18	11	251/251	1	$132,366	Running	5
3. UAW-DaimlerChrysler 400	Las Vegas	42	27	270/270	0	$118,916	Running	11
4. Golden Corral 500	Atlanta	26	3	325/325	0	$138,841	Running	7
5. Food City 500	Bristol	19	11	500/500	0	$124,516	Running	6
6. DIRECTV 500	Martinsville	29	4	500/500	0	$133,416	Running	6
7. Samsung/RadioShack 500	Texas	15	12	334/334	0	$154,816	Running	6
8. Subway Fresh 500	Phoenix	11	23	310/312	0	$102,291	Running	7
9. Aaron's 499	Talladega	27	31	151/188	8	$112,166	Engine	8
10. Crown Royal 400	Richmond	10	1	400/400	47	$239,166	Running	6

Race	Track	Start	Finish	Laps	Led	Winnings	Status	Rank
11. Dodge Charger 500	Darlington	22	5	367/367	0	$152,916	Running	5
12. Coca-Cola 600	Lowe's	34	11	400/400	0	$140,071	Running	5
13. Neigh. Excellence 400	Dover	11	10	400/400	1	$130,241	Running	4
14. Pocono 500	Pocono	11	14	200/200	0	$104,966	Running	6
15. 3M Performance 400	Michigan	6	3	129/129	3	$146,991	Running	4
16. Dodge/Save Mart 350	Infineon	26	26	110/110	0	$107,916	Running	5
17. Pepsi 400	Daytona	35	13	160/160	8	$134,716	Running	3
18. USG Sheetrock 400	Chicagoland	25	5	270/270	27	$164,591	Running	3
19. Lenox Industrial Tools 300	New Hamp.	25	43	134/308	0	$102,130	Engine	7
20. Pennsylvania 500	Pocono	26	43	115/200	0	$95,088	Accident	11
21. Allstate 400 at Brickyard	Indianapolis	31	6	160/160	0	$230,516	Running	10
22. AMD at the Glen	Watkins Glen	11	18	90/90	1	$99,966	Running	10
23. GFS Marketplace 400	Michigan	17	6	200/200	40	$137,116	Running	10
24. Sharpie 500	Bristol	40	3	500/500	35	$199,591	Running	9
25. Sony HD 500	California	6	2	250/250	0	$206,266	Running	6
26. Chevy Rock & Roll 400	Richmond	33	17	399/400	0	$104,666	Running	6
27. Sylvania 300	New Hamp.	13	13	300/300	0	$115,716	Running	7
28. Dover 400	Dover	13	21	397/400	0	$105,166	Running	7
29. Banquet 400	Kansas	12	10	267/267	18	$135,741	Running	7
30. UAW-Ford 500	Talladega	33	23	188/188	37	$115,866	Running	6
31. Bank of America 500	Lowe's	16	4	334/334	37	$154,916	Running	5
32. Subway 500	Martinsville	7	22	500/500	0	$104,591	Running	6
33. Bass Pro Shops 500	Atlanta	6	3	325/325	95	$215,991	Running	4
34. Dickies 500	Texas	10	6	339/339	1	$187,141	Running	3
35. Checker Auto Parts 500	Phoenix	4	9	312/312	0	$115,041	Running	5
36. Ford 400	Homestead	14	19	268/268	47	$113,216	Running	5

Eury Jr. and Earnhardt Jr.

99 FORD DRIVER PROFILE

Date of birth: August 15, 1979
Hometown: Columbia, Mo.
Resides: Mooresville, N.C.
Spouse: None **Children:** None
Height: 6-1 **Weight:** 185
Hobbies: Riding dirt bikes, remote-control cars, weightlifting

CARL EDWARDS

>>> **Crew chief:** Bob Osborne >>> >>> **Engine builder:** Roush-Yates Engines >>> >>> **Website:** www.roushracing.com >>>

>> NASCAR ACHIEVEMENTS

First NASCAR NEXTEL Cup Series start: August 22, 2004 (Michigan; started 23rd, finished 10th)
Best points finish: 3rd (2005)
Career victories: 4—2005: Atlanta (a,b), Pocono (a), Texas (b)
First victory: March 20, 2005 (Atlanta, career start No. 17)
Last victory: November 6, 2005 (Texas)
Career poles: 2—2005: California (b), Homestead
First pole: September 3, 2005 (California, career start No. 38)
Last pole: November 19, 2005 (Homestead)

>> CAREER HIGHLIGHTS

- His 2005 crew chief, Bob Osborne, was moved to Jamie McMurray's team early in 2006, and Edwards never strung together enough good finishes to be a contender. His strong finish at the night Bristol race suggested his short-track woes are behind him. He showed more emotion this season, getting into highly publicized disputes with Dale Earnhardt Jr. and Tony Stewart.
- Finished third in points in 2005, which was outstanding for a driver in his first full season. Edwards became the first driver to get his first wins in the NASCAR Busch Series and NASCAR NEXTEL Cup Series on the same weekend (spring Atlanta) and the first driver to finish in the top five in points in both series in the same season.
- Jumped from the NASCAR Craftsman Truck Series to the NASCAR NEXTEL Cup Series in August 2004, taking over the No. 99 Ford for Roush Racing after Jeff Burton left. Edwards posted three top 10s in his first four races. Because he ran more than seven NASCAR NEXTEL Cup Series races in 2004, he wasn't classified as a rookie in 2005.

>> FAST FACTS

- Exploded onto the NASCAR Craftsman Truck Series scene in 2003, snagging three wins and Raybestos Rookie of the Year while driving for Roush Racing. He spent the final 18 weeks of the season in the top 10 in points.
- Made seven NASCAR Craftsman Truck Series starts in 2002 and finished in the top 10 at Kansas Speedway. He also won the 2002 Baby Grand national title.

- Won NASCAR Dodge Weekly Racing Series championships at Capital Speedway, near Jefferson City, Mo., in modifieds in 1999 and pro modifieds in 2000.
- Began racing at 13, driving four-cylinder mini-sprints. He won 18 races in the mini-sprint series in four years. In 1997, Edwards switched to dirt-track racing in the IMCA modified division.
- Mike Edwards, his father, won more than 200 feature races at several Midwestern tracks in modifieds and midgets.
- Was a student at the University of Missouri and a part-time substitute teacher before signing with Roush Racing before the 2003 season.

CAREER STATISTICS

Year	Car owner	Races	Champ. finish	Wins	Top 5	Top 10	DNF	Poles	Money won
2004	Jack Roush	13	37	0	1	5	2	0	$1,454,380
2005	Jack Roush	36	3	4	13	18	1	2	$6,893,157
2006	Jack Roush	36	12	0	10	20	3	0	$5,353,629
TOTALS		**85**		**4**	**24**	**43**	**6**	**2**	**$13,701,166**

2006 RESULTS

Race	Track	Start	Finish	Laps	Led	Winnings	Status	Rank
1. Daytona 500	Daytona	5	43	78/203	0	$269,882	Accident	43
2. Auto Club 500	California	22	3	251/251	0	$165,550	Running	21
3. UAW-DaimlerChrysler 400	Las Vegas	21	26	270/270	0	$90,225	Running	23
4. Golden Corral 500	Atlanta	18	40	313/325	0	$85,700	Running	30
5. Food City 500	Bristol	3	4	500/500	0	$122,575	Running	22
6. DIRECTV 500	Martinsville	15	16	500/500	0	$89,100	Running	19
7. Samsung/RadioShack 500	Texas	37	36	256/334	50	$101,175	Accident	22
8. Subway Fresh 500	Phoenix	5	4	312/312	0	$126,685	Running	16
9. Aaron's 499	Talladega	3	8	188/188	7	$118,975	Running	15
10. Crown Royal 400	Richmond	9	7	400/400	0	$100,100	Running	13
11. Dodge Charger 500	Darlington	7	39	281/367	0	$86,550	Engine	17
12. Coca-Cola 600	Lowe's	22	3	400/400	11	$201,050	Running	14
13. Neigh. Excellence 400	Dover	25	15	400/400	2	$104,125	Running	14
14. Pocono 500	Pocono	40	25	199/200	1	$82,775	Running	13
15. 3M Performance 400	Michigan	31	2	129/129	25	$147,200	Running	13
16. Dodge/Save Mart 350	Infineon	20	6	110/110	0	$116,800	Running	13
17. Pepsi 400	Daytona	39	29	156/160	2	$100,650	Running	14
18. USG Sheetrock 400	Chicagoland	21	20	270/270	0	$106,725	Running	14
19. Lenox Industrial Tools 300	New Hamp.	17	2	308/308	0	$177,900	Running	13
20. Pennsylvania 500	Pocono	16	39	196/200	0	$80,125	Running	14
21. Allstate 400 at Brickyard	Indianapolis	22	9	160/160	0	$202,975	Running	14
22. AMD at the Glen	Watkins Glen	21	5	90/90	0	$110,725	Running	14
23. GFS Marketplace 400	Michigan	20	22	200/200	32	$90,750	Running	13
24. Sharpie 500	Bristol	39	7	500/500	16	$128,200	Running	13
25. Sony HD 500	California	24	4	250/250	2	$142,725	Running	12

──────── Carl Edwards continued ────────

2006 RESULTS

Race	Track	Start	Finish	Laps	Led	Winnings	Status	Rank
26. Chevy Rock & Roll 400	Richmond	9	35	397/400	0	$83,550	Running	13
27. Sylvania 300	New Hamp.	19	18	300/300	0	$91,525	Running	13
28. Dover 400	Dover	6	2	400/400	21	$172,850	Running	13
29. Banquet 400	Kansas	27	6	267/267	7	$124,350	Running	13
30. UAW-Ford 500	Talladega	17	9	188/188	0	$102,025	Running	12

Race	Track	Start	Finish	Laps	Led	Winnings	Status	Rank
31. Bank of America 500	Lowe's	28	8	334/334	12	$103,475	Running	12
32. Subway 500	Martinsville	27	12	500/500	0	$90,250	Running	12
33. Bass Pro Shops 500	Atlanta	12	7	325/325	1	$122,575	Running	12
34. Dickies 500	Texas	15	15	339/339	0	$120,050	Running	12
35. Checker Auto Parts 500	Phoenix	12	5	312/312	0	$120,425	Running	12
36. Ford 400	Homestead	31	8	268/268	0	$99,475	Running	12

TEAM FACTS >>> >>> **Primary sponsor:** M&M's >>> >>> **Owner:** Robert Yates >>> >>> **Team:** Robert Yates Racing >>>

38 FORD DRIVER PROFILE

Date of birth: April 1, 1976
Hometown: Chino Hills, Calif.
Resides: Concord, N.C.
Spouse: Michelle
Children: Todd, Taylor
Height: 5-9 **Weight:** 165
Hobbies: Spending time with family, boating

DAVID GILLILAND

>>> **Crew chief:** Todd Parrott >>> >>> **Engine builder:** Roush-Yates Engines >>> >>> **Website:** www.ryr.com >>> >>>

>> NASCAR ACHIEVEMENTS

First NASCAR NEXTEL Cup Series start: June 25, 2006 (Infineon; started 31st, finished 32nd)
Best points finish: 42nd (2006)
Career victories: 0
Best race finish: 15th (Twice, most recently, October 29, 2006, Atlanta)
Career poles: 1—2006: Talladega (b)
First pole: October 7, 2006 (Talladega, career start No. 9)

>> CAREER HIGHLIGHTS

- His NASCAR Busch Series win at Kentucky vaulted him to the top of many owners' wish lists during the 2006 season. In August, he took over the No. 38 Ford, replacing Elliott Sadler. Gilliland struggled at the NASCAR NEXTEL Cup Series level—he didn't finish on the lead lap until his ninth race—though he did score his first pole at Talladega.
- Made his NASCAR NEXTEL Cup Series debut for CJM Racing at Infineon Raceway in 2006. It was the first time a CJM Racing car had qualified for a NASCAR NEXTEL Cup Series event.

>> FAST FACTS

- Wowed the NASCAR world by winning the NASCAR Busch Series race at Kentucky in June 2006 while driving for Clay Andrews Racing, which dissolved later in the season.
- Made his debut in the NASCAR Busch Series in Phoenix in April 2005, starting 38th and finishing 43rd.
- Raced full-time in the NASCAR Grand National Division, AutoZone West Series in 2005 and finished fourth in the standings with one win and nine top fives. He also won the NASCAR Toyota All-Star Showdown at Irwindale Speedway.

- Won his first NASCAR Grand National Division, AutoZone West Series race in 2004 at Mesa Marin Speedway in Bakersfield, Calif. He also was the 2004 AutoZone West Series rookie of the year.
- Finished sixth in the standings for the NASCAR AutoZone Elite Division, Southwest Series in 2003 after winning five races and racking up eight top 10s.
- Is the son of former NASCAR NEXTEL Cup Series driver Butch Gilliland, who made 10 NASCAR NEXTEL Cup Series starts in the 1990s. David got his start in NASCAR in 1996 as his father's crew chief in the NASCAR Grand National Division, AutoZone West Series.

CAREER STATISTICS

Year	Car owner	Races	Champ. finish	Wins	Top 5	Top 10	DNF	Poles	Money won
2006	Robert Yates	14	42	0	0	0	1	1	$1,496,851
	Bryan Mullet	1		0	0	0	0	0	$68,050
TOTALS		**15**		**0**	**0**	**0**	**1**	**1**	**$1,564,901**

2006 RESULTS

Race	Track	Start	Finish	Laps	Led	Winnings	Status	Rank
16. Dodge/Save Mart 350	Infineon	31	32	108/110	0	$68,050	Running	58
23. GFS Marketplace 400	Michigan	26	38	145/200	0	$96,508	Running	57
24. Sharpie 500	Bristol	38	40	346/500	0	$109,758	Running	54
25. Sony HD 500	California	20	32	248/250	0	$112,208	Running	52
26. Chevy Rock & Roll 400	Richmond	24	36	396/400	0	$91,508	Running	49
27. Sylvania 300	New Hamp.	15	36	291/300	0	$95,808	Running	48
28. Dover 400	Dover	39	27	396/400	0	$96,758	Running	46
29. Banquet 400	Kansas	20	22	266/267	0	$114,033	Running	44
30. UAW-Ford 500	Talladega	1	15	188/188	0	$112,808	Running	43
31. Bank of America 500	Lowe's	35	33	161/334	0	$89,958	Accident	43
32. Subway 500	Martinsville	29	28	496/500	0	$96,243	Running	43
33. Bass Pro Shops 500	Atlanta	25	15	323/325	0	$122,558	Running	43
34. Dickies 500	Texas	7	21	338/339	0	$126,908	Running	42
35. Checker Auto Parts 500	Phoenix	13	16	312/312	1	$97,858	Running	42
36. Ford 400	Homestead	9	33	257/268	0	$90,483	Running	42

24 CHEVROLET DRIVER PROFILE

Date of birth: August 4, 1971
Hometown: Vallejo, Calif.
Resides: Charlotte and New York
Spouse: Ingrid **Children:** None
Height: 5-7 **Weight:** 150
Hobbies: Skiing, video games, golf, racquetball, scuba diving

JEFF GORDON

>>> **Crew chief:** Steve Letarte >>> >>> **Engine builder:** Hendrick Engines >>> >>> **Website:** www.hendrickmotorsports.com

>> NASCAR ACHIEVEMENTS

First NASCAR NEXTEL Cup Series start: November 15, 1992 (Atlanta; started 21st, finished 31st)

Best points finish: 1 (1995, 1997, 1998, 2001)

Career victories: 75—2006: Infineon, Chicagoland; 2005: Daytona (a), Martinsville (a,b), Talladega (a); 2004: California (a), Talladega (a), Infineon (a), Daytona (b), Indianapolis; 2003: Martinsville (a,b), Atlanta (b); 2002: Kansas, Bristol (b), Darlington (b); 2001: Las Vegas, Dover (a), Michigan (a), Indianapolis, Watkins Glen, Kansas; 2000: Talladega (a), Infineon, Richmond (b); 1999: Daytona (a), Atlanta (a), California, Infineon, Watkins Glen, Martinsville (b), Lowe's (b); 1998: Rockingham (a,b), Bristol (a), Lowe's (a), Infineon, Pocono (b), Indianapolis, Watkins Glen, Michigan (b), New Hampshire (b), Darlington (b), Daytona (b), Atlanta (b); 1997: Daytona (a), Rockingham (a), Bristol (a), Martinsville (a), Lowe's (a), Pocono (a), California, Watkins Glen, Darlington (b), New Hampshire (b); 1996: Richmond (a), Darlington (a,b), Bristol (a), Dover (a,b), Pocono (a), Talladega (b), Martinsville (b), North Wilkesboro; 1995: Rockingham (a), Atlanta (a), Bristol (a), Daytona (b), New Hampshire, Darlington (b), Dover (b); 1994: Lowe's (a), Indianapolis

First victory: May 29, 1994 (Lowe's, career start No. 42)

Last victory: July 9, 2006 (Chicagoland)

Career poles: 56—2006: Dover (b), Phoenix (b); 2005: Phoenix (a), Infineon; 2004: Martinsville (a), Michigan (a), Infineon, Daytona (b), Chicagoland, Bristol (b); 2003: Martinsville (a,b), Watkins Glen, Bristol (b); 2002: Bristol (a,b), Martinsville (a); 2001: Rockingham (a), Martinsville (a), Michigan (a), Infineon, New Hampshire (a), Richmond (b); 2000: Darlington (a), Lowe's (b), Atlanta (b); 1999: Daytona (a), Darlington (a),Richmond (a), Michigan (a), Infineon, New Hampshire (a), Indianapolis; 1998: California, Lowe's (a), Richmond (a),Pocono (a), Infineon, Watkins Glen, New Hampshire (b); 1997: Lowe's (a); 1996: Lowe's (a), Dover (a), Pocono (a), Daytona (b), Indianapolis; 1995: Darlington (a), Rockingham (a), Richmond (a), North Wilkesboro (a), Lowe's (a), Dover (a), Michigan (a), Indianapolis; 1994: Lowe's (a); 1993: Lowe's (b)

First pole: October 8, 1993 (Lowe's, career start No. 28)

Last pole: November 10, 2006 (Phoenix)

>> CAREER HIGHLIGHTS

- Had a good year in 2006—he qualified for the Chase for the NASCAR NEXTEL Cup and got married. Still, every season he doesn't win the championship is a disappointment. His team struggled with mid-race changes—good cars were not made great, and great cars were made good. He had championship hopes until consecutive bad finishes at Kansas and Talladega.
- After three wins in the first nine races of 2005, his season fell apart, and Gordon finished out of the top 10 for the first time since his rookie season. He struggled mightily on intermediate tracks. Robbie Loomis—only Gordon's second crew chief—left with 10 races remaining, and longtime crew member Steve Letarte took over atop the pitbox.
- Was near the top of the standings all season in 2004, showing a renewed focus and passion. He led the points going into the Chase for the NASCAR NEXTEL Cup but didn't win a race during the Chase or put together a streak necessary to win the title.
- A rough midseason stretch with five of six finishes outside of the top 20 left Gordon out of the championship race in 2003. But he led more laps than any other driver on the NASCAR NEXTEL Cup Series.
- A win at Darlington in 2002 pushed him up to second in points with 11 races to go, but four finishes of 36th or lower in the following seven races ended his shot at a fifth NASCAR NEXTEL Cup Series championship.
- Became part-owner, with Rick Hendrick, of Jimmie Johnson's No. 48 team in 2002.
- Bounced back from a down season in 2000 with his fourth NASCAR NEXTEL Cup Series championship in 2001, placing him third on the list of all-time champs behind seven-time winners Richard Petty and Dale Earnhardt. Gordon led the circuit in wins and poles with six, marking the sixth time in seven years he posted more wins than any other driver.
- Won the NASCAR All-Star race for the third time in his career in 2001, tying Dale Earnhardt for the most wins in the event. He also won the inaugural event at Kansas.
- Finished ninth in points in 2000, his lowest finish since 1993. He didn't have back-to-back wins for the first time since

———————————— Jeff Gordon continued ————————————

1995, and his three victories were his fewest since 1994.
- Holds the record for most consecutive years leading the series in wins with five (1995-1999).
- Won his third NASCAR NEXTEL Cup Series championship in 1998, his third in four seasons, and became the youngest three-time champ at 27. He tied Richard Petty's modern-era record for most wins in a season (13) and tied Cale Yarborough, Dale Earnhardt and Mark Martin for most consecutive wins with four (Pocono, Indianapolis, Watkins Glen, Michigan) during a season.
- Won his second NASCAR NEXTEL Cup Series championship in 1997. Also became the first driver to win more than $6 million in a season and the youngest driver, at 26, to win the Daytona 500.
- Mechanical problems in the 1996 season finale at Atlanta put him two laps down in the 10th lap and ended his chances to catch eventual champion Terry Labonte. Gordon finished second in series points, 37 behind Labonte.
- Became the youngest champion in the modern era, at 24, when he won his first NASCAR NEXTEL Cup Series championship in 1995. He won eight poles and won back-to-back races for the first time in his career.
- Won the inaugural Brickyard 400 in his adopted home state of Indiana in 1994.
- At 23, was the youngest driver in 30 years to win a Gatorade 125 qualifying race at Daytona in 1993.
- Was the first driver to have won Rookie of the Year honors in both the NASCAR Busch Series (1991) and NASCAR NEXTEL Cup Series when he was named the Raybestos Rookie of the Year in 1993.

- His first career race was the final race of the 1992 season at Atlanta, the last in the illustrious career of "The King," Richard Petty.

>>FAST FACTS

- Is ranked seventh in career NASCAR NEXTEL Cup Series wins with 75 and leads all-time money winnings with $82,358,526.
- Hosted Saturday Night Live on January 11, 2003, and has made several guest host appearances on Live with Regis and Kelly.
- Set the NASCAR Busch Series record with 11 poles in 1992; also won three races that season—all from the pole.
- Named NASCAR Busch Series Raybestos Rookie of the Year in 1991 following an 11th place finish in the points standings.
- Won the USAC Silver Crown Series championship in 1991.
- Was the 1990 USAC Midget champion at age 19, making him the youngest driver ever to win the title; was also the youngest driver ever awarded a USAC license at 16.
- Won three quarter-midget national championships and four karting titles.
- Won more than 600 short-track races as a youngster after beginning the sport in his native California at age 5; the family later relocated to Pittsboro, Ind., where he honed his skills.
- Is one of NASCAR's most active drivers on behalf of charitable causes. The Jeff Gordon Foundation, founded in 1999, primarily supports charities working on behalf of children in need. The Foundation supports the Leukemia & Lymphoma Society, the Make-A-Wish Foundation, the Hendrick Bone Marrow Foundation and Riley Hospital for Children in Indianapolis.

CAREER STATISTICS

Year	Car owner	Races	Champ. finish	Wins	Top 5	Top 10	DNF	Poles	Money won
1992	Rick Hendrick	1	81	0	0	0	1	0	$6,285
1993	Rick Hendrick	30	14	0	7	11	11	1	$765,168
1994	Rick Hendrick	31	8	2	7	14	10	1	$1,779,523
1995	Rick Hendrick	31	1	7	17	23	3	8	$4,347,343
1996	Rick Hendrick	31	2	10	21	24	5	5	$3,428,485
1997	Rick Hendrick	32	1	10	22	23	2	1	$6,375,658
1998	Rick Hendrick	33	1	13	26	28	2	7	$9,306,584
1999	Rick Hendrick	34	6	7	18	21	7	7	$5,858,633
2000	Rick Hendrick	34	9	3	11	22	2	3	$3,001,144
2001	Rick Hendrick	36	1	6	18	24	2	6	$10,879,757
2002	Rick Hendrick	36	4	3	13	20	3	3	$6,154,475
2003	Rick Hendrick	36	4	3	15	20	5	4	$6,622,002
2004	Rick Hendrick	36	3	5	16	25	4	6	$8,431,192
2005	Rick Hendrick	36	11	4	8	14	9	2	$7,930,830
2006	Rick Hendrick	36	6	2	14	18	7	2	$7,471,447
TOTALS		473		75	213	287	73	56	$82,358,526

2006 RESULTS

Race	Track	Start	Finish	Laps	Led	Winnings	Status	Rank
1. Daytona 500	Daytona	2	26	203/203	1	$334,879	Running	25
2. Auto Club 500	California	9	13	251/251	3	$127,261	Running	15
3. UAW-DaimlerChrysler 400	Las Vegas	13	5	270/270	0	$165,686	Running	9
4. Golden Corral 500	Atlanta	12	4	325/325	1	$137,236	Running	6
5. Food City 500	Bristol	11	21	500/500	3	$129,336	Running	7
6. DIRECTV 500	Martinsville	8	2	500/500	0	$153,461	Running	7
7. Samsung/RadioShack 500	Texas	11	22	332/334	0	$148,411	Running	8
8. Subway Fresh 500	Phoenix	19	10	312/312	0	$124,111	Running	6
9. Aaron's 499	Talladega	14	15	188/188	62	$151,311	Running	6
10. Crown Royal 400	Richmond	16	40	286/400	0	$110,861	Engine	9
11. Dodge Charger 500	Darlington	12	2	367/367	5	$223,161	Running	6
12. Coca-Cola 600	Lowe's	13	36	360/400	18	$133,111	Accident	7
13. Neigh. Excellence 400	Dover	3	12	400/400	81	$133,011	Running	9
14. Pocono 500	Pocono	6	34	189/200	0	$109,461	Accident	11
15. 3M Performance 400	Michigan	2	8	129/129	50	$137,436	Running	11
16. Dodge/Save Mart 350	Infineon	11	1	110/110	44	$325,061	Running	9
17. Pepsi 400	Daytona	4	40	154/160	27	$129,036	Accident	12
18. USG Sheetrock 400	Chicagoland	13	1	270/270	20	$327,761	Running	10
19. Lenox Industrial Tools 300	New Hamp.	7	15	308/308	1	$121,961	Running	9
20. Pennsylvania 500	Pocono	5	3	200/200	3	$175,961	Running	9
21. Allstate 400 at Brickyard	Indianapolis	16	16	160/160	0	$198,236	Running	8
22. AMD at the Glen	Watkins Glen	4	13	90/90	1	$113,736	Running	9
23. GFS Marketplace 400	Michigan	12	2	200/200	12	$161,061	Running	6
24. Sharpie 500	Bristol	13	5	500/500	41	$171,636	Running	5
25. Sony HD 500	California	5	5	250/250	42	$160,061	Running	4
26. Chevy Rock & Roll 400	Richmond	3	31	398/400	0	$112,611	Running	4
27. Sylvania 300	New Hamp.	2	3	300/300	34	$171,536	Running	4
28. Dover 400	Dover	1	3	400/400	0	$181,836	Running	2
29. Banquet 400	Kansas	11	39	238/267	0	$125,361	Fuel pump	6
30. UAW-Ford 500	Talladega	4	36	167/188	27	$117,636	Accident	6
31. Bank of America 500	Lowe's	41	24	301/334	2	$111,236	Engine	10
32. Subway 500	Martinsville	2	5	500/500	165	$148,686	Running	9
33. Bass Pro Shops 500	Atlanta	9	6	325/325	44	$158,561	Running	7
34. Dickies 500	Texas	23	9	339/339	0	$166,586	Running	6
35. Checker Auto Parts 500	Phoenix	1	4	312/312	0	$165,061	Running	6
36. Ford 400	Homestead	12	24	267/268	0	$112,786	Running	6

7 FORD
DRIVER PROFILE
Date of birth: January 2, 1969
Hometown: Bellflower, Calif.
Resides: Cornelius, N.C.
Spouse: None **Children:** None
Height: 5-10 **Weight:** 180
Hobbies: Mountain biking, water skiing, motorcycling, go-karting

ROBBY GORDON

Crew chief: Greg Erwin >>> >>> **Engine builder:** Roush-Yates Engines >>> >>> **Website:** www.robbygordon.com >>>

NASCAR ACHIEVEMENTS

First NASCAR NEXTEL Cup Series start: February 17, 1991 (Daytona; started 35th, finished 18th)
Best points finish: 16th (2003)
Career victories: 3—2003: Infineon, Watkins Glen; 2001: New Hampshire (b)
First victory: November 23, 2001 (New Hampshire, career start No. 62)
Last victory: August 10, 2003 (Watkins Glen)
Career poles: 1—1997: Atlanta (a)
First pole: March 7, 1997 (Atlanta, career start No. 11)

CAREER HIGHLIGHTS

- Put up solid results in 2006 for a self-owned team but was hurt by nine DNFs. Though he did not win a race and finished 30th in points, by qualifying for every race, Gordon showed vast improvement over 2005. He'll switch from Chevy to Ford for the 2007 season.
- Because of engine problems, he failed to qualify for several races in 2005, his first full season as owner/driver, and blew up too often when he made the show. He made headlines in a bad way at New Hampshire, when he threw his helmet at Michael Waltrip's car. He ran better the final couple of races after switching to Dale Earnhardt Inc. engines.
- Got into Richard Childress' doghouse in 2004 when he intentionally wrecked Greg Biffle at New Hampshire in the first race of the Chase for the NASCAR NEXTEL Cup—taking out Tony Stewart and Jeremy Mayfield in the process—and lost his No. 31 ride.
- Swept the road courses in 2003 (Infineon, Watkins Glen), and his two wins and 16th-place finish in points were career bests. The best stretch of his season—a win sandwiched between two sixth-place finishes—was followed by his worst stretch: In the last 13 races, his best finish was 12th; the rest of his finishes were 20th or worse.
- Has been at his best at road courses, getting his only top five in 1997 at Watkins Glen, two top 10s in 2000 at Infineon and Watkins Glen and his only top five in 2002 at Watkins Glen.
- Completed his first full season in the NASCAR NEXTEL Cup Series in 2002.
- Returned to NASCAR NEXTEL Cup Series racing in 2000 in a car he co-owned with Mike Held and John Menard after a one-year hiatus.
- Won his only career pole in 1997 in Atlanta.
- Had one start in 1993, and it was significant. He drove the No. 28 Texaco Havoline Ford at Talladega in that team's first race since the death of Davey Allison.
- Made only seven starts in the NASCAR NEXTEL Cup Series from his debut in 1991 through 1996, failing to produce any top 10s. He had five DNFs.

FAST FACTS

- Completed the Coca-Cola 600/Indianapolis 500 double in 2002 and 2003.
- Qualified third and led 22 laps in the 2001 Indianapolis 500.
- Perhaps his most famous moment came at the 1999 Indianapolis 500. After leading 33 laps, he ran out of fuel while leading on the race's final lap.
- Drove for his own CART series team in 1999 and for Arciero-Wells Racing in 1998.
- Finished second in the 1996 and 1997 IROC series.
- Won the 1996 SCORE Off-Road Trophy Truck Championship with four wins.
- Won CART races at Detroit and Phoenix in 1995 and finished fifth in the point standings.
- First full IndyCar season was in 1993, driving for the legendary A.J. Foyt.
- Won GTS class in IMSA 24 Hours of Daytona in 1993, his fourth straight victory in that event, all for car owner Jack Roush.
- Won Sports Car Club of America Trans-Am race at Long Beach, Calif., in 1992, also for Roush Racing.
- In 1991, won five IMSA GTO races in a Roush Racing Ford Mustang.
- Finished second in 1990 GTO season standings.
- Winner of the Baja 1000 in 1987 and 1989.
- Was the SCORE Off-Road champion for five straight years, beginning in 1985.

––––––––– Robby Gordon continued –––––––––

- Nickname is "Flash."
- His pre-race ritual is eating a turkey sandwich for lunch.
- Is an outstanding trick water skier.
- First job was working in his dad's feed yard raking chaff

(strands left over from bales of hay).
- Opened "Robby Gordon Off-Road," an off-road race shop for himself and off-road enthusiasts, in April 2003 in Anaheim.

CAREER STATISTICS

Year	Car owner	Races	Champ. finish	Wins	Top 5	Top 10	DNF	Poles	Money won
1991	Junie Donlavey	2	55	0	0	0	0	0	$27,265
1993	Robert Yates	1	94	0	0	0	1	0	$17,665
1994	Michael Kranefuss	1	76	0	0	0	1	0	$7,965
1996	Chip Ganassi	2	57	0	0	0	2	0	$29,115
	Teresa Earnhardt	1		0	0	0	1	0	$4,800
1997	Chip Ganassi	20	40	0	1	1	7	1	$622,439
1998	Buz McCall	1	67	0	0	0	1	0	$24,765
2000	M. Held/J. Menard	17	43	0	1	2	7	0	$620,781
2001	Richard Childress	10	44	1	1	2	1	0	$917,020
	Larry McClure	5		0	0	0	1	0	$287,545
	J. Smith/R. Evernham	2		0	1	1	0	0	$167,335
2002	Richard Childress	36	20	0	1	5	4	0	$3,342,703
2003	Richard Childress	36	16	2	4	10	2	0	$4,157,064
2004	Richard Childress	36	23	0	2	6	3	0	$4,225,719
2004	Richard Childress	36	23	0	2	6	3	0	$4,225,719
2005	Robby Gordon	29	37	0	1	2	13	0	$2,271,313
2006	Robby Gordon	36	30	0	1	3	9	0	$3,143,787
TOTALS		235		3	13	32	53	1	$19,867,281

2006 RESULTS

Race	Track	Start	Finish	Laps	Led	Winnings	Status	Rank
1. Daytona 500	Daytona	20	13	203/203	0	$269,558	Running	14
2. Auto Club 500	California	34	26	249/251	0	$95,075	Running	17
3. UAW-DaimlerChrysler 400	Las Vegas	32	12	270/270	0	$101,300	Running	14
4. Golden Corral 500	Atlanta	36	28	324/325	0	$69,810	Running	19
5. Food City 500	Bristol	37	26	497/500	0	$83,300	Running	20
6. DIRECTV 500	Martinsville	27	43	7/500	0	$64,384	Engine	27
7. Samsung/RadioShack 500	Texas	29	20	333/334	0	$109,275	Running	27
8. Subway Fresh 500	Phoenix	25	41	116/312	0	$60,560	Engine	31
9. Aaron's 499	Talladega	19	10	188/188	1	$103,350	Running	28
10. Crown Royal 400	Richmond	39	39	345/400	0	$62,650	Accident	32
11. Dodge Charger 500	Darlington	24	13	367/367	1	$85,225	Running	28
12. Coca-Cola 600	Lowe's	41	16	400/400	0	$98,075	Running	28
13. Neigh. Excellence 400	Dover	41	36	394/400	0	$73,525	Running	28
14. Pocono 500	Pocono	28	35	186/200	0	$60,975	Running	29
15. 3M Performance 400	Michigan	24	18	129/129	0	$76,025	Running	28
16. Dodge/Save Mart 350	Infineon	14	40	74/110	0	$67,125	Accident	29
17. Pepsi 400	Daytona	25	14	160/160	4	$97,475	Running	28
18. USG Sheetrock 400	Chicagoland	30	19	270/270	0	$88,125	Running	28
19. Lenox Industrial Tools 300	New Hamp.	34	19	308/308	0	$75,125	Running	28
20. Pennsylvania 500	Pocono	29	13	200/200	0	$74,725	Running	27
21. Allstate 400 at Brickyard	Indianapolis	9	35	160/160	0	$134,925	Running	27
22. AMD at the Glen	Watkins Glen	6	4	90/90	0	$108,100	Running	26
23. GFS Marketplace 400	Michigan	24	12	200/200	0	$78,800	Running	24
24. Sharpie 500	Bristol	42	27	498/500	0	$86,705	Running	24
25. Sony HD 500	California	25	43	193/250	0	$83,201	Transmission	26
26. Chevy Rock & Roll 400	Richmond	19	39	399/400	0	$69,300	Running	26
27. Sylvania 300	New Hamp.	9	15	300/300	2	$77,425	Running	25
28. Dover 400	Dover	14	41	98/400	0	$63,610	Accident	27
29. Banquet 400	Kansas	42	36	263/267	0	$77,650	Running	27
30. UAW-Ford 500	Talladega	36	16	188/188	0	$77,050	Running	27
31. Bank of America 500	Lowe's	19	25	300/334	0	$66,075	Running	28
32. Subway 500	Martinsville	26	37	416/500	0	$64,525	Rear end	28
33. Bass Pro Shops 500	Atlanta	29	10	325/325	0	$104,975	Running	28
34. Dickies 500	Texas	9	39	256/339	0	$92,050	Engine	30
35. Checker Auto Parts 500	Phoenix	40	32	307/312	0	$62,400	Running	30
36. Ford 400	Homestead	35	40	187/268	0	$60,175	Accident	30

TEAM FACTS >>> >>> **Primary sponsor:** Best Buy >>> >>> **Owner:** Gene Haas >>> >>> **Team:** Haas CNC Racing >>> >>>

66 CHEVROLET DRIVER PROFILE

Date of birth: September 6, 1962
Hometown: Owensboro, Ky.
Resides: Davidson, N.C.
Spouse: Michelle **Children:** None
Height: 5-8 **Weight:** 190
Hobbies: Hunting, radio-controlled cars

JEFF GREEN

Crew chief: Harold Holly >>> >>> **Engine builder:** Hendrick Engines >>> >>> **Website:** www.haasracing.com >>> >>>

>> NASCAR ACHIEVEMENTS

First NASCAR NEXTEL Cup Series start: September 10, 1994 (Richmond; started 34th, finished 36th)
Best points finish: 17th (2002)
Career victories: 0
Best race finish: 2nd (July 21, 2002, New Hampshire)
Career poles: 2—2003: Daytona (a); 2001: Bristol (b)
First pole: August 24, 2001 (Bristol, career start No. 55)
Last pole: February 9, 2003 (Daytona)

>> CAREER HIGHLIGHTS

- Green's best finish of the 2006 season, his first driving for Haas CNC Racing, was seventh, at the second Talladega race. It was one of two top 10s Green scored in 2006, which was Green's first season with multiple top 10 finishes since 2002.
- Struggled through a difficult 2005. A deal with Evernham Motorsports provided Petty Enterprises with better engines, and the cars were reliable, but they weren't fast. He had zero top 10 finishes and lost his ride with Petty.

- The No. 43 Petty Enterprises team didn't post its first top 10 in 2004 until the 32nd race and finished a disappointing 30th in points. The highlight was third-place qualifying runs at California and Richmond on back-to-back weekends.
- Raced for the big boys (Richard Childress Racing, Dale Earnhardt Inc. and Petty Enterprises) in 2003 but posted just one top 10 (Texas). His season started well, as he won the pole at the Daytona 500. But he was involved in an accident and finished 39th.
- Completed his first full NASCAR NEXTEL Cup Series season in 2002 and finished 17th in series points. He had a career-high four top fives, but qualifying problems hindered him— he qualified in the top 10 only twice.
- Made eight NASCAR NEXTEL Cup Series starts in 2001, all for Childress.
- Left the NASCAR Busch Series at midseason to drive for

Gary Bechtel in 1997. Green qualified fourth in his first race. He finished third for Raybestos Rookie of the Year behind Mike Skinner and his brother, David.

>> FAST FACTS
- Finished second in 2001 NASCAR Busch Series' points.
- Won the 2000 NASCAR Busch Series championship by a record 616 points over second-place Jason Keller.
- Green and brother David, the 1994 NASCAR Busch Series champion, were the first siblings both to win a major auto racing championship.
- Also competed in NASCAR late model stock cars, winning the 1990 track championship at Music City Metroplex in Nashville.
- First racing experience was in go-karts.
- With his brothers, Mark and David, began the Green Foundation, a charity organization, in 2002.

CAREER STATISTICS

Year	Car owner	Races	Champ. finish	Wins	Top 5	Top 10	DNF	Poles	Money won
1994	Earl Sadler	2	51	0	0	0	1	0	$11,455
	Junior Johnson	1		0	0	0	0	0	$8,815
1996	Gary Bechtel	2	49	0	0	0	0	0	$30,040
	Teresa Earnhardt	2		0	0	0	2	0	$16,835
1997	Gary Bechtel	20	39	0	1	2	4	0	$434,685
1998	Chip Ganassi	18	40	0	0	0	7	0	$449,611
	Gary Bechtel	3		0	0	0	0	0	$107,880
	Chuck Rider	1		0	0	0	0	0	$32,350
1999	Chip Ganassi	1	60	0	0	0	0	0	$62,921
2001	Richard Childress	8	48	0	0	1	3	1	$441,449
2002	Richard Childress	36	17	0	4	6	2	0	$2,531,339
2003	Teresa Earnhardt	12	34	0	0	2	0	0	$1,020,671
	Richard Childress	11		0	0	1	2	1	$987,249
	Petty Enterprises	8		0	0	0	2	0	$715,044
2004	Petty Enterprises	36	30	0	0	1	11	0	$3,443,537
2005	Petty Enterprises	36	29	0	0	0	2	0	$4,040,428
2006	Gene Haas	36	28	0	0	2	4	0	$3,767,754
TOTALS		**233**		**0**	**5**	**13**	**42**	**2**	**$18,112,531**

2006 RESULTS

Race	Track	Start	Finish	Laps	Led	Winnings	Status	Rank
1. Daytona 500	Daytona	21	42	156/203	0	$253,153	Running	42
2. Auto Club 500	California	26	24	250/251	0	$121,058	Running	35
3. UAW-DaimlerChrysler 400	Las Vegas	14	18	270/270	0	$119,508	Running	30
4. Golden Corral 500	Atlanta	39	26	324/325	0	$90,033	Running	31
5. Food City 500	Bristol	29	15	500/500	0	$113,458	Running	28
6. DIRECTV 500	Martinsville	34	25	491/500	0	$90,483	Running	28
7. Samsung/RadioShack 500	Texas	4	18	334/334	1	$133,833	Running	26
8. Subway Fresh 500	Phoenix	23	18	311/312	0	$91,808	Running	23
9. Aaron's 499	Talladega	39	14	188/188	1	$117,808	Running	21
10. Crown Royal 400	Richmond	25	18	399/400	0	$93,363	Running	21
11. Dodge Charger 500	Darlington	28	32	363/367	0	$75,975	Running	25
12. Coca-Cola 600	Lowe's	10	12	400/400	16	$131,033	Running	21
13. Neigh. Excellence 400	Dover	12	28	398/400	0	$99,958	Running	22
14. Pocono 500	Pocono	19	37	181/200	0	$68,575	Rear end	26
15. 3M Performance 400	Michigan	27	33	129/129	0	$77,300	Running	26
16. Dodge/Save Mart 350	Infineon	23	19	110/110	0	$102,833	Running	26
17. Pepsi 400	Daytona	36	26	160/160	0	$109,383	Running	25
18. USG Sheetrock 400	Chicagoland	22	27	269/270	0	$100,447	Running	26
19. Lenox Industrial Tools 300	New Hamp.	35	26	307/308	0	$90,647	Running	26
20. Pennsylvania 500	Pocono	32	35	199/200	0	$68,975	Running	28
21. Allstate 400 at Brickyard	Indianapolis	29	38	159/160	0	$142,625	Running	28
22. AMD at the Glen	Watkins Glen	22	15	90/90	0	$91,233	Running	28
23. GFS Marketplace 400	Michigan	35	27	200/200	0	$92,493	Running	27
24. Sharpie 500	Bristol	16	24	498/500	0	$96,975	Running	27
25. Sony HD 500	California	30	22	249/250	0	$113,783	Running	27
26. Chevy Rock & Roll 400	Richmond	34	41	273/400	0	$70,960	Parked	30
27. Sylvania 300	New Hamp.	20	43	2/300	0	$75,139	Accident	30
28. Dover 400	Dover	28	20	397/400	0	$92,883	Running	30
29. Banquet 400	Kansas	31	30	264/267	0	$87,350	Running	30
30. UAW-Ford 500	Talladega	37	7	188/188	0	$116,783	Running	30
31. Bank of America 500	Lowe's	20	16	332/334	0	$91,583	Running	29
32. Subway 500	Martinsville	8	8	500/500	0	$118,583	Running	27
33. Bass Pro Shops 500	Atlanta	28	23	322/325	0	$106,133	Running	27
34. Dickies 500	Texas	27	13	339/339	0	$130,058	Running	26
35. Checker Auto Parts 500	Phoenix	25	37	298/312	0	$69,750	Accident	27
36. Ford 400	Homestead	27	22	267/268	0	$89,458	Running	28

Green

TEAM FACTS >>> >>> **Primary sponsor:** FedEx >>> >>> **Owner:** Joe Gibbs >>> >>> **Team:** Joe Gibbs Racing >>> >>>

11 CHEVROLET DRIVER PROFILE

Date of birth: November 18, 1980
Hometown: Chesterfield, Va.
Resides: Davidson, N.C.
Spouse: None **Children:** None
Height: 6-0 **Weight:** 170
Hobbies: Online racing, spending time with family and friends

DENNY HAMLIN

Crew chief: Mike Ford >>> >>> **Engine builder:** Mark Cronquist >>> >>> **Website:** www.joegibbsracing.com >>> >>>

>> NASCAR ACHIEVEMENTS

First NASCAR NEXTEL Cup Series start: October 9, 2005 (Kansas; started 7th, finished 32nd)
Best points finish: 3rd (2006)
Career victories: 2—2006: Pocono (a,b)
First victory: June 11, 2006 (Pocono, career start No. 21)
Last victory: July 23, 2006 (Pocono)
Career poles: 4—2006: Pocono (a,b), Richmond (b); 2005: Phoenix (b)
First pole: November 12, 2005 (Phoenix, career start No. 6)
Last pole: September 8, 2006 (Richmond)

>> CAREER HIGHLIGHTS

- Stunned the sport in February 2006 with a win at the Budweiser Shootout at Daytona. Hamlin followed that up with two wins at Pocono, three poles and a Raybestos Rookie of the Year award. He also became the first rookie to qualify for the Chase for the NASCAR NEXTEL Cup. He showed remarkable consistency and versatility, racing well at every type of track. His third-place points finish was the best by a rookie in the modern era and best since James Hylton finished second in 1966.
- Hamlin's quick success in the NASCAR Busch Series in 2005 caught the attention of owner Joe Gibbs, who used Hamlin as a fill-in driver for the No. 11 NASCAR NEXTEL Cup Series car late in the season. Hamlin made the most of his starts, scoring three top 10s and a pole in seven races.

>> FAST FACTS

- Made his first NASCAR Busch Series start in 2004 at Darlington and finished eighth, a sign of things to come. Hamlin raced full-time in the NASCAR Busch Series in 2005, notched 11 top 10s and finished fifth in points. He had only three DNFs.
- Raced five NASCAR Craftsman Truck Series events in 2004, getting a top 10 at Indianapolis Raceway Park, for which he qualified seventh, and finishing 11th at New Hampshire.
- Won the Southern National Speedway Track Championship in 2003, posting 25 wins, 33 top fives and 30 poles that season. He won races at five different tracks in 2003: South Boston, Hickory, Southampton, Southern National and Coastal Plains.
- Began racing late models in 2000 and won rookie of the year at Southside Speedway.
- In his second season in the NASCAR Grand Stock Division (1999), he won the Most Popular Driver Award for his division after earning five feature wins and 17 top fives in 25 races.
- Moved to mini stock cars at age 16 and was the NASCAR Mini Stock Rookie of the Year at Southside and Langley Speedways in Virginia. He was the youngest driver to win a NASCAR Mini Stock track title at Langley Speedway.
- Started racing at age 7 in Junior Sportsman competition. Hamlin got off to a quick start; he won the first race he entered.
- Bill Elliott is his racing hero.
- Joins Dale Earnhardt Jr. as a NASCAR NEXTEL Cup Series driver whose favorite NFL team is the Redskins.

CAREER STATISTICS

Year	Car owner	Races	Champ. finish	Wins	Top 5	Top 10	DNF	Poles	Money won
2005	Joe Gibbs	7	41	0	0	3	0	1	$610,030
2006	Joe Gibbs	36	3	2	8	20	1	3	$6,607,932
TOTALS		**43**		**2**	**8**	**23**	**1**	**4**	**$7,217,962**

2006 RESULTS

Race	Track	Start	Finish	Laps	Led	Winnings	Status	Rank
1. Daytona 500	Daytona	17	30	203/203	0	$254,833	Running	31
2. Auto Club 500	California	5	12	251/251	0	$104,575	Running	20
3. UAW-DaimlerChrysler 400	Las Vegas	16	10	270/270	0	$109,650	Running	16
4. Golden Corral 500	Atlanta	7	31	323/325	16	$70,125	Running	20
5. Food City 500	Bristol	33	14	500/500	0	$88,000	Running	17
6. DIRECTV 500	Martinsville	41	37	307/500	0	$65,250	Accident	23
7. Samsung/RadioShack 500	Texas	8	4	334/334	41	$208,500	Running	14
8. Subway Fresh 500	Phoenix	6	34	289/312	0	$61,500	Running	18
9. Aaron's 499	Talladega	30	22	187/188	1	$84,625	Running	19
10. Crown Royal 400	Richmond	7	2	400/400	19	$165,200	Running	16
11. Dodge Charger 500	Darlington	5	10	367/367	0	$97,900	Running	13
12. Coca-Cola 600	Lowe's	8	9	400/400	25	$111,000	Running	11
13. Neigh. Excellence 400	Dover	7	11	400/400	0	$94,200	Running	11
14. Pocono 500	Pocono	1	1	200/200	83	$220,100	Running	9
15. 3M Performance 400	Michigan	21	12	129/129	0	$78,925	Running	9
16. Dodge/Save Mart 350	Infineon	40	12	110/110	0	$85,075	Running	11
17. Pepsi 400	Daytona	6	17	160/160	0	$93,700	Running	12
18. USG Sheetrock 400	Chicagoland	7	14	270/270	0	$91,525	Running	12
19. Lenox Industrial Tools 300	New Hamp.	12	6	308/308	1	$95,425	Running	12

2006 RESULTS

Race	Track	Start	Finish	Laps	Led	Winnings	Status	Rank
20. Pennsylvania 500	Pocono	1	1	200/200	151	$230,100	Running	8
21. Allstate 400 at Brickyard	Indianapolis	14	10	160/160	0	$177,225	Running	7
22. AMD at the Glen	Watkins Glen	10	10	90/90	0	$78,850	Running	8
23. GFS Marketplace 400	Michigan	9	9	200/200	0	$81,175	Running	8
24. Sharpie 500	Bristol	6	6	500/500	0	$111,800	Running	6
25. Sony HD 500	California	8	6	250/250	29	$107,000	Running	7
26. Chevy Rock & Roll 400	Richmond	1	15	399/400	19	$87,525	Running	5
27. Sylvania 300	New Hamp.	5	4	300/300	4	$113,050	Running	2
28. Dover 400	Dover	23	9	400/400	0	$80,875	Running	4
29. Banquet 400	Kansas	25	18	266/267	0	$88,925	Running	2
30. UAW-Ford 500	Talladega	12	21	188/188	1	$75,300	Running	5
31. Bank of America 500	Lowe's	22	28	265/334	0	$64,550	Running	6
32. Subway 500	Martinsville	3	2	500/500	28	$118,525	Running	4
33. Bass Pro Shops 500	Atlanta	4	8	325/325	0	$105,625	Running	3
34. Dickies 500	Texas	6	10	339/339	0	$121,200	Running	4
35. Checker Auto Parts 500	Phoenix	22	3	312/312	0	$139,800	Running	4
36. Ford 400	Homestead	33	3	268/268	0	$183,500	Running	3

TEAM FACTS >>> >>> **Primary sponsor:** Shell/Reese's >>> >>> **Owner:** Richard Childress >>> >>> **Team:** Richard Childress Racing

29 CHEVROLET
DRIVER PROFILE

Date of birth: December 8, 1975
Hometown: Bakersfield, Calif.
Resides: Winston-Salem, N.C.
Spouse: DeLana **Children:** None
Height: 5-10 **Weight:** 175
Hobbies: Radio-controlled racecars

KEVIN HARVICK

>>> >>> **Crew chief:** Todd Berrier >>> >>> **Engine builder:** Gary Wagner >>> >>> **Website:** www.rcrracing.com >>> >>>

>> NASCAR ACHIEVEMENTS

First NASCAR NEXTEL Cup Series start: February 26, 2001 (Rockingham; started 36th, finished 14th)

Best points finish: 4th (2006)

Career victories: 10—2006: Phoenix (a,b), Watkins Glen, Richmond (b), New Hampshire (b); 2005: Bristol (a); 2003: Indianapolis; 2002: Chicagoland; 2001: Atlanta (a), Chicagoland

First victory: March 11, 2001 (Atlanta, career start No. 3)

Last victory: November 12, 2006 (Phoenix)

Career poles: 5—2006: New Hampshire (b); 2005: Talladega (a), Richmond (b); 2003: Indianapolis; 2002: Daytona (b)

First pole: July 4, 2002 (Daytona, career start No. 51)

Last pole: September 15, 2006 (New Hampshire)

>> CAREER HIGHLIGHTS

- Had a historically good season—his 14 wins combined in the NASCAR Busch Series and NASCAR NEXTEL Cup Series are the most ever. He qualified for the Chase for the NASCAR NEXTEL Cup for the first time and was in contention for the championship through the final race. He won races at a wide variety of tracks, including his first at a road course (Watkins Glen).
- An early-season win at Bristol in 2005 suggested good things to come, but they never did. He failed to qualify for the Chase for the NASCAR NEXTEL Cup because he never found the consistency or horsepower to keep up with the Roush Racing and Hendrick Motorsports cars.
- Missed the Chase for the NASCAR NEXTEL Cup in 2004. He struggled through the middle of the season, usually his strong point. His usually reliable Richard Childress Racing cars broke down repeatedly.
- Finished a career-high fifth in points in a 2003 season plagued by inconsistency and slow starts. He finished 25th or worse in five of the first 14 races but got hot early in the second half of the season. Starting with a win from the pole August 3 at the Brickyard 400, Harvick had five straight top fives. Crew chief Todd Berrier replaced Gil Martin beginning in March at Bristol.
- Became the first driver in NASCAR NEXTEL Cup Series history to be forced to sit out of a race because of his actions on the track. Already on probation for rough driving, Harvick was suspended for the 2002 April race at Martinsville after he spun out another driver in a NASCAR Craftsman Truck Series race.
- Was the Raybestos Rookie of the Year in 2001 and won in only his third career NASCAR NEXTEL Cup Series start, at Atlanta, and won the inaugural race at Chicagoland.
- Ran in 35 NASCAR NEXTEL Cup Series races in 2001, taking over the Chevrolet owned by Richard Childress after the death of Dale Earnhardt in the Daytona 500.

>> FAST FACTS

- Owns a team, Kevin Harvick Inc., that fields entries in the NASCAR Busch Series and the NASCAR Craftsman Truck Series.
- Was the NASCAR Busch Series champion in 2006 and 2001. Finished the 2006 season with a record 32 top 10s and a record number of points (5,648).
- Got his first NASCAR Craftsman Truck Series win in his 75th start, at Phoenix, in 2002.
- Won the 2002 IROC championship.

— Kevin Harvick continued —

- Won the 1998 NASCAR Winston West Series championship.
- Was Rookie of the Year in the Featherlite Southwest Series in 1995, winning at Tucson and finishing 11th in points.
- Won the 1993 late model championship at Mesa Marin Raceway in his hometown of Bakersfield, Calif.

- Began racing go-karts at age 5, winning seven national titles and two Grand National championships.
- Kevin and his wife, DeLana, were married in Las Vegas in February 2001, two days after he made his NASCAR NEXTEL Cup Series debut at Rockingham.

CAREER STATISTICS

Year	Car owner	Races	Champ. finish	Wins	Top 5	Top 10	DNF	Poles	Money won
2001	Richard Childress	35	9	2	6	16	1	0	$4,302,202
2002	Richard Childress	35	21	1	5	8	6	1	$3,849,216
2003	Richard Childress	36	5	1	11	18	0	1	$6,237,119
2004	Richard Childress	36	14	0	5	14	4	0	$5,321,337
2005	Richard Childress	36	14	1	3	10	1	2	$5,630,358
2006	Richard Childress	36	4	5	15	20	1	1	$8,231,406
TOTALS		214		10	45	86	13	5	$33,571,638

2006 RESULTS

Race	Track	Start	Finish	Laps	Led	Winnings	Status	Rank
1. Daytona 500	Daytona	28	14	203/203	1	$302,244	Running	13
2. Auto Club 500	California	15	29	249/251	0	$116,611	Running	19
3. UAW-DaimlerChrysler 400	Las Vegas	29	11	270/270	0	$138,136	Running	17
4. Golden Corral 500	Atlanta	6	39	313/325	0	$102,876	Running	23
5. Food City 500	Bristol	14	2	500/500	8	$160,886	Running	13
6. DIRECTV 500	Martinsville	26	7	500/500	0	$115,011	Running	12
7. Samsung/RadioShack 500	Texas	24	5	334/334	1	$204,511	Running	9
8. Subway Fresh 500	Phoenix	15	1	312/312	10	$228,486	Running	8
9. Aaron's 499	Talladega	42	23	187/188	0	$121,811	Running	7
10. Crown Royal 400	Richmond	8	3	400/400	272	$169,386	Running	5
11. Dodge Charger 500	Darlington	14	37	350/367	0	$104,036	Running	9

Race	Track	Start	Finish	Laps	Led	Winnings	Status	Rank
12. Coca-Cola 600	Lowe's	12	34	373/400	0	$119,461	Running	9
13. Neigh. Excellence 400	Dover	5	3	400/400	0	$198,586	Running	8
14. Pocono 500	Pocono	12	13	200/200	0	$109,661	Running	8
15. 3M Performance 400	Michigan	19	10	129/129	0	$119,936	Running	8
16. Dodge/Save Mart 350	Infineon	3	24	110/110	5	$111,611	Running	10
17. Pepsi 400	Daytona	32	9	160/160	1	$140,386	Running	9
18. USG Sheetrock 400	Chicagoland	4	4	270/270	40	$184,586	Running	9
19. Lenox Industrial Tools 300	New Hamp.	14	5	308/308	0	$143,461	Running	8
20. Pennsylvania 500	Pocono	12	5	200/200	0	$134,436	Running	5
21. Allstate 400 at Brickyard	Indianapolis	10	3	160/160	18	$327,636	Running	4
22. AMD at the Glen	Watkins Glen	7	1	90/90	28	$223,161	Running	3
23. GFS Marketplace 400	Michigan	5	11	200/200	0	$117,661	Running	3
24. Sharpie 500	Bristol	11	11	500/500	0	$135,486	Running	3
25. Sony HD 500	California	15	15	250/250	0	$132,686	Running	3
26. Chevy Rock & Roll 400	Richmond	5	1	400/400	54	$234,136	Running	3
27. Sylvania 300	New Hamp.	1	1	300/300	196	$266,461	Running	1
28. Dover 400	Dover	25	32	366/400	0	$101,986	Engine	5
29. Banquet 400	Kansas	14	15	266/267	0	$129,011	Running	5
30. UAW-Ford 500	Talladega	14	6	188/188	0	$137,161	Running	4
31. Bank of America 500	Lowe's	5	18	332/334	0	$106,661	Running	3
32. Subway 500	Martinsville	12	9	500/500	0	$112,411	Running	2
33. Bass Pro Shops 500	Atlanta	2	31	321/325	9	$123,536	Running	6
34. Dickies 500	Texas	21	3	339/339	0	$254,186	Running	5
35. Checker Auto Parts 500	Phoenix	2	1	312/312	252	$245,761	Running	3
36. Ford 400	Homestead	7	5	268/268	0	$157,586	Running	4

TEAM FACTS >>> >>> **Primary sponsor:** UPS >>> >>> **Owner:** Michael Waltrip >>> >>> **Team:** Michael Waltrip Racing >>>

44 TOYOTA DRIVER PROFILE

Date of birth: November 26, 1956
Hometown: Hickory, N.C.
Resides: Hickory, N.C. **Spouse:** Kelley
Children: Jason, Natalee, Karsyn, Zachary **Height:** 6-2 **Weight:** 215
Hobbies: Golf, outdoor sports

DALE JARRETT

Crew chief: Matt Borland >>> >>> **Engine builder:** Toyota Racing Development >>> >>> **Website:** www.michaelwaltrip.com >>>

>> NASCAR ACHIEVEMENTS

First NASCAR NEXTEL Cup Series start: April 29, 1984 (Martinsville; started 24th, finished 14th)
Best points finish: 1st (1999)
Career victories: 32—2005: Talladega (b); 2003: Rockingham (a); 2002: Pocono (a), Michigan (b); 2001: Darlington (a), Texas, Martinsville (a), New Hampshire (a); 2000: Daytona (a), Rockingham (b); 1999: Richmond (a), Michigan (a), Daytona (b), Indianapolis; 1998: Darlington (a), Dover (a), Talladega (b); 1997: Atlanta (a), Darlington (a), Pocono (b), Bristol (b), Richmond (b), Lowe's (b), Phoenix; 1996: Daytona (a), Lowe's (a), Indianapolis, Michigan (b); 1995: Pocono (b); 1994: Lowe's (b); 1993: Daytona (a);

1991: Michigan (b)
First victory: August 18, 1991 (Michigan, career start No. 129)
Last victory: October 2, 2005 (Talladega)
Career poles: 16—2005: Daytona (a); 2002: Michigan (a); 2001: Las Vegas, Atlanta (a), Watkins Glen, Dover (b); 2000: Daytona (a,b), Atlanta (a); 1998: Las Vegas, Darlington (b); 1997: Darlington (a), Texas; 1996: Darlington (b), Rockingham (b); 1995: Daytona (a)
First pole: February 11, 1995 (Daytona, career start No. 229)
Last pole: February 12, 2005 (Daytona)

>> CAREER HIGHLIGHTS

- Had a disastrous 2006 season with Robert Yates Racing. The low point was the Coca-Cola 600, when he completed zero of 400 laps because of an accident. He didn't lead more than one lap in a race until the second Pocono race, when he led three. Jarrett will drive Toyota Camrys for Michael Waltrip Racing in 2007.

- A decent 2005 turned bad in the middle of the summer, as he faded from the top 10 and failed to make the Chase for the NASCAR NEXTEL Cup. A revolving door at crew chief continued to turn; Mike Ford was replaced by Billy Wilburn, who was replaced by Todd Parrott. A late-season win at Talladega got Jarrett off the schneid.
- A miserable 2003 carried over to 2004 until the Pocono 500, when Jarrett turned around his season and stopped his downward career spiral. Although he finished poorly in that race because his engine blew, his car was good. He scored his first top five of 2004 the next week. Jarrett climbed in the standings from there and had a shot at qualifying for the Chase for the NASCAR NEXTEL Cup but failed after a poor performance at Richmond.
- In 2003, had his worst season (26th in points) since 1987. For Jarrett, it was a disaster of a year filled with personnel changes, bad luck and ill-handling cars. He struggled even at tracks he usually thrived at; he finished 32nd and 23rd at Michigan, where he has four career wins.
- Made his 500th start in the 2003 spring Darlington race.
- Had a six-year streak of top five points finishes from 1996 to 2001. Jarrett finished in the top 10 in points from 1996 to 2002.
- Came close to his second NASCAR NEXTEL Cup Series championship in 2001, when a July victory at New Hampshire drew him even with Jeff Gordon in the standings. But Jarrett's hopes for a title unraveled with four finishes of 30th or worse in the next six races, and he finished fifth in the standings.
- Won the Daytona 500 three times, in 1993, 1996 and 2000. During his 1993 victory, his father was the commentator for CBS' national broadcast. He also won the 1999 Daytona summer race.
- Received a Driver of the Year ESPY in 1999, the same year he won the NASCAR NEXTEL Cup Series title. With his father, he became part of only the second father-son combination to win championships—joining Lee and Richard

Petty. He also led the circuit with 24 top fives and 29 top 10s in 1999.

- Joined Robert Yates Racing in 1995 and teamed with crew chief Todd Parrott from 1996 until 2001, winning 24 races and scoring 107 top fives and a NASCAR NEXTEL Cup Series title.
- Became the first NASCAR NEXTEL Cup Series driver for Joe Gibbs Racing in 1992 and got the company's first win, in the 1993 February Daytona 500.
- Got his first NASCAR NEXTEL Cup Series win at Michigan in 1991 after 128 starts, beating Davey Allison by only a few feet.
- Finished second to Davey Allison for Raybestos Rookie of the Year in 1987.

>> FAST FACTS

- Competed in IROC in eight seasons (1994, 1996, 1997, 1998, 1999, 2000, 2001 and 2002) and has two IROC wins, Daytona (2001) and Indianapolis (2002).
- Has 11 wins and 15 poles in the NASCAR Busch Series.
- Is considered one of the charter drivers in the NASCAR Busch Series, competing as a regular in 1982, the first year of competition for the division.
- Began racing in 1977 in the Limited Sportsman division at Hickory Motor Speedway, where his father, two-time NASCAR NEXTEL Cup champion Ned Jarrett, once was a track promoter.
- Was all-conference in football, basketball and golf at Newton-Conover (N.C.) High School. Also played baseball and was offered a full golf scholarship to the University of South Carolina.
- An excellent golfer, Jarrett has played some of America's most famous courses. If not for racing, he would have attempted a professional golf career.
- Won the USG Person of the Year Award in NASCAR in 2000 for his charity work on behalf of the Susan G. Komen Breast Cancer Foundation. Also was nominated for the award in 1996 for his fundraising efforts for Brenner Children's Hospital and for Carly Brayton, son of driver Scott Brayton, who was fatally injured in an accident during Indianapolis 500 practice that year.

CAREER STATISTICS

Year	Car owner	Races	Champ. finish	Wins	Top 5	Top 10	DNF	Poles	Money won
1984	Emanuel Zervakis	2	72	0	0	0	1	0	$2,350
	Jimmy Means	1		0	0	0	0	0	$4,995
1986	Mike Curb	1	108	0	0	0	1	0	$990
1987	Eric Freedlander	24	26	0	0	2	11	0	$143,405
1988	Cale Yarborough	19	23	0	0	1	8	0	$60,610
	Hoss Ellington	8		0	0	0	4	0	$51,655
	Buddy Arrington	1		0	0	0	1	0	$4,200
	Ralph Ball	1		0	0	0	1	0	$2,175
1989	Cale Yarborough	29	24	0	2	5	11	0	$232,317
1990	Wood Brothers	24	25	0	1	7	9	0	$214,495
1991	Wood Brothers	29	17	1	3	8	9	0	$444,256
1992	Joe Gibbs	29	19	0	2	8	5	0	$418,648
1993	Joe Gibbs	30	4	1	13	18	5	0	$1,242,394

Year	Car owner	Races	Champ. finish	Wins	Top 5	Top 10	DNF	Poles	Money won
1994	Joe Gibbs	30	16	1	4	9	7	0	$881,754
1995	Robert Yates	31	13	1	9	14	6	1	$1,363,158
1996	Robert Yates	31	3	4	17	21	3	2	$2,985,418
1997	Robert Yates	32	2	7	20	23	1	2	$3,240,542
1998	Robert Yates	33	3	3	19	22	3	2	$4,019,657
1999	Robert Yates	34	1	4	24	29	1	0	$6,649,596
2000	Robert Yates	34	4	2	15	24	2	3	$5,934,475
2001	Robert Yates	36	5	4	12	19	4	4	$5,377,742
2002	Robert Yates	36	9	2	10	18	5	1	$4,421,951
2003	Robert Yates	36	26	1	1	7	8	0	$4,121,487
2004	Robert Yates	36	15	0	6	14	3	0	$5,097,396
2005	Robert Yates	36	15	1	4	7	2	1	$5,338,232
2006	Robert Yates	36	23	0	1	4	5	0	$4,739,491
TOTALS		**639**		**32**	**163**	**260**	**116**	**16**	**$56,993,389**

— Dale Jarrett continued —

2006 RESULTS

Race	Track	Start	Finish	Laps	Led	Winnings	Status	Rank
1. Daytona 500	Daytona	25	10	203/203	0	$326,983	Running	10
2. Auto Club 500	California	19	17	251/251	0	$133,050	Running	11
3. UAW-DaimlerChrysler 400	Las Vegas	15	19	270/270	0	$124,325	Running	13
4. Golden Corral 500	Atlanta	31	9	325/325	0	$109,850	Running	9
5. Food City 500	Bristol	15	20	500/500	0	$119,475	Running	10
6. DIRECTV 500	Martinsville	28	15	500/500	1	$106,825	Running	11
7. Samsung/RadioShack 500	Texas	27	17	334/334	0	$143,350	Running	11
8. Subway Fresh 500	Phoenix	17	19	311/312	0	$99,325	Running	11
9. Aaron's 499	Talladega	4	12	188/188	1	$125,875	Running	10
10. Crown Royal 400	Richmond	26	21	399/400	0	$100,675	Running	12
11. Dodge Charger 500	Darlington	35	24	365/367	1	$106,750	Running	12
12. Coca-Cola 600	Lowe's	37	43	0/400	0	$113,817	Accident	16
13. Neigh. Excellence 400	Dover	40	24	399/400	0	$112,400	Running	17
14. Pocono 500	Pocono	27	38	181/200	0	$92,525	Running	19
15. 3M Performance 400	Michigan	40	20	129/129	0	$110,100	Running	19
16. Dodge/Save Mart 350	Infineon	22	34	104/110	0	$99,905	Accident	23
17. Pepsi 400	Daytona	7	22	160/160	1	$121,700	Running	21
18. USG Sheetrock 400	Chicagoland	41	31	269/270	0	$110,725	Running	24
19. Lenox Industrial Tools 300	New Hamp.	32	31	306/308	0	$101,025	Running	24
20. Pennsylvania 500	Pocono	38	28	200/200	3	$97,200	Running	25
21. Allstate 400 at Brickyard	Indianapolis	35	28	160/160	0	$172,825	Running	24
22. AMD at the Glen	Watkins Glen	39	26	90/90	0	$95,075	Running	24
23. GFS Marketplace 400	Michigan	37	36	166/200	0	$100,825	Engine	26
24. Sharpie 500	Bristol	32	15	499/500	0	$128,075	Running	26
25. Sony HD 500	California	36	10	250/250	0	$140,725	Running	24
26. Chevy Rock & Roll 400	Richmond	22	21	399/400	0	$103,275	Running	24
27. Sylvania 300	New Hamp.	37	28	299/300	0	$104,250	Running	24
28. Dover 400	Dover	34	15	398/400	0	$105,200	Running	24
29. Banquet 400	Kansas	32	4	267/267	0	$172,175	Running	24
30. UAW-Ford 500	Talladega	2	12	188/188	1	$125,475	Running	23
31. Bank of America 500	Lowe's	34	41	32/334	0	$92,085	Accident	24
32. Subway 500	Martinsville	39	16	500/500	0	$105,200	Running	24
33. Bass Pro Shops 500	Atlanta	23	11	325/325	0	$129,175	Running	22
34. Dickies 500	Texas	20	29	334/339	0	$126,150	Running	22
35. Checker Auto Parts 500	Phoenix	27	39	289/312	0	$93,575	Accident	23
36. Ford 400	Homestead	41	31	265/268	0	$96,625	Running	23

TEAM FACTS >>> >>> **Primary sponsor:** Lowe's >>> >>> **Owner:** Rick Hendrick >>> >>> **Team:** Hendrick Motorsports >>>

48 CHEVROLET DRIVER PROFILE

Date of birth: September 17, 1975
Hometown: El Cajon, Calif.
Resides: Charlotte
Spouse: Chandra **Children:** None
Height: 5-11 **Weight:** 175
Hobbies: Water sports, biking, snowboarding

JIMMIE JOHNSON

>>> **Crew chief:** Chad Knaus >>> >>> **Engine builder:** Hendrick Engines >>> >>> **Website:** www.hendrickmotorsports.com

NASCAR ACHIEVEMENTS

First NASCAR NEXTEL Cup Series start: October 7, 2001 (Lowe's; started 15th, finished 39th)
Best points finish: 1st (2006)
Career victories: 23—2006: Daytona (a), Las Vegas, Talladega (a), Indianapolis, Martinsville (b); 2005: Lowe's (a,b), Las Vegas, Dover (b); 2004: Darlington (a,b), Lowe's (a,b), Pocono (a,b), Martinsville (b), Atlanta (b); 2003: Lowe's (a), New Hampshire (a,b); 2002: California, Dover (a,b)
First victory: April 28, 2002 (California, career start No. 13)
Last victory: October 22, 2006 (Martinsville)
Career poles: 9—2006: Martinsville (a); 2005: Chicagoland; 2004: Lowe's (a); 2003: Pocono (a), Kansas (a); 2002: Daytona (a), Talladega (a), Lowe's (a), Richmond (b)
First pole: February 9, 2002 (Daytona, career start No. 4)
Last pole: March 31, 2006 (Martinsville)

CAREER HIGHLIGHTS

- Johnson finally closed the deal, winning his first NASCAR NEXTEL Cup Series championship. He was 156 points out of the lead after the fourth race in the Chase for the NASCAR NEXTEL Cup but rallied with finishes of 2-1-2-2-2-9. He started the season with a victory in the Daytona 500 and also won the Allstate 400 at the Brickyard. This time Johnson didn't fold or stress out in the Chase. His patience was the key to his comeback. His season started out with controversy, as his crew chief was suspended for the first four races for rules violations at Daytona.
- Spent the entire 2005 season in the top 10 in points. He never showed up at the track with a bad car. A blown tire and accident at Homestead dropped him from second to fifth in final points. It was a disappointing finish after he came so close to winning the title in 2004.
- After it appeared a pair of DNFs would knock him out of contention in the Chase for the NASCAR NEXTEL Cup in 2004, Johnson rallied with three consecutive victories and four in the next five races. He fell short to Kurt Busch for the championship by just eight points, the slimmest margin in NASCAR history. Johnson finished with eight wins, tops among all drivers, but had seven DNFs.
- A late-season charge in 2003—Johnson finished in the top three in the final six races—helped him end up second in points in only his second season. He finished the year two spots ahead of his car owner, Jeff Gordon. Johnson had at least one top 10 at a superspeedway, intermediate track,

short track and road course.
- His sweep at Dover in 2002 was the first by a rookie in NASCAR NEXTEL Cup Series history.
- Finished fifth in series points in 2002, one of the best rookie performances since Tony Stewart's three-win season in 1999. His first career NASCAR NEXTEL Cup Series win came in only his 13th NASCAR NEXTEL Cup Series start, and he led the NASCAR NEXTEL Cup Series standings for one week after the Kansas race in September.

>> FAST FACTS
- Named SPORTING NEWS' Driver of the Year in 2004 and 2006.
- Johnson and Jeff Gordon joined World Superbike champion Colin Edwards in Europe and won the 2002 Race of Champions Nations Cup, an annual event pitting the world's best rally, motorcycle and circuit racers against one another.

- Finished eighth in NASCAR Busch Series points in 2001, driving for Herzog Motorsports.
- Got his first career NASCAR Busch Series victory in 2001 at the series' inaugural race at Chicagoland Speedway.
- Won Rookie of the Year honors in the ASA ACDelco Challenge Series in 1998.
- Before racing stock cars, he won six off-road racing titles— the 1992, '93, and '94 Mickey Thompson Stadium Truck Series championships, the 1994 SCORE Desert championship and the 1996 and '97 SODA Winter Series championship.
- Competed in the 1995 SCORE Trophy Truck Series and the 1991 MTEG Series.
- Began racing in motocross events at age 4.
- Was selected as one of People's "Sexiest Men in the Fast Lane" in 2000, along with other NASCAR NEXTEL Cup Series and NASCAR Busch Series drivers.

CAREER STATISTICS

Year	Car owner	Races	Champ. finish	Wins	Top 5	Top 10	DNF	Poles	Money won
2001	Rick Hendrick	3	52	0	0	0	1	0	$122,320
2002	Rick Hendrick	36	5	3	6	21	3	4	$3,788,268
2003	Rick Hendrick	36	2	3	14	20	3	2	$7,745,530
2004	Rick Hendrick	36	2	8	20	23	7	1	$8,226,761
2005	Rick Hendrick	36	5	4	13	22	5	1	$8,336,712
2006	Rick Hendrick	36	1	5	13	24	1	1	$15,875,125
TOTALS		183		23	66	110	20	9	$44,134,716

2006 RESULTS

Race	Track	Start	Finish	Laps	Led	Winnings	Status	Rank
1. Daytona 500	Daytona	9	1	203/203	24	$1,505,120	Running	1
2. Auto Club 500	California	3	2	251/251	0	$235,936	Running	1
3. UAW-DaimlerChrysler 400	Las Vegas	3	1	270/270	1	$386,936	Running	1
4. Golden Corral 500	Atlanta	14	6	325/325	0	$121,761	Running	1
5. Food City 500	Bristol	5	30	487/500	0	$128,486	Running	3
6. DIRECTV 500	Martinsville	1	3	500/500	195	$150,361	Running	1
7. Samsung/RadioShack 500	Texas	16	11	334/334	0	$165,161	Running	1
8. Subway Fresh 500	Phoenix	10	7	312/312	0	$127,111	Running	2
9. Aaron's 499	Talladega	16	1	188/188	3	$326,061	Running	1
10. Crown Royal 400	Richmond	5	12	400/400	0	$118,361	Running	1
11. Dodge Charger 500	Darlington	25	4	367/367	81	$165,311	Running	1
12. Coca-Cola 600	Lowe's	3	2	400/400	24	$288,236	Running	1
13. Neigh. Excellence 400	Dover	42	6	400/400	0	$153,261	Running	1
14. Pocono 500	Pocono	10	10	200/200	0	$123,761	Running	1
15. 3M Performance 400	Michigan	4	6	129/129	0	$128,386	Running	1
16. Dodge/Save Mart 350	Infineon	16	10	110/110	2	$144,186	Running	1
17. Pepsi 400	Daytona	9	32	160/160	0	$130,386	Running	1
18. USG Sheetrock 400	Chicagoland	5	6	270/270	0	$154,286	Running	1
19. Lenox Industrial Tools 300	New Hamp.	6	9	308/308	0	$127,711	Running	1
20. Pennsylvania 500	Pocono	15	6	200/200	0	$133,661	Running	1
21. Allstate 400 at Brickyard	Indianapolis	5	1	160/160	33	$452,861	Running	1
22. AMD at the Glen	Watkins Glen	5	17	90/90	1	$110,111	Running	1
23. GFS Marketplace 400	Michigan	8	13	200/200	0	$123,586	Running	1
24. Sharpie 500	Bristol	18	10	500/500	0	$147,686	Running	1
25. Sony HD 500	California	16	11	250/250	0	$141,986	Running	2
26. Chevy Rock & Roll 400	Richmond	19	23	399/400	4	$114,836	Running	2
27. Sylvania 300	New Hamp.	7	39	233/300	0	$115,911	Running	9
28. Dover 400	Dover	18	13	399/400	0	$119,861	Running	8
29. Banquet 400	Kansas	3	14	267/267	105	$141,486	Running	8
30. UAW-Ford 500	Talladega	3	24	187/188	6	$120,086	Accident	8
31. Bank of America 500	Lowe's	10	2	334/334	72	$221,511	Running	7
32. Subway 500	Martinsville	9	1	500/500	245	$191,886	Running	3
33. Bass Pro Shops 500	Atlanta	3	2	325/325	27	$251,686	Running	2
34. Dickies 500	Texas	5	2	339/339	1	$364,236	Running	1
35. Checker Auto Parts 500	Phoenix	29	2	312/312	28	$212,211	Running	1
36. Ford 400	Homestead	15	9	268/268	2	$119,986	Running	1

Johnson

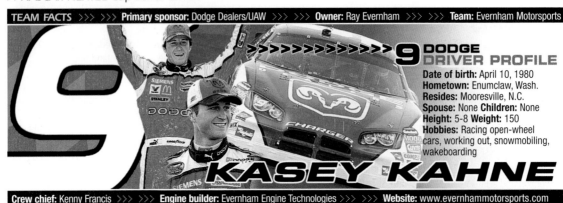

TEAM FACTS >>> >>> **Primary sponsor:** Dodge Dealers/UAW >>> >>> **Owner:** Ray Evernham >>> >>> **Team:** Evernham Motorsports

>>>>>>>>>>>>>> **9**

DODGE DRIVER PROFILE

Date of birth: April 10, 1980
Hometown: Enumclaw, Wash.
Resides: Mooresville, N.C.
Spouse: None **Children:** None
Height: 5-8 **Weight:** 150
Hobbies: Racing open-wheel cars, working out, snowmobiling, wakeboarding

KASEY KAHNE

Crew chief: Kenny Francis >>> >>> **Engine builder:** Evernham Engine Technologies >>> >>> **Website:** www.evernhammotorsports.com

>> NASCAR ACHIEVEMENTS

First NASCAR NEXTEL Cup Series start: February 15, 2004 (Daytona; started 27th, finished 41st)
Best points finish: 8th (2006)
Career victories: 7—2006: Atlanta (a), Texas (a), Lowe's (a,b), Michigan (a), California (b); 2005: Richmond (a)
First victory: May 14, 2005 (Richmond, career start No. 47)
Last victory: October 14, 2006 (Lowe's)
Career poles: 12—2006: Atlanta (a), Texas (a), Darlington, Michigan (a), Kansas, Homestead; 2005: Darlington, Richmond (a); 2004: Las Vegas, Darlington (a), California (a), Pocono (a)
First pole: March 5, 2004 (Las Vegas, career start No. 3)
Last pole: November 17, 2006 (Homestead)

>> CAREER HIGHLIGHTS

- Broke out big time in 2006, taking the checkered flag six times and sweeping the races at Lowe's Motor Speedway. But Kahne had to race his way into the Chase for the NASCAR NEXTEL Cup with a strong performance at Richmond because of inconsistency; almost every time he put together a string of good finishes, he followed it up with a string of bad ones. All of his 2006 wins came at intermediate tracks. To contend for a title, he needs to be strong everywhere.
- His first career win at Richmond in 2005 shed some light into an otherwise dark season. The sophomore driver and his team never got a good handle on the new Dodge Charger. Numerous blown right front tires suggest the team's setups were too aggressive.

- A veteran of the open-wheel USAC circuit, the Raybestos Rookie of the Year in 2004 combined incredible skill and incredible cars with incredibly bad luck. He lost sure wins with a blown tire and a wreck after slipping in oil left from a blown engine. He won four poles, which is remarkable considering how little experience he had at most tracks.
- Took over the No. 9 Dodge for Evernham Motorsports in 2004 after driver Bill Elliott announced he would run a partial schedule.

>> FAST FACTS

- Won back-to-back races in his first two starts in the NASCAR Craftsman Truck Series in 2004.
- Finished seventh in points in his only full season in the NASCAR Busch Series in 2003 and finished 33rd as a rookie in 2002.
- Won the "Night before the 500" Classic at Indianapolis Raceway Park in 2000 and 2001.
- Won 2000 USAC Midget championship and was named the USAC Rookie of the Year and Midget Driver of the Year.
- Second in the Northern Sprint Tour championship in 1997.
- Won the Mini-Sprint Class Hannigan (Wash.) Speedway championship and Northwest Mini-Sprint Car championship in 1996.
- Began racing Micro Midgets at age 14 in 1994.
- His hometown, Enumclaw, Wash., honored Kahne by making September 5, 2005, "Kasey Kahne Day" and presented him with the keys to the city. The town also renamed a city street "Kasey Kahne Drive."

Kahne

CAREER STATISTICS

Year	Car owner	Races	Champ. finish	Wins	Top 5	Top 10	DNF	Poles	Money won
2004	Ray Evernham	36	13	0	13	14	7	4	$5,415,611
2005	Ray Evernham	36	23	1	5	8	9	2	$5,183,697
2006	Ray Evernham	36	8	6	12	19	6	6	$7,695,378
TOTALS		108		7	30	41	22	12	$18,294,686

2006 RESULTS

Race	Track	Start	Finish	Laps	Led	Winnings	Status	Rank
1. Daytona 500	Daytona	27	11	203/203	0	$307,347	Running	12
2. Auto Club 500	California	13	4	251/251	1	$166,239	Running	4
3. UAW-DaimlerChrysler 400	Las Vegas	5	4	270/270	0	$186,714	Running	3
4. Golden Corral 500	Atlanta	1	1	325/325	85	$197,664	Running	2
5. Food City 500	Bristol	23	10	500/500	0	$125,864	Running	2
6. DIRECTV 500	Martinsville	5	35	374/500	0	$102,889	Engine	4
7. Samsung/RadioShack 500	Texas	1	1	334/334	63	$530,164	Running	3
8. Subway Fresh 500	Phoenix	22	6	312/312	0	$124,189	Running	3
9. Aaron's 499	Talladega	37	39	17/188	0	$112,989	Accident	4
10. Crown Royal 400	Richmond	6	34	396/400	0	$100,514	Running	7
11. Dodge Charger 500	Darlington	1	21	366/367	41	$126,439	Running	8
12. Coca-Cola 600	Lowe's	9	1	400/400	158	$428,114	Running	6
13. Neigh. Excellence 400	Dover	26	7	400/400	0	$135,039	Running	6
14. Pocono 500	Pocono	3	7	200/200	1	$117,189	Running	5
15. 3M Performance 400	Michigan	1	1	129/129	19	$205,364	Running	3
16. Dodge/Save Mart 350	Infineon	6	31	110/110	0	$110,914	Running	3
17. Pepsi 400	Daytona	38	25	160/160	0	$121,689	Running	4
18. USG Sheetrock 400	Chicagoland	3	23	267/267	0	$120,489	Running	5
19. Lenox Industrial Tools 300	New Hamp.	11	8	308/308	0	$119,689	Running	6
20. Pennsylvania 500	Pocono	3	31	199/200	0	$98,889	Running	7
21. Allstate 400 at Brickyard	Indianapolis	4	36	159/160	1	$173,689	Accident	11
22. AMD at the Glen	Watkins Glen	2	22	90/90	0	$103,189	Running	11
23. GFS Marketplace 400	Michigan	15	4	200/200	0	$131,439	Running	11
24. Sharpie 500	Bristol	31	12	500/500	0	$131,264	Running	11
25. Sony HD 500	California	9	1	250/250	130	$279,214	Running	11
26. Chevy Rock & Roll 400	Richmond	20	3	400/400	1	$158,639	Running	10
27. Sylvania 300	New Hamp.	33	16	300/300	0	$109,389	Running	9
28. Dover 400	Dover	21	38	172/400	0	$101,314	Accident	9
29. Banquet 400	Kansas	1	33	264/267	11	$132,414	Running	10
30. UAW-Ford 500	Talladega	25	2	188/188	7	$193,064	Running	9
31. Bank of America 500	Lowe's	2	1	334/334	134	$305,889	Running	8
32. Subway 500	Martinsville	32	7	500/500	0	$110,814	Running	8
33. Bass Pro Shops 500	Atlanta	8	38	255/325	0	$115,839	Accident	9
34. Dickies 500	Texas	4	33	328/339	2	$131,439	Engine	10
35. Checker Auto Parts 500	Phoenix	11	7	312/312	0	$118,239	Running	9
36. Ford 400	Homestead	1	4	268/268	90	$190,689	Running	8

TEAM FACTS >>> >>> **Primary sponsor:** DeWalt Tools >>> >>> **Owner:** Jack Roush >>> >>> **Team:** Roush Racing >>>

17 FORD

DRIVER PROFILE

Date of birth: March 10, 1972
Hometown: Cambridge, Wis.
Resides: Mooresville, N.C.
Spouse: Katie **Children:** Ross
Height: 5-9 **Weight:** 150
Hobbies: Motorcycles, boating, golf, computer games

MATT KENSETH

>>> **Crew chief:** Robbie Reiser >>> >>> **Engine builder:** Roush-Yates Engines >>> >>> **Website:** www.roushracing.com

>> NASCAR ACHIEVEMENTS

First NASCAR NEXTEL Cup Series start: September 20, 1998 (Dover; started 16th, finished 6th)
Best points finish: 1st (2003)
Career victories: 14—2006: California (a), Dover (a), Michigan (b), Bristol (b); 2005: Bristol (b); 2004: Rockingham, Las Vegas; 2003: Las Vegas; 2002: Rockingham (a), Texas, Michigan (a), Richmond (b), Phoenix; 2000: Lowe's
First victory: May 28, 2000 (Lowe's, career start No. 18)
Last victory: August 26, 2006 (Bristol)
Career poles: 3—2005: Bristol (b), Kansas; 2002: Dover (a)
First pole: May 31, 2002 (Dover, career start No. 89)
Last pole: October 8, 2005 (Kansas)

>> CAREER HIGHLIGHTS

- Was the driver to beat when the 2006 Chase for the NASCAR NEXTEL Cup started, but then the handling on his cars disappeared. It was a disappointing end to an otherwise strong season. He won four races and was in position to win several more—he was bumped out of the lead late at Chicagoland and Bristol and ran out of gas at Dover.
- Was assumed to be out of contention in 2005 after a horrendous start left him 24th in points after 14 races, but Kenseth stormed into the Chase for the NASCAR NEXTEL Cup with top 10 finishes in nine of 12 races.
- Determined to prove wrong those who criticized his 2003 championship as boring, Kenseth needed only three races in 2004 to double his win total from that season. He easily qualified for the Chase for the NASCAR NEXTEL Cup but neither his luck nor his car was consistently good.
- Although Kenseth had only one win in 2003 (Las Vegas), he built an insurmountable early-season points lead by finishing in the top 10 in 12 of the first 14 races. He finished the season as the NASCAR NEXTEL Cup Series champion, with a series-best 25 top 10s, and he never went more than three races without a top 10 finish. He set a modern-era record by assuming the points lead in the season's fourth race and holding it for 33 consecutive weeks.
- Won five races in 2002 (Rockingham, Texas, Michigan, Richmond, Phoenix), the most of any driver on the circuit.

— Matt Kenseth continued —

- Won the Raybestos Rookie of the Year Award in 2000 over Dale Earnhardt Jr. Kenseth's first career win was the Coca-Cola 600 at Lowe's, the circuit's longest race. He followed that victory with a second-place finish at Dover the next weekend.
- Made his NASCAR NEXTEL Cup Series debut in 1998 in the No. 94 Ford. He filled in for Bill Elliott so Elliott could attend his father's funeral. Kenseth finished sixth in the race.

>> FAST FACTS

- Finished third in 1999 NASCAR Busch Series standings with four wins and two poles.
- Was second in 1998 NASCAR Busch Series points race with three victories.
- Finished second in the 1997 NASCAR Busch Series Raybestos Rookie of the Year race despite starting only 21 races. His 1997 NASCAR Busch Series team Robbie Reiser, his current crew chief, owned.
- Was running second in the ASA standings when he left for the NASCAR Busch Series in 1997.

- Won one race and finished third in the Hooters ProCup Series in 1996.
- Made his NASCAR All-Pro Series debut in 1995, finishing in the top three in three of four starts.
- Won track titles at Madison International and Wisconsin International tracks in 1994 and a track title at Wisconsin International in 1995, with 15 wins in 60 races.
- Won the first Alan Kulwicki Memorial race in 1993 at Slinger Speedway shortly after fellow Wisconsin native Kulwicki died in a plane crash.
- Won ARTGO Challenge Series race at La Crosse, Wis., at age 19, becoming the youngest winner ever in that series. He broke the record held by Mark Martin.
- Began his short-track career at age 16, winning his first feature in his third race while he was a high school junior.
- Worked on his father's racecar for three years before starting to drive it.
- An avid Green Bay Packers fan, he exchanged helmets with quarterback Brett Favre at a 2003 Monday Night Football game at Lambeau Field.

CAREER STATISTICS

Year	Car owner	Races	Champ. finish	Wins	Top 5	Top 10	DNF	Poles	Money won
1998	Bill Elliott	1	57	0	0	1	0	0	$42,340
1999	Jack Roush	5	49	0	1	1	3	0	$143,561
2000	Jack Roush	34	14	1	4	11	5	0	$2,408,138
2001	Jack Roush	36	13	0	4	9	5	0	$2,565,579
2002	Jack Roush	36	8	5	11	19	3	1	$4,514,203
2003	Jack Roush	36	1	1	11	25	2	0	$9,422,764
2004	Jack Roush	36	8	2	8	16	6	0	$7,400,969
2005	Jack Roush	36	7	1	12	17	4	2	$7,034,134
2006	Jack Roush	36	2	4	15	21	1	0	$9,544,966
TOTALS		256		14	66	120	29	3	$43,076,654

2006 RESULTS

Race	Track	Start	Finish	Laps	Led	Winnings	Status	Rank
1. Daytona 500	Daytona	11	15	203/203	28	$302,549	Running	15
2. Auto Club 500	California	31	1	251/251	40	$324,991	Running	3
3. UAW-DaimlerChrysler 400	Las Vegas	9	2	270/270	146	$293,116	Running	2
4. Golden Corral 500	Atlanta	27	13	325/325	0	$118,616	Running	3
5. Food City 500	Bristol	7	3	500/500	124	$166,566	Running	1
6. DIRECTV 500	Martinsville	16	24	493/500	0	$113,491	Accident	3
7. Samsung/RadioShack 500	Texas	6	2	334/334	14	$362,491	Running	2
8. Subway Fresh 500	Phoenix	4	3	312/312	1	$168,116	Running	1
9. Aaron's 499	Talladega	12	6	188/188	23	$159,841	Running	2
10. Crown Royal 400	Richmond	11	38	351/400	0	$109,016	Running	3

Race	Track	Start	Finish	Laps	Led	Winnings	Status	Rank
11. Dodge Charger 500	Darlington	31	3	367/367	64	$205,291	Running	3
12. Coca-Cola 600	Lowe's	6	5	400/400	1	$180,366	Running	2
13. Neigh. Excellence 400	Dover	19	1	400/400	83	$323,591	Running	2
14. Pocono 500	Pocono	25	5	200/200	3	$141,641	Running	2
15. 3M Performance 400	Michigan	20	13	129/129	0	$121,416	Running	2
16. Dodge/Save Mart 350	Infineon	9	17	110/110	0	$120,791	Running	2
17. Pepsi 400	Daytona	10	5	160/160	1	$165,391	Running	2
18. USG Sheetrock 400	Chicagoland	8	22	270/270	112	$139,666	Running	2
19. Lenox Industrial Tools 300	New Hamp.	24	14	308/308	0	$119,716	Running	2
20. Pennsylvania 500	Pocono	11	14	200/200	0	$113,316	Running	2
21. Allstate 400 at Brickyard	Indianapolis	20	2	160/160	9	$361,141	Running	2
22. AMD at the Glen	Watkins Glen	30	21	90/90	0	$106,916	Running	2
23. GFS Marketplace 400	Michigan	3	1	200/200	87	$221,091	Running	2
24. Sharpie 500	Bristol	4	1	500/500	117	$336,516	Running	2
25. Sony HD 500	California	11	7	250/250	0	$146,641	Running	1
26. Chevy Rock & Roll 400	Richmond	10	8	400/400	39	$122,916	Running	1
27. Sylvania 300	New Hamp.	25	10	300/300	1	$130,466	Running	3
28. Dover 400	Dover	3	10	399/400	215	$136,816	Running	3
29. Banquet 400	Kansas	8	23	266/267	0	$129,516	Running	4
30. UAW-Ford 500	Talladega	19	4	188/188	21	$167,216	Running	2
31. Bank of America 500	Lowe's	11	14	332/334	1	$115,466	Running	2
32. Subway 500	Martinsville	20	11	500/500	0	$118,716	Running	1
33. Bass Pro Shops 500	Atlanta	1	4	325/325	0	$183,041	Running	1
34. Dickies 500	Texas	36	12	339/339	1	$152,791	Running	2
35. Checker Auto Parts 500	Phoenix	10	13	312/312	1	$114,941	Running	2
36. Ford 400	Homestead	19	6	268/268	0	$141,991	Running	2

The No. 17 team

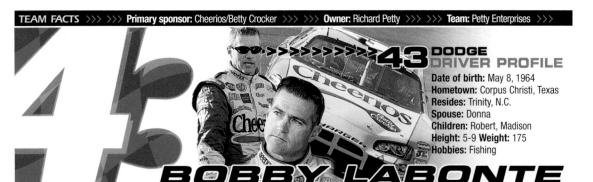

43 DODGE DRIVER PROFILE

Date of birth: May 8, 1964
Hometown: Corpus Christi, Texas
Resides: Trinity, N.C.
Spouse: Donna
Children: Robert, Madison
Height: 5-9 **Weight:** 175
Hobbies: Fishing

BOBBY LABONTE

>>> **Crew chief:** Paul Andrews >>> >>> **Engine builder:** Evernham Engine Technologies >>> >>> **Website:** www.pettyracing.com

>> NASCAR ACHIEVEMENTS

First NASCAR NEXTEL Cup Series start: June 2, 1991 (Dover; started 33rd, finished 34th)

Best points finish: 1st (2000)

Career victories: 21—2003: Atlanta (a), Homestead; 2002: Martinsville (a); 2001: Pocono (b), Atlanta (b); 2000: Rockingham (a), Indianapolis, Darlington (b), Lowe's (b); 1999: Dover (a), Pocono (a,b), Michigan (b), Atlanta (b); 1998: Atlanta (a), Talladega (a); 1997: Atlanta (b); 1996: Atlanta (b); 1995: Lowe's (a), Michigan (a,b)

First victory: May 28, 1995 (Lowe's, career start No. 74)

Last victory: November 16, 2003 (Homestead)

Career poles: 26—2004: Texas; 2003: Las Vegas, Texas, Michigan (a,b); 2001: California; 2000: Michigan (a), New Hampshire (b); 1999: Las Vegas, Atlanta (a), Lowe's (a,b), Dover (a); 1998: Daytona (a,b); Talladega (a); 1997: Dover (a), Darlington (b), Rockingham (b); 1996: Lowe's (b), Dover (b), Phoenix, Atlanta (b); 1995: Martinsville (a), Michigan (b); 1993: Richmond (b)

First pole: September 9, 1993 (Richmond, career start No. 25)

Last pole: April 2, 2004 (Texas)

>> CAREER HIGHLIGHTS

- Was hired to lead a resurgence of the legendary No. 43 car in 2006. The team boasted an impressive lineup of former champions with Labonte behind the wheel, Todd Parrott as crew chief and Robbie Loomis in a managerial role at Petty Enterprises, though Parrott left in August to return to Robert Yates Racing. Labonte had eight top 10s, the most for the 43 car since 1999 and more than Labonte had in 2005 with Joe Gibbs Racing.
- By Labonte's standards, 2005 was a disastrous season. He came close to winning only once but got passed in the final turn of the Coca-Cola 600. He left Joe Gibbs Racing at the end of the season for Petty Enterprises.
- A decent 2004 turned disastrous after the firing of crew chief Michael "Fatback" McSwain. After McSwain's departure following the 18th race of the season, Labonte did not finish in the top 10 again until the 34th race. His streak of consecutive seasons with at least one win ended at nine.

- Looked great early in the 2003 season with a streak of eight top 10s in nine races, but he faltered after that with seven consecutive finishes of 14th or worse. The season ended on a high note with a victory at Homestead.
- In 2002, snapped a run of five consecutive seasons of finishing among the top seven in points. His 16th-place finish was his worst since joining Joe Gibbs Racing in 1995.
- Won the NASCAR NEXTEL Cup Series championship in 2000. Bobby and Terry became the only brothers who each have won the title. Bobby grabbed the points lead after the third race of the season at Las Vegas and fell out of the top spot just once the rest of the way. He had only two finishes outside of the top 20.
- Broke his shoulder in 1999 during a NASCAR Busch Series practice in March at Darlington, but he did not miss a NASCAR NEXTEL Cup Series start and finished second in points to Dale Jarrett. He also swept the Pocono races.
- In 1996, got a win in the series finale at Atlanta, the same day Terry celebrated clinching the NASCAR NEXTEL Cup Series championship. Bobby won the series finale in Atlanta again in 1997.
- Moved from Bill Davis Racing to Joe Gibbs Racing in 1995 and enjoyed a breakthrough season, replacing Dale Jarrett in the No. 18 car. Labonte's first career win came in his 74th career start, at the Coca-Cola 600 at Charlotte. He also swept the Michigan races.
- Landed with Bill Davis Racing in 1993 and lost out to Jeff Gordon for the Raybestos Rookie of the Year award.

>> FAST FACTS

- Won the NASCAR Busch Series championship in 1991 and finished second in 1992 behind Joe Nemechek; Nemechek's winning margin of three points was tied for the closest in the history of NASCAR's three premier series.
- Raced late model stock cars at Caraway Speedway in Asheboro, N.C., winning the 1987 track championship with 12 victories in 23 races.
- Began his career in 1984 as a Hagan Racing crew member; Terry was the team's driver.

──────── Bobby Labonte continued ────────

- Ran quarter-midgets in Texas as a boy.
- Opened the first quarter-midget racetrack in North Carolina in May 2004.
- With brother Terry, was inducted into the Texas Sports Hall of Fame in 2001, nearly doubling the class of four inductees

from the racing community. The Labontes' class included Troy Aikman, Dick "Night Train" Lane, Bruce Matthews, Mike Munchak and Norm Cash.
- In 2001, Bobby and Terry had a park named in their honor, in their hometown of Corpus Christi, Texas.

CAREER STATISTICS

Year	Car owner	Races	Champ. finish	Wins	Top 5	Top 10	DNF	Poles	Money won
1991	Bobby Labonte	2	66	0	0	0	2	0	$8,350
1993	Bill Davis	30	19	0	0	6	6	1	$395,660
1994	Bill Davis	31	21	0	1	2	7	0	$550,305
1995	Joe Gibbs	31	10	3	7	14	6	2	$1,413,682
1996	Joe Gibbs	31	11	1	5	14	5	4	$1,475,196
1997	Joe Gibbs	32	7	1	9	18	1	3	$2,217,999
1998	Joe Gibbs	33	6	2	11	18	6	3	$2,980,052
1999	Joe Gibbs	34	2	5	2	6	1	5	$4,763,615
2000	Joe Gibbs	34	1	4	19	24	0	2	$7,361,386
2001	Joe Gibbs	36	6	2	9	20	6	1	$4,786,779
2002	Joe Gibbs	36	16	1	5	7	4	0	$4,183,715
2003	Joe Gibbs	36	8	2	12	17	5	4	$5,505,018
2004	Joe Gibbs	36	12	0	5	11	2	1	$5,201,397
2005	Joe Gibbs	36	24	0	4	7	10	0	$4,847,507
2006	Petty Enterprises	36	21	0	3	8	8	0	$4,949,058
TOTALS		474		21	113	192	69	26	$50,639,719

2006 RESULTS

Race	Track	Start	Finish	Laps	Led	Winnings	Status	Rank
1. Daytona 500	Daytona	8	35	197/203	0	$294,674	Accident	35
2. Auto Club 500	California	27	31	249/251	0	$116,186	Running	36
3. UAW-DaimlerChrysler 400	Las Vegas	17	30	270/270	1	$119,311	Running	36
4. Golden Corral 500	Atlanta	4	43	56/325	13	$103,725	Engine	38
5. Food City 500	Bristol	30	5	500/500	0	$138,836	Running	32
6. DIRECTV 500	Martinsville	13	32	429/500	0	$105,211	Running	35
7. Samsung/RadioShack 500	Texas	10	10	334/334	0	$164,211	Running	29
8. Subway Fresh 500	Phoenix	21	8	312/312	0	$117,661	Running	25
9. Aaron's 499	Talladega	31	29	163/188	0	$114,461	Engine	27
10. Crown Royal 400	Richmond	35	24	399/400	0	$104,761	Running	27
11. Dodge Charger 500	Darlington	11	22	366/367	0	$113,136	Running	27
12. Coca-Cola 600	Lowe's	5	17	400/400	1	$134,646	Running	26
13. Neigh. Excellence 400	Dover	28	13	400/400	0	$126,136	Running	24
14. Pocono 500	Pocono	23	12	200/200	0	$110,911	Running	23
15. 3M Performance 400	Michigan	5	28	129/129	0	$109,821	Running	25
16. Dodge/Save Mart 350	Infineon	21	35	104/110	0	$104,656	Accident	25
17. Pepsi 400	Daytona	34	42	146/160	0	$117,411	Accident	26
18. USG Sheetrock 400	Chicagoland	6	12	270/270	1	$132,136	Running	25
19. Lenox Industrial Tools 300	New Hamp.	27	23	308/308	0	$110,836	Running	25
20. Pennsylvania 500	Pocono	27	8	200/200	2	$122,561	Running	24
21. Allstate 400 at Brickyard	Indianapolis	38	40	135/160	0	$171,386	Engine	25
22. AMD at the Glen	Watkins Glen	36	24	90/90	0	$100,411	Running	25
23. GFS Marketplace 400	Michigan	25	19	200/200	0	$112,261	Running	25
24. Sharpie 500	Bristol	3	23	498/500	0	$126,886	Running	25
25. Sony HD 500	California	28	26	249/250	0	$124,861	Running	25
26. Chevy Rock & Roll 400	Richmond	27	22	399/400	0	$105,661	Running	25
27. Sylvania 300	New Hamp.	29	40	207/300	0	$104,161	Accident	27
28. Dover 400	Dover	26	7	400/400	0	$124,911	Running	25
29. Banquet 400	Kansas	16	17	266/267	0	$126,561	Running	25
30. UAW-Ford 500	Talladega	39	10	188/188	0	$130,036	Running	25
31. Bank of America 500	Lowe's	5	5	334/334	2	$151,436	Running	25
32. Subway 500	Martinsville	30	3	500/500	43	$137,661	Running	20
33. Bass Pro Shops 500	Atlanta	20	12	324/325	0	$134,336	Running	19
34. Dickies 500	Texas	13	16	338/339	0	$138,186	Running	19
35. Checker Auto Parts 500	Phoenix	15	27	311/312	0	$102,986	Running	19
36. Ford 400	Homestead	30	41	83/268	0	$96,911	Accident	21

TEAM FACTS >>> >>> **Primary sponsor:** Waste Management >>> >>> **Owner:** Bobby Ginn >>> >>> **Team:** Ginn Racing >>>

14 CHEVROLET DRIVER PROFILE

Date of birth: June 30, 1957
Hometown: Columbia, Tenn.
Resides: Franklin, Tenn.
Spouse: Paula **Children:** Steadman, Sutherlin **Height:** 6-0 **Weight:** 180
Hobbies: Collecting Civil War artifacts, watching University of Tennessee football

STERLING MARLIN

>>> **Crew chief:** Richard Labbe >>> >>> **Engine builder:** Hendrick Engines >>> >>> **Website:** www.ginnracing.com >>> >>>

>> NASCAR ACHIEVEMENTS

First NASCAR NEXTEL Cup Series start: May 8, 1976 (Nashville; started 30th, finished 29th)
Best points finish: 3rd (1995, 2001)
Career victories: 10—2002: Las Vegas, Darlington (a); 2001: Michigan (b), Lowe's (b); 1996: Talladega (a), Daytona (b); 1995: Daytona (a), Darlington (a), Talladega (b); 1994: Daytona (a)
First victory: February 20, 1994 (Daytona, career start No. 279)
Last victory: March 17, 2002 (Darlington)

Career poles: 11—2001: Daytona (b); 1999: Pocono (a); 1996: Talladega (a,b); 1995: Talladega (b); 1994: Phoenix; 1992: Daytona (a,b), Darlington (a,b); 1991: Daytona (b)
First pole: July 4, 1991 (Daytona, career start No. 205)
Last pole: July 5, 2001 (Daytona)

>> CAREER HIGHLIGHTS

- Saw his career continue to slide. Marlin finished on the lead lap in consecutive races twice during the 2006 season. He only once finished in the top 10 at a race, a ninth at

Richmond. He finished 34th in points, his worst in a full season. He piled up eight DNFs.

- A bad season turned terrible in 2005 when Chip Ganassi Racing decided not to bring back Marlin for another season. Marlin struggled constantly, but it wasn't all Marlin's fault; other Ganassi teams struggled, too.
- Never had consecutive top 10 finishes in 2004. A major reason is he didn't complete enough laps. He had DNFs because of accidents, engine failures, a brake failure and overheating.
- Finished 18th in points in 2003. He appeared on the verge of a strong season with eight top 10s in the first 15 races but never finished better than 10th the rest of the season. He made his 600th career start at Martinsville in October.
- Was having the most productive year of his career in 2002 when a neck injury that was a result of an accident at Kansas on September 29 ended his season. He had led in points for 25 consecutive races, from Rockingham, the second race of the season, through Richmond in September. Jamie McMurray replaced him.
- Was part of a bizarre incident during the 2002 Daytona 500, which was red-flagged while he was leading the race. While the cars were stopped, he got out of his car and began working on some body damage. He was penalized for the infraction and ultimately finished eighth.
- 2001 was Marlin's first season driving a Dodge, and he experienced a renaissance, finishing third in points with two wins (Michigan, Lowe's) and a career-best 12 top fives. The victory at Michigan was Marlin's first in five seasons. It also was Dodge's first victory since 1977.

- Had three mediocre seasons under Felix Sabates (1998 to 2000) that produced only three top fives. 2000 was his final season with Sabates, who sold the majority interests of the team to Chip Ganassi.
- Got his first NASCAR NEXTEL Cup Series win in the 1994 Daytona 500 in his 279th start. It was his first start with a new team, having moved from the Stavola Brothers to Morgan-McClure. The season began his best three-year stretch (1994-96), during which he posted six victories and 19 top fives and finished in the top 15 all three seasons, including a career-high finish of third in points in 1995.
- After not winning a pole for more than 200 career NASCAR NEXTEL Cup Series starts, Marlin won two poles in three races in 1991 (Daytona and Talladega).
- Was Raybestos Rookie of the Year in 1983. He didn't race another full season in the NASCAR NEXTEL Cup Series until 1987.
- Made his first NASCAR NEXTEL Cup Series start in 1976 at 18 at Nashville after his father, Coo Coo, suffered a broken shoulder and entered his son in the race in his place.

>> FAST FACTS

- Was named Professional Athlete of the Year in Tennessee in 1995 and 1996.
- Has two career victories in the NASCAR Busch Series, at Lowe's (1990) and Bristol (2000).
- Won three consecutive track championships at Nashville Raceway from 1980 to 1982.
- Was the team captain and an All Mid-State selection, playing quarterback and linebacker at Spring Hill (Tenn.) High School. He also played basketball in high school.

CAREER STATISTICS

Year	Car owner	Races	Champ. finish	Wins	Top 5	Top 10	DNF	Poles	Money won
1976	H.B. Cunningham	1	102	0	0	0	1	0	$565
1978	H.B. Cunningham	2	69	0	0	1	1	0	$10,170
1979	H.B. Cunningham	1	86	0	0	0	1	0	$505
1980	H.B. Cunningham	2	49	0	0	1	1	0	$18,750
	James D. Stacy	2		0	0	0	0	0	$6,725
	D. K. Ulrich	1		0	0	1	0	0	$4,335
1981	Coo Coo Marlin	1	93	0	0	0	1	0	$1,225
	D. K. Ulrich	1		0	0	0	1	0	$730
1982	Billy Matthews	1	115	0	0	0	1	0	$4,015
1983	Roger Hamby	30	18	0	0	1	11	0	$143,564
1984	Earl Sadler	11	37	0	0	2	7	0	$35,320
	Jimmy Means	1		0	0	0	0	0	$2,800
	Richard Bahre	1		0	0	0	1	0	$1,085
	Roger Hamby	1		0	0	0	0	0	$15,150
1985	Earl Sadler	7	37	0	0	0	5	0	$29,805
	Helen Rae Smith	1		0	0	0	0	0	$1,350
1986	Hoss Ellington	10	36	0	2	4	7	0	$113,070
1987	Billy Hagan	29	11	0	4	8	6	0	$306,412
1988	Billy Hagan	29	10	0	6	13	6	0	$521,464
1989	Billy Hagan	29	12	0	4	13	5	0	$473,267
1990	Billy Hagan	29	14	0	5	10	8	0	$369,167
1991	Junior Johnson	29	7	0	7	16	2	2	$633,690
1992	Junior Johnson	29	10	0	6	13	4	5	$649,048
1993	William Stavola	30	15	0	1	8	3	0	$628,835
1994	Morgan/McClure	31	14	1	5	11	7	1	$1,127,683
1995	Morgan/McClure	31	3	3	9	22	2	1	$2,253,502
1996	Morgan/McClure	31	8	2	5	10	6	0	$1,588,425
1997	Morgan/McClure	32	25	0	2	6	8	0	$1,301,370
1998	Chip Ganassi	32	13	0	0	6	1	0	$1,350,161
1999	Chip Ganassi	34	16	0	2	5	3	1	$1,797,416
2000	Chip Ganassi	34	19	0	1	7	4	0	$1,992,301
2001	Chip Ganassi	36	3	2	12	20	2	1	$4,517,634
2002	Chip Ganassi	29	18	2	8	14	3	0	$4,228,889
2003	Chip Ganassi	36	18	0	0	11	8	0	$4,384,491
2004	Chip Ganassi	36	21	0	3	7	9	0	$4,457,443
2005	Chip Ganassi	35	30	0	1	5	7	0	$4,080,118
2006	Bobby Ginn	36	34	0	0	1	8	0	$3,248,034
TOTALS		**711**		**10**	**83**	**216**	**142**	**11**	**$40,298,514**

2006 RESULTS

Race	Track	Start	Finish	Laps	Led	Winnings	Status	Rank
1. Daytona 500	Daytona	39	34	200/203	0	$248,713	Running	34
2. Auto Club 500	California	32	24	249/251	0	$88,592	Running	37
3. UAW-DaimlerChrysler 400	Las Vegas	31	36	258/270	0	$78,175	Engine	39
4. Golden Corral 500	Atlanta	33	34	322/325	0	$66,130	Running	39
5. Food City 500	Bristol	35	17	500/500	0	$101,783	Running	35
6. DIRECTV 500	Martinsville	6	14	500/500	9	$92,083	Running	32
7. Samsung/RadioShack 500	Texas	18	30	329/334	0	$89,325	Running	34
8. Subway Fresh 500	Phoenix	16	12	311/312	0	$90,883	Running	30
9. Aaron's 499	Talladega	9	37	91/188	0	$76,325	Accident	34
10. Crown Royal 400	Richmond	32	9	400/400	0	$96,783	Running	30
11. Dodge Charger 500	Darlington	27	28	364/367	0	$81,322	Running	33
12. Coca-Cola 600	Lowe's	26	28	396/400	0	$95,847	Running	33
13. Neigh. Excellence 400	Dover	23	31	398/400	0	$74,350	Running	33
14. Pocono 500	Pocono	16	42	18/200	0	$59,885	Engine	34
15. 3M Performance 400	Michigan	26	24	129/129	0	$85,658	Running	34
16. Dodge/Save Mart 350	Infineon	29	42	0/110	0	$66,900	Accident	34

— Sterling Marlin continued —

2006 RESULTS

Race	Track	Start	Finish	Laps	Led	Winnings	Status	Rank
17. Pepsi 400	Daytona	20	24	160/160	0	$104,383	Running	34
18. USG Sheetrock 400	Chicagoland	31	26	269/270	0	$95,158	Running	34
19. Lenox Industrial Tools 300	New Hamp.	23	16	308/308	0	$90,333	Running	32
20. Pennsylvania 500	Pocono	35	30	199/200	0	$74,372	Running	31
21. Allstate 400 at Brickyard	Indianapolis	33	31	160/160	0	$136,225	Running	32
22. AMD at the Glen	Watkins Glen	42	39	64/90	0	$57,750	Accident	33
23. GFS Marketplace 400	Michigan	10	29	199/200	0	$72,400	Running	33
24. Sharpie 500	Bristol	14	32	490/500	0	$85,255	Running	33
25. Sony HD 500	California	27	29	249/250	0	$99,108	Running	32
26. Chevy Rock & Roll 400	Richmond	28	30	398/400	0	$76,558	Running	32
27. Sylvania 300	New Hamp.	30	25	299/300	1	$83,347	Running	32
28. Dover 400	Dover	12	31	393/400	1	$65,225	Running	32
29. Banquet 400	Kansas	28	20	266/267	1	$103,983	Running	32
30. UAW-Ford 500	Talladega	7	40	145/188	0	$68,525	Accident	32
31. Bank of America 500	Lowe's	13	11	334/334	3	$106,133	Running	32
32. Subway 500	Martinsville	22	21	500/500	0	$81,508	Running	32
33. Bass Pro Shops 500	Atlanta	35	20	322/325	0	$105,433	Running	32
34. Dickies 500	Texas	31	40	208/339	1	$91,850	Accident	33
35. Checker Auto Parts 500	Phoenix	30	36	303/312	1	$61,875	Running	33
36. Ford 400	Homestead	18	37	213/268	0	$60,800	Engine	34

TEAM FACTS >>> >>> **Primary sponsor:** U.S. Army >>> >>> **Owner:** Bobby Ginn >>> >>> **Team:** Ginn Racing >>> >>>

01 CHEVROLET
DRIVER PROFILE

Date of birth: January 9, 1959
Hometown: Batesville, Ark.
Resides: Daytona Beach, Fla.
Spouse: Arlene **Children:** Amy, Rachel, Heather, Stacy, Matthew
Height: 5-6 **Weight:** 135
Hobbies: Weight training, quarter-midget racing with his son

MARK MARTIN

Crew chief: Ryan Pemberton >>> >>> **Engine builder:** Hendrick Engines >>> >>> **Website:** www.ginnracing.com >>> >>>

>> NASCAR ACHIEVEMENTS

First NASCAR NEXTEL Cup Series start: April 5, 1981 (North Wilkesboro; started 5th, finished 27th)
Best points finish: 2 (1990, 1994, 1998, 2002)
Career victories: 35—2005: Kansas; 2004: Dover (a); 2002: Lowe's (a); 2000: Martinsville (a); 1999: Rockingham (a), Dover (b); 1998: Las Vegas, Texas, California, Michigan (a), Bristol (b), Dover (b), Lowe's (b); 1997: Talladega (a), Infineon, Michigan (b), Dover (b); 1995: Talladega (a), Watkins Glen, Lowe's (b), North Wilkesboro (b); 1994: Watkins Glen, Atlanta (b); 1993: Watkins Glen, Michigan (b), Darlington (b), Bristol (b), Phoenix; 1992: Martinsville (a), Lowe's (b); 1991: Atlanta (b); 1990: Richmond (a), Michigan (b), North Wilkesboro (b); 1989: Rockingham (b)
First victory: October 22, 1989 (Rockingham, career start No. 113)
Last victory: October 9, 2005 (Kansas)
Career poles: 41—2001: Bristol (a), Richmond (a); 1999: Rockingham (b); 1998: Darlington (a), Dover (b), Rockingham (b); 1997: Rockingham (a), Infineon, Dover (b); 1996: Bristol (a,b), Pocono (b), Richmond (b); 1995: Watkins Glen, Bristol (a,b), New Hampshire; 1994: Watkins Glen; 1993: Rockingham (a,b), Watkins Glen, Bristol (b), New Hampshire; 1992: Atlanta (a); 1991: Martinsville (a,b), Lowe's (a,b), Pocono (a); 1990: North Wilkesboro (a), Pocono (b), Martinsville (b); 1989: Bristol (a), Darlington (a), Talladega (a,b), Dover (a), Daytona (b); 1988: Dover (b); 1981: Nashville (b), Richmond (b).
First pole: July 8, 1981 (Nashville, career start No. 3)
Last pole: May 4, 2001 (Richmond)

>> CAREER HIGHLIGHTS

- Made the Chase for the NASCAR NEXTEL Cup in 2006 for the third consecutive year. Martin did not win a race but ran consistently and competitively in his Roush Racing No. 6 Ford. Martin will run a partial schedule in 2007 for Ginn Racing (formerly MB2 Motorsports).
- Won the NASCAR NEXTEL All-Star Challenge and a points race at Kansas in 2005. He easily made the Chase for the NASCAR NEXTEL Cup, but an incident at Talladega ended his chances at the championship. He entered 2005 thinking it was his final year, but Jack Roush couldn't find a suitable driver for the No. 6 car, and Martin agreed to return in 2006.
- Had a resurgent year in 2004, driving the fastest car he has had since 1998. He stormed into the Chase for the NASCAR NEXTEL Cup, and although he didn't contend for the championship, he sure had fun along the way. He announced 2005 would be his last full-time season.
- In 2003, four engine failures and three accidents led to Martin completing only 89.4 percent of his laps on the way to a 17th-place points finish. He couldn't maintain positive momentum; he never had consecutive top fives and never had more than two straight top 10s.
- Finished second in 2002 for the fourth time in his NASCAR NEXTEL Cup Series career, 38 points behind champion Tony Stewart. His other second-place finishes: 1998, 364 points behind Jeff Gordon; 1994, 444 points behind Dale Earnhardt, and 1990, 26 points behind Earnhardt. The 2002 season was especially heartbreaking for Martin because he

held the points lead for two weeks late in the season.
- Made his 500th start in 2002, in March at Bristol.
- Had only three top fives in 2001, his fewest since 1988, his first season with Jack Roush. That contributed to a 12th-place finish in points, his lowest since 1988.
- Won the inaugural race at Las Vegas in 1998.
- Won the Watkins Glen race from the pole three consecutive seasons (1993-95)
- Tied a record for consecutive wins with four straight (Watkins Glen, Michigan, Bristol, Darlington) in 1993.
- Led the NASCAR NEXTEL Cup Series with five poles in 1991 (both Lowe's races, both Martinsville races, Pocono).
- Had a breakthrough season in 1989 and finished third in points. He got his first career win in his 113th start at Rockingham and won six poles, tying Alan Kulwicki for the series' season high. That year, he began a streak of 12 seasons with a top 10 finish in points. During that span, Martin had a seven-year streak of top five points finishes from 1993 to 1999.
- A win in the 1987 NASCAR Busch Series race at Dover grabbed the attention of Jack Roush, who was starting his own team the next season. Martin became Roush's first NASCAR NEXTEL Cup Series driver in 1988.
- Put in a second season as a driver/owner in 1982 and finished runner-up to Geoff Bodine for Raybestos Rookie of the Year. But Martin couldn't keep his team afloat and auctioned off his shop. He didn't compete full time in the NASCAR NEXTEL Cup Series racing again until 1988.
- Made a splash in his first NASCAR NEXTEL Cup Series season with five races as a driver/owner and a fifth-place finish at Martinsville in 1981. He also got his first career pole at Nashville in only his third career NASCAR NEXTEL Cup Series start.

>> FAST FACTS

- Has a series-leading 47 victories in the NASCAR Busch Series and was voted the NASCAR Busch Series' Greatest Driver by NASCAR fans and media during 2006, the 25th anniversary of the NASCAR Busch Series.
- Won a series-high six NASCAR Craftsman Truck Series races in 2006 and is expected to run a partial schedule in 2007.
- Grew up racing up short tracks throughout the Midwest.
- Won three consecutive ASA championships from 1978 to 1980 before moving to NASCAR; returned to ASA and won the 1986 title before switching back to NASCAR.
- Owns Mark Martin Performance, a company that sells quarter-midget racing chassis.
- Opened the Mark Martin Museum and auto dealership in 2006 in his hometown of Batesville, Ark. The museum houses several of Martin's past cars, including the No. 6 Ford he drove to a win at the Coca-Cola 600 in 2002.
- Helped build the quarter-midget track at the New Smyrna (Fla.) Speedway.

CAREER STATISTICS

Year	Car owner	Races	Champ. finish	Wins	Top 5	Top 10	DNF	Poles	Money won
1981	Mark Martin	5	42	0	1	2	2	2	$13,950
1982	Mark Martin	29	14	0	2	8	11	0	$124,215
	Bob Rogers	1		0	0	0	1	0	$2,440
1983	J.D. Stacy	7	30	0	1	2	3	0	$75,240
	D.K. Ulrich	2		0	0	0	2	0	$5,745
	Mark Martin	1		0	0	0	1	0	$1,640
	Morgan-McClure	6		0	0	1	2	0	$17,030
1986	Gerry Gunderman	5	48	0	0	0	2	0	$20,515
1987	Roger Hamby	1	101	0	0	0	1	0	$3,550
1988	Jack Roush	29	15	0	3	10	10	1	$223,630
1989	Jack Roush	29	3	1	14	18	4	6	$1,019,250
1990	Jack Roush	29	2	3	16	23	1	3	$1,302,958
1991	Jack Roush	29	6	1	14	17	5	5	$1,039,991
1992	Jack Roush	29	6	2	10	17	5	1	$1,000,571
1993	Jack Roush	30	3	5	12	19	5	5	$1,657,662
1994	Jack Roush	31	2	2	15	20	8	1	$1,628,906
1995	Jack Roush	31	4	4	13	22	1	4	$1,893,519
1996	Jack Roush	31	5	0	14	23	4	4	$1,887,396
1997	Jack Roush	32	3	4	16	24	3	3	$2,532,484
1998	Jack Roush	33	2	7	22	26	1	3	$4,309,006
1999	Jack Roush	34	3	2	19	26	3	1	$3,509,744
2000	Jack Roush	34	8	1	13	20	6	0	$3,098,874
2001	Jack Roush	36	12	0	3	15	4	2	$3,797,006
2002	Jack Roush	36	2	1	12	22	3	0	$7,004,893
2003	Jack Roush	36	17	0	5	10	7	0	$4,486,560
2004	Jack Roush	36	4	1	10	15	2	0	$5,479,004
2005	Jack Roush	36	4	1	12	19	2	0	$7,731,468
2006	Jack Roush	36	9	0	7	15	2	0	$5,568,748
TOTALS		**674**		**35**	**234**	**374**	**101**	**41**	**$59,428,575**

2006 RESULTS

Race	Track	Start	Finish	Laps	Led	Winnings	Status	Rank
1. Daytona 500	Daytona	10	12	203/203	19	$292,383	Running	11
2. Auto Club 500	California	10	9	251/251	1	$104,800	Running	6
3. UAW-DaimlerChrysler 400	Las Vegas	18	6	270/270	57	$122,950	Running	5
4. Golden Corral 500	Atlanta	11	2	325/325	0	$127,800	Running	4
5. Food City 500	Bristol	4	6	500/500	0	$105,825	Running	4
6. DIRECTV 500	Martinsville	30	13	500/500	0	$90,575	Running	2
7. Samsung/RadioShack 500	Texas	3	9	334/334	11	$151,850	Running	4
8. Subway Fresh 500	Phoenix	18	11	311/312	111	$98,425	Running	4
9. Aaron's 499	Talladega	10	35	101/188	0	$94,650	Running	5
10. Crown Royal 400	Richmond	2	11	400/400	1	$94,525	Running	4
11. Dodge Charger 500	Darlington	17	8	367/367	0	$105,625	Running	4
12. Coca-Cola 600	Lowe's	21	4	400/400	20	$166,100	Running	3
13. Neigh. Excellence 400	Dover	6	9	400/400	39	$107,950	Running	3
14. Pocono 500	Pocono	20	17	200/200	0	$82,275	Running	3
15. 3M Performance 400	Michigan	8	27	129/129	0	$88,035	Running	5
16. Dodge/Save Mart 350	Infineon	8	13	110/110	0	$96,725	Running	6
17. Pepsi 400	Daytona	24	33	160/160	0	$100,675	Running	6
18. USG Sheetrock 400	Chicagoland	9	18	270/270	1	$103,325	Running	6
19. Lenox Industrial Tools 300	New Hamp.	13	4	308/308	0	$124,700	Running	5
20. Pennsylvania 500	Pocono	30	19	200/200	0	$81,825	Running	6
21. Allstate 400 at Brickyard	Indianapolis	19	5	160/160	0	$239,150	Running	6
22. AMD at the Glen	Watkins Glen	20	20	90/90	0	$81,700	Running	6
23. GFS Marketplace 400	Michigan	14	5	200/200	0	$103,650	Running	4
24. Sharpie 500	Bristol	15	28	496/500	0	$101,195	Running	10
25. Sony HD 500	California	38	12	250/250	3	$110,625	Running	9
26. Chevy Rock & Roll 400	Richmond	4	5	400/400	0	$116,000	Running	7
27. Sylvania 300	New Hamp.	26	11	300/300	0	$95,975	Running	6
28. Dover 400	Dover	9	14	399/400	0	$87,075	Running	6
29. Banquet 400	Kansas	19	3	267/267	0	$181,525	Running	3
30. UAW-Ford 500	Talladega	30	8	188/188	2	$102,250	Running	3
31. Bank of America 500	Lowe's	7	30	239/334	0	$80,725	Accident	4
32. Subway 500	Martinsville	25	24	500/500	0	$83,900	Running	7
33. Bass Pro Shops 500	Atlanta	7	36	309/325	0	$96,900	Accident	8
34. Dickies 500	Texas	28	22	338/339	0	$113,475	Running	9
35. Checker Auto Parts 500	Phoenix	21	6	312/312	26	$104,725	Running	8
36. Ford 400	Homestead	26	18	268/268	0	$82,725	Running	9

TEAM FACTS >>> >>> **Primary sponsor:** 360 OTC >>> >>> **Owner:** Bill Davis >>> >>> **Team:** Bill Davis Racing >>>

36 TOYOTA DRIVER PROFILE

Date of birth: May 27, 1969
Hometown: Owensboro, Ky.
Resides: Mooresville, N.C.
Spouse: Shana **Children:** None
Height: 6-0 **Weight:** 190
Hobbies: Four-wheel vehicles, remote-control cars

JEREMY MAYFIELD

>>> **Crew chief:** Derrick Finley >>> >>> **Engine builder:** Terry Elledge >>> >>> **Website:** www.billdavisracing.com >>> >>>

>> NASCAR ACHIEVEMENTS

First NASCAR NEXTEL Cup Series start: October 10, 1993 (Lowe's; started 30th, finished 29th)
Best points finish: 7th (1998)
Career victories: 5—2005: Michigan (b); 2004: Richmond (b); 2000: California, Pocono (a); 1998: Pocono (a)
First victory: June 21, 1998 (Pocono, career start No. 125)
Last victory: August 21, 2005 (Michigan)
Career poles: 9—2004: Dover (a,b); 2003: Talladega (a); 2000: Talladega (a), Dover (b), Darlington (b), Rockingham (b); 1998: Texas; 1996: Talladega (b)
First pole: July 26, 1996 (Talladega, career start No. 66)
Last pole: September 24, 2004 (Dover)

>> CAREER HIGHLIGHTS

- The 2006 season started out bad and turned atrocious for Mayfield. He finished in the teens only four times. Mayfield had a falling out with team owner Ray Evernham and was fired after the Indianapolis race. Mayfield will drive a Toyota Camry for Bill Davis Racing in 2007.
- Made the Chase for the NASCAR NEXTEL Cup for the second consecutive season. His win at Michigan was just the second of the season for Dodge, but he struggled with the handling on the new Dodge Charger and ended the season ninth in the standings.
- Made a great comeback in 2004 and qualified for the Chase for the NASCAR NEXTEL Cup in dramatic fashion with a win at Richmond. He brought up the rear of the field when the Chase was over, finishing the season 10th.
- Was fired from Penske Racing's No. 12 Ford in October 2001, 28 races into the season. He landed with Evernham Motorsports for the 2002 season but had disappointing finishes with Evernham in 2002 (26th) and 2003 (19th).
- Had a roller-coaster 2000 that included a career-high two wins (Pocono, California) and four poles (Talladega, Darlington, Dover and Rockingham) but 11 DNFs. He missed two races after sustaining a head injury in a practice accident at the Brickyard 400.
- Won his first NASCAR NEXTEL Cup Series race in 1998 at Pocono, passing boyhood hero Darrell Waltrip for the lead 20 laps from the end. Led the points race four times in the first 16 races and finished the year seventh in points, a career high.
- First full season in NASCAR NEXTEL Cup Series was underwhelming, as Mayfield registered only one top 10 and finished 31st in points in 1995.

>> FAST FACTS

- Was the ARCA Rookie of the Year in 1993, with eight top fives and 10 top 10s, and made the jump from ARCA to the NASCAR NEXTEL Cup Series.
- Was the 1987 Kentucky Motor Speedway Rookie of the Year.
- Began racing go-karts in 1982 and then moved up through the weekly programs at tracks in central Tennessee, competing in street stocks, sportsman and late-model stocks.
- While competing in late models as a teen, Mayfield painted signs at the local racetrack and often painted the numbers on other drivers' cars to make ends meet.
- Moved to Nashville at 19 to work as a fabricator for Sadler Racing and ended up getting a late-model car from the Sadlers to compete.

CAREER STATISTICS

Year	Car owner	Races	Champ. finish	Wins	Top 5	Top 10	DNF	Poles	Money won
1993	Earl Sadler	1	75	0	0	0	0	0	$4,830
1994	Cale Yarborough	12	37	0	0	0	3	0	$137,865
	Earl Sadler	4		0	0	0	2	0	$48,255
	T. W. Taylor	4		0	0	0	0	0	$40,145
1995	Cale Yarborough	27	31	0	0	1	2	0	$436,805
1996	Michael Kranefuss	7	26	0	0	0	4	1	$128,990
1997	Michael Kranefuss	32	13	0	3	8	3	0	$1,067,203
1998	Roger Penske	33	7	1	12	16	2	1	$2,332,034

Year	Car owner	Races	Champ. finish	Wins	Top 5	Top 10	DNF	Poles	Money won
1999	Roger Penske	34	11	0	5	12	4	0	$2,125,227
2000	Roger Penske	32	24	2	6	12	11	4	$2,169,251
2001	Roger Penske	28	35	0	5	7	4	0	$2,682,603
2002	Ray Evernham	36	26	0	2	4	7	0	$2,494,583
2003	Ray Evernham	36	19	0	4	12	6	1	$3,371,879
2004	Ray Evernham	36	10	1	5	13	3	2	$4,915,842
2005	Ray Evernham	36	9	1	4	9	1	0	$5,741,090
2006	Ray Evernham	21	39	0	0	0	2	0	$2,582,057
	James Finch	1		0	0	0	1	0	$59,675
TOTALS		**403**		**5**	**48**	**96**	**59**	**9**	**$30,894,339**

2006 RESULTS

Race	Track	Start	Finish	Laps	Led	Winnings	Status	Rank
1. Daytona 500	Daytona	26	36	197/203	0	$278,049	Running	37
2. Auto Club 500	California	21	22	250/251	0	$116,916	Running	29
3. UAW-DaimlerChrysler 400	Las Vegas	24	25	270/270	0	$116,016	Running	28
4. Golden Corral 500	Atlanta	20	41	235/325	0	$95,846	Running	34
5. Food City 500	Bristol	10	16	500/500	0	$115,866	Running	34
6. DIRECTV 500	Martinsville	23	26	462/500	0	$100,066	Engine	33
7. Samsung/RadioShack 500	Texas	34	31	328/334	0	$116,891	Running	35
8. Subway Fresh 500	Phoenix	28	26	310/312	0	$95,841	Running	34
9. Aaron's 499	Talladega	36	13	188/188	1	$124,816	Running	32
10. Crown Royal 400	Richmond	38	32	397/400	0	$93,541	Running	34
11. Dodge Charger 500	Darlington	30	38	346/367	0	$96,866	Running	34
12. Coca-Cola 600	Lowe's	2	15	400/400	0	$134,116	Running	34
13. Neigh. Excellence 400	Dover	2	18	400/400	14	$120,316	Running	34
14. Pocono 500	Pocono	26	23	200/200	0	$97,266	Running	32
15. 3M Performance 400	Michigan	18	36	129/129	0	$98,991	Running	32
16. Dodge/Save Mart 350	Infineon	32	22	110/110	0	$105,441	Running	31
17. Pepsi 400	Daytona	42	36	159/160	0	$111,291	Running	32
18. USG Sheetrock 400	Chicagoland	16	24	270/270	0	$114,916	Running	32
19. Lenox Industrial Tools 300	New. Hamp.	37	29	306/308	0	$99,391	Running	33
20. Pennsylvania 500	Pocono	22	37	199/200	0	$90,566	Running	34
21. Allstate 400 at Brickyard	Indianapolis	15	41	82/160	0	$164,316	Suspension	34
36. Ford 400	Homestead	32	42	78/268	0	$59,675	Oil leak	39

TEAM FACTS >>> >>> **Primary sponsor:** Crown Royal/Irwin Tools >>> >>> **Owner:** Jack Roush >>> >>> **Team:** Roush Racing

26 FORD DRIVER PROFILE

Date of birth: June 3, 1976
Hometown: Joplin, Mo.
Resides: Statesville, N.C.
Spouse: None **Children:** None
Height: 5-8 **Weight:** 150
Hobbies: Home projects

JAMIE McMURRAY

>>> >>> **Crew chief:** TBA >>> >>> **Engine builder:** Roush-Yates Engines >>> >>> **Website:** www.roushracing.com >>> >>>

>> NASCAR ACHIEVEMENTS

First NASCAR NEXTEL Cup Series start: October 6, 2002
(Talladega; started 5th, finished 26th)
Best points finish: 11th (2004)
Career victories: 1—2002: Lowe's (b)
First victory: October 13, 2002 (Lowe's, career start No. 2)
Career poles: 2—2005: Pocono (b); 2003: Homestead
First pole: November 14, 2003 (Homestead, career start No. 42)
Last pole: July 23, 2005 (Pocono)

>> CAREER HIGHLIGHTS

- A change of scenery did not lead to a change in results in 2006 for McMurray. Big things were expected of him when he moved from Chip Ganassi Racing to Roush Racing, but he did not deliver. Though two of his Roush teammates qualified for the Chase for the NASCAR NEXTEL Cup, McMurray did not come close. His 25th-place finish in points was the worst in his career for a full season.
- Again missed the Chase for the NASCAR NEXTEL Cup. His cars often were decent but rarely competitive; in the first 26 races, he led one lap. He signed a contract to drive for Jack Roush for the 2007 season and openly lobbied to be let out of his deal with Chip Ganassi Racing in time for the 2006 season. That finally happened late in the season.
- Easily had the best 2004 season among drivers who did not make the Chase for the NASCAR NEXTEL Cup, and he had a better season overall then several who made the show. He didn't win a race, but his car was strong week in and week out.
- Won the Raybestos Rookie of the Year in the NASCAR NEXTEL Cup Series in 2003 with a consistent second half.

He finished outside of the top 20 just once in the last 13 races and grabbed his first pole in the season finale at Homestead.

- Became only the 11th driver to visit victory lane in only his second NASCAR NEXTEL Cup Series start, and he did it by holding off Bobby Labonte on the last lap in the 2002 October race at Lowe's Motor Speedway. McMurray was racing in place of Sterling Marlin for Chip Ganassi after a neck injury ended Marlin's season.

>> FAST FACTS

- Won his first NASCAR Craftsman Truck Series race in 2004 at Martinsville while driving for Jim Smith.
- NASCAR Busch Series victory on October 26, 2002, gave him the distinction of becoming the 100th driver to win a NASCAR Busch Series race.
- Ran in 69 NASCAR Busch Series races from 2000 to 2002, winning twice and earning six top fives.
- Finished third in the NASCAR Busch Series Raybestos Rookie of the Year standings in 2001.
- Finished 22nd in the 2000 NASCAR Craftsman Truck Series standings.
- Ran five NASCAR Craftsman Truck Series races in 1999 and also competed in the NASCAR RE/MAX Challenge Series.
- Ran in the NASCAR Dodge Weekly Series at several tracks in his home state of Missouri, most notably the I-44 Speedway, where he was track champion in 1997.
- Competed in the Grand American Late Model class from 1996 to 1998 and in the Grand American Modified division from 1994 to 1995.

─────────────── Jamie McMurray continued ───────────────

- Began racing late models in 1992 at age 16 and go-karts at age 8.
- Won four U.S. Go-Kart titles between 1986 to 1992 and was the World Go-Kart champion in 1991.
- Selected as one of only 10 Americans to represent the U.S. in an international karting event in the former Soviet Union in 1989.
- Became associated with 2002 NASCAR NEXTEL Cup Series champion Tony Stewart during their days on the go-kart circuit while Stewart was in the junior class and McMurray was in the rookie-junior class.

CAREER STATISTICS

Year	Car owner	Races	Champ. finish	Wins	Top 5	Top 10	DNF	Poles	Money won
2002	Chip Ganassi	6	46	1	1	2	1	0	$717,942
2003	Chip Ganassi	36	13	0	5	13	4	1	$3,258,806
2004	Chip Ganassi	36	11	0	9	23	6	0	$4,676,311
2005	Chip Ganassi	36	12	0	4	10	4	1	$4,639,303
2006	Jack Roush	36	25	0	3	7	7	0	$5,241,224
TOTALS		150		1	22	55	22	2	$18,533,586

2006 RESULTS

Race	Track	Start	Finish	Laps	Led	Winnings	Status	Rank
1. Daytona 500	Daytona	6	37	196/203	1	$287,183	Accident	36
2. Auto Club 500	California	25	6	251/251	0	$142,375	Running	18
3. UAW-DaimlerChrysler 400	Las Vegas	19	23	270/270	0	$113,625	Running	20
4. Golden Corral 500	Atlanta	34	14	325/325	0	$108,350	Running	16
5. Food City 500	Bristol	8	35	440/500	0	$125,275	Running	24
6. DIRECTV 500	Martinsville	2	9	500/500	6	$122,675	Running	17
7. Samsung/RadioShack 500	Texas	41	37	254/334	0	$127,100	Running	21
8. Subway Fresh 500	Phoenix	26	14	311/312	0	$112,750	Running	20
9. Aaron's 499	Talladega	8	5	188/188	18	$168,600	Running	17
10. Crown Royal 400	Richmond	31	19	399/400	0	$112,200	Running	17
11. Dodge Charger 500	Darlington	15	42	223/367	0	$113,200	Engine	20
12. Coca-Cola 600	Lowe's	33	8	400/400	0	$158,825	Running	18
13. Neigh. Excellence 400	Dover	9	2	400/400	95	$239,600	Running	15
14. Pocono 500	Pocono	8	18	200/200	0	$110,900	Running	14
15. 3M Performance 400	Michigan	41	23	129/129	0	$118,675	Running	15
16. Dodge/Save Mart 350	Infineon	2	18	110/110	0	$121,825	Running	16
17. Pepsi 400	Daytona	26	8	160/160	0	$148,475	Running	16
18. USG Sheetrock 400	Chicagoland	42	39	268/270	0	$123,850	Running	17
19. Lenox Industrial Tools 300	New Hamp.	33	33	303/308	0	$116,300	Running	17
20. Pennsylvania 500	Pocono	28	20	200/200	0	$113,225	Running	17
21. Allstate 400 at Brickyard	Indianapolis	18	26	160/160	0	$186,575	Running	19
22. AMD at the Glen	Watkins Glen	24	3	90/90	0	$163,225	Running	18
23. GFS Marketplace 400	Michigan	40	17	200/200	8	$119,150	Running	16
24. Sharpie 500	Bristol	37	29	496/500	0	$129,910	Running	18
25. Sony HD 500	California	31	20	250/250	0	$136,825	Running	17
26. Chevy Rock & Roll 400	Richmond	25	35	398/400	0	$112,275	Running	19
27. Sylvania 300	New Hamp.	42	29	298/300	0	$116,225	Running	19
28. Dover 400	Dover	32	17	398/400	0	$114,300	Running	18
29. Banquet 400	Kansas	41	42	128/267	0	$123,250	Accident	20
30. UAW-Ford 500	Talladega	8	37	160/188	22	$125,750	Accident	22
31. Bank of America 500	Lowe's	27	34	160/334	0	$107,800	Engine	22
32. Subway 500	Martinsville	24	19	500/500	0	$113,600	Running	22
33. Bass Pro Shops 500	Atlanta	22	40	244/325	0	$125,200	Running	24
34. Dickies 500	Texas	42	26	338/339	4	$141,500	Running	23
35. Checker Auto Parts 500	Phoenix	14	40	272/312	0	$108,175	Accident	24
36. Ford 400	Homestead	42	35	250/268	0	$108,050	Engine	25

TEAM FACTS >>> >>> Primary sponsor: GMAC/National Guard >>> >>> Owner: Rick Hendrick >>> >>> Team: Hendrick Motorsports

25 CHEVROLET DRIVER PROFILE

Date of birth: March 12, 1978
Hometown: Bakersfield, Calif.
Resides: Mooresville, N.C.
Spouse: None **Children:** None
Height: 5-8 **Weight:** 158 **Hobbies:** Wakeboarding, snowboarding

CASEY MEARS

>>> >>> Crew chief: Lance McGrew >>> >>> Engine builder: Hendrick Engines >>> >>> Website: www.hendrickmotorsports.com

>> NASCAR ACHIEVEMENTS

First NASCAR NEXTEL Cup Series start: February 16, 2003 (Daytona; started 29th, finished 27th)
Best points finish: 14th (2006)
Career victories: 0
Best race finish: 2nd (most recently, October 1, 2006, Kansas)
Career poles: 2—2004: Pocono (b), Indianapolis
First pole: July 30, 2004 (Pocono, career start No. 56)
Last pole: August 7, 2004 (Indianapolis)

>> CAREER HIGHLIGHTS

- Opened the 2006 season with three straight top 10s, hinting that his long-anticipated breakthrough season finally had arrived. But he didn't have his fourth top 10 until the 15th race of the season. He finished 14th in points, eight better than his previous best, but he led only three laps all season and wasn't competitive for victories. Mears will drive the No. 25 Hendrick Motorsports Chevy in 2007.
- Showed promise late in the season, leading a lot of laps at Texas and Homestead and finishing in the top 10 in four of the last seven races. Overall, however, he didn't finish enough laps in 2005, and on those he completed, he too often was in the back of the pack. He finished 22nd in points for the second consecutive season.
- Didn't win in 2004, but Mears had a strong enough car to do so several times. He qualified well, too. He clearly was more comfortable with the car and the rhythm of NASCAR

NEXTEL Cup Series racing.
- Struggled during his 2003 rookie season with 10 DNFs, and he finished 35th in points. Coming from open-wheel racing, Mears still was trying to figure out stock cars.

>> FAST FACTS
- Won first stock car race in an ARCA event June 14, 2003, at Michigan. Later that season, he won back-to-back ARCA races, July 25 and 26, at Pocono.
- Finished 21st in his rookie season in the NASCAR Busch Series in 2002, scoring one top five, at Talladega. It was announced in December 2002 that he would drive for Chip Ganassi in the NASCAR NEXTEL Cup Series in 2003.
- In 2001, had two top 10s in four starts in CART after replac-

ing Alex Zanardi, who was involved in a career-ending crash.
- In 2000, finished third in the Indy Lights Series, scoring his first win at the Grand Prix of Houston.
- Finished second in the Indy Lights Series in 1999, becoming only the fourth driver in series history to complete every lap.
- Won three races in off-road stadium SuperLites in 1996.
- Won the 1995 Jim Russell USAC Triple Crown championship at age 17.
- Was the second-youngest driver in USAC history to win a feature race (Mesa Marin, 1994) at age 16.
- Is the son of two-time Indy 500 starter and off-road legend Roger Mears.
- Is the nephew of four-time Indy 500 winner Rick Mears.

CAREER STATISTICS

Year	Car owner	Races	Champ. finish	Wins	Top 5	Top 10	DNF	Poles	Money won
2003	Chip Ganassi	36	35	0	0	0	10	0	$2,639,178
2004	Chip Ganassi	36	22	0	1	9	3	2	$3,462,623
2005	Chip Ganassi	36	22	0	3	9	3	0	$4,481,787
2006	Chip Ganassi	36	14	0	2	8	2	0	$6,128,449
TOTALS		**144**		**0**	**6**	**26**	**18**	**2**	**$16,712,037**

2006 RESULTS

Race	Track	Start	Finish	Laps	Led	Winnings	Status	Rank
1. Daytona 500	Daytona	14	2	203/203	0	$1,095,770	Running	2
2. Auto Club 500	California	20	7	251/251	0	$140,858	Running	2
3. UAW-DaimlerChrysler 400	Las Vegas	38	9	270/270	0	$147,383	Running	4
4. Golden Corral 500	Atlanta	10	21	324/325	0	$105,908	Running	5
5. Food City 500	Bristol	12	25	498/500	0	$118,083	Running	8
6. DIRECTV 500	Martinsville	32	27	456/500	0	$103,918	Running	10
7. Samsung/RadioShack 500	Texas	20	14	334/334	0	$150,233	Running	10
8. Subway Fresh 500	Phoenix	12	20	311/312	0	$103,983	Running	10
9. Aaron's 499	Talladega	25	20	188/188	2	$123,083	Running	11
10. Crown Royal 400	Richmond	3	17	399/400	0	$104,833	Running	10
11. Dodge Charger 500	Darlington	21	17	366/367	0	$113,908	Running	11
12. Coca-Cola 600	Lowe's	30	23	398/400	0	$124,933	Running	11
13. Neigh. Excellence 400	Dover	34	21	400/400	0	$116,983	Running	13
14. Pocono 500	Pocono	22	43	1/200	0	$94,255	Accident	15
15. 3M Performance 400	Michigan	37	7	129/129	0	$122,183	Running	14
16. Dodge/Save Mart 350	Infineon	34	20	110/110	0	$113,708	Running	15
17. Pepsi 400	Daytona	40	7	160/160	0	$150,833	Running	15
18. USG Sheetrock 400	Chicagoland	11	25	270/270	0	$118,783	Running	15
19. Lenox Industrial Tools 300	New Hamp.	29	21	308/308	0	$108,658	Running	15
20. Pennsylvania 500	Pocono	31	23	200/200	0	$101,333	Running	15
21. Allstate 400 at Brickyard	Indianapolis	39	23	160/160	0	$181,308	Running	15
22. AMD at the Glen	Watkins Glen	17	35	89/90	0	$92,483	Running	19
23. GFS Marketplace 400	Michigan	7	16	200/200	0	$110,633	Running	17
24. Sharpie 500	Bristol	11	17	499/500	0	$127,533	Running	16
25. Sony HD 500	California	33	14	250/250	0	$129,583	Running	15
26. Chevy Rock & Roll 400	Richmond	13	11	400/400	0	$110,208	Running	15
27. Sylvania 300	New Hamp.	24	21	300/300	0	$108,758	Running	15
28. Dover 400	Dover	24	22	397/400	0	$104,083	Running	15
29. Banquet 400	Kansas	33	2	267/267	0	$240,033	Running	15
30. UAW-Ford 500	Talladega	31	30	185/188	1	$104,683	Running	15
31. Bank of America 500	Lowe's	3	12	333/334	0	$113,158	Running	14
32. Subway 500	Martinsville	19	6	500/500	0	$113,233	Running	14
33. Bass Pro Shops 500	Atlanta	14	28	321/325	0	$114,333	Running	14
34. Dickies 500	Texas	25	7	339/339	0	$174,208	Running	14
35. Checker Auto Parts 500	Phoenix	17	26	312/312	0	$100,333	Running	15
36. Ford 400	Homestead	39	32	261/268	0	$95,983	Engine	14

15 CHEVROLET DRIVER PROFILE
Date of birth: August 21, 1980
Hometown: Eau Claire, Wis.
Resides: Mooresville, N.C.
Spouse: Single **Children:** None
Height: 5-10 **Weight:** 180
Hobbies: Ice racing, basketball, spending time with family, greyhound rescue

PAUL MENARD

>> NASCAR ACHIEVEMENTS
First NASCAR NEXTEL Cup Series start: August 10, 2003 (Watkins Glen; started 43rd, finished 29th)
Best points finish: 45th (2006)
Career victories: 0
Best race finish: 7th (March 19, 2006, Atlanta)

Career poles: 0
Best starting position: 22nd (March 17, 2006, Atlanta)

>> CAREER HIGHLIGHTS
- Showed flashes of being competitive in seven NASCAR NEXTEL Cup Series races in a Dale Earnhardt Inc. car in

—————————————— Paul Menard continued ——————————————

2006. He finished an impressive seventh at Atlanta and led at Talladega before getting caught up in a wreck. Menard will graduate to the NASCAR NEXTEL Cup Series full-time in 2007.
- Made a start at Watkins Glen in 2003 for Andy Petree and in 2005 for Dale Earnhardt Inc., finishing 29th and 27th, respectively.

>> FAST FACTS
- Won his first NASCAR Busch Series race in 2006, at Milwaukee, and finished sixth in the NASCAR Busch Series standings.
- Finished sixth in the NASCAR Busch Series standings in 2005 and posted 15 top 10s.
- Started the 2004 NASCAR Busch Series season racing for Andy Petree but switched to Dale Earnhardt Inc. in July. Menard finished second in the Raybestos Rookie of the Year standings and recorded his first career NASCAR Busch Series pole, at Kansas.
- Ran six NASCAR Busch Series races and five NASCAR Craftsman Truck Series races for Andy Petree in 2003, posting one top 10 in each series.
- Won in only his third ARCA start, at Talladega in 2003. It was his first event at the superspeedway.

- Competed in NASCAR AutoZone Elite Division, Midwest Series and Southwest Series events from 2000-02 and scored a Southwest Series victory at Phoenix in 2002.
- Began competing in go-karts at age 8 and started racing on ice in Wisconsin at age 15. Menard has won 10 International Ice Racing Association events.
- His family owns Menards, a home improvement store chain in the upper Midwest.

CAREER STATISTICS

Year	Car owner	Races	Champ. finish	Wins	Top 5	Top 10	DNF	Poles	Money won
2003	Andy Petree	1	66	0	0	0	0	0	$52,410
2005	Teresa Earnhardt	1	71	0	0	0	0	0	$58,755
2006	Teresa Earnhardt	7	45	0	0	1	2	0	$546,993
TOTALS		9		0	0	1	2	0	$658,158

2006 RESULTS

Race	Track	Start	Finish	Laps	Led	Winnings	Status	Rank
4. Golden Corral 500	Atlanta	22	7	325/325	0	$78,625	Running	41
12. Coca-Cola 600	Lowe's	36	14	400/400	0	$95,525	Running	44
22. AMD at the Glen	Watkins Glen	34	29	90/90	0	$59,250	Running	46
23. GFS Marketplace 400	Michigan	36	20	200/200	0	$72,475	Running	43
30. UAW-Ford 500	Talladega	24	34	173/188	1	$69,375	Accident	45
34. Dickies 500	Texas	32	41	194/339	0	$91,635	Engine	45
36. Ford 400	Homestead	28	17	268/268	1	$64,925	Accident	45

TEAM FACTS >>> **Primary sponsor:** Texaco/Havoline >>> **Owner:** Chip Ganassi >>> **Team:** Chip Ganassi Racing with Felix Sabates

42 DODGE DRIVER PROFILE

Date of birth: September 20, 1975
Hometown: Bogota, Colombia
Resides: Monte Carlo, Monaco
Spouse: Connie
Children: Sebastian, Paulina
Height: 5-6 **Weight:** 158
Hobbies: Computer games, snowboarding, windsurfing, golf

JUAN PABLO MONTOYA

>>> **Crew chief:** Donnie Wingo >>> >>> **Engine builder:** Ernie Elliott >>> >>> **Website:** www.chipganassiracing.com >>> >>>

>> NASCAR ACHIEVEMENTS
First NASCAR NEXTEL Cup Series start: November 19, 2006 (Homestead; started 29th, finished 34th)
Best points finish: 69th (2006)
Career victories: 0
Best race finish: 34th (November 19, 2006, Homestead)
Career poles: 0
Best starting position: 29th (November 19, 2006, Homestead)

>> CAREER HIGHLIGHTS
- Stunned the motorsports community with announcement that he would defect from Formula 1 to NASCAR in 2007. He spent the fall testing and racing stock cars for Chip Ganassi Racing.

>> FAST FACTS
- Is the first Formula 1 regular to make the permanent move to the NASCAR NEXTEL Cup Series.
- Spent six seasons (2001 to 2006) in Formula 1, racing for

WilliamsF1 during his first four seasons and Team McLaren during his last two. He posted seven wins in his F1 career and finished fifth or better in the standings in each of his full F1 seasons, including a career-high third in 2002 and 2003.
- Joined Graham Hill as the only two drivers to win both the Indianapolis 500 (2000) and Monaco Grand Prix (2003).
- Ran for Chip Ganassi in CART in 1999 and 2000. In 1999, Montoya posted seven wins, was named CART rookie of the year and became the youngest driver to win a CART championship. In 2000, Montoya posted three CART wins.
- Moved to North America in 1998 to join Ganassi's organization after winning the FIA International Formula 3000 Championship. He had finished second in the championship in 1997.
- Traveled to the United States to attend Skip Barber Racing School in 1992, and for the next five years, Montoya raced in South America, North America and Europe.
- Won Kart Junior World Championships in 1990 and 1991.
- Began racing karts in 1981 at age 6 in Colombia.

Year	Car owner	Races	Champ. finish	Wins	Top 5	Top 10	DNF	Poles	Money won
2006	Chip Ganassi	1	69	0	0	0	1	0	$61,425
TOTALS		**1**		**0**	**0**	**0**	**1**	**0**	**$61,425**

2006 RESULTS

Race	Track	Start	Finish	Laps	Led	Winnings	Status	Rank
36. Ford 400	Homestead	29	34	251/268	0	$61,425	Accident	69

TEAM FACTS >>> >>> **Primary sponsor:** TBA >>> >>> **Owner:** Bobby Ginn >>> >>> **Team:** Ginn Racing >>> >>>

13 CHEVROLET DRIVER PROFILE

Date of birth: September 26, 1963
Hometown: Lakeland, Fla.
Resides: Mooresville, N.C.
Spouse: Andrea **Children:** John, Blair, Kennedy
Height: 5-9 **Weight:** 185
Hobbies: Fishing, skiing

JOE NEMECHEK

Crew chief: Peter Sospenzo >>> >>> **Engine builder:** Hendrick Engines >>> >>> **Website:** www.ginnracing.com >>> >>>

>> NASCAR ACHIEVEMENTS

First NASCAR NEXTEL Cup Series start: July 11, 1993
(New Hampshire; started 15th, finished 36th)
Best points finish: 15th (2000)
Career victories: 4—2004: Kansas; 2003: Richmond (a);
2001: Rockingham (b); 1999: New Hampshire (b)
First victory: September 19, 1999 (New Hampshire, career start No. 180)
Last victory: October 10, 2004 (Kansas)
Career poles: 9—2005: Michigan (b); 2004: Kansas, Talladega (b); 2000: Talladega (b); 1999: Daytona (b), Talladega (b), Martinsville (b); 1997: California, Pocono (b)
First pole: June 20, 1997 (California, career start No. 105)
Last pole: August 20, 2005 (Michigan)

>> CAREER HIGHLIGHTS

- Nemechek's season was a mess from beginning to end. His team's owner sold the organization midway through the year, but Nemechek's results didn't change. He will turn the No. 01 Army car over to Mark Martin and Regan Smith next season and will drive the No. 13 car for owner Bobby Ginn.
- For the quality of cars Nemechek had week in and week out, his 2005 finishes were disappointing. Particularly difficult to handle was the Coca-Cola 600, in which he cut a tire and hit the wall while leading late. Two blown engines early dropped him out of the top 30, but he rallied to finish 16th in points.
- Won the NASCAR Busch Series race and the NASCAR NEXTEL Cup Series race, the latter from the pole, at Kansas Speedway in 2004. Using Hendrick Motorsports engines, his MB2 Chevy often was stout in 2004, but too many DNFs doomed his season. He completed just 86.7 percent of laps.
- Appeared to be on the way to a strong 2003 season after winning the spring Richmond race. But he had only three top 10s the rest of the way and eventually lost his job with Hendrick Motorsports. He ran the last four races of the season for MB2.

- Started his 300th career race at Pocono in June 2003.
- Began 2002 with Haas-Carter Motorsports, but the team ceased operations after only seven starts. He started one race as a replacement for the injured Johnny Benson, then replaced Jerry Nadeau in the No. 25 Hendrick Motorsports entry for the rest of the season. Despite the instability, Nemechek tied a career high with three top fives.
- Joined Andy Petree for the 2000 and 2001 seasons and had a career-high nine top 10s in 2000. He posted the second victory of his career at Rockingham in 2001.
- In 1999, won a career-best three poles (Daytona, Martinsville, Talladega) and got his first victory (New Hampshire) while driving for Felix Sabates.
- Ran two full seasons as a driver/owner in 1995 and 1996 after spending his first full NASCAR NEXTEL Cup Series season driving for Larry Hedrick in 1994.

>> FAST FACTS

- Owns his own NASCAR Busch Series team, NEMCO Motorsports, with his wife, Andrea. Has run races in the NASCAR Busch Series for 18 consecutive seasons, dating to 1989.
- Won the 1992 NASCAR Busch Series championship, edging Bobby Labonte by three points, the closest champion's margin in the history of NASCAR's three national series.
- Named the NASCAR Busch Series Raybestos Rookie of the Year in 1990.
- Won the championship and Rookie of the Year honors in NASCAR's All-Pro Series in 1989.
- Won the championship and Rookie of the Year honors in the United Stock Car Alliance series in 1988.
- Named Lakeland Interstate Speedway's Rookie of the Year in 1987.
- Began racing in 1983, in motocross; won more than 300 trophies in six years of competition.
- Attended the Florida Institute of Technology in Melbourne, Fla., before turning to racing full-time.

——————— Joe Nemechek continued ———————

CAREER STATISTICS

Year	Car owner	Races	Champ. finish	Wins	Top 5	Top 10	DNF	Poles	Money won
1993	Joe Nemechek	3	44	0	0	0	2	0	$24,300
	Morgan/McClure	2		0	0	0	0	0	$32,280
1994	Larry Hedrick	29	27	0	1	3	9	0	$389,565
1995	Joe Nemechek	29	28	0	1	4	5	0	$428,925
1996	Joe Nemechek	29	34	0	0	2	8	0	$666,247
1997	Felix Sabates	29	28	0	0	3	4	2	$679,954
	Phil Barkdoll	1		0	0	0	1	0	$52,240
1998	Felix Sabates	32	26	0	1	4	5	0	$1,343,991
1999	Felix Sabates	34	30	1	1	3	5	3	$1,634,946
2000	Andy Petree	34	15	0	3	9	6	1	$2,105,041
2001	Andy Petree	31	28	1	1	4	6	0	$2,543,660
2002	Rick Hendrick	25	34	0	3	3	8	0	$1,766,252
	Travis Carter	7		0	0	0	2	0	$612,062
	Tom Beard	1		0	0	0	0	0	$74,710
2003	Rick Hendrick	32	25	1	2	5	7	0	$2,355,059
	Tom Beard	4		0	0	1	0	0	$271,425
2004	Tom Beard	36	19	1	3	9	6	2	$4,345,554
2005	Tom Beard	36	16	0	2	9	2	1	$4,828,659
2006	Bobby Ginn	36	27	0	0	2	3	0	$4,099,914
TOTALS		**430**		**4**	**18**	**61**	**79**	**9**	**$28,256,242**

2006 RESULTS

Race	Track	Start	Finish	Laps	Led	Winnings	Status	Rank
1. Daytona 500	Daytona	38	33	200/203	0	$279,453	Running	33
2. Auto Club 500	California	8	27	249/251	0	$109,820	Running	32
3. UAW-DaimlerChrysler 400	Las Vegas	7	13	270/270	0	$126,295	Running	24
4. Golden Corral 500	Atlanta	13	17	325/325	0	$99,020	Running	22
5. Food City 500	Bristol	16	28	495/500	0	$109,255	Running	26
6. DIRECTV 500	Martinsville	22	23	495/500	0	$98,245	Running	25
7. Samsung/RadioShack 500	Texas	17	23	332/334	0	$129,070	Running	25
8. Subway Fresh 500	Phoenix	32	35	283/312	0	$87,720	Running	28
9. Aaron's 499	Talladega	6	27	173/188	5	$107,620	Accident	29
10. Crown Royal 400	Richmond	17	28	398/400	0	$93,445	Running	29
11. Dodge Charger 500	Darlington	36	16	366/367	0	$106,995	Running	29
12. Coca-Cola 600	Lowe's	19	18	399/400	0	$121,245	Running	29
13. Neigh. Excellence 400	Dover	13	35	396/400	0	$99,995	Running	29
14. Pocono 500	Pocono	21	29	198/200	0	$91,320	Running	29
15. 3M Performance 400	Michigan	7	26	129/129	0	$99,670	Running	29
16. Dodge/Save Mart 350	Infineon	10	25	110/110	0	$100,295	Running	28
17. Pepsi 400	Daytona	5	19	160/160	0	$118,370	Running	27
18. USG Sheetrock 400	Chicagoland	17	33	268/270	0	$105,545	Running	29
19. Lenox Industrial Tools 300	New Hamp.	16	41	199/308	0	$93,405	Accident	30
20. Pennsylvania 500	Pocono	10	17	200/200	0	$94,220	Running	30
21. Allstate 400 at Brickyard	Indianapolis	21	24	160/160	1	$171,845	Running	29
22. AMD at the Glen	Watkins Glen	37	42	61/90	0	$83,680	Accident	29
23. GFS Marketplace 400	Michigan	13	26	200/200	0	$110,395	Running	30
24. Sharpie 500	Bristol	41	26	498/500	0	$113,665	Running	31
25. Sony HD 500	California	13	25	249/250	0	$115,070	Running	31
26. Chevy Rock & Roll 400	Richmond	21	32	398/400	0	$90,495	Running	31
27. Sylvania 300	New Hamp.	17	32	295/300	0	$95,070	Running	31
28. Dover 400	Dover	5	26	396/400	0	$95,345	Running	31
29. Banquet 400	Kansas	18	27	265/267	0	$109,245	Running	31
30. UAW-Ford 500	Talladega	15	18	188/188	1	$102,845	Running	31
31. Bank of America 500	Lowe's	30	9	334/334	0	$108,095	Running	30
32. Subway 500	Martinsville	23	20	500/500	0	$98,795	Running	30
33. Bass Pro Shops 500	Atlanta	31	9	325/325	3	$132,845	Running	30
34. Dickies 500	Texas	16	18	338/339	0	$126,445	Running	29
35. Checker Auto Parts 500	Phoenix	5	19	312/312	0	$94,120	Running	29
36. Ford 400	Homestead	13	13	268/268	0	$107,645	Running	27

TEAM FACTS >>> >>> **Primary sponsor:** Alltel/Mobil 1 >>> >>> **Owner:** Roger Penske >>> >>> **Team:** Penske Racing >>>

12 DODGE DRIVER PROFILE

Date of birth: December 8, 1977
Hometown: South Bend, Ind.
Resides: Sherrills Ford, N.C.
Spouse: Krissie **Children:** None
Height: 5-11 **Weight:** 207
Hobbies: Fishing, restoring classic cars

RYAN NEWMAN

>>> **Crew chief:** Mike Nelson >>> >>> **Engine builder:** Penske-Jasper Engines >>> >>> **Website:** www.penskeracing.com

>> NASCAR ACHIEVEMENTS

First NASCAR NEXTEL Cup Series start: November 5, 2000 (Phoenix; started 10th, finished 41st)
Best points finish: 6th (2002, 2003, 2005)
Career victories: 12—2005: New Hampshire (b); 2004: Michigan (a), Dover (b); 2003: Texas, Dover (a,b), Chicagoland, Pocono (b), Michigan (b), Richmond (b), Kansas; 2002: New Hampshire (b)
First victory: September 15, 2002 (New Hampshire, career start No. 35)
Last victory: September 18, 2005 (New Hampshire)
Career poles: 37—2006: Dover (a), New Hampshire (a); 2005: Las Vegas, Atlanta (a,b), Texas (a,b), Lowe's (a), Michigan (a), Dover (a); 2004: Rockingham, Atlanta (a,b), Bristol (a), New Hampshire (a), Richmond (b), Lowe's (b), Martinsville (b), Phoenix; 2003: Atlanta (a,b), Bristol (a), Lowe's (a,b), Dover (a), Pocono (b), New Hampshire (b), Darlington (b), Rockingham (b), Phoenix; 2002: California, Chicagoland, New Hampshire (b), Martinsville (b), Rockingham (b), Phoenix; 2001: Lowe's (a)
First pole: May 24, 2001 (Lowe's, career start No. 3)
Last pole: July 14, 2006 (New Hampshire)

>> CAREER HIGHLIGHTS

- Stumbled through the worst season of his career in 2006. Normally the sport's best qualifier, Newman posted just two poles and managed just an 11.6 starting position, almost five spots worse than last year. His average finish took a similar dive. He did not come close to qualifying for the Chase for the NASCAR NEXTEL Cup.

- For the second straight season, Newman had to scramble to make the Chase for the NASCAR NEXTEL Cup in 2005. But once he made it, he stayed in the hunt until almost the end. The team struggled to get a handle on the new Dodge Charger during races but still was a crackerjack qualifier, leading the NASCAR NEXTEL Cup Series with eight poles.
- Won nine poles and two races in 2004, but his season was a bit of a disappointment. His car often was good, but the team couldn't sustain success and barely made it into the Chase for the NASCAR NEXTEL Cup. Still, Newman was the best qualifier in the series.
- Had more wins than any two drivers combined (eight) in 2003 and led the series in top fives (17) and poles (11). But Newman was inconsistent and unlucky early in the season, with five DNFs in the first half, and never could dig himself out of a points hole. In one stretch, he finished outside of the top 35 in five of seven races.
- Topped Jimmie Johnson for the 2002 Raybestos Rookie of the Year award. Newman also set a rookie record by tying Mark Martin's overall record for the most top 10s (22) in a season. He led the series with six poles, setting another rookie record for most poles in a season. He also tied series champion Tony Stewart in races led (22) and became the

second Raybestos Rookie of the Year to win the All-Star race.
- Scored his first pole in only his third career NASCAR NEXTEL Cup Series start, at the Coca-Cola 600 at Lowe's Motor Speedway in 2001, tying Mark Martin's record for earliest career pole.

>> FAST FACTS

- Made the most of his starts in the NASCAR Busch Series in 2005, winning six of nine races, including three consecutive (Watkins Glen, Michigan and Bristol) and the next two races he entered, at Dover and Lowe's.
- Graduated from Purdue University in August 2001 with a degree in Vehicle Structural Engineering.
- Made his stock car debut in an ARCA race at Michigan in 2000, then won the next race he entered at Pocono; also won ARCA races that year at Kentucky and Lowe's.
- Won the 1999 USAC Coors Light Silver Bullet Series national championship with two wins and 12 top 10s.
- Won seven times in midgets and once in sprint cars.
- Named Rookie of the Year in Sprint Cars (1999), USAC Silver Crown (1996) and USAC National Midgets (1995).
- Was the 1993 All-American Midget Series champion and Rookie of the Year.
- Is a member of the Quarter Midget Hall of Fame.
- Started racing quarter midgets at age 4.

CAREER STATISTICS

Year	Car owner	Races	Champ. finish	Wins	Top 5	Top 10	DNF	Poles	Money won
2000	Roger Penske	1	71	0	0	0	1	0	$37,825
2001	Roger Penske	7	49	0	2	2	2	1	$465,276
2002	Roger Penske	36	6	1	14	22	5	6	$5,346,651
2003	Roger Penske	36	6	8	17	22	7	11	$6,100,877
2004	Roger Penske	36	7	2	11	14	9	9	$6,349,146
2005	Roger Penske	36	6	1	8	16	3	8	$7,259,518
2006	Roger Penske	36	18	0	2	7	3	2	$5,960,473
TOTALS		**188**		**12**	**54**	**83**	**30**	**37**	**$31,519,766**

2006 RESULTS

Race	Track	Start	Finish	Laps	Led	Winnings	Status	Rank
1. Daytona 500	Daytona	18	3	203/203	23	$796,116	Running	3
2. Auto Club 500	California	11	20	250/251	0	$132,683	Running	7
3. UAW-DaimlerChrysler 400	Las Vegas	11	43	88/270	0	$112,125	Accident	18
4. Golden Corral 500	Atlanta	2	18	325/325	2	$115,033	Running	17
5. Food City 500	Bristol	6	9	500/500	0	$129,258	Running	12
6. DIRECTV 500	Martinsville	4	18	498/500	0	$114,358	Running	13
7. Samsung/RadioShack 500	Texas	14	40	200/334	0	$124,283	Accident	18
8. Subway Fresh 500	Phoenix	13	39	221/312	0	$106,258	Accident	22
9. Aaron's 499	Talladega	18	33	106/188	0	$122,308	Running	26
10. Crown Royal 400	Richmond	14	8	400/400	0	$120,658	Running	23
11. Dodge Charger 500	Darlington	2	6	367/367	2	$139,333	Running	19

Race	Track	Start	Finish	Laps	Led	Winnings	Status	Rank
12. Coca-Cola 600	Lowe's	18	35	369/400	0	$127,808	Running	22
13. Neigh. Excellence 400	Dover	1	14	400/400	0	$134,533	Running	19
14. Pocono 500	Pocono	14	11	200/200	1	$114,933	Running	18
15. 3M Performance 400	Michigan	42	15	129/129	0	$118,683	Running	17
16. Dodge/Save Mart 350	Infineon	4	2	110/110	11	$219,758	Running	17
17. Pepsi 400	Daytona	23	11	160/160	0	$140,088	Running	17
18. USG Sheetrock 400	Chicagoland	12	36	268/270	0	$123,058	Running	18
19. Lenox Industrial Tools 300	New Hamp.	1	39	279/308	16	$121,483	Running	19
20. Pennsylvania 500	Pocono	2	18	200/200	12	$109,483	Running	18
21. Allstate 400 at Brickyard	Indianapolis	8	13	160/160	0	$198,308	Running	18
22. AMD at the Glen	Watkins Glen	3	8	90/90	7	$116,708	Running	16
23. GFS Marketplace 400	Michigan	4	25	200/200	8	$115,783	Running	18
24. Sharpie 500	Bristol	21	8	500/500	0	$144,808	Running	15
25. Sony HD 500	California	12	33	248/250	0	$129,658	Running	16
26. Chevy Rock & Roll 400	Richmond	23	20	399/400	0	$111,733	Running	17
27. Sylvania 300	New Hamp.	4	12	300/300	0	$121,583	Running	16
28. Dover 400	Dover	4	24	397/400	28	$111,733	Running	17
29. Banquet 400	Kansas	15	24	266/267	3	$127,108	Running	17
30. UAW-Ford 500	Talladega	11	13	188/188	0	$94,983	Running	17
31. Bank of America 500	Lowe's	15	27	272/334	0	$107,658	Running	18
32. Subway 500	Martinsville	4	13	500/500	0	$114,658	Running	17
33. Bass Pro Shops 500	Atlanta	17	30	321/325	0	$125,258	Running	17
34. Dickies 500	Texas	24	34	328/339	0	$138,483	Running	18
35. Checker Auto Parts 500	Phoenix	7	15	312/312	0	$110,533	Running	18
36. Ford 400	Homestead	16	23	267/268	0	$109,108	Running	18

Newman

TEAM FACTS >>> >>> **Primary sponsor:** Wells Fargo/Marathon Oil >>> >>> **Owner:** Richard Petty >>> >>> **Team:** Petty Enterprises

45 DODGE DRIVER PROFILE

Date of birth: June 20, 1960
Hometown: Trinity, N.C.
Resides: Trinity, N.C.
Spouse: Pattie **Children:** Adam (deceased), Austin, Montgomery
Height: 6-2 **Weight:** 195
Hobbies: Reading, riding motorcycles

KYLE PETTY

>>> >>> **Crew chief:** Bill Wilburn >>> >>> **Engine builder:** Evernham Engine Technologies >>> >>> **Website:** www.pettyracing.com

>> NASCAR ACHIEVEMENTS

First NASCAR NEXTEL Cup Series start: August 5, 1979 (Talladega; started 18th, finished 9th)
Best points finish: 5th (1992, 1993)
Career victories: 8—1995: Dover (a); 1993: Pocono (a); 1992: Watkins Glen, Rockingham (b); 1991: Rockingham (a); 1990: Rockingham (a); 1987: Lowe's (a); 1986: Richmond (a)
First victory: February 23, 1986 (Richmond, career start No. 170)
Last victory: June 4, 1995 (Dover)
Career poles: 8—1993: Daytona (a); 1992: Rockingham (a,b), Martinsville (b); 1991: Rockingham (a,b); 1990: Rockingham (a), North Wilkesboro (b)
First pole: March 2, 1990 (Rockingham, career start No. 277)
Last pole: February 6, 1993 (Daytona)

>> CAREER HIGHLIGHTS

- Dropped after two years of improvement. Petty's average finish of 27.4 in 2006 was his worst since 2003. Though Petty matched his top 10 total from 2005 (two), he finished on the lead lap just 10 times. He remains more committed to turning around the No. 43 car than the No. 45.
- A strong showing in Speedweeks and an eighth-place finish at the first Bristol race hinted at a turnaround in 2005, but it never went much further. His engines—bought for the first time from Evernham Motorsports—were far better than in previous years, but his finishes were about the same.
- Made his 700th career start in 2004 but failed to notch a top 10 finish. Too often, he was just out there turning laps. He never started better than 18th, and his season-best finish was 12th, his only top 15.
- Made his 600th career NASCAR NEXTEL Cup Series start at the 2001 August Michigan race.
- Competed in 19 NASCAR NEXTEL Cup Series races in 2000 for Petty Enterprises before moving from his No. 44 NASCAR NEXTEL Cup Series car to his late son Adam's No. 45 car in the NASCAR Busch Series.
- Left owner Felix Sabates after the 1996 season after finishes of 30th and 27th in points the previous two seasons. He ran as an owner/driver in 1997 and shot up to 15th in

points but fell back down to 30th in 1998.
- Finished a career-high fifth in points in 1992 and 1993. In 1992, he made a late-season bid for the championship with seven top fives in the last 10 races.
- Sat out 11 races in 1991 after an accident in Talladega left him with a broken thigh bone.
- Finished 11th in points in 1990. He found victory lane once, at Rockingham, and Sabates was so elated, he presented Petty with a Rolls Royce. Petty won twice more at Rockingham in the next two seasons.
- Joined Sabates in 1989 and fell to 30th in points that season—even with two top 10s in the final three races.
- Became the first third-generation driver to win a NASCAR NEXTEL Cup Series race, following his father, Richard, and grandfather Lee with a victory at Richmond in 1986.
- Joined the Wood Brothers team in 1985. He finished ninth in points and won the Comeback Driver of the Year award.
- Made his NASCAR NEXTEL Cup Series debut in 1979, running five races for Petty Enterprises.

>> FAST FACTS

- Kyle and his wife, Pattie, were named recipients of the Myers Brothers Award, which recognizes individuals and/or groups who have provided outstanding contributions to the sport of stock car racing, in 2004. The Pettys turned a dream into reality in June of 2004, when the Victory Junction Gang Camp, a summer home for terminally and chronically ill children, officially opened its doors.
- Along with Tony Stewart, was named one of USA Weekend magazine's 2004 Most Caring Athletes.
- Petty, his father Richard and the entire Petty family were named Persons of the Year for 2000 by NASCAR Illustrated for their charitable work.
- Kyle Petty's Charity Ride Across America was founded in 1995. Petty also works with the Make-A-Wish Foundation, the Boy Scouts of America, the NASCAR NEXTEL Cup Racing Wives Auxiliary and the Victory Junction Gang Camp.
- Named NASCAR True Value Man of the Year in 1998 and 2002.
- Won the ARCA 200 at Daytona International Speedway in

February 1979. It was his first race on a closed course, and the victory led to the beginning of his NASCAR NEXTEL Cup Series career that same season.

- Petty was recruited by several colleges as a quarterback; others talked to him about a baseball scholarship.

CAREER STATISTICS

Year	Car owner	Races	Champ. finish	Wins	Top 5	Top 10	DNF	Poles	Money won
1979	Petty Enterprises	5	37	0	0	1	1	0	$10,810
1980	Petty Enterprises	14	28	0	0	6	5	0	$35,575
	B. Rahilly/B. Mock	1		0	0	0	0	0	$775
1981	Petty Enterprises	31	12	0	1	10	18	0	$112,289
1982	Petty Enterprises	23	15	0	2	4	13	0	$108,715
	Hoss Ellington	6		0	0	0	3	0	$12,015
1983	Petty Enterprises	30	13	0	0	2	10	0	$157,820
1984	Petty Enterprises	30	16	0	1	6	7	0	$324,555
1985	Wood Brothers	28	9	0	7	12	4	0	$296,367
1986	Wood Brothers	29	10	1	4	14	6	0	$403,242
1987	Wood Brothers	29	7	1	6	14	4	0	$544,437
1988	Wood Brothers	29	13	0	2	8	6	0	$377,092
1989	Felix Sabates	18	30	0	1	5	7	0	$111,022
	Rick Hendrick	1		0	0	0	0	0	$6,000
1990	Felix Sabates	29	11	1	2	14	5	2	$746,326
1991	Felix Sabates	18	31	1	2	4	5	2	$413,727
1992	Felix Sabates	29	5	2	9	17	5	3	$1,107,063
1993	Felix Sabates	30	5	1	9	15	5	1	$914,662
1994	Felix Sabates	31	15	0	2	7	3	0	$806,332
1995	Felix Sabates	30	30	1	1	5	10	0	$698,875
1996	Felix Sabates	28	27	0	0	2	4	0	$689,041
1997	Petty Enterprises	32	15	0	2	9	2	0	$984,314
1998	Petty Enterprises	33	30	0	0	2	8	0	$1,287,731
1999	Petty Enterprises	32	26	0	0	9	4	0	$1,278,953
2000	Petty Enterprises	18	41	0	0	1	6	0	$797,176
	Michael Kranefuss	1		0	0	0	0	0	$97,735
2001	Petty Enterprises	24	43	0	0	0	8	0	$1,008,919
2002	Petty Enterprises	36	22	0	0	1	1	0	$2,198,073
2003	Petty Enterprises	33	37	0	0	0	5	0	$2,293,222
2004	Petty Enterprises	35	33	0	0	0	9	0	$2,746,082
2005	Petty Enterprises	36	27	0	0	2	3	0	$3,465,687
2006	Petty Enterprises	36	32	0	0	2	5	0	$3,655,539
TOTALS		785		8	51	172	172	8	$27,724,220

2006 RESULTS

Race	Track	Start	Finish	Laps	Led	Winnings	Status	Rank
1. Daytona 500	Daytona	12	39	173/203	0	$256,833	Running	39
2. Auto Club 500	California	39	25	250/251	0	$107,333	Running	34
3. UAW-DaimlerChrysler 400	Las Vegas	39	29	270/270	1	$104,783	Running	33
4. Golden Corral 500	Atlanta	32	8	325/325	0	$108,133	Running	24
5. Food City 500	Bristol	28	18	500/500	0	$107,633	Running	25
6. DIRECTV 500	Martinsville	37	30	439/500	0	$77,550	Running	26
7. Samsung/RadioShack 500	Texas	19	39	248/334	0	$87,000	Engine	32
8. Subway Fresh 500	Phoenix	38	31	305/312	0	$72,400	Running	33
9. Aaron's 499	Talladega	28	18	188/188	0	$111,883	Running	31
10. Crown Royal 400	Richmond	12	26	398/400	0	$87,108	Running	31
11. Dodge Charger 500	Darlington	40	18	366/367	0	$103,133	Running	32
12. Coca-Cola 600	Lowe's	39	25	397/400	0	$108,308	Running	31
13. Neigh. Excellence 400	Dover	35	27	398/400	0	$102,608	Running	31
14. Pocono 500	Pocono	33	40	68/200	0	$68,175	Accident	33
15. 3M Performance 400	Michigan	35	35	129/129	1	$77,050	Running	33
16. Dodge/Save Mart 350	Infineon	33	21	110/110	0	$98,258	Running	30
17. Pepsi 400	Daytona	33	28	160/160	0	$102,597	Running	30
18. USG Sheetrock 400	Chicagoland	33	28	269/270	0	$89,800	Running	31
19. Lenox Industrial Tools 300	New Hamp.	41	28	306/308	0	$77,675	Running	31
20. Pennsylvania 500	Pocono	33	42	117/200	0	$67,885	Accident	33
21. Allstate 400 at Brickyard	Indianapolis	40	27	160/160	0	$161,508	Running	33
22. AMD at the Glen	Watkins Glen	38	30	90/90	1	$82,258	Running	32
23. GFS Marketplace 400	Michigan	42	31	199/200	1	$77,200	Running	32
24. Sharpie 500	Bristol	8	34	481/500	0	$90,535	Running	32
25. Sony HD 500	California	35	35	247/250	0	$92,150	Running	33
26. Chevy Rock & Roll 400	Richmond	38	34	397/400	0	$71,900	Running	33
27. Sylvania 300	New Hamp.	27	37	290/300	0	$75,700	Engine	33
28. Dover 400	Dover	17	25	396/400	0	$87,197	Running	33
29. Banquet 400	Kansas	24	29	265/267	0	$89,600	Running	33
30. UAW-Ford 500	Talladega	18	38	149/188	0	$76,800	Accident	33
31. Bank of America 500	Lowe's	32	22	330/334	0	$84,197	Running	33
32. Subway 500	Martinsville	14	10	500/500	0	$103,083	Running	33
33. Bass Pro Shops 500	Atlanta	37	17	323/325	0	$117,758	Running	33
34. Dickies 500	Texas	35	11	339/339	0	$144,808	Running	32
35. Checker Auto Parts 500	Phoenix	34	25	312/312	0	$86,458	Running	32
36. Ford 400	Homestead	38	28	266/268	0	$73,775	Running	32

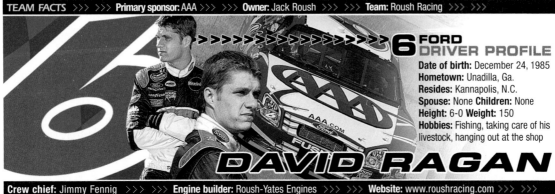

TEAM FACTS >>> >>> Primary sponsor: AAA >>> >>> Owner: Jack Roush >>> >>> Team: Roush Racing >>> >>>

6 FORD

DRIVER PROFILE

Date of birth: December 24, 1985
Hometown: Unadilla, Ga.
Resides: Kannapolis, N.C.
Spouse: None **Children:** None
Height: 6-0 **Weight:** 150
Hobbies: Fishing, taking care of his livestock, hanging out at the shop

DAVID RAGAN

Crew chief: Jimmy Fennig >>> >>> **Engine builder:** Roush-Yates Engines >>> >>> **Website:** www.roushracing.com >>> >>>

>> NASCAR ACHIEVEMENTS

First NASCAR NEXTEL Cup Series start: September 24, 2006 (Dover; started 37, finished 42)
Best points finish: 63rd (2006)
Career victories: 0
Best race finish: 25th (October 22, 2006, Martinsville)
Career poles: 0

Best starting position: 37th (September 24, 2006, Dover)

>> CAREER HIGHLIGHTS

- Will drive the No. 6 Ford for Roush Racing. Ragan replaces Mark Martin. Ragan finished just 47 of 400 laps in his NASCAR NEXTEL Cup Series debut at the second Dover race. He finished 42nd after spinning several times. He will be 21 when the 2007 season starts.

≫ FAST FACTS

- Shared Jack Roush's No. 6 NASCAR Craftsman Truck Series ride with Mark Martin and also piloted Roush's No. 50 truck in 2006. Ragan finished with one top five and six top 10s and scored his first pole in NASCAR's top three series at Gateway.
- Participated in Roush's Gong Show program in 2005. Ragan also ran seven ARCA races, winning one, and ran three NASCAR Busch Series races in 2005, with a season-high finish of 32nd.
- Made his NASCAR Busch Series and NASCAR Craftsman Truck Series debuts in 2004 and made seven ARCA starts

with one top five finish.
- Spent the summer of 2001 in North Carolina, working in Cam Strader's Goody's Dash shop and preparing two late model cars. Ragan raced late models in 2002 and 2003.
- Competed in legends cars in 2000. Ragan won 17 events and the Legends Semi-Pro Championship at Atlanta Motor Speedway.
- Began racing in the Bandolero Series at Atlanta Motor Speedway at age 11 in 1997. By 1999, he had won two division championships.
- Is the son of Ken Ragan, a former NASCAR NEXTEL Cup Series driver from 1983 to 1990.

CAREER STATISTICS

Year	Car owner	Races	Champ. finish	Wins	Top 5	Top 10	DNF	Poles	Money won
2006	Jack Roush	2	63	0	0	0	1	0	$129,610
TOTALS		2		0	0	0	1	0	$129,610

2006 RESULTS

Race	Track	Start	Finish	Laps	Led	Winnings	Status	Rank
28. Dover 400	Dover	37	42	46/400	0	$63,485	Accident	72
32. Subway 500	Martinsville	41	25	500/500	0	$66,125	Running	62

TEAM FACTS ≫ **Primary sponsor:** DLP/Texas Instruments ≫ **Owners:** Troy Aikman, Roger Staubach, Bill Saunders ≫ **Team:** Hall of Fame Racing

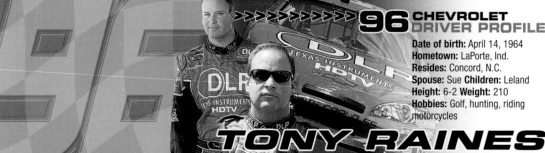

96 CHEVROLET DRIVER PROFILE

Date of birth: April 14, 1964
Hometown: LaPorte, Ind.
Resides: Concord, N.C.
Spouse: Sue **Children:** Leland
Height: 6-2 **Weight:** 210
Hobbies: Golf, hunting, riding motorcycles

TONY RAINES

≫≫ ≫≫ **Crew chief:** Brandon Thomas ≫≫ ≫≫ **Engine builder:** Joe Gibbs Racing ≫≫ ≫≫ **Website:** www.halloffameracing.com

≫ NASCAR ACHIEVEMENTS

First NASCAR NEXTEL Cup Series start: June 2, 2002 (Dover; started 17th, finished 31st)
Best points finish: 33rd (2003)
Career victories: 0
Best race finish: 6th (November 9, 2003, Rockingham)
Career poles: 0
Best starting position: 4th (November 9, 2003, Rockingham)

≫ CAREER HIGHLIGHTS

- Ran a partial season for Hall of Fame Racing in 2006. Terry Labonte ran the first five races and the road course events, and Raines ran the rest. He didn't post great results but ran well considering the No. 96 was a new, inexperienced team. His most impressive race was the second event at Lowe's Motor Speedway; he led three times and finished seventh. He will run the full schedule in 2007.
- In 2003, moved to the NASCAR NEXTEL Cup Series full-time with BACE Motorsports but managed just one top 10, a sixth-place finish at Rockingham.

≫ FAST FACTS

- Spent 2004 and 2005 racing in all three of NASCAR's premier series, posting nine top 10s in the NASCAR Busch Series in 2005 and finishing 20th in points.
- Picked by BACE Motorsports to drive in the NASCAR Busch Series in 1999 and won the Raybestos Rookie of the Year award after posting three top 10s.
- Graduated to the NASCAR Craftsman Truck Series in 1997 and won at I-70 Speedway. He won three more times in 1998 and finished fifth in points.
- Started racing in ASA full-time in 1989 and moved to the All-Pro Series in 1990, earning rookie of the year honors and finishing fourth in points. Raines moved back to ASA in 1991 and claimed the ASA championship in 1996.
- Spent much of his childhood following his father around racetracks in Indiana, helping out stock car teams.

Raines

CAREER STATISTICS

Year	Car owner	Races	Champ. finish	Wins	Top 5	Top 10	DNF	Poles	Money won
2002	Bill Baumgardner	7	51	0	0	0	3	0	$326,042
2003	Bill Baumgardner	35	33	0	0	1	5	0	$2,122,739
2004	Joe Auer	4	53	0	0	0	3	0	$245,239
	Bill Davis	1		0	0	0	1	0	$121,730
	James Finch	1		0	0	0	1	0	$60,025
2005	John Carter	5	50	0	0	0	1	0	$358,725
	Bob Jenkins	1		0	0	0	0	0	$61,775
2006	Bill Saunders	29	35	0	0	1	1	0	$2,358,230
TOTALS		**83**		**0**	**0**	**2**	**15**	**0**	**$5,654,505**

2006 RESULTS

Race	Track	Start	Finish	Laps	Led	Winnings	Status	Rank
6. DIRECTV 500	Martinsville	12	21	497/500	0	$67,850	Running	47
7. Samsung/RadioShack 500	Texas	36	24	332/334	0	$97,075	Running	42
8. Subway Fresh 500	Phoenix	36	17	311/312	0	$65,075	Running	42
9. Aaron's 499	Talladega	29	17	188/188	0	$84,675	Running	41
10. Crown Royal 400	Richmond	27	30	397/400	0	$64,300	Running	41
11. Dodge Charger 500	Darlington	42	20	366/367	0	$76,725	Running	39
12. Coca-Cola 600	Lowe's	42	40	264/400	0	$81,715	Engine	40
13. Neigh. Excellence 400	Dover	32	26	398/400	0	$79,100	Running	39
14. Pocono 500	Pocono	31	16	200/200	0	$68,275	Running	39
15. 3M Performance 400	Michigan	39	38	126/129	0	$68,850	Running	39
17. Pepsi 400	Daytona	21	21	160/160	0	$90,900	Running	38
18. USG Sheetrock 400	Chicagoland	39	40	267/270	0	$76,805	Running	38
19. Lenox Industrial Tools 300	New Hamp.	15	22	308/308	0	$74,200	Running	39
20. Pennsylvania 500	Pocono	19	21	200/200	0	$66,875	Running	38
21. Allstate 400 at Brickyard	Indianapolis	13	11	160/160	0	$168,825	Running	38
23. GFS Marketplace 400	Michigan	41	32	199/200	0	$69,125	Running	38
24. Sharpie 500	Bristol	34	25	498/500	0	$89,700	Running	38
25. Sony HD 500	California	42	37	247/250	0	$84,050	Running	38
26. Chevy Rock & Roll 400	Richmond	25	39	390/400	0	$63,225	Running	38
27. Sylvania 300	New Hamp.	28	26	299/300	0	$73,100	Running	37
28. Dover 400	Dover	41	23	397/400	0	$70,625	Running	37
29. Banquet 400	Kansas	38	28	265/267	0	$82,300	Running	37
30. UAW-Ford 500	Talladega	40	20	188/188	0	$78,500	Running	37
31. Bank of America 500	Lowe's	39	7	334/334	28	$95,375	Running	36
32. Subway 500	Martinsville	11	14	500/500	0	$73,575	Running	35
33. Bass Pro Shops 500	Atlanta	27	34	319/325	0	$79,200	Running	35
34. Dickies 500	Texas	41	19	338/339	0	$99,650	Running	35
35. Checker Auto Parts 500	Phoenix	41	21	312/312	0	$67,325	Running	35
36. Ford 400	Homestead	40	20	268/268	0	$70,700	Running	35

TEAM FACTS >>> Primary sponsor: Burger King/Domino's Pizza >>> Owner: Michael Waltrip >>> Team: Michael Waltrip Racing >>> >>>

00 TOYOTA

DRIVER PROFILE

Date of birth: March 2, 1970
Hometown: Zephyrhills, Fla.
Resides: Troutman, N.C.
Spouse: Lisa **Children:** Emilia
Height: 6-1 **Weight:** 170
Hobbies: Computer games, radio-controlled cars and planes

DAVID REUTIMANN

>>> Crew chief: TBA >>> >>> Engine builder: Toyota Racing Development >>> >>> Website: www.michaelwaltrip.com >>> >>>

>> NASCAR ACHIEVEMENTS

First NASCAR NEXTEL Cup Series start: October 15, 2005
(Lowe's; started 26th, finished 22th)
Best points finish: 70th (2005)
Career victories: 0
Best race finish: 22nd (October 15, 2005, Lowe's)
Career poles: 0
Best starting position: 26th (October 15, 2005, Lowe's)

>> CAREER HIGHLIGHTS

- Will drive for Michael Waltrip Racing full-time in the NASCAR Busch Series and NASCAR NEXTEL Cup Series. Reutimann finished 22nd racing for Michael Waltrip in his lone NASCAR NEXTEL Cup Series start, the second Lowe's event in 2005.

>> FAST FACTS

- Rode 15 top 10s to a third-place finish in points in the NASCAR Craftsman Truck Series in 2006. In 12 Busch Series races in 2006, he had an impressive four top 10 finishes.
- Competed full-time in the NASCAR Craftsman Truck Series in 2004 for Darrell Waltrip Racing and won rookie of the year

with two poles, four top fives and 10 top 10s. In 2005, Reutimann won his first NASCAR Craftsman Truck Series race, at Nashville, and finished with six top fives.
- Made 11 NASCAR Busch Series starts from 2002-2003, nine in a car owned by Joe Nemechek. In 2003, Reutimann collected two top fives, three top 10s and his first NASCAR Busch Series pole, at Memphis.
- Raced in the NASCAR AutoZone Elite Division, Southeast Series from 1997-2002, never finishing lower than seventh in the points standings. Reutimann was named rookie of the year in the series in 1997, won three races and finished a career-high second in points in 2002.
- Grew up racing in modifieds and late models.
- His father, Emil "Buzzie" Reutimann, competed in DIRT modifieds and ran one NASCAR NEXTEL Cup Series race, at Golden Gate Speedway in Tampa in 1963.

CAREER STATISTICS

Year	Car owner	Races	Champ. finish	Wins	Top 5	Top 10	DNF	Poles	Money won
2005	Michael Waltrip	1	70	0	0	0	0	0	$66,600
TOTALS		**1**		**0**	**0**	**0**	**0**	**0**	**$66,600**

TEAM FACTS >>> **Primary sponsor:** Valvoline/Stanley Tools >>> **Owner:** James Rocco >>> **Team:** Valvoline Evernham Racing

10 DODGE DRIVER PROFILE

Date of birth: January 1, 1971
Hometown: Bahama, N.C.
Resides: Bahama, N.C.
Spouse: Jai **Children:** Layne, Skyler **Height:** 5-6 **Weight:** 175
Hobbies: Motocross, motorcycling

SCOTT RIGGS

>>> **Crew chief:** Rodney Childers >>> **Engine builder:** Evernham Engine Technologies >>> **Website:** www.evernhammotorsports.com

>> NASCAR ACHIEVEMENTS

First NASCAR NEXTEL Cup Series start: February 15, 2004
(Daytona; started 36th, finished 34th)
Best points finish: 20th (2006)
Career victories: 0
Best race finish: 2nd (August 21, 2005, Michigan)
Career poles: 3—2006: Lowe's (a,b); 2005: Martinsville (a)
First pole: April 8, 2005 (Martinsville, career start No. 41)
Last pole: October 12, 2006 (Lowe's)

>> CAREER HIGHLIGHTS

- Failed to qualify for the 2006 Daytona 500 but turned in a strong season otherwise in his first season driving for Valvoline Evernham Racing. Riggs won the Nextel Open and had a car capable of winning the Coca-Cola 600, but a bad pit stop ended his chances of a good finish. He set career highs in most major categories and finished 20th in points; it was his first time finishing in the top 20.
- Doubled his previous season's top five and top 10 totals in 2005, but that only amounted to two and four, respectively. He had seven DNFs.
- In a frustrating 2004 season, Riggs never went five races

without a DNF and completed just 89.9 percent of his laps. In an era in which rookies are expected to produce right away, he wasn't a factor in the Raybestos Rookie of the Year race.

>> FAST FACTS

- Was voted the NASCAR Busch Series' 2003 Most Popular Driver by fans. He contended for the championship in 2003 and ultimately finished sixth in points, with two wins.
- Finished 10th in the 2002 NASCAR Busch Series, winning the Raybestos Rookie of the Year award.
- Finished fifth in the NASCAR Craftsman Truck Series in 2001, with five wins and 14 top fives; also ran in that series in 1999 and 2000.
- Was one of the top late model stock car drivers of NASCAR's Mid-Atlantic Region and a two-time champion at the Southern National Speedway in Kenley, N.C., where he has 60 victories.
- Competed in the NASCAR AutoZone Elite Division, Southeast Series, posting eight top 10s in 13 races during the 1998 season.
- Got his start in racing at age 14 when he began running dirt bikes in AMA Motocross competition. He finished third in the 1987 National AMA Competition.

CAREER STATISTICS

Year	Car owner	Races	Champ. finish	Wins	Top 5	Top 10	DNF	Poles	Money won
2004	James Rocco	35	29	0	1	2	8	0	$3,443,345
2005	James Rocco	36	34	0	2	4	7	1	$4,030,685
2006	James Rocco	35	20	0	1	8	2	2	$3,773,674
TOTALS		**106**		**0**	**4**	**14**	**17**	**3**	**$11,227,546**

2006 RESULTS

Race	Track	Start	Finish	Laps	Led	Winnings	Status	Rank
2. Auto Club 500	California	14	19	250/251	0	$88,925	Running	40
3. UAW-DaimlerChrysler 400	Las Vegas	22	28	270/270	0	$82,825	Running	38
4. Golden Corral 500	Atlanta	29	11	325/325	0	$74,650	Running	32
5. Food City 500	Bristol	38	41	344/500	0	$78,115	Running	36
6. DIRECTV 500	Martinsville	11	10	500/500	0	$76,700	Running	30
7. Samsung/RadioShack 500	Texas	22	7	334/334	0	$133,850	Running	28
8. Subway Fresh 500	Phoenix	24	28	229/312	0	$60,975	Running	29
9. Aaron's 499	Talladega	32	9	188/188	0	$97,975	Running	25
10. Crown Royal 400	Richmond	23	14	400/400	0	$69,250	Running	24
11. Dodge Charger 500	Darlington	19	31	363/367	0	$68,150	Running	26
12. Coca-Cola 600	Lowe's	1	13	400/400	90	$147,075	Running	25

Race	Track	Start	Finish	Laps	Led	Winnings	Status	Rank
13. Neigh. Excellence 400	Dover	15	20	400/400	0	$85,200	Running	25
14. Pocono 500	Pocono	17	8	200/200	1	$80,125	Running	21
15. 3M Performance 400	Michigan	16	29	129/129	0	$72,675	Running	23
16. Dodge/Save Mart 350	Infineon	25	27	110/110	0	$72,300	Running	24
17. Pepsi 400	Daytona	28	20	160/160	0	$93,425	Running	23
18. USG Sheetrock 400	Chicagoland	14	15	270/270	0	$91,325	Running	23
19. Lenox Industrial Tools 300	New Hamp.	42	10	308/308	0	$92,425	Running	21
20. Pennsylvania 500	Pocono	9	22	200/200	0	$66,575	Running	22
21. Allstate 400 at Brickyard	Indianapolis	12	21	160/160	0	$148,350	Running	21
22. AMD at the Glen	Watkins Glen	32	23	90/90	0	$64,700	Running	22
23. GFS Marketplace 400	Michigan	23	14	200/200	0	$77,700	Running	22
24. Sharpie 500	Bristol	23	4	500/500	0	$135,425	Running	19
25. Sony HD 500	California	4	17	250/250	0	$92,900	Running	19
26. Chevy Rock & Roll 400	Richmond	26	10	400/400	0	$81,750	Running	18
27. Sylvania 300	New Hamp.	23	35	291/300	0	$68,125	Running	21
28. Dover 400	Dover	2	34	295/400	0	$65,125	Accident	22
29. Banquet 400	Kansas	2	34	263/267	0	$78,050	Running	22
30. UAW-Ford 500	Talladega	41	19	188/188	34	$76,125	Running	21
31. Bank of America 500	Lowe's	1	17	332/334	0	$97,475	Running	20
32. Subway 500	Martinsville	17	30	495/500	0	$68,525	Running	19
33. Bass Pro Shops 500	Atlanta	19	22	322/325	0	$87,250	Running	20
34. Dickies 500	Texas	12	31	331/339	0	$93,675	Accident	20
35. Checker Auto Parts 500	Phoenix	42	22	312/312	0	$67,100	Running	21
36. Ford 400	Homestead	2	7	268/268	1	$91,100	Running	20

FORD
DRIVER PROFILE
Date of birth: September 12, 1956
Hometown: Chesapeake, Va.
Resides: Cornelius, N.C.
Spouse: Linda **Children:** Landon
Height: 5-8 **Weight:** 180
Hobbies: Flying, four-wheeling, water sports, snowmobiling

RICKY RUDD

>>> >>> **Crew chief:** Butch Hylton >>> >>> **Engine builder:** Yates-Roush >>> >>> **Website:** www.ryr.com >>> >>>

>> NASCAR ACHIEVEMENTS

First NASCAR NEXTEL Cup Series start: March 2, 1975 (Rockingham; started 26th, finished 11th)
Best points finish: 2nd (1991)
Career victories: 23—2002: Infineon; 2001: Pocono (a), Richmond (b); 1998: Martinsville (b); 1997: Dover (a), Indianapolis; 1996: Rockingham (b); 1995: Phoenix; 1994: New Hampshire; 1993: Michigan (a); 1992: Dover (b); 1991: Darlington (a); 1990: Watkins Glen; 1989: Infineon; 1988: Watkins Glen; 1987: Atlanta (b), Dover (b); 1986: Martinsville (a), Dover (b); 1985: Riverside (b); 1984: Richmond (b); 1983: Martinsville (b), Riverside (b)
First victory: June 5, 1983 (Riverside, career start No. 161)
Last victory: June 23, 2002 (Infineon)
Career poles: 29—2004: Talladega (a); 2002: Watkins Glen; 2001: Pocono (a); 2000: Las Vegas, Indianapolis; 1999: Rockingham (a); 1995: Infineon, Lowe's (b); 1994: Rockingham (b); 1992: Infineon; 1991: Infineon; 1990: Richmond (a), Infineon; 1988: Martinsville (a), Riverside (a); 1986: Dover (a); 1984: Bristol (a), North Wilkesboro (a), Dover (a), Nashville (b); 1983: Daytona (a), Richmond (a), Rockingham (a), Martinsville (a); 1982: Dover (b), Martinsville (b); 1981: Martinsville (a), Nashville (a), Dover (b)
First pole: April 24, 1981 (Martinsville, career start No. 96)
Last pole: April 23, 2004 (Talladega)

>> CAREER HIGHLIGHTS

- Rudd is reuniting with Robert Yates Racing in 2007 after taking 2006 off except for a relief driving appearance for Tony Stewart in the spring race at Dover. Most figured Rudd had retired. Rudd drove for Yates from 2000 to 2002 and revived his career with three consecutive top 10 finishes in points.
- Holds the record for consecutive NASCAR NEXTEL Cup Series starts with 788, which ran from the 1981 to 2005 seasons.
- Ranks third in NASCAR career starts (875) behind Richard Petty (1,184) and Dave Marcis (883).
- Was an owner-driver in the 1994-1999 seasons, when he won six races and had three top 10 points finishes.
- Best points finish was second in 1991, when he drove for Rick Hendrick and finished 195 points behind Dale Earnhardt.
- Never won more than two races in a season but won at least one race in 16 consecutive seasons (1983-1998).

>> FAST FACTS

- Started racing at age 9 and raced in motocross and go-karts as a teenager.
- Won the IROC championship in 1992.
- Father, Al Rudd Jr., owned an auto salvage business that led to Ricky's interest in cars.

CAREER STATISTICS

Year	Car owner	Races	Champ. finish	Wins	Top 5	Top 10	DNF	Poles	Money won
1975	Bill Champion	4	47	0	0	1	2	0	$4,345
1976	Al Rudd Sr.	4	53	0	0	1	2	0	$7,525
1977	Al Rudd Sr.	25	17	0	1	10	11	0	$68,448
1978	Al Rudd Sr.	13	31	0	0	4	7	0	$49,610
1979	Junie Donlavey	28	17	0	4	17	6	0	$146,302
1980	Nelson Malloch	7		0	0	1	4	0	$18,745
	D.K. Ulrich	3		0	0	0	1	0	$8,025
	Al Rudd Sr.	3	34	0	1	2	1	0	$23,515
1981	Bill Gardner	31	6	0	14	17	9	3	$381,968
1982	Richard Childress	30	9	0	6	13	13	2	$201,130
1983	Richard Childress	30	9	2	7	14	8	4	$257,585
1984	Bud Moore	30	7	1	7	16	6	4	$476,602
1985	Bud Moore	28	6	1	13	19	5	0	$512,441
1986	Bud Moore	29	5	2	11	17	7	1	$671,548
1987	Bud Moore	29	6	2	10	13	9	0	$653,508
1988	Kenny Bernstein	29	11	1	6	11	12	2	$410,954
1989	Kenny Bernstein	29	8	1	7	15	5	0	$534,824
1990	Rick Hendrick	29	7	1	8	15	5	2	$573,650
1991	Rick Hendrick	29	2	1	9	17	1	1	$1,093,765
1992	Rick Hendrick	29	7	1	9	18	4	1	$793,903
1993	Rick Hendrick	30	10	1	9	14	6	0	$752,562
1994	Ricky Rudd	31	5	1	6	15	2	1	$1,044,441
1995	Ricky Rudd	31	9	1	10	16	6	2	$1,337,703
1996	Ricky Rudd	31	6	1	5	16	1	0	$1,503,025
1997	Ricky Rudd	32	17	2	6	11	7	0	$1,975,981
1998	Ricky Rudd	33	22	1	1	5	7	0	$1,602,895
1999	Ricky Rudd	34	31	0	3	5	7	1	$1,632,011
2000	Robert Yates	34	5	0	12	19	1	2	$2,914,970
2001	Robert Yates	36	4	2	14	22	4	1	$4,878,027
2002	Robert Yates	36	10	1	8	12	4	1	$4,444,614
2003	Wood Brothers	36	23	0	4	5	9	0	$3,240,614
2004	Wood Brothers	36	24	0	1	3	6	1	$3,905,141
2005	Wood Brothers	36	21	0	2	5	5	0	$4,575,541
TOTALS		**875**		**23**	**194**	**373**	**184**	**29**	**$40,696,133**

TEAM FACTS >>> >>> **Primary sponsor:** Dodge Dealers/UAW >>> >>> **Owner:** Ray Evernham >>> >>> **Team:** Evernham Motorsports

19 DODGE DRIVER PROFILE

Date of birth: April 30, 1975
Hometown: Emporia, Va.
Resides: Emporia, Va.
Spouse: None **Children:** None
Height: 6-2 **Weight:** 195
Hobbies: Golf, hunting, basketball, water sports, video games

ELLIOTT SADLER

Crew chief: Josh Browne >>> **Engine builder:** Evernham Engine Technologies >>> **Website:** www.evernhammotorsports.com

>> NASCAR ACHIEVEMENTS

First NASCAR NEXTEL Cup Series start: May 24, 1998
(Lowe's; started 31st, finished 42nd)
Best points finish: 9th (2004)
Career victories: 3—2004: Texas, California (b); 2001: Bristol (a)
First victory: March 25, 2001 (Bristol, career start No. 75)
Last victory: September 5, 2004 (California)
Career poles: 7—2006: Talladega (a); 2005: Bristol (a), Indianapolis, Talladega (b), Lowe's (b); 2003: Darlington (a), Talladega (b)
First pole: March 14, 2003 (Darlington, career start No. 146)
Last pole: April 29, 2006 (Talladega)

>> CAREER HIGHLIGHTS

- Sadler was ninth in points after six races in 2006 but dropped precipitously after that and finished the season 22nd. After Watkins Glen, he left Robert Yates Racing to take over the No. 19 Evernham Motorsports Dodge, which he'll drive in 2007.
- Finished in the top 10 in points for the first time in his career in 2004. He won twice, a career high.
- Joined Robert Yates Racing in 2003 and shot up to 10th in points after 10 races. But consecutive finishes of 37th, 36th and 33rd pushed him out of the top 10 for good.
- Took the Wood Brothers to victory lane for the first time since 1993 with a win at Bristol in March 2001. It was Sadler's first career win.
- Was second to Tony Stewart for 1999 Raybestos Rookie of the Year.

>> FAST FACTS

- Along with brother Hermie, raises money for the Autism Society of America and the Victory Junction Gang Camp.
- Is a hunting guide. Raises Walker hunting dogs in the winter.
- Received a basketball scholarship to James Madison University to play for coach Lefty Driesell but suffered a knee injury that "allowed him to pursue a sit-down job."
- Began racing in go-karts at age 7 and won more than 200 races; he also won the 1983-84 Virginia State Karting Championship.

CAREER STATISTICS

Year	Car owner	Races	Champ. finish	Wins	Top 5	Top 10	DNF	Poles	Money won
1998	Gary Bechtel	2	59	0	0	0	1	0	$45,325
1999	Wood Brothers	34	24	0	0	1	2	0	$1,589,221
2000	Wood Brothers	33	29	0	0	1	5	0	$1,579,656
2001	Wood Brothers	36	20	1	2	2	2	0	$2,683,225
2002	Wood Brothers	36	23	0	2	7	6	0	$3,491,694
2003	Robert Yates	36	22	0	2	9	9	2	$3,795,174
2004	Robert Yates	36	9	2	8	14	1	0	$6,241,034
2005	Robert Yates	36	13	0	1	12	2	4	$5,811,941
2006	Robert Yates	22	22	0	1	5	3	1	$3,126,929
	Ray Evernham	14		0	0	2	4	0	$1,725,725
TOTALS		**285**		**3**	**16**	**53**	**35**	**7**	**$30,089,924**

2006 RESULTS

Race	Track	Start	Finish	Laps	Led	Winnings	Status	Rank
1. Daytona 500	Daytona	3	4	203/203	5	$684,076	Running	4
2. Auto Club 500	California	16	23	250/251	0	$115,083	Running	10
3. UAW-DaimlerChrysler 400	Las Vegas	26	14	270/270	1	$125,758	Running	8
4. Golden Corral 500	Atlanta	28	29	324/325	0	$97,433	Running	13
5. Food City 500	Bristol	13	13	500/500	0	$115,733	Running	11
6. DIRECTV 500	Martinsville	7	6	500/500	0	$120,808	Running	9
7. Samsung/RadioShack 500	Texas	25	33	286/334	1	$113,558	Engine	12
8. Subway Fresh 500	Phoenix	20	37	247/312	1	$89,008	Running	14
9. Aaron's 499	Talladega	1	16	188/188	23	$138,983	Running	13
10. Crown Royal 400	Richmond	37	13	400/400	0	$106,808	Running	14
11. Dodge Charger 500	Darlington	6	29	364/367	0	$99,483	Running	15
12. Coca-Cola 600	Lowe's	26	30	396/400	1	$113,958	Running	17
13. Neigh. Excellence 400	Dover	8	40	296/400	0	$100,933	Accident	20
14. Pocono 500	Pocono	13	20	200/200	0	$97,908	Running	20
15. 3M Performance 400	Michigan	32	22	129/129	0	$102,458	Running	21
16. Dodge/Save Mart 350	Infineon	24	8	110/110	0	$118,583	Running	19
17. Pepsi 400	Daytona	13	6	160/160	0	$144,083	Running	19
18. USG Sheetrock 400	Chicagoland	32	29	269/270	0	$107,008	Running	19
19. Lenox Industrial Tools 300	New Hamp.	18	25	307/308	5	$101,608	Running	20
20. Pennsylvania 500	Pocono	25	32	199/200	1	$89,433	Running	20
21. Allstate 400 at Brickyard	Indianapolis	27	43	3/160	0	$162,383	Accident	22
22. AMD at the Glen	Watkins Glen	12	7	90/90	0	$107,533	Running	20
23. GFS Marketplace 400	Michigan	2	10	200/200	0	$119,416	Running	20
24. Sharpie 500	Bristol	9	39	395/500	0	$111,951	Accident	21
25. Sony HD 500	California	18	13	250/250	8	$133,666	Running	21
26. Chevy Rock & Roll 400	Richmond	14	16	399/400	0	$99,966	Running	21
27. Sylvania 300	New Hamp.	14	6	300/300	0	$125,516	Running	20
28. Dover 400	Dover	35	16	398/400	30	$101,466	Running	20
29. Banquet 400	Kansas	9	40	228/267	0	$106,816	Running	19
30. UAW-Ford 500	Talladega	22	29	186/188	1	$102,691	Running	20
31. Bank of America 500	Lowe's	4	35	124/334	5	$95,816	Engine	21
32. Subway 500	Martinsville	34	38	412/500	0	$94,466	Engine	23
33. Bass Pro Shops 500	Atlanta	34	21	322/325	0	$118,666	Running	23
34. Dickies 500	Texas	2	37	310/339	0	$123,441	Running	24
35. Checker Auto Parts 500	Phoenix	16	17	312/312	0	$98,491	Running	22
36. Ford 400	Homestead	4	36	230/268	17	$90,991	Engine	22

70 CHEVROLET
DRIVER PROFILE

Date of birth: May 1, 1978
Hometown: Necedah, Wis.
Resides: Mooresville, N.C.
Spouse: Single **Children:** None
Height: 5-10 **Weight:** 185
Hobbies: Motorcycles, video games, radio-controlled cars

JOHNNY SAUTER

Crew chief: Robert Barker >>> >>> **Engine builder:** Hendrick Engines >>> >>> **Website:** www.haasracing.com

>> NASCAR ACHIEVEMENTS

First NASCAR NEXTEL Cup Series start: July 13, 2003
(Chicagoland; started 20th, finished 35th)
Best points finish: 36th (2004)
Career victories: 0
Best race finish: 9th (April 23, 2005, Phoenix)
Career poles: 0
Best starting position: 10th (March 28, 2004, Bristol)

>> CAREER HIGHLIGHTS

- Sauter moves up from the NASCAR Busch Series to drive a second car for Haas CNC Racing full-time in the NASCAR NEXTEL Cup Series in 2007. Sauter made one NASCAR NEXTEL Cup Series start in the car in 2006.
- Started the 2004 season driving for Richard Childress Racing's No. 30 team but lost the ride. He had three top 15 finishes in 13 races but finished on the lead lap only twice.

>> FAST FACTS

- Tied his career-high NASCAR Busch Series points finish of eighth and compiled nine top 10s in 2006.
- Captured a NASCAR Busch Series win from the pole for the first time at his home track of Milwaukee in 2005.

CAREER STATISTICS

Year	Car owner	Races	Champ. finish	Wins	Top 5	Top 10	DNF	Poles	Money won
2003	Larry McClure	5	51	0	0	0	0	0	$281,335
2004	Richard Childress	13	36	0	0	0	1	0	$1,164,266
	James Finch	3		0	0	0	1	0	$169,254
2005	James Finch	10	43	0	0	1	5	0	$749,453
2006	Gene Haas	1	77	0	0	0	0	0	$85,750
TOTALS		**32**		**0**	**0**	**1**	**7**	**0**	**$2,489,487**

2006 RESULTS

Race	Track	Start	Finish	Laps	Led	Winnings	Status	Rank
12. Coca-Cola 600	Lowe's	14	24	398/400	0	$85,750	Running	55

21 FORD
DRIVER PROFILE

Date of birth: May 29, 1955
Hometown: Fenton, Mo.
Resides: Concord, N.C.
Spouse: Ann **Children:** Dorothy, Sheldon **Height:** 5-9 **Weight:** 200
Hobbies: Driving in a number of racing series, riding dirt bikes and motorcycles

KEN SCHRADER

>>> **Crew chief:** Ernie Cope >>> **Engine builder:** Roush-Yates Engines >>> **Website:** www.woodbrothersracing.com >>>

>> NASCAR ACHIEVEMENTS

First NASCAR NEXTEL Cup Series start: July 14, 1984
(Nashville; started 27th, finished 19th)
Best points finish: 4th (1994)
Career victories: 4—1991: Atlanta (a), Dover (a); 1989: Lowe's (a); 1988: Talladega (b)
First victory: July 31, 1988 (Talladega, career start No. 108)
Last victory: June 2, 1991 (Dover)

Career poles: 23—1999: Talladega (a); 1998: Talladega (b), Phoenix; 1997: New Hampshire (a,b); 1995: Pocono (a); 1993: Richmond (a), Lowe's (a), Pocono (a,b), Michigan (a), Darlington (b); 1992: Pocono (a); 1990: Daytona (a), Lowe's (a), Rockingham (b); 1989: Daytona (a), Michigan (a), Pocono (b), Phoenix; 1988: Daytona (a), Darlington (a); 1987: Darlington (a)
First pole: March 27, 1987 (Darlington, career start No. 67)
Last pole: April 23, 1999 (Talladega)

— Ken Schrader continued —

>> CAREER HIGHLIGHTS

- Put up an uneven first season with Wood Brothers Racing in 2006. Schrader had a better average start and average finish in 2006 than in 2005, but he had fewer top 10s and led fewer laps.
- Didn't contend for any wins in 2005 but ran considerably better in his final season with BAM Racing (finishing with three top 10s and leading 34 laps) than he did in 2004.
- Finished the 2002 season 30th in series points, his first season outside of the top 20 in points since 1984. Nine DNFs didn't help; seven of them were mechanical.
- Made his 500th career start in 2001 at Martinsville. Topped the $2 million mark in winnings for the first time in his career.
- Bounced back into the top 10 in points in 1997 after joining Andy Petree Racing but never cracked the top 10 again with Petree.
- Was the teammate of Terry Labonte at Hendrick Motorsports in 1996, the year Labonte won his second championship. Schrader had three top fives and 10 top 10s.
- Joined Rick Hendrick and enjoyed a breakthrough season in 1988, finishing fifth in points with four top fives and 17 top 10s. He won the pole at the Daytona 500 in 1988 and won it again the next two seasons, 1989 and 1990.
- Broke into the top 10 in points in 1987, the same year he won his first pole (Darlington) and won one of the 125-mile qualifying races at Daytona.
- Was the 1985 Raybestos Rookie of the Year. Car owner Junie Donlavey, known for helping young drivers, gave Schrader his first full-time ride.
- Broke into the series in 1984 by renting Fords from owner Elmo Langley for his first three starts; Langley rewarded Schrader with two more starts after he took good care of the equipment.

>> FAST FACTS

- Will drive a Dodge truck for Bobby Hamilton in the NASCAR Craftsman Truck Series in 2007.
- Owns I-55 Raceway in Pevely, Mo., where he still competes when opportunities allow it. Is active in charitable events, most notably his "Night of Stars" event at Pevely.
- Has won races in the NASCAR NEXTEL Cup Series, NASCAR Busch Series, NASCAR Craftsman Truck Series and in three NASCAR Touring divisions—Busch North Series, Southwest Series and West Series.
- Won the 1983 United States Auto Club's 1983 Sprint Car championship and 1982 Silver Crown title.
- Won four USAC sprint races, six in the USAC Silver Crown division and 21 in USAC Midgets; won 24 midget races in other divisions.
- Named USAC's stock car Rookie of the Year in 1980.
- Began racing on local tracks around his home in Missouri in 1971, primarily in open-wheel competition.

CAREER STATISTICS

Year	Car owner	Races	Champ. finish	Wins	Top 5	Top 10	DNF	Poles	Money won
1984	Elmo Langley	5	53	0	0	0	0	0	$16,425
1985	Junie Donlavey	28	16	0	0	3	7	0	$211,523
1986	Junie Donlavey	29	16	0	0	4	9	0	$235,904
1987	Junie Donlavey	29	10	0	1	10	8	1	$375,918
1988	Rick Hendrick	28	5	1	4	17	1	2	$626,934
	Buddy Arrington	1	0	0	0	0	0	0	$4,610
1989	Rick Hendrick	29	5	1	10	14	6	4	$1,039,441
1990	Rick Hendrick	29	10	0	7	14	8	3	$769,934
1991	Rick Hendrick	29	9	2	10	18	6	0	$772,439
1992	Rick Hendrick	29	17	0	4	11	6	1	$639,679
1993	Rick Hendrick	30	9	0	9	15	4	6	$952,748
1994	Rick Hendrick	31	4	0	9	18	2	0	$1,171,062
1995	Rick Hendrick	31	17	0	2	10	9	1	$886,566
1996	Rick Hendrick	31	12	0	3	10	2	0	$1,089,603
1997	Andy Petree	32	10	0	2	8	1	2	$1,355,292
1998	Andy Petree	33	12	0	3	11	5	2	$1,887,399
1999	Andy Petree	34	15	0	0	6	1	1	$1,939,147
2000	Tom Beard	34	18	0	0	2	2	0	$1,711,476
2001	Tom Beard	36	19	0	0	5	2	0	$2,418,181
2002	Tom Beard	36	30	0	0	0	8	0	$2,460,140
2003	B.A. Morgenthau	32	36	0	0	2	8	0	$2,007,424
2004	B.A. Morgenthau	36	31	0	0	1	5	0	$2,519,393
2005	B.A. Morgenthau	36	31	0	0	3	7	0	$3,057,533
2006	Wood Brothers	36	31	0	0	2	8	0	$4,130,883
TOTALS		704		4	64	184	115	23	$32,422,853

2006 RESULTS

Race	Track	Start	Finish	Laps	Led	Winnings	Status	Rank
1. Daytona 500	Daytona	23	9	203/203	0	$328,897	Running	9
2. Auto Club 500	California	41	28	249/251	0	$109,589	Running	16
3. UAW-DaimlerChrysler 400	Las Vegas	23	41	187/270	0	$104,314	Engine	26
4. Golden Corral 500	Atlanta	25	24	324/325	0	$98,164	Running	26
5. Food City 500	Bristol	21	24	499/500	0	$111,014	Running	29
6. DIRECTV 500	Martinsville	19	40	164/500	0	$92,279	Overheating	31
7. Samsung/RadioShack 500	Texas	32	16	334/334	0	$140,089	Running	30
8. Subway Fresh 500	Phoenix	27	16	311/312	0	$95,389	Running	30
9. Aaron's 499	Talladega	35	42	8/188	0	$102,364	Accident	33
10. Crown Royal 400	Richmond	28	16	399/400	0	$97,564	Running	31
11. Dodge Charger 500	Darlington	23	15	366/367	0	$109,814	Running	30
12. Coca-Cola 600	Lowe's	40	26	397/400	0	$114,664	Running	30
13. Neigh. Excellence 400	Dover	38	33	397/400	0	$102,214	Running	30
14. Pocono 500	Pocono	29	30	197/200	0	$92,039	Running	30
15. 3M Performance 400	Michigan	22	42	30/129	0	$95,904	Accident	31
16. Dodge/Save Mart 350	Infineon	18	41	0/110	0	$94,214	Accident	33
17. Pepsi 400	Daytona	31	12	160/160	0	$125,464	Running	31
18. USG Sheetrock 400	Chicagoland	40	42	266/270	0	$103,644	Running	33
19. Lenox Industrial Tools 300	New Hamp.	34	43	303/308	0	$95,539	Running	31
20. Pennsylvania 500	Pocono	18	15	200/200	1	$96,939	Running	32
21. Allstate 400 at Brickyard	Indianapolis	11	14	160/160	0	$184,264	Running	31
22. AMD at the Glen	Watkins Glen	23	34	89/90	0	$85,689	Running	31
23. GFS Marketplace 400	Michigan	21	18	200/200	0	$102,939	Running	31
24. Sharpie 500	Bristol	17	13	500/500	0	$124,564	Running	30
25. Sony HD 500	California	29	23	249/250	0	$117,289	Running	30
26. Chevy Rock & Roll 400	Richmond	17	7	400/400	10	$121,039	Running	29
27. Sylvania 300	New Hamp.	10	33	295/300	0	$96,689	Running	29
28. Dover 400	Dover	36	19	397/400	0	$97,889	Running	29
29. Banquet 400	Kansas	36	13	267/267	0	$120,564	Running	29
30. UAW-Ford 500	Talladega	23	25	187/188	0	$101,664	Running	28
31. Bank of America 500	Lowe's	17	40	45/334	0	$87,364	Accident	31
32. Subway 500	Martinsville	10	41	331/500	0	$91,529	Accident	31
33. Bass Pro Shops 500	Atlanta	32	24	322/325	0	$113,839	Running	31
34. Dickies 500	Texas	18	42	173/339	0	$118,649	Accident	31
35. Checker Auto Parts 500	Phoenix	32	24	312/312	0	$93,839	Running	31
36. Ford 400	Homestead	37	29	266/268	0	$92,689	Running	31

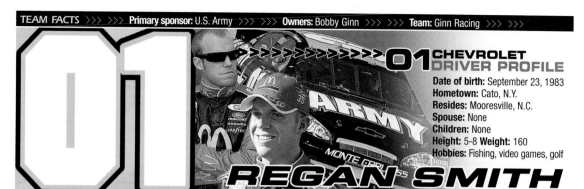

01 CHEVROLET
DRIVER PROFILE

Date of birth: September 23, 1983
Hometown: Cato, N.Y.
Resides: Mooresville, N.C.
Spouse: None
Children: None
Height: 5-8 **Weight:** 160
Hobbies: Fishing, video games, golf

REGAN SMITH

Crew chief: Ryan Pemberton >>> >>> **Engine builder:** Hendrick Engines >>> >>> **Website:** www.ginnracing.com >>> >>>

>> NASCAR ACHIEVEMENTS

No NASCAR NEXTEL Cup Series starts

>> CAREER HIGHLIGHTS

- Will split time with Mark Martin in the No. 01 Army Chevrolet for Ginn Racing (formerly MB2 Motorsports) in 2007.

>> FAST FACTS

- Competed full-time in the NASCAR Busch Series in 2006 for Team Rensi Motorsports. Smith scored his first top 10, at Lowe's in May and finished a career-high 20th in the NASCAR Busch Series standings.
- Competed in at least 10 NASCAR Busch Series races each season from 2003 to 2005. He also ran 10 NASCAR Craftsman Truck Series races in that span and scored a top 10 at Homestead-Miami.
- Made his first start in both the NASCAR Busch Series and NASCAR Craftsman Truck Series in 2002 but failed to finish at both.
- Set a record in the USAR Pro Cup Series, North Division with four consecutive poles in the 2001 season.
- Debuted in the Allison Legacy Series in 1998 and won the Allison Legacy Series championship, along with rookie of the year honors, in 1999.
- Won the WKA Grand National Championship in 1996 and the WKA Manufacturer's Cup in 1997.
- Moved to Mooresville, N.C., from upstate New York with his parents in 1994 to pursue a career in racing.
- Drove his first go-kart at age 4.
- Is the son of Ron and Lee Smith, former NASCAR Busch Series team owners.

41 DODGE
DRIVER PROFILE

Date of birth: February 5, 1986
Hometown: Peachtree City, Ga.
Resides: Concord, N.C.
Spouse: None **Children:** None
Height: 5-10 **Weight:** 165
Hobbies: Golfing, water sports, working out

REED SORENSON

>>> >>> **Crew chief:** Jimmy Elledge >>> >>> **Engine builder:** Ernie Elliott >>> >>> **Website:** www.chipganassiracing.com

>> NASCAR ACHIEVEMENTS

First NASCAR NEXTEL Cup Series start: October 30, 2005
  (Atlanta; started 22nd, finished 41st)
Best points finish: 24th (2006)
Career victories: 0
Best race finish: 5th (June 18, 2006, Michigan)
Career poles: 0
Best starting position: 7th (September 24, 2006, Dover)

>> CAREER HIGHLIGHTS

- Showed promise in the 2006 season. Sorenson, a Raybestos Rookie of the Year candidate, drove the No. 41 Dodge that was driven by Casey Mears the previous season. Sorenson was strong at Michigan and California. He struggled at restrictor-plate tracks, failing to finish at both Talladega events and finishing 29th and 34th at Daytona.
- Made his NASCAR NEXTEL Cup Series debut at Atlanta in

——————— Reed Sorenson continued ———————

October for Chip Ganassi Racing. It was an unspectacular start—a crash led to a 41st-place finish.

>> FAST FACTS

- Made a run at the NASCAR Busch Series title in the second half of 2005 before winding up fourth. He won two races, at Nashville and Gateway, and also won two poles. He had 12 top five finishes and 19 top 10s.
- Finished in the top 10 in three of his first five NASCAR Busch Series starts in 2004.
- Won in only his second start in the ARCA series, at Michigan in June 2004.
- Was the youngest driver ever to win ASA regional rookie of the year when he won the award in 2003 at age 17. He caught owner Chip Ganassi's eye, and Ganassi signed him to a driver development contract in 2003.
- Began racing at age 6 and won more than 250 races driving quarter midgets.

CAREER STATISTICS

Year	Car owner	Races	Champ. finish	Wins	Top 5	Top 10	DNF	Poles	Money won
2005	Chip Ganassi	1	67	0	0	0	1	0	$76,475
	James Finch	1		0	0	0	0	0	$61,100
2006	Chip Ganassi	36	24	0	1	5	4	0	$3,840,342
TOTALS		38		0	1	5	5	0	$3,702,767

2006 RESULTS

Race	Track	Start	Finish	Laps	Led	Winnings	Status	Rank
1. Daytona 500	Daytona	22	29	203/203	0	$262,908	Running	29
2. Auto Club 500	California	29	21	250/251	0	$97,875	Running	24
3. UAW-DaimlerChrysler 400	Las Vegas	36	40	206/270	0	$85,300	Running	32
4. Golden Corral 500	Atlanta	15	10	325/325	0	$89,225	Running	25
5. Food City 500	Bristol	22	22	499/500	0	$92,350	Running	27
6. DIRECTV 500	Martinsville	25	12	500/500	0	$85,925	Running	24
7. Samsung/RadioShack 500	Texas	13	13	334/334	0	$126,675	Running	19
8. Subway Fresh 500	Phoenix	34	40	206/312	0	$68,700	Running	24
9. Aaron's 499	Talladega	41	26	177/188	0	$89,825	Accident	24
10. Crown Royal 400	Richmond	24	23	399/400	0	$77,025	Running	26
11. Dodge Charger 500	Darlington	16	11	367/367	0	$94,375	Running	24
12. Coca-Cola 600	Lowe's	23	10	400/400	0	$119,275	Running	20
13. Neigh. Excellence 400	Dover	39	19	400/400	0	$91,600	Running	21
14. Pocono 500	Pocono	35	36	183/200	0	$68,750	Running	24
15. 3M Performance 400	Michigan	25	5	129/129	3	$98,350	Running	20
16. Dodge/Save Mart 350	Infineon	41	29	110/110	0	$79,500	Running	21
17. Pepsi 400	Daytona	37	34	160/160	1	$89,600	Running	24
18. USG Sheetrock 400	Chicagoland	18	7	270/270	6	$116,525	Running	21
19. Lenox Industrial Tools 300	New Hamp.	9	24	308/308	31	$92,550	Running	22
20. Pennsylvania 500	Pocono	23	26	200/200	0	$73,625	Running	23
21. Allstate 400 at Brickyard	Indianapolis	41	30	160/160	0	$147,725	Running	23
22. AMD at the Glen	Watkins Glen	40	12	90/90	2	$83,975	Running	23
23. GFS Marketplace 400	Michigan	28	8	200/200	0	$93,225	Running	21
24. Sharpie 500	Bristol	10	36	460/500	0	$90,315	Running	22
25. Sony HD 500	California	34	21	249/250	8	$98,175	Running	23
26. Chevy Rock & Roll 400	Richmond	29	14	400/400	0	$79,500	Running	22
27. Sylvania 300	New Hamp.	31	17	300/300	0	$83,625	Running	22
28. Dover 400	Dover	7	11	399/400	39	$102,125	Running	21
29. Banquet 400	Kansas	26	43	18/267	0	$84,566	Accident	23
30. UAW-Ford 500	Talladega	42	39	147/188	1	$76,675	Engine	24
31. Bank of America 500	Lowe's	9	36	115/334	0	$69,050	Accident	25
32. Subway 500	Martinsville	16	35	460/500	0	$72,625	Running	25
33. Bass Pro Shops 500	Atlanta	24	29	321/325	0	$88,000	Running	25
34. Dickies 500	Texas	19	17	338/339	0	$108,550	Running	25
35. Checker Auto Parts 500	Phoenix	28	29	310/312	0	$70,800	Running	25
36. Ford 400	Homestead	11	16	268/268	0	$76,925	Running	24

TEAM FACTS >>> >>> **Primary sponsor:** The Home Depot >>> >>> **Owner:** Joe Gibbs >>> >>> **Team:** Joe Gibbs Racing

20 CHEVROLET
DRIVER PROFILE

Date of birth: May 20, 1971
Hometown: Rushville, Ind.
Resides: Columbus, Ind.
Spouse: None **Children:** None
Height: 5-9 **Weight:** 170
Hobbies: Bowling, boating, fishing, scuba diving

TONY STEWART

>>> >>> **Crew chief:** Greg Zipadelli >>> >>> **Engine builder:** Mark Cronquist >>> >>> **Website:** www.joegibbsracing.com

>> NASCAR ACHIEVEMENTS

First NASCAR NEXTEL Cup Series start: February 14, 1999 (Daytona, started 2nd, finished 28th)

Best points finish: 1st (2002, 2005)

Career victories: 29—2006: Martinsville (a), Daytona (b), Kansas, Atlanta (b), Texas (b); 2005: Infineon, Daytona (b), New Hampshire (a), Indianapolis, Watkins Glen; 2004: Chicagoland, Watkins Glen; 2003: Pocono (a), Lowe's (b); 2002: Atlanta (a), Richmond (a), Watkins Glen; 2001: Richmond (a), Infineon, Bristol (b); 2000: Dover (a,b), Michigan (a), New Hampshire (a), Martinsville (b), Homestead; 1999: Richmond (b), Phoenix, Homestead

First victory: September 11, 1999 (Richmond, career start No. 25)

Last victory: November 5, 2006 (Texas)

Career poles: 10—2005: Daytona (b), New Hampshire (b), Martinsville (b); 2003: Chicagoland; 2002: Infineon, Indianapolis; 2000: Pocono (b), Martinsville (b); 1999: Martinsville (a), Bristol (b)

First pole: April 16, 1999 (Martinsville, career start No. 8)

Last pole: October 21, 2005 (Martinsville)

- Missing the Chase for the NASCAR NEXTEL Cup makes Stewart's 2006 a disappointment, and his 11th-place finish in points is his worst in his eight seasons. Stewart, the 2005 champion, fell out of the top 10 because he was inconsistent down the stretch. But his season wasn't all bad. He continued to prove he is the series' most versatile driver. He won at a short track (Martinsville), an intermediate track (Kansas) and a restrictor-plate track (Daytona) and finished second at a road course (Watkins Glen). He also won three of the final 10 races.
- Won his second NASCAR NEXTEL Cup Series championship and enjoyed the most dominant stretch of his career in 2005, peeling off 13 consecutive top 10 finishes, including five wins. He traced that success to a June test at Michigan, at which the team discovered a way to make the No. 20 Chevy faster. He won a points-paying restrictor-plate race for the first time at the July Daytona race, leading a race-record number of laps (151).
- Won two races in 2004 and led a ton of laps but never made a real run at the championship. He qualified easily for the Chase for the NASCAR NEXTEL Cup but wasn't a factor in the final 10 races.
- Struggled early in 2003 after switching from Pontiac to Chevrolet; he finished 40th or worse in three straight races in late April and early May. He salvaged his season with six straight top fives, starting at Dover on September 21 and ending at Atlanta on October 27.
- Won the NASCAR NEXTEL Cup Series championship in 2002, bouncing back after a last-place finish in the Daytona 500. His march to the top began at New Hampshire in July with the first of nine consecutive top 15s. The championship, along with Bobby Labonte's in 2000, gave owner Joe Gibbs his second title in three years.
- Won at Richmond in May 2002, giving him three victories there (1999, 2001, 2002) in four seasons.
- Won the 2001 Budweiser Shootout in Daytona, a non-points event, his first victory in restrictor-plate racing.
- Raced in the Indianapolis 500 and the Coca-Cola 600 on May 27, 2001, finishing sixth at Indianapolis and third at Lowe's Motor Speedway. He raced in both on the same day in 1999 as well, finishing ninth at Indy and fourth at Lowe's.
- Won the 1999 Raybestos Rookie of the Year award, winning three races (Phoenix, Richmond, Homestead) in the second half of the season. He became the first NASCAR NEXTEL Cup Series rookie to win three races.

>> **FAST FACTS**

- Donated $1 million to the Victory Junction Gang Camp, a facility for terminally and chronically ill children in Randleman, N.C., in 2003, 2005 and 2006. He was recognized for his philanthrophy in 2004 as NASCAR's USG Driver of the Year. Stewart donated the $100,000 award to the camp.
- Won the IROC championship in 2006.
- Named one of USA Weekend Magazine's 2004 Most Caring Athletes along with Kyle Petty.
- Purchased Eldora Speedway in Rossburg, Ohio, in November 2004.
- As a team owner, won the USAC Triple Crown—USAC Silver Crown, Sprint Car and Midget—with driver J.J. Yeley in 2003.
- Has a World of Outlaws sprint car team and won the series title in 2001 with driver Danny Lasoski.
- Ran a career-high 22 NASCAR Busch Series races for Joe Gibbs Racing in 1998, winning two poles and posting five top fives.
- Ran a full Indy Racing League schedule in 1998.
- Won the Indy Racing League championship in 1997 and was the IRL Rookie of the Year and the Indianapolis 500 Rookie of the Year in 1996.
- Swept the USAC Triple Crown in 1995, becoming first driver to do so.
- Was the 1994 USAC Midget national champion.
- Was the 1991 USAC Sprint Car Rookie of the Year.
- Won the 1987 World Karting Association national title.
- Won the 1983 International Karting Foundation Grand National title.
- Favorite driver is A.J. Foyt.

CAREER STATISTICS

Year	Car owner	Races	Champ. finish	Wins	Top 5	Top 10	DNF	Poles	Money won
1999	Joe Gibbs	34	4	3	12	21	1	2	$3,190,149
2000	Joe Gibbs	34	6	6	12	23	5	2	$3,642,348
2001	Joe Gibbs	36	2	3	15	22	4	0	$4,941,463
2002	Joe Gibbs	36	1	3	15	21	6	2	$9,163,761
2003	Joe Gibbs	36	7	2	12	18	5	1	$6,131,633
2004	Joe Gibbs	36	6	2	10	19	2	0	$7,824,927
2005	Joe Gibbs	36	1	5	17	25	1	3	$13,578,168
2006	Joe Gibbs	36	11	5	15	19	4	0	$8,801,569
TOTALS		284		29	108	168	28	10	$57,269,018

2006 RESULTS

Race	Track	Start	Finish	Laps	Led	Winnings	Status	Rank
1. Daytona 500	Daytona	15	5	203/203	20	$537,944	Running	5
2. Auto Club 500	California	12	43	214/251	28	$119,453	Engine	22
3. UAW-DaimlerChrysler 400	Las Vegas	2	21	2_0/270	54	$130,036	Running	19
4. Golden Corral 500	Atlanta	21	5	325/325	50	$154,961	Running	12
5. Food City 500	Bristol	1	12	500/500	245	$168,886	Running	9
6. DIRECTV 500	Martinsville	3	1	500/500	288	$220,786	Running	8
7. Samsung/RadioShack 500	Texas	40	3	334/334	99	$286,386	Running	5
8. Subway Fresh 500	Phoenix	3	2	312/312	6	$211,536	Running	5
9. Aaron's 499	Talladega	2	2	188/188	11	$260,136	Running	3
10. Crown Royal 400	Richmond	18	6	400/400	0	$139,661	Running	2
11. Dodge Charger 500	Darlington	13	12	367/367	0	$133,386	Running	2
12. Coca-Cola 600	Lowe's	32	42	32/400	0	$135,456	Accident	4
13. Neigh. Excellence 400	Dover	10	25	398/400	0	$130,786	Running	5
14. Pocono 500	Pocono	18	3	200/200	6	$182,311	Running	4
15. 3M Performance 400	Michigan	17	41	58/129	0	$122,666	Accident	6
16. Dodge/Save Mart 350	Infineon	12	28	110/110	1	$122,561	Running	7
17. Pepsi 400	Daytona	2	1	160/160	86	$369,586	Running	5
18. USG Sheetrock 400	Chicagoland	34	32	269/270	1	$132,386	Running	7
19. Lenox Industrial Tools 300	New Hamp.	5	37	285/308	28	$121,636	Running	11
20. Pennsylvania 500	Pocono	13	7	200/200	0	$132,461	Running	10
21. Allstate 400 at Brickyard	Indianapolis	32	8	160/160	0	$237,111	Running	9

––––––––––––––––––––––– Tony Stewart continued –––––––––––––––––––––––

2006 RESULTS

Race	Track	Start	Finish	Laps	Led	Winnings	Status	Rank
22. AMD at the Glen	Watkins Glen	8	2	90/90	7	$210,986	Running	7
23. GFS Marketplace 400	Michigan	33	3	200/200	0	$159,736	Running	5
24. Sharpie 500	Bristol	5	22	498/500	0	$140,761	Running	8
25. Sony HD 500	California	22	9	250/250	0	$149,611	Running	8
26. Chevy Rock & Roll 400	Richmond	40	18	399/400	0	$124,961	Running	11
27. Sylvania 300	New Hamp.	32	2	300/300	0	$220,686	Running	11
28. Dover 400	Dover	22	33	303/400	0	$119,786	Accident	11

Race	Track	Start	Finish	Laps	Led	Winnings	Status	Rank
29. Banquet 400	Kansas	21	1	267/267	5	$346,361	Running	11
30. UAW-Ford 500	Talladega	13	22	188/188	1	$125,636	Running	11
31. Bank of America 500	Lowe's	31	13	333/334	0	$125,336	Running	11
32. Subway 500	Martinsville	5	4	500/500	0	$141,211	Running	11
33. Bass Pro Shops 500	Atlanta	11	1	325/325	146	$373,286	Running	11
34. Dickies 500	Texas	8	1	339/339	278	$521,361	Running	11
35. Checker Auto Parts 500	Phoenix	23	14	312/312	0	$120,486	Running	11
36. Ford 400	Homestead	21	15	268/268	0	$120,411	Running	11

TEAM FACTS \>\>\> **Primary sponsor:** Coors Light/Lonestar \>\>\> **Owner:** Chip Ganassi \>\>\> **Team:** Chip Ganassi Racing with Felix Sabates

40 DODGE DRIVER PROFILE

Date of birth: June 19, 1977
Hometown: South Bend, Ind.
Resides: Davidson, N.C.
Spouse: None **Children:** None
Height: 5-9 **Weight:** 180
Hobbies: Boating, working on cars

DAVID STREMME

\>\>\> \>\>\> **Crew chief:** Steve Lane \>\>\> \>\>\> **Engine builder:** Ernie Elliott \>\>\> \>\>\> **Website:** www.chipganassiracing.com

\>\> NASCAR ACHIEVEMENTS

First NASCAR NEXTEL Cup Series start: July 10, 2005 (Chicagoland; started 31st, finished 16th)
Best points finish: 33rd (2006)
Career victories: 0
Best race finish: 11th (Twice, most recently, November 19, 2006, Homestead-Miami)
Career poles: 0
Best starting position: 3rd (July 1, 2006, Daytona)

\>\> CAREER HIGHLIGHTS

• Took over the No. 40 Dodge vacated by Sterling Marlin. Stremme struggled to stay in the top 35 throughout the first half of the 2006 season. He did not post a top 20 until the 15th race of the season. His best finish was 11th, at New Hampshire and in the final race at Homestead-Miami.

• Ran an impressive race at Chicagoland in his NASCAR NEXTEL Cup Series debut in 2005, finishing 16th. His three other NASCAR NEXTEL Cup Series races ended in crashes.

\>\> FAST FACTS

• Finished 13th in NASCAR Busch Series points in 2005, posting five top fives and 10 top 10s.

• Won his first pole in the NASCAR Busch Series in 2004 at Milwaukee. He also finished in the top 10 in points and doubled his top 10 finish total from 2003 with 17.

• Jumped to the NASCAR Busch Series in 2003, where he finished in the top 10 seven times and led six races to win the NASCAR Busch Series Raybestos Rookie of the Year award. He was the only rookie in 2003 to score three top fives.

• Was the 2002 ASA Rookie of the Year and finished in the top five in the ASA standings.

• Won his first Street Stock race at age 15 in 1993 in his mother's car at New Paris Speedway in Indiana. But his career was temporarily sidetracked after a few races when officials discovered his age.

• Inherited his love for racing from his parents, Lou and Cindy, who both were racers in the Midwest.

CAREER STATISTICS

Year	Car owner	Races	Champ. finish	Wins	Top 5	Top 10	DNF	Poles	Money won
2005	Chip Ganassi	4	57	0	0	0	3	0	$268,150
2006	Chip Ganassi	34	33	0	0	0	4	0	$3,456,113
TOTALS		38		0	0	0	7	0	$3,724,263

2006 RESULTS

Race	Track	Start	Finish	Laps	Led	Winnings	Status	Rank
1. Daytona 500	Daytona	32	28	203/203	0	$263,358	Running	28
2. Auto Club 500	California	40	33	248/251	0	$87,775	Running	33
3. UAW-DaimlerChrysler 400	Las Vegas	40	33	267/270	0	$97,272	Running	35

Race	Track	Start	Finish	Laps	Led	Winnings	Status	Rank
4. Golden Corral 500	Atlanta	38	33	322/325	0	$75,125	Running	35
5. Food City 500	Bristol	26	36	435/500	0	$86,400	Running	38
6. DIRECTV 500	Martinsville	38	38	299/500	0	$73,200	Accident	37
7. Samsung/RadioShack 500	Texas	28	21	333/334	0	$127,033	Running	37
8. Subway Fresh 500	Phoenix	29	29	308/312	0	$73,175	Running	36
9. Aaron's 499	Talladega	17	34	106/188	0	$85,725	Running	37
10. Crown Royal 400	Richmond	29	33	397/400	0	$72,375	Running	37
11. Dodge Charger 500	Darlington	4	25	365/367	0	$96,533	Running	36
12. Coca-Cola 600	Lowe's	25	31	396/400	0	$90,900	Running	37
13. Neigh. Excellence 400	Dover	29	41	290/400	1	$80,895	Overheating	37
14. Pocono 500	Pocono	32	26	199/200	0	$87,783	Running	37
15. 3M Performance 400	Michigan	30	19	129/129	0	$99,783	Running	36

2006 RESULTS

Race	Track	Start	Finish	Laps	Led	Winnings	Status	Rank
17. Pepsi 400	Daytona	3	16	160/160	2	$121,658	Running	36
18. USG Sheetrock 400	Chicagoland	20	21	270/270	0	$108,983	Running	36
19. Lenox Industrial Tools 300	New Hamp.	22	11	308/308	0	$109,233	Running	35
20. Pennsylvania 500	Pocono	42	29	199/200	0	$84,633	Running	35
21. Allstate 400 at Brickyard	Indianapolis	24	18	160/160	0	$179,033	Running	35
23. GFS Marketplace 400	Michigan	32	28	200/200	0	$90,132	Running	34
24. Sharpie 500	Bristol	36	35	468/500	0	$90,425	Running	34
25. Sony HD 500	California	32	36	247/250	0	$92,100	Running	34
26. Chevy Rock & Roll 400	Richmond	11	26	398/400	0	$92,058	Running	34
27. Sylvania 300	New Hamp.	6	20	300/300	0	$101,883	Running	34
28. Dover 400	Dover	20	18	398/400	3	$93,108	Running	34
29. Banquet 400	Kansas	40	26	265/267	0	$101,547	Running	34
30. UAW-Ford 500	Talladega	38	33	175/188	0	$78,500	Accident	34
31. Bank of America 500	Lowe's	12	15	332/334	0	$97,033	Running	34
32. Subway 500	Martinsville	13	15	500/500	0	$95,633	Running	34
33. Bass Pro Shops 500	Atlanta	33	39	246/325	0	$86,500	Accident	34
34. Dickies 500	Texas	17	24	338/339	1	$115,722	Running	34
35. Checker Auto Parts 500	Phoenix	36	18	312/312	0	$92,233	Running	34
36. Ford 400	Homestead	23	11	268/268	0	$94,508	Running	33

TEAM FACTS >>> >>> **Primary sponsor:** Bass Pro Shops >>> >>> **Owner:** Teresa Earnhardt >>> >>> **Team:** Dale Earnhardt Inc. >>>

1 CHEVROLET DRIVER PROFILE

Date of birth: June 29, 1980
Hometown: Mayetta, N.J.
Resides: Mooresville, N.C.
Spouse: None **Children:** None
Height: 5-11 **Weight:** 180
Hobbies: Fishing, hunting, riding four-wheelers

MARTIN TRUEX JR.

>>> **Crew chief:** Kevin Manion >>> >>> **Engine builder:** Dale Earnhardt Inc. >>> >>> **Website:** www.daleearnhardtinc.com >>>

>> NASCAR ACHIEVEMENTS

First NASCAR NEXTEL Cup Series start: October 31, 2004 (Atlanta; started 33rd, finished 37th)
Best points finish: 19th (2006)
Career victories: 0
Best race finish: 2nd (November 19, 2006, Homestead-Miami)
Career poles: 0
Best starting position: 5th (September 3, 2006, California)

>> CAREER HIGHLIGHTS

- 2006 was a disappointing rookie season for Truex in that many expected the two-time NASCAR Busch Series champ to win Raybestos Rookie of the Year. He ascended to the NASCAR NEXTEL Cup Series level with his entire NASCAR Busch Series team, and the No. 1 team's inexperience contributed to Truex's rough start. But Truex scored three of his five top 10s in the final 10 races and his best finish, second, in the final race at Homestead. Expect the improvement to continue in 2007.
- Ran nine total NASCAR NEXTEL Cup Series races in 2004 and 2005 to prepare for his full-time jump to the series in 2006. He scored one top 10, a seventh-place finish at Lowe's Motor Speedway in 2005.

>> FAST FACTS

- Became the first driver to win back-to-back NASCAR Busch Series championships (2004-2005) since Dale Earnhardt Jr. did it in 1998-1999. Truex won six races in 2005, led a series-high 19 races and beat runner-up Clint Bowyer by 68 points.
- Won the 2004 NASCAR Busch Series championship in just his first full season of competition. It was the first car owner title for the Chance 2 Motorsports team owned by Dale Earnhardt Jr. and Teresa Earnhardt. Truex won six races, including his first-ever NASCAR Busch Series win at Bristol, and led the standings for the season's final 20 weeks.
- Debuted in the NASCAR Busch Series in 2001 at Dover. Over the next two years, he ran 14 more NASCAR Busch Series races and finished in the top 10 three times.
- Joined the NASCAR Busch Series North Division in 2000 and won in his eighth start.
- Was the 1999 Turkey Derby Classic champion in 1999 for Modifieds at Wall Township Speedway in New Jersey.
- Raced go-karts at age 11 and moved to Modifieds at 18.
- Is the son of longtime NASCAR Busch Series North driver Martin Truex Sr.
- Follows Philadelphia sports teams: the Eagles, Phillies, Flyers and 76ers.

Truex Jr.

— Martin Truex Jr. continued —

CAREER STATISTICS

Year	Car owner	Races	Champ. finish	Wins	Top 5	Top 10	DNF	Poles	Money won
2004	Teresa Earnhardt	2	70	0	0	0	2	0	$116,150
2005	Teresa Earnhardt	7	47	0	0	1	5	0	$929,028
2006	Teresa Earnhardt	36	19	0	2	5	5	0	$4,759,248
TOTALS		45		0	2	6	12	0	$5,804,426

2006 RESULTS

Race	Track	Start	Finish	Laps	Led	Winnings	Status	Rank
1. Daytona 500	Daytona	19	16	203/203	0	$297,816	Running	16
2. Auto Club 500	California	23	15	251/251	0	$114,383	Running	13
3. UAW-DaimlerChrysler 400	Las Vegas	27	20	270/270	0	$113,558	Running	15
4. Golden Corral 500	Atlanta	35	19	324/325	0	$92,608	Running	15
5. Food City 500	Bristol	25	38	430/500	0	$86,300	Accident	21
6. DIRECTV 500	Martinsville	21	19	498/500	0	$94,208	Running	20
7. Samsung/RadioShack 500	Texas	9	8	334/334	2	$156,608	Running	15
8. Subway Fresh 500	Phoenix	9	22	311/312	0	$86,233	Running	15
9. Aaron's 499	Talladega	20	36	97/188	0	$84,500	Accident	20
10. Crown Royal 400	Richmond	22	41	285/400	0	$70,385	Engine	25
11. Dodge Charger 500	Darlington	39	14	367/367	0	$108,408	Running	22
12. Coca-Cola 600	Lowe's	27	21	399/400	0	$115,833	Running	23
13. Neigh. Excellence 400	Dover	21	22	399/400	0	$107,783	Running	23
14. Pocono 500	Pocono	15	24	199/200	0	$90,258	Running	25
15. 3M Performance 400	Michigan	11	16	129/129	0	$103,583	Running	24
16. Dodge/Save Mart 350	Infineon	39	15	110/110	0	$108,283	Running	22
17. Pepsi 400	Daytona	8	29	160/160	3	$90,325	Running	22
18. USG Sheetrock 400	Chicagoland	29	16	270/270	0	$116,283	Running	22
19. Lenox Industrial Tools 300	New Hamp.	8	18	308/308	0	$95,083	Running	23
20. Pennsylvania 500	Pocono	17	10	200/200	0	$105,383	Running	21
21. Allstate 400 at Brickyard	Indianapolis	23	19	160/160	0	$174,733	Running	21
22. AMD at the Glen	Watkins Glen	35	28	90/90	0	$84,583	Running	21
23. GFS Marketplace 400	Michigan	18	30	199/200	0	$80,325	Running	23
24. Sharpie 500	Bristol	24	18	499/500	0	$114,858	Running	23
25. Sony HD 500	California	5	18	250/250	0	$118,258	Running	22
26. Chevy Rock & Roll 400	Richmond	7	40	278/400	0	$71,100	Accident	23
27. Sylvania 300	New Hamp.	11	22	300/300	0	$96,458	Running	23
28. Dover 400	Dover	33	6	400/400	0	$123,283	Running	23
29. Banquet 400	Kansas	23	11	267/267	0	$123,358	Running	23
30. UAW-Ford 500	Talladega	16	5	188/188	2	$139,008	Running	19
31. Bank of America 500	Lowe's	26	31	216/334	0	$69,425	Running	19
32. Subway 500	Martinsville	18	36	453/500	0	$72,575	Running	21
33. Bass Pro Shops 500	Atlanta	21	37	305/325	0	$86,750	Accident	21
34. Dickies 500	Texas	34	14	339/339	0	$126,183	Running	21
35. Checker Auto Parts 500	Phoenix	26	12	312/312	0	$100,608	Running	19
36. Ford 400	Homestead	20	2	268/268	27	$260,458	Running	19

TEAM FACTS >>> >>> **Primary sponsor:** Red Bull >>> >>> **Owner:** Red Bull >>> >>> **Team:** Team Red Bull >>> >>>

83 TOYOTA DRIVER PROFILE

Date of birth: October 24, 1983
Hometown: Thomasville, N.C.
Resides: Thomasville, N.C.
Spouse: Single **Children:** None
Height: 5-11 **Weight:** 160
Hobbies: Video games, reading

BRIAN VICKERS

Crew chief: Doug Richert >>> >>> **Engine builder:** Toyota Racing Development >>> >>> **Website:** www.teamredbull.com >>>

>> NASCAR ACHIEVEMENTS

First NASCAR NEXTEL Cup Series start: October 11, 2003 (Lowe's; started 20th, finished 33rd)
Best points finish: 15th (2006)
Career victories: 1—2006: Talladega (b)
First victory: October 8, 2006 (Talladega, career start No. 107)
Career poles: 4—2006: Texas (b); 2005: New Hampshire (a); 2004: Richmond (a), California (b)
First pole: May 14, 2004 (Richmond, career start No. 16)
Last pole: November 3, 2006 (Texas)

>> CAREER HIGHLIGHTS

- Won his first NASCAR NEXTEL Cup Series race, the fall 2006 Talladega race, and it was a major controversy. He bumped teammate Jimmie Johnson, who turned into Dale Earnhardt Jr., on the race's final lap. As those two wrecked, Vickers drove to victory lane. That win came near the end of a tumultuous season. He asked for and was granted his release from Hendrick Motorsports and will drive a Toyota Camry for Team Red Bull in 2007.

- Didn't make the Chase for the NASCAR NEXTEL Cup but rebounded with a decent season in 2005 after a disappointing rookie year. Vickers led far more laps and was in contention for wins more often. He showed much more patience, especially when his car was fast. Vickers' No. 25 team worked well with a fellow Hendrick Motorsports team, the No. 5 team of Kyle Busch.

- Struggled in his rookie season in 2004. He rubbed fenders too often when he didn't intend to and didn't put together enough strong performances for his season to be anything but a disappointment.

- Qualified in the top five in four of the five NASCAR NEXTEL Cup Series races he entered in 2003.

>> FAST FACTS

- Ran a partial NASCAR Busch Series schedules in 2001 and 2002 before winning the NASCAR Busch Series championship in his first full season in 2003, becoming the youngest NASCAR champion ever at age 20.

- During 2002 NASCAR Busch Series season, he qualified for

the May race at Lowe's Motor Speedway on a Friday, hurried home for Trinity (N.C.) High School graduation ceremonies, then raced on Saturday.
- Earlier in the 2002 season, missed his high school prom because he was racing at Bristol.
- Had a 4.43 GPA in high school.

- Was the 2000 USAR Hooters ProCup Series Rookie of the Year and finished second in that series in 2001.
- Began racing late model stocks in the NASCAR Weekly Series in 1999.
- Was a three-time World Karting Association national champion in the mid-1990s. He began racing go-karts in 1994.

CAREER STATISTICS

Year	Car owner	Races	Champ. finish	Wins	Top 5	Top 10	DNF	Poles	Money won
2003	Rick Hendrick	5	49	0	0	0	1	0	$263,484
2004	Rick Hendrick	36	25	0	0	4	6	2	$3,135,886
2005	Rick Hendrick	36	17	0	5	10	4	1	$4,559,903
2006	Rick Hendrick	36	15	1	5	9	2	1	$4,602,990
TOTALS		**113**		**1**	**10**	**23**	**13**	**4**	**$12,557,263**

2006 RESULTS

Race	Track	Start	Finish	Laps	Led	Winnings	Status	Rank
1. Daytona 500	Daytona	35	7	203/203	21	$347,583	Running	7
2. Auto Club 500	California	28	18	250/251	0	$97,625	Running	9
3. UAW-DaimlerChrysler 400	Las Vegas	10	22	270/270	1	$97,150	Running	12
4. Golden Corral 500	Atlanta	37	23	324/325	0	$80,200	Running	14
5. Food City 500	Bristol	17	37	434/500	0	$86,350	Running	19
6. DIRECTV 500	Martinsville	24	8	500/500	0	$85,350	Running	15
7. Samsung/RadioShack 500	Texas	33	43	24/334	0	$86,847	Engine	20
8. Subway Fresh 500	Phoenix	14	13	311/312	0	$80,275	Running	19
9. Aaron's 499	Talladega	33	3	188/188	7	$172,300	Running	14
10. Crown Royal 400	Richmond	4	37	387/400	0	$70,900	Accident	19
11. Dodge Charger 500	Darlington	8	41	246/367	0	$74,475	Running	21
12. Coca-Cola 600	Lowe's	17	37	331/400	0	$90,050	Running	27
13. Neigh. Excellence 400	Dover	24	23	399/400	0	$89,925	Running	26
14. Pocono 500	Pocono	4	4	200/200	19	$117,850	Running	22
15. 3M Performance 400	Michigan	3	17	129/129	7	$96,175	Running	22
16. Dodge/Save Mart 350	Infineon	42	14	110/110	0	$89,025	Running	20
17. Pepsi 400	Daytona	17	18	160/160	13	$100,875	Running	20
18. USG Sheetrock 400	Chicagoland	2	13	270/270	0	$101,350	Running	20
19. Lenox Industrial Tools 300	New Hamp.	3	17	308/308	34	$90,525	Running	18
20. Pennsylvania 500	Pocono	4	4	200/200	0	$117,850	Running	16
21. Allstate 400 at Brickyard	Indianapolis	30	17	160/160	2	$161,675	Running	16
22. AMD at the Glen	Watkins Glen	19	16	90/90	0	$73,500	Running	15
23. GFS Marketplace 400	Michigan	27	15	200/200	0	$86,300	Running	15
24. Sharpie 500	Bristol	20	33	487/500	0	$91,595	Running	17
25. Sony HD 500	California	2	41	237/250	0	$97,340	Running	20
26. Chevy Rock & Roll 400	Richmond	37	24	398/400	0	$76,300	Running	20
27. Sylvania 300	New Hamp.	12	5	300/300	0	$118,625	Running	18
28. Dover 400	Dover	15	29	395/400	0	$73,550	Running	19
29. Banquet 400	Kansas	4	8	267/267	0	$110,525	Running	18
30. UAW-Ford 500	Talladega	9	1	188/188	17	$228,850	Running	16
31. Bank of America 500	Lowe's	25	10	334/334	0	$91,925	Running	15
32. Subway 500	Martinsville	21	17	500/500	0	$79,625	Running	15
33. Bass Pro Shops 500	Atlanta	15	19	323/325	0	$97,875	Running	15
34. Dickies 500	Texas	1	27	338/339	5	$125,175	Running	16
35. Checker Auto Parts 500	Phoenix	3	11	312/312	0	$83,350	Running	16
36. Ford 400	Homestead	6	21	267/268	0	$75,600	Running	15

TEAM FACTS >>> >>> **Primary sponsor:** Furniture Row >>> >>> **Owner:** Barney Visser >>> >>> **Team:** Furniture Row Racing

78 CHEVROLET DRIVER PROFILE

Date of birth: August 23, 1963
Hometown: St. Louis, Mo.
Resides: Concord, N.C.
Spouse: Kim
Children: Brooke, Brandy, Brittany
Height: 5-11 **Weight:** 172
Hobbies: video games, landscaping, following the St. Louis Cardinals

KENNY WALLACE

>>> >>> **Crew chief:** Jay Guy >>> >>> **Engine builder:** Dave Capriotti >>> >>> **Website:** www.furniturerowracing.com >>>

>> NASCAR ACHIEVEMENTS

First NASCAR NEXTEL Cup Series start: April 22, 1990 (North Wilkesboro; started 28th, finished 26th)
Best points finish: 22nd (1999)
Career victories: 0
Best race finish: 2nd (most recently, November 4, 2001, Rockingham)
Career poles: 3—2001: Rockingham (b); 1997: Martinsville (a); Bristol (b)
First pole: April 18, 1997 (Martinsville, career start No. 97)
Last pole: November 2, 2001 (Rockingham)

>> CAREER HIGHLIGHTS

- Ran a partial 2006 season for start-up team, Furniture Row Racing. Wallace's best finishes were 25th at Phoenix and Richmond. He had just one lead lap finish, at Indianapolis, where he finished 32nd.
- Ran the final two races of the 2005 season for Roush Racing after Jack Roush suspended Kurt Busch. In Busch's car, Wallace finished 16th at Phoenix and 21st at Homestead-Miami.
- Ran a full NASCAR NEXTEL Cup Series season for Bill Davis Racing in 2003 but finished the season with only one top 10, at the spring Bristol race.
- Took over Steve Park's ride for Dale Earnhardt Inc. in the 2001 Southern 500 after Park was injured in a crash during the NASCAR Busch Series race that weekend. Wallace finished the season with DEI with two top 10s. He ran the first four races of the 2002 season in Park's car before Park returned.

Kenny Wallace continued

- His 1999 season was his best in the NASCAR NEXTEL Cup Series. Wallace finished a career-high 22nd in points with three top fives and five top 10s in his first season driving for Andy Petree. One of those top fives was a career-best second-place finish at New Hampshire. Wallace has finished second twice since—at Talladega in 2000 and Rockingham in 2001—but has no NASCAR NEXTEL Cup Series wins.
- Finished second to his brother Rusty in the Budweiser Shootout in 1998.
- Notched his first top five finish (fourth) in 1994 at Martinsville while driving for the injured Ernie Irvan in Robert Yates Racing's No 28.
- Caught on with owner Felix Sabates after running six NASCAR NEXTEL Cup Series races in 1991 and 1992 for various owners. Wallace drove a full season for Sabates in 1993 and finished with three top 10s.

>> FAST FACTS
- Finished in the top 10 in NASCAR Busch Series points every season he ran a full NASCAR Busch Series schedule from 1989 through 2005.

- Made his NASCAR Craftsman Truck Series debut at Martinsville in 1995. In nine NASCAR Craftsman Truck Series races, Wallace has four top 10s.
- Won a career-high three NASCAR Busch Series races in 1994—at Bristol, Richmond and Martinsville.
- Won his first NASCAR Busch Series race in 1991, at Volusia County. He got one more win that season—at New Hampshire—and finished a career-high second in points.
- Was named rookie of the year and finished sixth in points in the NASCAR Busch Series in 1989.
- Got his first start in the NASCAR Busch Series in 1988 at Martinsville in a car owned by Dale Earnhardt. He started 26th and finished 11th.
- Nickname is Herman.
- Has appeared as an on-air personality for SPEED Channel on NASCAR RaceDay and NASCAR Victory Lane.
- His father was one of the most successful short-track drivers in the Midwest, and Kenny is the younger brother of Mike Wallace and former NASCAR NEXTEL Cup Series champion Rusty Wallace. His nephew Steve raced in the NASCAR Busch Series in 2006.

CAREER STATISTICS

Year	Car owner	Races	Champ. finish	Wins	Top 5	Top 10	DNF	Poles	Money won
1985	Richard Bahre	5	57	0	0	0	4	0	$9,540
1986	Richard Bahre	28	19	0	0	0	8	0	$108,767
1990	Randy Hope	1	82	0	0	0	1	0	$6,050
1991	Sam McMahon III	3	44	0	0	0	2	0	$11,425
	Chip Ganassi	2		0	0	0	0	0	$46,900
1993	Chip Ganassi	30	23	0	0	3	6	0	$330,325
1994	Robert Yates	10	40	0	1	2	1	0	$211,810
	Bill Elliott	1		0	0	1	0	0	$13,370
	Filbert Martocci	1		0	0	0	0	0	$9,825
1995	Filbert Martocci	11	42	0	0	0	3	0	$151,700
1996	Filbert Martocci	30	28	0	0	2	9	0	$457,665
1997	Filbert Martocci	31	33	0	0	2	11	2	$939,001
1998	Filbert Martocci	31	31	0	0	7	13	0	$1,019,861
1999	Andy Petree	34	22	0	3	5	7	0	$1,416,208
2000	Andy Petree	34	26	0	1	1	6	0	$1,723,966
2001	Jack Birmingham	12	39	0	0	0	5	0	$597,651
	Teresa Earnhardt	12		0	1	2	1	1	$965,030
2002	Bill Davis	10	39	0	0	0	0	0	$503,085
	Michael Waltrip	4		0	0	0	2	0	$54,570
	Teresa Earnhardt	4		0	0	1	0	0	$454,060
	Andy Petree	1		0	0	0	0	0	$44,775
	George Debidart	1		0	0	0	0	0	$240,635
	Richard Childress	1		0	0	0	0	0	$85,567
2003	Bill Davis	36	30	0	0	1	3	0	$2,480,492
2004	Michael Waltrip	4	50	0	0	0	2	0	$304,420
	Teresa Earnhardt	1		0	0	0	0	0	$61,735

CAREER STATISTICS

Year	Car owner	Races	Champ. finish	Wins	Top 5	Top 10	DNF	Poles	Money won
2005	Jack Roush	2	52	0	0	0	0	0	$221,300
	Michael Waltrip	2		0	0	0	1	0	$289,400
	Barney Visser	1		0	0	0	0	0	$63,275
2006	Barney Visser	17	43	0	0	0	3	0	$1,386,820
TOTALS		**327**		**0**	**6**	**27**	**76**	**3**	**$14,149,030**

2006 RESULTS

Race	Track	Start	Finish	Laps	Led	Winnings	Status	Rank
2. Auto Club 500	California	36	41	237/251	0	$77,400	Engine	48
3. UAW-DaimlerChrysler 400	Las Vegas	34	38	250/270	0	$77,750	Running	48
8. Subway Fresh 500	Phoenix	31	25	310/312	0	$63,075	Running	45
10. Crown Royal 400	Richmond	42	25	398/400	0	$64,875	Running	43
12. Coca-Cola 600	Lowe's	35	29	396/400	0	$83,175	Running	43
13. Neigh. Excellence 400	Dover	37	38	378/400	0	$73,265	Running	43
18. USG Sheetrock 400	Chicagoland	37	38	268/270	0	$77,225	Running	42
19. Lenox Industrial Tools 300	New Hamp.	19	42	184/308	0	$66,935	Accident	42
21. Allstate 400 at Brickyard	Indianapolis	28	32	160/160	1	$136,125	Running	42
24. Sharpie 500	Bristol	26	30	493/500	0	$83,475	Running	42
25. Sony HD 500	California	40	39	246/250	0	$83,940	Running	42
26. Chevy Rock & Roll 400	Richmond	41	37	395/400	0	$63,475	Running	42
29. Banquet 400	Kansas	43	31	264/267	0	$78,650	Running	42
30. UAW-Ford 500	Talladega	26	42	24/188	0	$68,260	Engine	42
32. Subway 500	Martinsville	40	29	496/500	0	$65,100	Running	42
33. Bass Pro Shops 500	Atlanta	43	35	319/325	0	$79,050	Running	42
34. Dickies 500	Texas	33	30	333/339	0	$94,375	Running	43

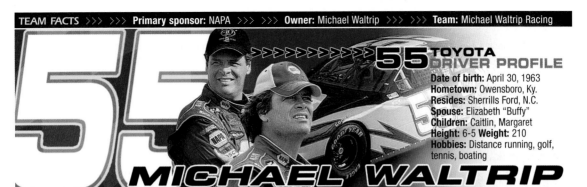

55 TOYOTA DRIVER PROFILE

Date of birth: April 30, 1963
Hometown: Owensboro, Ky.
Resides: Sherrills Ford, N.C.
Spouse: Elizabeth "Buffy"
Children: Caitlin, Margaret
Height: 6-5 **Weight:** 210
Hobbies: Distance running, golf, tennis, boating

MICHAEL WALTRIP

>>> **Crew chief:** David Hyder >>> >>> **Engine builder:** Toyota Racing Development >>> >>> **Website:** www.michaelwaltrip.com

>> NASCAR ACHIEVEMENTS

First NASCAR NEXTEL Cup Series start: May 26, 1985
(Lowe's; started 24th, finished 28th)
Best points finish: 12th (1994, 1995)
Career victories: 4—2003: Daytona (a), Talladega (b); 2002: Daytona (b); 2001: Daytona (a)
First victory: February 18, 2001 (Daytona, career start No. 463)
Last victory: September 28, 2003 (Talladega)
Career poles: 3—2005: Pocono (a); 1991: Dover (a), Michigan (a)
First pole: May 31, 1991 (Dover, career start No. 160)
Last pole: June 11, 2005 (Pocono)

>> CAREER HIGHLIGHTS

- It was a difficult 2006 season for Waltrip, who fell out of the top 35 in points and failed to qualify for races on speed. He finished 18th in the Daytona 500 and didn't best that until August. Things were much better off the track, as Michael Waltrip Racing prepared to run three Toyota Camry teams in the 2007 season.
- Streak of 270 consecutive races started ended at Indianapolis in 2006 when he failed to qualify.
- It was a typical Waltrip season in 2005—strong runs surrounded by mediocre runs. He had a new crew chief in Tony Eury Jr., and the two hit it off immediately. But a lack of consistency in the summer erased Waltrip's slim hopes of making the Chase for the NASCAR NEXTEL Cup, and Eury moved back to the No. 8 team.
- Was good at restrictor-plate races but not in many other situations in 2004. Toward the end of the season, he got a new crew chief, Pete Rondeau, and they worked hard to build positive momentum for 2005, but at the end of the season, a team shakeup sent Rondeau to be crew chief for Dale Earnhardt Jr. Tony Eury Jr., who was car chief for Earnhardt, became Waltrip's crew chief. Waltrip made his 600th start in 2004.
- Matched his career total in wins during the 2003 season, when he won two races (the Daytona 500 and Talladega). He became one of only eight drivers to win the Daytona 500

more than once. But his strong season (he was in the top 10 in points the first two-thirds of the season) fell apart starting with the 24th race at Bristol. From there, he finished out of the top 25 in 10 of 13 races. Still, he ended up 15th in points and had a career-high eight top fives.

- Got his 500th career NASCAR NEXTEL Cup Series start in 2002 in the February Rockingham race. He finished within the top 15 in points in 2002 for the first time in six seasons. He also won a 125 qualifying race at Daytona.
- Won his first NASCAR NEXTEL Cup Series points race in the 2001 Daytona 500, his 463rd career start. He finished second to Dale Earnhardt Jr. in the second Daytona race that year.
- Had his string of 387 consecutive starts snapped in 1998 when he failed to qualify at Phoenix.
- Won the 1996 NASCAR all-star race in his first year with Wood Brothers. He was the first to do so after transferring from the Open.
- Cracked the top 15 in points for the first time in 1991. He won his first two career NASCAR NEXTEL Cup Series poles that year in a four-race span (June 2 at Dover and June 23 at Michigan).
- Was runner-up for 1986 Raybestos Rookie of the Year to Alan Kulwicki.
- First NASCAR NEXTEL Cup Series start was in May at Lowe's Motor Speedway in 1985. He finished 28th; brother Darrell won the race.

>> FAST FACTS

- Becomes a NASCAR NEXTEL Cup Series team owner in 2007 when Michael Waltrip Racing makes its NASCAR NEXTEL Cup Series debut with Toyota.
- In 2005, he announced with his wife, Buffy, plans to build Waltrip Racing World, an interactive racing shop that will be accessible to the public in Cornelius, N.C., and is tentatively scheduled to open in mid-2007. Michael Waltrip Racing plans to relocate its NASCAR Busch Series and NASCAR NEXTEL Cup Series teams to the facility.
- Cites winning the All-Star race in 1996 and a NASCAR Busch Series race at Bristol in 1993 as top memories. After taking the first-ever backward victory lap in memory of Alan

─── Michael Waltrip continued ───

Kulwicki at Bristol, he proposed in victory lane to his wife.
- Still is a regular in the NASCAR Busch Series; owns, manages and drives the No. 99 Chevrolet in the NASCAR Busch Series.
- An avid distance runner, Waltrip has competed in several marathons including the prestigious Boston Marathon. He also had the honor of being a torch bearer in the 2002 Olympic Torch Relay to Salt Lake City.
- Won the Goody's Dash Series championship in 1983 and

was that series' Most Popular Driver in 1983 and 1984.
- Started in stock cars in 1981, when he was the Kentucky Motor Speedway champion in the Mini-Modified Division.
- Waltrip lived with Richard and Lynda Petty when he first moved to North Carolina from his native Kentucky in order to establish himself in NASCAR NEXTEL Cup Series racing.
- Began racing in go-karts in the mid-1970s and won numerous races.

CAREER STATISTICS

Year	Car owner	Races	Champ. finish	Wins	Top 5	Top 10	DNF	Poles	Money won
1985	Richard Bahre	5	57	0	0	0	4	0	$9,540
1986	Richard Bahre	28	19	0	0	0	8	0	$108,767
1987	Chuck Rider	29	20	0	0	1	8	0	$205,370
1988	Chuck Rider	28	18	0	1	3	8	0	$240,400
	Mueller Brothers	1		0	0	0	0	0	
1989	Chuck Rider	29	18	0	0	5	10	0	$249,233
1990	Chuck Rider	29	16	0	5	10	7	0	$395,507
1991	Chuck Rider	29	15	0	4	12	6	2	$440,812
1992	Chuck Rider	29	23	0	1	2	8	0	$410,545
1993	Chuck Rider	30	17	0	0	5	4	0	$529,923
1994	Chuck Rider	31	12	0	2	10	3	0	$706,426
1995	Chuck Rider	31	12	0	2	8	2	0	$898,338
1996	Wood Brothers	31	14	0	1	11	3	0	$1,182,811
1997	Wood Brothers	32	18	0	0	6	4	0	$1,138,599
1998	Wood Brothers	32	17	0	0	5	3	0	$1,508,680
1999	James Smith	34	29	0	1	3	10	0	$1,702,460
2000	James Smith	34	27	0	1	1	10	0	$1,690,821
2001	Teresa Earnhardt	36	24	1	3	3	6	0	$3,411,644
2002	Teresa Earnhardt	36	14	1	4	10	4	0	$3,185,969
2003	Teresa Earnhardt	36	15	2	8	11	6	0	$4,929,620
2004	Teresa Earnhardt	36	20	0	2	9	6	0	$4,694,564
2005	Teresa Earnhardt	36	25	0	3	7	10	1	$4,581,435
2006	Bill Davis	33	37	0	0	0	7	0	$2,971,978
TOTALS		**675**		**4**	**38**	**122**	**137**	**3**	**$35,193,442**

2006 RESULTS

Race	Track	Start	Finish	Laps	Led	Winnings	Status	Rank
1. Daytona 500	Daytona	30	18	203/203	0	$274,241	Running	18
2. Auto Club 500	California	33	36	247/251	0	$78,275	Running	27
3. UAW-DaimlerChrysler 400	Las Vegas	25	35	266/270	0	$78,375	Running	31
4. Golden Corral 500	Atlanta	24	20	324/325	1	$85,158	Running	29
5. Food City 500	Bristol	34	32	481/500	0	$88,147	Running	33
6. DIRECTV 500	Martinsville	33	29	445/500	0	$78,722	Running	34
7. Samsung/RadioShack 500	Texas	42	26	331/334	0	$108,833	Running	33
8. Subway Fresh 500	Phoenix	42	42	98/312	0	$60,435	Accident	35
9. Aaron's 499	Talladega	21	25	179/188	1	$92,447	Accident	35
10. Crown Royal 400	Richmond	30	31	397/400	0	$66,175	Running	35
11. Dodge Charger 500	Darlington	37	35	359/367	0	$67,450	Running	35
12. Coca-Cola 600	Lowe's	43	41	116/400	1	$81,605	Brakes	35
13. Neigh. Excellence 400	Dover	33	32	397/400	0	$74,200	Running	35
14. Pocono 500	Pocono	36	28	198/200	0	$74,672	Running	35
15. 3M Performance 400	Michigan	28	25	129/129	0	$83,622	Running	35
16. Dodge/Save Mart 350	Infineon	35	23	110/110	0	$87,433	Running	35
17. Pepsi 400	Daytona	19	38	158/160	0	$80,975	Running	35
18. USG Sheetrock 400	Chicagoland	36	30	269/270	0	$79,350	Running	35
19. Lenox Industrial Tools 300	New Hamp.	39	36	300/308	0	$67,900	Accident	36
20. Pennsylvania 500	Pocono	39	40	195/200	0	$60,175	Running	36
21. AMD at the Glen	Watkins Glen	36	36	89/90	1	$58,150	Running	36
22. GFS Marketplace 400	Michigan	22	23	200/200	0	$91,233	Running	36
23. Sharpie 500	Bristol	29	16	499/500	0	$110,183	Running	35
24. Sony HD 500	California	37	31	248/250	0	$93,897	Running	35
25. Sylvania 300	New Hamp.	35	23	299/300	0	$86,608	Running	35
28. Dover 400	Dover	29	28	396/400	0	$68,200	Running	35
29. Banquet 400	Kansas	35	35	263/267	0	$77,850	Running	36
30. UAW-Ford 500	Talladega	21	14	188/188	1	$120,033	Running	35
31. Bank of America 500	Lowe's	33	38	102/334	0	$60,400	Accident	35
32. Subway 500	Martinsville	33	34	472/500	0	$64,675	Running	36
33. Bass Pro Shops 500	Atlanta	39	33	319/325	0	$80,300	Running	36
34. Dickies 500	Texas	38	43	109/339	0	$91,564	Engine	36
35. Checker Auto Parts 500	Phoenix	19	42	234/312	0	$61,085	Engine	37

Jarrett and Waltrip

21 FORD DRIVER PROFILE

Date of birth: October 25, 1981
Hometown: Stuart, Va.
Resides: Mooresville, N.C.
Spouse: None Children: None
Height: 5-10 Weight: 145
Hobbies: Radio-controlled airplanes, golf, hunting

JON WOOD

>>> Crew chief: Ernie Cope >>> >>> Engine builder: Roush-Yates Engines >>> >>> Website: www.woodbrothersracing.com

>> NASCAR ACHIEVEMENTS

No NASCAR NEXTEL Cup Series starts

>> CAREER HIGHLIGHTS

- A member of the legendary Wood Brothers Racing family, he is being groomed to graduate to a full-time NASCAR NEXTEL Cup ride.

>> FAST FACTS

- Ran full NASCAR Busch Series seasons in 2005 and 2006 in a car owned by Wood Brothers and compiled three top fives and 11 top 10s. Two of his top fives came at super-speedways.
- Joined Roush Racing in 2001 and ran NASCAR Craftsman Truck Series races for Roush from 2001-2004. Wood's breakout season in the NASCAR Craftsman Truck Series came in 2003 when Wood finished with two wins, 10 top fives, 20 top 10s and two poles to finish fifth in series points.
- Competed in late models in 1999 and in the USAR Pro Cup Series in 2000.
- Won rookie of the year in the Allison Legacy Series in 1998.
- Raced in the champ-kart division in 1996 and 1997 and earned 27 victories, the 1996 WKA North Carolina Dirt Championship and 1997 WKA National Asphalt Championship.
- Ran go-karts by age 12 in equipment given to Wood by Dale Jarrett after Jarrett's son, Jason, had outgrown it. By 1995, Wood had collected 16 victories.
- Wood's racing career began with a big wheel race at Daytona Beach, Fla.
- Is a member of one of NASCAR's most famous families. Wood's team, Wood Brothers Racing, is owned and operated by his father, Eddie, and grandfather Glen and other family members.

---

18 CHEVROLET DRIVER PROFILE

Date of birth: October 5, 1976
Hometown: Phoenix
Resides: Davidson, N.C.
Spouse: Kristen Children: Faith
Height: 5-8 Weight: 165
Hobbies: Any kind of racing, golf

J.J. YELEY

>>> Crew chief: Steve Addington >>> >>> Engine builder: Mark Cronquist >>> >>> Website: www.joegibbsracing.com

>> NASCAR ACHIEVEMENTS

First NASCAR NEXTEL Cup Series start: September 5, 2004 (California, started 32nd, finished 41st)
Best points finish: 29th (2006)
Career victories: 0
Best race finish: 8th (September 17, 2006, New Hampshire)
Career poles: 0
Best starting position: 2nd (April 9, 2006, Texas)

>> CAREER HIGHLIGHTS

- Replaced Bobby Labonte in the No. 18 Chevrolet in 2006. Yeley showed flashes of talent, but he still was getting a feel for stock cars after learning to drive in open-wheel machines.
- Started six races for Joe Gibbs Racing during the 2004 and 2005 NASCAR NEXTEL Cup Series seasons. Yeley's best

—————————————————————— J.J. Yeley continued ——————————————————

showing was a 25th-place finish at Dover in 2005.

>> FAST FACTS

- Moved to the NASCAR Busch Series full-time in 2005, racing for Joe Gibbs. He finished 11th in points with four top fives and 12 top 10s. He improved on that in his second full NASCAR Busch Series season in 2006, with nine top fives, 22 top 10s and a fifth-place points finish.
- Followed in the footsteps of current Joe Gibbs Racing driver Tony Stewart by winning the USAC Triple Crown in 2003 with Silver Crown, Sprint Car and Midget championships. Yeley also set a record in USAC with 24 wins in a single season.

- Won the USAC Sprint Car championship in 2001. In 2002, he won the USAC Silver Crown championship.
- At age 21, he was the fastest rookie to qualify for the 1998 Indianapolis 500. He went on to finish ninth in the race.
- Started racing quarter-midgets at age 10 and moved to midgets by age 14.
- Given name is Christopher, but Yeley goes by J.J., which stands for "Jimy Jack"—a combination of his father's name (Jack) and his father's best friend's name (Jimy). Jack was a racer himself, winning the Arizona Midget championship seven times and World of Outlaws Midget championship twice.

CAREER STATISTICS

Year	Car owner	Races	Champ. finish	Wins	Top 5	Top 10	DNF	Poles	Money won
2004	Joe Gibbs	2	69	0	0	0	1	0	$144,040
2005	Joe Gibbs	4	56	0	0	0	0	0	$290,115
2006	Joe Gibbs	36	29	0	0	3	7	0	$4,336,547
TOTALS		**42**		**0**	**0**	**3**	**8**	**0**	**$4,770,602**

2006 RESULTS

Race	Track	Start	Finish	Laps	Led	Winnings	Status	Rank
1. Daytona 500	Daytona	36	41	157/203	0	$279,833	Running	41
2. Auto Club 500	California	4	8	251/251	2	$140,075	Running	23
3. UAW-DaimlerChrysler 400	Las Vegas	12	17	270/270	0	$129,025	Running	21
4. Golden Corral 500	Atlanta	5	15	325/325	0	$109,050	Running	18
5. Food City 500	Bristol	24	33	469/500	0	$114,075	Running	23
6. DIRECTV 500	Martinsville	18	20	497/500	1	$109,125	Running	22
7. Samsung/RadioShack 500	Texas	2	35	270/334	2	$118,075	Running	24
8. Subway Fresh 500	Phoenix	30	28	309/312	1	$99,975	Running	26
9. Aaron's 499	Talladega	11	11	188/188	1	$131,075	Running	22
10. Crown Royal 400	Richmond	34	22	399/400	0	$102,950	Running	22
11. Dodge Charger 500	Darlington	26	26	365/367	0	$107,775	Running	23
12. Coca-Cola 600	Lowe's	4	20	399/400	0	$132,575	Running	24
13. Neigh. Excellence 400	Dover	14	42	286/400	0	$107,385	Accident	27
14. Pocono 500	Pocono	24	15	200/200	0	$104,500	Running	27
15. 3M Performance 400	Michigan	14	40	80/129	0	$103,340	Running	27
16. Dodge/Save Mart 350	Infineon	38	33	104/110	0	$105,965	Accident	27
17. Pepsi 400	Daytona	11	37	158/160	1	$115,700	Running	29
18. USG Sheetrock 400	Chicagoland	10	10	270/270	0	$138,475	Running	27
19. Lenox Industrial Tools 300	New Hamp.	20	12	308/308	0	$114,950	Running	27
20. Pennsylvania 500	Pocono	21	11	200/200	0	$110,700	Running	26
21. Allstate 400 at Brickyard	Indianapolis	6	34	160/160	0	$170,500	Running	26
22. AMD at the Glen	Watkins Glen	26	33	90/90	0	$94,125	Running	27
23. GFS Marketplace 400	Michigan	31	37	158/200	0	$103,275	Accident	28
24. Sharpie 500	Bristol	25	31	492/500	0	$120,440	Running	28
25. Sony HD 500	California	19	19	250/250	0	$125,900	Running	28
26. Chevy Rock & Roll 400	Richmond	32	13	400/400	0	$108,325	Running	27
27. Sylvania 300	New Hamp.	36	8	300/300	4	$119,050	Running	26
28. Dover 400	Dover	42	30	395/400	0	$100,475	Running	28
29. Banquet 400	Kansas	5	41	194/267	0	$111,175	Accident	28
30. UAW-Ford 500	Talladega	10	32	177/188	0	$104,275	Accident	29
31. Bank of America 500	Lowe's	40	29	258/334	0	$96,425	Accident	28
32. Subway 500	Martinsville	36	31	494/500	0	$102,500	Running	29
33. Bass Pro Shops 500	Atlanta	30	16	323/325	0	$127,075	Running	29
34. Dickies 500	Texas	26	20	338/339	3	$136,675	Running	28
35. Checker Auto Parts 500	Phoenix	35	20	312/312	0	$104,925	Running	28
36. Ford 400	Homestead	8	30	265/268	0	$100,325	Gas	29

Yeley

MIKE BLISS

Date of birth: April 5, 1965 • **Hometown:** Milwaukie, Ore.

CAREER STATISTICS

Year	Car owner	Races	Champ. finish	Wins	Top 5	Top 10	DNF	Poles	Money won
1998	Buz McCall	2	58	0	0	0	0	0	$32,520
1999	Jack Birmingham	2	58	0	0	0	1	0	$42,475
2000	Jack Birmingham	24	39	0	0	1	8	0	$849,952
	A. J. Foyt	1		0	0	0	0	0	$103,996
2002	Chip Ganassi	1	64	0	0	0	0	0	$81,942
2003	Joe Gibbs	1	65	0	0	0	0	0	$65,300
2004	Gene Haas	2	49	0	0	1	1	0	$135,850
	Joe Gibbs	2		0	1	1	1	0	$148,555
2005	Gene Haas	36	28	0	0	2	8	0	$3,091,108
2006	Beth Ann Morgenthau	6	48	0	0	0	4	0	$471,458
TOTALS		77		0	1	5	23	0	$5,031,297

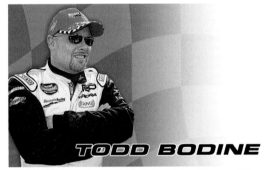

TODD BODINE

Date of birth: February 27, 1964 • **Hometown:** Chemung, N.Y.

CAREER STATISTICS

Year	Car owner	Races	Champ. finish	Wins	Top 5	Top 10	DNF	Poles	Money won
1992	Frank Cicci	1	87	0	0	0	1	0	$3,485
1993	B. Rahilly/B. Mock	10	40	0	0	0	5	0	$63,245
1994	Butch Mock	30	20	0	2	7	6	0	$494,316
1995	Butch Mock	28	33	0	1	3	10	0	$664,620
1996	Bill Elliott	4	40	0	0	1	1	0	$92,945
	David Blair	3		0	0	0	0	0	$32,800
	Andy Petree	3		0	0	0	0	0	$72,780
1997	Geoffrey Bodine	1	52	0	0	0	1	0	$25,400
	Rick Hendrick	1		0	0	0	0	0	$58,500
	Frank Cicci	1		0	0	0	1	1	$16,465
	Bob Hancher	1		0	0	0	1	0	$13,160
	Buz McCall	1		0	0	0	1	0	$12,270
1998	Joe Falk	7	41	0	1	1	1	0	$194,865
	Bob Hancher	7		0	0	1	1	0	$183,901
1999	Jack Birmingham	7	46	0	0	0	2	0	$208,382
2000	Joe Falk	2		0	0	1	1	0	$52,745
	Rick Hendrick	1	49	0	0	0	0	0	$117,260
	Travis Carter	1		0	0	0	0	0	$39,300
	Frank Cicci	1		0	0	0	1	0	$24,760
2001	Travis Carter	35	29	0	2	2	12	3	$1,740,315
2002	Travis Carter	24	38	0	1	4	9	1	$1,879,767
2003	Travis Carter	35	31	0	0	1	9	0	$2,521,724
2004	William Edwards	8		0	0	0	7	0	$455,749
	John Carter	2		0	0	0	2	0	$109,370
	Don Arnold	11	41	0	0	0	9	0	$710,411
2005	Larry McClure	1	68	0	0	0	0	0	$68,375
2006	Larry McClure	2	59	0	0	0	1	0	$145,875
TOTALS		228		0	7	21	81	5	$10,002,837

DERRIKE COPE

Date of birth: November 3, 1958 • **Hometown:** Spanaway, Wash.

CAREER STATISTICS

Year	Car owner	Races	Champ. finish	Wins	Top 5	Top 10	DNF	Poles	Money won
1982	George Jefferson	1	102	0	0	0	1	0	$625
1984	George Jefferson	3	57	0	0	0	1	0	$6,500
1985	George Jefferson	2	55	0	0	0	0	0	$7,100
1986	Warren Razore	5	47	0	0	1	2	0	$8,025
1987	Fred Stoke	11	37	0	0	0	8	0	$33,750
1988	James Testa	26	31	0	0	0	16	0	$132,835
1989	James Testa	3	28	0	0	0	3	0	$5,440
	Bob Whitcomb	20		0	0	4	9	0	$120,190
1990	Bob Whitcomb	29	18	2	2	6	10	0	$569,451
1991	Bob Whitcomb	28	28	0	1	2	14	0	$419,380
1992	Bob Whitcomb	29	21	0	0	3	6	0	$277,215
1993	Cale Yarborough	30	26	0	0	1	8	0	$402,515
1994	Cale Yarborough	16	30	0	0	0	7	0	$185,186
	T. W. Taylor	2		0	0	0	0	0	$35,110
	Bobby Allison	12		0	0	2	3	0	$178,140
1995	Bobby Allison	31	15	0	2	8	5	0	$683,075
1996	Bobby Allison	29	35	0	0	3	11	0	$675,781
1997	Tom Beard	31	27	0	1	2	6	0	$707,404
1998	Chuck Rider	28	37	0	0	0	9	1	$985,730
1999	Chuck Rider	11	44	0	0	0	3	0	$507,011
	Bud Moore	1		0	0	0	0	0	$19,740
	Larry Hedrick	3		0	0	0	1	0	$91,225
2000	Robert Fenley	3	57	0	0	0	1	0	$179,151
2001	Edward Campbell	1	60	0	0	0	0	0	$47,500
2002	Derrike Cope	2	63	0	0	0	1	0	$108,826
	B.A. Morgenthau	5		0	0	0	2	0	$224,390
2003	Derrike Cope	18	46	0	0	0	12	0	$1,030,691
2004	Don Arnold	12	40	0	0	0	3	0	$185,186
	Hermie Sadler	1		0	0	0	1	0	$35,110
	William Edwards	5		0	0	0	5	0	$178,140
2005	Raynard McGlynn	1	81	0	0	0	0	0	$64,375
2006	Raynard McGlynn	9	52	0	0	0	7	0	$632,185
TOTALS		408		2	6	32	155	1	$9,745,601

Cope

BILL ELLIOTT

Date of birth: October 8, 1955 • **Hometown:** Dawsonville, Ga.

CAREER STATISTICS

Year	Car owner	Races	Champ. finish	Wins	Top 5	Top 10	DNF	Poles	Money won
1976	George Elliott	4	41	0	0	0	4	0	$4,870
	William Champion	4		0	0	2	0	0	$6,765
1977	George Elliott	10	35	0	0	2	5	0	$19,925
1978	George Elliott	10	33	0	0	5	3	0	$42,065
1979	George Elliott	9	28	0	0	3	2	0	$50,475
	Roger Hamby	4		0	1	2	0	0	$6,975
1980	George Elliott	11	33	0	0	4	4	0	$42,545
1981	George Elliott	13	30	0	1	7	5	1	$68,570
1982	Harry/Mark Melling	21	25	0	8	9	6	1	$201,030
1983	Harry/Mark Melling	30	3	1	12	22	3	0	$318,500
1984	Harry/Mark Melling	30	3	3	13	24	3	4	$504,708
1985	Harry/Mark Melling	28	2	11	16	18	3	11	$1,015,468
1986	Harry/Mark Melling	29	4	2	8	16	6	4	$586,730
1987	Harry/Mark Melling	29	2	6	16	20	5	8	$978,500
1988	Harry/Mark Melling	29	1	6	15	22	1	6	$812,775
1989	Harry/Mark Melling	29	6	3	8	14	4	2	$694,962
1990	Harry/Mark Melling	29	4	1	12	16	2	2	$818,740
1991	Harry/Mark Melling	29	11	1	6	12	2	2	$586,370
1992	Junior Johnson	29	2	5	14	17	2	2	$1,197,555
1993	Junior Johnson	30	8	0	6	15	3	2	$755,050
1994	Junior Johnson	31	10	1	6	12	5	1	$812,260
1995	Bill Elliott	31	8	0	4	11	3	2	$745,640
1996	Bill Elliott	24	30	0	0	6	2	0	$716,506
1997	Bill Elliott	32	8	0	5	14	3	1	$1,287,518
1998	Bill Elliott	32	18	0	0	5	7	0	$1,341,465
1999	Bill Elliott	34	21	0	1	2	4	0	$1,538,151
2000	Bill Elliott	32	21	0	3	7	8	0	$2,217,957
2001	Ray Evernham	36	15	1	5	9	2	2	$3,303,071
2002	Ray Evernham	36	13	2	6	13	4	4	$3,644,871
2003	Ray Evernham	36	9	1	9	12	2	0	$4,108,355
2004	Ray Evernham	5	48	0	0	1	1	0	$453,475
	Bill Elliott	1		0	0	0	0	0	$75,425
2005	Ray Evernham	9	45	0	0	0	3	0	$773,568
2006	Michael Waltrip	5	44	0	0	0	0	0	$437,910
	John Carter	3		0	0	0	1	0	$227,330
	Nelson Bowers	1		0	0	0	0	0	$257,758
	Ray Evernham	1		0	0	0	0	0	$92,666
TOTALS		746		44	175	320	109	55	$38,860,357

Elliott

KEVIN LEPAGE

Date of birth: June 26, 1962 • **Hometown:** Shelburne, Vt.

CAREER STATISTICS

Year	Car owner	Races	Champ. finish	Wins	Top 5	Top 10	DNF	Poles	Money won
1997	Joe Falk	3	56	0	0	0	1	0	$1,557,720
1998	Jack Roush	13	35	0	0	2	5	0	$447,745
	Joe Falk	13		0	0	0	3	0	$384,591
	Buz McCall	1		0	0	0	1	0	$20,385
1999	Jack Roush	34	25	0	1	2	3	1	$1,587,841
2000	Jack Roush	32	28	0	1	3	5	0	$1,679,186
2001	Larry McClure	21	36	0	0	3	3	0	$987,976
	J. Smith/R. Evernham	8		0	0	1	0	0	$436,876
2002	Derrike Cope	2	62	0	0	0	2	0	$97,809
	Beth Ann Morgenthau	1		0	0	0	1	0	$44,650
2003	Larry McClure	8	43	0	0	0	1	0	$489,069
	Edward Campbell	2		0	0	0	0	0	$154,345
	Donna Lepage	1		0	0	0	0	0	$69,675
2004	John Carter	6	43	0	0	0	4	0	$352,092
	Larry McClure	6		0	0	0	1	0	$531,632
	Joe Auer	5		0	0	0	5	0	$299,996
2005	John Carter	14	39	0	0	1	1	0	$1,199,035
	Jeff Stec	7		0	0	0	2	0	$512,090
2006	Beth Ann Morgenthau	12	40	0	0	0	3	0	$856,814
	Jeff Stec	8		0	0	0	2	0	$784,183
	Bob Jenkins	2		0	0	0	2	0	$142,019
TOTALS		177		0	2	9	38	1	$11,333,842

BORIS SAID

Birth date: September 18, 1962 • **Hometown:** New York

CAREER STATISTICS

Year	Car owner	Races	Champ. finish	Wins	Top 5	Top 10	DNF	Poles	Money won
1999	Mark Simo	2	59	0	0	0	1	0	$68,657
2000	James Spencer	1	72	0	0	0	1	0	$36,940
2001	Doug Bawel	2	50	0	0	1	0	0	$124,340
2002	Doug Bawel	2	59	0	0	0	1	0	$87,400
2003	Nelson Bowers	2	55	0	0	1	0	1	$134,680
2004	Nelson Bowers	3	55	0	0	1	1	0	$208,440
2005	Robert Sutton	9	42	0	1	1	1	0	$964,965
2006	Mark Simo	3	47	0	1	2	1	1	$361,950
	Jeff Stec	1		0	0	0	0	0	$58,950
TOTALS		21		0	1	4	5	1	$2,132,035

NASCAR COMPETITION

>>> CAR MANUFACTURERS <<<

>>CHEVROLET >>>

Chevrolet won the 2006 NASCAR Manufacturer Championship, giving it four titles in a row and 30 overall. Chevrolet made its presence known in NASCAR racing for the first time in 1955 with the development of the small-block Chevy engine. Ironically, the same basic engine is the basis of today's NASCAR Chevrolet racing engine. Up to that time, the Chevrolet Division of General Motors used only non-competitive 6-cylinder engines in their products and these cars were not suitable for racing. Fonty Flock took the first of 532 Chevrolet wins in 1955 at Columbia, S.C. The first superspeedway Chevy win was Herb Thomas' victory in the 1955 Southern 500 at Darlington, S.C.

The brand showed its muscle in 1963 with the development of the fabled "mystery engine," which was the forerunner of the big-block Chevrolet engine of the 1960s and 70s. The team of Junior Johnson and car builder, Ray Fox, were dominant every time they entered an event during the '63 season. Chevy pulled its support of racing in 1964 and the brand competed only occasionally with independent teams until the early 1970s. Race promoter Richard Howard, car owner Junior Johnson and driver "Chargin' Charlie Glotzbach brought Chevy back into racing in 1971 with a winning Monte Carlo.

During the past 30-plus years, the Chevrolet Lumina and Monte Carlo brands have been strong competitors, with the Monte Carlo taking the title of the most successful model in NASCAR history. Hendrick Motorsports, Dale Earnhardt Inc., Joe Gibbs Racing and Richard Childress Racing are among Chevrolet's star roster of teams on today's circuit.

>>DODGE >>>

The first Dodge victory in NASCAR's premier division came in 1953 at West Palm Beach, Fla., with Lee Petty wheeling his Dodge Diplomat to victory. David Pearson won the 1966 championship driving a Cotton Owens-prepared Dodge Charger. The Charger was the first car NASCAR allowed to use a rear spoiler. It was found, in 1966, that the short trunk area of the streamlined hardtop would lift under high speed and a small strip of metal was added to the rear deck lid to increase stabilization.

The super aerodynamic Dodge Daytona, with its sloped nose and large rear stabilizing wing, was introduced at the inaugural race at

Talladega, Ala., in September of 1969. Plymouth countered with its 1970 model Superbird. The era of sophisticated factory-based aerodynamics had dawned over stock car racing with Bobby Isaac winning the 1970 championship piloting a Dodge.

Richard Petty and his Dodge Charger dominated the 1970s, racking up four championships during the decade. Dodge discontinued its involvement with NASCAR racing in 1977, save for an independent or two. In 2001, faithful Dodge fans were rewarded when Dodge returned to NASCAR. Bill Elliott—driving for car owner Ray Evernham—won the Daytona 500 pole in the brand's initial outing. In August that same year, Sterling Marlin recorded Dodge's first win since November 20, 1977 (Neil Bonnett, Ontario, Calif.) at Michigan. Many teams, such as Roger Penske, Chip Ganassi and Petty Enterprises have become part of the Dodge program in the past few years. The Dodge Charger returned to competition in 2005. Kasey Kahne's win in the Charger at Richmond International Raceway in May was the first for a Charger since Bonnett's 1977 victory.

>>FORD >>>

Although Ford had been involved with various forms of auto racing since the early 1900s, they came to NASCAR in the mid-1950s with a factory-backed team headed up by 1925 Indianapolis 500 winner, Pete DePaolo. The team's drivers consisted of the top talent of the day. John Holman and Ralph Moody took over the team in 1957 and for the next 15 years, the H-M team was considered among the very elite of American stock car racing.

David Pearson won back-to-back championships in 1968 and 1969 driving a factory-supported Ford. During this time, factory support was also given to the teams of Banjo Matthews, Jack Bowsher and Junior Johnson, with Bud Moore and Bill Stroppe handling the Mercury division. All were extremely successful.

Ford's Thunderbird was the dominant car on the superspeed-ways of the mid to late 1980s. The Ford Taurus was introduced to racing in 1998 and, like the Thunderbird, has been a force to reckon with on tracks of all sizes.

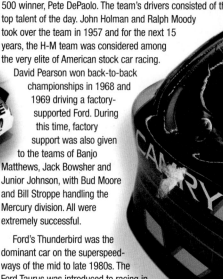

Today, Ford's top teams include Roush Racing, Robert Yates Racing and the famous Wood Brothers. Matt Kenseth, the 2003 champion, is among Ford's roster of star drivers. Fords have scored 553 victories in NASCAR's premier division since Jimmy Florian won at Dayton, Ohio in June 1950.

>> TOYOTA

Toyota will expand its NASCAR program by competing in the NASCAR NEXTEL Cup Series and the NASCAR Busch Series starting in 2007, fielding the Toyota Camry model. The expansion follows three years of Toyota competing in the NASCAR Craftsman Truck Series, and will result in all three of NASCAR's national series having four manufacturers competing, as Toyota joins Chevrolet, Dodge and Ford.

This year, Toyota is celebrating its 50th anniversary in the United States and its 25th year of participation in American professional auto racing. Toyota drivers and teams have won championships in IMSA, CART, IRL and off-road racing. They have

ALL-TIME MANUFACTURERS' CHAMPIONSHIPS

Chevrolet	30
Ford	15
Hudson	3
Dodge	2
Buick	2
Oldsmobile	1
Pontiac	1
Plymouth	1

won such historic events as the Rolex 24 at Daytona, the 12 Hours of Sebring, the Baja 1000 and the Indianapolis 500.

Toyota moved into NASCAR in 2000, fielding the Celica model in the NASCAR Goody's Dash Series. The following season, Robert Huffman gave Toyota its first NASCAR victory, at Kentucky Speedway. In 2003, Huffman gave Toyota its first NASCAR championship by capturing the NASCAR Goody's Dash title.

In 2004, Toyota entered the NASCAR Craftsman Truck Series with the Tundra—in the process becoming the first new manufacturer in one of NASCAR's top series in more than 50 years. In two seasons of NASCAR Craftsman Truck competition, Tundra drivers have recorded 13 victories and 18 poles.

Three full-time organizations will represent Toyota in the NASCAR NEXTEL Cup Series in 2007: Bill Davis Racing, Michael Waltrip Racing and Team Red Bull Racing.

>> TECHNICAL ELEMENTS <<

	NASCAR NEXTEL CUP SERIES	NASCAR BUSCH SERIES	NASCAR CRAFTSMAN TRUCK SERIES
Eligible models	Chevrolet Monte Carlo (a) Chevrolet Monte Carlo SS (a) Chevrolet Impala SS (a) Dodge Intrepid (b) Dodge Avenger (b) Ford Fusion (c) Ford Taurus (c) Toyota Camry	Chevrolet Monte Carlo Chevrolet Monte Carlo SS Dodge Charger (b) Dodge Intrepid (b) Ford Fusion (c) Ford Taurus (c) Toyota Camry	Chevrolet C1500 (Silverado) Dodge Ram 1500 Ford F-150 Toyota Tundra
Years	2005-2007	2005-2007	2005-2007
Engine	Cast iron 358 cubic inch (max.) V8 with aluminum cylinder heads	Cast iron 358 cubic inch (max.) V8 with aluminum cylinder heads	Cast iron 358 cubic inch (max.) V8 with aluminum cylinder heads
Horsepower*	850 @ 9,000 RPM	750 @ 8,400 RPM	750 @ 8,400 RPM
Compression ratio	12:1	12:1	12:1
Torque	550 ft/lb @ 7,500 RPM	535 ft/lb @ 6,500 RPM	535 ft/lb @ 6,500 RPM
Induction	One 4V Holley carburetor	One 4V Holley carburetor	One 4V Holley carburetor
Top Speed	200 MPH (est.)	195 MPH (est.)	190 MPH (est.)
Transmission	4-Speed	4-Speed	4-Speed
Fuel	Sunoco 112 octane 22-gallon capacity*	Sunoco 112 octane 22-gallon capacity*	Sunoco 112 octane 22-gallon capacity*
Front suspension	Independent coil springs Upper, lower "A" frames	Independent coil springs Upper, lower "A" frames	Independent coil springs Upper, lower "A" frames
Rear suspension	Trailing arms, coil springs, panhard bar	Trailing arms, coil springs, panhard bar	Trailing arms, coil springs, panhard bar
Chassis	Rectangular steel tubing w/integral roll cage	Rectangular steel tubing w/integral roll cage	Rectangular steel tubing w/integral roll cage
Body length	200.7 inches	200.7 inches	206 inches
Body width	72.5 inches	74.5 inches	75 inches
Height	51 inches (min.)	50.5 inches (min.)	59 inches (min.)
Weight	3,400 pounds w/o driver	3,400 pounds w/o driver	3,400 pounds w/o driver
Front air dam*	3.5 inches	4 inches	4 inches
Gear ratio	2.90 to 6.50	2.90 to 6.33:1	2.90 to 6.33:1
Spoiler*	55" wide x 4.5" high for all makes	57" wide x 5.75" high for all makes	66.75" wide x 8" high for all makes
Wheel base	110 inches	105 inches	112 inches
Wheels	Steel 15" x 9.5"	Steel 15" x 9.5"	Steel 15" x 9.5"
Tread width	60.5 inches (max.)	60.5 inches (max.)	60.5 inches (max.)
Front brakes	Disc	Disc	Disc
Rear brakes	Disc	Disc	Disc

(a) Eligible model year for the Chevrolet Monte Carlo is 2005, 2006-07 for the Monte Carlo SS and 2007 for the Impala SS.
(b) Eligible model year for the Dodge Intrepid is 2005 and 2006-07 for the Dodge Charger and 2007 for the Dodge Avenger.
(c) Eligible model year for the Ford Taurus is 2005 and 2006-07 for the Ford Fusion.
*Specifications may vary for restrictor-plate races. Note: Some information subject to change.

1 Front grill openings – These inlets allow air to pass through the radiator and ensure that the engine performs at the optimum temperature. Additional air ducts to the side help cool the brake systems.

2 Hood pins – There are four metal-and-wire hood pins with wire tethers that serve as a safety feature by keeping the hood closed.

3 Shock absorbers – These help control the compression and rebound of the suspension springs and provide a smooth and controlled ride to the driver.

4 Cowl induction – The housing for the air cleaner connects the air intake at the base of the windshield to the carburetor.

5 Jack post – This is the area where the jackman must place the jack on each side of the car during a pit stop. Some teams place a piece of fluorescent or bright-colored tape on the body of the car to indicate the specific area of the jack brace.

6 Impact data recorder – The impact data recorder, which records numerous measurements such as G Forces and Delta V (change in speed) from an accident, is located on the left side of the driver's seat.

7 Roll cage – A cage made of steel tubing inside the stock car's interior that is designed to protect the driver from impacts and rollovers. The roll cages must adhere to strict NASCAR safety guidelines and are inspected regularly.

8 Window net – This safety device is located on the driver's side window and is designed to keep his head and arms inside the car during an accident.

9 Windshield clips – The clips attach the windshield to the chassis and allow for easy removal should a driver need to be extricated from the vehicle.

10 Television camera – A miniature camera is mounted on the roof of the car that allows NASCAR fans a great view of their favorite drivers in race traffic.

11 Roof strips – The two half-inch tall aluminum strips which run length wise on the roof and help prevent the stock car from flipping when it is turned sideways during a spin or accident.

12 Roof flaps – The flaps, which were first used in NASCAR competition in 1994, are a safety feature that was developed to help prevent the stock car from becoming airborne when it is turned sideways or backward during a spin or accident.

13 Jacking bolt – This area is where the crew uses a tool to adjust the handling of the car by altering pressure on the rear springs. A wrench is inserted into a jack bolt attached to the springs and is used to adjust the preload on the springs and, in turn, the handling of the race car. Sometimes will hear the slang reference that the team is putting in a round (one turn) of wedge.

14 Rear spoiler – A metal blade that is attached to the deck lid of the car. The spoiler deflects the air coming off the roof and onto the rear deck lid which, in turn, creates rear downforce and more rear traction for the car.

15 Dry break fuel cell – The holding tank for a racecar's gasoline supply consists of a metal box containing a flexible, tear-resistant bladder and foam baffling, both of which are safety enhancements. The cell can hold 22 gallons of fuel. The Dry Break Inlet is a spring-loaded tube, allowing fast refueling without fuel spillage.

16 Deck lid – The term used for the trunk lid of a stock car.

17 Firewall – Sheet steel plate separates the engine compartment from the driver's compartment of the racecar. It's also used at the rear to separate the fuel cell compartment from the driver's compartment.

18 Track bar – A lateral bar that keeps the rear tires centered within the body of the car. The bar connects the frame on one side to the rear axle on the opposite side and can be adjusted in height to alter the handling of the car.

19 Sway or anti-roll bar – It's used to resist or counteract the rolling force of the car body through the turns.

20 Alternate exit – NASCAR issued a recommendation to teams in 2003 for an alternate exit, more commonly known as a roof hatch. The safety initiative provides drivers with an alternate exit through a "hatch" in the roof of the car in the event of an emergency situation.

>> INSIDE THE COCKPIT <<

The cockpit of a NASCAR NEXTEL Cup Series stock car serves as the "weekend office" for NASCAR NEXTEL Cup Series drivers. Configured uniquely by each team, it features extensive safety features, as well as instrument gauges that allow the driver to monitor the car's performance.

1 Main switch panel
Contains switches for starter, ignition and cooling fans

2 Tachometer
Monitors revolutions per minute (RPMs) of engine, assisting driver in selecting gears and monitoring engine power

3 Engine gauge cluster
Monitors engine oil pressure, water temperature, oil temperature, voltage and fuel pressure

4 Auxiliary switches
Can serve a number of purposes, including turning on the backup ignition system, ventilating fans or helmet cooling system

5 Master switch
Shuts down electrical system in emergency situations

6 Ignition kill switch
Shuts off engine in emergency situation

7 Radio button
Controls communication to pits and race spotter

8 Gearshift
Controls four-speed manual transmission

9 Safety seat
Provides extra support and protection for head, shoulders, ribs and lower extremities

10 Head and neck restraint
NASCAR mandates the use of a head and neck restraint system, the approved HANS Device, for all drivers competing in any of NASCAR's three national series (NASCAR NEXTEL Cup Series, NASCAR Busch Series, NASCAR Craftsman Truck Series), as well as its touring series

11 Window net
Keeps a driver's head and limbs inside the car during accidents

12 Rearview mirror

13 Fresh air vent
Directs outside air into the driving compartment

14 Main rearview mirror

15 Fire extinguisher

16 Seat belt harness

17 Fire extinguisher switch
Discharges fire-suppressing chemicals into the driving compartment

18 Fire extinguisher discharge nozzle

19 Helmet hook

>>CAR OF TOMORROW<<

Teams will use the newly-designed Car of Tomorrow for 16 events in 2007, beginning with the spring race at Bristol Motor Speedway. The Car of Tomorrow offers important safety and performance upgrades. It also addresses cost reduction, providing teams with a more efficient car to produce and tune.

"The Car of Tomorrow represents one of the sport's most significant innovations, and we feel everyone involved in NASCAR will experience the benefits," said NASCAR president Mike Helton. "No subject is more important than safety, and while the Car of Tomorrow was built around safety considerations, the competition and cost improvements will prove vital as well."

In addition to the Bristol races, teams will use the Car of Tomorrow in 2007 events at Phoenix International Raceway, Martinsville Speedway, Richmond International Raceway, Dover International Speedway and New Hampshire International Speedway. It also will be used at Darlington Raceway, the fall event at Talladega Superspeedway and road course events at Infineon Raceway and Watkins Glen International. With the exception of the 2.66-mile Talladega track and the two road courses, all tracks where the Car of Tomorrow will debut in 2007 are short tracks.

The 2008 Car of Tomorrow implementation schedule includes 26 events—adding both races at Daytona International Speedway, California Speedway, Pocono Raceway, Michigan International Speedway, the spring event at Talladega and Indianapolis Motor Speedway.

Teams will run the entire 2009 schedule with the Car of Tomorrow, adding both events at Atlanta Motor Speedway, Lowe's Motor Speedway and Texas Motor Speedway, plus events at Chicagoland Speedway, Kansas Speedway, Las Vegas Motor Speedway and Homestead-Miami Speedway. The rollout schedule could be sooner.

Of primary significance are the safety innovations: the Car of Tomorrow is 4 inches wider and 2 inches taller than current NASCAR race cars. The driver's compartment, or "roll cage," has been shifted 3 inches to the rear.

Where the COT will be used in 2007

Bristol (both races)
Martinsville (both races)
Phoenix (both races)
Richmond (both races)
Dover (both races)
New Hampshire (both races)
Darlington
Infineon Raceway
Watkins Glen
Talladega (fall race)

The driver's seat has been shifted 4 inches to the right, allowing more protection from a driver's side impact. More "crush-ability" is built into the car on both sides, ensuring even more protection.

The Car of Tomorrow exhaust system is another safety innovation. It runs through the body, diverting heat away from the driver and exiting on the right side.

Another important Car of Tomorrow feature is performance—how the car handles in traffic and reacts to downforce. The project represents the latest move by NASCAR to reduce current cars' aerodynamic dependence, and several innovations have addressed it:

>> The windshield is more upright, designed to increase the amount of drag, thereby slowing the cars.

>> The more box-like front bumper, which is three inches higher and thicker, catches air rather than deflecting it, another way to slow the car.

>> The air intake is below the front bumper, which eliminates the problem of overheating. Wind-blown trash can cover current car grilles, blocking air flow.

Several components will make the car easier to drive in traffic. Some are bolt-on, bolt-off pieces that teams can use to tune their cars, making them cost-efficient as well. Those include:

>> The "splitter," a flat shelf below the front bumper that can be adjusted.

>> A wing, like those commonly used in sports car series, fits on the car's rear deck lid, in the same spot where the spoiler is bolted.

>> The spoiler, a NASCAR staple, is a straight line on the Car of Tomorrow, rather than curved, as on current cars. A straight spoiler yields more stability in traffic.

>> TECHNICAL INSPECTION <<

NASCAR officials conduct inspections of all competitors' cars throughout a race weekend to enforce NASCAR rules and maintain competitive balance. Over the course of a weekend, NASCAR officials typically conduct three inspections before competition begins (initial, pre-qualifying, pre-race) and two following competition (post-qualifying and post-race).

An initial NASCAR NEXTEL Cup Series inspection, which occurs before any on-track activity on race weekend, typically involves approximately 50 officials, also known as inspectors, and is overseen by the NASCAR NEXTEL Cup Series director. The initial inspection process can range from four to 10 hours, depending on the event, for an entry list of 45-50 cars.

to measure each car to ensure it meets NASCAR requirements. Each car manufacturer—Chevrolet, Dodge, Ford and Toyota—has 14 unique templates that are used for their respective makes. The other 18 templates fit all four manufacturers' makes and are known as the aero-matched templates because they measure the key aerodynamic areas of the car.

The weight station has a steel platform that each car is rolled on, and it measures for the minimum weight requirement (3,400 pounds ready to compete—with fuel, oil, water, etc.—without driver) and also for the right side weight of 1,600 pounds. The height stick station has a raised horizontal bar with a graduated pin in the center that measures for the minimum height of each car.

Once a car passes inspection, it receives a round colored sticker that is adhered to the top center of the windshield. If a car fails inspection in this phase, the team must make the necessary adjustments and then formally present the car through inspection again for approval. If there are minor issues during inspection, NASCAR inspectors may allow teams to fix the problem at that time.

After passing initial inspection, all cars must pass another inspection before qualifying and the race. Both inspections are detailed but abbreviated in comparison to the initial inspection. Should NASCAR inspectors find an illegal part on a car, the part may be confiscated and put on display at the NASCAR NEXTEL Cup Series transporter for other teams to view. The team also may face additional fines or penalties.

Following qualifying, a post-qualifying inspection typically will be conducted for the top five cars in that

The inspection process is broken down into a multiple of groups that focus on different components of the racecar. During this process, inspectors will check the car's body, mandated safety features, undercarriage/chassis, engine, fuel cell, height, weight and measurements to ensure they meet NASCAR requirements as set forth in the rulebook. The inspection order is based on car owner points, with the highest-ranked car owner going through first.

In the template station, NASCAR inspectors utilize 32 templates

session as well as a few random selections. Following the race, the post-race inspection typically involves the top five finishers in the race as well as some random selections. The post-race inspection includes measurements of the car's height and weight, complete teardown of the engine to confirm the engine's compression ratios, re-inspection of a constantly changing variety of car components and on-board systems, cubic-inch displacement, as well as weight requirements and locations for specified internal engine components.

For any given NASCAR NEXTEL Cup Series event, it is unknown how many cars will enter. But one thing is certain: a maximum of 43 cars will start. NASCAR uses time trials, known as qualifying, to choose which teams make "The Show."

NASCAR officials use a draw to determine the qualifying order. Each team sends its crew chief or a representative to draw a number at the qualifying lottery, which is usually on the morning of qualifying. If 50 cars are entered, the NASCAR official will put Nos. 1-51 (always one more than there are entries) into a spinning ball. Each team representative draws one number, starting with the crew chief whose owner is highest in the owner point standings. After each team draws, officials record the number. When every team has drawn, the qualifying order is set.

To qualify for a race, drivers take one or two timed laps, depending on the track. Drivers receive one warmup lap before taking the green flag. The driver with the quickest qualifying time starts on the pole, which is the inside (left side) of the front row. The exception to this procedure is the Daytona 500, which follows a different qualifying method (see page 211).

>>PROVISIONAL SYSTEM

Starting positions 1 through 42 for a NASCAR NEXTEL Cup Series race are set by qualifying speed, and the highest-ranked 35 positions in NASCAR NEXTEL Cup Series owner points that enter an event before the entry deadline are assured one of those starting positions, providing they have made an attempt to qualify. The remaining seven spots will be assigned to drivers with the fastest qualifying speeds whose car owners are not among the highest-ranking 35.

The final starting position—the champion's provisional—can be utilized by a car owner whose driver is a current or past NASCAR NEXTEL Cup Series champion who participated as a driver during the 2006 NASCAR NEXTEL Cup season and was entered in the event for that owner in that car before the entry deadline. If there is more than one series champion vying for the position, it will be given to the most recent series champion.

If the final provisional starting position—43rd in the NASCAR NEXTEL Cup Series—is not filled by a current or past series champion, it will be assigned to the next eligible car owner according to qualifying results. Through the first five races of the season, the highest-ranking 35 in the 2006 owner points entered in the event before to the entry deadline will be assured one of the 42 starting positions, provided they have made an attempt to qualify.

From the sixth race on, the current owner championship points will be used to determine the highest-ranking 35 each race week.

A lottery is used to determine the order in which drivers make qualifying runs for each race.

>> RACING FLAGS / RACE PROCEDURES <<

NASCAR officials follow guidelines and rules, as any other sport or competition does. Race procedures include everything from the start of a race to flags, pit stops, restarts and, of course, the checkered flag. A pace or caution car leads the field before the start of a race.

>> PACE LAPS

Normally, the pace car completes three laps before turning onto pit road, allowing the field to begin the race. The pace laps serve several purposes, the first of which is to allow each car to warm up its engine and its tires. The pace laps also serve another purpose. Because pit road has a speed limit and drivers do not have speedometers in the cars—they have tachometers that gauge the engine's revolutions per minute, or rpms—the pace car drives the pit road speed limit the first time by the front stretch so drivers can locate that same speed on their tachometer.

>> FLAGS

NASCAR officials signal messages to drivers during races by waving an assortment of colored flags. The flagman, who is located on a stand high above the start/finish line, plays an important role.

Green flag: The green flag is displayed at the start of each race and for restarts during the race. Cars must maintain position as designated by NASCAR officials until they have crossed the start/finish line, and the No. 2 qualifier must not beat the No. 1 qualifier to the start/finish line. On restarts, the race will resume immediately when the green flag is waved.

Yellow flag: The yellow flag signifies caution and is given to the first car passing the starter immediately following the occurrence of the cause for caution. All cars receiving the yellow flag at the start/finish line shall slow down to a cautious pace, hold their position and form a single line behind the lead car.

Red flag: The red flag means the race must be stopped immediately, regardless of the position of the cars on the track. The red flag shall be used if, in the opinion of NASCAR officials, the race should be stopped. Cars should be brought to a stop in an area designated by NASCAR officials. Repairs, service of any nature, or refueling, whether on pit road or in the garage, will not be permitted when the race is halted due to a red flag unless the car has withdrawn from the event.

Black flag: The black flag means a car must go to the pits immediately and report to the NASCAR official at the car's pit area. It does not mean automatic disqualification. At the discretion of NASCAR officials, if the driver does not obey the black-flag directive, the driver might be given the **black flag with a white cross** at the start/finish line to inform the driver that any additional scoring of his or her car will be discontinued until further notice.

Blue flag with diagonal yellow stripe: This flag is displayed when drivers who are a lap down or significantly slower are about to be passed by lead-lap cars. Drivers who are shown the blue and diagonally yellow-striped flag must yield to the faster lead-lap cars.

White flag: The white flag waves when the driver in the lead begins his final lap.

Checkered flag: The most famous of all flags, the black and white checkered flag is displayed when the winner has crossed the finish line. All cars remaining on the track will take the checkered flag once.

>> PIT STOPS

Pit road is where drivers come for service to their cars. Teams choose their pit stall location according to how they qualify. The pole winner has the first choice, followed by the outside pole winner and so on. The pit stall is where teams store their equipment, such as tires, fuel and tools, used during the pits stops. When a driver enters pit road, he must enter into his designated pit box area. Drivers who come on to pit road for service usually arein need of fuel, new tires and perhaps a mechanical adjustment to improve the handling. Crews might also make minor repairs to the vehicle on pit road. Any major repairs must be made behind pit wall or in the garage area.

Green-flag pit stops: During green-flag competition, drivers are allowed to make pit stops as needed. However, drivers generally will try to stretch their fuel mileage as long as possible, hoping for a caution or yellow flag to make their pit stop.

Yellow-flag pit stops: During a caution period, NASCAR will make the determination to open and close pit road. A NASCAR official, in front of the entrance to pit road, will use an open/closed flag to communicate to drivers when the pits are open or closed. Once the pits are open, only the lead-lap cars are allowed to pit the first time around. Cars that are down a lap or more must wait until the second time around to make their pit stop. Once all cars exit pit road, they must rejoin the field behind the pace car.

>> RESTARTS

In 2003, NASCAR moved to prevent the practice of racing back to the start/finish line after a yellow flag is displayed. The rule provides for the first driver running one lap behind the leader when a caution is displayed to start in the last position on the lead lap when the race is restarted. All other cars one lap behind the leader will stay one lap behind the lead lap and in their respective positions from when the caution flag was displayed.

Following caution periods, NASCAR officials communicate to the drivers of a restart, when there is one lap to go before the green flag is waved. The flag man signals one lap to go at the start/finish line by holding up one finger. Generally, team spotters and crew chiefs help communicate to their drivers over the radio when there is one lap remaining before the restart.

For restarts during the race, except those during the final 25 laps, cars on the lead lap line up on the outside toward the wall while the lapped cars line up to the inside for a double-file restart.

NASCAR uses a 25-lap rule and a 10-lap rule for restarts late in the race. The 25-lap rule states that if a restart occurs with less than 25 laps remaining and more than 10 laps remaining, only lead-lap cars are permitted to restart in the outside line. The 10-lap rule states that if there are 10 or fewer laps remaining in an event, cars restart in single file with the leader of the race first in line and remaining lead-lap cars behind. All other cars must hold their respective track positions, regardless of running order.

When the green flag waves on restarts, all passing must be done on the righthand side until drivers cross the start/finish line.

>> GREEN-WHITE-CHECKERED FINISHES

In 2004, NASCAR worked to ensure that races would not finish under yellow-flag conditions by instituting a green-white-checkered system. The procedure consists of a restart of two laps—green flag for the first lap of the restart and the white flag signaling the final lap leading to the checkered flag. If a caution comes out on either lap, the race is completed under caution.

>> CHASE FOR THE NASCAR NEXTEL CUP <<

NASCAR implemented a new format to determine the NASCAR NEXTEL Cup Series champion in 2004 known as the Chase for the NASCAR NEXTEL Cup. The format has involved more drivers in the championship hunt and intensified fan interest and drama during the season's stretch run.

The first 26 championship-point events of the 36-race season determine which drivers will be eligible for the Chase for the NASCAR NEXTEL Cup and an opportunity to compete for the series championship.

Drivers who qualify for the Chase will participate against all other competitors during the season's final 10 races. Each week, all 43 drivers will vie for victories and prize money and continue to compete under the standard race points system.

The 2007 Chase begins September 16 at New Hampshire International Speedway and concludes November 18 at Homestead-Miami Speedway. The Chase driver who emerges atop the NASCAR NEXTEL Cup Series standings over the course of the 10-race stretch will be crowned the NASCAR NEXTEL Cup Series champion.

The 2004 Chase ended with the closest championship margin in NASCAR history—Kurt Busch edged Jimmie Johnson by eight points to win the NASCAR NEXTEL Cup Series championship. In 2005, Tony Stewart outlasted Greg Biffle and Carl Edwards by 35 points. Jimmy Johnson won his first NASCAR NEXTEL Cup Series title in 2006. He rallied from a 156-point deficit after four races into the Chase.

BACK ROW (*from left*): Dale Earnhardt Jr., Mark Martin, Matt Kenseth, Jeff Gordon, Jimmie Johnson, Kevin Harvick.
FRONT ROW (*from left*): Kasey Kahne, Jeff Burton, Kyle Busch, Denny Hamlin.

>> RACE SCHEDULE <<
2007 Chase for the NASCAR NEXTEL Cup

Race No.	Date	Track
Race **1**	September 16	New Hampshire International Speedway (1.058 miles)
Race **2**	September 23	Dover International Speedway (1 mile)
Race **3**	September 30	Kansas Speedway (1.5 miles)
Race **4**	October 7	Talladega Superspeedway (2.66 miles)
Race **5**	October 13	Lowe's Motor Speedway (1.5 miles)
Race **6**	October 21	Martinsville Speedway (.526 mile)
Race **7**	October 28	Atlanta Motor Speedway (1.54 miles)
Race **8**	November 4	Texas Motor Speedway (1.5 miles)
Race **9**	November 11	Phoenix International Raceway (1 mile)
Race **10**	November 18	Homestead-Miami Speedway (1.5 miles)

>>GLOSSARY OF RACING TERMS <<

Aerodynamics: As applied to racing, the study of airflow and the forces of resistance and pressure that result from the flow of air over, under and around a moving car.

A-frame: Either the upper or lower connecting suspension piece (in the shape of an A) locking the frame to the spindle.

Adhesion: The "stick" between two touching objects. Adhesion implies a static condition, while traction implies a dynamic (moving) condition.

Air box: Housing for the air cleaner that connects the air intake at the base of the windshield to the carburetor.

Air dam: A metal strip that hangs beneath the front grill, often just inches from the ground. The air dam helps provide aerodynamic downforce at the front of the car.

Air filter: Paper, gauze or synthetic fiber element used to prevent dirt particles from entering the engine. Located in the air box.

Air pressure: Force exerted by air within a tire, expressed in pounds per square inch (psi).

Alternator: A belt-driven device mounted on the front of the engine that recharges the battery while the engine is running.

A-post: The post extending from the roofline to the base of the windshield on either side of the car.

Apron: The paved portion of a racetrack that separates the racing surface from the (usually unpaved) infield.

Axle: Rotating shafts connecting the rear differential gears to the rear wheels.

Ball joint: A ball inside a socket that can turn and pivot in any direction. Used to allow suspension to travel while the driver steers the car.

Banking: The sloping of a racetrack, particularly at a curve or corner, from the apron to the outside wall. Degree of banking refers to the height of a track's slope at its outside edge.

Bear grease: Slang term used to describe any patching material used to fill cracks and holes or smooth bumps on a track's surface. Can also be used as a sealer on a track.

Bell housing: A cover, shaped like a bell, that surrounds the flywheel, clutch that connects the engine to the transmission.

Bias-ply: Layers of fabric within a tire that are woven in angles. Also used as a term to describe tires made in this manner.

Bite: (1) "Round of bite" describes the turning or adjusting of a car's jacking screws found at each wheel. "Weight jacking" distributes the car's weight at each wheel. (2) Adhesion of a tire to the track surface.

Bleeder valve: A valve in the wheel used to reduce air pressure in tires.

Blend line: Line painted on the track near the apron and extending from the pit road exit into the first turn. When leaving the pits, a driver must stay below it to safely blend back into traffic.

Blister: An overheating of the tread compound resulting in bubbles on the tire surface.

Blown motor: Major engine failure, for instance, when a connecting rod goes through the engine block. Usually produces a lot of smoke and steam.

Bodywork: The fabricated sheet metal that encloses the chassis.

Bore: Pistons travel up and down within each cylinder, or bore, in the engine block.

B-post: Post extending from the roofline to the base of the window behind the driver's head.

Brake caliper: The part of the braking system that, when applied by the driver, clamps the brake disk/rotor to slow or stop the car.

Camber: The amount a tire is tilted in or out from vertical. Described in degrees, either positive or negative.

Camshaft: A rotating shaft within the engine that opens and closes the intake and exhaust valves in the engine.

Carburetor: A device connected directly to the gas pedal and mounted on top of the intake manifold that controls the air/fuel mixture going to the engine.

Chassis: The steel structure or frame of the car.

Chute: A racetrack straightaway.

Compound: A formula or recipe of rubber composing a particular tire. Different tracks require different tire compounds. Left-side tires are considerably softer than right-side tires, and it's against the rules to run left sides on the right. There are four basic components: rubber polymers, carbon blacks, oils and curatives.

>> GLOSSARY OF RACING TERMS <<

Compression ratio: Amount that the air-fuel mixture is compressed as the piston reaches the top of the bore. The higher the compression, the more horsepower produced.

Contact patch: The portion of the tire that makes contact with the racing surface. The size of each tire's contact patch changes as the car is driven.

Cowl: A removable metal scoop at the base of the windshield and rear of the hood that directs air into the air box.

C-post: The post extending from the roofline of a race car to the base of the rear window to the top of the deck lid.

Crankcase: The area of the engine block that houses the crankshaft.

Crankshaft: The rotating shaft within the engine that delivers the power from the pistons to the flywheel, and from there to the transmission.

Cubic-inch displacement: The size of the engine measured in cubic inches.

Cut tire: A slice or puncture in the tread or sidewall due to high speed contact with debris on the racetrack or by contact with part of another racecar.

Cylinder head: Made of aluminum, it is bolted to the top of each side of the engine block. Cylinder heads hold the valves and spark plugs. Passages through the heads make up the intake and exhaust ports.

Deck lid: Slang term for the trunk lid of a racecar.

Dirty air: Aerodynamic term for the turbulent air currents caused by fast moving cars that can cause a particular car to lose control.

Donuts: Slang term for black, circular, dent-line marks on the side panels of stock cars, usually caused after rubbing against other cars at high speed.

Downforce: A combination of aerodynamic and centrifugal forces. The more downforce, the more grip a racecar has. But more downforce also means more drag, which can rob a racecar of speed.

Draft: Slang term for the aerodynamic effect that allows two or more cars traveling nose-to-tail to run faster than a single car. When one car follows another closely, the one in front cuts through the air, providing a cleaner path of air (that is, less resistance) for the car in back.

Drafting: The practice of two or more cars, running nose-to-tail, almost touching, while racing. The lead car, by displacing the air in front of it, creates a vacuum between its rear end and the nose of the following car, actually pulling the second car along with it.

Drag: The resistance a car experiences when passing through air at high speeds. A resisting force exerted on a car parallel to its airstream and opposite in direction to its motion.

Driveshaft: A steel tube that connects the transmission of a race car to the rear end housing.

Dyno: Shortened term for dynamometer, a machine used to measure an engine's horsepower.

Engine block: An iron casting from the manufacturer that envelopes the crankshaft, connecting rods and pistons.

Equalized: When the inner liner of a tire loses air pressure and that pressure becomes the same as that within the outer tire, creating a vibration. The inner shield should have a higher pounds per square inch than the outer tire.

Esses: Slang term used for a series of acute left- and right-hand turns on a road course, one turn immediately following another.

Fabricator: A person who specializes in creating the sheet metal body of a stock car. Most teams employ two or more.

Factory: A term designating the "Big Three" auto manufacturers: General Motors (GM), Ford and DaimlerChrysler. The "factory days" refer to the periods in the 1950s and '60s when the manufacturers actively and openly provided sponsorship money and technical support to some race teams.

Fan: An electrically or mechanically driven device that is used to pull air through the radiator or oil cooler. Heat is transferred from the hot oil or water in the radiator to the moving air.

Firewall: A solid metal plate that separates the engine compartment from the driver's compartment of the race car.

Flat-out: Slang term for racing a car as fast as possible under the given weather and track conditions.

Flywheel: A heavy metal rotating wheel that is part of the race car's clutch system, used to keep elements such as the crank shaft turning steadily.

In an effort to further ensure competitors' safety, NASCAR announced in September 2003 that racing back to the caution no longer would be permitted in the NASCAR NEXTEL Cup Series, NASCAR Busch Series and NASCAR Craftsman Truck Series. That led NASCAR to institute a new procedure in which the field is "frozen" on the racetrack once the caution flag is issued.

The cars' positions are determined by the previous timing-and-scoring line they passed on the race track. Example (see below): Cars Nos. 1 through 3 are scored by their running order when they passed timing and scoring line E; cars Nos. 4 and 5 are scored by their positions when they passed timing and scoring line D; cars 6 and 7 are scored by their positions when they passed timing and scoring line C.

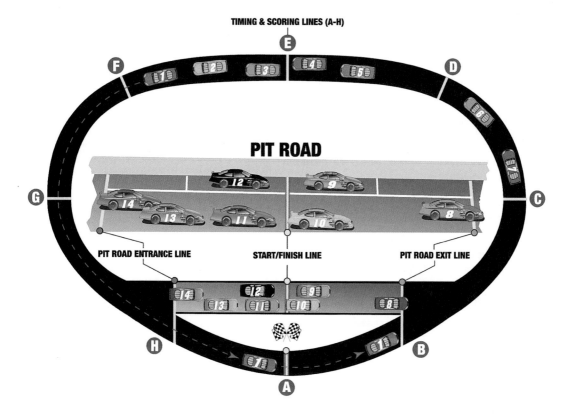

While the positions of the competitors on the race track will be "frozen," the pit lane, however, will remain active at this time with pit-road speed in effect.

The cars that are pitted from pit-road entrance to the start/finish line—cars 11, 12, 13 and 14—must reach the start/finish scoring line that extends across pit road before the race leader (No. 1 red car approaching scoring line A) reaches the same line on the race track. Should any of these cars on pit road reach that point first, they will not lose a lap to the leader. Should the leader reach scoring line A before cars 11-14, they would lose a lap to the leader. Those cars that are pitted from the start/finish line to the pit-road exit—cars 8, 9 and 10—must reach the pit-road exit scoring line before the leader (No. 1 red car approaching scoring line B) to avoid going a lap down. Example: car 8 would not go a lap down, while cars 9 and 10 would. Should a driver attempt to speed in pit lane to avoid going down a lap to the leader, that driver would lose a lap in addition to being moved to the end of the longest line. Should the race leader not slow immediately for the caution in an effort to put the pitted cars a lap down, the leader will be penalized by being sent to the end of the longest line and all pitted cars will retain their lap positions.

>>GLOSSARY OF RACING TERMS<<

Four-barrel: A type of carburetor.

Frame: The metal skeleton or structure of a race car, on which the sheet metal of the car's body is formed. Also referred to as a chassis.

Front clip: Beginning at the firewall, the frontmost section of a racecar. Holds the engine and its associated electrical, lubricating and cooling apparatus, as well as the braking, steering, and suspension mechanisms.

Front steer: A racecar in which the steering components are located ahead of the front axle.

Fuel cell: A holding tank for a race car's supply of gasoline. Consists of a metal box that contains a flexible, tear-resistant bladder and foam baffling. A product of aerospace technology, it's designed to eliminate or minimize fuel spillage. A fuel cell holds approximately 22 gallons.

Fuel pump: A device that pumps fuel from the fuel cell through the fuel line into the carburetor.

Gasket: A thin material, made of paper, metal, silicone or other synthetic materials, used as a seal between two similar machined metal surfaces, such as cylinder heads and the engine block.

Gauge: An instrument, usually mounted on the dashboard, used to monitor engine conditions, such as fuel pressure, oil pressure and temperature, water pressure and temperature, and RPM (revolutions per minute).

Gears: Circular, wheel-shaped parts with teeth along the edges. The interlocking of these two mechanisms enables one to turn the other.

Greenhouse: The upper area of the racecar that extends from the base of the windshield in the front, the tops of the doors on the sides and the base of the rear window in the back. Includes all of the A, B and C pillars, the entire glass area and the car's roof.

Groove: Slang term for the best route around the racetrack; the most efficient or quickest way around the track for a particular driver. The "high groove" takes a car closer to the outside wall for most of a lap, while the "low groove" takes a car closer to the apron than the outside wall. Road racers use the term "line". Drivers search for a fast groove, which has been known to change, depending on track and weather conditions.

Happy Hour: Slang term for the last official practice session held before an event. Usually takes place the day before the race.

Harmonic balancer: An element used to reduce vibrations in the crankshaft.

Handling: Generally, a racecar's performance while racing, qualifying and practicing. How a car handles is determined by its tires, suspension geometry, aerodynamics, and other factors.

Hauler: The 18-wheel tractor-trailer rig that teams use to transport two racecars, engines, tools and support equipment to the racetracks. Cars are stowed in the top section, while the bottom floor is used for work space.

Heat cycle: Each time a tire is raised to operating temperature.

High heat: Above normal (260 degrees) tire temperature.

Horsepower: A measurement of mechanical or engine power. Measured in the amount of power it takes to move 33,000 pounds one foot in a minute.

Ignition: An electrical system used to ignite the air-fuel mixture in an internal combustion engine.

Intake manifold: A housing that directs the air-fuel mixture through the port openings in the cylinder heads.

Intermediate track: Term describing a racetrack one mile or more, but less than two miles, in length.

Interval: The time-distance between two cars. Referred to roughly in car lengths, or precisely in seconds.

Jet: When air is sent at a high velocity through the carburetor, jets direct the fuel into the airstream. Jets are made slightly larger to make a richer mixture or slightly smaller to make a more lean mixture, depending on track and weather conditions.

Lapped traffic: Cars that have completed at least one full lap less than the race leader.

Air Flow

Draft

>> AERODYNAMICS

Study of airflow in regard to a stock car, including the effects of downforce and drag.

>> DRAG

The resistance a car experiences when passing through air at high speeds. An example of drag occurs when holding your hand outside the car window while traveling down the highway. Drag is what pushes your hand back—minimize the shape of your hand and the drag or force is less.

>> DOWNFORCE

A combination of aerodynamic and centrifugal forces at work. Downforce can be altered to improve the car's grip or traction by adjusting the spoiler as well as other aerodynamic changes to the car and its setup. As downforce is increased, the grip/traction is increased, as well as tire wear. Increasing downforce comes at the expense of creating more drag, which will reduce fuel efficiency.

Teams will tolerate any amount of drag for an increase in downforce at all tracks, with the exception of the two largest superspeedways, Daytona International Speedway and Talladega Superspeedway.

>> DRAFT

The aerodynamic effect that allows two or more cars traveling nose to tail to run faster than a single car. When one car follows another closely, the one in front punches through the air and provides a cleaner, less resistant path for the trailing cars.

>> DRAFTING

The practice, which is prevalent on superspeedways such as Daytona and Talladega, of two or more cars running nose to tail to create more speed for the group. The lead car displaces the air in front of it, creates a vacuum effect between its rear end and the nose of the second car and pulls the trailing cars along with it with less overall resistance. Two or more cars drafting will travel faster than a single car.

>> HANS DEVICE <<

As part of its continuing safety initiative, NASCAR became the world's first major auto racing sanctioning body to mandate the use of an approved head and neck restraint by all drivers on every type of race circuit, beginning with the 2002 season. The HANS Device helps to reduce extreme head motion during accidents and sudden stops. The device is required for use in NASCAR's three national series–the NASCAR NEXTEL Cup Series, NASCAR Busch Series, NASCAR Craftsman Truck Series–as well as its regional touring series. How the HANS Device works is illustrated:

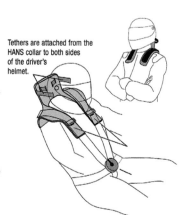

Tethers are attached from the HANS collar to both sides of the driver's helmet.

With HANS Device
Upon impact or sudden stop, the two tethers attached to a specially designed shoulder harness help keep the driver's head and neck in a stationary, upright position.

Without HANS Device
Unrestrained, the head and neck of the driver moves forward and/or to the side as the rest of his body and his car decelerate during impact or sudden stop.

>>GLOSSARY OF RACING TERMS<<

Lead lap: The lap that the race leader is on.

Line: See Groove

Loading: Weight at a given tire position on a car due to aerodynamics, vehicle weight and lateral G-forces in a turn.

Loose: Also known as "oversteer". When the rear tires of the car have trouble sticking in the corners. This causes the car to "fishtail" as the rear end swings outward during turns. A minor amount of this effect can be desirable on certain tracks.

Loose stuff: Debris such as sand, pebbles or small pieces of rubber that tend to collect on a track's apron or near the outside wall during a race.

Lug nuts: Large nuts applied with a high-pressure air wrench to wheel during a pit stop to secure the tires in place. All NASCAR cars use five lug nuts on each wheel, and penalties are assessed if a team fails to put all five on during a pit stop.

Magnaflux: Short for "magnetic particle inspection." A procedure for checking all ferrous (steel) parts (suspension pieces, connecting rods, cylinder heads, etc.) for cracks and other defects by utilizing a solution of metal particles and fluorescent dye and a black light. Surface cracks will appear as red lines.

Marbles: Excess rubber build-up above the upper groove on the racetrack.

Neutral: A term drivers use when referring to how their car is handling. When a car is neither loose nor pushing (tight).

Oil pump: This device pumps oil to lubricate all moving engine parts.

Panhard bar: A lateral bar that keeps the rear tires centered within the body of the car. It connects the frame on one side and the rear axle on the other. Also called the track bar.

Piston: A circular element that moves up and down in the cylinder, compressing the air-fuel mixture in the top of the chamber, helping to produce horsepower.

Pit road: The area where pit crews service the cars. Generally located along the front straightaway, but because of space limitations, some race tracks sport pit roads on both the front and back straightaways.

Pit stall: The area along pit road that is designated for a particular team's use during pit stops. Each car stops in the team's stall before being serviced.

Pole position: Term for the first position on the starting grid, awarded to the fastest qualifier.

Post-entry (PE): A team or driver who submits an entry blank for a race after the deadline for submission has passed. A post-entry receives no driver or owner points.

Push: See Tight.

Quarter-panel: The sheet metal on both sides of the car from the C-post to the rear bumper below the deck lid and above the wheel well.

Rear clip: The section of a race car that begins at the base of the rear windshield and extends to the rear bumper. Contains the car's fuel cell and rear suspension components.

Restart: The waving of the green flag following a caution period.

Restrictor plate: A thin metal plate with four holes that restrict airflow from the carburetor into the engine. Used to reduce horsepower and keep speeds down. The restrictor plates are currently used at Daytona International Speedway and Talladega Superspeedway, the two biggest and fastest tracks in NASCAR.

Ride height: The distance between the car's frame rails and the ground.

RPM: Short for revolutions per minute, a measurement of the speed of the engine's crankshaft.

Roll cage: The steel tubing inside the racecar's interior. Designed to protect the driver from impacts or rollovers, the roll cage must meet strict NASCAR safety guidelines and is inspected regularly.

Round: Slang term for a way of making chassis adjustments utilizing the racecar's springs. A wrench is inserted in a jack bolt attached to the springs and is used to tighten or loosen the amount of play in the spring. This in turn can loosen or tighten up the handling of a racecar.

>>TIGHT vs. LOOSE CONDITIONS <<

TIGHT: Also known as understeer. This occurs when the front wheels lose traction before the rear wheels. It causes the stock car to have trouble steering sharply and smoothly through the turns as the front end pushes toward the wall.

LOOSE: Also known as oversteer. This occurs when the rear tires of the stock car have trouble sticking in the corners. This causes the car to fishtail as the rear end swings outward while turning in the corners.

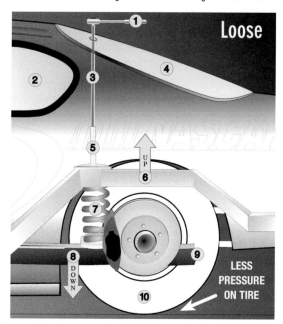

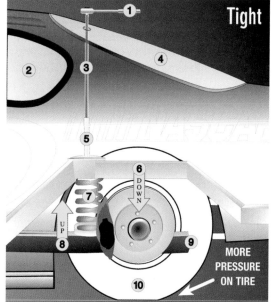

During a pit stop, one of the crewmen will sometimes add or subtract spring pressure by attaching a rachet and manually rotating it one way or the other. This tightens or loosens the spring and brings the frame and trailing arm forward or away from each other, applying more or less pressure on the tire when the car goes into a turn. This is known as adding or subtracting wedge.

1. Rachet inserted by crewman
2. Side window
3. Rachet extension
4. Rear window
5. Screw jack
6. Chassis frame
7. Coil spring
8. Trailing arm
9. Trailing arm end
10. Goodyear tire

>>GLOSSARY OF RACING TERMS<<

Scuffs: Slang term for tires that have been used at least once and saved for further racing. A lap or two is enough to "scuff" them in. Most often used in qualifying.

Setup: Slang term for the tuning and adjustments made to a racecar's suspension before and during a race.

Short track: Racetracks that are less than a mile in length.

Silly Season: Slang for the period that begins during the latter part of the current season, where in some teams announce driver, crew and/or sponsor changes for the following year.

Slick: A track condition where, for a number of reasons, it's hard for a car's tires to adhere to the surface or get a good "bite." A slick racetrack is not necessarily wet or slippery because of oil, water, etc. Temperature and the amount of rubber on a track are among factors that can create a slick track.

Slingshot: A maneuver in which a car following the leader in a draft suddenly steers around it, breaking the vacuum; this provides an extra burst of speed that allows the second car to take the lead. See Drafting.

Splash 'n' Go: A quick pit stop that involves nothing more than refueling the race car with the amount of fuel necessary to finish the race.

Spoiler: A metal blade attached to the rear deck lid of the car. It helps restrict airflow over the rear of the car, providing downforce and traction.

Stagger: The difference in size between the tires on the left and right sides of a car. Because of a tire's makeup, slight variations in circumference result. Stagger between right-side and left-side tires may range from less than a half inch to more than an inch. Stagger applies to only bias-ply tires and not radials.

Stick: Slang term used for tire traction, as in "the car's sticking to the track."

Stickers: Slang term for new tires. The name is derived from the manufacturer's stickers that are affixed to each new tire's contact surface.

Stop 'n' Go: A penalty, usually assessed for speeding on pit road or for unsafe driving. The car must be brought onto pit road at the appropriate speed and stopped for one full second in the team's pit stall before returning to the track.

Superspeedway: A racetrack of two miles or more in distance.

Racers refer to three types of oval tracks. Short tracks are under one mile, intermediate tracks are at least a mile but under two miles.

Sway bar: Sometimes called an "anti-roll bar." Bar used to resist or counteract the rolling force of the car body through the turns.

Template: A device used to check the body shape and size, to ensure compliance with the rules. The template closely resembles the shape of the factory version of the car.

Tight: Also known as "understeer." A car is said to be tight if the front wheels lose traction before the rear wheels do. A tight race car doesn't seem able to steer sharply enough through the turns. Instead, the front end continues toward the wall.

Toe: Looking at the car from the front, the amount the tires are turned in or out. If you imagine your feet to be the two front tires of a racecar, standing with your toes together would represent toe-in. Standing with your heels together would represent toe-out.

Track bar: See Panhard Bar.

Trading paint: Slang term used to describe aggressive driving involving a lot of bumping and rubbing.

Trailing arm: A rear suspension piece holding the rear axle firmly fore and aft yet allowing it to travel up and down.

Trioval: A racetrack that has a "hump" or "fifth turn" in addition to the standard four corners. Not to be confused with a triangle-shaped speedway, which has only three distinct corners.

200 mph tape: Also known as "racer's tape." Duct tape so strong it will hold a banged up racecar together long enough to finish a race.

Victory lane: Sometimes called the "winner's circle." The spot at each racetrack where the race winner parks for the celebration.

Wedge, round of: Adjusting the handling of the car by altering pressure on the rear springs.

Wedge: Term that refers to the cross weight adjustment on a racecar.

Window net: A woven mesh that hangs across the driver's side window, to prevent the driver's head and limbs from being exposed during an accident.

>> RACE TIRE vs. STREET TIRE <<

On a typical race weekend, a NASCAR NEXTEL Cup Series team will use between nine and 14 sets of tires depending on the length of the race and the type of track—short track, speedway, superspeedway or road course. By comparison, an average set of street tires gets replaced approximately every three years. NASCAR NEXTEL Cup Series racing tire specifications also differ from race to race depending upon the degree of track banking and the type of racing surface (asphalt, concrete or a mixture of both). Goodyear uses about 18 different tire codes to cover the needs of the NASCAR NEXTEL Cup Series during the course of a racing season.

Goodyear Lifeguard
Inner Liner Safety Spare

>> GOODYEAR EAGLE RACE TIRE vs. GOODYEAR EAGLE STREET TIRE <<

Estimated cost: $389 each / $150-200 each

Average life: 150 miles / 50,000 miles

Air pressure: (cold psi) 30 psi, left and 45 psi, right / all inflated to 35 psi

Inflated with: dry air or nitrogen / air

Weight: 24 pounds / 30 pounds

Tread thickness: ⅛ inch / ⅜ inch

Tread width: 11.5 inches / 9 inches

>> RACE TIRE SAFETY <<

Introduced in 1966, the Goodyear Lifeguard Inner Liner Safety Spare allows the car to return to the pits in the event of an air loss. Based on a tire-within-a-tire concept, it features a separate valve system that eliminates air equalization and prevents the tire and wheel assembly from becoming unbalanced.

>> GOODYEAR LIFEGUARD INNER LINER SAFETY SPARE <<

As a rule, the Goodyear Lifeguard inner liner safety spare is used on oval tracks one mile or more in length. It's also used on the right-side tires at Bristol Motor Speedway. The inner liner can be reused up to a dozen times if not damaged. It weighs 10 pounds and is generally inflated 12 to 25 pounds higher than the outer Goodyear Eagle race tire. The original version of this tire was first tested by drivers Richard Petty and Darel Dieringer and was used until 1992 before it was replaced by the current tubeless model.

>> ANATOMY OF A PIT STOP <<

Seven crew members are routinely allowed over the wall during pit stops per NASCAR rules. At times, NASCAR will inform teams that an eighth crew member will be allowed over the wall for a pit stop with the responsibility of cleaning the windshield. An average efficient pit stop that consists of the changing of all four tires and a full tank of fuel can take anywhere between 13 and 15 seconds. The amount of pit stops during a race vary because of numerous factors—race length, caution flags, fuel mileage, tire wear and pit strategy, to name a few. Below is a look at pit crew members and their responsibilities during a routine stop.

1 Rear tire carrier
Assists the rear tire changer by handing him a new right-side tire he has carried from behind the pit wall. May also adjust the rear jack bolt to change the car's handling.

2 Jackman
Operates a 20-pound hydraulic jack that is used to raise the car for tire changes. After new tires are bolted on to the right side of the car, he drops the car to the ground and repeats the process on the left side.

3 Rear tire changer
First removes and replaces right-rear tire using an airpowered impact wrench to loosen and tighten five lug nuts holding the tire rim in place. He then moves to the opposite side of the car to change the left-rear tire.

4 Front tire carrier
Assists the front tire changer by handing him a new, right-side tire that he has carried from behind the pit wall. He repeats the process on the left side of the car with a tire rolled to him by another crew member from behind the pit wall.

5 Front tire changer
First removes and replaces right-front tire using an air-powered impact wrench to loosen and tighten five lug nuts holding the tire rim in place. He then moves to the opposite side of the car to change the left-front tire.

6 Catch can man
Holds a can that collects overflow from the fuel cell as it is being filled. He also signals the rest of the team that the refueling process is finished by raising his hand.

7 Gas man
Empties two 12-gallon (81 pounds each) dump cans of fuel into the car's 22-gallon fuel cell.

8 Support crew
Assists the "over the wall" crew by rolling tires to them, handing them fuel, and retrieving air hoses and wrenches. According to NASCAR rules, support crew members must remain behind the pit wall during all stops.

9 Extra man
On occasion, and at the discretion of NASCAR officials, an eighth or "extra man" is allowed over the wall to clean the windshield and assist the driver if necessary.

10 NASCAR official
Watches for rules violations and helps maintain pit lane safety.

NASCAR TRACKS

NASCAR NEXTEL Cup Series:
Racing across America

The NASCAR NEXTEL Cup Series schedule includes 36 championship points events hosted at 22 tracks in 19 states. The Southeast remains the foundation of the series, but the NASCAR NEXTEL Cup Series has expanded to major markets throughout the country, particularly since the 1990s.

The Northeast–New England in particular–benefited first during that decade as the NASCAR NEXTEL Cup Series became a part of the area's sports scene in 1993 with the addition of the New Hampshire International Speedway. A year later, the NASCAR NEXTEL Cup Series laid a major footprint in the Midwest with the addition of Indianapolis Motor Speedway to the schedule.

The series, with events already in Arizona (Phoenix) and California (Sonoma), further expanded in the Southwest and West with the addition of the California Speedway near Los Angeles and Fort Worth's Texas Motor Speedway in 1997, and Las Vegas Motor Speedway a year later.

Florida–home of the world-famous Daytona International Speedway–added another venue near its southernmost tip in 1999 when Homestead-Miami Speedway hosted its inaugural NASCAR NEXTEL Cup Series event. The most recent additions came in 2001 and bolstered the Midwest with Chicagoland Speedway and Kansas Speedway joining the schedule.

In total–from the weekly and regional levels in the three national series that consist of the NASCAR NEXTEL Cup Series, NASCAR Busch Series and NASCAR Craftsman Truck Series–NASCAR sanctions more than 1,500 events at 108 tracks in 36 states and Canada.

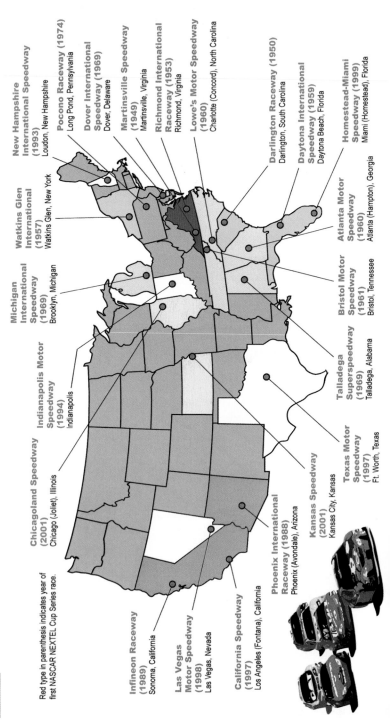

New Hampshire International Speedway (1993)
Loudon, New Hampshire

Pocono Raceway (1974)
Long Pond, Pennsylvania

Dover International Speedway (1969)
Dover, Delaware

Martinsville Speedway (1949)
Martinsville, Virginia

Richmond International Raceway (1953)
Richmond, Virginia

Lowe's Motor Speedway (1960)
Charlotte (Concord), North Carolina

Darlington Raceway (1950)
Darlington, South Carolina

Daytona International Speedway (1959)
Daytona Beach, Florida

Homestead-Miami Speedway (1999)
Miami (Homestead), Florida

Watkins Glen International (1957)
Watkins Glen, New York

Atlanta Motor Speedway (1960)
Atlanta (Hampton), Georgia

Michigan International Speedway (1969)
Brooklyn, Michigan

Bristol Motor Speedway (1961)
Bristol, Tennessee

Indianapolis Motor Speedway (1994)
Indianapolis

Talladega Superspeedway (1969)
Talladega, Alabama

Chicagoland Speedway (2001)
Chicago (Joliet), Illinois

Texas Motor Speedway (1997)
Ft. Worth, Texas

Kansas Speedway (2001)
Kansas City, Kansas

Red type in parenthesis indicates year of first NASCAR NEXTEL Cup Series race.

Phoenix International Raceway (1988)
Phoenix (Avondale), Arizona

Infineon Raceway (1988)
Sonoma, California

Las Vegas Motor Speedway (1998)
Las Vegas, Nevada

California Speedway (1997)
Los Angeles (Fontana), California

Decade First NASCAR NEXTEL Cup Race Held in State			
■ 1940s	□ 1960s	▨ 1980s	□ 2000s
▨ 1950s	□ 1970s	□ 1990s	

>>TRACK DISTANCES<<

Track	Distance	.5 Mile	1 Mile	1.5 Miles	2 Miles	2.5 Miles
Talladega Superspeedway	2.66-mile tri-oval					
Daytona International Speedway	2.5-mile oval					
Indianapolis Motor Speedway	2.5-mile oval					
Pocono Raceway	2.5-mile tri-oval					
Watkins Glen International	2.45-mile road course					
California Speedway	2-mile oval					
Michigan International Speedway	2-mile oval					
Infineon Raceway	1.99-mile road course					
Atlanta Motor Speedway	1.54-mile oval					
Chicagoland Speedway	1.5-mile tri-oval					
Homestead-Miami Speedway	1.5-mile oval					
Kansas Speedway	1.5-mile tri-oval					
Las Vegas Motor Speedway	1.5-mile oval					
Lowe's Motor Speedway	1.5-mile oval					
Texas Motor Speedway	1.5-mile oval					
Darlington Raceway	1.366 mile oval					
New Hampshire International Speedway	1.058-mile oval					
Dover International Speedway	1-mile oval					
Phoenix International Raceway	1-mile oval					
Richmond International Raceway	.75-mile oval					
Bristol Motor Speedway	.533-mile oval					
Martinsville Speedway	.526-mile oval					

TRACK FACTS

OLDEST
Martinsville Speedway—Martinsville, Va.,
first race: September 25, 1949

NEWEST
Kansas Speedway—Kansas City, Kan.,
first race: September 30, 2001

LONGEST
Talladega Superspeedway—Talladega, Ala.,
2.66-mile oval

SHORTEST
Martinsville Speedway—Martinsville, Va.,
.526-mile oval

LONGEST FRONT STRETCH
Talladega Superspeedway—Talladega, Ala.,
4,300 feet

SHORTEST FRONT STRETCH
Bristol Motor Speedway—Bristol, Tenn.,
650 feet

MOST BANKING IN TURNS
Bristol Motor Speedway—Bristol, Tenn.,
36 degrees

LEAST BANKING IN TURNS
Indianapolis Motor Speedway—Indianapolis,
9 degrees

LONGEST RACE DISTANCE
Lowe's Motor Speedway—Concord, N.C.,
600 miles

SHORTEST RACE DISTANCE
Infineon Raceway—Sonoma, Calif.,
218.9 miles

FASTEST OVAL QUALIFYING
Talladega Superspeedway—Talladega, Ala.,
212.809 mph (Bill Elliott, April 30, 1987)

FASTEST RACE AVERAGE SPEED
Talladega Superspeedway—Talladega, Ala.,
188.354 mph (Mark Martin, May 10, 1997)

>>ATLANTA MOTOR SPEEDWAY<<

TRACK FACTS >>> >>> **Location:** Hampton, Ga. >>> >>> **Owner:** Speedway Motorsports, Inc. >>> >>> **Track length:** 1.54 miles

ATLANTA
MOTOR SPEEDWAY
Real Racing. Real Fast.

>>> >>> **Grandstand seating:** 124,000 >>> >>> **Tickets:** (770) 946-4211 >>> >>> **Website:** www.atlantamotorspeedway.com

>>NASCAR NEXTEL CUP SERIES<<

>>TRACK RECORDS

Most wins: 9—Dale Earnhardt; **Most top fives:** 26—Dale Earnhardt; **Most top 10s:** 33—Richard Petty; **Oldest winner:** Morgan Shepherd, 51 years, 4 months, 27 days; March 20, 1993; **Youngest winner:** Jeff Gordon, 23 years, 7 months, 8 days; March 12, 1995; **Most lead changes:** 45—November 7, 1982; **Fewest lead changes:** 6—Three times, most recently, June 30, 1963; **Most leaders:** 17—March 12, 2000; **Fewest leaders:** 3—June 30, 1963; **Most laps led in a 400-mile race:** 167, Banjo Matthews, September 17, 1961; **Most laps led in a 500-mile race:** 308, Cale Yarborough, March 30, 1969; **Most cautions:** 11—Three times, most recently, November 14, 1993; **Fewest cautions:** 1—Twice, most recently, August 2, 1970; **Most caution laps:** 99—November 6, 1977; **Fewest caution laps:** 7—November 2, 1986; **Most on the lead lap:** 32—November 8, 1998; **Fewest on the lead lap:** 1—11 times, most recently, November 2, 1986; **Most running at the finish:** 41—March 20, 2005; **Fewest running at the finish:** 10—April 5, 1964; **Most laps led by a race winner:** 308—Cale Yarborough, March 30, 1969; **Fewest laps led by a race winner:** 1—David Pearson, September 17, 1961; **Closest margin of victory:** 0.006 seconds—Kevin Harvick defeated Jeff Gordon, March 11, 2001

>>QUALIFYING AND RACE RECORDS

QUALIFYING: Geoffrey Bodine, Ford; 197.478 mph (28.074 seconds), November 15, 1997
RACE: Bobby Labonte, Pontiac; 159.904 mph (3:07:48), November 16, 1997; **500 miles:** Bobby Labonte, Pontiac; 159.904 mph (3:07:48), November 16, 1997 (track size: 1.540 miles); Dale Earnhardt, Chevrolet; 163.633 mph (3:03:03), November 12, 1995 (track size: 1.522 miles); LeeRoy Yarbrough, 133.255 (3:45:35), August 10, 1969 (track size: 1.5 miles); **400 miles:** Richard Petty, Plymouth; 130.244 mph (3:04:30), August 7, 1966

24° Banking in Turns

Hampton
GEORGIA

First NASCAR NEXTEL Cup Series race:
July 31, 1960 (Fireball Roberts, winner)
Banking on straights: 5 degrees
Length of front stretch: 2,332 feet
Length of back stretch: 1,800 feet

2007 SCHEDULE
NASCAR NEXTEL Cup Series
Event: Golden Corral 500
Race: No. 4 of 36
Date: March 18 • **TV:** FOX • **Radio:** PRN

Event: Bass Pro Shops 500
Race: No. 33 of 36
Date: October 28 • **TV:** ABC • **Radio:** PRN

NASCAR Busch Series
Event: Nicorette 300
Race: No. 5 of 35 • **Date:** March 17
TV: ESPN2 • **Radio:** PRN

NASCAR Craftsman Truck Series
Event: John Deere 200
Race: No. 3 of 25
Date: March 16 • **TV:** SPEED • **Radio:** MRN

Event: EasyCare Vehicle Serivce Contracts 200
Race: No. 22 of 25
Date: October 27 • **TV:** SPEED • **Radio:** MRN
Race names subject to change

YEAR BY YEAR WINNERS

Year	Event	Race winner	Car make	Avg. speed	Start pos.	Car owner	Pole winner	Pole speed
2006	Bass Pro Shops 500	T. Stewart	Chevrolet	143.421	11	Joe Gibbs	None—conditions	
	Golden Corral 500	K. Kahne	Dodge	144.098	1	Ray Evernham	K. Kahne	192.553
2005	Bass Pro MBNA 500	C. Edwards	Ford	146.834	2	Jack Roush	R. Newman	193.928
	Golden Corral 500	C. Edwards	Ford	143.478	4	Jack Roush	R. Newman	194.690
2004	Bass/MBNA 500	Ji. Johnson	Chevrolet	145.847	8	Rick Hendrick	R. Newman	191.575
	Golden Corral 500	D.Earnhardt Jr.	Chevrolet	158.679	7	Teresa Earnhardt	R. Newman	193.575
2003	Bass/MBNA 500 (e)	J. Gordon	Chevrolet	127.769	19	Rick Hendrick	R. Newman	194.295
	Bass/MBNA 500	B. Labonte	Chevrolet	146.037	4	Joe Gibbs	R. Newman	191.417
2002	NAPA 500	Ku. Busch	Ford	127.519	8	Jack Roush	None—conditions	
	MBNA America 500	T. Stewart	Pontiac	148.443	9	Joe Gibbs	B. Elliott	191.542
2001	NAPA 500	B. Labonte	Pontiac	151.756	39	Joe Gibbs	D. Earnhardt Jr.	192.047
	Cracker Barrel 500	K. Harvick	Chevrolet	143.273	5	Richard Childress	D. Jarrett	192.748
2000	NAPA 500	J. Nadeau	Chevrolet	141.296	2	Rick Hendrick	J. Gordon	194.274
	Cracker Barrel 500	D. Earnhardt	Chevrolet	131.759	35	Richard Childress	D. Jarrett	192.574
1999	NAPA 500	B. Labonte	Pontiac	137.932	37	Joe Gibbs	K. Lepage	193.731
	Cracker Barrel 500	J. Gordon	Chevrolet	143.296	8	Rick Hendrick	B. Labonte	194.957

YEAR BY YEAR WINNERS continued

Year	Event	Race winner	Car make	Avg. speed	Start pos.	Car owner	Pole winner	Pole speed
1998	NAPA 500	J. Gordon	Chevrolet	114.915	21	Rick Hendrick	K. Irwin	193.461
	Primestar 500 (a)	B. Labonte	Pontiac	139.501	14	Joe Gibbs	J. Andretti	192.841
1997	NAPA 500 (c)	B. Labonte	Pontiac	159.904	21	Joe Gibbs	G. Bodine	197.478
	Primestar 500	D. Jarrett	Ford	132.731	9	Robert Yates	R. Gordon	186.507
1996	NAPA 500	B. Labonte	Chevrolet	134.661	1	Joe Gibbs	B. Labonte	185.887
	Purolator 500	D. Earnhardt	Chevrolet	161.298	18	Richard Childress	J. Benson	185.434
1995	NAPA 500	D. Earnhardt	Chevrolet	163.633	11	Richard Childress	D. Waltrip	185.046
	Purolator 500	J. Gordon	Chevrolet	150.115	3	Rick Hendrick	D. Earnhardt	185.077
1994	Hooters 500	M. Martin	Ford	148.982	5	Jack Roush	G. Sacks	185.830
	Purolator 500	E. Irvan	Ford	146.136	7	Robert Yates	L. Allen	180.207
1993	Hooters 500	R. Wallace	Pontiac	125.221	20	Roger Penske	H. Gant	176.902
	Motorcraft 500	M. Shepherd	Ford	150.442	7	Wood Brothers	R. Wallace	178.749
1992	Hooters 500	B. Elliott	Ford	133.322	11	Junior Johnson	R. Mast	180.183
	Motorcraft 500	B. Elliott	Ford	147.746	4	Junior Johnson	M. Martin	179.923
1991	Hardee's 500	M. Martin	Ford	137.968	4	Jack Roush	B. Elliott	177.937
	Motorcraft 500 (d)	K. Schrader	Chevrolet	140.470	5	Rick Hendrick	A. Kulwicki	174.413
1990	Atl. Journal 500	M. Shepherd	Ford	140.911	20	Bud Moore	R. Wallace	175.222
	Motorcraft 500	D. Earnhardt	Chevrolet	156.849	1	Richard Childress	None—conditions	
1989	Atl. Journal 500	D. Earnhardt	Chevrolet	140.229	3	Richard Childress	A. Kulwicki	179.112
	Motorcraft 500	D. Waltrip	Chevrolet	139.684	4	Rick Hendrick	A. Kulwicki	176.925
1988	Atl. Journal 500	R. Wallace	Pontiac	129.024	1	Raymond Beadle	R. Wallace	179.499
	Motorcraft 500	D. Earnhardt	Chevrolet	137.588	2	Richard Childress	G. Bodine	176.623
1987	Atl. Journal 500	B. Elliott	Ford	139.047	1	Harry Melling	B. Elliott	174.341
	Motorcraft 500	R. Rudd	Ford	133.689	6	Bud Moore	D. Earnhardt	175.497
1986	Atl. Journal 500	D. Earnhardt	Chevrolet	152.523	4	Richard Childress	B. Elliott	172.905
	Motorcraft 500	M. Shepherd	Buick	132.126	3	Jack Beebe	D. Earnhardt	170.713
1985	Atl. Journal 500	B. Elliott	Ford	139.597	3	Harry Melling	H. Gant	167.940
	Coca-Cola 500	B. Elliott	Ford	140.273	3	Harry Melling	N. Bonnett	170.278
1984	Atl. Journal 500	D. Earnhardt	Chevrolet	134.610	10	Richard Childress	B. Elliott	170.198
	Coca-Cola 500	B. Parsons	Chevrolet	144.945	8	Johnny Hayes	Buddy Baker	166.642
1983	Atl. Journal 500	N. Bonnett	Chevrolet	137.643	15	B. Rahilly/B. Mock	T. Richmond	168.151
	Coca-Cola 500	C. Yarborough	Chevrolet	124.055	22	Harry Ranier	G. Bodine	167.703
1982	Atl. Journal 500	B. Allison	Buick	130.884	9	DiProspero/Gardner	M. Shepherd	166.779
	Coca-Cola 500 (a)	D. Waltrip	Buick	124.824	14	Junior Johnson	D. Earnhardt	163.774
1981	Atl. Journal 500	N. Bonnett	Ford	130.391	5	Wood Brothers	H. Gant	163.266
	Coca-Cola 500	C. Yarborough	Buick	133.619	17	M.C. Anderson	T. Labonte	162.940
1980	Atl. Journal 500	C. Yarborough	Chevrolet	131.190	12	Junior Johnson	B. Allison	165.620
	Atlanta 500	D. Earnhardt	Chevrolet	134.808	31	Rod Osterlund	Buddy Baker	166.212
1979	Dixie 500	N. Bonnett	Mercury	140.120	4	Wood Brothers	Buddy Baker	164.813
	Atlanta 500	Buddy Baker	Oldsmobile	135.136	1	Ranier Racing	Buddy Baker	165.951
1978	Dixie 500	D. Allison	Chevrolet	124.312	13	Hoss Ellington	C. Yarborough	168.425
	Atlanta 500	B. Allison	Ford	142.520	4	Bud Moore	C. Yarborough	162.006
1977	Dixie 500	D. Waltrip	Chevrolet	110.052	8	DiProspero/Gardner	S. Sommers	160.229
	Atlanta 500	R. Petty	Dodge	144.093	1	Petty Enterprises	R. Petty	162.501
1976	Dixie 500	D. Marcis	Dodge	127.396	2	Nord Krauskopf	Buddy Baker	161.652
	Atlanta 500	D. Pearson	Mercury	128.904	2	Wood Brothers	D. Marcis	160.709
1975	Dixie 500	Buddy Baker	Ford	130.900	3	Bud Moore	D. Marcis	160.662
	Atlanta 500	R. Petty	Dodge	133.496	1	Petty Enterprises	R. Petty	159.029
1974	Dixie 500	R. Petty	Dodge	131.651	2	Petty Enterprises	C. Yarborough	156.750
	Atlanta 500	C. Yarborough	Chevrolet	136.910	9	Junior Johnson	D. Pearson	159.242
1973	Dixie 500	D. Pearson	Mercury	130.211	5	Wood Brothers	R. Petty	157.163
	Atlanta 500	D. Pearson	Mercury	139.351	9	Wood Brothers	None—conditions	
1972	Dixie 500	B. Allison	Chevrolet	131.295	3	Junior Johnson	D. Pearson	158.353
	Atlanta 500	B. Allison	Chevrolet	128.214	1	Junior Johnson	B. Allison	156.245
1971	Dixie 500	R. Petty	Plymouth	129.061	3	Petty Enterprises	Buddy Baker	155.796
	Atlanta 500	A.J. Foyt	Mercury	131.375	1	Wood Brothers	A.J. Foyt	155.152
1970	Dixie 500	R. Petty	Plymouth	142.712	6	Petty Enterprises	F. Lorenzen	157.625
	Atlanta 500 (b)	B. Allison	Dodge	139.554	9	Mario Rossi	C. Yarborough	159.929
1969	Dixie 500	L. Yarbrough	Ford	133.001	2	Junior Johnson	C. Yarborough	155.413
	Atlanta 500	C. Yarborough	Mercury	132.191	5	Wood Brothers	D. Pearson	156.794
1968	Dixie 500	L. Yarbrough	Mercury	127.068	5	Junior Johnson	Buddy Baker	153.361
	Atlanta 500	C. Yarborough	Mercury	125.564	4	Wood Brothers	L. Yarbrough	155.646
1967	Dixie 500	D. Hutcherson	Ford	132.286	8	Bondy Long	D. Dieringer	150.669
	Atlanta 500	C. Yarborough	Ford	131.238	1	Wood Brothers	C. Yarborough	148.996
1966	Dixie 400	R. Petty	Plymouth	130.244	5	Petty Enterprises	C. Turner	148.331
	Atlanta 500	J. Hurtubise	Plymouth	131.266	5	Norm Nelson	R. Petty	147.742
1965	Dixie 400	M. Panch	Ford	110.120	2	Wood Brothers	F. Lorenzen	143.407
	Atlanta 500	M. Panch	Ford	129.410	1	Wood Brothers	M. Panch	145.581
1964	Dixie 400	N. Jarrett	Ford	112.535	17	Bondy Long	Ju. Johnson	145.906
	Atlanta 500	F. Lorenzen	Ford	132.959	1	Holman-Moody	F. Lorenzen	146.470
1963	Dixie 400	Ju. Johnson	Chevrolet	121.139	2	Ray Fox	M. Panch	140.753
	Atlanta 500	F. Lorenzen	Ford	130.582	2	Holman-Moody	Ju. Johnson	141.038
1962	Dixie 400	R. White	Chevrolet	124.896	5	Rex White	F. Roberts	138.978
	Atlanta 500 (a)	F. Lorenzen	Ford	101.983	7	Holman-Moody	Matthews	137.640
1961	Dixie 400	D. Pearson	Pontiac	125.384	5	John Masoni	F. Roberts	136.294
	Festival 250	F. Lorenzen	Ford	118.007	5	Holman-Moody	F. Roberts	136.088
	Atlanta 500	B. Burdick	Pontiac	124.172	7	Roy Burdick	M. Panch	135.755
1960	Atlanta 500	B. Johns	Pontiac	134.596	5	Cotton Owens	F. Roberts	134.596
	Dixie 300	F. Roberts	Pontiac	112.653	1	John Hines	F. Roberts	133.870

KEY **(a)** Race shortened by rain. **(b)** Track remeasured from 1.5 miles to 1.522 miles. **(c)** Track reconfigured to 1.54 miles, with back stretch now the start-finish line. **(d)** First 47 laps run on March 17; final 281 laps run on March 18. **(e)** First 39 laps run on October 26; final 286 laps run on October 27.

ALL ATLANTA RACES

POLE WINNERS

Buddy Baker	7
Ryan Newman	6
Cale Yarborough	6
Bill Elliott	5
Fireball Roberts	5
Dale Earnhardt	4
Richard Petty	4
Geoffrey Bodine	3
Harry Gant	3
Alan Kulwicki	3
Fred Lorenzen	3
Marvin Panch	3
Rusty Wallace	3
Bobby Allison	2
Dale Jarrett	2
Junior Johnson	2
Bobby Labonte	2
Dave Marcis	2
David Pearson	2
Loy Allen	1
John Andretti	1
Johnny Benson	1
Neil Bonnett	1
Darel Dieringer	1
Dale Earnhardt Jr.	1
A.J. Foyt	1
Charlie Glotzbach	1
Jeff Gordon	1
Robby Gordon	1
Kenny Irwin	1
Kasey Kahne	1
Terry Labonte	1
Kevin Lepage	1
Mark Martin	1
Rick Mast	1
Banjo Mathews	1
Tim Richmond	1
Greg Sacks	1
Morgan Shepherd	1
Sam Sommers	1
Curtis Turner	1
Darrell Waltrip	1
LeeRoy Yarbrough	1

RACE WINNERS

Dale Earnhardt	9
Cale Yarborough	7
Bobby Labonte	6
Richard Petty	6
Bobby Allison	5
Bill Elliott	5
Jeff Gordon	4
Fred Lorenzen	4
David Pearson	4
Neil Bonnett	3
Morgan Shepherd	3
Darrell Waltrip	3
Buddy Baker	2
Carl Edwards	2
Mark Martin	2
Marvin Panch	2
Tony Stewart	2
Rusty Wallace	2
LeeRoy Yarbrough	2
Donnie Allison	1
Bob Burdick	1
Kurt Busch	1
Dale Earnhardt Jr.	1
A.J. Foyt	1
Kevin Harvick	1
Jim Hurtubise	1
Dick Hutcherson	1
Ernie Irvan	1
Dale Jarrett	1
Ned Jarrett	1
Bobby Johns	1
Jimmie Johnson	1
Junior Johnson	1
Kasey Kahne	1
Dave Marcis	1
Jerry Nadeau	1
Benny Parsons	1
Fireball Roberts	1
Ricky Rudd	1
Ken Schrader	1
Rex White	1

RACE 1

POLE WINNERS

Dale Earnhardt	4
Buddy Baker	3
Ryan Newman	3
Richard Petty	3
Cale Yarborough	3
Geoffrey Bodine	2
Dale Jarrett	2
Alan Kulwicki	2
Marvin Panch	2
Loy Allen Jr.	1
Bobby Allison	1
John Andretti	1
Johnny Benson	1
Neil Bonnett	1
Bill Elliott	1
A.J. Foyt	1
Charlie Glotzbach	1
Robby Gordon	1
Junior Johnson	1
Kasey Kahne	1
Bobby Labonte	1
Terry Labonte	1
Fred Lorenzen	1
Dave Marcis	1
Mark Martin	1
Banjo Mathews	1
David Pearson	1
Fireball Roberts	1
Rusty Wallace	1
LeeRoy Yarbrough	1

RACE WINNERS

Cale Yarborough	6
Dale Earnhardt	5
Bobby Allison	3
Fred Lorenzen	3
Bill Elliott	2
Jeff Gordon	2
Bobby Labonte	2
David Pearson	2
Richard Petty	2
Morgan Shepherd	2
Darrell Waltrip	2
Buddy Baker	1
Bob Burdick	1
Dale Earnhardt Jr.	1
Carl Edwards	1
A.J. Foyt	1
Kevin Harvick	1
Jim Hurtubise	1
Ernie Irvan	1
Dale Jarrett	1
Kasey Kahne	1
Marvin Panch	1
Benny Parsons	1
Fireball Roberts	1
Ricky Rudd	1
Ken Schrader	1
Tony Stewart	1

RACE 2

POLE WINNERS

Buddy Baker	4
Bill Elliott	4
Harry Gant	3
Ryan Newman	3
Fireball Roberts	3
Cale Yarborough	3
Fred Lorenzen	2
Rusty Wallace	2
Bobby Allison	1
Geoffrey Bodine	1
Darel Dieringer	1
Dale Earnhardt Jr.	1
Jeff Gordon	1
Kenny Irwin	1
Junior Johnson	1
Alan Kulwicki	1
Bobby Labonte	1
Kevin Lepage	1
Dave Marcis	1
Rick Mast	1
Marvin Panch	1
David Pearson	1
Richard Petty	1
Tim Richmond	1
Greg Sacks	1
Morgan Shepherd	1
Sam Sommers	1
Curtis Turner	1
Darrell Waltrip	1

RACE WINNERS

Dale Earnhardt	4
Bobby Labonte	4
Richard Petty	4
Neil Bonnett	3
Bill Elliott	3
Bobby Allison	2
Jeff Gordon	2
Mark Martin	2
David Pearson	2
Rusty Wallace	2
LeeRoy Yarbrough	2
Donnie Allison	1
Buddy Baker	1
Kurt Busch	1
Carl Edwards	1
Dick Hutcherson	1
Ned Jarrett	1
Bobby Johns	1
Jimmie Johnson	1
Junior Johnson	1
Dave Marcis	1
Jerry Nadeau	1
Marvin Panch	1
Morgan Shepherd	1
Tony Stewart	1
Darrell Waltrip	1
Rex White	1
Cale Yarborough	1

FESTIVAL 250

POLE WINNER

Fireball Roberts	1

RACE WINNER

Fred Lorenzen	1

>>ATLANTA MOTOR SPEEDWAY<<

>>NASCAR BUSCH SERIES<<

YEAR BY YEAR WINNERS

Year	Event	Race winner	Car make	Avg. speed	Start pos.	Pole winner	Pole speed
2006	Nicorette 300	J. Burton	Chevrolet	127.984	8	Ky. Busch	189.707
2005	Aaron's 312	C. Edwards	Ford	130.651	1	C. Edwards	191.364
2004	Aaron's 312	M. Kenseth	Ford	133.343	28	M. Bliss	188.867
2003	Aaron's 312	G. Biffle	Chevrolet	146.217	1	G. Biffle	192.300
2002	Aaron's 312	J. McMurray	Chevrolet	138.788	8	None—conditions	
2001	Aaron's 312	J. Nemechek	Chevrolet	143.954	3	R. Newman	191.661
2000	Aaron's 312	M. Martin	Ford	126.924	4	M. Kenseth	185.704
1999	Yellow Freight 300	M. Skinner	Chevrolet	117.178	17	D. Blaney	186.775
1998	Stihl 300	M. Martin	Ford	138.193	10	D. Trickle	186.673
1997	Stihl 300	M. Martin	Ford	151.751	13	T. Bender	179.835
1996	Busch Light 300	T. Labonte	Chevrolet	139.656	11	D. Trickle	177.544
1995	Busch Light 300	J. Benson	Chevrolet	145.767	10	M. Martin	176.623
1994	Busch Light 300	H. Gant	Chevrolet	127.649	23	S. Robinson	174.330
1993	Slick 50 300	W. Burton	Chevrolet	109.640	5	M. Martin	174.286
1992	Atlanta 300	J. Gordon	Chevrolet	124.412	1	J. Gordon	173.821

POLE WINNERS

Mark Martin	2
Dick Trickle	2
Tim Bender	1
Greg Biffle	1
Dave Blaney	1
Mike Bliss	1
Kyle Busch	1
Carl Edwards	1
Jeff Gordon	1
Matt Kenseth	1
Ryan Newman	1
Shawna Robinson	1

RACE WINNERS

Mark Martin	3
Johnny Benson	1
Greg Biffle	1
Jeff Burton	1
Ward Burton	1
Carl Edwards	1
Harry Gant	1
Jeff Gordon	1
Matt Kenseth	1
Terry Labonte	1
Jamie McMurray	1
Joe Nemechek	1
Mike Skinner	1

QUALIFYING RECORD: Greg Biffle, Chevrolet; 192.300 mph (28.830 seconds), October 25, 2003
RACE RECORD: Mark Martin, Ford; 151.751 mph (1:58:55), March 8, 1997

>>NASCAR CRAFTSMAN TRUCK SERIES<<

Bodine

YEAR BY YEAR WINNERS

Year	Event	Race winner	Car make	Avg. speed	Start pos.	Pole winner	Pole speed
2006	EasyCare 200	M. Bliss	Chevrolet	123.200	16	M. Skinner	180.993
	John Deere 200	T. Bodine	Toyota	133.388	1	T. Bodine	181.360
2005	EasyCare 200	Ky. Busch	Chevrolet	132.999	5	M. Skinner	182.591
	World Financial 200	R. Hornaday Jr.	Chevrolet	142.424	18	R. Crawford	182.735
2004	EasyCare 200	B. Hamilton	Dodge	123.675	12	D. Reutimann	179.452

POLE WINNERS

Mike Skinner	2
Todd Bodine	1
Rick Crawford	1
David Reutimann	1

RACE WINNERS

Mike Bliss	1
Todd Bodine	1
Kyle Busch	1
Bobby Hamilton	1
Ron Hornaday Jr.	1

QUALIFYING RECORD: Rick Crawford, Ford; 182.735 mph (30.339 seconds), March 18, 2005
RACE RECORD: Ron Hornaday Jr., Chevrolet; 142.424 mph (1:27:35), March 18, 2005

>>BRISTOL MOTOR SPEEDWAY<<

TRACK FACTS >>> >>> **Location:** Bristol, Tenn. >>> >>> **Owner:** Speedway Motorsports, Inc. >>> >>> **Track length:** .533 miles

>>> >>> **Grandstand seating:** 160,000 >>> >>> **Tickets:** (423) 764-1161 >>> >>> **Website:** www.bristolmotorspeedway.com

>>NASCAR NEXTEL CUP SERIES<<

>>TRACK RECORDS

Most wins: 12—Darrell Waltrip; **Most top fives:** 26—Richard Petty and Darrell Waltrip; **Most top 10s:** 37—Richard Petty; **Oldest winner:** Dale Earnhardt, 48 years, 3 months, 30 days; August 28, 1999; **Youngest winner:** Kurt Busch, 23 years, 7 months, 20 days; March 24, 2002; **Most lead changes:** 40—April 14, 1991; **Fewest lead changes:** 0—March 25, 1973; **Most leaders:** 16—April 9, 1995; **Fewest leaders:** 1—March 25, 1973; **Most cautions:** 20—Three times, most recently, August 23, 2003; **Fewest cautions:** 0—July 11, 1971; **Most caution laps:** 167—July 25, 1965; **Fewest caution laps:** 0—July 11, 1971; **Most on the lead lap:** 25—March 25, 2001; **Fewest on the lead lap:** 1—22 times, most recently, August 22, 1981; **Most running at the finish:** 40—April 11, 1999; **Fewest running at the finish:** 7—March 20, 1966; **Most laps led by a race winner:** 500—Cale Yarborough, March 25, 1973; **Fewest laps led by a race winner:** 1—Fred Lorenzen, July 26, 1964; **Closest margin of victory:** 0.10 seconds—Terry Labonte defeated Dale Earnhardt, August 26, 1995

>>QUALIFYING AND RACE RECORDS

QUALIFYING: Ryan Newman, Dodge; 128.709 mph (14.908 seconds), March 21, 2003
RACE: Charlie Glotzbach, Chevrolet; 101.074 mph (2:38:12), July 11, 1971

36° Banking in Turns   TENNESSEE Bristol

First NASCAR NEXTEL Cup Series race:
July 30, 1961 (Jack Smith, winner)
Banking on straights: 16 degrees
Length of front stretch: 650 feet
Length of back stretch: 650 feet

2007 SCHEDULE

NASCAR NEXTEL Cup Series
Event: Food City 500
Race: No. 5 of 36
Date: March 25 • **TV:** FOX • **Radio:** PRN

Event: Sharpie 500
Race: No. 24 of 36
Date: August 25 • **TV:** ESPN • **Radio:** PRN

NASCAR Busch Series
Event: Sharpie Mini 300
Race: No. 6 of 35 • **Date:** March 24
TV: ESPN2 • **Radio:** PRN

Event: Food City 250
Race: No. 26 of 35 • **Date:** August 24
TV: ESPN2 • **Radio:** PRN

NASCAR Craftsman Truck Series
Event: O'Reilly 200
Race: No. 16 of 25
Date: August 22 • **TV:** SPEED • **Radio:** MRN
Race names subject to change

YEAR BY YEAR WINNERS

Year	Event	Race winner	Car make	Avg. speed	Start pos.	Car owner	Pole winner	Pole speed
2006	Sharpie 500	M. Kenseth	Ford	90.025	4	Jack Roush	Ku. Busch	124.906
	Food City 500	Ku. Busch	Dodge	79.427	9	Roger Penske	None—conditions	
2005	Sharpie 500	M. Kenseth	Ford	84.678	1	Jack Roush	M. Kenseth	127.300
	Food City 500	K. Harvick	Chevrolet	77.496	13	Richard Childress	E. Sadler	127.733
2004	Sharpie 500	D. Earnhardt Jr.	Chevrolet	88.538	30	Teresa Earnhardt	J. Gordon	128.520
	Food City 500	Ku. Busch	Ford	82.607	13	Jack Roush	R. Newman	128.313
2003	Sharpie 500	Ku. Busch	Ford	77.421	5	Jack Roush	J. Gordon	127.597
	Food City 500	Ku. Busch	Ford	76.185	9	Jack Roush	R. Newman	128.709
2002	Sharpie 500	J. Gordon	Chevrolet	77.097	1	Rick Hendrick	J. Gordon	124.034
	Food City 500	Ku. Busch	Ford	82.281	27	Jack Roush	J. Gordon	127.216
2001	Sharpie 500	T. Stewart	Pontiac	85.106	18	Joe Gibbs	J. Green	123.674
	Food City 500	E. Sadler	Ford	86.949	38	Wood Brothers	M. Martin	126.303
2000	GoRacing.com 500	R. Wallace	Ford	85.394	1	Roger Penske	R. Wallace	125.477
	Food City 500	R. Wallace	Ford	88.018	6	Roger Penske	S. Park	126.370
1999	Goody's 500	D. Earnhardt	Chevrolet	91.276	26	Richard Childress	T. Stewart	124.589
	Food City 500	R. Wallace	Ford	93.363	1	Roger Penske	R. Wallace	125.142
1998	Goody's 500	M. Martin	Ford	86.918	4	Jack Roush	R. Wallace	125.554
	Food City 500	J. Gordon	Chevrolet	82.850	2	Rick Hendrick	R. Wallace	124.275
1997	Goody's 500	D. Jarrett	Ford	80.013	3	Robert Yates	K. Wallace	123.039
	Food City 500	J. Gordon	Chevrolet	75.035	5	Rick Hendrick	R. Wallace	123.586
1996	Goody's 500	R. Wallace	Ford	91.267	5	Roger Penske	M. Martin	124.857
	Food City 500 (a)	J. Gordon	Chevrolet	91.308	8	Rick Hendrick	M. Martin	123.578
1995	Goody's 500	T. Labonte	Chevrolet	81.979	2	Rick Hendrick	M. Martin	125.093
	Food City 500	J. Gordon	Chevrolet	92.011	2	Rick Hendrick	M. Martin	124.605

>>BRISTOL MOTOR SPEEDWAY<<

YEAR BY YEAR WINNERS continued

Year	Event	Race winner	Car make	Avg. speed	Start pos.	Car owner	Pole winner	Pole speed
1994	Goody's 500	R. Wallace	Ford	91.363	4	Roger Penske	H. Gant	124.186
	Food City 500	D. Earnhardt	Chevrolet	89.647	24	Richard Childress	C. Bown	124.946
1993	Bud 500	M. Martin	Ford	88.172	1	Jack Roush	M. Martin	121.405
	Food City 500	R. Wallace	Pontiac	84.730	1	Roger Penske	R. Wallace	120.938
1992	Bud 500 (d)	D. Waltrip	Chevrolet	91.198	9	Darrell Waltrip	E. Irvan	120.535
	Food City 500	A. Kulwicki	Ford	86.316	1	Alan Kulwicki	A. Kulwicki	122.474
1991	Bud 500	A. Kulwicki	Ford	82.028	5	Alan Kulwicki	B. Elliott	116.957
	Valleydale 500	R. Wallace	Pontiac	72.809	1	Roger Penske	R. Wallace	118.051
1990	Busch 500	E. Irvan	Chevrolet	91.782	6	Larry McClure	D. Earnhardt	115.604
	Valleydale 500	Da. Allison	Ford	87.258	19	Robert Yates	E. Irvan	116.157
1989	Busch 500	D. Waltrip	Chevrolet	78.775	9	Rick Hendrick	A. Kulwicki	117.043
	Valleydale 500	R. Wallace	Pontiac	76.034	8	Raymond Beadle	M. Martin	120.278
1988	Busch 500	D. Earnhardt	Chevrolet	78.775	5	Richard Childress	A. Kulwicki	116.893
	Valleydale 500	B. Elliott	Ford	83.115	13	Harry Melling	R. Wilson	117.552
1987	Busch 500	D. Earnhardt	Chevrolet	90.373	6	Richard Childress	T. Labonte	115.758
	Valleydale 500	D. Earnhardt	Chevrolet	75.621	3	Richard Childress	H. Gant	115.674
1986	Busch 500	D. Waltrip	Chevrolet	86.934	10	Junior Johnson	G. Bodine	114.665
	Valleydale 500	R. Wallace	Pontiac	89.747	14	Raymond Beadle	G. Bodine	114.850
1985	Busch 500	D. Earnhardt	Chevrolet	81.388	1	Richard Childress	D. Earnhardt	113.586
	Valleydale 500	D. Earnhardt	Chevrolet	81.790	12	Richard Childress	H. Gant	112.778
1984	Busch 500	T. Labonte	Chevrolet	85.365	6	Billy Hagan	G. Bodine	111.734
	Valleydale 500	D. Waltrip	Chevrolet	93.967	3	Junior Johnson	R. Rudd	111.390
1983	Busch 500 (a)	D. Waltrip	Chevrolet	89.430	2	Junior Johnson	J. Rutman	111.923
	Valleydale 500	D. Waltrip	Chevrolet	93.445	13	Junior Johnson	N. Bonnett	110.409
1982	Busch 500	D. Waltrip	Buick	94.318	8	Junior Johnson	T. Richmond	112.507
	Valleydale 500	D. Waltrip	Buick	94.025	1	Junior Johnson	D. Waltrip	111.068
1981	Busch 500	D. Waltrip	Buick	84.723	1	Junior Johnson	D. Waltrip	110.818
	Valleydale 500	D. Waltrip	Buick	89.530	1	Junior Johnson	D. Waltrip	112.125
1980	Busch Vol. 500	C. Yarborough	Chevrolet	86.973	1	Junior Johnson	C. Yarborough	110.990
	Valleydale SE 500	D. Earnhardt	Chevrolet	96.977	4	Rod Osterlund	C. Yarborough	111.688
1979	Volunteer 500	D. Waltrip	Chevrolet	91.493	5	DiProspero/Gardner	R. Petty	110.524
	Southeastern 500	D. Earnhardt	Chevrolet	91.033	9	Rod Osterlund	Buddy Baker	111.66
1978	Volunteer 500 (b)	C. Yarborough	Oldsmobile	88.628	4	Junior Johnson	L. Pond	110.958
	Southeastern 500	D. Waltrip	Chevrolet	92.401	7	DiProspero/Gardner	N. Bonnett	110.409
1977	Volunteer 400	C. Yarborough	Chevrolet	79.726	1	Junior Johnson	C. Yarborough	109.746
	Southeastern 500	C. Yarborough	Chevrolet	100.989	1	Junior Johnson	C. Yarborough	110.168
1976	Volunteer 400	C. Yarborough	Chevrolet	99.175	2	Junior Johnson	D. Waltrip	110.300
	Southeastern 400	C. Yarborough	Chevrolet	87.377	3	Junior Johnson	Buddy Baker	110.720
1975	Volunteer 500	R. Petty	Dodge	97.016	4	Petty Enterprises	C. Yarborough	110.162
	Southeastern 500	R. Petty	Dodge	97.053	2	Petty Enterprises	Buddy Baker	110.951
1974	Volunteer 500	C. Yarborough	Chevrolet	75.430	3	Junior Johnson	R. Petty	107.351
	Southeastern 500	C. Yarborough	Chevrolet	64.533	3	Junior Johnson	Do. Allison	107.785
1973	Volunteer 500	B. Parsons	Chevrolet	91.342	2	L.G. DeWitt	C. Yarborough	106.472
	Southeastern 500	C. Yarborough	Chevrolet	88.952	1	Junior Johnson	C. Yarborough	107.608
1972	Volunteer 500	B. Allison	Chevrolet	92.735	1	Junior Johnson	B. Allison	107.279
	Southeastern 500	B. Allison	Chevrolet	92.826	1	Junior Johnson	B. Allison	106.875
1971	Volunteer 500	C. Glotzbach	Chevrolet	101.074	2	Junior Johnson	R. Petty	104.589
	Southeastern 500	D. Pearson	Ford	91.704	1	Holman-Moody	D. Pearson	105.525
1970	Volunteer 500	B. Allison	Dodge	84.880	10	Bobby Allison	C. Yarborough	107.375
	Southeastern 500	Do. Allison	Ford	87.543	2	Banjo Matthews	D. Pearson	107.079
1969	Volunteer 500 (c)	D. Pearson	Ford	79.737	3	Holman-Moody	C. Yarborough	103.432
	Southeastern 500	B. Allison	Dodge	81.455	4	Mario Rossi	B. Isaac	88.669
1968	Volunteer 500	D. Pearson	Ford	76.310	6	Holman-Moody	L. Yarbrough	87.421
	Southeastern 500	D. Pearson	Ford	77.247	2	Holman-Moody	R. Petty	88.582
1967	Volunteer 500	R. Petty	Plymouth	78.705	1	Petty Enterprises	R. Petty	86.621
	Southeastern 500	D. Pearson	Dodge	75.930	14	Cotton Owens	D. Dieringer	87.124
1966	Volunteer 500	P. Goldsmith	Plymouth	77.963	4	Ray Nichels	C. Turner	84.309
	Southeastern 500	D. Hutcherson	Ford	69.952	6	Bondy Long	D. Pearson	86.248
1965	Volunteer 500	N. Jarrett	Ford	61.826	6	Bondy Long	F. Lorenzen	84.348
	Southeastern 500	Ju. Johnson	Ford	74.938	3	Rex Lovette	M. Panch	84.626
1964	Volunteer 500	F. Lorenzen	Ford	78.044	8	Holman-Moody	R. Petty	82.910
	Southeastern 500	F. Lorenzen	Ford	72.196	2	Holman-Moody	M. Panch	80.640
1963	Volunteer 500	F. Lorenzen	Ford	74.844	1	Holman-Moody	F. Lorenzen	82.229
	Southeastern 500	F. Roberts	Ford	76.910	3	Holman-Moody	F. Lorenzen	80.681
1962	Volunteer 500	J. Paschal	Plymouth	75.280	12	Petty Enterprises	F. Roberts	80.321
	Volunteer 500	B. Johns	Pontiac	73.320	6	Shorty Johns	F. Roberts	81.374
1961	Southeastern 500	J. Weatherly	Pontiac	72.450	2	Bud Moore	B. Johns	80.645
	Volunteer 500	J. Smith	Pontiac	68.370	12	Jack Smith	F. Lorenzen	79.225

KEY (a) Race shortened by rain. (b) First year in which the second race of the season was held at night. (c) Track was reconfigured from .5-miles to .533 miles and from 22 degrees to 36 degrees of banking in the turns. (d) Track surface is changed to concrete.

ALL ATLANTA RACES

POLE WINNERS

Cale Yarborough	9
Mark Martin	7
Rusty Wallace	6
Richard Petty	6
Jeff Gordon	4
Fred Lorenzen	4
Darrell Waltrip	4
Buddy Baker	3
Geoffrey Bodine	3
Harry Gant	3
Alan Kulwicki	3
David Pearson	3
Bobby Allison	3
Neil Bonnett	2
Dale Earnhardt	2
Ernie Irvan	2
Ryan Newman	2
Marvin Panch	2
Fireball Roberts	2
Donnie Allison	1
Chuck Bown	1
Kurt Busch	1
Darel Dieringer	1
Bill Elliott	1
Jeff Green	1
Bobby Isaac	1
Bobby Johns	1
Matt Kenseth	1
Terry Labonte	1
Steve Park	1
Lennie Pond	1
Tim Richmond	1
Ricky Rudd	1
Joe Ruttman	1
Elliott Sadler	1
Tony Stewart	1
Curtis Turner	1
Kenny Wallace	1
Rick Wilson	1
LeeRoy Yarbrough	1

RACE WINNERS

Darrell Waltrip	12
Dale Earnhardt	9
Rusty Wallace	9
Cale Yarborough	9
Kurt Busch	5
Jeff Gordon	5
David Pearson	5
Bobby Allison	4
Fred Lorenzen	3
Richard Petty	3
Matt Kenseth	2
Alan Kulwicki	2
Terry Labonte	2
Mark Martin	2
Davey Allison	1
Donnie Allison	1
Dale Earnhardt Jr.	1
Bill Elliott	1
Charlie Glotzbach	1
Paul Goldsmith	1
Kevin Harvick	1
Dick Hutcherson	1
Ernie Irvan	1
Dale Jarrett	1
Ned Jarrett	1
Bobby Johns	1
Junior Johnson	1
Benny Parsons	1
Jim Paschal	1
Fireball Roberts	1
Elliott Sadler	1
Jack Smith	1
Tony Stewart	1
Joe Weatherly	1

RACE 1

POLE WINNERS

Rusty Wallace	5
Mark Martin	4
Buddy Baker	3
David Pearson	3
Cale Yarborough	3
Neil Bonnett	2
Fred Lorenzen	2
Harry Gant	2
Ryan Newman	2
Marvin Panch	2
Darrell Waltrip	2
Bobby Allison	1
Donnie Allison	1
Geoffrey Bodine	1
Chuck Bown	1
Dale Earnhardt	1
Ernie Irvan	1
Jeff Gordon	1
Bobby Isaac	1
Alan Kulwicki	1
Steve Park	1
Richard Petty	1
Fireball Roberts	1
Ricky Rudd	1
Elliott Sadler	1
Rick Wilson	1

RACE WINNERS

Rusty Wallace	6
Dale Earnhardt	5
Darrell Waltrip	5
Kurt Busch	4
Jeff Gordon	4
Cale Yarborough	4
David Pearson	3
Bobby Allison	2
Davey Allison	1
Donnie Allison	1
Bill Elliott	1
Kevin Harvick	1
Dick Hutcherson	1
Bobby Johns	1
Junior Johnson	1
Alan Kulwicki	1
Fred Lorenzen	1
Richard Petty	1
Fireball Roberts	1
Elliott Sadler	1
Jack Smith	1

RACE 2

POLE WINNERS

Cale Yarborough	6
Richard Petty	5
Jeff Gordon	3
Mark Martin	3
Geoffrey Bodine	2
Dale Earnhardt	2
Alan Kulwicki	2
Fred Lorenzen	2
Rusty Wallace	2
Darrell Waltrip	2
Bobby Allison	1
Kurt Busch	1
Bill Elliott	1
Harry Grant	1
Jeff Green	1
Ernie Irvan	1
Bobby Johns	1
Matt Kenseth	1
Terry Labonte	1
Lennie Pond	1
Tim Richmond	1
Fireball Roberts	1
Joe Ruttman	1
Tony Stewart	1
Curtis Turner	1
Kenny Wallace	1
LeeRoy Yarbrough	1

RACE WINNERS

Darrell Waltrip	7
Cale Yarborough	5
Dale Earnhardt	4
Rusty Wallace	3
Bobby Allison	2
Matt Kenseth	2
Terry Labonte	2
Fred Lorenzen	2
Mark Martin	2
David Pearson	2
Richard Petty	2
Kurt Busch	1
Dale Earnhardt Jr.	1
Charlie Glotzbach	1
Paul Goldsmith	1
Jeff Gordon	1
Ernie Irvan	1
Dale Jarrett	1
Ned Jarrett	1
Alan Kulwicki	1
Benny Parsons	1
Jim Paschal	1
Tony Stewart	1
Joe Weatherly	1

>> NASCAR BUSCH SERIES <<

YEAR BY YEAR WINNERS

Year	Event	Race winner	Car make	Avg. speed	Start pos.	Pole winner	Pole speed	POLE WINNERS		RACE WINNERS	
2006	Food City 250	M. Kenseth	Ford	64.458	4	R. Newman	124.436	Jason Keller	3	Kevin Harvick	4
	Sharpie Mini 300	Ky. Busch	Chevrolet	71.606	20	None—conditions		Morgan Shepherd	3	Morgan Shepherd	4
2005	Food City 250	R. Newman	Dodge	58.810	3	Ky. Busch	125.404	Dale Earnhardt Jr.	2	Matt Kenseth	3
	Sharpie Pro. 250	K. Harvick	Chevrolet	59.534	38	None—conditions		Tommy Ellis	2	Brett Bodine	2
2004	Food City 250	D. Earnhardt Jr.	Chevrolet	64.872	1	D. Earnhardt Jr.	126.570	David Green	2	Todd Bodine	2
	Sharpie Pro. 250	M. Truex Jr.	Chevrolet	78.114	2	G. Biffle	127.132	Jeff Green	2	Steve Grissom	2
2003	Channellock 250	K. Harvick	Chevrolet	68.304	11	D. Green	126.495	Kevin Harvick	2	Mark Martin	2
	Food City 250	M. Waltrip	Chevrolet	71.951	4	J. Keller	126.021	Mark Martin	2	Larry Pearson	2
2002	Channellock 250	J. Green	Chevrolet	66.093	2	S. Riggs	126.270	Greg Biffle	1	Jimmy Spencer	2
	Food City 250	J. Spencer	Chevrolet	83.455	10	J. Keller	124.428	Brett Bodine	1	Michael Waltrip	2
2001	Cheez-It 250	M. Kenseth	Chevrolet	72.103	2	K. Harvick	125.264	Geoffrey Bodine	1	Sam Ard	1
	Food City 250	K. Harvick	Chefrolet	78.872	2	M. Skinner	124.460	Ron Bouchard	1	Jeff Burton	1
2000	Cheez-It 250	S. Marlin	Chevrolet	74.813	16	J. Green	124.428	Chuck Bown	1	Kyle Busch	1
	Food City 250	K. Harvick	Chevrolet	88.164	1	K. Harvick	123.356	Jeff Burton	1	Dale Earnhardt	1
1999	Moore's Snacks 250	J. Keller	Chevrolet	73.014	1	J. Keller	123.024	Ward Burton	1	Dale Earnhardt Jr.	1
	Food City 250	M. Kenseth	Chevrolet	83.761	3	J. Green	122.537	Kyle Busch	1	Jeff Fuller	1
1998	Moore's Snacks 250	E. Sadler	Chevrolet	75.484	3	D. Earnhardt Jr.	122.217	Dale Earnhardt	1	Harry Gant	1
	Ford City 250	K. Lepage	Chevrolet	76.887	5	S. Grissom	121.512	Carl Edwards	1	David Green	1
1997	Moore's Snacks 250	J. Burton	Ford	74.743	3	H. Sadler	120.938	Jeff Fuller	1	Jeff Green	1
	Food City 250	J. Spencer	Chevrolet	65.515	16	R. LaJoie	121.267	Harry Gant	1	Jack Ingram	1
1996	Goody's 250	M. Martin	Ford	85.783	10	C. Little	121.198	Steve Grissom	1	Dale Jarrett	1
	Food City 250	J. Fuller	Chevrolet	74.603	1	J. Fuller	121.029	Bobby Labonte	1	Jason Keller	1
1995	Goody's 250	S. Grissom	Chevrolet	89.664	18	D. Green	122.474	Randy LaJoie	1	Kevin Lepage	1
	Food City 250	S. Grissom	Chevrolet	87.234	28	S. Reeves	122.560	Chad Little	1	Bobby Labonte	1
1994	Goody's 250	D. Green	Chevrolet	81.085	3	M. Martin	123.746	Butch Miller	1	Sterling Marlin	1
	Food City 250	K. Wallace	Ford	87.616	7	H. Gant	123.364	Ryan Newman	1	Rick Mast	1
1993	Budweiser 250	M. Waltrip	Pontiac	77.911	9	W. Burton	122.945	Phil Parsons	1	Ryan Newman	1
	Food City 250	T. Bodine	Chevrolet	73.014	12	None—conditions		David Pearson	1	L.D. Ottinger	1
1992	Budweiser 250	H. Gant	Buick	92.929	18	B. Miller	121.267	Larry Pearson	1	Phil Parsons	1
	Food City 250	T. Bodine	Chevrolet	73.014	11	K. Wallace	118.189	Stevie Reeves	1	Elliott Sadler	1
1991	Budweiser 250	B. Labonte	Oldsmobile	92.839	21	J. Burton	117.286	Scott Riggs	1	Martin Truex	1
	Jay Johnson 250	D. Jarrett	Pontiac	71.822	11	C. Bown	116.737	Hermie Sadler	1	Kenny Wallace	1
1990	Budweiser 250	L. Ottinger	Oldsmobile	79.936	13	None—conditions		Mike Skinner	1	Darrell Waltrip	1
	Jay Johnson 250	R. Mast	Buick	85.447	12	B. Labonte	114.850	Kenny Wallace	1	Rick Wilson	1
1989	Budweiser 200	R. Wilson	Oldsmobile	85.776	1	R. Wilson	119.299	Rick Wilson	1		
	Jay Johnson 200	M. Martin	Ford	76.309	8	M. Shepherd	116.368				
1988	Budweiser 200	D. Earnhardt	Chevrolet	76.162	4	L. Pearson	117.057				
	Tri-City Pont. 200	L. Pearson	Chevrolet	70.609	7	T. Ellis	113.761				
1987	Budweiser 200	M. Shepherd	Buick	75.032	11	D. Earnhardt	117.653				
	Tri-City Pont. 200	L. Pearson	Chevroelt	70.609	4	M. Martin	117.754				
1986	Budweiser 200	M. Shepherd	Buick	75.032	2	G. Bodine	117.293				
	Tri-City Pont. 200	B. Bodine	Oldsmobile	76.293	1	B. Bodine	116.171				
1985	Budweiser 200	D. Waltrip	Chevrolet	74.372	16	T. Ellis	116.829				
	Tri-City Pont. 200	B. Bodine	Pontiac	71.331	4	R. Bouchard	116.964				
1984	No spring race held										
	Free Service 200	M. Shepherd	Buick	75.872	1	M. Shepherd	116.045				
1983	Southeastern 150	M. Shepherd	Oldsmobile	85.255	7	None—conditions					
	Free Service 150	S. Ard	Oldsmobile	85.255	2	P. Parsons	115.231				
1982	Southeastern 150	P. Parsons	Pontiac	80.848	7	D. Pearson	114.816				
	Pet Dairy 150	J. Ingram	Pontiac	79.923	6	M. Shepherd	115.132				

Kenseth

QUALIFYING RECORD: Greg Biffle, Ford; 127.132 mph (15.093 seconds), March 26, 2004
RACE RECORD: Harry Gant, Buick; 92.929 mph (1:26:02), April 4, 1992

>> NASCAR CRAFTSMAN TRUCK SERIES <<

YEAR BY YEAR WINNERS

Year	Event	Race winner	Truck make	Avg. speed	Start pos.	Pole winner	Pole speed	POLE WINNERS		RACE WINNERS	
2006	O'Reilly 200	M. Martin	Ford	72.081	1	M. Martin	125.248	Ron Hornaday Jr.	2	Ron Hornaday Jr.	2
2005	O'Reilly 200	M. Skinner	Toyota	83.390	2	D. Ruetimann	126.553	Mike Skinner	2	Rick Carelli	1
2004	O'Reilly 200	C. Edwards	Ford	74.495	5	K. Schrader	126.922	Greg Biffle	1	Carl Edwards	1
2003	O'Reilly 200	T. Kvapil	Chevrolet	88.813	12	T. Musgrave	123.562	Mark Martin	1	Travis Kvapil	1
1999	Coca-Cola 200	J. Sprague	Chevrolet	75.380	3	G. Biffle	120.831	Ted Musgrave	1	Mark Martin	1
1998	Loadhandler 200	R. Hornaday Jr.	Chevrolet	80.883	1	R. Hornaday	121.213	Dave Reutimann	1	Joe Ruttman	1
1997	Loadhandler 200	R. Hornaday Jr.	Chevrolet	70.583	1	R. Hornaday	119.910	Ken Schrader	1	Mike Skinner	1
1996	Coca-Cola 200	R. Carelli	Chevrolet	83.992	2	M. Skinner	117.805			Jack Sprague	1
1995	Pizza Plus 150	J. Ruttman	Ford	72.408	3	M. Skinner	118.738				

Martin

QUALIFYING RECORD: Ken Schrader, Chevrolet; 126.922 mph (15.118 seconds), August 25, 2004
RACE RECORD: Travis Kvapil, Chevrolet; 88.813 mph (1:12:01), August 20, 2003

>>CALIFORNIA SPEEDWAY<<

TRACK FACTS >>> >>> **Location:** Fontana, Calif. >>> >>> **Owner:** International Speedway Corp. >>> >>> **Track length:** 2.0 miles

>>> >>> **Grandstand seating:** 92,000 >>> >>> **Tickets:** (800) 944-7223 >>> >>> **Website:** www.californiaspeedway.com

>>NASCAR NEXTEL CUP SERIES<<

>>TRACK RECORDS

Most wins: 3—Jeff Gordon; **Most top fives:** 6—Jeff Gordon; **Most top 10s:** 6—Jeff Gordon and Rusty Wallace; **Oldest winner:** Rusty Wallace, 44 years, 8 months, 15 days; April 29, 2001; **Youngest winner:** Kyle Busch, 20 years, 4 months, 2 days; September 4, 2005; **Most lead changes:** 30—September 4, 2005; **Fewest lead changes:** 18—May 3, 1998; **Most leaders:** 15—Twice, most recently, May 2, 2004; **Fewest leaders:** 8—Twice, most recently, April 28, 2002; **Most cautions:** 11—Twice, most recently, September 4, 2005; **Fewest cautions:** 4—June 22, 1997; **Most caution laps:** 51—September 5, 2004; **Fewest caution laps:** 22—Twice, most recently, April 30, 2000; **Most on the lead lap:** 28—Twice, most recently, September 4, 2005; **Fewest on the lead lap:** 9—Twice, most recently, May 2, 1999; **Most running at the finish:** 42—September 3, 2006; **Fewest running at the finish:** 32—Twice, most recently, February 27, 2005; **Most laps led by a race winner:** 165—Mark Martin, May 3, 1998; **Fewest laps led by a race winner:** 26—Jeremy Mayfield, April 30, 2000; **Closest margin of victory:** 0.231 seconds—Greg Biffle defeated Jimmie Johnson, February 27, 2005

>>QUALIFYING AND RACE RECORDS

QUALIFYING: Kyle Busch, Chevrolet; 188.245 mph (38.248 seconds), February 26, 2005
RACE: Jeff Gordon, Chevrolet; 155.012 mph (3:12:32), June 22, 1997

Earnhardt Jr.

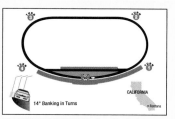

14° Banking in Turns

CALIFORNIA
Fontana

First NASCAR NEXTEL Cup Series race:
June 22, 1997 (Jeff Gordon, winner)
Banking in trioval: 11 degrees
Banking on back stretch: 3 degrees
Length of front stretch: 3,100 feet
Length of back stretch: 2,500 feet

2007 SCHEDULE

NASCAR NEXTEL Cup Series
Event: Auto Club 500
Race: No. 2 of 36
Date: February 25 • **TV:** FOX • **Radio:** MRN

Event: Sony HD 500
Race: No. 25 of 36
Date: September 2 • **TV:** ESPN • **Radio:** MRN

NASCAR Busch Series
Event: Stater Bros. 300
Race: No. 2 of 35 • **Date:** February 24
TV: ESPN2 • **Radio:** MRN

Event: Ameriquest 300
Race: No. 27 of 35 • **Date:** September 1
TV: ESPN2 • **Radio:** MRN

NASCAR Craftsman Truck Series
Event: RaceTickets.com 200
Race: No. 2 of 25
Date: February 23 • **TV:** SPEED • **Radio:** MRN

Race names subject to change

YEAR BY YEAR WINNERS

Year	Event	Race winner	Car make	Avg. speed	Start pos.	Car owner	Pole winner	Pole speed
2006	Sony HD 500	K. Kahne	Dodge	144.462	9	Ray Evernham	Ku. Busch	184.540
	Auto Club 500	M. Kenseth	Ford	147.852	31	Jack Roush	Ku. Busch	187.086
2005	Sony HD 500	Ky. Busch	Chevrolet	136.356	5	Rick Hendrick	C. Edwards	185.061
	Auto Club 500	G. Biffle	Ford	139.697	5	Jack Roush	Ky. Busch	188.245
2004	Pop Secret 500	E. Sadler	Ford	128.324	17	Robert Yates	B. Vickers	187.417
	Auto Club 500	J. Gordon	Chevrolet	137.268	16	Rick Hendrick	K. Kahne	186.940
2003	Auto Club 500	Ku. Busch	Ford	140.111	16	Jack Roush	S. Park	186.838
2002	NAPA Auto Parts 500	Ji. Johnson	Chevrolet	150.088	4	Rick Hendrick	R. Newman	187.432
2001	NAPA Auto Parts 500	R. Wallace	Ford	143.118	19	Roger Penske	B. Labonte	182.635
2000	NAPA Auto Parts 500	J. Mayfield	Ford	149.378	24	Roger Penske	M. Skinner	186.061
1999	California 500	J. Gordon	Chevrolet	150.276	5	Rick Hendrick	None—conditions	
1998	California 500	M. Martin	Ford	140.220	3	Jack Roush	J. Gordon	181.772
1997	California 500	J. Gordon	Chevrolet	155.012	3	Rick Hendrick	J. Nemechek	183.015

ALL CALIFORNIA RACES

POLE WINNERS	
Kurt Busch	2
Kyle Busch	1
Carl Edwards	1
Jeff Gordon	1
Kasey Kahne	1
Bobby Labonte	1
Joe Nemechek	1
Ryan Newman	1
Steve Park	1
Mike Skinner	1
Brian Vickers	1

RACE WINNERS	
Jeff Gordon	3
Greg Biffle	1
Kurt Busch	1
Kyle Busch	1
Jimmie Johnson	1
Kasey Kahne	1
Matt Kenseth	1
Mark Martin	1
Jeremy Mayfield	1
Elliott Sadler	1
Rusty Wallace	1

RACE 1

POLE WINNERS	
Kurt Busch	1
Kyle Busch	1
Jeff Gordon	1
Kasey Kahne	1
Bobby Labonte	1
Joe Nemechek	1
Ryan Newman	1
Steve Park	1
Mike Skinner	1

RACE WINNERS	
Jeff Gordon	3
Greg Biffle	1
Kurt Busch	1
Jimmie Johnson	1
Matt Kenseth	1
Mark Martin	1
Jeremy Mayfield	1
Rusty Wallace	1

RACE 2

POLE WINNERS	
Kurt Busch	1
Carl Edwards	1
Brian Vickers	1

RACE WINNERS	
Kyle Busch	1
Kasey Kahne	1
Elliott Sadler	1

>> NASCAR BUSCH SERIES <<

YEAR BY YEAR WINNERS

Year	Event	Race winner	Truck make	Avg. speed	Start pos.	Pole winner	Pole speed
2006	Ameriquest 300	K. Kahne	Dodge	137.160	4	C. Bowyer	179.399
	Stater Bros. 300	G. Biffle	Ford	147.501	3	C. Edwards	182.588
2005	Ameriquest 300	C. Edwards	Ford	139.104	4	C. Bowyer	181.330
	Stater Bros. 300	M. Martin	Ford	117.251	3	T. Stewart	185.941
2004	Target House 300	G. Biffle	Ford	147.844	14	C. Mears	182.890
	Stater Bros. 300	G. Biffle	Ford	138.978	15	J. Leffler	182.223
2003	1-800-PIT-SHOP.COM 300	M. Kenseth	Ford	129.419	19	K. Harvick	183.941
2002	Auto Club 300	S. Riggs	Ford	131.403	6	None—conditions	
2001	Auto Club 300	H. Parker Jr.	Chevrolet	155.957	26	B. Hamilton Jr.	179.198
2000	Auto Club 300	M. Kenseth	Chevrolet	126.375	8	J. Green	178.258
1999	Auto Club 300	M. Kenseth	Chevrolet	119.960	2	None—conditions	
1998	Kenwood 300	D. Earnhardt Jr.	Chevrolet	148.576	2	R. Pressley	174.073
1997	Kenwood 300	T. Bodine	Pontiac	145.083	28	S. Park	175.157

POLE WINNERS		RACE WINNERS	
Clint Bowyer	2	Greg Biffle	3
Carl Edwards	1	Matt Kenseth	3
Jeff Green	1	Todd Bodine	1
Bobby Hamilton Jr.	1	Dale Earnhardt Jr.	1
Kevin Harvick	1	Carl Edwards	1
Jason Leffler	1	Kasey Kahne	1
Casey Mears	1	Mark Martin	1
Steve Park	1	Hank Parker Jr.	1
Robert Pressley	1	Scott Riggs	1
Tony Stewart	1		

Kahne

QUALIFYING RECORD: Tony Stewart, Chevrolet; 185.941 mph (38.722 seconds), February 25, 2005
RACE RECORD: Hank Parker Jr., Chevrolet; 155.957 mph (1:55:25), April 28, 2001

>> NASCAR CRAFTSMAN TRUCK SERIES <<

Martin

YEAR BY YEAR WINNERS

Year	Event	Race winner	Car make	Avg. speed	Start pos.	Pole winner	Pole speed
2006	Racetickets.com 200	M. Martin	Ford	121.529	7	D. Reutimann	178.980
2005	Am. Racing Wheels 200	S. Park	Dodge	128.000	25	M. Skinner	178.218
2004	Am. Racing Wheels 200	T. Bodine	Toyota	127.141	9	T. Kvapil	178.669
2003	Am. Racing Wheels 200	T. Musgrave	Dodge	145.926	10	B. Gaughan	173.716
2002	Am. Racing Wheels 200	T. Musgrave	Dodge	140.296	11	D. Starr	175.850
2001	Auto Club 200	T. Musgrave	Dodge	113.297	12	S. Riggs	173.678
2000	Motorola 200	Ku. Busch	Ford	144.260	1	Ku. Busch	177.388
1999	NAPA Auto Parts 200	J. Sprague	Chevrolet	128.091	3	A. Houston	173.561
1998	The No Fear Challenge	J. Sprague	Chevrolet	141.844	10	A. Houston	172.022
1997	The No Fear Challenge	M. Bliss	Ford	137.195	1	M. Bliss	173.198

POLE WINNERS		RACE WINNERS	
Andy Houston	2	Ted Musgrave	3
Mike Bliss	1	Jack Sprague	2
Kurt Busch	1	Mike Bliss	1
Brendan Gaughan	1	Todd Bodine	1
Travis Kvapil	1	Kurt Busch	1
Scott Riggs	1	Mark Martin	1
David Reutimann	1	Steve Park	1
Mike Skinner	1		
David Starr	1		

QUALIFYING RECORD: David Reutimann, Toyota; 178.980 mph (40.228 seconds), February 24, 2006
RACE RECORD: Ted Musgrave, Dodge; 145.926 mph (1:22:14), September 20, 2003

>>CHICAGOLAND SPEEDWAY<<

TRACK FACTS >>> >>> **Location:** Joliet, Ill. >>> >>> **Owner:** Raceway Associates, LLC >>> >>> **Track length:** 1.5 miles >>>

>>> **Grandstand seating:** 75,000 >>> >>> **Tickets:** (815) 727-7223 >>> >>> **Website:** www.chicagolandspeedway.com >>>

>>NASCAR NEXTEL CUP SERIES<<

>> TRACK RECORDS

Most wins: 2—Kevin Harvick; **Most top fives:** 4—Jeff Gordon, Jimmie Johnson and Tony Stewart; **Most top 10s:** 5—Jimmie Johnson; **Oldest winner:** Jeff Gordon, 34 years, 11 months, 5 days, July 9, 2006 **Youngest winner:** Ryan Newman, 25 years, 7 months, 5 days, July 13, 2003; **Most lead changes:** 20 July 11, 2004; **Fewest lead changes:** 13—July 13, 2003; **Most leaders:** 13—July 11, 2004; **Fewest leaders:** 7—July 13, 2003; **Most cautions:** 10—Twice, most recently, July 11, 2005; **Fewest cautions:** 7—Twice, most recently, July 13, 2003; **Most caution laps:** 56—July 15, 2001; **Fewest caution laps:** 34—July 9, 2006; **Most on the lead lap:** 28—July 11, 2005; **Fewest on the lead lap:** 11—July 13, 2003; **Most running at the finish:** 42—July 9, 2006; **Fewest running at the finish:** 32—July 11, 2004; **Most laps led by a race winner:** 160—Tony Stewart, July 11, 2004; **Fewest laps led by a race winner:** 11—Dale Earnhardt Jr., July 11, 2005; **Closest margin of victory:** 0.291 seconds—Dale Earnhardt Jr. defeated Matt Kenseth, July 11, 2005

>> QUALIFYING AND RACE RECORDS

QUALIFYING: Jimmie Johnson, Chevrolet, 188.147 mph (28.701 seconds), July 8, 2005
RACE: Kevin Harvick, Chevrolet, 136.832 mph (2:55:37), July 14, 2002

18° Banking in Turns

First NASCAR NEXTEL Cup Series race:
July 15, 2001 (Kevin Harvick, winner)
Banking in trioval: 11 degrees
Banking on back stretch: 5 degrees
Length of front stretch: 2,400 feet
Length of back stretch: 1,700 feet

2007 SCHEDULE

NASCAR NEXTEL Cup Series
Event: USG Sheetrock 400
Race: No. 19 of 36
Date: July 15 • **TV:** TNT • **Radio:** MRN

NASCAR Busch Series
Event: USG Durock 300
Race: No. 20 of 35 • **Date:** July 14
TV: ESPN2 • **Radio:** MRN

Race names subject to change

YEAR BY YEAR WINNERS

Year	Event	Race winner	Car make	Avg. speed	Start pos.	Car owner	Pole winner	Pole speed	POLE WINNERS		RACE WINNERS	
2006	USG Sheetrock 400	J. Gordon	Chevrolet	132.077	13	Rick Hendrick	J. Burton	181.647	Todd Bodine	1	Kevin Harvick	2
2005	USG Sheetrock 400	D. Earnhardt Jr.	Chevrolet	127.638	25	Teresa Earnhardt	Ji. Johnson	188.147	Jeff Burton	1	Dale Earnhardt Jr.	1
2004	Tropicana 400	T. Stewart	Chevrolet	129.507	10	Joe Gibbs	J. Gordon	186.942	Jeff Gordon	1	Jeff Gordon	1
2003	Tropicana 400	R. Newman	Dodge	134.059	14	Roger Penske	T. Stewart	184.786	Jimmie Johnson	1	Ryan Newman	1
2002	Tropicana 400	K. Harvick	Chevrolet	136.832	32	Richard Childress	R. Newman	183.051	Ryan Newman	1	Tony Stewart	1
2001	Tropicana 400	K. Harvick	Chevrolet	131.759	6	Richard Childress	T. Bodine	183.717	Tony Stewart	1		

YEAR BY YEAR WINNERS

Year	Event	Race winner	Car make	Avg. speed	Start pos.	Pole winner	Pole speed
2006	USG Durock 300	C. Mears	Dodge	125.421	7	C. Edwards	176.528
2005	USG Durock 300	K. Harvick	Chevrolet	130.340	5	R. Newman	186.438
2004	Tropicana Twister 300	J. Labonte	Dodge	126.790	34	B. Hamilton Jr.	183.611
2003	Tropicana Twister 300	B. Hamilton Jr.	Ford	129.730	3	C. Mears	181.757
2002	Tropicana 300	Jo. Sauter	Chevrolet	128.008	20	T. Bodine	178.772
2001	Sam's Club 300	Ji. Johnson	Chevrolet	119.469	6	R. Newman	181.886

POLE WINNERS		RACE WINNERS	
Ryan Newman	2	Bobby Hamilton Jr.	1
Todd Bodine	1	Jimmie Johnson	1
Carl Edwards	1	Kevin Harvick	1
Bobby Hamilton Jr.	1	Justin Labonte	1
Casey Mears	1	Casey Mears	1
		Johnny Sauter	1

QUALIFYING RECORD: Ryan Newman, Dodge; 186.438 mph (28.964 seconds), July 8, 2005
RACE RECORD: Kevin Harvick, Chevrolet; 130.340 mph (2:18:06), July 9, 2005

≫ DARLINGTON RACEWAY ≪

TRACK FACTS ≫≫ ≫≫ **Location:** Darlington, S.C. ≫≫ ≫≫ **Owner:** International Speedway Corp. ≫≫ ≫≫ **Track length:** 1.366 miles

≫≫ ≫≫ **Grandstand seating:** 63,000 ≫≫ ≫≫ **Tickets:** (843) 395-8499 ≫≫ ≫≫ **Website:** www.darlingtonraceway.com ≫≫

≫ NASCAR NEXTEL CUP SERIES ≪

≫≫ TRACK RECORDS

Most wins: 10—David Pearson; **Most top fives:** 25—Richard Petty; **Most top 10s:** 35—Bill Elliott; **Oldest winner:** Harry Gant, 51 years, 7 months, 22 days; September 1, 1991; **Youngest winner:** Terry Labonte, 23 years, 9 months, 16 days; September 1, 1980; **Most lead changes:** 41—September 6, 1982; **Fewest lead changes:** 4—September 4, 1950; **Most leaders:** 20—September 4, 1994; **Fewest leaders:** 2—May 9, 1964; **Most laps led in a 500-mile race:** 351—Johnny Mantz, September 4, 1950; **Most laps led in a 400-mile race:** 281—Richard Petty, April 30, 1966; **Most cautions:** 15—March 26, 1995; **Fewest cautions:** 0—September 2, 1963; **Most caution laps:** 101—September 2, 1974; **Fewest caution laps:** 0—September 2, 1963; **Most on the lead lap:** 23—September 1, 2002; **Fewest on the lead lap:** 1—24 times, most recently, September 3, 1979; **Most running at the finish:** 41—March 21, 1999; **Fewest running at the finish:** 12—September 2, 1974; **Most laps led by a race winner:** 351—Johnny Mantz, September 4, 1950; **Fewest laps led by a race winner:** 1—Ricky Craven, March 16, 2003; **Closest margin of victory:** 0.002 seconds—Ricky Craven defeated Kurt Busch, March 16, 2003

≫≫ QUALIFYING AND RACE RECORDS

QUALIFYING: Ward Burton, Pontiac; 173.797 mph (28.295 seconds), March 22, 1996
RACE: Dale Earnhardt, Chevrolet; 139.958 mph (3:34:55), March 28, 1993. **500 miles:** Dale Earnhardt, Chevrolet; 139.958 mph (3:34:55), March 28, 1993. **400 miles:** David Pearson, Ford; 132.703 mph (3:00:54), May 11, 1968

Darlington • SOUTH CAROLINA

23° to 25° Banking in Turns

First NASCAR NEXTEL Cup Series race: September 4, 1950 (Johnny Mantz, winner)
Banking on front stretch: 3 degrees
Banking on back stretch: 2 degrees
Length of front stretch: 1,229 feet
Length of back stretch: 1,229 feet

2007 SCHEDULE

NASCAR NEXTEL Cup Series
Event: Dodge Charger 500
Race: No. 11 of 36
Date: May 12 • **TV:** FOX • **Radio:** MRN

NASCAR Busch Series
Event: Diamond Hill Plywood 200
Race: No. 12 of 35 • **Date:** May 11
TV: ESPN2 • **Radio:** MRN
Race names subject to change

>>DARLINGTON RACEWAY<<

YEAR BY YEAR WINNERS

Year	Event	Race winner	Car make	Avg. speed	Start pos.	Car owner	Pole winner	Pole speed
2006	Dodge Charger 500	G. Biffle	Ford	135.127	9	Jack Roush	K. Kahne	169.013
2005	Dodge Charger 500	G. Biffle	Ford	123.031	3	Jack Roush	K. Kahne	170.024
2004	Southern 500	Ji. Johnson	Chevrolet	125.044	4	Rick Hendrick	None—conditions	
	Car. Dodge Dlrs. 400	Ji. Johnson	Chevrolet	114.001	11	Rick Hendrick	K. Kahne	171.716
2003	Southern 500	T. Labonte	Chevrolet	120.744	3	Rick Hendrick	R. Newman	169.048
	Car. Dodge Dlrs. 400	R. Craven	Pontiac	126.214	31	Cal Wells	E. Sadler	170.147
2002	Southern 500	J. Gordon	Chevrolet	118.617	3	Rick Hendrick	None—conditions	
	Car. Dodge Dlrs. 400	S. Marlin	Dodge	126.070	11	Chip Ganassi	R. Craven	170.089
2001	Southern 500	W. Burton	Dodge	122.773	37	Bill Davis	Ku. Busch	168.048
	Car. Dodge Dlrs. 400	D. Jarrett	Ford	126.588	2	Robert Yates	None—conditions	
2000	Southern 500 (a)	B. Labonte	Pontiac	108.273	37	Joe Gibbs	J. Mayfield	169.444
	Mall.com 400	W. Burton	Pontiac	128.076	3	Bill Davis	J. Gordon	172.662
1999	Southern 500 (a)	J. Burton	Ford	107.816	15	Jack Roush	K. Irwin	170.970
	TranSouth 400 (a)	J. Burton	Ford	121.294	9	Jack Roush	J. Gordon	173.167
1998	Southern 500	J. Gordon	Chevrolet	139.031	5	Rick Hendrick	D. Jarrett	168.879
	TranSouth 400	D. Jarrett	Ford	127.962	3	Robert Yates	M. Martin	168.665
1997	Southern 500 (h)	J. Gordon	Chevrolet	121.149	7	Rick Hendrick	B. Labonte	170.661
	TranSouth 400	D. Jarrett	Ford	121.162	1	Robert Yates	D. Jarrett	171.095
1996	Southern 500	J. Gordon	Chevrolet	135.757	2	Rick Hendrick	D. Jarrett	170.934
	TranSouth 400	J. Gordon	Chevrolet	124.792	2	Rick Hendrick	W. Burton	173.797
1995	Southern 500	J. Gordon	Chevrolet	121.231	5	Rick Hendrick	J. Andretti	167.379
	TranSouth 400	S. Marlin	Chevrolet	111.392	5	Larry McClure	J. Gordon	170.833
1994	Southern 500	B. Elliott	Ford	127.952	9	Junior Johnson	G. Bodine	166.998
	TranSouth 400	D. Earnhardt	Chevrolet	132.432	9	Richard Childress	B. Elliott	165.553
1993	Southern 500	M. Martin	Ford	137.932	4	Jack Roush	K. Schrader	161.259
	TranSouth 500	D. Earnhardt	Chevrolet	139.958	1	Richard Childress	None—conditions	
1992	Southern 500	D. Waltrip	Chevrolet	129.114	5	Darrell Waltrip	S. Marlin	162.249
	TranSouth 500	B. Elliott	Ford	139.364	2	Junior Johnson	S. Marlin	163.067
1991	Southern 500	H. Gant	Oldsmobile	133.508	5	Leo Jackson	Da. Allison	162.506
	TranSouth 500	R. Rudd	Chevrolet	135.594	13	Rick Hendrick	G. Bodine	161.939
1990	Southern 500	D. Earnhardt	Chevrolet	123.141	1	Richard Childress	D. Earnhardt	158.448
	TranSouth 500	D. Earnhardt	Chevrolet	124.073	15	Richard Childress	G. Bodine	162.996
1989	Southern 500	D. Earnhardt	Chevrolet	135.462	10	Richard Childress	A. Kulwicki	160.156
	TranSouth 500	H. Gant	Oldsmobile	115.475	10	Leo/Richard Jackson	M. Martin	161.111
1988	Southern 500	B. Elliott	Ford	128.297	1	Harry Melling	B. Elliott	160.827
	TranSouth 500	L. Speed	Oldsmobile	131.284	8	Lake Speed	K. Schrader	162.657
1987	Southern 500 (a)	D. Earnhardt	Chevrolet	115.520	5	Richard Childress	Da. Allison	157.232
	TranSouth 500	D. Earnhardt	Chevrolet	122.540	2	Richard Childress	K. Schrader	158.387
1986	Southern 500	T. Richmond	Chevrolet	121.068	1	Rick Hendrick	T. Richmond	158.489
	TranSouth 500	D. Earnhardt	Chevrolet	128.994	4	Richard Childress	G. Bodine	159.197
1985	Southern 500	B. Elliott	Ford	121.254	1	Harry Melling	B. Elliott	156.641
	TranSouth 500	B. Elliott	Ford	126.295	1	Harry Melling	B. Elliott	157.454
1984	Southern 500	H. Gant	Chevrolet	128.270	1	Hal Needham	H. Gant	155.502
	TranSouth 500	D. Waltrip	Chevrolet	119.925	9	Junior Johnson	B. Parsons	156.328
1983	Southern 500	B. Allison	Buick	123.343	14	DiProspero/Gardner	Bonnett	157.187
	TranSouth 500	H. Gant	Buick	130.406	5	Hal Needham	Richmond	157.818
1982	Southern 500	C. Yarborough	Buick	115.224	9	M.C. Anderson	D. Pearson	155.739
	CRC Rebel 500	D. Earnhardt	Ford	123.554	5	Bud Moore	Buddy Baker	153.979
1981	Southern 500	N. Bonnett	Ford	126.410	3	Wood Brothers	H. Gant	152.693
	CRC Rebel 500	D. Waltrip	Buick	126.703	3	Junior Johnson	B. Elliott	153.896
1980	Southern 500	T. Labonte	Chevrolet	115.210	10	Billy Hagan	D. Waltrip	153.838
	CRC Rebel 500 (a)	D. Pearson	Chevrolet	112.397	2	Hoss Ellington	B. Parsons	155.866
1979	Southern 500	D. Pearson	Chevrolet	126.259	5	Rod Osterlund	B. Allison	154.880
	CRC Rebel 500	D. Waltrip	Chevrolet	121.721	2	DiProspero/Gardner	D. Allison	154.797
1978	Southern 500	C. Yarborough	Oldsmobile	116.828	6	Junior Johnson	D. Pearson	153.685
	Rebel 500	B. Parsons	Chevrolet	127.544	8	L.G. DeWitt	B. Allison	151.862
1977	Southern 500	D. Pearson	Mercury	106.797	5	Wood Brothers	D. Waltrip	153.493
	Rebel 500	D. Waltrip	Chevrolet	128.817	4	DiProspero/Gardner	D. Pearson	151.269
1976	Southern 500	D. Pearson	Mercury	120.534	1	Wood Brothers	D. Pearson	154.699
	Rebel 500	D. Pearson	Mercury	122.973	1	Wood Brothers	D. Pearson	154.171
1975	Southern 500	B. Allison	Matador	116.825	3	Roger Penske	D. Pearson	153.401
	Rebel 500	B. Allison	Matador	117.597	5	Roger Penske	D. Pearson	155.433
1974	Southern 500	C. Yarborough	Chevrolet	111.075	4	Junior Johnson	R. Petty	150.132
	Rebel 500 (d)	D. Pearson	Mercury	117.543	2	Wood Brothers	D. Allison	150.689
1973	Southern 500	C. Yarborough	Chevrolet	134.033	8	Junior Johnson	D. Pearson	150.366
	Rebel 500	D. Pearson	Mercury	122.655	1	Wood Brothers	D. Pearson	153.463
1972	Southern 500	B. Allison	Chevrolet	128.124	1	Junior Johnson	B. Allison	152.228
	Rebel 400	D. Pearson	Mercury	124.406	1	Wood Brothers	D. Pearson	148.209
1971	Southern 500	B. Allison	Mercury	131.398	1	Holman-Moody	B. Allison	147.915
	Rebel 400	Buddy Baker	Dodge	130.678	5	Petty Enterprises	D. Allison	149.826
1970	Southern 500 (c)	Buddy Baker	Dodge	128.817	2	Cotton Owens	D. Pearson	150.555
	Rebel 400	Pearson	Ford	129.668	3	Holman-Moody	C. Glotzbach	153.822
1969	Southern 500 (a)	L. Yarbrough	Ford	105.612	4	Junior Johnson	C. Yarborough	151.985
	Rebel 400	L. Yarbrough	Mercury	131.572	4	Junior Johnson	C. Yarborough	152.293
1968	Southern 500	C. Yarborough	Mercury	126.132	2	Wood Brothers	Glotzbach	144.830
	Rebel 400	D. Pearson	Ford	132.699	2	Holman-Moody	L. Yarbrough	148.850
1967	Southern 500	R. Petty	Plymouth	130.423	1	Petty Enterprises	R. Petty	143.436
	Rebel 400	R. Petty	Plymouth	125.738	2	Petty Enterprises	D. Pearson	144.536
1966	Southern 500	D. Dieringer	Mercury	114.830	3	Bud Moore	L. Yarbrough	140.058
	Rebel 400	R. Petty	Plymouth	131.993	1	Petty Enterprises	R. Petty	140.815
1965	Southern 500	N. Jarrett	Ford	115.878	10	Bondy Long	Ju. Johnson	137.571
	Rebel 300	Jr. Johnson	Ford	111.849	3	Rex Lovette	F. Lorenzen	138.133

ALL DARLINGTON RACES

POLE WINNERS

David Pearson	12
Fred Lorenzen	6
Fireball Roberts	6
Bill Elliott	5
Bobby Allison	4
Geoffrey Bodine	4
Richard Petty	4
Donnie Allison	3
Jeff Gordon	3
Dale Jarrett	3
Kasey Kahne	3
Ken Schrader	3
Davey Allison	2
Fonty Flock	2
Harry Gant	2
Charlie Glotzbach	2
Sterling Marlin	2
Mark Martin	2
Benny Parsons	2
Tim Richmond	2
Darrell Waltrip	2
Cale Yarborough	2
LeeRoy Yarbrough	2
John Andretti	1
Buddy Baker	1
Buck Baker	1
Neil Bonnett	1
Ward Burton	1
Kurt Busch	1
Ricky Craven	1
Dale Earnhardt	1
Kenny Irwin	1
Junior Johnson	1
Alan Kulwicki	1
Bobby Labonte	1
Jeremy Mayfield	1
Frank Mundy	1
Ryan Newman	1
Cotton Owens	1
Eddie Pagan	1
Elliott Sadler	1
Speedy Thompson	1
Curtis Turner	1

RACE WINNERS

David Pearson	10
Dale Earnhardt	9
Jeff Gordon	6
Bobby Allison	5
Bill Elliott	5
Darrell Waltrip	5
Cale Yarborough	5
Harry Gant	4
Buck Baker	3
Dale Jarrett	3
Richard Petty	3
Herb Thomas	3
Buddy Baker	2
Greg Biffle	2
Jeff Burton	2
Ward Burton	2
Jimmie Johnson	2
Terry Labonte	2
Fred Lorenzen	2
Sterling Marlin	2
Fireball Roberts	2
Nelson Stacy	2
Joe Weatherly	2
LeeRoy Yarbrough	2
Neil Bonnett	1
Ricky Craven	1
Darel Dieringer	1
Fonty Flock	1
Larry Frank	1
Ned Jarrett	1
Junior Johnson	1
Bobby Labonte	1
Johnny Mantz	1
Mark Martin	1
Benny Parsons	1
Dick Rathmann	1
Jim Reed	1
Tim Richmond	1
Ricky Rudd	1
Lake Speed	1
Speedy Thompson	1
Curtis Turner	1

RACE 1

POLE WINNERS

David Pearson	6
Fred Lorenzen	5
Donnie Allison	3
Geoffrey Bodine	3
Bill Elliott	3
Jeff Gordon	3
Kasey Kahne	3
Mark Martin	2
Benny Parsons	2
Ken Schrader	2
Bobby Allison	1
Buddy Baker	1
Ward Burton	1
Ricky Craven	1
Charlie Glotzbach	1
Dale Jarrett	1
Sterling Marlin	1
Richard Petty	1
Tim Richmond	1
Fireball Roberts	1
Elliott Sadler	1
Cale Yarborough	1
LeeRoy Yarbrough	1

RACE WINNERS

David Pearson	7
Dale Earnhardt	6
Darrell Waltrip	4
Dale Jarrett	3
Greg Biffle	2
Bill Elliott	2
Harry Gant	2
Fred Lorenzen	2
Sterling Marlin	2
Richard Petty	2
Joe Weatherly	2
Bobby Allison	1
Buddy Baker	1
Jeff Burton	1
Ward Burton	1
Ricky Craven	1
Jeff Gordon	1
Jimmie Johnson	1
Junior Johnson	1
Benny Parsons	1
Dick Rathmann	1
Ricky Rudd	1
Lake Speed	1
Nelson Stacy	1
LeeRoy Yarbrough	1

RACE 2

POLE WINNERS

David Pearson	6
Fireball Roberts	5
Bobby Allison	3
Richard Petty	3
Davey Allison	2
Bill Elliott	2
Fonty Flock	2
Harry Gant	2
Dale Jarrett	2
Darrell Waltrip	2
John Andretti	1
Buck Baker	1
Geoffrey Bodine	1
Neil Bonnett	1
Kurt Busch	1
Dale Earnhardt	1
Charlie Glotzbach	1
Kenny Irwin	1
Junior Johnson	1
Alan Kulwicki	1
Bobby Labonte	1
Fred Lorenzen	1
Sterling Marlin	1
Jeremy Mayfield	1
Frank Mundy	1
Ryan Newman	1
Cotton Owens	1
Eddie Pagan	1
Tim Richmond	1
Ken Schrader	1
Speedy Thompson	1
Curtis Turner	1
Cale Yarborough	1
LeeRoy Yarbrough	1

RACE WINNERS

Jeff Gordon	5
Cale Yarborough	5
Bobby Allison	4
Buck Baker	3
Dale Earnhardt	3
Bill Elliott	3
David Pearson	3
Herb Thomas	3
Harry Gant	2
Terry Labonte	2
Fireball Roberts	2
Buddy Baker	1
Neil Bonnett	1
Jeff Burton	1
Ward Burton	1
Darel Dieringer	1
Fonty Flock	1
Larry Frank	1
Ned Jarrett	1
Jimmie Johnson	1
Bobby Labonte	1
Johnny Mantz	1
Mark Martin	1
Richard Petty	1
Jim Reed	1
Tim Richmond	1
Nelson Stacy	1
Speedy Thompson	1
Curtis Turner	1
Darrell Waltrip	1
LeeRoy Yarbrough	1

YEAR BY YEAR WINNERS continued

Biffle

Year	Event	Race winner	Car make	Avg. speed	Start pos.	Car owner	Pole winner	Pole speed
1964	Southern 500	Buck Baker	Dodge	117.757	6	Ray Fox	R. Petty	136.815
	Rebel 300	F. Lorenzen	Ford	130.013	1	Holman-Moody	F. Lorenzen	135.727
1963	Southern 500	F. Roberts	Ford	129.784	9	Holman-Moody	F. Lorenzen	133.648
	Rebel 300 (e)	J. Weatherly	Pontiac	122.745	6	Bud Moore	F. Lorenzen	131.718
1962	Southern 500	L. Frank	Ford	117.965	10	Ratus Walters	F. Roberts	130.246
	Rebel 300 (g)	N. Stacy	Ford	117.429	3	Holman-Moody	F. Lorenzen	129.810
1961	Southern 500	N. Stacy	Ford	117.787	3	Dudley Farrell	F. Roberts	128.680
	Rebel 300	F. Lorenzen	Ford	119.520	1	Holman-Moody	F. Lorenzen	128.965
1960	Southern 500	Buck Baker	Pontiac	105.901	2	Jack Smith	F. Roberts	125.459
	Rebel 300 (f)	J. Weatherly	Ford	102.646	2	Holman-Moody	F. Roberts	127.750
1959	Southern 500	J. Reed	Chevrolet	111.836	14	Jim Reed	F. Roberts	123.734
1958	Southern 500	F. Roberts	Chevrolet	102.590	2	Frank Strickland	E. Pagan	116.952
1957	Southern 500	S. Thompson	Chevrolet	100.100	7	Speedy Thompson	C. Owens	117.416
1956	Southern 500	C. Turner	Ford	95.067	11	Charles Schwam	S. Thompson	119.659
1955	Southern 500	H. Thomas	Chevrolet	92.789	8	Herb Thomas	F. Roberts	110.682
1954	Southern 500	H. Thomas	Hudson	95.027	23	Herb Thomas	Buck Baker	108.261
1953	Southern 500 (b)	Buck Baker	Oldsmobile	92.881	7	Bobby Griffin	F. Flock	107.983
1952	Southern 500	F. Flock	Oldsmobile	74.513	1	Frank Christian	F. Flock	88.550
	Grand National 100	D. Rathmann	Hudson	83.818	4	Walt Chapman	None—conditions	
1951	Southern 500	H. Thomas	Hudson	76.907	2	Herb Thomas	F. Mundy	84.173
1950	Southern 500 (i)	J. Mantz	Plymouth	75.251	43	Bill France Sr.	C. Turner	82.034

KEY (a) Race shortened by rain. (b) Track reconfigured from 1.25 miles to 1.375 miles. (c) Track reconfigured from 1.375 miles to 1.366 miles. (d) Race shortened by 50 miles because of the energy shortage. (e) A 300-mile race divided into two 150-milers. (f) Race was halted after 57 laps and completed the following Saturday. (g) The last convertible race. (h) Front and back straightaway flip-flopped. (i) Bill France Sr., Hubert Westmoreland, Curtis Turner and Alvin Hawkins were co-owners of the car.

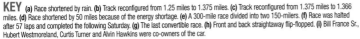

NASCAR BUSCH SERIES

YEAR BY YEAR WINNERS

Year	Event	Race winner	Car make	Avg. speed	Start pos.	Pole winner	Pole speed
2006	Diamond Hill Plywood 200	D. Hamlin	Chevrolet	106.999	1	D. Hamlin	167.670
2005	Diamond Hill Plywood 200	M. Kenseth	Ford	116.238	24	Ji. Johnson	168.186
2004	BI-LO 200	J. McMurray	Dodge	109.711	34	None—conditions	
	Diamond Hill Plywood 200	G. Biffle	Ford	120.141	4	Ky. Busch	168.619
2003	Darlingtonraceway.com 200	T. Bodine	Chevrolet	124.550	13	None—conditions	
	Winn-Dixie 200	B. Vickers	Chevrolet	114.744	4	K. Harvick	167.516
2002	Darlington.com 200	J. Burton	Ford	124.143	1	J. Burton	168.250
	Gatorade 200	J. Burton	Ford	92.525	33	None—conditions	
2001	SunCom 200	J. Green	Ford	128.742	13	R. Newman	170.301
	South Carolina 200	J. Burton	Ford	102.479	24	R. Newman	169.246
2000	SunCom 200	M. Martin	Ford	113.519	1	M. Martin	167.038
	Bumper to Bumper 200	M. Martin	Ford	118.215	1	M. Martin	164.965
1999	Diamond Hill 200	M. Kenseth	Chevrolet	121.945	9	M. Martin	166.568
	Dura Lube 200	M. Martin	Ford	132.227	2	W. Burton	167.676
1998	Diamond Hill 200	B. Labonte	Pontiac	100.443	9	J. Burton	162.577
	Dura Lube 200	D. Trickle	Chevrolet	123.233	4	M. McLaughlin	164.661
1997	Diamond Hill 200	R. LaJoie	Chevrolet	115.569	11	E. Sadler	166.051
	Dura Lube 200	J. Burton	Ford	118.080	10	M. Martin	163.745
1996	Dura Lube 200	M. Martin	Ford	120.763	2	J. Green	166.337
	Dura Lube 200	T. Labonte	Chevrolet	128.468	2	M. Martin	165.799
1995	Mark III Vans 200	L. Pearson	Chevrolet	108.087	36	T. Fedewa	162.905
	Gatorade 200	M. Martin	Ford	115.183	5	L. Pearson	161.429
1994	Mark III Vans 200	M. Martin	Ford	117.965	1	M. Martin	161.011
	Gatorade 200	M. Martin	Ford	124.824	2	R. LaJoie	161.022
1993	Mark III Vans 200	R. Pressley	Chevrolet	109.197	7	None—conditions	
	Gatorade 200	M. Martin	Ford	117.638	3	R. Craven	157.909
1992	Mark III Vans 200	R. Pressley	Oldsmobile	130.982	2	M. Martin	159.068
	Gatorade 200	M.Waltrip	Pontiac	138.140	15	M. Martin	159.652
1991	Pontiac 200	D. Jarrett	Pontiac	115.551	6	J. Hensley	158.894
	Gatorade 200	D. Earnhardt	Chevrolet	134.141	16	H. Gant	158.899
1990	Pontiac 200	H. Gant	Buick	129.689	3	K. Wallace	156.821
	Gatorade 200	D. Jarrett	Pontiac	136.342	28	G. Sacks	155.056
1989	Country Squire 200	G. Bodine	Chevrolet	118.681	1	G. Bodine	156.631
	Gatorade 200	H. Gant	Buick	119.170	3	K. Schrader	156.597
1988	Country Squire 200	G. Bodine	Chevrolet	115.514	1	G. Bodine	156.826
	Gatorade 200	H. Gant	Buick	136.009	2	M. Martin	156.422
1987	Country Squire 200	D. Earnhardt	Chevrolet	137.850	2	G. Bodine	157.646
	Gatorade 200	H. Gant	Buick	103.196	20	L. Pearson	154.978
1986	Dixie Cup 200	D. Waltrip	Pontiac	123.423	5	T. Richmond	157.298
	Gatorade 200	D. Earnhardt	Chevrolet	138.746	2	T. Richmond	154.749
1985	Dixie Cup 200	J. Ingram	Oldsmobile	108.460	11	D. Earnhardt	154.341
	Pontiac 200	D. Waltrip	Chevrolet	116.595	6	T. Richmond	155.704
1984	Dixie Cup 200	R. Bouchard	Pontiac	97.992	1	R. Bouchard	151.815
	Darlington 200	R. Bouchard	Pontiac	109.115	1	R. Bouchard	153.392
1983	Darlington 250	N. Bonnett	Pontiac	131.299	2	J. Ingram	152.630
1982	TranSouth 200	G. Bodine	Pontiac	129.018	3	H. Gant	154.259

POLE WINNERS		RACE WINNERS	
Mark Martin	8	Mark Martin	8
Geoffrey Bodine	4	Jeff Burton	4
Tim Richmond	3	Harry Gant	4
Ron Bouchard	2	Geoffrey Bodine	3
Jeff Burton	2	Dale Earnhardt	3
Harry Gant	2	Ron Bouchard	2
Ryan Newman	2	Dale Jarrett	2
Larry Pearson	2	Matt Kenseth	2
Ward Burton	1	Robert Pressley	2
Kyle Busch	1	Darrell Waltrip	2
Ricky Craven	1	Greg Biffle	1
Dale Earnhardt	1	Todd Bodine	1
Tim Fedewa	1	Neil Bonnett	1
Jeff Green	1	Jeff Green	1
Denny Hamlin	1	Denny Hamlin	1
Kevin Harvick	1	Jack Ingram	1
Jimmy Hensley	1	Bobby Labonte	1
Jack Ingram	1	Terry Labonte	1
Jimmie Johnson	1	Randy LaJoie	1
Randy LaJoie	1	Jamie McMurray	1
Mike McLaughlin	1	Larry Pearson	1
Greg Sacks	1	Dick Trickle	1
Elliott Sadler	1	Brian Vickers	1
Ken Schrader	1	Michael Waltrip	1
Kenny Wallace	1		

Hamlin

QUALIFYING RECORD: Ryan Newman, Ford; 170.301 mph (28.876), March 16, 2001
RACE RECORD: Michael Waltrip, Pontiac; 138.140 mph (1:27:13), September 5, 1992

>>DAYTONA INTERNATIONAL SPEEDWAY<<

TRACK FACTS >>> >>> **Location:** Daytona Beach, Fla. >>> >>> **Owner:** International Speedway Corp. >>> >>> **Track length:** 2.5 miles >>>

>>> **Grandstand seating:** 168,000 >>> >>> **Tickets:** (386) 253-7223 >>> >>> **Website:** www.daytonainternationalspeedway.com

>>NASCAR NEXTEL CUP SERIES<<

>>TRACK RECORDS

Most wins: 10—Richard Petty; **Most top fives:** 28—Richard Petty; **Most top 10s:** 37—Richard Petty; **Oldest winner:** Bobby Allison, 50 years, 2 months, 11 days; February 14, 1988; **Youngest winner:** Jeff Gordon, 23 years, 10 months, 27 days; July 1, 1995; **Most lead changes:** 60—February 17, 1974; **Fewest lead changes:** 0—February 12, 1960; **Most leaders:** 18—February 19, 2006; **Fewest leaders:** 1—Twice, most recently, February 22, 1963; **Most laps led in a 400-mile race:** 151—Tony Stewart, July 2, 2005; **Most laps led in a 500-mile race:** 184—Richard Petty, February 23, 1964; **Most cautions:** 12—July 1, 1989; **Fewest cautions:** 0—12 times, most recently, February 11, 1971; **Most caution laps:** 60—February 25, 1968; **Fewest caution laps:** 0—12 times, most recently February 11, 1971; **Most on the lead lap:** 34—July 1, 2006; **Fewest on the lead lap:** 1—Eight times, most recently, February 15, 1976; **Most running at the finish:** 40—Twice, most recently, July 1, 2006; **Fewest running at the finish:** 7—February 12, 1965; **Most laps led by a race winner:** 184—Richard Petty, February 23, 1964; **Fewest laps led by a race winner:** 1—Jimmy Spencer, July 2, 1994; **Closest margin of victory:** 0.029 seconds—John Andretti defeated Terry Labonte, July 5, 1997

>>QUALIFYING AND RACE RECORDS

QUALIFYING: Bill Elliott, Ford; 210.364 mph (42.783 seconds), February 9, 1987
RACE: Track: Buddy Baker, Oldsmobile; 177.602 mph (2:48:55), February 17, 1980; **500 miles:** Buddy Baker, Oldsmobile; 177.602 mph (2:48:55), February 17, 1980; **400 miles:** Bobby Allison, Mercury; 173.473 mph (2:18:21), July 4, 1980

31° Banking in Turns
Daytona Beach
FLORIDA

First NASCAR NEXTEL Cup Series race:
February 22, 1959 (Lee Petty, winner)
Banking in trioval: 18 degrees
Banking on back stretch: 3 degrees
Length of front stretch: 3,800 feet
Length of back stretch: 3,000 feet

YEAR BY YEAR WINNERS

Year	Event	Race winner	Car make	Avg. speed	Start pos.	Car owner	Pole winner	Pole speed
2006	Pepsi 400	T. Stewart	Chevrolet	153.143	2	Joe Gibbs	B. Said	186.143
	Daytona 500	Ji. Johnson	Chevrolet	142.667	9	Rick Hendrick	J. Burton	189.151
2005	Pepsi 400	T. Stewart	Chevrolet	131.016	1	Joe Gibbs	T. Stewart	185.582
	Daytona 500	J. Gordon	Chevrolet	135.173	15	Rick Hendrick	D. Jarrett	188.312
2004	Pepsi 400	J. Gordon	Chevrolet	145.117	1	Rick Hendrick	J. Gordon	188.660
	Daytona 500	D. Earnhardt Jr.	Chevrolet	156.345	3	Teresa Earnhardt	G. Biffle	188.387
2003	Pepsi 400	G. Biffle	Ford	166.109	30	Jack Roush	S. Park	184.752
	Daytona 500 (a)	M. Waltrip	Chevrolet	133.870	4	Teresa Earnhardt	J. Green	186.606
2002	Pepsi 400	M. Waltrip	Chevrolet	135.952	7	Teresa Earnhardt	K. Harvick	185.041
	Daytona 500	W. Burton	Dodge	142.971	19	Bill Davis	Ji. Johnson	185.831
2001	Pepsi 400	D. Earnhardt Jr.	Chevrolet	157.601	13	Teresa Earnhardt	S. Marlin	183.778
	Daytona 500	M. Waltrip	Chevrolet	161.783	19	Teresa Earnhardt	B. Elliott	183.565
2000	Pepsi 400	J. Burton	Ford	148.576	1	Jack Roush	D. Jarrett	187.547
	Daytona 500	D. Jarrett	Ford	155.669	1	Robert Yates	D. Jarrett	191.091
1999	Pepsi 400 (c)	D. Jarrett	Ford	169.213	12	Robert Yates	J. Nemechek	194.860
	Daytona 500	J. Gordon	Chevrolet	161.551	1	Rick Hendrick	J. Gordon	195.067
1998	Pepsi 400 (b)	J. Gordon	Chevrolet	144.549	8	Rick Hendrick	B. Labonte	193.611
	Daytona 500	D. Earnhardt	Chevrolet	172.712	4	Richard Childress	B. Labonte	192.415
1997	Pepsi 400	J. Andretti	Ford	167.791	3	Cale Yarborough	M. Skinner	189.777
	Daytona 500	J. Gordon	Chevrolet	148.295	6	Rick Hendrick	M. Skinner	189.813

2007 SCHEDULE

NASCAR NEXTEL Cup Series
Event: Daytona 500
Race: No. 1 of 36
Date: February 18 • **TV:** FOX • **Radio:** MRN

Event: Pepsi 400
Race: No. 18 of 36
Date: July 1 • **TV:** TNT • **Radio:** MRN

NASCAR Busch Series
Event: Hershey's Kissables 300
Race: No. 1 of 35 • **Date:** February 17
TV: ESPN2 • **Radio:** MRN

Event: Winn-Dixie 250
Race: No. 19 of 35 • **Date:** July 6
TV: ESPN2 • **Radio:** MRN

NASCAR Craftsman Truck Series
Event: GM Flex Fuel 250
Race: No. 1 of 25
Date: February 16 • **TV:** SPEED • **Radio:** MRN
Race names subject to change

YEAR BY YEAR WINNERS continued

Year	Event	Race winner	Car make	Avg. speed	Start pos.	Car owner	Pole winner	Pole speed
1996	Pepsi 400 (a)	S. Marlin	Chevrolet	161.602	2	Larry McClure	J. Gordon	188.869
	Daytona 500	D. Jarrett	Ford	154.308	7	Robert Yates	D. Earnhardt	189.510
1995	Pepsi 400	J. Gordon	Chevrolet	166.976	3	Rick Hendrick	D. Earnhardt	191.355
	Daytona 500	S. Marlin	Chevrolet	141.710	3	Larry McClure	D. Jarrett	193.498
1994	Pepsi 400	J. Spencer	Ford	155.558	3	Junior Johnson	D. Earnhardt	191.339
	Daytona 500	S. Marlin	Chevrolet	156.931	4	Larry McClure	L. Allen	190.158
1993	Pepsi 400	D. Earnhardt	Chevrolet	151.755	5	Richard Childress	E. Irvan	190.327
	Daytona 500	D. Jarrett	Chevrolet	154.972	2	Joe Gibbs	K. Petty	189.426
1992	Pepsi 400	E. Irvan	Chevrolet	170.457	6	Larry McClure	S. Marlin	189.366
	Daytona 500	Da. Allison	Ford	160.256	6	Robert Yates	S. Marlin	192.213
1991	Pepsi 400	B. Elliott	Ford	159.116	10	Harry Melling	S. Marlin	190.331
	Daytona 500	E. Irvan	Chevrolet	148.148	2	Larry McClure	Da. Allison	195.955
1990	Pepsi 400	D. Earnhardt	Chevrolet	160.894	3	Richard Childress	G. Sacks	195.533
	Daytona 500	D. Cope	Chevrolet	165.761	12	Bob Whitcomb	K. Schrader	196.515
1989	Pepsi 400	Da. Allison	Ford	132.207	8	Robert Yates	M. Martin	191.861
	Daytona 500	D. Waltrip	Chevrolet	148.466	2	Rick Hendrick	K. Schrader	196.996
1988	Pepsi 400	B. Elliott	Ford	163.302	38	Harry Melling	D. Waltrip	193.819
	Daytona 500	B. Allison	Buick	137.531	3	William Stavola	K. Schrader	193.823
1987	Pepsi 400	B. Allison	Buick	161.074	11	William Stavola	Da. Allison	198.085
	Daytona 500	B. Elliott	Ford	176.263	1	Harry Melling	B. Elliott	210.364
1986	Pepsi 400	T. Richmond	Chevrolet	131.916	9	Rick Hendrick	C. Yarborough	203.519
	Daytona 500	G. Bodine	Chevrolet	148.124	2	Rick Hendrick	B. Elliott	205.039
1985	Pepsi 400	G. Sacks	Chevrolet	158.730	9	DiProspero/Gardner	B. Elliott	201.523
	Daytona 500	B. Elliott	Ford	172.265	1	Harry Melling	B. Elliott	205.114
1984	Firecracker 400	R. Petty	Pontiac	171.204	6	Mike Curb	C. Yarborough	199.743
	Daytona 500	C. Yarborough	Chevrolet	150.994	1	Ranier Racing	C. Yarborough	201.848
1983	Firecracker 400	Buddy Baker	Ford	167.442	8	Wood Brothers	C. Yarborough	196.635
	Daytona 500	C. Yarborough	Pontiac	155.979	8	Harry Ranier	R. Rudd	198.864
1982	Firecracker 400	B. Allison	Buick	163.099	9	DiProspero/Gardner	G. Bodine	194.721
	Daytona 500	B. Allison	Buick	153.991	7	DiProspero/Gardner	B. Parsons	196.317
1981	Firecracker 400	C. Yarborough	Buick	142.588	1	M.C. Anderson	C. Yarborough	192.852
	Daytona 500	R. Petty	Buick	169.651	8	Petty Enterprises	B. Allison	194.624
1980	Firecracker 400	B. Allison	Mercury	173.473	14	Bud Moore	C. Yarborough	194.670
	Daytona 500	Buddy Baker	Oldsmobile	177.602	1	Harry Ranier	Buddy Baker	194.009
1979	Firecracker 400	N. Bonnett	Mercury	172.890	2	Wood Brothers	Buddy Baker	193.196
	Daytona 500	R. Petty	Oldsmobile	143.977	13	Petty Enterprises	Buddy Baker	196.049
1978	Firecracker 400	D. Pearson	Mercury	154.340	3	Wood Brothers	C. Yarborough	186.803
	Daytona 500	B. Allison	Ford	159.730	33	Bud Moore	C. Yarborough	187.536
1977	Firecracker 400	R. Petty	Dodge	142.716	5	Petty Enterprises	N. Bonnett	187.191
	Daytona 500	C. Yarborough	Chevrolet	153.218	4	Junior Johnson	Do. Allison	188.048
1976	Firecracker 400	C. Yarborough	Chevrolet	160.966	2	Junior Johnson	A. Foyt	183.090
	Daytona 500	D. Pearson	Mercury	152.181	7	Wood Brothers	R. Stott	183.456
1975	Firecracker 400	R. Petty	Dodge	158.381	13	Petty Enterprises	Do. Allison	186.737
	Daytona 500	B. Parsons	Chevrolet	153.649	32	L.G. DeWitt	Do. Allison	185.827
1974	Firecracker 400	D. Pearson	Mercury	138.301	1	Wood Brothers	D. Pearson	180.759
	Daytona 500 (d)	R. Petty	Dodge	140.894	2	Petty Enterprises	D. Pearson	185.817
1973	Firecracker 400	D. Pearson	Mercury	158.468	6	Wood Brothers	B. Allison	179.619
	Daytona 500	R. Petty	Dodge	157.205	7	Petty Enterprises	Buddy Baker	185.662
1972	Firecracker 400	D. Pearson	Mercury	160.821	2	Wood Brothers	B. Isaac	186.277
	Daytona 500	A. Foyt	Mercury	161.550	2	Wood Brothers	B. Isaac	186.632
1971	Firecracker 400	B. Isaac	Dodge	161.947	21	Nord Krauskopf	Do. Allison	183.228
	Daytona 500	R. Petty	Plymouth	144.462	5	Petty Enterprises	A. Foyt	182.744
1970	Firecracker 400	Do. Allison	Ford	162.235	15	Banjo Matthews	C. Yarborough	191.640
	Daytona 500	P. Hamilton	Plymouth	149.601	9	Petty Enterprises	C. Yarborough	194.015
1969	Firecracker 400	L. Yarbrough	Ford	160.875	9	Junior Johnson	C. Yarborough	190.706
	Daytona 500	L. Yarbrough	Ford	157.950	19	Junior Johnson	Buddy Baker	188.901
1968	Firecracker 400	C. Yarborough	Mercury	167.247	4	Wood Brothers	C. Glotzbach	188.901
	Daytona 500	C. Yarborough	Mercury	143.251	1	Wood Brothers	C. Yarborough	189.222
1967	Firecracker 400	C. Yarborough	Ford	143.583	2	Wood Brothers	D. Dieringer	179.802
	Daytona 500	M. Andretti	Ford	146.926	12	Holman-Moody	C. Turner	180.831
1966	Firecracker 400	S. McQuagg	Dodge	153.813	4	Ray Nichels	L. Yarbrough	176.660
	Daytona 500 (a)	R. Petty	Plymouth	160.627	1	Petty Enterprises	R. Petty	175.163
1965	Firecracker 400	A. Foyt	Ford	150.046	11	Banjo Matthews	M. Panch	171.510
	Daytona 500 (a)	F. Lorenzen	Ford	141.539	4	Holman-Moody	D. Dieringer	171.151
1964	Firecracker 400	A. Foyt	Dodge	151.451	19	Ray Nichels	D. Dieringer	172.678
	Daytona 500	R. Petty	Plymouth	154.334	2	Petty Enterprises	P. Goldsmith	174.910
1963	Firecracker 400	F. Roberts	Ford	150.927	3	Holman-Moody	Jr. Johnson	166.005
	Daytona 500	T. Lund	Ford	151.566	12	Wood Brothers	F. Roberts	160.943
1962	Firecracker 250	F. Roberts	Pontiac	153.688	4	Banjo Matthews	B. Matthews	160.499
	Daytona 500	F. Roberts	Pontiac	152.529	1	Jim Stephens	F. Roberts	156.999
1961	Firecracker 250	D. Pearson	Pontiac	154.294	2	John Masoni	F. Roberts	157.150
	Daytona 500	M. Panch	Pontiac	149.601	4	Smokey Yunick	F. Roberts	155.709
1960	Firecracker 250	J. Smith	Pontiac	146.842	1	Jack Smith	J. Smith	152.129
	Daytona 500	Jr. Johnson	Chevrolet	124.740	9	John Masoni	C. Owens	149.892
1959	Firecracker 250	F. Roberts	Pontiac	140.581	1	Jim Stephens	F. Roberts	144.997
	Daytona 500	L. Petty	Oldsmobile	135.521	15	Petty Enterprises	B. Welborn	140.581

KEY **(a)** Race shortened by rain. **(b)** First scheduled night race postponed until October because of fire. **(c)** First year in which second race was held at night. **(d)** Race shortened by 50 miles because of energy shortage.

ALL DAYTONA RACES

POLE WINNERS

Cale Yarborough	12
Buddy Baker	5
Bill Elliott	5
Fireball Roberts	5
Donnie Allison	4
Dale Jarrett	4
Sterling Marlin	4
Darel Dieringer	3
Dale Earnhardt	3
Jeff Gordon	3
Ken Schrader	3
Bobby Allison	2
Davey Allison	2
A.J. Foyt	2
Bobby Isaac	2
Bobby Labonte	2
David Pearson	2
Mike Skinner	2
Loy Allen	1
Greg Biffle	1
Geoffrey Bodine	1
Neil Bonnett	1
Jeff Burton	1
Charlie Glotzbach	1
Paul Goldsmith	1
Jeff Green	1
Kevin Harvick	1
Ernie Irvan	1
Jimmie Johnson	1
Junior Johnson	1
Mark Martin	1
Banjo Mathews	1
Joe Nemechek	1
Cotton Owens	1
Marvin Panch	1
Steve Park	1
Benny Parsons	1
Kyle Petty	1
Richard Petty	1
Ricky Rudd	1
Greg Sacks	1
Boris Said	1
Jack Smith	1
Tony Stewart	1
Ramo Stott	1
Curtis Turner	1
Darrell Waltrip	1
Bob Welborn	1
LeeRoy Yarbrough	1

RACE WINNERS

Richard Petty	10
Cale Yarborough	8
Bobby Allison	6
Jeff Gordon	6
David Pearson	6
Bill Elliott	4
Dale Jarrett	4
Fireball Roberts	4
Dale Earnhardt	3
A.J. Foyt	3
Sterling Marlin	3
Michael Waltrip	3
Davey Allison	2
Buddy Baker	2
Dale Earnhardt Jr.	2
Ernie Irvan	2
Tony Stewart	2
LeeRoy Yarbrough	2
Donnie Allison	1
John Andretti	1
Mario Andretti	1
Greg Biffle	1
Geoffrey Bodine	1
Neil Bonnett	1
Jeff Burton	1
Ward Burton	1
Derrike Cope	1
Pete Hamilton	1
Bobby Isaac	1
Jimmie Johnson	1
Junior Johnson	1
Fred Lorenzen	1
Tiny Lund	1
Sam McQuagg	1
Marvin Panch	1
Benny Parsons	1
Lee Petty	1
Tim Richmond	1
Greg Sacks	1
Jack Smith	1
Jimmy Spencer	1
Darrell Waltrip	1

RACE 1

POLE WINNERS

Buddy Baker	4
Bill Elliott	4
Cale Yarborough	4
Dale Jarrett	3
Fireball Roberts	3
Ken Schrader	3
Donnie Allison	2
Loy Allen	1
Bobby Allison	1
Davey Allison	1
Greg Biffle	1
Jeff Burton	1
Darel Dieringer	1
Dale Earnhardt	1
A.J. Foyt	1
Paul Goldsmith	1
Jeff Gordon	1
Jeff Green	1
Bobby Isaac	1
Jimmie Johnson	1
Bobby Labonte	1
Sterling Marlin	1
Cotton Owens	1
Benny Parsons	1
David Pearson	1
Kyle Petty	1
Richard Petty	1
Ricky Rudd	1
Mike Skinner	1
Ramo Stott	1
Curtis Turner	1
Bob Welborn	1

RACE WINNERS

Richard Petty	7
Cale Yarborough	4
Bobby Allison	3
Jeff Gordon	3
Dale Jarrett	3
Bill Elliott	2
Sterling Marlin	2
Michael Waltrip	2
Davey Allison	1
Mario Andretti	1
Buddy Baker	1
Geoffrey Bodine	1
Ward Burton	1
Derrike Cope	1
Dale Earnhardt	1
Dale Earnhardt Jr.	1
A.J. Foyt	1
Pete Hamilton	1
Ernie Irvan	1
Jimmie Johnson	1
Junior Johnson	1
Fred Lorenzen	1
Tiny Lund	1
Marvin Panch	1
Benny Parsons	1
David Pearson	1
Lee Petty	1
Fireball Roberts	1
Darrell Waltrip	1
LeeRoy Yarbrough	1

RACE 2

POLE WINNERS

Cale Yarborough	8
Sterling Marlin	3
Donnie Allison	2
Darel Dieringer	2
Dale Earnhardt	2
Jeff Gordon	2
Fireball Roberts	2
Bobby Allison	1
Davey Allison	1
Buddy Baker	1
Geoffrey Bodine	1
Neil Bonnett	1
Bill Elliott	1
A.J. Foyt	1
Charlie Glotzbach	1
Kevin Harvick	1
Ernie Irvan	1
Bobby Isaac	1
Dale Jarrett	1
Junior Johnson	1
Bobby Labonte	1
Mark Martin	1
Banjo Mathews	1
Joe Nemechek	1
Marvin Panch	1
Steve Park	1
David Pearson	1
Greg Sacks	1
Boris Said	1
Mike Skinner	1
Jack Smith	1
Tony Stewart	1
Darrell Waltrip	1
LeeRoy Yarbrough	1

RACE WINNERS

David Pearson	5
Cale Yarborough	4
Bobby Allison	3
Jeff Gordon	3
Richard Petty	3
Fireball Roberts	3
Dale Earnhardt	2
Bill Elliott	2
A.J. Foyt	2
Tony Stewart	2
Davey Allison	1
Donnie Allison	1
John Andretti	1
Buddy Baker	1
Greg Biffle	1
Neil Bonnett	1
Jeff Burton	1
Dale Earnhardt Jr.	1
Ernie Irvan	1
Bobby Isaac	1
Dale Jarrett	1
Sterling Marlin	1
Sam McQuagg	1
Tim Richmond	1
Greg Sacks	1
Jack Smith	1
Jimmy Spencer	1
Michael Waltrip	1
LeeRoy Yarbrough	1

>>DAYTONA INTERNATIONAL SPEEDWAY<<

>>NASCAR BUSCH SERIES<<

YEAR BY YEAR WINNERS

Year	Event	Race winner	Car make	Avg. speed	Start pos.	Pole winner	Pole speed
2006	Winn-Dixie 250	D. Earnhardt Jr.	Chevrolet	133.343	9	J. Yeley	183.509
	Hershey's Kissables 300	T. Stewart	Chevrolet	125.159	16	J. Yeley	183.094
2005	Winn-Dixie 250	M. Truex Jr.	Chevrolet	140.141	6	K. Harvick	182.515
	Hershey's Take 5 300	T. Stewart	Chevrolet	150.021	14	J. Nemechek	182.452
2004	Winn-Dixie 250	M. Wallace	Ford	135.014	16	M. Bliss	181.969
	Hershey's Kisses 300	D. Earnhardt Jr.	Chevrolet	127.179	8	M. Truex	181.138
2003	Daytona 250	D. Earnhardt Jr.	Chevrolet	153.715	1	D. Earnhardt Jr.	186.308
	Koolerz 300	D. Earnhardt Jr.	Chevrolet	143.770	2	J. Nemechek	186.050
2002	EAS/GNC 300	D. Earnhardt Jr.	Chevrolet	147.662	4	J. Nemechek	186.254
	Stacker/GNC 250	J. Nemechek	Pontiac	125.892	1	J. Nemechek	185.793
2001	NAPA Auto Parts 300	R. LaJoie	Pontiac	135.152	2	J. Nemechek	186.966
2000	Napa Auto Parts 300	M. Kenseth	Chevrolet	140.735	8	H. Stricklin	187.336
1999	Napa Auto Parts 300	R. LaJoie	Chevrolet	138.391	2	K. Schrader	189.865
1998	Napa Auto Parts 300	J. Nemechek	Chevrolet	137.213	1	M. McLaughlin	190.134
1997	Gargoyles 300	R. LaJoie	Chevrolet	149.688	14	E. Sadler	190.508
1996	Goody's 300	S. Grissom	Chevrolet	140.772	4	J. Purvis	189.733
1995	Goody's 300	C. Little	Ford	150.732	42	M. Waltrip	185.326
1994	Goody's 300	D. Earnhardt	Chevrolet	144.135	7	M. Waltrip	184.555
1993	Goody's 300	D. Earnhardt	Chevrolet	146.440	5	K. Schrader	186.513
1992	Goody's 300	D. Earnhardt	Chevrolet	132.434	4	M. Waltrip	186.556
1991	Goody's 300	D. Earnhardt	Chevrolet	144.192	3	D. Green	188.675
1990	Goody's 300	D. Earnhardt	Chevrolet	149.357	2	D. Waltrip	188.945
1989	Goody's 300	D. Waltrip	Chevrolet	131.211	9	K. Wallace	192.271
1988	Goody's 300	B. Allison	Buick	132.825	9	M. Swaim	189.825
1987	Goody's 300	G. Bodine	Chevrolet	155.106	5	T. Houston	194.389
1986	Goody's 300	D. Earnhardt	Pontiac	148.924	9	L. Pearson	191.310
1985	Goody's 300	G. Bodine	Pontiac	157.137	2	R. Wallace	187.438
1984	Goody's 300	D. Waltrip	Pontiac	156.613	12	L.D. Ottinger	187.682
1983	Goody's 300	D. Waltrip	Pontiac	147.642	5	S. Ard	185.774
1982	Goody's 300	D. Earnhardt	Pontiac	154.529	5	M. Porter	184.569

POLE WINNERS		RACE WINNERS	
Joe Nemechek	6	Dale Earnhardt	7
Michael Waltrip	3	Dale Earnhardt Jr.	5
Ken Schrader	2	Randy LaJoie	3
J.J. Yeley	2	Darrell Waltrip	3
Sam Ard	1	Geoffrey Bodine	2
Mike Bliss	1	Joe Nemechek	2
David Green	1	Tony Stewart	2
Kevin Harvick	1	Bobby Allison	1
Tommy Houston	1	Steve Grissom	1
L.D. Ottinger	1	Matt Kenseth	1
Larry Pearson	1	Chad Little	1
Mike Porter	1	Martin Truex	1
Jeff Purvis	1	Mike Wallace	1
Elliott Sadler	1		
Hut Stricklin	1		
Mike Swaim	1		
Martin Truex Jr.	1		
Kenny Wallace	1		
Rusty Wallace	1		
Darrell Waltrip	1		

QUALIFYING RECORD: Tommy Houston, Buick; 194.389 mph (46.298 seconds), February 10, 1987
RACE RECORD: Geoffrey Bodine, Pontiac; 157.137 mph (1:54:33), February 16, 1985

Earnhardt Jr.

>>NASCAR CRAFTSMAN TRUCK SERIES<<

YEAR BY YEAR WINNERS

Year	Event	Race winner	Car make	Avg. speed	Start pos.	Pole winner	Pole speed
2006	GM FlexFuel 250	M. Martin	Ford	146.622	1	M. Martin	178.628
2005	Fla. Dodge Dealers 250	B. Hamilton	Dodge	124.931	36	K. Earnhardt	182.475
2004	Fla. Dodge Dealers 250	C. Edwards	Ford	112.570	6	T. Cook	183.643
2003	Fla. Dodge Dealers 250	R. Crawford	Ford	127.642	19	J. Leffler	182.994
2002	Fla. Dodge Dealers 250	R. Pressley	Dodge	140.121	2	T. Musgrave	187.215
2001	Fla. Dodge Dealers 250	J. Ruttman	Dodge	129.407	1	J. Ruttman	186.123
2000	Daytona 250	M. Wallace	Ford	130.152	2	J. Ruttman	187.563

POLE WINNERS		RACE WINNERS	
Joe Ruttman	2	Rick Crawford	1
Terry Cook	1	Carl Edwards	1
Kerry Earnhardt	1	Bobby Hamilton	1
Jason Leffler	1	Mark Martin	1
Mark Martin	1	Robert Pressley	1
Ted Musgrave	1	Joe Ruttman	1
		Mike Wallace	1

QUALIFYING RECORD: Joe Ruttman, Dodge; 187.563 mph (47.984 seconds), February 16, 2000
RACE RECORD: Mark Martin, Ford; 146.622 mph (1:44:21), February 17, 2006

Hamilton

TRACK FACTS >>> >>> **Location:** Dover, Del. >>> >>> **Owner:** Dover Motorsports, Inc. >>> >>> **Track length:** 1 mile >>>

>>> **Grandstand seating:** 140,000 >>> >>> **Tickets:** (800) 441-7223 >>> >>> **Website:** www.doverspeedway.com >>> >>>

>>NASCAR NEXTEL CUP SERIES<<

>>TRACK RECORDS

Most wins: 7—Richard Petty and Bobby Allison; **Most top fives:** 19—Dale Earnhardt and Mark Martin; **Most top 10s:** 26—Richard Petty and Ricky Rudd; **Oldest winner:** Harry Gant, 52 years, 4 months, 21 days, May 31, 1992; **Youngest winner:** Jeff Gordon, 24 years, 1 month, 13 days, September 17, 1995; **Most lead changes:** 29—Twice, most recently, May 18, 1986; **Most lead changes:** 3—October 17, 1971; **Most leaders:** 13—Twice, most recently, September 24, 2000; **Fewest leaders:** 3—Five times, most recently, May 16, 1982; **Most laps led in a 400-mile race:** 381, Jeff Gordon, June 3, 2001; **Most laps led in a 500-mile race:** 491, Richard Petty, September 15, 1974; **Most cautions:** 16—September 19, 1993; **Fewest cautions:** 0—June 6, 1971; **Most caution laps:** 103—September 19, 1993; **Fewest caution laps:** 0—June 6, 1971; **Most on the lead lap:** 21—June 4, 2006; **Fewest on the lead lap:** 1—11 times, most recently, September 15, 1991; **Most running at the finish:** 39—June 2, 2002; **Fewest running at the finish:** 13—May 17, 1981; **Most laps led by a race winner:** 491—Richard Petty, September 15, 1974; **Fewest laps led by a race winner:** 6—Jeff Burton, September 24, 2006; **Closest margin of victory:** 0.080 seconds—Jimmie Johnson defeated Kyle Busch, September 25, 2005

>>QUALIFYING AND RACE RECORDS

QUALIFYING: Jeremy Mayfield, Dodge; 161.522 mph (22.288 seconds), June 4, 2004
RACE: Mark Martin, Ford; 132.719 mph (3:00:50), September 21, 1997; **400 miles:** Mark Martin, Ford; 132.719 mph (3:00:50), September 21, 1997; **500 miles:** Cale Yarborough, Chevrolet; 127.841 mph (3:54:40), May 19, 1974

First NASCAR NEXTEL Cup Series race:
July 6, 1969 (Richard Petty, winner)
Banking on straights: 9 degrees
Length of front stretch: 1,076 feet
Length of back stretch: 1,076 feet

YEAR BY YEAR WINNERS

Year	Event	Race winner	Car make	Avg. speed	Start pos.	Car owner	Pole winner	Pole speed
2006	Dover 400	J. Burton	Chevrolet	111.966	19	Richard Childress	J. Gordon	156.162
	Neighborhood Exc. 400	M. Kenseth	Ford	109.865	19	Jack Roush	R. Newman	154.633
2005	MBNA America 400	Ji. Johnson	Chevrolet	115.054	5	Rick Hendrick	R. Newman	158.102
	MBNA America 400	G. Biffle	Ford	122.626	2	Jack Roush	None—conditions	
2004	MBNA America 400	R. Newman	Dodge	119.067	2	Roger Penske	J. Mayfield	159.405
	MBNA America 400	M. Martin	Ford	97.042	7	Jack Roush	J. Mayfield	161.522
2003	MBNA America 400	R. Newman	Dodge	108.82	5	Roger Penske	None—conditions	
	MBNA Armed Forces 400	R. Newman	Dodge	106.896	1	Roger Penske	R. Newman	158.716
2002	MBNA Am. Heroes 400	Ji. Johnson	Chevrolet	120.805	19	Rick Hendrick	R. Wallace	156.822
	MBNA Platinum 400	Ji. Johnson	Chevrolet	117.551	10	Rick Hendrick	M. Kenseth	154.939
2001	MBNA Cal Ripken 400	D. Earnhardt Jr.	Chevrolet	101.559	27	Dale Earnhardt	D. Jarrett	154.919
	MBNA Platinum 400	J. Gordon	Chevrolet	120.361	2	Rick Hendrick	None—conditions	
2000	MBNA.com 400	T. Stewart	Pontiac	115.191	27	Joe Gibbs	J. Mayfield	159.872
	MBNA Platinum 400	T. Stewart	Pontiac	109.514	16	Joe Gibbs	R. Wallace	157.411
1999	MBNA Gold 400	M. Martin	Ford	127.434	8	Jack Roush	R. Wallace	159.964
	MBNA Platinum 400	B. Labonte	Pontiac	120.603	1	Joe Gibbs	B. Labonte	159.320
1998	MBNA Gold 400	M. Martin	Ford	113.834	1	Jack Roush	M. Martin	155.966
	MBNA Platinum 400	D. Jarrett	Ford	119.522	4	Robert Yates	R. Wallace	155.898

2007 SCHEDULE

NASCAR NEXTEL Cup Series
Event: Neighborhood Excellence 400
Race: No. 13 of 36
Date: June 3 • **TV:** FOX • **Radio:** MRN

Event: Dover 400
Race: No. 28 of 36
Date: September 23 • **TV:** ABC • **Radio:** MRN

NASCAR Busch Series
Event: StonebridgeRacing.com 200
Race: No. 14 of 35 • **Date:** June 2
TV: ESPN2 • **Radio:** MRN

Event: Dover 200
Race: No. 29 of 35 • **Date:** September 22
TV: ESPN2 • **Radio:** MRN

NASCAR Craftsman Truck Series
Event: AAA Insurance 200
Race: No. 8 of 25
Date: June 1 • **TV:** SPEED • **Radio:** MRN

Race names subject to change

>>DOVER INTERNATIONAL SPEEDWAY<<

YEAR BY YEAR WINNERS continued

Year	Event	Race winner	Car make	Avg. speed	Start pos.	Car owner	Pole winner	Pole speed
1997	MBNA 400	M. Martin	Ford	132.719	1	Jack Roush	M. Martin	152.033
	Miller 500	R. Rudd	Ford	114.635	13	Ricky Rudd	B. Labonte	152.788
1996	MBNA 500	J. Gordon	Chevrolet	105.646	3	Rick Hendrick	B. Labonte	155.086
	Miller 500	J. Gordon	Chevrolet	122.741	1	Rick Hendrick	J. Gordon	154.785
1995	MBNA 500	J. Gordon	Chevrolet	124.740	2	Rick Hendrick	R. Mast	153.446
	Miller 500	K. Petty	Pontiac	119.880	37	Felix Sabates	J. Gordon	153.669
1994	SpitFire 500	R. Wallace	Ford	112.556	10	Roger Penske	G. Bodine	152.840
	Budweiser 500	R. Wallace	Ford	102.529	6	Roger Penske	E. Irvan	151.956
1993	SpitFire 500	R. Wallace	Pontiac	100.334	1	Roger Penske	R. Wallace	151.564
	Budweiser 500	D. Earnhardt	Chevrolet	105.600	8	Richard Childress	E. Irvan	151.541
1992	Peak 500	R. Rudd	Chevrolet	115.289	6	Rick Hendrick	A. Kulwicki	145.267
	Budweiser 500	H. Gant	Oldsmobile	109.456	15	Leo Jackson	B. Bodine	147.408
1991	Peak 500	H. Gant	Oldsmobile	110.179	10	Leo Jackson	A. Kulwicki	146.825
	Budweiser 500	K. Schrader	Chevrolet	120.152	19	Rick Hendrick	M. Waltrip	143.392
1990	Peak 500	B. Elliot	Ford	125.945	1	Harry Melling	B. Elliott	144.928
	Budweiser 500	D. Cope	Chevrolet	123.960	15	Bob Whitcomb	D. Trickle	145.814
1989	Peak 500	D. Earnhardt	Chevrolet	122.909	15	Richard Childress	Da. Allison	146.169
	Budweiser 500	D. Earnhardt	Chevrolet	121.670	2	Richard Childress	M. Martin	144.387
1988	Delaware 500	B. Elliott	Ford	109.349	1	Harry Melling	M. Martin	148.075
	Budweiser 500	B. Elliott	Ford	118.726	17	Harry Melling	A. Kulwicki	146.681
1987	Delaware 500	R. Rudd	Ford	124.706	13	Bud Moore	A. Kulwicki	145.826
	Budweiser 500	Da. Allison	Ford	112.958	2	Harry Ranier	B. Elliott	145.056
1986	Delaware 500	R. Rudd	Ford	114.329	11	Bud Moore	G. Bodine	146.205
	Budweiser 500	G. Bodine	Chevrolet	115.009	3	Rick Hendrick	R. Rudd	138.217
1985	Delaware 500	H. Gant	Chevrolet	120.538	4	Hal Needham	B. Elliott	141.543
	Budweiser 500	B. Elliott	Ford	123.094	4	Melling Racing	T. Labonte	138.106
1984	Delaware 500	H. Gant	Chevrolet	111.856	4	Hal Needham	None—conditions	
	Budweiser 500	R. Petty	Pontiac	118.717	5	Mike Curb	R. Rudd	140.807
1983	Budweiser 500	B. Allison	Buick	116.077	7	DiProspero/Gardner	T. Labonte	139.573
	Mason-Dixon 500	B. Allison	Buick	114.847	10	DiProspero/Gardner	J. Ruttman	139.616
1982	CRC Chemicals 500	D. Waltrip	Buick	107.642	3	Junior Johnson	R. Rudd	139.384
	Mason-Dixon 500	B. Allison	Chevrolet	120.136	3	DiProspero/Gardner	D. Waltrip	139.308
1981	CRC Chemicals 500	N. Bonnett	Ford	119.561	3	Wood Brothers	R. Rudd	136.757
	Mason-Dixon 500	J. Ridley	Ford	116.595	11	Junie Donlavey	D. Pearson	138.425
1980	CRC Chemicals 500	D. Waltrip	Chevrolet	116.024	2	DiProspero/Gardner	C. Yarborough	137.583
	Mason-Dixon 500	B. Allison	Ford	113.866	8	Bud Moore	C. Yarborough	138.814
1979	CRC Chemicals 500	R. Petty	Chevrolet	114.366	4	Petty Enterprises	D. Earnhardt	135.726
	Mason-Dixon 500	N. Bonnett	Mercury	111.269	5	Wood Brothers	D. Waltrip	136.103
1978	Delaware 500	B. Allison	Ford	119.323	2	Bud Moore	J. McDuffie	135.480
	Mason-Dixon 500	D. Pearson	Mercury	114.664	3	Wood Brothers	Buddy Baker	135.452
1977	Delaware 500	B. Parsons	Chevrolet	114.708	7	L. G. DeWitt	N. Bonnett	134.233
	Mason-Dixon 500	C. Yarborough	Chevrolet	123.327	6	Junior Johnson	R. Petty	136.033
1976	Delaware 500	C. Yarborough	Chevrolet	115.740	1	Junior Johnson	C. Yarborough	133.377
	Mason-Dixon 500	B. Parsons	Chevrolet	115.436	7	L.G. DeWitt	D. Marcis	136.013
1975	Delaware 500	R. Petty	Dodge	111.372	3	Petty Enterprises	D. Marcis	133.953
	Mason-Dixon 500 (a)	D. Pearson	Mercury	100.820	1	Wood Brothers	D. Pearson	136.612
1974	Delaware 500	R. Petty	Dodge	113.640	2	Petty Enterprises	Buddy Baker	133.640
	Mason-Dixon 500 (b)	C. Yarborough	Chevrolet	115.057	3	Junior Johnson	D. Pearson	134.403
1973	Delaware 500	D. Pearson	Mercury	112.852	1	Wood Brothers	D. Pearson	124.649
	Mason-Dixon 500	D. Pearson	Mercury	119.745	1	Wood Brothers	D. Pearson	133.111
1972	Delaware 500	D. Pearson	Mercury	120.506	2	Wood Brothers	B. Allison	133.323
	Mason-Dixon 500	B. Allison	Chevrolet	118.019	2	Junior Johnson	B. Isaac	130.809
1971	Delaware 500	R. Petty	Plymouth	123.254	4	Petty Enterprises	B. Allison	132.811
	Mason-Dixon 500	B. Allison	Ford	123.119	2	Holman-Moody	R. Petty	129.486
1970	Mason-Dixon 300	R. Petty	Plymouth	112.103	2	Petty Enterprises	B. Isaac	129.538
1969	Mason-Dixon 300	R. Petty	Ford	115.772	3	Petty Enterprises	D. Pearson	130.430

KEY (a) First 140 miles run on Sunday May 18; final 360 miles run on Monday. (b) Race shortened by 50 miles because of the energy shortage.

ALL DOVER RACES

POLE WINNERS

David Pearson	6
Rusty Wallace	5
Alan Kulwicki	4
Mark Martin	4
Ricky Rudd	4
Bill Elliott	3
Jeff Gordon	3
Bobby Labonte	3
Jeremy Mayfield	3
Ryan Newman	3
Cale Yarborough	3
Bobby Allison	2
Buddy Baker	2
Geoffrey Bodine	2
Ernie Irvan	2
Bobby Isaac	2
Terry Labonte	2
Dave Marcis	2
Richard Petty	2
Darrell Waltrip	2
Davey Allison	1
Brett Bodine	1
Neil Bonnett	1
Dale Earnhardt	1
Dale Jarrett	1
Matt Kenseth	1
Rick Mast	1
J.D. McDuffie	1
Joe Ruttman	1
Dick Trickle	1
Michael Waltrip	1

RACE WINNERS

Bobby Allison	7
Richard Petty	7
David Pearson	5
Bill Elliott	4
Harry Gant	4
Jeff Gordon	4
Ricky Rudd	4
Dale Earnhardt	3
Jimmie Johnson	3
Ryan Newman	3
Rusty Wallace	3
Cale Yarborough	3
Neil Bonnett	2
Benny Parsons	2
Tony Stewart	2
Darrell Waltrip	2
Davey Allison	1
Greg Biffle	1
Geoffrey Bodine	1
Jeff Burton	1
Derrike Cope	1
Dale Earnhardt Jr.	1
Dale Jarrett	1
Matt Kenseth	1
Bobby Labonte	1
Kyle Petty	1
Jody Ridley	1
Ken Schrader	1

RACE 1

POLE WINNERS

David Pearson	5
Jeff Gordon	2
Ernie Irvan	2
Bobby Isaac	2
Bobby Labonte	2
Ryan Newman	2
Richard Petty	2
Ricky Rudd	2
Rusty Wallace	2
Darrell Waltrip	2
Buddy Baker	1
Brett Bodine	1
Bill Elliott	1
Matt Kenseth	1
Alan Kulwicki	1
Terry Labonte	1
Dave Marcis	1
Mark Martin	1
Jeremy Mayfield	1
Joe Ruttman	1
Dick Trickle	1
Michael Waltrip	1
Cale Yarborough	1

RACE WINNERS

Bobby Allison	5
David Pearson	3
Richard Petty	3
Dale Earnhardt	2
Bill Elliott	2
Jeff Gordon	2
Cale Yarborough	2
Davey Allison	1
Greg Biffle	1
Geoffrey Bodine	1
Neil Bonnett	1
Derrike Cope	1
Harry Gant	1
Dale Jarrett	1
Jimmie Johnson	1
Matt Kenseth	1
Bobby Labonte	1
Mark Martin	1
Ryan Newman	1
Benny Parsons	1
Kyle Petty	1
Jody Ridley	1
Ricky Rudd	1
Ken Schrader	1
Tony Stewart	1
Rusty Wallace	1

RACE 2

POLE WINNERS

Alan Kulwicki	3
Mark Martin	3
Rusty Wallace	3
Bobby Allison	2
Geoffrey Bodine	2
Bill Elliott	2
Jeremy Mayfield	2
Ricky Rudd	2
Cale Yarborough	2
Davey Allison	1
Buddy Baker	1
Neil Bonnett	1
Dale Earnhardt	1
Jeff Gordon	1
Dale Jarrett	1
Bobby Labonte	1
Terry Labonte	1
Dave Marcis	1
Rick Mast	1
Ryan Newman	1
David Pearson	1

RACE WINNERS

Richard Petty	4
Harry Gant	3
Mark Martin	3
Ricky Rudd	3
Bobby Allison	2
Bill Elliott	2
Jeff Gordon	2
Jimmie Johnson	2
David Pearson	2
Rusty Wallace	2
Darrell Waltrip	2
Neil Bonnett	1
Jeff Burton	1
Dale Earnhardt	1
Dale Earnhardt Jr.	1
Benny Parsons	1
Tony Stewart	1
Cale Yarborough	1

>>NASCAR BUSCH SERIES<<

YEAR BY YEAR WINNERS

Year	Event	Race winner	Car make	Avg. speed	Start pos.	Pole winner	Pole speed
2006	Dover 200	C. Bowyer	Chevrolet	96.908	16	S. Riggs	154.799
	Stonebridgeracing.com 200	J. Burton	Chevrolet	103.791	36	None—conditions	
2005	Dover 200	R. Newman	Dodge	115.644	1	R. Newman	156.419
	MBNA Racepoints 200	M. Truex Jr.	Chevrolet	97.258	5	None—conditions	
2004	MBNA America 200	G. Biffle	Ford	87.934	7	D. Green	157.916
	Stacker 2 Hundred	M. Truex Jr.	Chevrolet	122.013	2	K. Kahne	157.350
2003	MBNA Armed Forces 200	J. Nemechek	Chevrolet	104.651	1	J. Nemechek	156.747
	Stacker 200 by YJ Stinger	B. Vickers	Chevrolet	133.154	3	None—conditions	
2002	MBNA Platinum 200	G. Biffle	Ford	107.591	3	J. Green	155.347
	MBNA All-American 200	S. Wimmer	Pontiac	118.265	26	K. Lepage	155.767
2001	MBNA Platinum 200	J. Spencer	Chevrolet	91.394	21	None—conditions	
	MBNA.COM 200	J. Green	Ford	107.591	2	R. Newman	155.635
2000	MBNA Platinum 200	J. Keller	Chevrolet	99.709	22	K. Harvick	154.912
	MBNA.com 200	M. Kenseth	Chevrolet	109.041	14	M. Skinner	155.932

POLE WINNERS		RACE WINNERS	
Harry Gant	5	Todd Bodine	3
Dick Trickle	3	Greg Biffle	2
Ricky Craven	3	Dale Earnhardt Jr.	2
Bobby Labonte	2	Harry Gant	2
Kevin LePage	2	Matt Kenseth	2
Ryan Newman	2	Randy LaJoie	2
Mike Alexander	1	Robert Pressley	1
Brett Bodine	1	Martin Truex Jr.	1
Todd Bodine	1	Darrell Waltrip	1
Ron Bouchard	1	Michael Waltrip	1
Ward Burton	1	Sam Ard	1
Tommy Ellis	1	Casey Atwood	1
Jeff Gordon	1	Johnny Benson	1

Year	Event	Race winner	Car make	Avg. speed	Start pos.	Pole winner	Pole speed
1999	MBNA Platinum 200	D. Earnhardt Jr.	Chevrolet	91.324	15	D. Trickle	155.213
	MBNA Gold 200	C. Atwood	Chevrolet	91.382	5	M. Kenseth	155.293
1998	MBNA Platinum 200	D. Earnhardt Jr.	Chevrolet	130.152	16	K. Lepage	151.688
	MBNA Gold 200	M. Kenseth	Chevrolet	106.023	4	K. Grubb	153.498
1997	Goodw./Delco 200	B. Labonte	Pontiac	114.358	2	D. Trickle	148.926
	MBNA 200	J. Bessey	Chevrolet	94.912	6	D. Trickle	147.656
1996	Goodw./Delco 200	R. LaJoie	Chevrolet	96.308	16	B. Labonte	149.963
	MBNA 200	R. LaJoie	Chevrolet	118.343	24	R. Craven	150.069
1995	Goodw./Delco 200	M. McLaughlin	Chevrolet	102.887	5	T. Leslie	147.832
	MBNA 200	J. Rumley	Chevrolet	108.975	24	J. Keller	149.409
1994	Goodw./Delco 200	M. Wallace	Chevrolet	96.013	19	R. Craven	146.425
	Splitfire 200	J. Benson	Chevrolet	102.477	20	H. Gant	149.638
1993	Goodw./Delco 200	T. Bodine	Chevrolet	116.694	5	W. Burton	145.92
	Splitfire 200	T. Bodine	Chevrolet	104.545	22	T. Labonte	147.366
1992	Goodwrench 200	R. Pressley	Oldsmobile	89.408	4	T. Bodine	143.604
	Splitfire 200	R. Pressley	Oldsmobile	108.271	4	J. Gordon	143.079
1991	Budweiser 200	T. Bodine	Buick	118.323	9	D. Mader	142.510
	Splitfire 200	H. Gant	Buick	126.538	16	B. Miller	145.396
1990	Budweiser 200	M. Waltrip	Pontiac	108.091	4	B. Labonte	143.885
	Ames/Splitfire 200	H. Gant	Buick	123.097	3	T. Ellis	144.289
1989	Budweiser 200	R. Wilson	Oldsmobile	114.122	8	H. Gant	142.006
	Ames/Peak 200	K. Schrader	Chevrolet	111.300	14	M. Waltrip	143.209
1988	Budweiser 200	B. Hillin	Buick	112.236	15	M. Alexander	143.192
	Grand National 200	M. Waltrip	Chevrolet	116.073	5	H. Gant	143.896
1987	Budweiser 200	M. Martin	Ford	101.408	5	R. Mast	141.995
	Grand National 200	R. Mast	Buick	113.529	3	H. Gant	140.685
1986	Budweiser 200	D. Waltrip	Pontiac	107.914	2	B. Bodine	137.546
	Grand National 200	M. Shepherd	Buick	113.798	1	M. Shepherd	141.093
1985	Budweiser 200	D. Waltrip	Chevrolet	108.926	8	J. Ingram	135.941
1984	Budweiser 200	S. Ard	Oldsmobile	111.888	2	R. Bouchard	139.184
1983	Sportsman 200	R. Rudd	Oldsmobile	118.285	12	D. Pearson	137.504
1982	Sportsman 200	J. Ruttman	Pontiac	111.679	9	H. Gant	138.021

POLE WINNERS		RACE WINNERS	
David Green	1	Joe Bessey	1
Jeff Green	1	Clint Bowyer	1
Kevin Grubb	1	Jeff Burton	1
Kevin Harvick	1	Jeff Green	1
Jack Ingram	1	Bobby Hillin	1
Kasey Kahne	1	Jason Keller	1
Matt Kenseth	1	Bobby Labonte	1
Terry Labonte	1	Mark Martin	1
Tracy Leslie	1	Rick Mast	1
Dave Mader III	1	Mike McLaughlin	1
Rick Mast	1	Joe Nemechek	1
Butch Miller	1	Ryan Newman	1
Joe Nemechek	1	Ricky Rudd	1
David Pearson	1	Johnny Rumley	1
Scott Riggs	1	Joe Ruttman	1
Morgan Shepherd	1	Ken Schrader	1
Mike Skinner	1	Morgan Shepherd	1
Michael Waltrip	1	Jimmy Spencer	1
		Brian Vickers	1
		Mike Wallace	1
		Rick Wilson	1
		Scott Wimmer	1

Bowyer

QUALIFYING RECORD: David Green, Chevrolet; 157.916 mph (22.797 seconds), June 6, 2004
RACE RECORD: Dale Earnhardt Jr., Chevrolet; 130.152 mph (1:32:12), May 30, 1998

NASCAR CRAFTSMAN TRUCK SERIES
YEAR BY YEAR WINNERS

Year	Event	Race winner	Car make	Avg. speed	Start pos.	Pole winner	Pole speed
2006	AAA Auto Insurance 200	M. Martin	Ford	120.200	13	D. Reutimann	153.905
2005	MBNA RacePoints 200	Ky. Busch	Chevrolet	96.735	5	D. Starr	157.577
2004	MBNA America 200	C. Chaffin	Dodge	98.996	9	C. Edwards	152.892
2003	MBNA Armed Forces 200	J. Leffler	Dodge	97.232	26	None—conditions	
2002	MBNA America 200	T. Musgrave	Dodge	104.545	2	R. Crawford	150.414
2001	MBNA E-Commerce 200	S. Riggs	Dodge	99.256	1	S. Riggs	150.288
2000	MBNA E-Commerce.com 200	Ku. Busch	Ford	97.168	1	Ku. Busch	151.764

POLE WINNERS		RACE WINNERS	
Kurt Busch	1	Kurt Busch	1
Rick Crawford	1	Kyle Busch	1
Carl Edwards	1	Chad Chaffin	1
David Reutimann	1	Jason Leffler	1
Scott Riggs	1	Mark Martin	1
David Starr	1	Ted Musgrave	1
		Scott Riggs	1

Kyle Busch

QUALIFYING RECORD: David Starr, Chevrolet; 157.577 mph (22.846 seconds), June 3, 2005
RACE RECORD: Mark Martin, Ford; 120.200 mph (1:39:50), June 2, 2006

Kyle Busch

>>HOMESTEAD-MIAMI SPEEDWAY<<

TRACK FACTS >>> >>> **Location:** Homestead, Fla. >>> >>> **Owner:** International Speedway Corp. >>> >>> **Track length:** 1.5 miles

>>> >>> **Grandstand seating:** 65,000 >>> >>> **Tickets:** (305) 230-7223 >>> >>> **Website:** www.homesteadmiamispeedway.com

>>NASCAR NEXTEL CUP SERIES<<

>>TRACK RECORDS

Most wins: 3—Greg Biffle; **Most top fives:** 4—Mark Martin; **Most top 10s:** 6—Jeff Gordon; **Oldest winner:** Bill Elliott, 46 years, 1 month, 3 days, November 11, 2001; **Youngest winner:** Kurt Busch, 24 years, 3 months, 13 days, November 17, 2002; **Most lead changes:** 21—Twice, most recently November 20, 2005; **Fewest lead changes:** 12—November 17, 2002; **Most leaders:** 12—Twice, most recently November 20, 2005; **Fewest leaders:** 6—November 17, 2002; **Most cautions:** 14—November 21, 2004; **Fewest cautions:** 1—November 14, 1999; **Most caution laps:** 79—November 21, 2004; **Fewest caution laps:** 5—November 14, 1999; **Most on the lead lap:** 25—November 11, 2001; **Fewest on the lead lap:** 6—November 12, 2000; **Most running at the finish:** 42—November 11, 2001; **Fewest running at the finish:** 32—Three times, most recently, November 19, 2006; **Most laps led by a race winner:** 166—Tony Stewart, November 12, 2000; **Fewest laps led by a race winner:** 1—Bobby Labonte, November 16, 2003; **Closest margin of victory:** 0.017 seconds—Greg Biffle defeated Mark Martin, November 20, 2005

>>QUALIFYING AND RACE RECORDS

QUALIFYING: Jamie McMurray, Dodge; 181.111 mph (29.816 seconds), November 14, 2003
RACE: Tony Stewart, Pontiac; 140.335 mph (2:51:14), November 14, 1999

First NASCAR NEXTEL Cup Series race: November 14, 1999 (Tony Stewart, winner)
Banking on straights: 4 degrees
Length of front stretch: 1,760 feet
Length of back stretch: 1,760 feet

2007 SCHEDULE

NASCAR NEXTEL Cup Series
Event: Ford 400
Race: No. 36 of 36
Date: November 18
TV: ABC • **Radio:** MRN

NASCAR Busch Series
Event: Ford 300
Race: No. 35 of 35
Date: November 17
TV: ESPN2 • **Radio:** MRN

NASCAR Craftsman Truck Series
Event: Ford 300
Race: No. 25 of 35
Date: November 16
TV: SPEED • **Radio:** MRN
Race names subject to change

YEAR BY YEAR WINNERS

Year	Event	Race winner	Car make	Avg. speed	Start pos.	Car owner	Pole winner	Pole speed	POLE WINNERS		RACE WINNERS	
2006	Ford 400	G. Biffle	Ford	125.375	22	Jack Roush	K. Kahne	178.259	Kurt Busch	2	Greg Biffle	3
2005	Ford 400	G. Biffle	Ford	131.431	7	Jack Roush	C. Edwards	176.051	Bill Elliott	1	Tony Stewart	2
2004	Ford 400	G. Biffle	Ford	105.623	2	Jack Roush	Ku. Busch	179.319	Carl Edwards	1	Kurt Busch	1
2003	Ford 400	B. Labonte	Chevrolet	116.868	2	Joe Gibbs	J. McMurray	181.111	David Green	1	Bill Elliott	1
2002	Ford 400	Ku. Busch	Ford	116.462	1	Jack Roush	Ku. Busch	154.365	Kasey Kahne	1	Bobby Labonte	1
2001	Pennzoil Freedom 400	B. Elliott	Dodge	117.449	1	Ray Evernham	B. Elliott	155.226	Jamie McMurray	1		
2000	Pennzoil 400	T. Stewart	Pontiac	127.480	13	Joe Gibbs	S. Park	156.440	Steve Park	1		
1999	Pennzoil 400	T. Stewart	Pontiac	140.335	7	Joe Gibbs	D. Green	155.759				

>> NASCAR BUSCH SERIES <<

YEAR BY YEAR WINNERS

Year	Event	Race winner	Car make	Avg. speed	Start pos.	Pole winner	Pole speed	POLE WINNERS		RACE WINNERS	
2006	Ford 300	M. Kenseth	Ford	126.523	5	K. Harvick	174.272	Jeff Green	2	Joe Nemechek	3
2005	Ford 300	R. Newman	Dodge	124.410	1	R. Newman	174.548	Casey Atwood	1	Jeff Burton	1
2004	Ford 300	K. Harvick	Chevrolet	110.482	12	C. Mears	177.936	Greg Biffle	1	Jeff Gordon	1
2003	Ford 300	K. Kahne	Ford	121.376	3	G. Biffle	177.416	Bobby Hamilton Jr.	1	Kevin Harvick	1
2002	Ford 300	S. Wimmer	Pontiac	123.542	26	J. Green	152.031	Kevin Harvick	1	Dale Jarrett	1
2001	GNC Live Well 300	J. Nemechek	Chevrolet	132.191	20	J. Green	150.939	Bobby Labonte	1	Kasey Kahne	1
2000	Miami 300	J. Gordon	Chevrolet	125.450	6	B. Hamilton Jr.	151.490	Mike McLaughlin	1	Matt Kenseth	1
1999	Hotwheels.com 300	J. Nemechek	Chevrolet	124.596	12	H. Stricklin	149.456	Casey Mears	1	Kevin Lepage	1
1998	Jiffy Lube 300	J. Burton	Ford	129.605	23	C. Atwood	148.262	Joe Nemechek	1	Ryan Newman	1
1997	Jiffy Lube 300	J. Nemechek	Chevrolet	112.900	3	M. McLaughlin	147.771	Ryan Newman	1	Scott Wimmer	1
1996	Jiffy Lube 300	K. Lepage	Chevrolet	119.158	10	B. Labonte	139.074	Hut Stricklin	1		
1995	Jiffy Lube 300	D. Jarrett	Ford	92.229	26	J. Nemechek	134.628				

QUALIFYING RECORD: Casey Mears, Dodge; 177.936 mph (30.348), November 18, 2004
RACE RECORD: Joe Nemechek, Chevrolet; 132.191 mph (2:16:10), November 11, 2001

>> NASCAR CRAFTSMAN TRUCK SERIES <<

YEAR BY YEAR WINNERS

Year	Event	Race winner	Car make	Avg. speed	Start pos.	Pole winner	Pole speed	POLE WINNERS		RACE WINNERS	
2006	Ford 200	M. Martin	Ford	126.019	6	M. Skinner	171.856	David Reutimann	2	Todd Bodine	1
2005	Ford 200	T. Bodine	Toyota	119.920	9	D. Reutimann	173.116	Joe Ruttman	2	Rick Crawford	1
2004	Ford 200	K. Kahne	Dodge	114.930	13	D. Reutimann	171.255	Mike Bliss	1	Bobby Hamilton	1
2003	Ford 200	B. Hamilton	Dodge	120.439	1	B. Hamilton	169.252	Geoffrey Bodine	1	Ron Hornaday Jr.	1
2002	Ford 200	R. Hornaday Jr.	Chevrolet	133.260	5	M. Bliss	147.111	Bobby Hamilton	1	Andy Houston	1
2001	Fla. Dodge Dealers 400	T. Musgrave	Dodge	118.176	3	S. Riggs	146.017	Scott Riggs	1	Kenny Irwin	1
2000	Fla. Dodge Dealers 400	A. Houston	Chevrolet	129.755	3	J. Ruttman	146.727	Mike Skinner	1	Kasey Kahne	1
1999	Fla. Dodge Dealers 400	M. Wallace	Ford	109.813	10	R. Tolsma	149.813	Jack Sprague	1	Mark Martin	1
1998	Fla. Dodge Dealers 400	R. Crawford	Ford	114.475	12	J. Sprague	149.283	Randy Tolsma	1	Ted Musgrave	1
1997	Fla. Dodge Dealers 400	K. Irwin	Ford	98.565	5	J. Ruttman	140.221			Dave Rezendes	1
1996	Fla. Dodge Dealers 400	D. Rezendes	Ford	102.000	10	G. Bodine	135.598			Mike Wallace	1

QUALIFYING RECORD: David Reutimann, Toyota; 173.116 mph (31.193 seconds), November 20, 2005
RACE RECORD: Ron Hornaday Jr., Chevrolet; 133.260 mph (1:30:30), November 15, 2002

>>INDIANAPOLIS MOTOR SPEEDWAY<<

TRACK FACTS >>> >>> **Location:** Indianapolis >>> >>> **Owner:** Hulman-George Family >>> >>> **Track length:** 2.5 miles

>>> >>> **Grandstand seating:** 250,000 >>> >>> **Tickets:** (800) 822-4639 >>> >>> **Website:** www.brickyard400.com >>>

>>NASCAR NEXTEL CUP SERIES<<

>>TRACK RECORDS

Most wins: 4—Jeff Gordon; **Most top fives:** 7—Jeff Gordon; **Most top 10s:** 10—Jeff Gordon; **Oldest winner:** Bill Elliott, 46 years, 9 months, 27 days, August 4, 2002; **Youngest winner:** Jeff Gordon, 23 years, 2 days, August 6, 1994; **Most lead changes:** 21—August 6, 1994; **Fewest lead changes:** 9—Twice, most recently, August 8, 2004; **Most leaders:** 13—Twice, most recently, August 3, 1996; **Fewest leaders:** 5—August 5, 2000; **Most cautions:** 13—August 8, 2004; **Fewest cautions:** 1—August 5, 1995; **Most caution laps:** 47—August 8, 2004; **Fewest caution laps:** 4—August 5, 1995; **Most on the lead lap:** 35—August 6, 2006; **Fewest on the lead lap:** 14—August 5, 2000; **Most running at the finish:** 39—Twice, most recently, August 5, 2000; **Fewest running at the finish:** 27—August 8, 2004; **Most laps led by a race winner:** 124—Jeff Gordon, August 8, 2004; **Fewest laps led by a race winner:** 11—Dale Jarrett, August 3, 1996; **Closest margin of victory:** 0.183 seconds—Ricky Rudd defeated Bobby Labonte, August 2, 1997

>>QUALIFYING AND RACE RECORDS

QUALIFYING: Casey Mears, Dodge, 186.293 mph (48.311 seconds), August 7, 2004
RACE: Bobby Labonte, Pontiac, 155.912 mph (2:33:56), August 5, 2000

9° Banking in Turns
INDIANA
Indianapolis

First NASCAR NEXTEL Cup Series race:
August 6, 1994 (Jeff Gordon, winner)
Banking on straights: None
Length of front stretch: 3,300 feet
Length of back stretch: 3,300 feet
Length of short straightaways: 660 feet

2007 SCHEDULE

NASCAR NEXTEL Cup Series
Event: Allstate 400 at the Brickyard
Race: No. 20 of 36
Date: July 29 • **TV:** ESPN • **Radio:** IMS
Race name subject to change

YEAR BY YEAR WINNERS

Year	Event	Race winner	Car make	Avg. speed	Start pos.	Car owner	Pole winner	Pole speed
2006	Allstate 400	Ji. Johnson	Chevrolet	137.182	5	Rick Hendrick	J. Burton	182.778
2005	Allstate 400	T. Stewart	Chevrolet	118.782	22	Joe Gibbs	E. Sadler	184.116
2004	Brickyard 400	J. Gordon	Chevrolet	115.037	11	Rick Hendrick	C. Mears	186.293
2003	Brickyard 400	K. Harvick	Chevrolet	134.544	1	Richard Childress	K. Harvick	184.343
2002	Brickyard 400	B. Elliott	Dodge	125.033	2	Ray Evernham	T. Stewart	182.960
2001	Brickyard 400	J. Gordon	Chevrolet	130.790	27	Rick Hendrick	J. Spencer	179.666
2000	Brickyard 400	B. Labonte	Pontiac	155.912	3	Joe Gibbs	R. Rudd	181.068
1999	Brickyard 400	D. Jarrett	Ford	148.194	4	Robert Yates	J. Gordon	179.612
1998	Brickyard 400	J. Gordon	Chevrolet	126.770	3	Rick Hendrick	E Irvan	179.394
1997	Brickyard 400	R. Rudd	Ford	130.814	7	Ricky Rudd	E. Irvan	177.736
1996	Brickyard 400	D. Jarrett	Ford	139.508	24	Robert Yates	J. Gordon	176.419
1995	Brickyard 400	D. Earnhardt	Chevrolet	155.206	13	Richard Childress	J. Gordon	172.536
1994	Brickyard 400	J. Gordon	Chevrolet	131.977	3	Rick Hendrick	R. Mast	172.414

POLE WINNERS		RACE WINNERS	
Jeff Gordon	3	Jeff Gordon	4
Ernie Irvan	2	Dale Jarrett	2
Jeff Burton	1	Dale Earnhardt	1
Kevin Harvick	1	Bill Elliott	1
Rick Mast	1	Kevin Harvick	1
Casey Mears	1	Jimmie Johnson	1
Ricky Rudd	1	Bobby Labonte	1
Elliott Sadler	1	Ricky Rudd	1
Jimmy Spencer	1	Tony Stewart	1
Tony Stewart	1		

Johnson

>>INFINEON RACEWAY<<

TRACK FACTS >>> >>> **Location:** Sonoma, Calif. >>> >>> **Owner:** Speedway Motorsports, Inc. >>> >>> **Track length:** 1.99 miles

>>> >>> **Estimated capacity:** 102,000 >>> >>> **Tickets:** (800) 870-7223 >>> >>> **Website:** www.infineonraceway.com

>>NASCAR NEXTEL CUP SERIES<<

>>TRACK RECORDS

Most wins: 5—Jeff Gordon; **Most top fives:** 10—Ricky Rudd; **Most top 10s:** 13—Mark Martin; **Oldest winner:** Ricky Rudd, 45 years, 9 months, 11 days, June 23, 2002; **Youngest winner:** Jeff Gordon, 26 years, 10 months, 24 days, June 28, 1998; **Most lead changes:** 10—four times, most recently, June 23, 2002; **Fewest lead changes:** 3—June 11, 1989; **Most Leaders:** 9—Twice, most recently, June 23, 2002; **Fewest leaders:** 3—June 11, 1989; **Most cautions:** 9—June 10, 1990; **Fewest cautions:** 3—four times, most recently, June 23, 2002; **Most caution laps:** 26—June 27, 1999; **Fewest caution laps:** 7—June 7, 1992; **Most on the lead lap:** 34—June 26, 2005; **Fewest on the lead lap:** 14—twice, most recently, May 16, 1993; **Most running at the finish:** 42—Twice, most recently, June 26, 2005; **Fewest running at the finish:** 32— May 16, 1993; **Most laps led by a race winner:** 92—Jeff Gordon, June 27, 2004; **Fewest laps led by a race winner:** 2—Davey Allison June 9, 1991; **Closest margin of victory:** 0.05 seconds—Ricky Rudd defeated Rusty Wallace, June 11, 1989

>>QUALIFYING AND RACE RECORDS

QUALIFYING: Jeff Gordon, Chevrolet; 94.325 mph (75.950 seconds), June 26, 2005
RACE: Ricky Rudd, Ford; 81.007 mph (2:42:08), June 23, 2002
Note: Record for current track configuration

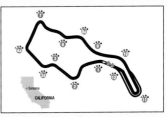

First NASCAR NEXTEL Cup Series race:
June 11, 1989 (Ricky Rudd, winner)
Banking: Varies
The chute: 890 feet

2007 SCHEDULE

NASCAR NEXTEL Cup Series
Event: Dodge/Save Mart 350
Race: No. 16 of 36
Date: June 25 • **TV:** FOX • **Radio:** PRN
Race name subject to change

YEAR BY YEAR WINNERS

Year	Event	Race winner	Car make	Avg. speed	Start pos.	Car owner	Pole winner	Pole speed
2006	Dodge/Save Mart 350	J. Gordon	Chevrolet	73.953	11	Rick Hendrick	Ku. Busch	93.055
2005	Dodge/Save Mart 350	T. Stewart	Chevrolet	72.845	7	Joe Gibbs	J. Gordon	94.325
2004	Dodge/Save Mart 350	J. Gordon	Chevrolet	77.456	1	Rick Hendrick	J. Gordon	94.303
2003	Dodge/Save Mart 350	R. Gordon	Chevrolet	73.821	2	Richard Childress	B. Said	93.620
2002	Dodge/Save Mart 350 (c)	R. Rudd	Ford	81.007	7	Robert Yates	T. Stewart	93.476
2001	Dodge/Save Mart 350	T. Stewart	Pontiac	75.889	3	Joe Gibbs	J. Gordon	93.699
2000	Save Mart/Kragen 350	J. Gordon	Chevrolet	78.789	5	Rick Hendrick	R. Wallace	99.309
1999	Save Mart 350 (a)	J. Gordon	Chevrolet	70.378	1	Rick Hendrick	J. Gordon	98.519
1998	Save Mart 350	J. Gordon	Chevrolet	72.387	1	Rick Hendrick	J. Gordon	98.711
1997	Save Mart 300	M. Martin	Ford	75.788	1	Jack Roush	M. Martin	92.807
1996	Save Mart 300	R. Wallace	Ford	77.673	7	Roger Penske	T. Labonte	92.524
1995	Save Mart 300	D. Earnhardt	Chevrolet	70.681	4	Richard Childress	R. Rudd	92.132
1994	Save Mart 300	E. Irvan	Ford	77.458	1	Robert Yates	E. Irvan	91.514
1993	Save Mart 300	G. Bodine	Ford	77.013	3	Bud Moore	D. Earnhardt	91.838
1992	Save Mart 300	E. Irvan	Chevrolet	81.413	2	Larry McClure	R. Rudd	90.985
1991	Banquet 300	Da. Allison	Ford	72.970	13	Robert Yates	R. Rudd	90.634
1990	Banquet 300	R. Wallace	Pontiac	69.245	11	Raymond Beadle	R. Rudd	99.743
1989	Banquet 300	R. Rudd	Buick	76.088	4	Kenny Bernstein	R. Wallace	90.041

POLE WINNERS		RACE WINNERS	
Jeff Gordon	5	Jeff Gordon	5
Ricky Rudd	4	Ernie Irvan	2
Rusty Wallace	2	Ricky Rudd	2
Kurt Busch	1	Tony Stewart	2
Dale Earnhardt	1	Rusty Wallace	2
Ernie Irvan	1	Davey Allison	1
Terry Labonte	1	Geoffrey Bodine	1
Mark Martin	1	Dale Earnhardt	1
Boris Said	1	Robby Gordon	1
Tony Stewart	1	Mark Martin	1

KEY (a) Track reconfigured from 2.52 miles to 1.949 miles. (b) Track reconfigured from 1.949 miles to 2 miles (c) Track reconfigured from 2 miles to 1.99 miles.

>>KANSAS SPEEDWAY<<

TRACK FACTS >>> >>> **Location:** Kansas City, Kan. >>> >>> **Owner:** International Speedway Corp. >>> >>> **Track length:** 1.5 miles

>>> >>> **Grandstand seating:** 81,687 >>> >>> **Tickets:** (913) 328-7223 >>> >>> **Website:** www.kansasspeedway.com >>>

>>NASCAR NEXTEL CUP SERIES<<

>>TRACK RECORDS

Most wins: 2—Jeff Gordon; **Most top fives:** 3—Jeff Gordon, Ryan Newman, Tony Stewart; **Most top 10s:** 5—Tony Stewart; **Oldest winner:** Mark Martin, 46 years, 9 months, October 9, 2005; **Youngest winner:** Ryan Newman, 25 years, 9 months, 27 days, October 5, 2003; **Most lead changes:** 24—October 10, 2004; **Fewest lead changes:** 13—September 29, 2002; **Most leaders:** 13—October 1, 2006; **Fewest leaders:** 10—September 29, 2002; **Most cautions:** 13—September 30, 2001; **Fewest cautions:** 7—October 9, 2005; **Most caution laps:** 70—September 30, 2001; **Fewest caution laps:** 28—October 9, 2005; **Most on the lead lap:** 25—October 9, 2005; **Fewest on the lead lap:** 9—September 29, 2002; **Most running at the finish:** 38—Twice, most recently, October 1, 2006; **Fewest running at the finish:** 27—September 29, 2002; **Most laps led by a race winner:** 139—Mark Martin, October 9, 2005; **Fewest laps led by a race winner:** 5—Tony Stewart, October 1, 2006; **Closest margin of victory:** 0.081 seconds—Joe Nemechek defeated Ricky Rudd, October 10, 2004

>>QUALIFYING AND RACE RECORDS

QUALIFYING: Matt Kenseth; 180.856 mph (29.858 seconds), October 8, 2005
RACE: Mark Martin, Ford; 137.774 mph (2:54:25), October 9, 2005

15° Banking in Turns — Kansas City • KANSAS

First NASCAR NEXTEL Cup Series race:
September 30, 2001 (Jeff Gordon, winner)
Banking on front stretch: 10.4 degrees
Banking on back stretch: 5 degrees
Length of front stretch: 2,685 feet
Length of back stretch: 2,207 feet

2007 SCHEDULE

NASCAR NEXTEL Cup Series
Event: Banquet 400
Race: No. 29 of 36
Date: September 30 • **TV:** ABC • **Radio:** MRN

NASCAR Busch Series
Event: Yellow Transportation 300
Race: No. 30 of 35 • **Date:** September 29
TV: ESPN2 • **Radio:** MRN

NASCAR Craftsman Truck Series
Event: O'Reilly Auto Parts 250
Race: No. 5 of 25
Date: April 28 • **TV:** SPEED • **Radio:** MRN
Race names subject to change

YEAR BY YEAR WINNERS

Year	Event	Race winner	Car make	Avg. speed	Start pos.	Car owner	Pole winner	Pole speed
2006	Banquet 400	T. Stewart	Chevrolet	121.753	21	J. Gibbs	K. Kahne	178.377
2005	Banquet 400	M. Martin	Ford	137.774	19	J. Roush	M. Kenseth	180.856
2004	Banquet 400	J. Nemechek	Chevrolet	128.058	1	N. Bowers	J. Nemechek	180.156
2003	Banquet 400	R. Newman	Dodge	121.630	11	R. Penske	Ji. Johnson	180.373
2002	Protection One 400	J. Gordon	Chevrolet	119.394	10	R. Hendrick	D. Earnhardt Jr.	177.924
2001	Protection One 400	J. Gordon	Chevrolet	110.576	2	R. Hendrick	J. Leffler	176.499

POLE WINNERS		RACE WINNERS	
Dale Earnhardt Jr.	1	Jeff Gordon	2
Jimmie Johnson	1	Mark Martin	1
Kasey Kahne	1	Joe Nemechek	1
Matt Kenseth	1	Ryan Newman	1
Jason Leffler	1	Tony Stewart	1
Joe Nemechek	1		

>> NASCAR BUSCH SERIES <<

Harvick

YEAR BY YEAR WINNERS

Year	Event	Race winner	Car make	Avg. speed	Start pos.	Pole winner	Pole speed
2006	Yellow Transport. 300	K. Harvick	Chevrolet	111.559	7	M. Kenseth	173.723
2005	United Way 300	K. Kahne	Dodge	117.328	4	M. Truex Jr.	178.938
2004	Mr. Goodcents 300	J. Nemechek	Chevrolet	117.504	19	P. Menard	176.062
2003	Mr. Goodcents 300	D. Green	Pontiac	113.148	3	M. Waltrip	178.365
2002	Mr. Goodcents 300	J. Burton	Ford	120.509	2	M. Waltrip	174.831
2001	Mr. Goodcents 300	J. Green	Ford	129.125	12	K. Lepage	174.210

POLE WINNERS		RACE WINNERS	
Michael Waltrip	2	Jeff Burton	1
Matt Kenseth	1	David Green	1
Kevin Lepage	1	Jeff Green	1
Paul Menard	1	Kevin Harvick	1
Martin Truex Jr.	1	Kasey Kahne	1
		Joe Nemechek	1

QUALIFYING RECORD: Michael Waltrip, Chevrolet; 178.365 mph (30.275), October 4, 2003
RACE RECORD: Jeff Green, Ford; 129.125 mph (2:19:24), September 29, 2001

>> NASCAR CRAFTSMAN TRUCK SERIES <<

Cook

YEAR BY YEAR WINNERS

Year	Event	Race winner	Car make	Avg. speed	Start pos.	Pole winner	Pole speed
2006	O'Reilly Auto Parts 250	T. Cook	Ford	111.581	5	M. Skinner	171.772
2005	O'Reilly Auto Parts 250	T. Bodine	Toyota	117.346	10	B. Lester	173.633
2004	O'Reilly Auto Parts 250	C. Edwards	Ford	105.994	2	None—conditions	
2003	O'Reilly Auto Parts 250	J. Wood	Ford	114.253	3	C. Chaffin	166.323
2002	O'Reilly Auto Parts 250	M. Bliss	Chevrolet	121.487	4	J. Leffler	165.812
2001	O'Reilly Auto Parts 250	R. Hendrick	Chevrolet	125.094	2	D. Setzer	162.411

POLE WINNERS		RACE WINNERS	
Chad Chaffin	1	Mike Bliss	1
Jason Leffler	1	Todd Bodine	1
Bill Lester	1	Terry Cook	1
Dennis Setzer	1	Carl Edwards	1
Mike Skinner	1	Ricky Hendrick	1
		Jon Wood	1

QUALIFYING RECORD: Bill Lester, Toyota; 173.633 mph (31.100 seconds), July 2, 2005
RACE RECORD: Ricky Hendrick, Chevrolet; 125.094 mph (2:00:09), July 7, 2001

>> LAS VEGAS MOTOR SPEEDWAY <<

TRACK FACTS >>> >>> **Location:** Las Vegas >>> >>> **Owner:** Speedway Motorsports, Inc. >>> >>> **Track length:** 1.5 miles

>>> >>> **Grandstand seating:** 142,000 >>> >>> **Tickets:** (702) 644-4444 >>> >>> **Website:** www.lvms.com >>> >>>

>> NASCAR NEXTEL CUP SERIES <<

>> TRACK RECORDS

Most wins: 2—Jeff Burton, Jimmie Johnson and Matt Kenseth; **Most top fives:** 4—Jeff Gordon, Mark Martin and Tony Stewart; **Most top 10s:** 6—Jeff Burton and Mark Martin; **Oldest winner:** Sterling Marlin, 44 years, 8 months, 1 day, March 3, 2002; **Youngest winner:** Jimmie Johnson, 29 years, 6 months, 24 days, March 13, 2005; **Most lead changes:** 25—Twice, most recently, March 13, 2005; **Fewest lead changes:** 13—March 5, 2000; **Most leaders:** 13—Twice, most recently, March 3, 2002; **Fewest leaders:** 7—March 5, 2000; **Most cautions:** 10—March 13, 2005; **Fewest cautions:** 2—Twice, most recently, March 5, 2000; **Most caution laps:** 46—March 13, 2005; **Fewest caution laps:** 9—March 1, 1998; **Most on the lead lap:** 30—March 12, 2006; **Fewest on the lead lap:** 10—Twice, most recently, March 7, 1999; **Most running at the finish:** 42—March 5, 2000; **Fewest running at the finish:** 33—March 7, 2004; **Most laps led by a race winner:** 123—Matt Kenseth, March 7, 2004; **Fewest laps led by a race winner:** 1—Jimmie Johnson, March 12, 2006; **Closest margin of victory:** 1.045 seconds—Jimmie Johnson defeated Matt Kenseth, March 12, 2006

First NASCAR NEXTEL Cup Series race:
March 1, 1998 (Mark Martin, winner)
Banking on straights: 9 degrees
Length of front stretch: 2,275 feet
Length of back stretch: 1,572 feet

>>LAS VEGAS MOTOR SPEEDWAY<<

>>QUALIFYING AND RACE RECORDS

QUALIFYING: Kasey Kahne, Dodge, 174.904 mph (30.874 seconds), March 5, 2003
RACE: Mark Martin, Ford, 146.554 mph (2:43:58), March 1, 1998

2007 SCHEDULE

NASCAR NEXTEL Cup Series
Event: UAW-DaimlerChrysler 400
Race: No. 3 of 36
Date: March 12 • **TV:** FOX • **Radio:** PRN

NASCAR Busch Series
Event: Sam's Town 300
Race: No. 4 of 35 • **Date:** March 10
TV: ESPN2 • **Radio:** PRN

NASCAR Craftsman Truck Series
Event: Smith's Las Vegas 350
Race: No. 19 of 25
Date: September 22 • **TV:** SPEED • **Radio:** MRN
Race names subject to change

YEAR BY YEAR WINNERS

Year	Event	Race winner	Car make	Avg. speed	Start pos.	Car owner	Pole winner	Pole speed
2006	UAW-DaimlerChrysler 400	Ji. Johnson	Chevrolet	133.358	3	Rick Hendrick	G. Biffle	172.403
2005	UAW-DaimlerChrysler 400	Ji. Johnson	Chevrolet	121.038	9	Rick Hendrick	R. Newman	173.745
2004	UAW-DaimlerChrysler 400	M. Kenseth	Ford	128.790	25	Jack Roush	K. Kahne	174.904
2003	UAW-DaimlerChrysler 400	M. Kenseth	Ford	132.934	17	Jack Roush	B. Labonte	173.016
2002	UAW-DaimlerChrysler 400	S. Marlin	Dodge	136.754	24	Chip Ganassi	T. Bodine	172.850
2001	UAW-DaimlerChrysler 400	J. Gordon	Chevrolet	135.546	24	Rick Hendrick	D. Jarrett	172.106
2000	CarsDirect.com 400 (a)	J. Burton	Ford	119.982	11	Jack Roush	R. Rudd	172.563
1999	Las Vegas 400	J. Burton	Ford	137.537	19	Jack Roush	B. Labonte	170.643
1998	Las Vegas 400	M. Martin	Ford	146.554	7	Jack Roush	D. Jarrett	168.224

KEY (a) Race shortened by rain.

POLE WINNERS		RACE WINNERS	
Dale Jarrett	2	Jeff Burton	2
Bobby Labonte	2	Jimmie Johnson	2
Greg Biffle	1	Matt Kenseth	2
Todd Bodine	1	Jeff Gordon	1
Kasey Kahne	1	Sterling Marlin	1
Ryan Newman	1	Mark Martin	1
Ricky Rudd	1		

>>NASCAR BUSCH SERIES<<

YEAR BY YEAR WINNERS

Year	Event	Race winner	Car make	Avg. speed	Start pos.	Pole winner	Pole speed
2006	Sam's Town 300	K. Kahne	Dodge	125.158	10	M. Kenseth	169.827
2005	Sam's Town 300	M. Martin	Ford	122.158	25	C. Edwards	170.951
2004	Sam's Town 300	K. Harvick	Chevrolet	122.172	11	M. Bliss	171.238
2003	Sam's Town 300	J. Nemechek	Chevrolet	115.582	29	None—conditions	
2002	Sam's Town 300	J. Burton	Ford	123.796	1	J. Burton	169.168
2001	Sam's Town 300	T. Bodine	Chevrolet	125.625	7	M. Kenseth	169.385
2000	Sam's Town 300	J. Burton	Ford	135.118	7	H. Parker Jr.	166.328
1999	Sam's Town 300	M. Martin	Ford	134.370	1	M. Martin	165.715
1998	Sam's Town 300	J. Spencer	Chevrolet	114.129	7	M. Martin	162.577
1997	Las Vegas 300	J. Green	Chevrolet	114.153	1	J. Green	159.311

POLE WINNERS		RACE WINNERS	
Matt Kenseth	2	Jeff Burton	2
Mark Martin	2	Mark Martin	2
Mike Bliss	1	Todd Bodine	1
Jeff Burton	1	Jeff Green	1
Carl Edwards	1	Kevin Harvick	1
Jeff Green	1	Kasey Kahne	1
Hank Parker Jr.	1	Joe Nemechek	1
		Jimmy Spencer	1

QUALIFYING RECORD: Mike Bliss, Chevrolet; 171.238 mph (31.535 seconds), March 5, 2004
RACE RECORD: Jeff Burton, Ford; 135.118 mph (2:13:13), March 4, 2000

Kahne

>>NASCAR CRAFTSMAN TRUCK SERIES<<

YEAR BY YEAR WINNERS

Year	Event	Race winner	Car make	Avg. speed	Start pos.	Pole winner	Pole speed
2006	Smith's Las Vegas 350	M. Skinner	Toyota	117.812	1	M. Skinner	178.065
2005	Las Vegas 350	T. Bodine	Toyota	126.238	3	M. Skinner	165.258
2004	Las Vegas 350	S. Hmiel	Chevrolet	123.865	21	M. Skinner	165.320
2003	Las Vegas 350	B. Gaughan	Dodge	123.826	1	B. Gaughan	162.152
2002	Las Vegas 350	D. Starr	Chevrolet	135.394	1	D. Starr	163.112
2001	The Orleans 350	T. Musgrave	Dodge	128.091	10	J. Sprague	161.803
1999	The Orleans 250	G. Biffle	Ford	127.229	5	S. Compton	161.796
1998	Sam's Town 250	J. Sprague	Chevrolet	130.801	1	J. Sprague	161.749
1997	Carquest Auto Parts 420K	J. Ruttman	Ford	125.849	8	J. Sprague	161.310
1996	Carquest Auto Parts 420K	J. Sprague	Chevrolet	120.782	3	B. Reffner	157.909

POLE WINNERS		RACE WINNERS	
Mike Skinner	3	Jack Sprague	2
Jack Sprague	3	Greg Biffle	1
Stacy Compton	1	Todd Bodine	1
Brendan Gaughan	1	Brendan Gaughan	1
Bryan Reffner	1	Shane Hmiel	1
David Starr	1	Ted Musgrave	1
		Joe Ruttman	1
		Mike Skinner	1
		David Starr	1

QUALIFYING RECORD: Mike Skinner, Toyota; 178.065 mph (30.326 seconds), September 23, 2006
RACE RECORD: David Starr, Chevrolet; 135.394 mph (1:37:03), October 13, 2002

Bodine

Johnson

>> LOWE'S MOTOR SPEEDWAY <<

TRACK FACTS >>> >>> **Location:** Concord, N.C. >>> >>> **Owner:** Speedway Motorsports, Inc. >>> >>> **Track length:** 1.5 miles

>>> >>> **Grandstand seating:** 165,000 >>> >>> **Tickets:** (704) 455-3267 >>> >>> **Website:** www.lowesmotorspeedway.com

>> NASCAR NEXTEL CUP SERIES <<

>> TRACK RECORDS

Most wins: 6—Bobby Allison and Darrell Waltrip; **Most top fives:** 23—Bobby Allison and Richard Petty; **Most top 10s:** 31—Richard Petty; **Oldest winner:** Cale Yarborough, 46 years, 6 months, 9 days, October 6, 1985; **Youngest winner:** Jeff Gordon, 22 years, 9 months, 25 days, May 29, 1994; **Most lead changes:** 59—May 27, 1979; **Fewest lead changes:** 2—May 21, 1961; **Most leaders:** 21—May 29, 2005; **Fewest leaders:** 3—May 21, 1961; **Most laps led in a 400-mile race:** 209—Junior Johnson, October 13, 1963; **Most laps led in a 500-mile race:** 328—Ernie Irvan, October 10, 1993; **Most laps led in a 600-mile race:** 335—Jim Paschal, May 28, 1967; **Most cautions:** 22—May 29, 2005; **Fewest cautions:** 0—May 21, 1961; **Most caution laps:** 113—May 25, 1980; **Fewest caution laps:** 0—May 21, 1961; **Most on the lead lap:** 24—October 15, 2005; **Fewest on the lead lap:** 1—14 times, most recently, May 24, 1987; **Most running at the finish:** 39—October 11, 2003; **Fewest running at the finish:** 10—May 21, 1961; **Most laps led by a race winner:** 335—Jim Paschal, May 28, 1967; **Fewest laps led by a race winner:** 3—Joe Weatherly, May 21, 1961; **Closest margin of victory:** 0.027 seconds—Jimmie Johnson defeated Bobby Labonte, May 29, 2005

>> QUALIFYING AND RACE RECORDS

QUALIFYING: Elliott Sadler, 193.216 mph (27.948 seconds), October 15, 2005
RACE: **Track:** Jeff Gordon, Chevrolet, 160.306 mph (3:07:31), October 11, 1999; **400 miles:** Fred Lorenzen, Ford; 134.559 mph (2:58:35), October 18, 1964; **500 miles:** Jeff Gordon, Chevrolet; 160.306 mph (3:07:31), October 11, 1999; **600 miles:** Bobby Labonte, Chevrolet; 151.952 mph (3:56:55), May 28, 1995

First NASCAR NEXTEL Cup Series race:
June 19, 1960 (Joe Lee Johnson, winner)
Banking on straights: 5 degrees
Length of front stretch: 1,980 feet
Length of back stretch: 1,500 feet

2007 SCHEDULE

NASCAR NEXTEL Cup Series
Event: NASCAR NEXTEL All-Star Challenge*
Date: May 19
TV: SPEED • **Radio:** MRN   *Non-points race

Event: Coca-Cola 600
Race: No. 12 of 36
Date: May 27 • **TV:** FOX • **Radio:** PRN

Event: Bank of America 500
Race: No. 31 of 36
Date: October 13 • **TV:** ABC • **Radio:** PRN

NASCAR Busch Series
Event: CarQuest Auto Parts 300
Race: No. 13 of 35 • **Date:** May 26
TV: ESPN2 • **Radio:** PRN

Event: Dollar General 300
Race: No. 31 of 35 • **Date:** October 12
TV: ESPN2 • **Radio:** PRN

NASCAR Craftsman Truck Series
Event: Quaker Steak & Lube 200
Race: No. 6 of 25 • **Date:** May 18 • **TV:** SPEED • **Radio:** MRN   *Race names subject to change*

YEAR BY YEAR WINNERS

Year	Event	Race winner	Car make	Avg. speed	Start pos.	Car owner	Pole winner	Pole speed
2006	Bank of America 500	K. Kahne	Dodge	132.142	2	Ray Evernham	S. Riggs	191.469
	Coca-Cola 600	K. Kahne	Dodge	128.840	9	Ray Evernham	S. Riggs	187.865
2005	UAW-GM Quality 500	Ji. Johnson	Chevrolet	120.334	3	Rick Hendrick	E. Sadler	193.216
	Coca-Cola 600	Ji. Johnson	Chevrolet	114.698	5	Rick Hendrick	R. Newman	192.988
2004	UAW-GM Quality 500	Ji. Johnson	Chevrolet	130.214	9	Rick Hendrick	R. Newman	188.877
	Coca-Cola 600	Ji. Johnson	Chevrolet	142.763	1	Rick Hendrick	Ji. Johnson	187.052
2003	UAW-GM Quality 500 (c)	T. Stewart	Chevrolet	142.871	6	Joe Gibbs	R. Newman	186.657
	Coca-Cola 600	Ji. Johnson	Chevrolet	126.198	37	Rick Hendrick	R. Newman	185.312
2002	UAW-GM Quality 500	J. McMurray	Dodge	141.481	5	Chip Ganassi	None—conditions	
	Coca-Cola 600	M. Martin	Ford	137.729	25	Jack Roush	J. Johnson	186.464
2001	UAW-GM Quality 500	S. Marlin	Dodge	139.006	13	Chip Ganassi	J. Spencer	185.147
	Coca-Cola 600	J. Burton	Ford	138.107	18	Jack Roush	R. Newman	185.217
2000	UAW-GM Quality 500	B. Labonte	Pontiac	133.630	2	Joe Gibbs	J. Gordon	185.561
	Coca-Cola 600	M. Kenseth	Ford	142.640	21	Jack Roush	D. Earnhardt Jr.	186.034
1999	UAW-GM Quality 500	J. Gordon	Chevrolet	160.306	22	Rick Hendrick	B. Labonte	185.682
	Coca-Cola 600	J. Burton	Ford	151.367	2	Jack Roush	B. Labonte	185.230

>>LOWE'S MOTOR SPEEDWAY<<

YEAR BY YEAR WINNERS continued

Year	Event	Race winner	Car make	Avg. speed	Start pos.	Car owner	Pole winner	Pole speed
1998	UAW-GM Quality 500	M. Martin	Ford	123.188	2	Jack Roush	D. Cope	181.690
	Coca-Cola 600	J. Gordon	Chevrolet	136.424	1	Rick Hendrick	J. Gordon	182.976
1997	UAW-GM Quality 500	D. Jarrett	Ford	144.323	5	Robert Yates	G. Bodine	184.256
	Coca-Cola 600 (a)	J. Gordon	Chevrolet	136.745	1	Rick Hendrick	J. Gordon	184.300
1996	UAW-GM Quality 500	T. Labonte	Chevrolet	143.143	16	Rick Hendrick	B. Labonte	184.068
	Coca-Cola 600	D. Jarrett	Ford	147.581	15	Robert Yates	J. Gordon	183.773
1995	UAW-GM Quality 500	M. Martin	Ford	145.358	5	Jack Roush	R. Rudd	180.578
	Coca-Cola 600	B. Labonte	Chevrolet	151.952	2	Joe Gibbs	J. Gordon	183.861
1994	Mello Yello 500	D. Jarrett	Chevrolet	145.922	22	Joe Gibbs	W. Burton	185.759
	Coca-Cola 600	J. Gordon	Chevrolet	139.445	1	Rick Hendrick	J. Gordon	181.439
1993	Mello Yello 500	E. Irvan	Ford	154.537	2	Robert Yates	J. Gordon	177.684
	Coca-Cola 600 (b)	D. Earnhardt	Chevrolet	145.504	14	Richard Childress	K. Schrader	177.352
1992	Mello Yello 500	M. Martin	Ford	153.537	4	Jack Roush	A. Kulwicki	179.027
	Coca-Cola 600	D. Earnhardt	Chevrolet	132.980	13	Richard Childress	B. Elliott	175.479
1991	Mello Yello 500	G. Bodine	Ford	138.984	6	Junior Johnson	M. Martin	176.499
	Coca-Cola 600	Da. Allison	Ford	138.951	10	Robert Yates	M. Martin	174.820
1990	Mello Yello 500	Da. Allison	Ford	137.428	5	Robert Yates	B. Bodine	174.385
	Coca-Cola 600	R. Wallace	Pontiac	137.650	9	Raymond Beadle	K. Schrader	173.963
1989	All Pro 500	K. Schrader	Chevrolet	149.863	2	Rick Hendrick	B. Elliott	174.081
	Coca-Cola 600	D. Waltrip	Chevrolet	144.077	4	Rick Hendrick	A. Kulwicki	173.021
1988	Oakwood 500	R. Wallace	Pontiac	130.677	3	Raymond Beadle	A. Kulwicki	175.896
	Coca-Cola 600	D. Waltrip	Chevrolet	124.460	5	Rick Hendrick	Da. Allison	173.594
1987	Oakwood 500	B. Elliott	Ford	128.443	7	Harry Melling	B. Allison	171.636
	Coca-Cola 600	K. Petty	Ford	131.483	7	Wood Brothers	B. Elliott	170.901
1986	Oakwood 500	D. Earnhardt	Chevrolet	132.403	3	Richard Childress	T. Richmond	167.078
	Coca-Cola 600	D. Earnhardt	Chevrolet	140.406	3	Richard Childress	G. Bodine	164.511
1985	Miller 500	C. Yarborough	Ford	136.761	7	Harry Ranier	H. Gant	166.139
	World 600	D. Waltrip	Chevrolet	141.807	4	Junior Johnson	B. Elliott	164.703
1984	Miller 500	B. Elliott	Ford	146.861	2	Harry Melling	B. Parsons	165.579
	World 600	B. Allison	Buick	129.233	16	DiProspero/Gardner	H. Gant	162.496
1983	Miller 500	R. Petty	Pontiac	139.998	20	Petty Enterprises	T. Richmond	163.073
	World 600	N. Bonnett	Chevrolet	140.707	5	B.Rahilly/B.Mock	Buddy Baker	162.841
1982	National 500	H. Gant	Buick	137.208	1	Hal Needham	H. Gant	164.694
	World 600	N. Bonnett	Ford	130.058	13	Wood Brothers	D. Pearson	162.511
1981	National 500	D. Waltrip	Buick	117.483	1	Junior Johnson	D. Waltrip	162.744
	World 600	B. Allison	Buick	129.326	7	Harry Ranier	N. Bonnett	158.115
1980	National 500	D. Earnhardt	Chevrolet	135.243	4	Rod Osterlund	Buddy Baker	165.634
	World 600	B. Parsons	Chevrolet	119.265	6	M.C. Anderson	C. Yarborough	165.194
1979	NAPA 500	C. Yarborough	Chevrolet	134.266	4	Junior Johnson	N. Bonnett	164.304
	World 600	D. Waltrip	Chevrolet	136.674	3	DiProspero/Gardner	N. Bonnett	160.125
1978	NAPA 500	B. Allison	Ford	141.826	8	Bud Moore	D. Pearson	161.355
	World 600	D. Waltrip	Chevrolet	138.355	17	DiProspero/Gardner	D. Pearson	160.551
1977	NAPA 500	B. Parsons	Chevrolet	142.780	8	L.G. DeWitt	D. Pearson	160.892
	World 600	R. Petty	Dodge	137.676	2	Petty Enterprises	D. Pearson	161.435
1976	National 500	Do. Allison	Chevrolet	141.226	15	Hoss Ellington	D. Pearson	161.223
	World 600	D. Pearson	Mercury	137.352	1	Wood Brothers	D. Pearson	159.132
1975	National 500	R. Petty	Dodge	132.209	9	Petty Enterprises	D. Pearson	161.701
	World 600	R. Petty	Dodge	145.327	3	Petty Enterprises	D. Pearson	159.353
1974	National 500	D. Pearson	Mercury	119.912	1	Wood Brothers	D. Pearson	158.749
	World 600	D. Pearson	Mercury	135.720	1	Wood Brothers	D. Pearson	157.498
1973	National 500	C. Yarborough	Chevrolet	145.240	2	Junior Johnson	D. Pearson	158.315
	World 600	Buddy Baker	Dodge	134.890	1	Nord Krauskopf	Buddy Baker	158.051
1972	National 500	B. Allison	Chevrolet	133.234	4	Junior Johnson	D. Pearson	158.539
	World 600	Buddy Baker	Dodge	142.255	6	Petty Enterprises	B. Allison	158.162
1971	National 500 (a)	B. Allison	Mercury	126.140	3	Holman-Moody	C. Glotzbach	157.085
	World 600	B. Allison	Mercury	140.442	2	Holman-Moody	C. Glotzbach	157.788
1970	National 500	L. Yarbrough	Mercury	123.246	5	Junior Johnson	C. Glotzbach	157.273
	World 600	D. Allison	Ford	129.680	9	Banjo Matthews	B. Isaac	159.277
1969	National 500	D. Allison	Ford	131.271	3	Banjo Matthews	C. Yarborough	162.162
	World 600	L. Yarbrough	Mercury	134.361	2	Junior Johnson	D. Allison	159.296
1968	National 500	C. Glotzbach	Dodge	135.324	1	Cotton Owens	C. Glotzbach	156.060
	World 600 (a)	Buddy Baker	Dodge	104.207	12	Ray Fox	D. Allison	159.223
1967	National 500	Buddy Baker	Dodge	130.317	4	Ray Fox	C. Yarborough	154.872
	World 600	J. Paschal	Plymouth	135.832	10	Tom Friedkin	C. Yarborough	154.385
1966	National 400	L. Yarbrough	Dodge	130.576	17	Jon Thorne	F. Lorenzen	150.533
	World 600	M. Panch	Plymouth	135.042	7	Petty Enterprises	R. Petty	148.637
1965	National 400	F. Lorenzen	Ford	119.117	1	Holman-Moody	F. Lorenzen	147.773
	World 600	F. Lorenzen	Ford	121.772	1	Holman-Moody	F. Lorenzen	145.268
1964	National 400	F. Lorenzen	Ford	134.475	3	Holman-Moody	R. Petty	150.711
	World 600	J. Paschal	Plymouth	125.772	12	Petty Enterprises	J. Pardue	144.346
1963	National 400	Ju. Johnson	Chevrolet	132.105	2	Ray Fox	M. Panch	143.017
	World 600	F. Lorenzen	Ford	132.417	2	Holman-Moody	Jr. Johnson	141.148
1962	National 400	Ju. Johnson	Pontiac	132.085	3	Ray Fox	F. Roberts	140.287
	World 600	N. Stacy	Ford	125.552	18	Holman-Moody	F. Roberts	140.150
1961	National 400	J. Weatherly	Pontiac	119.950	6	Bud Moore	D. Pearson	138.577
	World 600	D. Pearson	Pontiac	111.633	3	Ray Fox	R. Petty	131.611
1960	National 400	S. Thompson	Ford	112.905	3	Wood Brothers	F. Roberts	133.465
	World 600	J.L. Johnson	Chevrolet	107.735	20	Paul McDuffie	F. Roberts	133.904

KEY (a) Race shortened by rain. (b) First year in which first race began at twilight. (c) First year in which second race was held at night.

ALL LOWE'S RACES

POLE WINNERS	
David Pearson	14
Jeff Gordon	7
Ryan Newman	5
Bill Elliott	4
Charlie Glotzbach	4
Fireball Roberts	4
Cale Yarborough	4
Buddy Baker	3
Neil Bonnett	3
Harry Gant	3
Alan Kulwicki	3
Bobby Labonte	3
Fred Lorenzen	3
Richard Petty	3
Bobby Allison	2
Donnie Allison	2
Geoffrey Bodine	2
Jimmie Johnson	2
Mark Martin	2
Tim Richmond	2
Scott Riggs	2
Ken Schrader	2
Davey Allison	1
Brett Bodine	1
Ward Burton	1
Derrike Cope	1
Dale Earnhardt Jr.	1
Bobby Isaac	1
Junior Johnson	1
Marvin Panch	1
Jimmie Pardue	1
Benny Parsons	1
Ricky Rudd	1
Elliott Sadler	1
Jimmie Spencer	1
Darrell Waltrip	1

RACE WINNERS	
Bobby Allison	6
Darrell Waltrip	6
Dale Earnhardt	5
Jimmie Johnson	5
Buddy Baker	4
Jeff Gordon	4
Fred Lorenzen	4
Mark Martin	4
David Pearson	4
Richard Petty	4
Donnie Allison	3
Dale Jarrett	3
Cale Yarborough	3
LeeRoy Yarbrough	3
Davey Allison	2
Neil Bonnett	2
Jeff Burton	2
Bill Elliott	2
Junior Johnson	2
Kasey Kahne	2
Bobby Labonte	2
Benny Parsons	2
Jim Paschal	2
Rusty Wallace	2
Geoffrey Bodine	1
Harry Gant	1
Charlie Glotzbach	1
Ernie Irvan	1
Joe Lee Johnson	1
Matt Kenseth	1
Terry Labonte	1
Sterling Marlin	1
Jamie McMurray	1
Marvin Panch	1
Kyle Petty	1
Ken Schrader	1
Nelson Stacy	1
Tony Stewart	1
Speedy Thompson	1
Joe Weatherly	1

RACE 1

POLE WINNERS	
David Pearson	6
Jeff Gordon	5
Bill Elliott	3
Ryan Newman	3
Donnie Allison	2
Buddy Baker	2
Neil Bonnett	2
Jimmie Johnson	2
Richard Petty	2
Fireball Roberts	2
Ken Schrader	2
Cale Yarborough	2
Bobby Allison	1
Davey Allison	1
Geoffrey Bodine	1
Dale Earnhardt Jr.	1
Harry Gant	1
Charlie Glotzbach	1
Bobby Isaac	1
Junior Johnson	1
Alan Kulwicki	1
Bobby Labonte	1
Fred Lorenzen	1
Mark Martin	1
Jimmy Pardue	1
Scott Riggs	1

RACE WINNERS	
Darrell Waltrip	5
Bobby Allison	3
Buddy Baker	3
Dale Earnhardt	3
Jeff Gordon	3
Jimmie Johnson	3
David Pearson	3
Neil Bonnett	2
Jeff Burton	2
Fred Lorenzen	2
Jim Paschal	2
Richard Petty	2
Davey Allison	1
Donnie Allison	1
Dale Jarrett	1
Joe Lee Johnson	1
Kasey Kahne	1
Matt Kenseth	1
Bobby Labonte	1
Mark Martin	1
Marvin Panch	1
Benny Parsons	1
Kyle Petty	1
Nelson Stacy	1
Rusty Wallace	1
LeeRoy Yarbrough	1

RACE 2

POLE WINNERS	
David Pearson	8
Charlie Glotzbach	3
Harry Gant	2
Jeff Gordon	2
Alan Kulwicki	2
Bobby Labonte	2
Fred Lorenzen	2
Ryan Newman	2
Tim Richmond	2
Fireball Roberts	2
Cale Yarborough	2
Bobby Allison	1
Buddy Baker	1
Brett Bodine	1
Geoffrey Bodine	1
Neil Bonnett	1
Ward Burton	1
Derrike Cope	1
Bill Elliott	1
Mark Martin	1
Marvin Panch	1
Benny Parsons	1
Richard Petty	1
Scott Riggs	1
Ricky Rudd	1
Elliott Sadler	1
Jimmy Spencer	1
Darrell Waltrip	1

RACE WINNERS	
Bobby Allison	3
Mark Martin	3
Cale Yarborough	3
Donnie Allison	2
Dale Earnhardt	2
Bill Elliott	2
Dale Jarrett	2
Jimmie Johnson	2
Junior Johnson	2
Fred Lorenzen	2
Richard Petty	2
LeeRoy Yarbrough	2
Davey Allison	1
Buddy Baker	1
Geoffrey Bodine	1
Harry Gant	1
Charlie Glotzbach	1
Jeff Gordon	1
Ernie Irvan	1
Kasey Kahne	1
Bobby Labonte	1
Terry Labonte	1
Sterling Marlin	1
Jamie McMurray	1
Benny Parsons	1
David Pearson	1
Ken Schrader	1
Tony Stewart	1
Speedy Thompson	1
Rusty Wallace	1
Darrell Waltrip	1
Joe Weatherly	1

YEAR BY YEAR WINNERS

Year	Event	Race winner	Car make	Avg. speed	Start pos.	Pole winner	Pole speed
2006	Dollar General 300	D. Blaney	Chevrolet	106.999	23	C. Edwards	186.245
	Carquest Auto Parts 300	C. Edwards	Ford	110.735	9	M. Kenseth	184.011
2005	Dollar General 300	R. Newman	Dodge	102.506	2	Ji. Johnson	187.735
	Carquest Auto 300	Ky. Busch	Chevrolet	117.968	19	K. Kahne	186.735
2004	SpongeBob SquarePants 300	M. Bliss	Chevrolet	110.193	7	C. Mears	183.014
	Carquest Auto 300	Ky. Busch	Chevrolet	114.275	2	G. Biffle	183.542
2003	Carquest Auto 300	M. Kenseth	Ford	138.302	9	K. Harvick	184.445
	Little Trees 300	G. Biffle	Chevrolet	148.576	4	K. Harvick	184.313
2002	Carquest Auto 300	J. Green	Chevrolet	120.684	4	R. Hornaday	182.094
	Little Trees 300	J. Burton	Ford	142.443	2	M. Waltrip	180.343
2001	Carquest Auto 300	J. Green	Ford	128.205	2	None—conditions	
	Little Trees 300	G. Biffle	Ford	139.445	3	J. Burton	179.485
2000	Carquest Auto 300	J. Burton	Ford	121.759	4	D. Blaney	177.608
	All Pro 300	M. Kenseth	Chevrolet	145.064	1	M. Kenseth	178.956
1999	Carquest Auto 300	M. Martin	Ford	119.377	2	D. Green	176.569
	All Pro 300	M. Waltrip	Chevrolet	133.235	31	M. Kenseth	177.328
1998	Carquest Auto 300	M. Martin	Ford	133.449	6	B. Labonte	172.822
	All Pro 300	M. McLaughlin	Chevrolet	145.376	3	D. Blaney	177.247
1997	Carquest Auto 300	J. Nemechek	Chevrolet	126.954	2	M. Martin	175.012
	All Pro 300	J. Spencer	Chevrolet	127.089	4	J. Nemechek	176.378
1996	Red Dog 300	M. Martin	Ford	155.799	17	D. Jarrett	171.996
	All Pro 300	M. Martin	Ford	124.957	2	B. Labonte	174.272
1995	Red Dog 300	C. Little	Ford	131.707	7	R. Bickle	173.193
	All Pro 300	M. Martin	Ford	136.415	3	B. Dotter	172.051
1994	Champion 300	P. Parsons	Chevrolet	127.704	12	M. Skinner	172.480
	All Pro 300	T. Labonte	Chevrolet	134.831	16	M. Martin	176.696
1993	Champion 300	M. Waltrip	Pontiac	127.539	12	T. Leslie	172.574
	All Pro 300	M. Martin	Ford	113.960	5	B. Dotter	174.390
1992	Champion 300	J. Gordon	Ford	127.207	1	J. Gordon	170.638
	All Pro 300	J. Gordon	Ford	120.954	1	J. Gordon	173.566
1991	Champion 300	D. Earnhardt	Chevrolet	133.235	19	J. Sprague	167.167
	All Pro 300	H. Gant	Buick	121.937	33	W. Burton	172.574
1990	Champion 300	D. Jarrett	Pontiac	132.337	3	D. Trickle	168.219
	All Pro 300	S. Marlin	Oldsmobile	132.272	32	None—conditions	
1989	Champion 300	R. Moroso	Oldsmobile	136.450	4	G. Sacks	167.214
	All Pro 300	R. Moroso	Oldsmobile	126.035	4	M. Waltrip	168.993
1988	Winn-Dixie 300	D. Jarrett	Oldsmobile	139.969	6	G. Bodine	168.099
	All Pro 300	R. Moroso	Oldsmobile	123.683	13	H. Gant	169.710
1987	Winn-Dixie 300	H. Gant	Buick	139.643	16	B. Bodine	167.328
	All Pro 300	H. Gant	Buick	131.868	1	H. Gant	168.940
1986	Winn-Dixie 300	T. Richmond	Pontiac	139.715	1	T. Richmond	163.711
	All Pro 300	D. Earnhardt	Pontiac	138.746	1	D. Earnhardt	161.599
1985	Winn-Dixie 300	T. Richmond	Pontiac	119.284	1	T. Richmond	160.633
	Miller 400	T. Labonte	Pontiac	140.485	14	G. Bodine	162.656
1984	Mello Yello 300	B. Allison	Oldsmobile	126.198	8	L. Ottinger	162.421
	Miller Time 300	D. Waltrip	Pontiac	123.499	6	T. Richmond	163.676
1983	Mello Yello 300	D. Earnhardt	Pontiac	117.724	3	M. Shepherd	161.565
	Miller Time 300	S. Ard	Oldsmobile	141.269	10	L. Pearson	162.235
1982	Mello Yello 300	H. Gant	Pontiac	126.731	1	H. Gant	162.847
	Miller 300	D. Waltrip	Pontiac	123.485	3	P. Parsons	162.191

POLE WINNERS		RACE WINNERS	
Harry Gant	3	Mark Martin	6
Matt Kenseth	3	Harry Gant	4
Tim Richmond	3	Dale Earnhardt	3
Dave Blaney	2	Rob Moroso	3
Geoffrey Bodine	2	Greg Biffle	2
Bobby Dotter	2	Jeff Burton	2
Jeff Gordon	2	Kyle Busch	2
Kevin Harvick	2	Jeff Gordon	2
Mark Martin	2	Jeff Green	2
Bobby Labonte	2	Dale Jarrett	2
Michael Waltrip	2	Matt Kenseth	2
Rick Bickle	1	Terry Labonte	2
Greg Biffle	1	Tim Richmond	2
Brett Bodine	1	Darrell Waltrip	2
Jeff Burton	1	Michael Waltrip	2
Ward Burton	1	Bobby Allison	1
Dale Earnhardt	1	Sam Ard	1
Carl Edwards	1	Mike Bliss	1
David Green	1	Dave Blaney	1
Ron Hornaday	1	Carl Edwards	1
Dale Jarrett	1	Chad Little	1
Jimmie Johnson	1	Sterling Marlin	1
Kasey Kahne	1	Mike McLaughlin	1
Tracy Leslie	1	Joe Nemechek	1
Casey Mears	1	Ryan Newman	1
Joe Nemechek	1	Phil Parsons	1
L.D. Ottinger	1	Jimmy Spencer	1
Phil Parsons	1		
Larry Pearson	1		
Greg Sacks	1		
Morgan Shepherd	1		
Mike Skinner	1		
Jack Sprague	1		
Dick Trickle	1		

QUALIFYING RECORD: Kasey Kahne, Dodge; 186.735 mph (28.918 seconds), May 28, 2005
RACE RECORD: Mark Martin, Ford; 155.799 mph (1:55:32), May 25, 1996

Edwards

YEAR BY YEAR WINNERS

Year	Event	Race winner	Car make	Avg. speed	Start pos.	Pole winner	Pole speed
2006	Quaker Steak and Lube 200	Ky. Busch	Chevrolet	124.845	20	M. Skinner	179.378
2005	Quaker Steak and Lube 200	Ky. Busch	Chevrolet	104.571	3	M. Skinner	183.051
2004	Infineon 200	D. Setzer	Chevrolet	107.631	9	D. Starr	178.577
2003	Hardee's 200	T. Musgrave	Dodge	114.768	8	B. Lester	175.593

POLE WINNERS		RACE WINNERS	
Mike Skinner	2	Kyle Busch	2
Bill Lester	1	Ted Musgrave	1
David Starr	1	Dennis Setzer	1

QUALIFYING RECORD: Mike Skinner, Toyota; 183.051 mph (29.500 seconds), May 20, 2005
RACE RECORD: Kyle Busch, Chevrolet; 124.845 mph (1:36:36), May 19, 2006

Erin Crocker

>>MARTINSVILLE SPEEDWAY<<

TRACK FACTS >>> >>> **Location:** Martinsville, Va. >>> >>> **Owner:** International Speedway Corp. >>> >>> **Track length:** .526 miles

>>> >>> **Grandstand seating:** 65,000 >>> >>> **Tickets:** (877) 722-3849 >>> >>> **Website:** www.martinsvillespeedway.com

>>NASCAR NEXTEL CUP SERIES<<

>> TRACK RECORDS

Most wins: 15—Richard Petty; **Most top fives:** 30—Richard Petty; **Most top 10s:** 37—Richard Petty; **Oldest winner:** Harry Gant, 51 years, 8 months,12 days, September 22, 1991; **Youngest winner:** Richard Petty, 22 years, 9 months, 8 days, April 10, 1960; **Most lead changes:** 25—September 28, 1980; **Fewest lead changes:** 1—Three times, most recently, April 9, 1961; **Most leaders:** 14—October 15, 2001; **Fewest leaders:** 2—11 times, most recently, September 26, 1976; **Most laps led in a 500-lap race:** 493—Fred Lorenzen, September 27, 1964; **Most cautions:** 19—October 23, 2005; **Fewest cautions:** 1—Three times, most recently, April 25, 1971; **Most caution laps:** 119—October 19, 2003; **Fewest caution laps:** 3—April 25, 1971; **Most on the lead lap:** 26—Twice, most recently, October 22, 2006; **Fewest on the lead lap:** 1— 27 times, most recently, April 27, 1986; **Most running at the finish:** 42—April 18, 1999; **Fewest running at the finish:** 4—May 6, 1951; **Most laps led by a race winner:** 493—Fred Lorenzen, September 27, 1964; **Fewest laps led by a race winner:** 4—John Andretti, April 18, 1999; **Closest margin of victory:** 0.19 seconds— Geoffrey Bodine defeated Rusty Wallace, September 28, 1992

>> QUALIFYING AND RACE RECORDS

QUALIFYING: Tony Stewart, Chevrolet; 98.083 mph (19.306 seconds), October 21, 2005
RACE: Jeff Gordon, Chevrolet; 82.223 mph (3:11:55), September 22, 1996

12° Banking in Turns — VIRGINIA • Martinsville

First NASCAR NEXTEL Cup Series race: September 25, 1949 (Red Byron, winner)
Banking on straights: None
Length of front stretch: 800 feet
Length of back stretch: 800 feet

YEAR BY YEAR WINNERS

Year	Event	Race winner	Car make	Avg. speed	Start pos.	Car owner	Pole winner	Pole speed
2006	Subway 500	Ji. Johnson	Chevrolet	70.446	9	Rick Hendrick	Ku. Busch	97.568
	DIRECTV 500	T. Stewart	Chevrolet	72.741	3	Joe Gibbs	Ji. Johnson	96.736
2005	Subway 500	J. Gordon	Chevrolet	69.695	15	Rick Hendrick	T. Stewart	98.083
	Advance Auto Prts. 500	J. Gordon	Chevrolet	72.099	16	Rick Hendrick	S. Riggs	96.671
2004	Subway 500	Ji. Johnson	Chevrolet	66.103	18	Rick Hendrick	R. Newman	97.043
	Advance Auto Prts. 500	R. Wallace	Dodge	68.169	17	Roger Penske	J. Gordon	93.502
2003	Subway 500	J. Gordon	Chevrolet	67.658	1	Rick Hendrick	J. Gordon	93.650
	Virginia 500	J. Gordon	Chevrolet	75.557	1	Rick Hendrick	J. Gordon	94.307
2002	Old Dominion 500	K. Busch	Ford	74.651	36	Jack Roush	R. Newman	92.837
	Virginia 500	B. Labonte	Pontiac	73.951	15	Joe Gibbs	J. Gordon	94.181
2001	Old Dominion 500	R. Craven	Ford	75.750	6	Cal Wells	T. Bodine	93.724
	Virginia 500	D. Jarrett	Ford	70.799	13	Robert Yates	J. Gordon	94.087
2000	NAPA 500	T. Stewart	Pontiac	73.859	1	Joe Gibbs	T. Stewart	95.371
	Goody's 500	M. Martin	Ford	71.161	21	Jack Roush	R. Wallace	94.827
1999	NAPA 500 (e)	J. Gordon	Chevrolet	72.347	5	Rick Hendrick	J. Nemechek	95.223
	Goody's 500	J. Andretti	Pontiac	75.653	21	Petty Enterprises	T. Stewart	95.275
1998	NAPA 500	R. Rudd	Ford	73.350	2	Ricky Rudd	E. Irvan	93.600
	Goody's 500	B. Hamilton	Chevrolet	70.709	1	Larry McClure	B. Hamilton	93.175
1997	Hanes 500	J. Burton	Ford	73.078	10	Jack Roush	W. Burton	93.410
	Goody's 500	J. Gordon	Chevrolet	70.347	4	Rick Hendrick	K. Wallace	93.961
1996	Hanes 500	J. Gordon	Chevrolet	82.223	10	Rick Hendrick	B. Hamilton	94.120
	Goody's 500	R. Wallace	Ford	81.410	5	Roger Penske	R. Craven	93.079

2007 SCHEDULE

NASCAR NEXTEL Cup Series
Event: DIRECTV 500
Race: No. 6 of 36
Date: April 1 • **TV:** FOX • **Radio:** MRN

Event: Subway 500
Race: No. 32 of 36
Date: October 21 • **TV:** ABC • **Radio:** MRN

NASCAR Craftsman Truck Series
Event: Kroger 250
Race: No. 4 of 25
Date: March 31 • **TV:** SPEED • **Radio:** MRN

Event: Kroger 200
Race: No. 21 of 25
Date: October 20 • **TV:** SPEED • **Radio:** MRN
Race names subject to change

YEAR BY YEAR WINNERS continued

Year	Event	Race winner	Car make	Avg. speed	Start pos.	Car owner	Pole winner	Pole speed
1995	Goody's 500	D. Earnhardt	Chevrolet	73.946	2	Richard Childress	None—conditions	
	Hanes 500	R. Wallace	Ford	72.145	15	Roger Penske	B. Labonte	93.308
1994	Goody's 500	R. Wallace	Ford	77.139	7	Roger Penske	T. Musgrave	94.129
	Hanes 500	R. Wallace	Ford	76.700	1	Roger Penske	R. Wallace	92.942
1993	Goody's 500	E. Irvan	Ford	74.101	1	Robert Yates	E. Irvan	92.583
	Hanes 500	R. Wallace	Pontiac	79.078	5	Roger Penske	G. Bodine	93.887
1992	Goody's 500 (d)	G. Bodine	Ford	75.424	7	Bud Moore	K. Petty	92.497
	Hanes 500	M. Martin	Ford	78.086	12	Jack Roush	D. Waltrip	92.956
1991	Goody's 500	H. Gant	Oldsmobile	74.535	12	Leo Jackson	M. Martin	93.171
	Hanes 500	D. Earnhardt	Chevrolet	75.139	10	Richard Childress	M. Martin	91.949
1990	Goody's 500	G. Bodine	Ford	76.386	14	Junior Johnson	M. Martin	91.571
	Hanes 500	G. Bodine	Ford	77.423	1	Junior Johnson	G. Bodine	91.726
1989	Goody's 500	D. Waltrip	Chevrolet	76.571	2	Rick Hendrick	J. Hensley	91.913
	Pannill 500	D. Waltrip	Chevrolet	79.025	10	Rick Hendrick	G. Bodine	93.097
1988	Goody's 500	D. Waltrip	Chevrolet	74.988	20	Rick Hendrick	R. Wallace	91.372
	Pannill 500	D. Earnhardt	Chevrolet	74.740	14	Richard Childress	R. Rudd	91.328
1987	Goody's 500	D. Waltrip	Chevrolet	76.410	14	Rick Hendrick	G. Bodine	91.218
	Sovran Bank 500	D. Earnhardt	Chevrolet	72.808	4	Richard Childress	M. Shepherd	92.355
1986	Goody's 500	R. Wallace	Pontiac	73.191	8	Raymond Beadle	G. Bodine	90.599
	Sovran Bank 500	R. Rudd	Ford	76.882	4	Bud Moore	T. Richmond	90.716
1985	Goody's 500	D. Earnhardt	Chevrolet	70.694	11	Richard Childress	G. Bodine	90.521
	Sovran Bank 500	H. Gant	Chevrolet	73.072	13	Hal Needham	D. Waltrip	90.279
1984	Goody's 500	D. Waltrip	Chevrolet	75.532	3	Junior Johnson	G. Bodine	89.523
	Sovran Bank 500	G. Bodine	Chevrolet	73.264	6	Rick Hendrick	J. Ruttman	89.426
1983	Goody's 500	R. Rudd	Chevrolet	76.134	2	Richard Childress	D. Waltrip	89.342
	Va. Nat'l Bank 500	D. Waltrip	Chevrolet	66.460	3	Junior Johnson	R. Rudd	89.910
1982	Old Dominion 500	D. Waltrip	Buick	71.315	3	Junior Johnson	R. Rudd	89.132
	Va. Nat'l Bank 500	H. Gant	Buick	75.073	3	Hal Needham	T. Labonte	89.988
1981	Old Dominion 500	D. Waltrip	Buick	70.089	1	Junior Johnson	D. Waltrip	89.014
	Virginia 500	M. Shepherd	Pontiac	75.019	12	Cliff Stewart	R. Rudd	89.056
1980	Old Dominion 500	D. Earnhardt	Chevrolet	69.654	7	Rod Osterlund	Buddy Baker	88.500
	Virginia 500	D. Waltrip	Chevrolet	69.049	1	DiProspero/Gardner	D. Waltrip	88.566
1979	Old Dominion 500	Buddy Baker	Chevrolet	75.119	7	Harry Ranier	D. Waltrip	82.650
	Virginia 500	R. Petty	Chevrolet	76.562	2	Petty Enterprises	D. Waltrip	87.383
1978	Old Dominion 500	C. Yarborough	Oldsmobile	79.185	6	Junior Johnson	L. Pond	86.558
	Virginia 500	D. Waltrip	Chevrolet	78.119	3	DiProspero/Gardner	L. Pond	88.637
1977	Old Dominion 500	C. Yarborough	Chevrolet	73.447	3	Junior Johnson	N. Bonnett	87.637
	Virginia 500	C. Yarborough	Chevrolet	77.405	5	Junior Johnson	N. Bonnett	88.923
1976	Old Dominion 500	C. Yarborough	Chevrolet	75.370	4	Junior Johnson	D. Waltrip	88.484
	Virginia 500	D. Waltrip	Chevrolet	71.759	4	DiProspero/Gardner	D. Marcis	86.286
1975	Old Dominion 500	D. Marcis	Dodge	75.944	7	Nord Krauskopf	C. Yarborough	86.199
	Virginia 500	R. Petty	Dodge	69.282	6	Petty Enterprises	B. Parsons	85.789
1974	Old Dominion 500	E. Ross	Chevrolet	66.232	11	Junior Johnson	R. Petty	84.119
	Virginia 500 (c)	C. Yarborough	Chevrolet	77.855	1	Junior Johnson	C. Yarborough	84.362
1973	Old Dominion 500	R. Petty	Dodge	68.631	6	Petty Enterprises	C. Yarborough	85.922
	Virginia 500	D. Pearson	Mercury	70.251	1	Wood Brothers	D. Pearson	86.369
1972	Old Dominion 500	R. Petty	Plymouth	69.989	4	Petty Enterprises	B. Allison	85.890
	Virginia 500	R. Petty	Plymouth	72.657	3	Petty Enterprises	B. Allison	84.163
1971	Old Dominion 500	B. Isaac	Dodge	73.681	1	Nord Krauskopf	B. Isaac	83.635
	Virginia 500	R. Petty	Plymouth	77.077	3	Petty Enterprises	D. Allison	82.529
1970	Old Dominion 500	R. Petty	Plymouth	72.159	4	Petty Enterprises	B. Allison	82.167
	Virginia 500	B. Isaac	Dodge	68.512	2	Nord Krauskopf	L. Yarbrough	82.609
1969	Old Dominion 500	R. Petty	Ford	63.127	6	Petty Enterprises	D. Pearson	83.197
	Virginia 500 (b)	R. Petty	Ford	64.405	6	Petty Enterprises	B. Allison	78.260
1968	Old Dominion 500	R. Petty	Plymouth	72.159	6	Petty Enterprises	C. Yarborough	77.279
	Virginia 500	C. Yarborough	Mercury	66.686	3	Wood Brothers	D. Pearson	78.230
1967	Old Dominion 500	R. Petty	Plymouth	69.605	5	Petty Enterprises	C. Yarborough	77.386
	Virginia 500	R. Petty	Plymouth	67.446	2	Petty Enterprises	D. Dieringer	77.319
1966	Old Dominion 500	F. Lorenzen	Ford	69.177	2	Holman-Moody	Jr. Johnson	75.598
	Virginia 500	J. Paschal	Plymouth	69.156	1	Tom Friedkin	J. Paschal	76.345
1965	Old Dominion 500	Ju. Johnson	Ford	67.056	3	Rex Lovette	R. Petty	74.503
	Virginia 500	F. Lorenzen	Ford	66.765	2	Holman-Moody	Jr. Johnson	74.503
1964	Old Dominion 500	F. Lorenzen	Ford	67.320	1	Holman-Moody	F. Lorenzen	74.196
	Virginia 500	F. Lorenzen	Ford	70.098	1	Holman-Moody	F. Lorenzen	74.472
1963	Old Dominion 500	F. Lorenzen	Ford	67.487	2	Holman-Moody	Ju. Johnson	73.379
	Virginia 500	R. Petty	Plymouth	64.823	8	Petty Enterprises	R. White	72.000
1962	Old Dominion 500	N. Stacy	Ford	66.875	3	Holman-Moody	F. Roberts	71.513
	Virginia 500	R. Petty	Plymouth	66.426	7	Petty Enterprises	F. Lorenzen	71.287
1961	Old Dominion 500	J. Weatherly	Pontiac	62.586	4	Bud Moore	F. Lorenzen	70.730
	Virginia 500	Ju. Johnson	Pontiac	66.280	17	Rex Lovette	R. White	71.320
	Grand Nat'l. 200 (a)	F. Lorenzen	Ford	68.370	2	Holman-Moody	R. White	70.280
1960	Old Dominion 500	R. White	Chevrolet	60.440	2	Rex White	G. Wood	68.440
	Virginia 500	R. Petty	Plymouth	63.940	4	Petty Enterprises	G. Wood	69.150
1959	Old Dominion 500	R. White	Chevrolet	60.500	14	R.White/L.Clements	G. Wood	69.471
	Virginia 500	L. Petty	Oldsmobile	59.440	24	Petty Enterprises	B. Johns	66.030
1958	Old Dominion 500 (a)	F. Roberts	Chevrolet	64.340	4	Frank Strickland	G. Wood	67.950
	Virginia 500	B. Welborn	Chevrolet	61.160	20	J.H. Petty	Buck Baker	61.166
1957	Old Dominion 500	B. Welborn	Chevrolet	63.030	2	Bob Welborn	E. Pagan	65.837
	Virginia 500	Buck Baker	Chevrolet	57.138	6	Hugh Babb	P. Goldsmith	65.693
1956	Old Dominion 400	J. Smith	Dodge	61.140	23	Carl Kiekhaefer	Buck Baker	67.643
	Virginia 500	Buck Baker	Dodge	60.950	1	Carl Kiekhaefer	Buck Baker	N/A
1955	N/A	S. Thompson	Chrysler	59.603	17	Carl Kiekhaefer	None—conditions	
	N/A	T. Flock	Chrysler	52.555	4	Carl Kiekhaefer	J. Paschal	N/A
1954	N/A	L. Petty	Chrysler	44.548	1	Petty Enterprises	L. Petty	N/A
	N/A	J. Paschal	Oldsmobile	46.130	N/A	Bobby Griffin	None—conditions	

ALL MARTINSVILLE RACES

POLE WINNERS

Darrell Waltrip	8
Geoffrey Bodine	7
Buck Baker	5
Jeff Gordon	5
Cale Yarborough	5
Bobby Allison	4
Fred Lorenzen	4
Ricky Rudd	4
Glen Wood	4
Junior Johnson	3
Mark Martin	3
David Pearson	3
Tony Stewart	3
Rusty Wallace	3
Rex White	3
Neil Bonnett	2
Fonty Flock	2
Bobby Hamilton	2
Ernie Irvan	2
Ryan Newman	2
Jim Paschal	2
Richard Petty	2
Lennie Pond	2
Donnie Allison	1
Buddy Baker	1
Todd Bodine	1
Perk Brown	1
Ward Burton	1
Kurt Busch	1
Ricky Craven	1
Darel Dieringer	1
Tom Flock	1
Paul Goldsmith	1
Jimmy Hensley	1
Bobby Isaac	1
Bobby Johns	1
Jimmie Johnson	1
Bobby Labonte	1
Terry Labonte	1
Dave Marcis	1
Ted Musgrave	1
Joe Nemechek	1
Eddie Pagan	1
Benny Parsons	1
Kyle Petty	1
Lee Petty	1
Tim Richmond	1
Scott Riggs	1
Fireball Roberts	1
Joe Ruttman	1
Morgan Shepherd	1
Herb Thomas	1
Curtis Turner	1
Kenny Wallace	1
LeeRoy Yarbrough	1

RACE WINNERS

Richard Petty	15
Darrell Waltrip	11
Jeff Gordon	7
Rusty Wallace	7
Dale Earnhardt	6
Fred Lorenzen	6
Cale Yarborough	6
Geoffrey Bodine	4
Harry Gant	3
Jim Paschal	3
Lee Petty	3
Ricky Rudd	3
Buck Baker	2
Bobby Isaac	2
Jimmie Johnson	2
Junior Johnson	2
Mark Martin	2
Tony Stewart	2
Herb Thomas	2
Curtis Turner	2
Bob Welborn	2
Rex White	2
John Andretti	1
Buddy Baker	1
Jeff Burton	1
Kurt Busch	1
Red Byron	1
Ricky Craven	1
Tim Flock	1
Bobby Hamilton	1
Ernie Irvan	1
Dale Jarrett	1
Bobby Labonte	1
Dave Marcis	1
Frank Mundy	1
David Pearson	1
Dick Rathmann	1
Fireball Roberts	1
Earl Ross	1
Morgan Shepherd	1
Jack Smith	1
Nelson Stacy	1
Speedy Thompson	1
Joe Weatherly	1

RACE 1

POLE WINNERS

Buck Baker	4
Jeff Gordon	4
Darrell Waltrip	4
Geoffrey Bodine	3
Ricky Rudd	3
Bobby Allison	2
Fred Lorenzen	2
Jim Paschal	2
David Pearson	2
Rusty Wallace	2
Rex White	2
Donnie Allison	1
Neil Bonnett	1
Ricky Craven	1
Darel Dieringer	1
Tim Flock	1
Paul Goldsmith	1
Bobby Hamilton	1
Bobby Johns	1
Jimmie Johnson	1
Junior Johnson	1
Bobby Labonte	1
Terry Labonte	1
Dave Marcis	1
Mark Martin	1
Benny Parsons	1
Lennie Pond	1
Tim Richmond	1
Scott Riggs	1
Joe Ruttman	1
Morgan Shepherd	1
Tony Stewart	1
Kenny Wallace	1
Glen Wood	1
Cale Yarborough	1
LeeRoy Yarbrough	1

RACE WINNERS

Richard Petty	9
Rusty Wallace	5
Darrell Waltrip	5
Dale Earnhardt	3
Jeff Gordon	3
Cale Yarborough	3
Buck Baker	2
Geoffrey Bodine	2
Harry Gant	2
Fred Lorenzen	2
Mark Martin	2
Jim Paschal	2
Lee Petty	2
Curtis Turner	2
John Andretti	1
Tim Flock	1
Bobby Hamilton	1
Bobby Isaac	1
Dale Jarrett	1
Junior Johnson	1
Bobby Labonte	1
David Pearson	1
Dick Rathmann	1
Ricky Rudd	1
Tony Stewart	1
Morgan Shepherd	1
Bob Welborn	1

RACE 2

POLE WINNERS

Geoffrey Bodine	4
Darrell Waltrip	4
Cale Yarborough	4
Glen Wood	3
Bobby Allison	2
Fonty Flock	2
Ernie Irvan	2
Junior Johnson	2
Fred Lorenzen	2
Mark Martin	2
Ryan Newman	2
Richard Petty	2
Tony Stewart	2
Buck Baker	1
Buddy Baker	1
Todd Bodine	1
Neil Bonnett	1
Perk Brown	1
Ward Burton	1
Kurt Busch	1
Jeff Gordon	1
Bobby Hamilton	1
Jimmy Hensley	1
Bobby Isaac	1
Ted Musgrave	1
Joe Nemechek	1
Eddie Pagan	1
David Pearson	1
Kyle Petty	1
Lee Petty	1
Lennie Pond	1
Fireball Roberts	1
Ricky Rudd	1
Herb Thomas	1
Curtis Turner	1
Rusty Wallace	1

RACE WINNERS

Richard Petty	6
Darrell Waltrip	6
Jeff Gordon	4
Dale Earnhardt	3
Fred Lorenzen	3
Cale Yarborough	3
Geoffrey Bodine	2
Jimmie Johnson	2
Ricky Rudd	2
Herb Thomas	2
Rusty Wallace	2
Rex White	2
Buddy Baker	1
Jeff Burton	1
Kurt Busch	1
Red Byron	1
Ricky Craven	1
Harry Gant	1
Ernie Irvan	1
Bobby Isaac	1
Junior Johnson	1
Dave Marcis	1
Frank Mundy	1
Jim Paschal	1
Lee Petty	1
Fireball Roberts	1
Earl Ross	1
Jack Smith	1
Nelson Stacy	1
Tony Stewart	1
Speedy Thompson	1
Joe Weatherly	1
Bob Welborn	1

>>MARTINSVILLE SPEEDWAY<<

YEAR BY YEAR WINNERS continued

Year	Event	Race winner	Car make	Avg. speed	Start pos.	Car owner	Pole winner	Pole speed
1953	N/A	J. Paschal	Dodge	56.014	N/A	George Hutchens	F. Flock	N/A
	N/A	L. Petty	Dodge	N/A	N/A	Petty Enterprises	None—conditions	
1952	N/A	H. Thomas	Hudson	47.556	2	Herb Thomas	P. Brown	N/A
	N/A	D. Rathmann	Hudson	42.862	9	Walt Chapman	Buck Baker	N/A
1951	N/A	F. Mundy	Oldsmobile	N.A	3	Ted Chester	H. Thomas	N/A
	N/A	C. Turner	Oldsmobile	N/A	7	John Eanes	T. Flock	N/A
1950	N/A	H. Thomas	Plymouth	N/A	19	Herb Thomas	F. Flock	N/A
	N/A	C. Turner	Oldsmobile	N/A	N/A	John Eanes	Buck Baker	N/A
1949	N/A	R. Byron	Oldsmobile	N/A	3	Raymond Parks	C. Turner	N/A

KEY (a) Race shortened by rain. (b) Track reconfigured from .5 miles to .525 miles. (c) Race shortened by 26.25 miles because of energy shortage. (d) Race postponed until following day because of rain. (e) Pit road reconfigured to single pit road on front straightaway.

Stewart

>>NASCAR CRAFTSMAN TRUCK SERIES<<

Starr

YEAR BY YEAR WINNERS

Year	Event	Race winner	Car make	Avg. speed	Start pos.	Pole winner	Pole speed
2006	Kroger 200	J. Sprague	Toyota	60.172	1	J. Sprague	95.675
	Kroger 250	D. Starr	Toyota	59.219	15	B. Hamilton Jr.	95.180
2005	Kroger 200	R. Craven	Ford	64.332	9	R. Crawford	95.966
	Kroger 250	B. Labonte	Chevrolet	66.639	5	B. Hamilton	95.098
2004	Martinsville 200	J. McMurray	Chevrolet	60.819	18	None—conditions	
	Kroger 250	R. Crawford	Ford	61.490	3	J. Sprague	92.375
2003	Advance Auto Parts 200	J. Wood	Ford	72.069	2	C. Edwards	91.549
2003	Advance Auto Parts 200	D. Setzer	Chevrolet	66.921	5	T. Musgrave	91.297
2002	Advance Auto Parts 200	D. Setzer	Chevrolet	64.628	33	T. Musgrave	92.864
2001	Advance Auto Parts 200	S. Riggs	Dodge	70.836	2	J. Ruttman	92.411
2000	NAPA 250	B. Hamilton	Dodge	71.836	2	M. Wallace	93.070
1999	NAPA 250	J. Hensley	Dodge	74.294	9	M. Bliss	94.275
1998	NAPA 250	J. Sauter	Chevrolet	72.154	10	G. Biffle	91.891
1997	Hanes 250	R. Bickle	Chevrolet	72.297	1	R. Bickle	92.796
1996	Hanes 250	M. Skinner	Chevrolet	64.434	16	B. Hamilton	92.101
1995	Goody's 150	J. Ruttman	Ford	65.072	2	No trials held	

POLE WINNERS		RACE WINNERS	
Bobby Hamilton	2	Dennis Setzer	2
Ted Musgrave	2	Rich Bickle	1
Jack Sprague	2	Ricky Craven	1
Rich Bickle	1	Rick Crawford	1
Greg Biffle	1	Bobby Hamilton	1
Mike Bliss	1	Jimmy Hensley	1
Rick Crawford	1	Bobby Labonte	1
Carl Edwards	1	Jamie McMurray	1
Bobby Hamilton Jr.	1	Scott Riggs	1
Joe Ruttman	1	Joe Ruttman	1
Mike Wallace	1	Jay Sauter	1
		Mike Skinner	1
		Jack Sprague	1
		David Starr	1
		Jon Wood	1

QUALIFYING RECORD: Rick Crawford, Ford; 95.966 mph (19.732 seconds), October 22, 2005
RACE RECORD: 250 laps: Jimmy Hensley, Dodge; 74.294 mph (1:46:13), April 17, 1999; **200 laps:** Jon Wood, Ford; 72.069 mph (1:27:35); October 18, 2003.

>>MICHIGAN INTERNATIONAL SPEEDWAY<<

TRACK FACTS >>> >>> **Location:** Brooklyn, Mich. >>> >>> **Owner:** International Speedway Corp. >>> >>> **Track length:** 2 miles

>>> >>> **Grandstand seating:** 137,243 >>> >>> **Tickets:** (800) 354-1010 >>> >>> **Website:** www.mispeedway.com >>> >>>

>>NASCAR NEXTEL CUP SERIES<<

>>TRACK RECORDS

Most wins: 9—David Pearson; **Most top fives:** 21—Cale Yarborough; **Most top 10s:** 29—Bill Elliott; **Oldest winner:** Harry Gant, 52 years, 7 months, 6 days, August 16, 1992; **Youngest winner:** Kurt Busch, 24 years, 10 months, 11 days, June 15, 2003; **Most lead changes:** 65—August 16, 1981; **Fewest lead changes:** 7—August 12, 1984; **Most leaders:** 15—June 20, 1982; **Fewest leaders:** 5—Five times, most recently, August 12, 1984; **Most laps led in a 400-mile race:** 162—Rusty Wallace, August 20, 1989; **Most laps led in a 500-mile race:** 136—LeeRoy Yarbrough, June 15, 1969; **Most cautions:** 10—August 20, 2006; **Fewest cautions:** 0—Three times, most recently, June 13, 1999; **Most caution laps:** 63—August 24, 1975; **Fewest caution laps:** 0—Three times, most recently, June 13, 1999; **Most on the lead lap:** 32—August 18, 2002; **Fewest on the lead lap:** 2—Five times, most recently, June 15, 1975; **Most running at the finish:** 41—Three times, most recently, June 13, 1999; **Fewest running at the finish:** 14—June 16, 1974; **Most laps led by a race winner:** 162—Rusty Wallace, August 20, 1989; **Fewest laps led by a race winner:** 6—Jeremy Mayfield, August 21, 2005; **Closest margin of victory:** .085 seconds—Jeff Gordon defeated Ricky Rudd, June 10, 2001

>>QUALIFYING AND RACE RECORDS

QUALIFYING: Ryan Newman, Dodge; 194.232 mph (37.069 seconds), June 19, 2005
RACE: Dale Jarrett, Ford; 173.997 mph (2:17:56), June 13, 1999

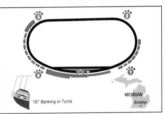

First NASCAR NEXTEL Cup Series race:
June 15, 1969 (Cale Yarborough, winner)
Banking on front stretch: 12 degrees
Banking on back stretch: 5 degrees
Length of front stretch: 3,600 feet
Length of back stretch: 2,242 feet

2007 SCHEDULE

NASCAR NEXTEL Cup Series
Event: 3M Performance 400
Race: No. 15 of 36
Date: June 17 • TV: TNT • Radio: MRN

Event: GFS Marketplace 400
Race: No. 23 of 36
Date: August 19 • TV: ESPN • Radio: MRN

NASCAR Busch Series
Event: CARFAX 250
Race: No. 25 of 35 • Date: August 18
TV: ESPN2 • Radio: MRN

NASCAR Craftsman Truck Series
Event: Con-Way Freight 200
Race: No. 10 of 25
Date: June 16
TV: SPEED • Radio: MRN

Race names subject to change

YEAR BY YEAR WINNERS

Year	Event	Race winner	Car make	Avg. speed	Start pos.	Car owner	Pole winner	Pole speed
2006	GFS Marketplace 400	M. Kenseth	Ford	135.097	3	Jack Roush	J. Burton	187.936
	3M Perform. 400 (a)	K. Kahne	Dodge	118.788	1	Ray Evernham	K. Kahne	185.644
2005	GFS Marketplace 400	J. Mayfield	Dodge	141.551	11	Ray Evernham	J. Nemechek	191.530
	Batman Begins 400	G. Biffle	Ford	150.596	25	Jack Roush	R. Newman	194.232
2004	GFS Marketplace 400	G. Biffle	Ford	139.063	24	Jack Roush	None—conditions	
	DHL 400	R. Newman	Dodge	139.292	4	Roger Penske	J. Gordon	190.865
2003	GFS Marketplace 400	R. Newman	Dodge	127.310	8	Roger Penske	B. Labonte	190.240
	Sirius 400	K. Busch	Ford	131.219	4	Jack Roush	B. Labonte	190.365
2002	Pepsi 400	D. Jarrett	Ford	140.566	8	Robert Yates	D. Earnhardt Jr.	189.668
	Sirius 400	M. Kenseth	Ford	154.822	20	Jack Roush	D. Jarrett	189.071
2001	Pepsi 400 (a)	S. Marlin	Dodge	140.513	15	Chip Ganassi	R. Craven	188.127
	Kmart 400	J. Gordon	Chevrolet	134.203	1	Rick Hendrick	J. Gordon	188.250
2000	Pepsi 400	R. Wallace	Ford	132.597	10	Roger Penske	D. Earnhardt Jr.	191.149
	Kmart 400 (a)	T. Stewart	Pontiac	143.926	28	Joe Gibbs	B. Labonte	189.883
1999	Pepsi 400	B. Labonte	Pontiac	144.332	19	Joe Gibbs	W. Burton	188.843
	Kmart 400	D. Jarrett	Ford	173.997	6	Robert Yates	J. Gordon	186.945
1998	Pepsi 400	J. Gordon	Chevrolet	151.995	3	Rick Hendrick	E. Irvan	183.416
	Miller 400	M. Martin	Ford	158.695	7	Jack Roush	W. Burton	181.561
1997	DeVilbiss 400	M. Martin	Ford	126.880	2	Jack Roush	J. Benson	183.332
	Miller 400	E. Irvan	Ford	153.338	20	Robert Yates	D. Jarrett	183.669

>>MICHIGAN INTERNATIONAL SPEEDWAY<<

YEAR BY YEAR WINNERS continued

Year	Event	Race winner	Car make	Avg. speed	Start pos.	Car owner	Pole winner	Pole speed
1996	Goodwrench 400	D. Jarrett	Ford	139.792	11	Robert Yates	J. Burton	185.395
	Miller 400	R. Wallace	Ford	166.033	18	Roger Penske	B. Hamilton	185.166
1995	Goodwrench 400	B. Labonte	Chevrolet	157.739	1	Joe Gibbs	B. Labonte	184.403
	Miller 400	B. Labonte	Chevrolet	134.141	19	Joe Gibbs	J. Gordon	186.611
1994	Goodwrench 400	G. Bodine	Ford	139.914	1	Geoffrey Bodine	G. Bodine	181.082
	Miller 400	R. Wallace	Ford	125.022	5	Roger Penske	L. Allen	180.641
1993	Champion 400	M. Martin	Ford	144.564	12	Jack Roush	K. Schrader	180.750
	Miller 400	R. Rudd	Chevrolet	148.484	2	Rick Hendrick	B. Bodine	175.456
1992	Champion 400	H. Gant	Oldsmobile	146.056	24	Leo Jackson	A. Kulwicki	178.196
	Miller 400	Da. Allison	Ford	152.672	1	Robert Yates	Da. Allison	176.258
1991	Champion 400	D. Jarrett	Ford	142.972	11	Wood Brothers	A. Kulwicki	173.431
	Miller 400	Da. Allison	Ford	160.912	4	Robert Yates	M. Waltrip	174.351
1990	Champion 400	M. Martin	Ford	138.822	5	Jack Roush	A. Kulwicki	174.982
	Miller 400	D. Earnhardt	Chevrolet	150.219	5	Richard Childress	None—conditions	
1989	Champion 400	R. Wallace	Pontiac	157.704	2	Raymond Beadle	G. Bodine	175.962
	Miller 400	B. Elliott	Ford	139.023	2	Harry Melling	K. Schrader	174.728
1988	Champion 400	Da. Allison	Ford	156.863	4	Harry Ranier	B. Elliott	174.940
	Miller 400	R. Wallace	Pontiac	153.551	5	Raymond Beadle	B. Elliott	172.687
1987	Champion 400	B. Elliott	Ford	138.648	3	Harry Melling	Da. Allison	170.705
	Miller Am. 400	D. Earnhardt	Chevrolet	148.454	5	Richard Childress	R. Wallace	170.746
1986	Champion 400	B. Elliott	Ford	135.376	3	Harry Melling	B. Parsons	171.924
	Miller Am. 400	B. Elliott	Ford	138.851	8	Harry Melling	T. Richmond	172.031
1985	Champion 400	B. Elliott	Ford	137.430	1	Harry Melling	B. Elliott	165.479
	Miller 400	B. Elliott	Ford	144.724	1	Harry Melling	None—conditions	
1984	Champion 400	D. Waltrip	Chevrolet	153.863	7	Junior Johnson	B. Elliott	165.217
	Miller 400	B. Elliott	Ford	134.705	1	Harry Melling	B. Elliott	164.339
1983	Champion 400	C. Yarborough	Chevrolet	147.511	7	Harry Ranier	T. Labonte	162.437
	Gabriel 400	C. Yarborough	Chevrolet	138.728	9	Harry Ranier	T. Labonte	161.965
1982	Champion 400	B. Allison	Buick	136.454	10	DiProspero/Gardner	B. Elliott	162.995
	Gabriel 400	C. Yarborough	Buick	118.110	4	M.C. Anderson	R. Bouchard	162.404
1981	Champion 400	R. Petty	Buick	123.457	7	Petty Enterprises	B. Elliott	161.501
	Gabriel 400	B. Allison	Buick	130.589	4	Harry Ranier	D. Waltrip	160.471
1980	Champion 400	C. Yarborough	Chevrolet	145.352	2	Junior Johnson	Buddy Baker	162.693
	Gabriel 400	B. Parsons	Chevrolet	131.808	1	M.C. Anderson	B. Parsons	163.662
1979	Champion 400	R. Petty	Chevrolet	130.376	5	Petty Enterprises	D. Pearson	162.992
	Gabriel 400	Buddy Baker	Chevrolet	135.798	3	Harry Ranier	N. Bonnett	162.371
1978	Champion 400	D.Pearson	Mercury	129.566	1	Wood Brothers	D.Pearson	164.073
	Gabriel 400	C. Yarborough	Oldsmobile	149.563	3	Junior Johnson	D.Pearson	163.936
1977	Champion 400	D. Waltrip	Chevrolet	137.944	3	DiProspero/Gardner	D.Pearson	160.346
	CAM2 400	C. Yarborough	Chevrolet	135.033	4	Junior Johnson	D.Pearson	159.175
1976	Champion 400	D.Pearson	Mercury	140.078	1	Wood Brothers	D.Pearson	160.875
	CAM2 400	D.Pearson	Mercury	141.148	8	Wood Brothers	R. Petty	158.569
1975	Champion 400	R. Petty	Dodge	107.583	4	Petty Enterprises	D.Pearson	159.798
	Motor State 400	D.Pearson	Mercury	131.398	3	Wood Brothers	C. Yarborough	158.541
1974	Yankee 400	D.Pearson	Mercury	133.045	1	Wood Brothers	D.Pearson	157.946
	Motor State 400 (c)	R. Petty	Dodge	127.987	4	Petty Enterprises	D.Pearson	156.426
1973	Motor State 400	D.Pearson	Mercury	153.485	2	Wood Brothers	Buddy Baker	158.273
1972	Yankee 400	D.Pearson	Mercury	134.416	4	Wood Brothers	R. Petty	157.607
	Motor State 400	D.Pearson	Mercury	146.639	3	Wood Brothers	B. Isaac	160.764
1971	Yankee 400 (b)	B. Allison	Mercury	149.862	2	Holman-Moody	P. Hamilton	161.901
	Motor State 400 (b)	B. Allison	Mercury	149.567	1	Holman-Moody	B. Allison	161.190
1970	Yankee 400 (b)	C. Glotzbach	Dodge	147.571	1	Ray Nichels	C. Glotzbach	157.363
	Motor State 400	C. Yarborough	Mercury	138.302	4	Wood Brothers	P. Hamilton	162.737
1969	Yankee 600 (a)	D. Pearson	Ford	115.508	1	Holman-Moody	D. Pearson	161.714
	Motor State 500	C. Yarborough	Mercury	139.254	4	Wood Brothers	Do. Allison	160.135

KEY (a) Race shortened by rain. (b) Track remeasured from 2 miles to 2.04 miles; ran 197-lap races. (c) Race shortened 40 miles because of energy shortage.

ALL MICHIGAN RACES

POLE WINNERS

David Pearson	10
Bill Elliott	6
Jeff Gordon	4
Bobby Labonte	4
Alan Kulwicki	3
Davey Allison	2
Buddy Baker	2
Geoffrey Bodine	2
Ron Bouchard	2
Jeff Burton	2
Ward Burton	2
Dale Earnhardt Jr. 2
Pete Hamilton	2
Dale Jarrett	2
Terry Labonte	2
Benny Parsons	2
Richard Petty	2
Ken Schrader	2
Loy Allen	1
Bobby Allison	1
Donnie Allison	1
Brett Bodine	1
Neil Bonnett	1
Ricky Craven	1
Charlie Glotzbach 1
Bobby Hamilton	1
Ernie Irvan	1
Bobby Isaac	1
Kasey Kahne	1
Joe Nemechek	1
Ryan Newman	1
Tim Richmond	1
Rusty Wallace	1
Darrell Waltrip	1
Michael Waltrip	1
Cale Yarborough 1

RACE WINNERS

David Pearson	9
Cale Yarborough	8
Bill Elliott	7
Rusty Wallace	5
Bobby Allison	4
Dale Jarrett	4
Mark Martin	4
Richard Petty	4
Davey Allison	3
Bobby Labonte	3
Greg Biffle	2
Dale Earnhardt	2
Jeff Gordon	2
Matt Kenseth	2
Ryan Newman	2
Darrell Waltrip	2
Buddy Baker	1
Geoffrey Bodine	1
Kurt Busch	1
Harry Gant	1
Charlie Glotzbach 1
Ernie Irvan	1
Kasey Kahne	1
Jeremy Mayfield	1
Benny Parsons	1
Ricky Rudd	1
Tony Stewart	1

RACE 1

POLE WINNERS

Jeff Gordon	4
David Pearson	3
Bill Elliott	2
Dale Jarrett	2
Bobby Labonte	2
Loy Allen	1
Bobby Allison	1
Davey Allison	1
Donnie Allison	1
Buddy Baker	1
Brett Bodine	1
Neil Bonnett	1
Ron Bouchard	1
Ward Burton	1
Bobby Hamilton	1
Pete Hamilton	1
Bobby Isaac	1
Kasey Kahne	1
Terry Labonte	1
Ryan Newman	1
Benny Parsons	1
Richard Petty	1
Tim Richmond	1
Ken Schrader	1
Rusty Wallace	1
Darrell Waltrip	1
Michael Waltrip	1
Cale Yarborough 1

RACE WINNERS

Cale Yarborough	6
Bill Elliott	4
David Pearson	4
Rusty Wallace	3
Bobby Allison	2
Davey Allison	2
Dale Earnhardt	2
Buddy Baker	1
Greg Biffle	1
Jeff Gordon	1
Kurt Busch	1
Ernie Irvan	1
Dale Jarrett	1
Kasey Kahne	1
Matt Kenseth	1
Bobby Labonte	1
Mark Martin	1
Ryan Newman	1
Benny Parsons	1
Richard Petty	1
Ricky Rudd	1
Tony Stewart	1

RACE 2

POLE WINNERS

David Pearson	7
Bill Elliott	4
Alan Kulwicki	3
Geoffrey Bodine	2
Jeff Burton	2
Dale Earnhardt Jr. 2
Bobby Labonte	2
Davey Allison	1
Buddy Baker	1
Johnny Benson	1
Ron Bouchard	1
Wart Burton	1
Ricky Craven	1
Charlie Glotzbach 1
Pete Hamilton	1
Ernie Irvan	1
Terry Labonte	1
Joe Nemechek	1
Benny Parsons	1
Richard Petty	1
Ken Schrader	1

RACE WINNERS

David Pearson	5
Bill Elliott	3
Dale Jarrett	3
Mark Martin	3
Richard Petty	2
Bobby Allison	2
Bobby Labonte	2
Rusty Wallace	2
Darrell Waltrip	2
Cale Yarborough	2
Davey Allison	1
Greg Biffle	1
Geoffrey Bodine	1
Harry Gant	1
Charlie Glotzbach 1
Jeff Gordon	1
Matt Kenseth	1
Sterling Marlin	1
Jeremy Mayfield	1
Ryan Newman	1

>>NASCAR BUSCH SERIES<<

YEAR BY YEAR WINNERS

Year	Event	Race winner	Car make	Avg. speed	Start pos.	Pole winner	Pole speed
2006	CARFAX 250	D. Earnhardt Jr.	Chevrolet	124.524	20	M. Martin	183.664
2005	Domino's Pizza 250	R. Newman	Dodge	136.986	38	None—conditions	
2004	Cabela's 250	Ky. Busch	Chevrolet	122.166	2	None—conditions	
2003	Cabela's 250	K. Harvick	Chevrolet	140.850	5	K. Kahne	186.490
2002	Cabela's 250	M. Waltrip	Chevrolet	135.644	2	K. Lepage	185.644
2001	NAPAonline.com 250	R. Newman	Ford	139.557	2	J. Spencer	184.824
2000	NAPAonline.com 250	T. Bodine	Chevrolet	162.749	16	B. Jones	184.786
1999	NAPA 200	D. Earnhardt Jr.	Chevrolet	158.975	3	D. Blaney	180.054
1998	Pepsi 200	J. Burton	Ford	167.910	1	J. Burton	177.052
1997	Detroit Gasket 200	S. Park	Chevrolet	159.681	4	H. Sadler	175.511
1996	Detroit Gasket 200	J. Purvis	Chevrolet	161.038	27	R. Craven	174.965
1995	Detroit Gasket 200	M. Martin	Ford	169.571	2	D. Jarrett	174.199
1994	Detroit Gasket 200	B. Labonte	Chevrolet	142.461	7	D. Cope	175.426

POLE WINNERS

Dave Blaney	1
Jeff Burton	1
Derrike Cope	1
Ricky Craven	1
Bill Elliott	1
Jeff Gordon	1
Dale Jarrett	1
Buckshot Jones	1
Kasey Kahne	1
Kevin Lepage	1
Mark Martin	1
Hermie Sadler	1
Jimmy Spencer	1

RACE WINNERS

Todd Bodine	2
Dale Earnhardt Jr.	2
Mark Martin	2
Ryan Newman	2
Jeff Burton	1
Kyle Busch	1
Kevin Harvick	1
Bobby Labonte	1
Jeff Purvis	1
Steve Park	1
Michael Waltrip	1

Earnhardt Jr.

YEAR BY YEAR WINNERS continued

Year	Event	Race winner	Car make	Avg. speed	Start pos.	Pole winner	Pole speed
1993	Detroit Gasket 200	M. Martin	Ford	124.611	2	B. Elliott	175.447
1992	Detroit Gasket 200	T. Bodine	Chevrolet	125.414	12	J. Gordon	173.135

QUALIFYING RECORD: Kasey Kahne, Ford; 186.490 mph (38.608 seconds), August 16, 2003
RACE RECORD: 250 miles: Todd Bodine, Chevrolet; 162.749 mph (1:32:10), August 19, 2000

>> NASCAR CRAFTSMAN TRUCK SERIES <<

YEAR BY YEAR WINNERS

Year	Event	Race winner	Car make	Avg. speed	Start pos.	Pole winner	Pole speed
2006	Con-way Freight 200	J. Benson	Toyota	116.534	5	M. Skinner	178.758
2005	Paramount Health 200	D. Setzer	Chevrolet	122.387	10	Ky. Busch	181.612
2004	Line-X 200	T. Kvapil	Toyota	125.479	8	None—conditions	
2003	Sears 200	B. Gaughan	Dodge	154.044	6	J. Leffler	178.037
2002	Michigan 200	R. Pressley	Dodge	142.208	8	None—conditions	
2000	Michigan 200	G. Biffle	Ford	138.408	2	J. McMurray	177.144
1999	goracing.com 200	G. Biffle	Ford	121.889	11	S. Compton	175.717

POLE WINNERS		RACE WINNERS	
Kyle Busch	1	Greg Biffle	2
Stacy Compton	1	Johnny Benson	1
Jamie McMurray	1	Brendan Gaughan	1
Jason Leffler	1	Travis Kvapil	1
Mike Skinner	1	Robert Pressley	1
		Dennis Setzer	1

Benson

QUALIFYING RECORD: Kyle Busch, Chevrolet; 181.612 mph (39.645 seconds), June 18, 2005
RACE RECORD: Brendan Gaughan, Dodge; 154.044 mph (1:17:54), July 26, 2003

>> NEW HAMPSHIRE INTERNATIONAL SPEEDWAY <<

TRACK FACTS >>> >>> **Location:** Loudon, N.H. >>> >>> **Owner:** Bob Bahre >>> >>> **Track length:** 1.058 miles >>>

>>> **Grandstand seating:** 91,000 >>> >>> **Tickets:** (603) 783-4931 >>> >>> **Website:** www.nhis.com >>> >>>

>> NASCAR NEXTEL CUP SERIES <<

>> TRACK RECORDS

Most wins: 4—Jeff Burton; **Most top fives:** 10—Jeff Gordon; **Most top 10s:** 14—Dale Jarrett; **Oldest winner:** Dale Jarrett, 44 years, 7 months, 26 days, July 22, 2001; **Youngest winner:** Kyle Busch, 21 years, 2 months, 14 days, July 16, 2006; **Most lead changes:** 23—Twice, most recently, July 21, 2002; **Fewest lead changes:** 1—September 17, 2000; **Most leaders:** 15—July 14, 1996; **Fewest leaders:** 1—September 17, 2000; **Most cautions:** 17—July 10, 1994; **Fewest cautions:** 2—July 13, 1997; **Most caution laps:** 78—July 10, 1994; **Fewest caution laps:** 10—July 13, 1997; **Most on the lead lap:** 30—July 21, 2002; **Fewest on the lead lap:** 7—July 11,19 93; **Most running at the finish:** 39—Three times, most recently, July 20, 2003; **Fewest running at the finish:** 30—Twice, most recently, September 17, 2000; **Most laps led by a race winner:** 300—Jeff Burton, September 17, 2000; **Fewest laps led by a race winner:** 2—Jeff Burton, July 11, 1999; **Closest margin of victory:** .292 seconds— Ryan Newman defeated Tony Stewart, September 18, 2005

>> QUALIFYING AND RACE RECORDS

QUALIFYING: Ryan Newman, Dodge; 133.357 mph (28.561 seconds), September 12, 2003
RACE: Jeff Burton, Ford; 117.134 mph (2:42:35), July 13, 1997

First NASCAR NEXTEL Cup Series race:
July 11, 1993 (Rusty Wallace, winner)
Banking on straights: 2 degrees
Length of front stretch: 1,500 feet
Length of back stretch: 1,500 feet

>>NEW HAMPSHIRE INTERNATIONAL SPEEDWAY<<

2007 SCHEDULE

NASCAR NEXTEL Cup Series
Event: Lenox Industrial Tools 300
Race: No. 17 of 36
Date: July 1 • **TV:** TNT • **Radio:** MRN

Event: Sylvania 300
Race: No. 27 of 36
Date: September 16 • **TV:** ABC • **Radio:** MRN

NASCAR Busch Series
Event: New England 200
Race: No. 18 of 35 • **Date:** June 30
TV: ESPN2 • **Radio:** MRN

NASCAR Craftsman Truck Series
Event: New Hampshire 200
Race: No. 18 of 25
Date: September 15 • **TV:** SPEED • **Radio:** MRN

Race names subject to change

YEAR BY YEAR WINNERS

Year	Event	Race winner	Car make	Avg. speed	Start pos.	Car owner	Pole winner	Pole speed
2006	Sylvania 300	K. Harvick	Chevrolet	102.195	1	Richard Childress	K. Harvick	132.282
	Lenox Ind. 300	Ky. Busch	Chevrolet	101.384	4	Rick Hendrick	R. Newman	129.683
2005	Sylvania 300	R. Newman	Dodge	95.891	13	Roger Penske	T. Stewart	131.143
	New England 300	T. Stewart	Chevrolet	102.608	13	Joe Gibbs	B. Vickers	130.327
2004	Sylvania 300	Ku. Busch	Ford	109.753	7	Jack Roush	None—conditions	
	Siemens 300	Ku. Busch	Ford	97.862	32	Jack Roush	R. Newman	132.360
2003	Sylvania 500	Ji. Johnson	Chevrolet	106.580	8	Rick Hendrick	R. Newman	133.357
	New England 300	Ji. Johnson	Chevrolet	96.924	6	Rick Hendrick	None—conditions	
2002	New Hampshire 300	R. Newman	Ford	105.081	1	Roger Penske	R. Newman	132.241
	New England 300	W. Burton	Dodge	92.342	31	Bill Davis	B. Elliott	131.469
2001	New Hampshire 300 (b)	R. Gordon	Chevrolet	103.594	31	Richard Childress	None—conditions	
	New England 300	D. Jarrett	Ford	102.131	9	Robert Yates	J. Gordon	131.770
2000	Dura-Lube/Kmart 300	J. Burton	Ford	102.003	2	Jack Roush	B. Labonte	127.632
	thatlook.com 300 (a)	T. Stewart	Pontiac	103.145	6	Joe Gibbs	R. Wallace	132.089
1999	Dura-Lube/Kmart 300	J. Nemechek	Chevrolet	100.673	11	Felix Sabates	R. Wallace	129.820
	Jiffy Lube 300	J. Burton	Ford	101.876	38	Jack Roush	J. Gordon	131.171
1998	CMT 300	J. Gordon	Chevrolet	112.078	1	Rick Hendrick	J. Gordon	129.033
	Jiffy Lube 300	J. Burton	Ford	102.996	5	Jack Roush	R. Craven	128.394
1997	CMT 300	J. Gordon	Chevrolet	100.364	13	Rick Hendrick	K. Schrader	129.182
	Jiffy Lube 300	J. Burton	Ford	117.134	15	Jack Roush	K. Schrader	129.423
1996	Jiffy Lube 300	E. Irvan	Ford	98.930	6	Robert Yates	R. Craven	129.379
1995	Slick 50 300	J. Gordon	Chevrolet	107.029	21	Rick Hendrick	M. Martin	128.815
1994	Slick 50 300	R. Rudd	Ford	87.599	3	Ricky Rudd	E. Irvan	127.197
1993	Slick 50 300	R. Wallace	Pontiac	105.947	33	Roger Penske	M. Martin	126.871

KEY (a) Race shortened by rain. (b) Race postponed to November 23 because of September 11 terrorist attacks.

ALL NEW HAMPSHIRE RACES

POLE WINNERS
Ryan Newman	4
Jeff Gordon	3
Ricky Craven	2
Mark Martin	2
Ken Schrader	2
Rusty Wallace	2
Bill Elliott	1
Kevin Harvick	1
Ernie Irvan	1
Bobby Labonte	1
Tony Stewart	1
Brian Vickers	1

RACE WINNERS
Jeff Burton	4
Jeff Gordon	3
Kurt Busch	2
Jimmy Johnson	2
Ryan Newman	2
Tony Stewart	2
Ward Burton	1
Kyle Busch	1
Robby Gordon	1
Kevin Harvick	1
Ernie Irvan	1
Dale Jarrett	1
Joe Nemechek	1
Ricky Rudd	1
Rusty Wallace	1

RACE 1

POLE WINNERS
Ricky Craven	2
Jeff Gordon	2
Mark Martin	2
Ryan Newman	2
Bill Elliott	1
Ernie Irvan	1
Ken Schrader	1
Brian Vickers	1
Rusty Wallace	1

RACE WINNERS
Jeff Burton	3
Tony Stewart	2
Ward Burton	1
Kurt Busch	1
Kyle Busch	1
Jeff Gordon	1
Ernie Irvan	1
Dale Jarrett	1
Jimmie Johnson	1
Ricky Rudd	1
Rusty Wallace	1

RACE 2

POLE WINNERS
Ryan Newman	2
Jeff Gordon	1
Kevin Harvick	1
Bobby Labonte	1
Ken Schrader	1
Tony Stewart	1
Rusty Wallace	1

RACE WINNERS
Jeff Gordon	2
Ryan Newman	2
Jeff Burton	1
Kurt Busch	1
Robby Gordon	1
Kevin Harvick	1
Jimmy Johnson	1
Joe Nemechek	1

>>NASCAR BUSCH SERIES<<

YEAR BY YEAR WINNERS

Year	Event	Race winner	Car make	Avg. speed	Start pos.	Pole winner	Pole speed
2006	New England 200	C. Edwards	Ford	105.624	9	Ky. Busch	128.204
2005	New England 200	M. Truex Jr.	Chevrolet	92.093	7	K. Harvick	130.336
2004	Siemens 200	M. Kenseth	Ford	93.709	21	J. McMurray	130.007
2003	New England 200	D. Green	Pontiac	108.005	37	None—conditions	
2002	Busch 200	B. Hamilton Jr.	Ford	110.368	2	S. Hmiel	129.406
2001	CVS Pharmacy 200	J. Keller	Ford	108.714	4	K. Harvick	130.716
2000	Busch 200	T. Fedewa	Chevrolet	89.366	1	T. Fedewa	130.247
1999	NASCAR Busch Series 200	E. Sawyer	Ford	103.324	2	J. Green	128.637
1998	Gumout 200	B. Jones	Pontiac	100.829	26	J. Bessey	127.701
1997	U.S. Cellular 200	M. McLaughlin	Chevrolet	76.752	12	None—conditions	
1996	Stanley 200 (a)	R. LaJoie	Chevrolet	96.953	2	None—conditions	
1995	NE Chevy 250	C. Little	Ford	104.972	9	M. McLaughlin	124.903
1994	NE Chevy 250	D. Cope	Ford	88.527	14	B. Labonte	124.871
1993	NE Chevy 250	R. Pressley	Chevrolet	89.560	3	J. Nemechek	124.875
1992	Budweiser 300	J. Burton	Oldsmobile	95.907	23	K. Wallace	122.532
	NE Chevy 250	J. Nemechek	Chevrolet	94.897	10	E. Irvan	122.422
1991	Budweiser 300	K. Wallace	Pontiac	109.093	3	J. Hensley	128.470
	NE Chevy 250	R. Craven	Chevrolet	90.832	1	R. Craven	121.800
1990	Budweiser 300	T. Ellis	Buick	85.797	4	J. Hensley	123.410
	NE Chevy 250	R. Mast	Buick	94.405	18	R. Craven	122.085

KEY (a) Race shortened to 200 laps.

QUALIFYING RECORD: Kevin Harvick, Chevrolet; 130.716 mph (29.138 seconds), May 11, 2001
RACE RECORD: Bobby Hamilton Jr., Ford; 110.368 mph (1:55:02), May 11, 2002

POLE WINNERS
Ricky Craven	2
Kevin Harvick	2
Jimmy Hensley	2
Joe Bessey	1
Kyle Busch	1
Tim Fedewa	1
Jeff Green	1
Shane Hmiel	1
Ernie Irvan	1
Bobby Labonte	1
Mike McLaughlin	1
Joe Nemechek	1
Kenny Wallace	1
Jamie McMurray	1

RACE WINNERS
Jeff Burton	1
Derrike Cope	1
Ricky Craven	1
Carl Edwards	1
Tommy Ellis	1
Tim Fedewa	1
David Green	1
Bobby Hamilton Jr.	1
Buckshot Jones	1
Jason Keller	1
Matt Kenseth	1
Randy LaJoie	1
Chad Little	1
Rick Mast	1
Mike McLaughlin	1
Joe Nemechek	1
Robert Pressley	1
Elton Sawyer	1
Martin Truex Jr.	1
Kenny Wallace	1

Edwards

>> NASCAR CRAFTSMAN TRUCK SERIES <<

Crawford

YEAR BY YEAR WINNERS

Year	Event	Race winner	Car make	Avg. speed	Start pos.	Pole winner	Pole speed
2006	Sylvania 200	J. Benson Jr.	Toyota	92.323	2	M. Skinner	129.626
2005	Sylvania 200	R. Crawford	Ford	101.244	5	M. Crafton	128.819
2004	New Hampshire 200	T. Kvapil	Toyota	89.482	3	J. Sprague	128.515
2003	New Hampshire 200	J. Spencer	Dodge	103.867	1	J. Spencer	127.346
2002	New England 200	T. Cook	Ford	103.549	2	J. Leffler	128.424
2001	New England 200	J. Sprague	Chevrolet	109.244	1	J. Sprague	128.091
2000	thatlook.com 200	K. Busch	Ford	98.491	5	J. Ruttman	127.885
1999	Pennzoil Tripleheader	D. Setzer	Dodge	101.810	10	S. Compton	126.745
1998	Pennzoil Tripleheader	A. Houston	Chevrolet	104.222	7	M. Wallace	126.994
1997	Pennzoil Tripleheader	J. Sauter	Chevrolet	97.138	26	J. Sprague	126.985
1996	Pennzoil Tripleheader	R. Hornaday Jr.	Chevrolet	97.129	8	M. Skinner	124.891

POLE WINNERS		RACE WINNERS	
Jack Sprague	3	Johnny Benson Jr.	1
Mike Skinner	2	Kurt Busch	1
Stacy Compton	1	Terry Cook	1
Matt Crafton	1	Rick Crawford	1
Jason Leffler	1	Ron Hornaday	1
Joe Ruttman	1	Andy Houston	1
Jimmy Spencer	1	Travis Kvapil	1
Mike Wallace	1	Jay Sauter	1
		Dennis Setzer	1
		Jimmy Spencer	1
		Jack Sprague	1

QUALIFYING RECORD: Mike Skinner, Toyota; 129.626 mph (29.383 seconds), September 16, 2006
RACE RECORD: Jack Sprague, Chevrolet; 109.244 mph (1:56:13), July 21, 2001

>> PHOENIX INTERNATIONAL RACEWAY <<

TRACK FACTS >>> >>> **Location:** Avondale, Ariz. >>> >>> **Owner:** International Speedway Corp. >>> >>> **Track length:** 1 mile

>>> >>> **Grandstand seating:** 76,812 >>> >>> **Tickets:** (602) 252-2227 >>> >>> **Website:** www.phoenixraceway.com >>> >>>

>> NASCAR NEXTEL CUP SERIES <<

>> TRACK RECORDS

Most wins: 2—Davey Allison, Jeff Burton, Dale Earnhardt Jr., Kevin Harvick; **Most top fives:** 8—Mark Martin; **Most top 10s:** 14—Mark Martin; **Oldest winner:** Rusty Wallace, 42 years, 2 months, 11 days, October 25, 1998; **Youngest winner:** Kyle Busch, 20 years, 6 months, 11 days, November 13, 2005; **Most lead changes:** 23—November 5, 2000; **Fewest lead changes:** 1—November 4, 1990; **Most leaders:** 16—October 29, 1995; **Fewest leaders:** 2—November 4, 1990; **Most cautions:** 11—November 7, 2004; **Fewest cautions:** 2—November 7, 1999; **Most caution laps:** 66—November 2, 2003; **Fewest caution laps:** 10—November 7, 1999; **Most on the lead lap:** 29—November 2, 2003; **Fewest on the lead lap:** 3—October 30, 1994; **Most running at the finish:** 41—Twice, most recently, November 7, 1999; **Fewest running at the finish:** 27—November 5, 1989; **Most laps led by a race winner:** 262—Dale Earnhardt, November 4, 1990; **Fewest laps led by a race winner:** 10—Kevin Harvick, April 22, 2006; **Closest margin of victory:** 0.17 seconds—Mark Martin defeated Ernie Irvan, October 31, 1993

>> QUALIFYING AND RACE RECORDS

QUALIFYING: Ryan Newman, Dodge, 135.854 mph (26.499 seconds), November 5, 2004
RACE: Tony Stewart, Pontiac; 118.132 mph (2:38:28), November 7, 1999

9° to 11° Banking in Turns

ARIZONA
Phoenix

First NASCAR NEXTEL Cup Series race:
November 6, 1988 (Alan Kulwicki, winner)
Banking on front stretch: 3 degrees
Banking on back stretch: 9 degrees
Length of front stretch: 1,179 feet
Length of back stretch: 1,551 feet

>>PHOENIX INTERNATIONAL RACEWAY <<

2007 SCHEDULE

NASCAR NEXTEL Cup Series
Event: Subway Fresh 500
Race: No. 8 of 36
Date: April 21 • **TV:** FOX • **Radio:** MRN

Event: Checker Auto Parts 500
Race: No. 35 of 36
Date: November 11 • **TV:** ABC • **Radio:** MRN

NASCAR Busch Series
Event: Bashas' Supermarkets 200
Race: No. 9 of 35 • **Date:** April 20
TV: ESPN2 • **Radio:** MRN

Event: Arizona Travel 200
Race: No. 34 of 35 • **Date:** November 10
TV: ESPN2 • **Radio:** MRN

NASCAR Craftsman Truck Series
Event: Casino Arizona 150
Race: No. 24 of 25 • **Date:** November 9
TV: SPEED • **Radio:** MRN
Race names subject to change

YEAR BY YEAR WINNERS

Year	Event	Race winner	Car make	Avg. speed	Start pos.	Car owner	Pole winner	Pole speed
2006	Checker Auto Parks 500	K. Harvick	Chevrolet	96.131	2	Richard Childress	J. Gordon	134..464
	Subway Fresh 500	K. Harvick	Chevrolet	107.063	15	Richard Childress	Ky. Busch	133.744
2005	Checker Auto Parts 500	Ky. Busch	Chevrolet	102.641	15	Rick Hendrick	D. Hamlin	134.173
	Subway Fresh 500	Ku. Busch	Ford	102.707	2	Jack Roush	J. Gordon	133.675
2004	Checker Auto Parts 500	D. Earnhardt. Jr.	Chevrolet	94.848	14	Teresa Earnhardt	R. Newman	135.854
2003	Checker Auto Parts 500	D. Earnhardt Jr.	Chevrolet	93.984	11	Teresa Earnhardt	R. Newman	133.675
2002	Checker Auto Parts 500	M. Kenseth	Ford	113.857	28	Jack Roush	R. Newman	132.655
2001	Checker Auto Parts 500	J. Burton	Ford	102.613	3	Jack Roush	C. Atwood	131.296
2000	Checker/Dura-Lube 500	J. Burton	Ford	105.041	2	Jack Roush	R. Wallace	134.178
1999	Dura-Lube 500	T. Stewart	Pontiac	118.132	11	Joe Gibbs	J. Andretti	132.670
1998	Dura-Lube 500 (a)	R. Wallace	Ford	108.211	6	Roger Penske	K. Schrader	131.234
1997	Dura-Lube 500	D. Jarrett	Ford	110.824	9	Robert Yates	B. Hamilton	130.933
1996	Dura-Lube 500	B. Hamilton	Pontiac	109.709	17	Petty Enterprises	B. Labonte	131.076
1995	Dura-Lube 500	R. Rudd	Ford	102.128	29	Ricky Rudd	B. Elliott	130.020
1994	Slick 50 500	T. Labonte	Chevrolet	107.463	19	Rick Hendrick	S. Marlin	129.833
1993	Slick 50 500	M. Martin	Ford	100.375	3	Jack Roush	B. Elliott	129.482
1992	Pyroil 500	Da. Allison	Ford	103.885	12	Robert Yates	R. Wallace	128.141
1991	Pyroil 500	Da. Allison	Ford	95.746	13	Robert Yates	G. Bodine	127.589
1990	Checker 500	D. Earnhardt	Chevrolet	96.786	3	Richard Childress	R. Wallace	124.443
1989	Autoworks 500	B. Elliott	Ford	105.683	13	Harry Melling	K. Schrader	124.645
1988	Checker 500	A. Kulwicki	Ford	90.457	21	Alan Kulwicki	G. Bodine	123.203

KEY (a) Race shortened by rain.

POLE WINNERS		RACE WINNERS	
Ryan Newman	3	Davey Allison	2
Rusty Wallace	3	Jeff Burton	2
Geoffrey Bodine	2	Dale Earnhardt Jr.	2
Bill Elliott	2	Kevin Harvick	2
Jeff Gordon	2	Kurt Busch	1
Ken Schrader	2	Kyle Busch	1
John Andretti	1	Dale Earnhardt	1
Casey Atwood	1	Bill Elliott	1
Kyle Busch	1	Bobby Hamilton	1
Bobby Hamilton	1	Dale Jarrett	1
Denny Hamlin	1	Matt Kenseth	1
Bobby Labonte	1	Alan Kulwicki	1
Sterling Marlin	1	Terry Labonte	1
		Mark Martin	1
		Ricky Rudd	1
		Tony Stewart	1
		Rusty Wallace	1

Gordon

>>NASCAR BUSCH SERIES<<

Biffle

YEAR BY YEAR WINNERS

Year	Event	Race winner	Car make	Avg. speed	Start pos.	Pole winner	Pole speed
2006	Arizona Travel 200	M. Kenseth	Ford	91.202	1	M. Kenseth	132.144
	Bashas' Supermarkets 200	K. Harvick	Chevrolet	92.250	14	J. Leffler	130.170
2005	Arizona 200	C. Edwards	Ford	97.893	1	C. Edwards	133.151
	Bashas' Supermarkets 200	G. Biffle	Ford	83.007	20	K. Kahne	132.091
2004	Bashas' Supermarkets 200	J. McMurray	Dodge	96.031	3	Ky. Busch	133.819
2003	Bashas' Supermarkets 200	B. Hamilton Jr.	Ford	96.734	4	K. Harvick	132.930
2002	Bashas' Supermarkets 200	S. Wimmer	Pontiac	96.709	18	G. Biffle	132.193
2001	Outback Steakhouse 200	G. Biffle	Ford	99.834	4	J. Spencer	131.339
2000	Outback Steakhouse 200	J. Burton	Ford	115.145	3	J. Leffler	130.957
1999	Outback Steakhouse 200	J. Gordon	Chevrolet	115.053	3	K. Schrader	129.580

POLE WINNERS		RACE WINNERS	
Jason Leffler	2	Greg Biffle	2
Carl Edwards	1	Jeff Burton	1
Greg Biffle	1	Carl Edwards	1
Kyle Busch	1	Jeff Gordon	1
Kevin Harvick	1	Bobby Hamilton Jr.	1
Kasey Kahne	1	Kevin Harvick	1
Matt Kenseth	1	Matt Kenseth	1
Ken Schrader	1	Jamie McMurray	1
Jimmy Spencer	1	Scott Wimmer	1

QUALIFYING RECORD: Kyle Busch, Chevrolet; 133.819 mph (26.902 seconds), November 4, 2004
RACE RECORD: Jeff Burton, Ford; 115.145 mph (1:44:13), November 4, 2000

>>NASCAR CRAFTSMAN TRUCK SERIES<<

YEAR BY YEAR WINNERS

Year	Event	Race winner	Car make	Avg. speed	Start pos.	Pole winner	Pole speed
2006	Casino Arizona 150	J. Benson Jr.	Toyota	86.221	1	J. Benson Jr.	132.660
2005	Chevy Silverado 150	T. Bodine	Toyota	96.515	6	B. Whitt	131.200
2004	Chevy Silverado 150	D. Starr	Chevrolet	90.756	5	J. Sprague	131.186
2003	Chevy Silverado 150	K. Harvick	Chevrolet	107.527	2	T. Musgrave	129.427
2002	Chevy Silverado 150	K. Harvick	Chevrolet	108.014	3	R. Crawford	128.329
2001	Chevy Silverado 150	G. Biffle	Ford	92.726	11	S. Compton	127.700
2000	Chevy Trucks NASCAR 150	J. Ruttman	Dodge	99.797	1	J. Ruttman	129.204
1999	Chevy Trucks NASCAR 150	R. Hornaday Jr.	Chevrolet	95.137	5	J. Sprague	128.402
1998	Chevy Trucks Desert Star	R. Hornaday Jr.	Chevrolet	101.714	4	S. Compton	127.596
	GM Goodwrench 300	M. Bliss	Ford	103.669	1	M. Bliss	127.155
1997	Chevy Trucks Desert Star	J. Sprague	Chevrolet	103.053	1	J. Sprague	121.236
	GM Goodwrench 300	J. Ruttman	Ford	103.942	7	M. Bliss	127.741
1996	Chevrolet Desert Star Cl.	J. Sprague	Chevrolet	84.780	2	M. Skinner	125.257
	GM Goodwrench 300	J. Sprague	Chevrolet	95.289	1	J. Sprague	126.957
1995	Skoal Copper World	M. Skinner	Chevrolet	87.565	16	R. Hornaday Jr.	123.665
	GM Goodwrench 200	M. Skinner	Chevrolet	91.102	3	J. Sprague	124.378

POLE WINNERS		RACE WINNERS	
Jack Sprague	5	Jack Sprague	3
Mike Bliss	2	Kevin Harvick	2
Stacy Compton	2	Ron Hornaday Jr.	2
Johnny Benson Jr.	1	Joe Ruttman	2
Rick Crawford	1	Mike Bliss	2
Ron Hornaday Jr.	1	Johnny Benson Jr.	1
Ted Musgrave	1	Greg Biffle	1
Joe Ruttman	1	Mike Bliss	1
Mike Skinner	1	Todd Bodine	1
Brandon Whitt	1	David Starr	1

Bodine

QUALIFYING RECORD: Johnny Benson Jr., Toyota; 132.660 mph (27.137 seconds), November 10, 2006
RACE RECORD: Kevin Harvick, Chevrolet; 108.014 mph (1:24:26), November 8, 2002

>>POCONO RACEWAY<<

TRACK FACTS >>> >>> **Location:** Long Pond, Pa. >>> >>> **Owner:** Pocono Raceway, Inc. >>> >>> **Track length:** 2.5 miles >>>

>>> **Estimated capacity:** 100,000 >>> >>> **Tickets:** (800) 722-3929 >>> >>> **Website:** www.poconoraceway.com >>> >>>

>>NASCAR NEXTEL CUP SERIES<<

>>TRACK RECORDS

Most wins: 5—Bill Elliott; **Most top fives:** 19—Mark Martin; **Most top 10s:** 27—Mark Martin; **Oldest winner:** Harry Gant, 50 years, 5 months, 7 days, June 7, 1990; **Youngest winner:** Jeff Gordon, 24 years, 10 months, 12 days, June 16, 1996; **Most lead changes:** 56—July 30, 1979; **Fewest lead changes:** 10—July 26, 1998; **Most leaders:** 16—Three times, most recently, June 13, 2004; **Fewest leaders:** 4—Twice, most recently, June 9, 1985; **Most cautions:** 13— Twice, most recently, July 24, 2005; **Fewest cautions:** 1—July 30, 1978; **Most caution laps:** 57—June 13, 2004; **Fewest caution laps:** 3—July 30, 1978; **Most on the lead lap:** 28— July 23, 2006; **Fewest on the lead lap:** 2—Twice, most recently, June 6, 1982; **Most running at the finish:** 41—July 23, 2006; **Fewest running at the finish:** 18—July 25, 1982; **Most laps led by a race winner:** 164—Jeff Gordon, July 26, 1998; **Fewest laps led by a race winner:** 4— Bobby Labonte, July 29, 2001; **Closest margin of victory:** 0.02 seconds—Bill Elliott defeated Harry Gant, June 9, 1985

>>QUALIFYING AND RACE RECORDS

QUALIFYING: Kasey Kahne, Dodge; 172.533 mph (52.164 seconds), June 11, 2004
RACE: Rusty Wallace, Ford; 144.892 mph (3:27:03), July 21, 1996

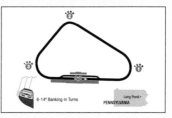

First NASCAR NEXTEL Cup Series race:
August 4, 1974 (Richard Petty, winner)
Banking on straights: None
Length of front stretch: 3,740 feet
Length of short stretch: 1,780 feet
Length of back stretch: 3,055 feet

2007 SCHEDULE

NASCAR NEXTEL Cup Series
Event: Pocono 500
Race: No. 14 of 36
Date: June 10
TV: TNT • Radio: MRN

Event: Pennsylvania 500
Race: No. 21 of 36
Date: August 5
TV: ESPN • Radio: MRN

Race names subject to change

YEAR BY YEAR WINNERS

Year	Event	Race winner	Car make	Avg. speed	Start pos.	Car owner	Pole winner	Pole speed
2006	Pennsylvania 500	D. Hamlin	Chevrolet	132.626	1	Joe Gibbs	D. Hamlin	169.827
	Pocono 500	D. Hamlin	Chevrolet	131.656	1	Joe Gibbs	D. Hamlin	169.638
2005	Pennsylvania 500	Ku. Busch	Ford	125.283	2	Jack Roush	J. McMurray	168.761
	Pocono 500	C. Edwards	Ford	129.177	29	Jack Roush	M. Waltrip	169.052
2004	Pennsylvania 500	J. Johnson	Chevrolet	126.271	14	Rick Hendrick	C. Mears	171.720
	Pocono 500	J. Johnson	Chevrolet	112.129	5	Rick Hendrick	K. Kahne	172.533
2003	Pennsylvania 500	R. Newman	Dodge	127.705	1	Roger Penske	R. Newman	170.358
	Pocono 500	T. Stewart	Chevrolet	134.892	4	Joe Gibbs	J. Johnson	170.645
2002	Pennsylvania 500	(a)B. Elliott	Dodge	125.809	1	Ray Evernham	B. Elliott	170.568
	Pocono 500	D. Jarrett	Ford	143.426	13	Robert Yates	None—conditions	
2001	Pennsylvania 500	B. Labonte	Pontiac	134.590	11	Joe Gibbs	T. Bodine	170.326
	Pocono 500	R. Rudd	Ford	134.389	1	Robert Yates	R. Rudd	170.503
2000	Pennsylvania 500	R. Wallace	Ford	130.662	2	Roger Penske	T. Stewart	172.391
	Pocono 500	J. Mayfield	Ford	139.741	22	Michael Kranefuss	R. Wallace	171.625
1999	Pennsylvania 500	B. Labonte	Pontiac	116.982	4	Joe Gibbs	M. Skinner	170.451
	Pocono 500	B. Labonte	Pontiac	118.898	3	Joe Gibbs	S. Marlin	170.506
1998	Pennsylvania 500	J. Gordon	Chevrolet	134.660	2	Rick Hendrick	W. Burton	168.805
	Pocono 500	J. Mayfield	Ford	117.809	3	Michael Kranefuss	J. Gordon	168.042
1997	Pennsylvania 500	D. Jarrett	Ford	142.068	4	Robert Yates	J. Nemechek	168.881
	Pocono 500	J. Gordon	Chevrolet	139.828	11	Rick Hendrick	B. Hamilton	168.089
1996	Miller 500	R. Wallace	Ford	144.892	13	Roger Penske	M. Martin	168.410
	Teamwork 500	J. Gordon	Chevrolet	139.104	1	Rick Hendrick	J. Gordon	169.725

Year	Event	Race winner	Car make	Avg. speed	Start pos.	Car owner	Pole winner	Pole speed
1995	Miller 500	D. Jarrett	Ford	134.038	15	Robert Yates	B. Elliott	162.496
	Teamwork 500	T. Labonte	Chevrolet	137.720	27	Rick Hendrick	K. Schrader	163.375
1994	Miller 500	G. Bodine	Ford	136.075	1	Geoffrey Bodine	G. Bodine	163.689
	Teamwork 500	R. Wallace	Ford	128.801	1	Roger Penske	R. Wallace	164.558
1993	Miller 500	D. Earnhardt	Chevrolet	133.343	11	Richard Childress	K. Schrader	162.934
	Champion SP 500	K. Petty	Pontiac	138.005	8	Felix Sabates	K. Schrader	162.816
1992	Miller 500	D. Waltrip	Chevrolet	134.058	8	Darrell Waltrip	Da. Allison	162.022
	Champion SP 500	A. Kulwicki	Ford	144.023	6	Alan Kulwicki	K. Schrader	162.499
1991	Miller 500 (a)	R. Wallace	Pontiac	115.459	10	Roger Penske	A. Kulwicki	161.473
	Champion SP 500	D. Waltrip	Chevrolet	122.666	13	Darrell Waltrip	M. Martin	161.996
1990	AC S. Plug 500	G. Bodine	Ford	124.070	4	Junior Johnson	M. Martin	158.264
	Miller Draft 500	H. Gant	Oldsmobile	120.600	16	Leo Jackson	E. Irvan	158.750
1989	AC S. Plug 500	B. Elliott	Ford	117.847	14	Harry Melling	K. Schrader	157.809
	Miller HL 500	T. Labonte	Ford	131.320	23	Junior Johnson	R. Wallace	157.489
1988	AC S. Plug 500	B. Elliott	Ford	122.866	2	Harry Melling	M. Shepherd	157.153
	Miller HL 500	G. Bodine	Chevrolet	126.147	3	Rick Hendrick	A. Kulwicki	158.806
1987	Summer 500	D. Earnhardt	Chevrolet	121.745	16	Richard Childress	T. Richmond	155.979
	Miller HL 500	T. Richmond	Chevrolet	122.166	3	Rick Hendrick	T. Labonte	155.502
1986	Summer 500 (a)	T. Richmond	Chevrolet	124.218	5	Rick Hendrick	H. Gant	154.392
	Miller HL 500	T. Richmond	Chevrolet	113.166	3	Rick Hendrick	G. Bodine	153.625
1985	Summer 500	B. Elliott	Ford	134.008	2	Harry Melling	B. Elliott	151.973
	Van Scoy 500	B. Elliott	Ford	138.974	1	Harry Melling	B. Elliott	152.563
1984	Like Cola 500	H. Gant	Chevrolet	121.351	3	Hal Needham	B. Elliott	152.184
	Van Scoy 500	C. Yarborough	Chevrolet	138.164	12	Harry Ranier	D. Pearson	150.921
1983	Like Cola 500	T. Richmond	Pontiac	114.818	1	Raymond Beadle	T. Richmond	151.981
	Van Scoy 500	B. Allison	Buick	128.636	7	DiProspero-Gardner	D. Waltrip	152.315
1982	Mt. Dew 500	B. Allison	Buick	115.496	4	DiProspero-Gardner	C. Yarborough	150.764
	Van Scoy 500	B. Allison	Buick	113.579	3	DiProspero-Gardner	None—conditions	
1981	Mt. Dew 500	D. Waltrip	Buick	119.111	1	Junior Johnson	D. Waltrip	150.148
1980	Coca-Cola 500	N. Bonnett	Mercury	124.395	2	Wood Brothers	C. Yarborough	151.469
1979	Coca-Cola 500	C. Yarborough	Chevrolet	115.207	2	Junior Johnson	H. Gant	148.711
1978	Coca-Cola 500	D. Waltrip	Chevrolet	142.540	4	DiProspero-Gardner	B. Parsons	149.235
1977	Coca-Cola 500	B. Parsons	Chevrolet	128.379	4	L.G. DeWitt	D. Waltrip	147.591
1976	Purolator 500	R. Petty	Dodge	115.875	5	Petty Enterprises	C. Yarborough	147.865
1975	Purolator 500	D. Pearson	Mercury	111.179	2	Wood Brothers	B. Allison	146.491
1974	Purolator 500	R. Petty	Dodge	115.593	3	Petty Enterprises	Buddy Baker	N/A

KEY (a) Race shortened by rain.

ALL POCONO RACES

POLE WINNERS

Bill Elliott	5
Ken Schrader	5
Mark Martin	3
Rusty Wallace	3
Darrell Waltrip	3
Geoffrey Bodine	2
Harry Gant	2
Jeff Gordon	2
Denny Hamlin	2
Alan Kulwicki	2
Tim Richmond	2
Bobby Allison	1
Davey Allison	1
Buddy Baker	1
Todd Bodine	1
Ward Burton	1
Bobby Hamilton	1
Ernie Irvan	1
Jimmy Johnson	1
Kasey Kahne	1
Terry Labonte	1
Sterling Marlin	1
Jamie McMurray	1
Casey Mears	1
Joe Nemechek	1
Ryan Newman	1
Benny Parsons	1
David Pearson	1
Ricky Rudd	1
Morgan Shepherd	1
Mike Skinner	1
Tony Stewart	1
Michael Waltrip	1

RACE WINNERS

Bill Elliott	5
Tim Richmond	4
Rusty Wallace	4
Darrell Waltrip	4
Bobby Allison	3
Geoffrey Bodine	3
Jeff Gordon	3
Dale Jarrett	3
Bobby Labonte	3
Dale Earnhardt	2
Harry Gant	2
Denny Hamlin	2
Jimmy Johnson	2
Terry Labonte	2
Jeremy Mayfield	2
Richard Petty	2
Cale Yarborough	2
Neil Bonnett	1
Kurt Busch	1
Carl Edwards	1
Alan Kulwicki	1
Ryan Newman	1
Benny Parsons	1
David Pearson	1
Kyle Petty	1
Ricky Rudd	1
Tony Stewart	1

RACE 1

POLE WINNERS

Ken Schrader	3
Rusty Wallace	3
Darrell Waltrip	3
Jeff Gordon	2
Cale Yarborough	2
Bobby Allison	1
Buddy Baker	1
Geoffrey Bodine	1
Bill Elliott	1
Harry Gant	1
Bobby Hamilton	1
Denny Hamlin	1
Ernie Irvan	1
Jimmy Johnson	1
Kasey Kahne	1
Alan Kulwicki	1
Terry Labonte	1
Sterling Marlin	1
Mark Martin	1
Benny Parsons	1
David Pearson	1
Ricky Rudd	1
Michael Waltrip	1

RACE WINNERS

Darrell Waltrip	3
Bobby Allison	2
Jeff Gordon	2
Terry Labonte	2
Jeremy Mayfield	2
Richard Petty	2
Tim Richmond	2
Cale Yarborough	2
Geoffrey Bodine	1
Neil Bonnett	1
Carl Edwards	1
Bill Elliott	1
Harry Gant	1
Denny Hamlin	1
Dale Jarrett	1
Jimmie Johnson	1
Alan Kulwicki	1
Bobby Labonte	1
Benny Parsons	1
David Pearson	1
Kyle Petty	1
Ricky Rudd	1
Tony Stewart	1
Rusty Wallace	1

RACE 2

POLE WINNERS

Bill Elliott	4
Mark Martin	2
Tim Richmond	2
Ken Schrader	2
Davey Allison	1
Geoffrey Bodine	1
Todd Bodine	1
Ward Burton	1
Harry Gant	1
Denny Hamlin	1
Alan Kulwicki	1
Jamie McMurray	1
Casey Mears	1
Joe Nemechek	1
Ryan Newman	1
Morgan Shepherd	1
Mike Skinner	1
Benny Parsons	1
Tony Stewart	1
Cale Yarborough	1

RACE WINNERS

Bill Elliott	4
Rusty Wallace	3
Geoffrey Bodine	2
Dale Earnhardt	2
Dale Jarrett	2
Bobby Labonte	2
Tim Richmond	2
Bobby Allison	1
Kurt Busch	1
Harry Gant	1
Jeff Gordon	1
Denny Hamlin	1
Jimmie Johnson	1
Ryan Newman	1
Darrell Waltrip	1

>>RICHMOND INTERNATIONAL RACEWAY<<

TRACK FACTS >>> >>> **Location:** Richmond, Va. >>> >>> **Owner:** International Speedway Corp. >>> >>> **Track length:** .750 miles

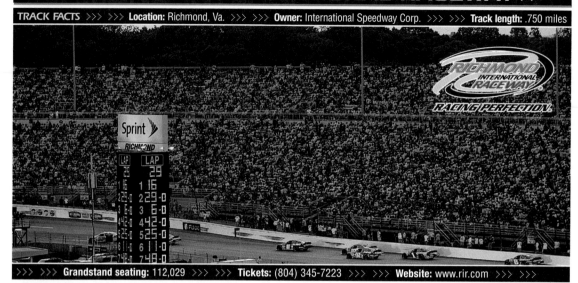

>>> >>> **Grandstand seating:** 112,029 >>> >>> **Tickets:** (804) 345-7223 >>> >>> **Website:** www.rir.com >>> >>>

>>NASCAR NEXTEL CUP SERIES<<

>> TRACK RECORDS

Most wins: 13—Richard Petty; **Most top fives:** 34—Richard Petty; **Most top 10s:** 41—Richard Petty; **Oldest winner:** Harry Gant, 51 Years, 7 months, 28 days, September 7, 1991; **Youngest winner:** Richard Petty, 23 years, 9 months, 21 days, April 23, 1961; **Most lead changes:** 25—Twice, most recently, March 3, 1996; **Fewest lead changes:** 2—Seven times, most recently, February 23, 1975; **Most leaders:** 16—September 10, 1994; **Fewest leaders:** 2—Eight times, most recently, March 11, 1979; **Most laps led in a 400-lap race:** 369, Bobby Allison, September 9, 1979; **Most cautions:** 15—May 3, 2003; **Fewest cautions:** 0—March 7, 1976; **Most caution laps:** 123—Twice, most recently, September 8, 1974; **Fewest caution laps:** 0—March 7, 1976; **Most on the lead lap:** 23—May 3, 2003; **Fewest on the lead lap:** 1—22 times, most recently, October 12, 1975; **Most running at the finish:** 39—Four times, most recently, September 9, 2006; **Fewest running at the finish:** 1—April 19, 1953; **Most laps led by a race winner:** 488—David Pearson, September 13, 1970; **Fewest laps led by a race winner:** 4—Kyle Petty, February 23, 1986; **Closest margin of victory:** 0.051 seconds—Jeff Burton defeated Jeff Gordon, September 12, 1998

>> QUALIFYING AND RACE RECORDS

QUALIFYING: Brian Vickers, Chevrolet; 129.983 mph (20.772 seconds), May 14, 2004
RACE: Dale Jarrett, Ford; 109.047 mph (2:45:04), September 6, 1997

14° Banking in Turns

VIRGINIA
Richmond ★

First NASCAR NEXTEL Cup Series race:
April 19, 1953 (Lee Petty, winner)
Banking on front stretch: 8 degrees
Banking on back stretch: 2 degrees
Length of front stretch: 1,290 feet
Length of back stretch: 860 feet

2007 SCHEDULE

NASCAR NEXTEL Cup Series
Event: Crown Royal 400
Race: No. 10 of 36
Date: May 5
TV: FOX • **Radio:** MRN

Event: Chevy Rock & Roll 400
Race: No. 26 of 36
Date: September 8
TV: ABC • **Radio:** MRN

NASCAR Busch Series
Event: Circuit City 250
Race: No. 11 of 35
Date: May 4 • **TV:** ESPN2 • **Radio:** MRN

Event: Emerson Radio 250
Race: No. 28 of 35
Date: September 7 • **TV:** ESPN2 • **Radio:** MRN
Race names subject to change

YEAR BY YEAR WINNERS

Year	Event	Race winner	Car make	Avg. speed	Start pos.	Car owner	Pole winner	Pole speed
2006	Chevy Rock & Roll 400	K. Harvick	Chevrolet	101.342	5	Richard Childress	D. Hamlin	127.986
	Crown Royal 400	D. Earnhardt Jr.	Chevrolet	97.061	10	Teresa Earnhardt	G. Biffle	127.395
2005	Chevy Rock & Roll 400	Ku. Busch	Ford	98.567	5	Jack Roush	K. Harvick	128.425
	Chevy Am. Revolution 400	K. Kahne	Dodge	100.316	1	Ray Evernham	K. Kahne	129.964
2004	Chevy Rock & Roll 400	J. Mayfield	Dodge	98.946	7	Ray Evernham	R. Newman	128.700
	Chevy Am. Revolution 400	D. Earnhardt Jr.	Chevrolet	98.253	4	Teresa Earnhardt	B. Vickers	129.983
2003	Chevrolet 400	R. Newman	Dodge	94.945	11	Roger Penske	M. Skinner	125.792
	Pontiac Excitement 400	J. Nemechek	Chevrolet	126.511	2	Joe Hendrick	T. Labonte	126.511
2002	Chevrolet 400	M. Kenseth	Ford	94.787	25	Jack Roush	Ji. Johnson	126.145
	Pontiac 400	T. Stewart	Pontiac	86.824	3	Joe Gibbs	W. Burton	127.389
2001	Chevrolet 400	R. Rudd	Ford	95.146	9	Robert Yates	J. Gordon	124.902
	Pontiac 400	T. Stewart	Pontiac	95.872	7	Joe Gibbs	M. Martin	124.613
2000	Chevrolet 400	J. Gordon	Chevrolet	99.871	13	Rick Hendrick	J. Burton	125.780
	Pontiac 400	D. Earnhardt Jr.	Chevrolet	99.374	5	Teresa Earnhardt	R. Wallace	124.740
1999	Exide Batteries 400	T. Stewart	Pontiac	104.006	2	Joe Gibbs	M. Skinner	125.465
	Pontiac 400	D. Jarrett	Ford	100.102	21	Robert Yates	J. Gordon	126.499
1998	Exide Batteries 400	J. Burton	Ford	91.985	3	Jack Roush	R. Wallace	125.377
	Pontiac 400	T. Labonte	Chevrolet	97.044	16	Rick Hendrick	J. Gordon	125.558
1997	Exide Batteries 400	D. Jarrett	Ford	109.047	23	Robert Yates	B. Elliott	124.723
	Pontiac 400	R. Wallace	Ford	108.499	7	Roger Penske	None—conditions	

YEAR BY YEAR WINNERS continued

Year	Event	Race winner	Car make	Avg. speed	Start pos.	Car owner	Pole winner	Pole speed
1996	Miller 400	E. Irvan	Ford	105.469	16	Robert Yates	M. Martin	122.744
	Pontiac 400	J. Gordon	Chevrolet	102.750	2	Rick Hendrick	T. Labonte	123.728
1995	Miller 400	R. Wallace	Ford	104.459	7	Roger Penske	D. Earnhardt	122.543
	Pontiac 400	T. Labonte	Chevrolet	106.425	24	Rick Hendrick	J. Gordon	124.757
1994	Miller 400	T. Labonte	Chevrolet	104.156	3	Rick Hendrick	T. Musgrave	124.052
	Pontiac 400	E. Irvan	Ford	98.334	7	Robert Yates	T. Musgrave	123.474
1993	Miller 400	R. Wallace	Pontiac	99.917	3	Roger Penske	B. Labonte	122.006
	Pontiac 400	Da. Allison	Ford	107.709	14	Robert Yates	K. Schrader	123.164
1992	Miller 400	R. Wallace	Pontiac	104.661	3	Roger Penske	E. Irvan	120.784
	Pontiac 400	B. Elliott	Ford	104.378	1	Junior Johnson	B. Elliott	121.337
1991	Miller 400	H. Gant	Oldsmobile	101.361	13	Leo Jackson	R. Wallace	120.590
	Pontiac 400	D. Earnhardt	Chevrolet	105.397	19	Richard Childress	Da. Allison	120.428
1990	Miller High Life 400	D. Earnhardt	Chevrolet	95.567	6	Richard Childress	E. Irvan	119.872
	Pontiac 400	M. Martin	Ford	92.158	6	Jack Roush	R. Rudd	119.617
1989	Miller High Life 400	R. Wallace	Pontiac	88.380	6	Raymond Beadle	B. Elliott	121.136
	Pontiac 400 (i)	R. Wallace	Pontiac	89.619	2	Raymond Beadle	G. Bodine	120.573
1988	Miller High Life 400 (g)	Da. Allison	Ford	95.770	1	Harry Ranier	Da. Allison	122.850
	Pontiac 400	N. Bonnett	Pontiac	66.401	3	B. Rahilly/B. Mock	M. Shepherd	94.645
1987	Wrangler Indigo 400	D. Earnhardt	Chevrolet	67.074	8	Richard Childress	A. Kulwicki	94.052
	Miller High Life 400	D. Earnhardt	Chevrolet	81.520	3	Richard Childress	A. Kulwicki	95.153
1986	Wrangler Indigo 400	T. Richmond	Chevrolet	70.161	4	Rick Hendrick	H. Gant	93.966
	Miller High Life 400	K. Petty	Ford	71.078	12	Wood Brothers	None—conditions	
1985	Wrangler SanforSet 400	D. Waltrip	Chevrolet	72.508	22	Junior Johnson	G. Bodine	94.535
	Miller High Life 400	D. Earnhardt	Chevrolet	67.945	4	Richard Childress	D. Waltrip	95.218
1984	Wrangler SanforSet 400	D. Waltrip	Chevrolet	74.780	1	Junior Johnson	D. Waltrip	92.518
	Miller High Life 400	R. Rudd	Ford	76.736	4	Bud Moore	D. Waltrip	93.817
1983	Wrangler SanforSet 400	B. Allison	Buick	79.381	6	DiProspero/Gardner	D. Waltrip	96.069
	Richmond 400	B. Allison	Chevrolet	79.584	6	DiProspero/Gardner	R. Rudd	93.439
1982	Wrangler SanforSet 400	B. Allison	Chevrolet	82.800	1	DiProspero/Gardner	B. Allison	93.435
	Richmond 400 (a)	D. Marcis	Chevrolet	72.914	6	Dave Marcis	D. Waltrip	93.256
1981	Wrangler SanforSet 400	B. Parsons	Ford	69.998	4	Bud Moore	M. Martin	93.435
	Richmond 400	D. Waltrip	Buick	76.570	7	Junior Johnson	M. Shepherd	92.821
1980	Capital City 400	B. Allison	Ford	79.722	2	Bud Moore	C. Yarborough	93.466
	Richmond 400	D. Waltrip	Chevrolet	67.703	1	DiProspero/Gardner	D. Waltrip	93.695
1979	Capital City 400	B. Allison	Ford	80.604	2	Bud Moore	D. Earnhardt	92.605
	Richmond 400	C. Yarborough	Oldsmobile	83.608	9	Junior Johnson	B. Allison	92.957
1978	Capital City 400	D. Waltrip	Chevrolet	79.568	1	DiProspero/Gardner	D. Waltrip	91.964
	Richmond 400	B. Parsons	Chevrolet	80.304	3	L.G. DeWitt	N. Bonnett	93.382
1977	Capital City 400	N. Bonnett	Dodge	80.644	2	Jim Stacy	B. Parsons	92.281
	Richmond 400 (a)	C. Yarborough	Chevrolet	73.084	7	Junior Johnson	N. Bonnett	93.632
1976	Capital City 400	C. Yarborough	Chevrolet	77.993	6	Junior Johnson	B. Parsons	92.460
	Richmond 400	D. Marcis	Dodge	72.792	2	Nord Krauskopf	B. Allison	92.715
1975	Capital City 500	D. Waltrip	Chevrolet	81.886	2	DiProspero/Gardner	B. Parsons	91.071
	Richmond 500	R. Petty	Dodge	74.913	1	Petty Enterprises.	R. Petty	93.340
1974	Capital City 500	R. Petty	Dodge	64.430	1	Petty Enterprises	R. Petty	88.852
	Richmond 500	B. Allison	Chevrolet	80.095	1	Bobby Allison	B. Allison	90.353
1973	Capital City 500	R. Petty	Dodge	63.215	5	Petty Enterprises	B. Allison	90.245
	Richmond 500	R. Petty	Dodge	74.764	8	Petty Enterprises	B. Allison	90.952
1972	Capital City 500	R. Petty	Plymouth	75.899	3	Petty Enterprises	B. Allison	89.669
	Richmond 500	R. Petty	Plymouth	76.258	3	Petty Enterprises	B. Allison	90.573
1971	Capital City 500	R. Petty	Plymouth	80.025	11	Petty Enterprises	B. Dennis	
	Richmond 500	R. Petty	Plymouth	79.836	28	Petty Enterprises	D. Marcis	87.178
1970	Capital City 500	R. Petty	Plymouth	81.476	1	Petty Enterprises	R. Petty	87.014
	Richmond 500 (f)	J. Hylton	Ford	82.044	3	James Hylton	R. Petty	89.137
1969	Capital City 500 (e)	B. Allison	Dodge	76.388	26	Mario Rossi	R. Petty	91.257
	Richmond 250 (d)	D. Pearson	Ford	73.752	1	Holman-Moody	D. Pearson	82.538
1968	Capital City 300 (c)	R. Petty	Plymouth	85.659	1	Petty Enterprises	R. Petty	103.178
	Richmond 250 (b)	D. Pearson	Ford	65.217	16	Holman-Moody	B. Isaac	67.822
1967	Capital City 300	R. Petty	Plymouth	57.631	2	Petty Enterprises	None—conditions	
	Richmond 250	R. Petty	Plymouth	65.982	1	Petty Enterprises	R. Petty	70.038
1966	Capital City 300	D. Pearson	Dodge	62.886	1	Cotton Owens	D. Pearson	70.644
	Richmond 250	D. Pearson	Dodge	66.539	4	Cotton Owens	T. Pistone	70.978
1965	Capital City 300	D. Pearson	Dodge	60.983	2	Cotton Owens	D. Hutcherson	67.340
	Richmond 250	Ju. Johnson	Ford	61.416	1	Rex Lovette	Ju. Johnson	67.847
1964	Capital City 300	C. Owens	Dodge	61.955	3	Cotton Owens	N. Jarrett	66.890
	Richmond 250	D. Pearson	Dodge	58.660	10	Cotton Owens	N. Jarrett	69.070
1963	Capital City 300	N. Jarrett	Ford	66.339	7	Charles Robinson	J. Weatherly	68.104
	Richmond 250	J. Weatherly	Pontiac	58.624	3	Bud Moore	R. White	69.151
1962	Capital City 300	J. Weatherly	Pontiac	64.980	2	Bud Moore	R. White	66.127
	Richmond 250 (h)	R. White	Chevrolet	51.360	20	Louis Clements	None—conditions	
1961	Capital City 250	J. Weatherly	Pontiac	61.677	7	Bud Moore	Ju. Johnson	65.010
	Richmond 200	R. Petty	Plymouth	62.456	1	Petty Enterprises	R. Petty	66.667
1960	Capital City 200	S. Thompson	Ford	63.739	3	Wood Brothers	N. Jarrett	64.410
	Richmond 300	L. Petty	Plymouth	62.251	10	Petty Enterprises	N. Jarrett	64.560
1959	Capital City 200	C. Owens	Ford	60.362	1	Cotton Owens	C. Owens	62.674
	Richmond 200	T. Pistone	Ford	56.881	12	Carl Rupert	Buck Baker	66.420
1958	Capital City 200	S. Thompson	Chevrolet	57.878	1	Speedy Thompson	S. Thompson	62.915
1957	Richmond 200	P. Goldsmith	Ford	62.445	7	Pete DePaolo	R. Hepler	64.239
1956	Richmond 200	Buck Baker	Dodge	56.232	1	Carl Kiekhafer	Buck Baker	67.091
1955	N/A	T. Flock	Chrysler	54.299	22	Carl Kiekhafer	None—conditions	
1953	N/A	L. Petty	Dodge	45.535	N/A	Petty Enterprises	Buck Baker	N/A

KEY **(a)** Race shortened by rain. **(b)** Last race as .5-mile dirt track. **(c)** Track paved and reconfigured to .625 miles. **(d)** Track remeasured from .625 miles to .5625 miles. **(e)** Track remeasured from .5625 miles to .5 miles. **(f)** Track remeasured from .5 miles to .542 miles. **(g)** Track reconfigured from .542 miles to .75 miles. **(h)** Race shortened by darkness. **(i)** Race postponed from February 26 to March 26 because of snow. **Note:** First year in which second race of the season was held at night was 1991; first season in which both events were held at night was 1999.

ALL RICHMOND RACES

POLE WINNERS

Bobby Allison	8
Richard Petty	8
Darrell Waltrip	7
Jeff Gordon	4
Ned Jarrett	4
Buck Baker	3
Bill Elliott	3
Mark Martin	3
Benny Parsons	3
Rusty Wallace	3
Davey Allison	2
Geoffrey Bodine	2
Neil Bonnett	2
Dale Earnhardt	2
Ernie Irvan	2
Junior Johnson	2
Alan Kulwicki	2
Terry Labonte	2
Ted Musgrave	2
David Pearson	2
Ricky Rudd	2
Morgan Shepherd	2
Mike Skinner	2
Rex White	2
Greg Biffle	1
Jeff Burton	1
Ward Burton	1
Bill Dennis	1
Harry Gant	1
Denny Hamlin	1
Kevin Harvick	1
Russ Hepler	1
Dick Hutcherson	1
Bobby Isaac	1
Jimmie Johnson	1
Kasey Kahne	1
Bobby Labonte	1
Dave Marcis	1
Ryan Newman	1
Cotton Owens	1
Tom Pistone	1
Ken Schrader	1
Speedy Thompson	1
Brian Vickers	1
Joe Weatherly	1
Cale Yarborough	1

RACE WINNERS

Richard Petty	13
Bobby Allison	7
David Pearson	6
Rusty Wallace	6
Darrell Waltrip	6
Dale Earnhardt	5
Dale Earnhardt Jr.	3
Terry Labonte	3
Tony Stewart	3
Joe Weatherly	3
Cale Yarborough	3
Davey Allison	2
Neil Bonnett	2
Jeff Gordon	2
Ernie Irvan	2
Dale Jarrett	2
Dave Marcis	2
Cotton Owens	2
Benny Parsons	2
Lee Petty	2
Speedy Thompson	2
Buck Baker	1
Jeff Burton	1
Kurt Busch	1
Bill Elliott	1
Tim Flock	1
Harry Gant	1
Paul Goldsmith	1
Kevin Harvick	1
James Hylton	1
Ned Jarrett	1
Junior Johnson	1
Kasey Kahne	1
Matt Kenseth	1
Mark Martin	1
Jeremy Mayfield	1
Joe Nemechek	1
Ryan Newman	1
Kyle Petty	1
Tom Pistone	1
Tim Richmond	1
Rex White	1

RACE 1

POLE WINNERS

Bobby Allison	5
Richard Petty	4
Darrell Waltrip	4
Buck Baker	3
Jeff Gordon	3
Neil Bonnett	2
Ned Jarrett	2
Terry Labonte	2
Ricky Rudd	2
Morgan Shepherd	2
Davey Allison	1
Greg Biffle	1
Geoffrey Bodine	1
Ward Burton	1
Bill Elliott	1
Russ Hepler	1
Bobby Isaac	1
Junior Johnson	1
Kasey Kahne	1
Alan Kulwicki	1
Dave Marcis	1
Mark Martin	1
Ted Musgrave	1
David Pearson	1
Tom Pistone	1
Ken Schrader	1
Brian Vickers	1
Rusty Wallace	1
Rex White	1

RACE WINNERS

Richard Petty	7
David Pearson	4
Dale Earnhardt	3
Dale Earnhardt Jr.	3
Bobby Allison	2
Terry Labonte	2
Dave Marcis	2
Lee Petty	2
Tony Stewart	2
Rusty Wallace	2
Darrell Waltrip	2
Cale Yarborough	2
Davey Allison	1
Buck Baker	1
Neil Bonnett	1
Bill Elliott	1
Tim Flock	1
Paul Goldsmith	1
Jeff Gordon	1
James Hylton	1
Ernie Irvan	1
Dale Jarrett	1
Junior Johnson	1
Kasey Kahne	1
Mark Martin	1
Joe Nemechek	1
Benny Parsons	1
Kyle Petty	1
Tom Pistone	1
Ricky Rudd	1
Joe Weatherly	1
Rex White	1

RACE 2

POLE WINNERS

Richard Petty	4
Bobby Allison	3
Benny Parsons	3
Darrell Waltrip	3
Dale Earnhardt	2
Bill Elliott	2
Ernie Irvan	2
Ned Jarrett	2
Mark Martin	2
Mike Skinner	2
Rusty Wallace	2
Davey Allison	1
Geoffrey Bodine	1
Jeff Burton	1
Bill Dennis	1
Harry Gant	1
Jeff Gordon	1
Denny Hamlin	1
Kevin Harvick	1
Dick Hutcherson	1
Jimmie Johnson	1
Junior Johnson	1
Alan Kulwicki	1
Bobby Labonte	1
Ted Musgrave	1
Ryan Newman	1
Cotton Owens	1
David Pearson	1
Speedy Thompson	1
Joe Weatherly	1
Rex White	1
Cale Yarborough	1

RACE WINNERS

Richard Petty	6
Bobby Allison	5
Rusty Wallace	4
Darrell Waltrip	4
Dale Earnhardt	2
Cotton Owens	2
David Pearson	2
Speedy Thompson	2
Joe Weatherly	2
Davey Allison	1
Neil Bonnett	1
Jeff Burton	1
Kurt Busch	1
Harry Gant	1
Jeff Gordon	1
Kevin Harvick	1
Ernie Irvan	1
Dale Jarrett	1
Ned Jarrett	1
Matt Kenseth	1
Terry Labonte	1
Jeremy Mayfield	1
Ryan Newman	1
Benny Parsons	1
Tim Richmond	1
Ricky Rudd	1
Tony Stewart	1
Cale Yarborough	1

>>RICHMOND INTERNATIONAL RACEWAY<<

>>NASCAR BUSCH SERIES<<

YEAR BY YEAR WINNERS

Year	Event	Race winner	Car make	Avg. speed	Start pos.	Pole winner	Pole speed
2006	Emerson Radio 250	K. Harvick	Chevrolet	85.627	5	J. Burton	126.357
	Circuit City 250	K. Harvick	Chevrolet	79.068	10	J. Leffler	126.334
2005	Emerson Radio 250	K. Harvick	Chevrolet	88.634	8	M. Martin	127.238
	Funai 250	C. Edwards	Ford	85.709	5	K. Kahne	128.977
2004	Funai 250	Ky. Busch	Chevrolet	85.023	1	Ky. Busch	129.348
	Emerson Radio 250	R. Gordon	Chevrolet	86.372	3	K. Kahne	127.678
2003	Hardee's 250	K. Harvick	Chevrolet	74.652	15	M. Waltrip	125.523
	Funai 250	Jo. Sauter	Chevrolet	99.543	30	None—conditions	
2002	Hardee's 250	J. Keller	Ford	80.138	2	None—conditions	
	Funai 250	D. Earnhardt Jr.	Chevrolet	78.089	1	D. Earnhardt Jr.	126.868
2001	Hardee's 250	J. Spencer	Chevrolet	84.028	3	M. Kenseth	125.780
	Autolite/Fram 250	J. Spencer	Chevrolet	90.156	3	J. Green	125.122
2000	Hardee's 250	J. Green	Chevrolet	81.023	1	J. Green	123.085
	Autolite/Fram 250	J. Burton	Ford	89.203	2	T. Bodine	123.768
1999	Hardee's 250	M. Martin	Ford	90.060	2	J. Keller	124.907
	Autolite 250	D. Earnhardt Jr.	Chevrolet	87.754	20	J. Burton	121.984
1998	Hardee's 250	J. Burton	Ford	95.799	8	W. Grubb	123.212
	Autolite 250	D. Earnhardt Jr.	Chevrolet	82.067	2	A. Santerre	123.604
1997	Hardee's 250	M. Martin	Ford	86.450	18	None—conditions	
	Autolite 250	S. Park	Chevrolet	77.747	2	M. Waltrip	122.227
1996	Hardee's 250	J. Purvis	Chevrolet	98.168	1	J. Purvis	121.114
	Autolite 250	K. Wallace	Ford	100.987	3	M. Waltrip	120.444
1995	Hardee's 250	K. Wallace	Ford	96.291	21	None—conditions	
	Autolite 250	D. Jarrett	Ford	104.928	6	R. LaJoie	119.846
1994	Hardee's 250	J. Nemechek	Chevrolet	91.253	3	D. Green	121.841
	Autolite 250	K. Wallace	Ford	97.487	6	J. Keller	121.968
1993	Hardee's 200	M. Martin	Ford	103.766	2	R. Mast	120.876
	Autolite 250	M. Martin	Ford	98.511	4	C. Bown	120.903
1992	Hardee's 200	H. Gant	Buick	97.561	28	J. Gordon	120.466
	Autolite 200	R. Pressley	Oldsmobile	95.373	14	T. Bodine	118.561
1991	Pontiac 200	H. Gant	Buick	92.156	11	J. Burton	118.848
	Autolite 200	H. Gant	Buick	86.719	29	B. Labonte	119.617
1990	Pontiac 200	M. Waltrip	Pontiac	88.091	1	M. Waltrip	118.561
	Autolite 200	R. Mast	Buick	99.759	22	M. Waltrip	118.974
1989	No spring race (snow)						
	Commonwealth 200	B. Hamilton	Oldsmobile	92.071	29	T. Ellis	118.953
1988	Commonwealth 200 (b)	H. Gant	Buick	89.434	1	H. Gant	121.218
1987	Freedlander 200	M. Martin	Ford	66.180	16	L. Pearson	98.312
1986	Freedlander 200	D. Earnhardt	Chevrolet	76.174	4	B. Bodine	98.218
1985	7-Eleven 150	T. Ellis	Pontiac	80.539	3	J. Hensley	97.638
1984	Wrangler 150	S. Ard	Oldsmobile	75.084	3	T. Ellis	97.814
	Miller Time 150	T. Ellis	Oldsmobile	65.199	1	T. Ellis	97.702
1983	Eastern 150	S. Ard	Oldsmobile	73.639	1	S. Ard	96.800
	Miller Time 150	M. Shepherd	Oldsmobile	63.848	3	T. Ellis	96.204
1982	Eastern 150	T. Houston	Chevrolet	57.667	15	G. Bodine	96.207
	Spring 220 (a)	B. Lindley	Pontiac	59.894	3	S. Ard	96.671
	Harvest 150	B. Lindley	Pontiac	76.839	7	T. Ellis	97.046

POLE WINNERS		RACE WINNERS	
Tommy Ellis	5	Mark Martin	5
Michael Waltrip	5	Harry Gant	4
Jeff Burton	3	Kevin Harvick	4
Sam Ard	2	Kenny Wallace	3
Todd Bodine	2	Sam Ard	2
Jeff Green	2	Jeff Burton	2
Kasey Kahne	2	Dale Earnhardt Jr.	2
Jason Keller	2	Tommy Ellis	2
Brett Bodine	1	Butch Lindley	2
Geoffrey Bodine	1	Jimmy Spencer	2
Chuck Bown	1	Kyle Busch	1
Kyle Busch	1	Dale Earnhardt	1
Dale Earnhardt Jr.	1	Carl Edwards	1
Harry Gant	1	Robby Gordon	1
Jeff Gordon	1	Jeff Green	1
David Green	1	Bobby Hamilton	1
Wayne Grubb	1	Tommy Houston	1
Jimmy Hensley	1	Dale Jarrett	1
Matt Kenseth	1	Jason Keller	1
Bobby Labonte	1	Rick Mast	1
Randy LaJoie	1	Joe Nemechek	1
Jason Leffler	1	Steve Park	1
Mark Martin	1	Robert Pressley	1
Rick Mast	1	Jeff Purvis	1
Larry Pearson	1	Johnny Sauter	1
Jeff Purvis	1	Morgan Shepherd	1
Andy Santerre	1	Kenny Wallace	1
		Michael Waltrip	1

KEY (a) Special, one-time race. **(b)** Track reconfigured to .75 miles.

QUALIFYING RECORD: Kyle Busch, Chevrolet; 129.348 mph (20.874 seconds), May 14, 2004
RACE RECORD: Dale Jarrett, Ford; 104.928 mph (1:47:13), September 8, 1995

>>TALLADEGA SUPERSPEEDWAY<<

TRACK FACTS >>> >>> **Location:** Talladega, Ala. >>> >>> **Owner:** International Speedway Corp. >>> >>> **Track length:** 2.66 miles

>>> >>> **Grandstand seating:** 143,231 >>> >>> **Tickets:** (877) 462-3342 >>> >>> **Website:** www.talladegasuperspeedway.com

>>NASCAR NEXTEL CUP SERIES<<

>>TRACK RECORDS

Most wins: 10—Dale Earnhardt; **Most top fives:** 23—Dale Earnhardt; **Most top 10s:** 27—Dale Earnhardt; **Oldest winner:** Harry Gant, 51 years, 3 months, 26 days, May 6, 1991; **Youngest winner:** Bobby Hillin Jr., 22 years, 1 month, 22 days, July 27, 1986; **Most lead changes:** 75—May 6, 1984; **Fewest lead changes:** 13—May 6, 1973; **Most leaders:** 26—Twice, most recently, April 22, 2001; **Fewest leaders:** 4—May 16, 1971; **Most cautions:** 11—April 25, 2004; **Fewest cautions:** 0—Three times, most recently, October 6, 2002; **Most caution laps:** 62—May 7, 1972; **Fewest caution laps:** 0—Three times, most recently, October 6, 2002; **Most on the lead lap:** 29—April 22, 2001; **Fewest on the lead lap:** 1—Twice, most recently, May 6, 1979; **Most running at the finish:** 40—April 22, 2001; **Fewest running at the finish:** 14—July 27, 1986; **Most laps led by a race winner:** 153—Pete Hamilton, August 23, 1970; **Fewest laps led by a race winner:** 2—Dale Jarrett, October 2, 2005; **Closest margin of victory:** 0.005 seconds—Dale Earnhardt defeated Ernie Irvan, July 25, 1993

>>QUALIFYING AND RACE RECORDS

QUALIFYING: Bill Elliott, Ford; 212.809 mph (44.998 seconds), April 30, 1987
RACE: Mark Martin, Ford; 188.354 mph (2:39:18), May 10, 1997

YEAR BY YEAR WINNERS

Year	Event	Race winner	Car make	Avg. speed	Start pos.	Car owner	Pole winner	Pole speed
2006	UAW-Ford 500	B. Vickers	Chevrolet	157.602	9	Rick Hendrick	D. Gilliland	191.712
	Aaron's 499	Ji. Johnson	Chevrolet	142.880	16	Rick Hendrick	E. Sadler	188.511
2005	UAW-Ford 500	D. Jarrett	Ford	143.818	2	Robert Yates	E. Sadler	189.260
	Aaron's 499	J. Gordon	Chevrolet	146.904	2	Rick Hendrick	K. Harvick	189.804
2004	EA Sports 500	D. Earnhardt Jr.	Chevrolet	156.929	10	Teresa Earnhardt	J. Nemechek	190.749
	Aaron's 499	J. Gordon	Chevrolet	129.396	11	Rick Hendrick	R. Rudd	191.180
2003	EA Sports 500	M. Waltrip	Chevrolet	156.045	18	Teresa Earnhardt	E. Sadler	189.943
	Aaron's 499	D. Earnhardt Jr.	Chevrolet	144.625	2	Teresa Earnhardt	J. Mayfield	186.489
2002	EA Sports 500	D. Earnhardt Jr.	Chevrolet	183.665	13	Teresa Earnhardt	None—conditions	
	Aaron's 499	D. Earnhardt Jr.	Chevrolet	159.022	4	Teresa Earnhardt	J. Johnson	186.532
2001	EA Sports 500	D. Earnhardt Jr.	Chevrolet	164.185	6	Teresa Earnhardt	S. Compton	185.240
	Talladega 500	B. Hamilton	Chevrolet	184.003	14	Andy Petree	S. Compton	184.861
2000	Winston 500	D. Earnhardt	Chevrolet	165.681	20	Richard Childress	J. Nemechek	190.279
	DieHard 500	J. Gordon	Chevrolet	161.157	36	Rick Hendrick	J. Mayfield	186.969
1999	Winston 500	D. Earnhardt	Chevrolet	166.632	27	Richard Childress	J. Nemechek	198.331
	DieHard 500	D. Earnhardt	Chevrolet	163.395	17	Richard Childress	K. Schrader	197.765
1998	Winston 500	D. Jarrett	Ford	159.318	3	Robert Yates	K. Schrader	196.153
	DieHard 500	B. Labonte	Pontiac	144.428	1	Joe Gibbs	B. Labonte	195.728
1997	DieHard 500	T. Labonte	Chevrolet	156.601	6	Rick Hendrick	E. Irvan	193.271
	Winston Select 500 (b)	M. Martin	Ford	188.354	18	Jack Roush	J. Andretti	193.627

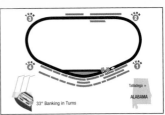

33° Banking in Turns

Talladega • ALABAMA

First NASCAR NEXTEL Cup Series race:
Sept. 14, 1969 (Richard Brickhouse, winner)
Banking in trioval: 18 degrees
Banking on back stretch: 2 degrees
Length of front stretch: 4,300 feet
Length of backstretch: 4,000 feet

2007 SCHEDULE

NASCAR NEXTEL Cup Series
Event: Aaron's 499
Race: No. 9 of 36
Date: April 29 • **TV:** FOX • **Radio:** MRN

Event: UAW-Ford 500
Race: No. 30 of 36
Date: October 7 • **TV:** ABC • **Radio:** MRN

NASCAR Busch Series
Event: Aaron's 312
Race: No. 10 of 35
Date: April 28 • **TV:** ESPN2 • **Radio:** MRN

NASCAR Craftsman Truck Series
Event: John Deere 250
Race: No. 20 of 25
Date: October 6 • **TV:** SPEED • **Radio:** MRN
Race names subject to change

>>TALLADEGA SUPERSPEEDWAY<<

YEAR BY YEAR WINNERS continued

Year	Event	Race winner	Car make	Avg. speed	Start pos.	Car owner	Pole winner	Pole speed
1996	DieHard 500 (a)	J. Gordon	Chevrolet	133.387	2	Rick Hendrick	J. Mayfield	192.370
	Winston Select 500	S. Marlin	Chevrolet	149.999	4	Larry McClure	E. Irvan	192.855
1995	DieHard 500	S. Marlin	Chevrolet	173.188	1	Larry McClure	S. Marlin	194.212
	Winston Select 500	M. Martin	Ford	178.902	3	Jack Roush	T. Labonte	196.532
1994	DieHard 500	J. Spencer	Ford	163.217	2	Junior Johnson	D. Earnhardt	193.470
	Winston Select 500	D. Earnhardt	Chevrolet	157.478	4	Richard Childress	E. Irvan	193.298
1993	DieHard 500	D. Earnhardt	Chevrolet	153.858	11	Richard Childress	B. Elliott	192.397
	Winston 500	E. Irvan	Chevrolet	155.412	16	Larry McClure	D. Earnhardt	192.355
1992	DieHard 500	E. Irvan	Chevrolet	176.309	7	Larry McClure	S. Marlin	190.586
	Winston 500	Da. Allison	Ford	167.609	2	Robert Yates	E. Irvan	192.831
1991	DieHard 500	D. Earnhardt	Chevrolet	147.383	4	Richard Childress	S. Marlin	192.085
	Winston 500	H. Gant	Oldsmobile	165.620	2	Leo Jackson	E. Irvan	195.186
1990	DieHard 500	D. Earnhardt	Chevrolet	174.430	1	Richard Childress	D. Earnhardt	192.513
	Winston 500	D. Earnhardt	Chevrolet	159.571	5	Richard Childress	B. Elliott	199.388
1989	DieHard 500	T. Labonte	Ford	157.354	5	Junior Johnson	M. Martin	194.800
	Winston 500	Da. Allison	Ford	155.869	2	Robert Yates	M. Martin	193.061
1988	Talladega DieHard 500	K. Schrader	Chevrolet	154.505	7	Rick Hendrick	D. Waltrip	196.274
	Winston 500	P. Parsons	Oldsmobile	156.547	3	Leo/Richard Jackson	Da. Allison	198.969
1987	Talladega 500	B. Elliott	Ford	171.293	1	Harry Melling	B. Elliott	203.827
	Winston 500 (a)	Da. Allison	Ford	154.228	3	Harry Ranier	B. Elliott	212.809
1986	Talladega 500	B. Hillin	Buick	151.552	13	William Stavola	B. Elliott	209.005
	Winston 500	B. Allison	Buick	157.698	2	William Stavola	B. Elliott	212.229
1985	Talladega 500	C. Yarborough	Ford	148.772	2	Harry Ranier	B. Elliott	207.578
	Winston 500	B. Elliott	Ford	186.288	1	Harry Melling	B. Elliott	209.398
1984	Talladega 500	D. Earnhardt	Chevrolet	155.485	3	Richard Childress	C. Yarborough	202.474
	Winston 500	C. Yarborough	Chevrolet	172.988	1	Harry Ranier	C. Yarborough	202.692
1983	Talladega 500	D. Earnhardt	Ford	170.611	4	Bud Moore	C. Yarborough	201.744
	Winston 500	R. Petty	Pontiac	153.936	15	Petty Enterprises	C. Yarborough	202.650
1982	Talladega 500	D. Waltrip	Buick	168.157	2	Junior Johnson	G. Bodine	199.400
	Winston 500	D. Waltrip	Buick	156.597	2	Junior Johnson	B. Parsons	200.176
1981	Talladega 500	R. Bouchard	Buick	156.737	10	Jack Beebe	H. Gant	195.897
	Winston 500	B. Allison	Buick	149.376	1	Harry Ranier	B. Allison	195.864
1980	Talladega 500	N. Bonnett	Mercury	166.894	2	Wood Brothers	Buddy Baker	198.545
	Winston 500	Buddy Baker	Oldsmobile	170.481	2	Harry Ranier	D. Pearson	197.704
1979	Talladega 500	D. Waltrip	Oldsmobile	161.229	8	DiProspero/Gardner	N. Bonnett	193.600
	Winston 500	B. Allison	Ford	154.770	12	Bud Moore	D. Waltrip	195.644
1978	Talladega 500	L. Pond	Oldsmobile	174.700	5	Harry Ranier	C. Yarborough	192.917
	Winston 500	C. Yarborough	Oldsmobile	159.699	1	Junior Johnson	C. Yarborough	191.904
1977	Talladega 500	Do. Allison	Chevrolet	162.524	2	Hoss Ellington	B. Parsons	192.684
	Winston 500	D. Waltrip	Chevrolet	164.877	11	DiProspero/Gardner	A. Foyt	192.424
1976	Talladega 500	D. Marcis	Dodge	157.547	1	Nord Krauskopf	D. Marcis	190.651
	Winston 500	Buddy Baker	Ford	169.887	12	Bud Moore	D. Marcis	189.197
1975	Talladega 500	Buddy Baker	Ford	130.892	2	Bud Moore	D. Marcis	191.340
	Winston 500	Buddy Baker	Ford	144.948	1	Bud Moore	Buddy Baker	189.947
1974	Talladega 500	R. Petty	Dodge	148.637	3	Petty Enterprises	D. Pearson	184.926
	Winston 500	D. Pearson	Mercury	130.220	1	Wood Brothers	D. Pearson	186.086
1973	Talladega 500	R. Brooks	Plymouth	145.454	24	Crawford Brothers	B. Allison	187.064
	Winston 500	D. Pearson	Mercury	131.956	2	Wood Brothers	Buddy Baker	193.435
1972	Talladega 500	J. Hylton	Mercury	148.728	22	James Hylton	B. Isaac	190.677
	Winston 500	D. Pearson	Mercury	134.400	2	Wood Brothers	B. Isaac	192.428
1971	Talladega 500	B. Allison	Mercury	145.945	2	Holman-Moody	Do. Allison	187.323
	Winston 500	Do. Allison	Mercury	147.419	1	Wood Brothers	Do. Allison	185.869
1970	Talladega 500	P. Hamilton	Plymouth	158.517	4	Petty Enterprises	B. Isaac	186.834
	Alabama 500	P. Hamilton	Plymouth	152.321	6	Petty Enterprises	B. Isaac	199.658
1969	Talladega 500	R. Brickhouse	Dodge	153.778	9	Ray Nichels	B. Isaac	196.386

KEY (a) Race shortened by darkness. (b) Race postponed from April 27 to May 10 because of rain.

ALL TALLADEGA RACES

POLE WINNERS

Name	
Bill Elliott	8
Cale Yarborough	6
Ernie Irvan	5
Bobby Isaac	5
Dale Earnhardt	3
Dave Marcis	3
Sterling Marlin	3
Jeremy Mayfield	3
Joe Nemechek	3
David Pearson	3
Elliott Sadler	3
Bobby Allison	2
Donnie Allison	2
Stacy Compton	2
Mark Martin	2
Benny Parsons	2
Ken Schrader	2
Darrell Waltrip	2
Davey Allison	1
John Andretti	1
Geoffrey Bodine	1
Neil Bonnett	1
A.J. Foyt	1
Harry Gant	1
David Gilliland	1
Kevin Harvick	1
Jimmie Johnson	1
Bobby Labonte	1
Terry Labonte	1
Ricky Rudd	1

RACE WINNERS

Name	
Dale Earnhardt	10
Dale Earnhardt Jr.	5
Bobby Allison	4
Buddy Baker	4
Jeff Gordon	4
Darrell Waltrip	4
Davey Allison	3
David Pearson	3
Cale Yarborough	3
Donnie Allison	2
Bill Elliott	2
Pete Hamilton	2
Ernie Irvan	2
Dale Jarrett	2
Terry Labonte	2
Sterling Marlin	2
Mark Martin	2
Richard Petty	2
Neil Bonnett	1
Ron Bouchard	1
Richard Brickhouse	1
Dick Brooks	1
Harry Gant	1
Bobby Hamilton	1
Bobby Hillin Jr.	1
James Hylton	1
Jimmie Johnson	1
Bobby Labonte	1
Dave Marcis	1
Phil Parsons	1
Lennie Pond	1
Ken Schrader	1
Jimmy Spencer	1
Brian Vickers	1
Michael Waltrip	1

RACE 1

POLE WINNERS

Name	
Bill Elliott	4
Ernie Irvan	4
Cale Yarborough	3
Buddy Baker	2
Bobby Isaac	2
Jeremy Mayfield	2
David Pearson	2
Bobby Allison	1
Davey Allison	1
Donnie Allison	1
Stacy Compton	1
Dale Earnhardt	1
A.J. Foyt	1
Harry Gant	1
Kevin Harvick	1
Jimmie Johnson	1
Bobby Labonte	1
Terry Labonte	1
Dave Marcis	1
Mark Martin	1
Benny Parsons	1
Ricky Rudd	1
Ken Schrader	1
Darrell Waltrip	1

RACE WINNERS

Name	
Bobby Allison	3
Buddy Baker	3
Dale Earnhardt	3
Jeff Gordon	3
David Pearson	3
Dale Earnhardt Jr.	2
Mark Martin	2
Darrell Waltrip	2
Cale Yarborough	2
Donnie Allison	1
Bill Elliott	1
Harry Gant	1
Bobby Hamilton	1
Pete Hamilton	1
Ernie Irvan	1
Jimmie Johnson	1
Bobby Labonte	1
Sterling Marlin	1
Phil Parsons	1
Richard Petty	1

RACE 2

POLE WINNERS

Name	
Bill Elliott	4
Bobby Isaac	3
Sterling Marlin	3
Joe Nemechek	3
Cale Yarborough	3
Dale Earnhardt	2
Dave Marcis	2
Elliott Sadler	2
Bobby Allison	1
Donnie Allison	1
Buddy Baker	1
Geoffrey Bodine	1
Neil Bonnett	1
Stacy Compton	1
Harry Gant	1
David Gilliland	1
Ernie Irvan	1
Mark Martin	1
Jeremy Mayfield	1
Benny Parsons	1
David Pearson	1
Ken Schrader	1
Darrell Waltrip	1

RACE WINNERS

Name	
Dale Earnhardt	7
Dale Earnhardt Jr.	3
Dale Jarrett	2
Terry Labonte	2
Darrell Waltrip	2
Bobby Allison	1
Donnie Allison	1
Buddy Baker	1
Neil Bonnett	1
Ron Bouchard	1
Richard Brickhouse	1
Dick Brooks	1
Bill Elliott	1
Jeff Gordon	1
Pete Hamilton	1
Bobby Hillin Jr.	1
James Hylton	1
Ernie Irvan	1
Dave Marcis	1
Sterling Marlin	1
Richard Petty	1
Lennie Pond	1
Ken Schrader	1
Jimmy Spencer	1
Brian Vickers	1
Michael Waltrip	1
Cale Yarborough	1

>>NASCAR BUSCH SERIES<<

YEAR BY YEAR WINNERS

Year	Event	Race winner	Car make	Avg. speed	Start pos.	Pole winner	Pole speed
2006	Aaron's 312	M. Truex Jr.	Chevrolet	149.785	12	J. Yeley	184.751
2005	Aaron's 312	M. Truex Jr.	Chevrolet	122.117	4	P. Menard	184.023
2004	Aaron's 312	M. Truex Jr.	Chevrolet	136.783	3	C. Bowyer	184.253
2003	Aaron's 312	D. Earnhardt Jr.	Chevrolet	114.768	3	J. Nemechek	188.649
2002	Aaron's 312	J. Keller	Ford	157.691	12	Jo. Sauter	188.764
2001	Subway 300	M. McLaughlin	Pontiac	131.258	14	J. Nemechek	189.729
2000	Touchstone Energy 300	J. Nemechek	Chevrolet	153.859	35	None—conditions	
1999	Touchstone Energy 300	T. Labonte	Chevrolet	150.793	16	K. Schrader	192.455
1998	Touchstone Energy 300	J. Nemechek	Chevrolet	118.196	1	J. Nemechek	189.628
1997	Easy Care 300	M. Martin	Ford	168.937	23	J. Nemechek	193.517
1996	Humminbird 500K	G. Sacks	Chevrolet	139.438	7	J. Nemechek	192.878
1995	Humminbird 500K	C. Little	Ford	122.904	7	J. Purvis	189.921
1994	Fram Filter 500K	K. Schrader	Chevrolet	167.473	17	J. Purvis	186.703
1993	Fram Filter 500K	D. Earnhardt	Chevrolet	146.801	22	B. Elliott	188.404
1992	Fram Filter 500K	E. Irvan	Chevrolet	158.359	2	D. Earnhardt	184.733

POLE WINNERS

Name	
Joe Nemechek	5
Jeff Purvis	2
Clint Bowyer	1
Dale Earnhardt	1
Bill Elliott	1
Paul Menard	1
Johnny Sauter	1
Ken Schrader	1
J.J. Yeley	1

RACE WINNERS

Name	
Martin Truex Jr.	3
Joe Nemechek	2
Dale Earnhardt	1
Dale Earnhardt Jr.	1
Ernie Irvan	1
Jason Keller	1
Terry Labonte	1
Chad Little	1
Mark Martin	1
Mike McLaughlin	1
Greg Sacks	1
Ken Schrader	1

QUALIFYING RECORD: Joe Nemechek, Chevrolet; 193.517 mph (49.494 seconds), April 24, 1997
RACE RECORD: Mark Martin, Ford; 168.937 mph (1:50:32), April 26, 1997

Truex Jr.

YEAR BY YEAR WINNERS

Year	Event	Race winner	Car make	Avg. speed	Start pos.	Pole winner	Pole speed	POLE WINNERS		RACE WINNERS	
2006	John Deere 250	M. Martin	Ford	138.207	1	M. Martin	182.320	Mark Martin	1	M. Martin	1

QUALIFYING RECORD: Mark Martin, Ford; 182.320 mph (52.523 seconds), October 7, 2006
RACE RECORD: Mark Martin, Ford; 138.207 mph (1:48:33), October 7, 2006

≫ TEXAS MOTOR SPEEDWAY ≪

TRACK FACTS ≫≫ ≫≫ **Location:** Fort Worth, Texas ≫≫ ≫≫ **Owner:** Speedway Motorsports, Inc. ≫≫ ≫≫ **Track length:** 1.5 miles

≫≫ ≫≫ **Grandstand seating:** 159,585 ≫≫ ≫≫ **Tickets:** (817) 215-8500 ≫≫ ≫≫ **Website:** www.texasmotorspeedway.com

≫ NASCAR NEXTEL CUP SERIES ≪

≫ TRACK RECORDS

Most wins: 1—Greg Biffle, Jeff Burton, Dale Earnhardt Jr.,Carl Edwards, Dale Jarrett, Kasey Kahne, Matt Kenseth, Terry Labonte, Mark Martin, Ryan Newman, Elliott Sadler, Tony Stewart; **Most top fives:** 4—Jeff Gordon, Mark Martin; **Most top 10s:** 7—Dale Earnhardt Jr., Tony Stewart; **Oldest winner:** Dale Jarrett, 44 years, 4 months, 6 days, April 1, 2001; **Youngest winner:** Ryan Newman, 25 years, 3 months, 22 days, March 30, 2003; **Most lead changes:** 29—April 2, 2000; **Fewest lead changes:** 18—April 1, 2001; **Most leaders:** 17—April 2, 2000; **Fewest leaders:** 7—April 1, 2001; **Most cautions:** 12—Twice, most recently, November 5, 2006; **Fewest cautions:** 6—November 6, 2005; **Most caution laps:** 73—April 6, 1997; **Fewest caution laps:** 27—November 6, 2005; **Most on the lead lap:** 25—November 6, 2005; **Fewest on the lead lap:** 8—April 6, 1997; **Most running at the finish:** 40—November 6, 2005; **Fewest running at the finish:** 29—Twice, most recently, April 5, 1998; **Most laps led by a race winner:** 278—Tony Stewart, November 5, 2006; **Fewest laps led by a race winner:** 37—Mark Martin, April 5, 1998; **Closest margin of victory:** 0.272 seconds—Tony Stewart defeated Jimmie Johnson, November 5, 2006

≫ QUALIFYING AND RACE RECORDS

QUALIFYING: Brian Vickers, Chevrolet; 196.235 mph (27.518 seconds), November 5, 2006
RACE: Carl Edwards, Ford; 151.055 mph (3:19:00), November 6, 2005

24° Banking in Turns

Fort Worth • TEXAS

First NASCAR NEXTEL Cup Series race: April 6, 1997 (Jeff Burton, winner)
Banking on straights: 5 degrees
Length of front stretch: 2,250 feet
Length of back stretch: 1,330 feet

>>TEXAS MOTOR SPEEDWAY<<

2007 SCHEDULE

NASCAR NEXTEL Cup Series
Event: Samsung/RadioShack 500
Race: No. 7 of 36
Date: April 15 • **TV:** FOX • **Radio:** PRN

Event: Dickies 500
Race: No. 34 of 36
Date: November 4 • **TV:** ABC • **Radio:** PRN

NASCAR Busch Series
Event: O'Reilly 300
Race: No. 8 of 35
Date: April 14 • **TV:** ESPN2 • **Radio:** PRN

Event: O'Reilly Challenge
Race: No. 33 of 35
Date: November 3 • **TV:** ESPN2 • **Radio:** PRN

NASCAR Craftsman Truck Series
Event: Sam's Town 400
Race: No. 9 of 25
Date: June 8 • **TV:** SPEED • **Radio:** MRN

Event: Silverado 350
Race: No. 23 of 25
Date: November 2 • **TV:** SPEED • **Radio:** MRN

Race names subject to change

YEAR BY YEAR WINNERS

Year	Event	Race winner	Car make	Avg. speed	Start pos.	Car owner	Pole winner	Pole speed
2006	Dickies 500	T. Stewart	Chevrolet	134.891	8	Joe Gibbs	B. Vickers	196.235
	Samsung/RadioShack 500	K. Kahne	Dodge	137.943	1	Ray Evernham	K. Kahne	190.315
2005	Dickies 500	C. Edwards	Ford	151.055	30	Jack Roush	R. Newman	192.947
	Samsung/RadioShack 500	G. Biffle	Ford	130.055	5	Jack Roush	R. Newman	192.582
2004	Samsung/RadioShack 500	E. Sadler	Ford	138.845	19	Robert Yates	B. Labonte	193.903
2003	Samsung/RadioShack 500	R. Newman	Dodge	134.517	3	Roger Penske	B. Labonte	193.514
2002	Samsung/RadioShack 500	M. Kenseth	Ford	142.453	31	Jack Roush	B. Elliott	194.224
2001	Harrah's 500	D. Jarrett	Ford	141.804	3	Robert Yates	D. Earnhardt Jr.	190.678
2000	DirecTV 500	D. Earnhardt Jr.	Chevrolet	131.152	4	Dale Earnhardt	T. Labonte	192.137
1999	Primestar 500	T. Labonte	Chevrolet	144.276	4	Rick Hendrick	K. Irwin	190.154
1998	Texas 500	M. Martin	Ford	136.771	7	Jack Roush	J. Mayfield	185.906
1997	Interstate Batteries 500	J. Burton	Ford	125.111	5	Jack Roush	None—conditions	

POLE WINNERS		RACE WINNERS	
Bobby Labonte	2	Greg Biffle	1
Ryan Newman	2	Jeff Burton	1
Dale Earnhardt Jr.	1	Dale Earnhardt Jr.	1
Bill Elliott	1	Carl Edwards	1
Kenny Irwin	1	Dale Jarrett	1
Kasey Kahne	1	Kasey Kahne	1
Terry Labonte	1	Matt Kenseth	1
Jeremy Mayfield	1	Terry Labonte	1
Brian Vickers	1	Mark Martin	1
		Ryan Newman	1
		Elliott Sadler	1
		Tony Stewart	1

>>NASCAR BUSCH SERIES<<

YEAR BY YEAR WINNERS

Year	Event	Race winner	Car make	Avg. speed	Start pos.	Pole winner	Pole speed
2006	O'Reilly Challenge 300	K. Harvick	Chevrolet	145.710	4	M. Martin	192.589
	O'Reilly 300	Ku. Busch	Dodge	129.984	7	D. Hamlin	187.905
2005	O'Reilly Challenge	K. Harvick	Chevrolet	138.019	3	R. Newman	189.500
	O'Reilly 300	K. Kahne	Dodge	126.746	25	S. Hmiel	189.840
2004	O'Reilly 300	M. Kenseth	Ford	115.482	15	Ky. Busch	189.847
2003	O'Reilly 300	J. Nemechek	Chevrolet	117.891	7	J. Keller	187.474
2002	O'Reilly 300	J. Purvis	Chevrolet	102.136	13	J. Green	193.483
2001	Jani-King 300	K. Harvick	Chevrolet	126.212	7	M. Kenseth	189.880
2000	Albertson's 300	M. Martin	Ford	108.130	2	J. Leffler	184.451
1999	Coca-Cola 300	M. Martin	Ford	127.417	2	D. Blaney	183.082
1998	Coca-Cola 300	D. Earnhardt Jr.	Chevrolet	120.174	16	E. Sadler	179.229
1997	Coca-Cola 300	M. Martin	Ford	122.993	20	J. Green	180.054

POLE WINNERS		RACE WINNERS	
Jeff Green	2	Kevin Harvick	3
Dave Blaney	1	Mark Martin	3
Kyle Busch	1	Kurt Busch	1
Denny Hamlin	1	Dale Earnhardt Jr.	1
Shane Hmiel	1	Kasey Kahne	1
Jason Keller	1	Matt Kenseth	1
Matt Kenseth	1	Joe Nemechek	1
Jason Leffler	1	Jeff Purvis	1
Mark Martin	1		
Ryan Newman	1		
Elliott Sadler	1		

Harvick

QUALIFYING RECORD: Jeff Green, Chevrolet; 193.493 mph (27.908 seconds), April 5, 2002
RACE RECORD: Kevin Harvick, Chevrolet; 145.710 mph (2:03:32), November 4, 2006

YEAR BY YEAR WINNERS

Year	Event	Race winner	Car make	Avg. speed	Start pos.	Pole winner	Pole speed
2006	Silverado 350K	C. Bowyer	Chevrolet	124.895	1	C. Bowyer	184.464
	Sam's Town 400	T. Bodine	Toyota	132.129	6	M. Skinner	183.206
2005	Silverado 350K	T. Bodine	Toyota	128.239	8	M. Skinner	182.593
	Chex 400K	J. Sprague	Chevrolet	144.844	7	M. Skinner	182.902
2004	O'Reilly 400K	D. Setzer	Chevrolet	148.959	4	T. Musgrave	180.971
	Silverado 350K	T. Bodine	Toyota	115.169	22	M. Skinner	182.174
2003	O'Reilly 400K	B. Gaughan	Dodge	140.621	5	None—conditions	
	Silverado 350	B. Gaughan	Dodge	122.727	7	A. Houston	181.531
2002	O'Reilly 400K	B. Gaughan	Dodge	129.569	10	J. Leffler	180.355
	Silverado 350	B. Gaughan	Dodge	137.736	5	M. Bliss	179.695
2001	O'Reilly 400K	J. Sprague	Chevrolet	133.620	3	None—conditions	
	Silverado 350	T. Kvapil	Chevrolet	112.020	7	S. Riggs	181.953
2000	Pronto Auto Parts 400	G. Biffle	Ford	126.932	1	G. Biffle	178.130
	O'Reilly 400	B. Reffner	Chevrolet	112.933	1	B. Reffner	180.373
1999	Pronto Auto Parts 400	D. Setzer	Dodge	122.805	3	J. Sauter	179.718
	O'Reilly 400	J. Sauter	Chevrolet	132.430	1	J. Sauter	179.152
1998	Pronto Auto Parts 400	T. Raines	Ford	111.018	12	J. Sprague	178.642
1997	Pronto Auto Parts 400	K. Irwin	Ford	131.823	5	M. Bliss	175.667

POLE WINNERS		RACE WINNERS	
Mike Skinner	3	Brendan Gaughan	4
Mike Bliss	2	Todd Bodine	2
Jay Sauter	2	Dennis Setzer	2
Greg Biffle	1	Jack Sprague	2
Clint Bowyer	1	Greg Biffle	1
Andy Houston	1	Clint Bowyer	1
Jason Leffler	1	Kenny Irwin	1
Ted Musgrave	1	Travis Kvapil	1
Bryan Reffner	1	Tony Raines	1
Scott Riggs	1	Bryan Reffner	1
Jack Sprague	1	Jay Sauter	1

QUALIFYING RECORD: Clint Bowyer, Chevrolet; 184.464 mph (29.274 seconds), November 3, 2006
RACE RECORD: 167 laps: Dennis Setzer, Chevrolet; 148.959 mph (1:40:54), June 11, 2004.
146 laps: Brendan Gaughan, Dodge; 137.736 mph (1:35:24), September 13, 2002

>>WATKINS GLEN INTERNATIONAL<<

TRACK FACTS >>> >>> **Location:** Watkins Glen, N.Y. >>> >>> **Owner:** International Speedway Corp. >>> >>> **Track length:** 2.45 miles

>>> >>> **Estimated capacity:** 85,000 >>> >>> **Tickets:** (866) 461-7223 >>> >>> **Website:** www.theglen.com >>> >>>

>>NASCAR NEXTEL CUP SERIES<<

>>TRACK RECORDS

Most wins: 4—Jeff Gordon; **Most top fives:** 12—Mark Martin; **Most top 10s:** 16—Mark Martin; **Oldest winner:** Geoffrey Bodine, 47 years, 3 months, 24 days, August 11, 1996; **Youngest winner:** Jeff Gordon, 26 years, 6 days, August 10, 1997; **Most lead changes:** 14—twice, most recently, August 13, 2006; **Fewest lead changes:** 0—August 4, 1957; **Most leaders:** 12—August 13, 1995; **Fewest leaders:** 1—August 4, 1957; **Most cautions:** 10—August 13, 2006; **Fewest cautions:** 0—July 18, 1965; **Most caution laps:** 36—August 14, 1988; **Fewest caution laps:** 0—July 18, 1965; **Most on the lead lap:** 34—August 14, 2005; **Fewest on the lead lap:** 2—Twice, most recently, July 18, 1965; **Most running at the finish:** 40—August 10, 2003; **Fewest running at the finish:** 11—July 18, 1965; **Most laps led by a race winner:** 75—Mark Martin, August 14, 1994; **Fewest laps led by a race winner:** 4—Ricky Rudd, August 14, 1988; **Closest margin of victory:** 0.172 seconds—Jeff Gordon defeated Jeff Burton, August 12, 2001

>>QUALIFYING AND RACE RECORDS

QUALIFYING: Jeff Gordon, Chevrolet; 124.580 mph (70.798 seconds), August 8, 2003
RACE: Mark Martin, Ford; 103.300 mph (2:11:54), August 13, 1995

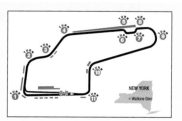

First NASCAR NEXTEL Cup Series race:
August 4, 1957 (Buck Baker, winner)
Banking: Varies
Length of pit road stretch: 2,141 feet
Length of back stretch: 1,839 feet

2007 SCHEDULE

NASCAR NEXTEL Cup Series
Event: AMD at the Glen
Race: No. 22 of 36
Date: August 12
TV: ESPN • **Radio:** MRN

NASCAR Busch Series
Event: ZIPPO 200
Race: No. 24 of 35
Date: August 11
TV: ESPN2 • **Radio:** MRN

Race names subject to change

YEAR BY YEAR WINNERS

Year	Event	Race winner	Car make	Avg. speed	Start pos.	Car owner	Pole winner	Pole speed
2006	AMD at the Glen	K. Harvick	Chevrolet	76.718	7	Richard Childress	Ku. Busch	122.966
2005	Sirius at the Glen	T. Stewart	Chevrolet	86.804	1	Joe Gibbs	None—conditions	
2004	Sirius at the Glen	T. Stewart	Chevrolet	92.249	4	Joe Gibbs	None—conditions	
2003	Sirius at the Glen	R. Gordon	Chevrolet	90.441	14	Richard Childress	J. Gordon	124.580
2002	Sirius at The Glen	T. Stewart	Pontiac	82.208	3	Joe Gibbs	R. Rudd	122.696
2001	G. Crossing at The Glen	J. Gordon	Chevrolet	89.081	13	Rick Hendrick	D. Jarrett	122.698
2000	G. Crossing at The Glen	S. Park	Chevrolet	91.336	18	Dale Earnhardt	None—conditions	
1999	Frontier at The Glen	J. Gordon	Chevrolet	87.722	3	Rick Hendrick	R. Wallace	121.234
1998	Bud at Glen	J. Gordon	Chevrolet	94.466	1	Rick Hendrick	J. Gordon	120.331
1997	Bud at Glen	J. Gordon	Chevrolet	91.294	11	Rick Hendrick	T. Bodine	120.505
1996	Bud at Glen	G. Bodine	Ford	92.334	13	Geoffrey Bodine	D. Earnhardt	120.733
1995	Bud at Glen	M. Martin	Ford	103.030	1	Jack Roush	M. Martin	120.411
1994	Bud at Glen	M. Martin	Ford	93.752	1	Jack Roush	M. Martin	118.326
1993	Bud at Glen	M. Martin	Ford	84.771	1	Jack Roush	M. Martin	119.118
1992	Bud at Glen (a)	K. Petty	Pontiac	88.980	2	Felix Sabates	D. Earnhardt	116.882
1991	Bud at Glen (b)	E. Irvan	Chevrolet	98.977	3	Larry McClure	T. Labonte	121.652
1990	Bud at Glen	R. Rudd	Chevrolet	92.452	12	Rick Hendrick	D. Earnhardt	121.190
1989	Bud at Glen	R. Wallace	Pontiac	87.242	13	Raymond Beadle	M. Shepherd	120.456
1988	Bud at Glen	R. Rudd	Buick	74.096	6	Kenny Bernstein	G. Bodine	120.541
1987	Bud at Glen	R. Wallace	Pontiac	90.682	2	Raymond Beadle	T. Labonte	117.956
1986	Bud at Glen	T. Richmond	Chevrolet	90.463	1	Rick Hendrick	T. Richmond	117.563
1965	The Glen 151.8	M. Panch	Ford	98.182	3	Wood Brothers	None—conditions	
1964	The Glen 151.8	B. Wade	Mercury	97.988	1	Bud Moore	B. Wade	102.222
1957	The Glen 101.2	Buck Baker	Chevrolet	83.064	1	Buck Baker	Buck Baker	87.071

KEY (a) Race shortened by rain. (b) Track reconfigured from 2.428 miles to 2.45 miles.

POLE WINNERS		RACE WINNERS	
Dale Earnhardt	3	Jeff Gordon	4
Mark Martin	3	Mark Martin	3
Jeff Gordon	2	Tony Stewart	3
Terry Labonte	2	Ricky Rudd	2
Buck Baker	1	Rusty Wallace	2
Geoffrey Bodine	1	Buck Baker	1
Todd Bodine	1	Geoffrey Bodine	1
Kurt Busch	1	Robby Gordon	1
Dale Jarrett	1	Kevin Harvick	1
Tim Richmond	1	Ernie Irvan	1
Ricky Rudd	1	Marvin Panch	1
Morgan Shepherd	1	Steve Park	1
Billy Wade	1	Kyle Petty	1
Rusty Wallace	1	Tim Richmond	1
		Billy Wade	1

>>NASCAR BUSCH SERIES<<

YEAR BY YEAR WINNERS

Kurt Busch

Year	Event	Race winner	Car make	Avg. speed	Start pos.	Pole winner	Pole speed
2005	ZIPPO 200	Ku. Busch	Dodge	89.221	1	Ku. Busch	121.526
2005	ZIPPO 200	R. Newman	Dodge	71.686	39	T. Stewart	121.069
2001	GNC Live Well 200	R. Fellows	Chevrolet	89.754	2	S. Pruett	121.052
2000	Lysol 200	R. Fellows	Chevrolet	90.586	1	R. Fellows	119.504
1999	Lysol 200	D.Earnhardt Jr.	Chevrolet	76.034	3	R. Fellows	117.060
1998	Lysol 200	R. Fellows	Chevrolet	70.183	2	B. Said	117.675
1997	Lysol 200	M. McLaughlin	Chevrolet	90.225	6	J. Nemechek	116.128
1996	Lysol 200	T. Labonte	Chevrolet	91.468	9	D. Green	115.995
1995	Lysol 200	T. Labonte	Chevrolet	84.186	1	T. Labonte	115.309
1994	Fay's 150	T. Labonte	Chevrolet	93.717	21	None—conditions	
1993	Fay's 150	B. Elliott	Ford	89.970	2	E. Irvan	114.632
1992	Fay's 150	E. Irvan	Chevrolet	93.991	22	None—conditions	
1991	Fay's 150	T. Labonte	Oldsmobile	94.003	1	T. Labonte	117.163

POLE WINNERS		RACE WINNERS	
Ron Fellows	2	Terry Labonte	4
Terry Labonte	2	Ron Fellows	3
Kurt Busch	1	Kurt Busch	1
David Green	1	Dale Earnhardt Jr.	1
Ernie Irvan	1	Bill Elliott	1
Joe Nemechek	1	Ernie Irvan	1
Scott Pruett	1	Mike McLaughlin	1
Boris Said	1	Ryan Newman	1
Tony Stewart	1		

QUALIFYING RECORD: Kurt Busch, Dodge; 121.526 mph (72.577 seconds), August 12, 2006
RACE RECORD: Terry Labonte, Chevrolet; 91.468 mph (2:22:47), June 30, 1996

>>TRACKS EXCLUSIVE TO THE NASCAR BUSCH SERIES AND NASCAR CRAFTSMAN TRUCK SERIES<<

>>AUTODROMO HERMANOS RODRIGUEZ<<

TRACK FACTS >>> >>> **Location:** Mexico City, Mexico >>> >>> **Owner:** Mexico City >>> >>> **Track length:** 2.518 miles >>> >>>

Grandstand seating: 90,000 >>> >>> **Tickets:** (5255) 5325-9000 >>> >>> **Website:** www.mexico200.com >>> >>>

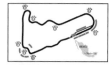

2007 SCHEDULE NASCAR Busch Series
Event: Telcel-Motorola Mexico 200 • **Race:** No. 3 of 35 • **Date:** March 4 • **TV:** ESPN2 • **Radio:** MRN
Race name subject to change

>>NASCAR BUSCH SERIES<<

YEAR BY YEAR WINNERS

Year	Event	Race winner	Car make	Avg. speed	Start pos.	Pole winner	Pole speed	POLE WINNERS		RACE WINNERS	
2006	Telcel-Motorola 200	D. Hamlin	Chevrolet	67.528	2	B. Said	102.665	Jorge Goeters	1	Denny Hamlin	1
2005	Telcel-Motorola 200	M. Truex Jr.	Chevrolet	67.591	3	J. Goeters	103.366	Boris Said	1	Martin Truex Jr.	1

QUALIFYING RECORD: Jorge Goeters, Ford; 103.366 mph (87.696 seconds), March 5, 2005
RACE RECORD: Martin Truex Jr., Chevrolet; 67.591 mph (2:58:49), March 6, 2005

>>CIRCUIT GILLES VILLENEUVE<<

TRACK FACTS >>> >>> **Location:** Montreal >>> >>> **Owner:** City of Montreal >>> >>> **Track length:** 2.709 miles >>> >>>

Estimated capacity: Varies >>> >>> **Tickets:** (514) 397-0007 >>> >>> **Website:** www.circuitgillesvilleneuve.ca >>> >>>

2007 SCHEDULE NASCAR Busch Series
Event: Montreal 200 (inaugural race) • **Race:** No. 23 of 35 • **Date:** August 4 • **TV:** ESPN2 • **Radio:** MRN
Race name subject to change

>> GATEWAY INTERNATIONAL RACEWAY <<

TRACK FACTS >>> **Location:** Madison, Ill. >>> >>> **Owner:** Dover Motorsports, Inc. >>> >>> **Track length:** 1.25 miles >>> >>>

Grandstand seating: 60,000 >>> >>> **Tickets:** (618) 875-7550 >>> >>> **Website:** www.gatewayraceway.com >>> >>>

Banking in Turns 1-2: 11 degrees • **Banking in Turns 3-4:** 9 degrees • **Length of front stretch:** 1,922 feet **Length of back stretch:** 1,976 feet

2007 SCHEDULE **NASCAR Busch Series** **Event:** Gateway 250 • **Race:** No. 21 of 35 • **Date:** July 21 **TV:** ESPN2 • **Radio:** MRN **Craftsman Truck Series** **Event:** Dodge Ram Tough 200 • **Race:** No. 17 of 25 **Date:** September 1 • **TV:** SPEED • **Radio:** MRN

>> NASCAR BUSCH SERIES <<

YEAR BY YEAR WINNERS

Year	Event	Race winner	Car make	Avg. speed	Start pos.	Pole winner	Pole speed
2006	Busch Silver Celebr. 250	C. Edwards	Ford	119.142	2	D. Hamlin	134.852
2005	Wallace Family Tribute 250	R. Sorenson	Dodge	103.318	2	M. Truex Jr.	135.021
2004	Charter Pipeline 250	M. Truex Jr.	Chevrolet	101.466	1	M. Truex Jr.	134.112
2003	Charter Pipeline 250	S. Riggs	Ford	92.870	8	A. Lewis	131.903
2002	Charter Pipeline 250	G. Biffle	Ford	106.926	7	R. LaJoie	131.911
2001	Carquest Auto Parts 250	K. Harvick	Chevrolet	103.448	2	G. Biffle	132.357
2000	Carquest Auto Parts 250	K. Harvick	Chevrolet	116.595	4	None—conditions	
1999	Carquest Auto Parts 250	D. Earnhardt Jr.	Chevrolet	104.227	18	C. Atwood	132.423
1998	Carquest Auto Parts 250	D. Earnhardt Jr.	Chevrolet	104.566	13	S. Hall	132.361
1997	Gateway 300	E. Sadler	Chevrolet	78.803	12	J. Bessey	130.993

POLE WINNERS		RACE WINNERS	
Martin Truex Jr.	2	Dale Earnhardt Jr.	2
Casey Atwood	1	Kevin Harvick	2
Joe Bessey	1	Greg Biffle	1
Greg Biffle	1	Carl Edwards	1
Shane Hall	1	Scott Riggs	1
Denny Hamlin	1	Elliott Sadler	1
Randy LaJoie	1	Reed Sorenson	1
Ashton Lewis Jr.	1	Martin Truex Jr.	1

QUALIFYING RECORD: Martin Truex Jr., Chevrolet; 135.021 mph (33.328 seconds), July 29, 2005
RACE RECORD: Carl Edwards, Ford; 119.142 mph (2:05:54), July 29, 2006

Edwards

>> NASCAR CRAFTSMAN TRUCK SERIES <<

YEAR BY YEAR WINNERS

Year	Event	Race winner	Car make	Avg. speed	Start pos.	Pole winner	Pole speed
2006	Ram Tough 200	T. Bodine	Toyota	84.966	3	None—conditions	
2005	Ram Tough 200	T. Musgrave	Dodge	100.854	1	T. Musgrave	135.159
2004	Ram Tough 200	D. Starr	Chevrolet	93.694	14	J. Sprague	133.227
2003	Ram Tough 200	B. Gaughan	Dodge	99.489	4	None—conditions	
2002	Ram Tough 200	T. Cook	Ford	109.323	8	M. Bliss	129.549
2001	Ram Tough 200	T. Musgrave	Dodge	112.237	1	T. Musgrave	129.971
2000	Ram Tough 200	J. Sprague	Chevrolet	113.726	2	G. Biffle	132.279
1999	Ram Tough 200	G. Biffle	Ford	111.853	5	S. Compton	133.093
1998	Ram Tough 200	R. Carelli	Chevrolet	99.764	4	G. Biffle	131.218

POLE WINNERS		RACE WINNERS	
Greg Biffle	2	Ted Musgrave	2
Ted Musgrave	2	Greg Biffle	1
Mike Bliss	1	Todd Bodine	1
Stacy Compton	1	Rick Carelli	1
Jack Sprague	1	Terry Cook	1
		Brendan Gaughan	1
		Jack Sprague	1
		David Starr	1

QUALIFYING RECORD: Ted Musgrave, Dodge; 135.159 mph (33.284 seconds), April 30, 2005
RACE RECORD: Jack Sprague, Chevrolet; 113.726 mph (1:35:31), May 7, 2000

Musgrave

>>KENTUCKY SPEEDWAY<<

TRACK FACTS >>> >>> **Location:** Sparta, Ky. >>> >>> **Owner:** Jerry Carroll >>> >>> **Track length:** 1.5 miles >>> >>>

Grandstand seating: 66,089 >>> >>> **Tickets:** (888) 652-7223 >>> >>> **Website:** www.kentuckyspeedway.com >>> >>>

Banking in turns: 14 degrees • **Banking on front stretch:** 8 degrees • **Banking on back stretch:** 4 degrees
Length of front stretch: 1,662 feet • **Length of back stretch:** 1,600 feet

2007 SCHEDULE **NASCAR Busch Series** Event: Meijer 300 • **Race:** No. 16 of 35 • **Date:** June 16
TV: ESPN2 • **Radio:** MRN **NASCAR Craftsman Truck Series** Event: Built Ford Tough 225
Race: No. 13 of 25 • **Date:** July 14 • **TV:** SPEED • **Radio:** MRN

>>NASCAR BUSCH SERIES<<

YEAR BY YEAR WINNERS

Year	Event	Race winner	Car make	Avg. speed	Start pos.	Pole winner	Pole speed	POLE WINNERS		RACE WINNERS	
2006	Meijer 300	D. Gilliland	Chevrolet	116.004	4	D. Hamlin	177.772	Stacy Compton	1	Todd Bodine	1
2005	Meijer 300	C. Edwards	Ford	117.111	1	C. Edwards	181.287	Carl Edwards	1	Kyle Busch	1
2004	Meijer 300	Ky. Busch	Chevrolet	126.642	2	M. Truex	180.102	Denny Hamlin	1	Carl Edwards	1
2003	Meijer 300	B. Hamilton Jr.	Ford	136.123	2	S. Compton	176.384	Scott Riggs	1	David Gilliland	1
2002	Kroger 300	T. Bodine	Chevrolet	127.164	6	S. Riggs	174.831	Jay Sauter	1	Bobby Hamilton Jr.	1
2001	Outback Steakhouse 300	K. Harvick	Chevrolet	118.590	11	Ja. Sauter	171.860	Martin Truex Jr.	1	Kevin Harvick	1

QUALIFYING RECORD: Carl Edwards, Ford; 181.287 mph (29.787seconds), June 18, 2005
RACE RECORD: Bobby Hamilton Jr., Ford; 136.123 mph (2:12:14), June 14, 2003

Gilliland

>>NASCAR CRAFTSMAN TRUCK SERIES<<

Setzer

YEAR BY YEAR WINNERS

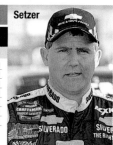

Year	Event	Race winner	Car make	Avg. speed	Start pos.	Pole winner	Pole speed	POLE WINNERS		RACE WINNERS	
2006	Built Ford Tough 225	R. Hornaday Jr.	Chevrolet	118.110	22	M. Ambrose	176.922	Marcos Ambrose	1	Greg Biffle	1
2005	Built Ford Tough 225	D. Setzer	Chevrolet	117.747	18	B. Lester	178.141	Jason Leffler	1	Mike Bliss	1
2004	Built Ford Tough 225	B. Hamilton	Dodge	122.600	3	None—conditions		Bill Lester	1	Carl Edwards	1
2003	Built Ford Tough 225	C. Edwards	Ford	122.393	5	J. Wood	169.641	Bryan Reffner	1	Bobby Hamilton	1
2002	Kroger 225	M. Bliss	Chevrolet	143.515	2	J. Leffler	168.303	Jack Sprague	1	Ron Hornaday Jr.	1
2001	Kroger 225	S. Riggs	Dodge	113.525	3	J. Sprague	167.115	Jon Wood	1	Scott Riggs	1
2000	Kroger 225	G. Biffle	Ford	98.385	2	B. Reffner	168.460			Dennis Setzer	1

QUALIFYING RECORD: Bill Lester, Toyota; 178.141 mph (30.313 seconds), July 9, 2005
RACE RECORD: Mike Bliss, Chevrolet; 143.515 mph (1:34:04), July 13, 2002

>>MANSFIELD MOTORSPORTS SPEEDWAY<<

TRACK FACTS >>> >>> **Location:** Mansfield, Ohio >>> >>> **Owner:** Michael Dzurilla >>> >>> **Track length:** .50 miles >>> >>>

Grandstand seating: 7,200 >>> >>> **Tickets:** (419) 525-7223 >>> >>> **Website:** www.mansfield-speedway.com >>> >>>

Banking in turns: compound, from 12 to 16 degrees • **Banking on straights:** 6 degrees
Length of front stretch: 545 feet • **Length of back stretch:** 545 feet
2007 SCHEDULE **NASCAR Craftsman Truck Series** **Event:** City of Mansfield 250 • **Race:** No. 7 of 25
Date: May 26 • **TV:** SPEED • **Radio:** MRN

>>NASCAR CRAFTSMAN TRUCK SERIES<<

Hornaday Jr.

YEAR BY YEAR WINNERS

Year	Event	Race winner	Car make	Avg. speed	Start pos.	Pole winner	Pole speed	POLE WINNERS		RACE WINNERS	
2006	City of Mansfield 250	R. Hornaday Jr.	Chevrolet	62.999	17	None—conditions		Ron Hornaday Jr.	1	Bobby Hamilton	1
2005	UAW/GM Ohio 250	B. Hamilton	Dodge	65.907	26	R. Hornaday Jr.	110.585			Ron Hornaday Jr.	1
2004	UAW/GM Ohio 250	J. Sprague	Chevrolet	54.706	1	None—conditions				Jack Sprague	1

QUALIFYING RECORD: Ron Hornaday Jr., Chevrolet; 110.585 mph (16.277 seconds), May 15, 2005
RACE RECORD: Bobby Hamilton, Dodge; 65.907 mph (1:55:37), May 15, 2005

>>MEMPHIS MOTORSPORTS PARK<<

TRACK FACTS >>> >>> **Location:** Memphis, Tenn. >>> >>> **Owner:** Dover Motorsports, Inc. >>> >>> **Track length:** .75 miles >>> >>>

Grandstand seating: 35,000 >>> >>> **Tickets:** (866) 407-7333 >>> >>> **Website:** www.memphismotorsportspark.com >>> >>>

Banking in turns: 11 degrees • **Banking on straights:** 4 degrees • **Length of front stretch:** 1,100 feet
Length of back stretch: 1,100 feet
2007 SCHEDULE **NASCAR Busch Series** **Event:** Sam's Town 250 • **Race:** No. 32 of 35
Date: October 27 • **TV:** ESPN2 • **Radio:** MRN   **NASCAR Craftsman Truck Series** **Event:** O'Reilly 200
Race: No. 12 of 25 • **Date:** June 30 • **TV:** SPEED • **Radio:** MRN

>>NASCAR BUSCH SERIES<<

YEAR BY YEAR WINNERS

Year	Event	Race winner	Car make	Avg. speed	Start pos.	Pole winner	Pole speed	POLE WINNERS		RACE WINNERS	
2006	Sam's Town 250	K. Harvick	Chevrolet	74.336	5	Jo. Sauter	118.614	Jeff Green	2	Kevin Harvick	2
2005	Sam's Town 250	C. Bowyer	Chevrolet	73.473	35	M. Truex	119.867	Greg Biffle	1	Clint Bowyer	1
2004	Sam's Town 250	M. Truex Jr.	Chevrolet	78.561	1	C. Bowyer	120.198	Clint Bowyer	1	Jeff Green	1
2003	Sam's Town 250	B. Hamilton Jr.	Ford	87.674	4	D. Reutimann	119.766	David Reutimann	1	Bobby Hamilton Jr.	1
2002	Sam's Town 250	S. Wimmer	Pontiac	79.337	6	G. Biffle	116.817	Johnny Sauter	1	Randy LaJoie	1
2001	Sam's Town 250	R. LaJoie	Chevrolet	75.050	16	None—conditions		Martin Truex Jr.	1	Martin Truex Jr.	1
2000	Sam's Town 250	K. Harvick	Chevrolet	92.352	2	J. Green	120.267			Scott Wimmer	1
1999	Sam's Town 250	J. Green	Chevrolet	76.583	1	J. Green	119.311				

QUALIFYING RECORD: Jeff Green, Chevrolet; 120.267 mph (22.450 seconds), October 28, 2000
RACE RECORD: Kevin Harvick, Chevrolet; 92.352 mph (2:01:49), October 29, 2000

>>NASCAR CRAFTSMAN TRUCK SERIES<<

Sprague

YEAR BY YEAR WINNERS

Year	Event	Race winner	Car make	Avg. speed	Start pos.	Pole winner	Pole speed	POLE WINNERS		RACE WINNERS	
2006	O'Reilly 200	J. Sprague	Toyota	88.367	1	J. Sprague	117.529	Jack Sprague	3	Jack Sprague	2
2005	O'Reilly 200	B. Whitt	Toyota	71.182	1	B. Whitt	118.801	Greg Biffle	2	Greg Biffle	1
2004	O'Reilly 200	B. Hamilton	Dodge	77.821	3	J. Sprague	118.917	Bobby Hamilton	1	Bobby Hamilton	1
2003	O'Reilly 200	T. Musgrave	Dodge	86.097	3	J. Wood	117.407	Jason Leffler	1	Ron Hornaday Jr.	1
2002	Memphis 200	T. Kvapil	Chevrolet	89.065	3	J. Leffler	117.971	Brandon Whitt	1	Travis Kvapil	1
2001	Memphis 200	D. Setzer	Chevrolet	82.279	4	J. Sprague	116.863	Jon Wood	1	Ted Musgrave	1
2000	Quaker State 200	J. Sprague	Chevrolet	85.565	5	B. Hamilton	118.043			Dennis Setzer	1
1999	Memphis 200	G. Biffle	Ford	75.303	1	G. Biffle	120.139			Brandon Whitt	1
1998	Memphis 200	R. Hornaday Jr.	Chevrolet	84.204	3	G. Biffle	118.901				

QUALIFYING RECORD: Greg Biffle, Ford; 120.139 mph (22.474 seconds), May 7, 1999
RACE RECORD: Travis Kvapil, Chevrolet; 89.065 mph (1:41:03), June 22, 2002

>>THE MILWAUKEE MILE<<

TRACK FACTS >>> >>> **Location:** West Allis, Wis. >>> >>> **Owner:** State of Wisconsin >>> >>> **Track length:** 1 mile

Grandstand seating: 40,000 >>> >>> **Tickets:** (414) 453-8277 >>> >>> **Website:** www.milwaukeemile.com >>> >>>

Banking in turns: 9.25 degrees • **Banking on straights:** 2.5 degrees • **Length of front stretch:** 1,265 feet
Length of back stretch: 1,265 feet

2007 SCHEDULE **NASCAR Busch Series** Event: AT&T 250 • **Race:** No. 17 of 35 • **Date:** June 23
TV: ESPN2 • **Radio:** MRN **Craftsman Truck Series** Event: Toyota Tundra Milwaukee 200 • **Race:** No. 11 of 25
Date: June 22 • **TV:** SPEED • **Radio:** MRN

>>NASCAR BUSCH SERIES<<

YEAR BY YEAR WINNERS

Menard

Year	Event	Race winner	Car make	Avg. speed	Start pos.	Pole winner	Pole speed
2006	AT&T 250	P. Menard	Chevrolet	82.042	3	A. Almirola	122.320
2005	SBC 250	Jo. Sauter	Dodge	97.403	1	Jo. Sauter	122.595
2004	Alan Kulwicki 250	R. Hornaday Jr.	Chevrolet	102.038	10	D. Stremme	122.553
2003	GNC 250	J. Keller	Ford	103.093	7	None—conditions	
2002	GNC Live Well 250	G. Biffle	Ford	94.182	1	G. Biffle	121.770
2001	GNC Live Well 250	G. Biffle	Ford	102.389	1	K. Harvick	122.474
2000	Sears Diehard 250	J. Green	Chevrolet	89.206	1	J. Green	121.572
1999	Diehard 250	C. Atwood	Chevrolet	97.858	1	C. Atwood	121.421
1998	Diehard 250	D. Earnhardt Jr.	Chevrolet	97.890	2	J. Purvis	119.904
1997	Sears Auto Center 250	R. LaJoie	Chevrolet	99.141	10	T. Fedewa	118.468
1996	Sears Auto Center 250	B. Jones	Ford	82.237	32	H. Sadler	118.320
1995	Sears Auto Center 250	D. Jarrett	Ford	95.379	12	D. Setzer	114.650
1994	Havoline 250	M. Wallace	Chevrolet	100.999	25	D. Green	115.407
1993	Havoline 250	S. Grissom	Chevrolet	89.003	14	B. Dotter	113.845
1985	Mil. Sentinel 200	J. Ingram	Pontiac	104.121	8	A. Kulwicki	112.711
1984	Red Carpet 200	S. Ard	Oldsmobile	97.206	3	D. Trickle	112.984

POLE WINNERS		RACE WINNERS	
Aric Almirola	1	Greg Biffle	2
Casey Atwood	1	Sam Ard	1
Greg Biffle	1	Casey Atwood	1
Bobby Dotter	1	Dale Earnhardt Jr.	1
Tim Fedewa	1	Jeff Green	1
David Green	1	Steve Grissom	1
Jeff Green	1	Ron Hornaday Jr.	1
Kevin Harvick	1	Jack Ingram	1
Alan Kulwicki	1	Dale Jarrett	1
Jeff Purvis	1	Buckshot Jones	1
Hermie Sadler	1	Jason Keller	1
Johnny Sauter	1	Randy LaJoie	1
Dennis Setzer	1	Paul Menard	1
David Stremme	1	Johnny Sauter	1
Dick Trickle	1	Mike Wallace	1

QUALIFYING RECORD: Johnny Sauter, Dodge; 122.595 mph (29.365 seconds), June 25, 2005
RACE RECORD: 250 miles: Jason Keller, Ford; 103.093 mph (2:25:30), June 29, 2003

>>NASCAR CRAFTSMAN TRUCK SERIES<<

YEAR BY YEAR WINNERS

Year	Event	Race winner	Car make	Avg. speed	Start pos.	Pole winner	Pole speed
2006	Toyota Tundra 200	J. Benson Jr.	Toyota	85.673	4	R. Hornaday Jr.	122.021
2005	Toyota Tundra 200	D. Setzer	Chevrolet	109.907	3	J. Sprague	121.980
2004	Black Cat 200	T. Musgrave	Dodge	83.230	1	T. Musgrave	121.980
2003	GNC 200	B. Gaughan	Dodge	109.689	2	T. Cook	119.996
2002	GNC Live Well 200	T. Cook	Ford	104.490	1	T. Cook	119.784
2001	GNC Live Well 200	T. Musgrave	Dodge	92.929	3	J. Sprague	120.692
2000	DieHard 200	K. Busch	Ford	89.264	1	K. Busch	120.518
1999	DieHard 200	G. Biffle	Ford	106.714	1	G. Biffle	121.102
1998	DieHard 200	M. Bliss	Ford	104.347	2	J. Sprague	120.530
1997	DieHard 200	R. Hornaday Jr.	Chevrolet	105.665	5	J. Sprague	119.178
1996	Sears Auto 200	J. Sprague	Chevrolet	87.816	8	M. Bliss	118.265
1995	Sears Auto 125	M. Skinner	Chevrolet	87.413	1	M. Skinner	112.535

POLE WINNERS		RACE WINNERS	
Jack Sprague	4	Ted Musgrave	2
Terry Cook	2	Johnny Benson Jr.	1
Greg Biffle	1	Greg Biffle	1
Mike Bliss	1	Mike Bliss	1
Kurt Busch	1	Kurt Busch	1
Ron Hornaday Jr.	1	Terry Cook	1
Ted Musgrave	1	Brendan Gaughan	1
Mike Sinner	1	Ron Hornaday Jr.	1
		Dennis Setzer	1
		Mike Skinner	1
		Jack Sprague	1

QUALIFYING RECORD: Ron Hornaday Jr., Chevrolet; 122.021 mph (29.503 seconds), June 23, 2006
RACE RECORD: Dennis Setzer, Chevrolet; 109.907 mph (1:49:11), June 24, 2005

Benson Jr.

TRACK FACTS >>> >>> **Location:** Nashville >>> >>> **Owner:** Dover Motorsports, Inc. >>> >>> **Track length:** 1.333 miles >>> >>>

Grandstand seating: 140,000 >>> >>> **Tickets:** (615) 547-7500 >>> >>> **Website:** www.nashvillesuperspeedway.com >>> >>>

Banking in turns: 14 degrees • **Banking on front stretch:** 9 degrees • **Banking on back stretch:** 6 degrees
Length of front stretch: 2,494 feet • **Length of back stretch:** 2,203 feet

2007 SCHEDULE **NASCAR Busch Series** Event 1: Pepsi 300 • **Race:** No. 7 of 35 • **Date:** April 7 • **TV:** ESPN2 • **Radio:** MRN **Event 2:** Federated Auto Parts 300 • **Race:** No. 15 of 35 • **Date:** June 9 • **TV:** ESPN2 • **Radio:** MRN **NASCAR Craftsman Truck Series** **Event:** Toyota Tundra 200 • **Race:** No. 16 of 25 • **Date:** August 12 • **TV:** SPEED • **Radio:** MRN

>>NASCAR BUSCH SERIES<<

YEAR BY YEAR WINNERS

Year	Event	Race winner	Car make	Avg. speed	Start pos.	Pole winner	Pole speed
2006	Federated Auto Parts 300	C. Edwards	Ford	123.511	13	T. Kluever	161.930
	Pepsi 300	K. Harvick	Chevrolet	111.820	7	D. Hamlin	165.282
2005	Pepsi 300	R. Sorenson	Dodge	124.436	1	R. Sorenson	165.928
	Federated Auto Parts 300	C. Bowyer	Chevrolet	122.141	5	None—conditions	
2004	Pepsi 300	M. Waltrip	Chevrolet	122.211	22	M. Truex	166.515
	Federated Auto Parts 300	J. Leffler	Chevrolet	114.708	2	M. Truex	163.569
2003	Pepsi 300	D. Green	Pontiac	122.724	7	R. LaJoie	163.324
	Trace Adkins Chr. 300	S. Riggs	Ford	118.547	3	None—conditions	
2002	Pepsi 300	S. Riggs	Ford	111.038	3	S. Hmiel	161.440
	Inside Traxx 300	J. Sprague	Chevrolet	125.244	5	G. Biffle	161.288
2001	Pepsi 300	G. Biffle	Ford	105.773	4	K. Harvick	159.678

POLE WINNERS		RACE WINNERS	
Martin Truex Jr.	2	Scott Riggs	2
Greg Biffle	1	Greg Biffle	1
Denny Hamlin	1	Clint Bowyer	1
Kevin Harvick	1	Carl Edwards	1
Shane Hmiel	1	David Green	1
Todd Kluever	1	Kevin Harvick	1
Randy LaJoie	1	Jason Leffler	1
		Jack Sprague	1
		Michael Waltrip	1

QUALIFYING RECORD: Martin Truex Jr., Chevrolet; 166.515 mph (28.819 seconds), April 9, 2004
RACE RECORD: Jack Sprague, Chevrolet; 125.244 mph (2:23:41), June 8, 2002

>>NASCAR CRAFTSMAN TRUCK SERIES<<

Reutimann

YEAR BY YEAR WINNERS

Year	Event	Race winner	Car make	Avg. speed	Start pos.	Pole winner	Pole speed
2006	Toyota Tundra 200	J. Benson Jr.	Toyota	108.704	22	E. Darnell	162.116
2005	Toyota Tundra 200	D. Reutimann	Toyota	109.246	6	M. Skinner	161.440
2004	Toyota Tundra 200	B. Hamilton	Dodge	124.068	15	B. Hamilton Jr.	160.990
2003	Federated Auto 200	C. Edwards	Ford	129.557	6	C. Chaffin	156.844
2002	Federated Auto 200	M. Bliss	Chevrolet	129.442	1	M. Bliss	157.322
2001	Federated Auto 200	S. Riggs	Dodge	132.466	1	S. Riggs	155.477

POLE WINNERS		RACE WINNERS	
Mike Bliss	1	Johnny Benson Jr.	1
Chad Chaffin	1	Mike Bliss	1
Erik Darnell	1	Carl Edwards	1
Bobby Hamilton Jr.	1	Bobby Hamilton	1
Scott Riggs	1	Scott Riggs	1
Mike Skinner	1	Dave Reutimann	1

QUALIFYING RECORD: Erik Darnell, Ford; 162.116 mph (29.601 seconds), August 12, 2006
RACE RECORD: Scott Riggs, Dodge; 132.466 mph (1:30:34), August 10, 2001

>>O'REILLY RACEWAY PARK AT INDIANAPOLIS<<

TRACK FACTS >>> >>> **Location:** Clermont, Ind. >>> >>> **Owner:** National Hot Rod Association >>> >>> **Track length:** .686 miles

Grandstand seating: 35,000 >>> >>> **Tickets:** (800) 884-6472 >>> >>> **Website:** www.oreillyracewaypark.com >>> >>>

Banking in turns: 7.5 degrees • **Banking on straights:** 2 degrees • **Length of front stretch:** 699 feet
Length of back stretch: 699 feet

2007 SCHEDULE **NASCAR Busch Series** **Event:** Kroger 200 • **Race:** No. 22 of 35 • **Date:** July 28 • **TV:** ESPN2
Radio: MRN **NASCAR Craftsman Truck Series** **Event:** Power Stroke Diesel 200 • **Race:** No. 14 of 25
Date: July 27 • **TV:** SPEED • **Radio:** MRN

>>NASCAR BUSCH SERIES<<

Harvick

YEAR BY YEAR WINNERS

Year	Event	Race winner	Car make	Avg. speed	Start pos.	Pole winner	Pole speed	POLE WINNERS		RACE WINNERS	
2006	Kroger 200	K. Harvick	Chevrolet	81.478	6	D. Hamlin	110.442	Randy LaJoie	2	Morgan Shepherd	3
2005	Kroger 200	M. Truex Jr.	Chevrolet	72.930	9	R. Sorenson	110.943	Mike Alexander	1	Kevin Harvick	2
2004	Kroger 200	Ky. Busch	Chevrolet	81.250	8	Jo. Sauter	111.248	Sam Ard	1	Jason Keller	2
2003	Kroger 200	B. Vickers	Chevrolet	90.049	3	S. Hmiel	110.690	Greg Biffle	1	Randy LaJoie	2
2002	Kroger 200	G. Biffle	Ford	81.788	1	G. Biffle	109.521	Brett Bodine	1	Greg Biffle	1
2001	Kroger 200	K. Harvick	Chevrolet	72.785	12	K. Wallace	110.635	Ward Burton	1	Kyle Busch	1
2000	Kroger 200	R. Hornaday	Chevrolet	79.626	16	J. Leffler	112.597	David Green	1	Dale Earnhardt Jr.	1
1999	Kroger 200	J. Keller	Chevrolet	73.293	1	J. Keller	112.352	Denny Hamlin	1	Steve Grissom	1
1998	Kroger 200	D. Earnhardt Jr.	Chevrolet	78.883	16	B. Jones	111.409	Jimmy Hensley	1	Jimmy Hensley	1
1997	Kroger 200	R. LaJoie	Chevrolet	59.652	1	R. LaJoie	111.193	Shane Hmiel	1	Ron Hornaday	1
1996	Kroger 200	R. LaJoie	Chevrolet	77.551	1	R. LaJoie	109.270	Ernie Irvan	1	Tommy Houston	1
1995	Kroger 200	J. Keller	Chevrolet	80.335	3	E. Sawyer	109.570	Buckshot Jones	1	Bobby Labonte	1
1994	Kroger 200	M. Wallace	Chevrolet	82.156	5	D. Green	113.461	Jason Keller	1	Tracy Leslie	1
1993	Kroger 200	T. Leslie	Chevrolet	69.792	10	E. Irvan	109.828	Jason Leffler	1	Butch Miller	1
1992	Kroger 200	J. Nemechek	Chevrolet	83.943	3	R. Pressley	109.265	Kelly Moore	1	Joe Nemechek	1
1991	Kroger 200	B. Labonte	Oldsmobile	76.034	3	W. Burton	110.516	L.D. Ottinger	1	Larry Pearson	1
1990	Kroger 200	S. Grissom	Oldsmobile	75.719	17	J. Hensley	110.260	Phil Parsons	1	Martin Truex Jr.	1
1989	Kroger 200	M. Waltrip	Pontiac	84.633	1	M. Waltrip	108.807	Robert Pressley	1	Brian Vickers	1
1988	Kroger 200	M. Shepherd	Buick	76.553	2	K. Moore	105.895	Johnny Sauter	1	Mike Wallace	1
1987	Kroger 200	L. Pearson	Pontiac	73.402	11	M. Alexander	104.387	Elton Sawyer	1	Michael Waltrip	1
1986	Kroger 200	B. Miller	Pontiac	75.431	18	D. Waltrip	104.910	Reed Sorenson	1		
1985	Kroger 200	J. Hensley	Oldsmobile	96.923	2	B. Bodine	105.121	Kenny Wallace	1		
1984	Kroger 200	M. Shepherd	Pontiac	88.579	3	L. Ottinger	104.246	Darrell Waltrip	1		
1983	Kroger 200	T. Houston	Chevrolet	79.600	7	P. Parsons	105.201	Michael Waltrip	1		
1982	Kroger 200	M. Shepherd	Oldsmobile	67.234	5	S. Ard	104.436				

QUALIFYING RECORD: David Green, Chevrolet; 113.461 mph (21.766 seconds), August 4, 1994
RACE RECORD: Jimmy Hensley, Oldsmobile; 96.923 mph (1:24:56), June 22, 1985

>>NASCAR CRAFTSMAN TRUCK SERIES<<

Crawford

YEAR BY YEAR WINNERS

Year	Event	Race winner	Car make	Avg. speed	Start pos.	Pole winner	Pole speed	POLE WINNERS		RACE WINNERS	
2006	Power Stroke 200	R. Crawford	Ford	75.789	3	D. Ragan	109.838	Terry Cook	2	Mike Skinner	2
2005	Power Stroke 200	D. Setzer	Chevrolet	84.910	1	None—conditions		Joe Ruttman	2	Jack Sprague	2
2004	Power Stroke 200	C. Chaffin	Dodge	77.007	5	J. Sprague	110.275	Mike Skinner	2	Greg Biffle	1
2003	Power Stroke 200	C. Edwards	Ford	88.121	5	T. Cook	107.777	Jimmy Hensley	1	Chad Chaffin	1
2002	Power Stroke 200	T. Cook	Ford	74.018	1	T. Cook	108.549	David Ragan	1	Terry Cook	1
2001	Power Stroke 200	J. Sprague	Chevrolet	80.745	2	J. Ruttman	109.043	Dennis Setzer	1	Rick Crawford	1
2000	Power Stroke 200	J. Ruttman	Dodge	75.064	1	J. Ruttman	111.843	Jack Sprague	1	Carl Edwards	1
1999	Power Stroke 200	G. Biffle	Ford	88.704	3	D. Setzer	111.133	Randy Tolsma	1	Ron Hornaday Jr.	1
1998	Cummins 200	J. Sprague	Chevrolet	77.235	3	R. Tolsma	110.829			Joe Ruttman	1
1997	Cummins 200	R. Hornaday Jr.	Chevrolet	81.753	2	J. Hensley	109.750			Dennis Setzer	1
1996	Cummins 200	M. Skinner	Chevrolet	85.720	1	M. Skinner	108.855				
1995	Action Packed 150	M. Skinner	Chevrolet	78.767	1	M. Skinner	108.387				

QUALIFYING RECORD: Joe Ruttman, Dodge; 111.843 mph (22.081 seconds), August 2, 2000
RACE RECORD: Greg Biffle, Ford; 88.704 mph (1:33:16), August 5, 1999

2006 SEASON REVIEW

2006 CHAMPION

48 JIMMIE JOHNSON

Car: No. 48 Chevrolet • **Car owner:** Rick Hendrick
Birth date: September 17, 1975 • **Hometown:** El Cajon, Calif.

NASCAR NEXTEL Cup Series Statistics

Seasons competed: 6 (1999-2006)
Career starts: 183   **Career wins:** 23   **Career poles:** 9
2006 championship season recap: The 2006 season was one of firsts for Johnson. After finishing second in points in 2003 and '04, Johnson got his first NASCAR NEXTEL Cup Series championship. Before that came his first Daytona 500 win in February, and then his first victory at the historic Indianapolis Motor Speedway in August. In between those milestones, he posted three more wins (Las Vegas, Talladega, Martinsville) and won the NASCAR NEXTEL All-Star Challenge at Lowe's Motor Speedway.

2006 CHAMPIONSHIP LINESCORE

Starts	Wins	Poles	Top 5	Top 10	Races Led	Laps Led	DNF
36	23	1	13	24	18	854	1

JIMMIE JOHNSON 2006 RACE BY RACE

No.	Race	Start	Finish	Points	Rank	Laps/ Completed	Money won	Status
1.	Daytona 500	9	1	185	1	203/203	$1,505,124	Running
2.	Auto Club 500	3	2	170	1	251/251	$235,936	Running
3.	UAW-DaimlerChrysler 400	3	1	185	1	270/270	$386,936	Running
4.	Golden Corral 500	14	6	150	1	325/325	$121,761	Running
5.	Food City 500	5	30	73	3	487/500	$128,486	Running
6.	DirecTV 500	1	3	170	1	500/500	$150,361	Running
7.	Samsung/RadioShack 500	16	11	130	1	334/334	$165,161	Running
8.	Subway Fresh 500	10	7	146	2	312/312	$127,111	Running
9.	Aaron's 499	16	1	185	1	188/188	$326,061	Running
10.	Crown Royal 400	5	12	127	1	400/400	$118,361	Running
11.	Dodge Charger 500	25	4	165	1	367/367	$165,311	Running
12.	Coca-Cola 600	3	2	175	1	400/400	$288,236	Running
13.	Neighborhood Excellence 400 presented by Bank of America	42	6	150	1	400/400	$153,261	Running
14.	Pocono 500	10	10	134	1	200/200	$123,761	Running
15.	3M Performance 400 pres. by Post-it Picture Paper	4	6	150	1	129/129	$128,386	Running
16.	Dodge/Save Mart 350	16	10	139	1	110/110	$144,186	Running
17.	Pepsi 400	9	32	67	1	160/160	$130,386	Running
18.	USG Sheetrock 400	5	6	150	1	270/270	$154,286	Running
19.	Lenox Industrial Tools 300	6	9	138	1	308/308	$127,711	Running
20.	Pennsylvania 500	15	6	150	1	200/200	$133,661	Running
21.	Allstate 400 at the Brickyard	5	1	185	1	160/160	$452,861	Running
22.	AMD at The Glen	5	17	117	1	90/90	$110,111	Running
23.	GFS Marketplace 400	8	13	124	1	200/200	$123,586	Running
24.	Sharpie 500	18	10	134	1	500/500	$147,686	Running
25.	Sony HD 500	16	11	130	2	250/250	$141,986	Running
26.	Chevy Rock & Roll 400	19	23	99	2	399/400	$114,836	Running
27.	Sylvania 300	7	39	46	9	233/300	$115,911	Running
28.	Dover 400	18	13	124	8	399/400	$119,861	Running
29.	Banquet 400 presented by ConAgra Foods	3	14	131	8	267/267	$141,486	Running
30.	UAW-Ford 500	3	24	96	8	187/188	$120,086	Accident
31.	Bank of America 500	10	2	175	7	334/334	$221,511	Running
32.	Subway 500	9	1	190	3	500/500	$191,886	Running
33.	Bass Pro Shops 500	3	2	175	2	325/325	$251,686	Running
34.	Dickies 500	5	2	175	1	339/339	$364,236	Running
35.	Checker Auto Parts 500 presented by Pennzoil	29	2	175	1	312/312	$212,211	Running
36.	Ford 400	15	9	143	1	268/268	$119,986	Running

11 DENNY HAMLIN

Car: No. 11 Chevrolet • **Car owner:** Joe Gibbs
Birth date: November 18, 1980 • **Hometown:** Chesterfield, Va.

NASCAR NEXTEL Cup Series Statistics

Seasons competed: 2 (2005-2006)
Career starts: 43   **Career wins:** 2   **Career poles:** 4
Rookie season recap: Hamlin's 2006 season was one of the best ever for a rookie in NASCAR NEXTEL Cup Series history. He swept the Pocono races, winning each from the pole, and became the first rookie to make the Chase for the NASCAR NEXTEL Cup. And Hamlin didn't just make the Chase—he was in contention for the NASCAR NEXTEL Cup Series championship until the season's final race. He ran away with the Raybestos Rookie of the Year award, winning the Raybestos Rookie of the Race 17 times in 36 races.

2006 LINESCORE

Starts	Wins	Poles	Top 5	Top 10	Races Led	Laps Led	DNF
36	2	3	8	20	13	418	1

RAYBESTOS ROOKIES OF THE YEAR

Year	Driver	Pts. Pos	Races	Poles	Wins	Top 5	Top 10	Winnings
2006	Denny Hamlin	3	36	3	2	8	20	$6,607,932
2005	Kyle Busch	20	36	1	2	9	13	$4,730,471
2004	Kasey Kahne	13	36	4	0	13	14	$5,415,611
2003	Jamie McMurray	13	36	1	0	5	13	$3,258,806
2002	Ryan Newman	6	36	6	1	14	22	$5,346,651
2001	Kevin Harvick	9	35	0	2	6	16	$4,302,202
2000	Matt Kenseth	14	34	0	1	4	11	$2,408,138
1999	Tony Stewart	4	34	2	3	12	21	$3,190,149
1998	Kenny Irwin	28	32	1	0	1	4	$1,459,967
1997	Mike Skinner	30	31	2	0	0	3	$900,569
1996	Johnny Benson	21	30	1	0	1	6	$932,580
1995	Ricky Craven	24	31	0	0	0	4	$597,054
1994	Jeff Burton	24	30	0	0	2	3	$594,700
1993	Jeff Gordon	14	30	1	0	7	11	$765,168
1992	Jimmy Hensley	28	22	0	0	0	4	$247,660
1991	Bobby Hamilton	22	28	0	0	0	4	$259,105
1990	Rob Moroso	30	25	0	0	0	1	$162,002
1989	Dick Trickle	15	28	0	0	6	9	$343,728
1988	Ken Bouchard	25	24	0	0	0	1	$109,410
1987	Davey Allison	21	22	5	2	9	10	$361,060
1986	Alan Kulwicki	21	23	0	0	1	4	$94,450
1985	Ken Schrader	16	28	0	0	0	3	$211,523
1984	Rusty Wallace	14	30	0	0	2	4	$196,617
1983	Sterling Marlin	19	30	0	0	0	1	$143,564
1982	Geoffrey Bodine	22	25	2	0	4	10	$258,500
1981	Ron Bouchard	22	22	1	1	5	12	$152,855
1980	Jody Ridley	7	31	0	0	2	18	$196,617
1979	Dale Earnhardt	7	27	4	1	11	17	$264,086
1978	Ronnie Thomas	18	27	0	0	0	2	$73,037
1977	Ricky Rudd	17	25	0	0	1	10	$68,448
1976	Skip Manning	18	27	0	0	0	4	$55,820
1975	Bruce Hill	16	26	0	0	3	11	$58,138
1974	Earl Ross	8	21	0	1	5	10	$64,830
1973	Lennie Pond	23	23	0	0	1	9	$25,155
1972	Larry Smith	23	23	0	0	0	7	$24,215
1971	Walter Ballard	10	41	0	0	3	11	$25,598
1970	Bill Dennis	25	25	0	0	0	5	$15,670
1969	Dick Brooks	21	28	0	0	3	12	$27,532
1968	Pete Hamilton	32	16	0	0	3	6	$8,239
1967	Donnie Allison	16	20	0	0	4	7	$16,440
1966	James Hylton	2	41	1	0	20	32	$29,575
1965	Sam McQuagg	24	15	0	0	2	5	$10,555
1964	Doug Cooper	21	39	0	0	4	11	$10,445
1963	Billy Wade	16	22	0	0	4	11	$8,710
1962	Tom Cox	18	40	0	0	12	20	$8,980
1961	Woody Wilson	41	5	0	0	0	1	$2,625
1960	David Pearson	23	22	1	0	3	7	$5,030
1959	Richard Petty	15	22	0	0	6	9	$7,630
1958	Shorty Rollins	4	21	0	1	10	17	$8,515
1957	Ken Rush	38	16	1	0	1	6	$2,045

>>2006 POINTS STANDINGS <<

NASCAR NEXTEL Cup Series

Rk. Driver	Points	Starts	Avg. start	Avg. finish	Wins	T5s	T10s	Laps led	DNFs	Poles	Rating	Money Won
1. Jimmie Johnson	6,475	36	10.8	9.7	5	13	24	854	1	1	101.9	$15,875,125
2. Matt Kenseth	6,419	36	14.6	9.8	4	15	21	1,132	1	0	101.7	$9,544,966
3. Denny Hamlin*	6,407	36	13.4	12.5	2	8	20	418	1	3	91.7	$6,607,932
4. Kevin Harvick	6,397	36	13.5	12.3	5	15	20	895	1	1	97.5	$8,231,406
5. Dale Earnhardt Jr.	6,328	36	19.2	13.5	1	10	17	444	3	0	95.3	$7,111,739
6. Jeff Gordon	6,256	36	10.0	14.9	2	14	18	690	7	2	98.5	$7,471,447
7. Jeff Burton	6,228	36	13.9	14.2	1	7	20	649	2	4	95.5	$6,439,995
8. Kasey Kahne	6,183	36	12.8	15.5	6	12	19	744	6	6	94.3	$7,695,378
9. Mark Martin	6,168	36	16.1	14.3	0	7	15	292	2	0	88.2	$5,568,748
10. Kyle Busch	6,027	36	14.9	15.5	1	10	18	571	2	1	91.6	$6,077,337
11. Tony Stewart	4,727	36	16.7	13.8	5	15	19	1,360	4	0	97.0	$8,801,569
12. Carl Edwards	4,428	36	19.3	15.3	0	10	20	189	3	0	87.6	$5,353,629
13. Greg Biffle	4,075	36	14.4	18.8	2	8	15	993	6	2	94.9	$5,347,623
14. Casey Mears	3,914	36	22.9	18.6	0	2	8	3	2	0	70.8	$6,128,449
15. Brian Vickers	3,906	36	16.8	19.3	1	5	9	126	2	1	76.6	$4,602,990
16. Kurt Busch	3,900	36	10.4	19.4	1	7	12	272	3	6	86.3	$5,681,655
17. Clint Bowyer*	3,833	36	20.3	19.7	0	4	11	112	4	0	74.9	$4,550,134
18. Ryan Newman	3,748	36	11.6	20.6	0	2	7	125	3	2	76.3	$5,960,473
19. Martin Truex Jr.*	3,673	36	21.2	20.8	0	2	5	34	5	0	71.3	$4,759,248
20. Scott Riggs	3,619	35	19.5	20.3	0	1	8	132	2	2	71.2	$3,773,674
21. Bobby Labonte	3,567	36	21.6	22.0	0	3	8	63	8	0	67.9	$4,949,058
22. Elliott Sadler	3,469	36	17.5	23.1	0	1	7	99	7	1	69.2	$4,852,654
23. Dale Jarrett	3,438	36	28.2	22.7	0	1	4	8	5	0	57.5	$4,739,491
24. Reed Sorenson*	3,434	36	25.6	23.1	0	1	5	91	4	0	68.4	$3,702,767
25. Jamie McMurray	3,405	36	25.3	23.6	0	3	7	154	7	0	67.4	$5,241,224
26. Dave Blaney	3,259	36	28.3	24.4	0	1	2	9	2	0	57.4	$3,479,643
27. Joe Nemechek	3,255	36	18.0	24.4	0	0	2	10	3	0	60.5	$4,109,394
28. Jeff Green	3,253	36	25.4	24.4	0	0	2	18	4	0	59.2	$3,767,754
29. J.J. Yeley*	3,220	36	21.3	25.0	0	0	3	23	7	0	66.5	$4,309,972
30. Robby Gordon	3,113	36	27.5	25.3	0	1	3	8	9	0	64.9	$3,143,787
31. Ken Schrader	3,049	36	25.6	26.3	0	0	2	11	8	0	57.2	$4,111,669
32. Kyle Petty	2,928	36	31.0	27.4	0	0	2	4	5	0	48.7	$3,655,539
33. David Stremme*	2,865	34	26.4	26.4	0	0	0	7	4	0	54.2	$3,480,188
34. Sterling Marlin	2,854	36	23.9	28.3	0	0	1	17	8	0	51.9	$3,248,034
35. Tony Raines	2,609	29	31.8	24.4	0	0	1	28	1	0	53.0	$2,358,230
36. Travis Kvapil	2,451	31	33.6	28.2	0	0	0	4	5	0	44.8	$2,867,087
37. Michael Waltrip	2,350	33	31.9	30.8	0	0	0	5	7	0	42.9	$2,971,978
38. Scott Wimmer	1,812	24	35.0	29.4	0	0	0	5	3	0	47.0	$1,904,783
39. Jeremy Mayfield	1,684	22	24.3	28.6	0	0	0	15	3	0	52.6	$2,641,732
40. Kevin Lepage	1,346	22	32.9	34.3	0	0	0	5	7	0	37.1	$1,823,351
41. Terry Labonte	1,278	17	35.7	29.3	0	1	1	23	3	0	44.5	$1,547,359
42. David Gilliland	1,178	15	22.1	28.3	0	0	0	1	1	1	53.4	$1,564,901
43. Kenny Wallace	984	17	34.8	34.2	0	0	0	1	3	0	33.0	$1,386,818
44. Bill Elliott	765	10	34.1	29.0	0	0	0	1	1	0	40.3	$1,056,041
45. Paul Menard	669	7	30.3	23.1	0	0	1	2	2	0	62.1	$547,018
46. Chad Chaffin	553	10	36.6	35.9	0	0	0	0	1	0	29.5	$819,218
47. Boris Said	415	4	16.0	21.5	0	1	2	10	1	1	66.4	$429,000
48. Mike Bliss	387	6	27.0	32.8	0	0	0	0	4	0	45.8	$471,458
49. Brent Sherman*	372	6	37.7	33.7	0	0	0	0	1	0	31.1	$637,056
50. Mike Wallace	355	4	28.3	24.8	0	0	0	0	0	0	63.2	$519,218
51. Stanton Barrett	343	7	36.7	38.0	0	0	0	0	5	0	28.8	$531,423
52. Derrike Cope	292	9	36.3	41.1	0	0	0	0	7	0	26.9	$652,168
53. Ward Burton	252	3	32.0	26.3	0	0	0	0	0	0	45.0	$232,450
54. Hermie Sadler	251	7	32.7	41.0	0	0	0	2	5	0	26.6	$716,355
55. Scott Pruett	223	2	20.0	18.0	0	0	1	0	0	0	77.4	$203,530
56. Todd Kluever	187	4	33.0	38.8	0	0	0	0	2	0	32.6	$283,127
57. Mike Skinner	184	4	33.0	39.0	0	0	0	0	2	0	30.0	$348,216
58. Kirk Shelmerdine	177	3	30.3	34.7	0	0	0	0	2	0	32.6	$445,624
59. Todd Bodine	143	2	27.0	30.5	0	0	0	0	1	0	37.4	$145,875

Rk.	Driver	Points	Starts	Avg. start	Avg. finish	Wins	T5s	T10s	Laps led	DNFs	Poles	Rating	Money Won
60.	Mike Garvey	138	4	35.0	39.5	0	0	0	0	3	0	31.5	$312,210
61.	Jimmy Spencer	122	2	38.5	34.0	0	0	0	0	0	0	30.2	$122,275
62.	Ron Fellows	119	2	17.5	34.5	0	0	0	0	0	0	65.7	$135,772
63.	David Ragan	88	2	41.5	40.5	0	0	0	1	1	0	30.8	$129,610
64.	Brandon Ash	88	2	39.0	33.5	0	0	0	0	1	0	40.9	$127,995
65.	Chad Blount	74	2	39.0	42.0	0	0	0	0	2	0	28.0	$147,678
66.	Morgan Shepherd	71	2	42.0	42.5	0	0	0	0	2	0	27.5	$149,407
67.	Eric McClure	70	1	27.0	31.0	0	0	0	0	0	0	30.1	$69,875
68.	Bill Lester	67	2	26.5	35.0	0	0	0	0	0	0	30.6	$135,360
69.	Juan Pablo Montoya	61	1	29.0	34.0	0	0	0	0	1	0	53.7	$61,425
70.	P.J. Jones	55	1	15.0	36.0	0	0	0	0	1	0	64.9	$67,610
71.	Carl Long	40	1	30.0	41.0	0	0	0	0	1	0	32.2	$101,433
72.	Ted Christopher	40	1	43.0	41.0	0	0	0	0	1	0	25.9	$67,060
73.	Brian Simo	40	1	43.0	41.0	0	0	0	0	1	0	41.6	$57,460
74.	Tom Hubert	34	1	37.0	43.0	0	0	0	0	1	0	25.3	$67,116
75.	Brandon Whitt	34	1	30.0	43.0	0	0	0	0	1	0	28.9	$61,286
76.	Marc Goossens	34	1	27.0	43.0	0	0	0	0	1	0	40.0	$57,537
77.	Johnny Sauter	0	1	36.0	33.0	0	0	0	0	0	0	38.6	$85,750
78.	Stephen Leicht	0	1	14.0	24.0	0	0	0	0	0	0	79.0	$62,275

*Raybestos Rookie of the Year contender

Driver rating: An average of these categories—Win, finish, top 15 finish, average running position on lead lap, average speed under green, fastest lap, led most laps, lead-lap finish. Maximum points: 150 per race.

»» 2006 CHASE BOXSCORE «

NASCAR NEXTEL Cup Series

Rk.	Driver	W	T5s	T10s	Avg. start	Avg. mid race	Avg. finish	Avg. pos	% fastest laps	% Laps t15s	% laps led	Rating	Pts.	Behind leader
1.	Jimmie Johnson	1	5	6	10.2	12.4	10.8	9.461	12.2	85.8	15	108.8	6,475	-
2.	Matt Kenseth	0	2	5	15.2	12.9	10.7	13.413	3.8	58.1	7.4	93.8	6,419	-56
3.	Denny Hamlin	0	4	7	15.5	15.9	10.6	15.984	2.4	57	1	85.6	6,407	-68
4.	Kevin Harvick	2	4	6	10.3	13.6	12.1	12.322	5.7	64.5	14.1	99.6	6,397	-78
5.	Dale Earnhardt Jr.	0	2	5	12.8	7.1	13	8.567	7.6	84.6	7.3	104.6	6,328	-147
6.	Jeff Gordon	0	4	6	10.6	9	15.3	10.503	6.8	81.2	8.5	99.2	6,256	-219
7.	Jeff Burton	1	3	5	17.6	15.4	16	14.087	3.7	66.3	2	91.7	6,228	-247
8.	Kasey Kahne	1	3	5	13.8	13	17.9	12.779	8.8	69.3	7.5	95.8	6,183	-292
9.	Mark Martin	0	1	3	19.8	15.1	17.2	15.64	1.4	58.9	0.9	80.8	6,168	-307
10.	Kyle Busch	0	1	3	12.8	17.6	22.7	18.553	4.3	56.5	3.2	82.5	6,027	-448

»» PASSES & LAPS BREAKDOWN «

NASCAR NEXTEL Cup Series, Top 15 drivers

Car No.	Driver	Green passes	Green times passed	Pass Diff.	Quality passes	% quality passes	Laps run	# fastest laps	% laps in T15
48	Jimmie Johnson	2,566	2,327	239	1,952	76.1	10,577	581	74.2
17	Matt Kenseth	2,726	2,287	439	1,820	66.8	10,600	485	74.6
11	Denny Hamlin	2,654	2,454	200	1,366	51.5	10,370	368	64.3
29	Kevin Harvick	2,500	2,363	137	1,429	57.2	10,560	457	69.9
8	Dale Earnhardt Jr.	2,881	2,509	372	1,890	65.6	10,358	538	73.2
24	Jeff Gordon	2,413	2,346	67	1,671	69.2	10,401	497	77.4
31	Jeff Burton	2,664	2,597	67	1,880	70.6	10,011	374	73.4
9	Kasey Kahne	2,628	2,645	-17	1,597	60.8	10,044	706	68.8
6	Mark Martin	2,341	2,257	84	1,363	58.2	10,455	312	67.3
5	Kyle Busch	2,579	2,209	370	1,672	64.8	10,013	489	68.2
20	Tony Stewart	2,748	2,129	619	1,436	52.3	10,057	633	61.9
99	Carl Edwards	3,045	2,692	353	1,870	61.4	10,347	343	59.6
16	Greg Biffle	2,465	2,456	9	1,454	59	9,851	645	63.5
42	Casey Mears	3,017	2,813	204	1,126	37.3	10,389	79	33.4
25	Brian Vickers	2,746	2,683	63	1,510	55.0	10,040	147	38.6

2006 Season review

III NASCAR® review

race-by-race

1 DAYTONA 500
Daytona International Speedway

Jimmie Johnson faced the same question all week: Could he race without his crew chief, Chad Knaus, who was ejected from Daytona after the No. 48 car failed a post-qualifying inspection? A trip to victory lane—Johnson's first Daytona 500 win and the biggest victory of his career—answered it. Willing himself to be patient when others around him went for broke and lost, Johnson held off strong challenges from Ryan Newman and Casey Mears in the closing laps.

2 AUTO CLUB 500
California Speedway

If somebody had to win this race at California, it might as well have been Matt Kenseth. Greg Biffle dominated the first three quarters of the race, leading 168 of the first 215 laps. But Biffle's engine failed. Next in line was Tony Stewart, but his engine failed, too. Finally, Kenseth held on to win, a bit of poetic justice considering Stewart had taken Kenseth out of contention in the Daytona 500 a week earlier.

3 UAW-DAIMLER CHRYSLER 400
Las Vegas Motor Speedway

Jimmie Johnson won without his crew chief for the second time in three races, this time at Las Vegas. Darian Grubb, the interim crew chief during Chad Knaus' suspension, continued to raise his profile while atop the No. 48's pit box. Johnson's last-lap pass of Matt Kenseth gave him a commanding lead in the points race and an unbelievable start to the season. Only a second-place finish at California kept Johnson from the season-opening hat trick.

4 GOLDEN CORRAL 500
Atlanta Motor Speedway

After a sophomore slump, Kasey Kahne had a junior jump. Kahne won the pole at Atlanta and then dominated at the end.

Second-place finisher Mark Martin caught Kahne and thought he had a chance at the win. But Kahne clearly was pacing himself, as he pulled away from Martin before Martin could attempt a pass.

5 FOOD CITY 500
Bristol Motor Speedway

Kurt Busch's first win in the No. 2 Dodge came exactly where you would have expected it: Bristol.

Busch replaced Rusty Wallace in the No. 2 after Wallace's retirement, and Busch's win came just as many of Wallace's did, with a late-race nudge of the leader, Matt Kenseth. It wasn't the only time Kenseth was pushed around that day. He walked up to Jeff Gordon to try to apologize for wrecking him on the final lap. But Gordon would have none of it and gave Kenseth a firm two-handed shove.

6 DIRECTV 500
Martinsville Speedway

Tony Stewart won the spring race at Martinsville and ended Hendrick Motorsports' three-race winning streak at the track. (Jimmie Johnson won the 2004 fall race, and Jeff Gordon swept in 2005.)

But Rick Hendrick's men didn't make it easy for Stewart. With 30 laps left—and with the crowd at its feet—Stewart fought Johnson for the lead. On his fourth try, Stewart finally got by Johnson. Gordon passed Johnson for second, but he couldn't catch Stewart before the checkered flag.

7 SAMSUNG/RADIOSHACK 500
Texas Motor Speedway

Strange but true: Through this race at Texas, Kasey Kahne had three wins in the NASCAR NEXTEL Cup Series, all three from the pole, and each on a different day. His first was on a Saturday in Richmond in 2005, his second on a Monday in Atlanta earlier in 2006. At Texas, he finally picked up a Sunday win.

Greg Biffle's horrible luck continued. He had the car to beat but wrecked after contact with Kurt Busch. The accident infuriated Biffle's girlfriend, who stormed Busch's pit box to confront his fiance. Seriously.

8 SUBWAY FRESH 500
Phoenix International Raceway

You could almost see Kevin Harvick in your mind's eye at Phoenix: Harvick, peering every few laps at his gas gauge, wondering when the thing would hit empty—and when his chances of winning would end. Greg Biffle and Mark Martin ran out of gas. Others veered onto pit lane for a quick fill up. But Harvick managed to complete the final 88 laps at Phoenix without pitting—and he was rewarded with a trip to victory lane.

9 AARON'S 499
Talladega Superspeedway

Jimmie Johnson figured out restrictor-plate racing. After causing wrecks at both Talladega races in 2005—and getting called an idiot by Dale Earnhardt Jr.—Johnson won the first two plate races in 2006.

The key, Johnson, learned, is patience. In the Aaron's 499, he was

12 COCA-COLA 600

content to ride around mid-pack until the end of the race, when he stormed to the front. He passed teammate Brian Vickers as the next-to-last lap became the final lap and drove on to victory.

10 CROWN ROYAL 400
Richmond International Raceway

Kevin Harvick dominated the spring race at Richmond, leading 272 of 400 laps, but bad pit strategy late in the race let Dale Earnhardt Jr. take the lead and drive to the win.

Earnhardt beat rookie Denny Hamlin to the line, an interesting juxtaposition considering Hamlin, before his career took off, once was Earnhardt's guest at Richmond.

11 DODGE CHARGER 500
Darlington Raceway

Greg Biffle finally got through a race without something bizarre happening, and the result was a trip to victory lane. Going into the race at Darlington, Biffle was in the top five in almost every significant racing statistic—except points. He had led a ton of laps, including the most in three races, but blown engines, wrecks and running out of gas doomed

Tony Stewart, who broke his shoulder blade in a wreck at Lowe's Motor Speedway the week before, started the race and stayed in the car until the first caution, when he gingerly got out and Ricky Rudd hopped in. Rudd finished 25th, two laps down—partly due to a speeding penalty.

14 POCONO 500
Pocono Raceway

Denny Hamlin's No. 11 Chevrolet at Pocono was the talk of the first half of the season. The car was so fast, one driver said more than a month later, Hamlin would have had to try not to win. That might be true, but give Hamlin credit, too, for overcoming adversity and staying patient in that fast car. A flat tire early in the race dropped him to the back of the field, and he made multiple pit stops to fix damage before roaring to his first career NASCAR NEXTEL Cup Series win.

15 3M PERFORMANCE 400
Michigan International Speedway

Kasey Kahne made a habit of winning from the pole. He won the first Michigan race from the pole—the third time he has done that this season. He got a little help this time from Mother Nature; the race was rained out 71 laps shy of the advertised 200. No matter, he was the class of the field all day.

He would have won whatever the distance was—just as long as it wasn't too short. He dropped to 38th and a lap down after debris on his grille caused overheating. But he fixed it and bided his time getting back to the front. He narrowly beat Carl Edwards coming out of the pits and held on for the win.

16 DODGE/SAVE MART 350
Infineon Raceway

It wasn't a bad weekend for Jeff Gordon. He announced his engagement to model Ingrid Vandebosch and then won the first road course race of the season at Infineon Raceway.

It was Gordon's first win of the season, and it propelled him into the top 10 in points. He passed an old and sometimes current teammate, Terry Labonte, for the win. Driving for Hall of Fame Racing in the No. 96 Chevrolet, Labonte's team used pit strategy to get to the front and wound up with a top five finish.

17 PEPSI 400
Daytona International Speedway

When the field for the Chase for the NASCAR NEXTEL Cup finally was set after the Richmond race, one driver likely looked back at the last 100 miles of the Pepsi 400 at Daytona as crucial. Greg Biffle—a driver on the Chase bubble late in the season—had a top 10 finish, if not top five, in his hip pocket before a late wreck took him out. Tony Stewart won the race for the second straight year, passing surprise leader Boris Said on Lap 158 of 160.

18 USG SHEETROCK 400
Chicagoland Speedway

Lost in all the controversy of how Jeff Gordon won the race at Chicagoland was that he won it with a great car. Gordon—who bumped leader Matt Kenseth with four laps to go, sending Kenseth spinning—had struggled at intermediate tracks in the recent past.

Kenseth dominated the second half of the race before the spin and finished 22nd after tangling with David Stremme and the finish line.

---

him to poor finishes. Not this night. He kept a charging Jeff Gordon at bay to win his second consecutive spring race at Darlington.

12 COCA-COLA 600
Lowe's Motor Speedway

Kasey Kahne's win in the Coca-Cola 600 was the fourth of his career—and the first that did not come from the pole. He started ninth; the polesitter, Kahne's teammate Scott Riggs, had a strong car but a bad pit stop late doomed him to a disappointing 13th-place finish. Jimmie Johnson, who had won the past four points races at Lowe's Motor Speedway, finished second.

13 NEIGHBORHOOD EXCELLENCE 400
Dover International Speedway

Matt Kenseth passed Jamie McMurray with three laps to go to pick up his first win at Dover International Speedway—the track where Kenseth made his NASCAR NEXTEL Cup Series debut. McMurray, winless since Octrober 2002, settled for second place.

19 NEW ENGLAND 300
New Hampshire International Speedway

Is it over yet? Kyle Busch won at New Hampshire in an event that never seemed to end. Because of late incidents—including an accident under caution—the race ran eight laps longer than advertised. Busch had enough gas—barely—to hold on for the win. Others were not so fortunate. Denny Hamlin ran out on the final lap, dropping to sixth. Elliott Sadler tried to coax more laps out of his No. 38 Ford than were reasonably possible; he ran out, too, and finished 25th.

20 PENNSYLVANIA 500
Pocono Raceway

Denny Hamlin was two for two in Pocono races, winning both from the pole. He dominated the second one, leading 151 of 200 laps in a race that for him was relatively uneventful.

But the race was crazy for just about everybody else. Tony Stewart sideswiped Clint Bowyer after Bowyer pinched Stewart into the wall. The contact sent Bowyer into Carl Edwards, who retaliated later by spinning Stewart on pit road. After the race, Edwards—who comes from the Jeff Gordon and Jimmie Johnson school of Don't Say Anything Controversial—said if it weren't for all the people watching, Stewart would be "bleeding."

21 ALLSTATE 400 AT THE BRICKYARD
Indianapolis Motor Speedway

Jimmie Johnson overcame a flat tire and a fire in his pit stall to win at the Brickyard. The win gave Johnson the checkered flag in NASCAR's two most prestigious races in the same year; he also won the Daytona 500. Jeff Burton dominated early but faded. Denny Hamlin claimed to have had the best-handling car, but he had engine and track position problems.

A gutsy decision not to pit late in the race gave Dale Earnhardt Jr. a sixth-place finish—and a bump up in points after two consecutive last-place finishes.

22 AMD AT THE GLEN
Watkins Glen International

Kevin Harvick picked up his first road race win in the NASCAR NEXTEL Cup Series after a fierce late-race duel with Tony Stewart. Stewart committed an uncharacteristic bobble with three laps to go, and Harvick took full advantage of it. Stewart held on for second. The story of the day was the bad luck of Kurt Busch. He was headed into the pits when the caution came out. The timing was awful. He was only a few feet from the commitment line and didn't have time to pull back onto the track. A resulting penalty forced him to the back of the pack, and he finished 19th.

23 GFS MARKETPLACE 400
Michigan International Speedway

All eyes were on Dale Earnhardt Jr. and Carl Edwards after they tangled in the NASCAR Busch Series race the day before, but they played nice. Polesitter Jeff Burton never led a lap, suffered a blown engine and finished 42nd, his first finish outside the top 15 in 17 races. Matt Kenseth won for the third time in 2006. Jeff Gordon finished second although he never got close enough to fight for the lead. That meant there was no repeat of the race at Chicagoland earlier in the season, when Gordon knocked Kenseth out of the way for the win.

33 BASS PRO SHOPS 500

24 SHARPIE 500
Bristol Motor Speedway

For a race expected to be intense and hard fought, this was a bit of a snoozer. There were no angry outbursts, no biting comments and nothing to distinguish what usually is the most entertaining race of the year. Not that winner Matt Kenseth complained. He won his fourth race of the season and second in a row. Jeff Burton dominated the first half of the race, but his car tightened up at the end. He faded to ninth.

25 SONY HD 500
California Speedway

Reed Sorenson ran out of gas with two laps left, allowing Kasey Kahne to drive to victory lane in a race he dominated. Kahne won his fifth race of the season, the most of anyone; more important, he moved closer to 10th in points. He sat 30 points behind Jeff Burton with one race left before the Chase for the NASCAR NEXTEL Cup. Kahne was the only driver outside the top 10 who mathematically had a chance to qualify for the Chase.

26 CHEVY ROCK & ROLL 400
Richmond International Raceway

Kevin Harvick sandbagged late in the cutoff race at Richmond, following leader Kyle Busch lap after lap. But with two laps left, Harvick passed Busch, seemingly with ease, and drove off to victory, his third of the year. Behind him, Chase for the NASCAR NEXTEL Cup drama unfolded in shocking fashion. Defending champion Tony Stewart, driving a backup car because he wrecked his primary car in practice, finished a disappointing 18th and failed to qualify for the Chase. Kasey Kahne, who started the race 11th, finished third in the race and grabbed Stewart's Chase spot.

27 SYLVANIA 300
New Hampshire International Speedway

For the first time in his NASCAR NEXTEL Cup Series career, Kevin Harvick won back-to-back races. He dominated the first race in the Chase for the NASCAR NEXTEL Cup, at New Hampshire, leading 196 of 300 laps

29 BANQUET 400
Kansas Speedway

With about half a lap to go at Kansas, Tony Stewart heard the noise he dreaded: He was out of gas. But the No. 20 had a 17-second lead, and if Stewart could just coast to the finish line, he'd win. When Stewart finally made it to the line—just ahead of second-place finisher Casey Mears, who also had run out of gas—he didn't know if any of the cars that had sped past him were for position. He radioed his crew to ask where he had finished. First, they told him.

Jeff Burton finished fifth and remained first in points, extending his lead over the second-place Denny Hamlin to 69 points.

30 UAW-FORD 500
Talladega Superspeedway

Brian Vickers' first win in the NASCAR NEXTEL Cup Series was the most controversial of the year. Vickers was running third, behind Hendrick Motorsports teammate Jimmie Johnson, who was running second to Dale Earnhardt Jr. Vickers hooked Johnson, who turned into Earnhardt. While Johnson and Earnhardt spun into the grass, Vickers sped to the checkered flag.

Jeff Burton's 27th-place finish because of a cut tire squeezed the points race. Burton left Talladega just six points ahead of Matt Kenseth, was was second in points.

31 BANK OF AMERICA 500
Lowe's Motor Speedway

The race was a mess of accidents, blown engines and pit stop after pit stop. Only 11 drivers finished on the lead lap, and only five of those drivers—Kasey Kahne (who won the race and completed the Lowe's sweep for the 2006 season), Jimmie Johnson, Jeff Burton, Dale Earnhardt Jr. and Kyle Busch—were competing in the Chase for the NASCAR NEXTEL Cup.

Denny Hamlin wrecked on the first lap, spent nearly 60 laps behind the wall and still finished 28th. Jeff Gordon finished 24th after his engine and slim championship hopes went up in smoke. Burton increased his lead in the points race by finishing third despite stalling on pit road and falling a lap down late in the race.

32 SUBWAY 500
Martinsville Speedway

Jimmie Johnson won a wild race at Martinsville that shuffled the points standings. Nine of the 10 Chase for the NASCAR NEXTEL Cup drivers changed positions, most notably Jeff Burton, whose blown engine and 42nd-place finish dropped him from first to fifth in points. Only Kasey Kahne—eighth in points—remained in the same position he was in before the race.

Matt Kenseth finished a solid 11th at Martinsville and headed to Atlanta atop the points list. The 2006 Chase was shaping up to be the tightest yet, with just 99 points separating first and eighth.

33 BASS PRO SHOPS 500
Atlanta Motor Speedway

Races at Atlanta always are big for Tony Stewart. His primary sponsor, The Home Depot, is headquartered nearby. But this race had an added incentive for Stewart: He loves to collect trophies, and the one for this race was unique—an 8-foot, 280-pound bronze grizzly bear. Stewart added it to

and assuming the points lead at the NASCAR NEXTEL Cup Series level, also a career first. Chasers Kyle Busch and Jimmie Johnson had horrible days, finishing 38th and 39th, respectively, and dropping to 10th and ninth in the points race. Tony Stewart, driving gingerly around Chase drivers, finished second.

28 DOVER 400
Dover International Speedway

Jeff Burton and Matt Kenseth waged a spirited, intense battle for the lead in the waning laps at Dover. Burton had the faster car, but Kenseth made him work for the pass. Once Burton did pass, he started to drive away, and Kenseth ran out of gas, anyway.

Burton led the final six laps—the only six he led all day—to pick up his first win since 2001. It vaulted him to the top of the points standings. Kasey Kahne (accident) and Kyle Busch (engine) finished 38th and 40th, respectively, digging themselves into an early hole in their first-ever Chase for the NASCAR NEXTEL Cup appearances.

his trophy room after holding off Jimmie Johnson for the win.

Johnson continued his resurrection in the Chase for the NASCAR NEXTEL Cup, finishing second in the race and creeping closer to points leader Matt Kenseth. Kenseth finished fourth, missing out on third by inches to Dale Earnhardt Jr., who sat fourth in points after the race. Rookie Denny Hamlin finished eighth (his second straight top 10 finish) and rose to third in points.

34 DICKIES 500
Texas Motor Speedway

Nobody could keep up with Tony Stewart at Texas, as he dominated a race at a 1.5-mile track for the second week in a row, leading 278 of 339 laps. Only Kasey Kahne and Jimmie Johnson appeared to be in Stewart's league, but they could only get to Stewart's bumper. And as soon as either got close, Stewart knuckled down and drove away.

Johnson finished second and took the points lead from Matt Kenseth, who struggled to a 12th-place finish. It was the latest in a season that Johnson had held the points lead. Dale Earnhardt Jr.'s sixth-place finish bumped him up to third in points.

35 CHECKER AUTO PARTS 500
Phoenix International Raceway

Kevin Harvick dominated the Checker Auto Parts 500, completing a sweep of Phoenix in 2006 and staving off elimination in the Chase for the NASCAR NEXTEL Cup.

Tied for third with Denny Hamlin after Phoenix, Harvick trailed points leader Jimmie Johnson, who finished second, by 90. Johnson drove a masterful race, weaving his way from 29th to fourth in the first 35 laps. He needed to finish 12th of better in the final race to win the championship. Matt Kenseth, second in points, finished 13th and all but conceded the title to Johnson. Kenseth's cars were horrible down the stretch.

36 FORD 400
Homestead-Miami Speedway

If he's racing at Homestead-Miami Speedway, Greg Biffle will find victory lane. Biffle won the season-ending race for the third straight season, taking the lead late and holding on until the end of a disjointed event.

Jimmie Johnson won the championship despite a harrowing day. He ran through debris on Lap 15, punching a hole in the front of his car. The team needed a long pit stop to fix it, and he restarted 39th.

By Lap 70, he reached 12th—the position he needed to be in to guarantee the championship. He cracked the top 10 on Lap 79 but not before pulling close enough behind Kevin Harvick to make you wonder if he knew what position he was in.

During a pit stop on Lap 118, a crew member dropped a lugnut that was supposed to be tightened onto the left front tire. Johnson started to pull away, but he stopped in time for the team to fix the problem. He dropped to 16th. From there, he largely mimicked whatever Matt Kenseth did. He followed Kenseth onto pit road and made the same two-tire decisions on pit stops. Johnson finished ninth, three spots behind Kenseth, and won the championship by 56 points.

36 FORD 400

Date	Race	Location	Winner	Owner	Pole	Time of race	Avg. speed	Victory margin	Race ldrs.	Lead chngs.	Cau. flags	Cau. laps	Cars ld.lap	DNFs
Feb. 19	Daytona 500	Daytona Beach, Fla.	Jimmie Johnson	Rick Hendrick	Jeff Burton	3:33:26	142.667	Under caution	18	32	11	39	31	5
Feb. 26	Auto Club 500	Fontana, Calif.	Matt Kenseth	Jack Roush	Kurt Busch	3:23:43	147.852	0.338 sec.	9	18	7	26	17	4
March 12	UAW-DaimlerChrysler 400	Las Vegas	Jimmie Johnson	Rick Hendrick	Greg Biffle	3:02:13	133.358	0.045 sec.	11	22	7	30	30	5
March 20	Golden Corral 500	Hampton, Ga.	Kasey Kahne	Ray Evernham	Kasey Kahne	3:28:24	144.098	1.928 sec.	12	27	8	43	18	2
March 26	Food City 500	Bristol, Tenn.	Kurt Busch	Roger Penske	None—conditions	3:21:19	79.427	0.179 sec.	8	19	18	104	21	5
April 2	DIRECTV 500	Martinsville, Va.	Tony Stewart	Joe Gibbs	Jimmie Johnson	3:36:56	72.741	1.083 sec.	6	12	16	87	16	10
April 9	Samsung/RadioShack 500	Fort Worth, Texas	Kasey Kahne	Ray Evernham	Kasey Kahne	3:37:55	137.943	5.229 sec.	12	22	9	43	18	8
April 22	Subway Fresh 500	Phoenix	Kevin Harvick	Richard Childress	Kyle Busch	2:54:51	107.063	2.774 sec.	11	20	7	29	10	4
May 1	Aaron's 499	Talladega, Ala.	Jimmie Johnson	Rick Hendrick	Elliott Sadler	3:30:00	142.880	0.120 sec.	22	56	8	34	21	14
May 6	Crown Royal 400	Richmond, Va.	Dale Earnhardt Jr.	Teresa Earnhardt	Greg Biffle	3:05:27	97.061	0.572 sec.	6	12	11	61	14	6
May 13	Dodge Charger 500	Darlington, S.C.	Greg Biffle	Jack Roush	Kasey Kahne	3:42:36	135.127	0.209 sec.	10	25	6	24	14	4
May 28	Coca-Cola 600	Concord, N.C.	Kasey Kahne	Ray Evernham	Scott Riggs	4:39:25	128.840	2.114 sec.	16	37	15	66	17	6
June 4	Neighborhood Excellence 400	Dover, Del.	Matt Kenseth	Jack Roush	Ryan Newman	3:38:27	109.865	0.787 sec.	12	23	9	51	21	5
June 11	Pocono 500	Long Pond, Pa.	Denny Hamlin*	Joe Gibbs	Denny Hamlin	3:47:52	131.656	1.328 sec.	13	25	7	28	23	7
June 18	3M Performance 400	Brooklyn, Mich.	Kasey Kahne	Ray Evernham	Kasey Kahne	2:10:19	118.788	Under caution	10	17	9	37	37	3
June 25	Dodge/Save Mart 350	Sonoma, Calif.	Jeff Gordon	Rick Hendrick	Kurt Busch	2:57:36	73.953	1.250 sec.	8	9	7	12	31	9
July 1	Pepsi 400	Daytona Beach, Fla.	Tony Stewart	Joe Gibbs	Boris Said	2:36:43	153.143	Under caution	15	29	6	19	34	3
July 9	USG Sheetrock 400	Joliet, Ill.	Jeff Gordon	Rick Hendrick	Jeff Burton	3:03:59	132.077	0.461 sec.	10	18	8	34	25	1
July 16	New England 300	Loudon, N.H.	Kyle Busch	Rick Hendrick	Ryan Newman	3:12:51	131.384	0.406 sec.	11	21	11	49	24	6
July 23	Pennsylvania 500	Long Pond, Pa.	Denny Hamlin	Joe Gibbs	Denny Hamlin	3:46:12	132.626	1.510 sec.	9	13	7	29	28	2
Aug. 6	Allstate 400 at the Brickyard	Indianapolis	Jimmie Johnson	Rick Hendrick	Jeff Burton	2:54:57	137.182	Under caution	9	18	8	24	35	5
Aug. 13	AMD at The Glen	Watkins Glen, N.Y.	Kevin Harvick	Richard Childress	Kurt Busch	2:52:27	76.718	0.892 sec.	11	14	10	22	33	5
Aug. 20	GFS Marketplace 400	Brooklyn, Mich.	Matt Kenseth	Jack Roush	Jeff Burton	2:57:39	135.097	0.622 sec.	11	26	10	36	28	7
Aug. 26	Sharpie 500	Bristol, Tenn.	Matt Kenseth	Jack Roush	Kurt Busch	2:57:37	90.025	0.591 sec.	7	18	10	62	14	4
Sept. 3	Sony HD 500	Fontana, Calif.	Kasey Kahne	Ray Evernham	Kurt Busch	3:27:40	144.462	3.427 sec.	10	26	6	29	20	1
Sept. 9	Chevy Rock & Roll 400	Richmond, Va.	Kevin Harvick	Richard Childress	Denny Hamlin	2:57:37	101.342	0.153 sec.	8	16	7	48	14	4
Sept. 17	Sylvania 300	Loudon, N.H.	Kevin Harvick	Richard Childress	Kevin Harvick	3:06:21	102.195	0.777 sec.	10	17	10	47	22	5
Sept. 24	Dover 400	Dover, Del.	Jeff Burton	Richard Childress	Jeff Gordon	3:34:21	111.966	7.955 sec.	9	12	10	48	9	12
Oct. 1	Banquet 400	Kansas City, Kan.	Tony Stewart	Joe Gibbs	Kasey Kahne	3:17:21	121.753	12.422 sec.	13	20	11	45	14	5
Oct. 8	UAW-Ford 500	Talladega, Ala.	Brian Vickers*	Rick Hendrick	David Gilliland	3:10:23	157.602	Under caution	23	63	6	22	23	13
Oct. 14	Bank of America 500	Concord, N.C.	Kasey Kahne	Ray Evernham	Scott Riggs	3:47:29	132.142	1.624 sec.	13	34	10	52	11	14
Oct. 22	Subway 500	Martinsville, Va.	Jimmie Johnson	Rick Hendrick	Kurt Busch	3:44:00	70.446	0.544 sec.	5	16	18	106	26	7
Oct. 29	Bass Pro Shops 500	Hampton, Ga.	Tony Stewart	Joe Gibbs	None—conditions	3:29:23	143.421	1.129 sec.	7	24	9	39	11	8
Nov. 5	Dickies 500	Fort Worth, Texas	Tony Stewart	Joe Gibbs	Brian Vickers	3:46:11	134.891	0.272 sec.	13	23	12	51	15	8
Nov. 12	Checker Auto Parts 500	Phoenix	Kevin Harvick	Richard Childress	Jeff Gordon	3:14:44	96.131	0.250 sec.	7	12	10	58	26	7
Nov. 19	Ford 400	Homestead, Fla.	Greg Biffle	Jack Roush	Kasey Kahne	3:12:23	125.375	0.389 sec.	10	15	11	43	20	11

*First-time race winner

Daytona International Speedway

Daytona Beach, Fla. • 2.5-mile banked paved trioval • February 19, 2006 • 500 miles, 200 laps • Purse: $18,029,052

Car	Driver	Make	Start	20 laps to go	Finish	Laps run	Laps led	Rating	Winnings
48	Jimmie Johnson	Chevrolet	9	5	1	203	24	118.4	$1,505,124
42	Casey Mears	Dodge	14	7	2	203	0	90.4	$1,095,766
12	Ryan Newman	Dodge	18	3	3	203	23	114.2	$796,116
38	Elliott Sadler	Ford	3	15	4	203	5	91.8	$684,076
20	Tony Stewart	Chevrolet	15	20	5	203	20	103.1	$537,944
07	Clint Bowyer*	Chevrolet	37	16	6	203	0	87.2	$411,683
25	Brian Vickers	Chevrolet	35	1	7	203	21	99.6	$347,583
8	Dale Earnhardt Jr.	Chevrolet	7	12	8	203	32	103.5	$377,694
21	Ken Schrader	Ford	23	33	9	203	0	67.3	$328,897
88	Dale Jarrett	Ford	25	27	10	203	0	69.6	$326,983
9	Kasey Kahne	Dodge	27	8	11	203	0	82.3	$307,347
6	Mark Martin	Ford	10	21	12	203	19	91.7	$292,383
7	Robby Gordon	Chevrolet	20	26	13	203	0	60.3	$269,558
29	Kevin Harvick	Chevrolet	28	17	14	203	1	84.6	$302,244
17	Matt Kenseth	Ford	11	34	15	203	28	87.9	$302,549
1	Martin Truex Jr.*	Chevrolet	19	23	16	203	0	63.8	$297,816
96	Terry Labonte	Chevrolet	43	28	17	203	0	57.9	$268,558
55	Michael Waltrip	Chevrolet	30	19	18	203	0	71.5	$274,241
36	Bill Elliott	Chevrolet	33	29	19	203	1	58.1	$257,758
27	Kirk Shelmerdine	Chevrolet	42	32	20	203	0	40.7	$272,008
49	Brent Sherman*	Dodge	29	31	21	203	0	41.5	$274,766
22	Dave Blaney	Dodge	34	11	22	203	0	84.8	$271,241
5	Kyle Busch	Chevrolet	4	4	23	203	5	89.3	$281,833
09	Mike Wallace	Dodge	24	6	24	203	0	71.2	$266,533
61	Kevin Lepage	Ford	31	30	25	203	1	47.3	$254,683
24	Jeff Gordon	Chevrolet	2	10	26	203	1	82.1	$334,879
32	Travis Kvapil	Chevrolet	40	36	27	203	1	51.1	$265,455
40	David Stremme*	Dodge	32	35	28	203	0	51.7	$263,358
41	Reed Sorenson*	Dodge	22	18	29	203	0	71.8	$262,908
11	Denny Hamlin*	Chevrolet	17	13	30	203	0	68.7	$254,833
16	Greg Biffle	Ford	16	24	31	203	1	69.1	$258,758
31	Jeff Burton	Chevrolet	1	22	32	202	18	75.0	$302,603
01	Joe Nemechek	Chevrolet	38	37	33	200	0	29.2	$279,453
14	Sterling Marlin	Chevrolet	39	2	34	200	0	61.3	$248,713
43	Bobby Labonte	Dodge	8	25	35	197	0	61.1	$294,674
19	Jeremy Mayfield	Dodge	26	38	36	197	0	48.9	$278,049
26	Jamie McMurray	Dodge	6	14	37	196	1	91.3	$287,183
2	Kurt Busch	Dodge	13	9	38	187	1	91.5	$280,366
45	Kyle Petty	Dodge	12	40	39	173	0	36.9	$256,833
00	Hermie Sadler	Ford	41	39	40	169	0	28.0	$245,633
18	J.J. Yeley*	Chevrolet	36	41	41	157	0	36.3	$279,833
66	Jeff Green	Chevrolet	21	42	42	156	0	31.9	$253,153
99	Carl Edwards	Ford	5	43	43	78	0	41.5	$269,882

POINT STANDINGS

Rk.	Driver	Pts.	Diff.
1.	Jimmie Johnson	185	—
2.	Ryan Newman	170	-15
3.	Casey Mears	170	-15
4.	Elliott Sadler	165	-20
5.	Tony Stewart	160	-25
6.	Dale Earnhardt Jr.	152	-33
7.	Brian Vickers	151	-34
8.	Clint Bowyer	150	-35
9.	Ken Schrader	138	-47
10.	Dale Jarrett	134	-51
11.	Mark Martin	132	-53
12.	Kasey Kahne	130	-55
13.	Kevin Harvick	126	-59
14.	Robby Gordon	124	-61
15.	Matt Kenseth	123	-62
16.	Martin Truex Jr.	115	-70
17.	Terry Labonte	112	-73
18.	Bill Elliott	111	-74
19.	Michael Waltrip	109	-76
20.	Kirk Shelmerdine	103	-82

*Rookie. **Time of race:** 3:33:26. **Average speed:** 142.667 mph. **Margin of victory:** Under caution. **Caution flags:** 11 for 39 laps: 18-20 (debris); 49-51 (debris); 80-84 (Cars 01, 18, 45, 66, 88, 99—accident, Turn 3); 92-95 (debris); 108-111 (Car 17—accident, Turn 3); 125-128 (Car 7—accident, Turn 2); 156-159 (debris); 177-180 (Car 32—accident, Turn 2); 188-190 (Cars 2, 14, 24, 26—accident, back-stretch); 198-201 (Cars 26, 31, 11—accident backstretch); 203-203 (Car 16—accident, Turn 4). **Lead changes:** 32 among 18 drivers: Burton 1-18; E. Sadler 19-23; J. Gordon 24; Kenseth 25-26; Earnhardt 27; Stewart 28-47; McMurray 48; Newman 49-57; Kenseth 58-80; Ku. Busch 81; Kvapil 82; Kenseth 83-84; Harvick 85; Earnhardt 86-90; Kenseth 91; Earnhardt 92-103; Martin 104-107; Johnson 108; Earnhardt 109-112; Biffle 113; Earnhardt 114-115; Ku. Busch 116-120; Johnson 121-125; Elliott 126; Martin 127-141; Earnhardt 142-143; Vickers 144-155; Johnson 156; Lepage 157; Earnhardt 158-163; Newman 164-177; Vickers 178-186; Johnson 187-203. **Note:** Green-white-checkered finish. **Fell out of race:** B. Labonte, McMurray, Ku. Busch, Edwards (accidents); H. Sadler (engine). **Pole:** Jeff Burton, 189.151 mph. **Dropped to rear:** Marlin (backup car); B. Labonte, Nemechek (engine change). **Failed to qualify:** Scott Riggs (10), Kenny Wallace (78), Scott Wimmer (4), Mike Skinner (23), Derrike Cope (74), Larry Gunselman (52), Chad Blount (37), Anthony Foyt (50), Andy Belmont (59), Randy LaJoie (64), Morgan Shepherd (89), Chad Chaffin (92), Carl Long (80), Paul Menard (15), Stanton Barrett (95). **Estimated attendance:** 200,000.

Driver rating: An average of these categories—Win, finish, top 15 finish, average running position on lead lap, average speed under green, fastest lap, led most laps, lead-lap finish. Maximum points: 150 per race.

California Speedway

Fontana, Calif. • 2-mile banked paved oval • February 26, 2006 • 500 miles, 250 laps • Purse: $5,934,504

Car	Driver	Make	Start	25 laps to go	Finish	Laps run	Laps led	Rating	Winnings
17	Matt Kenseth	Ford	31	1	1	251	40	123.0	$324,991
48	Jimmie Johnson	Chevrolet	3	2	2	251	0	112.7	$235,936
99	Carl Edwards	Ford	22	7	3	251	0	111.0	$165,550
9	Kasey Kahne	Dodge	13	4	4	251	1	102.7	$166,239
31	Jeff Burton	Chevrolet	6	8	5	251	0	106.0	$158,970
26	Jamie McMurray	Ford	25	9	6	251	0	100.4	$142,375
42	Casey Mears	Dodge	20	10	7	251	0	88.0	$140,858
18	J.J. Yeley*	Chevrolet	4	13	8	251	2	91.9	$140,075
6	Mark Martin	Ford	10	6	9	251	1	109.5	$104,800
5	Kyle Busch	Chevrolet	7	12	10	251	0	90.5	$105,225
8	Dale Earnhardt Jr.	Chevrolet	18	11	11	251	1	78.9	$132,366
11	Denny Hamlin*	Chevrolet	5	19	12	251	0	84.3	$104,575
24	Jeff Gordon	Chevrolet	9	5	13	251	3	86.2	$127,261
07	Clint Bowyer*	Chevrolet	32	14	14	251	0	70.6	$100,425
1	Martin Truex Jr.*	Chevrolet	23	16	15	251	0	72.0	$114,383
2	Kurt Busch	Dodge	1	17	16	251	7	88.9	$144,558
88	Dale Jarrett	Ford	19	15	17	251	0	73.6	$133,050
25	Brian Vickers	Chevrolet	28	20	18	250	0	82.7	$97,625
10	Scott Riggs	Dodge	14	23	19	250	0	70.0	$88,925
12	Ryan Newman	Dodge	11	24	20	250	0	68.1	$132,683
41	Reed Sorenson*	Dodge	29	18	21	250	0	77.6	$97,875
19	Jeremy Mayfield	Dodge	21	25	22	250	0	64.2	$116,916
38	Elliott Sadler	Ford	16	26	23	250	0	55.4	$115,083
66	Jeff Green	Chevrolet	26	21	24	250	0	57.4	$121,058
45	Kyle Petty	Dodge	39	22	25	250	0	58.2	$107,333
7	Robby Gordon	Chevrolet	34	27	26	249	0	63.4	$95,075
01	Joe Nemechek	Chevrolet	8	29	27	249	0	50.5	$109,820
21	Ken Schrader	Ford	41	32	28	249	0	52.0	$109,589
29	Kevin Harvick	Chevrolet	15	31	29	249	0	53.3	$116,611
22	Dave Blaney	Dodge	24	28	30	249	0	46.4	$91,583
43	Bobby Labonte	Dodge	27	30	31	249	0	49.1	$116,186
14	Sterling Marlin	Chevrolet	17	33	32	249	0	44.0	$88,592
40	David Stremme*	Dodge	40	34	33	248	0	41.4	$87,775
96	Terry Labonte	Chevrolet	43	36	34	248	0	36.9	$78,625
61	Kevin Lepage	Ford	37	37	35	248	0	34.6	$78,425
55	Michael Waltrip	Dodge	33	38	36	247	0	31.2	$78,275
49	Brent Sherman*	Dodge	42	40	37	247	0	29.4	$78,050
51	Mike Garvey	Chevrolet	35	39	38	247	0	31.0	$77,800
4	Scott Wimmer	Chevrolet	38	35	39	246	0	36.7	$77,680
95	Stanton Barrett	Chevrolet	30	42	40	242	0	26.3	$77,525
78	Kenny Wallace	Chevrolet	36	41	41	237	0	27.0	$77,400
16	Greg Biffle	Ford	2	3	42	229	168	120.1	$106,005
20	Tony Stewart	Chevrolet	12	43	43	214	28	101.9	$119,453

POINT STANDINGS

Rk.	Driver	Pts.	Diff.
1.	Jimmie Johnson	355	—
2.	Casey Mears	316	-39
3.	Matt Kenseth	308	-47
4.	Kasey Kahne	295	-60
5.	Dale Earnhardt Jr.	287	-68
6.	Mark Martin	275	-80
7.	Ryan Newman	273	-82
8.	Clint Bowyer	271	-84
9.	Brian Vickers	260	-95
10.	Elliott Sadler	259	-96
11.	Dale Jarrett	246	-109
12.	Martin Truex Jr.	233	-122
13.	Kyle Busch	233	-122
14.	Jeff Burton	227	-128
15.	Jeff Gordon	219	-136
16.	Ken Schrader	217	-138
17.	Robby Gordon	209	-146
18.	Jamie McMurray	207	-148
19.	Kevin Harvick	202	-153
20.	Denny Hamlin	200	-155

*Rookie. **Time of race:** 3:23:43. **Average speed:** 147.852 mph. **Margin of victory:** .338 seconds. **Caution flags:** 7 for 26 laps: 32-35 (debris); 89-92 (debris); 197-200 (debris); 215-218 (debris); 220-223 (Car 95—spin, Turn 4); 226-228 (Car 2—spin, Turn 4); 247-249 (oil on track). **Lap leaders:** 18 among 9 drivers: Ku. Busch 1-5; Biffle 6-35; Ku. Busch 36; Biffle 37-59; Stewart 60-79; Kenseth 80-81; Stewart 82-89; Kenseth 90-92; Ku. Busch 93; Kenseth 94-95; Biffle 96-135; Martin 136; Yeley 137-138; Biffle 139-182; Kahne 183; Earnhardt 184; Biffle 185-215; J. Gordon 216-218; Kenseth 219-251. **Note:** Green-white-checkered finish. **Fell out of race:** Stewart, Biffle, Wallace, Wimmer (engines). **Pole:** Kurt Busch, 187.086 mph. **Dropped to rear:** Sherman (backup car). **Failed to qualify:** Travis Kvapil (32), Hermie Sadler (00), Derrike Cope (74), Randy LaJoie (34), Morgan Shepherd (89). **Estimated attendance:** 85,000.

Driver rating: An average of these categories—Win, finish, top 15 finish, average running position on lead lap, average speed under green, fastest lap, led most laps, lead-lap finish. Maximum points: 150 per race.

>> UAW-DAIMLERCHRYSLER 400   race 3 of 36
Las Vegas Motor Speedway

Las Vegas • 1.5-mile banked paved oval • March 12, 2006 • 400.5 miles, 267 laps • Purse: $6,240,498

Car	Driver	Make	Start	27 laps to go	Finish	Laps run	Laps led	Rating	Winnings
48	Jimmie Johnson	Chevrolet	3	2	1	270	1	122.3	$386,936
17	Matt Kenseth	Ford	9	1	2	270	146	135.8	$293,116
5	Kyle Busch	Chevrolet	4	3	3	270	1	117.0	$204,775
9	Kasey Kahne	Dodge	5	5	4	270	0	107.7	$186,714
24	Jeff Gordon	Chevrolet	13	7	5	270	0	103.4	$165,686
6	Mark Martin	Ford	18	10	6	270	57	115.8	$122,950
31	Jeff Burton	Chevrolet	8	8	7	270	0	98.6	$145,270
16	Greg Biffle	Ford	1	11	8	270	6	106.1	$125,025
42	Casey Mears	Dodge	38	17	9	270	0	79.5	$147,383
11	Denny Hamlin*	Chevrolet	16	9	10	270	0	90.8	$109,650
29	Kevin Harvick	Chevrolet	29	6	11	270	0	95.3	$138,136
7	Robby Gordon	Chevrolet	32	12	12	270	0	78.0	$101,300
01	Joe Nemechek	Chevrolet	7	14	13	270	0	81.5	$126,295
38	Elliott Sadler	Ford	26	21	14	270	1	63.7	$125,758
07	Clint Bowyer*	Chevrolet	20	27	15	270	0	81.0	$105,800
2	Kurt Busch	Dodge	6	24	16	270	0	82.3	$126,583
18	J.J. Yeley*	Chevrolet	12	20	17	270	0	85.3	$129,025
66	Jeff Green	Chevrolet	14	16	18	270	0	75.2	$119,508
88	Dale Jarrett	Ford	15	18	19	270	0	71.1	$124,325
1	Martin Truex Jr.*	Chevrolet	27	29	20	270	0	62.0	$113,558
20	Tony Stewart	Chevrolet	2	4	21	270	54	116.4	$130,036
25	Brian Vickers	Chevrolet	10	19	22	270	1	67.4	$97,150
26	Jamie McMurray	Ford	19	23	23	270	0	77.5	$113,625
96	Terry Labonte	Chevrolet	35	30	24	270	1	50.1	$83,825
19	Jeremy Mayfield	Dodge	24	28	25	270	0	51.6	$116,016
99	Carl Edwards	Ford	21	25	26	270	0	57.0	$90,225
8	Dale Earnhardt Jr.	Chevrolet	42	13	27	270	0	65.4	$118,916
10	Scott Riggs	Dodge	22	15	28	270	0	79.3	$82,825
45	Kyle Petty	Dodge	39	26	29	270	1	51.7	$104,783
43	Bobby Labonte	Dodge	17	22	30	270	1	58.8	$119,311
22	Dave Blaney	Dodge	28	33	31	269	0	51.1	$90,833
4	Scott Wimmer	Chevrolet	37	32	32	269	0	42.2	$78,975
40	David Stremme*	Dodge	40	34	33	267	0	35.5	$97,272
49	Brent Sherman*	Dodge	41	36	34	266	0	30.4	$78,575
55	Michael Waltrip	Dodge	25	35	35	266	0	33.0	$78,375
14	Sterling Marlin	Chevrolet	31	31	36	258	0	41.7	$78,175
61	Kevin Lepage	Ford	30	38	37	251	0	37.3	$77,950
78	Kenny Wallace	Chevrolet	34	37	38	250	0	26.8	$77,750
32	Travis Kvapil	Chevrolet	33	39	39	216	0	33.7	$77,550
41	Reed Sorenson*	Dodge	36	41	40	206	0	53.0	$85,300
21	Ken Schrader	Ford	23	40	41	187	0	39.1	$104,314
34	Chad Chaffin	Chevrolet	43	42	42	157	0	24.9	$76,950
12	Ryan Newman	Dodge	11	43	43	88	0	34.2	$112,125

POINT STANDINGS

Rk.	Driver	Pts.	Diff.
1.	Jimmie Johnson	540	—
2.	Matt Kenseth	488	-52
3.	Kasey Kahne	455	-85
4.	Casey Mears	454	-86
5.	Mark Martin	430	-110
6.	Kyle Busch	403	-137
7.	Clint Bowyer	389	-151
8.	Elliott Sadler	385	-155
9.	Jeff Gordon	374	-166
10.	Jeff Burton	373	-167
11.	Dale Earnhardt Jr.	369	-171
12.	Brian Vickers	362	-178
13.	Dale Jarrett	352	-188
14.	Martin Truex Jr.	336	-204
15.	Robby Gordon	336	-204
16.	Denny Hamlin	334	-206
17.	Kevin Harvick	332	-208
18.	Ryan Newman	307	-233
19.	Tony Stewart	304	-236
20.	Jamie McMurray	301	-239

*Rookie. **Time of race:** 3:02:13. **Average speed:** 133.358 mph. **Margin of victory:** .045 seconds. **Caution flags:** 7 for 30 laps: 42-46 (Car 41—accident, Turn 2); 92-96 (Car 12—accident, Turn 2); 107-110 (Car 01—spin, frontstretch); 157-160 (debris); 188-191 (debris); 234-237 (debris); 265-268 (debris). **Lead changes:** 22 among 11 drivers: Biffle 1-2; Stewart 3-43; T. Labonte 44; Martin 45-91; Stewart 92; Vickers 93; Martin 94-96; Stewart 97-100; Kenseth 101; Stewart 102-107; Martin 108-114; Biffle 115-118; Kenseth 119-156; Stewart 157; E. Sadler 158; Kenseth 159-187; Ky. Busch 188; B. Labonte 189; Kenseth 190-233; Stewart 234; Petty 235; Kenseth 236-269; Johnson 270. **Note:** Green-white-checkered finish. **Fell out of race:** Marlin, Schrader, Chaffin (engine); Kvapil (electrical); Newman (accident). **Pole:** Greg Biffle, 172.403 mph. **Dropped to rear:** Newman, Wimmer (engine change); Mayfield, Wallace (backup car). **Failed to qualify:** Stanton Barrett (95), Hermie Sadler (00), Brandon Ash (02), Mike Skinner (37), Morgan Shepherd (89), Randy LaJoie (64). **Estimated attendance:** 156,000.

Driver rating: An average of these categories—Win, finish, top 15 finish, average running position on lead lap, average speed under green, fastest lap, led most laps, lead-lap finish. Maximum points: 150 per race.

Atlanta Motor Speedway

Hampton, Ga. • 1.54-mile banked paved oval • March 20, 2006 • 500.5 miles, 325 laps • Purse: $4,848,913

Car	Driver	Make	Start	33 laps to go	Finish	Laps run	Laps led	Rating	Winnings
9	Kasey Kahne	Dodge	1	1	1	325	85	126.6	$203,664
6	Mark Martin	Ford	11	3	2	325	0	107.3	$127,800
8	Dale Earnhardt Jr.	Chevrolet	26	7	3	325	0	96.7	$138,841
24	Jeff Gordon	Chevrolet	12	9	4	325	1	100.5	$137,236
20	Tony Stewart	Chevrolet	21	8	5	325	50	106.9	$154,961
48	Jimmie Johnson	Chevrolet	14	10	6	325	0	103	$121,761
15	Paul Menard	Chevrolet	22	11	7	325	0	76.5	$78,625
45	Kyle Petty	Dodge	32	17	8	325	0	69.8	$108,133
88	Dale Jarrett	Ford	31	14	9	325	0	82.6	$109,850
41	Reed Sorenson*	Dodge	15	13	10	325	0	81.1	$89,225
10	Scott Riggs	Dodge	29	18	11	325	0	63.5	$74,650
5	Kyle Busch	Chevrolet	17	12	12	325	0	84.4	$88,025
17	Matt Kenseth	Ford	27	2	13	325	0	99.7	$118,616
26	Jamie McMurray	Ford	34	20	14	325	0	74.7	$108,350
18	J.J. Yeley*	Chevrolet	5	15	15	325	0	89.6	$109,050
16	Greg Biffle	Ford	8	4	16	325	128	124.8	$104,175
01	Joe Nemechek	Chevrolet	13	19	17	325	0	70.9	$99,020
12	Ryan Newman	Dodge	2	24	18	325	2	62.8	$115,033
1	Martin Truex Jr. *	Chevrolet	35	23	19	324	0	66.5	$92,608
55	Michael Waltrip	Dodge	24	26	20	324	1	44.6	$85,158
42	Casey Mears	Dodge	10	27	21	324	0	54.7	$105,908
96	Terry Labonte	Chevrolet	43	28	22	324	5	45.9	$67,850
25	Brian Vickers	Chevrolet	37	21	23	324	0	62.9	$80,200
21	Ken Schrader	Ford	25	29	24	324	0	51.5	$98,164
31	Jeff Burton	Chevrolet	3	6	25	324	1	97.6	$97,870
66	Jeff Green	Chevrolet	39	30	26	324	0	61.7	$90,033
07	Clint Bowyer*	Chevrolet	16	16	27	324	0	62.9	$78,060
7	Robby Gordon	Chevrolet	36	5	28	324	0	85.5	$69,810
38	Elliott Sadler	Ford	28	25	29	324	0	65.1	$97,433
4	Scott Wimmer	Chevrolet	42	22	30	323	0	51.3	$69,900
11	Denny Hamlin*	Chevrolet	7	31	31	323	16	90.8	$70,125
22	Dave Blaney	Dodge	30	32	32	323	0	34.8	$75,797
40	David Stremme*	Dodge	38	33	33	322	0	35.5	$75,125
14	Sterling Marlin	Chevrolet	33	35	34	322	0	38.1	$66,130
61	Kevin Lepage	Ford	23	34	35	322	1	40.0	$66,190
49	Brent Sherman*	Dodge	40	36	36	322	0	28.5	$66,055
2	Kurt Busch	Dodge	9	37	37	321	22	78.8	$99,153
23	Bill Lester	Dodge	19	38	38	319	0	28.9	$65,985
29	Kevin Harvick	Chevrolet	6	40	39	313	0	62.8	$102,876
99	Carl Edwards	Ford	18	39	40	313	0	51.8	$85,700
19	Jeremy Mayfield	Dodge	20	41	41	235	0	34.1	$95,846
00	Hermie Sadler	Ford	41	42	42	166	0	25.9	$65,815
43	Bobby Labonte	Dodge	4	43	43	56	13	80.0	$103,725

POINT STANDINGS

Rk.	Driver	Pts.	Diff.
1.	Jimmie Johnson	690	—
2.	Kasey Kahne	640	-50
3.	Matt Kenseth	612	-78
4.	Mark Martin	600	-90
5.	Casey Mears	554	-136
6.	Jeff Gordon	539	-151
7.	Dale Earnhardt Jr.	534	-156
8.	Kyle Busch	530	-160
9.	Dale Jarrett	490	-200
10.	Clint Bowyer	471	-219
11.	Jeff Burton	466	-224
12.	Tony Stewart	464	-226
13.	Elliott Sadler	461	-229
14.	Brian Vickers	456	-234
15.	Martin Truex Jr.	442	-248
16.	Jamie McMurray	422	-268
17.	Ryan Newman	421	-269
18.	J.J. Yeley	417	-273
19.	Robby Gordon	415	-275
20.	Denny Hamlin	409	-281

*Rookie. **Time of race:** 3:28:24. **Average speed:** 144.098 mph. **Margin of victory:** 1.928 seconds. **Caution flags:** 8 for 43 laps: 16-19 (Car 12—spin, Turn 4); 43-47 (Car 5—accident, Turn 4); 68-73 (debris); 119-125 (Car 19—accident, Turn 2); 166-169 (debris); 189-197 (debris); 221-224 (Car 07—spin, Turn 2); 264-267 (debris). **Lead changes:** 27 among 12 drivers: Kahne 1; Newman 2-3; B. Labonte 4-16; Kahne 17-19; Biffle 20-43; Ku. Busch 44-63; Hamlin 64-67; Ku. Busch 68; Lepage 69; Hamlin 70-73; Biffle 74; Hamlin 75-79; Biffle 80-118; Ku. Busch 119; Stewart 120-141; Hamlin 142-144; Stewart 145-165; Burton 166; Waltrip 167; Stewart 168-171; Biffle 172-188; J. Gordon 189; T. Labonte 190-194; Stewart 195-197; Biffle 198-220; Kahne 221; Biffle 222-245; Kahne 246-325. **Fell out of race:** H. Sadler (suspension); B. Labonte (engine). **Pole:** Kasey Kahne, 192.533 mph. **Dropped to rear:** Vickers (engine change); Sherman (backup car). **Failed to qualify:** Mike Garvey (51), Stanton Barrett (95), Chad Chaffin (34), Derrike Cope (74), Kenny Wallace (78), Travis Kvapil (32), Mike Skinner (37), Greg Sacks (13), Chad Blount (92). **Estimated attendance:** 45,000.

Driver rating: An average of these categories—Win, finish, top 15 finish, average running position on lead lap, average speed under green, fastest lap, led most laps, lead-lap finish. Maximum points: 150 per race.

Bristol, Tenn. • .533-mile high-banked concrete oval • March 26, 2006 • 266.5 miles, 500 laps • Purse: $5,426,071

Car	Driver	Make	Start	50 laps to go	Finish	Laps run	Laps led	Rating	Winnings
2	Kurt Busch	Dodge	9	2	1	500	33	118.8	$175,858
29	Kevin Harvick	Chevrolet	14	3	2	500	8	117.0	$160,886
17	Matt Kenseth	Ford	7	1	3	500	124	130.2	$166,566
99	Carl Edwards	Ford	3	7	4	500	0	108.9	$122,575
43	Bobby Labonte	Dodge	30	6	5	500	0	91.9	$138,836
6	Mark Martin	Ford	4	8	6	500	0	103.6	$105,825
16	Greg Biffle	Ford	2	10	7	500	52	105.7	$105,150
5	Kyle Busch	Chevrolet	20	11	8	500	34	98.2	$102,450
12	Ryan Newman	Dodge	6	14	9	500	0	90.3	$129,258
9	Kasey Kahne	Dodge	23	15	10	500	0	89.8	$125,864
8	Dale Earnhardt Jr.	Chevrolet	19	12	11	500	0	95.8	$124,516
20	Tony Stewart	Chevrolet	1	5	12	500	245	126.2	$168,886
38	Elliott Sadler	Ford	13	9	13	500	0	88.8	$115,733
11	Denny Hamlin*	Chevrolet	33	18	14	500	0	76.0	$88,000
66	Jeff Green	Chevrolet	29	13	15	500	0	73.2	$113,458
19	Jeremy Mayfield	Dodge	10	16	16	500	0	77.8	$115,866
14	Sterling Marlin	Chevrolet	35	19	17	500	0	61.4	$97,783
45	Kyle Petty	Dodge	28	22	18	500	0	59.8	$107,633
4	Scott Wimmer	Chevrolet	40	21	19	500	0	52.8	$85,150
88	Dale Jarrett	Ford	15	17	20	500	0	77.4	$119,775
24	Jeff Gordon	Chevrolet	11	4	21	500	3	103.6	$129,336
41	Reed Sorenson*	Dodge	22	25	22	499	0	58.1	$92,450
22	Dave Blaney	Dodge	32	27	23	499	0	59.1	$96,783
21	Ken Schrader	Ford	21	24	24	499	0	75.7	$111,114
42	Casey Mears	Dodge	12	26	25	498	0	63.9	$118,183
7	Robby Gordon	Chevrolet	37	20	26	497	0	61.9	$83,400
96	Terry Labonte	Chevrolet	36	28	27	497	0	39.4	$80,060
01	Joe Nemechek	Chevrolet	16	29	28	495	0	52.1	$109,355
07	Clint Bowyer*	Chevrolet	27	23	29	495	0	54.6	$90,800
48	Jimmie Johnson	Chevrolet	5	30	30	487	0	38.3	$128,486
61	Kevin Lepage	Ford	39	31	31	485	1	40.2	$78,650
55	Michael Waltrip	Dodge	34	32	32	481	0	37.5	$88,147
18	J.J. Yeley*	Chevrolet	24	35	33	469	0	67.8	$117,075
31	Jeff Burton	Chevrolet	18	34	34	467	0	53.8	$107,345
26	Jamie McMurray	Ford	8	36	35	440	0	47.6	$117,275
40	David Stremme*	Dodge	26	37	36	435	0	35.5	$86,400
25	Brian Vickers	Chevrolet	17	38	37	434	0	58.1	$86,350
1	Martin Truex Jr.*	Chevrolet	25	33	38	430	0	48.0	$86,300
95	Stanton Barrett Jr.	Chevrolet	43	39	39	381	0	31.9	$78,240
32	Travis Kvapil	Chevrolet	41	40	40	349	0	41.0	$78,165
10	Scott Riggs	Dodge	38	42	41	344	0	40.0	$78,115
49	Brent Sherman*	Dodge	31	41	42	302	0	25.5	$78,060
00	Hermie Sadler	Chevrolet	42	43	43	96	0	23.3	$77,481

POINT STANDINGS

Rk.	Driver	Pts.	Diff.
1.	Matt Kenseth	782	—
2.	Kasey Kahne	774	-8
3.	Jimmie Johnson	763	-19
4.	Mark Martin	750	-32
5.	Kyle Busch	677	-105
6.	Dale Earnhardt Jr.	664	-118
7.	Jeff Gordon	644	-138
8.	Casey Mears	642	-140
9.	Tony Stewart	601	-181
10.	Dale Jarrett	593	-189
11.	Elliott Sadler	585	-197
12.	Ryan Newman	559	-223
13.	Kevin Harvick	553	-229
14.	Clint Bowyer	547	-235
15.	Greg Biffle	545	-237
16.	Kurt Busch	531	-251
17.	Denny Hamlin	530	-252
18.	Jeff Burton	527	-255
19.	Brian Vickers	508	-274
20.	Robby Gordon	500	-282

*Rookie. **Time of race:** 3:21:19. **Average speed:** 79.427 mph. **Margin of victory:** .179 seconds. **Caution flags:** 18 for 105 laps: 14-19 (Car 49—spin, backstretch); 74-77 (Car 45—spin, Turn 2); 109-115 (Car 95—accident, Turn 4); 119-123 (Car 10—spin, frontstretch); 127-131 (Cars 14, 55—accident, frontstretch); 161-167 (Car 31—spin, Turn 2); 188-199 (Cars 07, 22, 25, 40—accident, Turn 4); 207-212 (debris); 219-222 (debris); 250-253 (Car 49—spin, backstretch); 262-267 (Cars 12, 26, 41, 42—accident, frontstretch); 289-293 (Car 38—spin, Turn 2); 338-343 (Cars 20, 49—accident, Turn 4); 351-355 (Cars 19, 42—accident, backstretch); 408-412 (Car 61—accident, Turn 4); 415-419 (Cars 1, 18, 31—accident, Turn 4); 437-444 (Car 1—accident, Turn 3); 448-452 (Car 22—spin, Turn 2). **Note:** On Lap 193 (14 minutes, 10 seconds), the race was red-flagged for track clean-up. **Lead changes:** 19 among 8 drivers: Stewart 1-4; Biffle 5-56; Ku. Busch 57-60; Stewart 61-74; Lepage 75; Stewart 76-79; Kenseth 80-81; Stewart 82-134; Kenseth 135-141; Stewart 142-157; J. Gordon 158-160; Stewart 161; Ky. Busch 162-195; Kenseth 196-224; Stewart 225-331; Harvick 332-339; Stewart 340-385; Ku. Busch 386-409; Kenseth 410-495; Ku. Busch 496-500. **Fell out of race:** Truex, Kvapil, Sherman (accidents); Barrett (electrical); H. Sadler (handling). **Pole:** None—conditions. **Failed to qualify:** Chad Chaffin (34), Kenny Wallace (78), Mike Garvey (51), Mike Skinner (37), Morgan Shepherd (89), Chad Blount (92), Derrike Cope (74). **Estimated attendance:** 160,000.

Driver rating: An average of these categories—Win, finish, top 15 finish, average running position on lead lap, average speed under green, fastest lap, led most laps, lead-lap finish. Maximum points: 150 per race.

Martinsville Speedway

Martinsville, Va. • .526-mile paved oval • April 2, 2006 • 263 miles, 500 laps • Purse: $4,826,889

Car	Driver	Make	Start	50 laps to go	Finish	Laps run	Laps led	Rating	Winnings
20	Tony Stewart	Chevrolet	3	2	1	500	288	147.5	$220,786
24	Jeff Gordon	Chevrolet	8	5	2	500	0	111.8	$153,461
48	Jimmie Johnson	Chevrolet	1	1	3	500	195	129.8	$150,361
8	Dale Earnhardt Jr.	Chevrolet	29	9	4	500	0	95.4	$133,416
5	Kyle Busch	Chevrolet	17	3	5	500	0	117.2	$98,400
38	Elliott Sadler	Ford	7	4	6	500	0	108.4	$120,808
29	Kevin Harvick	Chevrolet	26	6	7	500	0	95.1	$115,011
25	Brian Vickers	Chevrolet	24	11	8	500	0	80.1	$85,350
26	Jamie McMurray	Ford	2	14	9	500	6	101.1	$122,675
10	Scott Riggs	Dodge	11	16	10	500	0	77.7	$76,700
2	Kurt Busch	Dodge	9	8	11	500	0	91.8	$111,683
41	Reed Sorenson*	Dodge	25	10	12	500	0	88.4	$85,925
6	Mark Martin	Ford	30	17	13	500	0	71.2	$90,575
14	Sterling Marlin	Chevrolet	6	15	14	500	9	77.6	$92,083
88	Dale Jarrett	Ford	28	20	15	500	1	67.2	$106,825
99	Carl Edwards	Ford	15	18	16	500	0	73.2	$89,100
22	Dave Blaney	Dodge	14	19	17	499	0	57.7	$89,233
12	Ryan Newman	Dodge	4	23	18	498	0	83.4	$114,358
1	Martin Truex Jr.*	Chevrolet	21	21	19	498	0	53.5	$94,208
18	J.J. Yeley*	Chevrolet	18	12	20	497	1	76.7	$109,125
96	Tony Raines	Chevrolet	12	24	21	497	0	59.0	$67,850
07	Clint Bowyer*	Chevrolet	42	25	22	496	0	43.2	$84,250
01	Joe Nemechek	Chevrolet	22	22	23	495	0	61.9	$98,245
17	Matt Kenseth	Ford	16	7	24	493	0	88.3	$113,491
66	Jeff Green	Chevrolet	34	26	25	491	0	56.4	$90,483
19	Jeremy Mayfield	Dodge	23	13	26	462	0	70.6	$100,066
42	Casey Mears	Dodge	32	27	27	456	0	50.9	$103,918
4	Scott Wimmer	Chevrolet	36	28	28	451	0	45.2	$69,460
55	Michael Waltrip	Dodge	33	29	29	445	0	41.9	$78,722
45	Kyle Petty	Dodge	37	30	30	439	0	49.1	$77,550
16	Greg Biffle	Ford	10	31	31	436	0	70.5	$86,100
43	Bobby Labonte	Dodge	13	32	32	429	0	54.4	$105,211
31	Jeff Burton	Chevrolet	20	33	33	426	0	74.4	$92,845
32	Travis Kvapil	Chevrolet	40	35	34	403	0	38.5	$65,425
9	Kasey Kahne	Dodge	5	34	35	374	0	83.1	$102,889
34	Chad Chaffin	Chevrolet	31	37	36	345	0	30.8	$65,325
11	Denny Hamlin*	Chevrolet	41	36	37	307	0	55.9	$65,250
40	David Stremme*	Dodge	38	39	38	299	0	39.0	$73,200
95	Stanton Barrett	Chevrolet	35	38	39	280	0	30.4	$65,140
21	Ken Schrader	Ford	19	40	40	164	0	58.9	$92,279
51	Mike Garvey	Chevrolet	39	41	41	93	0	35.6	$65,015
92	Chad Blount	Dodge	43	42	42	92	0	30.2	$64,960
7	Robby Gordon	Chevrolet	27	43	43	7	0	27.3	$64,384

POINT STANDINGS

Rk.	Driver	Pts.	Diff.
1.	Jimmie Johnson	933	—
2.	Mark Martin	874	-59
3.	Matt Kenseth	873	-60
4.	Kasey Kahne	832	-101
5.	Kyle Busch	832	-101
6.	Dale Earnhardt Jr.	824	-109
7.	Jeff Gordon	814	-119
8.	Tony Stewart	791	-142
9.	Elliott Sadler	735	-198
10.	Casey Mears	724	-209
11.	Dale Jarrett	716	-217
12.	Kevin Harvick	699	-234
13.	Ryan Newman	668	-265
14.	Kurt Busch	661	-272
15.	Brian Vickers	650	-283
16.	Clint Bowyer	644	-289
17.	Jamie McMurray	623	-310
18.	Greg Biffle	615	-318
19.	Carl Edwards	602	-331
20.	Martin Truex Jr.	597	-336

*Rookie. **Time of race:** 3:36:56. **Average speed:** 72.741 mph. **Margin of victory:** 1.083 seconds.
Caution flags: 16 for 87 laps: 3-9 (Cars 7, 8, 34—accident, Turn 2); 14-21 (Car 32—accident, Turn 2); 91-95 (Car 24—accident, Turns 3 and 4); 110-115 (Car 16—accident, backstretch); 135-139 (Car 40—accident, Turn 3); 172-175 (Car 6—accident, Turn 4); 227-231 (Car 31—accident, Turn 4); 289-294 (Car 01—accident, Turn 3); 309-313 (Car 11—spin, Turn 4); 318-323 (Car 8—accident, Turn 4); 336-339 (Car 01—accident, Turn 4); 366-370 (Car 66—accident, Turn 4); 427-432 (debris); 450-454 (Car 95—slow on track); 487-492 (Car 01—accident, Turn 1); 494-497 (Car 17—accident, Turn 1). **Lead changes:** 12 among 6 drivers: Johnson 1-27; McMurray 28-33; Stewart 34-172; Marlin 173-181; Yeley 182; Stewart 183-227; Johnson 228-290; Jarrett 291; Stewart 292-360; Johnson 361-371; Stewart 372-379; Johnson 380-473; Stewart 474-500. **Fell out of race:** Kenseth, Hamlin, Stremme (accident); Mayfield, Kahne, R. Gordon (engine); Barrrett, Garvey, Blount (brakes); Schrader (overheating). **Pole:** Jimmie Johnson, 96.736 mph.
Failed to qualify: Derrike Cope (74), Kevin Lepage (61), Kenny Wallace (78), Jimmy Spencer (49), Morgan Shepherd (89), Hermie Sadler (00). **Estimated attendance:** 65,000.

Driver rating: An average of these categories—Win, finish, top 15 finish, average running position on lead lap, average speed under green, fastest lap, led most laps, lead-lap finish. Maximum points: 150 per race.

>> SAMSUNG/RADIOSHACK 500   race 7 of 36

Texas Motor Speedway

Fort Worth, Texas • 1.5-mile banked paved oval • April 9, 2006 • 501 miles, 334 laps • Purse: $7,096,079

Car	Driver	Make	Start	34 laps to go	Finish	Laps run	Laps led	Rating	Winnings
9	Kasey Kahne	Dodge	1	2	1	334	63	131.4	$530,164
17	Matt Kenseth	Ford	6	4	2	334	14	104.5	$362,491
20	Tony Stewart	Chevrolet	40	1	3	334	99	125.5	$286,386
11	Denny Hamlin*	Chevrolet	8	8	4	334	41	123.1	$208,500
29	Kevin Harvick	Chevrolet	24	12	5	334	1	102.1	$204,511
31	Jeff Burton	Chevrolet	21	11	6	334	0	89.9	$172,220
10	Scott Riggs	Dodge	22	3	7	334	0	91.1	$133,850
1	Martin Truex Jr.*	Chevrolet	9	6	8	334	2	104.0	$156,608
6	Mark Martin	Ford	3	9	9	334	11	102.2	$151,850
43	Bobby Labonte	Dodge	10	10	10	334	0	92.4	$164,211
48	Jimmie Johnson	Chevrolet	16	15	11	334	0	75.4	$165,161
8	Dale Earnhardt Jr.	Chevrolet	15	14	12	334	0	82.3	$154,816
41	Reed Sorenson*	Dodge	13	5	13	334	0	90.7	$126,675
42	Casey Mears	Dodge	20	13	14	334	0	80.0	$150,233
5	Kyle Busch	Chevrolet	26	16	15	334	0	71.3	$129,725
21	Ken Schrader	Ford	32	19	16	334	0	66.9	$140,089
88	Dale Jarrett	Ford	27	20	17	334	0	64.3	$143,350
66	Jeff Green	Chevrolet	4	17	18	334	1	78.6	$133,833
07	Clint Bowyer*	Chevrolet	12	18	19	333	0	64.1	$116,075
7	Robby Gordon	Chevrolet	29	7	20	333	0	75.5	$109,275
40	David Stremme*	Dodge	28	21	21	333	0	52.9	$127,033
24	Jeff Gordon	Chevrolet	11	23	22	332	0	69.7	$148,411
01	Joe Nemechek	Chevrolet	17	24	23	332	0	49.3	$129,070
96	Tony Raines	Chevrolet	36	25	24	332	0	47.5	$97,075
44	Terry Labonte	Chevrolet	30	22	25	332	0	51.2	$95,975
55	Michael Waltrip	Dodge	42	27	26	331	0	46.9	$108,833
32	Travis Kvapil	Chevrolet	39	26	27	331	0	37.4	$105,122
4	Scott Wimmer	Chevrolet	43	28	28	330	0	52.7	$94,075
22	Dave Blaney	Dodge	31	29	29	330	0	39.4	$92,475
14	Sterling Marlin	Chevrolet	18	31	30	329	0	43.6	$89,325
19	Jeremy Mayfield	Dodge	34	30	31	328	0	41.2	$116,891
61	Kevin Lepage	Ford	35	32	32	328	0	31.3	$85,800
38	Elliott Sadler	Ford	25	33	33	286	1	66.8	$113,558
2	Kurt Busch	Dodge	7	35	34	286	0	72.4	$124,633
18	J.J. Yeley*	Chevrolet	2	38	35	270	2	85.7	$118,075
99	Carl Edwards	Ford	37	34	36	256	50	91.3	$101,175
26	Jamie McMurray	Ford	41	39	37	254	0	35.1	$127,100
51	Mike Garvey	Chevrolet	23	36	38	251	0	29.0	$79,125
45	Kyle Petty	Dodge	19	37	39	248	0	48.3	$87,000
12	Ryan Newman	Dodge	14	40	40	200	0	51.5	$124,283
74	Derrike Cope	Dodge	38	41	41	169	0	25.8	$78,760
16	Greg Biffle	Ford	5	42	42	81	49	90.0	$98,860
25	Brian Vickers	Chevrolet	33	43	43	24	0	32.2	$86,847

POINT STANDINGS

Rk.	Driver	Pts.	Diff.
1.	Jimmie Johnson	1,063	—
2.	Matt Kenseth	1,048	-15
3.	Kasey Kahne	1,017	-46
4.	Mark Martin	1,017	-46
5.	Tony Stewart	966	-97
6.	Dale Earnhardt Jr.	951	-112
7.	Kyle Busch	950	-113
8.	Jeff Gordon	911	-152
9.	Kevin Harvick	859	-204
10.	Casey Mears	845	-218
11.	Dale Jarrett	828	-235
12.	Elliott Sadler	804	-259
13.	Clint Bowyer	750	-313
14.	Denny Hamlin	747	-316
15.	Martin Truex Jr.	744	-319
16.	Jeff Burton	741	-322
17.	Kurt Busch	722	-341
18.	Ryan Newman	711	-352
19.	Reed Sorenson	701	-362
20.	Brian Vickers	684	-379

*Rookie. **Time of race:** 3:37:55. **Average speed:** 137.943 mph. **Margin of victory:** 5.229 seconds.
Caution flags: 9 for 43 laps: 65-68 (debris); 83-89 (Car 16—accident, Turn 3); 147-150 (debris); 161-164 (debris); 190-195 (Car 18—accident, Turn 4); 202-205 (Car 12—accident, Turn 1); 251-254 (oil on track); 258-263 (Car 99—accident, Turn 2); 314-317 (debris). **Note:** On Lap 86 (9 minutes, 27 seconds), the race was red-flagged for track repair. **Lead changes:** 22 among 12 drivers: Kahne—pole; Martin 1-11; Biffle 12-56; Green 57; Harvick 58; Truex 59-60; Biffle 61-64; Kahne 65-68; Yeley 69-70; Kahne 71-90; Hamlin 91; Stewart 92-146; Hamlin 148-158; Kenseth 159-161; E. Sadler 162; Edwards 163-166; Kenseth 167-177; Hamlin 178-206; Edwards 207-251; Kahne 252-263; Stewart 264-307; Kahne 308-334. **Fell out of race:** Sadler, Petty, Vickers (engine); Edwards, Garvey, Newman, Biffle (accident); Cope (electrical). **Pole:** Kasey Kahne, 190.315 mph. **Dropped to rear:** Kenseth (engine change); Cope, Wimmer (transmission change). **Failed to qualify:** Brent Sherman (49), Chad Blount (92), Kenny Wallace (78), Chad Chaffin (34), Stanton Barrett (95). **Estimated attendance:** 189,000.

Driver rating: An average of these categories—Win, finish, top 15 finish, average running position on lead lap, average speed under green, fastest lap, led most laps, lead-lap finish. Maximum points: 150 per race.

Avondale, Ariz. • 1-mile paved oval • April 22, 2006 • 312 miles, 312 laps • Purse: $4,866,887

Car	Driver	Make	Start	32 laps to go	Finish	Laps run	Laps led	Rating	Winnings
29	Kevin Harvick	Chevrolet	15	3	1	312	10	119.7	$228,486
20	Tony Stewart	Chevrolet	3	2	2	312	6	107.1	$211,536
17	Matt Kenseth	Ford	4	5	3	312	1	107.4	$168,116
99	Carl Edwards	Ford	5	6	4	312	0	98.9	$126,685
07	Clint Bowyer*	Chevrolet	8	8	5	312	21	114.5	$122,325
9	Kasey Kahne	Dodge	22	9	6	312	0	97.6	$124,189
48	Jimmie Johnson	Chevrolet	10	4	7	312	0	117.3	$127,111
43	Bobby Labonte	Dodge	21	10	8	312	0	91.5	$117,661
31	Jeff Burton	Chevrolet	37	13	9	312	0	80.1	$108,870
24	Jeff Gordon	Chevrolet	19	14	10	312	0	80.0	$124,111
6	Mark Martin	Ford	18	7	11	311	111	118.7	$98,425
14	Sterling Marlin	Chevrolet	16	16	12	311	0	81.1	$90,883
25	Brian Vickers	Chevrolet	14	17	13	311	0	83.2	$80,275
26	Jamie McMurray	Ford	26	15	14	311	0	73.3	$112,750
16	Greg Biffle	Ford	2	1	15	311	151	128.7	$102,350
21	Ken Schrader	Ford	27	20	16	311	0	72.6	$95,389
96	Tony Raines	Chevrolet	36	22	17	311	0	61.0	$65,075
66	Jeff Green	Chevrolet	23	21	18	311	0	68.6	$91,808
88	Dale Jarrett	Ford	17	23	19	311	0	64.7	$99,325
42	Casey Mears	Dodge	12	19	20	311	0	66.5	$103,983
32	Travis Kvapil	Chevrolet	39	24	21	311	0	45.7	$80,958
1	Martin Truex Jr.*	Chevrolet	9	12	22	311	0	88.0	$86,233
8	Dale Earnhardt Jr.	Chevrolet	11	18	23	310	0	86.5	$102,291
2	Kurt Busch	Dodge	7	11	24	310	0	83.0	$103,833
78	Kenny Wallace	Chevrolet	31	26	25	310	0	43.9	$63,075
19	Jeremy Mayfield	Dodge	28	27	26	310	0	46.5	$95,841
22	Dave Blaney	Dodge	41	25	27	309	2	56.7	$75,172
18	J.J. Yeley*	Chevrolet	30	29	28	309	1	51.9	$99,975
40	David Stremme*	Dodge	29	28	29	308	0	41.0	$73,175
4	Scott Wimmer	Chevrolet	33	30	30	307	0	46.2	$65,525
45	Kyle Petty	Dodge	38	31	31	305	0	37.5	$72,400
49	Brent Sherman*	Dodge	43	33	32	305	0	31.5	$61,750
95	Stanton Barrett Jr.	Chevrolet	35	32	33	301	0	30.5	$62,575
11	Denny Hamlin*	Chevrolet	6	34	34	289	0	47.5	$61,500
01	Joe Nemechek	Chevrolet	32	35	35	283	0	38.6	$87,720
5	Kyle Busch	Chevrolet	1	36	36	259	7	60.0	$84,425
38	Elliott Sadler	Ford	20	38	37	247	1	39.1	$89,008
10	Scott Riggs	Dodge	24	39	38	229	0	63.6	$60,975
12	Ryan Newman	Dodge	13	37	39	221	0	73.7	$106,258
41	Reed Sorenson*	Dodge	34	40	40	206	0	30.8	$68,700
7	Robby Gordon	Chevrolet	25	41	41	116	0	50.1	$60,560
55	Michael Waltrip	Dodge	42	42	42	98	0	40.2	$60,435
02	Brandon Ash	Dodge	40	43	43	98	1	29.4	$60,635

POINT STANDINGS

Rk.	Driver	Pts.	Diff.
1.	Matt Kenseth	1,218	—
2.	Jimmie Johnson	1,209	-9
3.	Kasey Kahne	1,167	-51
4.	Mark Martin	1,152	-66
5.	Tony Stewart	1,141	-77
6.	Jeff Gordon	1,045	-173
7.	Dale Earnhardt Jr.	1,045	-173
8.	Kevin Harvick	1,044	-174
9.	Kyle Busch	1,010	-208
10.	Casey Mears	948	-270
11.	Dale Jarrett	934	-284
12.	Clint Bowyer	910	-308
13.	Jeff Burton	879	-339
14.	Elliott Sadler	861	-357
15.	Martin Truex Jr.	841	-377
16.	Carl Edwards	822	-396
17.	Kurt Busch	813	-405
18.	Denny Hamlin	808	-410
19.	Brian Vickers	808	-410
20.	Jamie McMurray	796	-422

*Rookie. **Time of race:** 2:54:51. **Average speed:** 107.063 mph. **Margin of victory:** 2.774 seconds. **Caution flags:** 7 for 29 laps: 26-28 (debris); 55-57 (Car 22—accident, Turn 1); 89-92 (Car 10—accident, backstretch); 101-104 (Cars 5, 42—accident, Turn 2; Cars 01, 38, 45, 55—accident, Turn 4); 200-203 (debris); 213-216 (Cars 18, 49—accident, Turn 4); 224-230 (Cars 4, 6, 8, 10, 12, 45—accident, Turn 4). **Note:** On Lap 100 (9 minutes, 10 seconds), race was red-flagged for track clean-up. **Lead changes:** 20 among 11 drivers: Ky. Busch—pole; Biffle 1-26; Ash 27; Biffle 28-47; Ky. Busch 48-54; Biffle 55-65; Martin 66-88; Biffle 89; E. Sadler 90; Biffle 91-105; Martin 106-170; Bowyer 171-172; Kenseth 173; Blaney 174-175; Yeley 176; Martin 177-199; Bowyer 200-217; Stewart 218-223; Bowyer 224; Biffle 225-302; Harvick 303-312. **Fell out of race:** Newman, Waltrip (accident); R. Gordon (engine), Ash (transmission). **Pole:** Kyle Busch, 133.744 mph. **Dropped to rear:** Stewart (tire change). **Failed to qualify:** Chad Chaffin (34), Mike Garvey (51), Chad Blount (92), Kevin Lepage (61), Morgan Shepherd (89), Steve Portenga (52). **Estimated attendance:** 104,000.

Driver rating: An average of these categories—Win, finish, top 15 finish, average running position on lead lap, average speed under green, fastest lap, led most laps, lead-lap finish. Maximum points: 150 per race.

>>AARON'S 499

Talladega Superspeedway

Talladega, Ala. • 2.66-mile high-banked paved trioval • May 1, 2006 • 500 miles, 188 laps • Purse: $5,901,372

Car	Driver	Make	Start	19 laps to go	Finish	Laps run	Laps led	Rating	Winnings
48	Jimmie Johnson	Chevrolet	16	18	1	188	3	113.9	$326,061
20	Tony Stewart	Chevrolet	2	10	2	188	11	97.4	$260,136
25	Brian Vickers	Chevrolet	33	17	3	188	7	105.0	$172,300
31	Jeff Burton	Chevrolet	40	19	4	188	0	100.2	$176,745
26	Jamie McMurray	Ford	8	1	5	188	18	107.9	$168,600
17	Matt Kenseth	Ford	12	14	6	188	23	102.4	$159,841
2	Kurt Busch	Dodge	5	16	7	188	9	94.8	$143,233
99	Carl Edwards	Ford	3	5	8	188	7	92.0	$118,975
10	Scott Riggs	Dodge	32	2	9	188	0	91.6	$97,975
7	Robby Gordon	Chevrolet	19	20	10	188	1	100.1	$103,350
18	J.J. Yeley*	Chevrolet	11	15	11	188	1	84.0	$131,075
88	Dale Jarrett	Ford	4	11	12	188	1	74.5	$125,875
19	Jeremy Mayfield	Dodge	36	23	13	188	1	73.9	$124,816
66	Jeff Green	Chevrolet	39	22	14	188	1	87.7	$117,808
24	Jeff Gordon	Chevrolet	14	6	15	188	62	109.8	$151,311
38	Elliott Sadler	Ford	1	4	16	188	23	102.2	$138,983
96	Tony Raines	Chevrolet	29	12	17	188	0	72.7	$84,675
45	Kyle Petty	Dodge	28	24	18	188	0	56.4	$111,883
32	Travis Kvapil	Chevrolet	26	25	19	188	0	67.8	$101,083
42	Casey Mears	Dodge	25	27	20	188	2	70.2	$123,083
4	Scott Wimmer	Chevrolet	43	26	21	188	1	65.4	$85,350
11	Denny Hamlin*	Chevrolet	30	7	22	187	1	81.0	$84,625
29	Kevin Harvick	Chevrolet	42	28	23	187	0	44.2	$121,811
22	Dave Blaney	Dodge	38	13	24	183	1	65.3	$94,858
55	Michael Waltrip	Dodge	21	9	25	179	1	73.8	$92,447
41	Reed Sorenson*	Dodge	41	3	26	177	0	84.1	$89,825
01	Joe Nemechek	Chevrolet	6	21	27	173	5	84.1	$107,620
61	Kevin Lepage	Ford	23	8	28	173	1	60.9	$80,225
43	Bobby Labonte	Dodge	31	29	29	163	0	53.7	$114,461
34	Chad Chaffin	Chevrolet	34	31	30	152	0	36.2	$77,825
8	Dale Earnhardt Jr.	Chevrolet	27	30	31	151	8	86.5	$112,166
5	Kyle Busch	Chevrolet	13	32	32	150	0	43.6	$95,025
12	Ryan Newman	Dodge	18	33	33	106	0	46.0	$122,308
40	David Stremme*	Dodge	17	34	34	106	0	39.1	$85,725
6	Mark Martin	Ford	10	35	35	101	0	37.1	$94,650
1	Martin Truex Jr.*	Chevrolet	20	36	36	97	0	34.2	$84,500
14	Sterling Marlin	Chevrolet	9	37	37	91	0	38.9	$76,325
16	Greg Biffle	Ford	7	38	38	45	0	60.1	$96,175
9	Kasey Kahne	Dodge	37	39	39	17	0	33.8	$112,989
07	Clint Bowyer*	Chevrolet	15	40	40	16	0	32.9	$83,525
27	Kirk Shelmerdine	Chevrolet	22	41	41	9	0	31.8	$75,325
21	Ken Schrader	Ford	35	42	42	8	0	31.8	$102,364
00	Hermie Sadler	Ford	24	43	43	8	0	29.5	$75,308

POINT STANDINGS

Rk.	Driver	Pts.	Diff.
1.	Jimmie Johnson	1,394	—
2.	Matt Kenseth	1,373	-21
3.	Tony Stewart	1,316	-78
4.	Kasey Kahne	1,213	-181
5.	Mark Martin	1,210	-184
6.	Jeff Gordon	1,173	-221
7.	Kevin Harvick	1,138	-256
8.	Dale Earnhardt Jr.	1,120	-274
9.	Kyle Busch	1,077	-317
10.	Dale Jarrett	1,066	-328
11.	Casey Mears	1,056	-338
12.	Jeff Burton	1,039	-355
13.	Elliott Sadler	981	-413
14.	Brian Vickers	978	-416
15.	Carl Edwards	969	-425
16.	Kurt Busch	964	-430
17.	Jamie McMurray	956	-438
18.	Clint Bowyer	953	-441
19.	Denny Hamlin	910	-484
20.	Martin Truex Jr.	896	-498

*Rookie. **Time of race:** 3:30:00. **Average speed:** 142.880 mph. **Margin of victory:** 0.120 seconds. **Caution flags:** 8 for 34 laps: 10-15 (Cars 00, 1, 5, 6, 9, 12, 14, 21, 29, 34, 40, 41, 43—accident, Turn 3); 40-42 (debris); 89-92 (Car 8—accident, Turn 3); 111-114 (debris); 128-130 (Car 14—spin, frontstretch); 153-156 (Car 8—accident, Turn 4); 166-169 (oil on track); 174-179 (Cars 01, 12, 22, 32, 41, 55, 61—accident, frontstretch). **Lead changes:** 56 among 22 drivers: E. Sadler 1-2; Stewart 3-6; McMurray 7; J. Gordon 8-9; Green 10; Mayfield 11; Jarrett 12; Nemechek 13-17; Earnhardt 18-19; Vickers 20; Earnhardt 21-24; Ku. Busch 25; McMurray 26-34; Kenseth 35-39; Wimmer 40; Kenseth 41-43; E. Sadler 44-47; Mears 48-49; Edwards 50-53; J. Gordon 54-59; Edwards 60; J. Gordon 61-70; Earnhardt 71-72; Edwards 73-74; Kenseth 75-84; E. Sadler 85; Vickers 86-87; J. Gordon 88; R. Gordon 89; Waltrip 90; J. Gordon 91-101; E. Sadler 102-103; J. Gordon 104-110; Hamlin 111; J. Gordon 112-115; E. Sadler 116; J. Gordon 117-122; Johnson 123-124; E. Sadler 125-127; Yeley 128; Kenseth 129-132; J. Gordon 133-135; Kenseth 136; E. Sadler 137-146; J. Gordon 147-152; Blaney 153; Lepage 154; J. Gordon 155-157; Ku. Busch 158-165; McMurray 166-172; Stewart 173-179; J. Gordon 180; Vickers 181-183; McMurray 184; J. Gordon 185-186; Vickers 187; Johnson 188. **Fell out of race:** Waltrip, Sorenson, Nemechek, Lepage, Truex, Marlin, Kahne, Bowyer, Shelmerdine, Schrader, H. Sadler (accident); B. Labonte, Earnhardt, Biffle (engine). **Pole:** Elliott Sadler, 188.511 mph. **Dropped to rear:** Kenseth (unapproved impound adjustment). **Failed to qualify:** Morgan Shepherd (89), Stanton Barrett (95), Mike Wallace (09), Chad Blount (92), Brent Sherman (49), Kenny Wallace (78). **Estimated attendance:** 135,000.

Driver rating: An average of these categories—Win, finish, top 15 finish, average running position on lead lap, average speed under green, fastest lap, led most laps, lead-lap finish. Maximum points: 150 per race.

Richmond International Raceway

Richmond, Va. • .75-mile paved oval • May 6, 2006 • 300 miles, 400 laps • Purse: $4,931,502

Car	Driver	Make	Start	40 laps to go	Finish	Laps run	Laps led	Rating	Winnings
8	Dale Earnhardt Jr.	Chevrolet	10	1	1	400	47	129.5	$239,166
11	Denny Hamlin*	Chevrolet	7	4	2	400	19	118.5	$165,200
29	Kevin Harvick	Chevrolet	8	2	3	400	272	142.4	$169,386
16	Greg Biffle	Ford	1	6	4	400	54	115.4	$143,300
5	Kyle Busch	Chevrolet	21	3	5	400	7	101.6	$113,600
20	Tony Stewart	Chevrolet	18	5	6	400	0	96.2	$139,661
99	Carl Edwards	Ford	9	9	7	400	0	86.8	$100,100
12	Ryan Newman	Dodge	14	7	8	400	0	95.1	$120,658
14	Sterling Marlin	Chevrolet	32	15	9	400	0	80.8	$96,783
07	Clint Bowyer*	Chevrolet	20	8	10	400	0	87.7	$91,025
6	Mark Martin	Ford	2	14	11	400	1	102.7	$94,525
48	Jimmie Johnson	Chevrolet	5	17	12	400	0	76.6	$118,361
38	Elliott Sadler	Ford	37	12	13	400	0	73.0	$106,808
10	Scott Riggs	Dodge	23	11	14	400	0	74.9	$69,250
31	Jeff Burton	Chevrolet	15	13	15	399	0	96.0	$98,270
21	Ken Schrader	Ford	28	22	16	399	0	62.3	$97,564
42	Casey Mears	Dodge	3	18	17	399	0	70.8	$104,833
66	Jeff Green	Chevrolet	25	19	18	399	0	55.3	$93,363
26	Jamie McMurray	Ford	31	20	19	399	0	63.5	$112,200
22	Dave Blaney	Dodge	19	24	20	399	0	67.9	$85,808
88	Dale Jarrett	Ford	26	25	21	399	0	53.0	$100,675
18	J.J. Yeley*	Chevrolet	34	21	22	399	0	57.6	$102,950
41	Reed Sorenson*	Dodge	24	23	23	399	0	57.9	$77,025
43	Bobby Labonte	Dodge	35	16	24	399	0	68.8	$104,761
78	Kenny Wallace	Chevrolet	42	26	25	398	0	46.5	$64,875
45	Kyle Petty	Dodge	12	28	26	398	0	55.2	$87,108
32	Travis Kvapil	Chevrolet	36	27	27	398	0	44.6	$76,772
01	Joe Nemechek	Chevrolet	17	30	28	398	0	50.8	$93,445
2	Kurt Busch	Dodge	13	31	29	397	0	92.2	$105,008
96	Tony Raines	Chevrolet	27	34	30	397	0	42.6	$64,300
55	Michael Waltrip	Dodge	30	33	31	397	0	35.6	$66,175
19	Jeremy Mayfield	Dodge	38	32	32	397	0	32.9	$93,541
40	David Stremme*	Dodge	29	29	33	397	0	37.9	$72,375
9	Kasey Kahne	Dodge	6	35	34	396	0	80.6	$100,514
49	Mike Wallace	Dodge	43	36	35	395	0	38.1	$63,175
4	Scott Wimmer	Chevrolet	33	37	36	389	0	28.9	$63,025
25	Brian Vickers	Chevrolet	4	10	37	387	0	74.0	$70,900
17	Matt Kenseth	Ford	11	39	38	351	0	79.4	$109,016
7	Robby Gordon	Chevrolet	39	38	39	345	0	52.4	$62,650
24	Jeff Gordon	Chevrolet	16	40	40	286	0	71.8	$110,861
1	Martin Truex Jr.*	Chevrolet	22	41	41	285	0	50.6	$70,385
61	Kevin Lepage	Dodge	40	42	42	89	0	25.9	$62,260
74	Derrike Cope	Dodge	41	43	43	11	0	24.8	$62,473

POINT STANDINGS

Rk.	Driver	Pts.	Diff.
1.	Jimmie Johnson	1,521	—
2.	Tony Stewart	1,466	-55
3.	Matt Kenseth	1,422	-99
4.	Mark Martin	1,345	-176
5.	Kevin Harvick	1,313	-208
6.	Dale Earnhardt Jr.	1,305	-216
7.	Kasey Kahne	1,274	-247
8.	Kyle Busch	1,237	-284
9.	Jeff Gordon	1,216	-305
10.	Casey Mears	1,168	-353
11.	Jeff Burton	1,157	-364
12.	Dale Jarrett	1,141	-380
13.	Carl Edwards	1,115	-406
14.	Elliott Sadler	1,105	-416
15.	Clint Bowyer	1,087	-434
16.	Denny Hamlin	1,085	-436
17.	Jamie McMurray	1,062	-459
18.	Kurt Busch	1,040	-481
19.	Brian Vickers	1,030	-491
20.	Greg Biffle	999	-522

*Rookie. **Time of race:** 3:05:27. **Average speed:** 97.061 mph. **Margin of victory:** .572 seconds. **Caution flags:** 11 for 61 laps: 9-11 (Car 49—spin, backstretch); 21-23 (Car 4—accident, backstretch); 66-71 (Car 96—spin, frontstretch); 80-91 (Cars 66, 42—spin, frontstretch); 94-103 (Car 61—accident, Turn 3); 186-190 (Car 99—accident, Turn 4); 261-265 (Car 1—spin, frontstretch); 288-292 (oil on track); 347-352 (Car 7—accident, Turn 2); 387-390 (Cars 10, 25—accident, backstretch); 392-393 (Car 31—accident, backstretch). **Lead changes:** 12 among 6 drivers: Biffle 1; Martin 2; Biffle 3-49; Harvick 50-66; Biffle 67-72; Harvick 73-185; Earnhardt 186; Harvick 187-260; Earnhardt 261; Harvick 262-329; Hamlin 330-348; Ky. Busch 349-355; Earnhardt 356-400. **Fell out of race:** Vickers, R. Gordon (accident); J. Gordon, Truex, Lepage (engine); Cope (vibration). **Pole:** Greg Biffle, 127.395 mph. **Dropped to rear:** Jarrett (unapproved impound adjustment). **Failed to qualify:** Kertus Davis (89), Chad Chaffin (34), Stanton Barrett (95), Hermie Sadler (00). **Estimated attendance:** 107,000.

Driver rating: An average of these categories—Win, finish, top 15 finish, average running position on lead lap, average speed under green, fastest lap, led most laps, lead-lap finish. Maximum points: 150 per race.

Darlington, S.C. • 1.366-mile banked paved oval • May 13, 2006 • 501 miles, 367 laps • Purse: $5,400,769

Car	Driver	Make	Start	37 laps to go	Finish	Laps run	Laps led	Rating	Winnings
16	Greg Biffle	Ford	9	1	1	367	170	143.1	$290,175
24	Jeff Gordon	Chevrolet	12	3	2	367	5	111.4	$223,161
17	Matt Kenseth	Ford	31	2	3	367	64	119.1	$205,291
48	Jimmie Johnson	Chevrolet	25	4	4	367	81	122.2	$165,311
8	Dale Earnhardt Jr.	Chevrolet	22	5	5	367	0	107.1	$152,916
12	Ryan Newman	Dodge	2	6	6	367	2	117.0	$139,333
5	Kyle Busch	Chevrolet	29	7	7	367	1	92.4	$120,625
6	Mark Martin	Ford	17	8	8	367	0	95.5	$105,625
31	Jeff Burton	Chevrolet	20	9	9	367	0	91.7	$115,320
11	Denny Hamlin*	Chevrolet	5	10	10	367	0	100.7	$97,900
41	Reed Sorenson*	Dodge	16	11	11	367	0	82.2	$94,375
20	Tony Stewart	Chevrolet	13	13	12	367	0	83.2	$133,386
7	Robby Gordon	Chevrolet	24	16	13	367	1	93.5	$85,225
1	Martin Truex Jr.*	Chevrolet	39	12	14	367	0	76.2	$108,408
21	Ken Schrader	Ford	23	14	15	366	0	74.2	$109,814
01	Joe Nemechek	Chevrolet	36	20	16	366	0	69.1	$106,995
42	Casey Mears	Dodge	21	19	17	366	0	59.4	$113,908
45	Kyle Petty	Dodge	40	17	18	366	0	58.0	$103,133
2	Kurt Busch	Dodge	10	15	19	366	0	81.4	$115,633
96	Tony Raines	Chevrolet	42	21	20	366	0	58.5	$76,725
9	Kasey Kahne	Dodge	1	18	21	366	41	90.0	$126,439
43	Bobby Labonte	Dodge	11	22	22	366	0	71.1	$113,136
07	Clint Bowyer*	Chevrolet	3	23	23	365	0	72.2	$84,400
88	Dale Jarrett	Ford	35	25	24	365	1	48.1	$106,750
40	David Stremme*	Dodge	4	24	25	365	0	70.5	$96,533
18	J.J. Yeley*	Chevrolet	26	26	26	365	0	54.8	$107,775
22	Dave Blaney	Dodge	32	27	27	364	1	44.9	$84,158
14	Sterling Marlin	Chevrolet	27	28	28	364	0	38.6	$81,322
38	Elliott Sadler	Ford	6	30	29	364	0	58.3	$99,483
32	Travis Kvapil	Chevrolet	18	29	30	364	0	47.3	$71,400
10	Scott Riggs	Dodge	19	31	31	363	0	46.0	$68,150
66	Jeff Green	Chevrolet	28	32	32	363	0	41.5	$75,975
4	Scott Wimmer	Chevrolet	38	33	33	363	0	35.0	$68,750
44	Terry Labonte	Chevrolet	43	34	34	361	0	34.9	$67,675
55	Michael Waltrip	Dodge	37	35	35	359	0	37.3	$67,450
49	Kevin Lepage	Dodge	41	36	36	353	0	32.0	$67,300
29	Kevin Harvick	Chevrolet	14	37	37	350	0	61.4	$104,036
19	Jeremy Mayfield	Dodge	30	38	38	346	0	54.9	$96,866
99	Carl Edwards	Ford	7	39	39	281	0	77.0	$86,550
95	Stanton Barrett	Chevrolet	34	40	40	255	0	27.4	$66,600
25	Brian Vickers	Chevrolet	8	42	41	246	0	45.5	$74,475
26	Jamie McMurray	Ford	15	41	42	223	0	47.6	$113,200
74	Derrike Cope	Dodge	33	43	43	11	0	23.3	$66,577

POINT STANDINGS

Rk.	Driver	Pts.	Diff.
1.	Jimmie Johnson	1,686	—
2.	Tony Stewart	1,593	-93
3.	Matt Kenseth	1,592	-94
4.	Mark Martin	1,487	-199
5.	Dale Earnhardt Jr.	1,460	-226
6.	Jeff Gordon	1,391	-295
7.	Kyle Busch	1,388	-298
8.	Kasey Kahne	1,379	-307
9.	Kevin Harvick	1,365	-321
10.	Jeff Burton	1,295	-391
11.	Casey Mears	1,280	-406
12.	Dale Jarrett	1,237	-449
13.	Denny Hamlin	1,219	-467
14.	Greg Biffle	1,189	-497
15.	Elliott Sadler	1,181	-505
16.	Clint Bowyer	1,181	-505
17.	Carl Edwards	1,161	-525
18.	Kurt Busch	1,146	-540
19.	Ryan Newman	1,118	-568
20.	Jamie McMurray	1,099	-587

*Rookie. **Time of race:** 3:42:36. **Average speed:** 135.127 mph. **Margin of victory:** .209 seconds.
Caution flags: 6 for 24 laps: 28-31 (Car 25—accident, backstretch); 70-73 (debris); 96-99 (Cars 38, 66—accident, Turn 2); 151-154 (Car 20—spin, Turn 4); 213-216 (debris); 249-252 (Car 38—spin, Turn 1).
Lead changes: 25 among 10 drivers. Kahne 1-29; Blaney 30; Kahne 31-35; Biffle 36-96; Kahne 97-103; Biffle 104-113; Kenseth 114-115; Biffle 116-126; Kenseth 127-150; Newman 151; Jarrett 152; Kenseth 153-190; Johnson 191-212; Biffle 213; Johnson 214-248; Biffle 249; Johnson 250-264; Biffle 265-301; Johnson 302-307; J. Gordon 308; Johnson 309-311; J. Gordon 312-315; Newman 316; Ky. Busch 317; R. Gordon 318; Biffle 319-367. **Fell out of race:** Edwards, Barrett, McMurray (engine); Cope (oil pressure).
Pole: Kasey Kahne, 169.013 mph. **Dropped to rear:** Marlin, T. Labonte (engine change). **Failed to qualify:** Chad Chaffin (61), Kenny Wallace (78), Carl Long (37), Chad Blount (34). **Estimated attendance:** 75,000.

Driver rating: An average of these categories—Win, finish, top 15 finish, average running position on lead lap, average speed under green, fastest lap, led most laps, lead-lap finish. Maximum points: 150 per race.

Concord, N.C. • 1.5-mile high-banked paved trioval • May 28, 2006 • 600 miles, 400 laps • Purse: $6,432,681

Car	Driver	Make	Start	40 laps to go	Finish	Laps run	Laps led	Rating	Winnings
9	Kasey Kahne	Dodge	9	9	1	400	158	136.9	$428,114
48	Jimmie Johnson	Chevrolet	3	8	2	400	24	128.8	$288,236
99	Carl Edwards	Ford	22	1	3	400	11	92.3	$201,050
6	Mark Martin	Ford	21	12	4	400	20	107.9	$166,100
17	Matt Kenseth	Ford	6	11	5	400	1	100.5	$180,366
31	Jeff Burton	Chevrolet	11	16	6	400	12	110.6	$154,520
16	Greg Biffle	Ford	7	10	7	400	20	111.1	$134,650
26	Jamie McMurray	Ford	33	6	8	400	0	80.6	$158,825
11	Denny Hamlin*	Chevrolet	8	7	9	400	25	102.1	$111,000
41	Reed Sorenson*	Dodge	23	19	10	400	0	83.0	$119,275
8	Dale Earnhardt Jr.	Chevrolet	34	14	11	400	0	92.5	$140,071
66	Jeff Green	Chevrolet	10	3	12	400	16	96.3	$131,033
10	Scott Riggs	Dodge	1	2	13	400	90	117.2	$147,075
15	Paul Menard	Chevrolet	36	15	14	400	0	73.2	$95,525
19	Jeremy Mayfield	Dodge	2	4	15	400	0	81.8	$134,116
7	Robby Gordon	Chevrolet	41	17	16	400	0	61.5	$98,075
43	Bobby Labonte	Dodge	5	13	17	400	1	74.1	$134,646
01	Joe Nemechek	Chevrolet	19	5	18	399	0	54.0	$121,245
07	Clint Bowyer*	Chevrolet	15	22	19	399	0	59.1	$101,725
18	J.J. Yeley*	Chevrolet	4	23	20	399	0	79.4	$132,575
1	Martin Truex Jr.*	Chevrolet	27	18	21	399	0	60.7	$115,833
32	Travis Kvapil	Chevrolet	31	24	22	399	1	54.5	$104,908
42	Casey Mears	Dodge	30	20	23	398	0	78.2	$124,933
70	Johnny Sauter	Chevrolet	14	28	24	398	0	79.0	$85,750
45	Kyle Petty	Dodge	39	25	25	397	0	50.1	$108,308
21	Ken Schrader	Ford	40	31	26	397	0	42.6	$114,664
4	Scott Wimmer	Chevrolet	38	30	27	397	1	39.6	$86,825
14	Sterling Marlin	Chevrolet	16	29	28	396	0	53.5	$95,847
78	Kenny Wallace	Chevrolet	35	33	29	396	0	32.6	$83,175
38	Elliott Sadler	Ford	26	26	30	396	1	34.0	$113,958
40	David Stremme*	Dodge	25	27	31	396	0	62.6	$90,900
22	Dave Blaney	Dodge	29	32	32	395	0	45.5	$82,775
44	Terry Labonte	Chevrolet	24	34	33	393	0	44.4	$83,600
29	Kevin Harvick	Chevrolet	12	35	34	373	0	69.3	$119,461
12	Ryan Newman	Dodge	18	36	35	369	0	45.6	$127,808
24	Jeff Gordon	Chevrolet	13	21	36	360	18	64.2	$133,111
25	Brian Vickers	Chevrolet	17	38	37	331	0	52.4	$90,050
5	Kyle Busch	Chevrolet	28	37	38	313	0	79.0	$99,935
2	Kurt Busch	Dodge	20	40	39	290	0	49.0	$122,858
96	Tony Raines	Chevrolet	42	39	40	264	0	30.9	$81,715
55	Michael Waltrip	Dodge	43	41	41	116	1	25.9	$81,605
20	Tony Stewart	Chevrolet	32	42	42	32	0	31.9	$135,456
88	Dale Jarrett	Ford	37	43	43	0	0	26.8	$113,817

POINT STANDINGS

Rk.	Driver	Pts.	Diff.
1.	Jimmie Johnson	1,861	—
2.	Matt Kenseth	1,752	-109
3.	Mark Martin	1,652	-209
4.	Tony Stewart	1,630	-231
5.	Dale Earnhardt Jr.	1,590	-271
6.	Kasey Kahne	1,569	-292
7.	Jeff Gordon	1,451	-410
8.	Jeff Burton	1,450	-411
9.	Kevin Harvick	1,426	-435
10.	Kyle Busch	1,412	-449
11.	Casey Mears	1,374	-487
12.	Denny Hamlin	1,362	-499
13.	Greg Biffle	1,340	-521
14.	Carl Edwards	1,331	-530
15.	Clint Bowyer	1,287	-574
16.	Dale Jarrett	1,271	-590
17.	Elliott Sadler	1,259	-602
18.	Jamie McMurray	1,241	-620
19.	Kurt Busch	1,192	-669
20.	Reed Sorenson	1,187	-674

*Rookie. **Time of race:** 4:39:25. **Average speed:** 128.840 mph. **Margin of victory:** 2.114 seconds. **Caution flags:** 15 for 67 laps: 2-4 (Car 88—accident, Turn 3); 34-39 (Car 20—accident, Turn 2); 49-52 (Car 12—accident, Turn 4); 67-70 (Car 2—accident, Turn 2); 93-96 (debris); 113-115 (Car 15—spin, Turn 4); 130-134 (debris); 145-146 (Car 99—accident, Turn 2); 161-165 (Car 25—accident, Turn 4); 203-209 (debris); 236-239 (debris); 249-253 (Car 70—accident, Turn 1); 306-309 (debris); 314-320 (Cars 5, 42—accident, frontstretch); 364-367 (Car 24—accident, Turn 4). **Lead changes:** 37 among 16 drivers: Riggs 1-35; E. Sadler 36; Waltrip 37; Riggs 38-49; J. Gordon 50-67; Kvapil 68; Johnson 69-92; Biffle 93; Riggs 94-96; Green 97-109; Martin 110; Green 111-113; Martin 114-130; Burton 131; Riggs 132-144; Biffle 145-161; Wimmer 162; Hamlin 163-180; Kahne 181-200; Hamlin 201-203; Biffle 204; Kahne 205-235; Biffle 236; Hamlin 237-240; Kahne 241-248; Riggs 249; Kahne 250-289; Riggs 290-291; Kenseth 292; Kahne 293-305; Riggs 306; Burton 307-317; B. Labonte 318; Martin 319-320; Kahne 321-336; Riggs 337-359; Edwards 360-370; Kahne 371-400. **Fell out of race:** J. Gordon, Ky. Busch, Stewart, Jarrett (accident); Raines (engine); Waltrip (brakes). **Pole:** Scott Riggs, 187.865 mph. **Dropped to rear:** R. Gordon (engine change); Waltrip (driver change). **Failed to qualify:** Kevin Lepage (49); Hermie Sadler (00), Chad Chaffin (61); Michael Waltrip (55); Stanton Barrett (95); Mike Garvey (51); Chad Blount (34), Carl Long (37), Kirk Shelmerdine (27), Kertus Davis (72). **Estimated attendance:** 175,000.

Driver rating: An average of these categories—Win, finish, top 15 finish, average running position on lead lap, average speed under green, fastest lap, led most laps, lead-lap finish. Maximum points: 150 per race.

>> NEIGHBORHOOD EXCELLENCE 400
PRESENTED BY BANK OF AMERICA

Dover International Speedway

Dover, Del. • 1-mile banked concrete oval • June 4, 2006 • 400 miles, 400 laps • Purse: $5,667,009

Car	Driver	Make	Start	40 laps to go	Finish	Laps run	Laps led	Rating	Winnings
17	Matt Kenseth	Ford	19	5	1	400	83	132.5	$323,591
26	Jamie McMurray	Ford	9	1	2	400	95	96.5	$239,600
29	Kevin Harvick	Chevrolet	5	2	3	400	0	107.4	$198,586
31	Jeff Burton	Chevrolet	17	3	4	400	48	125.6	$164,245
5	Kyle Busch	Chevrolet	30	4	5	400	22	112.5	$132,925
48	Jimmie Johnson	Chevrolet	42	7	6	400	0	82.6	$153,261
9	Kasey Kahne	Dodge	26	6	7	400	0	98.3	$135,039
16	Greg Biffle	Ford	20	9	8	400	2	103.6	$112,800
6	Mark Martin	Ford	6	14	9	400	39	116.7	$107,950
8	Dale Earnhardt Jr.	Chevrolet	11	8	10	400	1	92.0	$130,241
11	Denny Hamlin*	Chevrolet	7	11	11	400	0	84.5	$94,200
24	Jeff Gordon	Chevrolet	3	13	12	400	81	110.0	$133,011
43	Bobby Labonte	Dodge	28	17	13	400	0	83.5	$126,136
12	Ryan Newman	Dodge	1	12	14	400	12	100.5	$134,533
99	Carl Edwards	Ford	25	15	15	400	2	75.9	$104,125
2	Kurt Busch	Dodge	4	10	16	400	0	76.1	$122,658
07	Clint Bowyer*	Chevrolet	22	16	17	400	0	85.8	$93,150
19	Jeremy Mayfield	Dodge	2	19	18	400	14	82.5	$120,316
41	Reed Sorenson*	Dodge	39	18	19	400	0	63.6	$91,600
10	Scott Riggs	Dodge	15	21	20	400	0	65.1	$85,200
42	Casey Mears	Dodge	34	20	21	400	0	71.9	$116,983
1	Martin Truex Jr.*	Chevrolet	21	22	22	399	0	67.9	$107,783
25	Brian Vickers	Chevrolet	24	23	23	399	0	63.3	$89,925
88	Dale Jarrett	Ford	40	24	24	399	0	47.0	$112,400
20	Tony Stewart	Chevrolet	10	25	25	398	0	59.7	$130,786
96	Tony Raines	Chevrolet	32	26	26	398	0	45.9	$79,100
45	Kyle Petty	Dodge	35	32	27	398	0	46.8	$102,608
66	Jeff Green	Chevrolet	12	27	28	398	0	55.8	$99,958
32	Travis Kvapil	Chevrolet	27	28	29	398	0	46.0	$89,308
22	Dave Blaney	Dodge	31	31	30	398	0	41.0	$87,047
14	Sterling Marlin	Chevrolet	23	29	31	398	0	52.9	$74,350
55	Michael Waltrip	Dodge	33	33	32	397	0	41.8	$74,200
21	Ken Schrader	Ford	38	30	33	397	0	44.1	$102,214
4	Scott Wimmer	Chevrolet	43	34	34	396	0	35.3	$73,850
01	Joe Nemechek	Chevrolet	13	35	35	396	0	47.5	$99,995
7	Robby Gordon	Chevrolet	41	36	36	394	0	33.2	$73,525
74	Derrike Cope	Dodge	36	37	37	393	0	31.9	$73,375
78	Kenny Wallace	Chevrolet	37	38	38	378	0	26.8	$73,265
49	Kevin Lepage	Dodge	18	39	39	299	0	34.9	$73,155
38	Elliott Sadler	Ford	8	40	40	296	0	71.8	$100,933
40	David Stremme*	Dodge	29	41	41	290	1	45.7	$80,895
18	J.J. Yeley*	Chevrolet	14	42	42	286	0	68.5	$107,385
00	Hermie Sadler	Chevrolet	16	43	43	136	0	25.8	$73,033

POINT STANDINGS

Rk.	Driver	Pts.	Diff.
1.	Jimmie Johnson	2,011	—
2.	Matt Kenseth	1,937	-74
3.	Mark Martin	1,795	-216
4.	Dale Earnhardt Jr.	1,729	-282
5.	Tony Stewart	1,718	-293
6.	Kasey Kahne	1,715	-296
7.	Jeff Burton	1,615	-396
8.	Kevin Harvick	1,591	-420
9.	Jeff Gordon	1,583	-428
10.	Kyle Busch	1,572	-439
11.	Denny Hamlin	1,492	-519
12.	Greg Biffle	1,487	-524
13.	Casey Mears	1,474	-537
14.	Carl Edwards	1,454	-557
15.	Jamie McMurray	1,421	-590
16.	Clint Bowyer	1,399	-612
17.	Dale Jarrett	1,362	-649
18.	Kurt Busch	1,307	-704
19.	Ryan Newman	1,302	-709
20.	Elliott Sadler	1,302	-709

*Rookie. **Time of race:** 3:38:27. **Average speed:** 109.865 mph. **Margin of victory:** .787 seconds. **Caution flags:** 9 for 51 laps: 37-41 (Car 96—spin, Turn 4); 116-120 (debris); 265-269 (debris); 275-278 (Cars 40, 48—accident, Turn 4); 285-288 (Car 18—accident, Turn 2); 291-295 (Car 18—accident, Turn 1); 301-312 (oil on track); 321-327 (oil in track); 346-349 (Car 7—spin, Turn 4). **Lead changes:** 23 among 12 drivers: Newman 1-12; Mayfield 13-26; Martin 27-37; J. Gordon 38-115; Kenseth 116; Stremme 117; J. Gordon 118-120; Kenseth 121-163; Burton 164-175; Kenseth 176-189; Burton 190-193; Kenseth 194-200; Burton 201-209; Ky. Busch 210; Biffle 211-212; Edwards 213-214; Burton 215-237; Martin 238-265; Earnhardt 266; Kenseth 267-279; Ky. Busch 280-300; Martin 301; McMurray 302-396; Kenseth 397-400. **Fell out of race:** Lepage (engine); E. Sadler, Yeley (accident); Stremme (overheating); H. Sadler (transmission). **Pole:** Ryan Newman, 154.633 mph. **Dropped to rear:** McMurray (engine change); Stewart (driver change). **Failed to qualify:** Stanton Barrett (95), Carl Long (34), Chad Chaffin (61), Donnie Neuenberger (52). **Estimated attendance:** 145,000.

Driver rating: An average of these categories—Win, finish, top 15 finish, average running position on lead lap, average speed under green, fastest lap, led most laps, lead-lap finish. Maximum points: 150 per race.

Pocono Raceway

Long Pond, Pa. • 2.5-mile banked triangular paved • June 11, 2006 • 500 miles, 200 laps • Purse: $4,841,521

Car	Driver	Make	Start	20 laps to go	Finish	Laps run	Laps led	Rating	Winnings
11	Denny Hamlin*	Chevrolet	1	1	1	200	83	137.1	$220,100
2	Kurt Busch	Dodge	2	3	2	200	31	127.1	$193,258
20	Tony Stewart	Chevrolet	18	4	3	200	6	116.4	$182,311
25	Brian Vickers	Chevrolet	4	5	4	200	19	115.9	$117,850
17	Matt Kenseth	Ford	25	6	5	200	3	99.5	$141,641
16	Greg Biffle	Ford	7	2	6	200	34	111.6	$106,425
9	Kasey Kahne	Dodge	3	9	7	200	1	102.0	$117,189
10	Scott Riggs	Dodge	17	8	8	200	1	79.2	$80,125
31	Jeff Burton	Chevrolet	5	15	9	200	11	113.4	$104,520
48	Jimmie Johnson	Chevrolet	10	12	10	200	0	90.1	$123,761
12	Ryan Newman	Dodge	14	7	11	200	1	87.7	$114,933
43	Bobby Labonte	Dodge	23	14	12	200	0	84.7	$110,911
29	Kevin Harvick	Chevrolet	12	16	13	200	0	84.2	$109,661
8	Dale Earnhardt Jr.	Chevrolet	11	11	14	200	0	96.3	$104,966
18	J.J. Yeley*	Chevrolet	24	19	15	200	0	72.5	$104,500
96	Tony Raines	Chevrolet	31	23	16	200	0	66.7	$68,275
6	Mark Martin	Ford	20	13	17	200	0	77.5	$82,275
26	Jamie McMurray	Ford	8	20	18	200	0	70.0	$110,900
32	Travis Kvapil	Chevrolet	38	22	19	200	1	50.5	$85,683
38	Elliott Sadler	Ford	13	21	20	200	0	68.1	$97,908
07	Clint Bowyer*	Chevrolet	42	18	21	200	8	71.3	$79,875
5	Kyle Busch	Chevrolet	9	10	22	200	0	87.1	$81,175
19	Jeremy Mayfield	Dodge	26	24	23	200	0	58.9	$97,266
1	Martin Truex Jr.*	Chevrolet	15	25	24	199	0	72.1	$90,258
99	Carl Edwards	Ford	40	26	25	199	1	85.2	$82,775
40	David Stremme*	Dodge	32	28	26	199	0	53.7	$87,783
22	Dave Blaney	Dodge	30	27	27	199	0	52.2	$77,033
55	Michael Waltrip	Dodge	36	31	28	198	0	37.7	$74,672
01	Joe Nemechek	Chevrolet	21	29	29	198	0	56.9	$91,320
21	Ken Schrader	Ford	29	30	30	197	0	44.2	$92,039
49	Kevin Lepage	Dodge	41	33	31	197	0	40.8	$61,675
78	Jimmy Spencer	Chevrolet	34	34	32	197	0	33.0	$61,525
61	Chad Chaffin	Ford	37	35	33	196	0	30.9	$62,275
24	Jeff Gordon	Chevrolet	6	17	34	189	0	74.9	$109,461
7	Robby Gordon	Chevrolet	28	36	35	186	0	48.9	$60,975
41	Reed Sorenson*	Dodge	35	37	36	183	0	42.5	$68,750
66	Jeff Green	Chevrolet	19	32	37	181	0	50.4	$68,575
88	Dale Jarrett	Ford	27	38	38	181	0	39.1	$92,525
44	Terry Labonte	Chevrolet	39	39	39	118	0	29.0	$60,325
45	Kyle Petty	Dodge	33	40	40	68	0	34.6	$68,175
51	Mike Garvey	Chevrolet	43	41	41	67	0	30.4	$60,035
14	Sterling Marlin	Chevrolet	16	42	42	18	0	46.1	$59,885
42	Casey Mears	Dodge	22	43	43	1	0	28.3	$94,255

POINT STANDINGS

Rk.	Driver	Pts.	Diff.
1.	Jimmie Johnson	2,145	—
2.	Matt Kenseth	2,097	-48
3.	Mark Martin	1,907	-238
4.	Tony Stewart	1,888	-257
5.	Kasey Kahne	1,866	-279
6.	Dale Earnhardt Jr.	1,850	-295
7.	Jeff Burton	1,758	-387
8.	Kevin Harvick	1,715	-430
9.	Denny Hamlin	1,682	-463
10.	Kyle Busch	1,669	-476
11.	Jeff Gordon	1,644	-501
12.	Greg Biffle	1,642	-503
13.	Carl Edwards	1,547	-598
14.	Jamie McMurray	1,530	-615
15.	Casey Mears	1,508	-637
16.	Clint Bowyer	1,504	-641
17.	Kurt Busch	1,482	-663
18.	Ryan Newman	1,437	-708
19.	Dale Jarrett	1,411	-734
20.	Elliott Sadler	1,405	-740

*Rookie. **Time of race:** 3:47:52. **Average speed:** 131.656 mph. **Margin of victory:** 1.328 seconds. **Caution flags:** 7 for 28 laps: 2-4 (Cars 42, 10—accident Turn 3); 22-24 (Car 41—accident); 52-57 (debris); 63-66 (debris); 70-73 (Car 45—accident, Turn 2); 142-145 (debris); 192-195 (Car 24—accident Turn 1). **Note:** On Lap 193 (13 minutes, 9 seconds), the race was red-flagged for track repair and clean-up. **Lead changes:** 25 among 13 drivers: Hamlin 1-21; Newman 22; Hamlin 23-50; Ku. Busch 51-52; Kvapil 53; Ku. Busch 54-58; Burton 59-69; Vickers 75-93; Ku. Busch 94; Edwards 95; Kahne 96; Stewart 97-102; Hamlin 103-104; Ku. Busch 105-120; Biffle 121-130; Ku. Busch 131; Hamlin 132-137; Kenseth 138-139; Biffle 140-163; Hamlin 164-165; Ku. Busch 166; Kenseth 167; Riggs 168; Bowyer 169-176; Hamlin 177-200. **Fell out of race:** J. Gordon, Petty, Mears (accident); Green (rear end); T. Labonte (brakes); Garvey (suspension); Marlin (engine). **Pole:** Denny Hamlin, 169.638 mph. **Failed to qualify:** Scott Wimmer (4), Derrike Cope (74), Stanton Barrett (95), Greg Sacks (34), Brent Sherman (72). **Estimated attendance:** 100,000.

Driver rating: An average of these categories—Win, finish, top 15 finish, average running position on lead lap, average speed under green, fastest lap, led most laps, lead-lap finish. Maximum points: 150 per race.

>> 3M PERFORMANCE 400

PRESENTED BY POST-IT PICTURE PAPER   race **15** of 36

Michigan International Speedway

Brooklyn, Mich. • 2-mile banked paved oval • June 18, 2006 • 400 miles, 200 laps • Purse: $5,037,040

Car	Driver	Make	Start	20 laps to go	Finish	Laps run	Laps led	Rating	Winnings
9	Kasey Kahne	Dodge	1	4	1	129	19	120.8	$205,364
99	Carl Edwards	Ford	31	1	2	129	25	115.5	$147,200
8	Dale Earnhardt Jr.	Chevrolet	6	3	3	129	3	121.5	$146,991
16	Greg Biffle	Ford	10	2	4	129	11	118.6	$115,300
41	Reed Sorenson*	Dodge	25	11	5	129	3	95.4	$98,350
48	Jimmie Johnson	Chevrolet	4	5	6	129	0	114.2	$128,386
42	Casey Mears	Dodge	37	7	7	129	0	96.4	$122,183
24	Jeff Gordon	Chevrolet	2	6	8	129	50	125.7	$137,436
2	Kurt Busch	Dodge	13	10	9	129	0	85.0	$117,583
29	Kevin Harvick	Chevrolet	19	8	10	129	0	96.2	$119,936
31	Jeff Burton	Chevrolet	12	12	11	129	0	98.3	$109,295
11	Denny Hamlin*	Chevrolet	21	16	12	129	0	86.0	$78,925
17	Matt Kenseth	Ford	20	17	13	129	0	75.7	$121,416
5	Kyle Busch	Chevrolet	15	15	14	129	9	86.8	$91,725
12	Ryan Newman	Dodge	42	21	15	129	0	75.3	$118,683
1	Martin Truex Jr.*	Chevrolet	11	20	16	129	0	80.7	$103,583
25	Brian Vickers	Chevrolet	3	9	17	129	7	99.2	$96,175
7	Robby Gordon	Chevrolet	24	25	18	129	0	65.3	$76,025
40	David Stremme*	Dodge	30	18	19	129	0	67.5	$99,783
88	Dale Jarrett	Ford	40	19	20	129	0	58.5	$110,100
32	Travis Kvapil	Chevrolet	23	23	21	129	0	68.7	$89,008
38	Elliott Sadler	Ford	32	29	22	129	0	51.7	$102,458
26	Jamie McMurray	Ford	41	31	23	129	0	58.0	$118,675
14	Sterling Marlin	Chevrolet	26	24	24	129	0	63.7	$85,658
55	Michael Waltrip	Dodge	28	33	25	129	0	46.1	$83,622
01	Joe Nemechek	Chevrolet	7	36	26	129	0	45.6	$99,670
6	Mark Martin	Ford	8	14	27	129	0	74.0	$88,035
43	Bobby Labonte	Dodge	5	13	28	129	0	74.7	$109,821
10	Scott Riggs	Dodge	16	22	29	129	0	63.8	$72,675
22	Dave Blaney	Dodge	33	26	30	129	0	49.9	$72,600
4	Scott Wimmer	Chevrolet	36	32	31	129	0	39.0	$69,450
23	Bill Lester	Dodge	34	35	32	129	0	32.2	$69,375
66	Jeff Green	Chevrolet	27	27	33	129	0	43.0	$77,300
49	Kevin Lepage	Dodge	29	28	34	129	1	42.6	$70,150
45	Kyle Petty	Dodge	35	30	35	129	1	37.3	$77,050
19	Jeremy Mayfield	Dodge	18	34	36	129	0	40.1	$98,991
34	Mike Skinner	Chevrolet	43	37	37	129	0	28.2	$68,950
96	Tony Raines	Chevrolet	39	38	38	126	0	47.5	$68,850
07	Clint Bowyer*	Chevrolet	9	39	39	86	0	43.7	$76,805
18	J.J. Yeley*	Chevrolet	14	40	40	80	0	58.4	$103,340
20	Tony Stewart	Chevrolet	17	41	41	58	0	40.5	$122,666
21	Ken Schrader	Ford	22	42	42	30	0	51.7	$95,904
74	Derrike Cope	Dodge	38	43	43	12	0	24.8	$68,127

POINT STANDINGS

Rk.	Driver	Pts.	Diff.
1.	Jimmie Johnson	2,295	—
2.	Matt Kenseth	2,221	-74
3.	Kasey Kahne	2,051	-244
4.	Dale Earnhardt Jr.	2,020	-275
5.	Mark Martin	1,989	-306
6.	Tony Stewart	1,928	-367
7.	Jeff Burton	1,888	-407
8.	Kevin Harvick	1,849	-446
9.	Denny Hamlin	1,809	-486
10.	Greg Biffle	1,807	-488
11.	Jeff Gordon	1,796	-499
12.	Kyle Busch	1,795	-500
13.	Carl Edwards	1,722	-573
14.	Casey Mears	1,654	-641
15.	Jamie McMurray	1,624	-671
16.	Kurt Busch	1,620	-675
17.	Ryan Newman	1,555	-740
18.	Clint Bowyer	1,550	-745
19.	Dale Jarrett	1,514	-781
20.	Reed Sorenson	1,508	-787

*Rookie. **Time of race:** 2:10:19. **Average speed:** 118.788 mph. **Margin of victory:** Under caution. **Caution flags:** 9 for 37 laps: 4-6 (Car 7—spin, Turn 2); 11-17 (rain); 23-25 (Cars 20, 66—accident, Turn 4); 32-35 (Cars 01, 18, 21—accident, backstretch); 55-58 (rain); 68-70 (Car 17—spin, Turn 2); 81-84 (debris); 112-115 (debris); 125-129 (rain). **Lead changes:** 17 among 10 drivers: Kahne 1; J. Gordon 2-22; Ky. Busch 23-31; Kahne 32-35; J. Gordon 36-45; Kahne 46; J. Gordon 47-55; Petty 56; J. Gordon 57-59; Earnhardt 60-61; J. Gordon 62-68; Biffle 69-79; Earnhardt 80; Vickers 81-87; Edwards 88-112; Lepage 113; Sorenson 114-116; Kahne 117-129. **Note:** Race shortened by rain. **Fell out of race:** Stewart, Schrader (accident); Cope (overheating). **Pole:** Kasey Kahne, 185.644 mph. **Dropped to rear:** Newman (transmission change). **Failed to qualify:** Carl Long (37), Mike Garvey (51), Chad Chaffin (61), Jimmy Spencer (78). **Estimated attendance:** 145,000.

Driver rating: An average of these categories—Win, finish, top 15 finish, average running position on lead lap, average speed under green, fastest lap, led most laps, lead-lap finish. Maximum points: 150 per race.

Sonoma, Calif. • 1.99-mile paved road course • June 25, 2006 • 218 miles, 110 laps • Purse: $5,371.771

Car	Driver	Make	Start	11 laps to go	Finish	Laps run	Laps led	Rating	Winnings
24	Jeff Gordon	Chevrolet	11	1	1	110	44	137.0	$325,661
12	Ryan Newman	Dodge	4	3	2	110	11	127.8	$219,758
96	Terry Labonte	Chevrolet	37	2	3	110	17	86.5	$155,825
16	Greg Biffle	Ford	7	4	4	110	0	113.5	$147,300
2	Kurt Busch	Dodge	1	5	5	110	29	121.8	$145,433
99	Carl Edwards	Ford	20	8	6	110	0	89.2	$116,800
31	Jeff Burton	Chevrolet	13	10	7	110	0	95.9	$122,120
38	Elliott Sadler	Ford	24	9	8	110	0	86.6	$118,583
60	Boris Said	Ford	5	6	9	110	1	107.7	$83,825
48	Jimmie Johnson	Chevrolet	16	11	10	110	2	98.4	$144,186
5	Kyle Busch	Chevrolet	19	7	11	110	0	88.8	$97,575
11	Denny Hamlin*	Chevrolet	40	15	12	110	0	74.5	$85,075
6	Mark Martin	Ford	8	12	13	110	0	93.4	$96,725
25	Brian Vickers	Chevrolet	42	14	14	110	0	77.7	$89,025
1	Martin Truex Jr.*	Chevrolet	39	13	15	110	0	75.2	$108,283
07	Clint Bowyer*	Chevrolet	28	23	16	110	0	63.2	$87,875
17	Matt Kenseth	Ford	9	24	17	110	0	83.5	$120,791
26	Jamie McMurray	Ford	2	17	18	110	0	61.3	$121,825
66	Jeff Green	Chevrolet	23	25	19	110	0	54.0	$102,833
42	Casey Mears	Dodge	34	18	20	110	0	53.6	$113,708
45	Kyle Petty	Dodge	33	21	21	110	0	47.1	$98,258
19	Jeremy Mayfield	Dodge	32	27	22	110	0	53.0	$105,441
55	Michael Waltrip	Dodge	35	31	23	110	0	43.2	$87,433
29	Kevin Harvick	Chevrolet	3	20	24	110	5	89.7	$111,611
01	Joe Nemechek	Chevrolet	10	26	25	110	0	72.0	$100,295
8	Dale Earnhardt Jr.	Chevrolet	26	32	26	110	0	66.3	$107,916
10	Scott Riggs	Dodge	25	34	27	110	0	38.1	$72,300
20	Tony Stewart	Chevrolet	12	16	28	110	1	95.5	$122,561
41	Reed Sorenson*	Dodge	41	30	29	110	0	37.9	$79,500
40	Scott Pruett	Dodge	27	33	30	110	0	57.1	$89,422
9	Kasey Kahne	Dodge	6	22	31	110	0	60.9	$110,914
72	David Gilliland	Dodge	31	36	32	108	0	36.0	$68,050
18	J.J. Yeley*	Chevrolet	38	19	33	104	0	49.2	$105,965
88	Dale Jarrett	Ford	22	29	34	104	0	45.5	$99,905
43	Bobby Labonte	Dodge	21	28	35	104	0	45.5	$104,656
4	P.J. Jones	Chevrolet	15	35	36	101	0	64.9	$67,610
32	Ron Fellows	Chevrolet	17	37	37	100	0	65.3	$67,475
02	Brandon Ash	Dodge	43	40	38	85	0	32.2	$67,360
22	Dave Blaney	Dodge	36	38	39	79	0	47.0	$67,250
7	Robby Gordon	Chevrolet	14	39	40	74	0	84.4	$67,125
21	Ken Schrader	Ford	18	41	41	0	0	31.9	$94,214
14	Sterling Marlin	Chevrolet	29	42	42	0	0	30.4	$66,900
27	Tom Hubert	Ford	30	43	43	0	0	28.9	$67,116

POINT STANDINGS

Rk.	Driver	Pts.	Diff.
1.	Jimmie Johnson	2,434	—
2.	Matt Kenseth	2,333	-101
3.	Kasey Kahne	2,121	-313
4.	Mark Martin	2,113	-321
5.	Dale Earnhardt Jr.	2,105	-329
6.	Jeff Burton	2,034	-400
7.	Tony Stewart	2,012	-422
8.	Jeff Gordon	1,986	-448
9.	Greg Biffle	1,967	-467
10.	Kevin Harvick	1,945	-489
11.	Denny Hamlin	1,936	-498
12.	Kyle Busch	1,925	-509
13.	Carl Edwards	1,872	-562
14.	Kurt Busch	1,780	-654
15.	Casey Mears	1,757	-677
16.	Jamie McMurray	1,733	-701
17.	Ryan Newman	1,730	-704
18.	Clint Bowyer	1,665	-769
19.	Elliott Sadler	1,644	-790
20.	Brian Vickers	1,619	-815

*Rookie. **Time of race:** 2:57:36. **Average speed:** 73.953 mph. **Margin of victory:** 1.250 seconds. **Caution flags:** 7 cautions for 12 laps. 2-3 (Cars 07, 14, 21, 27, 42—accident, Turn 8); 40-41 (Car 18—spin, Turn 3); 48 (Car 32—stalled on track); 60-61 (Car 01—spin, Turn 11); 98 (debris); 101-102 (debris); 106-107 (Cars 18, 41, 43, 88—accident, Turn 2). **Note:** On Lap 2 (12 minutes, 1 second) and Lap 105 (12 minutes, 40 seconds), the race was red-flagged for track clean-up. **Lead changes:** 9 among 8 drivers: Ku. Busch 1-29; Stewart 30; Said 31; Johnson 32; Harvick 33-37; Newman 38-48; J. Gordon 49-69; Johnson 70; T. Labonte 71-87; J. Gordon 88-110. **Fell out of race:** Yeley, Jarrett, B. Labonte, R. Gordon, Schrader, Marlin, Hubert (accident); Jones (rear end); Blaney (drive shaft). **Pole:** Kurt Busch, 93.055 mph. **Dropped to rear:** Truex (engine change). **Failed to qualify:** Johnny Miller (34), Chris Cook (49), Travis Kvapil (78), Stanton Barrett (95), Brian Simo (61). **Estimated attendance:** 102,000.

Driver rating: An average of these categories—Win, finish, top 15 finish, average running position on lead lap, average speed under green, fastest lap, led most laps, lead-lap finish. Maximum points: 150 per race.

Daytona International Speedway

Daytona Beach, Fla. • 2.5-mile high-banked paved trioval • July 1, 2006 • 400 miles, 160 laps • Purse: $6,074,820

Car	Driver	Make	Start	16 laps to go	Finish	Laps run	Laps led	Rating	Winnings
20	Tony Stewart	Chevrolet	2	1	1	160	86	137.0	$369,586
5	Kyle Busch	Chevrolet	14	9	2	160	0	108.9	$210,525
2	Kurt Busch	Dodge	16	6	3	160	0	101.2	$196,233
60	Boris Said	Ford	1	29	4	160	9	69.7	$143,900
17	Matt Kenseth	Ford	10	2	5	160	1	114.1	$165,391
38	Elliott Sadler	Ford	13	7	6	160	0	107.4	$144,083
42	Casey Mears	Dodge	40	35	7	160	0	56.5	$150,833
26	Jamie McMurray	Ford	26	14	8	160	0	96.6	$148,475
29	Kevin Harvick	Chevrolet	32	13	9	160	1	90.6	$140,386
07	Clint Bowyer*	Chevrolet	30	10	10	160	0	83.5	$114,875
12	Ryan Newman	Dodge	23	17	11	160	0	86.5	$140,083
21	Ken Schrader	Ford	31	23	12	160	0	79.6	$125,464
8	Dale Earnhardt Jr.	Chevrolet	35	19	13	160	8	82.1	$134,716
7	Robby Gordon	Chevrolet	25	24	14	160	4	68.1	$97,475
31	Jeff Burton	Chevrolet	39	20	15	160	0	72.4	$122,920
40	David Stremme*	Dodge	3	21	16	160	2	62.0	$121,658
11	Denny Hamlin*	Chevrolet	6	16	17	160	0	72.5	$93,700
25	Brian Vickers	Chevrolet	17	15	18	160	13	87.5	$100,875
01	Joe Nemechek	Chevrolet	5	27	19	160	0	64.1	$118,370
10	Scott Riggs	Dodge	28	36	20	160	0	48.3	$93,425
96	Tony Raines	Chevrolet	21	25	21	160	0	54.6	$90,900
88	Dale Jarrett	Ford	7	22	22	160	1	66.9	$121,700
9	Mike Wallace	Ford	18	26	23	160	0	66.7	$86,700
14	Sterling Marlin	Chevrolet	20	30	24	160	0	51.7	$104,383
9	Kasey Kahne	Dodge	38	34	25	160	0	56.5	$121,689
66	Jeff Green	Chevrolet	36	31	26	160	0	45.3	$109,383
22	Dave Blaney	Dodge	41	32	27	160	0	56.2	$97,833
45	Kyle Petty	Dodge	33	33	28	160	0	40.5	$102,597
1	Martin Truex Jr.*	Chevrolet	8	38	29	160	3	70.3	$90,325
32	Travis Kvapil	Chevrolet	15	37	30	160	0	37.2	$82,650
16	Greg Biffle	Ford	12	12	31	160	1	87.6	$102,175
48	Jimmie Johnson	Chevrolet	9	5	32	160	0	92.4	$130,386
6	Mark Martin	Ford	24	11	33	160	0	80.8	$100,675
41	Reed Sorenson*	Dodge	37	28	34	160	1	49.9	$89,600
61	Chad Chaffin	Chevrolet	43	39	35	159	0	30.7	$81,450
19	Jeremy Mayfield	Dodge	42	40	36	159	0	34.1	$111,291
18	J.J. Yeley*	Chevrolet	11	18	37	158	1	57.1	$115,700
55	Michael Waltrip	Dodge	19	41	38	158	0	37.2	$80,975
99	Carl Edwards	Ford	29	8	39	156	2	87.1	$100,650
24	Jeff Gordon	Chevrolet	4	4	40	154	27	94.7	$129,036
00	Hermie Sadler	Ford	22	42	41	154	0	25.4	$80,575
43	Bobby Labonte	Dodge	34	3	42	146	0	70.8	$117,411
27	Kirk Shelmerdine	Chevrolet	27	43	43	28	0	25.3	$80,681

POINT STANDINGS

Rk.	Driver	Pts.	Diff.
1.	Jimmie Johnson	2,501	—
2.	Matt Kenseth	2,493	-8
3.	Dale Earnhardt Jr.	2,234	-267
4.	Kasey Kahne	2,209	-292
5.	Tony Stewart	2,202	-299
6.	Mark Martin	2,177	-324
7.	Jeff Burton	2,152	-349
8.	Kyle Busch	2,095	-406
9.	Kevin Harvick	2,088	-413
10.	Denny Hamlin	2,048	-453
11.	Greg Biffle	2,042	-459
12.	Jeff Gordon	2,034	-467
13.	Kurt Busch	1,945	-556
14.	Carl Edwards	1,923	-578
15.	Casey Mears	1,903	-598
16.	Jamie McMurray	1,875	-626
17.	Ryan Newman	1,860	-641
18.	Clint Bowyer	1,799	-702
19.	Elliott Sadler	1,794	-707
20.	Brian Vickers	1,733	-768

*Rookie. **Time of race:** 2:36:43. **Average speed:** 153.143 mph. **Margin of victory:** Under caution. **Caution flags:** 6 for 19 laps: 9-11 (debris); 17-20 (Car 31—spin, Turn 2); 89-92 (debris); 148-151 (Cars 43, 48—accident, Turn 3); 155-157 (Cars 6, 16, 18, 24, 99—accident, Turn 2); 160-160 (debris). **Lead changes:** 29 among 15 drivers: Said—pole; Stewart 1-9; Truex 10-12; Biffle 13; J. Gordon 14-24; Kenseth 25; J. Gordon 26-32; Stewart 33-44; Edwards 45; R. Gordon 46-48; Jarrett 49; R. Gordon 50; Sorenson 51; Stremme 52; Stewart 53-80; Edwards 81; Earnhardt 82-85; Stremme 86; J. Gordon 87-89; Earnhardt 90-93; Yeley 94; J. Gordon 95-99; Vickers 100-110; Stewart 111-123; J. Gordon 124; Harvick 125; Vickers 126-127; Stewart 128-148; Said 149-157; Stewart 158-160. **Fell out of race:** J. Gordon, B. Labonte (accident); Shelmerdine (rear end). **Pole:** Boris Said, 186.143 mph. **Dropped to rear:** Waltrip, Kahne (unapproved impound adjustment). **Failed to qualify:** Scott Wimmer (4), Kevin Lepage (49), Kenny Wallace (78), Chad Blount (34), Kertus Davis (72). **Estimated attendance:** 150,000.

Driver rating: An average of these categories—Win, finish, top 15 finish, average running position on lead lap, average speed under green, fastest lap, led most laps, lead-lap finish. Maximum points: 150 per race.

Chicagoland

Joliet, Ill. • 1.5-mile banked paved oval • July 9, 2006 • 400 miles, 267 laps • Purse: $5,934,007

Car	Driver	Make	Start	27 laps to go	Finish	Laps run	Laps led	Rating	Winnings
24	Jeff Gordon	Chevrolet	13	2	1	270	20	131.7	$327,761
31	Jeff Burton	Chevrolet	1	3	2	270	60	124.1	$250,220
5	Kyle Busch	Chevrolet	23	7	3	270	2	107.6	$178,075
29	Kevin Harvick	Chevrolet	4	5	4	270	40	123.8	$184,586
8	Dale Earnhardt Jr.	Chevrolet	25	8	5	270	27	107.3	$164,591
48	Jimmie Johnson	Chevrolet	5	6	6	270	0	100.0	$154,286
41	Reed Sorenson*	Dodge	18	15	7	270	6	104.9	$116,525
2	Kurt Busch	Dodge	19	9	8	270	0	88.1	$138,958
07	Clint Bowyer*	Chevrolet	38	11	9	270	0	76.9	$114,425
18	J.J. Yeley*	Chevrolet	10	10	10	270	0	87.1	$138,475
16	Greg Biffle	Ford	27	18	11	270	0	91.2	$113,000
43	Bobby Labonte	Dodge	6	20	12	270	1	91.8	$132,136
25	Brian Vickers	Chevrolet	2	16	13	270	0	91.0	$101,350
11	Denny Hamlin*	Chevrolet	7	22	14	270	0	87.7	$91,525
10	Scott Riggs	Dodge	14	13	15	270	0	77.2	$91,325
1	Martin Truex Jr.*	Chevrolet	29	14	16	270	0	77.8	$116,283
22	Dave Blaney	Dodge	15	21	17	270	0	69.0	$106,233
6	Mark Martin	Ford	9	12	18	270	1	67.9	$103,325
7	Robby Gordon	Chevrolet	30	24	19	270	0	64.7	$88,125
99	Carl Edwards	Ford	21	23	20	270	0	58.8	$106,725
40	David Stremme*	Dodge	20	17	21	270	0	62.6	$108,983
17	Matt Kenseth	Ford	8	1	22	270	112	115.3	$139,666
9	Kasey Kahne	Dodge	3	19	23	270	0	72.6	$120,489
19	Jeremy Mayfield	Dodge	16	25	24	270	0	56.7	$114,916
42	Casey Mears	Dodge	11	26	25	270	0	74.5	$118,783
14	Sterling Marlin	Chevrolet	31	27	26	269	0	55.5	$95,158
66	Jeff Green	Chevrolet	22	28	27	269	0	62.9	$100,447
45	Kyle Petty	Dodge	33	29	28	269	0	47.4	$89,800
38	Elliott Sadler	Ford	32	31	29	269	0	46.6	$107,008
55	Michael Waltrip	Dodge	36	30	30	269	0	41.2	$79,350
88	Dale Jarrett	Ford	41	32	31	269	0	37.3	$110,725
20	Tony Stewart	Chevrolet	34	4	32	269	1	93.0	$132,386
01	Joe Nemechek	Chevrolet	17	35	33	268	0	44.0	$105,545
4	Scott Wimmer	Chevrolet	28	34	34	268	0	38.0	$78,050
00	Bill Elliott	Chevrolet	24	39	35	268	0	30.3	$77,850
12	Ryan Newman	Dodge	12	33	36	268	0	56.1	$123,058
32	Travis Kvapil	Chevrolet	43	38	37	268	0	35.5	$77,425
78	Kenny Wallace	Chevrolet	37	36	38	268	0	26.4	$77,225
26	Jamie McMurray	Ford	42	37	39	268	0	36.6	$123,850
96	Tony Raines	Chevrolet	39	40	40	267	0	36.5	$76,805
06	Todd Kluever	Ford	35	41	41	267	0	29.0	$76,605
21	Ken Schrader	Ford	40	42	42	266	0	44.6	$103,644
44	Terry Labonte	Chevrolet	26	43	43	167	0	33.4	$76,551

*Rookie. **Time of race:** 3:03:59. **Average speed:** 132.077 mph. **Margin of victory:** .461 seconds.
Caution flags: 8 for 34 laps: 69-72 (debris); 140-145 (debris); 172-175 (oil on track); 200-204 (Car 96—spin, backstretch); 217-220 (Car 38—spin, backstretch); 229-232 (Car 55—accident, Turn 2); 235-237 (Car 42—accident, Turn 2); 265-268 (Car 17—spin, Turn 2). **Lead changes:** 18 among 10 drivers: Burton 1-59; Ky. Busch 60-61; J. Gordon 62-69; Harvick 70-108; Earnhardt 109-124; J. Gordon 125-128; Burton 129; Kenseth 130; Stewart 131; Earnhardt 132-142; Sorenson 143-148; Kenseth 149-171; Harvick 172; Martin 173; Kenseth 174-199; J. Gordon 200; B. Labonte 201; Kenseth 202-263; J. Gordon 264-270. **Note:** Green-white-checkered finish. **Fell out of race:** Earnhardt (engine); Wallace, Nemechek, Waltrip, Kvapil (accidents); Barrett (oil pump). **Pole:** Jeff Burton, 181.647 mph. **Dropped to rear:** Elliott (engine change). **Failed to qualify:** Paul Menard (15), Kevin Lepage (49), Chad Blount (61), Brent Sherman (04), Mike Garvey (51), Derrike Cope (74), Carl Long (34). **Estimated attendance:** 80,000.

Driver rating: An average of these categories—Win, finish, top 15 finish, average running position on lead lap, average speed under green, fastest lap, led most laps, lead-lap finish. Maximum points: 150 per race.

POINT STANDINGS

Rk.	Driver	Pts.	Diff.
1.	Jimmie Johnson	2,651	—
2.	Matt Kenseth	2,600	-51
3.	Dale Earnhardt Jr.	2,394	-257
4.	Jeff Burton	2,327	-324
5.	Kasey Kahne	2,303	-348
6.	Mark Martin	2,291	-360
7.	Tony Stewart	2,274	-377
8.	Kyle Busch	2,265	-386
9.	Kevin Harvick	2,253	-398
10.	Jeff Gordon	2,219	-432
11.	Greg Biffle	2,172	-479
12.	Denny Hamlin	2,169	-482
13.	Kurt Busch	2,087	-564
14.	Carl Edwards	2,026	-625
15.	Casey Mears	1,991	-660
16.	Clint Bowyer	1,937	-714
17.	Jamie McMurray	1,921	-730
18.	Ryan Newman	1,915	-736
19.	Elliott Sadler	1,870	-781
20.	Brian Vickers	1,857	-794

>> LENOX INDUSTRIAL TOOLS 300 race 19 of 36

New Hampshire International Speedway

Loudon, N.H. • 1.058-mile flat paved oval • July 16, 2006 • 317 miles, 300 laps • Purse: $5,204,946

Car	Driver	Make	Start	30 laps to go	Finish	Laps run	Laps led	Rating	Winnings
5	Kyle Busch	Chevrolet	4	1	1	308	107	141.1	$242,175
99	Carl Edwards	Ford	17	8	2	308	0	106.7	$177,900
16	Greg Biffle	Ford	26	4	3	308	25	116.1	$142,950
6	Mark Martin	Ford	13	6	4	308	0	100.5	$124,700
29	Kevin Harvick	Chevrolet	14	9	5	308	0	104.6	$143,461
11	Denny Hamlin*	Chevrolet	12	3	6	308	1	107.8	$95,425
31	Jeff Burton	Chevrolet	2	14	7	308	37	105.5	$127,870
9	Kasey Kahne	Dodge	11	11	8	308	0	85.0	$119,689
48	Jimmie Johnson	Chevrolet	6	7	9	308	0	89.6	$127,711
10	Scott Riggs	Dodge	42	12	10	308	0	82.3	$92,425
40	David Stremme*	Dodge	22	16	11	308	0	74.2	$109,233
18	J.J. Yeley*	Chevrolet	20	17	12	308	0	75.5	$114,950
22	Dave Blaney	Dodge	28	23	13	308	0	72.7	$95,783
17	Matt Kenseth	Ford	24	24	14	308	0	65.0	$119,716
24	Jeff Gordon	Chevrolet	7	22	15	308	1	86.6	$121,961
14	Sterling Marlin	Chevrolet	23	26	16	308	0	61.5	$90,333
25	Brian Vickers	Chevrolet	3	13	17	308	34	94.5	$90,525
1	Martin Truex Jr.*	Chevrolet	8	20	18	308	0	70.0	$95,083
7	Robby Gordon	Chevrolet	34	18	19	308	0	65.5	$75,125
4	Scott Wimmer	Chevrolet	36	21	20	308	0	47.9	$77,625
42	Casey Mears	Dodge	29	15	21	308	0	61.8	$108,658
96	Tony Raines	Chevrolet	15	28	22	308	0	49.5	$74,200
43	Bobby Labonte	Dodge	27	25	23	308	0	53.3	$110,836
41	Reed Sorenson*	Dodge	9	5	24	308	31	106.1	$92,550
38	Elliott Sadler	Ford	18	2	25	307	5	71.3	$101,608
66	Jeff Green	Chevrolet	35	27	26	307	0	49.0	$90,647
07	Clint Bowyer*	Chevrolet	31	19	27	307	23	75.6	$80,375
45	Kyle Petty	Dodge	41	32	28	306	0	41.9	$77,675
19	Jeremy Mayfield	Dodge	37	10	29	306	0	51.6	$99,391
49	Kevin Lepage	Dodge	38	31	30	306	0	33.0	$69,650
88	Dale Jarrett	Ford	32	30	31	306	0	46.0	$101,025
00	Bill Elliott	Chevrolet	43	35	32	305	0	31.9	$68,725
26	Jamie McMurray	Ford	33	36	33	303	0	33.1	$116,300
21	Ken Schrader	Ford	21	29	34	303	0	37.4	$95,539
32	Travis Kvapil	Chevrolet	30	33	35	301	0	35.5	$68,125
55	Michael Waltrip	Dodge	39	34	36	300	0	38.2	$67,900
20	Tony Stewart	Chevrolet	5	38	37	285	28	89.9	$121,636
2	Kurt Busch	Dodge	10	37	38	285	0	62.6	$108,533
12	Ryan Newman	Dodge	1	39	39	279	16	75.7	$121,483
95	Stanton Barrett	Chevrolet	40	40	40	200	0	24.8	$67,225
01	Joe Nemechek	Chevrolet	16	41	41	199	0	72.3	$93,405
78	Kenny Wallace	Chevrolet	19	42	42	184	0	39.1	$66,935
8	Dale Earnhardt Jr.	Chevrolet	25	43	43	134	0	70.1	$102,130

POINT STANDINGS

Rk.	Driver	Pts.	Diff.
1.	Jimmie Johnson	2,789	—
2.	Matt Kenseth	2,721	-68
3.	Jeff Burton	2,478	-311
4.	Kyle Busch	2,455	-334
5.	Mark Martin	2,451	-338
6.	Kasey Kahne	2,445	-344
7.	Dale Earnhardt Jr.	2,428	-361
8.	Kevin Harvick	2,408	-381
9.	Greg Biffle	2,342	-447
10.	Jeff Gordon	2,342	-447
11.	Tony Stewart	2,331	-458
12.	Denny Hamlin	2,324	-465
13.	Carl Edwards	2,196	-593
14.	Kurt Busch	2,136	-653
15.	Casey Mears	2,091	-698
16.	Clint Bowyer	2,024	-765
17.	Jamie McMurray	1,985	-804
18.	Brian Vickers	1,974	-815
19.	Ryan Newman	1,966	-823
20.	Elliott Sadler	1,963	-826

*Rookie. **Time of race:** 3:12:51. **Average speed:** 101.384 mph. **Margin of victory:** .406 seconds.
Caution flags: 11 for 49 laps: 21-23 (Car 32—accident, Turn 3); 92-95 (Cars 12, 20—accident, Turn 4); 97-100 (Cars 12, 21, 24, 43—accident, Turn 2); 102-105 (Car 43—spin, Turn 2); 116-119 (debris); 188-194 (Car 78—accident, Turn 2); 201-204 (Cars 01, 25—accident, Turn 4); 211-214 (Car 66—accident, Turn 4); 235-238 (Car 2—accident, Turn 3); 268-271 (Car 21—accident, Turn 4); 300-306 (Cars 07, 25—accident, backstretch). **Lead changes:** 21 among 11 drivers: Newman 1-11; Vickers 12-20; Newman 21-25; Burton 26-62; Stewart 63-90; Vickers 91; J. Gordon 92; Vickers 93-106; Ky. Busch 107-108; Vickers 109-115; Ky. Busch 116-119, Sorenson 120-150; Biffle 151-173; Ky. Busch 174-180; Vickers 185-187; Hamlin 188; Ky. Busch 189-210; Biffle 211; Bowyer 212-234; E. Sadler 235-239; Ky. Busch 240-308. **Note:** Green-white-checkered finish. **Fell out of race:** Earnhardt (engine); Wallace, Nemechek, Waltrip, Kvapil (accidents); Barrett (oil pump). **Pole:** Ryan Newman, 129.683 mph. **Dropped to rear:** McMurray (engine change). **Failed to qualify:** Ted Christopher (61), Joey McCarthy (34), Derrike Cope (74), Morgan Shepherd (89). **Estimated attendance:** 100,000.

Driver rating: An average of these categories—Win, finish, top 15 finish, average running position on lead lap, average speed under green, fastest lap, led most laps, lead-lap finish. Maximum points: 150 per race.

Pocono Raceway

Pocono, Pa. • 2.5-mile banked triangular paved • July 23, 2006 • 500 miles, 200 laps • Purse: $4,836,658

Car	Driver	Make	Start	20 laps to go	Finish	Laps run	Laps led	Rating	Winnings
11	Denny Hamlin*	Chevrolet	1	5	1	200	151	149.0	$230,100
2	Kurt Busch	Dodge	7	7	2	200	4	122.4	$182,758
24	Jeff Gordon	Chevrolet	5	6	3	200	3	111.5	$175,961
25	Brian Vickers	Chevrolet	4	9	4	200	0	115.5	$117,850
29	Kevin Harvick	Chevrolet	12	8	5	200	0	110.9	$134,436
48	Jimmie Johnson	Chevrolet	15	11	6	200	0	104.4	$133,661
20	Tony Stewart	Chevrolet	13	14	7	200	0	95.9	$132,461
43	Bobby Labonte	Dodge	27	1	8	200	2	92.5	$122,561
31	Jeff Burton	Chevrolet	6	12	9	200	23	111.0	$105,720
1	Martin Truex Jr.*	Chevrolet	17	10	10	200	0	95.9	$105,383
18	J.J. Yeley*	Chevrolet	21	3	11	200	0	75.1	$110,700
5	Kyle Busch	Chevrolet	8	18	12	200	0	83.6	$86,275
7	Robby Gordon	Chevrolet	29	25	13	200	0	74.2	$74,725
17	Matt Kenseth	Ford	11	13	14	200	0	94.7	$113,316
21	Ken Schrader	Ford	18	2	15	200	1	77.5	$96,939
22	Dave Blaney	Dodge	24	20	16	200	0	67.1	$84,333
01	Joe Nemechek	Chevrolet	10	4	17	200	0	70.0	$94,220
12	Ryan Newman	Dodge	2	23	18	200	12	88.8	$109,483
6	Mark Martin	Ford	30	15	19	200	0	79.1	$81,825
26	Jamie McMurray	Ford	28	22	20	200	0	81.4	$113,225
96	Tony Raines	Chevrolet	19	28	21	200	0	61.1	$66,875
10	Scott Riggs	Dodge	9	16	22	200	0	72.8	$66,575
42	Casey Mears	Dodge	31	17	23	200	0	63.4	$101,333
16	Greg Biffle	Ford	20	26	24	200	0	72.7	$83,000
44	Terry Labonte	Chevrolet	37	27	25	200	0	53.6	$62,975
41	Reed Sorenson*	Dodge	23	24	26	200	0	56.4	$73,625
32	Travis Kvapil	Chevrolet	40	29	27	200	0	48.0	$79,533
88	Dale Jarrett	Ford	38	21	28	200	3	52.0	$97,200
40	David Stremme*	Dodge	42	30	29	199	0	45.6	$84,633
14	Sterling Marlin	Chevrolet	35	31	30	199	0	48.7	$74,372
9	Kasey Kahne	Dodge	3	19	31	199	0	62.8	$98,889
38	Elliott Sadler	Ford	25	33	32	199	1	35.9	$89,433
90	Stephen Leicht	Ford	36	37	33	199	0	38.6	$62,275
49	Kevin Lepage	Dodge	34	34	34	199	0	33.4	$61,125
66	Jeff Green	Chevrolet	32	32	35	199	0	41.9	$68,975
78	Jimmy Spencer	Chevrolet	43	35	36	199	0	27.3	$60,750
19	Jeremy Mayfield	Dodge	22	36	37	199	0	37.1	$90,566
4	Scott Wimmer	Chevrolet	41	38	38	196	0	30.7	$60,450
99	Carl Edwards	Ford	16	39	39	196	0	58.4	$80,125
55	Michael Waltrip	Dodge	39	40	40	195	0	28.5	$60,175
07	Clint Bowyer*	Chevrolet	14	41	41	194	0	42.0	$68,035
45	Kyle Petty	Dodge	33	43	42	117	0	36.7	$67,885
8	Dale Earnhardt Jr.	Chevrolet	26	42	43	115	0	53.9	$95,088

*Rookie. **Time of race:** 3:46:12. **Average speed:** 132.626 mph. **Margin of victory:** 1.510 seconds.
Caution flags: 7 for 29 laps: 22-24 (competition); 33-37 (Cars 07, 20, 99—accident, frontstretch); 67-71 (Car 45—accident, Turn 1); 77-79 (debris); 89-92 (Car 8—accident, Long Pond straight); 151-155 (debris); 181-184 (debris). **Lead changes:** 13 among 9 drivers: Hamlin 1-33; Newman 34-44; Burton 45-67; E. Sadler 68; J. Gordon 69-71; Newman 72; Hamlin 73-89; Jarrett 90-92; Hamlin 93-151; Schrader 152; Hamlin 153-174; Ku. Busch 175-178; B. Labonte 179-180; Hamlin 181-200. **Fell out of race:** Earnhardt, Petty (accidents). **Pole:** Denny Hamlin, 169.827 mph. **Failed to qualify:** Derrike Cope (74), Stanton Barrett (52), Greg Sacks (34), Chad Chaffin (61). **Estimated attendance:** 100,000.

Driver rating: An average of these categories—Win, finish, top 15 finish, average running position on lead lap, average speed under green, fastest lap, led most laps, lead-lap finish. Maximum points: 150 per race.

POINT STANDINGS

Rk.	Driver	Pts.	Diff.
1.	Jimmie Johnson	2,939	—
2.	Matt Kenseth	2,842	-97
3.	Jeff Burton	2,621	-318
4.	Kyle Busch	2,582	-357
5.	Kevin Harvick	2,563	-376
6.	Mark Martin	2,557	-382
7.	Kasey Kahne	2,515	-424
8.	Denny Hamlin	2,514	-425
9.	Jeff Gordon	2,512	-427
10.	Tony Stewart	2,477	-462
11.	Dale Earnhardt Jr.	2,462	-477
12.	Greg Biffle	2,433	-506
13.	Kurt Busch	2,311	-628
14.	Carl Edwards	2,242	-697
15.	Casey Mears	2,185	-754
16.	Brian Vickers	2,134	-805
17.	Jamie McMurray	2,088	-851
18.	Ryan Newman	2,080	-859
19.	Clint Bowyer	2,064	-875
20.	Elliott Sadler	2,035	-904

>>ALLSTATE 400 AT THE BRICKYARD race (21) of 36

Indianapolis Motor Speedway

Indianapolis • 2.5-mile semi-banked paved oval • August 6, 2006 • 400 miles, 160 laps • Purse: $9,325,620

Car	Driver	Make	Start	16 laps to go	Finish	Laps run	Laps led	Rating	Winnings
48	Jimmie Johnson	Chevrolet	5	8	1	160	33	124.3	$452,861
17	Matt Kenseth	Ford	20	7	2	160	9	117.7	$361,141
29	Kevin Harvick	Chevrolet	10	11	3	160	18	128.0	$327,636
07	Clint Bowyer*	Chevrolet	2	6	4	160	0	100.9	$271,900
6	Mark Martin	Ford	19	10	5	160	0	110.4	$239,150
8	Dale Earnhardt Jr.	Chevrolet	31	2	6	160	0	73.7	$230,516
5	Kyle Busch	Chevrolet	37	1	7	160	8	78.1	$209,825
20	Tony Stewart	Chevrolet	32	15	8	160	0	89.9	$237,111
99	Carl Edwards	Ford	22	9	9	160	0	107.9	$202,975
11	Denny Hamlin*	Chevrolet	14	5	10	160	0	99.0	$177,225
96	Tony Raines	Chevrolet	13	14	11	160	0	75.6	$168,825
2	Kurt Busch	Dodge	3	24	12	160	0	80.2	$211,933
12	Ryan Newman	Dodge	8	3	13	160	0	73.5	$198,308
21	Ken Schrader	Ford	11	21	14	160	0	85.2	$184,264
31	Jeff Burton	Chevrolet	1	16	15	160	87	121.7	$243,995
24	Jeff Gordon	Chevrolet	16	27	16	160	0	65.0	$198,236
25	Brian Vickers	Chevrolet	30	22	17	160	2	84.4	$161,675
40	David Stremme*	Dodge	24	25	18	160	0	69.7	$179,033
1	Martin Truex Jr.*	Chevrolet	23	19	19	160	0	58.9	$174,733
4	Scott Wimmer	Chevrolet	34	31	20	160	0	69.9	$152,275
10	Scott Riggs	Dodge	12	20	21	160	0	80.1	$148,350
00	Bill Elliott	Chevrolet	26	35	22	160	0	50.3	$143,850
42	Casey Mears	Dodge	39	26	23	160	0	73.7	$181,308
01	Joe Nemechek	Chevrolet	21	4	24	160	1	52.2	$171,845
32	Travis Kvapil	Chevrolet	36	13	25	160	0	59.5	$158,558
26	Jamie McMurray	Ford	18	33	26	160	0	75.5	$186,575
45	Kyle Petty	Dodge	40	23	27	160	0	46.2	$161,508
88	Dale Jarrett	Ford	35	32	28	160	0	50.7	$172,825
22	Dave Blaney	Dodge	42	28	29	160	0	49.3	$149,797
41	Reed Sorenson*	Dodge	41	34	30	160	0	43.1	$147,725
14	Sterling Marlin	Chevrolet	33	29	31	160	0	40.9	$136,225
78	Kenny Wallace	Chevrolet	28	36	32	160	1	36.0	$136,125
16	Greg Biffle	Ford	7	12	33	160	0	94.2	$156,625
18	J.J. Yeley*	Chevrolet	6	17	34	160	0	74.5	$170,500
7	Robby Gordon	Chevrolet	9	30	35	160	0	64.7	$134,925
9	Kasey Kahne	Dodge	4	18	36	159	1	83.7	$173,689
37	Mike Skinner	Dodge	17	38	37	159	0	33.2	$134,750
66	Jeff Green	Chevrolet	29	37	38	159	0	29.0	$142,625
34	Chad Chaffin	Dodge	25	39	39	158	0	28.6	$134,525
43	Bobby Labonte	Dodge	38	40	40	135	0	39.2	$171,386
19	Jeremy Mayfield	Dodge	15	41	41	82	0	38.9	$164,316
60	Boris Said	Ford	43	42	42	19	0	27.9	$134,225
38	Elliott Sadler	Ford	27	43	43	3	0	27.3	$162,383

POINT STANDINGS

Rk.	Driver	Pts.	Diff.
1.	Jimmie Johnson	3,124	—
2.	Matt Kenseth	3,017	-107
3.	Jeff Burton	2,749	-375
4.	Kyle Busch	2,733	-391
5.	Kevin Harvick	2,733	-391
6.	Mark Martin	2,712	-412
7.	Denny Hamlin	2,648	-476
8.	Jeff Gordon	2,627	-497
9.	Tony Stewart	2,619	-505
10.	Dale Earnhardt Jr.	2,612	-512
11.	Kasey Kahne	2,575	-549
12.	Greg Biffle	2,497	-627
13.	Kurt Busch	2,438	-686
14.	Carl Edwards	2,380	-744
15.	Casey Mears	2,279	-845
16.	Brian Vickers	2,251	-873
17.	Clint Bowyer	2,224	-900
18.	Ryan Newman	2,204	-920
19.	Jamie McMurray	2,173	-951
20.	Martin Truex Jr.	2,123	-1,001

*Rookie. **Time of race:** 2:54:57. **Average speed:** 137.182 mph. **Margin of victory:** Under caution. **Caution flags:** 8 for 24 laps: 4-6 (Cars 01, 38—accident, Turn 1); 17-19 (competition); 21-23 (Cars 41, 60—accident, Turn 3); 41-44 (competition); 58-60 (Car 19—accident, Turn 2); 87-89 (debris); 143-146 (debris); 160 (Car 9—accident, Turn 3). **Lap leaders:** 18 lead changes among 9 drivers: Burton 1-6; Kahne 7; Burton 8-41; Wallace 42; Burton 43-58; Vickers 59-60; Burton 61-69; Harvick 70; Burton 71-72; Harvick 73-89; Burton 90-109; Kenseth 110-116; Johnson 117-123; Kenseth 124-125; Ky. Busch 126; Nemechek 127; Johnson 128-143; Ky. Busch 144-150; Johnson 151-160. **Fell out of race:** Sadler, Said, Kahne (accidents); Mayfield (suspension); Labonte (engine). **Pole:** Jeff Burton, 182.778 mph. **Dropped to rear:** Ku. Busch (backup car); Chaffin, Jarrett (engine changes). **Failed to qualify:** Paul Menard (15), Michael Waltrip (55), Johnny Sauter (70), Kevin Lepage (49), Stephen Leicht (90), Bobby Hamilton Jr. (04), Derrike Cope (61). **Estimated attendance:** 280,000.

Driver rating: An average of these categories—Win, finish, top 15 finish, average running position on lead lap, average speed under green, fastest lap, led most laps, lead-lap finish. Maximum points: 150 per race.

Watkins Glen International

Watkins Glen, • N.Y. 2.45-mile paved road course • August 13, 2006 • 220.5 miles, 90 laps • Purse: $4,705,975

Car	Driver	Make	Start	9 laps to go	Finish	Laps run	Laps led	Rating	Winnings
29	Kevin Harvick	Chevrolet	7	1	1	90	28	126.4	$223,161
20	Tony Stewart	Chevrolet	8	2	2	90	7	130.1	$210,986
26	Jamie McMurray	Ford	24	3	3	90	0	103.6	$163,225
7	Robby Gordon	Chevrolet	6	4	4	90	0	119.0	$108,100
99	Carl Edwards	Ford	21	8	5	90	0	82.9	$110,725
40	Scott Pruett	Dodge	13	12	6	90	0	97.7	$114,108
38	Elliott Sadler	Ford	12	9	7	90	0	83.7	$107,533
12	Ryan Newman	Dodge	3	5	8	90	7	114.0	$116,708
5	Kyle Busch	Chevrolet	9	19	9	90	0	93.5	$88,025
11	Denny Hamlin*	Chevrolet	10	15	10	90	0	100.3	$78,850
31	Jeff Burton	Chevrolet	16	6	11	90	0	95.0	$97,445
41	Reed Sorenson*	Dodge	40	10	12	90	2	60.5	$83,975
24	Jeff Gordon	Chevrolet	4	20	13	90	1	99.1	$113,736
07	Clint Bowyer*	Chevrolet	14	24	14	90	0	79.7	$85,700
66	Jeff Green	Chevrolet	22	25	15	90	0	68.6	$91,233
25	Brian Vickers	Chevrolet	19	21	16	90	0	79.5	$73,500
48	Jimmie Johnson	Chevrolet	5	28	17	90	1	84.7	$110,111
8	Dale Earnhardt Jr.	Chevrolet	11	34	18	90	1	65.7	$99,966
2	Kurt Busch	Dodge	1	18	19	90	38	116.5	$117,333
6	Mark Martin	Ford	20	29	20	90	0	56.4	$81,700
17	Matt Kenseth	Ford	30	26	21	90	0	62.7	$106,916
9	Kasey Kahne	Dodge	2	14	22	90	0	74.1	$103,189
10	Scott Riggs	Dodge	32	17	23	90	0	46.9	$64,700
43	Bobby Labonte	Dodge	36	31	24	90	0	45.5	$100,411
4	Scott Wimmer	Chevrolet	28	27	25	90	3	51.6	$63,650
88	Dale Jarrett	Ford	39	33	26	90	0	38.6	$95,075
19	Bill Elliott	Dodge	31	32	27	90	0	44.2	$92,666
1	Martin Truex Jr.*	Chevrolet	35	30	28	90	0	58.7	$84,583
15	Paul Menard	Chevrolet	34	35	29	90	0	42.5	$59,250
45	Kyle Petty	Dodge	38	11	30	90	1	61.8	$82,258
60	Boris Said	Ford	15	7	31	90	0	60.1	$58,950
32	Ron Fellows	Chevrolet	18	16	32	90	0	66.0	$70,797
18	J.J. Yeley*	Chevrolet	26	13	33	90	0	50.7	$94,125
21	Ken Schrader	Ford	23	23	34	89	0	52.7	$85,689
42	Casey Mears	Dodge	17	36	35	89	0	77.0	$92,483
55	Michael Waltrip	Dodge	33	22	36	89	1	46.2	$58,150
96	Terry Labonte	Chevrolet	29	37	37	81	0	32.5	$58,025
16	Greg Biffle	Ford	41	38	38	75	0	35.9	$78,075
14	Sterling Marlin	Chevrolet	42	39	39	64	0	29.3	$57,750
22	Dave Blaney	Dodge	25	40	40	61	0	40.9	$57,600
34	Brian Simo	Chevrolet	43	41	41	61	0	41.6	$57,460
01	Joe Nemechek	Chevrolet	37	42	42	61	0	48.4	$83,680
90	Marc Goossens	Ford	27	43	43	58	0	40.0	$57,537

POINT STANDINGS

Rk.	Driver	Pts.	Diff.
1.	Jimmie Johnson	3,241	—
2.	Matt Kenseth	3,117	-124
3.	Kevin Harvick	2,918	-323
4.	Jeff Burton	2,879	-362
5.	Kyle Busch	2,871	-370
6.	Mark Martin	2,815	-426
7.	Tony Stewart	2,794	-447
8.	Denny Hamlin	2,782	-459
9.	Jeff Gordon	2,756	-485
10.	Dale Earnhardt Jr.	2,726	-515
11.	Kasey Kahne	2,672	-569
12.	Kurt Busch	2,554	-687
13.	Greg Biffle	2,546	-695
14.	Carl Edwards	2,535	-706
15.	Brian Vickers	2,366	-875
16.	Ryan Newman	2,351	-890
17.	Clint Bowyer	2,345	-896
18.	Jamie McMurray	2,338	-903
19.	Casey Mears	2,337	-904
20.	Elliott Sadler	2,215	-1,026

*Rookie. **Time of race:** 2:52:27. **Average speed:** 76.718 mph. **Margin of victory:** .892 seconds. **Caution flags:** 10 for 22 laps: 6-7 (Car 38—spin, backstretch); 29-30 (debris); 34-35 (Cars 60, 90—spin, inner loop); 40-41 (Car 19—spin, inner loop); 45-46 (debris); 55-56 (Car 01—spin, inner loop); 60-61 (Car 90—spin, Turn 4); 63-66 (Cars 01, 2, 4, 14, 17, 22, 34—accident, Turn 2); 80-81 (Car 42—stalled on track); 84-85 (Car 55—accident, Turn 7). **Lead changes:** 14 among 11 drivers: Ku. Busch—pole; Newman 1-7; Ku. Busch 8-21; J. Gordon 22; Johnson 23; Earnhardt 24; Wimmer 25-27; Waltrip 28; Petty 29; Ku. Busch 30-53; Stewart 54-55; Sorenson 56-57; Harvick 58-81; Stewart 82-86; Harvick 87-90. **Fell out of race:** Goossens, Nemechek, Simo, Blaney, Marlin (accidents). **Pole:** Kurt Busch, 122.966 mph. **Dropped to rear:** Martin, Goossens, Marlin (engine changes); Biffle (backup car). **Failed to qualify:** Chris Cook (49), Max Papis (78), Tom Hubert (27), David Murry (37), Dale Quarterley (72), Johnny Miller (92), Brandon Ash (02). **Estimated attendance:** 85,000.

Driver rating: An average of these categories—Win, finish, top 15 finish, average running position on lead lap, average speed under green, fastest lap, led most laps, lead-lap finish. Maximum points: 150 per race.

>> GFS MARKETPLACE 400

Michigan International Speedway

Brooklyn, Mich. • 2-mile banked paved oval • August 20, 2006 • 400 miles, 200 laps • Purse: $5,028,926

Car	Driver	Make	Start	20 laps to go	Finish	Laps run	Laps led	Rating	Winnings
17	Matt Kenseth	Ford	3	1	1	200	87	139.7	$221,091
24	Jeff Gordon	Chevrolet	12	3	2	200	12	119.6	$161,061
20	Tony Stewart	Chevrolet	33	4	3	200	0	102.5	$159,736
9	Kasey Kahne	Dodge	15	5	4	200	0	110.0	$131,439
6	Mark Martin	Ford	14	6	5	200	0	97.3	$103,650
8	Dale Earnhardt Jr.	Chevrolet	17	10	6	200	40	121.4	$137,116
16	Greg Biffle	Ford	6	7	7	200	0	108.0	$99,850
41	Reed Sorenson*	Dodge	28	9	8	200	0	92.5	$93,225
11	Denny Hamlin*	Chevrolet	9	11	9	200	0	91.2	$81,175
19	Elliott Sadler	Dodge	2	8	10	200	0	89.1	$119,416
29	Kevin Harvick	Chevrolet	5	16	11	200	0	84.7	$117,661
7	Robby Gordon	Chevrolet	24	13	12	200	0	67.5	$78,800
48	Jimmie Johnson	Chevrolet	8	12	13	200	0	85.3	$123,586
10	Scott Riggs	Dodge	23	19	14	200	0	59.0	$77,700
25	Brian Vickers	Chevrolet	27	17	15	200	0	63.4	$86,300
42	Casey Mears	Dodge	7	20	16	200	0	78.3	$110,633
26	Jamie McMurray	Ford	40	23	17	200	8	69.0	$119,150
21	Ken Schrader	Ford	21	15	18	200	0	69.2	$102,939
43	Bobby Labonte	Dodge	25	22	19	200	0	64.6	$112,261
15	Paul Menard	Chevrolet	36	25	20	200	0	56.7	$72,475
32	Travis Kvapil	Chevrolet	30	27	21	200	0	49.7	$94,558
99	Carl Edwards	Ford	20	18	22	200	32	98.5	$90,750
55	Michael Waltrip	Dodge	22	29	23	200	0	56.1	$91,233
22	Dave Blaney	Dodge	19	24	24	200	0	58.4	$87,983
12	Ryan Newman	Dodge	4	26	25	200	8	66.7	$115,783
01	Joe Nemechek	Chevrolet	13	28	26	200	0	70.0	$110,395
66	Jeff Green	Chevrolet	35	21	27	200	0	58.8	$92,493
40	David Stremme*	Dodge	32	30	28	200	0	40.2	$90,132
14	Sterling Marlin	Chevrolet	10	32	29	199	0	40.0	$72,400
1	Martin Truex Jr.*	Chevrolet	18	14	30	199	0	69.2	$80,325
45	Kyle Petty	Dodge	42	31	31	199	1	37.6	$77,200
96	Tony Raines	Chevrolet	41	33	32	199	0	41.9	$59,125
07	Clint Bowyer*	Chevrolet	29	2	33	197	6	83.7	$78,000
74	Derrike Cope	Dodge	34	34	34	197	0	30.3	$68,950
00	Hermie Sadler	Ford	43	35	35	197	2	28.4	$68,800
88	Dale Jarrett	Ford	37	36	36	166	0	49.2	$100,825
18	J.J. Yeley*	Chevrolet	31	37	37	158	0	63.2	$103,275
38	David Gilliland	Ford	26	39	38	145	0	34.9	$96,508
5	Kyle Busch	Chevrolet	11	40	39	132	3	79.0	$86,540
2	Kurt Busch	Dodge	16	38	40	127	1	74.8	$109,523
49	Kevin Lepage	Dodge	39	41	41	103	0	29.0	$68,440
31	Jeff Burton	Chevrolet	1	42	42	17	0	49.7	$100,530
06	Todd Kluever	Ford	38	43	43	10	0	25.6	$67,797

POINT STANDINGS

Rk.	Driver	Pts.	Diff.
1.	Jimmie Johnson	3,365	—
2.	Matt Kenseth	3,307	-58
3.	Kevin Harvick	3,048	-317
4.	Mark Martin	2,970	-395
5.	Tony Stewart	2,959	-406
6.	Jeff Gordon	2,931	-434
7.	Kyle Busch	2,922	-443
8.	Denny Hamlin	2,920	-445
9.	Jeff Burton	2,916	-449
10.	Dale Earnhardt Jr.	2,881	-484
11.	Kasey Kahne	2,832	-533
12.	Greg Biffle	2,692	-673
13.	Carl Edwards	2,637	-728
14.	Kurt Busch	2,602	-763
15.	Brian Vickers	2,484	-881
16.	Jamie McMurray	2,455	-910
17.	Casey Mears	2,452	-913
18.	Ryan Newman	2,444	-921
19.	Clint Bowyer	2,414	-951
20.	Elliott Sadler	2,349	-1,016

*Rookie. **Time of race:** 2:57:39. **Average speed:** 135.097 mph. **Margin of victory:** .622 seconds.
Caution flags: 10 for 36 laps: 6-8 (Car 7—spin, Turn 4); 12-14 (Cars 06, 40—accident, backstretch);
23-25 (Car 29—spin, Turn 4); 43-48 (Car 5—accident, Turn 2); 54-56 (debris); 63-65 (debris); 115-119
(Car 2—spin, Turn 2); 131-134 (Car 2—accident, Turn 3); 142-144 (debris); 161-163 (Car 18—accident,
Turn 3). **Lead changes:** 26 among 11 drivers: Burton—pole; Newman 1-8; Kenseth 9-23; McMurray
24-31; Ky. Busch 32-34; Earnhardt 35-43; Petty 44; H. Sadler 45-46; Edwards 47-48; J. Gordon 49-51;
Edwards 52; J. Gordon 53-56; Ku. Busch 57; Edwards 58-84; Edwards 85-92; Edwards 93-94; Earnhardt
95-105; Kenseth 106-110; J. Gordon 111-115; Earnhardt 116-125; Kenseth 126; Earnhardt 127-128;
Kenseth 129-161; Bowyer 162-164; Kenseth 165; Bowyer 166-168; Kenseth 169-200. **Fell out of race:**
Kluever, Lepage, Ku. Busch, Yeley (accidents); Burton, Jarrett, Bowyer (engines). **Pole:** Jeff Burton, 187.936 mph.
Dropped to rear: Gilliland (backup car). **Failed to qualify:** Scott Wimmer (4), Mike Skinner (34), Chad Chaffin
(61), Kenny Wallace (78). **Estimated attendance:** 145,000.

Driver rating: An average of these categories—Win, finish, top 15 finish, average running position on lead
lap, average speed under green, fastest lap, led most laps, lead-lap finish. Maximum points: 150 per race.

Bristol Motor Speedway

Bristol, Tenn. • .533-mile high-banked concrete oval • August 26, 2006 • 266.5 miles, 500 laps • Purse: $6,055,119

Car	Driver	Make	Start	50 laps to go	Finish	Laps run	Laps led	Rating	Winnings
17	Matt Kenseth	Ford	4	1	1	500	117	132.8	$336,516
5	Kyle Busch	Chevrolet	19	4	2	500	1	110.1	$202,375
8	Dale Earnhardt Jr.	Chevrolet	40	2	3	500	35	109.9	$199,591
10	Scott Riggs	Dodge	23	6	4	500	0	104.4	$135,425
24	Jeff Gordon	Chevrolet	13	5	5	500	41	116.4	$171,636
11	Denny Hamlin*	Chevrolet	6	7	6	500	0	102.1	$111,800
99	Carl Edwards	Ford	39	3	7	500	16	94.1	$128,200
12	Ryan Newman	Dodge	21	8	8	500	0	93.8	$144,808
31	Jeff Burton	Chevrolet	2	9	9	500	263	132.1	$145,720
48	Jimmie Johnson	Chevrolet	18	10	10	500	0	89.7	$147,686
29	Kevin Harvick	Chevrolet	7	12	11	500	0	96.7	$135,486
9	Kasey Kahne	Dodge	31	11	12	500	0	85.7	$131,264
21	Ken Schrader	Ford	17	13	13	500	0	79.4	$124,564
22	Dave Blaney	Dodge	22	16	14	500	0	69.4	$113,758
88	Dale Jarrett	Ford	32	14	15	499	0	65.6	$128,075
55	Michael Waltrip	Dodge	29	15	16	499	0	61.9	$110,183
42	Casey Mears	Dodge	11	19	17	499	0	75.0	$127,533
1	Martin Truex Jr.*	Chevrolet	24	21	18	499	0	69.8	$114,858
16	Greg Biffle	Ford	35	18	19	499	0	76.1	$108,775
32	Travis Kvapil	Chevrolet	28	22	20	499	0	54.9	$105,983
49	Kevin Lepage	Dodge	12	17	21	498	0	59.1	$96,922
20	Tony Stewart	Chevrolet	5	23	22	498	0	64.2	$140,761
43	Bobby Labonte	Dodge	3	20	23	498	0	71.5	$126,886
66	Jeff Green	Chevrolet	16	24	24	498	0	55.0	$96,975
96	Tony Raines	Chevrolet	34	26	25	498	0	42.3	$89,700
01	Joe Nemechek	Chevrolet	41	25	26	498	0	50.5	$113,665
7	Robby Gordon	Chevrolet	42	27	27	498	0	60.7	$86,705
6	Mark Martin	Ford	15	28	28	496	0	56.6	$101,195
26	Jamie McMurray	Ford	37	29	29	496	0	47.2	$129,910
78	Kenny Wallace	Chevrolet	26	30	30	493	0	31.9	$83,475
18	J.J. Yeley*	Chevrolet	25	31	31	492	0	43.2	$129,440
14	Sterling Marlin	Chevrolet	14	32	32	490	0	60.3	$85,255
25	Brian Vickers	Chevrolet	20	33	33	487	0	35.8	$91,595
45	Kyle Petty	Dodge	8	34	34	481	0	60.5	$90,535
40	David Stremme*	Dodge	36	35	35	468	0	41.0	$90,425
41	Reed Sorenson*	Dodge	10	36	36	460	0	50.8	$90,315
2	Kurt Busch	Dodge	1	37	37	446	27	86.8	$128,413
07	Clint Bowyer*	Chevrolet	27	39	38	415	0	44.0	$90,070
19	Elliott Sadler	Dodge	9	38	39	395	0	85.1	$111,951
38	David Gilliland	Ford	38	40	40	346	0	33.6	$109,758
34	Carl Long	Chevrolet	30	41	41	256	0	32.2	$81,700
4	Scott Wimmer	Chevrolet	43	42	42	209	0	36.2	$81,575
74	Derrike Cope	Dodge	33	43	43	7	0	24.8	$81,764

POINT STANDINGS

Rk.	Driver	Pts.	Diff.
1.	Jimmie Johnson	3,499	—
2.	Matt Kenseth	3,492	-7
3.	Kevin Harvick	3,178	-321
4.	Kyle Busch	3,097	-402
5.	Jeff Gordon	3,091	-408
6.	Denny Hamlin	3,070	-429
7.	Jeff Burton	3,064	-435
8.	Tony Stewart	3,056	-443
9.	Dale Earnhardt Jr.	3,051	-448
10.	Mark Martin	3,049	-450
11.	Kasey Kahne	2,959	-540
12.	Greg Biffle	2,798	-701
13.	Carl Edwards	2,788	-711
14.	Kurt Busch	2,659	-840
15.	Ryan Newman	2,586	-913
16.	Casey Mears	2,564	-935
17.	Brian Vickers	2,548	-951
18.	Jamie McMurray	2,531	-968
19.	Scott Riggs	2,477	-1,022
20.	Clint Bowyer	2,463	-1,036

*Rookie. **Time of race:** 2:57:37. **Average speed:** 90.025 mph. **Margin of victory:** .591 seconds. **Caution flags:** 10 for 62 laps: 62-67 (Car 14—accident, Turn 3); 89-93 (Car 45—accident, Turn 2); 115-119 (Car 38—accident, Turn 1); 203-207 (Car 29—accident, Turn 2); 211-216 (debris); 228-232 (Car 41—accident, frontstretch); 235-241 (Car 07—accident, Turn 4); 325-332 (Car 40—accident, Turn 4); 381-386 (Cars 01, 18, 19—accident, Turn 4); 446-454 (Car 19—accident, Turn 1). **Lead changes:** 18 among 7 drivers: Ku. Busch 1-11; Burton 12-53; Kenseth 54-61; Ku. Busch 62-76; Burton 77-115; Ku. Busch 116; Earnhardt 117-135; Edwards 136-151; Burton 152-179; J. Gordon 180-218; Burton 219-317; Kenseth 318-325; J. Gordon 326; Burton 327-381; J. Gordon 382; Earnhardt 383-398; Kenseth 399-448; Ky. Busch 449; Kenseth 450-500. **Fell out of race:** E. Sadler (accident); Long (electrical); Wimmer (engine); Cope (handling). **Pole:** Kurt Busch, 124.906 mph. **Failed to qualify:** Chad Chaffin (61), Hermie Sadler (00), Mike Wallace (09), Mike Skinner (37), Morgan Shepherd (89), Stanton Barrett (30). **Estimated attendance:** 160,000.

Driver rating: An average of these categories—Win, finish, top 15 finish, average running position on lead lap, average speed under green, fastest lap, led most laps, lead-lap finish. Maximum points: 150 per race.

>>SONY HD 500

race  of 36

California Speedway

Fontana, Calif. • 2-mile banked paved oval • September 3, 2006 • 500 miles, 250 laps • Purse: $5,963,974

Car	Driver	Make	Start	25 laps to go	Finish	Laps run	Laps led	Rating	Winnings
9	Kasey Kahne	Dodge	9	1	1	250	130	144.1	$279,214
8	Dale Earnhardt Jr.	Chevrolet	6	3	2	250	6	119.1	$206,266
07	Clint Bowyer*	Chevrolet	3	19	3	250	0	100.7	$167,950
99	Carl Edwards	Ford	24	9	4	250	2	96.5	$142,725
24	Jeff Gordon	Chevrolet	14	7	5	250	42	117.8	$160,061
11	Denny Hamlin*	Chevrolet	8	6	6	250	29	117.9	$107,000
17	Matt Kenseth	Ford	11	4	7	250	0	104.4	$146,641
5	Kyle Busch	Chevrolet	10	8	8	250	11	113.3	$114,775
20	Tony Stewart	Chevrolet	22	11	9	250	0	101.9	$149,611
88	Dale Jarrett	Ford	36	23	10	250	0	64.7	$140,725
48	Jimmie Johnson	Chevrolet	16	12	11	250	0	93.7	$141,986
6	Mark Martin	Ford	38	10	12	250	3	85.0	$110,625
19	Elliott Sadler	Dodge	18	2	13	250	8	80.1	$133,666
42	Casey Mears	Dodge	33	21	14	250	0	68.0	$129,583
29	Kevin Harvick	Chevrolet	15	13	15	250	0	90.4	$132,686
31	Jeff Burton	Chevrolet	7	16	16	250	0	90.3	$120,145
10	Scott Riggs	Dodge	4	5	17	250	0	76.2	$92,900
1	Martin Truex Jr.*	Chevrolet	5	17	18	250	0	74.6	$118,258
18	J.J. Yeley*	Chevrolet	19	18	19	250	0	77.6	$125,900
26	Jamie McMurray	Ford	31	20	20	250	0	67.5	$136,825
41	Reed Sorenson*	Dodge	34	15	21	249	8	80.9	$98,175
66	Jeff Green	Chevrolet	30	22	22	249	0	60.4	$113,783
21	Ken Schrader	Ford	29	24	23	249	0	52.0	$117,289
16	Greg Biffle	Ford	21	14	24	249	0	78.9	$105,650
01	Joe Nemechek	Chevrolet	13	28	25	249	0	63.5	$115,070
43	Bobby Labonte	Dodge	28	25	26	249	0	52.6	$124,861
2	Kurt Busch	Dodge	1	26	27	249	11	73.1	$135,918
22	Dave Blaney	Dodge	41	29	28	249	0	53.0	$101,718
14	Sterling Marlin	Chevrolet	27	34	29	249	0	41.4	$99,108
4	Scott Wimmer	Chevrolet	17	30	30	248	0	50.6	$87,400
55	Michael Waltrip	Dodge	37	33	31	248	0	40.6	$93,897
38	David Gilliland	Ford	20	31	32	248	0	36.3	$112,208
12	Ryan Newman	Dodge	12	32	33	248	0	51.5	$129,658
32	Travis Kvapil	Chevrolet	43	36	34	248	0	32.4	$85,150
45	Kyle Petty	Dodge	35	37	35	247	0	36.2	$92,150
40	David Stremme*	Dodge	32	38	36	247	0	40.7	$92,100
96	Tony Raines	Chevrolet	42	35	37	247	0	29.9	$84,050
49	Kevin Lepage	Dodge	39	39	38	247	0	32.6	$84,000
78	Kenny Wallace	Chevrolet	40	40	39	246	0	25.3	$83,940
44	Terry Labonte	Chevrolet	26	27	40	246	0	43.3	$83,890
25	Brian Vickers	Chevrolet	2	41	41	237	0	57.2	$97,340
00	Bill Elliott	Chevrolet	23	42	42	224	0	28.9	$83,785
7	Robby Gordon	Chevrolet	25	43	43	193	0	53.0	$83,201

POINT STANDINGS

Rk.	Driver	Pts.	Diff.
1.	Matt Kenseth	3,638	—
2.	Jimmie Johnson	3,629	-9
3.	Kevin Harvick	3,296	-342
4.	Jeff Gordon	3,251	-387
5.	Kyle Busch	3,244	-394
6.	Dale Earnhardt Jr.	3,226	-412
7.	Denny Hamlin	3,225	-413
8.	Tony Stewart	3,194	-444
9.	Mark Martin	3,181	-457
10.	Jeff Burton	3,179	-459
11.	Kasey Kahne	3,149	-489
12.	Carl Edwards	2,953	-685
13.	Greg Biffle	2,889	-749
14.	Kurt Busch	2,746	-892
15.	Casey Mears	2,685	-953
16.	Ryan Newman	2,634	-988
17.	Jamie McMurray	2,634	-1,004
18.	Clint Bowyer	2,628	-1,010
19.	Scott Riggs	2,589	-1,049
20.	Brian Vickers	2,588	-1,050

*Rookie. **Time of race:** 3:27:40. **Average speed:** 144.462 mph. **Margin of victory:** 3.427 seconds.
Caution flags: 7 for 29 laps: 11-13 (Car 7—spin, Turn 4); 29-31 (debris); 83-86 (debris); 111-115 (Car 25—accident, backstretch); 156-159 (debris); 173-178 (Car 38—spin, Turn 2); 192-195 (oil on track).
Lead changes: 26 among 10 drivers: Ku. Busch 1-11; Kahne 12-27; Hamlin 28-54; J. Gordon 55-75; Hamlin 76-77; Ky. Busch 78-79; J. Gordon 80-86; Ky. Busch 87; Kahne 88-117; Ky. Busch 118; Kahne 119; Ky. Busch 120-121; Kahne 122-156; J. Gordon 157-161; Ky. Busch 162-165; J. Gordon 166-174; Earnhardt 175-179; Kahne 180-181; Ky. Busch 182; Kahne 183-192; Martin 193-195; E. Sadler 196-203; Kahne 204-237; Earnhardt 238; Edwards 239-240; Sorenson 241-248; Kahne 249-250. **Fell out of race:** R. Gordon (transmission). **Pole:** Kurt Busch, 184.540 mph. **Dropped to rear:** Wimmer, Schrader (engine change); Stremme (transmission change). **Failed to qualify:** Todd Kluever (06), Kertus Davis (34), Chad Chaffin (61), Bill Lester (23). **Estimated attendance:** 102,000.

Driver rating: An average of these categories—Win, finish, top 15 finish, average running position on lead lap, average speed under green, fastest lap, led most laps, lead-lap finish. Maximum points: 150 per race.

Richmond International Raceway

Richmond, Va. • .75-mile paved oval • September 9, 2006 • 300 miles, 400 laps • Purse: $ 4,955,081

Car	Driver	Make	Start	40 laps to go	Finish	Laps run	Laps led	Rating	Winnings
29	Kevin Harvick	Chevrolet	5	2	1	400	54	134.8	$234,136
5	Kyle Busch	Chevrolet	12	1	2	400	248	138.4	$184,550
9	Kasey Kahne	Dodge	20	3	3	400	1	119.0	$158,639
22	Dave Blaney	Dodge	15	4	4	400	0	108.7	$130,983
6	Mark Martin	Ford	4	6	5	400	0	107.0	$116,000
16	Greg Biffle	Ford	8	5	6	400	0	100.4	$107,425
21	Ken Schrader	Ford	17	7	7	400	10	94.5	$121,039
17	Matt Kenseth	Ford	10	9	8	400	39	107.7	$122,916
31	Jeff Burton	Chevrolet	2	8	9	400	25	111.3	$104,995
10	Scott Riggs	Dodge	26	11	10	400	0	70.6	$81,750
42	Casey Mears	Dodge	13	10	11	400	0	82.8	$110,208
07	Clint Bowyer*	Chevrolet	16	12	12	400	0	90.4	$83,975
18	J.J. Yeley*	Chevrolet	32	13	13	400	0	80.9	$108,325
41	Reed Sorenson*	Dodge	29	14	14	400	0	71.7	$79,500
11	Denny Hamlin*	Chevrolet	1	15	15	399	19	97.1	$87,525
19	Elliott Sadler	Dodge	14	17	16	399	0	73.1	$99,966
8	Dale Earnhardt Jr.	Chevrolet	33	16	17	399	0	84.3	$104,666
20	Tony Stewart	Chevrolet	40	18	18	399	0	71.9	$124,961
7	Robby Gordon	Chevrolet	36	20	19	399	0	57.5	$69,300
12	Ryan Newman	Dodge	23	19	20	399	0	75.5	$111,733
88	Dale Jarrett	Ford	22	22	21	399	0	59.8	$103,275
43	Bobby Labonte	Dodge	27	21	22	399	0	57.7	$105,661
48	Jimmie Johnson	Chevrolet	19	25	23	399	4	70.4	$114,836
25	Brian Vickers	Chevrolet	37	23	24	398	0	52.9	$76,400
26	Jamie McMurray	Ford	30	24	25	398	0	49.3	$112,275
40	David Stremme*	Dodge	11	27	26	398	0	59.1	$92,058
2	Kurt Busch	Dodge	18	26	27	398	0	52.7	$105,808
32	Travis Kvapil	Chevrolet	31	28	28	398	0	42.7	$81,808
4	Scott Wimmer	Chevrolet	6	30	29	398	0	66.8	$67,025
14	Sterling Marlin	Chevrolet	28	31	30	398	0	48.6	$76,558
24	Jeff Gordon	Chevrolet	3	29	31	398	0	68.8	$112,611
01	Joe Nemechek	Chevrolet	21	32	32	398	0	43.5	$90,495
49	Kevin Lepage	Dodge	39	33	33	397	0	37.4	$74,522
45	Kyle Petty	Dodge	38	35	34	397	0	34.5	$71,900
99	Carl Edwards	Ford	9	34	35	397	0	45.5	$83,550
38	David Gilliland	Ford	24	36	36	396	0	57.3	$91,508
78	Kenny Wallace	Chevrolet	41	37	37	395	0	29.9	$63,475
61	Chad Chaffin	Dodge	42	38	38	392	0	28.0	$63,350
96	Tony Raines	Chevrolet	25	39	39	390	0	40.2	$63,225
1	Martin Truex Jr.*	Chevrolet	7	40	40	278	0	69.1	$71,100
66	Jeff Green	Chevrolet	34	41	41	273	0	53.1	$70,960
34	Chad Blount	Chevrolet	35	42	42	98	0	25.8	$62,835
89	Morgan Shepherd	Dodge	43	43	43	18	0	24.9	$62,689

POINT STANDINGS

Rk.	Driver	Pts.	Diff.
1.	Matt Kenseth	3,785	—
2.	Jimmie Johnson	3,728	-57
3.	Kevin Harvick	3,481	-10
4.	Kyle Busch	3,424	-15
5.	Denny Hamlin	3,348	-20
6.	Dale Earnhardt Jr.	3,338	-25
7.	Mark Martin	3,336	-30
8.	Jeff Burton	3,322	-35
9.	Jeff Gordon	3,321	-40
10.	Kasey Kahne	3,319	-45
11.	Tony Stewart	3,303	-1,747
12.	Greg Biffle	3,039	-2,011
13.	Carl Edwards	3,011	-2,039
14.	Kurt Busch	2,828	-2,222
15.	Casey Mears	2,815	-2,235
16.	Clint Bowyer	2,755	-2,295
17.	Ryan Newman	2,753	-2,297
18.	Scott Riggs	2,723	-2,327
19.	Jamie McMurray	2,722	-2,328
20.	Brian Vickers	2,679	-2,371

CHASE POINT STANDINGS

Rk.	Driver	Pts.	Diff.
1.	Matt Kenseth	5,050	—
2.	Jimmie Johnson	5,045	-5
3.	Kevin Harvick	5,040	-10
4.	Kyle Busch	5,035	-15
5.	Denny Hamlin	5,030	-20
6.	Dale Earnhardt Jr.	5,025	-25
7.	Mark Martin	5,020	-30
8.	Jeff Burton	5,015	-35
9.	Jeff Gordon	5,010	-40
10.	Kasey Kahne	5,005	-45

*Rookie. **Time of race:** 2:57:37. **Average speed:** 101.342 mph. **Margin of victory:** .153 seconds.
Caution flags: 7 for 48 laps: 36-40 (Car 14—spin, Turn 4); 82-86 (Cars 48, 99—accident, Turn 2); 121-125 (Cars 1, 38—accident, Turn 3); 129-137 (Car 1—accident, Turn 2); 221-228 (debris); 253-262 (Car 66—accident, Turn 2); 322-327 (Car 48—accident, Turn 2). **Lead changes:** 16 among 8 drivers: Hamlin 1-19; Harvick 20-36; Johnson 37-40; Harvick 41; Burton 42-66; Harvick 67-82; Kenseth 83-121; Ky. Busch 122-142; Harvick 143-153; Ky. Busch 154-215; Kahne 216; Ky. Busch 217-255; Schrader 256-265; Ky. Busch 266-333; Harvick 334-340; Ky. Busch 341-398; Harvick 399-400. **Fell out of race:** Truex (accident); Green (parked); Blount (suspension); Shepherd (brakes). **Pole:** Denny Hamlin, 127.986 mph. **Dropped to rear:** Blount (unapproved impound adjustment). **Failed to qualify:** Derrike Cope (74), Mike Wallace (09), Michael Waltrip (55), Hermie Sadler (00), Ted Christopher (27). **Estimated attendance:** 107,000.

Driver rating: An average of these categories—Win, finish, top 15 finish, average running position on lead lap, average speed under green, fastest lap, led most laps, lead-lap finish. Maximum points: 150 per race.

>>SYLVANIA 300

New Hampshire International Speedway

Loudon, N.H. • 1.058-mile flat paved oval • September 17, 2006 • 317.4 miles, 300 laps • Purse: $5,209,809

Car	Driver	Make	Start	30 laps to go	Finish	Laps run	Laps led	Rating	Winnings
29	Kevin Harvick	Chevrolet	1	1	1	300	196	148.9	$266,461
20	Tony Stewart	Chevrolet	32	8	2	300	0	109.5	$220,686
24	Jeff Gordon	Chevrolet	2	3	3	300	34	125.1	$171,536
11	Denny Hamlin*	Chevrolet	5	5	4	300	4	105.8	$113,050
25	Brian Vickers	Chevrolet	12	2	5	300	0	114.6	$118,625
19	Elliott Sadler	Dodge	14	7	6	300	0	80.0	$125,516
31	Jeff Burton	Chevrolet	22	4	7	300	52	117.0	$137,570
18	J.J. Yeley*	Chevrolet	36	6	8	300	4	78.0	$119,050
22	Dave Blaney	Dodge	21	9	9	300	5	85.2	$103,033
17	Matt Kenseth	Ford	25	10	10	300	1	91.0	$130,466
6	Mark Martin	Ford	26	14	11	300	1	98.4	$95,975
12	Ryan Newman	Dodge	4	13	12	300	0	97.2	$121,583
8	Dale Earnhardt Jr.	Chevrolet	13	12	13	300	0	104.3	$115,716
16	Greg Biffle	Ford	8	15	14	300	0	80.3	$93,675
7	Robby Gordon	Chevrolet	9	17	15	300	2	73.6	$77,425
9	Kasey Kahne	Dodge	33	11	16	300	0	84.4	$109,389
41	Reed Sorenson*	Dodge	31	16	17	300	0	85.4	$83,625
99	Carl Edwards	Ford	19	18	18	300	0	72.1	$91,525
2	Kurt Busch	Dodge	3	21	19	300	0	86.6	$114,058
40	David Stremme*	Dodge	6	19	20	300	0	77.6	$101,883
42	Casey Mears	Dodge	24	20	21	300	0	73.6	$108,758
1	Martin Truex Jr.*	Chevrolet	11	22	22	300	0	64.3	$96,458
55	Michael Waltrip	Dodge	35	25	23	299	0	57.9	$86,608
07	Clint Bowyer*	Chevrolet	18	29	24	299	0	57.7	$81,700
14	Sterling Marlin	Chevrolet	30	27	25	299	1	48.0	$83,347
96	Tony Raines	Chevrolet	28	23	26	299	0	58.5	$73,100
32	Travis Kvapil	Chevrolet	34	28	27	299	0	47.8	$72,875
88	Dale Jarrett	Ford	37	24	28	299	0	53.4	$104,250
26	Jamie McMurray	Ford	42	30	29	298	0	44.5	$116,225
49	Kevin Lepage	Dodge	40	32	30	297	0	38.8	$69,650
4	Scott Wimmer	Chevrolet	39	31	31	297	0	38.6	$68,950
01	Joe Nemechek	Chevrolet	17	34	32	295	0	45.7	$95,070
21	Ken Schrader	Ford	10	35	33	295	0	38.4	$96,689
61	Chad Chaffin	Dodge	38	36	34	293	0	31.0	$68,325
10	Scott Riggs	Dodge	23	33	35	291	0	52.8	$68,125
38	David Gilliland	Ford	15	37	36	291	0	55.1	$95,808
45	Kyle Petty	Dodge	27	26	37	290	0	39.2	$75,700
5	Kyle Busch	Chevrolet	16	38	38	276	0	41.8	$85,500
48	Jimmie Johnson	Chevrolet	7	40	39	233	0	59.2	$115,911
43	Bobby Labonte	Dodge	29	39	40	207	0	56.5	$104,161
27	Ted Christopher	Chevrolet	43	41	41	123	0	25.9	$67,060
89	Morgan Shepherd	Dodge	41	42	42	61	0	30.0	$66,935
66	Jeff Green	Chevrolet	20	43	43	2	0	29.3	$75,139

POINT STANDINGS

Rk.	Driver	Pts.	Diff.
1.	Kevin Harvick	5,230	—
2.	Denny Hamlin	5,195	-35
3.	Matt Kenseth	5,189	-41
4.	Jeff Gordon	5,180	-50
5.	Jeff Burton	5,166	-64
6.	Mark Martin	5,155	-75
7.	Dale Earnhardt Jr.	5,149	-81
8.	Kasey Kahne	5,120	-110
9.	Jimmie Johnson	5,091	-139
10.	Kyle Busch	5,084	-146
11.	Tony Stewart	3,473	-1,757
12.	Greg Biffle	3,160	-2,070
13.	Carl Edwards	3,120	-2,110
14.	Kurt Busch	2,934	-2,296
15.	Casey Mears	2,915	-2,315
16.	Ryan Newman	2,880	-2,350
17.	Clint Bowyer	2,846	-2,384
18.	Brian Vickers	2,834	-2,396
19.	Jamie McMurray	2,798	-2,432
20.	Elliott Sadler	2,789	-2,441

*Rookie. **Time of race:** 3:06:21. **Average speed:** 102.195 mph. **Margin of victory:** .777 seconds.
Caution flags: 10 for 47 laps: 4-8 (Cars 5, 66—accident, frontstretch); 30-33 (Car 01—spin, Turn 4);
81-85 (debris); 90-93 (Cars 14, 16, 48—accident, Turn 2); 98-103 (debris); 194-198 (debris); 200-203
(Car 5—accident, Turn 4); 209-215 (Car 43—accident, Turn 2); 267-270 (Car 10—accident, Turn 3);
294-296 (oil on track). **Lap leaders:** 17 among 10 drivers: Harvick 1-27; J. Gordon 28-29; Harvick 30;
Marlin 31; Hamlin 32-35; Harvick 36-52; J. Gordon 53-80; Harvick 81; J. Gordon 82-85; Burton 86-137;
Harvick 138-169; Martin 170; Kenseth 171; Yeley 172-175; R. Gordon 176-177; Harvick 178-211; Blaney
212-216; Harvick 217-300. **Fell out of race:** Petty (engine); B. Labonte, Green (accident); Christopher
(brakes); Shepherd (overheating). **Pole:** Kevin Harvick, 132.282 mph. **Failed to qualify:** Stanton Barrett (30),
Derrike Cope (74), Carl Long (46), Kenny Wallace (78), Chad Blount (34). **Estimated attendance:** 101,000.

Driver rating: An average of these categories—Win, finish, top 15 finish, average running position on lead
lap, average speed under green, fastest lap, led most laps, lead-lap finish. Maximum points: 150 per race.

Dover International Speedway

Dover, Del. • 1-mile banked concrete oval • September 24, 2006 • 400 miles, 400 laps • Purse: $5,028,146

Car	Driver	Make	Start	40 laps to go	Finish	Laps run	Laps led	Rating	Winnings
31	Jeff Burton	Chevrolet	19	2	1	400	6	105.1	$230,370
99	Carl Edwards	Ford	6	6	2	400	21	115.5	$172,850
24	Jeff Gordon	Chevrolet	1	7	3	400	0	103.4	$181,836
2	Kurt Busch	Dodge	10	3	4	400	0	116.2	$153,233
16	Greg Biffle	Ford	8	10	5	400	57	118.6	$123,825
1	Martin Truex Jr.*	Chevrolet	33	8	6	400	0	98.0	$123,283
43	Bobby Labonte	Dodge	26	9	7	400	0	80.9	$124,911
07	Clint Bowyer*	Chevrolet	16	5	8	400	0	101.4	$90,625
11	Denny Hamlin*	Chevrolet	23	11	9	400	0	74.1	$80,875
17	Matt Kenseth	Ford	3	1	10	399	215	132.1	$136,816
41	Reed Sorenson*	Dodge	7	4	11	399	39	112.5	$102,125
22	Dave Blaney	Dodge	38	13	12	399	0	65.1	$96,983
48	Jimmie Johnson	Chevrolet	18	14	13	399	0	86.5	$119,861
6	Mark Martin	Ford	9	15	14	399	0	85.2	$87,075
88	Dale Jarrett	Ford	34	18	15	398	0	64.1	$105,200
19	Elliott Sadler	Dodge	35	19	16	398	30	95.1	$101,466
26	Jamie McMurray	Ford	32	22	17	398	0	76.1	$114,300
40	David Stremme*	Dodge	20	21	18	398	3	69.8	$93,108
21	Ken Schrader	Ford	36	20	19	397	0	50.6	$97,889
66	Jeff Green	Chevrolet	28	23	20	397	0	55.4	$92,883
8	Dale Earnhardt Jr.	Chevrolet	13	24	21	397	0	87.5	$105,166
42	Casey Mears	Dodge	24	16	22	397	0	60.5	$104,083
96	Tony Raines	Chevrolet	41	25	23	397	0	49.7	$70,625
12	Ryan Newman	Dodge	4	17	24	397	28	92.3	$111,733
45	Kyle Petty	Dodge	17	26	25	396	0	45.5	$87,197
01	Joe Nemechek	Chevrolet	5	27	26	396	0	51.3	$95,345
38	David Gilliland	Ford	39	29	27	396	0	38.6	$96,758
55	Michael Waltrip	Dodge	29	28	28	396	0	47.0	$68,200
25	Brian Vickers	Chevrolet	15	30	29	395	0	60.8	$73,550
18	J.J. Yeley*	Chevrolet	42	31	30	395	0	58.0	$100,475
14	Sterling Marlin	Chevrolet	12	32	31	393	1	54.0	$65,225
29	Kevin Harvick	Chevrolet	25	12	32	366	0	65.7	$101,986
20	Tony Stewart	Chevrolet	22	33	33	303	0	47.6	$119,786
10	Scott Riggs	Dodge	2	34	34	295	0	67.8	$65,125
61	Stanton Barrett	Dodge	40	35	35	202	0	30.4	$64,500
4	Scott Wimmer	Chevrolet	43	36	36	199	0	45.2	$64,350
49	Kevin Lepage	Dodge	11	37	37	182	0	35.2	$64,225
9	Kasey Kahne	Dodge	21	38	38	172	0	36.7	$101,314
32	Travis Kvapil	Chevrolet	30	39	39	118	0	25.3	$63,975
5	Kyle Busch	Chevrolet	27	40	40	110	0	67.6	$81,800
7	Robby Gordon	Chevrolet	14	41	41	98	0	61.5	$63,610
06	David Ragan	Ford	37	42	42	46	0	31.9	$63,485
74	Derrike Cope	Dodge	31	43	43	39	0	26.4	$63,686

POINT STANDINGS

Rk.	Driver	Pts.	Diff.
1.	Jeff Burton	5,351	—
2.	Jeff Gordon	5,345	-6
3.	Matt Kenseth	5,333	-18
4.	Denny Hamlin	5,333	-18
5.	Kevin Harvick	5,297	-54
6.	Mark Martin	5,276	-75
7.	Dale Earnhardt Jr.	5,249	-102
8.	Jimmie Johnson	5,215	-136
9.	Kasey Kahne	5,169	-182
10.	Kyle Busch	5,127	-224
11.	Tony Stewart	3,537	-1,814
12.	Greg Biffle	3,320	-2,031
13.	Carl Edwards	3,295	-2,056
14.	Kurt Busch	3,094	-2,257
15.	Casey Mears	3,012	-2,339
16.	Clint Bowyer	2,988	-2,363
17.	Ryan Newman	2,976	-2,375
18.	Brian Vickers	2,910	-2,441
19.	Jamie McMurray	2,910	-2,441
20.	Elliott Sadler	2,909	-2,442

*Rookie. **Time of race:** 3:34:21. **Average speed:** 111.966 mph. **Margin of victories:** 7.955 seconds. **Caution flags:** 10 for 48 laps: 4-7 (Car 32—accident, frontstretch); 13-15 (Cars 9, 20—accident, Turn 4); 24-26 (Car 06—accident, Turn 4); 49-52 (Car 06—accident, Turn 3); 100-104 (Car 7—accident, Turn 3); 166-169 (debris); 186-189 (Car 49—accident, Turn 2); 206-213 (debris); 298-306 (Car 10—accident, Turn 3); 324-327 (Car 18—spin, frontstretch). **Lead changes:** 12 among 9 drivers: J. Gordon—pole; Newman 1-28; Edwards 29-49; Stremme 50-52; E. Sadler 53-73; Kenseth 74-113; E. Sadler 114-122; Kenseth 123-166; Marlin 167; Sorenson 168-206; Biffle 207-263; Kenseth 264-394; Burton 395-400. **Fell out of race:** Harvick, Wimmer, Ky. Busch, Cope (engine); Stewart, Riggs, Barrett, Lepage, Kahne, Kvapil, R. Gordon, Ragan (accident). **Pole:** Jeff Gordon, 156.162 mph. **Dropped to rear:** Riggs, Kvapil (engine change); Yeley (backup car). **Failed to qualify:** Morgan Shepherd (89), Kenny Wallace (78), Chad Blount (34), Donnie Neuenberger (52). **Estimated attendance:** 145,000.

Driver rating: An average of these categories—Win, finish, top 15 finish, average running position on lead lap, average speed under green, fastest lap, led most laps, lead-lap finish. Maximum points: 150 per race.

>>BANQUET 400 PRESENTED BY CONAGRA FOODS

race 29 of 36

Kansas Speedway

Kansas City, Kan. • 1.5-mile paved trioval • October 1, 2006 • 400 miles, 267 laps • Purse: $5,934,007

Car	Driver	Make	Start	27 laps to go	Finish	Laps run	Laps led	Rating	Winnings
20	Tony Stewart	Chevrolet	21	3	1	267	5	114.7	$346,361
42	Casey Mears	Dodge	33	7	2	267	0	91.1	$240,033
6	Mark Martin	Ford	19	11	3	267	0	93.1	$181,525
88	Dale Jarrett	Ford	32	12	4	267	0	86.1	$172,175
31	Jeff Burton	Chevrolet	10	2	5	267	1	117.8	$155,595
99	Carl Edwards	Ford	27	4	6	267	7	97.9	$124,350
5	Kyle Busch	Chevrolet	13	14	7	267	64	114.7	$128,625
25	Brian Vickers	Chevrolet	4	13	8	267	0	80.5	$110,525
07	Clint Bowyer*	Chevrolet	6	16	9	267	43	106.0	$109,425
8	Dale Earnhardt Jr.	Chevrolet	12	5	10	267	18	115.1	$135,741
1	Martin Truex Jr. *	Chevrolet	23	8	11	267	0	91.0	$123,358
16	Greg Biffle	Ford	29	6	12	267	2	98.4	$112,400
21	Ken Schrader	Ford	36	18	13	267	0	74.4	$120,564
48	Jimmie Johnson	Chevrolet	3	1	14	267	105	130.3	$141,486
29	Kevin Harvick	Chevrolet	14	10	15	266	0	75.1	$129,011
37	Bill Elliott	Dodge	39	23	16	266	0	50.0	$86,525
43	Bobby Labonte	Dodge	16	15	17	266	0	71.5	$126,561
11	Denny Hamlin*	Chevrolet	25	28	18	266	0	79.7	$88,925
32	Travis Kvapil	Chevrolet	37	25	19	266	1	52.5	$104,383
14	Sterling Marlin	Chevrolet	28	24	20	266	1	50.7	$103,983
22	Dave Blaney	Dodge	17	22	21	266	0	57.6	$98,983
38	David Gilliland	Ford	20	17	22	266	0	62.8	$114,033
17	Matt Kenseth	Ford	8	21	23	266	0	70.8	$129,516
12	Ryan Newman	Dodge	15	26	24	266	3	50.1	$127,108
2	Kurt Busch	Dodge	7	19	25	265	0	63.0	$122,133
40	David Stremme*	Dodge	40	32	26	265	0	46.9	$101,547
01	Joe Nemechek	Chevrolet	18	20	27	265	0	52.4	$109,245
96	Tony Raines	Chevrolet	38	30	28	265	0	39.6	$82,300
45	Kyle Petty	Dodge	24	27	29	265	0	60.2	$89,600
66	Jeff Green	Chevrolet	31	31	30	264	0	56.5	$87,350
78	Kenny Wallace	Chevrolet	43	33	31	264	0	30.9	$78,650
06	Todd Kluever	Ford	22	36	32	264	0	34.2	$78,450
9	Kasey Kahne	Dodge	1	9	33	264	11	91.0	$132,414
10	Scott Riggs	Dodge	2	34	34	263	6	83.0	$78,050
55	Michael Waltrip	Chevrolet	35	38	35	263	0	32.9	$77,850
7	Robby Gordon	Dodge	42	35	36	263	0	38.6	$77,650
61	Chad Chaffin	Dodge	34	39	37	261	0	26.3	$77,425
44	Terry Labonte	Chevrolet	30	37	38	253	0	36.8	$77,225
24	Jeff Gordon	Chevrolet	11	29	39	238	0	80.2	$125,361
19	Elliott Sadler	Dodge	9	40	40	228	0	40.7	$106,816
18	J.J. Yeley*	Chevrolet	5	41	41	194	0	69.1	$111,175
26	Jamie McMurray	Ford	41	42	42	128	0	42.2	$123,250
41	Reed Sorenson*	Dodge	26	43	43	18	0	38.2	$84,566

POINT STANDINGS

Rk.	Driver	Pts.	Diff.
1.	Jeff Burton	5,511	—
2.	Denny Hamlin	5,442	-69
3.	Mark Martin	5,441	-70
4.	Matt Kenseth	5,427	-84
5.	Kevin Harvick	5,415	-96
6.	Jeff Gordon	5,391	-120
7.	Dale Earnhardt Jr.	5,388	-123
8.	Jimmie Johnson	5,346	-165
9.	Kyle Busch	5,278	-233
10.	Kasey Kahne	5,238	-273
11.	Tony Stewart	3,722	-1,789
12.	Greg Biffle	3,452	-2,059
13.	Carl Edwards	3,450	-2,061
14.	Kurt Busch	3,182	-2,329
15.	Casey Mears	3,182	-2,329
16.	Clint Bowyer	3,131	-2,380
17.	Ryan Newman	3,072	-2,439
18.	Brian Vickers	3,052	-2,459
19.	Elliott Sadler	2,952	-2,559
20.	Jamie McMurray	2,947	-2,564

*Rookie. **Time of race:** 3:17:22. **Average speed:** 121.753 mph. **Margin of victory:** 12.422 seconds. **Caution flags:** 11 for 45 laps: 11-13 (Car 7—accident, Turn 4); 16-18 (Car 12—spin, Turn 4); 21-24 (Car 41—accident, Turn 4); 59-63 (debris); 69-72 (Car 38—spin, Turn 4); 131-136 (Car 26—accident, Turn 2); 146-149 (Car 19—accident, frontstretch); 154-157 (Car 11—accident, Turn 4); 173-176 (Car 07—accident, Turn 2); 182-185 (Car 12—spin, Turn 2); 196-199 (Cars 18, 40—accident, Turn 2). **Lead changes:** 20 among 13 drivers: Kahne 1-11; Newman 12-13; Johnson 14-28; Riggs 29-34; Bowyer 35-60; Kvapil 61; Earnhardt 62-79; Ky. Busch 80-124; Johnson 125-126; Newman 127; Ky. Busch 128-146; Marlin 147; Bowyer 148-157; Burton 158; Bowyer 159-165; Johnson 166-173; Edwards 174-180; Johnson 181-200; Biffle 201-202; Johnson 203-262; Stewart 263-267. **Fell out of race:** T. Labonte (suspension); J. Gordon (fuel pump); Yeley, McMurray, Sorenson (accident). **Pole:** Kasey Kahne, 178.377 mph. **Failed to qualify:** Scott Wimmer (4), Kevin Lepage (49), Chad Blount (34), Carl Long (46). **Estimated attendance:** 125,000.

Driver rating: An average of these categories—Win, finish, top 15 finish, average running position on lead lap, average speed under green, fastest lap, led most laps, lead-lap finish. Maximum points: 150 per race.

Talladega Superspeedway

Talladega, Ala. • 2.66-mile banked paved trioval • October 8, 2006 • 500 miles, 188 laps • Purse: $5,272,231

Car	Driver	Make	Start	19 laps to go	Finish	Laps run	Laps led	Rating	Winnings
25	Brian Vickers	Chevrolet	9	5	1	188	17	106.9	$228,850
9	Kasey Kahne	Dodge	25	2	2	188	7	99.2	$193,064
2	Kurt Busch	Dodge	29	4	3	188	3	105.6	$169,108
17	Matt Kenseth	Ford	19	10	4	188	21	120.2	$167,216
1	Martin Truex Jr.*	Chevrolet	16	6	5	188	2	91.3	$139,008
29	Kevin Harvick	Chevrolet	14	7	6	188	0	95.3	$137,161
66	Jeff Green	Chevrolet	37	23	7	188	0	83.9	$116,783
6	Mark Martin	Ford	30	12	8	188	2	85.0	$102,250
99	Carl Edwards	Ford	17	19	9	188	0	106.0	$102,025
43	Bobby Labonte	Dodge	39	28	10	188	0	51.2	$130,036
5	Kyle Busch	Chevrolet	6	27	11	188	10	87.3	$96,475
88	Dale Jarrett	Ford	2	9	12	188	1	57.1	$125,475
12	Ryan Newman	Dodge	11	17	13	188	0	86.4	$94,983
55	Michael Waltrip	Dodge	21	26	14	188	1	55.8	$120,033
38	David Gilliland	Ford	1	14	15	188	0	71.0	$112,808
7	Robby Gordon	Chevrolet	36	11	16	188	0	74.7	$77,050
09	Mike Wallace	Ford	28	24	17	188	0	76.7	$73,000
01	Joe Nemechek	Chevrolet	15	13	18	188	1	83.2	$102,845
10	Scott Riggs	Dodge	41	20	19	188	0	61.9	$76,125
96	Tony Raines	Chevrolet	40	25	20	188	0	52.4	$78,500
11	Denny Hamlin*	Chevrolet	12	22	21	188	1	66.8	$75,300
20	Tony Stewart	Chevrolet	13	16	22	188	1	69.1	$125,636
8	Dale Earnhardt Jr.	Chevrolet	33	1	23	188	37	85.5	$115,866
48	Jimmie Johnson	Chevrolet	3	3	24	187	6	81.3	$120,086
21	Ken Schrader	Ford	23	30	25	187	0	38.1	$101,664
49	Mike Bliss	Dodge	20	29	26	187	0	51.7	$82,358
31	Jeff Burton	Chevrolet	34	8	27	187	5	80.3	$99,945
22	Dave Blaney	Dodge	35	31	28	186	0	42.4	$82,897
19	Elliott Sadler	Dodge	22	32	29	186	1	61.8	$103,191
42	Casey Mears	Dodge	31	34	30	185	1	53.6	$107,183
4	Eric McClure	Chevrolet	27	33	31	182	0	30.1	$69,875
18	J.J. Yeley*	Chevrolet	10	15	32	177	0	47.0	$104,275
40	David Stremme*	Dodge	38	21	33	175	0	68.1	$78,500
15	Paul Menard	Dodge	24	18	34	173	1	68.8	$69,375
07	Clint Bowyer*	Chevrolet	32	35	35	171	5	54.2	$77,200
24	Jeff Gordon	Chevrolet	4	36	36	167	27	76.9	$117,636
26	Jamie McMurray	Ford	8	39	37	160	22	83.8	$125,750
45	Kyle Petty	Dodge	18	37	38	149	0	30.3	$76,800
41	Reed Sorenson*	Dodge	42	38	39	147	1	40.5	$76,675
14	Sterling Marlin	Chevrolet	7	40	40	145	0	50.9	$68,525
16	Greg Biffle	Ford	5	41	41	137	15	89.7	$88,735
78	Kenny Wallace	Chevrolet	26	42	42	24	0	45.9	$68,260
74	Derrike Cope	Dodge	43	43	43	9	0	30.0	$68,473

POINT STANDINGS

Rk.	Driver	Pts.	Diff.
1.	Jeff Burton	5,598	—
2.	Matt Kenseth	5,592	-6
3.	Mark Martin	5,588	-10
4.	Kevin Harvick	5,565	-33
5.	Denny Hamlin	5,547	-51
6.	Dale Earnhardt Jr.	5,492	-106
7.	Jeff Gordon	5,451	-147
8.	Jimmie Johnson	5,442	-156
9.	Kyle Busch	5,413	-185
10.	Kasey Kahne	5,413	-185
11.	Tony Stewart	3,824	-1,774
12.	Carl Edwards	3,588	-2,010
13.	Greg Biffle	3,497	-2,101
14.	Kurt Busch	3,352	-2,246
15.	Casey Mears	3,260	-2,338
16.	Brian Vickers	3,237	-2,361
17.	Ryan Newman	3,196	-2,402
18.	Clint Bowyer	3,194	-2,404
19.	Martin Truex Jr.	3,073	-2,525
20.	Elliott Sadler	3,033	-2,565

*Rookie. **Time of race:** 3:10:23. **Average speed:** 157.602 mph. **Margin of victory:** Under caution. **Caution flags:** 6 for 22 laps: 73-75 (debris); 131-134 (debris); 139-145 (Cars 07, 1, 11, 14, 16, 19, 24, 26, 29, 42, 43, 45, 99—accident, Turn 1); 150-152 (oil on track); 175-178 (Cars 11, 15, 18, 20, 40—accident, Turn 2); 188 (Cars 8, 48—accident, Turn 3). **Lead changes:** 63 among 23 drivers: Gilliland—pole; Jarrett 1; J. Gordon 2-3; McMurray 4-7; J. Gordon 8-17; McMurray 18-20; J. Gordon 21-24; McMurray 25-28; Biffle 29-35; Stewart 36; Ky. Busch 37-38; Earnhardt 39-41; Ky. Busch 42-44; Earnhardt 45; Ky. Busch 46; Kenseth 47-49; Ku. Busch 50; Kenseth 51; Ku. Busch 52; Earnhardt 53-59; E. Sadler 60; McMurray 61; Earnhardt 62; Kenseth 63-70; Biffle 71-76; J. Gordon 77-78; Biffle 79-80; J. Gordon 81-87; Earnhardt 88; J. Gordon 89; Ky. Busch 90-91; Earnhardt 92-93; McMurray 94-102; Vickers 103-108; McMurray 109; Martin 110-111; Vickers 112-114; Mears 115; Vickers 116-121; Ky. Busch 122-123; J. Gordon 124; Kenseth 125; Bowyer 126-127; Kenseth 128-129; Bowyer 130; Hamlin 131; Waltrip 132; Bowyer 133-134; Kenseth 135-138; Burton 139-143; Sorenson 144; Kenseth 145-146; Vickers 147; Johnson 148-149; Nemechek 150; Truex Jr. 151-152; Johnson 153; Menard 154; Johnson 155-157; Kahne 158-163; Ku. Busch 164; Kahne 165; Earnhardt 166-187; Vickers 188. **Fell out of race:** Johnson, Yeley, Stremme, Menard, Bowyer, J. Gordon, McMurray, Petty, Marlin, Biffle (accident); Sorenson, Wallace (engine); Cope (overheating). **Pole:** David Gilliland, 191.712 mph. **Failed to qualify:** Travis Kvapil (32), Chad Chaffin (61), Todd Bodine (4), Hermie Sadler (00), Kirk Shelmerdine (27), Kevin Lepage (34). **Estimated attendance:** 160,000.

Driver rating: An average of these categories—Win, finish, top 15 finish, average running position on lead lap, average speed under green, fastest lap, led most laps, lead-lap finish. Maximum points: 150 per race.

Lowe's Motor Speedway

Concord, N.C. • 1.5-mile high-banked paved trioval • October 14, 2006 • 501 miles, 334 laps • Purse: $5,078,500

Car	Driver	Make	Start	34 laps to go	Finish	Laps run	Laps led	Rating	Winnings
9	Kasey Kahne	Dodge	2	1	1	334	134	143.6	$305,889
48	Jimmie Johnson	Chevrolet	10	5	2	334	72	126.4	$221,511
31	Jeff Burton	Chevrolet	6	7	3	334	0	111.5	$176,870
8	Dale Earnhardt Jr.	Chevrolet	16	2	4	334	37	117.5	$154,916
43	Bobby Labonte	Dodge	21	8	5	334	2	90.6	$151,436
5	Kyle Busch	Chevrolet	18	6	6	334	1	105.6	$112,050
96	Tony Raines	Chevrolet	39	10	7	334	28	97.0	$95,375
99	Carl Edwards	Ford	28	3	8	334	12	101.4	$103,475
01	Joe Nemechek	Chevrolet	30	11	9	334	0	76.0	$108,095
25	Brian Vickers	Chevrolet	25	9	10	334	0	74.6	$91,925
14	Sterling Marlin	Chevrolet	13	12	11	334	3	85.2	$106,133
42	Casey Mears	Dodge	3	13	12	333	0	84.9	$113,158
20	Tony Stewart	Chevrolet	31	14	13	333	0	64.2	$125,336
17	Matt Kenseth	Ford	11	15	14	332	1	76.9	$115,466
40	David Stremme*	Dodge	12	16	15	332	0	80.1	$97,033
66	Jeff Green	Chevrolet	20	17	16	332	0	63.9	$91,583
10	Scott Riggs	Dodge	1	19	17	332	34	97.0	$97,475
29	Kevin Harvick	Chevrolet	5	18	18	332	0	82.4	$106,661
4	Todd Bodine	Chevrolet	14	20	19	331	0	50.9	$67,725
32	Travis Kvapil	Chevrolet	38	22	20	331	0	51.2	$81,783
44	Terry Labonte	Chevrolet	43	21	21	331	0	51.5	$63,725
45	Kyle Petty	Dodge	32	23	22	330	0	40.3	$84,197
07	Clint Bowyer*	Chevrolet	8	24	23	329	3	89.6	$75,700
24	Jeff Gordon	Chevrolet	41	4	24	301	2	97.6	$111,236
7	Robby Gordon	Chevrolet	19	25	25	300	0	72.5	$66,075
22	Dave Blaney	Dodge	36	27	26	278	0	36.5	$65,475
12	Ryan Newman	Dodge	15	29	27	272	0	65.2	$107,658
11	Denny Hamlin*	Chevrolet	22	30	28	265	0	32.9	$64,550
18	J.J. Yeley*	Chevrolet	40	26	29	258	0	56.4	$96,425
6	Mark Martin	Ford	7	28	30	239	0	84.1	$80,725
1	Martin Truex Jr.*	Chevrolet	26	31	31	216	0	39.4	$69,425
2	Kurt Busch	Dodge	42	32	32	208	0	50.5	$102,258
38	David Gilliland	Ford	35	33	33	161	0	38.6	$89,958
26	Jamie McMurray	Ford	27	34	34	160	0	54.2	$107,800
19	Elliott Sadler	Dodge	4	35	35	124	5	67.4	$95,816
41	Reed Sorenson*	Dodge	9	36	36	115	0	56.1	$69,050
16	Greg Biffle	Ford	33	37	37	111	0	64.3	$80,725
55	Michael Waltrip	Dodge	23	38	38	102	0	37.2	$60,400
06	Todd Kluever	Ford	37	39	39	45	0	41.5	$60,275
21	Ken Schrader	Ford	17	40	40	45	0	45.1	$87,364
88	Dale Jarrett	Ford	34	41	41	32	0	36.3	$92,085
49	Mike Bliss	Dodge	24	42	42	1	0	29.4	$59,885
72	Mike Skinner	Chevrolet	29	43	43	1	0	27.9	$60,093

POINT STANDINGS

Rk.	Driver	Pts.	Diff.
1.	Jeff Burton	5,763	—
2.	Matt Kenseth	5,718	-45
3.	Kevin Harvick	5,674	-89
4.	Mark Martin	5,661	-102
5.	Dale Earnhardt Jr.	5,657	-106
6.	Denny Hamlin	5,626	-137
7.	Jimmie Johnson	5,617	-146
8.	Kasey Kahne	5,603	-160
9.	Kyle Busch	5,568	-195
10.	Jeff Gordon	5,547	-216
11.	Tony Stewart	3,948	-1,815
12.	Carl Edwards	3,735	-2,028
13.	Greg Biffle	3,549	-2,214
14.	Kurt Busch	3,419	-2,344
15.	Casey Mears	3,387	-2,376
16.	Brian Vickers	3,371	-2,392
17.	Clint Bowyer	3,293	-2,470
18.	Ryan Newman	3,278	-2,485
19.	Martin Truex Jr.	3,143	-2,620
20.	Scott Riggs	3,131	-2,632

*Rookie. **Time of race:** 3:47:29. **Average speed:** 132.142 mph. **Margin of victory:** 1.624 seconds. **Caution flags:** 10 for 52 laps: 3-11 (Cars 1, 7, 11, 18, 26, 32, 45, 49, 72—accident, frontstretch); 18-21 (Car 22—accident, Turn 4); 35-38 (Car 88—accident, Turn 4); 47-52 (Cars 06, 21—accident, backstretch); 106-109 (Car 55—accident, Turn 4); 117-120 (Cars 2, 41—accident, Turn 2); 164-167 (Car 38—accident, backstretch); 243-251 (Cars 6, 7, 18—accident, Turn 4); 277-280 (debris); 303-306 (oil on track). **Lap leaders:** 34 among 13 drivers: Riggs—pole; Kahne 1-12; Riggs 13-18; Raines 19-30; Riggs 31-46; Earnhardt 47-77; Riggs 78-83; Bowyer 84-85; Ky. Busch 86; Johnson 87-88; Kenseth 89; Riggs 90-95; Kahne 96-117; Kahne 118-122; Raines 123-137; Kahne 138-153; Johnson 154-155; J. Gordon 156; B. Labonte 157-158; Raines 159; Kahne 160-164; Marlin 165-167; Johnson 168-202; Earnhardt 203-204; Bowyer 205; Kahne 206-210; Johnson 211-238; J. Gordon 239; Edwards 240; Earnhardt 241-244; Kahne 245; Edwards 246-256; Kahne 257-303; Johnson 304-308; Kahne 309-334. **Fell out of race:** Gordon, McMurray, Biffle (engine); Yeley, Martin, Gilliland, Sadler, Sorenson, Waltrip, Kluever, Jarrett, Bliss, Skinner (accident). **Pole:** Scott Riggs, 191.469 mph. **Dropped to rear:** Newman (backup car). **Failed to qualify:** Bill Elliott (83), Kevin Lepage (34), Derrike Cope (74), Chad Chaffin (61), Hermie Sadler (00), Kirk Shelmerdine (27), Carl Long (46), Kenny Wallace (78), Morgan Shepherd (89). **Estimated attendance:** 170,000.

Driver rating: An average of these categories—Win, finish, top 15 finish, average running position on lead lap, average speed under green, fastest lap, led most laps, lead-lap finish. Maximum points: 150 per race.

Martinsville, Va. • .526-mile paved oval • October 22, 2006 • 263 miles, 500 laps • Purse: $4,779,747

Car	Driver	Make	Start	50 laps to go	Finish	Laps run	Laps led	Rating	Winnings
48	Jimmie Johnson	Chevrolet	9	1	1	500	245	143.5	$191,886
11	Denny Hamlin*	Chevrolet	3	4	2	500	28	121.7	$118,525
43	Bobby Labonte	Dodge	30	2	3	500	43	85.0	$137,661
20	Tony Stewart	Chevrolet	5	9	4	500	0	108.6	$141,211
24	Jeff Gordon	Chevrolet	2	5	5	500	165	125.8	$148,686
42	Casey Mears	Dodge	19	3	6	500	0	88.0	$113,233
9	Kasey Kahne	Dodge	32	6	7	500	0	89.5	$110,814
66	Jeff Green	Chevrolet	8	10	8	500	0	98.7	$118,583
29	Kevin Harvick	Chevrolet	12	13	9	500	0	90.5	$112,411
45	Kyle Petty	Dodge	14	11	10	500	0	80.1	$103,083
17	Matt Kenseth	Ford	20	15	11	500	0	75.6	$118,716
99	Carl Edwards	Ford	27	12	12	500	0	79.6	$90,250
12	Ryan Newman	Dodge	4	17	13	500	0	71.8	$114,658
96	Tony Raines	Chevrolet	11	20	14	500	0	88.8	$73,575
40	David Stremme*	Dodge	13	21	15	500	0	70.1	$95,633
88	Dale Jarrett	Ford	39	18	16	500	0	60.2	$105,200
25	Brian Vickers	Chevrolet	21	14	17	500	0	70.6	$79,625
5	Kyle Busch	Chevrolet	15	25	18	500	0	92.4	$85,400
26	Jamie McMurray	Ford	24	23	19	500	0	56.2	$113,600
01	Joe Nemechek	Chevrolet	23	22	20	500	0	83.8	$98,795
14	Sterling Marlin	Chevrolet	22	19	21	500	0	64.7	$81,508
8	Dale Earnhardt Jr.	Chevrolet	7	7	22	500	0	101.3	$104,591
07	Clint Bowyer*	Chevrolet	37	8	23	500	0	64.5	$78,800
6	Mark Martin	Ford	25	16	24	500	0	78.9	$83,900
06	David Ragan	Ford	41	26	25	500	0	49.9	$66,125
4	Ward Burton	Chevrolet	35	24	26	500	0	51.7	$68,750
2	Kurt Busch	Dodge	1	28	27	496	19	96.9	$112,118
38	David Gilliland	Ford	29	27	28	496	0	40.3	$96,243
78	Kenny Wallace	Chevrolet	40	29	29	496	0	33.1	$65,100
10	Scott Riggs	Dodge	17	30	30	495	0	37.2	$68,525
18	J.J. Yeley*	Chevrolet	36	31	31	494	0	38.7	$102,500
16	Greg Biffle	Ford	38	32	32	486	0	47.3	$85,050
22	Dave Blaney	Dodge	6	33	33	485	0	63.7	$77,722
55	Michael Waltrip	Dodge	33	34	34	472	0	41.7	$64,675
41	Reed Sorenson*	Dodge	16	36	35	460	0	51.6	$72,625
1	Martin Truex Jr.*	Chevrolet	18	37	36	453	0	35.2	$72,575
7	Robby Gordon	Chevrolet	26	38	37	416	0	49.3	$64,525
19	Elliott Sadler	Dodge	34	35	38	412	0	66.2	$94,466
72	Mike Skinner	Chevrolet	43	39	39	341	0	30.5	$64,415
32	Travis Kvapil	Chevrolet	31	40	40	332	0	34.9	$64,365
21	Ken Schrader	Ford	10	41	41	331	0	81.7	$91,529
31	Jeff Burton	Chevrolet	28	42	42	217	0	41.1	$90,605
34	Kevin Lepage	Chevrolet	42	43	43	209	0	24.3	$63,657

POINT STANDINGS

Rk.	Driver	Pts.	Diff.
1.	Matt Kenseth	5,848	—
2.	Kevin Harvick	5,812	-36
3.	Jimmie Johnson	5,807	-41
4.	Denny Hamlin	5,801	-47
5.	Jeff Burton	5,800	-48
6.	Dale Earnhardt Jr.	5,754	-94
7.	Mark Martin	5,752	-96
8.	Kasey Kahne	5,749	-99
9.	Jeff Gordon	5,707	-141
10.	Kyle Busch	5,677	-171
11.	Tony Stewart	4,108	-1,740
12.	Carl Edwards	3,862	-1,986
13.	Greg Biffle	3,616	-2,232
14.	Casey Mears	3,537	-2,311
15.	Brian Vickers	3,483	-2,365
16.	Kurt Busch	3,456	-2,392
17.	Ryan Newman	3,402	-2,446
18.	Clint Bowyer	3,387	-2,461
19.	Scott Riggs	3,204	-2,644
20.	Bobby Labonte	3,203	-2,645

*Rookie. **Time of race:** 3:44:00. **Average speed:** 70.446 mph. **Margin of victory:** .544 seconds. **Caution flags:** 18 for 106 laps: 5-10 (Cars 1, 14, 45—accident, Turn 4); 66-72 (Car 42—spin, Turn 2); 156-161 (Car 40—spin, Turn 4); 205-209 (Car 55—accident, Turn 4); 223-227 (Car 4—accident, Turn 2); 233-238 (Cars 7, 29, 32, 41, 88—accident, Turn 3); 243-248 (Cars 32, 96—accident, Turn 3); 281-286 (Car 17—spin, Turn 4); 333-340 (Cars 06, 21, 88—accident, Turn 1); 347-352 (Car 72—accident, frontstretch); 357-361 (Car 06—spin, Turn 2); 365-371 (Car 2—accident, frontstretch); 401-406 (Car 26—spin, Turn 2); 449-453 (Cars 5, 06—accident, Turn 4); 462-467 (Cars 38, 42—accident, Turn 4); 470-476 (Car 07—accident, Turn 3); 478-482 (Cars 8, 9—accident, Turn 4); 491-494 (Car 78—spin, Turn 2). **Lead changes:** 16 among 5 drivers: Ku. Busch—pole; J. Gordon 1-144; Johnson 145; J. Gordon 146-152; Johnson 153-156; J. Gordon 157; Johnson 158-204; J. Gordon 205; Johnson 206-243; J. Gordon 244-255; Hamlin 256-282; Johnson 283-333; Ku. Busch 334-352; Johnson 353-400; Hamlin 401; B. Labonte 402-444; Johnson 445-500. **Fell out of race:** R. Gordon, Kvapil, Lepage (rear end); E. Sadler, J. Burton (engine); Skinner, Schrader (accident). **Pole:** Kurt Busch, 97.568 mph. **Dropped to rear:** Riggs, Wallace (engine change). **Failed to qualify:** Mike Bliss (49), Hermie Sadler (00), Chad Chaffin (61), Morgan Shepherd (89), Ted Christopher (27), Derrike Cope (74), Stanton Barrett (30). **Estimated attendance:** 65,000.

Driver rating: An average of these categories—Win, finish, top 15 finish, average running position on lead lap, average speed under green, fastest lap, led most laps, lead-lap finish. Maximum points: 150 per race.

>>BASS PRO SHOPS 500

Atlanta Motor Speedway

Hampton, Ga. • 1.54-mile banked paved oval • October 29, 2006 • 500.5 miles, 325 laps • Purse: $6,030,505

Car	Driver	Make	Start	33 laps to go	Finish	Laps run	Laps led	Rating	Winnings
20	Tony Stewart	Chevrolet	11	9	1	325	146	143.9	$373,286
48	Jimmie Johnson	Chevrolet	3	1	2	325	27	120.9	$251,686
8	Dale Earnhardt Jr.	Chevrolet	6	10	3	325	95	126.8	$215,991
17	Matt Kenseth	Ford	1	3	4	325	0	112.2	$183,041
16	Greg Biffle	Ford	13	2	5	325	0	96.9	$135,625
24	Jeff Gordon	Chevrolet	9	4	6	325	44	115.6	$158,561
99	Carl Edwards	Ford	12	5	7	325	1	99.8	$122,575
11	Denny Hamlin*	Chevrolet	4	8	8	325	0	88.8	$105,625
01	Joe Nemechek	Chevrolet	31	13	9	325	3	82.7	$132,845
7	Robby Gordon	Chevrolet	29	15	10	325	0	81.0	$104,975
88	Dale Jarrett	Ford	23	6	11	325	0	78.6	$129,175
43	Bobby Labonte	Dodge	20	20	12	324	0	86.2	$134,336
31	Jeff Burton	Chevrolet	5	19	13	323	0	99.7	$122,595
2	Kurt Busch	Dodge	16	17	14	323	0	79.4	$131,333
38	David Gilliland	Ford	25	24	15	323	0	71.1	$122,558
18	J.J. Yeley*	Chevrolet	30	22	16	323	0	57.7	$127,075
45	Kyle Petty	Dodge	37	18	17	323	0	51.9	$117,758
22	Dave Blaney	Dodge	26	21	18	323	0	70.4	$106,858
25	Brian Vickers	Chevrolet	15	25	19	323	0	60.5	$97,875
14	Sterling Marlin	Chevrolet	35	23	20	322	0	53.4	$105,433
19	Elliott Sadler	Dodge	34	29	21	322	0	53.3	$118,666
10	Scott Riggs	Dodge	19	26	22	322	0	65.7	$87,250
66	Jeff Green	Chevrolet	28	27	23	322	0	55.0	$106,133
21	Ken Schrader	Ford	32	28	24	322	0	53.5	$113,839
07	Clint Bowyer*	Chevrolet	18	12	25	322	0	79.9	$93,375
49	Mike Bliss	Dodge	41	16	26	321	0	58.0	$93,422
5	Kyle Busch	Chevrolet	10	33	27	321	0	45.0	$98,775
42	Casey Mears	Dodge	14	7	28	321	0	68.3	$114,333
41	Reed Sorenson*	Dodge	24	32	29	321	0	55.0	$88,000
12	Ryan Newman	Dodge	17	31	30	321	0	54.3	$125,258
29	Kevin Harvick	Chevrolet	2	30	31	321	9	81.9	$123,536
32	Travis Kvapil	Chevrolet	38	34	32	320	0	38.3	$79,525
55	Michael Waltrip	Dodge	39	37	33	319	0	38.3	$80,300
96	Tony Raines	Chevrolet	27	35	34	319	0	35.6	$79,200
78	Kenny Wallace	Chevrolet	43	36	35	319	0	29.9	$79,050
6	Mark Martin	Ford	7	14	36	309	0	73.8	$96,900
1	Martin Truex Jr.*	Chevrolet	21	11	37	305	0	82.6	$86,750
9	Kasey Kahne	Dodge	8	38	38	255	0	78.2	$115,839
40	David Stremme*	Dodge	33	39	39	246	0	40.0	$86,500
26	Jamie McMurray	Ford	22	40	40	244	0	49.2	$125,200
37	Bill Elliott	Dodge	36	41	41	146	0	31.2	$78,255
4	Todd Bodine	Chevrolet	40	42	42	144	0	23.8	$78,150
61	Kevin Lepage	Chevrolet	42	43	43	29	0	26.4	$78,362

POINT STANDINGS

Rk.	Driver	Pts.	Diff.
1.	Matt Kenseth	6,008	—
2.	Jimmie Johnson	5,982	-26
3.	Denny Hamlin	5,943	-65
4.	Jeff Burton	5,924	-84
5.	Dale Earnhardt Jr.	5,924	-84
6.	Kevin Harvick	5,887	-121
7.	Jeff Gordon	5,862	-146
8.	Mark Martin	5,807	-201
9.	Kasey Kahne	5,798	-210
10.	Kyle Busch	5,759	-249
11.	Tony Stewart	4,298	-1,710
12.	Carl Edwards	4,013	-1,995
13.	Greg Biffle	3,771	-2,237
14.	Casey Mears	3,616	-2,392
15.	Brian Vickers	3,589	-2,419
16.	Kurt Busch	3,577	-2,431
17.	Clint Bowyer	3,475	-2,533
18.	Ryan Newman	3,475	-2,533
19.	Bobby Labonte	3,330	-2,678
20.	Scott Riggs	3,301	-2,707

*Rookie. **Time of race:** 3:29:23. **Average speed:** 143.421 mph. **Margin of victory:** 1.129 seconds.
Caution flags: 9 for 39 laps: 5-7 (Car 5—spin, Turn 4); 83-86 (debris); 171-177 (Cars 24, 26—accident, Turn 2); 198-201 (debris); 244-247 (Car 12—accident, backstretch); 250-254 (Cars 9, 40—accident, Turn 1); 292-295 (debris); 306-309 (fluid on track); 311-314 (Cars 6, 14, 31, 42, 88—accident, Turn 1). **Lead changes:** 24 among 7 drivers: Kenseth—pole; Harvick 1-9; Earnhardt 10-23; Stewart 24-55; J. Gordon 56; Johnson 57-58; Nemechek 59-61; Earnhardt 62-82; J. Gordon 83; Earnhardt 84-114; J. Gordon 115-145; Edwards 146; J. Gordon 147-157; Stewart 158-170; Johnson 171; Stewart 172-177; Earnhardt 178-197; Johnson 198; Stewart 199-238; Johnson 239-260; Stewart 261-291; Johnson 292; Stewart 293-305; Earnhardt 306-314; Stewart 315-325. **Fell out of race:** Bliss, Elliott, Bodine, Lepage (engine); Martin, Truex, Kahne, Stremme (accident). **Pole:** None—conditions. **Dropped to rear:** R. Gordon, Schrader (engine change); Elliott (transmission change). **Failed to qualify:** Derrike Cope (74), Kirk Shelmerdine (27), Mike Skinner (72), A.J. Allmendinger (84). **Estimated attendance:** 115,000.

Driver rating: An average of these categories—Win, finish, top 15 finish, average running position on lead lap, average speed under green, fastest lap, led most laps, lead-lap finish. Maximum points: 150 per race.

Texas Motor Speedway

Fort Worth, Texas • 1.5-mile banked paved oval • November 5, 2006 • 508.5 miles, 339 laps • Purse: $7,089,515

Car	Driver	Make	Start	34 laps to go	Finish	Laps run	Laps led	Rating	Winnings
20	Tony Stewart	Chevrolet	8	1	1	339	278	149.7	$521,361
48	Jimmie Johnson	Chevrolet	5	3	2	339	1	121.6	$364,236
29	Kevin Harvick	Chevrolet	21	4	3	339	0	107.6	$254,186
5	Kyle Busch	Chevrolet	11	6	4	339	2	107.6	$204,250
07	Clint Bowyer*	Chevrolet	14	9	5	339	3	112.8	$176,625
8	Dale Earnhardt Jr.	Chevrolet	10	7	6	339	1	106.1	$187,141
42	Casey Mears	Dodge	25	10	7	339	0	90.0	$174,208
2	Kurt Busch	Dodge	3	13	8	339	37	99.0	$164,833
24	Jeff Gordon	Chevrolet	23	12	9	339	0	98.1	$166,586
11	Denny Hamlin*	Chevrolet	6	17	10	339	0	81.2	$121,200
45	Kyle Petty	Dodge	35	15	11	339	0	73.7	$144,808
17	Matt Kenseth	Ford	36	18	12	339	1	73.2	$152,791
66	Jeff Green	Chevrolet	27	16	13	339	0	68.4	$130,058
1	Martin Truex Jr.*	Chevrolet	34	8	14	339	0	91.3	$126,183
99	Carl Edwards	Ford	15	14	15	339	0	90.1	$120,050
43	Bobby Labonte	Dodge	13	23	16	338	0	71.4	$138,186
41	Reed Sorenson*	Dodge	19	21	17	338	0	77.7	$108,550
01	Joe Nemechek	Chevrolet	16	24	18	338	0	58.2	$126,445
96	Tony Raines	Chevrolet	41	19	19	338	0	55.7	$99,650
18	J.J. Yeley*	Chevrolet	26	22	20	338	3	56.8	$136,675
38	David Gilliland	Ford	7	26	21	338	0	75.6	$126,908
6	Mark Martin	Ford	28	25	22	338	0	45.4	$113,475
49	Mike Bliss	Dodge	22	29	23	338	0	49.0	$111,083
40	David Stremme*	Dodge	17	27	24	338	1	43.0	$115,722
4	Ward Burton	Chevrolet	37	28	25	338	0	43.3	$98,275
26	Jamie McMurray	Ford	42	31	26	338	4	55.2	$141,500
25	Brian Vickers	Chevrolet	1	20	27	338	5	73.5	$125,175
32	Travis Kvapil	Chevrolet	40	30	28	337	0	36.0	$96,775
88	Dale Jarrett	Ford	20	32	29	334	0	48.6	$126,150
78	Kenny Wallace	Chevrolet	33	33	30	333	0	29.8	$94,375
10	Scott Riggs	Dodge	12	5	31	331	0	86.4	$93,675
22	Dave Blaney	Dodge	30	34	32	330	0	40.4	$93,475
9	Kasey Kahne	Dodge	4	2	33	328	2	100.7	$131,439
12	Ryan Newman	Dodge	24	35	34	328	0	33.2	$138,483
16	Greg Biffle	Ford	39	11	35	324	0	63.6	$113,075
44	Terry Labonte	Chevrolet	43	36	36	316	0	28.4	$92,650
19	Elliott Sadler	Dodge	2	37	37	310	0	62.5	$123,441
31	Jeff Burton	Chevrolet	29	39	38	269	0	57.4	$118,595
7	Robby Gordon	Chevrolet	9	38	39	256	0	69.5	$92,050
14	Sterling Marlin	Chevrolet	31	40	40	208	1	39.9	$91,850
15	Paul Menard	Chevrolet	32	41	41	194	0	42.2	$91,635
21	Ken Schrader	Ford	18	42	42	173	0	52.0	$118,649
55	Michael Waltrip	Dodge	38	43	43	109	0	26.9	$91,564

Rk.	Driver	Pts.	Diff.
1.	Jimmie Johnson	6,157	—
2.	Matt Kenseth	6,140	-17
3.	Dale Earnhardt Jr.	6079	-78
4.	Denny Hamlin	6,077	-80
5.	Kevin Harvick	6,052	-105
6.	Jeff Gordon	6,000	-157
7.	Jeff Burton	5,973	-184
8.	Kyle Busch	5,924	-233
9.	Mark Martin	5,904	-253
10.	Kasey Kahne	5,867	-290
11.	Tony Stewart	4,488	-1,669
12.	Carl Edwards	4,131	-2,026
13.	Greg Biffle	3,829	-2,328
14.	Casey Mears	3,762	-2,395
15.	Kurt Busch	3,724	-2,433
16.	Brian Vickers	3,676	-2,481
17.	Clint Bowyer	3,635	-2,522
18.	Ryan Newman	3,536	-2,621
19.	Bobby Labonte	3,445	-2,712
20.	Scott Riggs	3,371	-2,786

*Rookie. **Time of race:** 3:46:11. **Average speed:** 134.891 mph. **Margin of victory:** .272 seconds. **Caution flags:** 12 for 51 laps: 1-4 (competition); 42-45 (competition); 90-94 (Car 31—accident, frontstretch); 136-140 (debris); 167-170 (Cars 07, 8—accident, Turn 4); 175-179 (Cars 6, 14, 21—accident, frontstretch); 182-185 (Car 7—accident, backstretch); 196-199 (oil on track); 233-236 (Car 41—spin, Turn 2); 258-261 (oil on track); 328-330 (Car 16—accident, Turn 1); 333-337 (Cars 1, 10, 17, 99—accident, Turn 4). **Lead changes:** 23 among 13 drivers: Vickers 1-4; Ku. Busch 5-41; Vickers 42; Stewart 43-89; Kahne 90; Stewart 91-136; Earnhardt 137; Marlin 138; Stewart 139-166; Bowyer 167; Kenseth 168; Stewart 169-195; Bowyer 196; McMurray 197-200; Stewart 201-232; Bowyer 233; Stewart 234-257; Kahne 258; Stremme 259; Stewart 260-317; Johnson 318; Ky. Busch 319-320; Yeley 321-323; Stewart 324-339. **Note:** Green-white-checkered finish. **Fell out of race:** Riggs, Biffle, Marlin, Schrader (accident); Kahne, R. Gordon, Menard, Waltrip (engine). **Pole:** Brian Vickers, 196.235 mph. **Dropped to rear:** Stremme, Martin (backup car). **Failed to qualify:** Chad Chaffin (34), Bill Elliott (37), Kevin Lepage (61), Mike Skinner (72), David Ragan (60), Derrike Cope (74), A.J. Allmendinger (84). **Estimated attendance:** 181,500.

Driver rating: An average of these categories—Win, finish, top 15 finish, average running position on lead lap, average speed under green, fastest lap, led most laps, lead-lap finish. Maximum points: 150 per race.

>>CHECKER AUTO PARTS 500

Phoenix International Raceway

Avondale, Ariz. • 1-mile paved oval • November 12, 2006 • 312 miles, 312 laps • Purse: $4,892,924

Car	Driver	Make	Start	32 laps to go	Finish	Laps run	Laps led	Rating	Winnings
29	Kevin Harvick	Chevrolet	2	2	1	312	252	150.0	$245,761
48	Jimmie Johnson	Chevrolet	29	3	2	312	28	123.1	$212,211
11	Denny Hamlin*	Chevrolet	22	7	3	312	0	108.7	$139,800
24	Jeff Gordon	Chevrolet	1	4	4	312	3	117.7	$165,061
99	Carl Edwards	Ford	12	5	5	312	0	117.6	$120,425
6	Mark Martin	Ford	21	1	6	312	26	96.5	$104,725
9	Kasey Kahne	Dodge	11	8	7	312	0	105.2	$118,239
2	Kurt Busch	Dodge	8	13	8	312	0	88.6	$116,083
8	Dale Earnhardt Jr.	Chevrolet	4	6	9	312	0	105.6	$115,041
31	Jeff Burton	Chevrolet	18	9	10	312	0	89.1	$108,845
25	Brian Vickers	Chevrolet	3	20	11	312	0	97.0	$83,350
1	Martin Truex Jr.*	Chevrolet	26	16	12	312	0	70.2	$100,608
17	Matt Kenseth	Ford	10	10	13	312	1	80.6	$114,941
20	Tony Stewart	Chevrolet	23	12	14	312	0	82.9	$120,486
12	Ryan Newman	Dodge	7	23	15	312	0	72.9	$110,533
38	David Gilliland	Ford	13	21	16	312	1	76.7	$97,858
19	Elliott Sadler	Dodge	16	22	17	312	0	59.6	$98,491
40	David Stremme*	Dodge	36	18	18	312	0	61.6	$92,233
01	Joe Nemechek	Chevrolet	5	25	19	312	0	71.5	$94,120
18	J.J. Yeley*	Chevrolet	35	14	20	312	0	63.0	$104,925
96	Tony Raines	Chevrolet	41	28	21	312	0	48.4	$67,325
10	Scott Riggs	Dodge	42	29	22	312	0	50.2	$67,100
22	Dave Blaney	Dodge	31	27	23	312	0	57.7	$81,983
21	Ken Schrader	Ford	32	19	24	312	0	49.9	$93,839
45	Kyle Petty	Dodge	34	30	25	312	0	45.9	$86,458
42	Casey Mears	Dodge	17	17	26	312	0	64.6	$100,333
43	Bobby Labonte	Dodge	15	31	27	311	0	52.4	$102,986
4	Ward Burton	Chevrolet	24	32	28	311	0	40.0	$65,425
41	Reed Sorenson*	Dodge	28	33	29	310	0	61.7	$70,800
32	Travis Kvapil	Chevrolet	33	34	30	310	0	34.5	$72,722
37	Bill Elliott	Dodge	43	35	31	309	0	31.4	$62,550
7	Robby Gordon	Dodge	40	36	32	307	0	39.1	$62,400
07	Clint Bowyer*	Chevrolet	20	11	33	306	0	73.2	$71,225
16	Greg Biffle	Ford	6	38	34	306	0	72.2	$82,350
61	Chad Chaffin	Dodge	39	37	35	306	0	27.9	$62,025
14	Sterling Marlin	Chevrolet	30	15	36	303	1	45.1	$61,875
66	Jeff Green	Chevrolet	25	26	37	298	0	59.6	$69,750
5	Kyle Busch	Chevrolet	9	40	38	291	0	72.5	$79,625
88	Dale Jarrett	Ford	27	24	39	289	0	56.3	$93,575
26	Jamie McMurray	Ford	14	39	40	272	0	81.0	$108,175
49	Mike Bliss	Dodge	38	41	41	262	0	37.5	$61,210
55	Michael Waltrip	Dodge	19	42	42	234	0	39.1	$61,085
72	Brandon Whitt	Chevrolet	37	43	43	123	0	25.3	$61,286

POINT STANDINGS

Rk.	Driver	Pts.	Diff.
1.	Jimmie Johnson	6,332	—
2.	Matt Kenseth	6,269	-63
3.	Kevin Harvick	6,242	-90
4.	Denny Hamlin	6,242	-90
5.	Dale Earnhardt Jr.	6,217	-115
6.	Jeff Gordon	6,165	-167
7.	Jeff Burton	6,107	-225
8.	Mark Martin	6,059	-273
9.	Kasey Kahne	6,013	-319
10.	Kyle Busch	5,973	-359
11.	Tony Stewart	4,609	-1,723
12.	Carl Edwards	4,286	-2,046
13.	Greg Biffle	3,890	-2,442
14.	Kurt Busch	3,866	-2,466
15.	Casey Mears	3,847	-2,485
16.	Brian Vickers	3,806	-2,526
17.	Clint Bowyer	3,699	-2,633
18.	Ryan Newman	3,654	-2,678
19.	Bobby Labonte	3,527	-2,805
20.	Martin Truex Jr.	3,498	-2,834

*Rookie. **Time of race:** 3:14:44. **Average speed:** 96.131 mph. **Margin of victory:** .250 seconds. **Caution flags:** 10 for 58 laps: 71-76 (debris); 151-157 (debris); 188-195 (oil on track); 227-230 (Cars 7, 61—accident, Turn 1); 253-257 (oil on track); 265-271 (Car 49—accident, backstretch); 274-281 (Cars 5, 12, 26, 66, 88—accident, Turn 1); 292-296 (Cars 14, 88—accident, Turn 4); 300-304 (Car 66—accident, Turn 1); 307-309 (Car 42—spin, Turn 2). **Note:** On Lap 307 (8 minutes, 58 seconds), the race was red-flagged for track clean-up. **Lead changes:** 12 among 7 drivers: J. Gordon 1-3; Harvick 4-71; Kenseth 72; Harvick 73-133; Johnson 134-151; Marlin 152; Johnson 153-161; Harvick 162-254; Gilliland 255; Martin 256-259; Johnson 260; Martin 261-282; Harvick 283-312. **Fell out of race:** Bowyer (oil line); Green, Jarrett, McMurray (accident); Bliss, Waltrip (engine); Whitt (rear end). **Pole:** Jeff Gordon, 134.464 mph. **Dropped to rear:** R. Gordon (engine change). **Failed to qualify:** Jason Leffler (71), Todd Kluever (06), Morgan Shepherd (89), Brandon Ash (02), Kevin Lepage (34), Kenny Wallace (78), Derrike Cope (74), Jeremy Mayfield (09). **Estimated attendance:** 106,000.

Driver rating: An average of these categories—Win, finish, top 15 finish, average running position on lead lap, average speed under green, fastest lap, led most laps, lead-lap finish. Maximum points: 150 per race.

Homestead-Miami Speedway

Homestead, Fla. • 1.5-mile paved oval • November 19, 2006 • 402 miles, 268 laps • Purse: $5,200,543

Car	Driver	Make	Start	27 laps to go	Finish	Laps run	Laps led	Rating	Winnings
16	Greg Biffle	Ford	22	1	1	268	47	133.5	$323,800
1	Martin Truex Jr.*	Chevrolet	20	6	2	268	27	114.6	$260,458
11	Denny Hamlin*	Chevrolet	33	3	3	268	0	96.3	$183,500
9	Kasey Kahne	Dodge	1	2	4	268	90	129.7	$190,689
29	Kevin Harvick	Chevrolet	7	7	5	268	0	98.6	$157,586
17	Matt Kenseth	Ford	19	5	6	268	0	104.9	$141,991
10	Scott Riggs	Dodge	2	4	7	268	1	111.4	$91,100
99	Carl Edwards	Ford	31	14	8	268	0	87.2	$99,475
48	Jimmie Johnson	Chevrolet	15	8	9	268	2	95.4	$119,986
07	Clint Bowyer*	Chevrolet	10	13	10	268	0	86.6	$85,400
40	David Stremme*	Dodge	23	10	11	268	0	81.8	$94,508
33	Scott Wimmer	Chevrolet	24	17	12	268	0	82.0	$65,950
01	Joe Nemechek	Chevrolet	13	18	13	268	0	79.3	$107,645
31	Jeff Burton	Chevrolet	5	9	14	268	0	97.8	$95,895
20	Tony Stewart	Chevrolet	21	12	15	268	0	68.7	$120,411
41	Reed Sorenson*	Dodge	11	19	16	268	0	70.1	$76,925
15	Paul Menard	Chevrolet	28	23	17	268	1	74.7	$64,925
6	Mark Martin	Ford	26	15	18	268	0	67.7	$82,725
8	Dale Earnhardt Jr.	Chevrolet	14	16	19	268	47	96.7	$113,216
96	Tony Raines	Chevrolet	40	26	20	268	0	47.1	$70,700
25	Brian Vickers	Chevrolet	6	25	21	267	0	57.6	$75,600
66	Jeff Green	Chevrolet	27	27	22	267	0	51.0	$89,458
12	Ryan Newman	Dodge	16	22	23	267	0	66.3	$109,108
24	Jeff Gordon	Chevrolet	12	24	24	267	0	51.4	$112,786
00	Bill Elliott	Chevrolet	43	28	25	267	0	46.4	$63,700
22	Dave Blaney	Dodge	25	30	26	266	0	57.4	$78,033
32	Travis Kvapil	Chevrolet	34	31	27	266	0	44.6	$75,622
45	Kyle Petty	Dodge	38	29	28	266	0	46.5	$73,775
21	Ken Schrader	Ford	37	32	29	266	0	38.1	$92,689
18	J.J. Yeley*	Chevrolet	8	20	30	265	8	75.4	$100,325
88	Dale Jarrett	Ford	41	33	31	265	0	35.7	$96,625
42	Casey Mears	Dodge	39	11	32	261	0	62.2	$95,983
38	David Gilliland	Ford	9	35	33	257	0	73.8	$90,483
30	Juan Pablo Montoya	Dodge	29	21	34	251	0	53.7	$61,425
26	Jamie McMurray	Ford	42	34	35	250	0	36.4	$108,050
19	Elliott Sadler	Dodge	4	36	36	230	17	78.4	$90,991
14	Sterling Marlin	Chevrolet	18	37	37	213	0	46.1	$60,800
5	Kyle Busch	Chevrolet	3	40	38	206	28	90.4	$78,600
49	Mike Bliss	Dodge	17	38	39	201	0	48.9	$60,400
7	Robby Gordon	Chevrolet	35	39	40	187	0	39.8	$60,175
43	Bobby Labonte	Dodge	30	41	41	83	0	24.3	$96,911
09	Jeremy Mayfield	Dodge	32	42	42	78	0	26.5	$59,675
2	Kurt Busch	Dodge	36	43	43	9	0	26.9	$100,506

POINT STANDINGS

Rk.	Driver	Pts.	Diff.
1.	Jimmie Johnson	6,475	—
2.	Matt Kenseth	6,419	-56
3.	Denny Hamlin	6,407	-68
4.	Kevin Harvick	6,397	-78
5.	Dale Earnhardt Jr.	6,328	-147
6.	Jeff Gordon	6,256	-219
7.	Jeff Burton	6,228	-247
8.	Kasey Kahne	6,183	-292
9.	Mark Martin	6,168	-307
10.	Kyle Busch	6,027	-448
11.	Tony Stewart	4,727	-1,748
12.	Carl Edwards	4,428	-2,047
13.	Greg Biffle	4,075	-2,400
14.	Casey Mears	3,914	-2,561
15.	Brian Vickers	3,906	-2,569
16.	Kurt Busch	3,900	-2,575
17.	Clint Bowyer	3,833	-2,642
18.	Ryan Newman	3,748	-2,727
19.	Martin Truex Jr.	3,673	-2,802
20.	Scott Riggs	3,619	-2,856

*Rookie. **Time of race:** 3:12:23. **Average speed:** 125.375 mph. **Margin of victory:** .389 seconds. **Caution flags:** 11 for 43 laps: 8-11 (Cars 2, 43—accident, backstretch); 16-18 (Car 2—accident, Turn 4); 46-49 (debris); 117-120 (Car 5—accident, Turn 2); 162-165 (debris); 175-178 (Car 38—accident, Turn 3); 190-193 (Car 7—accident, Turn 4); 206-209 (oil on track); 248-251 (Car 12—spin, backstretch); 263-266 (oil on track). **Note:** On Lap 253 (7 minutes, 58 seconds), the race was red-flagged for track clean-up. **Lead changes:** 15 among 10 drivers: Kahne 1-18; Ky. Busch 19-46; Kahne 47-104; Earnhardt 105-106; Johnson 107-108; Menard 109; Kahne 110-117; Earnhardt 118-162; Truex 163-189; Sadler 190-206; Kahne 207-209; Riggs 210; Kahne 211-213; Biffle 214-248; Yeley 249-256; Biffle 257-268. **Note:** Green-white checkered finish. **Fell out of race:** Yeley (out of gas); Mears, McMurray, Sadler, Marlin, Bliss (engine); Montoya, R.Gordon, Labonte, Ku. Busch (accident); Mayfield (oil leak). **Pole:** Kasey Kahne, 178.259 mph. **Dropped to rear:** Bowyer, R. Gordon (engine change). **Failed to qualify:** Ward Burton (4), Brandon Whitt (72), Casey Atwood (95), Kenny Wallace (78), Todd Klsuever (06), David Ragan (60), Michael Waltrip (55), Mike Skinner (27), Derrike Cope (74), Kevin Lepage (61), Carl Long (46), Chad Chaffin (34), Morgan Shepherd (89). **Estimated attendance:** 80,000.

Driver rating: An average of these categories—Win, finish, top 15 finish, average running position on lead lap, average speed under green, fastest lap, led most laps, lead-lap finish. Maximum points: 150 per race.

2007
BUDWEISER SHOOTOUT
AT DAYTONA

The 29th running of the Budweiser Shootout at Daytona will be run under the lights for the fourth consecutive year on Saturday, February 10, at Daytona International Speedway. The Budweiser Shootout traditionally kicks off Speedweeks and will be televised by FOX. The non-points event has jump-started the NASCAR NEXTEL Cup Series season since 1979. From 1979 to 1997, the event was known as the "Busch Clash," and in 1998 became the "Bud Shootout." The current name—"Budweiser Shootout at Daytona"—was adopted in 2001.

Dale Earnhardt leads all drivers with six victories in Budweiser Shootouts. The only drivers to win back-to-back Budweiser Shootouts are Neil Bonnett (1983-84), Ken Schrader (1989-90) and Tony Stewart (2001-02).

The Budweiser Shootout consists of drivers who earned a Bud Pole Award in the previous season and past champions of the event who did not earn a Bud Pole during the previous year but finished among the top 50 in the season's final championship standings. Past Budweiser Shootout champions who are eligible for the 2007 event are Dale Earnhardt Jr., Bill Elliott, Dale Jarrett, Mark Martin, Ken Schrader and Tony Stewart.

2006 BUD POLE WINNERS

Driver	Poles
Kurt Busch	6
Kasey Kahne	6
Jeff Burton	4
Denny Hamlin	3
Greg Biffle	2
Jeff Gordon	2
Ryan Newman	2
Scott Riggs	2
Kyle Busch	1
David Gilliland	1
Kevin Harvick	1
Jimmie Johnson	1
Elliott Sadler	1
Boris Said	1
Brian Vickers	1

PREVIOUS WINNERS

2006 – Denny Hamlin
2005 – Jimmie Johnson
2004 – Dale Jarrett
2003 – Dale Earnhardt Jr.
2002 – Tony Stewart
2001 – Tony Stewart
2000 – Dale Jarrett
1999 – Mark Martin
1998 – Rusty Wallace
1997 – Jeff Gordon
1996 – Dale Jarrett
1995 – Dale Earnhardt
1994 – Jeff Gordon
1993 – Dale Earnhardt
1992 – Geoffrey Bodine
1991 – Dale Earnhardt
1990 – Ken Schrader
1989 – Ken Schrader
1988 – Dale Earnhardt
1987 – Bill Elliott
1986 – Dale Earnhardt
1985 – Terry Labonte
1984 – Neil Bonnett
1983 – Neil Bonnett
1982 – Bobby Allison
1981 – Darrell Waltrip
1980 – Dale Earnhardt
1979 – Buddy Baker

GATORADE DUEL
AT DAYTONA

The Gatorade Duel at Daytona, scheduled for Thursday, February 15, is the largest-attended weekday sporting event in America. The two 150-mile qualifying races will determine the starting lineup for the Daytona 500, "The Great American Race."

From 1959-1968, the races were 100 miles in length; beginning in 1969, the distance was extended to 125 miles; and the current length was implemented in 2005.

The Daytona 500 uses a different qualifying procedure than any other race in the world. On Budweiser Pole Day, Sunday, February 11, the fastest two cars will solidify their starting spots for the Daytona 500, earning the pole and outside pole positions, respectively.

The fastest qualifier will earn the pole for both the Daytona 500 and the first 150-mile Gatorade Duel qualifying race. In addition to the polesitter, the odd-number positions (1st, 3rd, 5th, etc.) of the highest-ranked 35 finishers in the final 2006 NASCAR NEXTEL Cup Series car owner points standings will be assigned to the first qualifying race.

The second-fastest qualifier earns the outside pole for the Daytona 500 and will start on the pole for the second 150-mile Gatorade Duel qualifying race. In addition to the second-fastest qualifier, the even-number positions (2nd, 4th, 6th, etc.) of the highest-ranked 35 finishers in the final 2006 NASCAR NEXTEL Cup Series car owner points standings will be assigned to the second qualifying race.

The lineup for each qualifying race will be set based upon the qualifying speeds in the time trials for all cars, including those who are among the highest-ranked 35 in the final 2006 car owner point standings. The highest-ranked 35 designation does not determine the car's starting position, only the assignment of its 150-mile qualifying event.

Additional cars that were not among the highest-ranked 35 in the final 2006 car owner points will be alternated between the first and second 150-mile qualifying events using an odd-even format. The odd-number positions will be assigned to the first qualifying race, and the even-number positions will be assigned to the second qualifying race The odd-even positions are not determined by where a car qualified in the overall field, but its specific qualifying order among those cars not part of the highest-ranked 35 group.

A maximum of 66 cars will be permitted to compete between the two qualifying races, and all cars must compete in one of these events to be eligible for the Daytona 500.

Starting positions for the Daytona 500 will be designated for the highest-ranked 35 positions from the final 2006 car owner point standings from each qualifying race, the two-highest fin-ishing cars in each qualifying race not among that highest-ranked 35 group and the two front-row qualifiers.

The balance of the 43-car field will be filled by the fastest remaining qualifiers who have not earned a starting position, with the exception of the 43rd position, which will be assigned to an eligible former or current NASCAR NEXTEL Cup Series champion. Should there not be an eligible champion, the position will be assigned to the next fastest qualifier not in the field.

Dale Earnhardt leads all drivers with 12 victories in this event, including a remarkable 10-year winning streak from 1990-99. Cale Yarborough ranks second with six wins.

GATORADE DUEL WINNERS

Dale Earnhardt	12
Cale Yarborough	6
Bobby Allison	5
Darrell Waltrip	5
Bill Elliott	4
Bobby Isaac	4
Buddy Baker	3
Dale Earnhardt Jr.	3
Junior Johnson	3
Sterling Marlin	3
David Pearson	3
Fireball Roberts	3
Davey Allison	2
Neil Bonnett	2
Ernie Irvan	2
Ken Schrader	2
Joe Weatherly	2
Davey Allison	2
Elliott Sadler	2
Earl Balmer	1
Geoffrey Bodine	1
Darel Dieringer	1
A.J. Foyt	1
Charlie Glotzbach	1
Paul Goldsmith	1
Robby Gordon	1
Jeff Green	1
Pete Hamilton	1
Ernie Irvan	1
Dale Jarrett	1
Bobby Labonte	1
Terry Labonte	1
Fred Lorenzen	1
Coo Coo Marlin	1
Dave Marcis	1
Benny Parsons	1
Richard Petty	1
Ricky Rudd	1
Johnny Rutherford	1
Elliott Sadler	1
Mike Skinner	1
Jack Smith	1
Tony Stewart	1
Michael Waltrip	1
Bob Welborn	1
LeeRoy Yarbrough	1

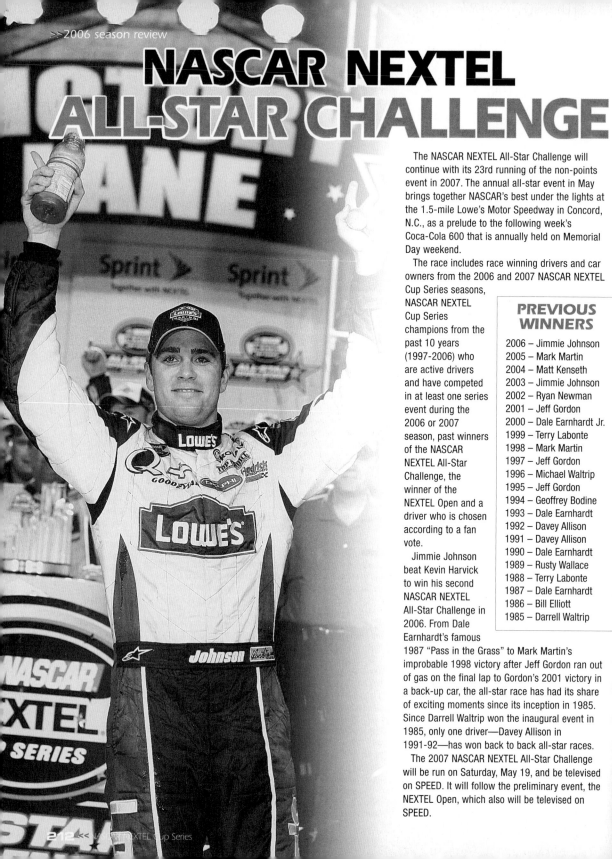

NASCAR NEXTEL
ALL-STAR CHALLENGE

The NASCAR NEXTEL All-Star Challenge will continue with its 23rd running of the non-points event in 2007. The annual all-star event in May brings together NASCAR's best under the lights at the 1.5-mile Lowe's Motor Speedway in Concord, N.C., as a prelude to the following week's Coca-Cola 600 that is annually held on Memorial Day weekend.

The race includes race winning drivers and car owners from the 2006 and 2007 NASCAR NEXTEL Cup Series seasons, NASCAR NEXTEL Cup Series champions from the past 10 years (1997-2006) who are active drivers and have competed in at least one series event during the 2006 or 2007 season, past winners of the NASCAR NEXTEL All-Star Challenge, the winner of the NEXTEL Open and a driver who is chosen according to a fan vote.

Jimmie Johnson beat Kevin Harvick to win his second NASCAR NEXTEL All-Star Challenge in 2006. From Dale Earnhardt's famous 1987 "Pass in the Grass" to Mark Martin's improbable 1998 victory after Jeff Gordon ran out of gas on the final lap to Gordon's 2001 victory in a back-up car, the all-star race has had its share of exciting moments since its inception in 1985. Since Darrell Waltrip won the inaugural event in 1985, only one driver—Davey Allison in 1991-92—has won back to back all-star races.

The 2007 NASCAR NEXTEL All-Star Challenge will be run on Saturday, May 19, and be televised on SPEED. It will follow the preliminary event, the NEXTEL Open, which also will be televised on SPEED.

PREVIOUS WINNERS

2006 – Jimmie Johnson
2005 – Mark Martin
2004 – Matt Kenseth
2003 – Jimmie Johnson
2002 – Ryan Newman
2001 – Jeff Gordon
2000 – Dale Earnhardt Jr.
1999 – Terry Labonte
1998 – Mark Martin
1997 – Jeff Gordon
1996 – Michael Waltrip
1995 – Jeff Gordon
1994 – Geoffrey Bodine
1993 – Dale Earnhardt
1992 – Davey Allison
1991 – Davey Allison
1990 – Dale Earnhardt
1989 – Rusty Wallace
1988 – Terry Labonte
1987 – Dale Earnhardt
1986 – Bill Elliott
1985 – Darrell Waltrip

NASCAR
TEAMS

>> TEAM OWNERS <<

NASCAR NEXTEL Cup Series

BAM RACING

Beth Ann Morgenthau

Years as NNCS owner: 5 • **Best points finish:** 31
Career victories: 0 • **Career poles:** 0

The former Beth Ann Coulter grew up a race fan, riding her bike to local short tracks in the Miami area and racing in go-karts and motorboats. In 1969, she married Tony Morgenthau, an investment banker who founded Morgenthau & Associates in 1972. Beth Ann and Tony began their trek as race team owners in ARCA. BAM settled on veteran Ken Schrader to drive the team's first full-time NASCAR NEXTEL Cup Series schedule in 2003. In 32 starts, Schrader registered the organization's first-ever top 10 finishes. In 2006, the team began the season with rookie Brent Sherman, but Sherman left the team because of poor results eight races into the season. The team ran veterans Kevin Lepage, Mike Wallace and Mike Bliss for the remainder of 2006.

CAREER NASCAR NEXTEL CUP SERIES STATISTICS

Year	Driver	Races	Won	Top 5	Top 10	DNF	Poles
2002	S. Robinson	7	0	0	0	4	0
	D. Cope	5	0	0	0	2	0
	S. Compton	2	0	0	0	1	0
	R. Hornaday	1	0	0	0	1	0
	S. Kirby	1	0	0	0	1	0
	K. Lepage	1	0	0	0	1	0
2003	K. Schrader	32	0	0	2	8	0
2004	K. Schrader	36	0	0	1	5	0
	K. Graf	1	0	0	0	0	0
2005	K. Schrader	36	0	0	3	7	0
2006	K. Lepage	12	0	0	0	3	0
	M. Bliss	6	0	0	0	4	0
	B. Sherman	6	0	0	0	1	0
	M. Wallace	1	0	0	0	0	0
TOTALS		147	0	0	6	38	0

CAREER NASCAR NEXTEL CUP SERIES STATISTICS

Year	Driver	Races	Won	Top 5	Top 10	DNF	Poles
1993	B. Labonte	30	0	0	6	6	1
1994	B. Labonte	31	0	1	2	7	0
1995	R. LaJoie	13	0	0	0	3	0
	W. Burton	9	1	3	4	2	0
	J. Hensley	5	0	0	0	2	0
	W. Dallenbach Jr.	1	0	1	1	0	0
1996	W. Burton	27	0	0	4	10	1
1997	W. Burton	31	0	0	7	7	1
1998	W. Burton	33	0	1	5	4	2
1999	W. Burton	34	0	6	16	3	1
	D. Blaney	5	0	0	0	2	0
2000	W. Burton	34	1	4	17	4	0
	D. Blaney	33	0	0	2	7	0
	S. Wimmer	1	0	0	0	0	0
2001	D. Blaney	36	0	0	6	6	0
	W. Burton	36	1	6	10	9	0
	H. Stricklin	1	0	0	0	0	0
2002	W. Burton	36	2	3	8	9	1
	H. Stricklin	22	0	0	0	5	0
	K. Wallace	10	0	0	0	0	0
	S. Wimmer	3	0	0	0	2	0
	G. Bodine	1	0	0	0	0	0
	T. Hubert	1	0	0	0	0	0
2003	K. Wallace	36	0	0	1	3	0
	W. Burton	32	0	0	4	4	0
	S. Wimmer	6	0	0	1	0	0
2004	S. Wimmer	35	0	1	2	7	0
	D. Blaney	6	0	0	0	2	0
	S. Hmiel	5	0	0	0	2	0
	T. Raines	1	0	0	0	1	0
2005	S. Wimmer	36	0	0	0	7	0
	M. Skinner	5	0	0	0	3	0
	J. Benson Jr.	1	0	0	0	0	0
2006	D. Blaney	36	0	1	2	2	0
	B. Lester	2	0	0	0	0	0
TOTALS		634	5	27	98	119	7

BILL DAVIS RACING

Bill Davis

Years as NNCS owner: 14
Best points finish: 9 • **Career victories:** 5
First victory: 1995, Rockingham • **Career poles:** 7
First pole: 1993, Richmond

Bill Davis became interested in racing in the 1980s through his long-time friend Julian Martin, whose son, Mark, was pursuing a racing career. Davis built an ASA car for Mark Martin to drive in the Midwest in 1987, and the relationship continued the following year even though Martin landed a ride with owner Jack Roush in NASCAR's top series. Davis began concentrating on the NASCAR Busch Series in 1988, where he fielded a part-time entry for Martin before hiring Jeff Gordon to run a full schedule in 1991. Davis joined NASCAR's premier series in 1993 with driver Bobby Labonte and finished a high of ninth in points with driver Ward Burton in 1999. In 2007, Davis will be one of three teams fielding Toyotas in the NASCAR NEXTEL Cup Series.

CHIP GANASSI RACING

Chip Ganassi, Felix Sabates

Years as NNCS ownership group: 7
Best points finish: 3 • **Career victories:** 5
First victory: 2001, Michigan • **Career poles:** 6
First pole: 2001, Daytona

Chip Ganassi, a successful owner in open-wheel racing, broke into NASCAR in the middle of the 2000 season when he purchased majority ownership of Felix Sabates' SABCO organization. Ganassi enjoyed immediate success in 2001 as Sterling Marlin finished third in the standings. In 2002, Ganassi pursued his first NASCAR NEXTEL Cup Series title with Marlin, who led the points for 25 weeks before his season was cut short by injury. Jamie McMurray took over for Marlin and won at Lowe's Motor Speedway in his second career start. In 2003, Ganassi expanded to three teams by adding driver Casey Mears. Ganassi signed former Formula 1 driver Juan Pablo Montoya to join second-year drivers Reed Sorenson and David Stremme in his NASCAR NEXTEL Cup Series lineup in 2007.

CAREER NASCAR NEXTEL CUP SERIES STATISTICS

Year	Driver	Races	Won	Top 5	Top 10	DNF	Poles
2000*	S. Marlin	34	0	1	7	4	0
	K. Irwin	17	0	1	1	2	0
	T. Musgrave	12	0	0	0	1	0
	B. Hamilton Jr.	1	0	0	0	0	0
	P. Jones	1	0	0	0	0	0
2001	S. Marlin	36	2	12	20	2	1
	J. Leffler	30	0	0	1	8	1
	S. Pruett	1	0	0	0	0	0
	D. Schroeder	1	0	0	0	0	0
2002	J. Spencer	34	0	2	6	7	0
	S. Marlin	29	2	8	14	3	0
	J. McMurray	6	1	1	2	1	0
	M. Bliss	1	0	0	0	0	0
	S. Pruett	1	0	0	1	0	0
2003	S. Marlin	36	0	0	11	8	0
	J. McMurray	36	0	5	13	4	1
	C. Mears	36	0	0	0	10	0
	S. Pruett	2	0	1	1	0	0
2004	S. Marlin	36	0	3	7	9	0
	J. McMurray	36	0	9	23	6	0
	C. Mears	36	0	1	9	3	2
	S. Pruett	1	0	1	1	0	0
2005	J. McMurray	36	0	4	10	4	1
	C. Mears	36	0	3	9	3	0
	S. Marlin	35	0	1	5	7	0
	D. Stremme	4	0	0	0	3	0
	S. Pruett	2	0	1	1	0	0
	R. Sorenson	1	0	0	0	1	0
2006	C. Mears	36	0	2	8	2	0
	R. Sorenson	36	0	1	5	4	0
	D. Stremme	34	0	0	0	4	0
	S. Pruett	2	0	0	1	0	0
	J. Montoya	1	0	0	0	1	0
*TOTALS		646	5	57	156	97	6

*Ganassi became primary owner following race No. 18 (New Hampshire) in 2000; Felix Sabates was owner before that date.

DALE EARNHARDT INC.
Teresa Earnhardt

Years as NNCS owner: 11 • **Best points finish:** 3
Career victories: 23 • **First victory:** 2000, Texas
Career poles: 11 • **First pole:** 2000, Bristol

Dale Earnhardt Inc., currently guided by Teresa Earnhardt, the widow of the late seven-time series champion Dale Earnhardt, began in 1996 with a limited three-race schedule. DEI ran Steve Park as its first full-season entry in 1999, the same season Dale Earnhardt Jr. made his first five career starts for the team as he was locking up his second consecutive NASCAR Busch Series championship. In 2000, DEI ran Park and Earnhardt Jr. as a two-car, full-season operation, and the drivers responded with three wins and four poles. DEI reached another milestone in 2003 as Earnhardt Jr. finished third in the standings, marking the first time one of the team's drivers had finished among the top five. Earnhardt Jr. then made the Chase for the NASCAR NEXTEL Cup in 2004 and 2006 and finished twice in the top five in points. DEI added two-time NASCAR Busch Series champion

Martin Truex Jr. to its NASCAR NEXTEL Cup Series lineup in 2006 and adds a third full-time team in 2007 with rookie Paul Menard.

CAREER NASCAR NEXTEL CUP SERIES STATISTICS

Year	Driver	Races	Won	Top 5	Top 10	DNF	Poles
1996	J. Green	2	0	0	0	2	0
	R. Gordon	1	0	0	0	1	0
1997	S. Park	4	0	0	0	1	0
1998	S. Park	17	0	0	0	5	0
	D. Waltrip	13	0	1	2	2	0
1999	S. Park	34	0	0	5	4	0
	D. Earnhardt Jr.	5	0	0	1	1	0
2000	D. Earnhardt Jr.	34	2	3	5	7	2
	S. Park	34	1	6	13	4	2
2001	D. Earnhardt Jr.	36	3	9	15	4	2
	M. Waltrip	36	1	3	3	6	0
	S. Park	24	1	5	12	2	0
	K. Wallace	12	0	1	2	1	1
2002	D. Earnhardt Jr.	36	2	11	16	3	2
	M. Waltrip	36	1	4	10	4	0
	S. Park	32	0	0	2	5	0
	K. Wallace	4	0	0	1	0	0
2003	D. Earnhardt Jr.	36	2	13	21	4	0
	M. Waltrip	36	2	8	11	6	0
	J. Green	12	0	0	0	2	0
	J. Andretti	11	0	0	0	2	0
	S. Park	11	0	0	1	3	1
	R. Fellows	2	0	0	1	1	0
	J. Keller	1	0	0	0	0	0
2004	D. Earnhardt Jr.	36	6	16	21	4	0
	M. Waltrip	36	0	2	9	6	0
	J. Andretti	5	0	0	0	1	0
	M. Truex Jr.	2	0	0	0	2	0
	R. Fellows	1	0	1	1	0	0
	K. Wallace	1	0	0	0	0	0
2005	D. Earnhardt Jr.	36	1	7	13	6	0
	M. Waltrip	36	0	3	7	10	1
	M. Truex Jr.	7	0	0	1	5	0
	P. Menard	1	0	0	0	0	0
2006	D. Earnhardt Jr.	36	1	10	17	3	0
	M. Truex Jr.	36	0	2	5	5	0
	P. Menard	7	0	0	1	2	0
TOTALS		709	23	105	196	114	11

EVERNHAM MOTORSPORTS
Ray Evernham

Years as NNCS owner: 7 • **Best points finish:** 8
Career victories: 13 • **First victory:** 2001, Homestead-Miami
Career poles: 24 • **First pole:** 2001, Daytona

After Ray Evernham earned three NASCAR NEXTEL Cup Series championships and 47 career wins as crew chief for Jeff Gordon at Hendrick Motorsports, he yearned for another challenge. It came with the formation of Evernham Motorsports, and then Dodge's return to the sport, which began with the 2001 Daytona 500. He fielded a two-car team and coupled veteran Bill Elliott with youngster Casey Atwood. Dodge made a splash in its return as Elliott won the pole for the Daytona 500 in 2001. Elliott then landed the organization's first victory at Homestead-Miami Speedway. In 2002, Jeremy Mayfield replaced Casey Atwood in Evernham's second full-time team. In 2003, Elliott finished ninth in the championship standings, marking the first time Evernham Motorsports had cracked the top 10. In 2004, Evernham added Kasey Kahne to his NASCAR NEXTEL Cup Series roster, and Kahne won rookie of the year honors. Evernham added a third full-time team in 2006, the No. 10 with driver Scott Riggs. Evernham has had a driver in every Chase for the NASCAR NEXTEL Cup—Mayfield in 2004 and 2005, Kahne in 2006—but neither driver finished higher than eighth in points. In 2006, Kahne lead the NASCAR NEXTEL Cup Series with nine wins. After Mayfield's departure during the 2006 season, Elliott Sadler took over in the No. 19 car and will continue with the team in 2007.

CAREER NASCAR NEXTEL CUP SERIES STATISTICS

Year	Driver	Races	Won	Top 5	Top 10	DNF	Poles
2000	C. Atwood	3	0	0	1	0	0
2001	B. Elliott	36	1	5	9	2	2
	C. Atwood	35	0	1	3	6	1
2002	B. Elliott	36	2	6	13	4	4
	J. Mayfield	36	0	2	4	7	0
	C. Atwood	1	0	0	0	0	0
	H. Parker	1	0	0	0	0	0
2003	B. Elliott	36	1	9	12	2	0
	J. Mayfield	36	0	4	12	6	1
	C. Atwood	2	0	0	0	1	0
2004	K. Kahne	36	0	13	14	7	4
	J. Mayfield	36	1	5	13	3	2
	B. Elliott	5	0	0	1	1	0
2005	K. Kahne	36	1	5	8	9	2
	J. Mayfield	36	1	4	9	1	0
	B. Elliott	9	0	0	0	3	0
2006	K. Kahne	36	6	12	19	5	6
	S. Riggs	35	0	1	8	2	2
	J. Mayfield	21	0	0	0	2	0
	E. Sadler	14	0	0	2	4	0
	B. Elliott	1	0	0	0	0	0
TOTALS		487	13	67	128	65	24

FRONT ROW MOTORSPORTS
Bob Jenkins

Years as NNCS owner: 2 • **Career victories:** 0
Career poles: 0

East Tennesseee native Bob Jenkins worked in support roles for race teams for several years before founding Front Row Motorsports in 2004. The team began with a full-time NASCAR Busch Series schedule, moved to the NASCAR NEXTEL Cup Series in 2005 and made its NASCAR NEXTEL Cup Series debut at Bristol with driver Stanton Barrett. The organization expanded to two full-time NASCAR NEXTEL Cup Series cars during the 2006 season. Jenkins, a restaurant entrepreneur, also is the principal owner of Charter Foods, a 40-unit chain of fast food restaurants primary made up of Taco Bells, and the principal owner of Oak Glove Co., which manufactures disposable vinyl gloves.

CAREER NASCAR NEXTEL CUP SERIES STATISTICS

Year	Driver	Races	Won	Top 5	Top 10	DNF	Poles
2005	S. Barrett	4	0	0	0	1	0
	H. Sadler	3	0	0	0	1	0
	B. Hamilton Jr.	2	0	0	0	1	0
	P.J. Jones	1	0	0	0	1	0
	J. McCarthy	1	0	0	0	0	0

Year	Driver	Races	Won	Top 5	Top 10	DNF	Poles
	J. Miller	1	0	0	0	0	0
	T. Raines	1	0	0	0	0	0
2006	C. Chaffin	6	0	0	0	1	0
	C. Blount	2	0	0	0	2	0
	K. Lepage	2	0	0	0	2	0
	C. Long	1	0	0	0	1	0
	B. Simo	1	0	0	0	1	0
	M. Skinner	1	0	0	0	0	0
TOTALS		26	0	0	0	11	0

FURNITURE ROW RACING
Barney Visser

Years as NNCS owner: 2 • **Career victories:** 0
Career poles: 0

Furniture Row Racing is one of the few sponsor-owned organizations in the NASCAR NEXTEL Cup Series, as well as one of the few that doesn't call North Carolina home. Furniture Row Companies owner Barney Visser of Cherry Hills, Colo., decided to get into NASCAR after meeting with a three other Colorado racing enthusiasts—driver Jerry Robertson, crew chief Joe Garone and engine builder Dave Capriotti—and built a race shop in an old waterbed store in Denver. Along with the No. 78 team in the NASCAR NEXTEL Cup Series, FRR also runs the No. 78 in the NASCAR Busch Series.

CAREER NASCAR NEXTEL CUP SERIES STATISTICS

Year	Driver	Races	Won	Top 5	Top 10	DNF	Poles
2005	J. Robertson	1	0	0	0	1	0
	K. Wallace	1	0	0	0	0	0
2006	K. Wallace	17	0	0	0	3	0
	J. Spencer	2	0	0	0	0	0
TOTALS		21	0	0	0	4	0

GINN RACING
Bobby Ginn

Years as NNCS owner: 1
Best points finish: 11 • **Career victories:** 2
First victory: 2002, Rockingham • **Career poles:** 9
First pole: 1998, Indianapolis

MB2 Motorsports, which was founded in 1996, began as a one-car team with Derrike Cope as the driver. MB2 expanded to a two-car team in 2000 with the addition of the Valvoline-sponsored No. 10 car and MBV Motorsports. It was an industry first—a sponsorship/ownership package. The 2006 season brought much change to the organization: Before the season, Valvoline left MB2/MBV Motorsports, and, in July, Nelson Bowers sold his majority ownership to real estate developer Bobby Ginn, who renamed the team. In 2007, veteran Mark Martin will share the No. 01 car with rookie Regan Smith, and former No. 01 driver Joe Nemechek moves to a third team, the No. 13.

CAREER NASCAR NEXTEL CUP SERIES STATISTICS

Year	Driver	Races	Won	Top 5	Top 10	DNF	Poles
1997	D. Cope	31	0	1	2	6	0
1998	E. Irvan	30	0	0	11	3	3
	R. Craven	3	0	0	0	0	0

Year	Driver	Races	Won	Top 5	Top 10	DNF	Poles
1999	E. Irvan	21	0	0	5	5	0
	J. Nadeau	12	0	0	0	2	0
	D. Trickle	1	0	0	0	0	0
2000	K. Schrader	34	0	0	2	2	0
	J. Benson	15	0	2	5	1	0
2001	J. Benson Jr.	36	0	6	14	8	0
	K. Schrader	36	0	0	5	2	0
2002	K. Schrader	36	0	0	0	8	0
	J. Benson Jr.	31	1	3	7	8	0
	J. Nadeau	3	0	0	0	0	0
	J. Nemechek	1	0	0	0	0	0
	M. Wallace	1	0	0	0	1	0
2003	J. Benson Jr.	36	0	2	4	6	0
	M. Skinner	11	0	0	0	2	1
	J. Nadeau	10	0	1	1	3	0
	M. Wallace	8	0	0	0	2	0
	J. Nemechek	4	0	0	1	0	0
	B. Said	2	0	0	1	0	1
	J. Keller	1	0	0	0	0	0
2004	J. Nemechek	36	1	3	9	6	2
	S. Riggs	35	0	1	2	8	0
	B. Said	3	0	0	1	1	0
2005	J. Nemechek	36	0	2	9	2	1
	S. Riggs	36	0	2	4	7	1
	B. Said	1	0	0	0	0	0
2006*	S. Marlin	36	0	0	1	8	0
	J. Nemechek	36	0	0	2	3	0
	B. Elliott	1	0	0	0	0	0
TOTALS		583	2	23	86	94	9

*Ginn became primary owner following race No. 20 (Pocono) in 2006; Nelson Bowers was owner before that date.

HAAS CNC RACING
Gene Haas

Years as NNCS owner: 5 • **Best points finish:** 28
Career victories: 0 • **Career poles:** 0

Gene Haas' company, Haas Automation Inc., a machine tool manufacturer, has been involved in partnerships with racing groups since 1995. In 2002, Haas started his own motorsports organization, Haas CNC Racing, which entered the NASCAR NEXTEL Cup Series full-time in 2003. He added a second full-time team in 2007. Not limited to off-track ownership responsibilities, Haas and co-driver Joe Custer drove to a best-in-class championship in the 2001 Best of the Desert Off-Road Truck Series.

CAREER NASCAR NEXTEL CUP SERIES STATISTICS

Year	Driver	Races	Won	Top 5	Top 10	DNF	Poles
2002	J. Sprague	3	0	0	0	1	0
2003	J. Sprague	18	0	0	0	4	0
	J. Leffler	10	0	0	0	0	0
	W. Burton	4	0	0	0	2	0
	J. Andretti	3	0	0	0	0	0
2004	W. Burton	34	0	0	3	8	0
	M. Bliss	2	0	0	1	1	0
	J. Leffler	1	0	0	0	1	0
2005	M. Bliss	36	0	0	2	8	0
2006	J. Green	36	0	0	2	4	0
	J. Sauter	1	0	0	0	0	0
TOTALS		148	0	0	8	29	0

HALL OF FAME RACING
Roger Staubach, Troy Aikman Bill Saunders

Years as NNCS owners: 1 • **Best points finish:** 35
Career victories: 0 • **Career poles:** 0

Winning on the gridiron wasn't enough for former quarterbacks Troy Aikman and Roger Staubach—they also want to win on the racetrack. The former Cowboys weren't avid NASCAR fans until 2003, when they decided to form a NASCAR NEXTEL Cup Series team. In 2005, Hall of Fame Racing was born, and the organization's NASCAR NEXTEL Cup Series team was ready for the 2006 Daytona 500. Terry Labonte and Tony Raines shared HOFR's No. 96 car during the 2006 season, and Labonte scored the organization's first top five finish, a third at Infineon, and Raines contributed a seventh-place finish at Lowe's Motor Speedway. In 2007, Raines will drive the car full-time.

CAREER NASCAR NEXTEL CUP SERIES STATISTICS

Year	Driver	Races	Won	Top 5	Top 10	DNF	Poles
2006	T. Raines	29	0	0	1	1	0
	T. Labonte	7	0	1	1	0	0
TOTALS		36	0	1	2	1	0

HENDRICK MOTORSPORTS
Rick Hendrick

Years as NNCS owner: 23 • **Best points finish:** 1
Career victories: 149 • **First victory:** 1984, Martinsville
Career poles: 133 • **First pole:** 1984, Bristol

Founded in 1984, Hendrick Motorsports now fields four full-time teams in NASCAR's premier series. It is the only organization to have won the series title in four consecutive seasons (Jeff Gordon in 1995, 1997 and 1998, Terry Labonte in 1996). Hendrick Motorsports started as a one-car operation for Rick Hendrick, who owned a championship drag racing boat team before coming to NASCAR. Hendrick founded "All-Star Racing" in 1984 with Geoffrey Bodine, driving 30 events and winning three. Hendrick eventually hooked up with Jeff Gordon, a rising open-wheel star. Gordon since has won four series championships, the third-best total of all-time. Ricky Hendrick, Rick's son, and nine other people were killed in a plane crash just outside Martinsville, Va., in 2004, rocking the Hendrick Motorsports family. The family also lost patriarch Papa Joe Hendrick in 2004—he died at age 84. Rick Hendrick had leukemia in 1996, but the disease now is in remission. Hendrick established the Hendrick Marrow Program in 1997 to aid patients who are suffering from leukemia or other life-threatening blood diseases.

CAREER NASCAR NEXTEL CUP SERIES STATISTICS

Year	Driver	Races	Won	Top 5	Top 10	DNF	Poles
1984	G. Bodine	30	3	7	14	8	3
1985	G. Bodine	28	0	10	14	5	3
	D. Brooks	1	0	0	1	0	0
1986	G. Bodine	29	2	10	15	12	8
	T. Richmond	29	7	13	17	2	8
	B. Bodine	1	0	0	0	0	0
1987	G. Bodine	29	0	3	10	10	2
	B. Parsons	29	0	6	9	12	0
	D. Waltrip	29	1	6	16	2	0
	T. Richmond	8	2	3	4	2	1

Year	Driver	Races	Won	Top 5	Top 10	DNF	Poles
	J. Fitzgerald	1	0	0	0	0	0
	R. Hendrick	1	0	0	0	1	0
1988	G. Bodine	29	1	10	16	4	3
	D. Waltrip	29	2	10	14	4	2
	K. Schrader	28	1	4	17	1	2
	R. Hendrick	1	0	0	0	0	0
	R. Moroso	1	0	0	0	0	0
1989	G. Bodine	29	1	9	11	7	3
	K. Schrader	29	1	10	14	6	4
	D. Waltrip	29	6	14	18	3	0
	B. Hamilton	1	0	0	0	1	0
	T. Kendall	1	0	0	0	1	0
	K. Petty	1	0	0	0	0	0
	G. Sacks	1	0	0	0	1	0
1990	R. Rudd	29	1	8	15	5	2
	K. Schrader	29	0	7	14	8	3
	D. Waltrip	23	0	5	12	0	0
	G. Sacks	16	0	2	4	5	0
	J. Horton	2	0	0	0	0	0
	S. Barrett	1	0	0	0	0	0
	H. Stricklin	1	0	0	0	1	0
	S. van der Merwe	1	0	0	0	1	0
1991	R. Rudd	29	1	9	17	1	1
	K. Schrader	29	2	10	18	6	0
1992	R. Rudd	29	1	9	18	4	1
	K. Schrader	29	0	4	11	6	1
	J. Gordon	1	0	0	0	1	0
1993	J. Gordon	30	0	7	11	11	1
	R. Rudd	30	1	9	14	6	0
	K. Schrader	30	0	9	15	4	6
	A. Unser Jr	1	0	0	0	1	0
1994	J. Gordon	31	2	7	14	10	1
	T. Labonte	31	3	6	14	4	0
	K. Schrader	31	0	9	18	2	0
1995	J. Gordon	31	7	17	23	3	8
	T. Labonte	31	3	14	17	3	1
	K. Schrader	31	0	2	10	9	1
	J. Purvis	1	0	0	0	0	0
1996	J. Gordon	31	10	21	24	5	5
	T. Labonte	31	2	21	24	3	4
	K. Schrader	31	0	3	10	2	0
1997	J. Gordon	32	10	22	23	2	1
	T. Labonte	32	1	8	20	3	0
	R. Craven	30	0	4	7	7	0
	T. Bodine	1	0	0	0	0	0
	J. Sprague	1	0	0	0	1	0
1998	J. Gordon	33	13	26	28	2	7
	T. Labonte	33	1	5	15	4	0
	W. Dallenbach Jr.	16	0	0	3	3	0
	R. LaJoie	9	0	1	3	3	0
	R. Craven	8	0	0	1	0	1
1999	W. Dallenbach Jr.	34	0	1	6	5	0
	J. Gordon	34	7	18	21	7	7
	T. Labonte	34	1	1	7	6	0
2000	J. Gordon	34	3	11	22	2	3
	J. Nadeau	34	1	3	5	9	0
	T. Labonte	32	0	3	6	3	1
	T. Bodine	1	0	0	0	0	0
	R. Hornaday	1	0	0	0	0	0
2001	J. Gordon	36	6	18	24	2	6
	T. Labonte	36	0	1	3	8	0
	J. Nadeau	36	0	4	10	8	0
	Ji. Johnson	3	0	0	0	1	0

Year	Driver	Races	Won	Top 5	Top 10	DNF	Poles
2002	J. Gordon	36	3	13	20	3	3
	Ji. Johnson	36	3	6	21	3	4
	T. Labonte	36	0	1	4	6	0
	J. Nemechek	25	0	3	3	8	0
	J. Nadeau	11	0	0	1	3	0
2003	J. Gordon	36	3	15	20	5	4
	Ji. Johnson	36	3	14	20	3	2
	T. Labonte	36	1	4	9	0	1
	J. Nemechek	32	1	2	5	7	0
	B. Vickers	5	0	0	0	1	0
	D. Green	2	0	0	0	1	0
2004	J. Gordon	36	5	16	25	4	6
	Ji. Johnson	36	8	20	23	7	1
	T. Labonte	36	0	0	6	5	0
	B. Vickers	36	0	0	4	6	2
	Ky. Busch	6	0	0	0	4	0
2005	Ky. Busch	36	2	9	13	8	1
	J. Gordon	36	4	8	14	9	2
	Ji. Johnson	36	4	13	22	5	1
	B. Vickers	36	0	5	10	4	1
	T. Labonte	9	0	0	0	5	0
2006	Ky. Busch	36	1	10	18	2	1
	J. Gordon	36	2	14	18	7	2
	Ji. Johnson	36	5	13	24	1	1
	B. Vickers	36	1	5	9	2	1
	T. Labonte	10	0	0	0	3	0
TOTALS		**2,242**	**149**	**591**	**986**	**371**	**133**

JOE GIBBS RACING
Joe Gibbs

Years as NNCS owner: 15 • **Best points finish:** 1
Career victories: 54 • **First victory:** 1993, Daytona
Career poles: 39 • **First pole:** 1995, Martinsville

The NFL lured Joe Gibbs back into its coaching fold in 2004, but that hasn't stopped Joe Gibbs Racing from thriving. JGR ran its first season in 1992, and Dale Jarrett scored JGR's first win in the 1993 Daytona 500 and an impressive fourth-place finish in the series championship. In 1995, Bobby Labonte scored three wins and the team's first pole. Setting a plan for the future, Gibbs signed open-wheel star Tony Stewart to run a limited NASCAR Busch Series schedule in 1997 and 1998—through a joint effort with Labonte's NASCAR Busch Series team—in preparation for 1999. Along with winning rookie of the year honors in the NASCAR NEXTEL Cup Series in 1999, Stewart scored three victories. Labonte brought JGR its first series championship in 2000, and, in 2002 and 2005, Stewart brought Gibbs his second and third series title. In 2006, JGR graduated two rookies to the NASCAR NEXTEL Cup Series, Denny Hamlin—the rookie of the year winner—and J.J. Yeley.

CAREER NASCAR NEXTEL CUP SERIES STATISTICS

Year	Driver	Races	Won	Top 5	Top 10	DNF	Poles
1992	D. Jarrett	29	0	2	8	5	0
1993	D. Jarrett	30	1	13	18	5	0
1994	D. Jarrett	30	1	4	9	7	0
1995	B. Labonte	31	3	7	14	6	2
1996	B. Labonte	31	1	5	14	5	4
1997	B. Labonte	32	1	9	18	1	3
1998	B. Labonte	33	2	11	18	6	3
1999	B. Labonte	34	5	23	26	1	5

Year	Driver	Races	Won	Top 5	Top 10	DNF	Poles
	T. Stewart	34	3	12	21	1	2
2000	B. Labonte	34	4	19	24	0	2
	T. Stewart	34	6	12	23	5	2
2001	B. Labonte	36	2	9	20	6	1
	T. Stewart	36	3	15	22	4	0
2002	B. Labonte	36	1	5	7	4	0
	T. Stewart	36	3	15	21	6	2
2003	B. Labonte	36	2	12	17	5	4
	T. Stewart	36	2	12	18	5	1
	M. Bliss	1	0	0	0	0	0
2004	B. Labonte	36	0	5	11	2	1
	T. Stewart	36	2	10	19	2	0
	M. Bliss	2	0	1	1	1	0
	J. Yeley	1	0	0	0	1	0
2005	B. Labonte	36	0	4	7	10	0
	T. Stewart	36	5	17	25	1	3
	J. Leffler	19	0	0	0	3	0
	D. Hamlin	7	0	0	3	0	1
	T. Labonte	5	0	0	1	1	0
	J. Yeley	4	0	0	0	0	0
2006	D. Hamlin	36	2	8	20	1	3
	T. Stewart	36	5	15	19	4	0
	J. Yeley	36	0	0	3	7	0
TOTALS		**861**	**54**	**245**	**407**	**105**	**39**

MICHAEL WALTRIP RACING

Michael Waltrip

Years as NNCS owner: 5 • **Career victories:** 0
Career poles: 0

Michael Waltrip Racing has been fielding a NASCAR Busch Series car for driver Michael Waltrip since 1996, and as a driver/owner in the NASCAR Busch Series, Waltrip has collected four wins and six poles. In 2002, the organization began running NASCAR NEXTEL Cup Series cars on a part-time basis, and the highlight of the organization's short NASCAR NEXTEL Cup Series history came when Buckshot Jones led 19 laps at Talladega in 2003. That should change in 2007, when MWR fields three cars full-time in the NASCAR NEXTEL Cup Series with Waltrip, Dale Jarrett and rookie David Reutimann as the drivers. Along with Bill Davis Racing and Team Red Bull, MWR will be one of three NASCAR NEXTEL Cup Series teams running the Toyota Camry in 2007. Waltrip Racing World, an interactive, high-tech race shop in Cornelius, N.C., will house the the organization's NASCAR Busch Series team and NASCAR NEXTEL Cup Series teams, and it is expected to be completed mid-2007.

CAREER NASCAR NEXTEL CUP SERIES STATISTICS

Year	Driver	Races	Won	Top 5	Top 10	DNF	Poles
2002	J. Nadeau	1	0	0	0	1	0
	K. Wallace	1	0	0	0	0	0
2003	B. Jones	1	0	0	0	1	0
	M. Skinner	1	0	0	0	1	0
2004	K. Wallace	4	0	0	0	2	0
2005	J. Benson Jr.	2	0	0	0	2	0
	D. Reutimann	1	0	0	0	0	0
	K. Wallace	2	0	0	0	1	0
2006	B. Elliott	5	0	0	0	0	0
TOTALS		**18**	**0**	**0**	**0**	**8**	**0**

MORGAN-McCLURE MOTORSPORTS

Larry McClure

Years as NNCS owner: 24 • **Best points finish:** 3
Career victories: 14 • **First victory:** 1990, Bristol
Career poles: 13 • **First pole:** 1988, Bristol

Morgan-McClure Motorsports was formed in 1983, when Larry McClure, Ed McClure, Jerry McClure, Teddy McClure and Tim Morgan bought a car from G.C. Spencer. Larry McClure and Morgan had been longtime business partners, operating a successful automobile dealership, which they continue today. One of the team's first drivers was 24-year-old Mark Martin. The team broke into the win column in 1990 with Ernie Irvan, marking the beginning of a nine-year run during which the team won 14 races. Among those were three at the Daytona 500, with Irvan in 1991 and Sterling Marlin in 1994 and 1995. The 1995 season by Marlin gave the organization its best points finish when he finished third.

CAREER NASCAR NEXTEL CUP SERIES STATISTICS

Year	Driver	Races	Won	Top 5	Top 10	DNF	Poles
1983	M. Martin	6	0	0	1	2	0
	C. Saylor	1	0	0	0	1	0
1984	T. Ellis	20	0	0	1	11	0
	L. Pond	4	0	0	0	2	0
	J. Ruttman	3	0	0	1	2	0
1985	J. Ruttman	16	0	1	4	10	0
1986	R. Wilson	17	0	0	4	8	0
	L. Speed	1	0	0	0	0	0
1987	R. Wilson	19	0	0	1	11	0
	A. Foyt	1	0	0	0	1	0
1988	R. Wilson	28	0	2	5	11	1
1989	R. Wilson	29	0	2	7	8	0
1990	E. Irvan	26	1	6	13	3	3
	P. Parsons	3	0	0	0	1	0
1991	E. Irvan	29	2	11	19	6	1
1992	E. Irvan	29	3	9	11	9	3
1993	E. Irvan	21	1	7	8	9	2
	J. Purvis	5	0	0	0	0	0
	J. Hensley	2	0	0	0	1	0
	J. Nemechek	2	0	0	0	0	0
1994	S. Marlin	31	1	5	11	7	1
1995	S. Marlin	31	3	9	22	2	1
1996	S. Marlin	31	2	5	10	6	0
1997	S. Marlin	32	0	2	6	8	0
1998	B. Hamilton	33	1	3	8	1	1
1999	B. Hamilton	34	0	1	10	3	0
2000	B. Hamilton	34	0	0	2	11	0
2001	K. Lepage	21	0	0	0	3	0
	B. Hamilton Jr.	7	0	0	0	2	0
	R. Gordon	5	0	0	0	1	0
	R. Bickle	1	0	0	0	0	0
2002	M. Skinner	36	0	0	1	6	0
2003	M. Skinner	14	0	0	0	4	0
	K. Lepage	8	0	0	0	1	0
	J. Sauter	5	0	0	0	0	0
	J. Miller	2	0	0	0	0	0
	S. Compton	1	0	0	0	0	0
	P. Jones	1	0	0	0	0	0
2004	J. Spencer	25	0	0	0	7	0
	K. Lepage	6	0	0	0	1	0
	M. Wallace	3	0	0	0	2	0
	E. McClure	1	0	0	0	0	0

Year	Driver	Races	Won	Top 5	Top 10	DNF	Poles
2005	M. Wallace	28	0	0	1	5	0
	P. Jones	2	0	0	0	1	0
	J. Andretti	1	0	0	0	0	0
	T. Bodine	1	0	0	0	0	0
2006	S. Wimmer	23	0	0	0	3	0
	W. Burton	3	0	0	0	0	0
	T. Bodine	2	0	0	0	1	0
	P.J. Jones	1	0	0	0	1	0
	E. McClure	1	0	0	0	0	0
TOTALS		**686**	**14**	**63**	**146**	**172**	**13**

PENSKE RACING
Roger Penske

Years as NNCS owner: 23 • **Best points finish:** 2
Career victories: 58 • **First victory:** 1973, Riverside
Career poles: 82 • **First pole:** 1974, Riverside

Roger Penske began racing himself in 1958, but he stopped in 1965 and began to build Penske Corporation. His first entry into NASCAR was in 1972 when he fielded a Matador for road-racing standout Mark Donohue at Riverside International Raceway. One year later, Donohue scored Penske's first NASCAR victory at Riverside. In 1980, Penske Racing put together a two-race deal with driver Rusty Wallace. The team displayed a promising future from the start, scoring a second-place finish to Dale Earnhardt at Atlanta. But with most of Penke's emphasis on his open-wheel interests, the two decided against teaming up. More than a decade passed before Penske returned to NASCAR, when Miller and Penske partnered with Wallace to form Penske Racing South in 1990. The team enjoyed its most success in 1993 when Wallace won 10 races and three poles and finished as series runner-up. After starting eight races for Penske between 2000-01, Ryan Newman teamed with Wallace for the 2002 season. After the 2005 season, Wallace retired, and Penske brought in 2004 NASCAR NEXTEL Cup Series champion Kurt Busch to replace Wallace in the No. 2 Dodge.

CAREER NASCAR NEXTEL CUP SERIES STATISTICS

Year	Driver	Races	Won	Top 5	Top 10	DNF	Poles
1972	D. Marcis	7	0	0	3	4	0
	M. Donohue	4	0	0	0	3	0
	D. Allison	1	0	1	1	0	0
1973	D. Marcis	4	0	1	1	3	0
	M. Donohue	2	1	1	1	1	0
1974	B. Allison	7	1	5	5	2	0
	G. Bettenhausen	5	0	1	3	1	0
	G. Follmer	1	0	0	0	1	1
	D. Marcis	1	0	0	1	0	0
1975	B. Allison	19	3	10	10	9	3
1976	B. Allison	30	0	15	19	9	2
	N. Bonnett*	0	0	0	0	0	1
1977	D. Marcis	12	0	5	7	3	0
1980	R. Wallace	2	0	1	1	0	0
1991	R. Wallace	29	2	9	14	10	2
1992	R. Wallace	29	1	5	12	5	1
1993	R. Wallace	30	10	19	21	5	3
1994	R. Wallace	31	8	17	20	5	2
1995	R. Wallace	31	2	15	19	4	0
1996	R. Wallace	31	5	8	18	6	0
1997	R. Wallace	32	1	8	12	11	1
1998	J. Mayfield	33	1	12	16	2	1
	R. Wallace	33	1	15	21	2	4

Year	Driver	Races	Won	Top 5	Top 10	DNF	Poles
1999	J. Mayfield	34	0	5	12	4	0
	R. Wallace	34	1	7	16	3	4
2000	R. Wallace	34	4	12	20	3	9
	J. Mayfield	32	2	6	12	11	4
	R. Newman	1	0	0	0	1	0
2001	R. Wallace	36	1	8	14	3	0
	J. Mayfield	28	0	5	7	4	0
	M. Wallace	8	0	1	2	1	0
	R. Newman	7	0	2	2	2	1
2002	R. Newman	36	1	14	22	5	6
	R. Wallace	36	0	7	17	1	1
2003	R. Newman	36	8	17	22	7	11
	R. Wallace	36	0	2	12	4	0
2004	B. Gaughan	36	0	1	4	8	0
	R. Newman	36	2	11	14	9	9
	R. Wallace	36	1	3	11	3	0
	T. Kvapil	3	0	0	0	1	0
	C. Blount	1	0	0	0	1	0
2005	T. Kvapil	36	0	0	2	7	0
	R. Newman	36	1	8	16	3	8
	R. Wallace	36	0	8	17	0	0
2006	Ku. Busch	36	1	7	12	3	6
	R. Newman	36	0	2	7	3	2
TOTALS		**1,024**	**58**	**274**	**446**	**173**	**82**

*Bonnett substituted in qualifying for Allison at Nashville and won the pole; Allison started the race with Bonnett relieving him after one lap.

PETTY ENTERPRISES
Richard Petty

Years as NNCS owner: 58 • **Best points finish:** 1
Career victories: 268
First victory: 1949, Heidelberg Speedway, Pittsburgh • **Career poles:** 155
First pole: 1954, Daytona Beach road course

Like NASCAR itself, Petty Enterprises traces its roots to the sands of Daytona Beach. Founded in 1949 by family patriarch Lee Petty, Petty Enterprises was there for the beginning of NASCAR's Grand National Division (now NASCAR NEXTEL Cup Series). Since then, Petty Enterprises has fielded cars for 45 drivers, including four generations of the Petty family. In a 25-year span from 1954-79, the team won 10 series championships. Richard Petty, who made his No. 43 car a household icon, holds seven series titles and remains highly active in the team's operations today. The organization took on its current shape in 1999 when Kyle Petty folded his own pe2 team into Petty Enterprises, forming a two-car team. In 2001, Petty Enterprises switched to Dodge when the manufacturer made its return to the series.

CAREER NASCAR NEXTEL CUP SERIES STATISTICS

Year	Driver	Races	Won	Top 5	Top 10	DNF	Poles
1949	L. Petty	6	1	3	5	2	0
1950	L. Petty	17	1	9	13	7	0
1951	L. Petty	32	1	11	19	18	0
1952	L. Petty	32	3	21	27	6	0
1953	L. Petty	36	5	26	32	7	0
	J. Lewallen	1	0	1	1	0	0
1954	L. Petty	33	7	23	31	3	3
	B. Welborn	6	0	0	1	3	0
1955	L. Petty	41	6	20	30	9	1
1956	L. Petty	47	2	17	28	15	1

Year	Driver	Races	Won	Top 5	Top 10	DNF	Poles
1957	L. Petty	41	4	20	33	6	3
	R. Earnhardt	8	0	0	3	4	0
	T. Lund	5	0	1	2	2	0
	J. Dodson	1	0	0	0	0	0
	B. Lutz	1	0	0	1	1	0
	B. Myers	1	0	0	0	1	0
1958	L. Petty	50	7	28	43	8	4
	R. Petty	9	0	0	1	5	0
	J. Linke	2	0	0	0	2	0
	J. Reed	1	0	0	0	1	0
	J. Thompson	1	0	1	1	0	0
	J. Weatherly	1	0	0	1	0	0
	B. Welborn	1	0	0	1	0	0
1959	L. Petty	42	11	27	35	8	2
	R. Petty	21	0	6	9	11	0
1960	R. Petty	40	3	16	30	8	2
	L. Petty	39	5	21	30	9	3
	J. Paschal	8	0	3	7	2	0
	M. Petty	2	0	0	2	0	0
	B. Johns	1	0	1	1	0	0
1961	R. Petty	42	2	18	23	19	2
	M. Petty	9	0	2	4	3	0
	L. Petty	3	1	2	2	1	1
	D. Dieringer	1	0	0	1	0	0
	A. Malone	1	0	0	1	0	0
	M. Panch	1	0	0	0	1	0
	J. Paschal	1	0	0	0	1	0
1962	R. Petty	52	8	32	39	11	4
	J. Paschal	9	3	5	8	0	0
	B. Blackburn	6	0	0	2	2	0
	M. Petty	5	0	2	3	2	0
	L. Petty	1	0	1	1	0	0
	S. Thompson	1	0	0	1	0	0
1963	R. Petty	54	14	30	39	12	8
	J. Paschal	29	5	15	18	10	1
	B. James	4	0	0	0	3	0
	M. Petty	4	0	1	2	2	0
	B. Welborn	4	0	3	3	1	0
	J. Hurtubise	3	0	0	0	3	0
	L. Petty	3	0	1	2	1	0
	J. Massey	2	0	0	0	2	0
	J. Weatherly	1	0	1	1	0	0
1964	R. Petty	61	9	37	43	20	9
	J. Paschal	13	1	7	8	5	0
	Buck Baker	6	0	3	4	1	0
	M. Petty	6	0	2	5	1	0
	L. Petty	2	0	0	0	2	0
1965	R. Petty	15	4	10	10	5	7
	J. Paschal	3	0	3	3	0	0
	L. Yarbrough	1	0	0	0	1	0
1966	R. Petty	39	8	20	22	17	16
	M. Panch	4	1	2	3	1	0
	D. Dieringer	1	0	0	0	1	0
	P. Lewis	1	0	0	0	1	0
	J. Paschal	1	0	0	0	1	0
1967	R. Petty	48	27	38	40	8	19
	T. Lund	4	0	3	3	2	0
	G. Spencer	3	0	2	2	1	0
1968	R. Petty	49	16	31	35	16	12
1969	R. Petty	50	10	31	38	15	6
	B. Baker	0	0	0	0	0	1
1970	R. Petty	38	16	25	29	10	9
	P. Hamilton	15	3	9	11	4	1
	D. Gurney	1	0	0	1	0	1
	J. Paschal	1	0	0	0	0	0

Year	Driver	Races	Won	Top 5	Top 10	DNF	Poles
1971	R. Petty	46	21	38	41	5	8
	Buddy Baker	18	1	12	15	3	1
1972	R. Petty	31	8	25	28	5	3
	Buddy Baker	10	1	3	4	6	0
1973	R. Petty	28	6	15	17	10	3
1974	R. Petty	30	10	22	23	8	7
	H. McGriff	4	0	0	1	2	0
1975	R. Petty	30	13	21	24	6	3
1976	R. Petty	30	3	19	22	9	1
1977	R. Petty	30	5	20	23	6	5
1978	R. Petty	30	0	11	17	12	0
1979	R. Petty	31	5	23	27	3	1
	K. Petty	5	0	0	1	1	0
1980	R. Petty	31	2	15	19	9	0
	K. Petty	14	0	0	6	5	0
1981	K. Petty	31	0	1	10	18	0
	R. Petty	31	3	12	16	14	0
1982	R. Petty	30	0	9	16	13	0
	K. Petty	23	0	2	4	13	0
1983	K. Petty	30	0	0	2	10	0
	R. Petty	30	3	9	21	5	0
1984	K. Petty	30	0	1	6	7	0
1985	D. Brooks	3	0	0	0	3	0
	M. Shepherd	1	0	0	0	0	0
1986	R. Petty	28	0	4	11	9	0
1987	R. Petty	29	0	9	14	6	0
1988	R. Petty	29	0	1	5	15	0
1989	R. Petty	25	0	0	0	12	0
1990	R. Petty	29	0	0	1	12	0
1991	R. Petty	29	0	0	1	10	0
1992	R. Petty	29	0	0	0	6	0
1993	R. Wilson	29	0	0	1	6	0
	J. Hensley	1	0	0	0	1	0
1994	W. Dallenbach Jr.	14	0	1	3	3	0
	J. Andretti	11	0	0	0	2	0
1995	B. Hamilton	31	0	4	10	2	0
1996	B. Hamilton	31	1	3	11	4	2
1997	B. Hamilton	32	1	6	8	4	2
	K. Petty	32	0	2	9	2	0
1998	J. Andretti	33	0	3	10	5	1
	K. Petty	33	0	0	2	8	0
1999	J. Andretti	34	1	3	10	10	1
	K. Petty	32	0	0	9	4	0
2000	J. Andretti	34	0	0	2	7	0
	K. Petty	18	0	0	1	6	0
	S. Grissom	5	0	0	0	0	0
	A. Petty	1	0	0	0	1	0
2001	J. Andretti	35	0	1	2	4	0
	B. Jones	30	0	0	0	10	0
	K. Petty	24	0	0	0	8	0
2002	J. Andretti	36	0	0	1	7	0
	K. Petty	36	0	0	1	1	0
	J. Nadeau	13	0	0	0	6	0
	S. Grissom	10	0	0	1	1	0
	B. Jones	7	0	0	0	2	0
	G. Biffle	2	0	0	0	0	0
	C. Fittipaldi	1	0	0	0	1	0
	T. Musgrave	1	0	0	0	0	0
2003	K. Petty	33	0	0	0	5	0
	J. Andretti	14	0	0	1	2	0
	C. Fittipaldi	14	0	0	0	6	0
	J. Green	8	0	0	0	2	0
2004	J. Green	36	0	0	1	11	0
	K. Petty	35	0	0	0	9	0

Year	Driver	Races	Won	Top 5	Top 10	DNF	Poles
2005	J. Green	36	0	0	0	2	0
	K. Petty	36	0	0	2	3	0
2006	B. Labonte	36	0	3	8	8	0
	K. Petty	36	0	0	2	5	0
TOTALS		2,749	268	889	1,264	725	154

PPI MOTORSPORTS
Cal Wells

Years as NNCS owner: 7 • **Best points finish:** 15
Career victories: 2 • **First victory:** 2001, Martinsville
Career poles: 3 • **First pole:** 2001, Michigan

With only three employees and a small garage in Westminster, Calif., in 1979, Cal Wells founded Precision Preparation Inc. (PPI)—a company specializing in servicing off-road racing teams. PPI eventually started fielding its own off-road competition efforts, which since has evolved into PPI Motorsports. Before coming to NASCAR, Wells was renowned for his efforts in stadium and off-road racing. In 1999, PPI moved into the NASCAR Busch Series and a year later began competing in NASCAR's premier series with Scott Pruett as the driver. In October 2001, the team captured its first victory, at Martinsville Speedway with Ricky Craven. In 2004, Craven lost his ride to Bobby Hamilton Jr., and in 2006, Travis Kvapil took over the No. 32.

CAREER NASCAR NEXTEL CUP SERIES STATISTICS

Year	Driver	Races	Won	Top 5	Top 10	DNF	Poles
2000	S. Pruett	28	0	0	1	11	0
	A. Houston	5	0	0	0	2	0
2001	R. Craven	36	1	4	7	9	1
	A. Houston	17	0	0	0	9	0
2002	R. Craven	36	0	3	9	4	2
2003	R. Craven	36	1	3	8	10	0
2004	R. Craven	25	0	0	0	8	0
	B. Hamilton Jr.	11	0	0	0	2	0
2005	B. Hamilton Jr.	31	0	0	0	8	0
	R. Fellows	2	0	0	1	0	0
2006	T. Kvapil	31	0	0	0	5	0
	R. Fellows	2	0	0	0	0	0
TOTALS		260	2	10	26	68	3

RICHARD CHILDRESS RACING
Richard Childress

Years as NNCS owner: 33 • **Best points finish:** 1
Career victories: 83 • **First victory:** 1983, Riverside
Career poles: 41 • **First pole:** 1982, Dover

Richard Childress was a driver before he was an owner, making his first start in 1969 at Talladega. In 1976, Childress drove the famed No. 3 through the 20th race of the 1981 season. Childress, then 35 and a veteran of 285 starts, turned the wheel over to Dale Earnhardt on August 16 at Michigan. Earnhardt drove the final 11 races of the season before the pair parted. In 1982, Ricky Rudd scored RCR its first pole, and in 1983, its first win. Earnhardt and Childress paired up again in 1984, and over the next 17 years, RCR recorded 67 wins and six NASCAR NEXTEL Cup Series titles. RCR was shaken February 18, 2001, when Dale Earnhardt died in an accident at the Daytona 500. The following week at

Rockingham, RCR's famed No. 3 was changed to No. 29 with Kevin Harvick taking over and earning rookie of the year honors for 2001. Harvick, working double-duty in the NASCAR NEXTEL Cup Series and the NASCAR Busch Series, won the 2001 NASCAR Busch Series title. RCR made its first appearance in the Chase for the NASCAR NEXTEL Cup when Kevin Harvick and Jeff Burton made the postseason in 2006.

CAREER NASCAR NEXTEL CUP SERIES STATISTICS

Year	Driver	Races	Won	Top 5	Top 10	DNF	Poles
1969	R. Childress	1	0	0	0	1	0
1972	R. Childress	14	0	0	0	12	0
1976	R. Childress	30	0	0	11	9	0
1977	R. Childress	30	0	0	11	9	0
1978	R. Childress	30	0	1	12	4	0
1979	R. Childress	31	0	1	11	5	0
1980	R. Childress	31	0	0	10	4	0
1981	R. Childress	20	0	1	1	7	0
	D. Earnhardt	11	0	2	6	4	0
1982	R. Rudd	30	0	6	13	13	2
1983	R. Rudd	30	2	7	14	9	4
1984	D. Earnhardt	30	2	12	22	2	0
1985	D. Earnhardt	28	4	10	16	9	1
1986	D. Earnhardt	29	5	16	23	4	1
1987	D. Earnhardt	29	11	21	24	2	1
1988	D. Earnhardt	29	3	13	19	1	0
	R. Combs	1	0	0	0	1	0
1989	D. Earnhardt	29	5	14	19	2	0
	J. Hensley	0	0	0	0	0	1
1990	D. Earnhardt	29	9	18	23	1	4
1991	D. Earnhardt	29	4	14	21	2	0
1992	D. Earnhardt	29	1	6	15	4	1
1993	D. Earnhardt	30	6	17	21	2	2
	N. Bonnett	2	0	0	0	2	0
1994	D. Earnhardt	31	4	20	25	3	2
1995	D. Earnhardt	31	5	19	23	2	3
1996	D. Earnhardt	31	2	13	17	2	2
	M. Skinner	5	0	0	0	1	0
1997	D. Earnhardt	32	0	7	16	0	0
	M. Skinner	31	0	0	3	7	2
1998	D. Earnhardt	33	1	5	13	3	0
	M. Skinner	30	0	4	9	3	0
	M. Shepherd	2	0	0	0	1	0
	M. Dillon	1	0	0	0	0	0
1999	D. Earnhardt	34	3	7	21	3	0
	M. Skinner	34	0	5	14	1	2
2000	D. Earnhardt	34	2	13	24	0	0
	M. Skinner	34	0	1	11	2	1
2001	K. Harvick	35	2	6	16	1	0
	M. Skinner	23	0	0	1	4	0
	R. Gordon	10	1	1	2	1	0
	J. Green	8	0	0	1	3	1
	D. Earnhardt	1	0	0	0	1	0
2002	R. Gordon	36	0	1	5	4	0
	J. Green	36	0	4	6	2	0
	K. Harvick	35	1	5	8	6	1
	K. Wallace	1	0	0	0	0	0
2003	R. Gordon	36	2	4	10	2	0
	K. Harvick	36	1	11	18	0	1
	S. Park	24	0	1	2	3	1
	J. Green	11	0	0	1	2	0
	J. Andretti	1	0	0	0	0	0
	R. Hornaday	1	0	0	0	0	0
2004	R. Gordon	36	0	2	6	3	0
	K. Harvick	36	0	5	14	4	0
	J. Burton	14	0	1	3	1	0

Year	Driver	Races	Won	Top 5	Top 10	DNF	Poles
	J. Sauter	13	0	0	0	1	0
	D. Blaney	8	0	0	0	1	0
	K. Earnhardt	3	0	0	0	1	0
	J. Inglebright	1	0	0	0	0	0
	M. Skinner	1	0	0	0	0	0
2005	K. Harvick	36	1	3	10	1	2
	D. Blaney	36	0	0	2	2	0
	J. Burton	36	0	3	6	3	0
	K. Earnhardt	3	0	0	0	2	0
	C. Bowyer	1	0	0	0	0	0
	B. Simo	1	0	0	1	0	0
2006	C. Bowyer	36	0	4	11	4	0
	J. Burton	36	1	7	20	2	4
	K. Harvick	36	5	15	20	1	1
	S. Wimmer	1	0	0	0	0	0
TOTALS		1,543	83	326	631	192	41

ROBBY GORDON MOTORSPORTS
Robby Gordon

Years as NNCS owner: 2 • **Best points finish:** 30
Career victories: 0 • **Career poles:** 0

The 2005 season marked the first solo ownership effort by Robby Gordon in the NASCAR NEXTEL Cup Series. Gordon began a NASCAR Busch Series team in 2004, competing in 25 races. In 2005, he brought the team up to the NASCAR NEXTEL Cup Series, and he switched his team from Chevrolet to Ford before the 2007 season.

CAREER NASCAR NEXTEL CUP SERIES STATISTICS

Year	Driver	Races	Won	Top 5	Top 10	DNF	Poles
2005	R. Gordon	29	0	1	2	13	0
2006	R. Gordon	36	0	1	3	9	0
TOTALS		65	0	2	5	22	0

ROBERT YATES RACING
Robert Yates

Years as NNCS owner: 18 • **Best points finish:** 1
Career victories: 57 • **First victory:** 1989, Talladega
Career poles: 47 • **First pole:** 1989, Dover

Robert Yates began his career at Holman-Moody Racing in 1968. By 1971, his reputation and skills with racing engines landed Yates a top job with Junior Johnson, where he provided power for legendary drivers Bobby Allison and Cale Yarborough. In 1988, Yates launched his own team, Robert Yates Racing, after taking over Harry Ranier's No. 28 team. In 1996, Yates' operation expanded to a two-car team with drivers Dale Jarrett and Ernie Irvan. Beginning with the 2003 season, Yates' famous No. 28 car was changed to No. 38 with the addition of sponsorship from M&M's and driver Elliot Sadler. During the 2006 season, Sadler left the team and was replaced by David Gilliland.

CAREER NASCAR NEXTEL CUP SERIES STATISTICS

Year	Driver	Races	Won	Top 5	Top 10	DNF	Poles
1989	D. Allison	29	2	7	13	6	1
1990	D. Allison	29	2	5	10	2	0
1991	D. Allison	29	5	12	16	4	3
1992	D. Allison	29	5	15	17	3	2

Year	Driver	Races	Won	Top 5	Top 10	DNF	Poles
1993	D. Allison	16	1	6	8	1	0
	E. Irvan	9	2	5	6	1	2
	L. Speed	3	0	0	1	0	0
	R. Gordon	1	0	0	0	1	0
1994	E. Irvan	20	3	13	15	3	5
	K. Wallace	10	0	1	2	1	0
1995	D. Jarrett	31	1	9	14	6	1
	E. Irvan	3	0	0	2	1	0
1996	E. Irvan	31	2	12	16	5	1
	D. Jarrett	31	4	17	21	3	2
1997	E. Irvan	32	1	5	13	8	2
	D. Jarrett	32	7	20	23	1	2
1998	D. Jarrett	33	3	19	22	3	2
	K. Irwin	32	0	1	4	8	1
1999	K. Irwin	34	0	2	6	5	2
	D. Jarrett	34	4	24	29	1	0
2000	D. Jarrett	34	2	15	24	2	3
	R. Rudd	34	0	12	19	1	2
2001	D. Jarrett	36	4	12	19	4	4
	R. Rudd	36	2	14	22	4	1
2002	D. Jarrett	36	2	10	18	5	1
	R. Rudd	36	1	8	12	4	1
2003	D. Jarrett	36	1	1	7	8	0
	E. Sadler	36	0	2	9	9	2
	J. Jarrett	1	0	0	0	0	0
2004	D. Jarrett	36	0	6	14	3	0
	E. Sadler	36	2	8	14	1	0
2005	D. Jarrett	36	1	4	7	2	1
	E. Sadler	36	0	1	12	2	4
2006	D. Jarrett	36	0	1	4	5	0
	E. Sadler	22	0	1	5	3	1
	D. Gilliland	14	0	0	0	1	1
	M. Goossens	1	0	0	0	1	0
S. Leight		1	0	0	0	0	0
TOTALS		971	57	268	424	118	47

ROUSH RACING
Jack Roush

Years as NNCS owner: 19 • **Best points finish:** 1
Career victories: 95 • **First victory:** 1989, Rockingham
Career poles: 58 • **First pole:** 1988, Dover

Almost a 20-year veteran owner in NASCAR's premier series, Jack Roush fielded back-to-back champions with Kurt Busch's victory in the inaugural Chase for the NASCAR NEXTEL Cup in 2004 and Matt Kenseth's NASCAR NEXTEL Cup Series title in 2003. A former graduate-level mathematician and grass-roots racer from Michigan, Roush began competing in NASCAR's premier series in 1988 with Mark Martin's team. Roush Racing also fields teams in the NASCAR Craftsman Truck Series and NASCAR Busch Series and supplies engines to other NASCAR teams. In 2005, Roush Racing was dominant, qualifying all five of its teams for the Chase for the NASCAR NEXTEL Cup. An avid pilot, Roush also owns Roush Industries, a Michigan-based company that supplies parts to the automotive and transportation industries.

CAREER NASCAR NEXTEL CUP SERIES STATISTICS

Year	Driver	Races	Won	Top 5	Top 10	DNF	Poles
1988	M. Martin	29	0	3	10	10	1
1989	M. Martin	29	1	14	18	4	6
1990	M. Martin	29	3	16	23	1	3
1991	M. Martin	29	1	14	17	5	5

Year	Driver	Races	Won	Top 5	Top 10	DNF	Poles
1992	W. Dallenbach Jr.	29	0	1	1	7	0
	M. Martin	29	2	10	17	5	1
1993	W. Dallenbach Jr.	30	0	1	4	7	0
	M. Martin	30	5	12	19	5	5
1994	M. Martin	31	2	15	20	8	1
	T. Musgrave	31	0	1	8	5	3
1995	M. Martin	31	4	13	22	1	4
	T. Musgrave	31	0	7	13	1	1
1996	M. Martin	31	0	14	23	4	4
	T. Musgrave	31	0	2	7	2	1
	J. Burton	30	0	6	12	1	1
1997	J. Burton	32	3	13	18	1	0
	M. Martin	32	4	16	24	3	3
	T. Musgrave	32	0	5	8	4	0
	C. Little	12	0	0	0	1	0
1998	J. Burton	33	2	18	23	4	0
	M. Martin	33	7	22	26	1	3
	J. Benson	32	0	3	10	5	0
	C. Little	32	0	1	7	7	0
	T. Musgrave	20	0	1	4	3	0
	K. Lepage	13	0	0	2	5	0
1999	J. Benson	34	0	0	2	5	0
	J. Burton	34	6	18	23	3	0
	K. Lepage	34	0	1	2	3	1
	C. Little	34	0	0	5	4	0
	M. Martin	34	2	19	26	3	1
	M. Kenseth	5	0	1	1	3	0
2000	J. Burton	34	4	15	22	2	1
	M. Kenseth	34	1	4	11	5	0
	M. Martin	34	1	13	20	6	0
	K. Lepage	32	0	1	3	5	0
	C. Little	27	0	0	1	3	0
	K. Busch	7	0	0	0	0	0
2001	J. Burton	36	2	8	16	1	0
	M. Kenseth	36	0	4	9	5	0
	M. Martin	36	0	3	15	4	2
	K. Busch	35	0	3	6	7	1
2002	J. Burton	36	0	5	14	5	0
	K. Busch	36	4	12	20	4	1
	M. Kenseth	36	5	11	19	3	1
	M. Martin	36	1	12	22	3	0
	G. Biffle	1	0	0	0	0	0
2003	J. Burton	36	0	3	11	4	0
	K. Busch	36	4	9	14	8	0
	M. Kenseth	36	1	11	25	2	0
	M. Martin	36	0	5	10	7	0
	G. Biffle	35	1	3	6	6	0
2004	G. Biffle	36	2	4	8	5	1
	K. Busch	36	3	10	21	3	1
	M. Kenseth	36	2	8	16	6	0
	M. Martin	36	1	10	15	2	0
	J. Burton	22	0	1	3	5	0
	C. Edwards	13	0	1	5	2	0
	D. Blaney	1	0	0	0	1	0
2005	G. Biffle	36	6	15	21	1	0
	C. Edwards	36	4	13	18	1	2
	M. Kenseth	36	1	12	17	4	2
	M. Martin	36	1	12	19	2	0
	K. Busch	34	3	9	18	3	0
	K. Wallace	2	0	0	0	0	0
2006	G. Biffle	36	2	8	15	6	2
	C. Edwards	36	0	10	20	3	0
	M. Kenseth	36	4	15	21	1	0

Year	Driver	Races	Won	Top 5	Top 10	DNF	Poles
	M. Martin	36	0	7	15	2	0
	J. McMurray	36	0	3	7	7	0
	T. Kluever	4	0	0	0	2	0
	D. Ragan	2	0	0	0	1	0
TOTALS		2,077	95	507	878	236	58

TEAM RED BULL
Red Bull

Years as NNCS owner: First

Team Red Bull might be a newcomer to the NASCAR NEXTEL Cup Series, but it isn't a newcomer to racing. Red Bull already owns and operates two Formula 1 teams and has been involved with teams and/or drivers in the NASCAR Busch Series, IndyCar and Champ Car, among other race series. The team is in experienced hands with general manager Marty Gaunt, a former late model driver and ARCA crew chief who has worked in the NASCAR NEXTEL Cup Series with Penske Racing. The organization will be one of three, along with Bill Davis Racing and Michael Waltrip Racing, that will run Toyota Camrys in the NASCAR NEXTEL Cup Series in 2007, and their driver lineup will feature 2003 NASCAR Busch Series champion Brian Vickers and rookie A.J. Allmendinger, a former Champ Car driver.

WOOD BROS. RACING
Glen, Len, Eddie Wood, Kim Wood Hall

Years as NNCS owner: 53 • **Best points finish:** 5
Career victories: 96 • **First victory:** 1960, Winston-Salem
Career poles: 119 • **First pole:** 1958, North Wilkesboro

Founded in 1953 by Glen Wood, Wood Brothers Racing is one of the most storied organizations in NASCAR. Its drivers' roll reads like a "Who's Who" of the sport, featuring some of racing's greatest names—David Pearson, Cale Yarborough, Marvin Panch, Tiny Lund, Fred Lorenzen, Dan Gurney, Bobby Rahal, Parnelli Jones, A.J. Foyt, Speedy Thompson, Donnie Allison, Buddy Baker, Morgan Shepherd, Dale Jarrett, Neil Bonnett, Michael Waltrip and Ricky Rudd. Glen Wood himself drove for his family operation from 1953-64. In 1963, Wood Brothers Racing took first place in the owner standings with five drivers. Wood Brothers Racing is credited with being the first team to truly grasp the importance of fast pit stops.

CAREER NASCAR NEXTEL CUP SERIES STATISTICS

Year	Driver	Races	Won	Top 5	Top 10	DNF	Poles
1953	G. Wood	2	0	0	0	2	0
1955	G. Wood	1	0	0	0	1	0
1956	G. Wood	1	0	0	0	1	0
1957	G. Wood	6	0	0	1	3	0
	J. Massey	2	0	1	2	0	0
1958	G. Wood	10	0	1	7	1	3
	J. Massey	1	0	1	1	0	0
	C. Turner	1	0	0	0	1	0
1959	G. Wood	18	0	8	11	6	3
	J. Johnson	2	0	1	1	1	0
	J. Beauchamp	1	0	0	0	0	0

Year	Driver	Races	Won	Top 5	Top 10	DNF	Poles
	J. Weatherly	1	0	0	1	0	0
1960	G. Wood	9	3	6	7	2	4
	J. Massey	3	0	2	2	1	0
	S. Thompson	3	2	3	3	0	0
	J. Johnson	2	0	1	1	1	1
	J. Weatherly	2	0	1	1	1	0
	F. Harb Jr.	1	0	0	0	1	0
	C. Turner	1	0	0	0	1	0
	B. Welborn	1	0	0	0	1	0
1961	C. Turner	7	0	1	1	6	0
	G. Wood	6	0	3	3	3	1
	B. Matthews	1	0	0	0	1	0
	S. Thompson	1	0	0	0	1	0
1962	M. Panch	14	0	5	8	5	0
1963	M. Panch	12	1	9	12	0	3
	T. Lund	7	1	5	6	1	0
	G. Wood	3	1	2	2	1	2
	T. Irwin	1	0	1	1	0	0
	F. Lorenzen	1	0	0	0	1	0
	D. MacDonald	1	0	1	1	0	0
1964	M. Panch	29	3	17	20	10	5
	D. Gurney	4	1	1	2	1	0
	G. Wood	2	0	1	1	1	1
	N. Stacy	1	0	0	0	1	0
1965	M. Panch	20	4	12	14	7	5
	C. Turner	4	1	3	3	1	0
	A. Foyt	1	0	0	0	1	0
	D. Gurney	1	1	1	1	0	0
1966	M. Panch	6	0	1	1	5	0
	C. Turner	6	0	2	2	3	0
	C. Yarborough	5	0	1	1	3	0
	D. Gurney	1	1	1	1	0	0
1967	C. Yarborough	15	2	7	8	8	4
	E. Balmer	1	0	0	0	1	0
1968	C. Yarborough	20	6	12	12	8	4
	D. Gurney	1	1	1	1	0	1
1969	C. Yarborough	19	2	7	8	11	6
	S. Savage	2	0	1	1	1	0
	D. Gurney	1	0	0	0	1	0
1970	C. Yarborough	18	3	11	13	7	5
	P. Jones	1	0	0	0	1	0
1971	D. Allison	11	1	7	8	4	5
	A. Foyt	4	2	4	4	0	4
1972	D. Pearson	14	6	11	12	3	4
	A. Foyt	6	2	5	5	1	3
1973	D. Pearson	18	11	14	14	4	8
1974	D. Pearson	19	7	15	15	4	11
1975	D. Pearson	21	3	13	14	8	7
1976	D. Pearson	22	10	16	18	4	8
1977	D. Pearson	22	2	16	16	6	5
1978	D. Pearson	22	4	11	11	11	7
1979	N. Bonnett	17	3	4	6	11	4
	D. Pearson	5	0	1	1	4	1
1980	N. Bonnett	22	2	10	13	10	0
1981	N. Bonnett	22	3	7	8	14	1
1982	N. Bonnett	22	1	6	8	11	0
1983	B. Baker	21	1	5	12	8	1
1984	B. Baker	21	0	4	12	7	1
	B. Rahal	1	0	0	0	1	0
1985	K. Petty	28	0	7	12	4	0
1986	K. Petty	29	1	4	14	6	0
1987	K. Petty	29	1	6	14	4	0
1988	K. Petty	29	0	2	8	6	0

Year	Driver	Races	Won	Top 5	Top 10	DNF	Poles
1989	N. Bonnett	26	0	0	11	5	0
	T. Ellis	3	0	0	0	1	0
1990	D. Jarrett	24	0	1	7	9	0
	N. Bonnett	5	0	0	0	3	0
1991	D. Jarrett	29	1	3	8	9	0
1992	M. Shepherd	29	0	3	11	3	0
1993	M. Shepherd	30	1	3	15	2	0
1994	M. Shepherd	31	0	9	16	2	0
1995	M. Shepherd	31	0	4	10	2	0
1996	M. Waltrip	31	0	1	11	3	0
1997	M. Waltrip	32	0	0	6	4	0
1998	M. Waltrip	32	0	0	5	3	0
1999	E. Sadler	34	0	0	1	2	0
2000	E. Sadler	33	0	0	1	5	0
2001	E. Sadler	36	1	2	2	2	0
2002	E. Sadler	36	0	2	7	6	0
2003	R. Rudd	36	0	4	5	9	0
2004	R. Rudd	36	0	1	3	6	1
2005	R. Rudd	36	0	2	9	5	0
2006	K. Schrader	36	0	0	2	8	0
TOTALS		1,271	96	334	516	334	119

Roush

>> CREW CHIEFS <<
NASCAR NEXTEL Cup Series

STEVE ADDINGTON

Date of birth: July 4, 1964
Hometown: Spartanburg, S.C.
Team: No. 18 Chevrolet
Years as crew chief with current team: 2
Overall seasons as NNCS crew chief: 2

THE ADDINGTON FILE

The 2005 season was Addington's first in the NASCAR NEXTEL Cup Series after being promoted within Joe Gibbs Racing. With Addington, Bobby Labonte scored seven top 10s. In 2006, rookie J.J. Yeley took over the car and finished with three top 10s. Before being promoted to the No. 18 team, Addington served as crew chief in 2004 for the No. 20 NASCAR Busch Series car, which Mike Bliss drove and finished fifth in points. Before moving to JGR, Addington was Jason Keller's crew chief in the NASCAR Busch Series, first at KEL Racing from 1991 to 1996 then at ppc Racing from 1999 to 2003.

PAUL ANDREWS

Date of birth: May 25, 1957
Hometown: Bangor, Maine
Team: No. 43 Dodge
Years as crew chief with current team: 1
Overall seasons as NNCS crew chief: 18

THE ANDREWS FILE

Andrews has experienced success as a crew chief. Leading Alan Kulwicki's NASCAR NEXTEL Cup Series team in 1992, he won the championship, and throughout his career as crew chief, he has compiled a dozen wins and more than 75 top fives. Andrews joined Petty Enterprises as crew chief for Kyle Petty's No. 45 car in 2005 after spending the 2004 season as the crew chief for Akins Motorsports' No. 38 NASCAR Busch Series team. He moved to the No. 43 team in September. Prior to working at Akins, Andrews was crew chief for Jeff Burton's NASCAR NEXTEL Cup Series team with Roush Racing and Steve Park's NASCAR NEXTEL Cup Series ride with Dale Earnhardt Inc.

TOMMY BALDWIN

Date of birth: October 27, 1966
Hometown: Bellport, N.Y.
Overall seasons as NNCS crew chief: 8

THE BALDWIN FILE

Baldwin learned to love racing at the side of his father, driver Tom Sr. Baldwin began working for Bill Davis Racing in 1998 and later won the 2002 Daytona 500 as Ward Burton's crew chief. In 2004, Baldwin began working with rookie driver Kasey Kahne and Evernham Motorsports. Under Baldwin, Kahne won the rookie of the year award in the NASCAR NEXTEL Cup Series in 2004. Baldwin left Evernham late in

the 2005 season and joined Robert Yates Racing as crew chief for the No. 38 team for the 2006 season but was let go before Indianapolis in 2006. He became competition director for Bill Davis shortly after.

ROBERT BARKER

Date of birth: March 2, 1971
Hometown: Brookneal, Va.
Team: No. 70 Chevrolet
Years as crew chief with current team: First
Overall seasons as NNCS crew chief: 3

THE BARKER FILE

"Bootie" Barker, who has an engineering degree from Old Dominion, began his NASCAR career in the NASCAR Craftsman Truck Series, working for Kurt Roehrig. From 1998 to 1999, he worked for Bill Davis Racing and Hendrick Motosports. In 2004 and 2005, Barker served as Ward Burton's and Mike Bliss' crew chief in Haas CNC Racing's No. 0. He stayed on in 2006 when Jeff Green took over the ride and the team changed to the No. 66. Before the 2007 season, Barker was named crew chief for Haas' second full-time team, the No. 70.

TODD BERRIER

Date of birth: May 29, 1970
Hometown: Kernersville, N.C.
Team: No. 29 Chevrolet
Years as crew chief with current team: 4
Overall seasons as NNCS crew chief: 4

THE BERRIER FILE

Berrier and Kevin Harvick's driver-crew chief bond was forged in the NASCAR Busch Series; they won the title in 2001 in their second year together. Berrier was reunited with Harvick in the NASCAR NEXTEL Cup Series in 2003 after working with driver Jeff Green in 2002 in the NASCAR NEXTEL Cup Series. In 2006, Harvick made the Chase for the NASCAR NEXTEL Cup, and Harvick finished a career-high fourth in points. Berrier also has crew chief experience in the NASCAR Craftsman Truck Series, guiding the No. 3 Richard Childress Racing team from midway through 1997 to 1999.

MATT BORLAND

Date of birth: September 2, 1971
Hometown: Haslett, Mich.
Team: No. 44 Toyota
Years as crew chief with current team: First
Overall seasons as NNCS crew chief: 7

THE BORLAND FILE

Borland, a mechanical engineer who has CART and research experience, and driver Ryan Newman worked together to build a resume of eight poles, two wins and 11 top 10s in an ARCA-Busch-Cup whirlwind before the pair came into the NASCAR NEXTEL Cup Series full time in 2002, when Borland guided Newman to six poles and a Raybestos Rookie of the Year award. In 2003, 2004 and 2005, Borland and Newman continued their pole-pounding ways. Borland helped Newman make the Chase for the NASCAR NEXTEL Cup in 2004 and 2005. The pair struggled in 2006, and Borland left his crew chief job with two races left in the season. He'll lead Dale Jarrett's No. 44 team in 2007.

JOSH BROWNE

Date of birth: August 5, 1971
Hometown: Philadelphia
Team: No. 19 Dodge
Years as crew chief with current team: 1
Overall seasons as NNCS crew chief: 1

THE BROWNE FILE

Browne spent four years with Evernham Motorsports before being promoted to team director for the No. 19 team when Elliott Sadler came on board in August 2006. Browne earned his engineering degree from Carnegie Mellon University and his master's degree in mechanical engineering from Oakland University. He joined Penske Racing as a simulation engineer in 1998. He left NASCAR two years later, but returned to manage Evernham's Dodge research and development program and later worked as the organization's director of vehicle dynamics before being promoted in 2006.

CHRIS CARRIER

Date of birth: April 6, 1960
Hometown: Bristol, Tenn.
Team: No. 4 Chevrolet
Years as crew chief with current team: 5
Overall seasons as NNCS crew chief: 5

THE CARRIER FILE

Carrier has been part of some impressive teams and drivers, including Morgan Shepherd, Dale Earnhardt, Bobby Allison and Harry Gant. Raised in Bristol Motor Speedway's neck of the woods, Carrier started working in NASCAR at age 14 and won his first race as a crew chief at 18. He become a crew chief for Morgan-McClure Motorsports in 2002 and guided Mike Skinner that season, Skinner and Stacy Compton in 2003 and Jimmy Spencer, Kevin Lepage and Mike Wallace in 2004. In 2005, he worked with Wallace and John Andretti, and Scott Wimmer, Ward Burton, Eric McClure and other racing veterans in 2006.

LARRY CARTER

Date of birth: September 21, 1962
Hometown: Raleigh, N.C.
Overall seasons as NNCS crew chief: 4

THE CARTER FILE

The nephew of team owner Travis Carter, Larry's first NASCAR NEXTEL Cup Series head wrench job came at Haas-Carter Motorsports. He then joined BACE Motorsports in 2003 as crew chief, working with rookie Tony Raines. Carter switched gears in 2004 when he worked with veteran Rusty Wallace and was part of the No. 2's victory at Martinsville that broke Wallace's 105-race winless streak. In 2005, he led Wallace through the "Rusty's Last Call" retirement tour and to the Chase for the NASCAR NEXTEL Cup, where Wallace finished eighth. He will team with rookie David Reutimann on the No. 00 team in 2007.

RODNEY CHILDERS

Date of birth: June 7, 1976
Hometown: Mooresville, N.C.
Team: No. 10 Dodge
Years as crew chief with current team: 2
Overall seasons as NNCS crew chief: 2

THE CHILDERS FILE

Childers started racing go-karts at age 12. After driving in the Hooters Cup and the NASCAR Busch Series, Childers decided to focus on becoming a NASCAR NEXTEL Cup Series crew chief in 2002. He began working for Penske Racing as head mechanic for the No. 77 in 2003 and became car chief for the No. 77 in 2004. In 2005, Childers moved to MBV Motorsports. After starting the season as car chief for the No. 10, Childers was promoted to crew chief midseason. He followed the No. 10 team to Evernham Motorsports and helped driver Scott Riggs earn a career-high eight top 10s in 2006.

ERNIE COPE

Date of birth: July 17, 1969
Hometown: Tacoma, Wash.
Team: No. 21 Ford
Years as crew chief with current team: First
Overall seasons as NNCS crew chief: 2

THE COPE FILE

Cope has served as crew chief for a number of part-time NASCAR NEXTEL Cup Series racers, including Andy Belmont, Hermie Sadler, Carl Long and his cousin Derrike Cope. Ernie Cope also has experience as a crew chief in the ARCA series. During the mid- to late 1990s, Cope made 11 starts in NASCAR's three premier series, including one NASCAR NEXTEL Cup Series start at Phoenix. He won the NASCAR West Series rookie of the year award in 1995. Cope will guide Wood Brothers Racing's No. 21 team in 2007.

JIMMY ELLEDGE

Date of birth: July 14, 1970
Hometown: Redding, Calif.
Team: No. 41 Dodge
Years as crew chief with current team: 4
Overall seasons as NNCS crew chief: 8

THE ELLEDGE FILE

Elledge originally intended to spend his career as a driver. In 1992, he decided to focus on the mechanical side of racing and learned the trade from Robert Yates, Richard Childress and Dale Earnhardt before joining Andy Petree Racing as the crew chief for Bobby Hamilton. Elledge moved to Chip Ganassi Racing in 2003, when he became the crew chief for Casey Mears. In his rookie season, Mears was 35th in points; in 2004 and 2005, Mears finished 22nd. In 2006, Elledge guided rookie Reed Sorenson to five top 10s.

GREG ERWIN

Date of birth: April 19, 1970
Hometown: Hatboro, Pa.
Team: No. 7 Chevrolet
Years as crew chief with current team: 2
Overall seasons as NNCS crew chief: 2

THE ERWIN FILE

Erwin, a mechanical engineering graduate of Clemson, has worked on Robby Gordon's teams at Team SABCO and Richard Childress Racing as an engineer and a mechanic. He also has worked as the lead engineer on XPress Motorsports' No. 16 NASCAR Craftsman Truck Series team. In April 2005, he replaced Bob Temple as crew chief for Gordon's fledgling Robby Gordon Motorsports' No. 7 team after the team's miserable start to the season—it missed four of the first 10 races. In 2006, Erwin's second season with the team, Gordon's average finish improved by about five spots (30.1 to 25.3).

TONY EURY JR.

Date of birth: January 3, 1973
Hometown: Kannapolis, N.C.
Team: No. 8 Chevrolet
Years as crew chief with current team: 2
Overall seasons as NNCS crew chief: 2

THE EURY FILE

Tony Eury Jr.'s father, Tony Eury Sr., served as crew chief on Dale Earnhardt Jr.'s No. 8 for five seasons, until 2004. During that time, Eury Jr. was the No. 8 team's car chief. After spending most of the 2005 season working as the crew chief for Dale Earnhardt Inc.'s No. 15 team, Eury Jr. moved back to crew chief the No. 8 team in the fall. The move reunited Earnhardt and Eury Jr., who are cousins, and helped the No. 8 team rebound from a 2005 season in which Earnhardt missed the Chase for the NASCAR NEXTEL Cup and finished 19th in points. In 2006, with Eury in charge, the No. 8 team finished fifth in points.

TONY EURY SR.

Date of Birth: December 11, 1953
Hometown: Kannapolis, N.C.
Team: No. 15 Chevrolet
Years as crew chief with current team: First
Overall seasons as NNCS crew chief: 5

THE EURY FILE

The Eury family has a long history with the Earnhardt family; Eury's father, Ralph, used to go racing and hunting with Ralph Earnhardt, Dale

Earnhardt Sr.'s father, in the 1960s. Eury Sr. was crew chief for Dale Earnhardt Jr. in the NASCAR Busch Series, and he helped Earnhardt Jr. win two NASCAR Busch Series championships in 1998 and 1999. Eury Sr. moved up with Earnhardt Jr. to the NASCAR NEXTEL Cup Series in 2000 until his son, Tony Eury Jr., took over the crew chief job in 2005. Eury Sr. then became director of competition at DEI. In 2007, Eury Sr. will return to the crew chief role and guide rookie Paul Menard.

JIMMY FENNIG

Date of birth: September 15, 1953
Hometown: Milwaukee
Team: No. 6 Ford
Years as crew chief with current team: First
Overall seasons as NNCS crew chief: 20

THE FENNIG FILE

Fennig got his start in the NASCAR NEXTEL Cup Series in 1984 with DiGard Racing and later spent time with Stavola Brothers Racing as Bobby Allison's crew chief. In 1990, Fennig joined Allison at Bobby Allison Motorsports, where he remained until he joined Roush Racing as the crew chief for Mark Martin in 1996. In 2002, Fennig moved to the No. 97 team as the crew chief for Kurt Busch and won a NASCAR NEXTEL Cup Series title in 2004. Fennig started 2006 as the crew chief for the No. 26 team with driver Jamie McMurray but became head of Roush's NASCAR Busch Series program after McMurray's tepid start. He'll work with rookie David Ragan in 2007.

DERRICK FINLEY

Date of birth: July 14, 1971
Hometown: Albuquerque, N.M.
Team: No. 36 Toyota
Years as crew chief with current team: First
Overall seasons as NNCS crew chief: 3

THE FINLEY FILE

Finley spent much of his childhood helping his father with his father's racecars. After graduating from the University of New Mexico with a mechanical engineering degree, he was hired by Dale Earnhardt to work at Dale Earnhardt Inc. as an engineer, and Finley helped DEI win two NASCAR Craftsman Truck Series championships and one NASCAR Busch Series championship. After a stint at Travis Carter Racing, Finley joined Bill Davis Racing, where he took over as crew chief for Scott Wimmer's No. 22 team late in 2004. He teamed with Michael Waltrip as crew chief to start the 2006 season but was switched to team engineer in May.

MIKE FORD

Date of birth: April 13, 1970
Hometown: Morristown, Tenn.
Team: No. 11 Chevrolet
Years as crew chief with current team: 2
Overall seasons as NNCS crew chief: 7

THE FORD FILE

Ford began his career in 1996 as a jackman for Dale Jarrett and helped Jarrett win the NASCAR NEXTEL Cup Series championship in 1999. He joined Evernham Motorsports in 2001—after serving as crew chief for Bill Elliott in Elliott's last year as a driver/owner—where he continued with Elliott as the crew chief on the No. 9 Dodge. Ford moved to Robert Yates Racing before the 2004 season to become Jarrett's crew chief and then to Joe Gibbs Racing's No. 11 team in the middle of the 2005 season. He guided 2006 Raybestos Rookie of the Year Denny Hamlin to a spot in the Chase for the NASCAR NEXTEL Cup in Hamlin's first full NASCAR NEXTEL Cup Series season.

KENNY FRANCIS

Date of birth: December 1, 1969
Hometown: Jacksonville, Fla.
Team: No. 9 Dodge
Years as crew chief with current team: 1
Overall seasons as NNCS crew chief: 4

THE FRANCIS FILE

Francis' career began as a child on the go-kart circuits near Jacksonville. He graduated to late model stock cars, and he continued racing while earning a degree in mechanical engineering at the University of Florida. In 1996, he made the move to the mechanical side of racing when he went to work in the NASCAR Busch Series. Two years later, he jumped to the NASCAR NEXTEL Cup Series and, in his second season, worked on Dale Jarrett's championship team. In 2001, Francis joined Evernham Motorsports as the team engineer for the No. 9 and moved to the No. 19 as crew chief in 2003. He moved back to the No. 9 to serve as team director for Kasey Kahne in 2006 and led Kahne to his first Chase for the NASCAR NEXTEL Cup.

ALAN GUSTAFSON

Date of birth: August 5, 1975
Hometown: Ormond Beach, Fla.
Team: No. 5 Chevrolet
Years as crew chief with current team: 2
Overall seasons as NNCS crew chief: 2

THE GUSTAFSON FILE

At age 8, Gustafson had begun his career in racing in Florida, working on go-karts at local tracks. After taking courses in mechanical engineering at Embry-Riddle Aeronautical University, he moved to North Carolina in 1996 and joined Hendrick Motorsports after the 1999 season. He was named lead engineer for the No. 5 NASCAR NEXTEL Cup Series team in 2002 and was promoted to crew chief when then-rookie Kyle Busch took over the ride in 2005. In 2006, Gustafson and Busch made their first Chase for the NASCAR NEXTEL Cup and finished 10th.

JAY GUY

Date of birth: May 22, 1973
Hometown: Troy, Pa.
Team: No. 78 Chevrolet
Years as crew chief with current team: First
Overall seasons as NNCS crew chief: 1

THE GUY FILE

Before he was hired by Furniture Row Racing to work on the No. 78 team in 2007, Guy was a NASCAR Busch Series crew chief with Wood Brothers/JTG Racing. He spent the 2005 season and the first half of the 2006 season with Jon Wood's No. 47 team and then switched to the No. 59 team with driver Stacy Compton. In 2004, Guy was a crew chief with FitzBradshaw Racing in the NASCAR Busch Series. In 2003, Guy crew chiefed Johnny Benson Jr.'s No. 10 team in the NASCAR NEXTEL Cup Series. Guy also has worked with Jamie McMurray, David Green, Hermie Sadler and Ted Musgrave in the NASCAR Busch Series and NASCAR Craftsman Truck Series.

KEVIN HAMLIN

Date of birth: June 17, 1959
Hometown: Kalamazoo, Mich.
Team: No. 22 Dodge
Years as crew chief with current team: 1
Overall seasons as NNCS crew chief: 16

THE HAMLIN FILE

Hamlin, who began his career as a drag racer in Michigan, has had success with several Richard Childress Racing drivers. He guided Kevin Harvick to the 2001 Raybestos Rookie of the Year title and led Dale Earnhardt before that. Hamlin joined the No. 31 team midway through the 2002 season. In 2004, he switched to the No. 30 team, which was a driver merry-go-round as Johnny Sauter departed and Dave Blaney and Jeff Burton cycled through. He rejoined the No. 31 team—with Burton as the driver—for the 2005 season. He moved to Bill Davis Racing and was reunited with Blaney on the No. 22 team before the 2006 season. In 2006, together Hamlin and Blaney scored Blaney's first top five finish (fourth at the fall Richmond race) since 2003.

HAROLD HOLLY

Date of Birth: March 14, 1967
Hometown: Pell City, Ala.
Team: No. 66 Chevrolet
Years as crew chief with current team: 1
Overall seasons as NNCS crew chief: 3

THE HOLLY FILE

Holly took over the No. 66 car, driven by Jeff Green, before the 2006 October trip to Martinsville. Green finished eighth—his second top 10 finish of the season. Green and Holly have a history of success; they teamed up to bring ppc Racing, where both worked from 1999-2001, a NASCAR Busch Series championship in 2000. Holly was born just down the road from Talladega Superspeedway, and at 19, he started working in the ARCA and ASA series. He got his first taste of the NASCAR NEXTEL Cup Series about a year later with Alan Kulwicki's team. He was crew chief for Bobby Hamilton Jr.'s team in the NASCAR Busch Series in 2004 and moved up with Hamilton to the No. 32 Chevrolet in the NASCAR NEXTEL Cup Series late in the 2004 season.

DAVID HYDER

Date of birth: August 19, 1967
Hometown: High Point, N.C.
Team: No. 55 Toyota
Years as crew chief with current team: First
Overall seasons as NNCS crew chief: 3

THE HYDER FILE

In 2007, Hyder joins Michael Waltrip Racing to lead team owner Michael Waltrip's No. 55 team. He spent the 2005 season as the crew chief for BAM Racing's No. 49 team, then switched to the Wood Brothers Racing's No. 21 team in 2006 and then moved back to the No. 49 in October 2006. Hyder first joined BAM after the fall Talladega race in 2004 as crew chief for Ken Schrader. Before that, Hyder spent more than four years with Petty Enterprises, serving as car chief for the No. 43 and No. 45 teams.

BUTCH HYLTON

Date of birth: October 27, 1965
Hometown: Chicago
Team: No. 28/88 Ford
Years as crew chief with current team: 1
Overall seasons as NNCS crew chief: 2

THE HYLTON FILE

Hylton joined Robert Yates Racing in June and took over as crew chief for the No. 88 in August, leading Dale Jarrett to six top 15 finishes in 2006. Hylton's first crew chief job in the NASCAR NEXTEL Cup Series came in 1998, when he guided a young Elliott Sadler for Diamond Ridge Motorsports. He was car chief for Roush Racing's No. 6 team from 1995 to 1997 and at Joe Gibbs Racing's No. 18 team from 1998 to 2001, winning a championship with Bobby Labonte in 2000. He worked as a crew chief in the NASCAR Busch Series for Richard Childress Racing and Kevin Harvick Inc. from 2002 to 2005.

CHAD KNAUS

Date of birth: August 5, 1971
Hometown: Rockford, Ill.
Team: No. 48 Chevrolet
Years as crew chief with current team: 5
Overall seasons as NNCS crew chief: 7

THE KNAUS FILE

Knaus grew up racing with his father in the Midwest, and he served as his dad's crew chief at age 14. He moved to North Carolina and eventually caught on with Hendrick Motorsports, where he spent five years with Jeff Gordon, working his way up from general fabricator to manager of the chassis and body construction. Knaus helped the No. 24 team win championships in 1995 and 1997. He left after the 1997 season and joined Dale Earnhardt Inc. as a car chief, then moved to Tyler Jet Motorsports and Melling Racing, where he was the crew chief for Stacy Compton in 2000. Knaus returned to Hendrick in December 2001 as the crew chief for Jimmie Johnson and led him to second-place points finishes in 2003 and 2004, a fifth-place spot in 2005 and a NASCAR NEXTEL Cup Series championship in 2006.

RICHARD LABBE

Date of birth: June 14, 1968
Hometown: Saco, Maine
Team: No. 14 Chevrolet
Years as crew chief with current team: 1
Overall seasons as NNCS crew chief: 7

THE LABBE FILE

"Slugger" Labbe worked in the NASCAR Busch Series North in the 1980s. In 1989, he went south to work with Tommy Houston and then Terry Labonte in the NASCAR Busch Series. Labbe was hired by Hendrick Motorsports and was car chief for Terry Labonte during his NASCAR NEXTEL Cup Series title year in 1996. He served with Robert Yates Racing as crew chief for Kenny Irwin during his 1998 rookie season and joined Dale Earnhardt Inc. as crew chief for Michael Waltrip in 2001. In 2004, Labbe left his crew chief position with Waltrip to assist the Chance 2 Motorsports and No. 8 teams at DEI. Labbe joined Evernham Motorsports as Jeremy Mayfield's crew chief for 2005 and led Mayfield to the Chase for the NASCAR NEXTEL Cup for the second consecutive season. He started the 2006 season as crew chief for RYR's No. 88 team but left in July. He then joined MB2 Motorsports and served as crew chief for Sterling Marlin.

STEVE LANE

Date of birth: November 15, 1971
Hometown: Winston-Salem, N.C.
Team: No. 40 Dodge
Years as crew chief with current team: 1
Overall seasons as NNCS crew chief: 3

THE LANE FILE

Lane and driver David Stremme enter their second NASCAR NEXTEL Cup Series season season together with high hopes after finishing 2006 with zero top 10s. Lane was promoted to crew chief for Stremme's No. 40 team in April of last season to replace Jeff Vadermoss. Before joining the No. 40 team, Lane had worked as the car chief on Chip Ganassi Racing's No. 41 team since 2004. Lane was crew chief for Petty Enterprises' No. 45 car for two seasons before hooking up with Ganassi Racing, and from 1997 to 2001, he was Jeremy Mayfield's car chief at Penske Racing.

STEVE LETARTE

Date of birth: May 14, 1979
Hometown: Portland, Maine
Team: No. 24 Chevrolet
Years as crew chief with current team: 2
Overall seasons as NNCS crew chief: 2

THE LETARTE FILE

Letarte has been part of Hendrick Motorsports' No. 24 team since he was 16, working under Ray Evernham, Brian Whitesell and Robbie Loomis and helping the team win four NASCAR NEXTEL Cup Series titles. Before that, he worked part-time for HMS while in high school. With the No. 24, Letarte first served as a tire specialist, mechanic and, until September 2005, the No. 24's car chief. In the midst of a disappointing season for driver Jeff Gordon in 2005, Letarte took over for Loomis as crew chief. Under Letarte in 2006, Gordon made the Chase for the NASCAR NEXTEL Cup and finished sixth.

PHILIPPE LOPEZ

Date of birth: January 28, 1963
Hometown: San Antonio, Texas
Overall seasons as NNCS crew chief: 13

THE LOPEZ FILE

Lopez, who studied mechanical engineering at Texas A&M, began his NASCAR NEXTEL Cup Series career in 1994, working with Ward Burton. Lopez also has worked as crew chief for Ron Hornaday, Darrell Waltrip, Hut Stricklin and Kenny Wallace. Lopez started the 2005 season as Dave Blaney's crew chief with the No. 07 car and then moved to Richard Childress Racing's research and development department. He spent the 2006 season leading Hall of Fame Racing's No. 96 team, which ran its first NASCAR NEXTEL Cup Series season in 2006 with drivers Tony Raines and Terry Labonte. In 2007, he takes over as HOFR's competition director.

KEVIN MANION

Date of birth: June 24, 1972
Hometown: Boylston, Mass.
Team: No. 1 Chevrolet
Years as crew chief with current team: 1
Overall seasons as NNCS crew chief: 1

THE MANION FILE

"Bono" Manion came up with Martin Truex Jr. to the NASCAR NEXTEL Cup Series and guided Truex to five top 10s in 2006 after winning championships in 2004 and 2005 with Truex's NASCAR Busch Series team. In 1993, before working with Truex, Manion hooked up with Steve Park in Modifieds and followed Park to Dale Earnhardt Inc. in 1997. He soon became the car chief for DEI's NASCAR NEXTEL Cup Series No. 1 team. When Chance 2 Motorsports started racing in 2003, Manion was named crew chief of its NASCAR Busch Series No. 8 team and won in the team's first race, with Dale Earnhardt Jr. at the wheel.

GIL MARTIN

Date of birth: September 17, 1960
Hometown: Nashville
Team: No. 07 Chevrolet
Years as crew chief with current team: 1
Overall seasons as NNCS crew chief: 7

THE MARTIN FILE

Martin is a fixture of Richard Childress Racing, and he guided RCR's newest NASCAR NEXTEL Cup Series driver, Clint Bowyer, to four top fives and 11 top 10s in 2006. Bowyer and Martin developed chemistry in 2005, when the pair led RCR's No. 2 NASCAR Busch Series team to

a second-place finish in the NASCAR Busch Series standings. Before 2005, Martin worked with Robby Gordon, Kerry Earnhardt and Kevin Harvick at RCR and was Harvick's crew chief for the first 23 races of 2002 before handing the reins to Todd Berrier.

ROY McCAULEY

Date of birth: March 10, 1970
Hometown: Davidsonville, Md.
Team: No. 2 Dodge
Years as crew chief with current team: 1
Overall seasons as NNCS crew chief: 2

THE McCAULEY FILE

McCauley graduated from the University of Maryland with a mechanical engineering degree. His first job out of college was in 1992 with the NASCAR NEXTEL Cup Series team of Alan Kulwicki, which won the championship that season. He worked in CART before joining PPI Motorsports in 2000. By late 2002, he was the No. 32's crew chief. In 2003, McCauley joined Penske Racing as an engineer. He served as Ryan Newman's crew chief in the NASCAR Busch Series in 2005 and as crew chief for former champion Kurt Busch in the No. 2 NASCAR NEXTEL Cup Series car in 2006.

LANCE McGREW

Date of birth: December 15, 1967
Hometown: Baton Rouge, La.
Team: No. 25 Chevrolet
Years as crew chief with current team: 2
Overall seasons as NNCS crew chief: 2

THE McGREW FILE

McGrew, who studied mechanical engineering at LSU, moved to North Carolina in 1993 to work on Jack Sprague's NASCAR Busch Series team. In 1999, he joined Hendrick Motorsports and won a NASCAR Busch Series championship in 2003 with driver Brian Vickers. He became crew chief for Vickers' NASCAR NEXTEL Cup Series No. 25 team for the 2005 season and led Vickers to five top five finishes. Vickers improved again in 2006, winning his first NASCAR NEXTEL Cup Series race at Talladega after announcing he would drive for Team Red Bull in 2007. McGrew will work with Casey Mears in 2007.

MICHAEL McSWAIN

Date of Birth: January 17, 1967
Hometown: Mount Holly, N.C.
Overall seasons as NNCS crew chief: 11

THE McSWAIN FILE

"Fatback" McSwain started his NASCAR NEXTEL Cup Series career as a fabricator for Lake Speed. He later worked for Jasper Racing and then for Ricky Rudd and Rudd Performance Motorsports. He followed Rudd to Robert Yates Racing in 2000 after Rudd sold his team. After the 2002 season, McSwain left RYR for Joe Gibbs Racing to crew chief the No. 18 car with driver Bobby Labonte. In August 2004, McSwain was reunited with Rudd at Wood Brothers

Racing as the crew chief for the No. 21 car. In December 2005, he was promoted to race director at Wood Brothers.

SCOTT MILLER

Date of birth: August 23, 1957
Hometown: Bardstown, Ky.
Team: No. 31 Chevrolet
Years as crew chief with current team: 2
Overall seasons as NNCS crew chief: 3

THE MILLER FILE

Miller joined Richard Childress Racing in 1997 as a chassis specialist for Dale Earnhardt's No. 3 team. After a short stint with PPI Motorsports and another with RCR, Miller served as crew chief for Ricky Craven with PPI in 2003. He spent the beginning of the 2005 season as a team manager/engineer on RCR's No. 29 team, and when the No. 29's crew chief, Todd Berrier, was suspended for the spring Bristol race, Miller filled in and helped driver Kevin Harvick win his only race of the season. In August, he took over as crew chief for the No. 07 car and then moved to the No. 31 car driven by Jeff Burton in November. In 2006, Miller helped Burton turn his career around, as the veteran made his first Chase for the NASCAR NEXTEL Cup and finished in the top seven in points for the first time since 2000.

MIKE NELSON

Date of birth: August 31, 1973
Hometown: Anderson, S.C.
Team: No. 12 Dodge
Years as crew chief with current team: 1
Overall seasons as NNCS crew chief: 1

THE NELSON FILE

Starting at age 14, Nelson competed regionally in the American Motorcyclist Association and won 10 races. He retired from racing at age 21 and joined Penske Racing's engineering department after graduating from Clemson University in 1998. Nelson became part of the No. 12 NASCAR NEXTEL Cup Series team's staff in time for the team's first season in 2000. Nelson eventually worked his way up to the No. 12's chief engineer position and "windshield" man on race days. Nelson became the No. 12's interim crew chief with two races left in the 2006 season when then-crew chief Matt Borland left the team.

BOB OSBORNE

Date of birth: June 5, 1973
Hometown: Chester, Pa.
Team: No. 99 Ford
Years as crew chief with current team: 3
Overall seasons as NNCS crew chief: 3

THE OSBORNE FILE

A mechanical engineer educated at Penn State, Osborne first caught on in the NASCAR NEXTEL Cup Series as a tire specialist in 1998. He was hired by Roush Racing the next year and eventually became director of engineers at Roush Racing. In 2004, he made his crew chief debut working with Jeff Burton. Osborne then guided Carl Edwards in the driver's first NASCAR NEXTEL Cup Series race in 2004. The pair built on their experience in 2005, as Edwards won his first NASCAR NEXTEL Cup Series race in only his 17th start and finished third in the Chase for the NASCAR NEXTEL Cup. In 2006, Osborne started the season with Edwards but was moved to the No. 26 car to jump-start Jamie McMurray's season after his team's slow start. In 2007, he'll be reunited with Edwards and the No. 99 team.

TODD PARROTT

Date of birth: February 9, 1964
Hometown: Charlotte
Team: No. 38 Ford
Years as crew chief with current team: 1
Overall seasons as NNCS crew chief: 11

THE PARROTT FILE

Parrott worked 20 years in the garage before getting his first shot at a crew chief job with Robert Yates Racing driver Ernie Irvan in 1995. The next season, Parrott moved to Dale Jarrett's team, where he spent seven seasons. Parrott and Jarrett drove to the top of the points standings in 1999. Parrott worked as director of competition for RYR in 2003 before taking over as crew chief for Elliott Sadler's No. 38 team. Parrott proved himself again in 2004, guiding Sadler to a spot in the inaugural Chase for the NASCAR NEXTEL Cup and to Sadler's highest points finish (ninth). In 2005, after Sadler barely missed the cut for the Chase, Parrott was moved back to Jarrett's No. 88 team and later left RYR. He joined Petty Enterprises and served as Bobby Labonte's crew chief until August 2006, when he left Petty to rejoin RYR and lead David Gilliland in the No. 38 car.

RYAN PEMBERTON

Date of birth: June 1, 1969
Hometown: Saratoga Springs, N.Y.
Team: No. 01 Chevrolet
Years as crew chief with current team: 3
Overall seasons as NNCS crew chief: 10

THE PEMBERTON FILE

Pemberton was offered a college basketball scholarship, but he passed it up to enter the racing world after high school. Just nine years later, in 1997, Pemberton became the crew chief for Derrike Cope in the NASCAR NEXTEL Cup Series. He rejoined MB2 Motorsports in 2003 after a stint with Jasper Motorsports and has been the crew chief for Joe Nemechek since the beginning of the 2004 season. The pairing proved successful, with Pemberton guiding Nemechek to the pole position in back-to-back races at Talladega and Kansas—and a trip to victory lane at Kansas—in 2004. Nemechek took a step back in 2005, with only one pole (Michigan) and no wins, and another in 2006, with no poles and no wins. In 2007, Pemberton will guide veteran Mark Martin and rookie Regan Smith in the No. 01 car.

DOUG RANDOLPH

Date of birth: October 17, 1965
Hometown: Morristown, Tenn.
Overall seasons as NNCS crew chief: 6

THE RANDOLPH FILE

Randolph began working in motorsports while in college at the University of Tennessee. He moved to Bill Davis Racing in 1999 and became crew chief for Dave Blaney in 2000. He found success as crew chief for driver Scott Riggs in the NASCAR Busch Series with ppc Racing, winning two races in 2003 and posting 17 top 10s. When Riggs joined MB2/MBV Motorsports for the 2004 season to race in the NASCAR NEXTEL Cup Series, Randolph came with him as his crew chief. Midway through 2005, Randolph was reassigned within MB2/MBV Motorsports. He became Sterling Marlin's crew chief in the No. 14 for 2006, but was reassigned in June and was moved to MB2's (now Ginn Racing's) NASCAR Busch Series team in late November.

ROBBIE REISER

Date of birth: June 27, 1963
Hometown: Allenton, Wis.
Team: No. 17 Ford
Years as crew chief with current team: 7
Overall seasons as NNCS crew chief: 7

THE REISER FILE

Reiser grew up with dreams of following in his father's footsteps as a driver, and he won a number of smaller late model championships before running a limited NASCAR Busch Series schedule in 1994 and 1995 with his own team, Reiser Enterprises. After working briefly with Hut Stricklin's NASCAR Busch Series team, Reiser became a full-time crew chief and owner, as Tim Bender drove his Reiser Enterprises NASCAR Busch Series ride in 1997. Soon after, Reiser teamed up with Matt Kenseth, and in 2000, the pair moved to Roush Racing and the NASCAR NEXTEL Cup Series. They made quick progress and in 2003 ran away with the NASCAR NEXTEL Cup Series championship. In 2006, Reiser led Kenseth to his third straight Chase for the NASCAR NEXTEL Cup.

DOUG RICHERT

Date of birth: June 14, 1960
Hometown: San Jose, Calif.
Team: No. 83 Toyota
Years as crew chief with current team: First
Overall seasons as NNCS crew chief: 22

THE RICHERT FILE

Richert started out building cars for short track racing in California. He began working in the NASCAR NEXTEL Cup Series in 1976 and became Dale Earnhardt's crew chief in 1980. Together they won their first NASCAR NEXTEL Cup Series title in 1980, when Richert was only 20. Richert joined PPI Motorsports in 2000 and worked with Joe Gibbs Racing before moving to Roush in 2003. He worked with Carl Edwards in the NASCAR Craftsman Truck Series and then became crew chief of Greg Biffle's No. 16 team in September 2003. Richert led Biffle to a second-place finish in points and six wins in

2005, but the pair's 2006 results were disappointing, as Biffle failed to make the Chase for the NASCAR NEXTEL Cup. He will be replaced as the No. 16 crew chief by Pat Tryson in 2007.

PETER SOSPENZO

Date of Birth: December 23, 1956
Hometown: Brooklyn, N.Y.
Team: No. 13 Chevrolet
Years as crew chief with current team: First
Overall seasons as NNCS crew chief: 7

THE SOSPENZO FILE

Sospenzo began working in NASCAR in 1979, but the veteran got his first crew chief job in 1999 when he was promoted to lead Penkse Racing's No. 12 car, piloted by Jeremy Mayfield. He got his first NASCAR NEXTEL Cup Series win as crew chief with Mayfield in 2000. In 2002, he moved to Hendrick Motorsports midseason to take over as crew chief for Joe Nemechek's No. 25 car. He stuck with the team when Brian Vickers took over the No. 25 in 2004, and in 2005, Hendrick paired him with veteran Terry Labonte on the No. 44. In 2007, he'll be reunited with Nemechek on Ginn Racing's new No. 13 team.

GREG STEADMAN

Date of birth: July 25, 1969
Hometown: Tampa
Overall seasons as NNCS crew chief: 7

THE STEADMAN FILE

Steadman competed in drag races as a teenager in Florida. He moved to North Carolina in 1994 and found a job at Petty Enterprises in 1995, and he has never left the organization. He had served as a crew chief for two of Richard Petty's NASCAR NEXTEL Cup Series teams before working as shop foreman for part of 2003, and he returned to crew chiefing with the No. 45 when he replaced Steve Lane. Steadman again was asked to become crew chief for Jeff Green in 2004 when a midseason change was made with the No. 43 team. He served as interim crew chief for the No. 43 and driver Bobby Labonte for a month in 2006 and then returned to his post as Petty's director of competition.

BRANDON THOMAS

Date of birth: April 17, 1974
Hometown: Kingsport, Tenn.
Team: No. 96 Chevrolet
Years as crew chief with current team: 1
Overall seasons as NNCS crew chief: 3

THE THOMAS FILE

Thomas earned his mechanical engineering degree from Virginia Tech in 1997 and soon after got his first racing job as an engineer in CART. In 1999, he moved to Penske Racing as an engineer for the No. 2 team and joined Joe Gibbs Racing's shocks department in 2001. In June 2002, he became crew chief for Petty Enterprises' No.

43 team. In 2003, he returned to Gibbs and served as the No. 18 team's engineer, then Gibbs' head of superspeedway research and development and briefly as crew chief for the No. 18 team in 2004. He joined Hall of Fame Racing as crew chief for the No. 96 team in October 2006.

PAT TRYSON

Date of birth: March 4, 1964
Hometown: Malvern, Pa.
Team: No. 16 Ford
Years as crew chief with current team: First
Overall seasons as NNCS crew chief: 10

THE TRYSON FILE

Tryson's father, Joe, built drag racing engines when Pat was growing up, and after Pat graduated from West Chester University, he went to work on Kenny Bernstein's top fuel dragster as his car chief/mechanic. Tryson has worked for several Roush Racing teams and has served as crew chief for Todd Bodine at ISM Motorsports, Geoffrey Bodine at Mattei Motorsports and Elliott Sadler at Wood Brothers Racing. He got his first win in 2001 with Sadler. In 2004, Tryson rejoined Roush Racing and helped lead Mark Martin to the Chase for the NASCAR NEXTEL Cup in 2004, 2005 and 2006. In 2007, he'll help Greg Biffle's No. 16 team try to rebound after a disappointing 2006 season.

RICK VIERS

Date of Birth: November 22, 1963
Hometown: Darlington, Md.
Team: No. 84 Toyota
Years as crew chief with current team: First
Overall seasons as NNCS crew chief: 2

THE VIERS FILE

A.J. Allmendinger and Team Red Bull might be new to NASCAR, but Viers is not. Viers' first racing job—with James Hylton Engineering—came in 1982, when Allmendinger was less than a year old. Since then Viers has worked for seven different racing organizations in various capacities, including Hendrick Motorsports and Richard Childress Racing. He was in his second stint at Bill Davis Racing when Allmendinger joined the organization as a NASCAR Craftsman Truck Series driver. Viers was Allmendinger's crew chief at BDR before joining him at Team Red Bull this season.

BILL WILBURN

Date of Birth: July 11, 1966
Hometown: Tempe, Ariz.
Team: No. 45 Dodge
Years as crew chief with current team: 1
Overall seasons as NNCS crew chief: 4

THE WILBURN FILE

The September 2006 hiring of Wilburn as crew chief for Petty Enterprises' No. 45 team is a homecoming of sorts for the 20-year Cup Series veteran. Early in his career he worked with Richard

Petty at Curb Motorsports and Petty Enterprises. But at the end of the 1990 season, Wilburn began a 14-year relationship with Penske Racing, and he climbed the ladder to become one of the lead mechanics on the No. 2 car before Rusty Wallace hand-selected him to lead the team in 2003. Wilburn left to lead Robert Yates Racing's No. 88 car in 2005, and he worked in the NASCAR Busch Series with David Gilliland before Clay Andrews Racing folded in August 2006.

DONNIE WINGO

Date of birth: February 13, 1960
Hometown: Spartanburg, S.C.
Team: No. 42 Dodge
Years as crew chief with current team: 4
Overall seasons as NNCS crew chief: 13

THE WINGO FILE

Wingo first was a NASCAR NEXTEL Cup Series crew chief in 1989 for Brett Bodine, and he got his first victory as a NASCAR NEXTEL Cup Series crew chief with Morgan Shepherd in 1990. He spent seven years as crew chief for Haas-Carter Motorsports—and most of those with Jimmy Spencer—before moving to Chip Ganassi Racing in 2003 to work with Jamie McMurray. Wingo's years of experience were crucial to the success of the team—McMurray had only six weeks of NASCAR NEXTEL Cup Series experience when the two joined forces on the No. 42 Dodge. Wingo led Casey Mears in the No. 42 in 2006 and will guide former Formula 1 star Juan Pablo Montoya's foray into NASCAR in 2007.

GREG ZIPADELLI

Date of birth: April 21, 1967
Hometown: Berlin, Conn.
Team: No. 20 Chevrolet
Years as crew chief with current team: 8
Overall seasons as NNCS crew chief: 8

THE ZIPADELLI FILE

Zipadelli's NASCAR ties go back to when he was a 7-year-old working on his father's NASCAR Featherlite Modified Tour car. At 14, Zipadelli had moved to working on cars for his family's Sherwood Racing team, and at 20, he was the crew chief for Modified Tour championship winner Mike McLaughlin. He moved to the NASCAR Busch North Series and won another championship with Mike Stefanik. He then joined Roush Racing on Jeff Burton's NASCAR NEXTEL Cup Series team before Joe Gibbs hired Zipadelli as the crew chief for Tony Stewart in the No. 20 car in 1999. Turns out Gibbs made a good decision: The duo won NASCAR NEXTEL Cup Series titles in 2002 and 2005. With Zipadelli, Stewart has finished outside of the top 10 in points only once—in 2006, when he missed the Chase for the NASCAR NEXTEL Cup and ended up 11th.

>> SERIES CHAMPIONS <<

NASCAR NEXTEL Cup Series

Year	Car No.	Driver	Car owner	Car make	Wins	Poles	Money won
1949	22	Red Byron	Raymond Parks	Oldsmobile	2	0	$5,800
1950	60	Bill Rexford	Julian Buesink	Oldsmobile	1	0	$6,175
1951	92	Herb Thomas	Herb Thomas	Hudson	7	4	$18,200
1952	91	Tim Flock	Ted Chester	Hudson	8	4	$20,210
1953	92	Herb Thomas	Herb Thomas	Hudson	11	10	$27,300
1954	92	—	Herb Thomas	Hudson	12	8	$27,540
1954	42	Lee Petty	—	Chrysler	7	3	$26,706
1955	300	Tim Flock	Carl Kiekhaefer	Chrysler	18	19	$33,750
1956	300B	Buck Baker	Carl Kiekhaefer	Chrysler	14	12	$29,790
1957	87	Buck Baker	Buck Baker	Chevrolet	10	5	$24,712
1958	42	Lee Petty	Petty Enterprises	Oldsmobile	7	4	$20,600
1959	42	Lee Petty	Petty Enterprises	Plymouth	10	2	$45,570
1960	4	Rex White	White-Clements	Chevrolet	6	3	$45,260
1961	11	Ned Jarrett	W.G. Holloway Jr.	Chevrolet	1	4	$27,285
1962	8	Joe Weatherly	Bud Moore	Pontiac	9	6	$56,110
1963	21	—	Wood Brothers	Ford	5	3	$77,636
1963	8	Joe Weatherly	—	Mercury	3	6	$58,110
1964	43	Richard Petty	Petty Enterprises	Plymouth	9	8	$98,810
1965	11	Ned Jarrett	Bondy Long	Ford	13	9	$77,966
1966	6	David Pearson	Cotton Owens	Dodge	14	7	$59,205
1967	43	Richard Petty	Petty Enterprises	Plymouth	27	18	$130,275
1968	17	David Pearson	Holman-Moody	Ford	16	12	$118,842
1969	17	David Pearson	Holman-Moody	Ford	11	14	$183,700
1970	71	Bobby Isaac	Nord Krauskopf	Dodge	11	13	$121,470
1971	43	Richard Petty	Petty Enterprises	Plymouth	21	9	$309,225
1972	43	Richard Petty	Petty Enterprises	Plymouth	8	3	$227,015
1973	72	Benny Parsons	L.G. DeWitt	Chevrolet	1	0	$114,345
1974	43	Richard Petty	Petty Enterprises	Dodge	10	7	$299,175
1975	43	Richard Petty	Petty Enterprises	Dodge	13	3	$378,865
1976	11	Cale Yarborough	Junior Johnson	Chevrolet	9	2	$387,173
1977	11	Cale Yarborough	Junior Johnson	Chevrolet	9	3	$477,499
1978	11	Cale Yarborough	Junior Johnson	Oldsmobile	10	8	$530,751
1979	43	Richard Petty	Petty Enterprises	Chevrolet	5	1	$531,292
1980	2	Dale Earnhardt	Rod Osterlund	Chevrolet	5	0	$588,926
1981	11	Darrell Waltrip	Junior Johnson	Buick	12	11	$693,342
1982	11	Darrell Waltrip	Junior Johnson	Buick	12	7	$873,118
1983	22	Bobby Allison	Bill Gardner	Buick	6	0	$828,355
1984	44	Terry Labonte	Billy Hagan	Chevrolet	2	2	$713,010
1985	11	Darrell Waltrip	Junior Johnson	Chevrolet	3	4	$1,318,735
1986	3	Dale Earnhardt	Richard Childress	Chevrolet	5	1	$1,783,880
1987	3	Dale Earnhardt	Richard Childress	Chevrolet	11	1	$2,099,243
1988	9	Bill Elliott	Harry Melling	Ford	6	6	$1,574,639
1989	27	Rusty Wallace	Raymond Beadle	Pontiac	6	4	$2,247,950
1990	3	Dale Earnhardt	Richard Childress	Chevrolet	9	4	$3,083,056
1991	3	Dale Earnhardt	Richard Childress	Chevrolet	4	0	$2,396,685
1992	7	Alan Kulwicki	Alan Kulwicki	Ford	2	6	$2,322,561
1993	3	Dale Earnhardt	Richard Childress	Chevrolet	6	2	$3,353,789
1994	3	Dale Earnhardt	Richard Childress	Chevrolet	4	2	$3,400,733
1995	24	Jeff Gordon	Rick Hendrick	Chevrolet	7	8	$4,347,343
1996	5	Terry Labonte	Rick Hendrick	Chevrolet	2	4	$4,030,648
1997	24	Jeff Gordon	Rick Hendrick	Chevrolet	10	1	$6,375,658
1998	24	Jeff Gordon	Rick Hendrick	Chevrolet	13	7	$9,306,584
1999	88	Dale Jarrett	Robert Yates	Ford	4	0	$6,649,596
2000	18	Bobby Labonte	Joe Gibbs	Pontiac	4	2	$7,361,387
2001	24	Jeff Gordon	Rick Hendrick	Chevrolet	6	6	$10,879,757
2002	20	Tony Stewart	Joe Gibbs	Pontiac	3	2	$9,163,761
2003	17	Matt Kenseth	Jack Roush	Ford	1	2	$9,422,764
2004	97	Kurt Busch	Jack Roush	Ford	3	1	$9,677,543
2005	20	Tony Stewart	Joe Gibbs	Chevrolet	5	3	$13,578,168
2006	48	Jimmie Johnson	Rick Hendrick	Chevrolet	5	1	$15,875,125

Note: In 1954 and 1963, the driver champion and car owner champion were on separate teams.

CHAMPION CREW CHIEFS

1949: Red Vogt; **1950:** Julian Buesink; **1951:** Smokey Yunick; **1952:** B.B. Blackburn; **1953:** Smokey Yunick; **1954:** Lee Petty; **1955:** Carl Kiekhafer; **1956:** Carl Kiekhafer; **1957:** Bud Moore; **1958:** Lee Petty; **1959:** Lee Petty; **1960:** Louis Clements; **1961:** Bud Allman; **1962:** Bud Moore; **1963:** Bud Moore; **1964:** Dale Inman; **1965:** John Ervin; **1966:** Cotton Owens; **1967:** Dale Inman; **1968:** Jake Elder; **1969:** Jake Elder; **1970:** Harry Hyde; **1971:** Dale Inman; **1972:** Dale Inman; **1973:** Travis Carter; **1974:** Dale Inman; **1975:** Dale Inman; **1976:** Herb Nab; **1977:** Herb Nab; **1978:** Tim Brewer/Travis Carter; **1979:** Dale Inman; **1980:** Doug Richert; **1981:** Tim Brewer; **1982:** Jeff Hammond; **1983:** Gary Nelson; **1984:** Dale Inman; **1985:** Jeff Hammond; **1986:** Kirk Shelmerdine; **1987:** Kirk Shelmerdine; **1988:** Ernie Elliott; **1989:** Barry Dodson; **1990:** Kirk Shelmerdine; **1991:** Kirk Shelmerdine; **1992:** Paul Andrews; **1993:** Andy Petree; **1994:** Andy Petree; **1995:** Ray Evernham; **1996:** Gary DeHart; **1997:** Ray Evernham; **1998:** Ray Evernham; **1999:** Todd Parrott; **2000:** Jimmy Makar; **2001:** Robbie Loomis; **2002:** Greg Zipadelli; **2003:** Robbie Reiser; **2004:** Jimmy Fennig; **2005:** Greg Zipadelli; **2006:** Chad Knaus.

CHAMPIONS AND RUNNERS-UP 1972-2006

Year	Champion	Runner-up	Points margin	Year	Champion	Runner-up	Points margin
1972	Richard Petty	Bobby Allison	127.90	1990	Dale Earnhardt	Mark Martin	26
1973	Benny Parsons	Cale Yarborough	67.15	1991	Dale Earnhardt	Ricky Rudd	195
1974	Richard Petty	Cale Yarborough	567.45	1992	Alan Kulwicki	Bill Elliott	10
1975	Richard Petty	Dave Marcis	722	1993	Dale Earnhardt	Rusty Wallace	80
1976	Cale Yarborough	Richard Petty	195	1994	Dale Earnhardt	Mark Martin	444
1977	Cale Yarborough	Richard Petty	386	1995	Jeff Gordon	Dale Earnhardt	34
1978	Cale Yarborough	Bobby Allison	474	1996	Terry Labonte	Jeff Gordon	37
1979	Richard Petty	Darrell Waltrip	11	1997	Jeff Gordon	Dale Jarrett	14
1980	Dale Earnhardt	Cale Yarborough	19	1998	Jeff Gordon	Mark Martin	364
1981	Darrell Waltrip	Bobby Allison	53	1999	Dale Jarrett	Bobby Labonte	201
1982	Darrell Waltrip	Bobby Allison	72	2000	Bobby Labonte	Dale Earnhardt	265
1983	Bobby Allison	Darrell Waltrip	47	2001	Jeff Gordon	Tony Stewart	349
1984	Terry Labonte	Harry Gant	65	2002	Tony Stewart	Mark Martin	38
1985	Darrell Waltrip	Bill Elliott	101	2003	Matt Kenseth	Jimmie Johnson	90
1986	Dale Earnhardt	Darrell Waltrip	288	2004*	Kurt Busch	Jimmie Johnson	8
1987	Dale Earnhardt	Bill Elliott	489	2005	Tony Stewart	Greg Biffle	35
1988	Bill Elliott	Rusty Wallace	24	2006	Jimmie Johnson	Matt Kenseth	56
1989	Rusty Wallace	Dale Earnhardt	12				

* Chase for the NASCAR NEXTEL Cup instituted.

TOP 10 CLOSEST CHAMPIONSHIP POINTS MARGINS

	Year	Champion	Runner-up	Points margin		Year	Champion	Runner-up	Points margin
1.	2004	Kurt Busch	Jimmie Johnson	8	6.	1980	Dale Earnhardt	Cale Yarborough	19
2.	1992	Alan Kulwicki	Bill Elliott	10	7.	1988	Bill Elliott	Rusty Wallace	24
3.	1979	Richard Petty	Darrell Waltrip	11	8.	1990	Dale Earnhardt	Mark Martin	26
4.	1989	Rusty Wallace	Dale Earnhardt	12	9.	1995	Jeff Gordon	Dale Earnhardt	34
5.	1997	Jeff Gordon	Dale Jarrett	14	10.	2005	Tony Stewart	Greg Biffle	35

CLOSEST POINTS BATTLES 1972-2006

SIX RACES TO GO: 1981—Darrell Waltrip led Bobby Allison by 2 points.
FIVE RACES TO GO: 2005—Tony Stewart and Jimmie Johnson were tied.
FOUR RACES TO GO: 2005—Tony Stewart led Jimmie Johnson by 15 points.
THREE RACES TO GO: 1996—Jeff Gordon led Terry Labonte by 1 point.
TWO RACES TO GO: 1979—Richard Petty led Darrell Waltrip by 8 points.
ONE RACE TO GO: 1979—Darrell Waltrip led Richard Petty by 2 points.

MULTIPLE CHAMPIONS 1972-2006

Titles	Driver	Years	Titles	Driver	Years
7	Dale Earnhardt	1994, '93, '91, '90, '87, '86, '80	2	Tony Stewart	2005, '02
	Richard Petty	1979 '75, '74, '72, '71, '67, '64		Terry Labonte	1996, '84
4	Jeff Gordon	2001, 1998, '97, '95		Ned Jarrett	1965, '61
3	Darrell Waltrip	1985, '82, '81		Joe Weatherly	1963, '62
	Cale Yarborough	1978, '77, '76		Buck Baker	1957, '56
	David Pearson	1969, '68, '66		Tim Flock	1955, '52
	Lee Petty	1959, '58, '54		Herb Thomas	1953, '51

>>INACTIVE CHAMPIONS<<

NASCAR NEXTEL Cup Series Champions

BOBBY ALLISON

Date of birth: December 3, 1937
Hometown: Hueytown, Ala.
Years of competition: 1961-88 (717 races)
NASCAR NEXTEL Cup Series titles: 1 (1983)
Victories: 84 **Poles:** 58
Career earnings: $7,102,233

Personal: Resides in Hueytown, Ala. ... Married (Judy). ... Career ended 13 races into the 1988 season because of injuries suffered in accident at Pocono Raceway. ... Son Davey Allison raced in NASCAR NEXTEL Cup Series before his 1993 death in a helicopter crash. Son Clifford Allison raced in ARCA and the NASCAR Busch Series before his 1992 death in a crash at Michigan International Speedway, during NASCAR Busch Series practice.

CAREER HIGHLIGHTS

84 race victories third on all-time list (tied with Darrell Waltrip). ... Won Daytona 500 three times—1978, '82, '88; in '88, son Davey Allison finished second. ... Brother Donnie Allison raced in the NASCAR NEXTEL Cup Series. ... Had best statistical season in 1972, driving for car owner Junior Johnson, winning 10 races, finishing second 12 times and taking 11 poles; finished second in series standings to Richard Petty. ... Member of NASCAR's famed "Alabama Gang." ... Inducted into International Motorsports Hall of Fame in 1993. ... Named one of NASCAR's 50 Greatest Drivers.

CHAMPIONSHIP SEASON RECAP

1983: Finished with six wins and 18 top fives in 30 starts. ... One of the most popular champions, he didn't win a series crown until more than two decades into his career. ... Won $883,000 in his title campaign. ... Allison wrapped up the championship at Riverside International Raceway, the season finale.

BUCK BAKER

Date of birth: March 4, 1919
Hometown: Charlotte
Years of competition: 1949-76 (636 races)
NASCAR NEXTEL Cup Series titles: 2 (1956, 1957)
Victories: 46 **Poles:** 44
Career earnings: $325,570

Personal: Deceased April 14, 2002. ... Full name Elzie Wylie Baker. ... Son Buddy also was a NASCAR NEXTEL Cup standout. ... Drove a bus before deciding to try auto racing in 1939. ... Founded high-performance driving schools at Atlanta Motor Speedway, Bristol Motor Speedway, Darlington Raceway and North Carolina Speedway.

CAREER HIGHLIGHTS

First driver to win consecutive NASCAR NEXTEL Cup Series titles. ... Finished second in NASCAR NEXTEL Cup Series points standings twice (1955, '58). ... Known for versatility. Won races in NASCAR's Modified, Speedway, Grand American and NASCAR NEXTEL Cup Series. ... Career victory total of 46 is 13th-best all-time. ... Inducted into International Motorsports Hall of Fame in 1990. ... Named one of NASCAR's 50 Greatest Drivers.

CHAMPIONSHIP SEASONS RECAP

1956: Won first title driving for Carl Kiekhaefer. ... Finished with 14 wins and 39 top 10s in 48 starts. ... Had $34,076 in race winnings.
1957: Won second title driving his own car. ... Finished with 10 wins and 30 top fives in 40 starts. ... Claimed $30,763 in race winnings.

RED BYRON

Date of birth: March 12, 1915
Hometown: Anniston, Ala
Years of competition: 1949-51 (15 races)
NASCAR NEXTEL Cup Series titles: 1 (1949)
Victories: 2 **Poles:** 2
Career earnings: $10,100

Personal: Deceased, November 7, 1960. ... Real name was Robert. ... Bomber tail-gunner during World War II. ... Health problems led to early exit from racing.

CAREER HIGHLIGHTS

Won first NASCAR-sanctioned race, in 1948, on the Daytona Beach road-beach course. ... Was one of key early supporters of Bill France Sr.'s formation of NASCAR. ... After retiring from stock car racing, became interested in sports cars; at the time of his death, was striving to develop an American car capable of winning the 24 Hours of LeMans. ... Named one of NASCAR's 50 Greatest Drivers.

CHAMPIONSHIP SEASON RECAP

1949: Season had only eight races and won the title on the strength of two wins and four top five finishes in six starts. ... Finished with $5,800 in race winnings. ... Drove with a special brace fastened to the clutch to support his leg, which was wounded during World War II.

DALE EARNHARDT

Date of birth: April 29, 1951
Hometown: Kannapolis, N.C.
Years of competition: 1975-2001 (676 races)
NASCAR NEXTEL Cup Series titles: 7 (1980, 1986, 1987,1990, 1991, 1993, 1994)
Victories: 76 **Poles:** 22
Career earnings: $41,742,384

Personal: Deceased February 18, 2001, in accident on last lap of Daytona 500. ... Son Dale Jr. races in NASCAR NEXTEL Cup Series. Son Kerry races in NASCAR Busch Series. ... Father Ralph Earnhardt raced in NASCAR NEXTEL Cup Series. ... Full name Ralph Dale Earnhardt. ... Had two nicknames during career, "Ironhead" and "The Intimidator."

CAREER HIGHLIGHTS

Co-holder of record for most NASCAR NEXTEL Cup Series championships with Richard Petty. ... Victory total sixth-best all-time. ... Ranks among top 10 all-time money winners in NASCAR NEXTEL Cup Series. ... Won Daytona 500 in 1998; all-time leader in race victories at Daytona International Speedway, with 34. ... Finished second in NASCAR NEXTEL Cup Series points three times, including 2000 season.

... Named NASCAR's 2001 Most Popular Driver posthumously. ... First NASCAR NEXTEL Cup Series start was in 1975 World 600 at Charlotte. Finished 22nd, one spot ahead of future car owner Richard Childress. ... Named one of NASCAR's 50 Greatest Drivers.

CHAMPIONSHIP SEASONS RECAP

1980: Won first title driving for Rod Osterlund. ... Won by 19 points over Cale Yarborough, the fifth-closest championship battle in history. ... Finished with five wins and 24 top 10s in 31 starts. ... Earned $671,990 in race winnings.

1986: Earned his second championship and first with owner Richard Childress. ... Finished with five wins and 23 top 10s in 29 starts. ... $1,768,879 in race winnings.

1987: Won back-to-back titles and third crown overall. ... Clinched championship at Rockingham, three races from season's end. ... Finished with 11 wins and 24 top 10s in 29 starts. ... $2,069,243 in race winnings.

1990: Fourth title was controversial as runner-up Mark Martin forfeited 46 points earlier in the season because of a rules infraction. ... Earnhardt's margin of victory was 24 points. ... Finished with nine wins and 18 top fives in 29 starts. ... $3,308,056 in race winnings.

1991: Won consecutive titles for the second time in his career. ... Finished with four wins and 21 top 10s in 29 starts. ... $2,416,685 in race winnings.

1993: Clinched sixth title in final race of the year at Atlanta. ... Finished with six wins and 21 top 10s in 30 starts. ... $3,353,789 in prize money.

1994: Seventh title tied Richard Petty for most championships. ... Third time in his career he posted consecutive series titles. ... Won four races, including title-clincher at Rockingham. ... $3,300,733 in prize money.

TIM FLOCK

Date of birth: May 11, 1924
Hometown: Fort Payne, Ala.
Years of competition: 1949-61 (189 races)
NASCAR NEXTEL Cup Series titles: 2 (1952, 1955)
Victories: 40 **Poles:** 39
Career earnings: $103,515

Personal: Deceased March 31, 1998. ... Father Carl Flock was a tightrope walker. ... Tim, brothers Bob and Fonty and sister Ethel all were in a race in the 1950s, the only time four siblings have been in the same NASCAR NEXTEL Cup Series race. Ethel finished ahead of her brothers.

CAREER HIGHLIGHTS

Won 18 races in 1955, a victory record that stood until Richard Petty won 27 in 1967. ... Winning percentage of 21.2 (40 wins in 189 starts) is highest in NASCAR NEXTEL Cup Series history. ... Won NASCAR's only sports car race, in 1955, driving a Mercedes-Benz 300 SL. ... Occasionally drove with a monkey named Jocko Flocko as a "co-pilot." ... Said "I always thought you could do both—win and have fun." ... Inducted into International Motorsports Hall of Fame in 1991. ... Named one of NASCAR's 50 Greatest Drivers.

CHAMPIONSHIP SEASONS RECAP

1952: Won first title driving Ted Chester's Hudson Hornet. ... Finished with eight wins and 22 top fives in 33 starts. ... $22,890 in race winnings.

1955: Won second title driving Carl Kiekhaefer's Chrysler. ... Dominated with 18 wins in 38 races. ... $37,779 in race winnings.

BOBBY ISAAC

Date of birth: August 1, 1932
Hometown: Catawba, N.C.
Years of competition: 1964-79 (308 races)
NASCAR NEXTEL Cup Series titles: 1 (1970)
Victories: 37 **Poles:** 50.
Career earnings: $585,297

Personal: Deceased August 14, 1977. ... After parents died, quit school as teenager to work in a sawmill. ... Died after suffering a heart attack during a Late Model Sportsman race at Hickory (N.C.) Speedway.

CAREER HIGHLIGHTS

In 1964, his first full season, led every race entered. ... Won 11 races in championship season, driving futuristic-looking Dodge Daytonas. ... 50-pole total for his career is seventh-best all-time. ... Holds record for most poles in a season, with 20 in 1969. ... Set a then-record speed of 201.104 mph in a closed-course test at Talladega in 1970. ... Inducted into International Motorsports Hall of Fame in 1996. ... Named one of NASCAR's 50 Greatest Drivers.

CHAMPIONSHIP SEASON RECAP

1970: Finished with 11 wins and 32 top 10 finishes in 47 starts. ... Won championship over Bobby Allison by 51 points. ... Best known for his winged, orange No. 71 Dodge Daytona. ... $199,600 in race winnings.

NED JARRETT

Date of birth: October 12, 1932
Hometown: Newton, N.C.
Years of competition: 1953-66 (352 races)
NASCAR NEXTEL Cup Series titles: 2 (1961, 1965)
Victories: 50 **Poles:** 38
Career earnings: $289,146

Personal: Resides in Hickory, N.C. ... Married (Martha). ... Nicknamed "Gentleman Ned" during career. ... Since retiring, has become recognized as one of NASCAR's greatest ambassadors and is considered instrumental to NASCAR's growth because of his television work. ... Son Dale competes in NASCAR NEXTEL Cup Series, and won the series championship in 1999.

CAREER HIGHLIGHTS

50 race victories 10th on all-time list (tied with Junior Johnson). ... 48 victories on short tracks; short-track victory total third-best all-time. ... Won total of 28 races during 1964 and '65 seasons. ... Became television commentator. Remembered for emotional call of son Dale's winning Daytona 500 in 1993. ... Inducted into International Motorsports Association Hall of Fame in 1991. ... Named one of NASCAR's 50 Greatest Drivers.

CHAMPIONSHIP SEASONS RECAP

1961: Won his first championship driving a Chevrolet for B.G. Holloway. ... Finished with only one victory, but posted 34 top 10s in 46 starts. ... $41,055 in race winnings.

1965: Won second title driving for DuPont heir, Bondy Long. ... Finished with 13 wins and 42 top fives in 54 starts. ... Won the 1965 Southern 500 at Darlington by 14 laps, (17.5 miles), the largest margin of victory in NASCAR history. ... $93,624 in race winnings. ... Won title despite a back injury sustained at Greenville, S.C.

ALAN KULWICKI

Date of birth: December 14, 1954
Hometown: Greenfield, Wis.
Years of competition: 1985-93 (207 races)
NASCAR NEXTEL Cup Series titles: 1 (1992)
Victories: 5 **Poles:** 24
Career earnings: $5,059,052

Personal: Deceased April 1, 1993, in plane crash, en route to NASCAR NEXTEL Cup Series race at Bristol Motor Speedway. ... Held degree in mechanical engineering from the University of Wisconsin.

CAREER HIGHLIGHTS

First Northern driver to win the NASCAR NEXTEL Cup Series title since New York's Bill Rexford in 1950. ... Won title by second-closest margin in series history, 10 points ahead of Bill Elliott. Was 278 points out of first place with six races remaining in season. ... Inducted into International Motorsports Hall of Fame in 2002. ... Named one of NASCAR's 50 Greatest Drivers.

CHAMPIONSHIP SEASON RECAP

1992: Recorded just two wins during his championship season but thrived on consistency with 17 top 10 finishes. ... $2,322,561 in race winnings. ... Although courted by top teams, always drove his own car.

TERRY LABONTE

Date of birth: November 16, 1956
Hometown: Corpus Christi, Texas
Years of competition: 1978-2006 (848 races)
NASCAR NEXTEL Cup Series titles: 2 (1984, 1996)
Victories: 22 **Poles:** 27
Career earnings: $40,559,678

Personal: Married (Kim). ... Resides in Thomasville, N.C. .... Was inducted into the Texas Sports Hall of Fame in 2001. Labonte and his brother, Bobby, are among four auto racing inductees, including Carroll Shelby and Johnny Rutherford. ... Brother Bobby won the NASCAR NEXTEL Cup Series title in 2000, making the Labontes the first brothers to win series championships. ... Labonte's son, Justin, (February 5, 1981) competes in the NASCAR Busch Series. ... Loves to hunt and fish.

CAREER HIGHLIGHTS

Is one of 13 drivers in NASCAR NEXTEL Cup Series history to win multiple series titles. ... Has won races in all three of NASCAR's elite series—NASCAR NEXTEL Cup Series, NASCAR Busch Series and NASCAR Craftsman Truck Series. ... Was the 1989 International Race of Champions (IROC) series champion. ... Held the "Iron Man" streak of consecutive starts with 655 until Ricky Rudd broke it in May 2002 at Charlotte. ... Last victory came in the last Labor Day weekend race at Darlington in 2003. His first NASCAR NEXTEL Cup Series victory came at in 1980 at Darlington in the Southern 500 ...

CHAMPIONSHIP SEASONS RECAP

1984: Won two races in a season for the first time in his career, from the pole in June at Riverside and the summer race at Bristol. ... Accumulated six second- and third-place finishes and 24 top 10s. ... Beat Harry Gant by 58 points. ... $713,010 in race winnings driving a Chevrolet for Billy Hagan. ...

1996: Won two races, North Wilkesboro in April and Infineon in May. ... Finished second a career-high seven times and tied a personal best with six third-place finishes. Matched his personal best of 24 top 10s in his 1984 title season. ... Driving a Rick Hendrick Chevrolet, beat teammate Jeff Gordon by 37 points. ... $4,030,648 in season winnings. ... Broke Richard Petty's record with his 514th consecutive start, in April at Martinsville.

BENNY PARSONS

Date of birth: July 12, 1941
Hometown: Detroit
Years of competition: 1970-88 (526 races)
NASCAR NEXTEL Cup Series titles: 1 (1973)
Victories: 21 **Poles:** 20
Career earnings: $3,926,539

Personal: Married (Terri). ... Resides in Concord, N.C. .... Avid golfer. ... Does television commentary for NASCAR events on NBC and TNT. ... Nicknamed the "Taxi Cab Driver from Detroit," for listing it as his occupation on race entry forms.

CAREER HIGHLIGHTS

First driver to qualify a stock car at more than 200 mph (200.176 mph), at 1982 Winston 500 at Talladega Superspeedway. ... Won 1975 Daytona 500. ... Finished in the top 10 in 283 of 526 events (54 percent) ... Inducted into International Motorsports Hall of Fame in 1994. ... Named one of NASCAR's 50 Greatest Drivers.

CHAMPIONSHIP SEASON RECAP

1973: Finished with 21 top 10s in 28 starts. ... One of four drivers to win only one event during a championship season. ... Involved in one of NASCAR's most dramatic clinching scenarios. ... An early incident during the final race at Rockingham in 1973 seemed to dash his title hopes, but several teams came to his aid and rebuilt his car for him to finish the race and clinch the championship. ... Won the title by 67 points over Cale Yarborough. ... Collected $182,321 in race winnings.

DAVID PEARSON

Date of birth: December 22, 1934
Hometown: Spartanburg, S.C.
Years of competition: 1960-86 (574 races)
NASCAR NEXTEL Cup Series titles: 3 (1966, 1968, 1969)
Victories: 105 **Poles:** 113
Career earnings: $2,482,596

Personal: Resides in Spartanburg, S.C. ... Nicknamed "The Silver Fox" during racing career. ... Son, Larry, is a former NASCAR Busch Series champion.

CAREER HIGHLIGHTS

105 victories second-best total all-time. ... During 1968-69, had combined totals of 27 victories and 30 runner-up finishes. ... Won career-high 16 races in 1968. ... Won Daytona 500 only once, in 1976, but had six victories overall at Daytona International Speedway (tied for third all-time with Bobby Allison) via five Firecracker 400 victories. ... Drove for legendary Wood Brothers from 1972-79. ... Inducted into International Motorsports Hall of Fame in 1993. ... Named one of NASCAR's 50 Greatest Drivers.

1966: Won his first title driving a Cotton Owens Dodge. ... Finished with 15 victories and 33 top 10s in 42 races. ... $78,193 in race winnings.
1968: Won a career-high 16 races. ... Title came with Holman-Moody organization, his first of two in a row. ... Posted 36 top five finishes in 47 starts. ... $133,064 in race winnings.
1969: Won his second consecutive title—and third overall—for Holman Moody. ... Finished with 11 wins and 42 top fives in 51 races. ... $229,760 in race winnings.

LEE PETTY

Date of birth: March 14, 1914
Hometown: Level Cross, N.C.
Years of competition: 1949-64 (429 races)
NASCAR NEXTEL Cup Series titles: 3 (1954, 1958, 1959)
Victories: 54 **Poles:** 18
Career earnings: $209,780

Personal: Deceased April 5, 2000. ... Father of seven-time NASCAR NEXTEL Cup Series champion Richard Petty, grandfather of NASCAR NEXTEL Cup Series driver Kyle Petty. ... Helped develop racecar safety innovations such as roll bars and window nets.

CAREER HIGHLIGHTS

First driver to win three NASCAR NEXTEL Cup Series titles. ... Won the first Daytona 500, edging Johnny Beauchamp in a photo finish; the result took three days to be determined. ... Upon retirement, 54 victories was best all-time total. Son Richard broke that record in 1967. Now ninth all-time. ... Inducted into International Motorsports Hall of Fame in 1990. ... Named one of NASCAR's 50 Greatest Drivers.

CHAMPIONSHIP SEASONS RECAP

1954: Finished with seven wins and 32 top 10s in 34 starts. ... $21,101 in race winnings.
1958: Finished with seven wins and 44 top 10s in 50 starts. ... $26,565 in race winnings. Son Richard began his driving career during Lee's second title season.
1959: Finished with 11 wins and 35 top 10s in 42 races. ... $49,219 in race winnings.

RICHARD PETTY

Date of birth: July 2, 1937
Hometown: Randleman, N.C.
Years of competition: 1958-92 (1,184 races)
NASCAR NEXTEL Cup Series titles: 7 (1964, 1967, 1971, 1972, 1974, 1975, 1979)
Victories: 200 **Poles:** 127
Career earnings: $7,755,409

Personal: Married (Lynda). ... Resides in Level Cross, N.C. ... Father Lee Petty won three NASCAR NEXTEL Cup Series championships. ... Nicknamed "The King."

CAREER HIGHLIGHTS

Co-holds record for most NASCAR NEXTEL Cup Series championships (seven) with the late Dale Earnhardt. ... Holds records for most NASCAR NEXTEL Cup Series victories (200), poles (127), vic-

tories in a season (27, 1967), consecutive victories (10, 1967) and starts (1,184). ... Last victory came in Firecracker 400 at Daytona International Speedway on July 4, 1984, with President Ronald Reagan in attendance. ... Won Daytona 500 a record seven times. ... Now heads multicar Petty Enterprises team in NASCAR NEXTEL Cup Series, with son Kyle Petty as lead driver. ... Inducted into International Motorsports Hall of Fame in 1997. ... Named one of NASCAR's 50 Greatest Drivers.

CHAMPIONSHIP SEASONS RECAP

1964: Finished with nine wins, 37 top fives and 43 top 10s in 61 starts. ... Won first Daytona 500, dominating with help from Chrysler's Hemi-head engine.
1967: Many consider this the greatest single-season performance in NASCAR history. ... Finished with 27 wins (including 10 in a row), and 38 top fives in 48 starts. ... Broke father Lee Petty's record for most career wins of 54 with a win at Darlington in May.
1971: Finished with 21 wins and 38 top fives in 46 starts. ... Captured third of seven Daytona 500 wins. Seven victories came on superspeedways.
1972: Finished with eight wins and 25 top fives in 31 starts. ... Won the first race—Riverside—while carrying the logo of his new sponsor, STP. Relationship between Petty and STP lasted nearly 30 seasons.
1974: Finished with 10 wins and 22 top fives in 30 races. ... Won fifth Daytona 500.
1975: Won the series title by a 722-point margin over runner-up Dave Marcis. ... Finished with 13 wins in 30 starts. ... Swept both races at Charlotte, North Wilkesboro and Bristol.
1979: Won seventh and final series title, a record that later was tied when Dale Earnhardt won his seventh title in 1994. ... Petty won his sixth Daytona 500 in an Oldsmobile but drove a Chevrolet most of the season. ... Daytona 500 win was punctuated by a last-lap altercation between Cale Yarborough and Bobby Allison, an event generally regarded as a turning point in national television attention for NASCAR. ... Finished with five wins, the least amount in any of his championship seasons. ... Also had 23 top fives in 31 starts. ... Topped $500,000 in season winnings for the first time.

BILL REXFORD

Date of birth: March 14, 1927
Hometown: Conowango Valley, N.Y.
Years of competition: 1949-53 (36 races)
NASCAR NEXTEL Cup Series titles: 1 (1950)
Victories: 1 **Poles:** 1
Career earnings: $7,535

Personal: Deceased April 18, 1994. ... Stopped racing at the age of 26. ... Lived in California after retirement.

CAREER HIGHLIGHTS

Youngest driver–23–to win a NASCAR NEXTEL Cup Series championship. ... Championship came in controversial manner; benefited from NASCAR penalizing Red Byron and Lee Petty (deducting points) for running in non-NASCAR events.

CHAMPIONSHIP SEASON RECAP

1950: Finished with one win and 11 top 10s in 17 starts. ... Drove for New York car dealer Julian Buesink. ... $6,175 in race winnings.

HERB THOMAS

Date of birth: April 6, 1923
Hometown: Sanford, N.C.
Years of competition: 1949-62 (230 races)
NASCAR NEXTEL Cup Series titles: 2 (1951, 1953)
Victories: 48 **Poles:** 39
Career earnings: $126,570

Personal: Deceased August 8, 2000. ... Survived near-fatal racing accident in October 1956 that curtailed career. ... After several comeback attempts, retired from racing, founded a trucking company and ran a sawmill.

CAREER HIGHLIGHTS

First two-time NASCAR NEXTEL Cup Series champion. ... First three-time (1951, 1954, 1955) winner of the Southern 500. ... 48 career victories 12th-best total all-time. ... Series runner-up twice (1952, 1954). ... Inducted into International Motorsports Hall of Fame in 1994. ... Named one of NASCAR's 50 Greatest Drivers.

CHAMPIONSHIP SEASONS RECAP

1951: Finished with seven wins and 16 top fives in 33 races. ... $21,025 in race winnings. ... Drove a Hudson Hornet for owner Marshall Teague.
1953: Finished with 12 wins and 31 top 10s in 37 races. ... $28,909 in race winnings. ... Won second title driving a Hudson Hornet.

RUSTY WALLACE

Date of birth: August 14, 1956
Hometown: St. Louis
Years of competition: 1980-2005 (706 races)
NASCAR NEXTEL Cup Series titles: 1 (1989)
Victories: 55 **Poles:** 36
Career earnings: $49,741,326

Personal: Married (Patti). ... An avid aviator who owns his own airplanes and helicopter.... Also a jet-rated pilot. ... Also a golf and boating enthusiast. ... Youngest son Stephen (August 18, 1987) competes in the NASCAR Busch Series. ... Became a NASCAR Busch Series car owner in 2004. ... 2005 was his last season as an active driver.

CAREER HIGHLIGHTS

Ranks eighth on all-time victories list. ... Ranks fourth in all-time money won. ... Tied for second all-time—with Ricky Rudd—for most consecutive seasons with at least one win (16). Streak ended in 2002. ... 1984 series Raybestos Rookie of the Year. ... 1991 International Race of Champions (IROC) champion. ...Named one of NASCAR's 50 Greatest Drivers.

CHAMPIONSHIP SEASON RECAP

1989: Finished with six wins, 13 top fives and 20 top 10 finishes in 29 events. ... Edged Dale Earnhardt by 12 points, the fourth-closest championship margin in history. ... Posted first $2 million season, with $1,120,090 in race winnings and $1,117,860 in postseason bonuses.

DARRELL WALTRIP

Date of birth: February 5, 1947
Hometown: Owensboro, Ky.
Years of competition: 1972-2000 (809 races)
NASCAR NEXTEL Cup Series titles: 3 (1981, 1982, 1985)
Victories: 84 **Poles:** 59
Career earnings: $19,416,618

Personal: Married (Stevie). ... Resides in Franklin, Tenn. ... Nicknamed "Jaws" during his career because of outspoken demeanor. ... Younger brother Michael competes in NASCAR NEXTEL Cup Series.

CAREER HIGHLIGHTS

84 career victories third all-time (tied with Bobby Allison), behind Richard Petty (200) and David Pearson (105). ... ... Won his three series titles driving for the legendary driver/owner Junior Johnson. ... Was first driver in a Tide-sponsored car. "Tide Machine" Chevrolet started one of NASCAR's longest-running and most well-known sponsorships ... Ended career-long frustration by finally winning Daytona 500 in 1989, driving Rick Hendrick-owned Chevrolet. ... Now works as television commentator on FOX Network's NASCAR NEXTEL Cup Series broadcasts. ... Named one of NASCAR's 50 Greatest Drivers.

CHAMPIONSHIP SEASONS RECAP

1981: Finished with 12 wins and 21 top fives in 31 races. ... $799,134 in race winnings. ... Swept both races at Rockingham and Bristol. ... Won title by 67 points over Bobby Allison.
1982: Finished with 12 wins and 20 top 10s in 30 races. ... Swept both races at Nashville, Bristol, Talladega and North Wilkesboro. ... $923,150 in race winnings.
1985: Finished with three wins and 21 top 10s in 28 races. ... $1,318,374 in race winnings. .... Became first driver to win more than $1million in a season.

JOE WEATHERLY

Date of birth: May 29, 1922
Hometown: Norfolk, Va.
Years of competition: 1960-64 (230 races)
NASCAR NEXTEL Cup Series titles: 2 (1962, 1963)
Victories: 25 **Poles:** 19
Career earnings: $193,620

Personal: Deceased January 19, 1964, in racing accident at Riverside, Calif. ... One of first NASCAR "personalities" who attracted fans to the sport. ... Raced motorcycles before moving to stock cars. ... Nicknamed "Little Joe" and the "Clown Prince of Stock Car Racing" during his career.

CAREER HIGHLIGHTS

One of seven two-time NASCAR NEXTEL Cup Series champions. ... Accumulated 25 victories in only five seasons. ... Won 101 races in the 1952 and '53 seasons in NASCAR Modified division, winning division title in '53. ... From 1956-59, drove in NASCAR Convertible division. ... 1962 NASCAR NEXTEL Cup Series title was first for legendary car owner/crew chief Bud Moore. ... Inducted into International Motorsports Hall of Fame in 1994. ... Named one of NASCAR's 50 Greatest Drivers.

1962: Finished with nine wins and 45 top 10s in 45 races. ... $70,742 in race winnings. ... Drove for owner Bud Moore.
1963: With no permanent ride, took the title by driving for a record nine different teams during the year. ... Finished with three wins in 53 starts. ... $74,623 in race winnings.

REX WHITE

Date of birth: August 17, 1929
Hometown: Spartanburg, S.C.
Years of competition: 1956-64 (233 races)
NASCAR NEXTEL Cup Series titles: 1 (1960)
Victories: 28 **Poles:** 35
Career earnings: $190,283

Personal: Resides in Forest Park, Ga. ... Drove for a trucking company after leaving racing; retired in summer of 2001–at the age of 72. ... Often mistaken during his racing days for popular comedian George Gobel.

CAREER HIGHLIGHTS

In championship season, finished 3,936 points ahead of runner-up Richard Petty. ... Career victory total of 28 is 20th-best all-time. ... Series runner-up in 1961. ... Finished in series standings top 10 in six of nine years. ... Consistency was hallmark of career. Finished in top five in 110 of 233 races; finished outside of the top 10 only 30 percent of the time. ... A short-track expert; only one victory came on a big speedway, the 1962 Dixie 400 at Atlanta Motor Speedway. ... Named one of NASCAR's 50 Greatest Drivers.

CHAMPIONSHIP SEASON RECAP

1960: Finished with six wins and 35 top 10s in 40 starts. ... Drove

for his own team, becoming one of just five owner/drivers in history to capture the series championship. ... $57,524 in race winnings.

CALE YARBOROUGH

Date of birth: March 27, 1940
Hometown: Sardis, S.C.
Years of competition: 1957-88 (559 races)
NASCAR NEXTEL Cup Series titles: 3 (1976, 1977, 1978)
Victories: 83 **Poles:** 70
Career earnings: $5,003,616

Personal: Resides in Sardis, S.C. ... Married (Betty Jo). ... Full name William Caleb Yarborough. ... Runs car dealership in Florence, S.C.

CAREER HIGHLIGHTS

83 race victories fifth-best total all-time. ... Only driver to win three consecutive NASCAR NEXTEL Cup Series championships. ... Finished second in series standings three times. ... Won Daytona 500 four times (1968, '77, '83, '84), second behind Richard Petty's seven victories. ... Tied with Buddy Baker and Bill Elliott for most Daytona 500 poles (four). ... Holds record for most poles overall at Daytona International Speedway (12). ... Inducted into International Motorsports Hall of Fame in 1993. ... Named one of NASCAR's 50 Greatest Drivers.

CHAMPIONSHIP SEASONS RECAP

1976: Finished with nine wins and 22 top fives in 30 starts. ... $453,404 in race winnings.
1977: Finished with nine wins and 25 top fives in 30 starts. ... $561,641 in race winnings.
1978: Finished with 10 wins and 23 top fives in 30 races. ... $623,505 in race winnings.

≫ NOTABLE DRIVERS ≪

NASCAR NEXTEL Cup Series Drivers

DAVEY ALLISON

Date of birth: February 25, 1961
Hometown: Hueytown, Ala.
Years of competition: 1985-93 (191 races)
Victories: 19
Poles: 14
Career winnings: $6,726,974

Personal: Deceased July 13, 1993, after a helicopter crash the day before in the Talladega Superspeedway infield. ... First job was sweeping floors at his father's auto shop, Bobby Allison Racing, in Hueytown, Ala. ... Brother Clifford Allison raced in NASCAR until his death in a 1992 NASCAR Busch Series practice crash at Michigan International Speedway. ... Father Bobby won the 1983 NASCAR NEXTEL Cup championship.

CAREER HIGHLIGHTS

Helped make the No. 28 Texaco/Havoline-sponsored Ford popular among NASCAR fans. ... Finished second in 1988 Daytona 500 behind father Bobby. ... Won 1992 Daytona 500. ... 1987 Raybestos Rookie of the Year, becoming first rookie to win two races. ... In 1987, became first rookie to qualify on front row (outside pole) for Daytona 500. ... Had 66 top-five finishes and 92 top 10 finishes. ... Inducted into International Motorsports Hall of Fame in 1998. ... Named one of NASCAR's 50 Greatest Drivers.

DONNIE ALLISON

Date of birth: September 7, 1939
Hometown: Hueytown, Ala.
Years of competition: 1966-88 (242 races)
Victories: 10
Poles: 17
Career winnings: $1,034,923

Personal: Resides in Salisbury, N.C. ... Married (Pat). ... Original member of stock car racing's "Alabama Gang." ... Perhaps best remembered for his involvement in his and brother Bobby's nationally televised fight with Cale Yarborough after the 1979 Daytona 500.

CAREER HIGHLIGHTS

In 1970, won the World 600 on May 24 and six days later finished fourth in the Indianapolis 500, taking Indy Rookie of the Year honors. ... Career curtailed after accident in 1981 World 600. Competed in only 13 races from that point, with his final race at Michigan International Speedway in August 1988. ... Had 115 top 10 finishes.

BUDDY BAKER

Date of birth: January 25, 1941
Hometown: Charlotte
Years of competition: 1959-92 (699 races)

Victories: 19
Poles: 40
Career winnings: $3,640,371

Personal: Resides in Sherrills Ford, N.C. ... At 6-6, one of tallest drivers in history. ... Nicknamed "Leadfoot" and the "Gentle Giant" during career. ... Did television race commentary after retiring from competition. ... Son of racing legend Buck Baker, who won NASCAR NEXTEL Cup titles in 1956 and 1957. ... Full name Elzie Wylie Baker Jr.

CAREER HIGHLIGHTS

Won 1980 Daytona 500. Average speed of 177.602 mph is still the race record. ... Won consecutive (1972-73) World 600s. ... Finished career-high fifth in 1977 NASCAR NEXTEL Cup points. ... Inducted into International Motorsports Association Hall of Fame in 1997. ... Named one of NASCAR's 50 Greatest Drivers.

NEIL BONNETT

Date of birth: July 30, 1946
Hometown: Bessemer, Ala
Years of competition: 1974-93 (362 races)

Victories: 18
Poles: 20
Career winnings: $3,861,661

Personal: Deceased February 11, 1994, in accident at Daytona International Speedway, in practice for the Daytona 500. ... Original "Alabama Gang" member. ... Became television commentator in latter stages of racing career and hosted his own race show on The Nashville Network. ... Was out of action for three years after April 1990 crash at Darlington Raceway. ... Full name Lawrence Neil Bonnett.

CAREER HIGHLIGHTS

Won consecutive World 600s in 1982 and '83. ... Finished a career-high fourth in series points in 1985. .... Had 156 top 10 finishes. ... Won consecutive Busch Clash titles at Daytona International Speedway in 1983 and '84. ... Named one of NASCAR's 50 Greatest Drivers.

FONTY FLOCK

Date of birth: March 21, 1921
Hometown: Decatur, Ga.
Years of competition: 1949-57 (153 races).

Victories: 19
Poles: 33
Career winnings: $73,758

Personal: Deceased July 15, 1972. Full name Truman Fontello Flock. ... Younger brother Tim Flock won NASCAR NEXTEL Cup championships in 1952 and '55. ... Older brother Bob Flock won four NASCAR NEXTEL Cup races between 1949-52. ... Sister Ethel also raced.

CAREER HIGHLIGHTS

Biggest victory came in 1952 Southern 500. ... Finished a career-high

second in series points in 1951. ... Had 20 runner-up finishes in career. ... Won Raleigh 300 in May 1953 after starting 43rd. ... Started on the pole in nine of his 19 victories.

A.J. FOYT

Date of birth: January 16, 1935
Hometown: Houston
Years of competition: 1963-94 (128 races)

Victories: 7
Poles: 10
Career winnings: $706,684

Personal: Resides in Hockley, Texas. ... Married (Lucy). ... Son Larry Foyt, a NASCAR Busch Series rookie in 2002, drove in the NASCAR NEXTEL Cup Series in 2003 and still makes occasional starts. ... Inducted into International Motorsports Hall of Fame in 2000.

CAREER HIGHLIGHTS

Never raced more than seven times in a NASCAR NEXTEL Cup season; concentrated on legendary IndyCar career that included four Indianapolis 500 victories. ... Won 1972 Daytona 500; also won the Firecracker 400 at Daytona International Speedway in 1964 and 1965. ... Had six second-place finishes and four third-place finishes.

HARRY GANT

Date of birth: January 10, 1940
Hometown: Taylorsville, N.C.
Years of competition: 1973-94 (474 races)

Victories: 18
Poles: 17
Career winnings: $8,456,104

Personal: Resides in Taylorsville, N.C. ... Married (Peggy). ... Nicknamed "Handsome Harry" for years, then "Mr. September" after September 1991 run of four consecutive victories.

CAREER HIGHLIGHTS

Runner-up in 1984 series championship standings. ... Won four consecutive races in September 1991 (Darlington, Richmond, Dover and Martinsville) ... Three-time runner-up in NASCAR Busch Series standings (1969, '76, '77). ... Named one of NASCAR's 50 Greatest Drivers.

JANET GUTHRIE

Date of birth: March 7, 1938
Hometown: Iowa City, Iowa
Years of competition: 1976-78, 1980 (33 races)

Victories: None
Poles: None
Career winnings: $75,309

Personal: Resides in Miami. ... Married (Warren Levene). ... Earned her pilot's license by age 17 and was able to fly more than 20 types of aircraft. ... Graduated from University of Michigan in 1960 with a degree in physics. ... Worked as aviation engineer and qualified for

NASA astronaut program but was disqualified when a Ph.D. was subsequently made a requirement. ... Also served as a flight instructor.

CAREER HIGHLIGHTS

In 1977, became first woman to qualify for the Daytona 500 and finished 12th; placed 11th in her only other appearance, in 1980. ... Only woman to lead a NASCAR NEXTEL Cup race (Ontario, 1977). ...Career-best finish was sixth at Bristol. ... Finished in the top 15 in 17 of her 33 career races, with five top 10s. ... First woman to qualify for a NASCAR NEXTEL Cup race since Louise Smith in 1949 when she finished 15th at Charlotte in 1976. ... Did not succeed in her first attempt to become the first woman to qualify for the Indianapolis 500 in 1976 but did qualify in 1977 and had a career-best finish of ninth in 1978. ... Inducted into Women's Sports Hall of Fame in 1980.

ERNIE IRVAN

Date of birth: January 13, 1959
Hometown: Salinas. Calif.
Years of competition: 1987-99 (313 races)
Victories: 15
Poles: 22
Career winnings: $11,625,817

Personal: Resides in Mooresville, N.C. ... Married (Kim). ... Retired from racing in September 1999, after an August 20 accident at Michigan—five years to the day after his previous bad accident at the track.

CAREER HIGHLIGHTS

Won 1991 Daytona 500 ... Finished career-best fifth in points, in 1991. ... Was polesitter in consecutive years (1997 and '98) for the Brickyard 400 at Indianapolis Motor Speedway. ... Made remarkable comeback from serious August 20, 1994, accident at Michigan International Speedway, returning to racing in October 1995 and finishing sixth at North Wilkesboro Speedway. ... Followed late Davey Allison as driver of popular No. 28 Texaco/Havoline Ford. ... Four of 15 career victories came in restrictor-plate events (two at Daytona International Speedway, two at Talladega Superspeedway). ... Named one of NASCAR's 50 Greatest Drivers.

JUNIOR JOHNSON

Date of birth: June 28, 1931
Hometown: Ronda, N.C.
Years of competition: 1953-66 (313 races)
Victories: 50
Poles: 47
Career winnings: $275,910

Personal: Resides in Wilkesboro, N.C. ... Full name Robert Glenn Johnson. ... Married (Lisa).

CAREER HIGHLIGHTS

Won second annual Daytona 500 in 1960. ... Victory total (50) ties for 10th (with Ned Jarrett) on all-time list. ... Poles total (47) ninth all-time. ... After retiring from driving, added to legend as car owner. His drivers won 132 races and six NASCAR NEXTEL Cup championships. ... Car owner victory total of 132 ranks second all-time. ... Inducted into International Motorsports Hall of Fame in 1990. ... Named one of NASCAR's 50 Greatest Drivers.

FRED LORENZEN

Date of birth: December 30, 1934
Hometown: Elmhurst, Ill.
Years of competition: 1956-72 (158 races)
Victories: 26
Poles: 33
Career winnings: $496,574

Personal: Resides in Oakwood, Ill. ... Immensely popular with fans. Had several nicknames, including "Golden Boy," "Fearless Freddie" and the "Elmhurst Express." ... Stopped racing full-time in 1967 at age of 33, became successful in real estate. ... returned to NASCAR 1970-72.

CAREER HIGHLIGHTS

First NASCAR NEXTEL Cup driver to win more than $100,000 in a season, winning $113,570 in 1963. ... Won 1965 Daytona 500. ... Won World 600 in 1965 after starting on the pole. ... Excelled at Martinsville Speedway, winning five of seven races there between 1963-66. ... Inducted into International Motorsports Hall of Fame in 1990. ... Named one of NASCAR's 50 Greatest Drivers.

TINY LUND

Date of birth: November 14, 1929
Hometown: Harlan, Iowa
Years of competition: 1955-75 (303 races)
Victories: 5
Poles: 6
Career winnings: $185,703

Personal: Deceased August 17, 1975, in racing accident at Talladega Superspeedway. ... Full name DeWayne Louis Lund. ... His stature—6-5, 250 pounds—belied his nickname.

CAREER HIGHLIGHTS

Recorded one of the most dramatic victories in racing history in 1963 Daytona 500. During practice for race, rescued fellow driver Marvin Panch from a burning car. Panch asked Lund to replace him in his Wood Brothers-owned Ford. Lund agreed and went on to win the race. Lund was awarded Carnegie Medal For Heroism, for saving Panch. ... Inducted into International Motorsports Hall of Fame in 1994. ... Named one of NASCAR's 50 Greatest Drivers.

DAVE MARCIS

Date of birth: March 1, 1941
Hometown: Wausau, Wis.
Years of competition: 1968-2002 (883 races)
Victories: 5
Poles: 14
Career winnings: $7,349,818

Personal: Resides in Avery's Creek, N.C. ... Married (Helen). ... Retired from driving after the 2002 Daytona 500.

CAREER HIGHLIGHTS

An independent for most of his career, Marcis always chose to do things his way—from the shoestring budget he operated on as an owner/driver to the wing tips he preferred over state-of-the-art driving shoes. ... Had his best season driving Nord Krauskopf's No. 71 K&K Insurance Dodge in 1976, when he notched three of his five career victories and won seven poles. A victory in the Talladega 500, in which he finished 29.5 seconds ahead of Buddy Baker, was Marcis' first on a superspeedway. ... His best points finish was second, to Richard Petty, in 1975. Marcis had 16 top five finishes that season.

HERSHEL McGRIFF

Date of birth: December 14, 1927
Hometown: Bridal Veil, Ore.
Years of competition: 1950-93 (85 races)
Victories: 4
Poles: 5
Career winnings: $130,190

Personal: Married (Sheri). ... Resides in Green Valley, Ariz.

CAREER HIGHLIGHTS

Had three stints in NASCAR NEXTEL Cup—1950-54, 1971-78, 1980-93. ... Finished sixth in series standings in 1954, when he won four of the season's last nine races. ... Retired at end of 2001 season, in which he competed in NASCAR West Series, at the age of 74. ... Finished 12th in his last race, at Irwindale Speedway. ... Named one of NASCAR's 50 Greatest Drivers.

TIM RICHMOND

Date of birth: June 7, 1955
Hometown: Ashland, Ohio
Years of competition: 1980-87 (185 races)
Victories: 13
Poles: 14
Career winnings: $2,310,018

Personal: Deceased August 13, 1989. ... Considered one of NASCAR's most colorful personalities. ... Also was a talented open-wheel driver and twice competed in the Indianapolis 500. ... Was named Indy 500 Rookie of the Year in 1980 when he finished ninth.

CAREER HIGHLIGHTS

It's arguable that no other driver has made such an impression on NASCAR in such a short period. ... In 1986 season, won a series-high seven races, finishing a career-high third in the series standings. ... Won 1986 Southern 500 after starting on the pole. ... Four victories came at Riverside International Raceway, including first career victory in 1982 and last career victory in 1987. ... Inducted into International Motorsports Hall of Fame in 2002. ... Named one of NASCAR's 50 Greatest Drivers.

FIREBALL ROBERTS

Date of birth: January 20, 1929
Hometown: Daytona Beach, Fla.
Years of competition: 1950-64 (206 races)
Victories: 33

Poles: 36
Career winnings: $290,309

Personal: Deceased July 2, 1964, 39 days after a fiery crash at Charlotte seven laps into the World 600 and is buried near Turn 3 of Daytona International Speedway in Daytona Memorial Park. ... Full name Edward Glenn Roberts; nicknamed "Fireball" from his days as a hard-throwing pitcher in high school. ... Thought of as one of NASCAR's smartest drivers, Roberts was one of the first to utilize a fitness regimen.

CAREER HIGHLIGHTS

Perhaps the greatest driver never to win a NASCAR title and arguably stock car racing's first superstar, Roberts won some of NASCAR's most-famous events—the Daytona 500 (1962), the Southern 500 (1958, '63) and the Firecracker 400 (1959, '62, '63). ... Accumulated 93 top five and 122 top 10 finishes along with 36 career poles. ... Was second in the points standings in his rookie season, and placed in the top 10 five other times. ... Despite running only 10 NASCAR races in 1958, Roberts had six wins, one second and a third and finished 11th in points. ... Inducted into International Motorsports Hall of Fame in 1990. ... Named one of NASCAR's 50 Greatest Drivers.

Roberts

WENDELL SCOTT

Date of birth: August 29, 1921
Hometown: Danville, Va.
Years of competition: 1961-1973 (495 races)
Victories: 1
Poles: 1
Career winnings: $180,629

Personal: Deceased December 22, 1990 ... Forced to end career because of a broken pelvis suffered in 1973 crash at Talladega Superspeedway. ... Former cab driver was an Army mechanic in World War II and ran his own garage upon his return from the war, fixing cars and perfecting his driving skills on Virginia tracks.

First African-American driver to compete in NASCAR NEXTEL Cup regularly. ... Had 20 top five and 147 top 10 finishes. ... Finished in the top 10 in championship points four consecutive seasons, with his best effort a sixth-place showing in 1966 ... Only victory came at Turkey Day 200 in 1964 at Jacksonville Speedway ... Inducted into the International Motorsports Hall of Fame in 1999.

CURTIS TURNER

Date of birth: April 12, 1924
Hometown: Roanoke, Va.
Years of competition: 1949-68 (184 races)
Victories: 17
Poles: 16
Career winnings: $122,155

Personal: Deceased October 4, 1970, in airplane crash. ... *Sports Illustrated* called him the "Babe Ruth of Stock Car Racing."

CAREER HIGHLIGHTS

Won fourth race of NASCAR's first season—1949. ... Had 73 top 10 finishes in 184 starts. ...Started on the pole in five of his victories. ... Inducted into International Motorsports Hall of Fame in 1992. ...

Named one of NASCAR's 50 Greatest Drivers.

LEEROY YARBROUGH

Date of birth: September 17, 1938
Hometown: Jacksonville
Years of competition: 1960-72 (198 races)
Victories: 14
Poles: 11
Career winnings: $450,329

Personal: Deceased December 7, 1984.

CAREER HIGHLIGHTS

Most successful season was in 1969, with seven wins, all on super-speedways. ... Became the first driver to win NASCAR's "Triple Crown"—the Daytona 500, the World 600 and the Southern 500—in the same year. ... His seven superspeedway victories set the record for big track wins at the time. ... Also posted career highs with 16 top five and 21 top 10 finishes that year. ... Accumulated 65 top five finishes in addition to 92 top 10 efforts despite averaging only 16.5 races per year. ... Also drove in three Indianapolis 500s. ... Named one of NASCAR's 50 Greatest Drivers in 1998.

≫ INACTIVE DRIVERS WITH 50+ VICTORIES ≪

NASCAR NEXTEL Cup Series Drivers

BOBBY ALLISON

Year	Car owner	Races	Won	2nd	3rd	4th	5th	6-10th	11-43rd	DNF	Poles	Outside poles	Money won
1961	Bobby Allison	4	0	0	0	0	0	0	2	2	0	0	$650
1965	Bobby Allison	8	0	0	0	0	0	3	1	4	0	0	$4,780
1966	Bobby Allison	34	3	0	3	1	2	5	3	17	4	1	$21,850
1967	Bobby Allison	28	3	2	2	3	2	4	1	11	1	2	$12,840
	Cotton Owens	9	1	2	3	1	0	1	0	1	0	2	$16,130
	Bud Moore	4	0	0	0	0	0	1	1	2	0	0	$2,520
	Nord Krauskopf	2	0	0	0	0	0	0	0	2	0	0	$2,375
	Holman-Moody	2	2	0	0	0	0	0	0	0	1	0	$19,550
1968	Bobby Allison	22	1	2	3	3	1	2	0	10	0	1	$21,263
	Bondy Long	8	0	0	1	1	0	0	0	6	0	0	$17,433
	Bill Ellis	5	0	1	0	2	1	0	0	1	2	0	$7,795
	Holman-Moody	2	1	1	0	0	0	0	0	0	0	2	$3,900
1969	Mario Rossi	23	4	3	1	1	2	1	0	11	1	2	$64,710
	Bill Ellis	2	1	0	0	0	0	0	0	1	0	0	$1,275
	Bobby Allison	2	0	0	0	0	0	1	0	1	0	0	$790
1970	Mario Rossi	20	1	6	4	1	0	2	2	4	2	3	$95,495
	Bobby Allison	26	2	9	4	3	0	3	2	3	3	2	$36,470
1971	Holman-Moody	22	8	5	3	2	0	1	0	3	6	5	$194,665
	Bobby Allison	18	2	1	0	3	1	3	2	6	3	2	$44,630
1972	Junior Johnson	31	10	12	2	1	0	2	1	3	11	8	$271,395
1973	Bobby Allison	27	2	2	6	4	1	1	1	10	6	6	$101,380
1974	Bobby Allison	17	1	3	4	1	2	0	0	6	3	2	$74,915
	Roger Penske	10	1	0	1	1	3	0	0	4	0	3	$42,485
1975	Roger Penske	19	3	3	1	2	1	0	0	9	3	2	$122,435
1976	Roger Penske	30	0	2	6	5	2	4	2	9	2	4	$210,377
1977	Bobby Allison	30	0	1	0	2	2	10	3	12	0	2	$87,740
1978	Bud Moore	30	5	3	4	0	2	8	1	7	1	5	$335,636
1979	Bud Moore	31	5	7	2	3	0	4	3	7	3	6	$403,014
1980	Bud Moore	31	4	2	4	1	1	6	0	13	2	2	$356,050
1981	Ranier Racing	31	5	7	4	3	2	5	2	3	2	5	$644,311
1982	DiGard Racing	30	8	2	1	2	1	5	3	8	1	3	$726,562
1983	DiGard Racing	30	6	5	6	1	0	7	3	2	0	0	$828,355
1984	DiGard Racing	30	2	1	2	4	4	6	7	4	0	0	$627,637

Year	Car owner	Races	Won	2nd	3rd	4th	5th	6-10th	11-43rd	DNF	Poles	Outside poles	Money won
1985	DiGard Racing	15	0	0	3	2	1	3	4	2	0	1	$217,690
	Bobby Allison	13	0	0	0	1	0	1	5	6	0	0	$54,846
1986	Stavola Brothers	29	1	2	1	1	1	8	9	6	0	1	$503,095
1987	Stavola Brothers	29	1	1	0	1	1	9	7	9	1	2	$515,894
1988	Stavola Brothers	13	1	1	0	0	1	3	6	1	0	0	$409,295
TOTALS		717	84	86	71	56	34	109	71	206	58	74	$7,102,233

DALE EARNHARDT

Year	Car owner	Races	Won	2nd	3rd	4th	5th	6-10th	11-43rd	DNF	Poles	Outside poles	Money won
1975	Ed Negre	1	0	0	0	0	0	0	1	0	0	0	$1,925
1976	Walter Ballard	1	0	0	0	0	0	0	0	1	0	0	$1,725
	Johnny Ray	1	0	0	0	0	0	0	0	1	0	0	$1,360
1977	Henley Gray	1	0	0	0	0	0	0	0	1	0	0	$1,375
1978	Will Cronkrite	4	0	0	0	0	0	1	3	0	0	0	$13,245
	Rod Osterlund	1	0	0	0	1	0	0	0	0	0	0	$6,900
1979	Rod Osterlund	27	1	1	3	4	2	6	6	4	4	0	$264,086
1980	Rod Osterlund	31	5	3	4	3	4	4	4	4	0	1	$588,926
1981	Rod Osterlund	16	0	2	3	0	2	3	2	4	0	1	$220,085
	Jim Stacy	4	0	0	0	0	0	1	1	2	0	0	$34,300
	Richard Childress	11	0	0	0	2	0	4	1	4	0	2	$92,728
1982	Bud Moore	30	1	1	3	2	0	5	0	18	1	0	$375,325
1983	Bud Moore	30	2	3	0	3	1	5	3	13	0	1	$446,272
1984	Richard Childress	30	2	4	2	0	4	10	6	2	0	1	$616,788
1985	Richard Childress	28	4	0	0	4	2	6	3	9	1	0	$546,596
1986	Richard Childress	29	5	5	3	1	2	7	2	4	1	3	$1,783,880
1987	Richard Childress	29	11	5	1	2	2	3	3	2	1	4	$2,099,243
1988	Richard Childress	29	3	2	3	3	2	6	9	1	0	5	$1,214,089
1989	Richard Childress	29	5	3	5	1	0	5	8	2	0	1	$1,435,730
1990	Richard Childress	29	9	3	3	1	2	5	5	1	4	2	$3,083,056
1991	Richard Childress	29	4	3	4	1	2	7	6	2	0	1	$2,396,685
1992	Richard Childress	29	1	2	2	1	0	9	10	4	1	1	$915,463
1993	Richard Childress	30	6	5	3	3	0	4	7	2	2	1	$3,353,789
1994	Richard Childress	31	4	7	6	1	2	5	3	3	2	2	$3,300,733
1995	Richard Childress	31	5	6	5	1	2	4	6	2	3	2	$3,154,241
1996	Richard Childress	31	2	3	3	4	1	4	12	2	2	0	$2,285,926
1997	Richard Childress	32	0	4	1	1	1	9	16	0	0	1	$2,151,909
1998	Richard Childress	33	1	0	1	2	1	8	17	3	0	1	$2,990,749
1999	Richard Childress	34	3	3	0	0	1	14	10	3	0	0	$3,149,536
2000	Richard Childress	34	2	5	4	2	0	11	10	0	0	0	$4,918,886
2001	Richard Childress	1	0	0	0	0	0	0	0	1	0	0	$296,833
TOTALS		676	76	70	59	43	33	146	154	95	22	30	$41,742,384

NED JARRETT

Year	Car owner	Races	Won	2nd	3rd	4th	5th	6-10th	11-43rd	DNF	Poles	Outside poles	Money won
1953	Ned Jarrett	2	0	0	0	0	0	0	0	2	0	0	$125
1954	Ned Jarrett	2	0	0	0	0	0	0	1	1	0	0	$25
1955	Mellie Bernard	3	0	0	0	0	0	0	1	2	0	0	$260
1956	Ned Jarrett	2	0	0	0	0	0	0	1	1	0	0	$60
1957	Ned Jarrett	1	0	0	0	0	0	0	0	1	0	0	$50
1959	Paul Spaulding	1	0	1	0	0	0	0	0	0	0	0	$525
	Ned Jarrett	16	2	0	1	0	0	2	3	8	2	0	$3,285
1960	Ned Jarrett	40	5	3	4	4	4	6	2	12	5	2	$20,540
1961	Ned Jarrett	2	0	0	0	0	0	0	0	2	0	0	$110
	W.G. Holloway	44	1	4	8	4	6	10	2	9	4	3	$27,125
1962	W.G. Holloway	51	6	2	3	3	5	13	5	14	4	4	$34,890
	J.C. Parker	1	0	0	0	0	0	1	0	0	0	0	$430
1963	W.G. Holloway	2	0	0	0	0	0	0	0	2	0	0	$200
	Burton-Robinson	50	8	7	5	7	4	7	3	9	5	6	$38,265
	Herman Beam	1	0	0	0	0	1	0	0	0	0	0	$275
1964	Burton-Robinson	4	1	0	0	0	1	0	0	2	1	0	$3,275
	Bondy Long	55	14	7	4	5	3	2	0	20	8	9	$60,055
1965	Bondy Long	54	13	13	10	4	2	2	1	9	9	6	$77,966
1966	Bondy Long	8	0	0	1	1	1	2	0	3	0	0	$8,685
	Henley Gray	2	0	0	0	0	0	0	0	2	0	0	$2,375
	Larry Hess	10	0	0	2	0	0	0	1	7	0	0	$9,720
	Bernard Alvarez	1	0	0	0	0	0	0	0	1	0	0	$905
TOTALS		352	50	37	38	28	27	45	20	107	38	30	$289,146

JUNIOR JOHNSON

Year	Car owner	Races	Won	2nd	3rd	4th	5th	6-10th	11-43rd	DNF	Poles	Outside poles	Money won
1953	Gwyn Staley	1	0	0	0	0	0	0	0	1	0	0	$110
1954	George Miller	1	0	0	0	0	1	0	0	0	0	0	$300
	Paul Whiteman	3	0	0	0	0	0	0	1	2	1	0	$250
1955	Junior Johnson	1	0	0	0	0	0	0	0	1	0	0	$25
	Buchan-Lowe	33	5	0	2	1	3	5	1	16	2	3	$9,280
	Henry Ford	1	0	0	0	0	0	0	0	1	0	0	$50
	Bob Welborn	1	0	1	0	0	0	0	0	0	0	0	$700
1956	A.L. Bumgarner	8	0	0	0	0	0	0	0	8	1	0	$200
	Jim Stephens	1	0	0	0	0	0	0	0	1	0	0	$50
	Carl Kiekhaefer	1	0	1	0	0	0	0	0	0	0	1	$700
	Pete DePaolo	2	0	0	0	0	0	0	0	2	0	0	$200
	Smokey Yunick	1	0	0	0	0	0	0	1	0	0	0	$200
1957	A.L. Bumgarner	1	0	0	0	0	0	0	0	1	0	0	$50
1958	Paul Spaulding	26	6	2	3	1	0	3	1	10	0	2	$12,205
	Dick Beaty	1	0	0	0	0	0	1	0	0	0	0	$215
1959	Paul Spaulding	26	5	1	3	2	2	1	3	9	1	0	$8,330
	Wood Brothers	2	0	0	0	1	0	0	0	1	0	0	$275
1960	Paul Spaulding	2	0	0	0	0	0	0	0	2	1	0	$50
	John Masoni	2	1	0	0	0	1	0	0	0	0	0	$19,875
	Wood Brothers	2	0	0	0	1	0	0	0	1	0	0	$345
	Rex Lovette	26	2	2	4	1	2	4	1	10	1	4	$10,320
	Bob Welborn	1	0	0	0	0	0	0	0	1	0	0	$75
	Tom Pistone	1	0	0	0	0	0	0	0	1	0	0	$110
1961	Rex Lovette	40	7	2	2	3	1	3	2	20	9	9	$24,785
	John Masoni	1	0	1	0	0	0	0	0	0	1	0	$525
1962	Rex Lovette	11	0	0	2	1	1	0	0	7	1	3	$3,960
	Buck Baker	1	0	0	0	0	0	0	0	1	0	0	$50
	Ray Nichels	1	0	0	0	0	0	0	0	1	0	0	$200
	Cotton Owens	4	0	1	0	0	0	1	0	2	0	1	$7,345
	Ray Fox	6	1	1	0	0	0	0	0	4	1	1	$22,385
1963	Ray Fox	2	1	0	0	0	0	0	0	1	0	1	$3,200
	Rex Lovette	30	6	2	2	0	0	0	0	20	9	6	$61,210
	Bill Stroppe	1	0	0	0	1	0	0	0	0	0	0	$1,300
1964	Rex Lovette	2	0	0	0	0	0	0	0	2	0	1	$675
	Ray Fox	9	1	1	0	3	0	1	0	3	0	1	$8,265
	Banjo Matthews	17	2	1	4	0	0	0	0	10	4	1	$16,460
	Holman-Moody	1	0	0	0	0	0	0	0	1	1	0	$100
1965	Rex Lovette	36	13	2	1	1	0	0	0	19	10	9	$57,925
1966	Junior Johnson	7	0	0	0	0	1	0	0	6	3	2	$3,610
TOTALS		**313**	**50**	**18**	**23**	**15**	**13**	**19**	**10**	**165**	**47**	**45**	**$275,910**

DAVID PEARSON

Year	Car owner	Races	Won	2nd	3rd	4th	5th	6-10th	11-43rd	DNF	Poles	Outside poles	Money won
1960	David Pearson	22	0	1	0	1	1	2	6	11	1	0	$5,030
1961	Ray Fox Sr.	7	3	0	1	0	0	0	0	3	1	2	$47,790
	David Pearson	12	0	0	1	1	1	0	3	6	0	0	$1,790
1962	Ray Fox Sr.	6	0	0	0	0	0	3	0	3	0	1	$8,315
	Cotton Owens	4	0	0	0	1	0	0	1	2	0	1	$5,185
	David Pearson	2	0	0	0	0	0	1	0	1	0	1	$2,075
1963	Cotton Owens	41	0	3	2	5	3	6	6	16	2	1	$21,160
1964	Cotton Owens	61	9	8	3	7	2	9	1	22	12	10	$38,175
1965	Cotton Owens	14	2	2	1	1	0	1	0	7	1	2	$8,925
1966	Cotton Owens	42	14	5	4	1	0	8	2	8	7	10	$59,205
1967	Holman-Moody	12	0	5	1	1	0	0	0	5	2	0	$53,650
	Cotton Owens	10	2	0	1	1	0	2	0	4	0	4	$16,260
1968	Holman-Moody	48	16	12	4	2	2	2	1	9	12	17	$118,842
1969	Holman-Moody	51	11	18	7	2	2	2	0	9	14	11	$183,700
1970	Holman-Moody	19	1	2	2	3	1	1	0	9	2	4	$87,118
1971	Holman-Moody	10	2	3	1	2	0	0	0	2	2	2	$25,950
	Chris Vallo	7	0	0	0	0	0	1	0	6	0	0	$6,085
1972	Wood Brothers	14	6	1	3	1	0	0	0	3	4	6	$131,415
	Bud Moore	2	0	0	0	1	0	0	0	1	0	0	$5,860
	Junie Donlavey	1	0	0	0	0	0	0	0	1	0	0	$430
1973	Wood Brothers	18	11	2	1	0	0	0	0	4	8	5	$213,966
1974	Wood Brothers	19	7	5	2	1	0	0	0	4	11	1	$221,615

Year	Car owner	Races	Won	2nd	3rd	4th	5th	6-10th	11-43rd	DNF	Poles	Outside poles	Money won
1975	Wood Brothers	21	3	6	2	2	0	0	0	8	7	5	$179,208
1976	Wood Brothers	22	10	3	2	1	0	2	0	4	8	5	$283,686
1977	Wood Brothers	22	2	7	2	2	3	0	0	6	5	1	$180,999
1978	Wood Brothers	22	4	2	1	1	3	0	0	11	7	1	$151,837
1979	Wood Brothers	5	0	1	0	0	0	0	0	4	1	0	$22,815
	Rod Osterlund	4	1	1	0	1	0	1	0	0	1	1	$64,865
1980	Hoss Ellington	9	1	2	1	0	0	1	0	4	1	3	$94,330
1981	Joel Halpern	4	0	0	0	0	0	1	0	3	0	0	$9,625
	Kennie Childers	1	0	0	0	0	0	0	0	1	1	0	$2,675
	Hoss Ellington	1	0	0	0	0	0	1	0	0	0	0	$4,850
1982	Bobby Hawkins	6	0	0	1	0	1	0	0	4	2	0	$47,945
1983	Bobby Hawkins	10	0	0	1	0	0	3	0	6	0	0	$59,720
1984	Bobby Hawkins	11	0	0	0	0	0	3	1	7	1	0	$54,125
1985	Hoss Ellington	8	0	0	0	0	0	1	1	6	0	1	$48,090
	David Pearson	4	0	0	0	0	0	0	0	4	0	1	$7,535
1986	David Pearson	2	0	0	0	0	0	1	0	1	0	0	$8,405
TOTALS		**574**	**105**	**89**	**44**	**38**	**19**	**52**	**22**	**205**	**113**	**96**	**$2,482,596**

LEE PETTY

Year	Car owner	Races	Won	2nd	3rd	4th	5th	6-10th	11-43rd	DNF	Poles	Outside poles	Money won
1949	Petty Enterprises	8	1	2	0	0	0	4	0	1	0	0	$3,475
1950	Petty Enterprises	18	1	1	2	3	1	4	1	4	0	1	$7,375
1951	Petty Enterprises	32	1	4	2	1	3	8	7	6	0	0	$7,225
1952	Petty Enterprises	32	3	6	5	5	2	5	0	6	0	0	$15,620
1953	Petty Enterprises	36	5	4	10	4	3	5	2	3	0	2	$17,225
1954	Petty Enterprises	33	7	5	4	3	3	8	0	3	3	3	$18,775
	Gary Drake	1	0	0	0	1	0	0	0	0	0	0	$350
1955	Petty Enterprises	41	6	4	5	4	1	9	3	9	1	4	$16,760
	Henry Ford	1	0	0	0	0	0	0	0	1	0	0	$50
1956	Petty Enterprises	46	2	1	6	2	5	10	5	15	1	3	$13,380
	Fred Frazier	1	0	0	0	0	0	0	1	0	0	0	$175
1957	Petty Enterprises	41	4	4	3	3	6	12	3	6	3	3	$15,670
1958	Petty Enterprises	49	7	5	3	9	3	13	4	5	4	6	$20,600
1959	Petty Enterprises	42	11	5	7	4	0	6	1	8	2	5	$43,590
1960	Petty Enterprises	39	5	7	2	6	1	8	1	9	3	3	$26,650
1961	Petty Enterprises	3	1	0	1	0	0	0	0	1	1	0	$1,260
1962	Petty Enterprises	1	0	0	0	0	1	0	0	0	0	0	$750
1963	Petty Enterprises	3	0	0	0	1	0	1	0	1	0	0	$600
1964	Petty Enterprises	2	0	0	0	0	0	0	0	2	0	0	$250
TOTALS		**429**	**54**	**48**	**50**	**46**	**29**	**93**	**28**	**80**	**18**	**30**	**$209,780**

RICHARD PETTY

Year	Car owner	Races	Won	2nd	3rd	4th	5th	6-10th	11-43rd	DNF	Poles	Outside poles	Money won
1958	Petty Enterprises	9	0	0	0	0	0	1	3	5	0	0	$645
1959	Petty Enterprises	21	0	1	2	1	1	3	2	11	0	1	$5,605
1960	Petty Enterprises	40	3	7	3	3	1	13	2	8	2	3	$35,180
1961	Petty Enterprises	42	2	4	4	5	3	4	2	18	2	2	$22,671
1962	Petty Enterprises	52	8	9	8	5	2	6	3	11	5	7	$52,885
1963	Petty Enterprises	54	14	10	2	4	1	8	4	12	8	7	$47,765
1964	Petty Enterprises	61	9	14	11	0	2	5	1	19	9	17	$98,810
1965	Petty Enterprises	14	4	4	2	0	0	0	0	4	7	4	$16,450
1966	Petty Enterprises	39	8	9	3	0	0	1	1	17	16	6	$78,840
1967	Petty Enterprises	48	27	7	2	1	1	1	1	8	19	15	$130,275
1968	Petty Enterprises	49	16	6	5	2	2	2	0	16	12	12	$89,003
1969	Petty Enterprises	50	10	9	9	0	3	4	0	15	6	10	$109,180
1970	Petty Enterprises	40	18	5	0	0	2	4	1	10	9	8	$138,969
1971	Petty Enterprises	46	21	8	7	2	0	3	0	5	9	11	$309,225
1972	Petty Enterprises	31	8	9	5	2	1	2	0	4	3	6	$227,015
1973	Petty Enterprises	28	6	6	1	2	0	1	2	10	3	3	$159,655
1974	Petty Enterprises	30	10	8	4	0	0	1	0	7	7	8	$299,175
1975	Petty Enterprises	30	13	5	3	0	0	3	0	6	3	5	$378,865
1976	Petty Enterprises	30	3	9	3	4	0	3	0	8	1	5	$338,265
1977	Petty Enterprises	30	5	6	6	2	1	3	1	6	5	5	$345,886
1978	Petty Enterprises	30	0	3	3	3	2	6	1	12	0	1	$215,491
1979	Petty Enterprises	31	5	7	2	4	5	4	1	3	1	2	$531,292

Year	Car owner	Races	Won	2nd	3rd	4th	5th	6-10th	11-43rd	DNF	Poles	Outside poles	Money won
1980	Petty Enterprises	31	2	4	3	2	4	3	3	10	0	0	$374,092
1981	Petty Enterprises	31	3	1	4	3	1	4	1	14	0	0	$389,214
1982	Petty Enterprises	30	0	5	2	1	1	7	1	13	0	0	$453,832
1983	Petty Enterprises	30	3	1	1	1	3	12	4	5	0	0	$491,022
1984	Mike Curb	30	2	0	0	2	1	8	10	7	0	0	$251,226
1985	Mike Curb	28	0	0	1	0	0	12	3	12	0	0	$306,142
1986	Petty Enterprises	29	0	1	2	1	0	7	8	10	0	1	$280,657
1987	Petty Enterprises	29	0	1	3	2	3	5	10	6	0	0	$468,602
1988	Petty Enterprises	29	0	0	1	0	0	4	9	15	0	0	$190,155
1989	Petty Enterprises	25	0	0	0	0	0	0	13	12	0	0	$133,050
1990	Petty Enterprises	29	0	0	0	0	0	1	16	12	0	0	$169,465
1991	Petty Enterprises	29	0	0	0	0	0	1	18	10	0	0	$268,035
1992	Petty Enterprises	29	0	0	0	0	0	0	24	5	0	1	$348,870
TOTALS		**1,184**	**200**	**156**	**102**	**52**	**40**	**144**	**143**	**347**	**127**	**140**	**$7,755,409**

RUSTY WALLACE

Year	Car owner	Races	Won	2nd	3rd	4th	5th	6-10th	11-43rd	DNF	Poles	Outside poles	Money won
1980	Roger Penske	2	0	1	0	0	0	0	1	0	0	0	$22,760
1981	John Childs	2	0	0	0	0	0	1	1	1	0	0	$8,650
	Ron Benfield	2	0	0	0	0	0	0	2	2	0	0	$4,245
1982	John Childs	3	0	0	0	0	0	0	0	3	0	0	$7,655
1984	Cliff Stewart	30	0	0	0	1	1	2	17	9	0	0	$195,927
1985	Cliff Stewart	28	0	0	0	0	2	6	8	12	0	0	$233,670
1986	Raymond Beadle	29	2	0	0	2	0	12	9	4	0	0	$557,354
1987	Raymond Beadle	29	2	3	2	1	1	7	6	7	1	2	$690,652
1988	Raymond Beadle	29	6	5	4	2	2	4	4	2	2	4	$1,411,567
1989	Raymond Beadle	29	6	4	0	2	1	7	5	4	4	2	$2,247,950
1990	Raymond Beadle	29	2	3	2	0	2	7	5	8	2	1	$954,129
1991	Roger Penske	29	2	0	3	2	2	5	5	10	2	2	$502,073
1992	Roger Penske	29	1	2	1	1	0	7	12	5	1	1	$657,925
1993	Roger Penske	30	10	4	2	1	2	2	4	5	3	1	$1,702,154
1994	Roger Penske	31	8	3	1	4	1	3	6	5	2	2	$1,914,072
1995	Roger Penske	31	2	4	6	2	1	4	8	4	0	0	$1,642,837
1996	Roger Penske	31	5	1	0	1	1	10	7	6	0	1	$1,665,315
1997	Roger Penske	32	1	3	2	0	2	4	9	11	1	1	$1,705,625
1998	Roger Penske	33	1	2	5	3	4	6	10	2	4	3	$2,667,889
1999	Roger Penske	34	1	0	1	3	2	9	15	3	4	3	$2,454,050
2000	Roger Penske	34	4	1	1	3	3	8	11	3	9	2	$3,621,468
2001	Roger Penske	36	1	0	2	2	3	6	19	3	0	3	$4,788,652
2002	Roger Penske	36	0	4	1	1	1	10	19	1	1	0	$4,785,134
2003	Roger Penske	36	0	0	1	0	1	10	24	4	0	1	$4,246,547
2004	Roger Penske	36	1	1	0	0	1	8	25	3	0	2	$4,981,100
2005	Roger Penske	36	0	1	1	2	4	9	19	0	0	0	$6,070,826
TOTALS		**706**	**55**	**42**	**35**	**33**	**37**	**147**	**251**	**117**	**36**	**31**	**$49,741,326**

DARRELL WALTRIP

Year	Car owner	Races	Won	2nd	3rd	4th	5th	6-10th	11-43rd	DNF	Poles	Outside poles	Money won
1972	Darrell Waltrip	5	0	0	1	0	0	2	0	2	0	0	$8,615
1973	Darrell Waltrip	14	0	1	0	0	0	3	3	7	0	0	$27,775
	Bud Moore	5	0	0	0	0	0	1	0	4	0	1	$5,691
1974	Darrell Waltrip	16	0	1	3	2	1	4	0	5	1	0	$57,690
1975	Darrell Waltrip	17	1	2	0	3	2	2	0	7	2	1	$79,762
	Bill Gardner	11	1	0	2	0	0	1	0	7	0	3	$20,430
1976	Bill Gardner	30	1	3	4	1	1	2	2	16	3	1	$191,501
1977	Bill Gardner	30	6	4	3	1	2	6	1	7	3	3	$276,312
1978	Bill Gardner	30	6	6	4	1	1	1	2	9	2	7	$343,367
1979	Bill Gardner	31	7	4	6	2	1	3	7	1	5	3	$523,691
1980	Bill Gardner	31	5	3	2	6	0	1	2	12	5	5	$382,138
1981	Junior Johnson	31	12	6	3	0	0	4	2	4	11	4	$693,342
1982	Junior Johnson	30	12	1	3	0	1	2	3	8	7	6	$873,118
1983	Junior Johnson	30	6	8	4	2	2	3	1	4	7	3	$824,858
1984	Junior Johnson	30	7	2	3	1	0	7	7	3	4	2	$703,876

Year	Car owner	Races	Won	2nd	3rd	4th	5th	6-10th	11-43rd	DNF	Poles	Outside poles	Money won
1985	Junior Johnson	28	3	6	6	2	1	3	2	5	4	1	$1,318,735
1986	Junior Johnson	29	3	2	4	6	6	1	1	6	1	4	$1,099,735
1987	Rick Hendrick	29	1	1	1	2	1	10	11	2	0	2	$511,768
1988	Rick Hendrick	29	2	1	1	2	4	4	11	4	2	1	$731,659
1989	Rick Hendrick	29	6	2	2	2	2	4	8	3	0	6	$1,323,079
1990	Rick Hendrick	23	0	1	1	2	1	7	11	0	0	0	$530,420
1991	Darrell Waltrip	29	2	2	1	0	0	12	6	6	0	0	$604,854
1992	Darrell Waltrip	29	3	2	3	0	2	3	12	4	1	0	$876,492
1993	Darrell Waltrip	30	0	0	2	1	1	6	15	5	0	0	$746,646
1994	Darrell Waltrip	31	0	0	2	2	0	9	17	1	0	0	$835,680
1995	Darrell Waltrip	31	0	0	1	3	0	4	12	11	1	0	$850,632
1996	Darrell Waltrip	31	0	0	0	0	0	2	18	11	0	0	$740,185
1997	Darrell Waltrip	31	0	0	0	0	1	3	22	5	0	0	$958,679
1998	Darrell Waltrip	5	0	0	0	0	0	0	3	2	0	0	$222,865
	Dale Earnhardt	13	0	0	0	0	1	1	9	2	0	0	$398,615
	T. Beverly	15	0	0	0	0	0	0	14	1	0	0	$434,995
1999	Travis Carter	27	0	0	0	0	0	0	23	4	0	0	$973,133
2000	Travis Carter	29	0	0	0	0	0	0	11	7	0	1	$1,246,280
TOTALS		**809**	**84**	**58**	**62**	**41**	**31**	**111**	**236**	**177**	**59**	**54**	**$19,416,618**

CALE YARBOROUGH

Year	Car owner	Races	Won	2nd	3rd	4th	5th	6-10th	11-43rd	DNF	Poles	Outside poles	Money won
1957	Bob Weatherly	1	0	0	0	0	0	0	0	1	0	0	$100
1959	Cale Yarborough	1	0	0	0	0	0	0	0	1	0	0	$150
1960	Cale Yarborough	1	0	0	0	0	0	0	0	1	0	0	$85
1961	Cale Yarborough	1	0	0	0	0	0	0	0	1	0	0	$200
1962	Cale Yarborough	8	0	0	0	0	0	1	1	6	0	0	$2,725
1963	Herman Beam	14	0	0	0	0	3	4	7	0	0	0	$4,100
	Cale Yarborough	4	0	0	0	0	0	0	2	2	0	0	$1,450
1964	Herman Beam	20	0	0	0	0	1	4	5	10	0	0	$7,680
	Cale Yarborough	4	0	0	0	0	0	2	0	2	0	0	$1,615
1965	Cale Yarborough	21	0	0	1	0	0	5	1	14	0	0	$6,540
	Ken Myler	18	1	1	0	5	3	2	2	4	0	0	$6,305
	Banjo Matthews	7	0	2	0	0	0	0	0	5	0	1	$12,295
1966	Banjo Matthews	8	0	2	0	0	0	3	0	3	0	0	$18,290
	Ken Myler	1	0	0	0	0	0	1	0	0	0	0	$390
	Wood Brothers	5	0	0	0	1	0	0	1	3	0	0	$4,350
1967	Wood Brothers	16	2	3	1	1	0	0	0	9	4	2	$56,685
1968	Wood Brothers	21	6	2	1	0	3	0	0	9	4	2	$136,786
1969	Wood Brothers	19	2	2	1	2	0	1	0	11	6	2	$74,240
1970	Wood Brothers	18	3	4	2	0	1	1	0	7	5	1	$114,675
	Banjo Matthews	1	0	0	0	0	0	0	0	1	0	0	$1,200
1971	Cale Yarborough	4	0	0	0	0	0	1	0	3	0	0	$3,869
1972	Cale Yarborough	5	0	0	0	0	1	3	0	1	0	0	$11,332
1973	Junior Johnson	28	4	6	4	1	1	3	1	8	5	4	$162,235
1974	Junior Johnson	30	10	4	5	1	1	1	1	7	3	6	$255,525
1975	Junior Johnson	27	3	3	3	3	1	0	0	14	3	0	$139,258
1976	Junior Johnson	30	9	6	3	1	2	1	3	5	2	3	$387,173
1977	Junior Johnson	30	9	6	4	3	3	2	3	0	3	7	$477,499
1978	Junior Johnson	30	10	6	1	5	1	1	4	2	8	7	$530,751
1979	Junior Johnson	31	4	2	6	4	2	3	4	6	1	4	$413,872
1980	Junior Johnson	31	6	4	4	4	1	3	4	5	14	6	$537,358
1981	M.C. Anderson	18	2	1	2	0	1	3	2	7	2	3	$150,840
1982	M.C. Anderson	16	3	2	1	2	0	0	0	8	2	0	$219,090
1983	Harry Ranier	16	4	0	0	0	0	4	0	8	3	1	$254,535
1984	Harry Ranier	16	3	1	3	1	2	0	4	2	4	0	$385,853
1985	Harry Ranier	16	2	2	2	0	0	1	0	9	0	4	$310,465
1986	Harry Ranier	16	0	0	2	0	0	3	1	10	1	0	$137,010
1987	Cale Yarborough	16	0	0	0	1	1	2	3	9	0	0	$111,025
1988	Cale Yarborough	10	0	0	0	0	0	3	3	4	0	0	$66,065
TOTALS		**559**	**83**	**59**	**46**	**35**	**28**	**58**	**52**	**198**	**70**	**53**	**$5,003,616**

NASCAR HISTORY

>> ALL-TIME RACE WINNERS <<
NASCAR NEXTEL Cup Series

1.	* Richard Petty	200
2.	* David Pearson	105
3.	* Bobby Allison	84
	* Darrell Waltrip	84
5.	* Cale Yarborough	83
6.	# Dale Earnhardt	76
7.	Jeff Gordon	75
8.	* Rusty Wallace	55
9.	# Lee Petty	54
10.	* Ned Jarrett	50
	* Junior Johnson	50
12.	# Herb Thomas	48
13.	# Buck Baker	46
14.	Bill Elliott	44
15.	# Tim Flock	40
16.	# Bobby Isaac	37
17.	Mark Martin	35
18.	#† Fireball Roberts	33
19.	Dale Jarrett	32
20.	Tony Stewart	29
21.	*† Rex White	28
22.	* Fred Lorenzen	26
23.	# Jim Paschal	25
	# Joe Weatherly	25
25.	Jimmie Johnson	23
	* Ricky Rudd	23
27.	* Terry Labonte	22
28.	Bobby Labonte	21
	* Benny Parsons	21
	# Jack Smith	21
31.	# Speedy Thompson	20
32.	# Davey Allison	19
	* Buddy Baker	19
	# Fonty Flock	19
35.	Geoffrey Bodine	18
	# Neil Bonnett	18
	Jeff Burton	18
	* Harry Gant	18
39.	Dale Earnhardt Jr.	17
	* Marvin Panch	17
	# Curtis Turner	17
42.	Kurt Busch	15
	* Ernie Irvan	15
44.	# Dick Hutcherson	14

	Matt Kenseth	14
	# Lee Roy Yarbrough	14
47.	# Dick Rathmann	13
	# Tim Richmond	13
49.	Ryan Newman	12
50.	Greg Biffle	11
51.	* Donnie Allison	10
	Kevin Harvick	10
	Sterling Marlin	10
54.	* Paul Goldsmith	9
	* Cotton Owens	9
	# Bob Welborn	9
57.	Kyle Petty	8
58.	# Darel Dieringer	7
	* A.J. Foyt	7
	Kasey Kahne	7
	* Jim Reed	7
	# Marshall Teague	7
63.	Ward Burton	5
	* Dan Gurney	5
	# Alan Kulwicki	5
	# Tiny Lund	5
	* Dave Marcis	5
	Jeremy Mayfield	5
	* Ralph Moody	5
70.	* Lloyd Dane	4
	Carl Edwards	4
	# Bob Flock	4
	* Charlie Glotzbach	4
	* Eddie Gray	4
	Bobby Hamilton	4
	* Pete Hamilton	4
	* Parnelli Jones	4
	* Hershel McGriff	4
	Joe Nemechek	4
	# Eddie Pagan	4
	Ken Schrader	4
	Morgan Shepherd	4
	# Nelson Stacy	4
	# Billy Wade	4
	Michael Waltrip	4
	* Glen Wood	4
87.	# Bill Blair	3
	Kyle Busch	3

	Robby Gordon	3
	# Dick Linder	3
	* Frank Mundy	3
	Elliott Sadler	3
	# Gwyn Staley	2
94.	John Andretti	2
	* Johnny Beauchamp	2
	# Red Byron	2
	Derrike Cope	2
	Ricky Craven	2
	* Ray Elder	2
	Denny Hamlin	2
	* James Hylton	2
	* Bobby Johns	2
	* Joe Lee Johnson	2
	# Al Keller	2
	# Elmo Langley	2
	* Danny Letner	2
	# Billy Myers	2
	# Jimmy Pardue	2
	Steve Park	2
	* Tom Pistone	2
	# Marvin Porter	2
	# Gober Sosebee	2
	Jimmy Spencer	2
	# Emanuel Zervakis	2
115.	* Johnny Allen	1
	# Bill Amick	1
	* Mario Andretti	1
	* Earl Balmer	1
	Johnny Benson	1
	* Brett Bodine	1
	* Ron Bouchard	1
	* Richard Brickhouse	1
	# Dick Brooks	1
	* Bob Burdick	1
	* Marvin Burke	1
	* Neil Cole	1
	* Jim Cook	1
	# Mark Donohue	1
	# Joe Eubanks	1
	# Lou Figaro	1
	# Jimmy Florian	1
	* Larry Frank	1

	* Danny Graves	1
	* Royce Hagerty	1
	* Bobby Hillin Jr.	1
	# Jim Hurtubise	1
	* John Kieper	1
	* Harold Kite	1
	* Paul Lewis	1
	# Johnny Mantz	1
	Jamie McMurray	1
	* Sam McQuagg	1
	* Lloyd Moore	1
	* Jerry Nadeau	1
	* Norm Nelson	1
	* Bill Norton	1
	* Phil Parsons	1
	* Dick Passwater	1
	* Lennie Pond	1
	* Bill Rexford	1
	# Jody Ridley	1
	# Shorty Rollins	1
	# Jim Roper	1
	* Earl Ross	1
	* John Rostek	1
	* Johnny Rutherford	1
	Greg Sacks	1
	* Leon Sales	1
	* Frankie Schneider	1
	# Wendell Scott	1
	# Buddy Shuman	1
	* John Soares Jr.	1
	* Lake Speed	1
	# Chuck Stevenson	1
	# Donald Thomas	1
	* Tommy Thompson	1
	Brian Vickers	1
	* Art Watts	1
	* Danny Weinberg	1
	* Jack White	1

* Retired
# Deceased
† Rex White and Fireball Roberts had two convertible wins not included in totals.

>> WINS MODERN ERA <<
NASCAR NEXTEL Cup Series 1972-2006

1.	* Darrell Waltrip		84
2.	# Dale Earnhardt		76
3.	Jeff Gordon		75
4.	* Cale Yarborough		69
5.	* Richard Petty		60
6.	* Bobby Allison		55
	* Rusty Wallace		55
8.	* David Pearson		45
9.	Bill Elliott		44
10.	Mark Martin		35
11.	Dale Jarrett		32
12.	Tony Stewart		29
13.	Jimmie Johnson		23
	* Ricky Rudd		23
15.	* Terry Labonte		22
16.	Bobby Labonte		21
17.	* Benny Parsons		20
18.	# Davey Allison		19
19.	Geoffrey Bodine		18
	# Neil Bonnett		18
	Jeff Burton		18
	* Harry Gant		18
23.	Dale Earnhardt Jr.		17
24.	* Buddy Baker		15
	Kurt Busch		15
	* Ernie Irvan		15

SPEEDWAY WINNERS
NASCAR NEXTEL Cup Series

Driver	Wins	Driver	Wins	Driver	Wins	Driver	Wins	Driver	Wins	Driver	Wins
1. Richard Petty	55	19. Harry Gant	13	Kasey Kahne	6	Bobby Isaac	3	Mario Andretti	1	Hershel McGriff	1
2. Jeff Gordon	51	D. Earnhardt Jr.	13	Kyle Petty	6	Alan Kulwicki	3	Johnny Benson	1	Jamie McMurray	1
3. David Pearson	49	21. Fred Lorenzen	12	Tim Richmond	6	Joe Nemechek	3	Ron Bouchard	1	Sam McQuagg	1
4. Dale Earnhardt	48	Benny Parsons	12	40. Ward Burton	5	Morgan Shepherd	3	R. Brickhouse	1	Ralph Moody	1
5. Bobby Allison	47	Ricky Rudd	12	Junior Johnson	5	Nelson Stacy	3	Dick Brooks	1	Jerry Nadeau	1
Cale Yarborough	47	24. Greg Biffle	11	Herb Thomas	5	S. Thompson	3	Bob Burdick	1	Eddie Pagan	1
7. Bill Elliott	40	Matt Kenseth	11	43. Buck Baker	4	Joe Weatherly	3	Ricky Craven	1	Steve Park	1
8. Darrell Waltrip	32	Terry Labonte	11	Carl Edwards	4	62. Derrike Cope	2	Darel Dieringer	1	Phil Parsons	1
9. Dale Jarrett	28	Ryan Newman	11	Jeremy Mayfield	4	Charlie Glotzbach	2	Larry Frank	1	Lennie Pond	1
10. Rusty Wallace	24	Fireball Roberts	11	Marvin Panch	4	Denny Hamlin	2	Robby Gordon	1	Marvin Porter	1
11. Mark Martin	24	L. Yarborough	11	Ken Schrader	4	Ned Jarrett	2	Bobby Hillin Jr.	1	Dick Rathmann	1
12. Jimmie Johnson	21	30. Sterling Marlin	10	Michael Waltrip	4	Dave Marcis	2	Dick Hutcherson	1	Jim Reed	1
13. Bobby Labonte	20	31. Donnie Allison	9	49. Kyle Busch	3	Jim Paschal	2	Jim Hurtubise	1	Jody Ridley	1
14. Tony Stewart	18	32. Kurt Busch	8	Fonty Flock	3	Lee Petty	2	James Hylton	1	Greg Sacks	1
15. Buddy Baker	17	Ernie Irvan	8	Tim Flock	3	Elliott Sadler	2	Bobby Johns	1	Lake Speed	1
Jeff Burton	16	34. Geoff Bodine	7	Paul Goldsmith	3	Jimmy Spencer	2	Joe Lee Johnson	1	Jack Smith	1
17. Neil Bonnett	15	Kevin Harvick	7	Bobby Hamilton	3	Curtis Turner	2	Tiny Lund	1	T. Thompson	1
18. Davey Allison	14	36. A.J. Foyt	6	Pete Hamilton	3	72. John Andretti	1	Johnny Mantz	1	Brian Vickers	1
										Rex White	1

SHORT TRACK WINNERS
NASCAR NEXTEL Cup Series

Driver	Wins	Driver	Wins	Driver	Wins	Driver	Wins	Driver	Wins	Driver	Wins
1. Richard Petty	139	24. Fred Lorenzen	14	Ralph Moody	4	Tiny Lund	2	Lou Figaro	1	Bill Rexford	1
2. David Pearson	52	25. Dick Hutcherson	13	Glen Wood	4	Billy Myers	2	Jimmy Florian	1	Shorty Rollins	1
Lee Petty	52	26. Dick Rathmann	12	49. Neil Bonnett	3	Jimmy Pardue	2	Danny Graves	1	Jim Roper	1
4. Ned Jarrett	48	27. Marvin Panch	11	Lloyd Dane	3	Tom Pistone	2	Royce Hagerty	1	Earl Ross	1
5. Darrell Waltrip	47	28. Terry Labonte	9	Eddie Gray	3	Tim Richmond	2	Bobby Hamilton	1	John Rostek	1
6. Junior Johnson	45	29. Geoff Bodine	8	Matt Kenseth	3	Gober Sosebee	2	Pete Hamilton	1	J. Rutherford	1
7. Herb Thomas	43	Cotton Owens	8	Dick Linder	3	Gwyn Staley	2	James Hylton	1	Leon Sales	1
8. Buck Baker	41	Benny Parsons	8	Dave Marcis	3	Billy Wade	2	Bobby Johns	1	Morgan Shepherd	1
9. Tim Flock	34	32. Kurt Busch	7	Hershel McGriff	3	Emanuel Zervakis	2	Parnelli Jones	1	Elliot Sadler	1
Bobby Isaac	34	Mark Martin	7	Frank Mundy	3	79. Johnny Allen	1	Kasey Kahne	1	Frankie Schneider	1
11. C. Yarborough	33	Bob Welborn	7	Eddie Pagan	3	Donnie Allison	1	Al Keller	1	Wendell Scott	1
12. Bobby Allison	31	35. Jim Reed	6	L. Yarborough	3	Bill Amick	1	John Kieper	1	Buddy Shuman	1
13. Dale Earnhardt	27	Tony Stewart	6	59. Buddy Baker	2	John Andretti	1	Bobby Labonte	1	John Soares Jr.	1
14. Rusty Wallace	25	37. Darel Dieringer	5	J. Beauchamp	2	Earl Balmer	1	Paul Lewis	1	Nelson Stacy	1
Rex White	25	Harry Gant	5	Bill Blair	2	Brett Bodine	1	Jeremy Mayfield	1	Donald Thomas	1
16. Jim Paschal	23	Paul Goldsmith	5	Jeff Burton	2	Marvin Burke	1	Lloyd Moore	1	Art Watts	1
17. Joe Weatherly	21	Ricky Rudd	5	Bill Elliott	2	Red Byron	1	Norm Nelson	1	Danny Weinberg	1
18. Fireball Roberts	19	Marshall Teague	5	Charlie Glotzbach	2	June Cleveland	1	Joe Nemechek	1	Jack White	1
Jack Smith	19	42. Davey Allison	4	Kevin Harvick	2	Neil Cole	1	Ryan Newman	1		
20. S. Thompson	17	Dale Earnhardt Jr.	4	Jimmie Johnson	2	Jim Cook	1	Bill Norton	1		
21. Fonty Flock	16	Bob Flock	4	Alan Kulwicki	2	B. Courtwright	1	Dick Passwater	1		
22. Jeff Gordon	15	Ernie Irvan	4	Elmo Langley	2	Ricky Craven	1	Kyle Petty	1		
Curtis Turner	15	Dale Jarrett	4	Danny Letner	2	Joe Eubanks	1	Marvin Porter	1		

ROAD COURSE WINNERS
NASCAR NEXTEL Cup Series

Driver	Wins	Driver	Wins	Driver	Wins	Driver	Wins	Driver	Wins	Driver	Wins
1. Jeff Gordon	9	Darrell Waltrip	5	Robby Gordon	2	Buck Baker	1	A.J. Foyt	1	Benny Parsons	1
2. Bobby Allison	6	10. Mark Martin	4	Parnelli Jones	2	Bill Blair	1	Paul Goldsmith	1	Kyle Petty	1
Richard Petty	6	David Pearson	4	Terry Labonte	2	Red Byron	1	Eddie Gray	1	Lee Petty	1
Ricky Rudd	6	12. Geoff Bodine	3	Marvin Panch	2	Lloyd Dane	1	Kevin Harvick	1	Jack Smith	1
Rusty Wallace	6	Tim Flock	3	Fireball Roberts	2	Darel Dieringer	1	Al Keller	1	Chuck Stevenson	1
6. Dan Gurney	5	Ernie Irvan	3	Marshall Teague	2	Mark Donohue	1	Harold Kite	1		
Tim Richmond	5	Cale Yarborough	3	Billy Wade	2	Dale Earnhardt	1	Cotton Owens	1		
Tony Stewart	5	16. Ray Elder	2	24. Davey Allison	1	Bill Elliott	1	Steve Park	1		

>> ALL-TIME WINS BY CAR NUMBER <<

NASCAR NEXTEL Cup Series

Car #	Wins	Driver (Wins)
0	2	Jim Cook (1), Darel Dieringer (1)
01	1	Joe Nemechek
06	1	Cale Yarborough (1)
1	14	Donnie Allison (4), Billy Wade (4), Steve Park (2), Lloyd Dane (1), Eddie Gray (1), Paul Lewis (1), David Pearson (1)
2	59	Rusty Wallace (37), Bobby Allison (7), Dale Earnhardt (6), Bill Blair (3), Tim Richmond (2), Kurt Busch (1), Herb Thomas (1), Jim Paschal (1), David Pearson (1)
3	97	Dale Earnhardt (67), Junior Johnson (9), Paul Goldsmith (5), David Pearson (3), Dick Rothmann (3), Buck Baker (2), Buddy Baker (2), Ricky Rudd (2), Earl Balmer (1), Charlie Glotzbach (1), Danny Letner (1), Fireball Roberts (1)
4	44	Rex White (26), Ernie Irvan (7), Sterling Marlin (6), Bobby Hamilton (1), Al Keller (1), Billy Myers (1), John Soares(1), Bob Welborn (1)
5	32	Terry Labonte (12), Geoffrey Bodine (7), Ricky Rudd (4), Kyle Busch (3), Cotton Owens (3), Neil Bonnett (2), Bobby Johns (1), Morgan Sheperd (1)
6	82	Mark Martin (35), David Pearson (27), Marshall Teague (7), Cotton Owens (6), Bobby Allison (1), Buddy Baker (1), Joe Eubanks (1), Charlie Glotzbach (1), Pete Hamilton (1), Danny Letner (1), Herb Thomas (1)
7	23	Jim Reed (7), Alan Kulwicki (5), Geoffrey Bodine (4), Bob Flock (4), Fonty Flock (1), Frank Mundy (1), Kyle Petty (1)
8	38	Joe Weatherly (20), Dale Earnhardt Jr. (17), Bobby Hillin (1)
9	47	Bill Elliot (38), Kasey Kahne (7), Donald Thomas (1), Herb Thomas (1)
10	10	Ricky Rudd (6), Derrike Cope (2), Johnny Benson, Jr. (1), Greg Sacks (1)
11	182	Cale Yarborough (55), Ned Jarrett (49), Darrell Waltrip (43), Junior Johnson (11), Bill Elliot (6), Geoffrey Bodine (4), Terry Labonte (4), Bobby Allison (3), Buddy Baker (2), Denny Hamlin (2), Mario Andretti (1), A.J. Foyt (1), Parnelli Jones (1)
12	55	Bobby Allison (25), Ryan Newman (12), Ralph Moody (5), Neil Bonnett (3), Jerry Mayfield (3), Joe Weatherly (3), LeeRoy Yarbrough (2), Paul Goldsmith (1), Marvin Porter (1)
13	1	Johnny Rutherford (1)
14	26	Fonty Flock (14), Jim Paschal (7), Hershel McGriff (4), Bobby Allison (1)
15	40	Bobby Allison (14), Ricky Rudd (6), Buddy Baker (5), Michael Waltrip (4), Geoffrey Bodine (3), Dale Earnhardt (3), Penny Parsons (3), Tim Flock (1), Morgan Shepherd (1)
16	23	Greg Biffle (11), Darel Dieringer (5), Bobby Allison (3), Glen Wood (3), Mike Donohue (1), Joe Weatherly (1)
17	59	David Pearson (30), Darrell Waltrip (15), Matt Kenseth (14)
18	23	Bobby Labonte (21), Dale Jarrett (2)
19	3	Jeremy Mayfield (2), John Rostek (1)
20	30	Tony Stewart (29), Marvin Panch (1)
21	90	David Pearson (43), Cale Yarborough (13), Neil Bonnett (9), Marvin Panch (8), A.J. Foyt (4), Speedy Thompson (2), Donnie Allison (1), Buddy Baker (1), Tim Flock (1), Dale Jarrett (1), Harold Kite (1), Tiny Lund (1), Kyle Petty (1), Elliot Sadler (1), Morgan Shepherd (1), Curtis Turner (1), Glen Wood (1)
22	56	Fireball Roberts (30), Bobby Allison (17), Ward Burton (5), Red Byron (2), Dick Brooks (1), Chuck Stevenson (1)
23	3	Frank Mundy (2), Al Keller (1)
24	75	Jeff Gordon (75)
25	20	Tim Richmond (9), Ken Schrader (4), Dick Linder (3), Jerry Nadeau (1), Joe Nemechek (1), Brian Vickers (1), Jack White (1)
26	20	Junior Johnson (12), Ricky Rudd (2), Chris Turner (2), Brett Bodine (1), Darel Dieringer (1), Bobby Isaac (1), Fred Lorenzen (1)
27	51	Rusty Wallace (18), Junior Johnson (13), Donnie Allison (8), Benny Parsons (5), Cale Yarborough (5), Jimmy Spencer (2), Tim Richmond (2), Jimmy Florian (1)
28	76	Fred Lorenzen (25), Davey Allison (19), Cale Yarborough (9), Ernie Irvan (8), Bobby Allison (5), Buddy Baker (5), Ricky Rudd (3), Dan Gurney (1), Dale Jarrett (1)
29	27	Dick Hutcherson (13), Kevin Harvick (10), Nelson Stacy (4)
30	1	Speedy Thompson (1)
31	4	Robby Gordon (3), Jeff Burton (1)
32	2	Ricky Craven (2)
33	20	Harry Gant (18), Lou Figaro (1), Joe Nemechek (1)
34	2	Jim Roper (1), Wendell Scott (1)
37	1	Bobby Isaac (1)
38	7	Gwyn Staley (3), Elliott Sadler (2), Ned Jarrett (1), Bob Welborn (1)
40	9	Sterling Marlin (4), Pete Hamilton (3), Jamie McMurray (1), Tommy Thompson (1)
41	22	Curtis Turner (12), Richard Petty (6), Jim Paschal (3), A.J. Foyt (1)
42	67	Lee Petty (53), Kyle Petty (6), Jim Paschal (4), Richard Petty (2), Marvin Panch (1), Joe Nemechek (1)
43	198	Richard Petty (192), Bobby Hamilton (2), Jim Paschal (2), John Andretti (1), Lee Petty (1)
44	13	Terry Labonte (6), Rex White (2), Lloyd Dane (2), Jim Paschal (1), Curtis Turner (1), Bob Welborn (1)
45	6	Eddie Pagan (4), LeeRoy Yarbrough (2)
46	11	Speedy Thompson (8), Jack Smith (2), Bob Welborn (1)
47	24	Jack Smith (18), Buck Baker (1), Ron Bouchard (1), Fonty Flock (1), A.J. Foyt (1), Dick Hutcherson (1), Morgan Shepherd (1)
48	26	Jimmie Johnson (23), James Hylton (2), Bill Norton (1)
49	7	Bob Welborn (5), Bobby Allison (1), Jim Paschal (1)
51	2	Gober Sosebee (2)
52	2	Neil Cole (1), Earl Ross (1)
53	1	Bob Burdick (1)
54	3	Jimmy Pardue (2), Lennie Pond (1)
55	12	Junior Johnson (5), Tiny Lund (4), Bobby Hamilton (1), Benny Parsons (1), Phil Parsons (1)
56	1	Jim Hurtubise (1)
58	1	Johnny Allen (1)
59	3	Tom Pistone (2), Lloyd Moore (1)
60	1	Bill Rexford (1)
62	1	Frankie Schneider (1)
64	2	Elmo Langley (2)
66	1	Larry Frank (1)
71	44	Bobby Isaac (35), Dave Marcis (1), Buddy Baker (3), Fireball Roberts (1)
72	14	Benny Parsons (12), Bobby Johns (1), Joe Weatherly (1)
73	2	J. Beauchamp (2)
75	6	Neil Bonnett (4), Jim Paschal (1), Fireball Roberts (1)
77	1	Joe Lee Johnson (1)
78	4	Jim Paschal (3), Dick Passwater (1)
80	1	Jim Paschal (1)
81	1	Danny Graves (1)
83	1	Lake Speed (1)
85	2	E. Zervakis (2)
86	1	Buck Baker (1)
87	27	Buck Baker (26), Jim Paschal (1)
88	65	Dale Jarrett (28), Darrell Waltrip (26), Bobby Allison (8), Buck Baker (2)
89	4	Buck Baker (2), Joe Lee Johnson (1), Buddy Shuman (1)
90	1	Jody Ridley (1)
91	16	Tim Flock (16)
92	43	Herb Thomas (42), Marvin Panch (1)
96	2	Ray Elder (2)
97	17	Kurt Busch (14), Parnelli Jones (2), Bill Amick (1)
98	25	LeeRoy Yarbrough (10), Marvin Panch (6), Eddie Gray (3), John Andretti (1), John Kieper (1), Johnny Mantz (1), Sam McQuagg (1), Marvin Porter (1), Leon Sales (1)
99	28	Jeff Burton (17), Carl Edwards (4), Paul Goldsmith (3), Charlie Glotzbach (2), Richard Brickhouse (1), Shorty Rollins (1), Curtis Turner (1)
115	1	Parnelli Jones (1)
120	10	Dick Rathmann (10)
121	3	Dan Gurney (3)
225	1	Lloyd Dane (1)
297	1	Speedy Thompson (1)
299	1	Norm Nelson (1)
300	29	Tim Flock (17), Buck Baker (6), Speedy Thompson (6)
301	5	Tim Flock (4), Buck Baker (1)
500	5	Buck Baker (3), Speedy Thompson (2)
502	1	Buck Baker (1)

≫ DRIVER RECORDS ≪

NASCAR NEXTEL Cup Series

ALL RACES

Most wins, career—200, Richard Petty (1958-92).
Most wins, season—27, Richard Petty (1967).
Most consecutive wins—10, Richard Petty (1967).
Most wins from pole, career—61, Richard Petty (1958-92).
Most wins from pole, season—15, Richard Petty (1967).
Oldest driver to win a race—Harry Gant, 52 years, 219 days (August 16, 1992).
Youngest driver to win a race—Kyle Busch, 20 years, 125 days (September 4, 2005).
Most consecutive races won from pole—4, Richard Petty (1967) and Darrell Waltrip (1981).
Most years won at least one race from pole—16, Richard Petty (1958-92).
Most consecutive wins at one track—7, Richard Petty, Richmond International Raceway (1970-73), and Darrell Waltrip, Bristol Motor Speedway (1981-84).

MODERN ERA RECORDS ▪ 1972-2005

Most wins—84, Darrell Waltrip (1972-2000).

Most wins, season—13, Richard Petty (1975), Jeff Gordon (1998).
Most consecutive wins—4, Cale Yarborough (1976), Darrell Waltrip (1981), Dale Earnhardt (1987), Harry Gant (1991), Bill Elliott (1992), Mark Martin (1993), Jeff Gordon (1998).
Most wins from pole, career—24, Darrell Waltrip (1972-2000).
Most wins from pole, season—8, Darrell Waltrip (1981).
Most consecutive races won from pole—4, Darrell Waltrip (1981).
Most years won at least one race from pole—9, Darrell Waltrip (1972-2000).
Most consecutive years won at least one race from pole—7, Darrell Waltrip (1978-84).
Most consecutive wins at one track—7, Darrell Waltrip, Bristol Motor Speedway (1981-84).
Most races, career—1,184, Richard Petty, 1958-92.
Most years leading circuit in wins—7, Richard Petty, 1958-92.
Most consecutive years leading circuit in wins—5, Jeff Gordon, 1995-99.
Best winning percentage, career (at least 10 wins, 100 starts)—21.1, Herb Thomas (48 wins, 228 starts), 1949-1962.
Most races started without a win—653, J.D. McDuffie, 1963-91.

≫ ALL-TIME MONEY LEADERS ≪

NASCAR NEXTEL Cup Series

Rank	Driver	Career starts	Career winnings	Average per start
1.	Jeff Gordon	473	$82,358,526	$174,119
2.	Mark Martin	674	$59,428,575	$88,172
3.	Tony Stewart	284	$57,269,018	$201,651
4.	Dale Jarrett	639	$56,993,389	$89,191
5.	Bobby Labonte	474	$50,639,719	$106,834
6.	Rusty Wallace	706	$49,741,326	$70,455
7.	Jeff Burton	439	$46,898,336	$106,829
8.	Jimmie Johnson	183	$44,134,716	$241,173
9.	Matt Kenseth	256	$43,076,654	$168,268
10.	Dale Earnhardt Jr.	255	$42,945,535	$168,413
11.	Dale Earnhardt	676	$41,742,384	$61,749
12.	Ricky Rudd	875	$40,696,133	$46,509
13.	Terry Labonte	848	$40,559,678	$47,829
14.	Sterling Marlin	711	$40,298,514	$56,678
15.	Bill Elliott	756	$38,860,357	$51,402
16.	Kurt Busch	220	$36,194,280	$164,519
17.	Michael Waltrip	675	$35,193,442	$52,138
18.	Kevin Harvick	214	$33,571,638	$156,876
19.	Ken Schrader	704	$32,422,853	$46,055
20.	Ryan Newman	188	$31,519,766	$167,658
21.	Jeremy Mayfield	403	$30,894,339	$76,660
22.	Elliott Sadler	285	$30,089,924	$105,578
23.	Joe Nemechek	430	$28,256,242	$65,712
24.	Kyle Petty	785	$27,724,220	$35,317
25.	Ward Burton	359	$24,256,185	$67,565
26.	Greg Biffle	150	$20,994,998	$139,966
27.	Jimmy Spencer	478	$20,336,358	$42,607
28.	Robby Gordon	235	$19,867,281	$84,541
29.	Darrell Waltrip	809	$19,416,618	$24,000
30.	Jamie McMurray	150	$18,533,586	$123,557
31.	John Andretti	340	$18,350,754	$53,972
32.	Kasey Kahne	108	$18,294,686	$169,395
33.	Jeff Green	233	$18,112,531	$77,736
34.	Dave Blaney	235	$17,435,743	$74,194
35.	Johnny Benson	271	$16,833,410	$62,116
36.	Casey Mears	144	$16,712,037	$116,055
37.	Geoffrey Bodine	570	$16,528,725	$28,997
38.	Bobby Hamilton	371	$15,464,030	$41,682
39.	Ricky Craven	278	$15,209,281	$54,709
40.	Mike Skinner	244	$14,601,642	$59,842

Career winnings include race winnings, postseason awards, non-points race winnings and special bonuses.

>>ALL-TIME POLE WINNERS<<

NASCAR NEXTEL Cup Series

	Driver	Poles		Driver	Poles		Driver	Poles
1.	Richard Petty	126		Dale Earnhardt Jr.	6	135.	Casey Atwood	1
2.	David Pearson	113		Tiny Lund	6		Dick Bailey	1
3.	Cale Yarborough	70		Eddie Pagan	6		Larry Baumel	1
4.	Darrell Waltrip	59		Mike Skinner	6		Bill Blair	1
5.	Bobby Allison	57	72.	Bill Amick	5		Dave Blaney	1
6.	Jeff Gordon	56		Brett Bodine	5		Al Bonnell	1
7.	Bill Elliott	55		Todd Bodine	5		Chuck Bown	1
8.	Bobby Isaac	51		Bobby Hamilton	5		Perk Brown	1
9.	Junior Johnson	47		Kevin Harvick	5		Wally Campbell	1
10.	Buck Baker	44		Dick Linder	5		Neil Cole	1
11.	Mark Martin	41		Hershel McGriff	5		Jim Cook	1
12.	Buddy Baker	40		Ralph Moody	5		Derrike Cope	1
13.	Tim Flock	39		Ted Musgrave	5		Doug Cox	1
	Herb Thomas	39		Tom Pistone	5		Lloyd Dane	1
15.	Geoff Bodine	37		Lennie Pond	5		Bill Dennis	1
	Ryan Newman	37		Jim Reed	5		Bob Duell	1
17.	Rusty Wallace	36		Billy Wade	5		Ralph Earnhardt	1
18.	Ned Jarrett	35		Art Watts	5		Lou Figaro	1
	Fireball Roberts	35	86.	John Andretti	4		Jimmy Florian	1
	Rex White	35		Denny Hamlin	4		George Follmer	1
21.	Fonty Flock	33		James Hylton	4		David Gilliland	1
	Fred Lorenzen	33		Rick Mast	4		Robby Gordon	1
23.	Ricky Rudd	29		Frank Mundy	4		Danny Graves	1
24.	Terry Labonte	27		Steve Park	4		Eddie Gray	1
25.	Bobby Labonte	26		Matt Kenseth	4		David Green	1
26.	Alan Kulwicki	24		Gober Sosebee	4		Royce Hagerty	1
	Jack Smith	24		Brian Vickers	4		Jimmy Hensley	1
28.	Ken Schrader	23	95.	Johnny Allen	3		Russ Hepler	1
29.	Dale Earnhardt	22		Loy Allen Jr	3		Jim Hunter	1
	Dick Hutcherson	22		Greg Biffle	3		Possum Jones	1
	Ernie Irvan	22		Ron Bouchard	3		Al Keller	1
32.	Marvin Panch	21		Joe Eubanks	3		Pat Kirkwood	1
33.	Neil Bonnett	20		Pete Hamilton	3		Elmo Langley	1
	Benny Parsons	20		Kenny Irwin Jr	3		Jason Leffler	1
35.	Speedy Thompson	19		Parnelli Jones	3		Kevin Lepage	1
	Joe Weatherly	19		John Kieper	3		Danny Letner	1
37.	Lee Petty	18		Banjo Matthews	3		Jimmie Lewallen	1
38.	Donnie Allison	17		Jimmy Pardue	3		Paul Lewis	1
	Harry Gant	17		Scott Riggs	3		Joe Littlejohn	1
	Curtis Turner	17		Joe Ruttman	3		Chuck Mahoney	1
41.	Dale Jarrett	16		Jimmy Spencer	3		Jim Massey	1
42.	Davey Allison	14		Marshall Teague	3		J.D McDuffie	1
	Dave Marcis	14		Kenny Wallace	3		Joe Millikan	1
	Tim Richmond	14		Michael Waltrip	3		Tommy Moon	1
	Glen Wood	14	112.	Johnny Benson	2		Paul "Bud" Moore	1
46.	Dick Rathmann	13		Bob Burdick	2		Billy Myers	1
47.	Charlie Glotzbach	12		Kyle Busch	2		Norm Nelson	1
	Kasey Kahne	12		Red Byron	2		Andy Pierce	1
	Jim Paschal	12		Billy Carden	2		Bob Pronger	1
50.	Darel Dieringer	11		Stacy Compton	2		Bill Rexford	1
	Sterling Marlin	11		Carl Edwards	2		Bob Ross	1
	Cotton Owens	11		Bob Flock	2		John Rostek	1
	Lee Roy Yarbrough	11		Jeff Green	2		Frankie Schneider	1
54.	A.J. Foyt	10		Dan Gurney	2		Wendell Scott	1
	Tony Stewart	10		Friday Hassler	2		Frank Secrist	1
56.	Kurt Busch	9		Tommy Irwin	2		Lloyd Shaw	1
	Jimmie Johnson	9		Bobby Johns	2		Slick Smith	1
	Jeremy Mayfield	9		Mel Larson	2		Sam Sommers	1
	Joe Nemechek	9		Jamie McMurray	2		G.C. Spencer	1
60.	Paul Goldsmith	8		Casey Mears	2		Ramo Stott	1
	Kyle Petty	8		Ken Rush	2		Hut Stricklin	1
	Elliott Sadler	8		Greg Sacks	2		Donald Thomas	1
63.	Ward Burton	7		Boris Said	2		Dick Trickle	1
	Morgan Shepherd	7		John Sears	2		Ken Wagner	1
	Bob Welborn	7		Gwyn Staley	2		Danny Weinberg	1
66.	Jeff Burton	6		Doug Yates	2		Dink Widenhouse	1
	Ricky Craven	6		Emanuel Zervakis	2		Rick Wilson	1

>> SPEEDWAY POLE WINNERS <<

NASCAR NEXTEL Cup Series

Driver	Poles	Driver	Poles	Driver	Poles	Driver	Poles	Driver	Poles	Driver	Poles
1. David Pearson	58	21. Ernie Irvan	13	Marvin Panch	6	Pete Hamilton	3	Scott Riggs	2	Lee Petty	1
2. Bill Elliott	48	Terry Labonte	13	Junior Johnson	6	Denny Hamlin	3	Greg Sacks	2	Dick Rathmann	1
3. C. Yarborough	46	Ricky Rudd	13	Elliott Sadler	6	Kenny Irwin Jr.	3	Morgan Shepherd	2	Bob Ross	1
4. Jeff Gordon	36	24. Davey Allison	12	L. Yarbrough	6	Cotton Owens	3	Jimmy Spencer	2	Joe Ruttman	1
5. Ryan Newman	32	Dale Earnhardt	12	45. Jeff Burton	5	Steve Park	3	85. Casey Atwood	1	Boris Said	1
6. Buddy Baker	29	Harry Gant	12	Ward Burton	5	Curtis Turner	3	Dave Blaney	1	Frankie Schneider	1
7. Bobby Labonte	24	27. Neil Bonnett	11	Kurt Busch	5	Brian Vickers	3	Derrike Cope	1	Frank Secrist	1
8. Richard Petty	23	C. Glotzbach	11	Fonty Flock	5	Michael Waltrip	3	Tim Flock	1	Jack Smith	1
9. Mark Martin	22	Kasey Kahne	11	Tony Stewart	5	69. J. Benson	2	David Gilliland	1	Slick Smith	1
Ken Schrader	22	Sterling Marlin	11	50. John Andretti	4	Greg Biffle	2	Robby Gordon	1	Sam Sommers	1
11. Geoff Bodine	21	31. Benny Parsons	10	Darel Dieringer	4	Ron Bouchard	2	David Green	1	Ramo Stott	1
12. Fireball Roberts	20	32. Dave Marcis	9	Kevin Harvick	4	Kyle Busch	2	Jeff Green	1	Hut Stricklin	1
13. Rusty Wallace	19	Jeremy Mayfield	9	Rick Mast	4	Stacy Compton	2	Friday Hassler	1	Marshall Teague	1
14. Bobby Allison	18	Tim Richmond	9	Mike Skinner	4	Carl Edwards	2	Dick Hutcherson	1	S. Thompson	1
15. Alan Kulwicki	17	35. Joe Nemechek	8	Herb Thomas	4	Paul Goldsmith	2	Jason Leffler	1	Dick Trickle	1
16. Donnie Allison	15	36. Rick Craven	7	56. Loy Allen Jr.	3	Matt Kenseth	2	Kevin Lepage	1	Kenny Wallace	1
Bobby Isaac	15	A.J. Foyt	7	John Andretti	3	Banjo Matthews	2	J.D. McDuffie	1	Bob Welborn	1
Dale Jarrett	15	Jimmie Johnson	7	Buck Baker	3	Jamie McMurray	2	Hershel McGriff	1		
Darrell Waltrip	15	39. Dale Earnhardt Jr.	6	Todd Bodine	3	Casey Mears	2	Frank Mundy	1		
20. Fred Lorenzen	14	Kyle Petty	6	Bobby Hamilton	3	Eddie Pagan	2	Jimmy Pardue	1		

>> SHORT TRACK POLE WINNERS <<

NASCAR NEXTEL Cup Series

Driver	Wins	Driver	Wins	Driver	Wins	Driver	Wins	Driver	Wins	Driver	Wins
1. Richard Petty	97	Dick Rathmann	12	Hershel McGriff	4	Mel Larson	2	Doug Cox	1	Chuck Mahoney	1
2. David Pearson	47	29. Buddy Baker	11	Eddie Pagan	4	Frank Mundy	2	Ricky Craven	1	Jim Massey	1
3. Junior Johnson	40	Glenn Wood	11	M. Shepherd	4	Jimmy Pardue	2	Bill Dennis	1	Joe Millikan	1
4. Buck Baker	38	31. Benny Parsons	10	Tony Stewart	4	Kyle Petty	2	Bob Duell	1	Tommy Moon	1
5. Bobby Isaac	36	Ricky Rudd	10	Billy Wade	4	Ken Rush	2	Glenn Dunaway	1	Paul "Bud" Moore	1
6. Tim Flock	35	33. Neil Bonnett	9	Art Watts	4	Joe Ruttman	2	Ralph Earnhardt	1	Billy Myers	1
Ned Jarrett	35	34. Ernie Irvan	8	61. Johnny Allen	3	John Sears	2	Lou Figaro	1	Norm Nelson	1
Herb Thomas	35	Cotton Owens	8	Bob Flock	3	Mike Skinner	2	Jimmy Florian	1	Joe Nemechek	1
Darrell Waltrip	35	36. Darrell Dieringer	7	Paul Goldsmith	3	Gwyn Staley	2	A.J. Foyt	1	Steve Park	1
Rex White	35	Bill Elliott	7	Jim Reed	3	Marshall Teague	2	Charlie Glotzbach	1	Andy Pierce	1
11. Bobby Allison	34	Terry Labonte	7	Tim Richmond	3	Kenny Wallace	2	Danny Graves	1	Don Porter	1
12. Fonty Flock	29	Tiny Lund	6	Gober Sosebee	3	Doug Yates	2	Jeff Green	1	Bill Rexford	1
13. Jack Smith	22	Alan Kulwicki	7	67. Davey Allison	2	E. Zervakis	2	Royce Hagerty	1	Scott Riggs	1
C. Yarborough	22	Bob Welborn	6	Donnie Allison	2	95. Dick Bailey	1	Denny Hamlin	1	John Rostek	1
15. D. Hutcherson	20	42. Bill Amick	5	Brett Bodine	2	Larry Baumel	1	Kevin Harvick	1	Elliott Sadler	1
16. Joe Weatherly	19	Dale Earnhardt	5	Bob Burdick	2	Bill Benson	1	Friday Hassler	1	Ken Schrader	1
17. S. Thompson	18	Joe Eubanks	5	Ward Burton	2	Greg Biffle	1	Jimmy Hensley	1	Wendell Scott	1
18. Fred Lorenzen	17	Harry Gant	5	Kurt Busch	2	Bill Blair	1	Russ Hepler	1	Lloyd Shaw	1
19. Lee Petty	16	Dick Linder	5	Red Byron	2	Todd Bodine	1	Jim Hunter	1	G.C. Spencer	1
20. Mark Martin	15	Dave Marcis	5	Billy Carden	2	Al Bonnell	1	Possum Jones	1	Jimmy Spencer	1
Fireball Roberts	15	Ralph Moody	5	Bobby Hamilton	2	Ron Bouchard	1	Kasey Kahne	1	Lyle Tadlock	1
22. Geoff Bodine	14	Ted Musgrave	5	Tommy Irwin	2	Chuck Bown	1	Al Keller	1	Donald Thomas	1
Jeff Gordon	14	Ryan Newman	5	Bobby Johns	2	Perk Brown	1	Matt Kenseth	1	Brian Vickers	1
Marvin Panch	14	Tom Pistone	5	Jimmie Johnson	2	Jeff Burton	1	Elmo Langley	1	Ken Wagner	1
Curtis Turner	14	Lennie Pond	5	Parnelli Jones	2	Wally Campbell	1	Danny Letner	1	Danny Weinberg	1
Rusty Wallace	14	L. Yarbrough	5	John Kieper	2	Neil Cole	1	Jimmie Lewallen	1	Dink Widenhouse	1
27. Jim Paschal	12	54. James Hylton	4	Bobby Labonte	2	Jim Cook	1	Paul Lewis	1	Rick Wilson	1

>> ROAD COURSE POLE WINNERS <<

NASCAR NEXTEL Cup Series

Driver	Wins	Driver	Wins	Driver	Wins	Driver	Wins	Driver	Wins	Driver	Wins
1. Darrell Waltrip	9	9. Mark Martin	4	Dan Gurney	2	Eddie Gray	1	Joe Littlejohn	1	Jack Smith	1
2. Terry Labonte	8	10. Buck Baker	3	Fred Lorenzen	2	Dick Hutcherson	1	Banjo Matthews	1	Gober Sosebee	1
David Pearson	8	Tim Flock	3	Tim Richmond	2	Ernie Irvan	1	Marvin Panch	1	Billy Wade	1
4. Jeff Gordon	7	Paul Goldsmith	3	Tony Stewart	2	Dale Jarrett	1	Lee Petty	1	Art Watts	1
5. Richard Petty	6	Rusty Wallace	3	Cale Yarborough	2	Jimmie Johnson	1	Bob Pronger	1		
Ricky Rudd	6	14. Geoff Bodine	2	21. Todd Bodine	1	Junior Johnson	1	Jim Reed	1		
7. Bobby Allison	5	Kurt Busch	2	George Follmer	1	Parnelli Jones	1	Boris Said	1		
Dale Earnhardt	5	A.J. Foyt	2	Danny Graves	1	Pat Kirkwood	1	Morgan Shepherd	1		

>> POLES MODERN ERA <<

NASCAR NEXTEL Cup Series 1972-2006

1.	* Darrell Waltrip	59	
2.	* David Pearson	57	
3.	Jeff Gordon	56	
4.	Bill Elliott	55	
5.	* Cale Yarborough	51	
6.	Mark Martin	41	
7.	* Geoffrey Bodine	37	
	Ryan Newman	37	
9.	* Rusty Wallace	36	
10.	* Bobby Allison	35	
11.	* Buddy Baker	30	
12.	* Ricky Rudd	29	
13.	Terry Labonte	27	
14.	Bobby Labonte	26	
15.	# Alan Kulwicki	24	
16.	* Richard Petty	23	
	Ken Schrader	23	
18.	# Dale Earnhardt	22	
	* Ernie Irvan	22	
20.	# Neil Bonnett	21	
21.	* Benny Parsons	19	
22.	* Harry Gant	17	
23.	Dale Jarrett	16	
24.	# Davey Allison	14	
	# Tim Richmond	14	

>> RACES WON FROM THE POLE <<

NASCAR NEXTEL Cup Series

1.	Richard Petty	61	21.	Marvin Panch	6		Glen Wood	3
2.	David Pearson	37		Fireball Roberts	6	42.	Davey Allison	2
3.	Darrell Waltrip	24		Jack Smith	6		Donnie Allison	2
4.	Bobby Isaac	21		Joe Weatherly	6		Darel Dieringer	2
5.	Bobby Allison	20	25.	Buddy Baker	4		Harry Gant	2
6.	Herb Thomas	19		Dick Hutcherson	4		Charlie Glotzbach	2
7.	Jeff Gordon	17		Kasey Kahne	4		Paul Goldsmith	2
8.	Tim Flock	16		Bobby Labonte	4		Denny Hamlin	2
	Cale Yarborough	16		Terry Labonte	4		Kevin Harvick	2
10.	Bill Elliott	15		Jim Paschal	4		Ernie Irvan	2
11.	Buck Baker	12		Tim Richmond	4		Dale Jarrett	2
	Junior Johnson	12		Curtis Turner	4		Dick Linder	2
13.	Ned Jarrett	11	33.	Geoff Bodine	3		Eddie Pagan	2
	Fred Lorenzen	11		Dale Earnhardt	3		Jim Reed	2
15.	Fonty Flock	9		A.J. Foyt	3		Tony Stewart	2
	Rusty Wallace	9		Hershel McGriff	3		Bob Welborn	2
17.	Mark Martin	7		Ryan Newman	3	57.	Kurt Busch	1
	Lee Petty	7		Cotton Owens	3		Neil Cole	1
	Speedy Thompson	7		Kyle Petty	3		Jim Cook	1
	Rex White	7		Billy Wade	3		Lou Figaro	1

Danny Graves	1
Dan Gurney	1
Bobby Hamilton	1
Jimmie Johnson	1
Parnelli Jones	1
Matt Kenseth	1
Alan Kulwicki	1
Dave Marcis	1
Sterling Marlin	1
Ralph Moody	1
Frank Mundy	1
Norm Nelson	1
Joe Nemechek	1
Benny Parsons	1
Ricky Rudd	1
Gwyn Staley	1
Marshall Teague	1
Donald Thomas	1
Art Watts	1
Lee Roy Yarbrough	1

>> DRIVER RECORDS QUALIFYING <<

NASCAR NEXTEL Cup Series

ALL RACES

Most poles, career—126, Richard Petty (1958-92).

Most poles, season—20, Bobby Isaac (1969).

Most consecutive poles—5, Bobby Allison (1972); Cale Yarborough (1980); Bill Elliott (1985).

Most years won at least one pole—23, David Pearson (1960-86).

Most consecutive years won at least one pole—20, David Pearson (1963-82).

Most consecutive poles won at one track—11, David Pearson (1973-78), Lowe's Motor Speedway.

Most poles at one track—14, David Pearson, Lowe's Motor Speedway.

QUALIFYING RECORDS MODERN ERA 1972-2006

Most poles, career—59, Darrell Waltrip (1972-00).

Most poles, season—14, Cale Yarborough (1980).

Most consecutive poles—5, Bobby Allison (1972); Cale Yarborough (1980); Bill Elliott (1985).

Most years won at least one pole—16, Darrell Waltrip (1972-2000).

Most consecutive years won at least one pole—14, Jeff Gordon (1993-2006).

Most consecutive poles won at one track—11, David Pearson

ALL-TIME STARTS

NASCAR NEXTEL Cup Series

	Driver	Total starts			Driver	Total starts
1.	* Richard Petty	1,184	14.		Michael Waltrip	675
2.	* Dave Marcis	883	15.		Mark Martin	674
3.	* Ricky Rudd	875	16.	*	J.D. McDuffie	653
4.	* Terry Labonte	848	17.		Dale Jarrett	639
5.	* Darrell Waltrip	809	18.	*	Buck Baker	631
6.	Kyle Petty	785	19.	*	James Hylton	602
7.	Bill Elliott	756	20.	*	David Pearson	574
8.	* Bobby Allison	717	21.		Geoffrey Bodine	570
9.	Sterling Marlin	711	22.	*	Buddy Arrington	563
10.	* Rusty Wallace	706	23.	*	Cale Yarborough	559
11.	Ken Schrader	704	24.	*	Elmo Langley	536
12.	* Buddy Baker	698	25.	*	Benny Parsons	526
13.	# Dale Earnhardt	676				

STARTS MODERN ERA

NASCAR NEXTEL Cup Series 1972-2006

	Driver				Driver	
1.	* Ricky Rudd	875	14.	*	Richard Petty	619
2.	Terry Labonte	848	15.		Geoffrey Bodine	570
3.	* Darrell Waltrip	809	16.		Morgan Shepherd	513
4.	Kyle Petty	785	17.	*	Brett Bodine	480
5.	* Dave Marcis	760	18.		Jimmy Spencer	478
6.	Bill Elliott	756	19.	*	Bobby Allison	476
7.	Sterling Marlin	711	20.	*	Harry Gant	474
8.	* Rusty Wallace	706			Bobby Labonte	474
9.	Ken Schrader	704	22.	*	Jimmy Means	455
10.	# Dale Earnhardt	676	23.	*	J.D. McDuffie	443
11.	Michael Waltrip	675	24.	*	Benny Parsons	441
12.	Mark Martin	674	25.	*	Buddy Arrington	427
13.	Dale Jarrett	639				

DRIVERS WITH AT LEAST 300 CONSECUTIVE STARTS

NASCAR NEXTEL Cup Series

Rank	Driver	Start	End	Races
1.	* Ricky Rudd	January 11, 1981	November 20, 2005	788
2.	* Rusty Wallace	February 19, 1984	November 20, 2005	697
3.	* Terry Labonte	January 14, 1979	August 5, 2000	655
4.	# Dale Earnhardt	September 9, 1979	February 25, 2001	648
5.	Mark Martin	February 14, 1988	—	617
6.	Ken Schrader	February 17, 1985	August 3, 2003	579
7.	* Richard Petty	November 14, 1971	March 19, 1989	513
8.	Jeff Gordon	November 12, 1992	—	473
9.	Bobby Labonte	February 14, 1993	—	472
10.	* Darrell Waltrip	January 18, 1976	June 24, 1990	431
11.	Michael Waltrip	February 23, 1986	October 17, 1998	421
12.	Dale Jarrett	October 9, 1994	—	415
13.	Bill Elliott	October 31, 1982	April 28, 1996	395
14.	* Bobby Allison	November 9, 1975	June 19, 1988	374
15.	Jeff Burton	March 24, 1996	—	340
16.	Sterling Marlin	February 15, 1987	March 1, 1998	332
17.	* Benny Parsons	November 14, 1971	July 4, 1982	321

>> 2006 SEASON <<

Race No.	Location	Date	Winner	Car owner
1.	Daytona Beach, Fla.	Feb. 19	Jimmie Johnson	Rick Hendrick
2.	Fontana, Calif.	Feb. 26	Matt Kenseth	Jack Roush
3.	Las Vegas	March 12	Jimmie Johnson	Rick Hendrick
4.	Hampton, Ga.	March 19	Kasey Kahne	Ray Evernham
5.	Bristol, Tenn.	March 26	Kurt Busch	Roger Penske
6.	Martinsville, Va.	April 2	Tony Stewart	Joe Gibbs
7.	Fort Worth, Texas	April 9	Kasey Kahne	Ray Evernham
8.	Phoenix	April 22	Kevin Harvick	Richard Childress
9.	Talladega, Ala.	April 30	Jimmie Johnson	Rick Hendrick
10.	Richmond, Va.	May 6	Dale Earnhardt Jr.	Teresa Earnhardt
11.	Darlington, S.C.	May 13	Greg Biffle	Jack Roush
12.	Concord, N.C.	May 28	Kasey Kahne	Ray Evernham
13.	Dover, Del.	June 4	Matt Kenseth	Jack Roush
14.	Pocono, Pa.	June 11	Denny Hamlin	Joe Gibbs
15.	Brooklyn, Mich.	June 18	Kasey Kahne	Ray Evernham
16.	Sonoma, Calif.	June 25	Jeff Gordon	Rick Hendrick
17.	Daytona Beach, Fla.	July 1	Tony Stewart	Joe Gibbs
18.	Joliet, Ill.	July 9	Jeff Gordon	Rick Hendrick
19.	Loudon, N.H.	July 16	Kyle Busch	Rick Hendrick
20.	Pocono, Pa.	July 23	Denny Hamlin	Joe Gibbs
21.	Indianapolis	Aug. 6	Jimmie Johnson	Rick Hendrick
22.	Watkins Glen, N.Y.	Aug. 13	Kevin Harvick	Richard Childress
23.	Brooklyn, Mich.	Aug. 20	Matt Kenseth	Jack Roush
24.	Bristol, Tenn.	Aug. 26	Matt Kenseth	Jack Roush
25.	Fontana, Calif.	Sept. 3	Kasey Kahne	Ray Evernham
26.	Richmond, Va.	Sept. 9	Kevin Harvick	Richard Childress
27.	Loudon, N.H.	Sept. 17	Kevin Harvick	Richard Childress
28.	Dover, Del.	Sept. 24	Jeff Burton	Richard Childress
29.	Kansas City, Kan.	Oct. 1	Tony Stewart	Joe Gibbs
30.	Talladega, Ala.	Oct. 8	Brian Vickers	Rick Hendrick
31.	Concord, N.C.	Oct. 14	Kasey Kahne	Ray Evernham
32.	Martinsville, Va.	Oct. 22	Jimmie Johnson	Rick Hendrick
33.	Hampton, Ga.	Oct. 29	Tony Stewart	Joe Gibbs
34.	Fort Worth, Texas	Nov. 5	Tony Stewart	Joe Gibbs
35.	Phoenix	Nov. 12	Kevin Harvick	Richard Childress
36.	Homestead, Fla.	Nov. 19	Greg Biffle	Jack Roush

>> TOP 20 PERFORMANCE CHART

Rk	Driver	Points	Starts	Poles	Wins	Top 5s	Top 10s	DNF
1.	Jimmie Johnson	6,475	36	1	5	13	24	1
2.	Matt Kenseth	6,419	36	0	4	15	21	1
3.	Denny Hamlin	6,407	36	3	2	8	20	1
4.	Kevin Harvick	6,397	36	1	5	15	20	1
5.	Dale Earnhardt Jr.	6,328	36	0	1	10	17	3
6.	Jeff Gordon	6,256	36	2	2	14	18	7
7.	Jeff Burton	6,228	36	4	1	7	20	2
8.	Kasey Kahne	6,183	36	6	6	12	19	6
9.	Mark Martin	6,168	36	0	0	7	15	2
10.	Kyle Busch	6,027	36	1	1	10	18	2
11.	Tony Stewart	4,727	36	0	5	15	19	4
12.	Carl Edwards	4,428	36	0	0	10	20	3
13.	Greg Biffle	4,075	36	2	2	8	15	6
14.	Casey Mears	3,914	36	0	0	2	8	2
15.	Brian Vickers	3,906	36	1	1	5	9	2
16.	Kurt Busch	3,900	36	6	1	7	12	3
17.	Clint Bowyer	3,833	36	0	0	4	11	4
18.	Ryan Newman	3,748	36	2	0	2	7	3
19.	Martin Truex Jr.	3,673	36	0	0	2	5	5
20.	Scott Riggs	3,619	35	2	0	1	8	2

>> POINTS STANDINGS

1. Jimmie Johnson 6,475
2. Matt Kenseth 6,419
3. Denny Hamlin 6,407
4. Kevin Harvick 6,397
5. Dale Earnhardt Jr. 6,328
6. Jeff Gordon 6,256
7. Jeff Burton 6,228
8. Kasey Kahne 6,183
9. Mark Martin 6,168
10. Kyle Busch 6,027

>> RACE WINNERS   14

1. Kasey Kahne 6
2. Kevin Harvick 5
   Jimmie Johnson 5
   Tony Stewart 5
6. Matt Kenseth 4
7. Greg Biffle 2
   Jeff Gordon 2
   Denny Hamlin 2
10. Jeff Burton 1
   Kurt Busch 1
   Kyle Busch 1
   Dale Earnhardt Jr. 1
   Brian Vickers 1

>> MONEY WON LEADERS

1. Jimmie Johnson $15,875,125
2. Matt Kenseth...............................9,544,966
3. Tony Stewart...............................8,801,569
4. Kevin Harvick 8,231,406
5. Kasey Kahne...............................7,695,378
6. Jeff Gordon.................................7,471,447
7. Dale Earnhardt Jr. 7,111,739
8. Denny Hamlin..............................6,607,932
9. Jeff Burton 6,439,995
10. Casey Mears 6,128,449

>> POLE WINNERS   15

1. Kurt Busch 6
   Kasey Kahne 6
3. Jeff Burton 4
4. Denny Hamlin 3
5. Greg Biffle..2
   Jeff Gordon 2
   Ryan Newman 2
   Scott Riggs 2
9. Kyle Busch 1
   David Gilliland 1
   Kevin Harvick 1
   Jimmie Johnson 1
   Elliott Sadler 1
   Boris Said 1
   Brian Vickers 1

2005 SEASON

SMOKIN' THE COMPETITION

A midseason tear helps Stewart win his second title

For a guy obsessed with racing, Tony Stewart doesn't like driving much. He once said that if he had to drive the length of a NASCAR NEXTEL Cup Series race in a regular car without listening to music or stopping for a Coke, he would "want to commit arson" when he got out of the car. And it's not just regular driving that bores him. He hates testing his racecar.

Yet it was a test early in the year at Michigan that led to the best season of Stewart's career.

The difference before and after the Michigan test was so stark, it was as if Stewart's crew chief, Greg Zipadelli, gave Stewart an entirely different car.

Before the first Michigan race, Stewart's average finish was 16.1. From that race on, it was 6.0, including a stretch in which he won five of seven races.

Stewart rode that momentum into the Chase for the NASCAR NEXTEL Cup. He finished 15th at Homestead-Miami and won his second NASCAR NEXTEL Cup Series title. Not bad for a guy who doesn't like to drive.

>> 2005 SEASON <<

Race No.	Location	Date	Winner	Car owner
1.	Daytona Beach, Fla.	Feb. 20	Jeff Gordon	Rick Hendrick
2.	Fontana, Calif.	Feb. 27	Greg Biffle	Jack Roush
3.	Las Vegas	March 13	Jimmie Johnson	Rick Hendrick
4.	Hampton, Ga.	March 20	Carl Edwards	Jack Roush
5.	Bristol, Tenn.	April 3	Kevin Harvick	Richard Childress
6.	Martinsville, Va.	April 10	Jeff Gordon	Rick Hendrick
7.	Fort Worth, Texas	April 17	Greg Biffle	Jack Roush
8.	Phoenix	April 23	Kurt Busch	Jack Roush
9.	Talladega, Ala.	May 1	Jeff Gordon	Rick Hendrick
10.	Darlington, S.C.	May 7	Greg Biffle	Jack Roush
11.	Richmond, Va.	May 14	Kasey Kahne	Ray Evernham
12.	Concord, N.C.	May 29	Jimmie Johnson	Rick Hendrick
13.	Dover, Del.	June 5	Greg Biffle	Jack Roush
14.	Pocono, Pa.	June 12	Carl Edwards	Jack Roush
15.	Brooklyn, Mich.	June 19	Greg Biffle	Jack Roush
16.	Sonoma, Calif.	June 26	Tony Stewart	Joe Gibbs
17.	Daytona Beach, Fla.	July 2	Tony Stewart	Joe Gibbs
18.	Joliet, Ill.	July 10	Dale Earnhardt Jr.	Teresa Earnhardt
19.	Loudon, N.H.	July 17	Tony Stewart	Joe Gibbs
20.	Pocono, Pa.	July 24	Kurt Busch	Jack Roush
21.	Indianapolis	Aug. 7	Tony Stewart	Joe Gibbs
22.	Watkins Glen, N.Y.	Aug. 14	Tony Stewart	Joe Gibbs
23.	Brooklyn, Mich.	Aug. 21	Jeremy Mayfield	Ray Evernham
24.	Bristol, Tenn.	Aug. 27	Matt Kenseth	Jack Roush
25.	Fontana, Calif.	Sept. 4	Kyle Busch	Rick Hendrick
26.	Richmond, Va.	Sept. 10	Kurt Busch	Jack Roush
27.	Loudon, N.H.	Sept. 18	Ryan Newman	Roger Penske
28.	Dover, Del.	Sept. 25	Jimmie Johnson	Rick Hendrick
29.	Talladega, Ala.	Oct. 2	Dale Jarrett	Robert Yates
30.	Kansas City, Kan.	Oct. 9	Mark Martin	Jack Roush
31.	Concord, N.C.	Oct. 15	Jimmie Johnson	Rick Hendrick
32.	Martinsville, Va.	Oct. 23	Jeff Gordon	Rick Hendrick
33.	Hampton, Ga.	Oct. 30	Carl Edwards	Jack Roush
34.	Fort Worth, Texas	Nov. 6	Carl Edwards	Jack Roush
35.	Phoenix	Nov. 13	Kyle Busch	Rick Hendrick
36.	Homestead, Fla.	Nov. 20	Greg Biffle	Jack Roush

>> TOP 20 PERFORMANCE CHART

Rk	Driver	Points	Starts	Poles	Wins	Top 5s	Top 10s	DNF
1.	Tony Stewart	6,533	36	3	5	17	25	1
2.	Greg Biffle	6,498	36	0	6	15	21	1
3.	Carl Edwards	6,498	36	2	4	13	18	1
4.	Mark Martin	6,428	36	0	1	12	19	2
5.	Jimmie Johnson	6,406	36	1	4	13	22	5
6.	Ryan Newman	6,359	36	8	1	8	16	3
7.	Matt Kenseth	6,352	36	2	1	12	17	4
8.	Rusty Wallace	6,140	36	0	0	8	17	0
9.	Jeremy Mayfield	6,073	36	0	1	4	9	1
10.	Kurt Busch	5,974	34	0	3	9	18	3
11.	Jeff Gordon	4,174	36	2	4	8	14	9
12.	Jamie McMurray	4,130	36	1	0	4	10	4
13.	Elliott Sadler	4,084	36	4	0	1	12	2
14.	Kevin Harvick	4,072	36	2	1	3	10	1
15.	Dale Jarrett	3,960	36	1	1	4	7	2
16.	Joe Nemechek	3,953	36	1	0	2	9	2
17.	Brian Vickers	3,847	36	1	0	5	10	4
18.	Jeff Burton	3,803	36	0	0	3	6	3
19.	Dale Earnhardt Jr.	3,780	36	0	1	7	13	6
20.	Kyle Busch	3,753	36	1	2	9	13	8

>> POINTS STANDINGS

1. Tony Stewart 6,533
2. Greg Biffle 6,498
3. Carl Edwards 6,498
4. Mark Martin 6,428
5. Jimmie Johnson 6,406
6. Ryan Newman 6,359
7. Matt Kenseth 6,352
8. Rusty Wallace 6,140
9. Jeremy Mayfield 6,073
10. Kurt Busch 5,974

>> RACE WINNERS   15

1. Greg Biffle 6
2. Tony Stewart 5
3. Carl Edwards 4
   Jeff Gordon 4
   Jimmie Johnson 4
6. Kurt Busch 3
7. Kyle Busch 2
8. Dale Earnhardt Jr. 1
   Kevin Harvick 1
   Dale Jarrett 1
   Kasey Kahne 1
   Matt Kenseth 1
   Jeremy Mayfield 1
   Mark Martin 1
   Ryan Newman 1

>> MONEY WON LEADERS

1. Tony Stewart $13,578,168
2. Greg Biffle 8,354,052
3. Jimmie Johnson 8,336,712
4. Jeff Gordon 7,930,830
5. Mark Martin 7,731,468
6. Kurt Busch 7,667,861
7. Ryan Newman 7,259,518
8. Matt Kenseth 7,034,134
9. Carl Edwards 6,893,157
10. Dale Earnhardt Jr. 6,284,577

>> POLE WINNERS   17

1. Ryan Newman 8
2. Elliott Sadler 4
3. Tony Stewart 3
4. Carl Edwards 2
   Kevin Harvick 2
   Kasey Kahne 2
   Matt Kenseth 2
   Jeff Gordon 2
9. Kyle Busch 1
   Dale Jarrett 1
   Jimmie Johnson 1
   Denny Hamlin 1
   Jamie McMurray 1
   Joe Nemechek 1
   Scott Riggs 1
   Brian Vickers 1
   Michael Waltrip 1

>> 2004 SEASON <<

Race No.	Location	Date	Winner	Car owner
1.	Daytona Beach, Fla.	Feb. 15	Dale Earnhardt Jr.	Teresa Earnhardt
2.	Rockingham, N.C.	Feb. 22	Matt Kenseth	Jack Roush
3.	Las Vegas	March 7	Matt Kenseth	Jack Roush
4.	Hampton, Ga.	March 14	Dale Earnhardt Jr.	Teresa Earnhardt
5.	Darlington, S.C.	March 21	Jimmie Johnson	Rick Hendrick
6.	Bristol, Tenn.	March 28	Kurt Busch	Jack Roush
7.	Forth Worth, Texas	April 4	Elliott Sadler	Robert Yates
8.	Martinsville, Va.	April 18	Rusty Wallace	Roger Penske
9.	Talladega, Ala.	April 25	Jeff Gordon	Rick Hendrick
10.	Fontana, Calif.	May 2	Jeff Gordon	Rick Hendrick
11.	Richmond, Va.	May 15	Dale Earnhardt Jr.	Teresa Earnhardt
12.	Concord, N.C.	May 30	Jimmie Johnson	Rick Hendrick
13.	Dover, Del.	June 6	Mark Martin	Jack Roush
14.	Long Pond, Pa.	June 13	Jimmie Johnson	Rick Hendrick
15.	Brooklyn, Mich.	June 20	Ryan Newman	Roger Penske
16.	Sonoma, Calif.	June 27	Jeff Gordon	Rick Hendrick
17.	Daytona Beach, Fla.	July 3	Jeff Gordon	Rick Hendrick
18.	Joliet, Ill.	July 11	Tony Stewart	Joe Gibbs
19.	Loudon, N.H.	July 25	Kurt Busch	Jack Roush
20.	Long Pond, Pa.	Aug. 1	Jimmie Johnson	Rick Hendrick
21.	Indianapolis	Aug. 8	Jeff Gordon	Rick Hendrick
22.	Watkins Glen, N.Y.	Aug. 15	Tony Stewart	Joe Gibbs
23.	Brooklyn, Mich.	Aug. 22	Greg Biffle	Jack Roush
24.	Bristol, Tenn.	Aug. 28	Dale Earnhardt Jr.	Teresa Earnhardt
25.	Fontana, Calif.	Sept. 5	Elliott Sadler	Robert Yates
26.	Richmond, Va.	Sept. 11	Jeremy Mayfield	Ray Evernham
27.	Loudon, N.H.	Sept. 19	Kurt Busch	Jack Roush
28.	Dover, Del.	Sept. 26	Ryan Newman	Roger Penske
29.	Talladega, Ala.	Oct. 3	Dale Earnhardt Jr.	Teresa Earnhardt
30.	Kansas City, Kan.	Oct. 10	Joe Nemechek	Nelson Bowers
31.	Concord, N.C.	Oct. 16	Jimmie Johnson	Rick Hendrick
32.	Martinsville, Va.	Oct. 24	Jimmie Johnson	Rick Hendrick
33.	Hampton, Ga.	Oct. 31	Jimmie Johnson	Rick Hendrick
34.	Phoenix	Nov. 7	Dale Earnhardt Jr.	Teresa Earnhardt
35.	Darlington, S.C.	Nov. 14	Jimmie Johnson	Rick Hendrick
36.	Homestead, Fla.	Nov. 21	Greg Biffle	Jack Roush

>> TOP 20 PERFORMANCE CHART

Rk	Driver	Points	Starts	Poles	Wins	Top 5s	Top 10s	DNF
1.	Kurt Busch	6,506	36	1	3	10	21	3
2.	Jimmie Johnson	6,498	36	1	8	20	23	7
3.	Jeff Gordon	6,490	36	6	5	16	25	4
4.	Mark Martin	6,399	36	0	1	10	15	2
5.	Dale Earnhardt Jr.	6,368	36	0	6	16	21	4
6.	Tony Stewart	6,326	36	0	2	10	19	2
7.	Ryan Newman	6,180	36	9	2	11	14	9
8.	Matt Kenseth	6,069	36	0	2	8	16	6
9.	Elliott Sadler	6,024	36	0	2	8	14	1
10.	Jeremy Mayfield	6,000	36	2	1	5	13	3
11.	Jamie McMurray	4,597	36	0	0	9	23	6
12.	Bobby Labonte	4,277	36	1	0	5	11	2
13.	Kasey Kahne	4,274	36	4	0	13	14	7
14.	Kevin Harvick	4,228	36	0	0	5	14	4
15.	Dale Jarrett	4,214	36	0	0	6	14	3
16.	Rusty Wallace	3,960	36	0	1	3	11	3
17.	Greg Biffle	3,902	36	1	2	4	8	5
18.	Jeff Burton	3,902	36	0	0	2	6	6
19.	Joe Nemechek	3,878	36	2	1	3	9	6
20.	Michael Waltrip	3,878	36	0	0	2	9	6

>> POINTS STANDINGS

1. Kurt Busch 6,506
2. Jimmie Johnson 6,498
3. Jeff Gordon 6,490
4. Mark Martin 6,399
5. Dale Earnhardt Jr. 6,368
6. Tony Stewart 6,326
7. Ryan Newman 6,180
8. Matt Kenseth 6,069
9. Elliott Sadler 6,024
10. Jeremy Mayfield 6,000

>> RACE WINNERS   13

1. Jimmie Johnson 8
2. Dale Earnhardt Jr. 6
3. Jeff Gordon 5
4. Kurt Busch..3
5. Greg Biffle 2
   Matt Kenseth 2
   Ryan Newman 2
   Elliott Sadler 2
   Tony Stewart 2
10. Mark Martin...1
   Jeremy Mayfield 1
   Joe Nemechek..1
   Rusty Wallace 1

>> MONEY WON LEADERS

1. Kurt Busch $9,661,513
2. Dale Earnhardt Jr. 8,906,860
3. Jeff Gordon 8,431,192
4. Jimmie Johnson............................8,266,761
5. Tony Stewart 7,824,927
6. Matt Kenseth 7,400,969
7. Ryan Newman 6,349,146
8. Elliott Sadler.................................6,241,034
9. Mark Martin 5,471,584
10. Kasey Kahne 5,415,611

>> POLE WINNERS   12

1. Ryan Newman 9
2. Jeff Gordon 6
3. Kasey Kahne 4
4. Jeremy Mayfield 2
   Casey Mears 2
   Joe Nemechek..2
   Brian Vickers 2
8. Greg Biffle 1
   Kurt Busch..1
   Jimmie Johnson...1
   Bobby Labonte..1
   Ricky Rudd 1

>>2003 SEASON<<

Race No.	Location	Date	Winner	Car owner
1.	Daytona Beach, Fla.	Feb. 16	Michael Waltrip	Teresa Earnhardt
2.	Rockingham, N.C.	Feb. 23	Dale Jarrett	Robert Yates
3.	Las Vegas	March 2	Matt Kenseth	Jack Roush
4.	Hampton, Ga.	March 9	Bobby Labonte	Joe Gibbs
5.	Darlington, S.C.	March 16	Ricky Craven	Cal Wells III
6.	Bristol, Tenn.	March 23	Kurt Busch	Jack Roush
7.	Forth Worth, Texas	March 30	Ryan Newman	Roger Penske
8.	Talladega, Ala.	April 6	Dale Earnhardt Jr.	Teresa Earnhardt
9.	Martinsville, Va.	April 13	Jeff Gordon	Rick Hendrick
10.	Fontana, Calif.	April 27	Kurt Busch	Jack Roush
11.	Richmond, Va.	May 3	Joe Nemechek	Rick Hendrick
12.	Concord, N.C.	May 25	Jimmie Johnson	Rick Hendrick
13.	Dover, Del.	June 1	Ryan Newman	Roger Penske
14.	Long Pond, Pa.	June 8	Tony Stewart	Joe Gibbs
15.	Brooklyn, Mich.	June 15	Kurt Busch	Jack Roush
16.	Sonoma, Calif.	June 22	Robby Gordon	Richard Childress
17.	Daytona Beach, Fla.	July 5	Greg Biffle	Jack Roush
18.	Joliet, Ill.	July 13	Ryan Newman	Roger Penske
19.	Loudon, N.H.	July 20	Jimmie Johnson	Rick Hendrick
20.	Long Pond, Pa.	July 27	Ryan Newman	Roger Penske
21.	Indianapolis	Aug. 3	Kevin Harvick	Richard Childress
22.	Watkins Glen, N.Y.	Aug. 10	Robby Gordon	Richard Childress
23.	Brooklyn, Mich.	Aug. 17	Ryan Newman	Roger Penske
24.	Bristol, Tenn.	Aug. 23	Kurt Busch	Jack Roush
25.	Darlington, S.C.	Aug. 31	Terry Labonte	Rick Hendrick
26.	Richmond, Va.	Sept. 6	Ryan Newman	Roger Penske
27.	Loudon, N.H.	Sept. 14	Jimmie Johnson	Rick Hendrick
28.	Dover, Del.	Sept. 21	Ryan Newman	Roger Penske
29.	Talladega, Ala.	Sept. 28	Michael Waltrip	Teresa Earnhardt
30.	Kansas City, Kan.	Oct. 5	Ryan Newman	Roger Penske
31.	Concord, N.C.	Oct. 11	Tony Stewart	Joe Gibbs
32.	Martinsville, Va.	Oct. 19	Jeff Gordon	Rick Hendrick
33.	Hampton, Ga.	Oct. 27	Jeff Gordon	Rick Hendrick
34.	Phoenix	Nov. 2	Dale Earnhardt Jr.	Teresa Earnhardt
35.	Rockingham, N.C.	Nov. 9	Bill Elliott	Ray Evernham
36.	Homestead, Fla.	Nov. 16	Bobby Labonte	Joe Gibbs

>>TOP 20 PERFORMANCE CHART

Rk	Driver	Points	Starts	Poles	Wins	Top 5s	Top 10s	DNF
1.	Matt Kenseth	5,022	36	0	1	11	25	3
2.	Jimmie Johnson	4,932	36	2	3	14	20	3
3.	Dale Earnhardt Jr.	4,815	36	0	2	13	21	4
4.	Jeff Gordon	4,785	36	4	3	15	20	5
5.	Kevin Harvick	4,770	36	1	1	11	18	0
6.	Ryan Newman	4,711	36	11	8	17	22	7
7.	Tony Stewart	4,549	36	1	2	12	18	5
8.	Bobby Labonte	4,377	36	4	2	12	17	5
9.	Bill Elliott	4,303	36	0	1	9	12	2
10.	Terry Labonte	4,162	36	1	1	4	9	0
11.	Kurt Busch	4,150	36	0	4	9	14	8
12.	Jeff Burton	4,109	36	0	0	3	11	4
13.	Jamie McMurray	3,965	36	1	0	5	13	4
14.	Rusty Wallace	3,950	36	0	0	2	12	4
15.	Michael Waltrip	3,934	36	0	2	8	11	6
16.	Robby Gordon	3,856	36	0	2	4	10	2
17.	Mark Martin	3,769	36	0	0	5	10	7
18.	Sterling Marlin	3,745	36	0	0	0	11	8
19.	Jeremy Mayfield	3,736	36	1	0	4	12	6
20.	Greg Biffle	3,696	35	0	1	3	6	6

>>POINTS STANDINGS

1. Matt Kenseth 5,022
2. Jimmie Johnson.......................4,932
3. Dale Earnhardt Jr......................4,815
4. Jeff Gordon 4,785
5. Kevin Harvick 4,770
6. Ryan Newman 4,711
7. Tony Stewart 4,549
8. Bobby Labonte 4,377
9. Bill Elliott 4,303
10. Terry Labonte 4,162

>>RACE WINNERS   17

1. Ryan Newman................................8
2. Kurt Busch...................................4
3. Jeff Gordon 3
   Jimmie Johnson 3
5. Dale Earnhardt Jr...........................2
   Robby Gordon 2
   Bobby Labonte 2
   Tony Stewart 2
   Michael Waltrip 2
10. Greg Biffle 1
   Ricky Craven 1
   Bill Elliott 1
   Kevin Harvick 1
   Dale Jarrett 1
   Matt Kenseth 1
   Terry Labonte 1
   Joe Nemechek 1

>>MONEY WON LEADERS

1. Matt Kenseth.................$9,422,764
2. Jimmie Johnson 7,745,530
3. Dale Earnhardt Jr. 6,880,807
4. Jeff Gordon 6,622,002
5. Kevin Harvick 6,237,119
6. Tony Stewart 6,131,633
7. Ryan Newman.................6,100,877
8. Bobby Labonte 5,505,018
9. Bill Elliott......................5,008,530
10. Terry Labonte 4,283,625

>>POLE WINNERS   15

1. Ryan Newman...............................11
2. Jeff Gordon 4
   Bobby Labonte 4
4. Jimmie Johnson 2
   Steve Park.....................................2
   Elliott Sadler 2
7. Dave Blaney 1
   Jeff Green 1
   Kevin Harvick 1
   Terry Labonte 1
   Jeremy Mayfield 1
   Jamie McMurray 1
   Boris Said 1
   Mike Skinner 1
   Tony Stewart 1

BY A NOSE

Craven and Busch duel to the closest finish in NASCAR history

When the guy who won doesn't even realize it, you know the finish is close. In fact, at Darlington on March 16, 2003, it was the closest in NASCAR history.

After Ricky Craven and Kurt Busch took the checkered flag nearly simultaneously, Craven radioed to his crew members to find out whether to celebrate or cry. They didn't know, either. Only when Craven saw his number atop the scoring pole did he realize he'd won.

The margin: .002 seconds. You could watch the TV replay 100 times and never see who won.

Busch and Craven beat on each other over two laps, and for the final run to the checkered flag, they were rubbing against each other, trying to will the other to yield just the slightest bit. Neither did.

"This is exactly what you dream of," Craven said. "It's the perfect way to win a race at the perfect track."

Though the two nearly wrecked each other, there were no hard feelings. Busch visited Craven in victory lane.

"It's a bit stale that I was on the wrong end of it, but it was just an awesome duel," Busch said. "This is something where we'll slap high-fives and drink a couple of beers to later on."

>>2002 SEASON<<

Race No.	Location	Date	Winner	Car owner
1.	Daytona Beach, Fla.	Feb. 17	Ward Burton	Bill Davis
2.	Rockingham, N.C.	Feb. 24	Matt Kenseth	Jack Roush
3.	Las Vegas	March 3	Sterling Marlin	Chip Ganassi
4.	Hampton, Ga.	March 10	Tony Stewart	Joe Gibbs
5.	Darlington, S.C.	March 17	Sterling Marlin	Chip Ganassi
6.	Bristol, Tenn.	March 24	Kurt Busch	Jack Roush
7.	Forth Worth, Texas	April 7	Matt Kenseth	Jack Roush
8.	Martinsville, Va.	April 14	Bobby Labonte	Joe Gibbs
9.	Talladega, Ala.	April 21	Dale Earnhardt Jr.	Teresa Earnhardt
10.	Fontana, Calif.	April 28	Jimmie Johnson	Rick Hendrick
11.	Richmond, Va.	May 4	Tony Stewart	Joe Gibbs
12.	Concord, N.C.	May 26	Mark Martin	Jack Roush
13.	Dover, Del.	June 2	Jimmie Johnson	Rick Hendrick
14.	Long Pond, Pa.	June 9	Dale Jarrett	Robert Yates
15.	Brooklyn, Mich.	June 16	Matt Kenseth	Jack Roush
16.	Sonoma, Calif.	June 23	Ricky Rudd	Robert Yates
17.	Daytona Beach, Fla.	July 6	Michael Waltrip	Teresa Earnhardt
18.	Joliet, Ill.	July 14	Kevin Harvick	Richard Childress
19.	Loudon, N.H.	July 21	Ward Burton	Bill Davis
20.	Long Pond, Pa.	July 28	Bill Elliott	Ray Evernham
21.	Indianapolis	Aug. 4	Bill Elliott	Ray Evernham
22.	Watkins Glen, N.Y.	Aug. 11	Tony Stewart	Joe Gibbs
23.	Brooklyn, Mich.	Aug. 18	Dale Jarrett	Robert Yates
24.	Bristol, Tenn.	Aug. 24	Jeff Gordon	Rick Hendrick
25.	Darlington, S.C.	Sept. 1	Jeff Gordon	Rick Hendrick
26.	Richmond, Va.	Sept. 7	Matt Kenseth	Jack Roush
27.	Loudon, N.H.	Sept. 15	Ryan Newman	Roger Penske
28.	Dover, Del.	Sept. 22	Jimmie Johnson	Rick Hendrick
29.	Kansas City, Kan.	Sept. 29	Jeff Gordon	Rick Hendrick
30.	Talladega, Ala.	Oct. 6	Dale Earnhardt Jr.	Teresa Earnhardt
31.	Concord, N.C.	Oct. 13	Jamie McMurray	Chip Ganassi
32.	Martinsville, Va.	Oct. 20	Kurt Busch	Jack Roush
33.	Hampton, Ga.	Oct. 27	Kurt Busch	Jack Roush
34.	Rockingham, N.C.	Nov. 3	Johnny Benson	Nelson Bowers
35.	Phoenix	Nov. 10	Matt Kenseth	Jack Roush
36.	Homestead, Fla.	Nov. 17	Kurt Busch	Jack Roush

>>TOP 20 PERFORMANCE CHART

Rk	Driver	Points	Starts	Poles	Wins	Top 5s	Top 10s	DNF
1.	Tony Stewart	4,800	36	2	3	15	21	8
2.	Mark Martin	4,762	36	0	1	12	22	7
3.	Kurt Busch	4,641	36	1	4	12	20	8
4.	Jeff Gordon	4,607	36	3	3	13	20	7
5.	Jimmie Johnson	4,600	36	4	3	6	21	6
6.	Ryan Newman	4,593	36	6	1	14	22	8
7.	Rusty Wallace	4,574	36	1	0	7	17	5
8.	Matt Kenseth	4,432	36	1	5	11	19	7
9.	Dale Jarrett	4,415	36	1	2	10	18	8
10.	Ricky Rudd	4,323	36	1	1	8	12	8
11.	Dale Earnhardt Jr.	4,270	36	2	2	11	16	7
12.	Jeff Burton	4,259	36	0	0	5	14	7
13.	Bill Elliott	4,158	36	4	2	6	13	8
14.	Michael Waltrip	3,985	36	0	1	4	10	7
15.	Ricky Craven	3,888	36	2	0	3	9	8
16.	Bobby Labonte	3,810	36	0	1	5	7	8
17.	Jeff Green	3,704	36	0	0	4	6	6
18.	Sterling Marlin	3,703	29	0	2	8	14	6
19.	Dave Blaney	3,670	36	0	0	0	5	6
20.	Robby Gordon	3,632	36	0	0	1	5	8

>>POINTS STANDINGS

1. Tony Stewart 4,800
2. Mark Martin 4,762
3. Kurt Busch 4,641
4. Jeff Gordon 4,607
5. Jimmie Johnson 4,600
6. Ryan Newman 4,593
7. Rusty Wallace 4,574
8. Matt Kenseth 4,432
9. Dale Jarrett 4,415
10. Ricky Rudd..................................4,323

>>RACE WINNERS   18

1. Matt Kenseth 5
2. Kurt Busch...4
3. Jeff Gordon 3
   Jimmie Johnson 3
   Tony Stewart 3
6. Ward Burton 2
   Dale Earnhardt Jr. 2
   Bill Elliott...2
   Dale Jarrett 2
   Sterling Marlin 2
11. Johnny Benson 1
   Kevin Harvick 1
   Bobby Labonte 1
   Mark Martin 1
   Jamie McMurray 1
   Ryan Newman 1
   Ricky Rudd 1
   Michael Waltrip 1

>>MONEY WON LEADERS

1. Tony Stewart $9,163,761
2. Mark Martin......................7,004,893
3. Jeff Gordon 6,154,475
4. Ryan Newman 5,346,651
5. Kurt Busch........................5,105,394
6. Dale Earnhardt Jr. 4,970,034
7. Ward Burton 4,899,884
8. Rusty Wallace 4,785,134
9. Matt Kenseth 4,514,203
10. Ricky Rudd 4,444,614

>>POLE WINNERS   15

1. Ryan Newman.....................................6
2. Bill Elliott...4
   Jimmie Johnson 4
4. Jeff Gordon 3
5. Ricky Craven 2
   Dale Earnhardt Jr. 2
   Tony Stewart 2
8. Todd Bodine 1
   Ward Burton 1
   Kurt Busch..1
   Kevin Harvick 1
   Dale Jarrett 1
   Matt Kenseth 1
   Ricky Rudd 1
   Rusty Wallace 1

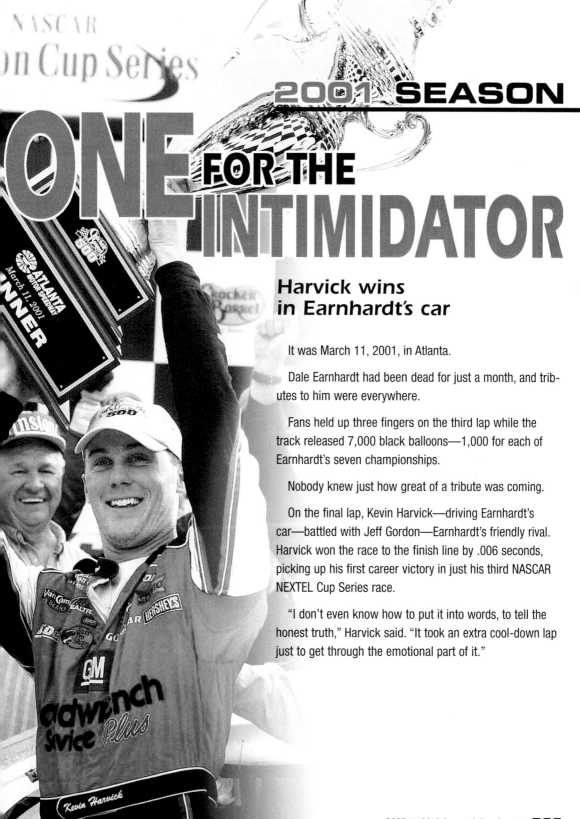

ONE FOR THE INTIMIDATOR

Harvick wins in Earnhardt's car

It was March 11, 2001, in Atlanta.

Dale Earnhardt had been dead for just a month, and tributes to him were everywhere.

Fans held up three fingers on the third lap while the track released 7,000 black balloons—1,000 for each of Earnhardt's seven championships.

Nobody knew just how great of a tribute was coming.

On the final lap, Kevin Harvick—driving Earnhardt's car—battled with Jeff Gordon—Earnhardt's friendly rival. Harvick won the race to the finish line by .006 seconds, picking up his first career victory in just his third NASCAR NEXTEL Cup Series race.

"I don't even know how to put it into words, to tell the honest truth," Harvick said. "It took an extra cool-down lap just to get through the emotional part of it."

>>> 2001 SEASON <<<

Race No.	Location	Date	Winner	Car owner
1.	Daytona Beach, Fla.	Feb. 18	Michael Waltrip	Teresa Earnhardt
2.	Rockingham, N.C.	Feb. 25	Steve Park	Teresa Earnhardt
3.	Las Vegas	March 4	Jeff Gordon	Rick Hendrick
4.	Atlanta	March 11	Kevin Harvick	Richard Childress
5.	Darlington, S.C.	March 18	Dale Jarrett	Robert Yates
6.	Bristol, Tenn.	March 25	Elliott Sadler	Glen Wood
7.	Forth Worth, Texas	April 1	Dale Jarrett	Robert Yates
8.	Martinsville, Va.	April 8	Dale Jarrett	Robert Yates
9.	Talladega, Ala.	April 22	Bobby Hamilton	Andy Petree
10.	Los Angeles	April 29	Rusty Wallace	Roger Penske
11.	Richmond, Va.	May 5	Tony Stewart	Joe Gibbs
12.	Concord, N.C.	May 27	Jeff Burton	Jack Roush
13.	Dover, Del.	June 3	Jeff Gordon	Rick Hendrick
14.	Brooklyn, Mich.	June 10	Jeff Gordon	Rick Hendrick
15.	Long Pond, Pa.	June 17	Ricky Rudd	Robert Yates
16.	Sonoma, Calif.	June 24	Tony Stewart	Joe Gibbs
17.	Daytona Beach, Fla.	July 7	Dale Earnhardt Jr.	Teresa Earnhardt
18.	Joliet, Ill.	July 15	Kevin Harvick	Richard Childress
19.	Loudon, N.H.	July 22	Dale Jarrett	Robert Yates
20.	Long Pond, Pa.	July 29	Bobby Labonte	Joe Gibbs
21.	Indianapolis	Aug. 5	Jeff Gordon	Rick Hendrick
22.	Watkins Glen, N.Y.	Aug. 12	Jeff Gordon	Rick Hendrick
23.	Brooklyn, Mich.	Aug. 19	Sterling Marlin	Chip Ganassi
24.	Bristol, Tenn.	Aug. 25	Tony Stewart	Joe Gibbs
25.	Darlington, S.C.	Sept. 2	Ward Burton	Bill Davis
26.	Richmond, Va.	Sept. 8	Ricky Rudd	Robert Yates
27.	Dover, Del.	Sept. 23	Dale Earnhardt Jr.	Teresa Earnhardt
28.	Kansas City, Kan.	Sept. 30	Jeff Gordon	Rick Hendrick
29.	Concord, N.C.	Oct. 7	Sterling Marlin	Chip Ganassi
30.	Martinsville, Va.	Oct. 14	Ricky Craven	Cal Wells III
31.	Talladega, Ala.	Oct. 21	Dale Earnhardt Jr.	Teresa Earnhardt
32.	Phoenix	Oct. 28	Jeff Burton	Jack Roush
33.	Rockingham, N.C.	Nov. 4	Joe Nemechek	Andy Petree
34.	Miami	Nov. 11	Bill Elliott	Ray Evernham
35.	Atlanta	Nov. 18	Bobby Labonte	Joe Gibbs
36.	Loudon, N.H.	Nov. 23	Robby Gordon	Richard Childress

>> TOP 20 PERFORMANCE CHART

Rk	Driver	Points	Starts	Poles	Wins	Top 5s	Top 10s	DNF
1.	Jeff Gordon	5,112	36	6	6	18	24	2
2.	Tony Stewart	4,763	36	0	3	15	22	4
3.	Sterling Marlin	4,741	36	1	2	12	20	2
4.	Ricky Rudd	4,706	36	1	2	14	22	4
5.	Dale Jarrett	4,612	36	4	4	12	19	4
6.	Bobby Labonte	4,561	36	1	2	9	20	6
7.	Rusty Wallace	4,481	36	0	1	8	14	3
8.	Dale Earnhardt Jr.	4,460	36	2	3	9	15	4
9.	Kevin Harvick	4,406	35	0	2	6	16	1
10.	Jeff Burton	4,394	36	0	2	8	16	1
11.	Johnny Benson	4,152	36	0	0	6	14	8
12.	Mark Martin	4,095	36	2	0	3	15	4
13.	Matt Kenseth	3,982	36	0	0	4	9	5
14.	Ward Burton	3,846	36	0	1	6	10	9
15.	Bill Elliott	3,824	36	2	1	5	9	2
16.	Jimmy Spencer	3,782	36	2	0	3	8	7
17.	Jerry Nadeau	3,675	36	0	0	4	10	8
18.	Bobby Hamilton	3,575	36	0	1	3	7	0
19.	Ken Schrader	3,480	36	0	0	0	5	2
20.	Elliott Sadler	3,471	36	0	1	2	2	2

>> POINTS STANDINGS

1. Jeff Gordon 5,112
2. Tony Stewart 4,763
3. Sterling Marlin 4,741
4. Ricky Rudd..................4,706
5. Dale Jarrett 4,612
6. Bobby Labonte 4,561
7. Rusty Wallace 4,481
8. Dale Earnhardt Jr. 4,460
9. Kevin Harvick 4,406
10. Jeff Burton 4,394

>> RACE WINNERS 19

1. Jeff Gordon 6
2. Dale Jarrett 4
3. Dale Earnhardt Jr. 3
   Tony Stewart 3
5. Jeff Burton 2
   Kevin Harvick 2
   Bobby Labonte 2
   Sterling Marlin................2
   Ricky Rudd 2
10. Ward Burton 1
   Ricky Craven 1
   Bill Elliott 1
   Robby Gordon 1
   Bobby Hamilton 1
   Joe Nemechek 1
   Steve Park 1
   Elliott Sadler 1
   Rusty Wallace 1
   Michael Waltrip 1

>> MONEY WON LEADERS

1. Jeff Gordon $10,879,757
2. Dale Earnhardt Jr. 5,827,542
3. Dale Jarrett 5,377,742
4. Tony Stewart...........4,941,463
5. Ricky Rudd 4,828,027
6. Rusty Wallace 4,788,652
7. Bobby Labonte 4,786,779
8. Sterling Marlin.........4,517,634
9. Kevin Harvick 4,302,202
10. Jeff Burton 4,230,737

>> POLE WINNERS 18

1. Jeff Gordon 6
2. Dale Jarrett 4
3. Todd Bodine 3
4. Stacy Compton 2
   Dale Earnhardt Jr. 2
   Bill Elliott 2
   Mark Martin 2
   Jimmy Spencer 2
9. Casey Atwood 1
   Kurt Busch 1
   Ricky Craven 1
   Jeff Green 1
   Bobby Labonte 1
   Jason Leffler 1
   Sterling Marlin 1
   Ryan Newman 1
   Ricky Rudd 1
   Kenny Wallace 1

Race No.	Location	Date	Winner	Car owner
1.	Daytona Beach, Fla,	Feb. 20	Dale Jarrett	Robert Yates
2.	Rockingham, N.C.	Feb. 27	Bobby Labonte	Joe Gibbs
3.	Las Vegas	March 5	Jeff Burton	Jack Roush
4.	Hampton, Ga.	March 12	Dale Earnhardt	Richard Childress
5.	Darlington, S.C.	March 19	Ward Burton	Bill Davis
6.	Bristol, Tenn.	March 26	Rusty Wallace	Roger Penske
7.	Forth Worth, Texas	April 2	Dale Earnhardt Jr.	Dale Earnhardt
8.	Martinsville, Va.	April 9	Mark Martin	Jack Roush
9.	Talladega, Ala.	April 16	Jeff Gordon	Rick Hendrick
10.	Fontana, Calif.	April 30	Jeremy Mayfield	Michael Kranefuss
11.	Richmond, Va.	May 6	Dale Earnhardt Jr.	Dale Earnhardt
12.	Concord, N.C.	May 28	Matt Kenseth	Mark Martin
13.	Dover, Del.	June 4	Tony Stewart	Joe Gibbs
14.	Brooklyn, Mich.	June 11	Tony Stewart	Joe Gibbs
15.	Long Pond, Pa.	June 19	Jeremy Mayfield	Michael Kranefuss
16.	Sonoma, Calif.	June 25	Jeff Gordon	Rick Hendrick
17.	Daytona Beach, Fla.	July 1	Jeff Burton	Jack Roush
18.	Loudon, N.H.	July 9	Tony Stewart	Joe Gibbs
19.	Long Pond, Pa.	July 23	Rusty Wallace	Roger Penske
20.	Indianapolis	Aug. 5	Bobby Labonte	Joe Gibbs
21.	Watkins Glen, N.Y.	Aug. 13	Steve Park	Dale Earnhardt
22.	Brooklyn, Mich.	Aug. 20	Rusty Wallace	Roger Penske
23.	Bristol, Tenn.	Aug. 26	Rusty Wallace	Roger Penske
24.	Darlington, S.C.	Sept. 3	Bobby Labonte	Joe Gibbs
25.	Richmond, Va.	Sept. 9	Jeff Gordon	Rick Hendrick
26.	Loudon, N.H.	Sept. 17	Jeff Burton	Robert Corn
27.	Dover, Del.	Sept. 24	Tony Stewart	Joe Gibbs
28.	Martinsville, Va.	Oct. 1	Tony Stewart	Joe Gibbs
29.	Concord, N.C.	Oct. 8	Bobby Labonte	Joe Gibbs
30.	Talladega, Ala.	Oct. 15	Dale Earnhardt	Richard Childress
31.	Rockingham, N.C.	Oct. 22	Dale Jarrett	Robert Yates
32.	Phoenix	Nov. 5	Jeff Burton	Jack Roush
33.	Homestead, Fla.	Nov. 12	Tony Stewart	Joe Gibbs
34.	Hampton, Ga.	Nov. 20	Jerry Nadeau	Rick Hendrick

>> TOP 20 PERFORMANCE CHART

Rk	Driver	Points	Starts	Poles	Wins	Top 5s	Top 10s	DNF
1.	Bobby Labonte	5,130	34	2	4	19	24	0
2.	Dale Earnhardt	4,865	34	0	2	13	24	0
3.	Jeff Burton	4,836	34	1	4	15	22	2
4.	Dale Jarrett	4,684	34	3	2	15	24	2
5.	Ricky Rudd	4,575	34	2	0	12	19	1
6.	Tony Stewart	4,570	34	2	6	12	23	5
7.	Rusty Wallace	4,544	34	9	4	12	20	3
8.	Mark Martin	4,410	34	0	1	13	20	6
9.	Jeff Gordon	4,361	34	3	3	11	22	2
10.	Ward Burton	4,152	34	0	1	4	17	4
11.	Steve Park	3,934	34	2	1	6	13	4
12.	Mike Skinner	3,898	34	1	0	1	11	2
13.	Johnny Benson	3,716	33	0	0	3	7	3
14.	Matt Kenseth	3,711	34	0	1	4	11	5
15.	Joe Nemechek	3,534	34	1	0	3	9	6
16.	Dale Earnhardt Jr.	3,516	34	2	2	3	5	7
17.	Terry Labonte	3,433	32	1	0	3	6	3
18.	Ken Schrader	3,398	34	0	0	0	2	2
19.	Sterling Marlin	3,363	34	0	0	1	7	4
20.	Jerry Nadeau	3,273	34	0	1	3	5	9

>> POINTS STANDINGS

1. Bobby Labonte 5,130
2. Dale Earnhardt 4,865
3. Jeff Burton 4,836
4. Dale Jarrett..................................4,684
5. Ricky Rudd 4,575
6. Tony Stewart 4,570
7. Rusty Wallace 4,544
8. Mark Martin 4,410
9. Jeff Gordon..................................4,361
10. Ward Burton 4,152

>> RACE WINNERS   14

1. Tony Stewart 6
2. Jeff Burton 4
   Bobby Labonte...................................4
   Rusty Wallace 4
5. Jeff Gordon 3
6. Dale Earnhardt....................................2
   Dale Earnhardt Jr. 2
   Dale Jarrett 2
   Jeremy Mayfield 2
10. Ward Burton 1
   Matt Kenseth 1
   Mark Martin 1
   Jerry Nadeau 1
   Steve Park 1

>> MONEY WON LEADERS

1. Bobby Labonte...................$7,361,386
2. Jeff Burton............................5,959,439
3. Dale Jarrett...........................5,934,475
4. Dale Earnhardt.....................4,918,886
5. Tony Stewart 3,642,348
6. Rusty Wallace 3,621,468
7. Mark Martin 3,098,874
8. Jeff Gordon 3,001,144
9. Ricky Rudd 2,914,970
10. Dale Earnhardt Jr. 2,801,880

>> POLE WINNERS   13

1. Rusty Wallace 9
2. Jeremy Mayfield 4
3. Jeff Gordon 3
   Dale Jarrett 3
5. Dale Earnhardt Jr. 2
   Bobby Labonte...................................2
   Steve Park 2
   Ricky Rudd 2
   Tony Stewart 2
10. Jeff Burton..1
   Terry Labonte 1
   Joe Nemechek 1
   Mike Skinner 1

>> 1999 SEASON <<

Race No.	Location	Date	Winner	Car owner
1.	Daytona Beach, Fla.	Feb. 14	Jeff Gordon	Rick Hendrick
2.	Rockingham, N.C.	Feb. 21	Mark Martin	Jack Roush
3.	Las Vegas	March 7	Jeff Burton	Jack Roush
4.	Hampton, Ga.	March 14	Jeff Gordon	Rick Hendrick
5.	Darlington, S.C.	March 21	Jeff Burton	Jack Roush
6.	Forth Worth, Texas	March 28	Terry Labonte	Rick Hendrick
7.	Bristol, Tenn.	April 11	Rusty Wallace	Roger Penske
8.	Martinsville, Va.	April 18	John Andretti	Richard Petty
9.	Talladega, Ala.	April 25	Dale Earnhardt	Richard Childress
10.	Fontana, Calif.	May 2	Jeff Gordon	Rick Hendrick
11.	Richmond, Va.	May 15	Dale Jarrett	Robert Yates
12.	Concord, N.C.	May 30	Jeff Burton	Rick Hendrick
13.	Dover, Del.	June 6	Bobby Labonte	Joe Gibbs
14.	Brooklyn, Mich.	June 13	Dale Jarrett	Robert Yates
15.	Long Pond, Pa.	June 20	Bobby Labonte	Joe Gibbs
16.	Sonoma, Calif.	June 27	Jeff Gordon	Rick Hendrick
17.	Daytona Beach, Fla.	July 3	Dale Jarrett	Robert Yates
18.	Loudon, N.H.	July 11	Jeff Burton	Jack Roush
19.	Long Pond, Pa.	July 25	Bobby Labonte	Joe Gibbs
20.	Indianapolis	Aug. 8	Dale Jarrett	Robert Yates
21.	Watkins Glen, N.Y.	Aug. 15	Jeff Gordon	Rick Hendrick
22.	Brooklyn, Mich.	Aug. 22	Bobby Labonte	Joe Gibbs
23.	Bristol, Tenn.	Aug. 28	Dale Earnhardt	Richard Childress
24.	Darlington, S.C.	Sept. 5	Jeff Burton	Jack Roush
25.	Richmond, Va.	Sept. 11	Tony Stewart	Joe Gibbs
26.	Loudon, N.H.	Sept. 19	Joe Nemechek	Felix Sabates
27.	Dover, Del.	Sept. 26	Mark Martin	Jack Roush
28.	Martinsville, Va.	Oct. 3	Jeff Gordon	Rick Hendrick
29.	Concord, N.C.	Oct. 11	Jeff Gordon	Rick Hendrick
30.	Talladega, Ala.	Oct. 17	Dale Earnhardt	Richard Childress
31.	Rockingham, N.C.	Oct. 24	Jeff Burton	Jack Roush
32.	Phoenix	Nov. 7	Tony Stewart	Joe Gibbs
33.	Homestead, Fla.	Nov. 14	Tony Stewart	Joe Gibbs
34.	Hampton, Ga.	Nov. 21	Bobby Labonte	Joe Gibbs

>> POINTS STANDINGS

1.	Dale Jarrett	5,262
2.	Bobby Labonte	5,061
3.	Mark Martin	4,943
4.	Tony Stewart	4,774
5.	Jeff Burton	4,733
6.	Jeff Gordon	4,620
7.	Dale Earnhardt	4,492
8.	Rusty Wallace	4,155
9.	Ward Burton	4,062
10.	Mike Skinner	4,003

>> RACE WINNERS   11

1.	Jeff Gordon	7
2.	Jeff Burton	6
3.	Bobby Labonte	5
4.	Dale Jarrett	4
5.	Dale Earnhardt	3
	Tony Stewart	3
7.	Mark Martin	2
8.	John Andretti	1
	Terry Labonte	1
	Joe Nemechek	1
	Rusty Wallace	1

>> MONEY WON LEADERS

1.	Dale Jarrett	$6,649,596
2.	Jeff Gordon	5,858,633
3.	Jeff Burton	5,725,399
4.	Bobby Labonte	4,763,615
5.	Mark Martin	3,509,744
6.	Tony Stewart	3,190,149
7.	Dale Earnhardt	3,048,236
8.	Mike Skinner	2,499,877
9.	Terry Labonte	2,475,365
10.	Rusty Wallace	2,454,050

>> TOP 20 PERFORMANCE CHART

Rk	Driver	Points	Starts	Poles	Wins	Top 5s	Top 10s	DNF
1.	Dale Jarrett	5,262	34	0	4	24	29	1
2.	Bobby Labonte	5,061	34	5	5	23	26	1
3.	Mark Martin	4,943	34	1	2	19	26	3
4.	Tony Stewart	4,774	34	2	3	12	21	1
5.	Jeff Burton	4,733	34	0	6	18	23	3
6.	Jeff Gordon	4,620	34	7	7	18	21	7
7.	Dale Earnhardt	4,492	34	0	3	7	21	3
8.	Rusty Wallace	4,155	34	4	1	7	16	3
9.	Ward Burton	4,062	34	1	0	6	16	3
10.	Mike Skinner	4,003	34	2	0	5	14	1
11.	Jeremy Mayfield	3,743	34	0	0	5	12	4
12.	Terry Labonte	3,580	34	0	1	1	7	6
13.	Bobby Hamilton	3,564	34	0	0	1	10	3
14.	Steve Park	3,481	34	0	0	0	5	4
15.	Ken Schrader	3,479	34	1	0	0	6	1
16.	Sterling Marlin	3,397	34	1	0	2	5	3
17.	John Andretti	3,394	34	1	1	3	10	10
18.	Wally Dallenbach Jr	3,367	34	0	0	1	6	5
19.	Kenny Irwin	3,338	34	2	0	2	6	5
20.	Jimmy Spencer	3,312	34	0	0	2	4	6

>> POLE WINNERS   15

1.	Jeff Gordon	7
2.	Bobby Labonte	5
3.	Rusty Wallace	4
4.	Joe Nemechek	3
5.	Kenny Irwin	2
	Mike Skinner	2
	Tony Stewart	2
8.	John Andretti	1
	Ward Burton	1
	David Green	1
	Kevin Lepage	1
	Sterling Marlin	1
	Mark Martin	1
	Ricky Rudd	1
	Ken Schrader	1

>> 1998 SEASON <<

Race No.	Location	Date	Winner	Car owner
1.	Daytona Beach, Fla.	Feb. 15	Dale Earnhardt	Richard Childress
2.	Rockingham, N.C.	Feb. 22	Jeff Gordon	Rick Hendrick
3.	Las Vegas	March 1	Mark Martin	Jack Roush
4.	Hampton, Ga.	March 9	Bobby Labonte	Joe Gibbs
5.	Darlington, S.C.	March 22	Dale Jarrett	Robert Yates
6.	Bristol, Tenn.	March 29	Jeff Gordon	Rick Hendrick
7.	Forth Worth, Texas	April 5	Mark Martin	Jack Roush
8.	Martinsville, Va.	April 20	Bobby Hamilton	Larry McClure
9.	Talladega, Ala.	April 26	Bobby Labonte	Joe Gibbs
10.	Fontana, Calif.	May 3	Mark Martin	Jack Roush
11.	Concord, N.C.	May 24	Jeff Gordon	Rick Hendrick
12.	Dover, Del.	May 31	Dale Jarrett	Robert Yates
13.	Richmond, Va.	June 6	Terry Labonte	Rick Hendrick
14.	Brooklyn, Mich.	June 14	Mark Martin	Jack Roush
15.	Long Pond, Pa.	June 21	Jeremy Mayfield	Michael Kranefuss
16.	Sonoma, Calif.	June 28	Jeff Gordon	Rick Hendrick
17.	Loudon, N.H.	July 12	Jeff Burton	Jack Roush
18.	Long Pond, Pa.	July 26	Jeff Gordon	Rick Hendrick
19.	Indianapolis	Aug. 1	Jeff Gordon	Rick Hendrick
20.	Watkins Glen, N.Y.	Aug. 9	Jeff Gordon	Rick Hendrick
21.	Brooklyn, Mich.	Aug. 16	Jeff Gordon	Rick Hendrick
22.	Bristol, Tenn.	Aug. 22	Mark Martin	Jack Roush
23.	Loudon, N.H.	Aug. 30	Jeff Gordon	Rick Hendrick
24.	Darlington, S.C.	Sept. 6	Jeff Gordon	Rick Hendrick
25.	Richmond, Va.	Sept. 12	Jeff Burton	Jack Roush
26.	Dover, Del.	Sept. 20	Mark Martin	Jack Roush
27.	Martinsville, Va.	Sept. 27	Ricky Rudd	Ricky Rudd
28.	Concord, N.C.	Oct. 4	Mark Martin	Jack Roush
29.	Talladega, Ala.	Oct. 11	Dale Jarrett	Robert Yates
30.	Daytona Beach, Fla.	Oct. 17	Jeff Gordon	Rick Hendrick
31.	Phoenix	Oct. 25	Rusty Wallace	Roger Penske
32.	Rockingham, N.C.	Nov. 1	Jeff Gordon	Rick Hendrick
33.	Hampton, Ga.	Nov. 8	Jeff Gordon	Rick Hendrick

>> TOP 20 PERFORMANCE CHART

Rk	Driver	Points	Starts	Poles	Wins	Top 5s	Top 10s	DNF
1.	Jeff Gordon	5,328	33	7	13	26	28	2
2.	Mark Martin	4,964	33	3	7	22	26	1
3.	Dale Jarrett	4,619	33	2	3	19	22	3
4.	Rusty Wallace	4,501	33	4	1	15	21	2
5.	Jeff Burton	4,415	33	0	2	18	23	4
6.	Bobby Labonte	4,180	33	3	2	11	18	6
7.	Jeremy Mayfield	4,157	33	1	1	12	16	2
8.	Dale Earnhardt	3,928	33	0	1	5	13	3
9.	Terry Labonte	3,901	33	0	1	5	15	4
10.	Bobby Hamilton	3,786	33	1	1	3	8	1
11.	John Andretti	3,682	33	1	0	3	10	5
12.	Ken Schrader	3,675	33	2	0	3	11	5
13.	Sterling Marlin	3,530	32	0	0	0	6	1
14.	Jimmy Spencer	3,464	31	0	0	3	8	2
15.	Chad Little	3,423	32	0	0	1	7	7
16.	Ward Burton	3,352	33	2	0	1	5	4
17.	Michael Waltrip	3,340	32	0	0	0	5	3
18.	Bill Elliott	3,305	32	0	0	0	5	7
19.	Ernie Irvan	3,262	30	3	0	0	11	3
20.	Johnny Benson	3,160	32	0	0	3	10	5

>> POINTS STANDINGS

1. Jeff Gordon 5,328
2. Mark Martin 4,964
3. Dale Jarrett 4,619
4. Rusty Wallace 4,501
5. Jeff Burton 4,415
6. Bobby Labonte 4,180
7. Jeremy Mayfield 4,157
8. Dale Earnhardt 3,928
9. Terry Labonte 3,901
10. Bobby Hamilton 3,786

>> RACE WINNERS   11

1. Jeff Gordon 13
2. Mark Martin 7
3. Dale Jarrett 3
4. Jeff Burton.....................................2
   Bobby Labonte...............................2
6. Dale Earnhardt 1
   Bobby Hamilton 1
   Terry Labonte 1
   Jeremy Mayfield 1
   Ricky Rudd 1
   Rusty Wallace 1

>> MONEY WON LEADERS

1. Jeff Gordon $9,306,584
2. Mark Martin......................4,309,006
3. Dale Jarrett 4,019,657
4. Dale Earnhardt.................2,990,749
5. Bobby Labonte.................2,980,052
6. Rusty Wallace..................2,667,889
7. Jeff Burton......................2,626,987
8. Jeremy Mayfield 2,332,034
9. Bobby Hamilton 2,089,566
10. Terry Labonte..................2,054,163

>> POLE WINNERS   15

1. Jeff Gordon 7
2. Rusty Wallace 4
3. Ernie Irvan 3
   Bobby Labonte...............................3
   Mark Martin....................................3
6. Ward Burton 2
   Dale Jarrett.....................................2
   Ken Schrader..................................2
9. John Andretti 1
   Derrike Cope 1
   Ricky Craven 1
   Bobby Hamilton 1
   Kenny Irwin 1
   Rick Mast 1
   Jeremy Mayfield 1

>> 1997 SEASON <<

Race No.	Location	Date	Winner	Car owner
1.	Daytona Beach, Fla.	Feb. 16	Jeff Gordon	Rick Hendrick
2.	Rockingham, N.C.	Feb. 23	Jeff Gordon	Rick Hendrick
3.	Richmond, Va.	March 2	Rusty Wallace	Roger Penske
4.	Hampton, Ga.	March 9	Dale Jarrett	Robert Yates
5.	Darlington, S.C.	March 23	Dale Jarrett	Robert Yates
6.	Forth Worth, Texas	April 6	Jeff Burton	Jack Roush
7.	Bristol, Tenn.	April 13	Jeff Gordon	Rick Hendrick
8.	Martinsville, Va.	April 20	Jeff Gordon	Rick Hendrick
9.	Sonoma, Calif.	May 5	Mark Martin	Jack Roush
10.	Talladega, Ala.	May 10	Mark Martin	Jack Roush
11.	Concord, N.C.	May 25	Jeff Gordon	Rick Hendrick
12.	Dover, Del.	June 1	Ricky Rudd	Ricky Rudd
13.	Long Pond, Pa.	June 8	Jeff Gordon	Rick Hendrick
14.	Brooklyn, Mich.	June 15	Ernie Irvan	Robert Yates
15.	Fontana, Calif.	June 22	Jeff Gordon	Rick Hendrick
16.	Daytona Beach, Fla.	July 5	John Andretti	Cale Yarborough
17.	Loudon, N.H.	July 13	Jeff Burton	Jack Roush
18.	Long Pond, Pa.	July 20	Dale Jarrett	Robert Yates
19.	Indianapolis	Aug. 2	Ricky Rudd	Ricky Rudd
20.	Watkins Glen, N.Y.	Aug. 10	Jeff Gordon	Rick Hendrick
21.	Brooklyn, Mich.	Aug. 17	Mark Martin	Jack Roush
22.	Bristol, Tenn.	Aug. 23	Dale Jarrett	Robert Yates
23.	Darlington, S.C.	Aug. 31	Jeff Gordon	Rick Hendrick
24.	Richmond, Va.	Sept.6	Dale Jarrett	Robert Yates
25.	Loudon, N.H.	Sept. 14	Jeff Gordon	Rick Hendrick
26.	Dover, Del.	Sept. 21	Mark Martin	Jack Roush
27.	Martinsville, Va.	Sept. 29	Jeff Burton	Jack Roush
28.	Concord, N.C.	Oct. 5	Dale Jarrett	Robert Yates
29.	Talladega, Ala.	Oct. 12	Terry Labonte	Rick Hendrick
30.	Rockingham, N.C.	Oct. 27	Bobby Hamilton	Richard Petty
31.	Phoenix	Nov. 2	Dale Jarrett	Robert Yates
32.	Hampton, Ga.	Nov. 16	Bobby Labonte	Joe Gibbs

>> POINTS STANDINGS

1. Jeff Gordon 4,710
2. Dale Jarrett 4,696
3. Mark Martin 4,681
4. Jeff Burton 4,285
5. Dale Earnhardt 4,216
6. Terry Labonte 4,177
7. Bobby Labonte 4,101
8. Bill Elliott 3,836
9. Rusty Wallace 3,598
10. Ken Schrader 3,576

>> RACE WINNERS 11

1. Jeff Gordon 10
2. Dale Jarrett 7
3. Mark Martin 4
4. Jeff Burton 3
5. Ricky Rudd 2
6. John Andretti 1
   Bobby Hamilton 1
   Ernie Irvan 1
   Bobby Labonte 1
   Terry Labonte 1
   Rusty Wallace 1

>> MONEY WON LEADERS

1. Jeff Gordon $6,375,658
2. Dale Jarrett.....................3,240,542
3. Mark Martin 2,532,484
4. Jeff Burton 2,296,614
5. Terry Labonte 2,270,144
6. Bobby Labonte 2,217,999
7. Dale Earnhardt 2,151,909
8. Ricky Rudd 1,975,981
9. Rusty Wallace 1,705,625
10. Ernie Irvan 1,614,281

>> TOP 20 PERFORMANCE CHART

Rk	Driver	Points	Starts	Poles	Wins	Top 5s	Top 10s	DNF
1.	Jeff Gordon	4,710	32	1	10	22	23	2
2.	Dale Jarrett	4,696	32	2	7	20	23	1
3.	Mark Martin	4,681	32	3	4	16	24	3
4.	Jeff Burton	4,285	32	0	3	13	18	1
5.	Dale Earnhardt	4,216	32	0	0	7	16	0
6.	Terry Labonte	4,177	32	0	1	8	20	3
7.	Bobby Labonte	4,101	32	3	1	9	18	1
8.	Bill Elliott	3,836	32	1	0	5	14	3
9.	Rusty Wallace	3,598	32	1	1	8	12	11
10.	Ken Schrader	3,576	32	2	0	2	8	1
11.	Johnny Benson	3,575	32	1	0	0	8	2
12.	Ted Musgrave	3,556	32	0	0	5	8	4
13.	Jeremy Mayfield	3,547	32	0	0	3	8	3
14.	Ernie Irvan	3,534	32	2	1	5	13	8
15.	Kyle Petty	3,455	32	0	0	2	9	2
16.	Bobby Hamilton	3,450	32	2	1	6	8	4
17.	Ricky Rudd	3,330	32	0	2	6	11	7
18.	Michael Waltrip	3,173	32	0	0	0	6	4
19.	Ricky Craven	3,108	30	0	0	4	7	7
20.	Jimmy Spencer	3,079	32	0	0	1	4	6

>> POLE WINNERS 18

1. Bobby Labonte 3
   Mark Martin 3
3. Geoffrey Bodine 2
   Bobby Hamilton 2
   Ernie Irvan 2
   Dale Jarrett................................2
   Joe Nemechek 2
   Ken Schrader 2
   Mike Skinner 2
   Kenny Wallace 2
11. John Andretti 1
   Johnny Benson 1
   Todd Bodine 1
   Ward Burton 1
   Bill Elliott...................................1
   Jeff Gordon 1
   Robby Gordon 1
   Rusty Wallace 1

CONQUERING HIS FEARS

Irvan returns from head injuries to win at Michigan

Ernie Irvan's worst memory of racing at Michigan International Speedway really isn't even a memory. He has no recollection of the crash that nearly killed him during a practice in 1994.

His best memory of the track, thankfully, is more vivid. His win there in 1997 stirred incredible emotions in Irvan and throughout the sport.

Head injuries suffered in that practice wreck kept Irvan out of racing for almost 14 months, but he returned to pilot the No. 28 Ford for Robert Yates Racing in 1996. The win at Michigan was his third since climbing back into a racecar.

"It's real hard to drive with tears in your eyes," Irvan said. "I kept going through Turn 2 thinking, 'Man, this is where the wreck happened.' "

>> **1996 SEASON** <<

Race No.	Location	Date	Winner	Car owner
1.	Daytona Beach, Fla.	Feb. 18	Dale Jarrett	Robert Yates
2.	Rockingham, N.C.	Feb. 25	Dale Earnhardt	Richard Childress
3.	Richmond, Va.	March 3	Jeff Gordon	Rick Hendrick
4.	Hampton, Ga.	March 10	Dale Earnhardt	Richard Childress
5.	Darlington, S.C.	March 24	Jeff Gordon	Rick Hendrick
6.	Bristol, Tenn.	March 31	Jeff Gordon	Rick Hendrick
7.	N. Wilkesboro, N.C.	April 14	Terry Labonte	Rick Hendrick
8.	Martinsville, Va.	April 21	Rusty Wallace	Roger Penske
9.	Talladega, Ala.	April 28	Sterling Marlin	Morgan-McClure
10.	Sonoma, Calif.	May 5	Rusty Wallace	Roger Penske
11.	Concord, N.C.	May 26	Dale Jarrett	Robert Yates
12.	Dover, Del.	June 2	Jeff Gordon	Rick Hendrick
13.	Long Pond, Pa.	June 16	Jeff Gordon	Rick Hendrick
14.	Brooklyn, Mich.	June 23	Rusty Wallace	Roger Penske
15.	Daytona Beach, Fla.	July 6	Sterling Marlin	Morgan-McClure
16.	Loudon, N.H.	July 14	Ernie Irvan	Robert Yates
17.	Long Pond, Pa.	July 21	Rusty Wallace	Roger Penske
18.	Talladega, Ala.	July 28	Jeff Gordon	Rick Hendrick
19.	Indianapolis	Aug. 3	Dale Jarrett	Robert Yates
20.	Watkins Glen, N.Y.	Aug. 11	Geoffrey Bodine	Geoffrey Bodine
21.	Brooklyn, Mich.	Aug. 18	Dale Jarrett	Robert Yates
22.	Bristol, Tenn.	Aug. 24	Rusty Wallace	Roger Penske
23.	Darlington, S.C.	Sept. 1	Jeff Gordon	Rick Hendrick
24.	Richmond, Va.	Sept. 7	Ernie Irvan	Robert Yates
25.	Dover, Del.	Sept. 15	Jeff Gordon	Rick Hendrick
26.	Martinsville, Va.	Sept. 22	Jeff Gordon	Rick Hendrick
27.	N. Wilkesboro, N.C.	Sept. 29	Jeff Gordon	Rick Hendrick
28.	Concord, N.C.	Oct. 6	Terry Labonte	Rick Hendrick
29.	Rockingham, N.C.	Oct. 20	Ricky Rudd	Ricky Rudd
30.	Phoenix	Oct. 27	Bobby Hamilton	Richard Petty
31.	Hampton, Ga.	Nov. 10	Bobby Labonte	Joe Gibbs

>> POINTS STANDINGS

1. Terry Labonte 4,657
2. Jeff Gordon..4,620
3. Dale Jarrett 4,568
4. Dale Earnhardt 4,327
5. Mark Martin 4,278
6. Ricky Rudd 3,845
7. Rusty Wallace 3,717
8. Sterling Marlin 3,682
9. Bobby Hamilton 3,639
10. Ernie Irvan 3,632

>> RACE WINNERS 11

1. Jeff Gordon 10
2. Rusty Wallace 5
3. Dale Jarrett 4
4. Dale Earnhardt...2
   Ernie Irvan 2
   Terry Labonte 2
   Sterling Marlin 2
8. Geoffrey Bodine 1
   Bobby Hamilton 1
   Bobby Labonte 1
   Ricky Rudd 1

>> MONEY WON LEADERS

1. Terry Labonte $4,030,648
2. Jeff Gordon..................................3,428,485
3. Dale Jarrett 2,985,418
4. Dale Earnhardt...........................2,285,926
5. Mark Martin 1,887,396
6. Ernie Irvan...................................1,683,313
7. Rusty Wallace 1,665,315
8. Sterling Marlin 1,588,425
9. Ricky Rudd 1,503,025
10. Bobby Labonte 1,475,196

>> POLE WINNERS 14

1. Jeff Gordon 5
2. Bobby Labonte 4
   Terry Labonte 4
   Mark Martin..4
5. Ricky Craven 2
   Dale Earnhardt...2
   Bobby Hamilton 2
   Dale Jarrett 2
9. Johnny Benson 1
   Jeff Burton 1
   Ward Burton 1
   Ernie Irvan 1
   Jeremy Mayfield 1
   Ted Musgrave 1

>> TOP 20 PERFORMANCE CHART

Rk	Driver	Points	Starts	Poles	Wins	Top 5s	Top 10s	DNF
1.	Terry Labonte	4,657	31	4	2	21	24	3
2.	Jeff Gordon	4,620	31	5	10	21	24	5
3.	Dale Jarrett	4,568	31	2	4	17	21	3
4.	Dale Earnhardt	4,327	31	2	2	13	17	2
5.	Mark Martin	4,278	31	4	0	14	23	4
6.	Ricky Rudd	3,845	31	0	1	5	16	1
7.	Rusty Wallace	3,717	31	0	5	8	18	6
8.	Sterling Marlin	3,682	31	0	2	5	10	6
9.	Bobby Hamilton	3,639	31	2	1	3	11	4
10.	Ernie Irvan	3,632	31	1	2	12	16	5
11.	Bobby Labonte	3,590	31	4	1	5	14	5
12.	Ken Schrader	3,540	31	0	0	3	10	2
13.	Jeff Burton	3,538	30	1	0	6	12	1
14.	Michael Waltrip	3,535	31	0	0	1	11	3
15.	Jimmy Spencer	3,476	31	0	0	2	9	2
16.	Ted Musgrave	3,466	31	1	0	2	7	2
17.	Geoffrey Bodine	3,218	31	0	1	2	6	5
18.	Rick Mast	3,190	31	0	0	1	5	6
19.	Morgan Shepherd	3,133	31	0	0	1	5	3
20.	Ricky Craven	3,078	31	2	0	3	5	7

Race No.	Location	Date	Winner	Car owner
1.	Daytona Beach, Fla.	Feb. 19	Sterling Marlin	Morgan-McClure
2.	Rockingham, N.C.	Feb. 26	Jeff Gordon	Rick Hendrick
3.	Richmond, Va.	March 5	Terry Labonte	Rick Hendrick
4.	Hampton, Ga.	March 12	Jeff Gordon	Rick Hendrick
5.	Darlington, S.C.	March 26	Sterling Marlin	Morgan-McClure
6.	Bristol, Tenn.	April 2	Jeff Gordon	Rick Hendrick
7.	N. Wilkesboro, N.C.	April 9	Dale Earnhardt	Richard Childress
8.	Martinsville, Va.	April 23	Rusty Wallace	Roger Penske
9.	Talladega, Ala.	April 30	Mark Martin	Jack Roush
10.	Sonoma, Calif.	May 7	Dale Earnhardt	Richard Childress
11.	Concord, N.C.	May 28	Bobby Labonte	Joe Gibbs
12.	Dover, Del.	June 4	Kyle Petty	Felix Sabates
13.	Long Pond, Pa.	June 11	Terry Labonte	Rick Hendrick
14.	Brooklyn, Mich.	June 18	Bobby Labonte	Joe Gibbs
15.	Daytona Beach, Fla.	July 1	Jeff Gordon	Rick Hendrick
16.	Loudon, N.H.	July 9	Jeff Gordon	Rick Hendrick
17.	Long Pond, Pa.	July 16	Dale Jarrett	Robert Yates
18.	Talladega, Ala.	July 23	Sterling Marlin	Morgan-McClure
19.	Indianapolis	Aug. 5	Dale Earnhardt	Richard Childress
20.	Watkins Glen, N.Y.	Aug. 13	Mark Martin	Jack Roush
21.	Brooklyn, Mich.	Aug. 20	Bobby Labonte	Joe Gibbs
22.	Bristol, Tenn.	Aug. 26	Terry Labonte	Rick Hendrick
23.	Darlington, S.C.	Sept. 3	Jeff Gordon	Rick Hendrick
24.	Richmond, Va.	Sept. 9	Rusty Wallace	Roger Penske
25.	Dover, Del.	Sept. 17	Jeff Gordon	Rick Hendrick
26.	Martinsville, Va.	Sept. 24	Dale Earnhardt	Richard Childress
27.	N. Wilkesboro, N.C.	Oct. 1	Mark Martin	Jack Roush
28.	Concord, N.C.	Oct. 8	Mark Martin	Jack Roush
29.	Rockingham, N.C.	Oct. 22	Ward Burton	Bill Davis
30.	Phoenix	Oct. 29	Ricky Rudd	Ricky Rudd
31.	Hampton, Ga.	Nov. 12	Dale Earnhardt	Richard Childress

>> POINTS STANDINGS

1. Jeff Gordon 4,614
2. Dale Earnhardt 4,580
3. Sterling Marlin 4,361
4. Mark Martin 4,320
5. Rusty Wallace 4,240
6. Terry Labonte 4,146
7. Ted Musgrave 3,949
8. Bill Elliott 3,746
9. Ricky Rudd 3,734
10. Bobby Labonte 3,718

>> RACE WINNERS 11

1. Jeff Gordon 7
2. Dale Earnhardt..5
3. Mark Martin 4
4. Bobby Labonte..3
   Terry Labonte..3
   Sterling Marlin...3
7. Rusty Wallace 2
8. Ward Burton 1
   Dale Jarrett..1
   Kyle Petty...1
   Ricky Rudd 1

>> MONEY WON LEADERS

1. Jeff Gordon $4,347,343
2. Dale Earnhardt...................................3,154,241
3. Sterling Marlin 2,253,502
4. Mark Martin 1,893,519
5. Rusty Wallace 1,642,837
6. Terry Labonte 1,558,659
7. Bobby Labonte 1,413,682
8. Dale Jarrett 1,363,158
9. Ricky Rudd 1,337,703
10. Ted Musgrave 1,147,445

>> TOP 20 PERFORMANCE CHART

Rk	Driver	Points	Starts	Poles	Wins	Top 5s	Top 10s	DNF
1.	Jeff Gordon	4,614	31	8	7	17	23	3
2.	Dale Earnhardt	4,580	31	3	5	19	23	2
3.	Sterling Marlin	4,361	31	1	3	9	22	2
4.	Mark Martin	4,320	31	4	4	13	22	1
5.	Rusty Wallace	4,240	31	0	2	15	19	4
6.	Terry Labonte	4,146	31	1	3	14	17	3
7.	Ted Musgrave	3,949	31	1	0	7	13	1
8.	Bill Elliott	3,746	31	2	0	4	11	3
9.	Ricky Rudd	3,734	31	2	1	10	16	6
10.	Bobby Labonte	3,718	31	2	3	7	14	6
11.	Morgan Shepherd	3,618	31	0	0	4	10	2
12.	Michael Waltrip	3,601	31	0	0	2	8	2
13.	Dale Jarrett	3,584	31	1	1	9	14	6
14.	Bobby Hamilton	3,576	31	0	0	4	10	2
15.	Derrike Cope	3,384	31	0	0	2	8	5
16.	Geoffrey Bodine	3,357	31	0	0	1	4	5
17.	Ken Schrader	3,221	31	1	0	2	10	9
18.	John Andretti	3,140	31	1	0	1	5	7
19.	Darrell Waltrip	3,078	31	1	0	4	8	11
20.	Brett Bodine	2,988	31	0	0	0	2	3

>> POLE WINNERS 15

1. Jeff Gordon 8
2. Mark Martin 4
3. Dale Earnhardt..3
4. Bill Elliott 2
   Bobby Labonte..2
   Ricky Rudd 2
7. John Andretti 1
   Dale Jarrett..1
   Terry Labonte..1
   Sterling Marlin...1
   Rick Mast..1
   Ted Musgrave 1
   Ken Schrader 1
   Hut Stricklin 1
   Darrell Waltrip 1

>> 1994 SEASON <<

Race No.	Location	Date	Winner	Car owner
1.	Daytona Beach, Fla.	Feb. 20	Sterling Marlin	Larry McClure
2.	Rockingham, N.C.	Feb. 27	Rusty Wallace	Roger Penske
3.	Richmond, Va.	March 6	Ernie Irvan	Robert Yates
4.	Hampton, Ga.	March 13	Ernie Irvan	Robert Yates
5.	Darlington, S.C.	March 27	Dale Earnhardt	Richard Childress
6.	Bristol, Tenn.	April 10	Dale Earnhardt	Richard Childress
7.	N. Wilkesboro, N.C.	April 17	Terry Labonte	Rick Hendrick
8.	Martinsville, Va.	April 24	Rusty Wallace	Roger Penske
9.	Talladega, Ala.	May 1	Dale Earnhardt	Richard Childress
10.	Sonoma, Calif.	May 15	Ernie Irvan	Robert Yates
11.	Concord, N.C.	May 29	Jeff Gordon	Rick Hendrick
12.	Dover, Del.	June 5	Rusty Wallace	Roger Penske
13.	Long Pond, Pa.	June 12	Rusty Wallace	Roger Penske
14.	Brooklyn, Mich.	June 19	Rusty Wallace	Roger Penske
15.	Daytona Beach, Fla.	July 2	Jimmy Spencer	Junior Johnson
16.	Loudon, N.H.	July 10	Ricky Rudd	Ricky Rudd
17.	Long Pond, Pa.	July 17	Geoffrey Bodine	Geoffrey Bodine
18.	Talladega, Ala.	July 24	Jimmy Spencer	Junior Johnson
19.	Indianapolis	Aug. 6	Jeff Gordon	Rick Hendrick
20.	Watkins Glen, N.Y.	Aug. 14	Mark Martin	Jack Roush
21.	Brooklyn, Mich.	Aug. 21	Geoffrey Bodine	Geoffrey Bodine
22.	Bristol, Tenn.	Aug. 27	Rusty Wallace	Roger Penske
23.	Darlington, S.C.	Sept. 4	Bill Elliott	Junior Johnson
24.	Richmond, Va.	Sept. 10	Terry Labonte	Rick Hendrick
25.	Dover, Del.	Sept. 18	Rusty Wallace	Roger Penske
26.	Martinsville, Va.	Sept. 25	Rusty Wallace	Roger Penske
27.	N. Wilkesboro, N.C.	Oct. 2	Geoffrey Bodine	Geoffrey Bodine
28.	Concord, N.C.	Oct. 9	Dale Jarrett	Joe Gibbs
29.	Rockingham, N.C.	Oct. 23	Dale Earnhardt	Richard Childress
30.	Phoenix	Oct. 30	Terry Labonte	Rick Hendrick
31.	Hampton, Ga.	Nov. 13	Mark Martin	Jack Roush

>> POINTS STANDINGS

1. Dale Earnhardt 4,694
2. Mark Martin 4,250
3. Rusty Wallace...............................4,207
4. Ken Schrader 4,060
5. Ricky Rudd 4,050
6. Morgan Shepherd.............................4,029
7. Terry Labonte 3,876
8. Jeff Gordon 3,776
9. Darrell Waltrip 3,688
10. Bill Elliott 3,617

>> RACE WINNERS   12

1. Rusty Wallace 8
2. Dale Earnhardt 4
3. Geoffrey Bodine 3
     Ernie Irvan....................................3
     Terry Labonte 3
6. Jeff Gordon 2
     Mark Martin 2
     Jimmy Spencer 2
9. Bill Elliott.....................................1
     Dale Jarrett 1
     Sterling Marlin 1
     Ricky Rudd 1

>> MONEY WON LEADERS

1. Dale Earnhardt $3,300,733
2. Rusty Wallace 1,914,072
3. Jeff Gordon 1,779,523
4. Mark Martin 1,628,906
5. Geoffrey Bodine 1,276,126
6. Ken Schrader 1,171,062
7. Sterling Marlin.....................1,127,683
8. Terry Labonte 1,125,921
9. Morgan Shepherd 1,089,038
10. Ricky Rudd 1,044,441

>> TOP 20 PERFORMANCE CHART

Rk	Driver	Points	Starts	Poles	Wins	Top 5s	Top 10s	DNF
1.	Dale Earnhardt	4,694	31	2	4	20	25	3
2.	Mark Martin	4,250	31	1	2	15	20	8
3.	Rusty Wallace	4,207	31	2	8	17	20	5
4.	Ken Schrader	4,060	31	0	0	9	18	2
5.	Ricky Rudd	4,050	31	1	1	6	15	2
6.	Morgan Shepherd	4,029	31	0	0	9	16	2
7.	Terry Labonte	3,876	31	0	3	6	14	4
8.	Jeff Gordon	3,776	31	1	2	7	14	10
9.	Darrell Waltrip	3,688	31	0	0	4	13	1
10.	Bill Elliott	3,617	31	1	1	6	12	5
11.	Lake Speed	3,565	31	0	0	4	9	4
12.	Michael Waltrip	3,512	31	0	0	2	10	3
13.	Ted Musgrave	3,477	31	3	0	1	8	5
14.	Sterling Marlin	3,443	31	1	1	5	11	7
15.	Kyle Petty	3,339	31	0	0	2	7	3
16.	Dale Jarrett	3,298	30	0	1	4	9	7
17.	Geoffrey Bodine	3,297	31	5	3	7	10	15
18.	Rick Mast	3,238	31	1	0	4	10	10
19.	Brett Bodine	3,159	31	0	0	1	6	7
20.	Todd Bodine	3,048	30	0	0	2	7	6

>> POLE WINNERS   17

1. Geoffrey Bodine.................................5
     Ernie Irvan....................................5
3. Loy Allen 3
     Ted Musgrave 3
5. Dale Earnhardt 2
     Rusty Wallace 2
7. Chuck Bown 1
     Ward Burton 1
     Bill Elliott...................................1
     Harry Gant 1
     Jeff Gordon 1
     Sterling Marlin 1
     Mark Martin 1
     Rick Mast 1
     Ricky Rudd 1
     Greg Sacks 1
     Jimmy Spencer 1

NO.7 FOR NO.3

Earnhardt's final championship is a model of consistency

It was a pivotal year in the history of NASCAR. A young kid named Jeff Gordon, fresh off winning rookie of the year honors the season before, won two races and began introducing NASCAR to legions of new fans in 1994.

But the old guard wouldn't go quietly. Dale Earnhardt won his seventh championship in a dominating fashion. He beat the second-place finisher, Mark Martin, by 444 points, an unbelievable margin.

Earnhardt set a career mark with 25 top 10s, including 20 top fives, in 31 races. By comparison, Matt Kenseth's 2003 season, oft noted for its consistency, also featured 25 top 10s, but that season was five races longer. Kenseth had only 11 top fives.

Earnhardt scored four wins in 1994—at Darlington, Bristol, Talladega and Rockingham.

Earnhardt would not win another championship. The closest he came was 1995, when he finished second to Gordon by 34 points. He finished second again in 2000 to Bobby Labonte, by 265.

>> 1993 SEASON <<

Race No.	Location	Date	Winner	Car owner
1.	Daytona Beach, Fla.	Feb. 14	Dale Jarrett	Joe Gibbs
2.	Rockingham, N.C.	Feb. 28	Rusty Wallace	Roger Penske
3.	Richmond, Va.	March 7	Davey Allison	Robert Yates
4.	Hampton, Ga.	March 20	Morgan Shepherd	Wood Brothers
5.	Darlington, S.C.	March 28	Dale Earnhardt	Richard Childress
6.	Bristol, Tenn.	April 4	Rusty Wallace	Roger Penske
7.	N. Wilkesboro, N.C.	April 18	Rusty Wallace	Roger Penske
8.	Martinsville, Va.	April 25	Rusty Wallace	Roger Penske
9.	Talladega, Ala.	May 2	Ernie Irvan	Larry McClure
10.	Sonoma, Calif.	May 16	Geoffrey Bodine	Bud Moore
11.	Concord, N.C.	May 30	Dale Earnhardt	Richard Childress
12.	Dover, Del.	June 6	Dale Earnhardt	Richard Childress
13.	Long Pond, Pa.	June 13	Kyle Petty	Felix Sabates
14.	Brooklyn, Mich.	June 20	Ricky Rudd	Rick Hendrick
15.	Daytona Beach, Fla.	July 3	Dale Earnhardt	Richard Childress
16.	Loudon, N.H.	July 11	Rusty Wallace	Roger Penske
17.	Long Pond, Pa.	July 18	Dale Earnhardt	Richard Childress
18.	Talladega, Ala.	July 25	Dale Earnhardt	Richard Childress
19.	Watkins Glen, N.Y.	Aug. 8	Mark Martin	Jack Roush
20.	Brooklyn, Mich.	Aug. 15	Mark Martin	Jack Roush
21.	Bristol, Tenn.	Aug. 28	Mark Martin	Jack Roush
22.	Darlington, S.C.	Sept. 5	Mark Martin	Jack Roush
23.	Richmond, Va.	Sept. 11	Rusty Wallace	Roger Penske
24.	Dover, Del.	Sept. 19	Rusty Wallace	Roger Penske
25.	Martinsville, Va.	Sept. 26	Ernie Irvan	Robert Yates
26.	N. Wilkesboro, N.C.	Oct. 3	Rusty Wallace	Roger Penske
27.	Concord, N.C.	Oct. 10	Ernie Irvan	Robert Yates
28.	Rockingham, N.C.	Oct. 24	Rusty Wallace	Roger Penske
29.	Phoenix	Oct. 31	Mark Martin	Jack Roush
30.	Hampton, Ga.	Nov. 14	Rusty Wallace	Roger Penske

>> POINTS STANDINGS

1. Dale Earnhardt 4,526
2. Rusty Wallace 4,446
3. Mark Martin 4,150
4. Dale Jarrett 4,000
5. Kyle Petty 3,860
6. Ernie Irvan 3,834
7. Morgan Shepherd 3,807
8. Bill Elliott 3,774
9. Ken Schrader 3,715
10. Ricky Rudd 3,644

>> RACE WINNERS   10

1. Rusty Wallace 10
2. Dale Earnhardt 6
3. Mark Martin 5
4. Ernie Irvan 3
5. Davey Allison 1
   Geoffrey Bodine 1
   Dale Jarrett 1
   Kyle Petty 1
   Ricky Rudd 1
   Morgan Shepherd 1

>> MONEY WON LEADERS

1. Dale Earnhardt $3,353,789
2. Rusty Wallace 1,702,154
3. Mark Martin 1,657,662
4. Ernie Irvan 1,400,468
5. Dale Jarrett 1,242,394
6. Bill Elliott 955,859
7. Ken Schrader 952,748
8. Kyle Petty 914,662
9. Geoffrey Bodine 783,762
10. Morgan Shepherd 782,523

>> POLE WINNERS   12

1. Ken Schrader 6
2. Mark Martin 5
3. Ernie Irvan 4
4. Rusty Wallace 3
5. Brett Bodine 2
   Dale Earnhardt 2
   Bill Elliott 2
8. Geoffrey Bodine 1
   Harry Gant 1
   Jeff Gordon 1
   Bobby Labonte 1
   Kyle Petty 1

>> TOP 20 PERFORMANCE CHART

Rk	Driver	Points	Starts	Poles	Wins	Top 5s	Top 10s	DNF
1.	Dale Earnhardt	4,526	30	2	6	17	21	2
2.	Rusty Wallace	4,446	30	3	10	19	21	5
3.	Mark Martin	4,150	30	5	5	12	19	5
4.	Dale Jarrett	4,000	30	0	1	13	18	5
5.	Kyle Petty	3,860	30	1	1	9	15	5
6.	Ernie Irvan	3,834	30	4	3	12	14	10
7.	Morgan Shepherd	3,807	30	0	1	3	15	2
8.	Bill Elliott	3,774	30	2	0	6	15	3
9.	Ken Schrader	3,715	30	6	0	9	15	4
10.	Ricky Rudd	3,644	30	0	1	9	14	6
11.	Harry Gant	3,524	30	1	0	4	12	6
12.	Jimmy Spencer	3,496	30	0	0	5	10	4
13.	Darrell Waltrip	3,479	30	0	0	4	10	4
14.	Jeff Gordon	3,447	30	1	0	7	11	11
15.	Sterling Marlin	3,355	30	0	0	1	8	3
16.	Geoffrey Bodine	3,338	30	1	1	2	9	9
17.	Michael Waltrip	3,291	30	0	0	0	5	4
18.	Terry Labonte	3,280	30	0	0	0	10	6
19.	Bobby Labonte	3,221	30	1	0	0	6	6
20.	Brett Bodine	3,183	29	2	0	3	9.	6

>> 1992 SEASON <<

Race No.	Location	Date	Winner	Car owner
1.	Daytona Beach, Fla.	Feb. 16	Davey Allison	Robert Yates
2.	Rockingham, N.C.	March 1	Bill Elliott	Junior Johnson
3.	Richmond, Va.	March 8	Bill Elliott	Junior Johnson
4.	Hampton, Ga.	March 15	Bill Elliott	Junior Johnson
5.	Darlington, S.C.	March 29	Bill Elliott	Junior Johnson
6.	Bristol, Tenn.	April 5	Alan Kulwicki	Alan Kulwicki
7.	N. Wilkesboro, N.C.	April 12	Davey Allison	Robert Yates
8.	Martinsville, Va.	April 26	Mark Martin	Jack Roush
9.	Talladega, Ala.	May 3	Davey Allison	Robert Yates
10.	Concord, N.C.	May 24	Dale Earnhardt	Richard Childress
11.	Dover, Del.	May 31	Harry Gant	Leo Jackson
12.	Sonoma, Calif.	June 7	Ernie Irvan	Larry McClure
13.	Long Pond, Pa.	June 14	Alan Kulwicki	Alan Kulwicki
14.	Brooklyn, Mich.	June 21	Davey Allison	Robert Yates
15.	Daytona Beach, Fla.	July 4	Ernie Irvan	Larry McClure
16.	Long Pond, Pa.	July 19	Darrell Waltrip	Darrell Waltrip
17.	Talladega, Ala.	July 26	Ernie Irvan	Morgan-McClure
18.	Watkins Glen, N.Y.	Aug. 9	Kyle Petty	Felix Sabates
19.	Brooklyn, Mich.	Aug. 16	Harry Gant	Leo Jackson
20.	Bristol, Tenn.	Aug. 29	Darrell Waltrip	Darrell Waltrip
21.	Darlington, S.C.	Sept. 6	Darrell Waltrip	Darrell Waltrip
22.	Richmond, Va.	Sept. 12	Rusty Wallace	Roger Penske
23.	Dover, Del.	Sept. 20	Ricky Rudd	Rick Hendrick
24.	Martinsville, Va.	Sept. 28	Geoffrey Bodine	Bud Moore
25.	N. Wilkesboro, N.C.	Oct. 5	Geoffrey Bodine	Bud Moore
26.	Concord, N.C.	Oct. 11	Mark Martin	Jack Roush
27.	Rockingham, N.C.	Oct. 25	Kyle Petty	Felix Sabates
28.	Phoenix	Nov. 1	Davey Allison	Robert Yates
29.	Hampton, Ga.	Nov. 15	Bill Elliott	Junior Johnson

>> POINTS STANDINGS

1. Alan Kulwicki 4,078
2. Bill Elliott 4,068
3. Davey Allison 4,015
4. Harry Gant 3,955
5. Kyle Petty 3,945
6. Mark Martin 3,887
7. Ricky Rudd 3,735
8. Terry Labonte 3,674
9. Darrell Waltrip 3,659
10. Sterling Marlin 3,063

>> RACE WINNERS   12

1. Davey Allison..5
   Bill Elliott..5
3. Ernie Irvan...3
   Darrell Waltrip..3
5. Geoffrey Bodine..2
   Harry Gant..2
   Alan Kulwicki 2
   Mark Martin 2
   Kyle Petty 2
10. Dale Earnhardt 1
    Ricky Rudd 1
    Rusty Wallace 1

>> MONEY WON LEADERS

1. Alan Kulwicki....................................$2,322,561
2. Davey Allison...............................1,955,628
3. Bill Elliott.....................................1,692,381
4. Harry Gant....................................1,122,776
5. Kyle Petty 1,107,063
6. Mark Martin 1,000,571
7. Ernie Irvan...996,885
8. Dale Earnhardt 915,463
9. Darrell Waltrip 876,492
10. Ricky Rudd 793,903

>> TOP 20 PERFORMANCE CHART

Rk	Driver	Points	Starts	Poles	Wins	Top 5s	Top 10s	DNF
1.	Alan Kulwicki	4,078	29	6	2	11	17	2
2.	Bill Elliott	4,068	29	2	5	14	17	2
3.	Davey Allison	4,015	29	2	5	15	17	3
4.	Harry Gant	3,955	29	0	2	10	15	3
5.	Kyle Petty	3,945	29	3	2	9	17	5
6.	Mark Martin	3,887	29	1	2	10	17	5
7.	Ricky Rudd	3,735	29	1	1	9	18	4
8.	Terry Labonte	3,674	29	0	0	4	16	3
9.	Darrell Waltrip	3,659	29	1	3	10	13	4
10.	Sterling Marlin	3,603	29	5	0	6	13	4
11.	Ernie Irvan	3,580	29	3	3	9	11	9
12.	Dale Earnhardt	3,574	29	1	1	6	15	4
13.	Rusty Wallace	3,556	29	1	1	5	12	5
14.	Morgan Shepherd	3,549	29	0	0	3	11	3
15.	Brett Bodine	3,491	29	1	0	2	13	4
16.	Geoffrey Bodine	3,437	29	0	2	7	11	7
17.	Ken Schrader	3,404	29	1	0	4	11	6
18.	Ted Musgrave	3,315	29	0	0	1	7	3
19.	Dale Jarrett	3,251	29	0	0	2	8	5
20.	Dick Trickle	3,097	29	0	0	3	9	6

>> POLE WINNERS   14

1. Alan Kulwicki..6
2. Sterling Marlin..5
3. Ernie Irvan...3
   Kyle Petty 3
5. Davey Allison..2
   Bill Elliott..2
7. Brett Bodine 1
   Dale Earnhardt 1
   Mark Martin 1
   Rick Mast 1
   Ricky Rudd 1
   Ken Schrader 1
   Rusty Wallace 1
   Darrell Waltrip 1

>> 1991 SEASON <<

Race No.	Location	Date	Winner	Car owner
1.	Daytona Beach, Fla.	Feb. 17	Ernie Irvan	Larry McClure
2.	Richmond, Va.	Feb. 24	Dale Earnhardt	Richard Childress
3.	Rockingham, N.C.	March 3	Kyle Petty	Felix Sabates
4.	Hampton, Ga.	March 17	Ken Schrader	Rick Hendrick
5.	Darlington, S.C.	April 7	Ricky Rudd	Rick Hendrick
6.	Bristol, Tenn.	April 14	Rusty Wallace	Roger Penske
7.	N. Wilkesboro, N.C.	April 21	Darrell Waltrip	Darrell Waltrip
8.	Martinsville, Va.	April 28	Dale Earnhardt	Richard Childress
9.	Talladega, Ala.	May 6	Harry Gant	Leo Jackson
10.	Concord, N.C.	May 26	Davey Allison	Robert Yates
11.	Dover, Del.	June 2	Ken Schrader	Rick Hendrick
12.	Sonoma, Calif.	June 9	Davey Allison	Robert Yates
13.	Long Pond, Pa.	June 16	Darrell Waltrip	Darrell Waltrip
14.	Brooklyn, Mich.	June 23	Davey Allison	Robert Yates
15.	Daytona Beach, Fla.	July 6	Bill Elliott	Harry Melling
16.	Long Pond, Pa.	July 21	Rusty Wallace	Roger Penske
17.	Talladega, Ala.	July 28	Dale Earnhardt	Richard Childress
18.	Watkins Glen, N.Y.	Aug. 11	Ernie Irvan	Larry McClure
19.	Brooklyn, Mich.	Aug. 18	Dale Jarrett	Wood Brothers
20.	Bristol, Tenn.	Aug. 24	Alan Kulwicki	Alan Kulwicki
21.	Darlington, S.C.	Sept. 1	Harry Gant	Leo Jackson
22.	Richmond, Va.	Sept. 7	Harry Gant	Leo Jackson
23.	Dover, Del.	Sept. 15	Harry Gant	Leo Jackson
24.	Martinsville, Va.	Sept. 22	Harry Gant	Leo Jackson
25.	N. Wilkesboro, N.C.	Sept. 29	Dale Earnhardt	Richard Childress
26.	Concord, N.C.	Oct. 6	Geoffrey Bodine	Junior Johnson
27.	Rockingham, N.C.	Oct. 20	Davey Allison	Robert Yates
28.	Phoenix	Nov. 3	Davey Allison	Robert Yates
29.	Hampton, Ga.	Nov. 17	Mark Martin	Jack Roush

>> POINTS STANDINGS

1. Dale Earnhardt 4,287
2. Ricky Rudd 4,092
3. Davey Allison 4,088
4. Harry Gant 3,985
5. Ernie Irvan 3,925
6. Mark Martin 3,914
7. Sterling Marlin 3,839
8. Darrell Waltrip 3,711
9. Ken Schrader 3,690
10. Rusty Wallace 3,582

>> RACE WINNERS   14

1. Davey Allison 5
   Harry Gant 5
3. Dale Earnhardt...............................4
4. Ernie Irvan 2
   Ken Schrader 2
   Rusty Wallace 2
   Darrell Waltrip 2
8. Geoffrey Bodine 1
   Bill Elliott 1
   Dale Jarrett 1
   Alan Kulwicki 1
   Mark Martin 1
   Kyle Petty...................................1
   Ricky Rudd 1

>> MONEY WON LEADERS

1. Dale Earnhardt..................$2,396,685
2. Davey Allison 1,732,924
3. Harry Gant 1,194,033
4. Ricky Rudd 1,093,765
5. Ernie Irvan 1,079,017
6. Mark Martin........................1,039,991
7. Ken Schrader 722,434
8. Bill Elliott 705,605
9. Sterling Marlin 633,690
10. Geoffrey Bodine 625,256

>> TOP 20 PERFORMANCE CHART

Rk	Driver	Points	Starts	Poles	Wins	Top 5s	Top 10s	DNF
1.	Dale Earnhardt	4,287	29	0	4	14	21	2
2.	Ricky Rudd	4,092	29	1	1	9	17	1
3.	Davey Allison	4,088	29	3	5	12	16	4
4.	Harry Gant	3,985	29	1	5	15	17	2
5.	Ernie Irvan	3,925	29	1	2	11	19	6
6.	Mark Martin	3,914	29	5	1	14	17	5
7.	Sterling Marlin	3,839	29	2	0	7	16	2
8.	Darrell Waltrip	3,711	29	0	2	5	17	6
9.	Ken Schrader	3,690	29	0	2	10	18	6
10.	Rusty Wallace	3,582	29	2	2	9	14	10
11.	Bill Elliott	3,535	29	2	1	6	12	2
12.	Morgan Shepherd	3,438	29	0	0	4	14	6
13.	Alan Kulwicki	3,354	29	4	1	4	11	7
14.	Geoffrey Bodine	3,277	27	2	1	6	12	7
15.	Michael Waltrip	3,254	29	2	0	4	12	6
16.	Hut Stricklin	3,199	29	0	0	3	7	7
17.	Dale Jarrett	3,124	29	0	1	3	8	9
18.	Terry Labonte	3,024	29	1	0	1	7	8
19.	Brett Bodine	2,980	29	1	0	2	6	13
20.	Joe Ruttman	2,938	29	0	0	1	4	2

>> POLE WINNERS   14

1. Mark Martin...................................5
2. Alan Kulwicki 4
3. Davey Allison 3
4. Geoffrey Bodine 2
   Bill Elliott 2
   Sterling Marlin 2
   Kyle Petty...................................2
   Rusty Wallace 2
   Michael Waltrip 2
10. Brett Bodine.................................1
    Harry Gant 1
    Ernie Irvan 1
    Terry Labonte................................1
    Ricky Rudd 1

Race No.	Location	Date	Winner	Car owner
1.	Daytona Beach, Fla.	Feb. 18	Derrike Cope	Bob Whitcomb
2.	Richmond, Va.	Feb. 25	Mark Martin	Jack Roush
3.	Rockingham, N.C.	March 4	Kyle Petty	Felix Sabates
4.	Hampton, Ga.	March 18	Dale Earnhardt	Richard Childress
5.	Darlington, S.C.	April 1	Dale Earnhardt	Richard Childress
6.	Bristol, Tenn.	April 8	Davey Allison	Robert Yates
7.	N. Wilkesboro, N.C.	April 22	Brett Bodine	Kenny Bernstein
8.	Martinsville, Va.	April 29	Geoffrey Bodine	Junior Johnson
9.	Talladega, Ala.	May 6	Dale Earnhardt	Richard Childress
10.	Concord, N.C.	May 27	Rusty Wallace	Raymond Beadle
11.	Dover, Del.	June 3	Derrike Cope	Bob Whitcomb
12.	Sonoma, Calif.	June 10	Rusty Wallace	Raymond Beadle
13.	Long Pond, Pa.	June 17	Harry Gant	Leo Jackson
14.	Brooklyn, Mich.	June 24	Dale Earnhardt	Richard Childress
15.	Daytona Beach, Fla.	July 7	Dale Earnhardt	Richard Childress
16.	Long Pond, Pa.	July 22	Geoffrey Bodine	Junior Johnson
17.	Talladega, Ala.	July 29	Dale Earnhardt	Richard Childress
18.	Watkins Glen, N.Y.	Aug. 12	Ricky Rudd	Rick Hendrick
19.	Brooklyn, Mich.	Aug. 19	Mark Martin	Jack Roush
20.	Bristol, Tenn.	Aug. 25	Ernie Irvan	Larry McClure
21.	Darlington, S.C.	Sept. 2	Dale Earnhardt	Richard Childress
22.	Richmond, Va.	Sept. 9	Dale Earnhardt	Richard Childress
23.	Dover, Del.	Sept. 16	Bill Elliott	Harry Melling
24.	Martinsville, Va.	Sept. 23	Geoffrey Bodine	Junior Johnson
25.	N. Wilkesboro, N.C.	Sept. 30	Mark Martin	Jack Roush
26.	Concord N.C.	Oct. 7	Davey Allison	Robert Yates
27.	Rockingham, N.C.	Oct. 21	Alan Kulwicki	Alan Kulwicki
28.	Phoenix	Nov. 4	Dale Earnhardt	Richard Childress
29.	Hampton, Ga.	Nov. 18	Morgan Shepherd	Bud Moore

>> POINTS STANDINGS

1. Dale Earnhardt 4,430
2. Mark Martin 4,404
3. Geoffrey Bodine 4,017
4. Bill Elliott 3,999
5. Morgan Shepherd 3,689
6. Rusty Wallace 3,676
7. Ricky Rudd 3,601
8. Alan Kulwicki 3,599
9. Ernie Irvan 3,593
10. Ken Schrader 3,572

>> RACE WINNERS 14

1. Dale Earnhardt.............9
2. Geoffrey Bodine 3
   Mark Martin 3
4. Davey Allison 2
   Derrike Cope 2
   Rusty Wallace 2
7. Brett Bodine.............1
   Bill Elliott 1
   Harry Gant 1
   Ernie Irvan 1
   Alan Kulwicki 1
   Kyle Petty 1
   Ricky Rudd 1
   Morgan Shepherd 1

>> MONEY WON LEADERS

1. Dale Earnhardt.............$3,083,056
2. Mark Martin.............1,302,958
3. Geoffrey Bodine 1,131,222
4. Bill Elliott 1,090,730
5. Rusty Wallace 954,129
6. Ken Schrader 769,934
7. Kyle Petty 746,326
8. Morgan Shepherd 666,915
9. Davey Allison 640,684
10. Ricky Rudd 573,650

>> TOP 20 PERFORMANCE CHART

Rk	Driver	Points	Starts	Poles	Wins	Top 5s	Top 10s	DNF
1.	Dale Earnhardt	4,430	29	4	9	18	23	1
2.	Mark Martin	4,404	29	3	3	16	23	1
3.	Geoffrey Bodine	4,017	29	2	3	11	19	3
4.	Bill Elliott	3,999	29	2	1	12	16	2
5.	Morgan Shepherd	3,689	29	0	1	7	16	6
6.	Rusty Wallace	3,676	29	2	2	9	16	8
7.	Ricky Rudd	3,601	29	2	1	8	15	5
8.	Alan Kulwicki	3,599	29	1	1	5	13	6
9.	Ernie Irvan	3,593	29	3	1	6	13	5
10.	Ken Schrader	3,572	29	3	0	7	14	8
11.	Kyle Petty	3,501	29	2	1	2	14	5
12.	Brett Bodine	3,440	29	1	1	5	9	5
13.	Davey Allison	3,423	29	0	2	5	10	2
14.	Sterling Marlin	3,387	29	0	0	5	10	8
15.	Terry Labonte	3,371	29	0	0	4	9	5
16.	Michael Waltrip	3,251	29	0	0	5	10	7
17.	Harry Gant	3,182	28	0	1	6	9	6
18.	Derrike Cope	3,140	29	0	2	2	6	10
19.	Bobby Hillin Jr	3,048	29	0	0	1	4	8
20.	Darrell Waltrip	3,013	23	0	0	5	12	0

>> POLE WINNERS 13

1. Dale Earnhardt.............4
2. Ernie Irvan.............3
   Mark Martin.............3
   Ken Schrader.............3
5. Geoffrey Bodine 2
   Bill Elliott 2
   Kyle Petty 2
   Ricky Rudd 2
   Rusty Wallace 2
10. Brett Bodine.............1
    Alan Kulwicki 1
    Greg Sacks 1
    Dick Trickle 1

>> 1989 SEASON <<

Race No.	Location	Date	Winner	Car owner
1.	Daytona Beach, Fla.	Feb. 19	Darrell Waltrip	Rick Hendrick
2.	Rockingham, N.C.	Mar. 5	Rusty Wallace	Raymond Beadle
3.	Hampton, Ga.	March 19	Darrell Waltrip	Rick Hendrick
4.	Richmond, Va.	March 26	Rusty Wallace	Raymond Beadle
5.	Darlington, S.C.	April 2	Harry Gant	Leo Jackson
6.	Bristol, Tenn.	April 9	Rusty Wallace	Raymond Beadle
7.	N. Wilkesboro, N.C.	April 16	Dale Earnhardt	Richard Childress
8.	Martinsville, Va.	April 23	Darrell Waltrip	Rick Hendrick
9.	Talladega, Ala.	May 7	Davey Allison	Robert Yates
10.	Concord, N.C.	May 28	Darrell Waltrip	Rick Hendrick
11.	Dover, Del.	June 4	Dale Earnhardt	Richard Childress
12.	Sonoma, Calif.	June 11	Ricky Rudd	Kenny Bernstein
13.	Long Pond, Pa.	June 18	Terry Labonte	Junior Johnson
14.	Brooklyn, Mich.	June 25	Bill Elliott	Harry Melling
15.	Daytona Beach, Fla.	July 1	Davey Allison	Robert Yates
16.	Long Pond, Pa.	July 23	Bill Elliott	Harry Melling
17.	Talladega, Ala.	July 30	Terry Labonte	Junior Johnson
18.	Watkins Glen, N.Y.	Aug. 13	Rusty Wallace	Raymond Beadle
19.	Brooklyn, Mich.	Aug. 20	Rusty Wallace	Raymond Beadle
20.	Bristol, Tenn.	Aug. 26	Darrell Waltrip	Rick Hendrick
21.	Darlington, S.C.	Sept. 3	Dale Earnhardt	Richard Childress
22.	Richmond, Va.	Sept. 10	Rusty Wallace	Raymond Beadle
23.	Dover, Del.	Sept. 17	Dale Earnhardt	Richard Childress
24.	Martinsville, Va.	Sept. 24	Darrell Waltrip	Rick Hendrick
25.	Concord, N.C.	Oct. 8	Ken Schrader	Rick Hendrick
26.	N. Wilkesboro, N.C.	Oct. 15	Geoffrey Bodine	Rick Hendrick
27.	Rockingham, N.C.	Oct. 22	Mark Martin	Jack Roush
28.	Phoenix	Nov. 5	Bill Elliott	Harry Melling
29.	Hampton, Ga.	Nov. 19	Dale Earnhardt	Richard Childress

>> POINTS STANDINGS

1. Rusty Wallace 4,176
2. Dale Earnhardt 4,164
3. Mark Martin 4,053
4. Darrell Waltrip 3,971
5. Ken Schrader 3,786
6. Bill Elliott 3,774
7. Harry Gant 3,610
8. Ricky Rudd 3,608
9. Geoffrey Bodine 3,600
10. Terry Labonte 3,569

>> RACE WINNERS   11

1. Rusty Wallace 6
   Darrell Waltrip 6
3. Dale Earnhardt 5
4. Bill Elliott 3
5. Davey Allison 2
   Terry Labonte 2
7. Geoffrey Bodine 1
   Harry Gant 1
   Mark Martin 1
   Ricky Rudd 1
   Ken Schrader 1

>> MONEY WON LEADERS

1. Rusty Wallace $2,247,950
2. Dale Earnhardt 1,435,730
3. Darrell Waltrip 1,323,079
4. Ken Schrader 1,039,441
5. Mark Martin 1,019,250
6. Bill Elliott 854,570
7. Terry Labonte 704,806
8. Harry Gant 641,092
9. Davey Allison 640,956
10. Geoffrey Bodine 620,594

>> POLE WINNERS   9

1. Alan Kulwicki 6
   Mark Martin 6
3. Ken Schrader 4
   Rusty Wallace 4
5. Geoffrey Bodine 3
   Bill Elliott 2
7. Davey Allison 1
   Jimmy Hensley 1
   Morgan Shepherd 1

>> TOP 20 PERFORMANCE CHART

Rk	Driver	Points	Starts	Poles	Wins	Top 5s	Top 10s	DNF
1.	Rusty Wallace	4,176	29	4	6	13	20	4
2.	Dale Earnhardt	4,164	29	0	5	14	19	2
3.	Mark Martin	4,053	29	6	1	14	18	4
4.	Darrell Waltrip	3,971	29	0	6	14	18	3
5.	Ken Schrader	3,786	29	4	1	10	14	6
6.	Bill Elliott	3,774	29	2	3	8	14	4
7.	Harry Gant	3,610	29	0	1	9	14	4
8.	Ricky Rudd	3,608	29	0	1	7	15	5
9.	Geoffrey Bodine	3,600	29	3	1	9	11	7
10.	Terry Labonte	3,569	29	0	2	9	11	6
11.	Davey Allison	3,481	29	1	2	7	13	6
12.	Sterling Marlin	3,422	29	0	0	4	13	5
13.	Morgan Shepherd	3,403	29	1	0	5	13	9
14.	Alan Kulwicki	3,236	29	6	0	5	9	11
15.	Bobby Hillin Jr	3,139	28	0	0	1	7	7
16.	Rick Wilson	3,119	29	0	0	2	7	8
17.	Dick Trickle	3,079	28	0	0	6	9	8
18.	Michael Waltrip	3,057	29	0	0	0	5	10
19.	Brett Bodine	3,051	29	0	0	1	6	9
20.	Neil Bonnett	2,995	26	0	0	0	11	5

ALL IN THE FAMILY

Allisons' 1-2 finish at Daytona is special for father and son

When Bobby Allison pulled away from the second place car to win the 1988 Daytona 500 by two car lengths, he beat of one of the men with whom he competed most fiercely: his son, Davey.

NASCAR historians can find only one other time that a father-son combo finished 1-2, when Richard and Lee Petty did it in 1960. June Allison, Bobby's wife and Davey's mom, was asked who she wanted to win. "Bobby. He's the one who pays my bills," she said. Said Bobby after the race: "It was a great feeling to look back and see someone you think is the best coming-up driver and know it's your son." Davey considered it the best day of his career, even better than when he won the Daytona 500, in 1992.

But the emotional high of that day in 1988 would not last. Tragedy soon would strike the Allison family, again and again. A wreck at Pocono later that season nearly killed Bobby and ultimately ended his career. Clifford Allison died four years later in a practice crash at Michigan, and Davey died in a helicopter crash in 1993.

>> 1988 SEASON <<

Race No.	Location	Date	Winner	Car owner
1.	Daytona Beach, Fla.	Feb. 14	Bobby Allison	Stavola Brothers
2.	Richmond, Va.	Feb. 21	Neil Bonnett	Rahilly-Mock
3.	Rockingham, N.C.	March 6	Neil Bonnett	Rahilly-Mock
4.	Hampton, Ga.	March 20	Dale Earnhardt	Richard Childress
5.	Darlington, S.C.	March 27	Lake Speed	Lake Speed
6.	Bristol, Tenn.	April 10	Bill Elliott	Harry Melling
7.	N. Wilkesboro, N.C.	April 17	Terry Labonte	Junior Johnson
8.	Martinsville, Va.	April 24	Dale Earnhardt	Richard Childress
9.	Talladega, Ala.	May 1	Phil Parsons	Jackson Brothers
10.	Concord, N.C.	May 29	Darrell Waltrip	Rick Hendrick
11.	Dover, Del.	June 5	Bill Elliott	Harry Melling
12.	Riverside, Calif.	June 12	Rusty Wallace	Raymond Beadle
13.	Long Pond, Pa.	June 19	Geoffrey Bodine	Rick Hendrick
14.	Brooklyn, Mich.	June 26	Rusty Wallace	Raymond Beadle
15.	Daytona Beach, Fla.	July 2	Bill Elliott	Harry Melling
16.	Long Pond, Pa.	July 24	Bill Elliott	Harry Melling
17.	Talladega, Ala.	July 31	Ken Schrader	Rick Hendrick
18.	Watkins Glen, N.Y.	Aug. 14	Ricky Rudd	Kenny Bernstein
19.	Brooklyn, Mich.	Aug. 21	Davey Allison	Harry Ranier
20.	Bristol, Tenn.	Aug. 27	Dale Earnhardt	Richard Childress
21.	Darlington, S.C.	Sept. 4	Bill Elliott	Harry Melling
22.	Richmond, Va.	Sept. 11	Davey Allison	Harry Ranier
23.	Dover, Del.	Sept. 18	Bill Elliott	Harry Melling
24.	Martinsville, Va.	Sept. 25	Darrell Waltrip	Rick Hendrick
25.	Concord, N.C.	Oct. 9	Rusty Wallace	Raymond Beadle
26.	N. Wilkesboro, N.C.	Oct. 16	Rusty Wallace	Raymond Beadle
27.	Rockingham, N.C.	Oct. 23	Rusty Wallace	Raymond Beadle
28.	Phoenix	Nov. 6	Alan Kulwicki	Alan Kulwicki
29.	Hampton, Ga.	Nov. 20	Rusty Wallace	Raymond Beadle

>> POINTS STANDINGS

1. Bill Elliott 4,488
2. Rusty Wallace 4,464
3. Dale Earnhardt 4,256
4. Terry Labonte 4,007
5. Ken Schrader 3,858
6. Geoffrey Bodine 3,799
7. Darrell Waltrip 3,764
8. Davey Allison 3,631
9. Phil Parsons 3,630
10. Sterling Marlin 3,621

>> RACE WINNERS   14

1. Bill Elliott 6
   Rusty Wallace 6
3. Dale Earnhardt..........................3
4. Davey Allison 2
   Neil Bonnett...............................2
   Darrell Waltrip 2
7. Bobby Allison 1
   Geoffrey Bodine 1
   Alan Kulwicki 1
   Terry Labonte 1
   Phil Parsons 1
   Ricky Rudd 1
   Ken Schrader..............................1
   Lake Speed 1

>> MONEY WON LEADERS

1. Bill Elliott $1,574,639
2. Rusty Wallace 1,411,567
3. Dale Earnhardt...................1,214,089
4. Terry Labonte 950,781
5. Davey Allison 844,532
6. Darrell Waltrip 731,659
7. Ken Schrader 631,544
8. Geoffrey Bodine 570,643
9. Phil Parsons 532,043
10. Sterling Marlin 521,464

>> POLE WINNERS   12

1. Bill Elliott 6
2. Alan Kulwicki 4
3. Davey Allison 3
   Geoffrey Bodine 3
5. Ricky Rudd 2
   Ken Schrader..............................2
   Morgan Shepherd 2
   Rusty Wallace 2
   Darrell Waltrip 2
10. Terry Labonte 1
   Mark Martin................................1
   Rick Wilson 1

>> TOP 20 PERFORMANCE CHART

Rk	Driver	Points	Starts	Poles	Wins	Top 5s	Top 10s	DNF
1.	Bill Elliott	4,488	29	6	6	15	22	1
2.	Rusty Wallace	4,464	29	2	6	19	23	2
3.	Dale Earnhardt	4,256	29	0	3	13	19	1
4.	Terry Labonte	4,007	29	1	1	11	18	3
5.	Ken Schrader	3,858	29	2	1	4	17	1
6.	Geoffrey Bodine	3,799	29	3	1	10	16	4
7.	Darrell Waltrip	3,764	29	2	2	10	14	4
8.	Davey Allison	3,631	29	3	2	12	16	7
9.	Phil Parsons	3,630	29	0	1	6	15	6
10.	Sterling Marlin	3,621	29	0	0	6	13	6
11.	Ricky Rudd	3,547	29	2	1	6	11	12
12.	Bobby Hillin Jr	3,446	29	0	0	1	7	2
13.	Kyle Petty	3,296	29	0	0	2	8	6
14.	Alan Kulwicki	3,176	29	4	1	7	9	12
15.	Mark Martin	3,142	29	1	0	3	10	10
16.	Neil Bonnett	3,035	27	0	2	3	7	5
17.	Lake Speed	2,979	29	0	1	4	7	11
18.	Michael Waltrip	2,949	29	0	0	1	3	8
19.	Dave Marcis	2,854	29	0	0	0	2	7
20.	Brett Bodine	2,833	29	0	0	2	5	11

>> 1987 SEASON <<

Race No.	Location	Date	Winner	Car owner
1.	Daytona Beach, Fla.	Feb. 15	Bill Elliott	Harry Melling
2.	Rockingham, N.C.	March 1	Dale Earnhardt	Richard Childress
3.	Richmond, Va.	March 8	Dale Earnhardt	Richard Childress
4.	Hampton, Ga.	March 15	Ricky Rudd	Bud Moore
5.	Darlington, S.C.	March 29	Dale Earnhardt	Richard Childress
6.	N. Wilkesboro, N.C.	April 5	Dale Earnhardt	Richard Childress
7.	Bristol, Tenn.	April 12	Dale Earnhardt	Richard Childress
8.	Martinsville, Va.	April 26	Dale Earnhardt	Richard Childress
9.	Talladega, Ala.	May 3	Davey Allison	Harry Ranier
10.	Concord, N.C.	May 24	Kyle Petty	Wood Brothers
11.	Dover, Del.	May 31	Davey Allison	Harry Ranier
12.	Long Pond, Pa.	June 14	Tim Richmond	Rick Hendrick
13.	Riverside, Calif.	June 21	Tim Richmond	Rick Hendrick
14.	Brooklyn, Mich.	June 28	Dale Earnhardt	Richard Childress
15.	Daytona Beach, Fla.	July 4	Bobby Allison	Stavola Brothers
16.	Long Pond, Pa.	July 19	Dale Earnhardt	Richard Childress
17.	Talladega, Ala.	July 26	Bill Elliott	Harry Melling
18.	Watkins Glen, N.Y.	Aug. 10	Rusty Wallace	Raymond Beadle
19.	Brooklyn, Mich.	Aug. 16	Bill Elliott	Harry Melling
20.	Bristol, Tenn.	Aug. 22	Dale Earnhardt	Richard Childress
21.	Darlington, S.C.	Sept. 6	Dale Earnhardt	Richard Childress
22.	Richmond, Va.	Sept. 13	Dale Earnhardt	Richard Childress
23.	Dover, Del.	Sept. 20	Ricky Rudd	Bud Moore
24.	Martinsville, Va.	Sept. 27	Darrell Waltrip	Rick Hendrick
25.	N. Wilkesboro, N.C.	Oct. 4	Terry Labonte	Junior Johnson
26.	Concord, N.C.	Oct. 11	Bill Elliott	Harry Melling
27.	Rockingham, N.C.	Oct. 25	Bill Elliott	Harry Melling
28.	Riverside, Calif.	Nov. 8	Rusty Wallace	Raymond Beadle
29.	Hampton, Ga.	Nov. 22	Bill Elliott	Harry Melling

>> POINTS STANDINGS

1. Dale Earnhardt 4,696
2. Bill Elliott.......................................4,207
3. Terry Labonte 4,007
4. Darrell Waltrip 3,911
5. Rusty Wallace 3,818
6. Ricky Rudd 3,742
7. Kyle Petty 3,737
8. Richard Petty 3,708
9. Bobby Allison 3,525
10. Ken Schrader 3,405

>> RACE WINNERS   10

1. Dale Earnhardt...............................11
2. Bill Elliott..6
3. Davey Allison 2
   Tim Richmond 2
   Ricky Rudd 2
   Rusty Wallace 2
7. Bobby Allison 1
   Terry Labonte..................................1
   Kyle Petty...1
   Darrell Waltrip 1

>> MONEY WON LEADERS

1. Dale Earnhardt.....................$2,099,243
2. Bill Elliott 1,619,210
3. Terry Labonte 825,369
4. Rusty Wallace 690,652
5. Ricky Rudd 653,508
6. Benny Parsons 566,484
7. Kyle Petty 544,437
8. Bobby Allison 515,894
9. Darrell Waltrip 511,768
10. Richard Petty 468,702

>> TOP 20 PERFORMANCE CHART

Rk	Driver	Points	Starts	Poles	Wins	Top 5s	Top 10s	DNF
1.	Dale Earnhardt	4,696	29	1	11	21	24	2
2.	Bill Elliott	4,207	29	8	6	16	20	5
3.	Terry Labonte	4,007	29	4	1	13	22	5
4.	Darrell Waltrip	3,911	29	0	1	6	16	2
5.	Rusty Wallace	3,818	29	1	2	9	16	7
6.	Ricky Rudd	3,742	29	0	2	10	13	9
7.	Kyle Petty	3,737	29	0	1	6	14	4
8.	Richard Petty	3,708	29	0	0	9	14	6
9.	Bobby Allison	3,525	29	1	1	4	13	9
10.	Ken Schrader	3,405	29	1	0	1	10	8
11.	Sterling Marlin	3,381	29	0	0	4	8	6
12.	Neil Bonnett	3,352	26	0	0	5	15	4
13.	Geoffrey Bodine	3,328	29	2	0	3	10	10
14.	Phil Parsons	3,327	29	0	0	1	7	5
15.	Alan Kulwicki	3,238	29	3	0	3	9	11
16.	Benny Parsons	3,215	29	0	0	6	9	12
17.	Morgan Shepherd	3,099	29	1	0	7	11	13
18.	Dave Marcis	3,080	29	0	0	2	7	10
19.	Bobby Hillin Jr	3,027	29	0	0	1	4	12
20.	Michael Waltrip	2,840	29	0	0	0	1	8

>> POLE WINNERS   12

1. Bill Elliott 8
2. Davey Allison 5
3. Terry Labonte...................................4
4. Alan Kulwicki 3
5. Geoffrey Bodine 2
6. Bobby Allison 1
   Dale Earnhardt 1
   Harry Gant 1
   Tim Richmond 1
   Ken Schrader 1
   Morgan Shepherd 1
   Rusty Wallace 1

>> 1986 SEASON <<

Race No.	Location	Date	Winner	Car owner
1.	Daytona Beach, Fla.	Feb. 16	Geoffrey Bodine	Rick Hendrick
2.	Richmond, Va.	Feb. 23	Kyle Petty	Wood Brothers
3.	Rockingham, N.C.	March 2	Terry Labonte	Billy Hagan
4.	Hampton, Ga.	March 16	Morgan Shepherd	Jack Beebe
5.	Bristol, Tenn.	April 6	Rusty Wallace	Raymond Beadle
6.	Darlington, S.C.	April 13	Dale Earnhardt	Richard Childress
7.	N. Wilkesboro, N.C.	April 20	Dale Earnhardt	Richard Childress
8.	Martinsville, Va.	April 27	Ricky Rudd	Bud Moore
9.	Talladega, Ala.	May 4	Bobby Allison	Stavola Brothers
10.	Dover, Del.	May 18	Geoffrey Bodine	Rick Hendrick
11.	Concord, N.C.	May 25	Dale Earnhardt	Richard Childress
12.	Riverside, Calif.	June 1	Darrell Waltrip	Junior Johnson
13.	Long Pond, Pa.	June 8	Tim Richmond	Rick Hendrick
14.	Brooklyn, Mich.	June 15	Bill Elliott	Harry Melling
15.	Daytona Beach, Fla.	July 4	Tim Richmond	Rick Hendrick
16.	Long Pond, Pa.	July 20	Tim Richmond	Rick Hendrick
17.	Talladega, Ala.	July 27	Bobby Hillin, Jr.	Stavola Brothers
18.	Watkins Glen, N.Y.	Aug. 10	Tim Richmond	Rick Hendrick
19.	Brooklyn, Mich.	Aug. 17	Bill Elliott	Harry Melling
20.	Bristol, Tenn.	Aug. 23	Darrell Waltrip	Junior Johnson
21.	Darlington, S.C.	Aug. 31	Tim Richmond	Rick Hendrick
22.	Richmond, Va.	Sept. 7	Tim Richmond	Rick Hendrick
23.	Dover, Del.	Sept. 14	Ricky Rudd	Bud Moore
24.	Martinsville, Va.	Sept. 21	Rusty Wallace	Raymond Beadle
25.	N. Wilkesboro, N.C.	Sept. 28	Darrell Waltrip	Junior Johnson
26.	Concord, N.C.	Oct. 5	Dale Earnhardt	Richard Childress
27.	Rockingham, N.C.	Oct. 19	Neil Bonnett	Junior Johnson
28.	Hampton, Ga.	Nov. 2	Dale Earnhardt	Richard Childress
29.	Riverside, Calif.	Nov.16	Tim Richmond	Rick Hendrick

>> POINTS STANDINGS

1. Dale Earnhardt 4,468
2. Darrell Waltrip 4,180
3. Tim Richmond 4,174
4. Bill Elliott 3,844
5. Ricky Rudd 3,823
6. Rusty Wallace 3,757
7. Bobby Allison 3,698
8. Geoffrey Bodine 3,678
9. Bobby Hillin Jr. 3,541
10. Kyle Petty 3,537

>> RACE WINNERS   13

1. Tim Richmond 7
2. Dale Earnhardt 5
3. Darrell Waltrip 3
4. Geoffrey Bodine 2
    Bill Elliott 2
    Ricky Rudd 2
    Rusty Wallace 2
8. Bobby Allison 1
    Neil Bonnett 1
    Bobby Hillin Jr. 1
    Terry Labonte 1
    Kyle Petty 1
    Morgan Shepherd 1

>> MONEY WON LEADERS

1. Dale Earnhardt $1,768,880
2. Darrell Waltrip 1,099,735
3. Bill Elliott 1,049,142
4. Tim Richmond 973,221
5. Geoffrey Bodine 795,111
6. Ricky Rudd 671,548
7. Harry Gant 583,024
8. Rusty Wallace 557,354
9. Terry Labonte 522,235
10. Bobby Allison 503,095

>> TOP 20 PERFORMANCE CHART

Rk	Driver	Points	Starts	Poles	Wins	Top 5s	Top 10s	DNF
1.	Dale Earnhardt	4,468	29	1	5	16	23	4
2.	Darrell Waltrip	4,180	29	1	3	21	22	7
3.	Tim Richmond	4,174	29	8	7	13	17	2
4.	Bill Elliott	3,844	29	4	2	8	16	6
5.	Ricky Rudd	3,823	29	1	2	11	17	7
6.	Rusty Wallace	3,757	29	0	2	4	16	4
7.	Bobby Allison	3,698	29	0	1	6	15	6
8.	Geoffrey Bodine	3,678	29	8	2	10	15	12
9.	Bobby Hillin Jr.	3,541	29	0	1	4	14	5
10.	Kyle Petty	3,537	29	0	1	4	14	6
11.	Harry Gant	3,498	29	2	0	9	13	14
12.	Terry Labonte	3,473	29	1	1	5	10	11
13.	Neil Bonnett	3,369	28	0	1	6	12	10
14.	Richard Petty	3,314	29	0	0	4	11	10
15.	Joe Ruttman	3,295	29	0	0	5	14	9
16.	Ken Schrader	3,052	29	0	0	0	4	9
17.	Dave Marcis	2,912	29	0	0	1	4	14
18.	Morgan Shepherd	2,896	27	0	1	4	8	15
19.	Michael Waltrip	2,853	28	0	0	0	0	8
20.	Buddy Arrington	2,776	26	0	0	0	0	3

>> POLE WINNERS   10

1. Geoffrey Bodine 8
    Tim Richmond 8
3. Bill Elliott 4
4. Harry Gant 2
5. Dale Earnhardt 1
    Terry Labonte 1
    Benny Parsons 1
    Ricky Rudd 1
    Darrell Waltrip 1
    Cale Yarborough 1

>> 1985 SEASON <<

Race No.	Location	Date	Winner	Car owner
1.	Daytona Beach, Fla.	Feb. 17	Bill Elliott	Harry Melling
2.	Richmond, Va.	Feb. 24	Dale Earnhardt	Richard Childress
3.	Rockingham, N.C.	March 3	Neil Bonnett	Junior Johnson
4.	Hampton, Ga.	March 17	Bill Elliott	Harry Melling
5.	Bristol, Tenn.	April 6	Dale Earnhardt	Richard Childress
6.	Darlington, S.C.	April 14	Bill Elliott	Harry Melling
7.	N. Wilkesboro, N.C.	April 21	Neil Bonnett	Junior Johnson
8.	Martinsville, Va.	April 28	Harry Gant	Needham-Reynolds
9.	Talladega, Ala.	May 5	Bill Elliott	Harry Melling
10.	Dover, Del.	May 19	Bill Elliott	Harry Melling
11.	Concord, N.C.	May 26	Darrell Waltrip	Junior Johnson
12.	Riverside, Calif.	June 2	Terry Labonte	Billy Hagan
13.	Long Pond, Pa.	June 9	Bill Elliott	Harry Melling
14.	Brooklyn, Mich.	June 16	Bill Elliott	Harry Melling
15.	Daytona Beach, Fla.	July 4	Greg Sacks	Bill Gardner
16.	Long Pond, Pa.	July 21	Bill Elliott	Harry Melling
17.	Talladega, Ala.	July 28	Cale Yarborough	Harry Ranier
18.	Brooklyn, Mich.	Aug. 11	Bill Elliott	Harry Melling
19.	Bristol, Tenn.	Aug. 24	Dale Earnhardt	Richard Childress
20.	Darlington, S.C.	Sept. 1	Bill Elliott	Harry Melling
21.	Richmond, Va.	Sept. 8	Darrell Waltrip	Junior Johnson
22.	Dover, Del.	Sept. 15	Harry Gant	Needham-Reynolds
23.	Martinsville, Va.	Sept. 22	Dale Earnhardt	Richard Childress
24.	N. Wilkesboro, N.C.	Sept. 29	Harry Gant	Needham-Reynolds
25.	Concord, N.C.	Oct. 6	Cale Yarborough	Harry Ranier
26.	Rockingham, N.C.	Oct. 20	Darrell Waltrip	Junior Johnson
27.	Hampton, Ga.	Nov. 3	Bill Elliott	Harry Melling
28.	Riverside, Calif.	Nov. 17	Ricky Rudd	Bud Moore

>> POINTS STANDINGS

1. Darrell Waltrip 4,292
2. Bill Elliott 4,191
3. Harry Gant 4,028
4. Neil Bonnett 3,897
5. Geoffrey Bodine 3,862
6. Ricky Rudd 3,857
7. Terry Labonte 3,683
8. Dale Earnhardt 3,561
9. Kyle Petty 3,523
10. Lake Speed....................................3,507

>> RACE WINNERS   9

1. Bill Elliott 11
2. Dale Earnhardt 4
3. Harry Gant 3
   Darrell Waltrip 3
5. Neil Bonnett 2
   Cale Yarborough................................2
7. Terry Labonte....................................1
   Ricky Rudd 1
   Greg Sacks 1

>> MONEY WON LEADERS

1. Bill Elliott $2,383,187
2. Darrell Waltrip 1,318,735
3. Harry Gant 804,287
4. Terry Labonte 694,510
5. Geoffrey Bodine 565,865
6. Dale Earnhardt 546,596
7. Neil Bonnett 530,145
8. Ricky Rudd 512,441
9. Cale Yarborough 310,465
10. Richard Petty 306,142

>> POLE WINNERS   7

1. Bill Elliott 11
2. Terry Labonte....................................4
   Darrell Waltrip 4
4. Geoffrey Bodine 3
   Harry Gant 3
6. Neil Bonnett.......................................1
   Dale Earnhardt....................................1

>> TOP 20 PERFORMANCE CHART

Rk	Driver	Points	Starts	Poles	Wins	Top 5s	Top 10s	DNF
1.	Darrell Waltrip	4,292	28	4	3	18	21	5
2.	Bill Elliott	4,191	28	11	11	16	18	3
3.	Harry Gant	4,028	28	3	3	14	19	6
4.	Neil Bonnett	3,897	28	1	2	11	18	5
5.	Geoffrey Bodine	3,862	28	3	0	10	14	5
6.	Ricky Rudd	3,857	28	0	1	13	19	5
7.	Terry Labonte	3,683	28	4	1	8	17	8
8.	Dale Earnhardt	3,561	28	1	4	10	16	9
9.	Kyle Petty	3,523	28	0	0	7	12	4
10.	Lake Speed	3,507	28	0	0	2	14	4
11.	Tim Richmond	3,413	28	0	0	3	13	7
12.	Bobby Allison	3,312	28	0	0	7	11	8
13.	Ron Bouchard	3,267	28	0	0	5	12	10
14.	Richard Petty	3,140	28	0	0	1	13	12
15.	Bobby Hillin Jr	3,091	28	0	0	0	5	5
16.	Ken Schrader	3,024	28	0	0	0	3	7
17.	Buddy Baker	2,986	28	0	0	2	7	13
18.	Dave Marcis	2,871	28	0	0	0	5	11
19.	Rusty Wallace	2,867	28	0	0	2	8	12
20.	Buddy Arrington	2,780	26	0	0	0	1	5

>> 1984 SEASON <<

Race No.	Location	Date	Winner	Car owner
1.	Daytona Beach, Fla.	Feb. 19	Cale Yarborough	Harry Ranier
2.	Richmond, Va.	Feb. 26	Ricky Rudd	Bud Moore
3.	Rockingham, N.C.	March 4	Bobby Allison	Bill Gardner
4.	Hampton, Ga.	March 18	Benny Parsons	Johnny Hayes
5.	Bristol, Tenn.	April 1	Darrell Waltrip	Junior Johnson
6.	N. Wilkesboro, N.C.	April 8	Tim Richmond	Raymond Beadle
7.	Darlington, S.C.	April 15	Darrell Waltrip	Junior Johnson
8.	Martinsville, Va.	April 29	Geoffrey Bodine	Rick Hendrick
9.	Talladega, Ala.	May 6	Cale Yarborough	Harry Ranier
10.	Nashville	May 12	Darrell Waltrip	Junior Johnson
11.	Dover, Del.	May 20	Richard Petty	Mike Curb
12.	Concord, N.C.	May 27	Bobby Allison	Bill Gardner
13.	Riverside, Calif.	June 3	Terry Labonte	Billy Hagan
14.	Long Pond, Pa.	June 10	Cale Yarborough	Harry Ranier
15.	Brooklyn, Mich.	June 17	Bill Elliott	Harry Melling
16.	Daytona Beach, Fla.	July 4	Richard Petty	Mike Curb
17.	Nashville	July 14	Geoffrey Bodine	Rick Hendrick
18.	Long Pond, Pa.	July 22	Harry Gant	Needham-Reynolds
19.	Talladega, Ala.	July 29	Dale Earnhardt	Richard Childress
20.	Brooklyn, Mich.	Aug. 12	Darrell Waltrip	Junior Johnson
21.	Bristol, Tenn.	Aug. 25	Terry Labonte	Billy Hagan
22.	Darlington, S.C.	Sept. 2	Harry Gant	Needham-Reynolds
23.	Richmond, Va.	Sept. 9	Darrell Waltrip	Junior Johnson
24.	Dover, Del.	Sept. 16	Harry Gant	Needham-Reynolds
25.	Martinsville, Va.	Sept. 23	Darrell Waltrip	Junior Johnson
26.	Concord, N.C.	Oct. 7	Bill Elliott	Harry Melling
27.	N. Wilkesboro, N.C.	Oct. 14	Darrell Waltrip	Junior Johnson
28.	Rockingham, N.C.	Oct. 21	Bill Elliott	Harry Melling
29.	Hampton, Ga.	Nov. 11	Dale Earnhardt	Richard Childress
30.	Riverside, Calif.	Nov. 18	Geoffrey Bodine	Rick Hendrick

>> POINTS STANDINGS

1. Terry Labonte 4,508
2. Harry Gant 4,443
3. Bill Elliott 4,377
4. Dale Earnhardt 4,265
5. Darrell Waltrip 4,230
6. Bobby Allison 4,094
7. Ricky Rudd 3,918
8. Neil Bonnett 3,802
9. Geoffrey Bodine 3,734
10. Richard Petty 3,643

>> RACE WINNERS   12

1. Darrell Waltrip 7
2. Geoffrey Bodine 3
   Bill Elliott 3
   Harry Gant 3
   Cale Yarborough 3
6. Bobby Allison 2
   Dale Earnhardt 2
   Terry Labonte 2
   Richard Petty 2
10. Benny Parsons 1
   Tim Richmond 1
   Ricky Rudd 1

>> MONEY WON LEADERS

1. Terry Labonte $713,010
2. Darrell Waltrip 703,876
3. Bill Elliott 660,226
4. Harry Gant 650,707
5. Bobby Allison 627,637
6. Dale Earnhardt 616,788
7. Ricky Rudd 476,602
8. Geoffrey Bodine 393,924
9. Cale Yarborough 385,853
10. Dave Marcis 330,766

>> TOP 20 PERFORMANCE CHART

Rk	Driver	Points	Starts	Poles	Wins	Top 5s	Top 10s	DNF
1.	Terry Labonte	4,508	30	2	2	17	24	3
2.	Harry Gant	4,443	30	3	3	15	23	4
3.	Bill Elliott	4,377	30	4	3	13	24	3
4.	Dale Earnhardt	4,265	30	0	2	12	22	2
5.	Darrell Waltrip	4,235	30	4	7	13	20	3
6.	Bobby Allison	4,094	30	0	2	13	19	4
7.	Ricky Rudd	3,918	30	4	1	7	16	6
8.	Neil Bonnett	3,797	30	0	0	7	14	6
9.	Geoffrey Bodine	3,734	30	3	3	7	14	8
10.	Richard Petty	3,643	30	0	2	5	13	7
11.	Ron Bouchard	3,609	30	0	0	5	10	8
12.	Tim Richmond	3,505	30	0	1	6	11	12
13.	Dave Marcis	3,416	30	0	0	3	9	7
14.	Rusty Wallace	3,316	30	0	0	2	4	9
15.	Dick Brooks	3,265	30	0	0	1	5	11
16.	Kyle Petty	3,159	30	0	0	1	6	7
17.	Trevor Boys	3,040	30	0	0	0	1	8
18.	Joe Ruttman	2,945	29	1	0	0	8	14
19.	Greg Sacks	2,545	29	0	0	0	1	14
20.	Buddy Arrington	2,504	26	0	0	0	0	9

>> POLE WINNERS   11

1. Bill Elliott 4
   Ricky Rudd 4
   Darrell Waltrip 4
   Cale Yarborough 4
5. Geoffrey Bodine 3
   Harry Gant 3
7. Terry Labonte 2
   Benny Parsons 2
9. Buddy Baker 1
   David Pearson 1
   Joe Ruttman 1

1983 SEASON

Race No.	Location	Date	Winner	Car owner
1.	Daytona Beach, Fla.	Feb. 20	Cale Yarborough	Harry Ranier
2.	Richmond, Va.	Feb. 27	Bobby Allison	Bill Gardner
3.	Rockingham, N.C.	March 13	Richard Petty	Petty Enterprises
4.	Hampton, Ga.	March 27	Cale Yarborough	Harry Ranier
5.	Darlington, S.C.	April 10	Harry Gant	Needham-Reynolds
6.	N. Wilkesboro, N.C.	April 17	Darrell Waltrip	Junior Johnson
7.	Martinsville, Va.	April 24	Darrell Waltrip	Junior Johnson
8.	Talladega, Ala.	May 1	Richard Petty	Petty Enterprises
9.	Nashville	May 7	Darrell Waltrip	Junior Johnson
10.	Dover, Del.	May 15	Bobby Allison	Bill Gardner
11.	Bristol, Tenn.	May 21	Darrell Waltrip	Junior Johnson
12.	Concord, N.C.	May 29	Neil Bonnett	Rahilly-Mock
13.	Riverside, Calif.	June 5	Ricky Rudd	Richard Childress
14.	Long Pond, Pa.	June 12	Bobby Allison	Bill Gardner
15.	Brooklyn, Mich.	June 19	Cale Yarborough	Harry Ranier
16.	Daytona Beach, Fla.	July 4	Buddy Baker	Wood Brothers
17.	Nashville	July 16	Dale Earnhardt	Bud Moore
18.	Long Pond, Pa.	July 24	Tim Richmond	Raymond Beadle
19.	Talladega, Ala.	July 31	Dale Earnhardt	Bud Moore
20.	Brooklyn, Mich.	Aug. 21	Cale Yarborough	Harry Ranier
21.	Bristol, Tenn.	Aug. 27	Darrell Waltrip	Junior Johnson
22.	Darlington, S.C.	Sept. 5	Bobby Allison	Bill Gardner
23.	Richmond, Va.	Sept. 11	Bobby Allison	Bill Gardner
24.	Dover, Del.	Sept. 18	Bobby Allison	Bill Gardner
25.	Martinsville, Va.	Sept. 25	Ricky Rudd	Richard Childress
26.	N. Wilkesboro, N.C.	Oct. 2	Darrell Waltrip	Junior Johnson
27.	Concord, N.C.	Oct. 9	Richard Petty	Petty Enterprises
28.	Rockingham, N.C.	Oct. 30	Terry Labonte	Billy Hagan
29.	Hampton, Ga.	Nov. 6	Neil Bonnett	Rahilly-Mock
30.	Riverside, Calif.	Nov. 20	Bill Elliott	Harry Melling

>> POINTS STANDINGS

1. Bobby Allison 4,667
2. Darrell Waltrip 4,620
3. Bill Elliott 4,279
4. Richard Petty 4,042
5. Terry Labonte 4,009
6. Neil Bonnett 3,837
7. Harry Gant 3,790
8. Dale Earnhardt 3,732
9. Ricky Rudd 3,693
10. Tim Richmond..............................3,592

>> RACE WINNERS   12

1. Bobby Allison 6
   Darrell Waltrip 6
3. Cale Yarborough 4
4. Richard Petty 3
5. Neil Bonnett 2
   Dale Earnhardt 2
   Ricky Rudd 2
8. Buddy Baker 1
   Bill Elliott 1
   Harry Gant 1
   Terry Labonte.....................................1
   Tim Richmond 1

>> MONEY WON LEADERS

1. Bobby Allison $828,355
2. Darrell Waltrip 824,858
3. Richard Petty 491,022
4. Bill Elliott............................479,965
5. Neil Bonnett 455,662
6. Dale Earnhardt 446,272
7. Harry Gant 390,189
8. Terry Labonte 362,790
9. Dave Marcis 306,355
10. Morgan Shepherd 270,851

>> TOP 20 PERFORMANCE CHART

Rk	Driver	Points	Starts	Poles	Wins	Top 5s	Top 10s	DNF
1.	Bobby Allison	4,667	30	0	6	18	25	2
2.	Darrell Waltrip	4,620	30	7	6	22	25	4
3.	Bill Elliott	4,279	30	0	1	12	22	3
4.	Richard Petty	4,042	30	0	3	9	21	5
5.	Terry Labonte	4,009	30	3	1	11	20	7
6.	Neil Bonnett	3,837	30	4	2	10	17	7
7.	Harry Gant	3,790	30	0	1	10	16	9
8.	Dale Earnhardt	3,732	30	0	2	9	14	13
9.	Ricky Rudd	3,693	30	4	2	7	14	9
10.	Tim Richmond	3,592	30	4	1	10	15	13
11.	Dave Marcis	3,361	30	0	0	0	7	11
12.	Joe Ruttman	3,342	30	2	0	4	10	13
13.	Kyle Petty	3,261	30	0	0	0	2	10
14.	Buddy Arrington	3,158	30	0	0	0	2	10
15.	Ron Bouchard	3,113	28	1	0	1	7	11
16.	Geoffrey Bodine	3,019	28	1	0	5	9	15
17.	Jimmy Means	2,983	28	0	0	0	3	7
18.	Sterling Marlin	2,980	30	0	0	0	1	11
19.	Dick Brooks	2,946	30	0	0	2	6	12
20.	Morgan Shepherd	2,818	26	0	0	3	13	11

>> POLE WINNERS   10

1. Darrell Waltrip 7
2. Neil Bonnett 4
   Tim Richmond 4
   Ricky Rudd 4
5. Terry Labonte.....................................3
   Cale Yarborough 3
7. Joe Ruttman 2
8. Buddy Baker 1
   Geoffrey Bodine 1
   Ron Bouchard 1

>> 1982 SEASON <<

Race No.	Location	Date	Winner	Car owner
1.	Daytona Beach, Fla.	Feb. 14	Bobby Allison	Bill Gardner
2.	Richmond, Va.	Feb. 21	Dave Marcis	Dave Marcis
3.	Bristol, Tenn.	March 14	Darrell Waltrip	Junior Johnson
4.	Hampton, Ga.	March 21	Darrell Waltrip	Junior Johnson
5.	Rockingham, N.C.	March 28	Cale Yarborough	M.C. Anderson
6.	Darlington, S.C.	April 4	Dale Earnhardt	Bud Moore
7.	N. Wilkesboro, N.C.	April 18	Darrell Waltrip	Junior Johnson
8.	Martinsville, Va.	April 25	Harry Gant	Needham-Reynolds
9.	Talladega, Ala.	May 2	Darrell Waltrip	Junior Johnson
10.	Nashville	May 8	Darrell Waltrip	Junior Johnson
11.	Dover, Del.	May 16	Bobby Allison	Bill Gardner
12.	Concord, N.C.	May 30	Neil Bonnett	Wood Brothers
13.	Long Pond, Pa.	June 6	Bobby Allison	Bill Gardner
14.	Riverside, Calif.	June 13	Tim Richmond	Jim Stacy
15.	Brooklyn, Mich.	June 20	Cale Yarborough	M.C. Anderson
16.	Daytona Beach, Fla.	July 4	Bobby Allison	Bill Gardner
17.	Nashville	July 10	Darrell Waltrip	Junior Johnson
18.	Long Pond, Pa.	July 25	Bobby Allison	Bill Gardner
19.	Talladega, Ala.	Aug. 1	Darrell Waltrip	Junior Johnson
20.	Brooklyn, Mich.	Aug. 22	Bobby Allison	Bill Gardner
21.	Bristol, Tenn.	Aug. 28	Darrell Waltrip	Junior Johnson
22.	Darlington, S.C.	Sept. 6	Cale Yarborough	M.C. Anderson
23.	Richmond, Va.	Sept. 12	Bobby Allison	Bill Gardner
24.	Dover, Del.	Sept. 19	Darrell Waltrip	Junior Johnson
25.	N. Wilkesboro, N.C.	Oct. 3	Darrell Waltrip	Junior Johnson
26.	Concord, N.C.	Oct. 10	Harry Gant	Needham-Reynolds
27.	Martinsville, Va.	Oct. 17	Darrell Waltrip	Junior Johnson
28.	Rockingham, N.C.	Oct. 31	Darrell Waltrip	Junior Johnson
29.	Hampton, Ga.	Nov. 7	Bobby Allison	Bill Gardner
30.	Riverside, Calif.	Nov. 21	Tim Richmond	Jim Stacy

>> POINTS STANDINGS

1. Darrell Waltrip 4,489
2. Bobby Allison 4,417
3. Terry Labonte 4,211
4. Harry Gant 3,877
5. Richard Petty 3,814
6. Dave Marcis 3,666
7. Buddy Arrington 3,642
8. Ron Bouchard 3,545
9. Ricky Rudd 3,537
10. Morgan Shepherd 3,451

>> RACE WINNERS   8

1. Darrell Waltrip 12
2. Bobby Allison 8
3. Cale Yarborough 3
4. Harry Gant 2
   Tim Richmond 2
6. Neil Bonnett 1
   Dale Earnhardt......................................1
   Dave Marcis 1

>> MONEY WON LEADERS

1. Darrell Waltrip $873,118
2. Bobby Allison 726,562
3. Richard Petty 453,832
4. Dale Earnhardt 375,325
5. Terry Labonte 363,970
6. Ron Bouchard 356,582
7. Harry Gant 311,769
8. Jody Ridley 304,960
9. Geoffrey Bodine 258,500
10. Buddy Baker...........................253,675

>> POLE WINNERS   15

1. Darrell Waltrip 7
2. Benny Parsons 3
3. Geoffrey Bodine 2
   Terry Labonte 2
   David Pearson 2
   Ricky Rudd 2
   Morgan Shepherd 2
   Cale Yarborough 2
9. Bobby Allison..1
   Buddy Baker 1
   Ron Bouchard 1
   Dale Earnhardt......................................1
   Bill Elliott 1
   Harry Gant 1
   Tim Richmond 1

>> TOP 20 PERFORMANCE CHART

Rk	Driver	Points	Starts	Poles	Wins	Top 5s	Top 10s	DNF
1.	Darrell Waltrip	4,489	30	7	12	17	20	8
2.	Bobby Allison	4,417	30	1	8	14	20	8
3.	Terry Labonte	4,211	30	2	0	17	21	8
4.	Harry Gant	3,877	30	1	2	9	16	10
5.	Richard Petty	3,814	30	0	0	9	16	13
6.	Dave Marcis	3,666	30	0	1	2	14	7
7.	Buddy Arrington	3,642	30	0	0	0	8	2
8.	Ron Bouchard	3,545	30	1	0	3	15	10
9.	Ricky Rudd	3,537	30	2	0	6	13	13
10.	Morgan Shepherd	3,451	29	2	0	6	13	14
11.	Jimmy Means	3,423	30	0	0	0	2	5
12.	Dale Earnhardt	3,402	30	1	1	7	12	18
13.	Jody Ridley	3,333	30	0	0	0	10	12
14.	Mark Martin	3,042	30	0	0	2	8	12
15.	Kyle Petty	3,024	29	0	0	2	4	16
16.	Joe Ruttman	3,021	29	0	0	5	7	15
17.	Neil Bonnett	2,966	25	0	1	7	10	12
18.	Benny Parsons	2,892	23	3	0	10	13	10
19.	J.D. McDuffie	2,886	30	0	0	0	1	14
20.	Lake Speed	2,853	30	0	0	0	5	19

>> 1981 SEASON <<

Race No.	Location	Date	Winner	Car owner
1.	Riverside, Calif.	Jan. 11	Bobby Allison	Harry Ranier
2.	Daytona Beach, Fla.	Feb. 15	Richard Petty	Petty Enterprises
3.	Richmond, Va.	Feb. 22	Darrell Waltrip	Junior Johnson
4.	Rockingham, N.C.	March 1	Darrell Waltrip	Junior Johnson
5.	Hampton, Ga.	March 15	Cale Yarborough	M.C. Anderson
6.	Bristol, Tenn.	March 29	Darrell Waltrip	Junior Johnson
7.	N. Wilkesboro, N.C.	April 5	Richard Petty	Petty Enterprises
8.	Darlington, S.C.	April 12	Darrell Waltrip	Junior Johnson
9.	Martinsville, Va.	April 26	Morgan Shepherd	Cliff Stewart
10.	Talladega, Ala.	May 3	Bobby Allison	Harry Ranier
11.	Nashville	May 9	Benny Parsons	Bud Moore
12.	Dover, Del.	May 17	Jody Ridley	Junie Donlavey
13.	Concord, N.C.	May 24	Bobby Allison	Harry Ranier
14.	Bryan, Texas	June 7	Benny Parsons	Bud Moore
15.	Riverside, Calif.	June 14	Darrell Waltrip	Junior Johnson
16.	Brooklyn, Mich.	June 21	Bobby Allison	Harry Ranier
17.	Daytona Beach, Fla.	July 4	Cale Yarborough	M.C. Anderson
18.	Nashville	July 11	Darrell Waltrip	Junior Johnson
19.	Long Pond, Pa.	July 26	Darrell Waltrip	Junior Johnson
20.	Talladega, Ala.	Aug. 2	Ron Bouchard	Jack Beebe
21.	Brooklyn, Mich.	Aug. 16	Richard Petty	Petty Enterprises
22.	Bristol, Tenn.	Aug. 22	Darrell Waltrip	Junior Johnson
23.	Darlington, S.C.	Sept. 7	Neil Bonnett	Wood Brothers
24.	Richmond, Va.	Sept. 13	Benny Parsons	Bud Moore
25.	Dover, Del.	Sept. 20	Neil Bonnett	Wood Brothers
26.	Martinsville, Va.	Sept. 27	Darrell Waltrip	Junior Johnson
27.	N. Wilkesboro, N.C.	Oct. 4	Darrell Waltrip	Junior Johnson
28.	Concord, N.C.	Oct. 11	Darrell Waltrip	Junior Johnson
29.	Rockingham, N.C.	Nov. 1	Darrell Waltrip	Junior Johnson
30.	Hampton, Ga.	Nov. 8	Neil Bonnett	Wood Brothers
31.	Riverside, Calif.	Nov. 22	Bobby Allison	Harry Ranier

>> POINTS STANDINGS

1. Darrell Waltrip 4,880
2. Bobby Allison 4,827
3. Harry Gant 4,213
4. Terry Labonte 4,052
5. Jody Ridley 4,002
6. Ricky Rudd 3,991
7. Dale Earnhardt 3,978
8. Richard Petty 3,882
9. Dave Marcis 3,510
10. Benny Parsons 3,452

>> RACE WINNERS   9

1. Darrell Waltrip 12
2. Bobby Allison 5
3. Neil Bonnett 3
   Benny Parsons 3
   Richard Petty 3
6. Cale Yarborough 2
7. Ron Bouchard 1
   Jody Ridley 1
   Morgan Shepherd 1

>> MONEY WON LEADERS

1. Darrell Waltrip.............$693,352
2. Bobby Allison 644,311
3. Richard Petty 389,214
4. Ricky Rudd 381,968
5. Dale Earnhardt 347,113
6. Terry Labonte 334,987
7. Benny Parsons 287,949
8. Harry Gant 280,047
9. Jody Ridley 257,318
10. Neil Bonnett 181,670

>> POLE WINNERS   13

1. Darrell Waltrip 11
2. Harry Gant 3
   Ricky Rudd 3
4. Bobby Allison...................2
   Terry Labonte...................2
   Mark Martin......................2
   Cale Yarborough.............2
8. Neil Bonnett.....................1
   Ron Bouchard 1
   Bill Elliott..........................1
   Dave Marcis 1
   David Pearson 1
   Morgan Shepherd 1

>> TOP 20 PERFORMANCE CHART

Rk	Driver	Points	Starts	Poles	Wins	Top 5s	Top 10s	DNF
1.	Darrell Waltrip	4,880	31	11	12	21	25	4
2.	Bobby Allison	4,827	31	2	5	21	26	3
3.	Harry Gant	4,213	31	3	0	13	18	9
4.	Terry Labonte	4,052	31	2	0	8	17	7
5.	Jody Ridley	4,002	31	0	1	3	18	8
6.	Ricky Rudd	3,991	31	3	0	14	17	9
7.	Dale Earnhardt	3,978	31	0	0	9	17	10
8.	Richard Petty	3,882	31	0	3	12	16	14
9.	Dave Marcis	3,510	31	1	0	4	9	15
10.	Benny Parsons	3,452	31	0	3	10	12	17
11.	Buddy Arrington	3,384	31	0	0	0	7	7
12.	Kyle Petty	3,335	31	0	0	1	10	18
13.	Morgan Shepherd	3,264	29	1	1	3	10	13
14.	Jimmy Means	3,145	30	0	0	0	2	6
15.	Tommy Gale	3,143	30	0	0	0	0	5
16.	Tim Richmond	3,094	29	0	0	0	6	12
17.	J.D. McDuffie	3,000	28	0	0	0	1	8
18.	Lake Speed	2,820	27	0	0	0	6	12
19.	James Hylton	2,756	28	0	0	0	0	11
20.	Joe Millikan	2,682	23	0	0	3	10	6

>> 1980 SEASON <<

Race No.	Location	Date	Winner	Car owner
1.	Riverside, Calif.	Jan. 19	Darrell Waltrip	Bill Gardner
2.	Daytona Beach, Fla.	Feb. 17	Buddy Baker	Harry Ranier
3.	Richmond, Va.	Feb. 24	Darrell Waltrip	Bill Gardner
4.	Rockingham, N.C.	March 9	Cale Yarborough	Junior Johnson
5.	Hampton, Ga.	March 16	Dale Earnhardt	Rod Osterlund
6.	Bristol, Tenn.	March 30	Dale Earnhardt	Rod Osterlund
7.	Darlington, S.C.	April 13	David Pearson	Hoss Ellington
8.	N. Wilkesboro, N.C.	April 20	Richard Petty	Petty Enterprises
9.	Martinsville, Va.	April 27	Darrell Waltrip	Bill Gardner
10.	Talladega, Ala.	May 4	Buddy Baker	Harry Ranier
11.	Nashville	May 10	Richard Petty	Petty Enterprises
12.	Dover, Del.	May 18	Bobby Allison	Bud Moore
13.	Concord, N.C.	May 25	Benny Parsons	M.C. Anderson
14.	Bryan, Texas	June 1	Cale Yarborough	Junior Johnson
15.	Riverside, Calif.	June 8	Darrell Waltrip	Bill Gardner
16.	Brooklyn, Mich.	June 15	Benny Parsons	M.C. Anderson
17.	Daytona Beach, Fla.	July 4	Bobby Allison	Bud Moore
18.	Nashville	July 12	Dale Earnhardt	Rod Osterlund
19.	Long Pond, Pa.	July 27	Neil Bonnett	Wood Brothers
20.	Talladega, Ala.	Aug. 3	Neil Bonnett	Wood Brothers
21.	Brooklyn, Mich.	Aug. 17	Cale Yarborough	Junior Johnson
22.	Bristol, Tenn.	Aug. 23	Cale Yarborough	Junior Johnson
23.	Darlington, S.C.	Sept. 1	Terry Labonte	Billy Hagan
24.	Richmond, Va.	Sept. 7	Bobby Allison	Bud Moore
25.	Dover, Del.	Sept. 14	Darrell Waltrip	Bill Gardner
26.	N. Wilkesboro, N.C.	Sept. 21	Bobby Allison	Bud Moore
27.	Martinsville, Va.	Sept. 28	Dale Earnhardt	Rod Osterlund
28.	Concord, N.C.	Oct. 5	Dale Earnhardt	Rod Osterlund
29.	Rockingham, N.C.	Oct. 19	Cale Yarborough	Junior Johnson
30.	Hampton, Ga.	Nov. 2	Cale Yarborough	Junior Johnson
31.	Fontana, Calif.	Nov. 15	Benny Parsons	M.C. Anderson

>> POINTS STANDINGS

1. Dale Earnhardt 4,661
2. Cale Yarborough 4,642
3. Benny Parsons 4,278
4. Richard Petty 4,255
5. Darrell Waltrip 4,239
6. Bobby Allison 4,020
7. Jody Ridley 3,972
8. Terry Labonte 3,766
9. Dave Marcis 3,745
10. Richard Childress 3,742

>> RACE WINNERS   10

1. Cale Yarborough 6
2. Dale Earnhardt 5
   Darrell Waltrip 5
4. Bobby Allison 4
5. Benny Parsons 3
6. Buddy Baker 2
   Neil Bonnett 2
   Richard Petty 2
9. Terry Labonte 1
   David Pearson 1

>> MONEY WON LEADERS

1. Dale Earnhardt $588,926
2. Cale Yarborough 537,358
3. Benny Parsons 385,140
4. Darrell Waltrip 382,138
5. Richard Petty 374,092
6. Bobby Allison 356,050
7. Buddy Baker 264,200
8. Terry Labonte 215,889
9. Neil Bonnett 210,547
10. Jody Ridley 196,617

>> POLE WINNERS   7

1. Cale Yarborough 14
2. Buddy Baker 6
3. Darrell Waltrip 5
4. Bobby Allison 2
   Benny Parsons 2
6. Donnie Allison 1
   David Pearson 1

>> TOP 20 PERFORMANCE CHART

Rk	Driver	Points	Starts	Poles	Wins	Top 5s	Top 10s	DNF
1.	Dale Earnhardt	4,661	31	0	5	19	24	4
2.	Cale Yarborough	4,642	31	14	6	19	22	5
3.	Benny Parsons	4,278	31	2	3	16	21	10
4.	Richard Petty	4,255	31	0	2	15	19	9
5.	Darrell Waltrip	4,239	31	5	5	16	17	12
6.	Bobby Allison	4,020	31	2	4	12	18	13
7.	Jody Ridley	3,972	31	0	0	2	18	4
8.	Terry Labonte	3,766	31	0	1	6	16	12
9.	Dave Marcis	3,745	31	0	0	4	14	8
10.	Richard Childress	3,742	31	0	0	0	10	4
11.	Harry Gant	3,703	31	0	0	9	14	10
12.	Buddy Arrington	3,461	31	0	0	0	7	8
13.	James Hylton	3,449	31	0	0	0	4	3
14.	Ronnie Thomas	3,066	30	0	0	0	4	13
15.	Cecil Gordon	2,993	29	0	0	0	3	6
16.	J.D. McDuffie	2,968	31	0	0	0	3	15
17.	Jimmy Means	2,947	28	0	0	0	0	8
18.	Tommy Gale	2,885	29	0	0	0	0	8
19.	Neil Bonnett	2,865	22	0	2	10	13	10
20.	Roger Hamby	2,606	26	0	0	0	0	9

>> 1979 SEASON <<

Race No.	Location	Date	Winner	Car owner
1.	Riverside, Calif.	Jan. 14	Darrell Waltrip	Bill Gardner
2.	Daytona Beach, Fla.	Feb. 18	Richard Petty	Petty Enterprises
3.	Rockingham, N.C.	March 4	Bobby Allison	Bud Moore
4.	Richmond, Va.	March 11	Cale Yarborough	Junior Johnson
5.	Hampton, Ga.	March 18	Buddy Baker	Harry Ranier
6.	N. Wilkesboro, N.C.	March 25	Bobby Allison	Bud Moore
7.	Bristol, Tenn.	April 1	Dale Earnhardt	Rod Osterlund
8.	Darlington, S.C.	April 8	Darrell Waltrip	Bill Gardner
9.	Martinsville, Va.	April 22	Richard Petty	Petty Enterprises
10.	Talladega, Ala.	May 6	Bobby Allison	Bud Moore
11.	Nashville	May 12	Cale Yarborough	Junior Johnson
12.	Dover, Del.	May 20	Neil Bonnett	Wood Brothers
13.	Concord, N.C.	May 27	Darrell Waltrip	Bill Gardner
14.	Bryan, Texas	June 3	Darrell Waltrip	Bill Gardner
15.	Riverside, Calif.	June 10	Bobby Allison	Bud Moore
16.	Brooklyn, Mich.	June 17	Buddy Baker	Harry Ranier
17.	Daytona Beach, Fla.	July 4	Neil Bonnett	Wood Brothers
18.	Nashville	July 14	Darrell Waltrip	Bill Gardner
19.	Long Pond, Pa.	July 30	Cale Yarborough	Junior Johnson
20.	Talladega, Ala.	Aug. 5	Darrell Waltrip	Bill Gardner
21.	Brooklyn, Mich.	Aug. 19	Richard Petty	Petty Enterprises
22.	Bristol, Tenn.	Aug. 25	Darrell Waltrip	Bill Gardner
23.	Darlington, S.C.	Sept. 3	David Pearson	Rod Osterlund
24.	Richmond, Va.	Sept. 9	Bobby Allison	Bud Moore
25.	Dover, Del.	Sept. 16	Richard Petty	Petty Enterprises
26.	Martinsville, Va.	Sept. 23	Buddy Baker	Harry Ranier
27.	Concord, N.C.	Oct. 7	Cale Yarborough	Junior Johnson
28.	N. Wilkesboro, N.C.	Oct. 14	Benny Parsons	M.C. Anderson
29.	Rockingham, N.C.	Oct. 21	Richard Petty	Petty Enterprises
30.	Hampton, Ga.	Nov. 4	Neil Bonnett	Wood Brothers
31.	Fontana, Calif.	Nov. 18	Benny Parsons	M.C. Anderson

>> POINTS STANDINGS

1. Richard Petty 4,830
2. Darrell Waltrip................4,819
3. Bobby Allison.................4,633
4. Cale Yarborough.............4,604
5. Benny Parsons................4,256
6. Joe Millikan...................4,014
7. Dale Earnhardt................3,749
8. Richard Childress............3,735
9. Ricky Rudd....................3,642
10. Terry Labonte................3,615

>> RACE WINNERS   9

1. Darrell Waltrip 7
2. Bobby Allison 5
   Richard Petty 5
4. Cale Yarborough................4
5. Buddy Baker 3
   Neil Bonnett 3
7. Benny Parsons.................2
8. Dale Earnhardt.................1
   David Pearson 1

>> MONEY WON LEADERS

1. Richard Petty $531,292
2. Darrell Waltrip..........523,691
3. Cale Yarborough........413,872
4. Bobby Allison............403,014
5. Buddy Baker 287,552
6. Dale Earnhardt 264,086
7. Benny Parsons 241,205
8. Joe Millikan..............222,053
9. Ricky Rudd 146,302
10. Donnie Allison..........144,770

>> POLE WINNERS   12

1. Buddy Baker 7
2. Darrell Waltrip..................5
3. Neil Bonnet 4
   Dale Earnhardt..................4
5. Bobby Allison...................3
6. David Pearson 2
7. Donnie Allison..................1
   Harry Gant 1
   Joe Millikan......................1
   Benny Parsons.................1
   Richard Petty 1
   Cale Yarborough...............1

>> TOP 20 PERFORMANCE CHART

Rk	Driver	Points	Starts	Poles	Wins	Top 5s	Top 10s	DNF
1.	Richard Petty	4,830	31	1	5	23	27	3
2.	Darrell Waltrip	4,819	31	5	7	19	22	2
3.	Bobby Allison	4,633	31	3	5	18	22	7
4.	Cale Yarborough	4,604	31	1	4	19	22	6
5.	Benny Parsons	4,256	31	1	2	16	21	7
6.	Joe Millikan	4,014	31	1	0	5	20	8
7.	Dale Earnhardt	3,749	27	4	1	11	17	4
8.	Richard Childress	3,735	31	0	0	1	11	5
9.	Ricky Rudd	3,642	28	0	0	4	17	6
10.	Terry Labonte	3,615	31	0	0	2	13	10
11.	Buddy Arrington	3,589	31	0	0	1	7	9
12.	D.K. Ulrich	3,508	31	0	0	0	5	5
13.	J.D. McDuffie	3,473	31	0	0	1	7	11
14.	James Hylton	3,405	30	0	0	0	5	7
15.	Buddy Baker	3,249	26	7	3	12	15	11
16.	Frank Warren	3,199	31	0	0	0	3	10
17.	Ronnie Thomas	2,912	30	0	0	0	3	15
18.	Tommy Gale	2,795	28	0	0	0	1	9
19.	Cecil Gordon	2,737	28	0	0	0	0	9
20.	Dave Marcis	2,736	25	0	0	1	6	12

>> 1978 SEASON <<

Race No.	Location	Date	Winner	Car owner
1.	Riverside, Calif.	Jan. 22	Cale Yarborough	Junior Johnson
2.	Daytona Beach, Fla.	Feb. 19	Bobby Allison	Bud Moore
3.	Richmond, Va.	Feb. 26	Benny Parsons	L.G. DeWitt
4.	Rockingham, N.C.	March 5	David Pearson	Wood Brothers
5.	Hampton, Ga.	March 19	Bobby Allison	Bud Moore
6.	Bristol, Tenn.	April 2	Darrell Waltrip	Bill Gardner
7.	Darlington, S.C.	April 9	Benny Parsons	L.G. DeWitt
8.	N. Wilkesboro, N.C.	April 16	Darrell Waltrip	Bill Gardner
9.	Martinsville, Va.	April 23	Darrell Waltrip	Bill Gardner
10.	Talladega, Ala.	May 14	Cale Yarborough	Junior Johnson
11.	Dover, Del.	May 21	David Pearson	Wood Brothers
12.	Concord, N.C.	May 28	Darrell Waltrip	Bill Gardner
13.	Nashville	June 3	Cale Yarborough	Junior Johnson
14.	Riverside, Calif.	June 11	Benny Parsons	L.G. DeWitt
15.	Brooklyn, Mich.	June 18	Cale Yarborough	Junior Johnson
16.	Daytona Beach, Fla.	July 4	David Pearson	Wood Brothers
17.	Nashville	July 15	Cale Yarborough	Junior Johnson
18.	Long Pond, Pa.	July 30	Darrell Waltrip	Bill Gardner
19.	Talladega, Ala.	Aug. 6	Lennie Pond	Harry Ranier
20.	Brooklyn, Mich.	Aug. 20	David Pearson	Wood Brothers
21.	Bristol, Tenn.	Aug. 26	Cale Yarborough	Junior Johnson
22.	Darlington, S.C.	Sept. 4	Cale Yarborough	Junior Johnson
23.	Richmond, Va.	Sept. 10	Darrell Waltrip	Bill Gardner
24.	Dover, Del.	Sept. 17	Bobby Allison	Bud Moore
25.	Martinsville, Va.	Sept. 24	Cale Yarborough	Junior Johnson
26.	N. Wilkesboro, N.C.	Oct. 1	Cale Yarborough	Junior Johnson
27.	Concord, N.C.	Oct. 8	Bobby Allison	Bud Moore
28.	Rockingham, N.C.	Oct. 22	Cale Yarborough	Junior Johnson
29.	Hampton, Ga.	Nov. 5	Donnie Allison	Hoss Ellington
30.	Fontana, Calif.	Nov. 19	Bobby Allison	Bud Moore

>> POINTS STANDINGS

1. Cale Yarborough 4,841
2. Bobby Allison 4,367
3. Darrell Waltrip 4,362
4. Benny Parsons 4,350
5. Dave Marcis 4,335
6. Richard Petty 3,949
7. Lennie Pond 3,794
8. Dick Brooks 3,769
9. Buddy Arrington 3,626
10. Richard Childress 3,566

>> RACE WINNERS 7

1. Cale Yarborough...10
2. Darrell Waltrip 6
3. Bobby Allison 5
4. David Pearson 4
5. Benny Parsons 3
6. Donnie Allison 1
   Lennie Pond...1

>> MONEY WON LEADERS

1. Cale Yarborough $530,751
2. Darrell Waltrip 343,367
3. Bobby Allison 335,635
4. Benny Parsons 288,458
5. Richard Petty 215,491
6. Dave Marcis 178,725
7. Lennie Pond 160,627
8. Neil Bonnett 155,875
9. David Pearson.................................151,837
10. Dick Brooks 131,474

>> POLE WINNERS 9

1. Cale Yarborough..8
2. David Pearson 7
3. Lennie Pond..5
4. Neil Bonnet 3
5. Benny Parsons...2
   Darrell Waltrip 2
7. Bobby Allison 1
   Buddy Baker 1
   J.D. McDuffie...1

>> TOP 20 PERFORMANCE CHART

Rk	Driver	Points	Starts	Poles	Wins	Top 5s	Top 10s	DNF
1.	Cale Yarborough	4,841	30	8	10	23	24	2
2.	Bobby Allison	4,367	30	1	5	14	22	7
3.	Darrell Waltrip	4,362	30	2	6	19	20	9
4.	Benny Parsons	4,350	30	2	3	15	21	4
5.	Dave Marcis	4,335	30	0	0	14	24	2
6.	Richard Petty	3,949	30	0	0	11	17	12
7.	Lennie Pond	3,794	28	5	1	11	19	8
8.	Dick Brooks	3,769	30	0	0	5	17	8
9.	Buddy Arrington	3,626	30	0	0	1	7	2
10.	Richard Childress	3,566	30	0	0	1	12	4
11.	J.D. McDuffie	3,255	30	1	0	1	6	11
12.	Neil Bonnett	3,129	30	3	0	7	12	18
13.	Tighe Scott	3,110	29	0	0	0	7	11
14.	Frank Warren	3,036	30	0	0	0	0	7
15.	Dick May	2,936	28	0	0	0	2	7
16.	David Pearson	2,756	22	7	4	11	11	11
17.	Jimmy Means	2,756	27	0	0	0	2	11
18.	Ronnie Thomas	2,733	27	0	0	0	2	11
19.	Cecil Gordon	2,641	26	0	0	0	1	8
20.	Tommy Gale	2,639	26	0	0	0	0	7

≫ 1977 SEASON ≪

Race No.	Location	Date	Winner	Car owner
1.	Riverside, Calif.	Jan. 16	David Pearson	Wood Brothers
2.	Daytona Beach, Fla.	Feb. 20	Cale Yarborough	Junior Johnson
3.	Richmond, Va.	Feb. 27	Cale Yarborough	Junior Johnson
4.	Rockingham, N.C.	March 13	Richard Petty	Petty Enterprises
5.	Hampton, Ga.	March 20	Richard Petty	Petty Enterprises
6.	N. Wilkesboro, N.C	March 27	Cale Yarborough	Junior Johnson
7.	Darlington, S.C.	April 3	Darrell Waltrip	Bill Gardner
8.	Bristol, Tenn.	April 17	Cale Yarborough	Junior Johnson
9.	Martinsville, Va.	April 24	Cale Yarborough	Junior Johnson
10.	Talladega, Ala.	May 1	Darrell Waltrip	Bill Gardner
11.	Nashville	May 7	Benny Parsons	L.G. DeWitt
12.	Dover, Del.	May 15	Cale Yarborough	Junior Johnson
13.	Concord, N.C.	May 29	Richard Petty	Petty Enterprises
14.	Riverside, Calif.	June 12	Richard Petty	Petty Enterprises
15.	Brooklyn, Mich.	June 19	Cale Yarborough	Junior Johnson
16.	Daytona Beach, Fla.	July 4	Richard Petty	Petty Enterprises
17.	Nashville	July 16	Darrell Waltrip	Bill Gardner
18.	Long Pond, Pa.	July 31	Benny Parsons	L.G. DeWitt
19.	Talladega, Ala.	Aug. 7	Donnie Allison	Hoss Ellington
20.	Brooklyn, Mich.	Aug. 22	Darrell Waltrip	Bill Gardner
21.	Bristol, Tenn.	Aug. 28	Cale Yarborough	Junior Johnson
22.	Darlington, S.C.	Sept. 5	David Pearson	Wood Brothers
23.	Richmond, Va.	Sept. 11	Neil Bonnett	Jim Stacy
24.	Dover, Del.	Sept. 18	Benny Parsons	L.G. DeWitt
25.	Martinsville, Va.	Sept. 25	Cale Yarborough	Junior Johnson
26.	N. Wilkesboro, N.C	Oct. 2	Darrell Waltrip	Bill Gardner
27.	Concord, N.C.	Oct. 9	Benny Parsons	L.G. DeWitt
28.	Rockingham, N.C.	Oct. 23	Donnie Allison	Hoss Ellington
29.	Hampton, Ga.	Nov. 6	Darrell Waltrip	Bill Gardner
30.	Fontana, Calif.	Nov. 20	Neil Bonnett	Jim Stacy

≫ POINTS STANDINGS

1. Cale Yarborough 5,000
2. Richard Petty 4,614
3. Benny Parsons 4,570
4. Darrell Waltrip.............................4,498
5. Buddy Baker 3,961
6. Dick Brooks 3,742
7. James Hylton 3,476
8. Bobby Allison 3,467
9. Richard Childress 3,463
10. Cecil Gordon 3,294

≫ RACE WINNERS   7

1. Cale Yarborough.............................9
2. Darrell Waltrip..............................6
3. Richard Petty...............................5
4. Benny Parsons..............................4
5. Donnie Allison 2
   Neil Bonnett 2
   David Pearson 2

≫ MONEY WON LEADERS

1. Cale Yarborough $477,498
2. Richard Petty 345,886
3. Benny Parsons 297,421
4. Darrell Waltrip...................276,312
5. Buddy Baker 205,803
6. David Pearson...................180,999
7. Dick Brooks 141,421
8. Donnie Allison 124,785
9. Neil Bonnett 110,672
10. James Hylton 108,398

≫ POLE WINNERS   9

1. Neil Bonnett................................6
2. David Pearson 5
   Richard Petty 5
4. Donnie Allison 3
   Benny Parsons 3
   Darrell Waltrip 3
   Cale Yarborough............................3
8. A.J. Foyt 1
   Sam Sommers...............................1

≫ TOP 20 PERFORMANCE CHART

Rk	Driver	Points	Starts	Poles	Wins	Top 5s	Top 10s	DNF
1.	Cale Yarborough	5,000	30	3	9	25	27	0
2.	Richard Petty	4,614	30	5	5	20	23	6
3.	Benny Parsons	4,570	30	3	4	20	22	6
4.	Darrell Waltrip	4,498	30	3	6	16	24	7
5.	Buddy Baker	3,961	30	0	0	9	20	9
6.	Dick Brooks	3,742	29	0	0	7	20	10
7.	James Hylton	3,476	30	0	0	0	11	5
8.	Bobby Allison	3,467	30	0	0	5	15	12
9.	Richard Childress	3,463	30	0	0	0	11	9
10.	Cecil Gordon	3,294	30	0	0	0	2	5
11.	Buddy Arrington	3,247	28	0	0	0	5	2
12.	J.D. McDuffie	3,236	30	0	0	0	4	12
13.	David Pearson	3,227	22	5	2	16	16	6
14.	Skip Manning	3,120	28	0	0	1	8	11
15.	D.K. Ulrich	2,901	30	0	0	0	0	12
16.	Frank Warren	2,876	29	0	0	0	1	12
17.	Ricky Rudd	2,810	25	0	0	1	10	11
18.	Neil Bonnett	2,649	23	6	2	5	9	11
19.	Jimmy Means	2,640	26	0	0	0	6	12
20.	Tighe Scott	2,628	26	0	0	1	1	15

>> 1976 SEASON <<

Race No.	Location	Date	Winner	Car owner
1.	Riverside, Calif.	Jan. 18	David Pearson	Wood Brothers
2.	Daytona Beach, Fla.	Feb. 15	David Pearson	Wood Brothers
3.	Rockingham, N.C.	Feb. 29	Richard Petty	Petty Enterprises
4.	Richmond, Va.	March 7	Dave Marcis	Nord Krauskopf
5.	Bristol, Tenn.	March 14	Cale Yarborough	Junior Johnson
6.	Hampton, Ga.	March 21	David Pearson	Wood Brothers
7.	N. Wilkesboro, N.C.	April 4	Cale Yarborough	Junior Johnson
8.	Darlington, S.C.	April 11	David Pearson	Wood Brothers
9.	Martinsville, Va.	April 25	Darrell Waltrip	Bill Gardner
10.	Talladega, Ala.	May 2	Buddy Baker	Bud Moore
11.	Nashville	May 8	Cale Yarborough	Junior Johnson
12.	Dover, Del.	May 16	Benny Parsons	L.G. DeWitt
13.	Concord, N.C.	May 30	David Pearson	Wood Brothers
14.	Riverside, Calif.	June 13	David Pearson	Wood Brothers
15.	Brooklyn, Mich.	June 20	David Pearson	Wood Brothers
16.	Daytona Beach, Fla.	July 4	Cale Yarborough	Junior Johnson
17.	Nashville	July 17	Benny Parsons	L.G. DeWitt
18.	Long Pond, Pa.	Aug. 1	Richard Petty	Petty Enterprises
19.	Talladega, Ala.	Aug. 8	Dave Marcis	Nord Krauskopf
20.	Brooklyn, Mich.	Aug. 22	David Pearson	Wood Brothers
21.	Bristol, Tenn.	Aug. 29	Cale Yarborough	Junior Johnson
22.	Darlington, S.C.	Sept. 6	David Pearson	Wood Brothers
23.	Richmond, Va.	Sept. 12	Cale Yarborough	Junior Johnson
24.	Dover, Del.	Sept. 19	Cale Yarborough	Junior Johnson
25.	Martinsville, Va.	Sept. 26	Cale Yarborough	Junior Johnson
26.	N. Wilkesboro, N.C.	Oct. 3	Cale Yarborough	Junior Johnson
27.	Concord, N.C.	Oct. 10	Donnie Allison	Hoss Ellington
28.	Rockingham, N.C.	Oct. 24	Richard Petty	Petty Enterprises
29.	Hampton, Ga.	Nov. 7	Dave Marcis	Nord Krauskopf
30.	Fontana, Calif.	Nov. 21	David Pearson	Wood Brothers

>> POINTS STANDINGS

1. Cale Yarborough 4,644
2. Richard Petty...................................4,449
3. Benny Parsons 4,304
4. Bobby Allison 4,097
5. Lennie Pond 3,930
6. Dave Marcis 3,875
7. Buddy Baker 3,745
8. Darrell Waltrip 3,505
9. David Pearson 3,483
10. Dick Brooks 3,447

>> RACE WINNERS   8

1. David Pearson 10
2. Cale Yarborough 9
3. Dave Marcis..3
   Richard Petty 3
5. Benny Parsons 2
6. Donnie Allison 1
   Buddy Baker 1
   Darrell Waltrip

>> MONEY WON LEADERS

1. Cale Yarborough $387,173
2. Richard Petty...........................338,265
3. David Pearson 283,686
4. Benny Parsons 242,970
5. Buddy Baker 214,439
6. Bobby Allison 210,376
7. Dave Marcis 198,199
8. Darrell Waltrip 191,501
9. Lennie Pond 159,701
10. Dick Brooks 105,917

>> POLE WINNERS   11

1. David Pearson 8
2. Dave Marcis..7
3. Darrell Waltrip 3
4. Bobby Allison 2
   Buddy Baker 2
   Benny Parsons 2
   Cale Yarborough 2
8. Neil Bonnett..1
   A.J. Foyt...1
   Richard Petty 1
   Ramo Stott...1

>> TOP 20 PERFORMANCE CHART

Rk	Driver	Points	Starts	Poles	Wins	Top 5s	Top 10s	DNF
1.	Cale Yarborough	4,644	30	2	9	22	23	5
2.	Richard Petty	4,449	30	1	3	19	22	9
3.	Benny Parsons	4,304	30	2	2	18	23	5
4.	Bobby Allison	4,097	30	2	0	15	19	9
5.	Lennie Pond	3,930	30	0	0	10	19	9
6.	Dave Marcis	3,875	30	7	3	9	16	11
7.	Buddy Baker	3,745	30	2	1	16	16	14
8.	Darrell Waltrip	3,505	30	3	1	10	12	16
9.	David Pearson	3,483	22	8	10	16	18	4
10.	Dick Brooks	3,447	28	0	0	3	18	10
11.	Richard Childress	3,428	30	0	0	0	11	9
12.	J.D. McDuffie	3,400	30	0	0	1	8	10
13.	James Hylton	3,380	30	0	0	2	5	8
14.	D.K. Ulrich	3,280	30	0	0	0	2	7
15.	Cecil Gordon	3,247	30	0	0	0	5	10
16.	Frank Warren	3,240	30	0	0	0	3	6
17.	Dave Sisco	2,994	28	0	0	0	7	9
18.	Skip Manning	2,931	27	0	0	0	4	10
19.	Ed Negre	2,709	28	0	0	0	2	14
20.	Buddy Arrington	2,573	25	0	0	0	3	10

1976 SEASON

SECRET'S IN THE SHOES

Wins at three types of tracks make Marcis' ninth season his finest

If you don't like Dave Marcis, you don't like people.

Marcis, a classic pulled-himself-up-by-his-boot-straps, drove-the-family-car driver, endeared himself to legions of fans with hard work, good nature and wing tips.

Yes, Marcis raced in his trademark wing tips, not the fancy racing shoes of most of his competitors. Those wing tips might as well have been made of lead in 1976.

Coming off a second-place points finish in 1975, Marcis won three races and seven poles, both career highs. His wins came at three wildly different tracks: Richmond, Talladega and Atlanta.

In his long career, Marcis made 883 starts, second most to Richard Petty. He won five races and sat on 14 poles. HIs final start came in 2002, when he was 60.

>> 1975 SEASON <<

Race No.	Location	Date	Winner	Car owner
1.	Riverside, Calif.	Jan. 19	Bobby Allison	Roger Penske
2.	Daytona Beach, Fla.	Feb. 16	Benny Parsons	L.G. DeWitt
3.	Richmond, Va.	Feb. 23	Richard Petty	Petty Enterprises
4.	Rockingham, N.C.	March 2	Cale Yarborough	Junior Johnson
5.	Bristol, Tenn.	March 16	Richard Petty	Petty Enterprises
6.	Hampton, Ga.	March 23	Richard Petty	Petty Enterprises
7.	N. Wilkesboro, N.C.	April 6	Richard Petty	Petty Enterprises
8.	Darlington, S.C.	April 13	Bobby Allison	Roger Penske
9.	Martinsville, Va.	April 27	Richard Petty	Petty Enterprises
10.	Talladega, Ala.	May 4	Buddy Baker	Bud Moore
11.	Nashville	May 10	Darrell Waltrip	Darrell Waltrip
12.	Dover, Del.	May 19	David Pearson	Wood Brothers
13.	Concord, N.C.	May 25	Richard Petty	Petty Enterprises
14.	Riverside, Calif.	June 8	Richard Petty	Petty Enterprises
15.	Brooklyn, Mich.	June 15	David Pearson	Wood Brothers
16.	Daytona Beach, Fla.	July 4	Richard Petty	Petty Enterprises
17.	Nashville	July 20	Cale Yarborough	Junior Johnson
18.	Long Pond, Pa.	Aug. 3	David Pearson	Wood Brothers
19.	Talladega, Ala.	Aug. 17	Buddy Baker	Bud Moore
20.	Brooklyn, Mich.	Aug. 24	Richard Petty	Petty Enterprises
21.	Darlington, S.C.	Sept. 1	Bobby Allison	Roger Penske
22.	Dover, Del.	Sept. 14	Richard Petty	Petty Enterprises
23.	N. Wilkesboro, N.C.	Sept. 21	Richard Petty	Petty Enterprises
24.	Martinsville, Va.	Sept. 28	Dave Marcis	Nord Krauskopf
25.	Concord, N.C.	Oct. 5	Richard Petty	Petty Enterprises
26.	Richmond, Va.	Oct. 12	Darrell Waltrip	Bill Gardner
27.	Rockingham, N.C.	Oct. 19	Cale Yarborough	Junior Johnson
28.	Bristol, Tenn.	Nov. 2	Richard Petty	Petty Enterprises
29.	Hampton, Ga.	Nov. 9	Buddy Baker	Bud Moore
30.	Fontana, Calif.	Nov. 23	Buddy Baker	Bud Moore

>> POINTS STANDINGS

1. Richard Petty 4,783
2. Dave Marcis 4,061
3. James Hylton 3,914
4. Benny Parsons 3,820
5. Richard Childress 3,818
6. Cecil Gordon 3,702
7. Darrell Waltrip 3,462
8. Elmo Langley 3,399
9. Cale Yarborough 3,295
10. Dick Brooks 3,182

>> RACE WINNERS 8

1. Richard Petty 13
2. Buddy Baker 4
3. Bobby Allison 3
   David Pearson 3
   Cale Yarborough 3
6. Darrell Waltrip 2
7. Dave Marcis 1
   Benny Parsons 1

>> MONEY WON LEADERS

1. Richard Petty $378,865
2. David Pearson.............................179,207
3. Buddy Baker 169,917
4. Dave Marcis 149,202
5. Benny Parsons 140,199
6. Cale Yarborough 139,257
7. Bobby Allison 122,435
8. James Hylton 101,141
9. Darrell Waltrip.............................100,191

>> POLE WINNERS 9

1. David Pearson 7
2. Dave Marcis 4
3. Bobby Allison 3
   Buddy Baker 3
   Benny Parsons...3
   Richard Petty 3
   Cale Yarborough..3
8. Donnie Allison 2
   Darrell Waltrip 2

>> TOP 20 PERFORMANCE CHART

Rk	Driver	Points	Starts	Poles	Wins	Top 5s	Top 10s	DNF
1.	Richard Petty	4,783	30	3	13	21	24	6
2.	Dave Marcis	4,061	30	4	1	16	18	12
3.	James Hylton	3,914	30	0	0	2	16	3
4.	Benny Parsons	3,820	30	3	1	11	17	13
5.	Richard Childress	3,818	30	0	0	2	15	4
6.	Cecil Gordon	3,702	30	0	0	7	16	10
7.	Darrell Waltrip	3,462	28	2	2	11	14	15
8.	Elmo Langley	3,399	29	0	0	2	7	9
9.	Cale Yarborough	3,295	27	3	3	13	13	14
10.	Dick Brooks	3,182	25	0	0	6	15	8
11.	Walter Ballard	3,151	30	0	0	0	3	16
12.	Frank Warren	3,148	28	0	0	0	0	6
13.	Dave Sisco	3,116	28	0	0	2	7	13
14.	David Pearson	3,057	21	7	3	13	14	8
15.	Buddy Baker	3,050	23	3	4	12	13	10
16.	Bruce Hill	3,002	26	0	0	3	11	10
17.	Ed Negre	2,982	29	0	0	0	4	12
18.	Buddy Arrington	2,766	25	0	0	0	3	4
19.	J.D. McDuffie	2,746	26	0	0	1	6	11
20.	Coo Coo Marlin	2,584	23	0	0	4	11	10

1974 SEASON

UNSOLVED MYSTERY

Sand, soft drinks and fuel cells are a winning mix for Petty at Talladega

If you get to the track early enough, you can see it every week: Bleary-eyed crew members, wearing jeans, sponsor shirts and sneakers, staggering into the garage area to begin work on the cars.

They expect to find the cars exactly how they left them, and the last thing they do Sunday before the race is go over a detailed checklist to make sure they didn't forget anything.

On August 11, 1974, they couldn't believe what they found when they arrived at the garage at Talladega. It's easy to imagine their eyes, half-closed with sleep, suddenly looking like saucers. Up to 20 cars had been vandalized. Someone had cut belts and tires and had dumped sand, water, dirt and soda into gas tanks. No one ever was charged, and all the teams put their cars back together. Richard Petty scored his first Talladega victory that day.

>> 1974 SEASON <<

Race No.	Location	Date	Winner	Car owner
1.	Riverside, Calif.	Jan. 26	Cale Yarborough	Junior Johnson
2.	Daytona Beach, Fla.	Feb. 17	Richard Petty	Petty Enterprises
3.	Richmond, Va.	Feb. 24	Bobby Allison	Bobby Allison
4.	Rockingham, N.C.	March 3	Richard Petty	Petty Enterprises
5.	Bristol, Tenn.	March 17	Cale Yarborough	Junior Johnson
6.	Hampton, Ga.	March 24	Cale Yarborough	Junior Johnson
7.	Darlington, S.C.	April 7	David Pearson	Wood Brothers
8.	N. Wilkesboro, N.C.	April 21	Richard Petty	Petty Enterprises
9.	Martinsville, Va.	April 28	Cale Yarborough	Junior Johnson
10.	Talladega, Ala.	May 5	David Pearson	Wood Brothers
11.	Nashville	May 11	Richard Petty	Petty Enterprises
12.	Dover, Del.	May 19	Cale Yarborough	Junior Johnson
13.	Concord, N.C.	May 26	David Pearson	Wood Brothers
14.	Riverside, Calif.	June 9	Cale Yarborough	Junior Johnson
15.	Brooklyn, Mich.	June 16	Richard Petty	Petty Enterprises
16.	Daytona Beach, Fla.	July 4	David Pearson	Wood Brothers
17.	Bristol, Tenn.	July 14	Cale Yarborough	Junior Johnson
18.	Nashville	July 20	Cale Yarborough	Junior Johnson
19.	Hampton, Ga.	July 28	Richard Petty	Petty Enterprises
20.	Long Pond, Pa.	Aug. 4	Richard Petty	Petty Enterprises
21.	Talladega, Ala.	Aug. 11	Richard Petty	Petty Enterprises
22.	Brooklyn, Mich.	Aug. 25	David Pearson	Wood Brothers
23.	Darlington, S.C.	Sept. 2	Cale Yarborough	Junior Johnson
24.	Richmond, Va.	Sept. 8	Richard Petty	Petty Enterprises
25.	Dover, Del.	Sept. 15	Richard Petty	Petty Enterprises
26.	N. Wilkesboro, N.C.	Sept. 22	Cale Yarborough	Junior Johnson
27.	Martinsville, Va.	Sept. 29	Earl Ross	Allan Brooke
28.	Concord, N.C.	Oct. 6	David Pearson	Wood Brothers
29.	Rockingham, N.C.	Oct. 20	David Pearson	Wood Brothers
30.	Fontana, Calif.	Nov. 24	Bobby Allison	Roger Penske

>> POINTS STANDINGS

1. Richard Petty 5,037.75
2. Cale Yarborough..............4,470.30
3. David Pearson 2,389.25
4. Bobby Allison 2,019.19
5. Benny Parsons...............1,591.50
6. Dave Marcis 1,378.20
7. Buddy Baker 1,016.88
8. Earl Ross 1,009.47
9. Cecil Gordon 1,000.65
10. David Sisco 956.20

>> RACE WINNERS   5

1. Richard Petty 10
   Cale Yarborough................10
3. David Pearson 7
4. Bobby Allison 2
5. Earl Ross 1

>> MONEY WON LEADERS

1. Richard Petty $330,347
2. Cale Yarborough 272,946
3. David Pearson 233,567
4. Bobby Allison 129,768

>> POLE WINNERS   8

1. David Pearson 11
2. Richard Petty 7
3. Bobby Allison 3
   Cale Yarborough................3
5. Donnie Allison 2
   Buddy Baker 2
7. George Follmer 1
   Darrell Waltrip 1

>> TOP 20 PERFORMANCE CHART

Rk	Driver	Points	Starts	Poles	Wins	Top 5s	Top 10s	DNF
1.	Richard Petty	5,037	30	7	10	22	23	8
2.	Cale Yarborough	4,470	30	3	10	21	22	7
3.	David Pearson	2,389	19	11	7	15	15	4
4.	Bobby Allison	2,019	27	3	2	17	17	10
5.	Benny Parsons	1,591	30	0	0	11	14	16
6.	Dave Marcis	1,378	30	0	0	6	18	8
7.	Buddy Baker	1,016	19	2	0	11	12	8
8.	Earl Ross	1,009	21	0	1	5	10	6
9.	Cecil Gordon	1,000	30	0	0	1	10	10
10.	David Sisco	956	28	0	0	2	9	11
11.	James Hylton	924	29	0	0	1	8	14
12.	J.D. McDuffie	920	30	0	0	0	7	15
13.	Frank Warren	820	29	0	0	1	2	12
14.	Richie Panch	775	28	0	0	2	7	17
15.	Walter Ballard	748	27	0	0	1	6	13
16.	Richard Childress	735	29	0	0	0	3	19
17.	Donnie Allison	728	21	2	0	6	10	11
18.	Lennie Pond	723	22	0	0	5	11	9
19.	Darrell Waltrip	609	16	1	0	7	11	5
20.	Tony Bettenhausen	601	0	0	0	0	0	0

>> 1973 SEASON <<

Race No.	Location	Date	Winner	Car owner
1.	Riverside, Calif.	Jan. 21	Mark Donohue	Roger Penske
2.	Daytona Beach, Fla.	Feb. 18	Richard Petty	Petty Enterprises
3.	Richmond, Va.	Feb. 25	Richard Petty	Petty Enterprises
4.	Rockingham, N.C.	March 18	David Pearson	Wood Brothers
5.	Bristol, Tenn.	March 25	Cale Yarborough	Junior Johnson
6.	Hampton, Ga.	April 1	David Pearson	Wood Brothers
7.	N. Wilkesboro, N.C.	April 8	Richard Petty	Petty Enterprises
8.	Darlington, S.C.	April 15	David Pearson	Wood Brothers
9.	Martinsville, Va.	April 29	David Pearson	Wood Brothers
10.	Talladega, Ala.	May 6	David Pearson	Wood Brothers
11.	Nashville	May 12	Cale Yarborough	Junior Johnson
12.	Concord, N.C.	May 27	Buddy Baker	Nord Krauskopf
13.	Dover, Del.	June 3	David Pearson	Wood Brothers
14.	Bryan, Texas	June 10	Richard Petty	Petty Enterprises
15.	Riverside, Calif.	June 17	Bobby Allison	Bobby Allison
16.	Brooklyn, Mich.	June 24	David Pearson	Wood Brothers
17.	Daytona Beach, Fla.	July 4	David Pearson	Wood Brothers
18.	Bristol, Tenn.	July 8	Benny Parsons	L.G. DeWitt
19.	Hampton, Ga.	July 22	David Pearson	Wood Brothers
20.	Talladega, Ala.	Aug. 12	Dick Brooks	Crawford Brothers
21.	Nashville	Aug. 25	Buddy Baker	Nord Krauskopf
22.	Darlington, S.C.	Sept. 3	Cale Yarborough	Junior Johnson
23.	Richmond, Va.	Sept. 9	Richard Petty	Petty Enterprises
24.	Dover, Del.	Sept. 16	David Pearson	Wood Brothers
25.	N. Wilkesboro, N.C.	Sept. 23	Bobby Allison	Bobby Allison
26.	Martinsville, Va.	Sept. 30	Richard Petty	Petty Enterprises
27.	Concord, N.C.	Oct. 7	Cale Yarborough	Junior Johnson
28.	Rockingham, N.C.	Oct. 21	David Pearson	Wood Brothers

>> POINTS STANDINGS

1. Benny Parsons 7,173.80
2. Cale Yarborough 7,106.65
3. Cecil Gordon 7,046.80
4. James Hylton 6,972.75
5. Richard Petty......................................6,877.95
6. Buddy Baker 6,327.60
7. Bobby Allison......................................6,272.30
8. Walter Ballard 5,955.70
9. Elmo Langley......................................5,826.85
10. J.D. McDuffie 5,743.90

>> RACE WINNERS   8

1. David Pearson 11
2. Richard Petty 6
3. Cale Yarborough 4
4. Bobby Allison..2
    Buddy Baker 2
6. Dick Brooks 1
    Mark Donohue......................................1
    Benny Parsons 1

>> MONEY WON LEADERS

1. David Pearson $216,737
2. Cale Yarborough 181,574
3. Richard Petty 171,122
4. Buddy Baker............................132,988
5. Benny Parsons 114,345
6. Bobby Allison 107,299

>> POLE WINNERS   5

1. David Pearson 8
2. Bobby Allison..6
3. Buddy Baker 5
    Cale Yarborough 5
5. Richard Petty...3

>> TOP 20 PERFORMANCE CHART

Rk	Driver	Points	Starts	Poles	Wins	Top 5s	Top 10s	DNF
1.	Benny Parsons	7,173	28	0	1	15	21	7
2.	Cale Yarborough	7,106	28	5	4	16	19	8
3.	Cecil Gordon	7,046	28	0	0	8	18	5
4.	James Hylton	6,972	28	0	0	1	11	2
5.	Richard Petty	6,877	28	3	6	15	17	10
6.	Buddy Baker	6,327	27	5	2	16	20	7
7.	Bobby Allison	6,272	27	6	2	15	16	11
8.	Walter Ballard	5,955	28	0	0	0	4	8
9.	Elmo Langley	5,826	27	0	0	0	4	7
10.	J.D. McDuffie	5,743	27	0	0	3	10	10
11.	Jabe Thomas	5,637	25	0	0	0	1	6
12.	Buddy Arrington	5,483	26	0	0	1	4	9
13.	David Pearson	5,382	18	8	11	14	14	4
14.	Henley Gray	5,215	24	0	0	0	4	4
15.	Richard Childress	5,169	25	0	0	1	2	11
16.	Frank Warren	4,992	26	0	0	0	0	9
17.	Dave Sisco	4,986	23	0	0	2	6	11
18.	Ed Negre	4,942	24	0	0	1	2	9
19.	Dean Dalton	4,712	26	0	0	0	2	11
20.	Charlie Roberts	4,695	24	0	0	0	0	7

>> 1972 SEASON <<

Race No.	Location	Date	Winner	Car owner
1.	Riverside, Calif.	Jan. 23	Richard Petty	Petty Enterprises
2.	Daytona Beach, Fla.	Feb. 20	A.J. Foyt	Wood Brothers
3.	Richmond, Va.	Feb. 27	Richard Petty	Petty Enterprises
4.	Fontana, Calif.	March 5	A.J. Foyt	Wood Brothers
5.	Rockingham, N.C.	March 12	Bobby Isaac	Nord Krauskopf
6.	Hampton, Ga.	March 26	Bobby Allison	Junior Johnson
7.	Bristol, Tenn.	April 9	Bobby Allison	Junior Johnson
8.	Darlington, S.C.	April 16	David Pearson	Wood Brothers
9.	N. Wilkesboro, N.C.	April 23	Richard Petty	Petty Enterprises
10.	Martinsville, Va.	April 30	Richard Petty	Petty Enterprises
11.	Talladega, Ala.	May 7	David Pearson	Wood Brothers
12.	Concord, N.C.	May 28	Buddy Baker	Petty Enterprises
13.	Dover, Del.	June 4	Bobby Allison	Junior Johnson
14.	Brooklyn, Mich.	June 11	David Pearson	Wood Brothers
15.	Riverside, Calif.	June 18	Ray Elder	Fred Elder
16.	Bryan, Texas	June 25	Richard Petty	Petty Enterprises
17.	Daytona Beach, Fla.	July 4	David Pearson	Wood Brothers
18.	Bristol, Tenn.	July 9	Bobby Allison	Junior Johnson
19.	Trenton, N.J.	July 16	Bobby Allison	Junior Johnson
20.	Hampton, Ga.	July 23	Bobby Allison	Junior Johnson
21.	Talladega, Ala.	Aug. 6	James Hylton	James Hylton
22.	Brooklyn, Mich.	Aug. 20	David Pearson	Wood Brothers
23.	Nashville	Aug. 26	Bobby Allison	Junior Johnson
24.	Darlington, S.C.	Sept. 4	Bobby Allison	Junior Johnson
25.	Richmond, Va.	Sept. 10	Richard Petty	Petty Enterprises
26.	Dover, Del.	Sept. 17	David Pearson	Wood Brothers
27.	Martinsville, Va.	Sept. 24	Richard Petty	Petty Enterprises
28.	N. Wilkesboro, N.C.	Oct. 1	Richard Petty	Petty Enterprises
29.	Concord, N.C.	Oct. 8	Bobby Allison	Junior Johnson
30.	Rockingham, N.C.	Oct. 22	Bobby Allison	Junior Johnson
31.	Bryan, Texas	Nov. 12	Buddy Baker	Nord Krauskopf

>> POINTS STANDINGS

1. Richard Petty 8,701.40
2. Bobby Allison 8,573.50
3. James Hylton 8,158.70
4. Cecil Gordon 7,326.05
5. Benny Parsons.........................6,844.15
6. Walter Ballard 6,781.45
7. Elmo Langley 6,656.25
8. John Sears 6,298.50
9. Dean Dalton 6,295.05
10. Ben Arnold.............................6,179.00

>> RACE WINNERS   8

1. Bobby Allison 10
2. Richard Petty 8
3. David Pearson 6
4. Buddy Baker 2
   A.J. Foyt 2
6. Ray Elder 1
   James Hylton 1
   Bobby Isaac 1

>> MONEY WON LEADERS

1. Bobby Allison $284,467
2. Richard Petty 265,460
3. David Pearson....................139,599
4. James Hylton 113,705

>> POLE WINNERS   6

1. Bobby Allison 11
2. Bobby Isaac 9
3. David Pearson 4
4. A.J. Foyt 3
   Richard Petty 3
6. Buddy Baker 1

>> TOP 20 PERFORMANCE CHART

Rk	Driver	Points	Starts	Poles	Wins	Top 5s	Top 10s	DNF
1.	Richard Petty	8,701	31	3	8	25	28	5
2.	Bobby Allison	8,573	31	11	10	25	27	3
3.	James Hylton	8,158	31	0	1	9	23	4
4.	Cecil Gordon	7,326	31	0	0	4	16	6
5.	Benny Parsons	6,844	31	0	0	10	19	11
6.	Walter Ballard	6,781	31	0	0	0	7	6
7.	Elmo Langley	6,656	30	0	0	1	9	9
8.	John Sears	6,298	28	0	0	2	7	9
9.	Dean Dalton	6,295	29	0	0	0	4	9
10.	Ben Arnold	6,179	26	0	0	0	7	6
11.	Frank Warren	5,788	30	0	0	0	2	13
12.	Jabe Thomas	5,772	28	0	0	0	4	12
13.	Bill Champion	5,470	29	0	0	0	4	11
14.	Ray Williams	5,712	28	0	0	0	5	9
15.	Dave Marcis	5,459	27	0	0	5	11	11
16.	Charlie Roberts	5,354	26	0	0	0	1	7
17.	Henley Gray	5,093	28	0	0	0	2	10
18.	J.D. McDuffie	5,075	27	0	0	1	2	12
19.	Bobby Isaac	5,050	27	9	1	10	10	16
20.	David Pearson	4,718	17	4	6	12	13	5

>> 1971 SEASON <<

Race No.	Location	Date	Winner	Car owner
1.	Riverside, Calif.	Jan. 10	Ray Elder	Fred Elder
2.	Daytona Beach, Fla.	Feb. 11	Pete Hamilton	Cotton Owens
3.	Daytona Beach, Fla.	Feb. 11	David Pearson	Holman-Moody
4.	Daytona Beach, Fla.	Feb. 14	Richard Petty	Petty Enterprises
5.	Ontario, Calif.	Feb. 28	A.J. Foyt	Wood Brothers
6.	Richmond, Va.	March 7	Richard Petty	Petty Enterprises
7.	Rockingham, N.C.	March 14	Richard Petty	Petty Enterprises
8.	Hickory, N.C.	March 21	Richard Petty	Petty Enterprises
9.	Bristol, Tenn.	March 28	David Pearson	Holman-Moody
10.	Hampton, Ga.	April 4	A.J. Foyt	Wood Brothers
11.	Columbia, S.C.	April 8	Richard Petty	Petty Enterprises
12.	Greenville, S.C.	April 10	Bobby Isaac	Nord Krauskopf
13.	Maryville, Tenn.	April 15	Richard Petty	Petty Enterprises
14.	N. Wilkesboro, N.C.	April 18	Richard Petty	Petty Enterprises
15.	Martinsville, Va.	April 25	Richard Petty	Petty Enterprises
16.	Darlington, S.C.	May 2	Buddy Baker	Petty Enterprises
17.	South Boston, Va.	May 9	Benny Parsons	L.G. DeWitt
18.	Talladega, Ala.	May 16	Donnie Allison	Wood Brothers
19.	Asheville, N.C.	May 21	Richard Petty	Petty Enterprises
20.	Kingsport, Tenn.	May 23	Bobby Isaac	Nord Krauskopf
21.	Concord, N.C.	May 30	Bobby Allison	Holman-Moody
22.	Dover, Del.	Jun. 6	Bobby Allison	Holman-Moody
23.	Brooklyn, Mich.	June 13	Bobby Allison	Holman-Moody
24.	Riverside, Calif.	June 20	Bobby Allison	Bobby Allison
25.	Houston	June 23	Bobby Allison	Bobby Allison
26.	Greenville, S.C.	June 26	Richard Petty	Petty Enterprises
27.	Daytona Beach, Fla.	July 4	Bobby Isaac	Nord Krauskopf
28.	Bristol, Tenn.	July 11	Charlie Glotzbach	Junior Johnson
29.	Malta, N.Y.	July 14	Richard Petty	Petty Enterprises
30.	Islip, N.Y.	July 15	Richard Petty	Petty Enterprises
31.	Trenton, N.J.	July 18	Richard Petty	Petty Enterprises
32.	Nashville	July 24	Richard Petty	Petty Enterprises
33.	Hampton, Ga.	Aug. 1	Richard Petty	Petty Enterprises
34.	Winston-Salem, N.C.	Aug. 6	Bobby Allison	Melvin Joseph
35.	Ona, W.Va.	Aug. 8	Richard Petty	Petty Enterprises
36.	Brooklyn, Mich.	Aug. 15	Bobby Allison	Holman-Moody
37.	Talladega, Ala.	Aug. 22	Bobby Allison	Holman-Moody
38.	Columbia, S.C.	Aug. 27	Richard Petty	Petty Enterprises
39.	Hickory, N.C.	Aug. 28	Tiny Lund	Ronnie Hopkins
40.	Darlington, S.C.	Sept. 6	Bobby Allison	Holman-Moody
41.	Martinsville, Va.	Sept. 26	Bobby Isaac	Nord Krauskopf
42.	Concord, N.C.	Oct. 10	Bobby Allison	Holman-Moody
43.	Dover, Del.	Oct. 17	Richard Petty	Petty Enterprises
44.	Rockingham, N.C.	Oct. 24	Richard Petty	Petty Enterprises
45.	Macon, Ga.	Nov. 7	Bobby Allison	Holman-Moody
46.	Richmond, Va.	Nov. 14	Richard Petty	Petty Enterprises
47.	N. Wilkesboro, N.C.	Nov. 22	Tiny Lund	Ronnie Hopkins
48.	College Station, Texas	Dec. 12	Richard Petty	Petty Enterprises

>> POINTS STANDINGS

1. Richard Petty 4,435
2. James Hylton 4,071
3. Cecil Gordon 3,677
4. Bobby Allison 3,636
5. Elmo Langley 3,356
6. Jabe Thomas 3,200
7. Bill Champion 3,058
8. Frank Warren 2,886
9. J.D. McDuffie 2,862
10. Walter Ballard 2,633

>> RACE WINNERS   12

1. Richard Petty 21
2. Bobby Allison 11
3. Bobby Isaac 4
4. A.J. Foyt 2
    Tiny Lund 2
    David Pearson 2
7. Donnie Allison 1
    Buddy Baker 1
    Ray Elder 1
    Charlie Glotzbach 1
    Pete Hamilton 1
    Benny Parsons 1

>> MONEY WON LEADERS

1. Richard Petty $269,225
2. Bobby Allison 235,795
3. Buddy Baker 115,150
4. Bobby Isaac 106,426
5. Donnie Allison 69,995
6. Pete Hamilton 60,440
7. James Hylton 55,860
8. Benny Parsons 48,517
9. Fred Lorenzen 45,100
10. Cecil Gordon 42,949

>> POLE WINNERS   14

1. Bobby Allison 9
    Richard Petty 9
3. Donnie Allison 5
    Bobby Isaac 5
5. A.J. Foyt 4
    Charlie Glotzbach 4
7. Pete Hamilton 2
    Friday Hassler 2
    Dave Marcis 2
    David Pearson 2
11. Buddy Baker 1
    Bill Dennis 1
    James Hylton 1
    Fred Lorenzen 1

>> 1970 SEASON <<

Race No.	Location	Date	Winner	Car owner
1.	Riverside, Calif.	Jan. 18	A.J. Foyt	Jack Bowsher
2.	Daytona Beach, Fla.	Feb. 19	Cale Yarborough	Wood Brothers
3.	Daytona Beach, Fla.	Feb. 19	Charlie Glotzbach	Ray Nichels
4.	Daytona Beach, Fla.	Feb. 22	Pete Hamilton	Petty Enterprises
5.	Richmond, Va.	March 1	James Hylton	James Hylton
6.	Rockingham, N.C.	March 8	Richard Petty	Petty Enterprises
7.	Savannah, Ga.	March 15	Richard Petty	Petty Enterprises
8.	Hampton, Ga.	March 29	Bobby Allison	Mario Rossi
9.	Bristol, Tenn.	April 5	Donnie Allison	Banjo Matthews
10.	Talladega, Ala.	April 12	Pete Hamilton	Petty Enterprises
11.	N. Wilkesboro, N.C.	April 18	Richard Petty	Petty Enterprises
12.	Columbia, S.C.	April 30	Richard Petty	Donald Robertson
13.	Darlington, S.C.	May 9	David Pearson	Holman-Moody
14.	Beltsville, Md.	May 15	Bobby Isaac	Nord Krauskopf
15.	Hampton, Va.	May 18	Bobby Isaac	Nord Krauskopf
16.	Concord, N.C.	May 24	Donnie Allison	Banjo Matthews
17.	Maryville, Tenn.	May 28	Bobby Isaac	Nord Krauskopf
18.	Martinsville, Va.	May 31	Bobby Isaac	Nord Krauskopf
19.	Brooklyn, Mich.	June 7	Cale Yarborough	Wood Brothers
20.	Riverside, Calif.	June 14	Richard Petty	Petty Enterprises
21.	Hickory, N.C.	June 20	Bobby Isaac	Nord Krauskopf
22.	Kingsport, Tenn.	June 26	Richard Petty	Petty Enterprises
23.	Greenville, S.C.	June 27	Bobby Isaac	Nord Krauskopf
24.	Daytona Beach, Fla.	July 4	Donnie Allison	Banjo Matthews
25.	Malta, N.Y.	July 7	Richard Petty	Petty Enterprises
26.	Thompson, Conn.	July 9	Bobby Isaac	Nord Krauskopf
27.	Trenton, N.J.	July 12	Richard Petty	Petty Enterprises
28.	Bristol, Tenn.	July 19	Bobby Allison	Bobby Allison
29.	Maryville, Tenn.	July 24	Richard Petty	Petty Enterprises
30.	Nashville	July 25	Bobby Isaac	Nord Krauskopf
31.	Hampton, Ga.	Aug. 2	Richard Petty	Petty Enterprises
32.	Columbia, S.C.	Aug. 6	Bobby Isaac	Nord Krauskopf
33.	Ona, W.Va.	Aug. 11	Richard Petty	Petty Enterprises
34.	Brooklyn, Mich.	Aug. 16	Charlie Glotzbach	Ray Nichels
35.	Talladega, Ala.	Aug. 23	Pete Hamilton	Petty Enterprises
36.	Winston-Salem, N.C.	Aug. 28	Richard Petty	Petty Enterprises
37.	South Boston, Va.	Aug. 29	Richard Petty	Petty Enterprises
38.	Darlington, S.C.	Sept. 7	Buddy Baker	Cotton Owens
39.	Hickory, N.C.	Sept. 11	Bobby Isaac	Nord Krauskopf
40.	Richmond, Va.	Sept. 13	Richard Petty	Petty Enterprises
41.	Dover, Del.	Sept. 20	Richard Petty	Petty Enterprises
42.	Raleigh, N.C.	Sept. 30	Richard Petty	Donald Robertson
43.	N. Wilkesboro, N.C.	Oct. 4	Bobby Isaac	Nord Krauskopf
44.	Concord, N.C.	Oct. 11	LeeRoy Yarbrough	Junior Johnson
45.	Martinsville, Va.	Oct. 18	Richard Petty	Petty Enterprises
46.	Macon, Ga.	Nov. 8	Richard Petty	Petty Enterprises
47.	Rockingham, N.C.	Nov. 15	Cale Yarborough	Wood Brothers
48.	Hampton, Va.	Nov. 22	Bobby Allison	Bobby Allison

>> POINTS STANDINGS

1. Bobby Isaac 3,911
2. Bobby Allison 3,860
3. James Hylton 3,788
4. Richard Petty 3,447
5. Neil Castles............3,158
6. Elmo Langley 3,154
7. Jabe Thomas 3,120
8. Benny Parsons 2,993
9. Dave Marcis 2,820
10. Frank Warren 2,697

>> RACE WINNERS   12

1. Richard Petty 18
2. Bobby Isaac 11
3. Bobby Allison 3
   Donnie Allison 3
   Pete Hamilton 3
   Cale Yarborough....................3
7. Charlie Glotzbach 2
8. Buddy Baker 1
   A.J. Foyt 1
   James Hylton 1
   David Pearson 1
   LeeRoy Yarbrough 1

>> MONEY WON LEADERS

1. Richard Petty $138,969
2. Bobby Allison 131,965
3. Pete Hamilton 131,406
4. Bobby Isaac 121,470
5. Cale Yarborough 115,875
6. Donnie Allison..............92,606
7. David Pearson..............87,118
8. Buddy Baker 62,928
9. LeeRoy Yarbrough 61,930
10. James Hylton 59,705

>> POLE WINNERS   16

1. Bobby Isaac.......................13
2. Richard Petty 9
3. Bobby Allison 5
   Cale Yarborough....................5
5. Charlie Glotzbach 4
6. David Pearson 2
7. Donnie Allison 1
   Buddy Baker 1
   Larry Baumel 1
   Dan Gurney 1
   Pete Hamilton 1
   James Hylton 1
   Fred Lorenzen 1
   Benny Parsons......................1
   John Sears 1
   LeeRoy Yarbrough 1

>> 1969 SEASON <<

Race No.	Location	Date	Winner	Car owner
1.	Macon, Ga.	Nov. 17	Richard Petty	Petty Enterprises
2.	Montgomery, Ala.	Dec. 8	Bobby Allison	Mario Rossi
3.	Riverside, Calif.	Feb. 1	Richard Petty	Petty Enterprises
4.	Daytona Beach, Fla.	Feb. 20	David Pearson	Holman-Moody
5.	Daytona Beach, Fla.	Feb. 20	Bobby Isaac	Nord Krauskopf
6.	Daytona Beach, Fla.	Feb. 23	LeeRoy Yarbrough	Junior Johnson
7.	Rockingham, N.C.	March 9	David Pearson	Holman-Moody
8.	Augusta, Ga.	March 16	David Pearson	Holman-Moody
9.	Bristol, Tenn.	March 23	Bobby Allison	Mario Rossi
10.	Hampton, Ga.	March 30	Cale Yarborough	Wood Brothers
11.	Columbia, S.C.	April 3	Bobby Isaac	Nord Krauskopf
12.	Hickory, N.C.	April 6	Bobby Isaac	Nord Krauskopf
13.	Greenville, S.C.	April 8	Bobby Isaac	Nord Krauskopf
14.	Richmond, Va.	April 13	David Pearson	Holman-Moody
15.	N. Wilkesboro, N.C.	April 20	Bobby Allison	Mario Rossi
16.	Martinsville, Va.	April 27	Richard Petty	Petty Enterprises
17.	Weaverville, N.C.	May 4	Bobby Isaac	Nord Krauskopf
18.	Darlington, S.C.	May 10	LeeRoy Yarbrough	Junior Johnson
19.	Beltsville, Md.	May 16	Bobby Isaac	Nord Krauskopf
20.	Hampton, Va.	May 17	David Pearson	Holman-Moody
21.	Concord, N.C.	May 25	LeeRoy Yarbrough	Junior Johnson
22.	Macon, Ga.	June 1	Bobby Isaac	Nord Krauskopf
23.	Maryville, Tenn.	June 5	Bobby Isaac	Nord Krauskopf
24.	Brooklyn, Mich.	June 15	Cale Yarborough	Wood Brothers
25.	Kingsport, Tenn.	June 19	Richard Petty	Petty Enterprises
26.	Greenville, S.C.	June 21	Bobby Isaac	Nord Krauskopf
27.	Raleigh, N.C.	June 26	David Pearson	Holman-Moody
28.	Daytona Beach, Fla.	July 4	LeeRoy Yarbrough	Junior Johnson
29.	Dover, Del.	July 6	Richard Petty	Petty Enterprises
30.	Thompson, Conn.	July 10	David Pearson	Holman-Moody
31.	Trenton, N.J.	July 13	David Pearson	Holman-Moody
32.	Beltsville, Md.	July 15	Richard Petty	Petty Enterprises
33.	Bristol, Tenn.	July 20	David Pearson	Holman-Moody
34.	Nashville	July 26	Richard Petty	Petty Enterprises
35.	Maryville, Tenn.	July 27	Richard Petty	Petty Enterprises
36.	Hampton, Ga.	Aug. 10	LeeRoy Yarbrough	Junior Johnson
37.	Brooklyn, Mich.	Aug. 17	David Pearson	Holman-Moody
38.	South Boston, Va.	Aug. 21	Bobby Isaac	Nord Krauskopf
39.	Winston-Salem, N.C.	Aug. 22	Richard Petty	Petty Enterprises
40.	Weaverville, N.C.	Aug. 24	Bobby Isaac	Nord Krauskopf
41.	Darlington, S.C.	Sept. 1	LeeRoy Yarbrough	Junior Johnson
42.	Hickory, N.C.	Sept. 5	Bobby Isaac	Nord Krauskopf
43.	Richmond, Va.	Sept. 7	Bobby Allison	Mario Rossi
44.	Talladega, Ala.	Sept. 14	Richard Brickhouse	Ray Nichels
45.	Columbia, S.C.	Sept. 18	Bobby Isaac	Nord Krauskopf
46.	Martinsville, Va.	Sept. 28	Richard Petty	Petty Enterprises
47.	N. Wilkesboro, N.C.	Oct. 5	David Pearson	Holman-Moody
48.	Concord, N.C.	Oct. 12	Donnie Allison	Banjo Matthews
49.	Savannah, Ga.	Oct. 17	Bobby Isaac	Nord Krauskopf
50.	Augusta, Ga.	Oct. 19	Bobby Isaac	Nord Krauskopf
51.	Rockingham, N.C.	Oct. 26	LeeRoy Yarbrough	Junior Johnson
52.	Jefferson, Ga.	Nov. 2	Bobby Isaac	Nord Krauskopf
53.	Macon, Ga.	Nov. 9	Bobby Allison	Mario Rossi
54.	College Station, Texas	Dec. 7	Bobby Isaac	Nord Krauskopf

>> POINTS STANDINGS

1. David Pearson...4,170
2. Richard Petty 3,813
3. James Hylton 3,750
4. Neil Castles..3,530
5. Elmo Langley 3,383
6. Bobby Isaac 3,301
7. John Sears...3,166
8. Jabe Thomas 3,103
9. Wendell Scott 3,015
10. Cecil Gordon 3,002

>> RACE WINNERS   8

1 Bobby Isaac 17
2 David Pearson..11
3. Richard Petty 10
4. LeeRoy Yarbrough 7
5. Bobby Allison 5
6. Cale Yarborough..2
7. Donnie Allison 1
   Richard Brickhouse 1

>> MONEY WON LEADERS

1. LeeRoy Yarbrough $188,105
2. David Pearson....................................183,700
3. Richard Petty 109,180
4. Bobby Isaac 80,560
5. Donnie Allison 74,255
6. Cale Yarborough 73,540
7. Bobby Allison 66,775
8. Buddy Baker 57,910
9. James Hylton 55,992
10. Richard Brickhouse.............................45,312

>> POLE WINNERS   9

1. Bobby Isaac 20
2. David Pearson 13
3. Richard Petty 6
   Cale Yarborough.......................................6
5. Buddy Baker 3
6. Donnie Allison 2
   Charlie Glotzbach......................................2
8. Bobby Allison 1
   A.J. Foyt...1

>> 1968 SEASON <<

Race No.	Location	Date	Winner	Car owner
1.	Macon, Ga.	Nov. 12	Bobby Allison	Holman-Moody
2.	Montgomery, Ala.	Nov. 26	Richard Petty	Petty Enterprises
3.	Riverside, Calif.	Jan. 21	Dan Gurney	Wood Brothers
4.	Daytona Beach, Fla.	Feb. 25	Cale Yarborough	Wood Brothers
5.	Bristol, Tenn.	March 17	David Pearson	Holman-Moody
6.	Richmond, Va.	March 24	David Pearson	Holman-Moody
7.	Hampton, Ga.	March 31	Cale Yarborough	Wood Brothers
8.	Hickory, N.C.	April 7	Richard Petty	Petty Enterprises
9.	Greenville, S.C.	April 13	Richard Petty	Petty Enterprises
10.	Columbia, S.C.	April 18	Bobby Isaac	Nord Krauskopf
11.	N. Wilkesboro, N.C.	April 21	David Pearson	Holman-Moody
12.	Martinsville, Va.	April 28	Cale Yarborough	Wood Brothers
13.	Augusta, Ga.	May 3	Bobby Isaac	Nord Krauskopf
14.	Weaverville, N.C.	May 5	David Pearson	Holman-Moody
15.	Darlington, S.C.	May 11	David Pearson	Holman-Moody
16.	Beltsville, Md.	May 17	David Pearson	Holman-Moody
17.	Hampton, Va.	May 18	David Pearson	Holman-Moody
18.	Concord, N.C.	May 26	Buddy Baker	Raymond Fox
19.	Asheville, N.C.	May 31	Richard Petty	Petty Enterprises
20.	Macon, Ga.	June 2	David Pearson	Holman-Moody
21.	Maryville, Tenn.	June 6	Richard Petty	Petty Enterprises
22.	Birmingham, Ala.	June 8	Richard Petty	Petty Enterprises
23.	Rockingham, N.C.	June 16	Donnie Allison	Banjo Matthews
24.	Greenville, S.C.	June 22	Richard Petty	Petty Enterprises
25.	Daytona Beach, Fla.	July 4	Cale Yarborough	Wood Brothers
26.	Islip, N.Y.	July 7	Bobby Allison	Bobby Allison
27.	Oxford, Maine	July 9	Richard Petty	Petty Enterprises
28.	Fonda, N.Y.	July 11	Richard Petty	Petty Enterprises
29.	Trenton, N.J.	July 14	LeeRoy Yarbrough	Junior Johnson
30.	Bristol, Tenn.	July 21	David Pearson	Holman-Moody
31.	Maryville, Tenn.	July 25	Richard Petty	Petty Enterprises
32.	Nashville	July 27	David Pearson	Holman-Moody
33.	Hampton, Ga.	Aug. 4	LeeRoy Yarbrough	Junior Johnson
34.	Columbia, S.C.	Aug. 8	David Pearson	Holman-Moody
35.	Winston-Salem, N.C.	Aug. 10	David Pearson	Holman-Moody
36.	Weaverville, N.C.	Aug. 18	David Pearson	Holman-Moody
37.	South Boston, Va.	Aug. 23	Richard Petty	Petty Enterprises
38.	Hampton, Va.	Aug. 24	David Pearson	Holman-Moody
39.	Darlington, S.C.	Sept. 2	Cale Yarborough	Wood Brothers
40.	Hickory, N.C.	Sept. 6	David Pearson	Holman-Moody
41.	Richmond, Va.	Sept. 8	Richard Petty	Petty Enterprises
42.	Beltsville, Md.	Sept. 13	Bobby Isaac	Nord Krauskopf
43.	Hillsboro, N.C.	Sept. 15	Richard Petty	Petty Enterprises
44.	Martinsville, Va.	Sept. 22	Richard Petty	Petty Enterprises
45.	N. Wilkesboro, N.C.	Sept. 29	Richard Petty	Petty Enterprises
46.	Augusta, Ga.	Oct. 5	David Pearson	Holman-Moody
47.	Concord, N.C.	Oct. 20	Charlie Glotzbach	Cotton Owens
48.	Rockingham, N.C.	Oct. 27	Richard Petty	Petty Enterprises
49.	Jefferson, Ga.	Nov. 3	Cale Yarborough	Wood Brothers

>> POINTS STANDINGS

1. David Pearson 3,499
2. Bobby Isaac 3,373
3. Richard Petty 3,123
4. Clyde Lynn 3,041
5. John Sears 3,017
6. Elmo Langley 2,823
7. James Hylton 2,719
8. Jabe Thomas 2,687
9. Wendell Scott 2,685
10. Roy Tyner 2,504

>> RACE WINNERS   10

1. David Pearson 16
    Richard Petty 16
3. Cale Yarborough............6
4. Bobby Isaac 3
5. Bobby Allison 2
    LeeRoy Yarbrough 2
7. Donnie Allison 1
    Buddy Baker 1
    Charlie Glotzbach............1
    Dan Gurney 1

>> MONEY WON LEADERS

1. Cale Yarborough $134,136
2. David Pearson............118,487
3. Richard Petty 89,103
4. LeeRoy Yarbrough............86,604
5. Buddy Baker 54,125
6. Donnie Allison 50,815
7. Bobby Allison 50,391
8. Bobby Isaac 44,530
9. Charlie Glotzbach 41,835
10. James Hylton 27,865

>> POLE WINNERS   11

1. David Pearson 12
    Richard Petty 12
3. LeeRoy Yarbrough 6
4. Buddy Baker 4
    Cale Yarborough............4
6. Charlie Glotzbach............3
    Bobby Isaac 3
8. Bobby Allison 3
9. Donnie Allison 1
    Darel Dieringer 1
    Dan Gurney 1

>> 1967 SEASON <<

Race No.	Location	Date	Winner	Car owner
1.	Augusta, Ga.	Nov. 13	Richard Petty	Petty Enterprises
2.	Riverside, Calif.	Jan. 29	Parnelli Jones	William Stroppe
3.	Daytona Beach, Fla.	Feb. 24	LeeRoy Yarbrough	Jon Thorne
4.	Daytona Beach, Fla.	Feb. 24	Fred Lorenzen	Holman-Moody
5.	Daytona Beach, Fla.	Feb. 26	Mario Andretti	Holman-Moody
6.	Weaverville, N.C.	March 5	Richard Petty	Petty Enterprises
7.	Bristol, Tenn.	March 19	David Pearson	Cotton Owens
8.	Greenville, S.C.	March 25	David Pearson	Cotton Owens
9.	Winston-Salem, N.C.	March 27	Bobby Allison	Bobby Allison
10.	Hampton, Ga.	April 2	Cale Yarborough	Wood Brothers
11.	Columbia, S.C.	April 6	Richard Petty	Petty Enterprises
12.	Hickory, N.C.	April 9	Richard Petty	Petty Enterprises
13.	N. Wilkesboro, N.C.	April 16	Darel Dieringer	Junior Johnson
14.	Martinsville, Va.	April 23	Richard Petty	Petty Enterprises
15.	Savannah, Ga.	April 28	Bobby Allison	Bobby Allison
16.	Richmond, Va.	April 30	Richard Petty	Petty Enterprises
17.	Darlington, S.C.	May 13	Richard Petty	Petty Enterprises
18.	Beltsville, Md.	May 19	Jim Paschal	Thomas Friedkin
19.	Hampton, Va.	May 20	Richard Petty	Petty Enterprises
20.	Concord, N.C.	May 28	Jim Paschal	Thomas Friedkin
21.	Asheville, N.C.	June 2	Jim Paschal	Thomas Friedkin
22.	Macon, Ga.	June 6	Richard Petty	Petty Enterprises
23.	Maryville, Tenn.	June 8	Richard Petty	Petty Enterprises
24.	Birmingham, Ala.	June 10	Bobby Allison	Cotton Owens
25.	Rockingham, N.C.	June 18	Richard Petty	Petty Enterprises
26.	Greenville, S.C.	June 24	Richard Petty	Petty Enterprises
27.	Montgomery, Ala.	June 27	Jim Paschal	Thomas Friedkin
28.	Daytona Beach, Fla.	July 4	Cale Yarborough	Wood Brothers
29.	Trenton, N.J.	July 9	Richard Petty	Petty Enterprises
30.	Oxford, Maine	July 11	Bobby Allison	Bobby Allison
31.	Fonda, N.Y.	July 13	Richard Petty	Petty Enterprises
32.	Islip, N.Y.	July 15	Richard Petty	Petty Enterprises
33.	Bristol, Tenn.	July 23	Richard Petty	Petty Enterprises
34.	Maryville, Tenn.	July 27	Dick Hutcherson	Bondy Long
35.	Nashville	July 29	Richard Petty	Petty Enterprises
36.	Hampton, Ga.	Aug. 6	Dick Hutcherson	Bondy Long
37.	Winston-Salem, N.C.	Aug. 12	Richard Petty	Petty Enterprises
38.	Columbia, S.C.	Aug. 17	Richard Petty	Petty Enterprises
39.	Savannah, Ga.	Aug. 25	Richard Petty	Petty Enterprises
40.	Darlington, S.C.	Sept. 4	Richard Petty	Petty Enterprises
41.	Hickory, N.C.	Sept. 8	Richard Petty	Petty Enterprises
42.	Richmond, Va.	Sept. 10	Richard Petty	Petty Enterprises
43.	Beltsville, Md.	Sept. 15	Richard Petty	Petty Enterprises
44.	Hillsboro, N.C.	Sept. 17	Richard Petty	Petty Enterprises
45.	Martinsville, Va.	Sept. 24	Richard Petty	Petty Enterprises
46.	N. Wilkesboro, N.C.	Oct. 1	Richard Petty	Petty Enterprises
47.	Concord, N.C.	Oct. 15	Buddy Baker	Raymond Fox
48.	Rockingham, N.C.	Oct. 29	Bobby Allison	Holman-Moody
49.	Weaverville, N.C.	Nov. 5	Bobby Allison	Holman-Moody

>> POINTS STANDINGS

1. Richard Petty 42,472
2. James Hylton 36,444
3. Dick Hutcherson 33,658
4. Bobby Allison 30,812
5. John Sears 29,078
6. Jim Paschal 27,624
7. David Pearson.............................26,302
8. Neil Castles.................................23,218
9. Elmo Langley 22,286
10. Wendell Scott 20,700

>> RACE WINNERS   12

1. Richard Petty 27
2. Bobby Allison 6
3. Jim Paschal 4
4. Dick Hutcherson............................2
   David Pearson.................................2
   Cale Yarborough............................2
7. Mario Andretti 1
   Buddy Baker 1
   Darel Dieringer...............................1
   Parnelli Jones 1
   Fred Lorenzen 1
   LeeRoy Yarbrough 1

>> MONEY WON LEADERS

1. Richard Petty $130,275
2. Dick Hutcherson 75,965
3. David Pearson.........................69,585
4. Cale Yarborough 56,685
5. Bobby Allison 53,415
6. Jim Paschal 53,380
7. Buddy Baker 45,110
8. James Hylton 39,005
9. Paul Goldsmith 35,360
10. Darel Dieringer 32,870

>> POLE WINNERS   11

1. Richard Petty 19
2. Dick Hutcherson.............................9
3. Darel Dieringer...............................6
4. Cale Yarborough............................4
5. Bobby Allison 2
   David Pearson.................................2
   Curtis Turner 2
8. James Hunter 1
   James Hylton 1
   Jim Paschal 1
   John Sears.......................................1

>> 1966 SEASON <<

Race No.	Location	Date	Winner	Car owner
1.	Augusta, Ga.	Nov. 14	Richard Petty	Petty Enterprises
2.	Riverside, Calif.	Jan. 23	Dan Gurney	Wood Brothers
3.	Daytona Beach, Fla.	Feb. 25	Paul Goldsmith	Ray Nichels
4.	Daytona Beach, Fla.	Feb. 25	Earl Balmer	Raymond Fox
5.	Daytona Beach, Fla.	Feb. 27	Richard Petty	Petty Enterprises
6.	Rockingham, N.C.	March 13	Paul Goldsmith	Ray Nichels
7.	Bristol, Tenn.	March 20	Dick Hutcherson	Holman-Moody
8.	Hampton, Ga.	March 27	Jim Hurtubise	Norm Nelson
9.	Hickory, N.C.	April 3	David Pearson	Cotton Owens
10.	Columbia, S.C.	April 7	David Pearson	Cotton Owens
11.	Greenville, S.C.	April 9	David Pearson	Cotton Owens
12.	Winston-Salem, N.C.	April 11	David Pearson	Cotton Owens
13.	N. Wilkesboro, N.C.	April 17	Jim Paschal	Thomas Friedkin
14.	Martinsville, Va.	April 24	Jim Paschal	Thomas Friedkin
15.	Darlington, S.C.	April 30	Richard Petty	Petty Enterprises
16.	Hampton, Va.	May 7	Richard Petty	Petty Enterprises
17.	Macon, Ga.	May 10	Richard Petty	Petty Enterprises
18.	Monroe, N.C.	May 13	Darel Dieringer	Reid Shaw
19.	Richmond, Va.	May 15	David Pearson	Cotton Owens
20.	Concord, N.C.	May 22	Marvin Panch	Petty Enterprises
21.	Moyock, N.C.	May 29	David Pearson	Cotton Owens
22.	Asheville, N.C.	June 3	David Pearson	Cotton Owens
23.	Spartanburg, S.C.	June 4	Elmo Langley	Langley/Woodfield
24.	Maryville, Tenn.	June 9	David Pearson	Cotton Owens
25.	Weaverville, N.C.	June 12	Richard Petty	Petty Enterprises
26.	Beltsville, Md.	June 15	Tiny Lund	Lyle Stelter
27.	Greenville, S.C.	June 25	David Pearson	Cotton Owens
28.	Daytona Beach, Fla.	July 4	Sam McQuagg	Ray Nichels
29.	Manassas, Va.	July 7	Elmo Langley	Langley/Woodfield
30.	Bridgehampton, N.Y.	July 10	David Pearson	Cotton Owens
31.	Oxford, Maine	July 12	Bobby Allison	Bobby Allison
32.	Fonda, N.Y.	July 14	David Pearson	Cotton Owens
33.	Islip, N.Y.	July 16	Bobby Allison	Bobby Allison
34.	Bristol, Tenn.	July 24	Paul Goldsmith	Ray Nichels
35.	Maryville, Tenn.	July 28	Paul Lewis	Paul Lewis
36.	Nashville	July 30	Richard Petty	Petty Enterprises
37.	Hampton, Ga.	Aug. 7	Richard Petty	Petty Enterprises
38.	Columbia, S.C.	Aug. 18	David Pearson	Cotton Owens
39.	Weaverville, N.C.	Aug. 21	Darel Dieringer	Walter "Bud" Moore
40.	Beltsville, Md.	Aug. 24	Bobby Allison	Bobby Allison
41.	Winston-Salem, N.C.	Aug. 27	David Pearson	Cotton Owens
42.	Darlington, S.C.	Sept. 5	Darel Dieringer	Walter "Bud" Moore
43.	Hickory, N.C.	Sept. 9	David Pearson	Cotton Owens
44.	Richmond, Va.	Sept. 11	David Pearson	Cotton Owens
45.	Hillsboro, N.C.	Sept. 18	Dick Hutcherson	Bondy Long
46.	Martinsville, Va.	Sept. 25	Fred Lorenzen	Holman-Moody
47.	N. Wilkesboro, N.C.	Oct. 2	Dick Hutcherson	Bondy Long
48.	Concord, N.C.	Oct. 16	LeeRoy Yarbrough	Jon Thorne
49.	Rockingham, N.C.	Oct. 30	Fred Lorenzen	Holman-Moody

>> POINTS STANDINGS

1. David Pearson 35,638
2. James Hylton 33,688
3. Richard Petty 22,952
4. Henley Gray 22,468
5. Paul Goldsmith 22,078
6. Wendell Scott 21,702
7. John Sears 21,432
8. J.T. Putney 21,208
9. Neil Castles................................20,446
10. Bobby Allison 19,910

>> RACE WINNERS   17

1. David Pearson 15
2. Richard Petty 8
3. Bobby Allison 3
   Darel Dieringer 3
   Paul Goldsmith................................3
   Dick Hutcherson 3
7. Elmo Langley 2
   Fred Lorenzen 2
   Jim Paschal 2
10. Earl Balmer 1
   Dan Gurney 1
   Jim Hurtubise 1
   Paul Lewis 1
   Tiny Lund................................1
   Sam McQuagg 1
   Marvin Panch 1
   LeeRoy Yarbrough 1

>> MONEY WON LEADERS

1. Richard Petty $78,840
2. David Pearson................................59,205
3. Darel Dieringer 50,960
4. Paul Goldsmith 48,075
5. Marvin Panch 37,385
6. Fred Lorenzen 36,310
7. James Hylton 29,575
8. Jim Paschal 29,415
9. Sam McQuagg 27,960
10. G.C. Spencer................................25,675

>> POLE WINNERS   15

1. Richard Petty 16
2. David Pearson 7
3. Bobby Allison 4
   Tom Pistone 4
5. Junior Johnson 3
6. Dick Hutcherson 2
   Fred Lorenzen 2
   Jim Paschal 2
   Curtis Turner 2
   LeeRoy Yarbrough 2
11. Buddy Baker 1
   Paul Goldsmith................................1
   James Hylton 1
   Elmo Langley 1
   Tiny Lund................................1

>> 1965 SEASON <<

Race No.	Location	Date	Winner	Car owner
1.	Riverside, Calif.	Jan. 17	Dan Gurney	Wood Brothers
2.	Daytona Beach, Fla.	Feb. 12	Darel Dieringer	Walter "Bud" Moore
3.	Daytona Beach, Fla.	Feb. 12	Junior Johnson	Rex Lovette
4.	Daytona Beach, Fla.	Feb. 14	Fred Lorenzen	Holman-Moody
5.	Spartanburg, S.C.	Feb. 27	Ned Jarrett	Bondy Long
6.	Weaverville, N.C.	Feb. 28	Ned Jarrett	Bondy Long
7.	Richmond, Va.	March 7	Junior Johnson	Rex Lovette
8.	Hillsboro, N.C.	March 14	Ned Jarrett	Bondy Long
9.	Hampton, Ga.	April 11	Marvin Panch	Wood Brothers
10.	Greenville, S.C.	April 17	Dick Hutcherson	Holman-Moody
11.	N. Wilkesboro, N.C.	April 18	Junior Johnson	Rex Lovette
12.	Martinsville, Va.	April 25	Fred Lorenzen	Holman-Moody
13.	Columbia, S.C.	April 28	Tiny Lund	Lyle Stelter
14.	Bristol, Tenn.	May 2	Junior Johnson	Rex Lovette
15.	Darlington, S.C.	May 8	Junior Johnson	Rex Lovette
16.	Hampton, Va.	May 14	Ned Jarrett	Bondy Long
17.	Winston-Salem, N.C.	May 15	Junior Johnson	Rex Lovette
18.	Hickory, N.C.	May 16	Junior Johnson	Rex Lovette
19.	Concord, N.C.	May 23	Fred Lorenzen	Holman-Moody
20.	Shelby, N.C.	May 27	Ned Jarrett	Bondy Long
21.	Asheville, N.C.	May 29	Junior Johnson	Rex Lovette
22.	Harris, N.C.	May 30	Ned Jarrett	Bondy Long
23.	Nashville	June 3	Dick Hutcherson	Holman-Moody
24.	Birmingham, Ala.	June 6	Ned Jarrett	Bondy Long
25.	Hampton, Ga.	June 13	Marvin Panch	Wood Brothers
26.	Greenville, S.C.	June 19	Dick Hutcherson	Holman-Moody
27.	Myrtle Beach, S.C.	June 24	Dick Hutcherson	Holman-Moody
28.	Valdosta, Ga.	June 27	Cale Yarborough	Kenny Myler
29.	Daytona Beach, Fla.	July 4	A.J. Foyt	Wood Brothers
30.	Manassas, Va.	July 8	Junior Johnson	Rex Lovette
31.	Old Bridge, N.J.	July 9	Junior Johnson	Rex Lovette
32.	Islip, N.Y.	July 14	Marvin Panch	Wood Brothers
33.	Watkins Glen, N.Y.	July 18	Marvin Panch	Wood Brothers
34.	Bristol, Tenn.	July 25	Ned Jarrett	Bondy Long
35.	Nashville	July 31	Richard Petty	Petty Enterprises
36.	Shelby, N.C.	Aug. 5	Ned Jarrett	Bondy Long
37.	Weaverville, N.C.	Aug. 8	Richard Petty	Petty Enterprises
38.	Maryville, Tenn.	Aug. 13	Dick Hutcherson	Holman-Moody
39.	Spartanburg, S.C.	Aug. 14	Ned Jarrett	Bondy Long
40.	Augusta, Ga.	Aug. 15	Dick Hutcherson	Holman-Moody
41.	Columbus, Ga.	Aug. 19	David Pearson	Cotton Owens
42.	Moyock, N.C.	Aug. 24	Dick Hutcherson	Holman-Moody
43.	Beltsville, Md.	Aug. 25	Ned Jarrett	Bondy Long
44.	Winston-Salem, N.C.	Aug. 28	Junior Johnson	Rex Lovette
45.	Darlington, S.C.	Sept. 6	Ned Jarrett	Bondy Long
46.	Hickory, N.C.	Sept. 10	Richard Petty	Petty Enterprises
47.	New Oxford, Pa.	Sept. 14	Dick Hutcherson	Holman-Moody
48.	Manassas, Va.	Sept. 17	Richard Petty	Petty Enterprises
49.	Richmond, Va.	Sept. 18	David Pearson	Cotton Owens
50.	Martinsville, Va.	Sept. 26	Junior Johnson	Rex Lovette
51.	N. Wilkesboro, N.C.	Oct. 3	Junior Johnson	Rex Lovette
52.	Concord, N.C.	Oct. 17	Fred Lorenzen	Holman-Moody
53.	Hillsboro, N.C.	Oct. 24	Dick Hutcherson	Holman-Moody
54.	Rockingham, N.C.	Oct. 31	Curtis Turner	Wood Brothers
55.	Moyock, N.C.	Nov. 7	Ned Jarrett	Bondy Long

>> POINTS STANDINGS

1. Ned Jarrett 38,824
2. Dick Hutcherson 35,790
3. Darel Dieringer 24,696
4. G.C. Spencer 24,314
5. Marvin Panch 22,798
6. Bob Derrington 21,394
7. J.T. Putney 20,928
8. Neil Castles 20,848
9. Buddy Baker 20,672
10. Cale Yarborough 20,192

>> RACE WINNERS 13

1. Ned Jarrett 13
   Junior Johnson 13
3. Dick Hutcherson 9
4. Fred Lorenzen 4
   Marvin Panch...4
   Richard Petty...4
7. David Pearson 2
8. Darel Dieringer 1
   A.J. Foyt 1
   Dan Gurney 1
   Tiny Lund..1
   Curtis Turner 1
   Cale Yarborough...1

>> MONEY WON LEADERS

1. Ned Jarrett $77,966
2. Fred Lorenzen..................................77,115
3. Junior Johnson 57,925
4. Marvin Panch 54,045
5. Dick Hutcherson 49,420
6. Darel Dieringer 47,775
7. Buddy Baker 25,390
8. Cale Yarborough 24,040
9. Bobby Johns 23,695
10. G.C. Spencer...................................23,030

>> POLE WINNERS 13

1. Junior Johnson 10
2. Dick Hutcherson 9
   Ned Jarrett 9
4. Richard Petty 7
5. Fred Lorenzen 6
6. Marvin Panch..5
7. Darel Dieringer 2
8. Bobby Isaac 1
   Paul Lewis..1
   Bud Moore..1
   David Pearson 1
   Tom Pistone..1
   G.C. Spencer 1

>> 1964 SEASON <<

Race No.	Location	Date	Winner	Car owner
1.	Concord, N.C.	Nov. 10	Ned Jarrett	Charles Robinson
2.	Augusta, Ga.	Nov. 17	Fireball Roberts	Holman-Moody
3.	Jacksonville, Fla.	Dec. 1	Wendell Scott	Wendell Scott
4.	Savannah, Ga.	Dec. 29	Richard Petty	Petty Enterprises
5.	Riverside, Calif.	Jan. 19	Dan Gurney	Wood Brothers
6.	Daytona Beach, Fla.	Feb. 21	Junior Johnson	Raymond Fox
7.	Daytona Beach, Fla.	Feb. 21	Bobby Isaac	Ray Nichels
8.	Daytona Beach, Fla.	Feb. 23	Richard Petty	Petty Enterprises
9.	Richmond, Va.	March 10	David Pearson	Cotton Owens
10.	Bristol, Tenn.	March 22	Fred Lorenzen	Holman-Moody
11.	Greenville, S.C.	March 28	David Pearson	Cotton Owens
12.	Winston-Salem, N.C.	March 30	Marvin Panch	Wood Brothers
13.	Hampton, Ga.	April 5	Fred Lorenzen	Holman-Moody
14.	Weaverville, N.C.	April 11	Marvin Panch	Wood Brothers
15.	Hillsboro, N.C.	April 12	David Pearson	Cotton Owens
16.	Spartanburg, S.C.	April 14	Ned Jarrett	Bondy Long
17.	Columbia, S.C.	April 16	Ned Jarrett	Bondy Long
18.	N. Wilkesboro, N.C.	April 19	Fred Lorenzen	Holman-Moody
19.	Martinsville, Va.	April 26	Fred Lorenzen	Holman-Moody
20.	Savannah, Ga.	May 1	LeeRoy Yarbrough	Louie Weathersby
21.	Darlington, S.C.	May 9	Fred Lorenzen	Holman-Moody
22.	Hampton, Va.	May 15	Ned Jarrett	Bondy Long
23.	Hickory, N.C.	May 16	Ned Jarrett	Bondy Long
24.	South Boston, Va.	May 17	Richard Petty	Petty Enterprises
25.	Concord, N.C.	May 24	Jim Paschal	Petty Enterprises
26.	Greenville, S.C.	May 30	LeeRoy Yarbrough	Louie Weathersby
27.	Asheville, N.C.	May 31	Ned Jarrett	Bondy Long
28.	Hampton, Ga.	June 7	Ned Jarrett	Bondy Long
29.	Concord, N.C.	June 11	Richard Petty	Petty Enterprises
30.	Nashville	June 14	Richard Petty	Petty Enterprises
31.	Chattanooga	June 19	David Pearson	Cotton Owens
32.	Birmingham, Ala.	June 21	Ned Jarrett	Bondy Long
33.	Valdosta, Ga.	June 23	Buck Baker	Raymond Fox
34.	Spartanburg, S.C.	June 26	Richard Petty	Petty Enterprises
35.	Daytona Beach, Fla.	July 4	A.J. Foyt	Ray Nichels
36.	Manassas, Va.	July 8	Ned Jarrett	Bondy Long
37.	Old Bridge, N.J.	July 10	Billy Wade	Bud Moore
38.	Bridgehampton, N.Y.	July 12	Billy Wade	Bud Moore
39.	Islip, N.Y.	July 15	Billy Wade	Bud Moore
40.	Watkins Glen, N.Y.	July 19	Billy Wade	Bud Moore
41.	New Oxford, Pa.	July 21	David Pearson	Cotton Owens
42.	Bristol, Tenn.	July 26	Fred Lorenzen	Holman-Moody
43.	Nashville	Aug. 2	Richard Petty	Petty Enterprises
44.	Myrtle Beach, S.C.	Aug. 7	David Pearson	Cotton Owens
45.	Weaverville, N.C.	Aug. 9	Ned Jarrett	Bondy Long
46.	Moyock, N.C.	Aug. 13	Ned Jarrett	Bondy Long
47.	Huntington, W.Va.	Aug. 16	Richard Petty	Petty Enterprises
48.	Columbia, S.C.	Aug. 21	David Pearson	Cotton Owens
49.	Winston-Salem, N.C.	Aug. 22	Junior Johnson	Banjo Matthews
50.	Roanoke, Va.	Aug. 23	Junior Johnson	Banjo Matthews
51.	Darlington, S.C.	Sept. 7	Buck Baker	Raymond Fox
52.	Hickory, N.C.	Sept. 11	David Pearson	Cotton Owens
53.	Richmond, Va.	Sept. 14	Cotton Owens	Cotton Owens
54.	Manassas, Va.	Sept. 18	Ned Jarrett	Bondy Long
55.	Hillsboro, N.C.	Sept. 20	Ned Jarrett	Bondy Long
56.	Martinsville, Va.	Sept. 27	Fred Lorenzen	Holman-Moody
57.	Savannah, Ga.	Oct. 9	Ned Jarrett	Bondy Long
58.	N. Wilkesboro, N.C.	Oct. 11	Marvin Panch	Wood Brothers
59.	Concord, N.C.	Oct. 18	Fred Lorenzen	Holman-Moody
60.	Harris, N.C.	Oct. 25	Richard Petty	Petty Enterprises
61.	Augusta, Ga.	Nov. 1	Darel Dieringer	Bud Moore
62.	Jacksonville, N.C.	Nov. 8	Ned Jarrett	Bondy Long

>> POINTS STANDINGS

1. Richard Petty 40,252
2. Ned Jarrett 34,950
3. David Pearson................32,146
4. Billy Wade 28,474
5. Jimmy Pardue................26,570
6. Curtis Crider 25,606
7. Jim Paschal 22,450
8. Larry Thomas................22,950
9. Buck Baker 22,366
10. Marvin Panch 21,480

>> RACE WINNERS　　17

1. Ned Jarrett 15
2. Richard Petty 9
3. Fred Lorenzen 8
　 David Pearson 8
5. Billy Wade 4
6. Junior Johnson 3
　 Marvin Panch.................3
8. Buck Baker 2
　 LeeRoy Yarbrough 2
10. Darel Dieringer 1
　 A.J. Foyt 1
　 Dan Gurney 1
　 Bobby Isaac 1
　 Cotton Owens 1
　 Jim Paschal 1
　 Fireball Roberts 1
　 Wendell Scott 1

>> MONEY WON LEADERS

1. Richard Petty $98,810
2. Fred Lorenzen 72,385
3. Ned Jarrett 63,330
4. Jim Paschal 54,960
5. Buck Baker..............41,080
6. David Pearson...........38,175
7. Jimmy Pardue...........36,440
8. Marvin Panch 32,135
9. Billy Wade 29,710
10. Fireball Roberts..........28,345

>> POLE WINNERS　　14

1. David Pearson 12
2. Ned Jarrett 9
　 Richard Petty 9
4. Fred Lorenzen 7
5. Junior Johnson 5
　 Marvin Panch...............5
　 Billy Wade 5
8. Paul Goldsmith.............2
　 Dick Hutcherson 2
　 Jimmy Pardue 2
11. Darel Dieringer 1
　 Jack Smith 1
　 Glen Wood 1
　 Doug Yates.................1

RACING PIONEER

Scott laps the field—twice—for his first NASCAR win

Wendell Scott is the only African-American to win a NASCAR race, but he never got to celebrate in victory lane.

The win was erroneously—some say intentionally—given to Buck Baker at first. Only after the celebration was over did officials officially acknowledge Scott was the winner. He didn't just win—he dominated, finishing ahead of Baker by two laps.

The event was at a half-mile track in Jacksonville, Fla. Though the race was run December 1, 1963, it was considered part of the 1964 season.

Scott got his start in the sport like many others, by making bootleg runs. Running on a tight budget, he won 128 local races. At the NASCAR NEXTEL Cup Series level, Scott made 495 starts, compiled 147 top 10s and finished in the top 10 in points four times.

He drove the No. 34, and his family always was right there with him. His sons worked on the pit crew, his daughter kept score and his wife occasionally drove the truck that hauled the car. His career was the basis for a movie, *Greased Lightning*, starring Richard Pryor.

Scott died in 1990 at 69 and was inducted into the International Motorsports Hall of Fame in 1999.

>> 1963 SEASON <<

Race No.	Location	Date	Winner	Car owner
1.	Birmingham, Ala.	Nov. 4	Jim Paschal	Petty Enterprises
2.	Tampa, Fla.	Nov. 11	Richard Petty	Petty Enterprises
3.	Randleman, N.C.	Nov. 22	Jim Paschal	Petty Enterprises
4.	Riverside, Calif.	Jan. 20	Dan Gurney	Holman-Moody
5.	Daytona Beach, Fla.	Feb. 22	Junior Johnson	Raymond Fox
6.	Daytona Beach, Fla.	Feb. 22	Johnny Rutherford	Smokey Yunick
7.	Daytona Beach, Fla.	Feb. 24	Tiny Lund	Wood Brothers
8.	Spartanburg, S.C.	March 2	Richard Petty	Petty Enterprises
9.	Weaverville, N.C.	March 3	Richard Petty	Petty Enterprises
10.	Hillsboro, N.C.	March 10	Junior Johnson	Raymond Fox
11.	Hampton, Ga.	March 17	Fred Lorenzen	Holman-Moody
12.	Hickory, N.C.	March 24	Junior Johnson	Raymond Fox
13.	Bristol, Tenn.	March 31	Fireball Roberts	Holman-Moody
14.	Augusta, Ga.	April 4	Ned Jarrett	Charles Robinson
15.	Richmond, Va.	April 7	Joe Weatherly	Bud Moore
16.	Greenville, S.C.	April 13	Buck Baker	Buck Baker
17.	South Boston, Va.	April 14	Richard Petty	Petty Enterprises
18.	Winston-Salem, N.C.	April 15	Jim Paschal	Petty Enterprises
19.	Martinsville, Va.	April 21	Richard Petty	Petty Enterprises
20.	N. Wilkesboro, N.C.	April 28	Richard Petty	Petty Enterprises
21.	Columbia, S.C.	May 2	Richard Petty	Petty Enterprises
22.	Randleman, N.C.	May 5	Jim Paschal	Petty Enterprises
23.	Darlington, S.C.	May 11	Joe Weatherly	Bud Moore
24.	Manassas, Va.	May 18	Richard Petty	Petty Enterprises
25.	Richmond, Va.	May 19	Ned Jarrett	Charles Robinson
26.	Concord, N.C.	June 2	Fred Lorenzen	Holman-Moody
27.	Birmingham, Ala.	June 9	Richard Petty	Petty Enterprises
28.	Hampton, Ga.	June 30	Junior Johnson	Raymond Fox
29.	Daytona Beach, Fla.	July 4	Fireball Roberts	Holman-Moody
30.	Myrtle Beach, S.C.	July 7	Ned Jarrett	Charles Robinson
31.	Savannah, Ga.	July 10	Ned Jarrett	Charles Robinson
32.	Moyock, N.C.	July 11	Jimmy Pardue	Peter Stewart
33.	Winston-Salem, N.C.	July 13	Glen Wood	Wood Brothers
34.	Asheville, N.C.	July 14	Ned Jarrett	Charles Robinson
35.	Old Bridge, N.J.	July 19	Fireball Roberts	Holman-Moody
36.	Bridgehampton, N.Y.	July 21	Richard Petty	Petty Enterprises
37.	Bristol, Tenn.	July 28	Fred Lorenzen	Holman-Moody
38.	Greenville, S.C.	July 30	Richard Petty	Petty Enterprises
39.	Nashville	Aug. 4	Jim Paschal	Petty Enterprises
40.	Columbia, S.C.	Aug. 8	Richard Petty	Petty Enterprises
41.	Weaverville, N.C.	Aug. 11	Fred Lorenzen	Holman-Moody
42.	Spartanburg, S.C.	Aug. 14	Ned Jarrett	Charles Robinson
43.	Winston-Salem, N.C.	Aug. 16	Junior Johnson	Raymond Fox
44.	Huntington, W.Va.	Aug. 18	Fred Lorenzen	Holman-Moody
45.	Darlington, S.C.	Sept. 2	Fireball Roberts	Holman-Moody
46.	Hickory, N.C.	Sept. 6	Junior Johnson	Raymond Fox
47.	Richmond, Va.	Sept. 8	Ned Jarrett	Charles Robinson
48.	Martinsville, Va.	Sept. 22	Fred Lorenzen	Holman-Moody
49.	Moyock, N.C.	Sept. 24	Ned Jarrett	Charles Robinson
50.	N. Wilkesboro, N.C.	Sept. 29	Marvin Panch	Wood Brothers
51.	Randleman, N.C.	Oct. 5	Richard Petty	Petty Enterprises
52.	Concord, N.C.	Oct. 13	Junior Johnson	Raymond Fox
53.	South Boston, Va.	Oct. 20	Richard Petty	Petty Enterprises
54.	Hillsboro, N.C.	Oct. 27	Joe Weatherly	Bud Moore
55.	Riverside, Calif.	Nov. 3	Darel Dieringer	William Stroppe

>> POINTS STANDINGS

1. Joe Weatherly 33,398
2. Richard Petty 31,170
3. Fred Lorenzen 29,684
4. Ned Jarrett 27,214
5. Fireball Roberts 22,642
6. Jimmy Pardue....................................22,228
7. Darel Dieringer 21,418
8. David Pearson 21,156
9. Rex White 20,976
10. Tiny Lund 19,624

>> RACE WINNERS   15

1. Richard Petty 14
2. Ned Jarrett 8
3. Junior Johnson 7
4. Fred Lorenzen 6
5. Jim Paschal 5
6. Fireball Roberts 4
7. Joe Weatherly 3
8. Buck Baker 1
    Darel Dieringer 1
    Dan Gurney 1
    Tiny Lund..1
    Marvin Panch.....................................1
    Jimmy Pardue 1
    Johnny Rutherford 1
    Glen Wood 1

>> MONEY WON LEADERS

1. Fred Lorenzen....................................$113,570
2. Fireball Roberts..................................67,320
3. Junior Johnson...................................65,710
4. Joe Weatherly....................................57,710
5. Richard Petty 47,765
6. Tiny Lund 40,930
7. Ned Jarrett 38,740
8. Marvin Panch......................................37,461
9. Darel Dieringer 25,575
10. Rex White 24,235

>> POLE WINNERS   15

1. Junior Johnson 9
    Fred Lorenzen 9
3. Richard Petty 8
4. Joe Weatherly 6
5. Ned Jarrett 4
6. Marvin Panch......................................3
    Rex White 3
8. David Pearson 2
    Fireball Roberts 2
    Jack Smith 2
    Glen Wood 2
12. Paul Goldsmith....................................1
    Jimmy Pardue 1
    Jim Paschal 1
    LeeRoy Yarbrough 1

Race No.	Location	Date	Winner	Car owner
1.	Concord, N.C.	Nov. 5	Jack Smith	Jack Smith
2.	Weaverville, N.C.	Nov. 12	Rex White	Rex White
3.	Daytona Beach, Fla.	Feb. 16	Fireball Roberts	Jim Stephens
4.	Daytona Beach, Fla.	Feb. 16	Joe Weatherly	Bud Moore
5.	Daytona Beach, Fla.	Feb. 18	Fireball Roberts	Jim Stephens
6.	Concord, N.C.	Feb. 25	Joe Weatherly	Bud Moore
7.	Weaverville, N.C.	March 4	Joe Weatherly	Bud Moore
8.	Savannah, Ga.	March 17	Jack Smith	Jack Smith
9.	Hillsboro, N.C.	March 18	Rex White	Rex White
10.	Richmond, Va.	April 1	Rex White	Rex White
11.	Columbia, S.C.	April 13	Ned Jarrett	Bee Gee Holloway
12.	N. Wilkesboro, N.C.	April 15	Richard Petty	Petty Enterprises
13.	Greenville, S.C.	April 19	Ned Jarrett	Bee Gee Holloway
14.	Myrtle Beach, S.C.	April 21	Jack Smith	Jack Smith
15.	Martinsville, Va.	April 22	Richard Petty	Petty Enterprises
16.	Winston-Salem, N.C.	April 23	Rex White	Rex White
17.	Bristol, Tenn.	April 29	Bobby Johns	Shorty Johns
18.	Richmond, Va.	May 4	Jimmy Pardue	Jimmy Pardue
19.	Hickory, N.C.	May 5	Jack Smith	Jack Smith
20.	Concord, N.C.	May 6	Joe Weatherly	Bud Moore
21.	Darlington, S.C.	May 12	Nelson Stacy	Holman-Moody
22.	Spartanburg, S.C.	May 19	Ned Jarrett	Bee Gee Holloway
23.	Concord, N.C.	May 27	Nelson Stacy	Holman-Moody
24.	Hampton, Ga.	June 10	Fred Lorenzen	Holman-Moody
25.	Winston-Salem, N.C.	June 16	Johnny Allen	Fred Lovette
26.	Augusta, Ga.	June 19	Joe Weatherly	Bud Moore
27.	Richmond, Va.	June 22	Jim Paschal	Cliff Stewart
28.	South Boston, Va.	June 23	Rex White	Rex White
29.	Daytona Beach, Fla.	July 4	Fireball Roberts	Banjo Matthews
30.	Columbia, S.C.	July 7	Rex White	Rex White
31.	Asheville, N.C.	July 13	Jack Smith	Jack Smith
32.	Greenville, S.C.	July 14	Richard Petty	Petty Enterprises
33.	Augusta, Ga.	July 17	Joe Weatherly	Bud Moore
34.	Savannah, Ga.	July 20	Joe Weatherly	Bud Moore
35.	Myrtle Beach, S.C.	July 21	Ned Jarrett	Bee Gee Holloway
36.	Bristol, Tenn.	July 29	Jim Paschal	Petty Enterprises
37.	Chattanooga, Tenn.	Aug. 3	Joe Weatherly	Bud Moore
38.	Nashville	Aug. 5	Jim Paschal	Petty Enterprises
39.	Huntsville, Ala.	Aug. 8	Richard Petty	Petty Enterprises
40.	Weaverville, N.C.	Aug. 12	Jim Paschal	Petty Enterprises
41.	Roanoke, Va.	Aug. 15	Richard Petty	Petty Enterprises
42.	Winston-Salem, N.C.	Aug. 18	Richard Petty	Petty Enterprises
43.	Spartanburg, S.C.	Aug. 21	Richard Petty	Petty Enterprises
44.	Valdosta, Ga.	Aug. 25	Ned Jarrett	Bee Gee Holloway
45.	Darlington, S.C.	Sept. 3	Larry Frank	Ratus Walters
46.	Hickory, N.C.	Sept. 7	Rex White	Rex White
47.	Richmond, Va.	Sept. 9	Joe Weatherly	Bud Moore
48.	Moyock, N.C.	Sept. 11	Ned Jarrett	Bee Gee Holloway
49.	Augusta, Ga.	Sept. 13	Fred Lorenzen	Mamie Reynolds
50.	Martinsville, Va.	Sept. 23	Nelson Stacy	Holman-Moody
51.	N. Wilkesboro, N.C.	Sept. 30	Richard Petty	Petty Enterprises
52.	Concord, N.C.	Oct. 14	Junior Johnson	Raymond Fox
53.	Hampton, Ga.	Oct. 28	Rex White	Rex White

>> POINTS STANDINGS

1. Joe Weatherly 30,836
2. Richard Petty 28,440
3. Ned Jarrett 25,336
4. Jack Smith 22,870
5. Rex White 19,424
6. Jim Paschal 18,128
7. Fred Lorenzen 17,554
8. Fireball Roberts 16,380
9. Marvin Panch 15,138
10. David Pearson 14,404

>> RACE WINNERS   14

1. Joe Weatherly 9
2. Richard Petty 8
   Rex White 8
4. Ned Jarrett 6
5. Jack Smith 5
6. Jim Paschal 4
7. Fireball Roberts 3
   Nelson Stacy 3
9. Fred Lorenzen 2
10. Johnny Allen 1
   Larry Frank 1
   Bobby Johns 1
   Junior Johnson 1
   Jimmy Pardue 1

>> MONEY WON LEADERS

1. Joe Weatherly $55,055
2. Richard Petty 52,885
3. Fireball Roberts 51,790
4. Fred Lorenzen 42,948
5. Nelson Stacy 42,515
6. Ned Jarrett 35,320
7. Junior Johnson 33,940
8. Larry Frank 31,410
9. Rex White 30,643
10. Jack Smith 28,485

>> POLE WINNERS   13

1. Fireball Roberts 9
   Rex White 9
3. Jack Smith 7
   Joe Weatherly 7
5. Ned Jarrett 4
   Richard Petty 4
7. Fred Lorenzen 3
8. Junior Johnson 2
   Banjo Matthews 2
10. Johnny Allen 1
   Darel Dieringer 1
   Cotton Owens 1
   Wendell Scott 1

>> 1961 SEASON <<

Race No.	Location	Date	Winner	Car owner
1.	Charlotte	Nov. 6	Joe Weatherly	Bradford White
2.	Jacksonville, Fla.	Nov. 20	Lee Petty	Petty Enterprises
3.	Daytona Beach, Fla.	Feb. 24	Fireball Roberts	Jim Stephens
4.	Daytona Beach, Fla.	Feb. 24	Joe Weatherly	Bud Moore
5.	Daytona Beach, Fla.	Feb. 26	Marvin Panch	Smokey Yunick
6.	Spartanburg, S.C.	March 4	Cotton Owens	Cotton Owens
7.	Weaverville, N.C.	March 5	Rex White	Rex White
8.	Hanford, Calif.	March 12	Fireball Roberts	J.D. Braswell
9.	Hampton, Ga.	March 26	Bob Burdick	Roy Burdick
10.	Greenville, S.C.	April 1	Emanuel Zervakis	Monroe Shook
11.	Hillsboro, N.C.	April 2	Cotton Owens	Cotton Owens
12.	Winston-Salem, N.C.	April 3	Rex White	Rex White
13.	Martinsville, Va.	April 9	Fred Lorenzen	Holman-Moody
14.	N. Wilkesboro, N.C.	April 16	Rex White	Rex White
15.	Columbia, S.C.	April 20	Cotton Owens	Cotton Owens
16.	Hickory, N.C.	April 22	Junior Johnson	Rex Lovette
17.	Richmond, Va.	April 23	Richard Petty	Petty Enterprises
18.	Martinsville, Va.	April 30	Junior Johnson	Rex Lovette
19.	Darlington, S.C.	May 6	Fred Lorenzen	Holman-Moody
20.	Concord, N.C.	May 21	Richard Petty	Petty Enterprises
21.	Concord, N.C.	May 21	Joe Weatherly	Bud Moore
22.	Riverside, Calif.	May 21	Lloyd Dane	Lloyd Dane
23.	Los Angles, Calif.	May 27	Eddie Gray	Eddie Gray
24.	Concord, N.C.	May 28	David Pearson	John Masoni
25.	Spartanburg, S.C.	June 2	Jim Paschal	J.H. Petty
26.	Birmingham, Ala.	June 4	Ned Jarrett	Bee Gee Holloway
27.	Greenville, S.C.	June 8	Jack Smith	Jack Smith
28.	Winston-Salem, N.C.	June 10	Rex White	Rex White
29.	Norwood, Mass.	June 17	Emanuel Zervakis	Monroe Shook
30.	Hartsville, S.C.	June 23	Buck Baker	Buck Baker
31.	Roanoke, Va.	June 24	Junior Johnson	Rex Lovette
32.	Daytona Beach, Fla.	July 4	David Pearson	John Masoni
33.	Hampton, Ga.	July 9	Fred Lorenzen	Holman-Moody
34.	Columbia, S.C.	July 20	Cotton Owens	Cotton Owens
35.	Myrtle Beach, S.C.	July 22	Joe Weatherly	Bud Moore
36.	Bristol, Tenn.	July 30	Jack Smith	Jack Smith
37.	Nashville	Aug. 6	Jim Paschal	J.H. Petty
38.	Winston-Salem, N.C.	Aug. 9	Rex White	Rex White
39.	Weaverville, N.C.	Aug. 13	Junior Johnson	Rex Lovette
40.	Richmond, Va.	Aug. 18	Junior Johnson	Rex Lovette
41.	South Boston, Va.	Aug. 27	Junior Johnson	Rex Lovette
42.	Darlington, S.C.	Sept. 4	Nelson Stacy	Dudley Farrell
43.	Hickory, N.C.	Sept. 8	Rex White	Rex White
44.	Richmond, Va.	Sept. 10	Joe Weatherly	Bud Moore
45.	Sacramento, Calif.	Sept. 10	Eddie Gray	Eddie Gray
46.	Hampton, Ga.	Sept. 17	David Pearson	John Masoni
47.	Martinsville, Va.	Sept. 24	Joe Weatherly	Bud Moore
48.	N. Wilkesboro, N.C.	Oct. 1	Rex White	Rex White
49.	Concord, N.C.	Oct. 15	Joe Weatherly	Bud Moore
50.	Bristol, Tenn.	Oct. 22	Joe Weatherly	Bud Moore
51.	Greenville, S.C.	Oct. 28	Junior Johnson	Rex Lovette
52.	Hillsboro, N.C.	Oct. 29	Joe Weatherly	Bud Moore

>> POINTS STANDINGS

1. Ned Jarrett 27,272
2. Rex White 26,442
3. Emanuel Zervakis 22,312
4. Joe Weatherly 17,894
5. Fireball Roberts...17,600
6. Junior Johnson 17,178
7. Jack Smith 15,186
8. Richard Petty 14,984
9. Jim Paschal 13,922
10. Buck Baker 13,746

>> RACE WINNERS   19

1. Joe Weatherly 9
2. Junior Johnson 7
   Rex White 7
4. Cotton Owens 4
5. Fred Lorenzen 3
   David Pearson 3
7. Eddie Gray 2
   Jim Paschal 2
   Richard Petty 2
   Fireball Roberts 2
   Jack Smith 2
   Emanuel Zervakis 2
13. Buck Baker 1
   Bob Burdick 1
   Lloyd Dane 1
   Ned Jarrett 1
   Marvin Panch...1
   Lee Petty 1
   Nelson Stacy 1

>> MONEY WON LEADERS

1. David Pearson.....................................$49,580
2. Rex White 48,830
3. Joe Weatherly 39,965
4. Fireball Roberts......................................38,300
5. Fred Lorenzen..29,655
6. Marvin Panch...28,865
7. Ned Jarrett 27,235
8. Nelson Stacy...26,760
9. Junior Johnson 25,310
10. Richard Petty 22,671

>> POLE WINNERS   21

1. Junior Johnson 10
2. Rex White 7
3. Fireball Roberts 6
4. Ned Jarrett 4
   Fred Lorenzen 4
   Joe Weatherly 4
7. Cotton Owens 2
   Richard Petty 2
9. Johnny Allen, Bill Amick, Buck Baker, Eddie Gray, Bobby Johns, Marvin Panch, Jim Paschal, David Pearson, Lee Petty, Bob Ross, Danny Weinberg, Glen Wood, Emanuel Zervakis 1

Race No.	Location	Date	Winner	Car owner
1.	Charlotte	Nov. 8	Jack Smith	Jack Smith
2.	Columbia, S.C.	Nov. 26	Ned Jarrett	Ned Jarrett
3.	Daytona Beach, Fla.	Feb. 12	Fireball Roberts	John Hines
4.	Daytona Beach, Fla.	Feb. 12	Jack Smith	Jack Smith
5.	Daytona Beach, Fla.	Feb. 14	Junior Johnson	John Masoni
6.	Charlotte, N.C.	Feb. 28	Richard Petty	Petty Enterprises
7.	N. Wilkesboro, N.C.	March 27	Lee Petty	Petty Enterprises
8.	Phoenix	April 3	John Rostek	John Rostek
9.	Columbia, S.C.	April 5	Rex White	Rex White
10.	Martinsville, Va.	April 10	Richard Petty	Petty Enterprises
11.	Hickory, N.C.	April 16	Joe Weatherly	Holman-Moody
12.	Wilson, N.C.	April 17	Joe Weatherly	Holman-Moody
13.	Winston-Salem, N.C.	April 18	Glen Wood	Wood Brothers
14.	Greenville, S.C.	April 23	Ned Jarrett	Ned Jarrett
15.	Weaverville, N.C.	April 24	Lee Petty	Petty Enterprises
16.	Darlington, S.C.	May 14	Joe Weatherly	Holman-Moody
17.	Spartanburg, S.C.	May 28	Ned Jarrett	Ned Jarrett
18.	Hillsboro, N.C.	May 29	Lee Petty	Petty Enterprises
19.	Richmond, Va.	June 5	Lee Petty	Petty Enterprises
20.	Hanford, Calif.	June 12	Marvin Porter	Vel Miletich
21.	Concord, N.C.	June 19	Joe Lee Johnson	Paul McDuffie
22.	Winston-Salem, N.C.	June 26	Glen Wood	Wood Brothers
23.	Daytona Beach, Fla.	July 4	Jack Smith	Jack Smith
24.	Heidelburg, Pa.	July 10	Lee Petty	Petty Enterprises
25.	Montgomery, N.Y.	July 17	Rex White	Rex White
26.	Myrtle Beach, S.C.	July 23	Buck Baker	Buck Baker
27.	Hampton, Ga.	July 31	Fireball Roberts	John Hines
28.	Birmingham, Ala.	Aug. 3	Ned Jarrett	Ned Jarrett
29.	Nashville	Aug. 7	Johnny Beauchamp	Dale Swanson
30.	Weaverville, N.C.	Aug. 14	Rex White	Rex White
31.	Spartanburg, S.C.	Aug. 16	Cotton Owens	Cotton Owens
32.	Columbia, S.C.	Aug. 18	Rex White	Rex White
33.	South Boston, Va.	Aug. 20	Junior Johnson	John Masoni
34.	Winston-Salem, N.C.	Aug. 23	Glen Wood	Wood Brothers
35.	Darlington, S.C.	Sept. 5	Buck Baker	Jack Smith
36.	Hickory, N.C.	Sept. 9	Junior Johnson	John Masoni
37.	Sacramento	Sept. 11	Jim Cook	Floyd Johnson
38.	Sumter, S.C.	Sept. 15	Ned Jarrett	Ned Jarrett
39.	Hillsboro, N.C.	Sept. 18	Richard Petty	Petty Enterprises
40.	Martinsville, Va.	Sept. 25	Rex White	Rex White
41.	N. Wilkesboro, N.C.	Oct. 2	Rex White	Rex White
42.	Concord, N.C.	Oct. 16	Speedy Thompson	Wood Brothers
43.	Richmond, Va.	Oct. 23	Speedy Thompson	Wood Brothers
44.	Hampton, Ga.	Oct. 30	Bobby Johns	Cotton Owens

>> POINTS STANDINGS

1. Rex White 21,164
2. Richard Petty 17,228
3. Bobby Johns 14,964
4. Buck Baker 14,674
5. Ned Jarrett 14,660
6. Lee Petty 14,510
7. Junior Johnson 9,932
8. Emanuel Zervakis 9,720
9. Jim Paschal 8,968
10. Banjo Matthews 8,458

>> RACE WINNERS   18

1. Rex White 6
2. Ned Jarrett 5
    Lee Petty 5
4. Junior Johnson 3
    Richard Petty 3
    Jack Smith 3
    Joe Weatherly 3
    Glen Wood 3
9. Buck Baker 2
    Fireball Roberts 2
    Speedy Thompson 2
12. Johnny Beauchamp 1
    Jim Cook 1
    Bobby Johns 1
    Joe Lee Johnson 1
    Cotton Owens 1
    Marvin Porter 1
    John Rostek 1

>> MONEY WON LEADERS

1. Rex White $45,280
2. Bobby Johns.........................40,840
3. Richardy Petty 35,180
4. Buck Baker..........................33,915
5. Joe Lee Johnson 33,388
6. Junior Johnson 30,775
7. Lee Petty 26,650
8. Jack Smith 23,590
9. Ned Jarrett 20,540
10. Fireball Roberts...................19,895

>> POLE WINNERS   19

1. Fireball Roberts 6
2. Ned Jarrett 5
3. Jack Smith 4
    Glen Wood 4
5. Junior Johnson 3
    Cotton Owens 3
    Lee Petty 3
    Rex White 3
9. Buck Baker 2
    Richard Petty 2
11. Jim Cook 1
    Tommy Irwin 1
    Mel Larson..................................1
    David Pearson 1
    John Rostek................................1
    Frank Secrist 1
    Curtis Turner 1
    Doug Yates..................................1
    Emanuel Zervakis 1

>> 1959 SEASON <<

Race No.	Location	Date	Winner	Car owner
1.	Fayetteville, N.C.	Nov. 9	Bob Welborn	J.H. Petty
2.	Daytona Beach, Fla.	Feb. 20	Bob Welborn	W.J. Ridgeway
3.	Daytona Beach, Fla.	Feb. 22	Lee Petty	Petty Enterprises
4.	Hillsboro, N.C.	March 1	Curtis Turner	Bradford White
5.	Concord, N.C.	March 8	Curtis Turner	Bradford White
6.	Atlanta	March 22	Johnny Beauchamp	Roy Burdick
7.	Wilson, N.C.	March 29	Junior Johnson	Paul Spaulding
8.	Winston-Salem, N.C.	March 30	Jim Reed	Jim Reed
9.	Columbia, S.C.	April 4	Jack Smith	Jack Smith
10.	N. Wilkesboro, N.C.	April 5	Lee Petty	Petty Enterprises
11.	Reading, Pa.	April 26	Junior Johnson	Paul Spaulding
12.	Hickory, N.C.	May 2	Junior Johnson	Paul Spaulding
13.	Martinsville, Va.	May 3	Lee Petty	Petty Enterprises
14.	Trenton, N.J.	May 17	Tom Pistone	Carl Rupert
15.	Charlotte, N.C.	May 22	Lee Petty	Petty Enterprises
16.	Nashville	May 24	Rex White	Rex White
17.	Los Angles	May 30	Parnelli Jones	Vel Miletich
18.	Spartanburg, S.C.	June 5	Jack Smith	Jack Smith
19.	Greenville, S.C.	June 13	Junior Johnson	Paul Spaulding
20.	Atlanta	June 14	Lee Petty	Petty Enterprises
21.	Columbia, S.C.	June 18	Lee Petty	Petty Enterprises
22.	Wilson, N.C.	June 20	Junior Johnson	Paul Spaulding
23.	Richmond, Va.	June 21	Tom Pistone	Carl Rupert
24.	Winston-Salem, N.C.	June 27	Rex White	Rex White
25.	Weaverville, N.C.	June 28	Rex White	Rex White
26.	Daytona Beach, Fla.	July 4	Fireball Roberts	Jim Stephens
27.	Pittsburgh	July 21	Jim Reed	Jim Reed
28.	Charlotte	July 26	Jack Smith	Jack Smith
29.	Myrtle Beach, S.C.	Aug. 1	Ned Jarrett	Ned Jarrett
30.	Charlotte	Aug. 2	Ned Jarrett	Ned Jarrett
31.	Nashville	Aug. 9	Joe Lee Johnson	Joe Lee Johnson
32.	Weaverville, N.C.	Aug. 16	Bob Welborn	Bob Welborn
33.	Winston-Salem, N.C.	Aug. 21	Rex White	Rex White
34.	Greenville, S.C.	Aug. 22	Buck Baker	Lynton Tyson
35.	Columbia, S.C.	Aug. 29	Lee Petty	Petty Enterprises
36.	Darlington, S.C.	Sept. 7	Jim Reed	Jim Reed
37.	Hickory, N.C.	Sept. 11	Lee Petty	Petty Enterprises
38.	Richmond, Va.	Sept. 13	Cotton Owens	Cotton Owens
39.	Sacramento	Sept. 13	Eddie Gray	Vel Miletich
40.	Hillsboro, N.C.	Sept. 20	Lee Petty	Petty Enterprises
41.	Martinsville, Va.	Sept. 27	Rex White	White-Clements
42.	Weaverville, N.C.	Oct. 11	Lee Petty	Petty Enterprises
43.	N. Wilkesboro, N.C.	Oct. 18	Lee Petty	Petty Enterprises
44.	Concord, N.C.	Oct. 25	Jack Smith	Jack Smith

>> POINTS STANDINGS

1. Lee Petty 11,792
2. Cotton Owens.........................9,962
3. Speedy Thompson 7,684
4. Herman Beam 7,396
5. Buck Baker 7,170
6. Tom Pistone 7,050
7. L.D. Austin 6,519
8. Jack Smith 6,150
9. Jim Reed 5,744
10. Rex White 5,526

>> RACE WINNERS 16

1. Lee Petty 11
2. Junior Johnson 5
   Rex White 5
4. Jack Smith 4
5. Jim Reed 3
   Bob Welborn 3
7. Ned Jarrett 2
   Tom Pistone 2
   Curtis Turner 2
10. Buck Baker 1
   Johnny Beauchamp 1
   Eddie Gray 1
   Joe Lee Johnson 1
   Parnelli Jones 1
   Cotton Owens 1
   Fireball Roberts 1

>> MONEY WON LEADERS

1. Lee Petty $43,590
2. Jim Reed 22,784
3. Cotton Owens....................11,925
4. Jack Smith 11,850
5. Rex White 11,560
6. Tom Pistone 10,885
7. Fireball Roberts 10,865
8. Bob Burdick 10,050
9. Buck Baker............................9,540
10. Joe Weatherly.....................9,495

>> POLE WINNERS 16

1. Bob Welborn 5
   Rex White 5
3. Buck Baker 4
4. Fireball Roberts 3
   Jack Smith 3
   Glen Wood 3
7. Bob Burdick..................................2
   Cotton Owens 2
   Lee Petty 2
10. Dick Bailey 1
   Tommy Irwin 1
   Bobby Johns 1
   Junior Johnson 1
   Jim Reed 1
   Speedy Thompson 1
   Curtis Turner 1

1958 SEASON

Race No.	Location	Date	Winner	Car owner
1.	Fayetteville, N.C.	Nov. 3	Rex White	J.H. Petty
2.	Daytona Beach, Fla.	Feb. 23	Paul Goldsmith	Smokey Yunick
3.	Concord, N.C.	March 2	Lee Petty	Petty Enterprises
4.	Fayetteville, N.C.	March 15	Curtis Turner	Holman-Moody
5.	Wilson, N.C.	March 16	Lee Petty	Petty Enterprises
6.	Hillsboro, N.C.	March 23	Buck Baker	Buck Baker
7.	Fayetteville, N.C.	April 5	Bob Welborn	J.H. Petty
8.	Columbia, S.C.	April 10	Speedy Thompson	Speedy Thompson
9.	Spartanburg, S.C.	April 12	Speedy Thompson	Speedy Thompson
10.	Atlanta	April 13	Curtis Turner	Holman-Moody
11.	Charlotte	April 18	Curtis Turner	Holman-Moody
12.	Martinsville, Va.	April 20	Bob Welborn	J.H. Petty
13.	Manassas, Va.	April 25	Frankie Schneider	Frankie Schneider
14.	Old Bridge, N.J.	April 27	Jim Reed	Jim Reed
15.	Greenville, S.C.	May 3	Jack Smith	Jack Smith
16.	Greensboro, N.C.	May 11	Bob Welborn	J.H. Petty
17.	Roanoke, Va.	May 15	Jim Reed	Jim Reed
18.	N. Wilkesboro, N.C.	May 18	Junior Johnson	Paul Spaulding
19.	Winston-Salem, N.C.	May 24	Bob Welborn	J.H. Petty
20.	Trenton, N.J.	May 30	Fireball Roberts	Frank Strickland
21.	Riverside, Calif.	June 1	Eddie Gray	Eddie Gray
22.	Columbia, S.C.	June 5	Junior Johnson	Paul Spaulding
23.	Bradford, Pa.	June 12	Junior Johnson	Paul Spaulding
24.	Reading, Pa.	June 15	Junior Johnson	Paul Spaulding
25.	New Oxford, Pa.	June 25	Lee Petty	Petty Enterprises
26.	Hickory, N.C.	June 28	Lee Petty	Petty Enterprises
27.	Weaverville, N.C.	June 29	Rex White	J.H. Petty
28.	Raleigh, N.C.	July 4	Fireball Roberts	Frank Strickland
29.	Asheville, N.C.	July 12	Jim Paschal	J.H. Petty
30.	Busti, N.Y.	July 16	Shorty Rollins	Shorty Rollins
31.	Toronto	July 18	Lee Petty	Petty Enterprises
32.	Buffalo, N.Y.	July 19	Jim Reed	Jim Reed
33.	Rochester, N.Y.	July 25	Cotton Owens	Jim Stephens
34.	Belmar, N.J.	July 26	Jim Reed	Jim Reed
35.	Bridgehampton, N.Y.	Aug. 2	Jack Smith	Jack Smith
36.	Columbia, S.C.	Aug. 7	Speedy Thompson	Speedy Thompson
37.	Nashville	Aug. 10	Joe Weatherly	Holman-Moody
38.	Weaverville, N.C.	Aug. 17	Fireball Roberts	Frank Strickland
39.	Winston-Salem, N.C.	Aug. 22	Lee Petty	Petty Enterprises
40.	Myrtle Beach, S.C.	Aug. 23	Bob Welborn	J.H. Petty
41.	Darlington, S.C.	Sept. 1	Fireball Roberts	Frank Strickland
42.	Charlotte	Sept. 5	Buck Baker	Buck Baker
43.	Birmingham, Ala.	Sept. 7	Fireball Roberts	Frank Strickland
44.	Sacramento	Sept. 7	Parnelli Jones	Vel Miletich
45.	Gastonia, N.C.	Sept. 12	Buck Baker	Buck Baker
46.	Richmond, Va.	Sept. 14	Speedy Thompson	Speedy Thompson
47.	Hillsboro, N.C.	Sept. 28	Joe Eubanks	Jim Stephens
48.	Salisbury, N.C.	Oct. 5	Lee Petty	Petty Enterprises
49.	Martinsville, Va.	Oct. 12	Fireball Roberts	Frank Strickland
50.	N. Wilkesboro, N.C.	Oct. 19	Junior Johnson	Paul Spaulding
51.	Atlanta	Oct. 26	Junior Johnson	Paul Spaulding

>> POINTS STANDINGS

1. Lee Petty 12,232
2. Buck Baker 11,588
3. Speedy Thompson 8,792
4. Shorty Rollins 8,124
5. Jack Smith 7,666
6. L.D. Austin 6,972
7. Rex White 6,552
8. Junior Johnson 6,380
9. Eddie Pagan 4,910
10. Jim Reed 4,762

>> RACE WINNERS 19

1. Lee Petty..........................7
2. Junior Johnson 6
   Fireball Roberts 6
4. Bob Welborn 5
5. Jim Reed..........................4
   Speedy Thompson...............4
7. Buck Baker 3
   Curtis Turner 3
9. Jack Smith 2
   Rex White 2
11. Joe Eubanks 1
    Paul Goldsmith 1
    Eddie Gray 1
    Parnelli Jones 1
    Jim Paschal 1
    Cotton Owens 1
    Shorty Rollins 1
    Frankie Schneider 1
    Joe Weatherly 1

>> MONEY WON LEADERS

1. Fireball Roberts $31,755
2. Buck Baker 22,740
3. Lee Petty 21,550
4. Speedy Thompson 12,985
5. Junior Johnson 12,420
6. Shorty Rollins 11,315
7. Jack Smith ....11,090.
8. Rex White 11,075
9. Curtis Turner 9,720
10. Jim Reed 8,795

>> POLE WINNERS 23

1. Speedy Thompson..................7
   Rex White 7
3. Lee Petty.............................4
   Jack Smith 4
5. Buck Baker 3
   Glen Wood 3
7. Parnelli Jones 2
   Tiny Lund 2
   Cotton Owens 2
   Eddie Pagan 2
   Marvin Panch 2
   Jim Reed 2
13. Bob Duell 1
    George Dunn 1
    Paul Goldsmith 1
    Possum Jones........................1
    Jimmy Massey 1
    Jim Paschal 1
    Ken Rush 1
    Gober Sosebee 1
    Curtis Turner 1
    Joe Weatherly 1
    Bob Welborn 1

>> 1957 SEASON <<

Race No.	Location	Date	Winner	Car owner
1.	Lancaster, Calif.	Nov. 11	Marvin Panch	Pete DePaolo
2.	Concord, N.C.	Dec. 2	Marvin Panch	Pete DePaolo
3.	Titusville, Fla.	Dec. 30	Fireball Roberts	Pete DePaolo
4.	Daytona Beach, Fla.	Feb. 17	Cotton Owens	Ray Nichels
5.	Concord, N.C.	March 3	Jack Smith	Hugh Babb
6.	Wilson, N.C.	March 17	Ralph Moody	Pete DePaolo
7.	Hillsboro, N.C.	March 24	Buck Baker	Hugh Babb
8.	Weaverville, N.C.	March 31	Buck Baker	Hugh Babb
9.	North Wilkesboro, N.C.	April 7	Fireball Roberts	Pete DePaolo
10.	Langhorne, Pa.	April 14	Fireball Roberts	Pete DePaolo
11.	Charlotte	April 19	Fireball Roberts	Pete DePaolo
12.	Spartanburg, S.C.	April 27	Marvin Panch	Pete DePaolo
13.	Greensboro, N.C.	April 28	Paul Goldsmith	Smokey Yunick
14.	Portland	April 28	Art Watts	Al Schmidhamer
15.	Shelby, N.C.	May 4	Fireball Roberts	Pete DePaolo
16.	Richmond, Va.	May 5	Paul Goldsmith	Pete DePaolo
17.	Martinsville, Va.	May 19	Buck Baker	Hugh Babb
18.	Portland	May 26	Eddie Pagan	Eddie Pagan
19.	Eureka, Calif.	May 30	Lloyd Dane	Lloyd Dane
20.	New Oxford, Pa.	May 30	Buck Baker	Hugh Babb
21.	Lancaster, S.C.	June 1	Paul Goldsmith	Smokey Yunick
22.	Los Angeles	June 8	Eddie Pagan	Eddie Pagan
23.	Newport, Tenn.	June 15	Fireball Roberts	Fireball Roberts
24.	Columbia, S.C.	June 20	Jack Smith	Jack Smith
25.	Sacramento	June 22	Bill Amick	William Amick
26.	Spartanburg, S.C.	June 29	Lee Petty	Petty Enterprises
27.	Jacksonville, N.C.	June 30	Buck Baker	Buck Baker
28.	Raleigh, N.C.	July 4	Paul Goldsmith	Smokey Yunick
29.	Charlotte	July 12	Marvin Panch	Marvin Panch
30.	LeHi, Ark.	July 14	Marvin Panch	Herb Thomas
31.	Portland	July 14	Eddie Pagan	Eddie Pagan
32.	Hickory, N.C.	July 20	Jack Smith	Jack Smith
33.	Norfolk, Va.	July 24	Buck Baker	Buck Baker
34.	Lancaster, S.C.	July 30	Speedy Thompson	Speedy Thompson
35.	Watkins Glen, N.Y.	Aug. 4	Buck Baker	Buck Baker
36.	Bremerton, Wash.	Aug. 4	Parnelli Jones	Oscar Maples
37.	New Oxford, Pa.	Aug. 10	Marvin Panch	Marvin Panch
38.	Old Bridge, N.J.	Aug. 16	Lee Petty	Petty Enterprises
39.	Myrtle Beach, S.C.	Aug. 26	Gwyn Staley	J.H. Petty
40.	Darlington, S.C.	Sept. 2	Speedy Thompson	Speedy Thompson
41.	Syracuse, N.Y.	Sept. 5	Gwyn Staley	J.H. Petty
42.	Weaverville, N.C.	Sept. 8	Lee Petty	Petty Enterprises
43.	Sacramento	Sept. 8	Danny Graves	Danny Graves
44.	San Jose, Calif.	Sept. 15	Marvin Porter	Marvin Porter
45.	Langhorne, Pa.	Sept. 15	Gwyn Staley	J.H. Petty
46.	Columbia, S.C.	Sept. 19	Buck Baker	Buck Baker
47.	Shelby, N.C.	Sept. 21	Buck Baker	Buck Baker
48.	Charlotte	Oct. 5	Lee Petty	Petty Enterprises
49.	Martinsville, Va.	Oct. 6	Bob Welborn	Bob Welborn
50.	Newberry, S.C.	Oct. 12	Fireball Roberts	Fireball Roberts
51.	Concord, N.C.	Oct. 13	Fireball Roberts	Fireball Roberts
52.	N. Wilkesboro, N.C.	Oct. 20	Jack Smith	Jack Smith
53.	Greensboro, N.C.	Oct. 27	Buck Baker	Buck Baker

>> POINTS STANDINGS

1. Buck Baker 10,716
2. Marvin Panch 9,956
3. Speedy Thompson 8,580
4. Lee Petty 8,528
5. Jack Smith 8,464
6. Fireball Roberts 8,268
7. Johnny Allen 7,068
8. L.D. Austin 6,532
9. Brownie King 5,740
10. Jim Paschal 5,136

>> RACE WINNERS   18

1. Buck Baker 10
2. Fireball Roberts 8
3. Marvin Panch 6
4. Paul Goldsmith 4
   Lee Petty 4
   Jack Smith 4
7. Eddie Pagan 3
   Gwyn Staley 3
9. Speedy Thompson 2
10. Bill Amick 1
    Lloyd Dane 1
    Danny Graves 1
    Parnelli Jones 1
    Ralph Moody 1
    Cotton Owens 1
    Marvin Porter 1
    Art Watts 1
    Bob Welborn 1

>> MONEY WON LEADERS

1. Buck Baker...............................$25,665
2. Speedy Thompson 24,710
3. Marvin Panch 19,980
4. Fireball Roberts 17,425
5. Lee Petty 15,945
6. Cotton Owens 12,325
7. Paul Goldsmith 11,950
8. Jack Smith 11,335
9. Johnny Allen 8,075
10. Bill Amick 8,030

>> POLE WINNERS   24

1. Buck Baker 6
2. Art Watts 5
3. Paul Goldsmith 4
   Marvin Panch 4
   Fireball Roberts 4
   Speedy Thompson 4
7. Tiny Lund 3
   Lee Petty 3
9. Bill Amick 2
   Eddie Pagan 2
   Jack Smith 2
   Gwyn Staley 2
13. Johnny Allen 1
    Lloyd Dane 1
    Danny Graves 1
    Russ Hepler 1
    Parnelli Jones 1
    Mel Larson 1
    Banjo Matthews.....................................1
    Cotton Owens 1
    Ken Rush 1
    Frankie Schneider 1
    Curtis Turner 1
    Rex White 1

Race No.	Location	Date	Winner	Car owner
1.	Hickory, N.C.	Nov. 13	Tim Flock	Carl Kiekhafer
2.	Charlotte	Nov. 20	Fonty Flock	Carl Kiekhafer
3.	Lancaster, Calif.	Nov. 20	Chuck Stevenson	Carl Dane
4.	W. Palm Beach, Fla.	Dec. 11	Herb Thomas	Herb Thomas
5.	Phoenix	Jan. 22	Buck Baker	Carl Kiekhafer
6.	Daytona Beach, Fla.	Feb. 26	Tim Flock	Carl Kiekhafer
7.	W. Palm Beach, Fla.	March 4	Billy Myers	William Stroppe
8.	Wilson, N.C.	March 18	Herb Thomas	Smokey Yunick
9.	Atlanta	March 25	Buck Baker	Carl Kiekhafer
10.	N. Wilkesboro, N.C.	April 8	Tim Flock	Carl Kiekhafer
11.	Langhorne, Pa.	April 22	Buck Baker	Carl Kiekhafer
12.	Richmond, Va.	April 29	Buck Baker	Carl Kiekhafer
13.	Columbia, S.C.	May 5	Speedy Thompson	Carl Kiekhafer
14.	Concord, N.C.	May 6	Speedy Thompson	Carl Kiekhafer
15.	Greenville, S.C.	May 10	Buck Baker	Carl Kiekhafer
16.	Hickory, N.C.	May 12	Speedy Thompson	Carl Kiekhafer
17.	Hillsboro, N.C.	May 13	Buck Baker	Carl Kiekhafer
18.	Martinsville, Va.	May 20	Buck Baker	Carl Kiekhafer
19.	New Oxford, Pa.	May 25	Buck Baker	Carl Kiekhafer
20.	Charlotte, N.C.	May 27	Speedy Thompson	Carl Kiekhafer
21.	Portland	May 27	Herb Thomas	Carl Kiekhafer
22.	Eureka, Calif.	May 30	Herb Thomas	Carl Kiekhafer
23.	Syracuse, N.Y.	May 30	Buck Baker	Carl Kiekhafer
24.	Merced, Calif.	June 3	Herb Thomas	Carl Kiekhafer
25.	LeHi, Ark.	June 10	Ralph Moody	Pete DePaolo
26.	Charlotte	June 15	Speedy Thompson	Carl Kiekhafer
27.	Rochester, N.Y.	June 22	Speedy Thompson	Carl Kiekhafer
28.	Portland, Ore.	June 24	John Kieper	John Kieper
29.	Weaverville, N.C.	June 1	Lee Petty	Petty Enterprises
30.	Raleigh, N.C.	July 4	Fireball Roberts	Pete DePaolo
31.	Spartanburg, S.C.	July 7	Lee Petty	Petty Enterprises
32.	Sacramento	July 8	Lloyd Dane	Lloyd Dane
33.	Chicago	July 21	Fireball Roberts	Pete DePaolo
34.	Shelby, N.C.	July 27	Speedy Thompson	Carl Kiekhafer
35.	Montgomery, Ala.	July 29	Marvin Panch	Tom Harbison
36.	Oklahoma City	Aug. 3	Jim Paschal	Frank Hayworth
37.	Elkhart Lakes, Wis.	Aug. 12	Tim Flock	William Stroppe
38.	Old Bridge, N.J.	Aug. 17	Ralph Moody	Pete DePaolo
39.	San Mateo, Calif.	Aug. 19	Eddie Pagan	Eddie Pagan
40.	Norfolk, Va.	Aug. 22	Billy Myers	William Stroppe
41.	Spartanburg, S.C.	Aug. 23	Ralph Moody	Pete DePaolo
42.	Myrtle Beach, S.C.	Aug. 25	Fireball Roberts	Pete DePaolo
43.	Portland	Aug. 26	Royce Haggerty	Curly Weida
44.	Darlington, S.C.	Sept. 3	Curtis Turner	Charles Schwam
45.	Montgomery, Ala.	Sept. 9	Buck Baker	Carl Kiekhafer
46.	Charlotte	Sept. 12	Ralph Moody	Pete DePaolo
47.	Langhorne, Pa.	Sept. 23	Paul Goldsmith	Smokey Yunick
48.	Portland	Sept. 23	Lloyd Dane	Lloyd Dane
49.	Columbia, S.C.	Sept. 29	Buck Baker	Carl Kiekhafer
50.	Hillsboro, N.C.	Sept. 30	Fireball Roberts	Pete DePaolo
51.	Newport, Tenn.	Oct. 7	Fireball Roberts	Pete DePaolo
52.	Charlotte	Oct. 17	Buck Baker	Carl Kiekhafer
53.	Shelby, N.C.	Oct. 23	Buck Baker	Carl Kiekhafer
54.	Martinsville, Va.	Oct. 28	Jack Smith	Carl Kiekhafer
55.	Hickory, N.C.	Nov. 11	Speedy Thompson	Carl Kiekhafer
56.	Wilson, N.C.	Nov. 18	Buck Baker	Carl Kiekhafer

>> POINTS STANDINGS

1. Buck Baker 9,272
2. Herb Thomas 8,568
3. Speedy Thompson 8,328
4. Lee Petty 8,324
5. Jim Paschal 7,878
6. Billy Myers 6,920
7. Fireball Roberts 5,794
8. Ralph Moody 5,548
9. Tim Flock 5,062
10. Marvin Panch 4,680

>> RACE WINNERS   19

1. Buck Baker 14
2. Speedy Thompson 8
3. Fireball Roberts 5
   Herb Thomas 5
5. Tim Flock 4
   Ralph Moody 4
7. Lloyd Dane 2
   Billy Myers 2
   Lee Petty 2
10. Fonty Flock 1
    Paul Goldsmith 1
    Royce Haggerty 1
    John Kieper 1
    Eddie Pagan 1
    Marvin Panch 1
    Jim Paschal 1
    Jack Smith 1
    Chuck Stevenson 1
    Curtis Turner 1

>> MONEY WON LEADERS

1. Buck Baker $29,140
2. Speedy Thompson 24,670
3. Herb Thomas 17,695
4. Jim Paschal 16,540
5. Tim Flock 15,409
6. Billy Myers 15,320
7. Ralph Moody 14,545
8. Fireball Roberts 14,395
9. Curtis Turner 14,295
10. Lee Petty 13,455

>> POLE WINNERS   22

1. Buck Baker 11
2. Speedy Thompson 7
3. Tim Flock 5
   Ralph Moody 5
5. John Kieper 3
   Fireball Roberts 3
   Herb Thomas 3
8. Joe Eubanks 2
   Fonty Flock 2
   Eddie Pagan 2
   Jim Reed 2
12. Doug Cox 1
    Ralph Earnhardt 1
    Royce Haggerty 1
    Junior Johnson 1
    Frank Mundy 1
    Billy Myers 1
    Marvin Panch 1
    Jim Paschal 1
    Lee Petty 1
    Joe Weatherly 1
    Rex White 1

>> 1955 SEASON <<

Race No.	Location	Date	Winner	Car owner
1.	High Point, N.C.	Nov. 7	Lee Petty	Petty Enterprises
2.	W. Palm Beach, Fla.	Feb. 6	Herb Thomas	Herb Thomas
3.	Jacksonville, Fla.	Feb. 13	Lee Petty	Petty Enterprises
4.	Daytona Beach, Fla.	Feb. 27	Tim Flock	Carl Kiekhafer
5.	Savannah, Ga.	March 6	Lee Petty	Petty Enterprises
6.	Columbia, S.C.	March 26	Fonty Flock	Frank Christian
7.	Hillsboro, N.C.	March 27	Jim Paschal	Ernest Woods
8.	N. Wilkesboro, N.C.	April 3	Buck Baker	Bobby Griffin
9.	Montgomery, Ala.	April 17	Tim Flock	Carl Kiekhafer
10.	Langhorne, Pa.	April 24	Tim Flock	Carl Kiekhafer
11.	Charlotte	May 1	Buck Baker	Buck Baker
12.	Hickory, N.C.	May 7	Junior Johnson	Beckham/Lowe
13.	Phoenix	May 8	Tim Flock	Carl Kiekhafer
14.	Tucson, Ariz.	May 15	Danny Letner	Cos Concilla
15.	Martinsville, Va.	May 15	Tim Flock	Carl Kiekhafer
16.	Richmond, Va.	May 22	Tim Flock	Carl Kiekhafer
17.	Raleigh, N.C.	May 28	Junior Johnson	Beckham/Lowe
18.	Winston-Salem, N.C.	May 29	Lee Petty	Petty Enterprises
19.	New Oxford, Pa.	June 10	Junior Johnson	Beckham/Lowe
20.	Rochester, N.Y.	June 17	Tim Flock	Carl Kiekhafer
21.	Fonda, N.Y.	June 18	Junior Johnson	Beckham/Lowe
22.	Plattsburg, N.Y.	June 19	Lee Petty	Petty Enterprises
23.	Charlotte	June 24	Tim Flock	Carl Kiekhafer
24.	Spartanburg, S.C.	July 6	Tim Flock	Carl Kiekhafer
25.	Columbia, S.C.	July 9	Jim Paschal	Ernest Woods
26.	Weaverville, N.C.	July 10	Tim Flock	Carl Kiekhafer
27.	Morristown, N.J.	July 15	Tim Flock	Carl Kiekhafer
28.	Altamont, N.Y.	July 29	Junior Johnson	Beckham/Lowe
29.	Syracuse, N.Y.	July 30	Tim Flock	Carl Kiekhafer
30.	San Mateo, Calif.	July 31	Tim Flock	Carl Kiekhafer
31.	Charlotte	Aug. 5	Jim Paschal	Ernest Woods
32.	Winston-Salem, N.C.	Aug. 7	Lee Petty	Petty Enterprises
33.	LeHi, Ark.	Aug. 14	Fonty Flock	Carl Kiekhafer
34.	Raleigh, N.C.	Aug. 20	Herb Thomas	Herb Thomas
35.	Darlington, S.C.	Sept. 5	Herb Thomas	Herb Thomas
36.	Montgomery, Ala.	Sept. 11	Tim Flock	Carl Kiekhafer
37.	Langhorne, Pa.	Sept. 18	Tim Flock	Carl Kiekhafer
38.	Raleigh, N.C.	Sept. 30	Fonty Flock	Carl Kiekhafer
39.	Greenville, S.C.	Oct. 6	Tim Flock	Carl Kiekhafer
40.	LeHi, Ark.	Oct. 9	Speedy Thompson	Pete DePaolo
41.	Columbia, S.C.	Oct. 15	Tim Flock	Carl Kiekhafer
42.	Martinsville, Va.	Oct. 16	Speedy Thompson	Carl Kiekhafer
43.	Las Vegas	Oct. 16	Norm Nelson	Carl Kiekhafer
44.	N. Wilkesboro, N.C.	Oct. 23	Buck Baker	Pete DePaolo
45.	Hillsboro, N.C.	Oct. 30	Tim Flock	Carl Kiekhafer

>> POINTS STANDINGS

1. Tim Flock 9,596
2. Buck Baker 8,088
3. Lee Petty 7,194
4. Bob Welborn 5,460
5. Herb Thomas 5,186
6. Junior Johnson 4,810
7. Eddie Skinner 4,652
8. Jim Paschal 4,572
9. Jimmy Lewallen 4,526
10. Gwyn Staley 4,360

>> RACE WINNERS   10

1. Tim Flock....................................18
2. Lee Petty 6
3. Junior Johnson 5
4. Buck Baker 3
    Fonty Flock 3
    Jim Paschal 3
    Herb Thomas 3
8. Speedy Thompson 2
9. Danny Letner 1
    Norm Nelson 1

>> MONEY WON LEADERS

1. Tim Flock $33,275
2. Buck Baker 17,590
3. Lee Petty 16,775
4. Herb Thomas 16,320
5. Fonty Flock 12,690
6. Junior Johnson 10,055
7. Jim Paschal 9,700
8. Bob Welborn 8,275
9. Speedy Thompson 6,680
10. Gwyn Staley 5,815

>> POLE WINNERS   14

1. Tim Flock....................................18
2. Fonty Flock 6
3. Dick Rathmann 3
4. Bill Amick 2
    Buck Baker 2
    Junior Johnson 2
    Jim Paschal 2
    Herb Thomas 2
9. Jimmy Lewallen 1
    Norm Nelson 1
    Lee Petty 1
    Fireball Roberts 1
    Bob Welborn 1
    Dink Widenhouse 1

>> 1954 SEASON <<

Race No.	Location	Date	Winner	Car owner
1.	W. Palm Beach, Fla.	Feb. 7	Herb Thomas	Herb Thomas
2.	Daytona Beach, Fla.	Feb. 21	Lee Petty	Petty Enterprises
3.	Jacksonville, Fla.	March 7	Herb Thomas	Herb Thomas
4.	Atlanta	March 21	Herb Thomas	Herb Thomas
5.	Savannah, Ga.	March 28	Al Keller	George Miller
6.	Oakland, Calif.	March 28	Dick Rathmann	Ray Erickson
7.	N. Wilkesboro, N.C.	April 4	Dick Rathmann	John Ditz
8.	Hillsboro, N.C.	April 18	Herb Thomas	Herb Thomas
9.	Macon, Ga.	April 25	Gober Sosebee	Gober Sosebee
10.	Langhorne, Pa.	May 2	Herb Thomas	Herb Thomas
11.	Wilson, N.C.	May 9	Buck Baker	Ernest Woods
12.	Martinsville, Va.	May 16	Jim Paschal	Bobby Griffin
13.	Sharon, Pa.	May 23	Lee Petty	Petty Enterprises
14.	Raleigh, N.C.	May 29	Herb Thomas	Herb Thomas
15.	Charlotte	May 30	Buck Baker	Bobby Griffin
16.	Gardena, Calif.	May 30	John Soares	Charles Vance
17.	Columbia, S.C.	June 6	Curtis Turner	Elmer Brooks
18.	Linden, N.J.	June 13	Al Keller	Paul Whiteman
19.	Mechanicsburg, Pa.	June 17	Herb Thomas	Herb Thomas
20.	Hickory, N.C.	June 19	Herb Thomas	Herb Thomas
21.	Rochester, N.Y.	June 25	Lee Petty	Petty Enterprises
22.	Spartanburg, S.C.	July 3	Herb Thomas	Herb Thomas
23.	Weaverville, N.C.	July 4	Herb Thomas	Herb Thomas
24.	Willow Springs, Ill.	July 10	Dick Rathmann	John Ditz
25.	Grand Rapids, Mich.	July 11	Lee Petty	Petty Enterprises
26.	Morristown, N.J.	July 30	Buck Baker	Ernest Woods
27.	Oakland, Calif.	Aug. 1	Danny Letner	Joseph Bearscheck
28.	Charlotte	Aug. 13	Lee Petty	Petty Enterprises
29.	San Mateo, Calif.	Aug. 22	Hershel McGriff	Frank Christian
30.	Corbin, Ky.	Aug. 29	Lee Petty	Petty Enterprises
31.	Darlington, S.C.	Sept. 6	Herb Thomas	Herb Thomas
32.	Macon, Ga.	Sept. 12	Hershel McGriff	Frank Christian
33.	Charlotte	Sept. 24	Hershel McGriff	Frank Christian
34.	Langhorne, Pa.	Sept. 26	Herb Thomas	Herb Thomas
35.	LeHi, Ark.	Oct. 10	Buck Baker	Bobby Griffin
36.	Martinsville, Va.	Oct. 17	Lee Petty	Petty Enterprises
37.	N. Wilkesboro, N.C.	Oct. 24	Hershel McGriff	Frank Christian

>> POINTS STANDINGS

1. Lee Petty 8,649
2. Herb Thomas 8,366
3. Buck Baker 6,893
4. Dick Rathmann 6,760
5. Joe Eubanks 5,467
6. Hershel McGriff 5,137
7. Jim Paschal 3,903
8. Jimmy Lewallen 3,233
9. Curtis Turner 2,994
10. Ralph Liguori 2,905

>> RACE WINNERS 11

1. Herb Thomas 12
2. Lee Petty 7
3. Buck Baker.....................................4
   Hershel McGriff..............................4
5. Dick Rathmann...............................3
6. Al Keller 2
7. Danny Letner 1
   Jim Paschal 1
   John Soares.....................................1
   Gober Sosebee 1
   Curtis Turner....................................1

>> MONEY WON LEADERS

1. Herb Thomas $27,540
2. Lee Petty 19,125
3. Buck Baker................................18,015
4. Dick Rathmann 14,910
5. Hershel McGriff 11,625
6. Curtis Turner................................9,820
7. Joe Eubanks 7,160
8. Jim Paschal.................................4,585
9. Marvin Panch 4,530
10. Jimmy Lewallen 3,965

>> POLE WINNERS 13

1. Herb Thomas 8
2. Buck Baker.......................................7
3. Hershel McGriff................................5
4. Dick Rathmann................................4
5. Lee Petty 3
6. Jim Paschal 2
7. Tim Flock 1
   Junior Johnson.................................1
   Al Keller 1
   Danny Letner 1
   Marvin Panch 1
   Gober Sosebee 1
   Curtis Turner......................................1

>> 1953 SEASON <<

Race No.	Location	Date	Winner	Car owner
1.	W. Palm Beach, Fla.	Feb. 1	Lee Petty	Petty Enterprises
2.	Daytona Beach, Fla.	Feb. 15	Bill Blair	Bill Blair
3.	Spring Lake, N.C.	March 8	Herb Thomas	Herb Thomas
4.	N. Wilkesboro, N.C.	March 29	Herb Thomas	Herb Thomas
5.	Charlotte	April 5	Dick Passwater	Frank Arford
6.	Richmond, Va.	April 19	Lee Petty	Petty Enterprises
7.	Macon, Ga.	April 26	Dick Rathmann	Walt Chapman
8.	Langhorne, Pa.	May 3	Buck Baker	Bobby Griffin
9.	Columbia, S.C.	May 9	Buck Baker	Bobby Griffin
10.	Hickory, N.C.	May 16	Tim Flock	Ted Chester
11.	Martinsville, Va.	May 17	Lee Petty	Petty Enterprises
12.	Columbus, Ohio	May 24	Herb Thomas	Herb Thomas
13.	Raleigh, N.C.	May 30	Fonty Flock	Frank Christian
14.	Shreveport, La.	June 7	Lee Petty	Petty Enterprises
15.	Pensacola, Fla.	June 14	Herb Thomas	Herb Thomas
16.	Langhorne, Pa.	June 21	Dick Rathmann	Walt Chapman
17.	High Point, N.C.	June 26	Herb Thomas	Herb Thomas
18.	Wilson, N.C.	June 28	Fonty Flock	Frank Christian
19.	Rochester, N.Y.	July 3	Herb Thomas	Herb Thomas
20.	Spartanburg, S.C.	July 4	Lee Petty	Petty Enterprises
21.	Morristown, N.J.	July 10	Dick Rathmann	Walt Chapman
22.	Atlanta	July 12	Herb Thomas	Herb Thomas
23.	Rapid City, S.D.	July 22	Herb Thomas	Herb Thomas
24.	North Platte, Neb.	July 26	Dick Rathmann	Walt Chapman
25.	Davenport, Iowa	Aug. 2	Herb Thomas	Herb Thomas
26.	Hillsboro, N.C.	Aug. 9	Curtis Turner	Frank Christian
27.	Weaverville, N.C.	Aug. 16	Fonty Flock	Frank Christian
28.	Norfolk, Va.	Aug. 23	Herb Thomas	Herb Thomas
29.	Hickory, N.C.	Aug. 29	Fonty Flock	Frank Christian
30.	Darlington, S.C.	Sept. 7	Buck Baker	Bobby Griffin
31.	Macon, Ga.	Sept. 13	Speedy Thompson	Buckshot Morris
32.	Langhorne, Pa.	Sept. 20	Dick Rathmann	Walt Chapman
33.	Bloomsburg, Pa.	Oct. 3	Herb Thomas	Herb Thomas
34.	Wilson, N.C.	Oct. 4	Herb Thomas	Herb Thomas
35.	N. Wilkesboro, N.C.	Oct. 11	Speedy Thompson	Buckshot Morris
36.	Martinsville, Va.	Oct. 13	Jim Paschal	George Hutchens
37.	Atlanta	Nov. 1	Buck Baker	Bobby Griffin

>> POINTS STANDINGS

1. Herb Thomas 8,460
2. Lee Petty 7,814
3. Dick Rathmann..........................7,362
4. Buck Baker 6,713
5. Fonty Flock 6,174
6. Tim Flock 5,011
7. Jim Paschal.............................4,211
8. Joe Eubanks............................3,603
9. Jimmy Lewallen 3,508
10. Curtis Turner 3,373

>> RACE WINNERS 11

1. Herb Thomas 12
2. Lee Petty 5
   Dick Rathmann 5
4. Buck Baker 4
   Fonty Flock 4
6. Speedy Thompson 2
7. Bill Blair.................................1
   Tim Flock...............................1
   Jim Paschal 1
   Dick Passwater 1
   Curtis Turner 1

>> MONEY WON LEADERS

1. Herb Thomas $24,300
2. Dick Rathmann........................19,205
3. Lee Petty 17,225
4. Fonty Flock.............................16,440
5. Buck Baker..............................16,220
6. Tim Flock 7,365
7. Speedy Thompson 6,150
8. Jim Paschal 4,935
9. Joe Eubanks............................4,725
10. Bill Blair.................................3,970

>> POLE WINNERS 11

1. Herb Thomas 11
2. Buck Baker 4
3. Fonty Flock 3
   Tim Flock................................3
   Curtis Turner 3
6. Dick Rathmann 2
7. Joe Eubanks 1
   Jim Paschal.............................1
   Bob Pronger 1
   Lloyd Shaw 1
   Slick Smith 1

The field prepares to take the green flag during the early '50s at Hickory (N.C.) Speedway. The historic track opened in 1951 and still is operating today.

Tim Flock 1953 SEASON

MONKEYING AROUND

Flock adds a co-pilot

You could call Tim Flock eccentric. He ran eight races in 1953 with his pet monkey, Jocko Flocko, riding shotgun. No word on whether Jocko wore a HANS device.

You could call Flock controversial. He was banned for life from NASCAR for trying to form a drivers' union.

You could call Flock dominant. He won 40 races in 189 starts, a 21.2 winning percentage that dwarfs Richard Petty's and Jeff Gordon's and is second only to Herb Thomas' for drivers with enough races and wins to count.

Whatever you call Flock, you have to call him a two-time champion. He won the first of his two titles in 1952, despite missing one event and flipping his car in the final race. He won his second title in 1955, though he ran in just 39 of 45 races.

You could call Flock a legend, too.

>> 1952 SEASON <<

Race No.	Location	Date	Winner	Car owner
1.	W. Palm Beach, Fla.	Jan. 20	Tim Flock	Ted Chester
2.	Daytona Beach, Fla.	Feb. 10	Marshall Teague	Marshall Teague
3.	Jacksonville, Fla.	March 6	Marshall Teague	Marshall Teague
4.	N. Wilkesboro, N.C.	March 30	Herb Thomas	Herb Thomas
5.	Martinsville, Va.	April 6	Dick Rathmann	Walt Chapman
6.	Columbia, S.C.	April 12	Buck Baker	B.A. Pless
7.	Atlanta	April 20	Bill Blair	George Hutchens
8.	Macon, Ga.	April 27	Herb Thomas	Herb Thomas
9.	Langhorne, Pa.	May 4	Dick Rathmann	Walt Chapman
10.	Darlington, S.C.	May 10	Dick Rathmann	Walt Chapman
11.	Dayton, Ohio	May 18	Dick Rathmann	Walt Chapman
12.	Canfield, Ohio	May 30	Herb Thomas	Herb Thomas
13.	Augusta, Ga.	June 1	Gober Sosebee	Sam Knox
14.	Toledo, Ohio	June 1	Tim Flock	Ted Chester
15.	Hillsboro, N.C.	June 8	Tim Flock	Ted Chester
16.	Charlotte	June 15	Herb Thomas	Herb Thomas
17.	Detroit	June 29	Tim Flock	Ted Chester
18.	Niagara Falls, Ontario	July 1	Buddy Shuman	B.A. Pless
19.	Oswego, N.Y.	July 4	Tim Flock	Ted Chester
20.	Monroe, Mich.	July 6	Tim Flock	Ted Chester
21.	Morristown, N.J.	July 11	Lee Petty	Petty Enterprises
22.	South Bend, Ind.	July 20	Tim Flock	Ted Chester
23.	Rochester, N.Y.	Aug. 15	Tim Flock	Ted Chester
24.	Weaverville, N.C.	Aug. 17	Bob Flock	Ted Chester
25.	Darlington, S.C.	Sept. 1	Fonty Flock	Frank Christian
26.	Macon, Ga.	Sept. 7	Lee Petty	Petty Enterprises
27.	Langhorne, Pa.	Sept. 14	Lee Petty	Petty Enterprises
28.	Dayton, Ohio	Sept. 21	Dick Rathmann	Walt Chapman
29.	Wilson, N.C.	Sept. 28	Herb Thomas	Herb Thomas
30.	Hillsboro, N.C.	Oct. 12	Fonty Flock	Frank Christian
31.	Martinsville, Va.	Oct. 19	Herb Thomas	Herb Thomas
32.	N. Wilkesboro, N.C.	Oct. 26	Herb Thomas	Herb Thomas
33.	Atlanta	Nov. 16	Donald Thomas	Herb Thomas
34.	W. Palm Beach, Fla.	Nov. 30	Herb Thomas	Herb Thomas

>> POINTS STANDINGS

1. Tim Flock.............................6,858.5
2. Herb Thomas......................6,752.5
3. Lee Petty............................6,498.5
4. Fonty Flock........................5,183.5
5. Dick Rathmann 3,952.5
6. Bill Blair.............................3,499.0
7. Joe Eubanks.......................3,090.5
8. Ray Duhigg........................2,986.5
9. Donald Thomas 2,574.0
10. Buddy Shuman 2,483.0

>> RACE WINNERS   12

1. Tim Flock.................................8
   Herb Thomas 8
3. Dick Rathmann 5
4. Lee Petty.................................3
5. Fonty Flock 2
   Marshall Teague 2
7. Buck Baker..............................1
   Bill Blair..................................1
   Bob Flock................................1
   Buddy Shuman 1
   Gober Sosebee 1
   Donald Thomas 1

>> MONEY WON LEADERS

1. Tim Flock $20,210
2. Fonty Flock 18,040
3. Herb Thomas 17,625
4. Lee Petty..........................15,670
5. Dick Rathmann 10,309
6. Bill Blair.............................7,095
7. Buddy Shuman 4,210
8. Donald Thomas...................4,075
9. Johnny Patterson 3,350
10. Ray Duhigg........................3,275

>> POLE WINNERS   12

1. Herb Thomas 10
2. Fonty Flock 7
3. Tim Flock.................................4
4. Buck Baker..............................2
   Dick Rathmann 2
6. Bill Blair..................................1
   Perk Brown 1
   Pat Kirkwood 1
   Tommy Moon.............................1
   Jack Smith 1
   Marshall Teague 1
   Donald Thomas 1

The Flock brothers, left to right, Bob, Tim and Fonty, were a colorful and successful trio. All three won races in 1952, and Tim won the championship.

Race No.	Location	Date	Winner	Car owner
1.	Daytona Beach, Fla.	Feb. 11	Marshall Teague	Marshall Teague
2.	Charlotte	April 1	Curtis Turner	Nash Motor Company
3.	Mobile, Ala.	April 8	Tim Flock	Ted Chester
4.	Gardena, Calif.	April 8	Marshall Teague	Marshall Teague
5.	Hillsboro, N.C.	April 15	Fonty Flock	Frank Christian
6.	Phoenix	April 22	Marshall Teague	Marshall Teague
7.	N. Wilkesboro, N.C.	April 29	Fonty Flock	Frank Christian
8.	Martinsville, Va.	May 6	Curtis Turner	John Eanes
9.	Canfield, Ohio	May 30	Marshall Teague	Marshall Teague
10.	Columbus, Ga.	June 10	Tim Flock	Ted Chester
11.	Columbia, S.C.	June 16	Frank Mundy	Perry Smith
12.	Dayton, Ohio	June 24	Curtis Turner	John Eanes
13.	Gardena, Calif.	June 30	Lou Figaro	Jack Gaynor
14.	Grand Rapids, Mich.	July 1	Marshall Teague	Marshall Teague
15.	Bainbridge, Ohio	July 8	Fonty Flock	Frank Christian
16.	Carnegie, Pa.	July 15	Herb Thomas	Hubert Westmoreland
17.	Weaverville, N.C.	July 29	Fonty Flock	Frank Christian
18.	Rochester, N.Y.	July 31	Lee Petty	Petty Enterprises
19.	Altamont, N.Y.	Aug. 1	Fonty Flock	Frank Christian
20.	Detroit	Aug. 12	Tommy Thompson	Tommy Thompson
21.	Toledo, Ohio	Aug. 19	Tim Flock	Ted Chester
22.	Morristown, N.J.	Aug. 24	Tim Flock	Ted Chester
23.	Greenville, S.C.	Aug. 25	Bob Flock	Ted Chester
24.	Darlington, S.C.	Sept. 3	Herb Thomas	Herb Thomas
25.	Columbia, S.C.	Sept. 7	Tim Flock	Ted Chester
26.	Macon, Ga.	Sept. 8	Herb Thomas	Herb Thomas
27.	Langhorne, Pa.	Sept. 15	Herb Thomas	Herb Thomas
28.	Charlotte	Sept. 23	Herb Thomas	Herb Thomas
29.	Dayton, Ohio	Sept. 23	Fonty Flock	Frank Christian
30.	Wilson, N.C.	Sept. 30	Fonty Flock	Frank Christian
31.	Hillsboro, N.C.	Oct. 7	Herb Thomas	Herb Thomas
32.	Thompson, Conn.	Oct. 12	Neil Cole	John Golabek
33.	Shippenville, Pa.	Oct. 14	Tim Flock	Ted Chester
34.	Martinsville, Va.	Oct. 14	Frank Mundy	Ted Chester
35.	Oakland, Calif.	Oct. 14	Marvin Burke	Bob Phillippi
36.	N. Wilkesboro, N.C.	Oct. 21	Fonty Flock	Ted Chester
37.	Hanford, Calif.	Oct. 28	Danny Weinberg	Tony Sampo
38.	Jacksonville, Fla.	Nov. 4	Herb Thomas	Marshall Teague
39.	Atlanta	Nov. 11	Tim Flock	Ted Chester
40.	Gardena, Calif.	Nov. 11	Bill Norton	Larry Bettinger
41.	Mobile, Ala.	Nov. 25	Frank Mundy	Perry Smith

>> POINTS STANDINGS

1. Herb Thomas 4,208.45
2. Fonty Flock 4,062.25
3. Tim Flock 3,722.50
4. Lee Petty 2,392.25
5. Frank Mundy 1,963.50
6. Buddy Shuman 1,368.75
7. Jesse James Taylor 1,214.00
8. Dick Rathmann 1,040.00
9. Bill Snowden 1.009.25
10. Joe Eubanks 1,005.50

>> RACE WINNERS   14

1. Fonty Flock 8
2. Tim Flock 7
   Herb Thomas 7
4. Marshall Teague 5
5. Frank Mundy 3
   Curtis Turner 3
7. Marvin Burke 1
   Neil Cole 1
   Lou Figaro 1
   Bob Flock 1
   Bill Norton 1
   Lee Petty 1
   Tommy Thompson 1
   Danny Weinberg 1

>> MONEY WON LEADERS

1. Herb Thomas $19,425
2. Fonty Flock 14,770
3. Tim Flock 14,670
4. Lee Petty 7,250
5. Frank Mundy 6,470
6. Tommy Thompson 5,225
7. Bob Flock 3,375
8. Jesse James Taylor 3,175
9. Dick Rathmann 3,105
10. Joe Eubanks 3,085

>> POLE WINNERS   12

1. Fonty Flock 12
2. Tim Flock 6
3. Frank Mundy 4
   Herb Thomas 4
5. Billy Carden 2
6. Neil Cole 1
   Lou Figaro 1
   Bob Flock 1
   Andy Pierce 1
   Bill Rexford 1
   Gober Sosebee 1
   Marshall Teague 1

>> 1950 SEASON <<

Race No.	Location	Date	Winner	Car owner
1.	Daytona Beach, Fla.	Feb. 5	Harold Kite	Harold Kite
2.	Charlotte	April 2	Tim Flock	Harold Kite
3.	Langhorne, Pa.	April 16	Curtis Turner	John Eanes
4.	Martinsville, Va.	May 21	Curtis Turner	John Eanes
5.	Canfield, Ohio	May 30	Bill Rexford	Julian Buesink
6.	Vernon, N.Y.	June 18	Bill Blair	Sam Rice
7.	Dayton, Ohio	June 25	Jimmy Florian	Jimmy Florian
8.	Rochester, N.Y.	July 2	Curtis Turner	John Eanes
9.	Charlotte	July 23	Curtis Turner	John Eanes
10.	Hillsboro, N.C.	Aug. 13	Fireball Roberts	Sam Rice
11.	Dayton, Ohio	Aug. 20	Dick Linder	Don Rogalla
12.	Hamburg, N.Y.	Aug. 27	Dick Linder	Don Rogalla
13.	Darlington, S.C.	Sept. 4	Johnny Mantz	Westmoreland/ France Sr.
14.	Langhorne, Pa.	Sept. 17	Fonty Flock	Frank Christian
15.	N. Wilkesboro, N.C.	Sept. 24	Leon Sales	Hubert Westmoreland
16.	Vernon, N.Y.	Oct. 1	Dick Linder	Don Rogalla
17.	Martinsville, Va.	Oct. 15	Herb Thomas	Herb Thomas
18.	Winchester, Ind.	Oct. 15	Lloyd Moore	Julian Buesink
19.	Hillsboro, N.C.	Oct. 29	Lee Petty	Petty Enterprises

>> POINTS STANDINGS

1. Bill Rexford 1,959.0
2. Fireball Roberts 1,848.5
3. Lee Petty 1,590.0
4. Lloyd Moore...1,398.0
5. Curtis Turner 1,375.5
6. Johnny Mantz 1,282.0
7. Chuck Mahoney...................................1,217.5
8. Dick Linder 1,121.0
9. Jimmy Florian...801.0
10. Bill Blair 766.0

>> RACE WINNERS   14

1. Curtis Turner 4
2. Dick Linder 3
3. Bill Blair 1
   Fonty Flock 1
   Tim Flock...1
   Jimmy Florian 1
   Harold Kite 1
   Johnny Mantz 1
   Lloyd Moore 1
   Lee Petty 1
   Bill Rexford 1
   Fireball Roberts 1
   Leon Sales...1
   Herb Thomas 1

>> MONEY WON LEADERS

1. Johnny Mantz.........................$10,560
2. Curtis Turner 7,195
3. Fireball Roberts.........................6,475
4. Lee Petty 6,375
5. Dick Linder 5,450
6. Lloyd Moore 5,300
7. Bill Rexford...............................5,175
8. Bill Blair 4,200
9. Tim Flock 3,975
10. Herb Thomas 2,825

>> POLE WINNERS   11

1. Dick Linder 5
2. Curtis Turner 4
3. Fonty Flock 2
4. Buck Baker 1
   Red Byron 1
   Wally Campbell 1
   Tim Flock...1
   Jimmy Florian 1
   Joe Littlejohn 1
   Chuck Mahoney...1
   Fireball Roberts 1

Seventy-five drivers took the green flag for the first Southern 500 on Labor Day in 1950 at Darlington. Several of them drove their cars to the race, then raced them. Johnny Mantz emerged as the winner.

Race No.	Location	Date	Winner	Car owner
1.	Charlotte	June 19	Jim Roper	R.B. McIntosh
2.	Daytona Beach, Fla.	July 10	Red Byron	Raymond Parks
3.	Hillsboro, N.C.	Aug. 7	Bob Flock	Frank Christian
4.	Langhorne, Pa.	Sept. 11	Curtis Turner	Hubert Westmoreland
5.	Hamburg, N.Y.	Sept. 18	Jack White	Dailey Moyer
6.	Martinsville, Va.	Sept. 25	Red Byron	Raymond Parks
7.	Carnegie, Pa.	Oct. 2	Lee Petty	Petty Enterprises
8.	N. Wilkesboro, N.C.	Oct. 16	Bob Flock	Frank Christian

>> POINTS STANDINGS

1. Red Byron 842.5
2. Lee Petty 725.0
3. Bob Flock 704.0
4. Bill Blair................................567.5
5. Fonty Flock 554.5
6. Curtis Turner 430.0
7. Ray Erickson 422.0
8. Tim Flock...............................421.0
9. Glenn Dunnaway 384.0
10. Frank Mundy 370.0

>> RACE WINNERS   6

1. Red Byron.................................2
   Bob Flock.................................2
3. Lee Petty 1
   Jim Roper.................................1
   Curtis Turner.............................1
   Jack White 1

>> MONEY WON LEADERS

1. Red Byron $4,800
2. Bob Flock 4,550
3. Lee Petty 3,375
4. Curtis Turner...................... 2,475
5. Jim Roper.......................... 2,050
6. Fonty Flock........................ 1,775
7. Jack White 1,500
8. Tim Flock 1,350
9. Gober Sosebee 1,225
10. Frank Murphy 1,000

>> POLE WINNERS   6

1. Red Byron.................................2
2. Al Bonnell 1
   Bob Flock 1
   Gober Sosebee 1
   Curtis Turner.............................1
   Ken Wagner 1

THE WINNER WHO WASN'T

NASCAR's premier series officially debuts in Charlotte

Impress your friends with the answer to this trivia question: The first driver to take the checkered flag in an official NASCAR NEXTEL Cup Series race in Charlotte was not named the winner. Name him and the official winner.

Glenn Dunnaway was leading as the race ended, but he later was disqualified for adjustments to the chassis. Jim Roper, who finished three laps down, became the winner.

The race was held at Charlotte Speedway, a 3⁄4-mile dirt track.

Lee Petty borrowed a car and rolled it, finishing 17th as his 9-year-old son, Richard, sold programs in the infield. Petty won $25. Roper won $2,000. Other big names in the race: the Flock brothers, Red Byron, Curtis Turner and Herb Thomas.

>> 1948 SEASON <<

Location	Date	Winner	Car owner
Daytona Beach, Fla.	Feb.15	Red Byron	Raymond Parks
Jacksonville, Fla.	Feb. 24	Fonty Flock	Babb/Fields
Atlanta	March 27	Fonty Flock	Babb/Fields
Macon, Ga.	April 4	Fonty Flock	Babb/Fields
Augusta, Ga.	April 11	Bob Flock	Raymond Parks
Jacksonville, Fla.	April 18	Skimp Hersey	Mac Richardson
Greensboro, N.C.	April 18	Fonty Flock	Babb/Fields
N. Wilkesboro, N.C.	April 25	Red Byron	Raymond Parks
Lexington, N.C.	May 2	Red Byron	Raymond Parks
Wadesboro, N.C.	May 9	Red Byron	Raymond Parks
Richmond, Va.	May 16	Red Byron	Raymond Parks
Macon, Ga.	May 23	Gober Sosebee	Gober Sosebee
Danville, Va.	May 23	Bill Blair	Bill Blair
Dover, N.J.	May 23	Johnny Rogers	N/A
Greensboro, N.C.	May 29	Bob Flock	Raymond Parks
N. Wilkesboro, N.C.	May 30	Marshall Teague	Marshall Teague
Jacksonville, Fla.	May 30	Paul Pappy	N/A
Danville, Va.	June 4	Bob Flock	Raymond Parks
Greensboro, N.C.	June 5	Red Byron	Raymond Parks
Lexington, N.C.	June 6	Bob Flock	Raymond Parks
Wadesboro, N.C.	June 13	Fonty Flock	Babb/Fields
Birmingham, Ala.	June 20	Fonty Flock	Babb/Fields
Columbus, Ga.	June 20	Bob Flock	Raymond Parks
Greensboro, N.C.	June 20	Tim Flock	Charlie Mobley
Occoneechee, N.C.	June 27	Fonty Flock	Babb/Fields
Martinsville, Va.	July 4	Fonty Flock	Babb/Fields
Charlotte	July 11	Red Byron	Raymond Parks
N. Wilkesboro, N.C.	July 18	Curtis Turner	Bob Smith
Greensboro, N.C.	July 25	Curtis Turner	Bob Smith
Columbus, Ga.	July 25	Billy Carden	N/A
Lexington, N.C.	Aug. 1	Curtis Turner	Bob Smith
Daytona Beach, Fla.	Aug. 8	Fonty Flock	Babb/Fields
Langhorne, Pa.	Aug. 15	Al Keller	N/A
Columbus, Ga.	Sept. 5	Gober Sosebee	Gober Sosebee
N. Wilkesboro, N.C. (1)	Sept. 5	Curtis Turner	Bob Smith
N. Wilkesboro, N.C. (2)	Sept. 5	Curtis Turner	Bob Smith
Charlotte (1)	Sept. 12	Curtis Turner	Bob Smith
Charlotte (2)	Sept. 12	Buddy Shuman	Shuman-Thompson
Occoneechee, N.C. (1)	Sept. 19	Fonty Flock	Babb/Fields
Occoneechee, N.C. (2)	Sept. 19	Fonty Flock	Babb/Fields
Lexington, N.C. (1)	Sept. 26	Fonty Flock	Babb/Fields
Lexington, N.C. (2)	Sept. 26	Gober Sosebee	Gober Sosebee
Elkin, N.C. (1)	Oct.3	Buddy Shuman	Shuman-Thompson
Elkin, N.C. (2)	Oct. 3	Curtis Turner	Bob Smith
Macon, Ga. (1)	Oct. 3	Billy Carden	N/A
Macon, Ga. (2)	Oct. 3	Red Byron	Raymond Parks
Greensboro, N.C.	Oct. 10	Fonty Flock	Joe Wolf
Greensboro, N.C.	Oct. 16	Fonty Flock	Joe Wolf
N. Wilkesboro, N.C.	Oct. 17	Red Byron	Raymond Parks
Charlotte	Oct. 24	Red Byron	Raymond Parks
Winston-Salem, N.C.	Oct. 31	Fonty Flock	Joe Wolf
Columbus, Ga.	Nov.14	Red Byron	Raymond Parks

>> POINTS STANDINGS

1.	Red Byron	2996.50
2.	Fonty Flock	2963.75
3.	Tim Flock	1759.50
4.	Curtis Turner	1540.50
5.	Buddy Shuman	1350.00
6.	Bill Blair	1188.50
7.	Bob Flock	1181.50
8.	Marshall Teague	1134.25
9.	Bill Snowden	1092.50
10.	Buck Baker	952.50
11.	Billy Carden	866.50
12.	Johnny Grubb	733.00
13.	Speedy Thompson	623.00
14.	Roscoe Thompson	471.00
15.	Jimmy Lewallen	437.00
16.	Al Keller	415.00
17.	Jimmy Thompson	386.00
18.	Jack Smith	384.75
19.	Pee Wee Martin	354.00
20.	Fred Mahon	353.00

>> RACE WINNERS   14

1.	Fonty Flock	15
2.	Red Byron	11
3.	Curtis Turner	7
4.	Bob Flock	5
5.	Gober Sosebee	3
6.	Billy Carden	2
	Buddy Shuman	2
8.	Bill Blair	1
	Tim Flock	1
	Skimp Hersey	1
	Al Keller	1
	Paul Pappy	1
	Johnny Rogers	1
	Marshall Teague	1

>> MONEY WON LEADERS

1.	Red Byron	$1,250
2.	Fonty Flock	600
3.	Tim Flock	400
4.	Curtis Turner	350
5.	Buddy Shuman	300
6.	Bill Blair	250
7.	Bob Flock	200
8.	Marshall Teague	150
	Bill Snowden	150
	Buck Baker	150
	Billy Carden	150
	Johnny Grubb	150
	Speedy Thompson	150
14.	Jimmy Lewallen	100
	Al Keller	100
	Jimmy Thompson	100
	Jack Smith	100
	Pee Wee Martin	100
	Fred Mahon	100

NASCAR BUSCH SERIES

NASCAR BUSCH SERIES
MILESTONES

The NASCAR Busch Series, which enters its 26th season in 2007, has established itself as the No. 2 motorsports series in the United States, second only to the NASCAR NEXTEL Cup Series.

The NASCAR Busch Series represents the middle rung in NASCAR's national series, situated between the NASCAR NEXTEL Cup Series and NASCAR Craftsman Truck Series. The NASCAR Busch Series has proved to be an outstanding series for competitors who aspire to become NASCAR NEXTEL Cup Series drivers, with many of today's premier drivers having competed in the series over the years. Many drivers also have chosen to spend their entire careers in this division because of the competitive nature and popularity of the series.

The series was formed in 1982 when NASCAR consolidated the old Late Model Sportsman division into a touring series of nearly 30 races per year. The series, however, has roots dating back more than five decades. It debuted in 1950 as the NASCAR Sportsman Division and remained so until 1968 before being renamed the NASCAR Late Model Sportsman Division. In 1982, Anheuser-Busch, Inc. joined with NASCAR to create the evolving touring circuit now commonly known as the NASCAR Busch Series.

Truex Jr.

SOME OF THE MILESTONES IN THE HISTORY OF THE SERIES:

1950 The origin of the NASCAR Busch Series traces back to this year when the series was known as the NASCAR Sportsman Division. Drivers would frequently compete in three to four races per week—approximately 60 races per year—throughout the East Coast region of the United States. Some of the notable names that claimed championships in this division during these early years were Ralph Earnhardt (1956) and Ned Jarrett (1957-58), fathers of future NASCAR NEXTEL Cup Series champions Dale Earnhardt and Dale Jarrett.

1968 The NASCAR Sportsman Division undergoes its first name change, now known as the NASCAR Late Model Sportsman Division.

1982 NASCAR Late Model Sportsman Division is consolidated into a national touring series and renamed the NASCAR Budweiser Late Model Sportsman Series. The inaugural season consisted of 29 races.

February 13, 1982 The first race of the new touring series—Goody's 300—was held at Daytona International Speedway. Mike Porter took the pole and Dale Earnhardt won the inaugural race in a Pontiac. This race also marked the series' first superspeedway event.

February 20, 1982 Tommy Houston wins the series' first short track race, the Eastern 150 at Richmond International Raceway.

March 28, 1982 Diane Teel becomes the first female driver to start a NASCAR Busch Series race, competing at Martinsville (Va.) Speedway and finishing 26th.

October 31, 1982 The series championship comes down to the final race of the season at Martinsville Speedway between Jack Ingram and Sam Ard. Ingram, despite a 26th-place finish, holds off Ard, who finished sixth, to claim the first series title by 49 points.

October 8, 1983 Sam Ard establishes a series record with four consecutive wins during the season. Ard won at South Boston (Va.) Speedway (Sept. 17); Martinsville Speedway (September 24); Orange County (N.C.) Speedway (October 1); and Lowe's Motor Speedway (October 8). The series record still stands.

1984 One of the most important milestones in series history as Anheuser-Busch switches its series sponsorship from its Budweiser brand to Busch. The NASCAR Budweiser Late Model Sportsman Series is renamed the NASCAR Busch Grand National Series.

May 26-27, 1984 Bobby Allison becomes the first driver to sweep a race weekend, winning the NASCAR Busch Series and NASCAR NEXTEL Cup Series races at Charlotte Motor Speedway. He won the NASCAR Busch race—the Mello Yello 300—on Saturday and came back the next day to win the NASCAR NEXTEL Cup Series event, the World 600.

October 20, 1984 Sam Ard clinches his second consecutive series title, becoming the first driver in history to win back-to-back championships. He also becomes the first multiple champion in the series.

1985 Jack Ingram captures his second series title, joining two-time champ Ard as the only champions in the four-year-old series.

July 6, 1986 The series' first road course race is held at Road Atlanta in Braselton, Ga. The race was won by Darrell Waltrip.

1987 Larry Pearson, son of the legendary David Pearson, wins his second consecutive series championship, joining Sam Ard (1983-84) as the only drivers at this stage to win back-to-back titles.

1989 The Raybestos Rookie of the Year award is established, with Kenny Wallace claiming the inaugural honor. Wallace edged Bobby Hamilton for the award, posting 16 top 10 finishes in 29 starts en route to a sixth-place finish in the championship. ... Jack Ingram is the first driver in the series to earn $1 million in his career.

1992 Joe Nemechek earns the series championship in the closest battle in series history. Nemechek defeated runner-up Bobby Labonte by just three points for the crown. The margin remains the closest in series history. ... Jeff Gordon becomes the first driver to win $100,000 in a NASCAR Busch Series race at Charlotte Motor Speedway.

1995 The series name is altered slightly, changing to the present NASCAR Busch Series, Grand National Division.

October 19, 1996 Tommy Houston, a 15-year series veteran, makes his final series start at the season finale at North Carolina Speedway in Rockingham, N.C. Houston, who finished 39th that day, concludes his career with a series-record 417 starts.

1997 Randy LaJoie becomes the third driver in history to win back-to-back series championships, joining Sam Ard (1983-84) and Larry Pearson (1986-87). LaJoie also enjoyed another piece of history, becoming the first driver to earn $1 million in a single season.

March 16, 1997 The NASCAR Busch Series travels west for the Las Vegas 300 at Las Vegas Motor Speedway, marking the first race west of the Mississippi River in series history. California Speedway, Texas Motor Speedway and Gateway International Raceway near St. Louis also were added to the series schedule that season.

September 5, 1998 Dick Trickle, at 56 years, 11 months, becomes the oldest driver to win a NASCAR Busch Series race, at Darlington (S.C.) Raceway.

October 17, 1998 The Petty racing legacy is extended to a fourth generation as Adam Petty, son of Kyle, makes his NASCAR Busch Series debut at Gateway International Raceway in Madison, Ill. Petty finished 27th.

November 13, 1998 NASCAR and Anheuser-Busch announce a multi-year renewal of the Busch beer title sponsorship. With this announcement came an increase in the series' point fund ($650,000 to $1.5 million); a Busch beer marketing campaign and an integrated, media-driven marketing plan which included: a new series logo; aggressive national and market-specific public relations efforts; comprehensive coverage on NASCAR's website; and additional inclusion on licensed TV, radio and print media.

January 1999 Final attendance figures are announced for the 1998 season and the numbers reveal that more than 2 million attended races that year.

June 27, 1999 At Watkins Glen (N.Y.) International, Bill Lester makes history as the first African-American driver to start a NASCAR Busch Series race. Lester finished 21st after starting 24th.

July 4, 1999 Casey Atwood, at 18 years, 11 months, wins at The Milwaukee Mile, becoming the youngest winner of a NASCAR Busch Series race in history. Atwood easily eclipses the mark set by Rob Moroso, who was 19 years, nine months old when he won previously at Myrtle Beach (S.C.) Speedway on July 2, 1988.

November 11, 1999 NASCAR announces a six-year television contract with NBC Sports and Turner Sports (a joint venture) and an eight-year agreement with FOX and its FX cable network, beginning with the 2001 NASCAR NEXTEL Cup Series and NASCAR Busch Series seasons.

November 13, 1999 Dale Earnhardt Jr. is crowned the 1999 series champion, becoming the fourth driver to win consecutive titles and second in a row. Earnhardt Jr. joins Sam Ard (1983-84), Larry Pearson (1986-87) and Randy LaJoie (1996-97).

November 2000 Jeff Green earns his first NASCAR Busch Series championship and enhances the family racing legacy. Coupled with his brother David's series title in 1994, the Greens become the first brothers to win NASCAR Busch Series titles. ... For the first time in NASCAR Busch Series history, three rookies (Kevin Harvick, Ron Hornaday and Jimmie Johnson) finish in the top 10 in the final driver points standings.

2001 As a result of increased broadcast and cable coverage on NBC/TNT and FOX/FX, the NASCAR Busch Series enjoys tremendous increases in television ratings and viewership. The number of households tuning in to watch NASCAR Busch Series races increases 33 percent compared to the previous year. The NASCAR Busch Series is establishing itself as the No. 2 motorsports series in the United States.

November 3, 2001 Kevin Harvick becomes the 15th different NASCAR Busch Series champion since 1982 in an incredible season. While chasing the title, team owner Richard Childress asks Harvick to take over the team's NASCAR NEXTEL Cup Series ride of Dale Earnhardt, who was involved in a fatal accident in the season opener. Harvick responded by finishing ninth in the NASCAR NEXTEL Cup Series championship and capturing the NASCAR NEX-TEL Cup Series Raybestos Rookie of the Year award. ... Childress becomes the only car owner ever to win championships in all three of NASCAR's national series: NASCAR NEXTEL Cup Series (1986-87, '90-91, '93-94 with Dale Earnhardt); NASCAR Craftsman Truck Series (1995 with Mike Skinner); and NASCAR Busch Series with Harvick.

2002 Greg Biffle of Roush Racing captures the NASCAR Busch Series crown, becoming the first driver in history to win titles in the NASCAR Craftsman Truck Series and this series. Biffle becomes the first driver in NASCAR Busch Series history to top $2 million in single-season earnings.

2003 Brian Vickers is NASCAR's youngest champion ever at 20 years old. He edges runner-up David Green by 14 points. The No. 5 Chevrolet that Vickers drives is fielded by Hendrick Motorsports, which joins Roush Racing and Richard Childress Racing as the only teams to have won championships in each of NASCAR's top three series—NASCAR Craftsman Truck Series, NASCAR Busch Series and what becomes NASCAR NEXTEL Cup Series.

2004 19-year-old Kyle Busch challenges Brian Vickers' record but finishes second in the points standings to Martin Truex Jr. However, Busch does become the series' youngest Raybestos Rookie of the Year. Busch also is the first rookie to lead the most miles in the series (1,390.89).

2005 Martin Truex Jr. becomes the first driver to win back-to-back NASCAR Busch Series titles since his co-owner Dale Earnhardt Jr. did it in 1998-1999. Carl Edwards wins Raybestos Rookie of the Year and became the first driver in history to finish in the top five in final points in the NASCAR Busch Series and NASCAR NEXTEL Cup Series. He finished third in both. The NASCAR Busch Series also runs NASCAR's first race in Mexico. Truex wins the Telcel Motorola 200 on March 6 at Autodromo Hermanos Rodriguez.

2006 The NASCAR Busch Series celebrates its 25th anniversary during the 2006 season, and fans and media vote Mark Martin as the greatest NASCAR Busch Series driver. Kevin Harvick tallies nine wins and 32 top 10s and wins the championship by a huge margin—824 points, the largest ever in the NASCAR Busch Series— over second-place finisher Carl Edwards. Harvick's 32 top 10s are the most ever in a season for a NASCAR Busch Series driver.

>>2007 SCHEDULE<<

NASCAR Busch Series

Date	Race	Track	TV/Radio	Time (Eastern)	2006 winner
February 17	Hershey's Kissables 300	Daytona International Speedway	ESPN2/MRN	1:20 p.m.	Tony Stewart
February 24	Stater Bros. 300	California Speedway	ESPN2/MRN	6:30 p.m.	Greg Biffle
March 4	Telcel-Motorola Mexico 200	Autodromo Hermanos Rodriguez	ESPN2/MRN	2:05 p.m.	Denny Hamlin
March 10	Sam's Town 300	Las Vegas Motor Speedway	ESPN2/PRN	6:10 p.m.	Kasey Kahne
March 17	Nicorette 300	Atlanta Motor Speedway	ESPN2/PRN	3:05 p.m.	Jeff Burton
March 24	Sharpie Mini 300	Bristol Motor Speedway	ESPN2/PRN	3:15 p.m.	Kyle Busch
April 7	Pepsi 300	Nashville Superspeedway	ESPN2/MRN	4:05 p.m.	Kevin Harvick
April 14	O'Reilly 300	Texas Motor Speedway	ESPN2/PRN	3:05 p.m.	Kurt Busch
April 20	Bashas' Supermarkets 200	Phoenix International Raceway	ESPN2/MRN	9 p.m.	Kevin Harvick
April 28	Aaron's 312	Talladega Superspeedway	ESPN2/MRN	3:15 p.m.	Martin Truex Jr.
May 4	Circuit City 250	Richmond International Raceway	ESPN2/MRN	8 p.m.	Kevin Harvick
May 11	Diamond Hill Plywood 200	Darlington Raceway	ESPN2/MRN	7:55 p.m.	Denny Hamlin
May 26	CARQUEST Auto Parts 300	Lowe's Motor Speedway	ESPN2/PRN	8 p.m.	Carl Edwards
June 2	StonebridgeRacing.com 200	Dover International Speedway	ESPN2/MRN	3:30 p.m.	Jeff Burton
June 9	Federated Auto Parts 300	Nashville Superspeedway	ESPN2/MRN	8:05 p.m.	Carl Edwards
June 16	Meijer 300	Kentucky Speedway	ESPN2/MRN	7:55 p.m.	David Gilliland
June 23	AT&T 250	The Milwaukee Mile	ESPN2/MRN	9:05 p.m.	Paul Menard
June 30	New England 200	New Hampshire International Speedway	ESPN2/MRN	3 p.m.	Carl Edwards
July 6	Winn-Dixie 250	Daytona International Speedway	ESPN2/MRN	7:55 p.m.	Dale Earnhardt Jr.
July 14	USG Durock 300	Chicagoland Speedway	ESPN2/MRN	4:05 p.m.	Casey Mears
July 21	Gateway 250	Gateway International Raceway	ESPN2/MRN	8:15 p.m.	Carl Edwards
July 28	KROGER 200	O'Reilly Raceway Park	ESPN2/MRN	9:05 p.m.	Kevin Harvick
August 4	Montreal 200	Circuit Gilles Villeneuve	ESPN2/MRN	TBD	Inaugural event
August 11	ZIPPO 200	Watkins Glen International	ESPN2/MRN	2 p.m.	Kurt Busch
August 18	CARFAX 250	Michigan International Speedway	ESPN2/MRN	3 p.m.	Dale Earnhardt Jr.
August 24	Food City 250	Bristol Motor Speedway	ESPN2/PRN	7:50 p.m.	Matt Kenseth
September 1	Ameriquest 300	California Speedway	ESPN2/MRN	10:10 p.m.	Kasey Kahne
September 7	Emerson Radio 250	Richmond International Raceway	ESPN2/MRN	7:50 p.m.	Kevin Harvick
September 22	Dover 200	Dover International Speedway	ESPN2/MRN	3:05 p.m.	Clint Bowyer
September 29	Yellow Transportation 300	Kansas Speedway	ESPN2/MRN	3:05 p.m.	Kevin Harvick
October 12	Dollar General 300	Lowe's Motor Speedway	ESPN2/PRN	8 p.m.	Dave Blaney
October 27	Sam's Town 250	Memphis Motorsports Park	ESPN2/MRN	2:10 p.m.	Kevin Harvick
November 3	O'Reilly Challenge	Texas Motor Speedway	ESPN2/MRN	2 p.m.	Kevin Harvick
November 10	Arizona Travel 200	Phoenix International Raceway	ESPN2/MRN	3:30 p.m.	Matt Kenseth
November 17	Ford 300	Homestead-Miami Speedway	ESPN2/MRN	7:10 p.m.	Matt Kenseth

NOTE: Race names, TV information and start times are subject to change. ABC will televise selected races.

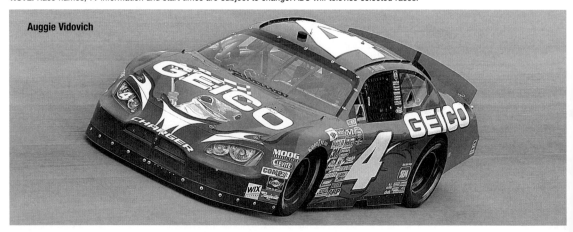

Auggie Vidovich

ARIC ALMIROLA

Car: Chevrolet • **Date of birth:** 3/14/84
Hometown: Tampa, Fla. • **Owner/Team:** Joe Gibbs

CAREER STATISTICS

Year	Rank	Starts	Wins	Poles	T5	T10	Races led	Laps led
2006	51	9	0	0	0	0	1	13
Totals		9	0	0	0	0	1	13

MARCOS AMBROSE

Car: No. 59 Ford • **Date of birth:** 9/1/76
Hometown: Launceston, Tasmania • **Owner/Team:** Tad Geschicker

No career NASCAR Busch Series Statistics

JOHN ANDRETTI

Date of birth: 3/12/63 • **Hometown:** Bethlehem, Pa.
Owner/Team: Greg Pollex

CAREER STATISTICS

Year	Rank	Starts	Wins	Poles	T5	T10	Races led	Laps led
1998	96	1	0	0	0	0	0	0
2006	12	35	0	0	1	4	3	3
Totals		36	0	0	1	4	3	3

CASEY ATWOOD

Date of birth: 8/25/80
Hometown: Antioch, Tenn.

CAREER STATISTICS

Year	Rank	Starts	Wins	Poles	T5	T10	Races led	Laps led
1998	38	13	0	2	1	1	2	129
1999	13	31	2	2	5	9	5	244
2000	8	32	0	2	0	8	3	108
2003	37	14	0	0	0	4	0	0
2004	19	29	0	0	1	7	4	97
2005	76	4	0	0	0	1	0	0
2006	52	8	0	0	0	0	1	1
Totals		131	2	6	7	30	15	579

GREG BIFFLE

Car: No. 16 Ford • **Date of birth:** 12/23/69
Hometown: Vancouver, Wash. • **Owner/Team:** Jack Roush

CAREER STATISTICS

Year	Rank	Starts	Wins	Poles	T5	T10	Races led	Laps led
1996	77	2	0	0	0	0	0	0
2001	4	33	5	2	16	21	19	948
2002	1	34	4	5	20	25	22	1061
2003	35	14	2	2	3	4	4	222
2004	3	34	5	2	15	21	18	553
2005	10	27	1	0	16	21	15	543
2006	9	30	1	0	9	18	9	170
Totals		174	18	11	79	110	87	3497

DAVE BLANEY

Car: No. 32 Toyota • **Date of birth:** 10/24/62
Hometown: Hartford, Ohio • **Owner/Team:** Braun Racing

CAREER STATISTICS

Year	Rank	Starts	Wins	Poles	T5	T10	Races led	Laps led
1998	29	20	0	1	0	3	1	5
1999	7	31	0	4	5	12	6	139
2000	46	8	0	1	2	4	1	24
2001	155	1	0	0	0	0	0	0
2002	114	1	0	0	0	0	1	3
2003	43	10	0	0	0	3	0	0
2004	60	6	0	0	0	0	1	42
2005	56	9	0	0	0	0	0	0
2006	47	7	1	0	1	2	2	6
Totals		93	1	6	8	24	12	219

MIKE BLISS

Date of birth: 4/5/65
Hometown: Milwaukie, Ore.

CAREER STATISTICS

Year	Rank	Starts	Wins	Poles	T5	T10	Races led	Laps led
1998	71	2	0	0	0	1	0	0
1999	84	3	0	0	0	0	0	0
2000	100	1	0	0	0	0	0	0
2001	143	1	0	0	0	0	0	0
2003	10	34	0	0	8	14	3	136
2004	5	34	1	3	6	14	7	109
2005	130	1	0	0	0	0	0	0
2006	62	8	0	0	0	0	0	0
Totals		84	1	3	14	29	10	245

CLINT BOWYER

Car: No. 2 Chevrolet • **Date of birth:** 5/30/79
Hometown: Emporia, Kan. • **Owner/Team:** Richard Childress

CAREER STATISTICS

Year	Rank	Starts	Wins	Poles	T5	T10	Races led	Laps led
2004	29	17	0	1	4	7	2	108
2005	2	35	2	2	12	22	12	565
2006	3	35	1	2	12	17	17	579
Totals		87	3	5	28	46	31	1252

JEFF BURTON

Car: No. 29 Chevrolet • **Date of birth:** 6/29/67
Hometown: South Boston, Va. • **Owner/Team:** Richard Childress

CAREER STATISTICS								
Year	Rank	Starts	Wins	Poles	T5	T10	Races led	Laps led
1988	44	5	0	0	0	0	0	0
1989	13	27	0	0	2	6	1	14
1990	15	31	1	1	3	5	4	154
1991	12	31	1	2	3	10	4	210
1992	9	31	1	0	4	10	7	101
1993	14	28	1	0	3	10	6	330
1996	113	1	0	0	0	0	0	0
1997	26	13	2	1	9	10	9	714
1998	30	13	3	2	7	9	7	441
1999	25	14	1	1	7	12	4	116
2000	29	14	4	0	11	13	9	833
2001	33	11	1	1	4	9	4	163
2002	31	13	5	2	8	9	7	586
2003	76	4	0	0	0	0	1	24
2004	57	4	0	0	2	3	2	28
2005	58	5	0	0	2	3	3	131
2006	28	16	2	1	7	10	9	212
Totals		261	22	11	72	119	77	4057

KURT BUSCH

Car: No. 39 Dodge • **Date of birth:** 8/4/78
Hometown: Las Vegas • **Owner/Team:** Roger Penske

CAREER STATISTICS								
Year	Rank	Starts	Wins	Poles	T5	T10	Races led	Laps led
2006	39	7	2	1	5	6	7	303
Totals		7	2	1	5	6	7	303

KYLE BUSCH

Car: No. 5 Chevrolet • **Date of birth:** 5/2/85
Hometown: Las Vegas • **Owner/Team:** Rick Hendrick

CAREER STATISTICS								
Year	Rank	Starts	Wins	Poles	T5	T10	Races led	Laps led
2003	48	7	0	0	2	3	2	39
2004	2	34	5	5	16	22	21	1108
2005	44	14	1	1	2	3	7	159
2006	7	34	1	2	4	12	10	200
Totals		89	7	8	24	40	40	1506

BRAD COLEMAN

Car: No. 18 Chevrolet • **Date of birth:** 2/26/88
Hometown: Martinsville, Va. • **Owner/Team:** Joe Gibbs

CAREER STATISTICS								
Year	Rank	Starts	Wins	Poles	T5	T10	Races led	Laps led
2006	108	2	0	0	0	0	0	0
Totals		2	0	0	0	0	0	0

MATT CRAFTON

Date of birth: 6/11/76
Hometown: Tulare, Calif.
No career NASCAR Busch Series Statistics

ERIN CROCKER

Date of birth: 3/23/8
Hometown: Wilbraham, Mass.

CAREER STATISTICS								
Year	Rank	Starts	Wins	Poles	T5	T10	Races led	Laps led
2005	90	4	0	0	0	0	0	0
2006	67	6	0	0	0	0	0	0
Totals		10	0	0	0	0	0	0

KERTUS DAVIS

Car: No. 77 Chevrolet • **Date of birth:** 2/26/81
Hometown: Gaffney, S.C. • **Owner/Team:** Kevin Harvick Inc.

CAREER STATISTICS								
Year	Rank	Starts	Wins	Poles	T5	T10	Races led	Laps led
2001	80	4	0	0	0	0	0	0
2002	67	5	0	0	0	0	0	0
2004	93	3	0	0	0	0	0	0
2005	31	28	0	0	0	1	1	3
2006	40	22	0	0	0	1	1	1
Totals		62	0	0	0	1	2	4

DALE EARNHARDT JR.

Car: Chevrolet • **Date of birth:** 10/10/74
Hometown: Kannapolis, N.C. • **Owner/Team:** Dale Earnhardt Inc.

CAREER STATISTICS								
Year	Rank	Starts	Wins	Poles	T5	T10	Races led	Laps led
1996	79	1	0	0	0	0	0	0
1997	47	8	0	0	0	1	1	22
1998	1	31	7	3	16	22	19	1615
1999	1	32	6	3	18	22	23	725
2001	118	1	0	0	0	0	0	0
2002	60	3	2	1	2	2	2	249
2003	66	3	3	1	3	3	3	227
2004	49	4	2	1	3	3	4	203
2005	75	4	0	0	1	2	2	23
2006	53	5	2	0	2	3	3	146
Totals		92	22	9	45	58	57	3210

CARL EDWARDS

Car: No. 60 Ford • **Date of birth:** 8/15/79
Hometown: Columbia, Mo. • **Owner/Team:** Jack Roush

CAREER STATISTICS								
Year	Rank	Starts	Wins	Poles	T5	T10	Races led	Laps led
2002	117	1	0	0	0	0	0	0

Year	Rank	Starts	Wins	Poles	T5	T10	Races led	Laps led
2004	116	1	0	0	0	0	0	0
2005	3	34	5	4	15	21	14	525
2006	2	35	4	3	15	25	17	662
Totals		71	9	7	30	46	31	1187

Year	Rank	Starts	Wins	Poles	T5	T10	Races led	Laps led
2004	21	25	1	0	6	10	9	152
2005	78	4	0	0	1	2	1	13
2006	64	4	0	0	2	3	2	21
Totals		36	1	0	10	16	14	217

AARON FIKE

Date of birth: 11/24/82
Hometown: Galesburg, Ill.

CAREER STATISTICS

Year	Rank	Starts	Wins	Poles	T5	T10	Races led	Laps led
2004	46	13	0	0	0	0	0	0
2005	27	24	0	0	0	1	0	0
2006	43	15	0	0	0	0	0	0
Totals		52	0	0	0	1	0	0

CALE GALE

Car: Chevrolet • **Date of birth:** 3/5/85
Hometown: Mobile, Ala. • **Owner/Team:** Kevin Harvick Inc.

CAREER STATISTICS

Year	Rank	Starts	Wins	Poles	T5	T10	Races led	Laps led
2006	81	4	0	0	0	0	1	2
Totals		4	0	0	0	0	1	2

DAVID GILLILAND

Car: No. 25 Ford • **Date of birth:** 4/1/76
Hometown: Chino, Calif. • **Owner/Team:** Ed Rensi

CAREER STATISTICS

Year	Rank	Starts	Wins	Poles	T5	T10	Races led	Laps led
2005	127	2	0	0	0	0	0	0
2006	56	9	1	0	1	1	1	11
Totals		11	1	0	1	1	1	11

JORGE GOETERS

Date of birth: 6/26/70 • **Hometown:** San Luis Potosi, Mexico
Owner/Team: Star Motorsports

CAREER STATISTICS

Year	Rank	Starts	Wins	Poles	T5	T10	Races led	Laps led
2005	82	3	0	1	0	1	1	24
2006	82	4	0	0	0	0	0	0
Totals		7	0	1	0	1	1	24

ROBBY GORDON

Car: No. 55 Ford • **Date of birth:** 1/2/69
Hometown: Orange, Calif. • **Owner/Team:** Robby Gordon

CAREER STATISTICS

Year	Rank	Starts	Wins	Poles	T5	T10	Races led	Laps led
2001	60	3	0	0	1	1	2	31

DAVID GREEN

Date of birth: 1/28/58
Hometown: Owensboro, Ken.

CAREER STATISTICS

Year	Rank	Starts	Wins	Poles	T5	T10	Races led	Laps led
1989	96	1	0	0	0	0	0	0
1990	85	2	0	0	0	0	0	0
1991	13	29	1	1	6	9	5	210
1993	3	28	0	0	6	16	5	94
1994	1	28	1	9	10	14	11	380
1995	12	26	1	4	4	6	7	271
1996	2	26	2	4	13	18	10	501
1998	26	19	0	0	7	8	1	32
1999	27	17	0	1	1	7	0	0
2000	9	32	0	0	2	11	6	88
2001	13	33	0	0	0	6	1	1
2002	40	12	0	0	3	4	1	9
2003	2	34	3	2	11	21	10	122
2004	7	34	0	1	6	16	4	81
2005	8	35	1	0	3	6	5	24
2006	23	27	0	0	0	2	1	1
Totals		383	9	22	72	144	67	1814

BOBBY HAMILTON JR.

Car: No. 35 Ford • **Date of birth:** 1/8/78
Hometown: White House, Tenn. • **Owner/Team:** Ed Rensi

CAREER STATISTICS

Year	Rank	Starts	Wins	Poles	T5	T10	Races led	Laps led
1998	83	2	0	0	0	0	1	4
1999	39	18	0	0	0	1	1	1
2000	19	32	0	1	1	3	0	0
2001	17	33	0	1	2	5	3	40
2002	8	34	1	0	6	15	11	357
2003	4	34	4	1	13	22	13	643
2004	22	23	0	1	7	12	9	425
Totals		176	5	4	29	58	38	1470

DENNY HAMLIN

Car: No. 29 Chevrolet • **Date of birth:** 11/18/80
Hometown: Chesterfield, Va. • **Owner/Team:** Joe Gibbs

CAREER STATISTICS

Year	Rank	Starts	Wins	Poles	T5	T10	Races led	Laps led
2004	103	1	0	0	0	1	0	0
2005	5	35	0	0	1	11	7	177
2006	4	35	2	6	12	23	14	595
Totals		71	2	6	13	35	21	772

KEVIN HARVICK

Car: Chevrolet • **Date of birth:** 12/8/75 • **Hometown:** Bakersfield, Calif. • **Owner/Team:** Richard Childress, Kevin Harvick Inc.

CAREER STATISTICS								
Year	Rank	Starts	Wins	Poles	T5	T10	Races led	Laps led
1999	138	1	0	0	0	0	0	0
2000	3	31	3	2	8	16	11	665
2001	1	33	5	4	20	24	18	1265
2002	64	4	0	0	0	1	2	54
2003	16	19	3	5	12	18	15	971
2004	20	22	2	0	10	15	10	311
2005	18	21	4	2	14	15	14	621
2006	1	35	9	1	23	32	20	1220
Totals		166	26	14	87	121	90	5107

RON HORNADAY JR.

Date of birth: 6/20/58
Hometown: Palmdale, Calif.

CAREER STATISTICS								
Year	Rank	Starts	Wins	Poles	T5	T10	Races led	Laps led
1998	61	4	0	0	0	1	0	0
1999	68	4	0	0	0	1	1	98
2000	5	32	2	0	6	13	8	246
2001	36	12	0	0	1	3	2	26
2002	18	30	0	1	5	8	6	231
2003	3	34	1	0	8	17	12	403
2004	4	34	1	0	7	16	10	153
2005	57	8	0	0	0	0	1	36
2006	35	14	0	0	3	5	0	0
Totals		172	4	1	30	64	40	1193

SAM HORNISH JR.

Car: No. 39 Dodge • **Date of birth:** 7/2/79
Hometown: Bryan, Ohio • **Owner/Team:** Roger Penske

CAREER STATISTICS								
Year	Rank	Starts	Wins	Poles	T5	T10	Races led	Laps led
2006	117	2	0	0	0	0	0	0
Totals		2	0	0	0	0	0	0

SHANE HUFFMAN

Car: No. 88 Chevrolet • **Date of birth:** 12/30/73
Hometown: Hickory, N.C. • **Owner/Team:** JR Motorsports

CAREER STATISTICS								
Year	Rank	Starts	Wins	Poles	T5	T10	Races led	Laps led
2001	108	1	0	0	0	0	0	0
2006	49	10	0	0	1	2	1	17
Totals		11	0	0	1	2	1	17

RICHARD JOHNS

Car: No. 25 Ford • **Age:** 25
Hometown: Lawrenceville, Ga. • **Owner/Team:** Ed Rensi
No career NASCAR Busch Series Statistics

P.J. JONES

Date of birth: 4/23/69
Hometown: Torrance, Calif.

CAREER STATISTICS								
Year	Rank	Starts	Wins	Poles	T5	T10	Races led	Laps led
2000	38	20	0	0	0	1	2	11
2001	65	4	0	0	0	0	0	0
2002	115	1	0	0	0	0	0	0
2006	75	5	0	0	0	0	0	0
Totals		30	0	0	0	1	2	11

MICHEL JOURDAIN JR.

Date of birth: 9/2/76
Hometown: Mexico City, Mexico

CAREER STATISTICS								
Year	Rank	Starts	Wins	Poles	T5	T10	Races led	Laps led
2005	37	20	0	0	0	1	1	1
2006	91	3	0	0	0	0	2	11
Totals		23	0	0	1	3		12

KASEY KAHNE

Car: No. 9 Dodge • **Date of birth:** 4/10/80
Hometown: Enumclaw, Wash. • **Owner/Team:** Ray Evernham

CAREER STATISTICS								
Year	Rank	Starts	Wins	Poles	T5	T10	Races led	Laps led
2002	33	20	0	0	0	1	0	0
2003	7	34	1	1	4	14	6	47
2004	11	30	0	2	9	14	8	320
2005	21	22	2	3	6	6	10	245
2006	31	17	2	0	4	6	5	221
Totals		123	5	6	23	41	29	833

JOEL KAUFFMAN

Date of birth: 12/9/85
Hometown: LaGrange, Ind.

CAREER STATISTICS								
Year	Rank	Starts	Wins	Poles	T5	T10	Races led	Laps led
2005	67	7	0	0	0	0	0	0
2006	57	11	0	0	0	0	0	0
Totals		18	0	0	0	0	0	0

JASON KELLER

Date of birth: 4/23/70
Hometown: Greenville, S.C.

CAREER STATISTICS								
Year	Rank	Starts	Wins	Poles	T5	T10	Races led	Laps led
1991	105	1	0	0	0	0	0	0
1992	53	5	0	0	0	0	0	0

Year	Rank	Starts	Wins	Poles	T5	T10	Races led	Laps led
1993	33	12	0	0	0	1	0	0
1994	17	27	0	3	1	7	3	99
1995	4	26	1	1	6	12	4	176
1996	6	26	0	0	3	10	1	1
1997	13	29	0	0	2	9	1	26
1998	16	31	0	0	2	8	1	1
1999	8	32	2	3	5	12	8	503
2000	2	32	1	0	13	19	6	104
2001	3	33	1	0	14	22	6	106
2002	2	34	4	2	17	22	15	785
2003	5	34	1	2	10	17	8	145
2004	6	34	0	0	6	12	2	60
2005	9	35	0	0	1	6	4	9
2006	41	10	0	0	0	0	1	1
Totals		401	10	11	80	157	60	2016

MATT KENSETH

Car: Ford • **Date of birth:** 3/10/72
Hometown: Cambridge, Wis. • **Owner/Team:** Jack Roush

CAREER STATISTICS

Year	Rank	Starts	Wins	Poles	T5	T10	Races led	Laps led
1996	101	1	0	0	0	0	0	0
1997	22	21	0	0	2	7	2	29
1998	2	31	3	1	17	23	10	437
1999	3	32	4	2	14	20	15	874
2000	17	20	4	2	10	17	12	331
2001	18	23	1	3	12	14	13	413
2002	77	4	0	0	1	2	0	0
2003	24	14	2	0	7	9	8	515
2004	25	16	3	0	8	11	9	443
2005	24	15	1	0	5	12	4	78
2006	18	21	3	4	15	18	16	798
Totals		198	21	12	91	133	89	3918

BRAD KESELOWSKI

Car: No. 23 Chevrolet • **Date of birth:** 2/12/84
Hometown: Rochester Hills, Mich. • **Owner/Team:** Keith Coleman

CAREER STATISTICS

Year	Rank	Starts	Wins	Poles	T5	T10	Races led	Laps led
2006	72	7	0	0	0	0	1	2
Totals		7	0	0	0	0	1	2

KRAIG KINSER

Car: Chevrolet • **Date of birth:** 10/8/84
Hometown: Bloomington, Ind. • **Owner/Team:** Ginn Racing
No career NASCAR Busch Series Statistics

TODD KLUEVER

Car: No. 16 Ford • **Date of birth:** 7/6/78
Hometown: Sun Prairie, Wis. • **Owner/Team:** Jack Roush

CAREER STATISTICS

Year	Rank	Starts	Wins	Poles	T5	T10	Races led	Laps led
2006	17	35	0	1	0	4	1	17
Totals		35	0	1	0	4	1	17

BOBBY LABONTE

Car: No. 77 Chevrolet • **Date of birth:** 5/8/64
Hometown: Corpus Christi, Texas • **Owner/Team:** Kevin Harvick Inc.

CAREER STATISTICS

Year	Rank	Starts	Wins	Poles	T5	T10	Races led	Laps led
1982	163	1	0	0	0	0	0	0
1985	68	2	0	0	0	0	0	0
1988	55	6	0	0	0	0	0	0
1989	41	7	0	0	1	3	0	0
1990	4	31	0	2	6	17	6	206
1991	1	31	2	2	10	21	10	299
1992	2	31	3	0	13	19	8	393
1993	62	2	0	1	1	1	1	153
1994	35	12	1	1	2	3	3	10
1996	19	16	1	3	9	13	7	208
1997	27	16	1	0	4	8	6	275
1998	54	5	1	1	2	3	3	40
1999	103	1	0	0	0	0	0	0
2004	68	3	0	0	0	1	1	13
2005	55	7	0	0	0	4	0	0
2006	54	7	0	0	0	2	0	0
Totals		178	9	10	48	95	45	1597

BURNEY LAMAR

Date of birth: 8/21/81
Hometown: West Sacramento, Calif.

CAREER STATISTICS

Year	Rank	Starts	Wins	Poles	T5	T10	Races led	Laps led
2005	110	2	0	0	0	0	0	0
2006	22	29	0	0	1	3	0	0
Totals		31	0	0	1	3	0	0

JASON LEFFLER

Car: No. 38 Toyota • **Date of birth:** 9/16/75
Hometown: Long Beach, Calif. • **Owner/Team:** Braun Racing

CAREER STATISTICS

Year	Rank	Starts	Wins	Poles	T5	T10	Races led	Laps led
1999	74	4	0	0	0	0	0	0
2000	20	31	0	3	2	4	3	47
2003	52	6	0	0	1	1	2	6
2004	12	27	1	1	8	17	6	115
2005	30	15	0	0	2	7	1	9
2006	13	35	0	2	3	7	6	199
Totals		118	1	6	16	36	18	376

STEPHEN LEICHT

Car: No. 90 Ford • **Date of birth:** 1/9/87
Hometown: Asheville, N.C. • **Owner/Team:** Robert Yates

CAREER STATISTICS

Year	Rank	Starts	Wins	Poles	T5	T10	Races led	Laps led
2005	86	2	0	0	0	0	0	0
2006	32	20	0	0	0	1	1	8
Totals		22	0	0	0	1	1	8

KEVIN LEPAGE

Date of birth: 6/26/62
Hometown: Shelburne, Vt.

CAREER STATISTICS

Year	Rank	Starts	Wins	Poles	T5	T10	Races led	Laps led
1986	88	1	0	0	0	0	0	0
1994	24	21	0	0	0	1	1	7
1995	18	22	0	0	0	5	1	4
1996	8	26	1	0	3	10	5	141
1997	12	30	0	0	3	6	3	102
1998	14	24	1	1	6	10	7	75
1999	35	14	0	0	2	6	1	24
2000	42	10	0	0	1	2	0	0
2001	31	16	0	1	1	4	3	105
2002	25	24	0	2	3	6	3	89
2004	42	11	0	0	0	0	0	0
2005	64	6	0	0	0	1	0	0
2006	65	7	0	0	0	0	0	0
Totals		212	2	4	19	51	24	547

ASHTON LEWIS JR.

Date of birth: 1/22/72
Hometown: Chesapeake, Va.

CAREER STATISTICS

Year	Rank	Starts	Wins	Poles	T5	T10	Races led	Laps led
1993	107	1	0	0	0	0	0	0
1994	93	1	0	0	0	0	0	0
1995	92	1	0	0	0	0	0	0
1998	53	8	0	0	1	1	1	3
2000	51	11	0	0	0	0	0	0
2001	20	32	0	0	2	3	0	0
2002	17	34	0	0	1	7	2	12
2003	12	34	0	1	2	10	2	45
2004	8	34	0	0	3	8	3	43
2005	14	35	0	0	1	5	3	12
2006	15	35	0	0	2	3	2	28
Totals		226	0	1	12	37	13	143

MARK MARTIN

Date of birth: 1/9/59
Hometown: Batesville, Ark.

CAREER STATISTICS

Year	Rank	Starts	Wins	Poles	T5	T10	Races led	Laps led
1982	162	1	0	0	0	0	0	0
1987	8	27	3	6	5	13	8	257
1988	29	13	1	0	2	6	1	5

Year	Rank	Starts	Wins	Poles	T5	T10	Races led	Laps led
1989	20	17	1	1	6	8	8	353
1990	32	12	1	0	3	5	3	216
1991	102	1	0	0	0	0	0	0
1992	21	14	1	2	5	9	9	429
1993	24	14	7	1	7	7	11	990
1994	20	15	3	3	8	11	14	1120
1995	22	15	3	1	9	11	11	851
1996	21	14	6	2	11	12	14	991
1997	24	15	6	3	10	12	11	598
1998	27	15	2	1	6	9	8	211
1999	26	14	6	3	9	10	12	746
2000	27	13	5	4	12	13	12	969
2004	56	5	0	0	1	4	1	4
2005	43	8	2	1	5	6	6	164
2006	44	7	0	2	5	5	3	98
Totals		220	47	30	104	141	132	8002

MATT McCALL

Date of birth: 7/31/81
Hometown: Denver, N.C.

CAREER STATISTICS

Year	Rank	Starts	Wins	Poles	T5	T10	Races led	Laps led
2006	79	5	0	0	0	0	0	0
Totals		5	0	0	0	0	0	0

ERIC McCLURE

Car: No. 0 Chevrolet • **Date of birth:** 12/11/78
Hometown: Chilhowie, Va. • **Owner/Team:** Davis Motorsports

CAREER STATISTICS

Year	Rank	Starts	Wins	Poles	T5	T10	Races led	Laps led
2003	130	1	0	0	0	0	0	0
2004	82	4	0	0	0	0	0	0
2005	72	8	0	0	0	0	0	0
2006	125	2	0	0	0	0	0	0
Totals		15	0	0	0	0	0	0

MARK McFARLAND

Date of birth: 2/1/78
Hometown: Winchester, Va.

CAREER STATISTICS

Year	Rank	Starts	Wins	Poles	T5	T10	Races led	Laps led
1998	69	4	0	0	0	0	0	0
2000	114	1	0	0	0	0	0	0
2001	103	1	0	0	0	0	0	0
2004	73	3	0	0	0	0	0	0
2005	148	1	0	0	0	0	0	0
2006	30	21	0	0	0	1	0	0
Totals		31	0	0	0	1	0	0

JAMIE MCMURRAY

Car: No. 37 Ford • **Date of birth:** 6/3/76
Hometown: Joplin, Mo. • **Owner/Team:** Brewco Motorsports

CAREER STATISTICS								
Year	Rank	Starts	Wins	Poles	T5	T10	Races led	Laps led
2000	93	2	0	0	0	0	0	0
2001	16	33	0	0	0	3	1	1
2002	6	34	2	0	6	14	9	87
2003	20	19	2	0	6	10	4	400
2004	32	14	3	1	6	8	6	170
2005	36	16	0	0	2	5	1	22
2006	25	20	0	0	4	8	7	106
Totals		138	7	1	24	48	28	786

CASEY MEARS

Date of birth: 3/12/78
Hometown: Bakersfield, Calif.

CAREER STATISTICS								
Year	Rank	Starts	Wins	Poles	T5	T10	Races led	Laps led
2001	114	1	0	0	0	0	0	0
2002	21	34	0	0	1	2	2	5
2003	34	14	0	1	1	4	1	2
2004	34	13	0	3	2	6	6	133
2005	116	1	0	0	0	0	0	0
2006	38	9	1	0	4	5	5	128
Totals		72	1	4	8	17	14	268

PAUL MENARD

Car: No. 11 Chevrolet • Date of birth: 8/21/80
Hometown: EauClaire, Wis. • Owner/Team: Dale Earnhardt Inc.

CAREER STATISTICS								
Year	Rank	Starts	Wins	Poles	T5	T10	Races led	Laps led
2003	60	6	0	0	0	1	0	0
2004	23	27	0	1	0	0	0	0
2005	6	35	0	1	6	15	10	188
2006	6	35	1	0	7	16	9	180
Totals		103	1	2	13	32	19	368

JUAN PABLO MONTOYA

Car: No. 42 Dodge • Date of birth: 9/20/75
Hometown: Bogota, Columbia • Owner/Team: Chip Ganassi

CAREER STATISTICS								
Year	Rank	Starts	Wins	Poles	T5	T10	Races led	Laps led
2006	68	4	0	0	0	0	1	1
Totals		4	0	0	0	0	1	1

DONNIE NEUENBERGER

Date of birth: 8/10/62
Hometown: Brandywine, Md.

CAREER STATISTICS								
Year	Rank	Starts	Wins	Poles	T5	T10	Races led	Laps led
2002	103	1	0	0	0	0	0	0
2003	74	6	0	0	0	0	0	0

Year	Rank	Starts	Wins	Poles	T5	T10	Races led	Laps led
2004	75	6	0	0	0	0	0	0
2005	101	3	0	0	0	0	0	0
2006	96	4	0	0	0	0	0	0
Totals		20	0	0	0	0	0	0

RYAN NEWMAN

Car: No. 39 Dodge • Date of birth: 12/8/77
Hometown: South Bend, Ind. • Owner/Team: Roger Penske

CAREER STATISTICS								
Year	Rank	Starts	Wins	Poles	T5	T10	Races led	Laps led
2001	28	15	1	6	2	8	8	416
2005	34	9	6	4	8	8	9	800
2006	60	6	0	1	2	3	4	121
Totals		30	7	11	12	19	21	1337

DANNY O'QUINN JR.

Date of birth: 5/7/85
Hometown: Coeburn, Va.

CAREER STATISTICS								
Year	Rank	Starts	Wins	Poles	T5	T10	Races led	Laps led
2006	19	33	0	0	1	5	0	0
Totals		33	0	0	1	5	0	0

MAX PAPIS

Date of birth: 10/3/69
Hometown: Como, Italy

CAREER STATISTICS								
Year	Rank	Starts	Wins	Poles	T5	T10	Races led	Laps led
2006	97	2	0	0	0	0	0	0
Totals		2	0	0	0	0	0	0

STEVE PARK

Date of birth: 8/23/67
Hometown: East Northport, N.Y.

CAREER STATISTICS								
Year	Rank	Starts	Wins	Poles	T5	T10	Races led	Laps led
1990	101	1	0	0	0	0	0	0
1995	109	1	0	0	0	0	0	0
1996	98	1	0	0	0	0	0	0
1997	3	30	3	1	12	20	14	477
2000	43	9	0	0	0	3	2	25
2001	46	7	0	0	2	5	1	40
2003	102	1	0	0	1	1	0	0
2006	77	6	0	0	0	0	0	0
Totals		56	3	1	15	29	17	542

TIMOTHY PETERS

Car: Chevrolet • Date of birth: 8/29/80
Hometown: Providence, N.C. • Owner/Team: Richard Childress

Year	Rank	Starts	Wins	Poles	T5	T10	Races led	Laps led
2006	105	1	0	0	0	0	0	0
Totals		1	0	0	0	0	0	0

DAVID RAGAN

Car: No. 6 Ford • **Date of birth:** 12/24/85
Hometown: Unadilla, Ga. • **Owner/Team:** Jack Roush

CAREER STATISTICS

Year	Rank	Starts	Wins	Poles	T5	T10	Races led	Laps led
2004	130	1	0	0	0	0	0	0
2005	97	3	0	0	0	0	0	0
2006	92	3	0	0	0	0	0	0
Totals		7	0	0	0	0	0	0

DAVID REUTIMANN

Car: No. 99 Toyota • **Date of birth:** 3/2/70
Hometown: Zephyrhills, Fla. • **Owner/Team:** Michael Waltrip

CAREER STATISTICS

Year	Rank	Starts	Wins	Poles	T5	T10	Races led	Laps led
2002	63	4	0	0	0	0	1	12
2003	50	7	0	0	2	3	1	22
2004	70	4	0	0	0	0	0	0
2005	118	1	0	0	0	0	0	0
2006	34	15	0	0	0	4	0	0
Totals		31	0	0	2	7	2	34

SCOTT RIGGS

Car: No. 9 Dodge • **Date of birth:** 1/1/71
Hometown: Bahama, N.C. • **Owner/Team:** Ray Evernham

CAREER STATISTICS

Year	Rank	Starts	Wins	Poles	T5	T10	Races led	Laps led
2002	10	34	2	2	8	13	12	415
2003	6	34	2	0	11	17	14	505
2005	111	1	0	0	0	0	0	0
2006	48	7	0	1	0	3	1	40
Totals		76	4	3	19	33	27	960

ELLIOTT SADLER

Car: No. 9 Dodge • **Date of birth:** 4/30/75
Hometown: Emporia, Va. • **Owner/Team:** Ray Evernham

CAREER STATISTICS

Year	Rank	Starts	Wins	Poles	T5	T10	Races led	Laps led
1995	70	2	0	0	0	1	0	0
1996	35	13	0	0	1	3	1	2
1997	5	30	3	4	6	10	9	317
1998	8	31	2	1	5	10	7	256
1999	36	15	0	0	1	3	2	34
2000	80	3	0	0	0	0	0	0
2003	144	1	0	0	0	0	0	0

Year	Rank	Starts	Wins	Poles	T5	T10	Races led	Laps led
2005	28	16	0	0	5	9	4	64
2006	63	7	0	0	0	0	0	0
Totals		118	5	5	18	36	23	673

JAY SAUTER

Date of birth: 6/22/62
Hometown: West Salem, Wis.

CAREER STATISTICS

Year	Rank	Starts	Wins	Poles	T5	T10	Races led	Laps led
1997	86	1	0	0	0	0	0	0
2000	16	31	0	0	1	8	3	25
2001	19	31	0	1	2	7	2	13
2002	36	14	0	0	1	4	4	47

Year	Rank	Starts	Wins	Poles	T5	T10	Races led	Laps led
2003	49	10	0	0	0	1	1	2
2004	63	6	0	0	0	0	0	0
2005	139	1	0	0	0	0	0	0
2006	21	33	0	0	0	3	1	6
Totals		127	0	1	4	23	11	93

Year	Rank	Starts	Wins	Poles	T5	T10	Races led	Laps led
2003	8	34	1	0	6	14	10	231
2004	18	34	0	1	4	8	7	193
2005	12	35	1	1	5	11	8	326
2006	8	35	0	1	2	9	1	85
Totals		176	3	4	21	49	32	934

JOHNNY SAUTER

Car: No. 00 Chevrolet • **Date of birth:** 5/01/78
Hometown: Necedah, Wis. • **Owner/Team:** Gene Haas

CAREER STATISTICS								
Year	Rank	Starts	Wins	Poles	T5	T10	Races led	Laps led
2001	55	5	0	0	1	1	1	13
2002	15	33	1	1	3	6	5	86

TIM SAUTER

Date of birth: 10/13/64
Hometown: Necedah, Wis.

CAREER STATISTICS								
Year	Rank	Starts	Wins	Poles	T5	T10	Races led	Laps led
2000	73	3	0	0	0	0	0	0
2001	32	18	0	0	0	2	0	0

Year	Rank	Starts	Wins	Poles	T5	T10	Races led	Laps led
2002	13	34	0	0	0	7	4	12
2003	46	12	0	0	0	0	1	4
2004	79	4	0	0	0	0	0	0
2005	49	12	0	0	0	0	0	0
2006	27	28	0	0	0	0	2	7
Totals		111	0	0	0	9	7	23

REGAN SMITH

Car: Chevrolet • **Date of birth:** 9/23/83
Hometown: Cato, N.Y. • **Owner/Team:** Ginn Racing

CAREER STATISTICS

Year	Rank	Starts	Wins	Poles	T5	T10	Races led	Laps led
2002	118	1	0	0	0	0	0	0
2003	38	18	0	0	0	0	0	0
2004	45	10	0	0	0	0	0	0
2005	33	21	0	0	0	0	1	5
2006	20	35	0	0	0	1	2	6
Totals		85	0	0	0	1	3	11

REED SORENSON

Car: No. 41 Dodge • **Date of birth:** 2/5/86
Hometown: Peachtree City, Ga. • **Owner/Team:** Chip Ganassi

CAREER STATISTICS

Year	Rank	Starts	Wins	Poles	T5	T10	Races led	Laps led
2004	52	5	0	0	1	3	1	47
2005	4	35	2	2	12	19	12	403
2006	10	34	0	0	5	14	4	31
Totals		74	2	2	18	36	17	481

TONY STEWART

Car: Chevrolet • **Date of birth:** 5/20/71 • **Hometown:** Rushville, Ind.
Owner/Team: Joe Gibbs, Kevin Harvick Inc.

CAREER STATISTICS

Year	Rank	Starts	Wins	Poles	T5	T10	Races led	Laps led
1996	49	9	0	0	0	0	0	0
1997	58	5	0	0	1	2	0	0
1998	21	22	0	2	5	5	6	157
2003	109	1	0	0	0	0	1	86
2004	58	4	0	0	2	2	3	129
2005	39	12	1	2	4	4	6	132
2006	37	12	1	0	3	5	6	89
Totals		65	2	4	15	18	22	593

DAVID STREMME

Car: No. 41 Dodge • **Date of birth:** 6/19/77
Hometown: South Bend, Ind. • **Owner/Team:** Chip Ganassi

CAREER STATISTICS

Year	Rank	Starts	Wins	Poles	T5	T10	Races led	Laps led
2003	22	18	0	0	3	7	6	86
2004	10	34	0	1	5	14	1	75
2005	13	35	0	0	5	10	6	120

Year	Rank	Starts	Wins	Poles	T5	T10	Races led	Laps led
2006	118	1	0	0	0	0	0	0
Totals		88	0	1	13	31	13	281

PAUL TRACY

Date of birth: 12/17/68
Hometown: Scarborough, Ontario

CAREER STATISTICS

Year	Rank	Starts	Wins	Poles	T5	T10	Races led	Laps led
2006	76	6	0	0	0	0	0	0
Totals		6	0	0	0	0	0	0

MARTIN TRUEX JR.

Car: Chevrolet • **Date of birth:** 6/29/80
Hometown: Mayetta, N.J. • **Owner/Team:** Dale Earnhardt Inc.

CAREER STATISTICS

Year	Rank	Starts	Wins	Poles	T5	T10	Races led	Laps led
2001	133	1	0	0	0	0	0	0
2002	65	4	0	0	0	0	0	0
2003	40	10	0	0	2	3	1	11
2004	1	34	6	7	17	26	21	954
2005	1	35	6	3	15	22	19	705
2006	50	6	1	0	2	4	2	113
Totals		90	13	10	36	55	43	1783

AUGGIE VIDOVICH

Car: No. 4 Toyota • **Date of birth:** 2/20/81
Hometown: Lakeside, Calif. • **Owner/Team:** Biagi-DenBeste Racing

CAREER STATISTICS

Year	Rank	Starts	Wins	Poles	T5	T10	Races led	Laps led
2006	33	21	0	0	0	0	1	3
Totals		21	0	0	0	0	1	3

MIKE WALLACE

Car: No. 7 Chevrolet • **Date of birth:** 3/10/59
Hometown: St. Louis • **Owner/Team:** James Finch

CAREER STATISTICS

Year	Rank	Starts	Wins	Poles	T5	T10	Races led	Laps led
1990	82	1	0	0	0	1	0	0
1991	39	9	0	0	1	2	1	4
1992	22	17	0	0	1	3	1	110
1993	12	28	0	0	1	9	1	4
1994	19	22	3	0	6	9	7	338
1995	20	19	0	0	4	9	8	148
1996	26	17	0	0	2	5	0	0
1997	59	6	0	0	0	0	0	0
1998	57	6	0	0	0	1	0	0
1999	136	1	0	0	0	0	0	0
2000	59	8	0	0	0	0	0	0
2001	50	8	0	0	0	1	0	0
2002	37	17	0	0	0	0	2	10

Year	Rank	Starts	Wins	Poles	T5	T10	Races led	Laps led
2003	13	32	0	0	1	3	0	0
2004	17	34	1	0	1	4	8	33
2005	40	12	0	0	1	3	1	5
2006	24	23	0	0	2	3	3	35
Totals		260	4	0	20	53	32	687

STEVE WALLACE

Car: No. 66 Dodge • **Date of birth:** 8/18/87
Hometown: Greensboro, N.C. • **Owner/Team:** Rusty Wallace

CAREER STATISTICS

Year	Rank	Starts	Wins	Poles	T5	T10	Races led	Laps led
2005	105	1	0	0	0	0	0	0
2006	36	17	0	0	0	0	1	3
Totals		18	0	0	0	0	1	3

MICHAEL WALTRIP

Car: Toyota • **Date of birth:** 4/30/63
Hometown: Owensboro, Ky. • **Owner/Team:** Michael Waltrip

CAREER STATISTICS

Year	Rank	Starts	Wins	Poles	T5	T10	Races led	Laps led
1988	41	5	1	0	2	2	2	44
1989	22	14	1	4	5	8	6	201
1990	30	13	2	2	4	4	5	306
1991	34	10	0	0	5	5	5	75
1992	26	11	1	1	3	6	4	83
1993	30	10	2	0	4	5	8	194
1994	41	9	0	1	2	4	5	47
1995	48	6	0	1	2	2	3	56
1996	34	13	0	1	3	3	5	66
1997	29	16	0	1	4	5	5	36
1998	34	15	0	0	1	6	2	29
1999	29	15	1	0	3	7	2	27
2000	37	12	0	0	2	4	2	19
2001	41	12	0	0	1	3	1	55
2002	27	19	1	2	6	11	9	389
2003	18	20	1	2	8	13	9	419
2004	13	31	1	0	3	9	9	79
2005	35	17	0	0	0	4	1	24
2006	26	21	0	0	1	3	4	28
Totals		269	11	15	59	104	87	2177

SCOTT WIMMER

Car: No. 29 Chevrolet • **Date of birth:** 1/26/76
Hometown: Wausau, Wis. • **Owner/Team:** Richard Childress

CAREER STATISTICS

Year	Rank	Starts	Wins	Poles	T5	T10	Races led	Laps led
2000	78	3	0	0	0	0	1	2
2001	11	33	0	0	2	8	6	53
2002	3	34	4	0	11	17	7	191
2003	9	34	1	0	4	12	6	133
2006	29	19	0	0	0	4	3	28
Totals		123	5	0	17	41	23	407

JON WOOD

Car: No. 47 Ford • **Date of birth:** 10/25/81
Hometown: Stuart, Va. • **Owner/Team:** ST Motorsports

CAREER STATISTICS

Year	Rank	Starts	Wins	Poles	T5	T10	Races led	Laps led
2002	88	1	0	0	0	1	0	0
2003	122	1	0	0	0	0	0	0
2005	15	35	0	0	2	6	1	1
2006	14	35	0	0	1	4	1	2
Totals		72	0	0	3	11	2	3

J.J. YELEY

Car: No. 1 Chevrolet • **Date of birth:** 10/5/76
Hometown: Phoenix • **Owner/Team:** Phoenix Racing

CAREER STATISTICS

Year	Rank	Starts	Wins	Poles	T5	T10	Races led	Laps led
2004	30	17	0	0	0	4	2	42
2005	11	35	0	0	4	12	5	100
2006	5	35	0	3	9	22	8	86
Totals		87	0	3	13	38	15	228

Yeley

>>2006 POINTS STANDINGS <<

NASCAR Busch Series

Pos.	Driver	Points	Behind	Starts	Wins	Top 5	Top 10	DNFs	Poles	Money won
1.	Kevin Harvick	5,648	—	35	9	23	32	0	1	$2,850,864
2.	Carl Edwards	4,824	-824	35	4	15	25	3	3	$1,878,844
3.	Clint Bowyer	4,683	-965	35	1	12	17	0	2	$1,715,649
4.	Denny Hamlin	4,667	-981	35	2	12	23	1	6	$1,757,309
5.	J.J. Yeley	4,487	-1,161	35	0	9	22	3	3	$1,504,366
6.	Paul Menard	4,075	-1,573	35	1	7	16	5	0	$1,723,218
7.	Kyle Busch	3,921	-1,727	34	1	4	12	4	2	$1,182,182
8.	Johnny Sauter	3,794	-1,854	35	0	2	9	2	1	$1,561,164
9.	Greg Biffle	3,789	-1,859	30	1	9	18	4	0	$928,356
10.	Reed Sorenson	3,670	-1,978	34	0	5	14	9	0	$1,068,468
11.	Kenny Wallace	3,626	-2,022	35	0	0	4	2	0	$1,122,350
12.	John Andretti*	3,562	-2,086	35	0	1	4	1	0	$1,113,596
13.	Jason Leffler	3,554	-2,094	35	0	3	7	8	2	$1,182,579
14.	Jon Wood	3,381	-2,267	35	0	1	4	5	0	$1,025,040
15.	Ashton Lewis Jr.	3,376	-2,272	35	0	2	3	2	0	$1,005,295
16.	Stacy Compton	3,339	-2,309	35	0	1	2	3	0	$1,005,566
17.	Todd Kluever*	3,304	-2,344	35	0	0	4	7	1	$980,632
18.	Matt Kenseth	3,221	-2,427	21	3	15	18	1	4	$835,166
19.	Danny O'Quinn Jr.*	3,163	-2,485	33	0	1	5	3	0	$931,506
20.	Regan Smith	3,136	-2,512	35	0	0	1	4	0	$953,682
21.	Jay Sauter	2,879	-2,769	33	0	0	3	7	0	$776,565
22.	Burney Lamar*	2,710	-2,938	29	0	1	3	6	0	$925,969
23.	David Green	2,573	-3,075	27	0	0	2	1	0	$915,223
24.	Mike Wallace	2,479	-3,169	23	0	2	3	1	0	$755,183
25.	Jamie McMurray	2,297	-3,351	20	0	4	8	5	0	$522,060
26.	Michael Waltrip	2,126	-3,522	21	0	1	3	3	0	$570,535
27.	Tim Sauter	2,109	-3,539	28	0	0	0	5	0	$662,833
28.	Jeff Burton	2,040	-3,608	16	2	7	10	5	1	$558,650
29.	Scott Wimmer	2,002	-3,646	19	0	0	4	2	0	$505,593
30.	Mark McFarland*	1,975	-3,673	21	0	0	1	1	0	$565,624
31.	Kasey Kahne	1,954	-3,694	17	2	4	6	4	0	$593,892
32.	Stephen Leicht*	1,790	-3,858	20	0	0	1	2	0	$449,048
33.	Auggie Vidovich	1,628	-4,020	21	0	0	0	4	0	$533,398
34.	David Reutimann	1,598	-4,050	15	0	0	4	3	0	$394,878
35.	Ron Hornaday Jr.	1,536	-4,112	14	0	3	5	1	0	$389,366
36.	Steve Wallace	1,528	-4,120	17	0	0	0	0	0	$375,487
37.	Tony Stewart	1,461	-4,187	12	1	3	5	2	0	$427,052
38.	Casey Mears	1,200	-4,448	9	1	4	5	2	0	$290,430
39.	Kurt Busch	1,160	-4,488	7	2	5	6	0	1	$236,250
40.	Kertus Davis	1,119	-4,529	22	0	0	0	15	0	$418,390
41.	Jason Keller	1,116	-4,532	10	0	0	0	0	0	$373,410
42.	Brian Vickers	1,062	-4,586	8	0	2	4	1	0	$239,895
43.	Aaron Fike	1,004	-4,644	15	0	0	0	4	0	$383,644
44.	Mark Martin	973	-4,675	7	0	5	5	1	2	$192,215
45.	Mark Green	934	-4,714	11	0	0	1	2	0	$320,586
46.	Mike Skinner	874	-4,774	9	0	0	1	1	0	$170,795
47.	Dave Blaney	854	-4,794	7	1	1	2	1	0	$179,020
48.	Scott Riggs	850	-4,798	7	0	0	3	1	1	$163,020
49.	Shane Huffman	841	-4,807	10	0	1	2	3	0	$241,982
50.	Martin Truex Jr.	835	-4,813	6	1	2	4	1	0	$166,007
51.	Aric Almirola	833	-4,815	9	0	0	0	2	1	$163,700
52.	Casey Atwood	814	-4,834	8	0	0	0	0	0	$223,084
53.	Dale Earnhardt Jr	761	-4,887	5	2	2	3	0	0	$221,580
54.	Bobby Labonte	755	-4,893	7	0	0	2	0	0	$177,684
55.	Tracy Hines*	752	-4,896	11	0	0	0	3	0	$263,777
56.	David Gilliland*	733	-4,915	9	1	1	1	3	0	$258,175
57.	Joel Kauffman*	716	-4,932	11	0	0	0	2	0	$238,789
58.	Boris Said	663	-4,985	6	0	1	2	1	1	$203,361
59.	Ken Schrader	662	-4,986	8	0	0	0	0	0	$197,127
60.	Ryan Newman	659	-4,989	6	0	2	3	2	1	$140,850
61.	Stanton Barrett	606	-5,042	9	0	0	0	3	0	$159,125
62.	Mike Bliss	596	-5,052	8	0	0	0	2	0	$158,960
63.	Elliott Sadler	550	-5,098	7	0	0	0	0	0	$146,490
64.	Robby Gordon	526	-5,122	4	0	2	3	1	0	$114,174
65.	Kevin Lepage	523	-5,125	7	0	0	0	3	0	$141,841
66.	Jerry Robertson	477	-5,171	9	0	0	0	5	0	$159,920
67.	Erin Crocker	474	-5,174	6	0	0	0	1	0	$139,736
68.	Juan Pablo Montoya	438	-5,210	4	0	0	0	0	0	$79,205
69.	Carlos Contreras	437	-5,211	6	0	0	0	1	0	$144,665
70.	Shane Hall	422	-5,226	9	0	0	0	7	0	$153,184
71.	Ted Musgrave	418	-5,230	5	0	0	0	0	0	$87,040
72.	Brad Keselowski	414	-5,234	7	0	0	0	3	0	$127,055
73.	Kevin Grubb	413	-5,235	5	0	0	1	1	0	$100,017
74.	A.J. Foyt IV*	400	-5,248	7	0	0	0	2	0	$237,835

#	Name									
75.	P.J. Jones	376	-5,272	5	0	0	0	1	0	$101,367
76.	Paul Tracy	372	-5,276	6	0	0	0	2	0	$183,120
77.	Steve Park	351	-5,297	6	0	0	0	3	0	$102,450
78.	Chris Cook	316	-5,332	4	0	0	0	0	0	$96,920
79.	Matt McCall	314	-5,334	5	0	0	0	1	0	$93,505
80.	Justin Diercks	311	-5,337	7	0	0	0	2	0	$120,852
81.	Cale Gale	309	-5,339	4	0	0	0	1	0	$110,002
82.	Jorge Goeters*	295	-5,353	4	0	0	0	2	0	$100,552
83.	Derrike Cope	287	-5,361	5	0	0	0	3	0	$65,900
84.	Jimmie Johnson	283	-5,365	3	0	0	1	1	0	$58,935
85.	Steadman Marlin	281	-5,367	5	0	0	0	4	0	$116,710
86.	Kevin Conway*	253	-5,395	4	0	0	0	1	0	$74,231
87.	Adrian Fernandez	239	-5,409	2	0	0	0	0	0	$57,800
88.	Jason White	229	-5,419	4	0	0	0	3	0	$70,555
89.	Carl Long	224	-5,424	5	0	0	0	4	0	$84,533
90.	Chad Chaffin	216	-5,432	3	0	0	0	0	0	$48,150
91.	Michel Jourdain Jr.	214	-5,434	3	0	0	0	2	0	$76,515
92.	David Ragan	204	-5,444	3	0	0	0	2	0	$56,555
93.	David Odell	204	-5,444	3	0	0	0	1	0	$51,720
94.	Ron Fellows	202	-5,446	2	0	0	1	1	0	$65,692
95.	Morgan Shepherd	194	-5,454	6	0	0	0	6	0	$91,551
96.	Donnie Neuenberger	180	-5,468	4	0	0	0	1	0	$103,855
97.	Max Papis	164	-5,484	2	0	0	0	1	0	$34,060
98.	Steve Grissom	148	-5,500	2	0	0	0	1	0	$72,136
99.	Marc Goossens	143	-5,505	1	0	0	1	0	0	$46,000
100.	Brent Sherman	140	-5,508	2	0	0	0	0	0	$43,420
101.	Randy LaJoie	138	-5,510	3	0	0	0	3	0	$73,695
102.	Joe Nemechek	137	-5,511	2	0	0	0	1	0	$64,695
103.	Willie Allen	137	-5,511	2	0	0	0	1	0	$39,965
104.	Scott Pruett	134	-5,514	1	0	0	1	0	0	$29,520
105.	Timothy Peters	124	-5,524	1	0	0	0	0	0	$21,400
106.	Chris Wimmer*	123	-5,525	3	0	0	0	3	0	$48,196
107.	Jeff Fuller	122	-5,526	2	0	0	0	1	0	$33,050
108.	Brad Coleman	116	-5,532	2	0	0	0	1	0	$39,887
109.	Peyton Sellers	116	-5,532	2	0	0	0	1	0	$32,455
110.	Ron Young	110	-5,538	2	0	0	0	1	0	$39,975
111.	Todd Bodine	107	-5,541	2	0	0	0	1	0	$40,615
112.	Chris Horn	101	-5,547	3	0	0	0	3	0	$50,765
113.	Brian Simo	97	-5,551	1	0	0	0	0	0	$17,500
114.	Jeff Green	97	-5,551	1	0	0	0	0	0	$17,050
115.	Justin Labonte	97	-5,551	1	0	0	0	0	0	$25,515
116.	Butch Leitzinger	91	-5,557	1	0	0	0	0	0	$15,350
117.	Sam Hornish Jr.	89	-5,559	2	0	0	0	2	0	$42,679
118.	David Stremme	85	-5,563	1	0	0	0	0	0	$20,457
119.	Matt Kobyluck	83	-5,565	2	0	0	0	2	0	$29,700
120.	Kevin Hamlin	82	-5,566	1	0	0	0	0	0	$28,150
121.	D.J. Kennington	82	-5,566	1	0	0	0	0	0	$17,475
122.	Darrell Waltrip	79	-5,569	1	0	0	0	0	0	$23,858
123.	Rogelio Lopez	76	-5,572	1	0	0	0	0	0	$40,400
124.	Ryan Moore	76	-5,572	1	0	0	0	0	0	$16,700
125.	Eric McClure	74	-5,574	2	0	0	0	2	0	$37,133
126.	Brad Baker	73	-5,575	1	0	0	0	0	0	$17,200
127.	Patrick Goeters	70	-5,578	1	0	0	0	0	0	$42,285
128.	Dwayne Leik	67	-5,581	1	0	0	0	0	0	$20,025
129.	Dexter Bean	67	-5,581	1	0	0	0	0	0	$17,290
130.	Caleb Holman	64	-5,584	1	0	0	0	0	0	$14,390
131.	Jeremy Mayfield	63	-5,585	1	0	0	0	0	0	$26,812
132.	Spencer Clark	58	-5,590	1	0	0	0	0	0	$21,540
133.	Jamie Mosley	58	-5,590	1	0	0	0	0	0	$17,535
134.	Joey Miller	55	-5,593	1	0	0	0	0	0	$21,958
135.	Chase Pistone	52	-5,596	1	0	0	0	1	0	$17,970
136.	Randy MacDonald	49	-5,599	3	0	0	0	2	0	$48,118
137.	Brad Teague	49	-5,599	1	0	0	0	1	0	$13,835
138.	Jimmy Morales	46	-5,602	1	0	0	0	1	0	$39,970
139.	Ricky Craven	46	-5,602	1	0	0	0	1	0	$17,800
140.	Kim Crosby	43	-5,605	1	0	0	0	1	0	$13,715
141.	Shelby Howard	43	-5,605	1	0	0	0	1	0	$16,985
142.	James Hylton	40	-5,608	1	0	0	0	1	0	$13,680
143.	Carlos Pardo	37	-5,611	1	0	0	0	1	0	$41,730
144.	Justin Ashburn	37	-5,611	1	0	0	0	1	0	$17,595
145.	Jeff Spraker	37	-5,611	1	0	0	0	1	0	$19,415
146.	Sean Caisse	37	-5,611	1	0	0	0	1	0	$19,664
147.	Josh Richeson	34	-5,614	1	0	0	0	1	0	$21,482
148.	Jennifer Cobb	34	-5,614	1	0	0	0	1	0	$20,896
149.	Brian Keselowski	34	-5,614	1	0	0	0	1	0	$19,463
150.	Tim Schendel	34	-5,614	1	0	0	0	1	0	$16,828
151.	Scott Lynch	34	-5,614	1	0	0	0	1	0	$14,900
152.	John Hayden	0	-5,648	1	0	0	0	1	0	$14,450
153.	Jerick Johnson	0	-5,648	1	0	0	0	1	0	$13,870
154.	Joey McCarthy	0	-5,648	1	0	0	0	1	0	$15,045

*Rookie

>>> 2006 RACE RESULTS <<<

NASCAR Busch Series

No.	Date	Race	Track	Winner	Pole
1.	February 18	Hershey's Kissables 300	Daytona International Speedway	Tony Stewart	J.J. Yeley
2.	February 25	Stater Bros. 300	California Speedway	Greg Biffle	Carl Edwards
3.	March 5	Telcel-Motorola 200 presented by Banamex	Autodromo Hermanos Rodriguez	Denny Hamlin	Boris Said
4.	March 11	Sam's Town 300	Las Vegas Motor Speedway	Kasey Kahne	Matt Kenseth
5.	March 18	Nicorette 300	Atlanta Motor Speedway	Jeff Burton	Kyle Busch
6.	March 25	Sharpie Mini 300	Bristol Motor Speedway	Kyle Busch	Kevin Harvick
7.	April 8	O'Reilly 300	Texas Motor Speedway	Kurt Busch	Denny Hamlin
8.	April 15	Pepsi 300	Nashville Superspeedway	Kevin Harvick	Denny Hamlin
9.	April 21	Bashas' Supermarkets 200	Phoenix International Raceway	Kevin Harvick	Jason Leffler
10.	April 29	Aaron's 312	Talladega Superspeedway	Martin Truex Jr.	J.J. Yeley
11.	May 5	Circuit City 250 presented by FUNAI	Richmond International Raceway	Kevin Harvick	Jason Leffler
12.	May 12	Diamond Hill Plywood 200	Darlington Raceway	Denny Hamlin	Denny Hamlin
13.	May 27	Carquest Auto Parts 300	Lowe's Motor Speedway	Carl Edwards	Matt Kenseth
14.	June 3	Stonebridgeracing.com 200	Dover International Speedway	Jeff Burton	Kevin Harvick
15.	June 10	Federated Auto Parts 300	Nashville Superspeedway	Carl Edwards	Todd Kluever
16.	June 17	Meijer 300 presented by Oreo	Kentucky Speedway	David Gilliland	Denny Hamlin
17.	June 24	AT&T 250	The Milwaukee Mile	Paul Menard	Aric Almirola
18.	June 30	Winn-Dixie 250 presented by PepsiCo	Daytona International Speedway	Dale Earnhardt Jr.	J.J. Yeley
19.	July 8	USG Durock 300	Chicagoland Speedway	Casey Mears	Carl Edwards
20.	July 15	New England 200	New Hampshire International Speedway	Carl Edwards	Kyle Busch
21.	July 22	Goody's 250	Martinsville Raceway	Kevin Harvick	Clint Bowyer
22.	July 29	Busch Silver Celebration 250 presented by Shop and Save	Gateway International Raceway	Carl Edwards	Denny Hamlin
23.	August 5	Kroger 200 benefiting Riley Hospital for Children	O'Reilly Raceway Park	Kevin Harvick	Denny Hamlin
24.	August 12	Zippo 200	Watkins Glen International	Kurt Busch	Kurt Busch
25.	August 19	Carfax 250	Michigan International Speedway	Dale Earnhardt Jr.	Mark Martin
26.	August 25	Food City 250	Bristol Motor Speedway	Matt Kenseth	Ryan Newman
27.	September 2	Ameriquest 300	California Speedway	Kasey Kahne	Clint Bowyer
28.	September 8	Emerson Radio 250	Richmond International Raceway	Kevin Harvick	Jeff Burton
29.	September 23	Dover 200	Dover International Speedway	Clint Bowyer	Scott Riggs
30.	September 30	Yellow Transportation 300	Kansas Speedway	Kevin Harvick	Matt Kenseth
31.	October 13	Dollar General 300	Lowe's Motor Speedway	Dave Blaney	Carl Edwards
32.	October 28	Sam's Town 250	Memphis Motorsports Park	Kevin Harvick	Johnny Sauter
33.	November 4	O'Reilly Challenge	Texas Motor Speedway	Kevin Harvick	Mark Martin
34.	November 11	Arizona Travel 200	Phoenix International Raceway	Matt Kenseth	Matt Kenseth
35.	November 18	Ford 300	Homestead-Miami Speedway	Matt Kenseth	Kevin Harvick

Paul Menard

⭐ 21 KEVIN HARVICK

Car: No. 21 Chevrolet • **Car owner:** Richard Childress
Birth date: December 8, 1975 • **Hometown:** Bakersfield, Calif.

NASCAR Busch Series Statistics

Seasons competed: 8 (1999-2006)
Career starts: 166   **Career wins:** 26   **Career poles:** 14

2006 championship season recap: Harvick arguably had the most successful NASCAR Busch Series season ever in 2006. He broke Sam Ard's record for most top 10s in a season with 32, and he came one win short of tying Ard's record for most wins in a season. The points race wasn't even close; Harvick jumped to the top of the standings after the season's second race and never fell, finishing 824 points ahead of second-place finisher Carl Edwards. It was the largest margin of victory in NASCAR Busch Series history.

2006 CHAMPIONSHIP LINESCORE

Starts	Wins	Poles	Top 5	Top 10	Races Led	Laps Led	DNF
35	9	1	23	32	20	1,197	0

KEVIN HARVICK 2006 RACE BY RACE

No.	Race	Start	Finish	Points	Rank	Laps/ Completed	Money won	Status
1.	Hershey's Kissables 300	17	5	155	5	120/120	$58,875	Running
2.	Stater Bros. 300	28	8	147	1	150/150	$27,300	Running
3.	Telcel-Motorola 200	11	3	165	1	80/80	$61,125	Running
4.	Sam's Town 300	4	3	175	1	206/206	$51,225	Running
5.	Nicorette 300	30	11	130	1	195/195	$17,125	Running
6.	Sharpie Mini 300	1	2	180	1	300/300	$38,675	Running
7.	O'Reilly 300	21	8	147	1	206/206	$25,025	Running
8.	Pepsi 300	7	1	185	1	225/225	$43,875	Running
9.	Bashas' Supermarkets 200	14	1	185	1	206/206	$67,450	Running
10.	Aaron's 312	19	2	170	1	117/117	$38,425	Running
11.	Circuit City 250	10	1	185	1	250/250	$38,725	Running
12.	Diamond Hill Plywood 200	17	7	146	1	147/147	$15,985	Running
13.	Carquest Auto Parts 300	5	8	147	1	200/200	$20,800	Running
14.	StonebridgeRacing.com 200	1	13	129	1	200/200	$16,150	Running
15.	Federated Auto Parts 300	12	3	165	1	225/225	$28,250	Running
16.	Meijer 300	13	6	155	1	200/200	$26,625	Running
17.	AT&T 250	18	19	106	1	258/258	$16,150	Running
18.	Winn-Dixie 250	42	3	165	1	103/103	$46,125	Running
19.	USG Durock 300	9	4	160	1	200/200	$36,850	Running
20.	New England 200	4	2	170	1	200/200	$33,850	Running
21.	Goody's 250	6	1	190	1	250/250	$74,925	Running
22.	Busch Silver Celebration 250	3	5	155	1	200/200	$29,725	Running
23.	Kroger 200	6	1	190	1	200/200	$42,075	Running
24.	Zippo 200	3	7	151	1	83/83	$17,800	Running
25.	Carfax 250	9	8	142	1	128/128	$18,570	Running
26.	Food City 250	30	2	175	1	250/250	$36,625	Running
27.	Ameriquest 300	3	2	175	1	150/150	$62,850	Running
28.	Emerson Radio 250	5	1	190	1	250/250	$39,025	Running
29.	Dover 200	24	3	165	1	202/202	$24,250	Running
30.	Yellow Transportation 300	7	1	185	1	200/200	$78,800	Running
31.	Dollar General 300	8	9	138	1	202/203	$20,150	Running
32.	Sam's Town 250	5	1	185	1	252/252	$53,150	Running
33.	O'Reilly Challenge	4	1	190	1	200/200	$65,625	Running
34.	Arizona Travel 200	6	2	170	1	203/203	$39,475	Running
35.	Ford 300	1	6	155	1	200/200	$34,075	Running

>>SERIES CHAMPIONS <<

NASCAR Busch Series

The NASCAR Busch Series started in 1982, but the circuit's roots date back more than five decades. Originally formed as the NASCAR Sportsman Division in 1950, the series competed until 1968 under that name before becoming the NASCAR Late Model Sportsman Division. Fourteen years later, Anheuser-Busch, Inc. joined with NASCAR to create what is now known as the NASCAR Busch Series.

ALL-TIME TITLE WINNERS

1950: Mike Klapak *	**1962:** Rene Charland	**1974:** Jack Ingram	**1986:** Larry Pearson	**1998:** Dale Earnhardt Jr.
1951: Mike Klapak	**1963:** Rene Charland	**1975:** L.D. Ottinger	**1987:** Larry Pearson	**1999:** Dale Earnhardt Jr.
1952: Mike Klapak	**1964:** Rene Charland	**1976:** L.D. Ottinger	**1988:** Tommy Ellis	**2000:** Jeff Green
1953: Johnny Roberts	**1965:** Rene Charland	**1977:** Butch Lindley	**1989:** Rob Moroso	**2001:** Kevin Harvick
1954: Danny Graves	**1966:** Don MacTavish	**1978:** Butch Lindley	**1990:** Chuck Bown	**2002:** Greg Biffle
1955: Billy Myers	**1967:** Pete Hamilton	**1979:** Gene Glover	**1991:** Bobby Labonte	**2003:** Brian Vickers ^
1956: Ralph Earnhardt	**1968:** Joe Thurman †	**1980:** Morgan Shepherd	**1992:** Joe Nemechek	**2004:** Martin Truex Jr.
1957: Ned Jarrett	**1969:** Red Farmer	**1981:** Tommy Ellis	**1993:** Steve Grissom	**2005:** Martin Truex Jr.
1958: Ned Jarrett	**1970:** Red Farmer	**1982:** Jack Ingram ‡	**1994:** David Green	**2006:** Kevin Harvick
1959: Rick Henderson	**1971:** Red Farmer	**1983:** Sam Ard	**1995:** Johnny Benson §	
1960: Bill Wimble	**1972:** Jack Ingram	**1984:** Sam Ard ∞	**1996:** Randy LaJoie	
1961: Dick Nephew	**1973:** Jack Ingram	**1985:** Jack Ingram	**1997:** Randy LaJoie	

*   NASCAR Sportsman Division was formed in 1950
†   Series changed name to NASCAR Late Model Sportsman Division in 1968
‡   Series changed name to NASCAR Budweiser Late Model Sportsman Series in 1982
∞   Series changed name to NASCAR Busch Grand National Series in 1984
§   Series changed name to NASCAR Busch Series, Grand National Division in 1995
^   Series changed name to NASCAR Busch Series in 2003

>>SEASON BY SEASON CHAMPIONS <<

NASCAR Busch Series

Year	No.	Driver	Owner	Make	Wins	Poles	Winnings	Runner-up	Points behind
1982	11	Jack Ingram	Aline Ingram	Olds./Pont.	7	1	$122,100	Sam Ard	49
1983	00	Sam Ard	Howard Thomas	Oldsmobile	10	10	$192,362	Jack Ingram	87
1984	00	Sam Ard	Howard Thomas	Oldsmobile	8	7	$217,531	Jack Ingram	426
1985	11	Jack Ingram	Aline Ingram	Pontiac	5	2	$164,710	Jimmy Hensley	29
1986	21	Larry Pearson	David Pearson	Pontiac	1	1	$184,344	Brett Bodine	20
1987	21	Larry Pearson	David Pearson	Chevrolet	6	3	$256,372	Jimmy Hensley	382
1988	99	Tommy Ellis	John Jackson	Buick	3	5	$200,003	Rob Moroso	239
1989	25	Rob Moroso	Dick Moroso	Oldsmobile	4	6	$346,739	Tommy Houston	55
1990	63	Chuck Bown	Hubert Hensley	Pontiac	6	4	$323,399	Jimmy Hensley	200
1991	44	Bobby Labonte	Bobby Labonte	Oldsmobile	2	2	$246,368	Kenny Wallace	74
1992	87	Joe Nemechek	Joe Nemechek	Chevrolet	2	1	$285,008	Bobby Labonte	3
1993	31	Steve Grissom	Wayne Grissom	Chevrolet	2	0	$336,432	Ricky Craven	253
1994	44	David Green	Bobby Labonte	Chevrolet	1	9	$391,670	Ricky Craven	46
1995	74	Johnny Benson	William Baumgardner	Chevrolet	2	0	$469,129	Chad Little	404
1996	74	Randy LaJoie	William Baumgardner	Chevrolet	5	2	$532,823	David Green	29
1997	74	Randy LaJoie	William Baumgardner	Chevrolet	5	2	$1,105,201	Todd Bodine	266
1998	3	Dale Earnhardt Jr.	Dale Earnhardt	Chevrolet	5	3	$1,332,701	Matt Kenseth	48
1999	3	Dale Earnhardt Jr.	Dale Earnhardt	Chevrolet	6	3	$1,680,549	Jeff Green	280
2000	10	Jeff Green	Greg Pollex	Chevrolet	6	7	$1,929,937	Jason Keller	616
2001	2	Kevin Harvick	Richard Childress	Chevrolet	5	5	$1,833,570	Jeff Green	124
2002	60	Greg Biffle	Jack Roush	Ford	4	5	$2,337,255	Jason Keller	264
2003	5	Brian Vickers	Ricky Hendrick	Chevrolet	3	1	$1,987,255	David Green	14
2004	8	Martin Truex Jr.	Teresa Earnhardt and Dale Earnhardt Jr.	Chevrolet	6	7	$2,537,171	Kyle Busch	230
2005	8	Martin Truex Jr.	Teresa Earnhardt and Dale Earnhardt Jr.	Chevrolet	6	3	$3,143,692	Clint Bowyer	68
2006	21	Kevin Harvick	Richard Childress	Chevrolet	9	1	$2,850,864	Carl Edwards	824

8 MARTIN TRUEX JR.

Car: No. 8 Chevrolet • **Car owners:** Teresa Earnhardt
Birth date: June 5, 1979 • **Hometown:** Mayetta, N.J.

NASCAR Busch Series Statistics

Seasons competed: 6 (2001-2006)
Career starts: 90   **Career wins:** 13   **Career poles:** 10

2005 championship season recap: Truex became the first driver to win back to back NASCAR Busch Series championships since Chance 2 Motorsports co-owner Dale Earnhardt Jr. did it in 1998-1999. Truex and Ryan Newman led all NASCAR Busch Series drivers with six victories. Truex entered the final race at Homestead with a 64-point lead over Clint Bowyer and wound up beating Bowyer by 68 points. Truex led the most races (19) and had an average finishing position of 10.46.

2005 CHAMPIONSHIP LINESCORE

Starts	Wins	Poles	Top 5	Top 10	Races Led	Laps Led	DNF
35	6	3	15	22	19	705	2

2004 championship season recap: In winning his first NASCAR Busch Series championship, Truex became the first to complete a championship season without a DNF. He clinched the title with a fourth-place finish at Darlington in the second-to-last race of the season. He topped seven statistical categories in 2004, including wins (six), poles (seven), points (5,173), top fives (17), top 10s (26), races led (21) and average finish (7.6). He beat runner-up Kyle Busch by 230 points.

2004 CHAMPIONSHIP LINESCORE

Starts	Wins	Poles	Top 5	Top 10	Races Led	Laps Led	DNF
34	6	7	17	26	21	954	0

5 BRIAN VICKERS

Car: Chevrolet • **Car owner:** Ricky Hendrick
Birth date: October 24, 1983 • **Hometown:** Thomasville, N.C.

NASCAR Busch Series Statistics

Seasons Competed: 5 (2001-2003, 2005-2006)
Career starts: 73   **Career wins:** 3   **Career poles:** 1

2003 championship season recap: Vickers became the youngest winner ever of a NASCAR series title by capturing the NASCAR Busch Series crown at 20 years old. In a close battle for the points championship, Vickers finished 11th in the last race of the season at Homestead-Miami Speedway after gaining back a lost lap. That kept Vickers just 14 points ahead of 1994 series champion David Green, who finished ninth at Homestead. It was the second-closest title race in series history.

2003 CHAMPIONSHIP LINESCORE

Starts	Wins	Poles	Top 5	Top 10	Races Led	Laps Led	DNF
34	3	1	13	21	14	623	3

Brian Vickers

2002 CHAMPION

60 GREG BIFFLE

Car: Ford • **Car owner:** Jack Roush
Birth date: December 23, 1969 • **Hometown:** Vancouver, Wash.

NASCAR Busch Series Statistics

Seasons competed: 7 (1996, 2001-2006)
Career starts: 174   **Career wins:** 18   **Career poles:** 11

2002 championship season recap: Biffle became the first driver to win the crown in the NASCAR Busch Series and the NASCAR Craftsman Truck Series (2000), both with Roush Racing. He was a model of consistency en route to the title, posting a series-leading 25 top 10 finishes in 34 starts, including four wins. He also led the series in top five efforts (20) and laps led (1,061). He beat runner-up Jason Keller by 264 points.

2002 CHAMPIONSHIP LINESCORE

Starts	Wins	Poles	Top 5	Top 10	Races Led	Laps Led	DNF
34	4	5	20	25	22	1,061	5

2001 CHAMPION

2 KEVIN HARVICK

Car: No. 2 Chevrolet • **Car owner:** Richard Childress
Birth date: December 8, 1975 • **Hometown:** Bakersfield, Calif.

NASCAR Busch Series Statistics

Seasons competed: 8 (1999-2006)
Career starts: 166   **Career wins:** 26   **Career poles:** 14

2001 championship season recap: Harvick followed up his rookie-of-the-year campaign with a championship. He was powered by five wins, four poleand 20 top five finishes for a 124-point margin over runner-up and defending series champion Jeff Green. Harvick never fell outside the top three in the championship race and took the lead after the 15th race and did not relinquish it the remainder of the season.

2001 CHAMPIONSHIP LINESCORE

Starts	Wins	Poles	Top 5	Top 10	Races Led	Laps Led	DNF
33	5	4	20	24	18	1,265	1

2000 CHAMPION

10 JEFF GREEN

Car: Ford • **Car owner:** Jack Roush
Birth date: December 23, 1969 • **Hometown:** Vancouver, Wash.

NASCAR Busch Series Statistics

Seasons competed: 16 (1990-2003, 2005-2006)
Career starts: 251   **Career wins:** 16   **Career poles:** 24

2000 championship season recap: Green constructed the most dominant preformance in NASCAR Busch Series history. He led in wins (6), poles (7), top 5s (25) and top 10s (27) en route to the largest points differential ever, 616 over runner-up Jason Keller. Matt Kenseth led the points for the first seven races; Todd Bodine took over after the eighth, with Green in third. Green finished fifth in the next race at Talladega, gained the points lead and kept it..

2000 CHAMPIONSHIP LINESCORE

Starts	Wins	Poles	Top 5	Top 10	Races Led	Laps Led	DNF
34	4	5	20	25	22	1,061	5

⭐3 DALE EARNHARDT JR.

Car: Chevrolet • **Car Owner:** Dale Earnhardt
Birth date: October 10, 1974 • **Hometown:** Kannapolis, N.C.

NASCAR Busch Series Statistics

Seasons competed: 10 (1996-99, 2001-2006)
Career starts: 92   **Career wins:** 22   **Career poles:** 9

1999 championship season recap: Earnhardt became the fourth driver—and second in a row—in NASCAR Busch Series history to win consecutive championships. He followed up Randy LaJoie's feat in 1996-97 and joined the company of Sam Ard (1983-84) and Larry Pearson (1986-87) as a back-to-back champion. Earnhardt led the series in wins (6), top 5s (18) and top 10s (22) and rolled to a 280-point advantage over runner-up Jeff Green.

1999 CHAMPIONSHIP LINESCORE

Starts	Wins	Poles	Top 5	Top 10	Races Led	Laps Led	DNF
32	6	3	18	22	23	725	4

1998 championship season recap: Earnhardt, after just nine career starts in the previous two seasons, stormed into title contention. Earnhardt led the series in wins (7) and poles (3) and ranked second in top five (16) and top 10 (22) finishes. Earnhardt's win at California Speedway handed him the championship lead and kept Matt Kenseth at bay the rest of the way. His second-place finish at Atlanta gave him a 166-point lead heading into the season finale, and he needed it. He finished 42nd because of an engine failure while Kenseth finished fourth, but Earnhardt had enough cushion to secure the title.

1998 CHAMPIONSHIP LINESCORE

Starts	Wins	Poles	Top 5	Top 10	Races Led	Laps Led	DNF
31	7	3	16	22	19	1,576	3

⭐74 RANDY LaJOIE

Car: Chevrolet • **Car owner:** William Baumgardner
Birth date: August 28, 1961 • **Hometown:** South Norwalk, Conn.

NASCAR Busch Series Statistics

Seasons competed: 19 (1986-90, 1993-2006)
Career starts: 350   **Career wins:** 15   **Career poles:** 9

1997 championship season recap: LaJoie was the third driver to win consecutive NASCAR Busch Series titles and fourth multiple champion. LaJoie led the series with 15 top five finishes and was second in wins (5) and top 10 efforts (21), coasting by runner-up Todd Bodine by 266 points. LaJoie earned $1,105,201, becoming the first NASCAR Busch Series champion to top the $1 million mark in season winnings.

1997 CHAMPIONSHIP LINESCORE

Starts	Wins	Poles	Top 5	Top 10	Races Led	Laps Led	DNF
30	5	2	15	21	13	1,037	1

1996 championship season recap: LaJoie slipped by 1994 NASCAR Busch Series champion David Green by 29 points. LaJoie was paced by five wins, which ranked second in the series, and a series-leading 20 top 10 efforts. LaJoie overtook Green for the points lead by virtue of a sixth-place finish at Charlotte with two races left. LaJoie held a 33-point lead going into the season-ending race at Miami, and used a 10th-place finish to offset a ninth-place performance by Green to secure the title.

1996 CHAMPIONSHIP LINESCORE

Starts	Wins	Poles	Top 5	Top 10	Races Led	Laps Led	DNF
26	5	2	11	20	12	800	4

1995 CHAMPION

74 JOHNNY BENSON JR.

Car: Chevrolet • **Car Owner:** William Baumgardner
Birth date: June 27, 1963 • **Hometown:** Grand Rapids, Mich.

NASCAR Busch Series Statistics

Seasons competed: 9 (1993-1996, 1998-1999, 2002-2005)
Career starts: 90   **Career wins:** 3   **Career poles:** 1
1995 championship season recap: Benson posted just a pair or wins, but his consistency in placing among the top 10 let him roll to a NASCAR Busch Series crown. He recorded 19 top 10 finishes—12 among the top five—to outdistance runner-up Chad Little by 404 points, the third-largest margin in series history. Benson won the fourth race of the season, Atlanta, to grab the points lead from Terry Labonte and relinquished the top spot just once the rest of the season.

1995 CHAMPIONSHIP LINESCORE

Starts	Wins	Poles	Top 5	Top 10	Races Led	Laps Led	DNF
26	2	0	12	19	13	564	1

1994 CHAMPION

44 DAVID GREEN

Car: Chevrolet • **Car owner:** Bobby Labonte
Birth date: January 28, 1958 • **Hometown:** Owensboro, Ky.

NASCAR Busch Series Statistics

Seasons competed: 16 (1989-91,1993-96, 1998-2006)
Career starts: 383   **Career wins:** 9   **Career poles:** 22
1994 championship season recap: Green became only the second driver to register just one victory yet still win the championship. Green edged Ricky Craven by 46 points. Green's fourth-place finish at South Boston in the 17th race pushed him past Craven as the leader, and he maintained the lead. Green was boosted by 10 top five finishes and just one DNF. He had a series-leading nine poles.

1994 CHAMPIONSHIP LINESCORE

Starts	Wins	Poles	Top 5	Top 10	Races Led	Laps Led	DNF
28	1	9	10	14	11	380	1

1993 CHAMPION

31 STEVE GRISSOM

Car: Chevrolet • **Car owner:** Wayne Grissom
Birth date: June 26, 1963 • **Hometown:** Gadsden, Ala.

NASCAR Busch Series Statistics

Seasons competed: 21 (1986-2006)
Career starts: 306   **Career wins:** 11   **Career poles:** 4
1993 championship season recap: Grissom's consistency paved the way to a championship. His series-leading 11 top five finishes boosted him to a 253-point spread over runner-up Ricky Craven. Grissom took the lead from David Green with a fourth-place finish at Michigan, the 17th race of the season, and held the top spot for the rest of the year.

1993 CHAMPIONSHIP LINESCORE

Starts	Wins	Poles	Top 5	Top 10	Races Led	Laps Led	DNF
28	2	0	11	18	7	120	4

87 JOE NEMECHEK

Car: Chevrolet • **Car owner:** Joe Nemechek
Birth date: September 26, 1963 • **Hometown:** Lakeland, Fla.

NASCAR Busch Series Statistics

Seasons competed: 18 (1989-2006)
Career starts: 271   **Career wins:** 16   **Career poles:** 18

1992 championship season recap: Nemechek took on the defending series champion, Bobby Labonte, and outlasted him in the closest championship battle in NASCAR Busch Series history. Nemechek wrestled the lead from Todd Bodine with three races remaining. Labonte won two of the final three races, including the season finale at Hickory, but Nemechek finished sixth at Hickory to edge him by three points.

1992 CHAMPIONSHIP LINESCORE

Starts	Wins	Poles	Top 5	Top 10	Races Led	Laps Led	DNF
31	2	1	13	18	8	241	2

44 BOBBY LABONTE

Car: Oldsmobile • **Car owner:** Bobby Labonte
Birth date: May 8, 1964 •**Hometown:** Corpus Christi, Texas

NASCAR Busch Series Statistics

Seasons competed: 16 (1982, 1985, 1988-94, 1996-1999, 2004-2006)
Career starts: 178   **Career wins:** 9   **Career poles:** 10

1991 championship season recap: Kenny Wallace took the lead from Labonte with three races to go, but Labonte overcame the 33-point deficit. Labonte had a pair of top five finishes and an eighth-place effort, while Wallace cracked the top 20 just once in that span with a third-place finish at Rockingham.

1991 CHAMPIONSHIP LINESCORE

Starts	Wins	Poles	Top 5	Top 10	Races Led	Laps Led	DNF
31	2	2	10	21	10	306	3

63 CHUCK BOWN

Car: Pontiac • **Car owner:** Hubert Hensley
Birth date: February 2, 1954 • **Hometown:** Portland

NASCAR Busch Series Statistics

Seasons competed: 11 (1986-93, 1995-96, 1999)
Career starts: 187   **Career wins:** 11   **Career poles:** 13

1990 championship season recap: Bown, buoyed by a series-high six wins, earned his NASCAR Busch Series title by a 200-point margin over Jimmy Hensley. Bown took the lead after a win at Hickory in the 11th race of the season and never relinquished the top spot.

1990 CHAMPIONSHIP LINESCORE

Starts	Wins	Poles	Top 5	Top 10	Races Led	Laps Led	DNF
31	6	4	13	18	14	1,224	2

1989 CHAMPION

25 ROB MOROSO

Car: Oldsmobile • **Car owner:** Dick Moroso
Birth date: September 28, 1968 • **Hometown:** Madison, Conn.

NASCAR Busch Series Statistics

Seasons competed: 4 (1986-1989)
Career starts: 86   **Career wins:** 6   **Career poles:** 8

1989 championship season recap: Moroso overcame Tommy Houston to capture his NASCAR Busch Series crown. Moroso topped Houston by 55 points but was trailing him down the stretch. Houston came into the season finale at Martinsville with a 19-point lead but lost the title when he finished 24th because of engine failure as Moroso finished third. Moroso had a series-leading four wins and series-high six poles.

1989 CHAMPIONSHIP LINESCORE

Starts	Wins	Poles	Top 5	Top 10	Races Led	Laps Led	DNF
29	4	6	12	16	11	566	3

1988 CHAMPION

99 TOMMY ELLIS

Car: Buick • **Car Owner:** John Jackson
Birth date: August 8, 1947 • **Hometown:** Richmond, Va.

NASCAR Busch Series Statistics

Seasons competed: 14 (1982-1995)
Career starts: 235   **Career wins:** 22   **Career poles:** 28

1988 championship season recap: Ellis, after a stint in the NASCAR NEXTEL Cup Series, returned to the NASCAR Busch Series and captured his first championship. He posted a 239-point spread over runner-up Rob Moroso. Ellis was tied for second in the series in wins with three, trailing only Harry Gant (five)—and notched 20 top 10 finishes in 30 starts. He also had a series-leading five poles.

1988 CHAMPIONSHIP LINESCORE

Starts	Wins	Poles	Top 5	Top 10	Races Led	Laps Led	DNF
30	3	5	12	20	13	740	4

1986-87 CHAMPION

21 LARRY PEARSON

Car: Pontiac/Chevrolet • **Car owner:** David Pearson
Birth date: November 2, 1953 • **Hometown:** Spartanburg, S.C.

NASCAR Busch Series Statistics

Seasons competed: 16 (1982-90, 1993-99)
Career starts: 259   **Career wins:** 15   Career poles: 11

1987 championship season recap: Pearson became the second driver to win consecutive NASCAR Busch Series crowns and the third multiple champion in the series. While his first title run was one of the closest in history, he rolled to his second as he outdistanced runner-up Jimmy Hensley by 382 points. Pearson led the series with six wins and registered 20 top 10 finishes.

1987 CHAMPIONSHIP LINESCORE

Starts	Wins	Poles	Top 5	Top 10	Races Led	Laps Led	DNF
27	6	3	16	20	13	720	3

1986 championship season recap: Pearson rallied late to claim his first NASCAR Busch Series title, edging Brett Bodine by 20 points. The points battle would become the second closest in series history. Bodine led Pearson by 19 points with five races to go, but two races later, Pearson grabbed the lead by six points. Pearson extended the lead to 30 heading into the season finale at Martinsville and clinched with a runner-up showing while Bodine made a final gasp with a victory.

1986 CHAMPIONSHIP LINESCORE

Starts	Wins	Poles	Top 5	Top 10	Races Led	Laps Led	DNF
31	1	1	17	24	7	200	2

1982 & 85 CHAMPION

11 JACK INGRAM

Car: Pontiac/Oldsmobile • **Car owner:** Aline Ingram
Birth date: December 28, 1936 • **Hometown:** Asheville, N.C.

NASCAR Busch Series Statistics

Seasons competed: 10 (1982-1991)
Career starts: 274   **Career wins:** 31   **Career poles:** 5

1985 championship season recap: Ingram joined Sam Ard as a multiple champion in the NASCAR Busch Series, adding this crown to the one he captured in the inaugural 1982 season. Ingram had another tough battle en route to this title as well, edging Jimmy Hensley by 29 points. Ingram owned a 39-point lead with one to go and iced it with a fifth-place finish in the season finale at Martinsville.

1985 CHAMPIONSHIP LINESCORE

Starts	Wins	Poles	Top 5	Top 10	Races Led	Laps Led	DNF
27	5	2	17	22	15	770	4

1982 championship season recap: Ingram became the inaugural NASCAR Busch Series champion, edging Sam Ard by 49 points. Ingram had an incredible run of consistency as he posted 23 top five finishes, including a series-leading seven victories. Ard, with four wins, was trailing by 58 points with three races remaining but never was able to get closer to Ingram than 43 points over that span.

1982 CHAMPIONSHIP LINESCORE

Starts	Wins	Poles	Top 5	Top 10	Races Led	Laps Led	DNF
29	7	1	23	24	N/A	N/A	4

1983-84 CHAMPION

00 SAM ARD

Car: Oldsmobile • **Car owner:** Howard Thomas
Birth date: February 14, 1939 • **Hometown:** Asheboro, N.C.

NASCAR Busch Series Statistics

Seasons competed: 3 (1982-84)
Career starts: 92   **Career wins:** 22   **Career poles:** 25

1984 championship season recap: Ard and Jack Ingram had squared off for the championship the first two seasons, with each earning a title, but the third battle between the two was no contest. Ard became the series' first multiple and back-to-back champion by rolling to a 426-point spread over Ingram. Ard and Ingram tied for the series lead in wins with eight each, but it was Ard's consistency that allowed him to coast to the crown.

1984 CHAMPIONSHIP LINESCORE

Starts	Wins	Poles	Top 5	Top 10	Races Led	Laps Led	DNF
28	8	7	24	26	26	2,099	1

1983 championship season recap: It was a battle between the top two contenders—Ard and defending champion Jack Ingram—from the inaugural 1982 season, but this time Ard prevailed. He needed a NASCAR Busch Series-record 10 victories to fend off Ingram and claim the title by 87 points. He also led the series with 10 poles. Ingram stayed in the hunt behind five wins and 29 top 10 efforts but could not run down the dominating Ard in the end.

1983 CHAMPIONSHIP LINESCORE

Starts	Wins	Poles	Top 5	Top 10	Races Led	Laps Led	DNF
35	10	10	23	30	N/A	1,862	3

50 DANNY O'QUINN JR.

Car: Ford • **Car owner:** Jack Roush
Birth date: May 7, 1985 • **Hometown:** Coeburn, Va.

NASCAR Busch Series Statistics

Seasons competed: 1 (2006)
Career starts: 33   **Career wins:** 0   **Career poles:** 0

2006 season recap: O'Quinn beat out racing veteran John Andretti for the NASCAR Busch Series Raybestos Rookie of the Year award. O'Quinn, just 21 years old, finished with one top five in 33 races and showed his versatility with top 10s coming at two short tracks (O'Reilly Raceway Park and Memphis), a superspeedway (Nashville), an intermediate track (Lowe's Motor Speedway) and a 1-mile track (Milwaukee). O'Quinn finished the 2006 season ranked 19th in NASCAR Busch Series points.

2006 LINESCORE

Starts	Wins	Poles	Top 5	Top 10	Races Led	Laps Led	DNF
33	0	0	1	5	0	0	3

RAYBESTOS ROOKIES OF THE YEAR

Year	Driver	Points	Finish	Races	Poles	Wins	Top 5	Top 10	Winnings	Hometown
1989	Kenny Wallace	3,750	6	29	3	0	4	16	$88,423	St. Louis
1990	Joe Nemechek	3,022	17	28	0	0	2	5	$70,279	Lakeland, Fla.
1991	Jeff Gordon	3,582	11	30	1	0	5	10	$111,608	Pittsboro, Ind.
1992	Ricky Craven	3,456	14	31	1	0	0	5	$167,618	Newburgh, Maine
1993	Hermie Sadler	3,362	10	28	0	1	4	8	$149,596	Emporia, Va.
1994	Johnny Benson Jr.	3,303	6	28	0	1	6	9	$190,011	Grand Rapids, Mich
1995	Jeff Fuller	2,845	10	26	1	0	1	6	$174,950	Auburn, Mass.
1996	Glenn Allen	2,593	14	26	0	0	0	2	$176,372	Cincinnati
1997	Steve Park	4,080	3	30	1	3	12	20	$677,921	East Northport, N.Y.
1998	Andy Santerre	2,598	20	29	1	0	1	2	$307,835	Cherryfield, Maine
1999	Tony Raines	3,142	12	31	0	0	1	3	$657,220	LaPorte, Ind.
2000	Kevin Harvick	4,113	3	31	2	3	8	16	$995,274	Bakersfield, Calif.
2001	Greg Biffle	4,509	4	33	2	5	16	21	$1,623,546	Vancouver, Wash.
2002	Scott Riggs	4,023	10	34	2	2	8	13	$1,170,846	Bahama, N.C.
2003	David Stremme	2,354	22	18	0	0	3	7	$443,537	South Bend, Ind.
2004	Kyle Busch	4,943	2	34	5	5	16	22	$2,027,050	Las Vegas
2005	Carl Edwards	4,601	3	34	4	5	15	21	$1,759,782	Columbia, Mo.
2006	Danny O'Quinn Jr.	3,163	19	33	0	0	1	5	$931,506	Coeburn, Va.

MISCELLANEOUS RECORDS

Most races started: 417—Tommy Houston, 1982-1996
Most wins, season: 10—Sam Ard, 1983
Most wins, career: 47—Mark Martin, 1982-2006
Most superspeedway wins, season: 5—Dale Earnhardt Jr., 1998; Mark Martin, 1993, '96, '97, 2000; Chad Little, 1995; Greg Biffle, 2001, '04
Most superspeedway wins, career: 38—Mark Martin, 1982-2005
Most short track wins, season: 9—Sam Ard, 1983
Most short track wins, career: 29—Jack Ingram, 1982-1991
Most years winning at least one race: 14, Mark Martin
Most different race winners, season: 18—1988, '89
Most wins at one track: 11—Mark Martin, Rockingham
Most races won from pole, career: 9—Sam Ard, 1982-84; Mark Martin, 1987-2000
Most races won from pole, season: 4—Sam Ard, 1983
Oldest driver to win: Dick Trickle (56 years, 11 months), Darlington, Sept. 5, 1998
Youngest driver To win: Casey Atwood (18 years, 10 months), Milwaukee, July 4, 1999
Most races started without winning: 208—Ed Berrier, 1984-1997
Most top five finishes, season: 25—Jeff Green, 2000
Most top five finishes, career: 123—Tommy Houston, 1982-1996
Most top 10 finishes, season: 32—Kevin Harvick, 2006
Most top 10 finishes, career: 198—Tommy Houston, 1982-1996
Most poles, season: 11—Jeff Gordon, 1992
Most poles, career: 30—Mark Martin, 1982-2006
Most years winning at least one pole: 13—Mark Martin
Most different pole winners, season: 24—1998
Most poles at one track: 7—Tommy Ellis, Hickory; Mark Martin, Darlington
Most money won, season: $3,143,692—Martin Truex Jr., 2005
Most money won, career: $10,843,511—Jason Keller, 1991-2006
Most money won, race: $132,400—Denny Hamlin, March 5, 2006
Largest purse, superspeedway: $2,629,362—Daytona, February 18, 2006
Largest purse, short track: $1,434,019—Bristol, March 6, 2006
Largest purse, road course: $2,452,988—Mexico City, March 5, 2006
Largest margin of victory by series champion: 824 points—Kevin Harvick over Carl Edwards, 2006
Smallest margin of victory by series champion: 3 points—Joe Nemechek over Bobby Labonte, 1992

SERIES RACE RECORDS

Longest race, distance: 400 miles—Charlotte, October 5, 1985
Longest race, time: 3 hrs., 48 min., 25 sec.—Gateway, July 26, 1997
Shortest race, distance: 56.25 miles—Orange County, 1985-1988
Shortest race, time: 38 min., 4 sec.—Orange County, June 14, 1986
Fastest average speed: 169.571 mph—Michigan, August 19, 1995
Slowest average speed: 48.842 mph—Orange County, August 13, 1982
Most caution flags, race: 26—Hickory, April 18, 1992
Most caution laps, race: 132—Hickory, April 18, 1992
Fewest caution flags, race: 0, five times—most recent, Michigan, August 15, 1998
Fewest caution laps, race: 0, five times—most recent, Michigan, August 15, 1998
Most lead changes, race: 35, three times—most recent, Rockingham, February 22, 1997
Most cars finishing on lead lap, race: 34—Daytona, July 1, 2005
Fewest cars finishing on lead lap: 1, 12 times—most recent, Orange County, August 10, 1991
Largest starting field: 47—Oxford, Maine, July 10, 1988
Smallest starting field: 17—Hampton, Va., May 8, 1982
Most cars running at finish: 43—Michigan, August 15, 1998
Fewest DNFs, race: 0—Michigan, August 15, 1998
Fewest cars running at finish: 10—North Wilkesboro, April 8, 1983
Most DNFs, race: 26—Lowe's Motor Speedway, November 10, 1987

RECORDS SET IN CONSECUTIVE YEARS

Most consecutive starts: 360—Tommy Houston, February 13, 1982-February 26, 1994
Most consecutive races won: 4—Sam Ard, 1983
Most consecutive races in first place, season: 34—Kevin Harvick, 2006
Most consecutive years winning at least one race: 10—Dale Earnhardt, 1985-1994
Most consecutive different race winners, season: 13—1988
Most consecutive wins at one track: 5—Dale Earnhardt, Daytona, 1990-1994; Jack Ingram, South Boston, 1985-1986
Most consecutive races running at finish: 74—Ron Hornaday, October 12, 2002-November 20, 2004
Most consecutive poles: 3, four drivers—most recent, Jeff Gordon, 1992
Most consecutive different pole winners, season: 15—1995
Most consecutive poles at one track: 4—David Green, Hickory, 1994-1996; Joe Nemechek, Daytona, 2001-2003
Most consecutive years winning at least one pole: 9—Mark Martin, 1992-2000

SERIES FIRSTS

First race: Daytona International Speedway, February 13, 1982
First winner: Dale Earnhardt
First pole winner: Mike Porter, Daytona, February 9, 1982
First superspeedway race: Daytona, February 13, 1982
First superspeedway winner: Dale Earnhardt
First short track race: Richmond, February 20, 1982
First short track winner: Tommy Houston
First road course race: Road Atlanta, July 6, 1986
First road course winner: Darrell Waltrip
First Chevrolet win: Tommy Houston, Richmond, February 20, 1982
First Dodge win: Hank Parker Jr., Pikes Peak, July 27, 2002
First Ford win: Mark Martin, Dover, May 30, 1987
First driver to win $100,000 in a race: Jeff Gordon, 1992
First driver to win $1 million in a career: Jack Ingram, 1989
First driver to win $1 million in a season: Randy LaJoie, 1997
First driver to win $10 million in a career: Jason Keller, 2005
First brothers to win championships: David Green, 1994; Jeff Green, 2000

>> ALL-TIME RACE WINNERS <<
NASCAR Busch Series

DRIVER	WINS	DRIVER	WINS	DRIVER	WINS	DRIVER	WINS	DRIVER	WINS
Mark Martin	47	Terry Labonte	11	Ward Burton	4	Phil Parsons	2	David Gilliland	1
Jack Ingram	31	Michael Waltrip	11	Ricky Craven	4	Tim Richmond	2	Robby Gordon	1
Kevin Harvick	26	Jason Keller	10	Tim Fedewa	4	Johnny Rumley	2	Bobby Hamilton	1
Tommy Houston	24	Robert Pressley	10	Ron Hornaday Jr.	4	Hermie Sadler	2	Denny Hamlin	1
Sam Ard	22	Carl Edwards	9	Jeff Purvis	4	Elton Sawyer	2	Jimmie Johnson	1
Jeff Burton	22	David Green	9	Scott Riggs	4	Ken Schrader	2	Justin Labonte	1
Dale Earnhardt Jr.	22	Jimmy Hensley	9	Mike Wallace	4	Dennis Setzer	2	Jason Leffler	1
Tommy Ellis	22	Bobby Labonte	9	Johnny Benson Jr.	3	Ronnie Silver	2	Tracy Leslie	1
Dale Earnhardt	21	Rick Mast	9	Clint Bowyer	3	Reed Sorenson	2	Dick McCabe	1
Harry Gant	21	Kenny Wallace	9	Ron Fellows	3	Tony Stewart	2	Casey Mears	1
Matt Kenseth	21	Kyle Busch	7	Ernie Irvan	3	Dick Trickle	2	Paul Menard	1
Greg Biffle	18	Jamie McMurray	7	L.D. Ottinger	3	Rick Wilson	2	David Pearson	1
Jeff Green	16	Ryan Newman	7	Steve Park	3	Jamie Aube	1	Larry Pollard	1
Joe Nemechek	16	Geoffrey Bodine	6	Johnny Sauter	3	Ed Berrier	1	Ricky Rudd	1
Todd Bodine	15	Butch Lindley	6	Brian Vickers	3	Joe Bessey	1	Joe Ruttman	1
Randy LaJoie	15	Chad Little	6	Mike Alexander	2	Dave Blaney	1	Greg Sacks	1
Larry Pearson	15	Mike McLaughlin	6	Bobby Allison	2	Mike Bliss	1	Andy Santerre	1
Morgan Shepherd	15	Rob Moroso	6	Casey Atwood	2	Neil Bonnett	1	John Settlemyre	1
Martin Truex Jr.	13	Brett Bodine	5	Ron Bouchard	2	Kurt Busch	1	Mike Skinner	1
Darrell Waltrip	13	Jeff Gordon	5	Bobby Hillin	2	Ronald Cooper	1	Jack Sprague	1
Jimmy Spencer	12	Bobby Hamilton Jr.	5	Buckshot Jones	2	Derrike Cope	1	Brad Teague	1
Chuck Bown	11	Kasey Kahne	5	Kevin Lepage	2	Bobby Dotter	1		
Steve Grissom	11	Elliott Sadler	5	Butch Miller	2	Bill Elliott	1		
Dale Jarrett	11	Scott Wimmer	5	Hank Parker Jr.	2	Jeff Fuller	1		

>> ALL-TIME POLE WINNERS <<
NASCAR Busch Series

DRIVER	POLES	DRIVER	POLES	DRIVER	POLES	DRIVER	POLES	DRIVER	POLES
Tommy Ellis	28	Ricky Craven	8	Steve Grissom	4	Paul Menard	2	Alan Kulwicki	1
Mark Martin	30	Rob Moroso	8	Bobby Hamilton Jr.	4	Kelly Moore	2	Ashton Lewis	1
Sam Ard	24	Todd Bodine	7	Shane Hmiel	4	Mike Porter	2	Chad Little	1
Jeff Green	23	Ward Burton	7	Terry Labonte	4	Greg Sacks	2	Curtis Markham	1
David Green	22	Dale Earnhardt	7	Kevin Lepage	4	Boris Said	2	Sterling Marlin	1
Tommy Houston	18	Carl Edwards	7	Casey Mears	4	Elton Sawyer	2	Jamie McMurray	1
Joe Nemechek	18	Denny Hamlin	7	Butch Miller	4	Reed Sorenson	2	Gary Niece	1
Brett Bodine	16	Dick Trickle	7	L.D. Ottinger	4	Hut Stricklin	2	Steve Park	1
Jimmy Hensley	15	Casey Atwood	6	Johnny Sauter	4	Brad Teague	2	Hank Parker Jr.	1
Michael Waltrip	15	Dave Blaney	6	Tony Stewart	4	Rusty Wallace	2	Randy Porter	1
Harry Gant	14	Kasey Kahne	6	Darrell Waltrip	4	Aric Almirola	1	Scott Pruett	1
Kevin Harvick	14	Jason Leffler	6	Mike Alexander	3	Tim Bender	1	Tony Raines	1
Dale Jarrett	14	Phil Parsons	6	Mike Bliss	3	Johnny Benson	1	Stevie Reeves	1
Geoffrey Bodine	13	Robert Pressley	6	Buckshot Jones	3	Ed Berrier	1	David Reutimann	1
Chuck Bown	12	Jeff Purvis	6	David Pearson	3	Rich Bickle	1	Shawna Robinson	1
Jeff Gordon	12	Tim Richmond	6	Scott Riggs	3	Jim Bown	1	Johnny Rumley	1
Matt Kenseth	12	Morgan Shepherd	6	Hermie Sadler	3	Kurt Busch	1	Andy Santerre	1
Greg Biffle	11	Clint Bowyer	5	Mike Skinner	3	Stacy Compton	1	Jay Sauter	1
Jeff Burton	11	Jack Ingram	5	Jimmy Spencer	3	Derrike Cope	1	Dennis Setzer	1
Jason Keller	11	Ernie Irvan	5	J.J. Yeley	3	Dave Dion	1	Bob Shreeves	1
Ryan Newman	11	Butch Lindley	5	Davey Allison	2	Eddie Falk	1	Jack Sprague	1
Larry Pearson	11	Rick Mast	5	Joe Bessey	2	Jeff Fuller	1	David Stremme	1
Bobby Labonte	10	Mike McLaughlin	5	Bill Elliott	2	Jorge Goeters	1	Mike Swaim	1
Martin Truex Jr.	10	Elliott Sadler	5	Ron Fellows	2	Kevin Grubb	1	Brian Vickers	1
Kenny Wallace	10	Ken Schrader	5	Shane Hall	2	Wayne Grubb	1	Rick Wilson	1
Dale Earnhardt Jr.	9	Ron Bouchard	4	Jimmie Johnson	2	Ron Hornaday Jr.	1		
Randy LaJoie	9	Bobby Dotter	4	Tracy Leslie	2	Robert Ingram	1		
Kyle Busch	8	Tim Fedewa	4	Dave Mader III	2	Todd Kluever	1		

>> 2006 SEASON <<

Pos.	Driver	Points	Starts	Poles	Wins	Top 5	Top 10	Winnings
1.	Kevin Harvick	5,648	35	1	9	23	32	$2,850,864
2.	Carl Edwards	4,824	35	3	4	15	25	$1,878,844
3.	Clint Bowyer	4,683	35	2	1	12	17	$1,715,649
4.	Denny Hamlin	4,667	35	6	2	12	23	$1,757,309
5.	J.J. Yeley	4,487	35	3	0	9	22	$1,504,366
6.	Paul Menard	4,075	35	0	1	7	16	$1,723,218
7.	Kyle Busch	3,921	34	2	1	4	12	$1,182,182
8.	Johnny Sauter	3,794	35	1	0	2	9	$1,561,164
9.	Greg Biffle	3,789	30	0	1	9	18	$928,356
10.	Reed Sorenson	3,670	34	0	0	5	14	$1,068,468

>> RACE WINNERS 17

Kevin Harvick	9
Carl Edwards	4
Matt Kenseth	3
Jeff Burton	2
Kurt Busch	2
Dale Earnhardt Jr.	2
Denny Hamlin	2
Kasey Kahne	2
Greg Biffle	1
Dave Blaney	1
Clint Bowyer	1
Kyle Busch	1
David Gilliland	1
Casey Mears	1
Paul Menard	1
Tony Stewart	1
Martin Truex Jr.	1

>> MONEY WON LEADERS

Kevin Harvick	$2,850,864
Carl Edwards	$1,878,844
Denny Hamlin	$1,757,309
Paul Menard	$1,723,218
Clint Bowyer	$1,715,649
Johnny Sauter	$1,561,164
J.J. Yeley	$1,504,366
Jason Leffler	$1,182,579
Kyle Busch	$1,182,182
Kenny Wallace	$1,122,350

>> POLE WINNERS 16

Denny Hamlin	7
Matt Kenseth	4
Carl Edwards	3
J.J. Yeley	3
Clint Bowyer	2
Kyle Busch	2
Jason Leffler	2
Mark Martin	2
Jeff Burton	1
Kurt Busch	1
Kevin Harvick	1
Todd Kluever	1
Ryan Newman	1
Scott Riggs	1
Boris Said	1
Johnny Sauter	1

Jason Leffler

>> 2005 SEASON <<

Pos.	Driver	Points	Starts	Poles	Wins	Top 5	Top 10	Winnings
1.	Martin Truex Jr.	4,937	35	3	6	15	22	$3,143,692
2.	Clint Bowyer	4,869	35	2	2	12	22	$2,114,592
3.	Carl Edwards #	4,601	34	4	5	15	21	$1,759,782
4.	Reed Sorenson #	4,453	35	2	2	12	19	$1,800,178
5.	Denny Hamlin #	4,143	35	0	0	1	11	$1,494,198
6.	Paul Menard	4,101	35	1	0	6	15	$1,310,560
7.	Kenny Wallace	4,068	35	0	0	5	11	$1,275,584
8.	David Green	3,908	35	0	1	3	6	$1,252,051
9.	Jason Keller	3,866	35	0	0	1	6	$1,074,477
10	Greg Biffle	3,865	27	0	1	16	21	$1,212,275

Raybestos Rookie of the Year candidate

>> RACE WINNERS 14

Ryan Newman...6
Martin Truex Jr. 6
Carl Edwards...5
Kevin Harvick..4
Clint Bowyer...2
Kasey Kahne...2
Mark Martin..2
Reed Sorenson...2
Greg Biffle..1
Kyle Busch...1
David Green...1
Matt Kenseth..1
Johnny Sauter..1
Tony Stewart..1

>> MONEY WON LEADERS

Martin Truex Jr. $3,143,692
Clint Bowyer $2,114,592
Reed Sorenson $1,800,178
Carl Edwards.................................$1,759,782
Denny Hamlin $1,494,198
Paul Menard $1,310,560
Kenny Wallace $1,275,584
Johnny Sauter $1,260,880
David Green $1,252,051
Greg Biffle $1,212,275

>> POLE WINNERS 16

Carl Edwards...4
Ryan Newman...4
Kasey Kahne...3
Martin Truex Jr. 3
Clint Bowyer...2
Kevin Harvick..2
Jimmie Johnson..2
Reed Sorenson...2
Tony Stewart...2
Kyle Busch...1
Kevin Hamlin..1
Shane Hmiel...1
Mark Martin..1
Paul Menard...1
Joe Nemechek..1
Johnny Sauter..1

>> 2004 SEASON <<

Pos.	Driver	Points	Starts	Poles	Wins	Top 5	Top 10	Winnings
1.	Martin Truex Jr.	5,173	34	7	6	17	26	$2,537,171
2.	Kyle Busch #	4,943	34	5	5	16	22	$2,027,050
3.	Greg Biffle	4,568	34	2	5	15	21	$1,568,712
4.	Ron Hornaday Jr.	4,258	34	0	1	7	16	$1,539,519
5.	Mike Bliss	4,115	34	3	1	6	14	$1,298,784
6.	Jason Keller	4,088	34	0	0	6	12	$1,345,009
7.	David Green	4,082	34	1	0	6	16	$1,318,024
8.	Ashton Lewis	3,892	34	0	0	3	8	$1,013,987
9.	Kenny Wallace	3,851	34	0	0	0	10	$952,076
10	David Stremme	3,738	34	1	0	5	14	$1,017,952

Raybestos Rookie of the Year candidate

>> RACE WINNERS 15

Martin Truex Jr. 6
Greg Biffle..5
Kyle Busch...5
Matt Kenseth..3
Jamie McMurray 3
Dale Earnhardt Jr. 2
Kevin Harvick..2
Mike Bliss..1
Robby Gordon...1
Ron Hornaday Jr..1
Justin Labonte..1
Jason Leffler...1
Joe Nemechek..1
Mike Wallace..1
Michael Waltrip...1

>> MONEY WON LEADERS

Martin Truex Jr. $2,537,171
Kyle Busch $2,027,050
Greg Biffle $1,568,712
Ron Hornaday Jr. $1,539,519
Jason Keller $1,345,009
David Green $1,318,024
Mike Bliss.....................................$1,298,784
Jason Leffler $1,168,779
David Stremme $1,017,952
Ashton Lewis................................$1,013,987

>> POLE WINNERS 16

Carl Edwards...4
Martin Truex Jr. 7
Kyle Busch...5
Mike Bliss..3
Casey Mears...3
Greg Biffle..2
Kasey Kahne...2
Johnny Benson..1
Clint Bowyer...1
Dale Earnhardt Jr. 1
David Green...1
Bobby Hamilton Jr. 1
Jason Leffler...1
Jamie McMurray 1
Paul Menard...1
Johnny Sauter..1
David Stremme..1

>> 2003 SEASON <<

Pos.	Driver	Points	Starts	Poles	Wins	Top 5	Top 10	Winnings
1.	Brian Vickers	4,637	34	1	3	13	21	$1,987,255
2.	David Green	4,623	34	2	3	11	21	$1,721,860
3.	Ron Hornaday Jr.	4,591	34	0	1	8	17	$1,441,770
4.	Bobby Hamilton Jr.	4,588	34	1	4	13	22	$1,619,965
5.	Jason Keller	4,528	34	1	1	10	17	$1,488,340
6.	Scott Riggs	4,462	34	0	2	11	17	$1,435,530
7.	Kasey Kahne	4,104	34	1	1	4	14	$1,073,665
8.	Johnny Sauter	4,098	34	0	1	6	14	$1,143,460
9.	Scott Wimmer	4,059	34	0	1	4	12	$1,159,160
10	Mike Bliss	3,932	34	0	0	8	14	$935,035

 # Raybestos Rookie of the Year candidate

>> RACE WINNERS 17

Bobby Hamilton Jr. 4
Dale Earnhardt Jr. 3
David Green 3
Kevin Harvick 3
Joe Nemechek 3
Brian Vickers 3
Greg Biffle 2
Matt Kenseth...2
Jamie McMurray 2
Scott Riggs 2
Todd Bodine 1
Ron Hornaday Jr, ...1
Kasey Kahne 1
Jason Keller 1
Johnny Sauter 1
Michael Waltrip 1
Scott Wimmer 1

>> MONEY WON LEADERS

Brian Vickers $1,987,255
David Green $1,721,860
Bobby Hamilton Jr. $1,619,965
Jason Keller $1,488,340
Ron Hornaday Jr. $1,441,770
Scott Riggs $1,435,530
Scott Wimmer $1,159,160
Johnny Sauter $1,143,460
Kasey Kahne $1,073,665
Mike Bliss..........................$935,035

>> POLE WINNERS 16

Kevin Harvick 5
Joe Nemechek 3
Greg Biffle 2
David Green 2
Randy LaJoie..2
Michael Waltrip 2
Stacy Compton 1
Dale Earnhardt Jr. 1
Bobby Hamilton Jr. 1
Shane Hmiel 1
Kasey Kahne 1
Jason Keller 1
Ashton Lewis Jr. 1
Casey Mears 1
David Reutimann 1
Brian Vickers 1

>> 2002 SEASON <<

Pos.	Driver	Points	Starts	Poles	Wins	Top 5	Top 10	Winnings
1.	Greg Biffle	4,919	34	5	4	20	25	$2,337,254
2.	Jason Keller	4,655	34	2	4	17	22	$1,669,642
3.	Scott Wimmer	4,488	34	0	4	11	17	$1,332,409
4.	Mike McLaughlin	4,253	34	0	0	7	17	$1,281,356
5.	Jack Sprague	4,206	34	0	1	9	15	$1,103,989
6.	Jamie McMurray	4,147	34	0	2	6	14	$1,044,282
7.	Kenny Wallace	4,078	34	0	0	2	13	$882,800
8.	Bobby Hamilton Jr.	4,058	34	0	1	6	15	$1,072,280
9.	Stacy Compton	4,042	34	0	0	5	11	$861,924
10.	Scott Riggs #	4,023	34	2	2	8	13	$1,170,846

 # Raybestos Rookie of the Year candidate

>> RACE WINNERS 17

Jeff Burton 5
Greg Biffle...4
Jason Keller 4
Scott Wimmer 4
Dale Earnhardt Jr. 2
Jeff Green 2
Jamie McMurray 2
Scott Riggs 2
Todd Bodine 1
Bobby Hamilton Jr. 1
Joe Nemechek 1
Hank Parker Jr. 1
Jeff Purvis..1
Johnny Sauter 1
Jimmy Spencer 1
Jack Sprague 1
Michael Waltrip 1

>> MONEY WON LEADERS

Greg Biffle $2,337,254
Jason Keller $1,669,642
Scott Wimmer $1,332,409
Mike McLaughlin................$1,281,356
Scott Riggs $1,170,846
Bobby Hamilton Jr. $1,072,280
Jamie McMurray $1,044,282
Randy LaJoie $1,018,629
Johnny Sauter $991,534
Kenny Wallace $882,800

>> POLE WINNERS 14

Greg Biffle 5
Jeff Green 5
Jeff Burton 2
Shane Hmiel 2
Jason Keller 2
Kevin Lepage..2
Joe Nemechek 2
Scott Riggs 2
Michael Waltrip 2
Todd Bodine 1
Dale Earnhardt Jr. 1
Ron Hornaday Jr. 1
Randy LaJoie..1
Johnny Sauter 1

>> 2001 SEASON <<

Pos.	Driver	Points	Starts	Poles	Wins	Top 5	Top 10	Winnings
1.	Kevin Harvick	4,813	33	5	5	20	24	$1,833,570
2.	Jeff Green	4,689	33	2	4	16	26	$1,797,836
3.	Jason Keller	4,637	33	0	1	14	22	$1,519,811
4.	Greg Biffle #	4,509	33	2	5	16	21	$1,623,546
5.	Elton Sawyer	4,100	33	0	0	6	19	$1,079,093
6.	Tony Raines	3,975	33	1	0	4	13	$921,777
7.	Mike McLaughlin	3,962	33	0	1	5	12	$951,682
8.	Jimmie Johnson	3,871	33	0	1	4	9	$920,192
9.	Chad Little	3,846	33	0	0	2	6	$690,321
10.	Kenny Wallace	3,799	33	2	1	7	13	$821,665

Raybestos Rookie of the Year candidate

>> RACE WINNERS 17

Greg Biffle	5
Kevin Harvick	5
Jeff Green	4
Jimmy Spencer	3
Todd Bodine	2
Randy LaJoie	2
Joe Nemechek	2
Jeff Burton	1
Ron Fellows	1
Jimmie Johnson	1
Jason Keller	1
Matt Kenseth	1
Mike McLaughlin	1
Rayn Newman	1
Hank Parker Jr.	1
Jeff Purvis	1
Kenny Wallace	1

>> MONEY WON LEADERS

Kevin Harvick	$1,833,570
Jeff Green	$1,797,836
Greg Biffle	$1,623,546
Jason Keller	$1,519,811
Elton Sawyer	$1,079,093
Mike McLaughlin	$951,682
Hank Parker Jr.	$936,819
Tony Raines	$921,777
Jimmie Johnson	$920,192
Randy LaJoie	$917,791

>> POLE WINNERS 15

Ryan Newman	6
Kevin Harvick	5
Matt Kenseth	3
Greg Biffle	2
Jeff Green	2
Joe Nemechek	2
Kenny Wallace	2
Jeff Burton	1
Bobby Hamilton Jr.	1
Kevin Lepage	1
Scott Pruett	1
Tony Raines	1
Jay Sauter	1
Mike Skinner	1
Jimmy Spencer	1

>> 2000 SEASON <<

Pos.	Driver	Points	Starts	Poles	Wins	Top 5	Top 10	Winnings
1.	Jeff Green	5,005	32	7	6	25	27	$1,929,937
2.	Jason Keller	4,389	32	0	1	13	19	$1,174,448
3.	Kevin Harvick #	4,113	31	2	3	8	16	$995,274
4.	Todd Bodine	4,075	32	1	1	14	19	$935,269
5.	Ron Hornaday Jr. #	3,870	32	0	2	6	13	$958,836
6.	Elton Sawyer	3,776	32	0	0	5	14	$925,919
7.	Randy LaJoie	3,670	32	0	1	4	9	$873,179
8.	Casey Atwood	3,404	32	2	0	0	8	$775,615
9.	David Green	3,316	32	0	0	2	11	$759,269
10.	Jimmie Johnson #	3,264	31	0	0	0	6	$549,271

Raybestos Rookie of the Year candidate

>> RACE WINNERS 14

Jeff Green	6
Mark Martin	5
Jeff Burton	4
Matt Kenseth	4
Kevin Harvick	3
Ron Hornaday Jr.	2
Todd Bodine	1
Tim Fedewa	1
Ron Fellows	1
Jeff Gordon	1
Jason Keller	1
Randy LaJoie	1
Sterling Marlin	1
Joe Nemechek	1

>> MONEY WON LEADERS

Jeff Green	$1,929,937
Jason Keller	$1,174,448
Kevin Harvick	$995,274
Ron Hornaday Jr.	$958,836
Todd Bodine	$935,269
Elton Sawyer	$925,919
Randy LaJoie	$873,179
Matt Kenseth	$839,305
Casey Atwood	$775,615
David Green	$759,269

>> POLE WINNERS 16

Mark Martin	4
Jason Leffler	3
Casey Atwood	2
Kevin Harvick	2
Matt Kenseth	2
Dave Blaney	1
Todd Bodine	1
Tim Fedewa	1
Ron Fellows	1
Bobby Hamilton Jr.	1
Buckshot Jones	1
Hank Parker Jr.	1
Jeff Purvis	1
Hut Stricklin	1
Mike Skinner	1

>> 1999 SEASON <<

Pos.	Driver	Points	Starts	Poles	Wins	Top 5	Top 10	Winnings
1.	Dale Earnhardt Jr.	4,647	32	3	6	18	22	$985,195
2.	Jeff Green	4,367	31	3	3	15	19	$735,040
3.	Matt Kenseth	4,327	32	2	4	14	20	$859,660
4.	Todd Bodine	4,029	32	0	0	10	21	$541,860
5.	Elton Sawyer	3,891	32	0	1	4	14	$599,105
6.	Jeff Purvis	3,658	32	0	0	4	12	$631,416
7.	Dave Blaney	3,582	31	4	0	5	12	$499,660
8.	Jason Keller	3,537	32	3	2	5	12	$631,850
9.	Mike McLaughlin	3,478	32	0	0	3	8	$631,950
10.	Randy LaJoie	3,379	32	0	1	6	7	$695,210

Raybestos Rookie of the Year candidate

>> RACE WINNERS 15

Dale Earnhardt Jr.	6
Mark Martin	6
Matt Kenseth	4
Jeff Green	3
Casey Atwood	2
Jason Keller	2
Jeff Burton	1
Jeff Gordon	1
Terry Labonte	1
Randy LaJoie	1
Joe Nemechek	1
Andy Santerre	1
Elton Sawyer	1
Mike Skinner	1
Michael Waltrip	1

>> MONEY WON LEADERS

Dale Earnhardt Jr.	$985,195
Matt Kenseth	$859,660
Jeff Green	$735,040
Randy LaJoie	$695,210
Mike McLaughlin	$631,950
Jason Keller	$631,850
Jeff Purvis	$631,416
Elton Sawyer	$599,105
Tony Raines	$555,820
Todd Bodine	$541,860

>> POLE WINNERS 14

Dave Blaney	4
Dale Earnhardt Jr.	3
Jeff Green	3
Jason Keller	3
Mark Martin	3
Ken Schrader	3
Casey Atwood	2
David Green	2
Matt Kenseth	2
Jeff Burton	1
Ward Burton	1
Ron Fellows	1
Hut Stricklin	1
Dick Trickle	1
Jimmy Spencer	1

>> 1998 SEASON <<

Pos.	Driver	Points	Starts	Poles	Wins	Top 5	Top 10	Winnings
1.	Dale Earnhardt Jr.	4469	31	3	7	16	22	$1,332,701
2.	Matt Kenseth	4421	31	1	3	17	23	$991,965
3.	Mike McLaughlin	4045	31	1	2	11	16	$828,313
4.	Randy LaJoie	3543	31	0	1	7	12	$783,703
5.	Elton Sawyer	3533	31	0	0	4	10	$576,089
6.	Phil Parsons	3525	31	0	0	5	9	$550,352
7.	Tim Fedewa	3515	31	1	2	4	10	$526,520
8.	Elliott Sadler	3470	31	1	2	5	10	$635,058
9.	Buckshot Jones	3453	31	1	1	6	9	$484,932
10.	Hermie Sadler	3340	31	0	0	2	5	$405,691

Raybestos Rookie of the Year candidate

>> RACE WINNERS 16

Dale Earnhardt Jr.	7
Jeff Burton	3
Matt Kenseth	3
Tim Fedewa	2
Mark Martin	2
Mike McLaughlin	2
Joe Nemechek	2
Elliott Sadler	2
E Berrier	1
Ron Fellows	1
Buckshot Jones	1
Bobby Labonte	1
Randy LaJoie	1
Kevin Lepage	1
Jimmy Spencer	1
Dick Trickle	1

>> MONEY WON LEADERS

Dale Earnhardt Jr.	$1,332,701
Matt Kenseth	$991,965
Mike McLaughlin	$828,313
Randy LaJoie	$783,703
Elliott Sadler	$635,058
Elton Sawyer	$576,089
Phil Parsons	$550,352
Jeff Purvis	$536,415
Tim Fedewa	$526,520
Buckshot Jones	$484,932

>> POLE WINNERS 24

Greg Biffle	5
Dale Earnhardt Jr.	3
Casey Atwood	2
Jeff Burton	2
Robert Pressley	2
Joe Nemechek	2
Tony Stewart	2
Joe Bessey	1
Dave Blaney	1
Tim Fedewa	1
Steve Grissom	1
Kevin Grubb	1
Wayne Grubb	1
Shane Hall	1
Buckshot Jones	1
Matt Kenseth	1
Bobby Labonte	1
Kevin Lepage	1
Mark Martin	1
Mike McLaughlin	1
Jeff Purvis	1
Elliott Sadler	1
Boris Said	1
Andy Santerre	1
Dick Trickle	1

>> 1997 SEASON <<

Pos.	Driver	Points	Starts	Poles	Wins	Top 5	Top 10	Winnings
1.	Randy LaJoie	4,381	30	2	5	15	21	$1,105,201
2.	Todd Bodine	4,115	30	0	1	9	22	$658,295
3.	Steve Park #	4,080	30	1	3	12	20	$677,921
4.	Mike McLaughlin	3,614	30	2	2	7	14	$585,173
5.	Elliott Sadler	3,534	30	4	3	6	10	$556,372
6.	Phil Parsons	3,523	30	0	0	5	12	$411,026
7.	Buckshot Jones	3,437	30	0	0	5	14	$446,637
8.	Elton Sawyer	3,419	30	0	0	6	9	$349,229
9.	Tim Fedewa	3,398	30	1	0	4	11	$346,424
10.	Hermie Sadler	3,340	30	2	0	2	7	$328,154

Raybestos Rookie of the Year candidate

>> RACE WINNERS 13

Mark Martin	6
Randy LaJoie	5
Steve Park	3
Elliott Sadler	3
Jeff Burton	2
Mike McLaughlin	2
Joe Nemechek	2
Jimmy Spencer	2
Joe Bessey	1
Todd Bodine	1
Jeff Green	1
Bobby Labonte	1
Dick Trickle	1

>> MONEY WON LEADERS

Randy LaJoie	$1,105,201
Steve Park	$677,921
Todd Bodine	$658,295
Mike McLaughlin	$585,173
Elliott Sadler	$556,372
Buckshot Jones	$446,637
Phil Parsons	$411,026
Kevin Lepage	$396,937
Mark Martin	$373,469
Jason Keller	$372,681

>> POLE WINNERS 15

Elliott Sadler	4
Mark Martin	3
Joe Nemechek	3
Jeff Green	2
Randy LaJoie	2
Mike McLaughlin	2
Hermie Sadler	2
Dick Trickle	2
Tim Bender	1
Joe Bessey	1
Jeff Burton	1
Tim Fedewa	1
Shane Hall	1
Steve Park	1
Michael Waltrip	11

>> 1996 SEASON <<

Pos.	Driver	Points	Starts	Poles	Wins	Top 5	Top 10	Winnings
1.	Randy LaJoie	3,714	26	2	5	11	20	$532,823
2.	David Green	3,685	26	4	2	13	18	$469,118
3.	Todd Bodine	3,064	26	0	1	3	9	$281,616
4.	Jeff Green	3,059	26	1	0	5	13	$369,285
5.	Chad Little	2,984	26	1	0	2	7	$317,394
6.	Jason Keller	2,900	26	0	0	3	10	$281,902
7.	Jeff Purvis	2,894	26	2	2	4	7	$266,026
8.	Kevin Lepage	2,870	26	0	1	3	10	$254,925
9.	Phil Parsons	2,854	26	0	0	5	6	$215,023
10.	Mike McLaughlin	2,853	26	0	0	7	10	$290,701

Raybestos Rookie of the Year candidate

>> RACE WINNERS 13

Mark Martin	6
Randy LaJoie	5
Terry Labonte	3
David Green	2
Jeff Purvis	2
Todd Bodine	1
Jeff Fuller	1
Steve Grissom	1
Buckshot Jones	1
Bobby Labonte	1
Kevin Lepage	1
Greg Sacks	1
Kenny Wallace	1

>> MONEY WON LEADERS

Randy LaJoie	$532,823
David Green	$469,118
Chad Little	$317,394
Mike McLaughlin	$290,701
Jason Keller	$281,902
Todd Bodine	$281,616
Jeff Green	$269,285
Jeff Purvis	$266,026
Kevin Lepage	$254,925
Hermie Sadler	$238,511

>> POLE WINNERS 16

David Green	4
Bobby Labonte	3
Ricky Craven	2
Randy LaJoie	2
Mark Martin	2
Jeff Purvis	2
Jeff Fuller	1
Jeff Green	1
Dale Jarrett	1
Buckshot Jones	1
Chad Little	1
Sterling Marlin	1
Joe Nemechek	1
Hermie Sadler	1
Dick Trickle	1
Michael Waltrip	1

>> 1995 SEASON <<

Pos.	Driver	Points	Starts	Poles	Wins	Top 5	Top 10	Winnings
1.	Johnny Benson	3,688	26	0	2	12	19	$469,129
2.	Chad Little	3,284	26	0	6	11	13	$529,056
3.	Mike McLaughlin	3,273	26	1	1	9	14	$317,075
4.	Jason Keller	3,211	26	1	1	6	12	$257,880
5.	Jeff Green	3,182	26	1	0	6	12	$241,187
6.	Larry Pearson	3,029	26	1	2	5	8	$276,057
7.	Tim Fedewa	3,022	26	1	1	4	4	$253,907
8.	Phil Parsons	2,985	26	0	0	3	9	$177,358
9.	Elton Sawyer	2,952	26	1	0	2	9	$250,833
10.	Jeff Fuller #	2,845	26	0	0	1	6	$174,950

Raybestos Rookie of the Year candidate

>> RACE WINNERS 14

Chad Little.............................6
Dale Jarrett...........................3
Mark Martin...........................3
Johnny Benson......................2
Steve Grissom.......................2
Larry Pearson........................2
Todd Bodine..........................1
Tim Fedewa...........................1
David Green...........................1
Jason Keller...........................1
Terry Labonte........................1
Mike McLaughlin....................1
Johnny Rumley.......................1
Kenny Wallace........................1

>> MONEY WON LEADERS

Chad Little $529,056
Johnny Benson $469,129
Mike McLaughlin $317,075
Larry Pearson $276,057
David Green $274,628
Jason Keller $257,880
Tim Fedewa $253,907
Elton Sawyer $250,833
Jeff Green $241,187
Mark Martin $210,475

>> POLE WINNERS 21

Dave Blaney 4
David Green 4
Rich Bickle 1
Bobby Dotter 1
Tim Fedewa.................................1
Jeff Green 1
Dale Jarrett 1
Jason Keller 1
Terry Labonte 1
Randy LaJoie 1
Tracy Leslie 1
Curtis Markham 1
Mark Martin.................................1
Mike McLaughlin 1
Joe Nemechek 1
Larry Pearson 1
Jeff Purvis 1
Stevie Reeves 1
Elton Sawyer 1
Dennis Setzer 1
Darrell Waltrip 1
Michael Waltrip 1

>> 1994 SEASON <<

Pos.	Driver	Points	Starts	Poles	Wins	Top 5	Top 10	Winnings
1.	David Green	3,725	28	9	1	10	14	$391,670
2.	Ricky Craven	3,679	28	1	2	8	16	$273,000
3.	Chad Little	3,662	28	0	0	10	14	$234,022
4.	Kenny Wallace	3,554	28	1	3	11	15	$307,017
5.	Hermie Sadler	3,466	28	0	1	6	11	$238,204
6.	Johnny Benson #	3,303	28	0	1	6	9	$190,011
7.	Bobby Dotter	3,299	28	0	0	2	8	$176,093
8.	Larry Pearson	3,277	27	0	0	3	12	$161,859
9.	Dennis Setzer #	3,273	28	0	2	4	11	$214,246
10.	Tim Fedewa	3,125	28	0	0	1	8	$142,034

Raybestos Rookie of the Year candidate

>> RACE WINNERS 17

Terry Labonte 4
Mark Martin 3
Kenny Wallace............................3
M Wallace 3
Ricky Craven 2
Dennis Setzer 2
Johnny Benson 1
Derrike Cope 1
Dale Earnhardt 1
Harry Gant 1
David Green 1
Bobby Labonte 1
Joe Nemechek 1
Phil Parsons 1
Hermie Sadler 1
Elton Sawyer 1
Ken Schrader 1

>> MONEY WON LEADERS

David Green $391,670
Kenny Wallace $307,017
Ricky Craven $273,000
Hermie Sadler $238,204
Chad Little $234,022
Terry Labonte $215,438
Dennis Setzer $214,246
Mark Martin $200,608
Johnny Benson $190,011
Tracy Leslie $188,567

>> POLE WINNERS 14

David Green 9
Jason Keller 3
Mark Martin 3
Harry Gant 2
Derrike Cope 1
Ricky Craven 1
Bobby Labonte 1
Randy LaJoie 1
Robert Pressley 1
Jeff Purvis 1
Shawna Robinson 1
Mike Skinner 1
Kenny Wallace 1
Ken Wallace 1

Pos.	Driver	Points	Starts	Poles	Wins	Top 5	Top 10	Winnings
1.	Steve Grissom	3,846	28	0	2	11	18	$336,432
2.	Ricky Craven	3,593	28	1	0	6	17	$197,829
3.	David Green	3,584	28	0	0	6	16	$225,747
4.	Chuck Bown	3,532	28	1	1	5	13	$195,961
5.	Joe Nemechek	3,443	28	3	0	8	11	$254,346
6.	Ward Burton	3,413	28	4	3	9	10	$293,622
7.	Bobby Dotter	3,406	28	2	0	3	8	$160,003
8.	Robert Pressley	3,389	28	0	3	8	13	$254,723
9.	Todd Bodine	3,387	28	1	3	9	13	$240,899
10.	Hermie Sadler #	3,362	28	0	1	4	8	$149,596

 # Raybestos Rookie of the Year candidate

>> **RACE WINNERS** 13

Mark Martin 7
Todd Bodine 3
Ward Burton 3
Robert Pressley 3
Dale Earnhardt 2
Steve Grissom 2
Michael Waltrip 2
Chuck Bown 1
Jeff Burton 1
Bill Elliott 1
Tracy Leslie 1
Johnny Rumley 1
Hermie Sadler 1

>> **MONEY WON LEADERS**

Steve Grissom $336,432
Ward Burton $293,622
Robert Pressley $254,723
Joe Nemechek $254,346
Todd Bodine $240,899
Mark Martin $230,703
David Green $225,747
Jeff Burton $212,843
Ricky Craven $197,829
Chuck Bown $195,961

>> **POLE WINNERS** 16

Ward Burton 4
Ernie Irvan 3
Joe Nemechek 3
Bobby Dotter 2
Bill Elliott 2
Todd Bodine 1
Chuck Bown 1
Ricky Craven 1
Jeff Green 1
Bobby Labonte 1
Terry Labonte 1
Tracy Leslie 1
Mark Martin 1
Rick Mast 1
Butch Miller 1
Ken Schrader 1

Pos.	Driver	Points	Starts	Poles	Wins	Top 5	Top 10	Winnings
1.	Joe Nemechek	4,275	31	1	2	13	18	$285,008
2.	Bobby Labonte	4,272	31	0	3	13	19	$329,985
3.	Todd Bodine	4,212	31	2	3	11	19	$284,284
4.	Jeff Gordon	4,053	31	11	3	10	15	$412,293
5.	Robert Pressley	3,988	31	2	5	11	16	$299,303
6.	Kenny Wallace	3,966	31	2	1	7	15	$166,167
7.	Butch Miller	3,725	31	2	0	4	10	$131,991
8.	Ward Burton	3,648	31	0	1	3	10	$203,116
9.	Jeff Burton	3,609	31	0	1	4	10	$202,775
10.	Tommy Houston	3,599	31	0	1	2	10	$133,065

 # Raybestos Rookie of the Year candidate

>> **RACE WINNERS** 17

Robert Pressley 5
Todd Bodine 3
Jeff Gordon 3
Bobby Labonte 3
Harry Gant 2
Ernie Irvan 2
Joe Nemechek 2
Jimmy Spencer 2
Jeff Burton 1
Ward Burton 1
Bobby Dotter 1
Dale Earnhardt 1
Steve Grissom 1
Tommy Houston 1
Mark Martin 1
Kenny Wallace 1
Michael Waltrip 1

>> **MONEY WON LEADERS**

Jeff Gordon $412,293
Bobby Labonte $329,985
Robert Pressley $299,303
Joe Nemechek $285,008
Todd Bodine $284,284
Ward Burton $203,116
Jeff Burton $202,775
Steve Grissom $170,716
Chuck Bown $169,513
Kenny Wallace $166,167

>> **POLE WINNERS** 14

Jeff Gordon 11
Todd Bodine 2
Mark Martin 2
Butch Miller 2
Robert Pressley 2
Kenny Wallace 2
Jim Bown 1
Ricky Craven 1
Dale Earnhardt 1
Steve Grissom 1
Ernie Irvan 1
Joe Nemechek 1
Johnny Rumley 1
Michael Waltrip 1

>> 1991 SEASON <<

Pos.	Driver	Points	Starts	Poles	Wins	Top 5	Top 10	Winnings
1.	Bobby Labonte	4,264	31	2	2	10	21	$246,368
2.	Kenny Wallace	4,190	31	1	2	11	17	$274,506
3.	Robert Pressley	3,929	31	1	1	8	15	$171,256
4.	Chuck Bown	3,922	31	5	3	9	14	$244,739
5.	Jimmy Hensley	3,916	31	4	3	9	17	$227,739
6.	Joe Nemechek	3,902	31	0	0	5	16	$124,255
7.	Todd Bodine	3,825	31	2	1	7	15	$136,273
8.	Tommy Houston	3,777	31	0	0	5	11	$163,827
9.	Tom Peck	3,746	31	0	0	2	13	$163,189
10.	Steve Grissom	3,689	31	1	1	7	13	$152,206

Raybestos Rookie of the Year candidate

>> RACE WINNERS 16

Harry Gant	5
Chuck Bown	3
Dale Earnhardt	3
Jimmy Hensley	3
Dale Jarrett	3
Ricky Craven	2
Bobby Labonte	2
Kenny Wallace	2
Todd Bodine	1
Jeff Burton	1
David Green	1
Steve Grissom	1
Ernie Irvan	1
Terry Labonte	1
Butch Miller	1
Robert Pressley	1

>> MONEY WON LEADERS

Kenny Wallace	$274,506
Bobby Labonte	$246,368
Chuck Bown	$244,739
Jimmy Hensley	$227,969
Robert Pressley	$171,256
Tommy Houston	$163,827
Tom Peck	$163,189
Steve Grissom	$152,206
Jeff Burton	$144,798
Todd Bodine	$136,273

>> POLE WINNERS 20

Chuck Bown	5
Jimmy Hensley	4
Todd Bodine	2
Jeff Burton	2
Bobby Labonte	2
Ward Burton	1
Ricky Craven	1
Dale Earnhardt	1
Harry Gant	1
Jeff Gordon	1
David Green	1
Steve Grissom	1
Ernie Irvan	1
Terry Labonte	1
Dave Mader	1
Butch Miller	1
Robert Pressley	1
Elton Sawyer	1
Jack Sprague	1
Kenny Wallace	1

>> 1990 SEASON <<

Pos.	Driver	Points	Starts	Poles	Wins	Top 5	Top 10	Winnings
1.	Chuck Bown	4,372	31	4	6	13	18	$323,399
2.	Jimmy Hensley	4,172	31	4	1	9	17	$201,877
3.	Steve Grissom	3,982	31	1	4	11	15	$166,842
4.	Bobby Labonte	3,977	31	2	0	6	17	$136,936
5.	Tom Peck	3,868	31	0	0	2	12	$109,821
6.	Tommy Ellis	3,829	31	3	1	5	13	$205,863
7.	Kenny Wallace	3,829	31	1	0	4	14	$112,781
8.	L.D. Ottinger	3,693	31	0	1	5	7	$156,674
9.	Tommy Houston	3,667	31	0	4	9	14	$200,350
10.	Rick Mast	3,617	31	1	3	8	10	$127,965

Raybestos Rookie of the Year candidate

>> RACE WINNERS 13

Chuck Bown	6
Steve Grissom	4
Tommy Houston	4
Rick Mast	3
Harry Gant	2
Dale Jarrett	2
Michael Waltrip	2
Jeff Burton	1
Tommy Ellis	1
Jimmy Hensley	1
Sterling Marlin	1
Mark Martin	1
L.D. Ottinger	1

>> MONEY WON LEADERS

Chuck Bown	$323,399
Tommy Ellis	$205,863
Jimmy Hensley	$201,877
Tommy Houston	$200,350
Steve Grissom	$166,842
L .D. Ottinger	$156,674
Bobby Hamilton	$156,281
Elton Sawyer	$144,699
Bobby Labonte	$136,936
Rick Mast	$127,965

>> POLE WINNERS 17

Chuck Bown	4
Jimmy Hensley	4
Tommy Ellis	3
Ricky Craven	2
Bobby Labonte	2
Michael Waltrip	2
Davey Allison	1
Ed Berrier	1
Jeff Burton	1
Harry Gant	1
Steve Grissom	1
Dave Mader	1
Rick Mast	1
Greg Sacks	1
Dick Trickle	1
Kenny Wallace	1
Darrell Waltrip	1

>> 1989 SEASON <<

Pos.	Driver	Points	Starts	Poles	Wins	Top 5	Top 10	Winnings
1.	Rob Moroso	4,001	29	6	4	12	16	$346,849
2.	Tommy Houston	3,946	29	1	3	12	17	$184,734
3.	Tommy Ellis	3,945	29	1	3	11	19	$202,141
4.	L.D. Ottinger	3,916	29	0	1	7	16	$109,821
5.	Jack Ingram	3,802	29	0	0	7	14	$144,436
6.	Kenny Wallace #	3,750	29	3	0	4	16	$88,423
7.	Rick Mast	3,558	29	2	2	9	13	$127,028
8.	Ronald Cooper	3,557	29	0	1	4	10	$106,068
9.	Chuck Bown	3,349	29	2	0	5	12	$103,294
10.	Tom Peck	3,171	28	0	0	2	7	$58,441

Raybestos Rookie of the Year candidate

>> RACE WINNERS 18

Rob Moroso 4
Tommy Ellis 3
Tommy Houston 3
Jimmy Spencer..3
Dale Earnhardt 2
Harry Gant 2
Rick Mast 2
Rick Wilson 2
Geoffrey Bodine 1
Ronald Cooper 1
Bobby Hamilton 1
Bobby Hillin 1
Mark Martin 1
L.D. Ottinger 1
Robert Pressley...1
Ken Schrader 1
Darrell Waltrip...1
Michael Waltrip 1

>> MONEY WON LEADERS

Rob Moroso $346,849
Tommy Ellis $202,141
Tommy Houston $184,735
Jack Ingram $144,436
Rick Mast $127,028
L.D. Ottinger $109,821
Ronaled Cooper $106,068
Jimmy Spencer $103,726
Chuck Bown $103,294
Michael Waltrip............................$90,487

>> POLE WINNERS 17

Ronald Moroso 6
Michael Waltrip 4
Kenny Wallace...3
Chuck Bown 2
Rick Mast 2
Geoffrey Bodine 1
Tommy Ellis 1
Harry Gant 1
Jimmy Hensley 1
Tommy Houston 1
Dale Jarrett 1
Mark Martin 1
Greg Sacks 1
Ken Schrader 1
Jimmy Spencer 1
Morgan Shepherd 1
Rick Wilson 1

>> 1988 SEASON <<

Pos.	Driver	Points	Starts	Poles	Wins	Top 5	Top 10	Winnings
1.	Tommy Ellis	4,310	30	5	3	12	20	$200,003
2.	Rob Moroso	4,071	30	2	2	10	19	$181,618
3.	Mike Alexander	4,053	30	1	1	10	17	$151,303
4.	Larry Pearson	4,050	30	5	3	13	16	$164,593
5.	Tommy Houston	4,042	30	2	3	11	17	$123,385
6.	Jimmy Hensley	3,904	30	0	1	7	13	$125,615
7.	Jimmy Spencer	3,839	30	0	0	5	13	$64,112
8.	Rick Mast	3,809	30	0	2	5	13	$116,557
9.	L.D. Ottinger	3,732	30	1	0	5	11	$66,640
10.	Jack Ingram	3,610	30	0	0	10	12	$100,497

Raybestos Rookie of the Year candidate

>> RACE WINNERS 18

Harry Gant...5
Tommy Ellis 3
Tommy Houston...3
Larry Pearson 3
Rick Mast 2
Ronald Moroso 2
Mike Alexander 1
Bobby Allison 1
Geoffrey Bodine...1
Dale Earnhardt..1
Jimmy Hensley 1
Bobby Hillin 1
Dale Jarrett 1
Mark Martin..1
Dick McCabe 1
Morgan Shepherd 1
Darrell Waltrip 1
Michael Waltrip 1

>> MONEY WON LEADERS

Tommy Ellis $200,003
Ronald Moroso $181,618
Larry Pearson $164,593
Mike Alexander $151,303
Jimmy Hensley............................$125,615
Tommy Houston $123,385
Rick Mast..................................$116,557
Jack Ingram $100,497
Harry Gant $88,847
L.D. Ottinger...............................$66,640

>> POLE WINNERS 12

Tommy Ellis 5
Larry Pearson 5
Harry Gant 4
Geoffrey Bodine 3
Tommy Houston...2
Ronald Moroso 2
Mike Alexander 1
Bobby Dotter 1
Dale Earnhardt 1
Dale Jarrett 1
L.D. Ottinger 1
Mike Swaim 1

>> 1987 SEASON <<

Pos.	Driver	Points	Starts	Poles	Wins	Top 5	Top 10	Winnings
1.	Larry Pearson	3,999	27	3	6	16	20	$185,124
2.	Jimmy Hensley	3,617	27	2	1	8	14	$66,505
3.	Brett Bodine	3,611	27	5	0	8	17	$115,889
4.	Jack Ingram	3,598	27	0	1	6	14	$105,530
5.	Mike Alexander	3,497	27	1	1	8	13	$51,598
6.	Dale Jarrett	3,444	27	0	1	5	11	$84,025
7.	Brad Teague	3,391	27	0	1	1	9	$94,960
8.	Mark Martin	3,349	27	6	3	5	13	$65,208
9.	Rick Mast	3,319	27	1	2	4	9	$69,704
10.	L.D. Ottinger	3,318	27	0	0	6	10	$95,440

 # Raybestos Rookie of the Year candidate

>> RACE WINNERS 15

Larry Pearson	6
Harry Gant	3
Mark Martin	3
Morgan Shepherd	3
Rick Mast	2
Mike Alexander	1
Jamie Aube	1
Geoffrey Bodine	1
Dale Earnhardt	1
Tommy Ellis	1
Jimmy Hensley	1
Jack Ingram	1
Dale Jarrett	1
Larry Pollard	1
Brad Teague	1

>> MONEY WON LEADERS

Larry Pearson	$256,372
Brett Bodine	$138,551
Jack Ingram	$124,929
Brad Teague	$106,172
L.D. Ottinger	$102,702
Dale Jarrett	$97,499
Jimmy Hensley	$94,504
Tommy Houston	$90,340
Harry Gant	$85,722
Darrell Waltrip	$77,684

>> POLE WINNERS 13

Mark Martin	6
Brett Bodine	5
Larry Pearson	3
Harry Gant	2
Jimmy Hensley	2
Tommy Houston	2
Mike Alexander	1
Geoffrey Bodine	1
Dave Dion	1
Dale Earnhardt	1
Robert Ingram	1
Rick Mast	1
Rusty Wallace	1

>> 1986 SEASON <<

Pos.	Driver	Points	Starts	Poles	Wins	Top 5	Top 10	Winnings
1.	Larry Pearson	4,551	31	1	1	17	24	$127,488
2.	Brett Bodine	4,531	31	8	2	16	24	$146,233
3.	Jack Ingram	4,301	29	1	5	16	22	$152,229
4.	Dale Jarrett	4,261	31	5	1	14	19	$71,463
5.	L.D. Ottinger	4,153	31	0	1	12	20	$79,363
6.	Tommy Houston	4,121	31	4	4	12	18	$108,038
7.	Ronnie Silver	3,967	31	0	1	9	12	$85,584
8.	Jimmy Hensley	3,950	31	0	0	3	9	$86,019
9.	Charlie Luck	3,847	31	0	0	1	14	$51,518
10.	Larry Pollard	3,726	30	0	0	1	11	$45,029

 # Raybestos Rookie of the Year candidate

>> RACE WINNERS 17

Robert Pressley	5
Dale Earnhardt	5
Jack Ingram	5
Tommy Houston	4
Morgan Shepherd	4
Darrell Waltrip	4
Brett Bodine	2
Chuck Bown	1
Dale Jarrett	1
Butch Miller	1
L.D. Ottinger	1
Larry Pearson	1
Tim Richmond	1
Ronnie Silver	1

>> MONEY WON LEADERS

Larry Pearson	$184,344
Jack Ingram	$174,482
Brett Bodine	$173,181
Dale Earnhardt	$150,558
Tommy Houston	$121,706
L.D. Ottinger	$96,476
Ronnie Silver	$96,262
Jimmy Hensley	$95,148
Dale Jarrett	$90,701
Darrell Waltrip	$87,873

>> POLE WINNERS 14

Brett Bodine	8
Dale Jarrett	5
Tommy Houston	4
Tim Richmond	3
Darrell Waltrip	2
Mike Alexander	1
Davey Allison	1
Geoffrey Bodine	1
Dale Earnhardt	1
Jack Ingram	1
Terry Labonte	1
Larry Pearson	1
Randy Porter	1
Morgan Shepherd	1

>> 1985 SEASON <<

Pos.	Driver	Points	Starts	Poles	Wins	Top 5	Top 10	Winnings
1.	Jack Ingram	4,106	27	2	5	17	22	$115,798
2.	Jimmy Hensley	4,077	27	4	3	15	23	$92,808
3.	Larry Pearson	3,951	27	0	2	15	19	$101,438
4.	Tommy Houston	3,936	27	4	1	17	21	$81,258
5.	Dale Jarrett	3,774	27	0	0	9	17	$51,323
6.	L.D. Ottinger	3,732	27	0	0	6	19	$65,748
7.	Rick Mast	3,589	27	0	0	5	15	$52,380
8.	Ronnie Silver	3,425	27	0	1	3	13	$49,758
9.	Larry Pollard	3,197	24	0	0	2	12	$30,235
10.	Eddie Falk	3,044	27	0	0	0	4	$30,145

Raybestos Rookie of the Year candidate

>> RACE WINNERS 12

Tommy Ellis	5
Jack Ingram	5
Brett Bodine	3
Jimmy Hensley	3
Darrell Waltrip	3
Larry Pearson	2
Geoffrey Bodine	1
Dale Earnhardt	1
Tommy Houston	1
Terry Labonte	1
Tim Richmond	1
Ronnie Silver	1

>> MONEY WON LEADERS

Jack Ingram	$164,709
Larry Pearson	$120,453
Jimmy Hensley	$115,963
Tommy Houston	$97,932
L.D. Ottinger	$77,291
Tommy Ellis	$73,936
Geoffrey Bodine	$71,433
Dale Jarrett	$65,566
Rick Mast	$61,977
Ronnie Silver	$57,470

>> POLE WINNERS 13

Jimmy Hensley	4
Tommy Houston	4
Brett Bodine	3
Tommy Ellis	3
Geoffrey Bodine	2
Jack Ingram	2
Tim Richmond	2
Brad Teague	2
Ron Bouchard	1
Dale Earnhardt	1
Alan Kulwicki	1
Mike Porter	1
Rusty Wallace	1

>> 1984 SEASON <<

Pos.	Driver	Points	Starts	Poles	Wins	Top 5	Top 10	Winnings
1.	Sam Ard	4,552	28	7	8	24	26	$217,531
2.	Jack Ingram	4,126	29	0	8	17	19	$122,953
3.	Tommy Houston	4,070	29	4	2	15	22	$104,778
4.	Dale Jarrett	4,014	29	1	0	9	19	$72,503
5.	Ronnie Silver	3,398	26	0	0	8	14	$52,133
6.	Joe Thurman	3,221	27	0	0	2	8	$51,383
7.	Charlie Luck	3,172	26	0	0	1	9	$40,279
8.	L.D. Ottinger	3,069	26	3	0	3	10	$43,264
9.	Jeff Hensley	3,032	26	0	0	1	7	$29,629
10.	Bob Shreeves	2,869	25	0	0	0	7	$33,739

Raybestos Rookie of the Year candidate

>> RACE WINNERS 10

Sam Ard	8
Jack Ingram	8
Morgan Shepherd	3
Ron Bouchard	2
Tommy Houston	2
Darrell Waltrip	2
Bobby Allison	1
Geoffrey Bodine	1
Tommy Ellis	1
Larry Pearson	1

>> MONEY WON LEADERS

Sam Ard	$217,531
Jack Ingram	$122,953
Tommy Houston	$104,778
Dale Jarrett	$72,503
Ronnie Silver	$52,133
J Thurman	$51,383
Darrel Waltrip	$50,280
L.D. Ottinger	$43,264
Geoffrey Bodine	$42,950
Charlie Luck	$40,279

>> POLE WINNERS 11

Sam Ard	7
Tommy Ellis	4
Tommy Houston	4
Geoffrey Bodine	3
Ron Bouchard	3
L.D. Ottinger	3
Eddie Falk	1
Dale Jarrett	1
Tim Richmond	1
Morgan Shepherd	1
Dick Trickle	1

>> 1983 SEASON <<

Pos.	Driver	Points	Starts	Poles	Wins	Top 5	Top 10	Winnings
1.	Sam Ard	5,454	35	10	10	23	30	$192,362
2.	Jack Ingram	5,367	35	1	5	23	29	$126,956
3.	Tommy Houston	4,933	35	1	4	14	22	$104,561
4.	Tommy Ellis	4,929	35	7	7	16	21	$97,251
5.	Dale Jarrett	4,837	35	4	0	17	21	$55,360
6.	Ronnie Silver	4,058	32	0	0	6	16	$35,705
7.	Pete Silva	3,945	31	0	0	6	13	$42,900
8.	Jimmy Hensley	3,716	29	0	0	5	16	$26,305
9.	Eddie Falk	3,617	30	0	0	1	13	$21,162
10.	Jeff Hensley	3,444	28	0	0	1	9	$18,875

Raybestos Rookie of the Year candidate

>> RACE WINNERS 10

Sam Ard 10
Tommy Ellis 7
Jack Ingram 5
Tommy Houston 4
Dale Earnhardt 2
Butch Lindley 2
Morgan Shepherd 2
Neil Bonnett 1
Ricky Rudd 1
Darrell Waltrip 1

>> MONEY WON LEADERS

Sam Ard $192,362
Jack Ingram $126,956
Tommy Houston $104,561
Tommy Ellis $97,251
Dale Jarrett $55,360
Butch Lindley $44,488
Pete Silva $42,900
Phil Parsons $40,976
Morgan Shepherd..........................$36,570
Ronnie Silver $35,705

>> POLE WINNERS 11

Sam Ard 10
Tommy Ellis 7
Dale Jarrett 4
Phil Parsons 4
Butch Lindley 3
Dale Earnhardt 1
Tommy Houston 1
Jack Ingram 1
David Pearson 1
Larry Pearson 1
Morgan Shepherd 1

>> 1982 SEASON <<

Pos.	Driver	Points	Starts	Poles	Wins	Top 5	Top 10	Winnings
1.	Jack Ingram	4,495	29	1	7	23	24	$122,100
2.	Sam Ard	4,446	29	7	4	20	23	$122,099
3.	Tommy Ellis	3,873	29	5	1	13	16	$78,782
4.	Tommy Houston	3,827	29	0	2	11	18	$67,792
5.	Phil Parsons	3,783	29	2	1	5	18	$62,839
6.	Dale Jarrett	3,332	29	0	0	1	15	$27,260
7.	Pete Silva	2,349	18	0	0	5	8	$18,127
8.	Jimmy Lawson	2,106	18	0	0	0	5	$12,458
9.	Bob Shreeves	1,928	15	1	0	5	8	$13,785
10.	Butch Lindley	1,581	14	2	4	9	10	$38,170

Raybestos Rookie of the Year candidate

>> RACE WINNERS 14

Jack Ingram 7
Sam Ard 4
Butch Lindley..4
Dale Earnhardt..2
Tommy Houston...2
Morgan Shepherd 2
Geoffrey Bodine 1
Tommy Ellis 1
Harry Gant 1
Phil Parsons 1
David Pearsons 1
Joe Ruttman 1
John Settlemyre 1
Darrell Waltrip 1

>> MONEY WON LEADERS

Jack Ingram $122,100
Sam Ard $122,099
Tommy Ellis $78,782
Tommy Houston $67,792
Phil Parsons $62,839
Butch Lindley $38,170
Dale Earnhardt $29,980
Geoffrey Bodine $29,005
Dale Jarrett $27,260
Morgan Shepherd..........................$23,955

>> POLE WINNERS 12

Sam Ard 7
Tommy Ellis..5
Harry Gant..3
Geoffrey Bodine 2
Butch Lindley 2
Phil Parsons 2
David Pearson 2
Morgan Shepherd 2
Jack Ingram 1
Gary Neice 1
Mike Porter 1
Bob Shreeves 1

NASCAR
CRAFTSMAN
TRUCK SERIES

NASCAR CRAFTSMAN TRUCK SERIES
MILESTONES

1993 Four off-road racing enthusiasts—Dick Landfield, Jimmy Smith, Jim Venable and Frank "Scoop" Vessels—build a prototype racing pickup truck.

February 1994 The group seeks a NASCAR sanction for truck racing.

May 14, 1994 NASCAR President Bill France announces the creation of the NASCAR Craftsman Truck Series, then titled NASCAR SuperTruck Series, during a news conference at Infineon Raceway in Sonoma, Calif.

July 30, 1994 The first of four demonstration races is held at Mesa Marin Raceway in Bakersfield, Calif. P.J. Jones is the first NASCAR Craftsman Truck Series winner, in a Ford owned by Frank "Scoop" Vessels.

Late 1994 Craftsman agrees to present the series. A 20-race schedule is released. Total posted awards of $1.6 million are announced, along with a complete national television package.

November 20, 1994 Rick Carelli wins the first of three preview races held at Tucson Raceway Park. Each is broadcast live by TNN as a part of its Winter Heat package.

February 5, 1995 The NASCAR Craftsman Truck Series begins at Phoenix International Raceway. Mike Skinner, driving the GM Goodwrench Service Chevrolet, is the first winner, beating former NASCAR NEXTEL Cup Series champ Terry Labonte by 0.09 seconds.

June 3, 1995 Mike Skinner's Ford Credit 200 victory at Louisville Motor Speedway makes him the first in the series to win consecutive races.

June 23, 1995 Joe Ruttman and Irvan-Simo Racing give Ford its first series win, in the Pizza Plus 150 at Bristol Motor Speedway.

July 15, 1995 Butch Miller, in the Raybestos Ford, edges Mike Skinner in the closest finish to date—0.0001 seconds—at Colorado National Speedway.

July 29, 1995 Ron Hornaday Jr. drives Teresa Earnhardt's Papa John's Pizza Chevrolet to victory in the series' first road race, at Heartland Park Topeka.

August 17, 1995 Ron Hornaday Jr.'s win at Flemington Speedway clinches the first series manufacturer championship for Chevrolet.

September 7, 1995 Geoffrey Bodine (second) and Todd Bodine (sixth) set the record for the best finishes by brothers in the NASCAR Craftsman Truck Series at the Fas Mart Supertruck Shootout at Richmond International Raceway.

October 27, 1995 Mike Skinner wins the first NASCAR Craftsman Truck Series championship at Phoenix by 126 points over

Ron Hornaday Jr.

Joe Ruttman. The championship is worth $428,096.

November 18, 1995 A second season of 24 races is announced during an awards banquet at the Fairmont Hotel in San Francisco. The total posted awards increase to $4 million.

February 1996 Sears Craftsman agrees to become the title sponsor of the NASCAR Craftsman Truck Series under a new, three-year agreement.

March 17, 1996 Dave Rezendes wins a then-record $44,550 with a victory in the Florida Dodge Dealers 400 at Homestead-Miami Speedway.

May 3, 1996 Rich Bickle, qualifying for the Craftsman 200 at Portland Speedway, drives a Richard Petty-owned Cummins Engine Company Dodge to the company's first pole since the late 1970s in a major NASCAR series.

June 9, 1996 Mike Skinner's road racing victory at Heartland Park Topeka completes the first three-wins-in-a-row streak in series history.

September 8, 1996 Ron Hornaday Jr.'s New Hampshire International Speedway victory makes him the first in the series to win on a short track, road course and superspeedway in a single season.

October 26, 1996 A crowd of 58,000 for the GM Goodwrench/Delco Battery 300 at Phoenix International Raceway sets a series attendance record.

November 16, 1996 Ron Hornaday Jr., celebrating his 1996 NASCAR Craftsman Truck Series championship at Fairmont Hotel, sets a season winnings mark of $625,634. Mike Skinner's third-place award make him the first series millionaire. A 26-race schedule is announced for the 1997 season, including events at Walt Disney World Speedway, California Speedway and Texas Motor Speedway.

January 19, 1997 Walt Disney World Speedway near Orlando hosts the opening race of the third season, the Chevy Trucks Challenge. Tammy Jo Kirk, the first female driver in the NASCAR Craftsman Trucks Series, finishes 24th in the No. 07 Ford after qualifying ninth.

March 1, 1997 Ron Hornaday Jr.'s win at Tucson Raceway Park makes him the first competitor to win in all three seasons of the NASCAR Craftsman Truck Series.

March 16, 1997 Kenny Irwin becomes the first Rookie of the Year candidate to win a race, capturing the Florida Dodge Dealers 400 at Homestead-Miami Speedway.

May 24, 1997 Dodge gets its first victory in the NASCAR Craftsman Truck Series as Tony Raines wins the Western Auto/Parts America 200 at I-70 Speedway in Kansas City, Mo.

November 9, 1997 Jack Sprague becomes the third different NASCAR Craftsman Truck Series champion by a record 232 points over Rich Bickle. Joe Ruttman's victory in the Carquest Auto Parts 420K is worth a record $83,000.

December 13, 1997 Jack Sprague boosts the single-season, money record to $880,835. He also becomes the tour's all-time leading money winner. Five drivers—Sprague, Ron Hornaday Jr., Joe Ruttman, Mike Skinner and Mike Bliss—now have won more than $1 million during their NASCAR Craftsman Truck Series careers.

January 18, 1998 Ron Hornaday Jr. becomes the first driver to win a race in all four years of the NASCAR Craftsman Truck Series.

July 25, 1998 The series adopts a "live" pit stop format for most venues.

September 19, 1998 Jack Sprague finishes fourth at Gateway International Raceway to become the tour's first $2 million career winner.

October 10, 1998 Tom Hubert wins the Bud Pole for the

Kragen/Exide 151 at Infineon Raceway. He's the record 15th different driver to record a fast time.

October 24, 1998 Mike Bliss wins the GM Goodwrench Service Plus/AC Delco 300 at Phoenix International Raceway to become the series' 12th consecutive different winner.

November 8, 1998 Ron Hornaday Jr. becomes the first two-time NASCAR Craftsman Truck Series champion, beating Jack Sprague by three points—the closest margin of victory in series history. The pair finishes one-two in the season-ending Sam's Town 250 at Las Vegas Motor Speedway, with Sprague winning a race record $84,725.

December 11, 1998 Ron Hornaday Jr. collects nearly $400,000 in postseason awards to set career and single-season money won records of $2,442,586 and $915,407, respectively.

March 20, 1999 The CART FedEx Championship Series and NASCAR Craftsman Truck Series share a weekend for the first time, at Homestead-Miami Speedway.

March 27, 1999 Ron Hornaday Jr. becomes the first driver to win in all five seasons of the series when he captures the Chevy Trucks NASCAR 150 at Phoenix International Raceway.

April 3, 1999 Ron Hornaday Jr. wins the series' 100th race at Evergreen Speedway near Seattle and the $100,000 Craftsman bonus award.

June 11, 1999 Dodge scores its first NASCAR Craftsman Truck Series superspeedway victory when Dennis Setzer captures Pronto Auto Parts 400 at Texas Motor Speedway.

July 24, 1999 The NASCAR Craftsman Truck Series visits Michigan Speedway for the first time. Greg Biffle wins the goracing.com 200.

September 13, 1999 Chevrolet, Dodge and Ford drivers participate in a NASCAR test at Daytona International Speedway to lay the groundwork for a Speedweeks visit to the historic venue in 2000.

September 24, 1999 Greg Biffle's victory in The Orleans 250 at Las Vegas Motor Speedway hands Ford its first series manufacturer championship. Biffle's ninth win of the year sets a single-season record.

October 30, 1999 Three drivers—Greg Biffle, Jack Sprague and Dennis Setzer—enter the season finale just 25 points apart in the series' closest three-way showdown. Sprague wins NAPA Auto Parts 200 to clinch his second NASCAR Craftsman Truck Series title and post his 100th lead lap finish. His eight-point cushion, over Biffle, was the tour's second-tightest.

December 10, 1999 Postseason awards distributed at the fifth annual champion's banquet make Jack Sprague and Ron Hornaday Jr. the first drivers to win $3 million in the NASCAR Craftsman Truck Series.

February 18, 2000 Daytona International Speedway hosts its first NASCAR Craftsman Truck Series event. The lead changes 31 times before Mike Wallace drafts past Andy Houston entering the final set of turns of the 100th and final lap.

June 17, 2000 The NASCAR Craftsman Truck Series opens Kentucky Speedway to the delight of a sellout crowd.

July 8, 2000 Kurt Busch becomes the first rookie to win back-to-back races in the series.

October 13, 2000 Greg Biffle closes out the

championship race for the first time prior to the final race of the season. He is the first champion to drive a Ford to the title. It is the first NASCAR championship for team owner Jack Roush.

November 2, 2000 Greg Biffle is the first one-season millionaire, winning $1,002,510. He is the youngest champion at 30 years, nine months, 22 days and the first who didn't compete on the tour in 1995.

April 4, 2001 The series celebrates its 150th race at Martinsville Speedway. Scott Riggs scores the first NASCAR Craftsman Truck Series victory for Jim Smith, an owner who has fielded at least one entry in every event.

June 2, 2001 Dodge's eighth consecutive victory, at Dover International Speedway, matches a NASCAR Craftsman Trucks Series record set in 1995 by Chevrolet.

June 8, 2001 In winning for the first time at Texas Motor Speedway, Jack Sprague becomes the only competitor to win in six consecutive seasons on the NASCAR Craftsman Truck Series.

June 29, 2001 Jack Sprague records his 16th career Bud Pole at The Milwaukee Mile to become the series' all-time qualifying leader. He extends the mark to 20 by season's end.

July 7, 2001 Ricky Hendrick becomes the youngest winner in NASCAR Craftsman Truck Series history (21 years, three months, five days) with his victory at Kansas Speedway.

July 14, 2001 Jack Sprague finishes third at Kentucky Speedway and becomes the first $4 million winner in series history.

September 28, 2001 Ted Musgrave's victory at South Boston Speedway gives Dodge its first NASCAR Craftsman Truck Series manufacturer title.

November 3, 2001 By starting the final race of the season at California Speedway, Jack Sprague wraps up an unprecedented third NASCAR Craftsman Truck Series championship..

February 15, 2002 Robert Pressley becomes the second competitor (and the first since the series' inaugural race) to win in his first NASCAR Craftsman Truck Series appearance. Pressley wins the Florida Dodge Dealers 250 at Daytona International Speedway.

April 15, 2002 Winning from the 33rd starting position at Martinsville Speedway, Dennis Setzer races to victory from the deepest in the field for a series race. Setzer is only the second provisional starter to win in the series.

September 13, 2002 Brendan Gaughan, the Raybestos Rookie of the Year, completes a sweep of two series races held at Texas Motor Speedway. Gaughan is the first NASCAR driver to do so at the 1.5-mile superspeedway.

October 13, 2002 David Starr's victory at Las Vegas Motor Speedway gives owner Wayne Spears his first win in the team's 187th series appearance. That's the longest any owner has waited for win.

November 15, 2002 Mike Bliss becomes the fifth series champion with a fifth-place finish at Homestead-Miami Speedway. Xpress Motorsports is the first championship team without a NASCAR NEXTEL Cup Series owner or driver affiliation.

February 12, 2003 NASCAR announces that Toyota will join the Craftsman Truck Series in 2004, marking the first time a NASCAR series will include a foreign automaker.

March 25, 2003 Dennis Setzer wins the Lucas Oil 250 at Mesa Marin Raceway to match the NASCAR Craftsman Truck Series record for victories in consecutive seasons. Setzer wins for the sixth straight season, matching the mark set by Jack Sprague in 2001. Setzer continued the streak through the 2005 season, with wins in eight straight seasons.

October 11, 2003 Brendan Gaughan makes series history, winning his fourth consecutive race at Texas Motor Speedway and completing his second straight season sweep at the track.

November 14, 2003 Travis Kvapil, 27, is the youngest driver to win the NASCAR Craftsman Truck Series championship. Kvapil set another NASCAR Craftsman Truck Series record by completing all but a single lap in 2003—and that on the half-mile Mesa Marin Raceway. Xpress Motorsports' Steve Coulter becomes the first owner to win consecutive championships in the NASCAR Craftsman Truck Series.

March 13, 2004 David Reutimann wins Toyota's first pole in the NASCAR Craftsman Truck Series in his No. 17 Tundra at the Easycare Vehicle Service Contracts 200 at Atlanta Motor Speedway.

July 31, 2004 Toyota earns its first NASCAR Craftsman Truck Series win when Travis Kvapil captures the checkered flag in his No. 24 Bang Racing Line-X Tundra in the Line-X Spray-on Truck Bedliners 200 at Michigan International Speedway.

September 9, 2004 With an eighth-place finish at Richmond International Raceway, Jack Sprague becomes the NASCAR Craftsman Truck Series' first $5 million career winner.

November 19, 2004 Bobby Hamilton, 47, clinches the 2004 NASCAR Craftsman Truck Series championship with a 16th-place finish at Homestead, becoming the first driver/owner champion in series history. Fellow Dodge driver Kasey Kahne wins the race to become the first driver in NASCAR Craftsman Truck Series history to win in each of his first two series starts.

February 18, 2005 Bobby Hamilton makes 2005's Daytona race even more memorable by coming back from a 36th-place start to win. It is the furthest back a truck has ever come from to win in the NASCAR Craftsman Truck Series.

November 19, 2005 Ted Musgrave wins the 2005 NASCAR Craftsman Truck Series championship at Homestead. It's the first NASCAR Craftsman Truck Series championship for Musgrave, who had finished second or third in points the four previous seasons. In an appropriate ending to a season that celebrated 10 years of truck racing, the NASCAR Craftsman Truck Series' first three champions—Mike Skinner (1995), Ron Hornaday (1996) and Jack Sprague (1997)—finish in the top 10 in points.

November 17, 2006 The title drought for NASCAR's Bodine brothers ends in 2006 when Todd Bodine wins the NASCAR Craftsman Truck Series championship. Brett Bodine had finished second in the NASCAR Busch Series standings in 1986, and Geoffrey Bodine had finished third in the NASCAR NEXTEL Cup Series standings in 1990. Todd Bodine's championship is the first NASCAR series title for Toyota.

NASCAR Craftsman Truck Series

Date	Race	Track	TV/Radio	Time (Eastern)	2006 winner
February 16	GM Flex Fuel 250	Daytona International Speedway	SPEED/MRN	8:15 p.m.	Mark Martin
February 23	RaceTickets.com 200	California Speedway	SPEED/MRN	9:15 p.m.	Mark Martin
March 16	John Deere 200	Atlanta Motor Speedway	SPEED/MRN	9:15 p.m.	Todd Bodine
March 31	Kroger 250	Martinsville Speedway	SPEED/MRN	3:15 p.m.	David Starr
April 28	O'Reilly Auto Parts 250	Kansas Speedway	SPEED/MRN	3:15 p.m.	Terry Cook
May 18	Quaker Steak & Lube 200	Lowe's Motor Speedway	SPEED/MRN	8:45 p.m.	Kyle Busch
May 26	City of Mansfield 250	Mansfield Motorsports Speedway	SPEED/MRN	2:15 p.m.	Ron Hornaday
June 1	AAA Insurance 200	Dover International Speedway	SPEED/MRN	8:30 p.m.	Mark Martin
June 8	Sam's Town 400	Texas Motor Speedway	SPEED/MRN	9:15 p.m.	Todd Bodine
June 16	Con-Way Freight 200	Michigan International Speedway	SPEED/MRN	3:15 p.m.	Johnny Benson
June 22	Toyota Tundra Milwaukee 200	The Milwaukee Mile	SPEED/MRN	9:15 p.m.	Johnny Benson
June 30	O'Reilly 200	Memphis MotorSports Park	SPEED/MRN	9:15 p.m.	Jack Sprague
July 14	Built Ford Tough 225	Kentucky Speedway	SPEED/MRN	8:15 p.m.	Ron Hornaday
July 27	Power Stroke Diesel 200	O'Reilly Raceway Park	SPEED/MRN	8:45 p.m.	Rick Crawford
August 11	Toyota Tundra 200	Nashville Superspeedway	SPEED/MRN	5:15 p.m.	Johnny Benson
August 22	O'Reilly 200	Bristol Motor Speedway	SPEED/MRN	9:15 p.m.	Mark Martin
September 1	Dodge Ram Tough 200	Gateway International Raceway	SPEED/MRN	8:15 p.m.	Todd Bodine
September 15	New Hampshire 200	New Hampshire International Speedway	SPEED/MRN	2:15 p.m.	Johnny Benson
September 22	Smith's Las Vegas 350	Las Vegas Motor Speedway	SPEED/MRN	9:15 p.m.	Mike Skinner
October 6	John Deere 250	Talladega Superspeedway	SPEED/MRN	3:15 p.m.	Mark Martin
October 20	Kroger 200	Martinsville Speedway	SPEED/MRN	1:15 p.m.	Jack Sprague
October 27	EasyCare Contracts 200	Atlanta Motor Speedway	SPEED/MRN	5:15 p.m.	Mike Bliss
November 2	Silverado 350	Texas Motor Speedway	SPEED/MRN	9:15 p.m.	Clint Bowyer
November 9	Casino Arizona 150	Phoenix International Raceway	SPEED/MRN	8:15 p.m.	Johnny Benson
November 16	Ford 200	Homestead-Miami Speedway	SPEED/MRN	8:15 p.m.	Mark Martin

NOTE: Race names, TV information and start times are subject to change. FOX will televise two races.

Johnny Benson

>> 2007 DRIVERS <<

NASCAR Craftsman Truck Series

WILLIE ALLEN

Date of birth: 6/15/80
Hometown: Aqua, Tenn.

Year	Rank	Starts	Wins	Poles	T5	T10	Races led	Laps led
CAREER STATISTICS								
2005	63	2	0	0	0	1	0	0
2006	89	1	0	0	0	0	0	0
Totals		3	0	0	0	1	0	0

JUSTIN ALLGAIER

Date of birth: 6/6/86
Hometown: Riverton, Ill.

Year	Rank	Starts	Wins	Poles	T5	T10	Races led	Laps led
CAREER STATISTICS								
2005	58	4	0	0	0	0	0	0
2006	56	3	0	0	0	0	0	0
Totals		7	0	0	0	0	0	0

T.J. BELL

Date of birth: 8/25/80
Hometown: Reno, Nev.

Year	Rank	Starts	Wins	Poles	T5	T10	Races led	Laps led
CAREER STATISTICS								
2003	26	12	0	0	0	0	0	0
2005	75	1	0	0	0	0	0	0
2006	77	1	0	0	0	0	1	1
Totals		14	0	0	0	0	1	1

JOHNNY BENSON

Truck: No. 23 Toyota • **Date of birth:** 6/27/63
Hometown: Grand Rapids, Mich. • **Owner/Team:** Bill Davis Racing

Year	Rank	Starts	Wins	Poles	T5	T10	Races led	Laps led
CAREER STATISTICS								
1995	26	7	0	0	2	5	0	0
1996	37	4	0	1	1	4	2	119
1997	121	1	0	0	0	0	0	0
2004	25	13	0	0	5	8	1	5
2005	10	25	0	0	6	10	8	79
2006	2	25	5	1	13	17	9	315
Totals		75	5	2	27	44	20	518

KELLY BIRES

Truck: No. 21 Ford • **Date of birth:** 8/25/84
Hometown: Mauston, Wis. • **Owner/Team:** Wood Brothers

Year	Rank	Starts	Wins	Poles	T5	T10	Races led	Laps led
CAREER STATISTICS								
2006	76	1	0	0	0	0	0	0
Totals		1	0	0	0	0	0	0

BLAKE BJORKLUND

Truck: No. 06 Chevrolet • **Date of birth:** 9/8/85
Hometown: Isanti, Minn. • **Owner/Team:** MRD Motorsports
No career NASCAR Craftsman Truck Series statistics

MIKE BLISS

Date of birth: 4/5/65
Hometown: Milwaukie, Ore.

Year	Rank	Starts	Wins	Poles	T5	T10	Races led	Laps led
CAREER STATISTICS								
1995	8	19	1	0	5	12	1	21
1996	5	24	2	2	9	11	4	347
1997	4	26	1	6	11	18	11	686
1998	10	27	2	4	5	9	11	826
1999	9	25	1	2	6	13	9	157
2001	86	1	0	0	0	1	0	0
2002	1	22	5	4	13	18	13	389
2005	41	5	0	0	1	2	1	8
2006	11	25	1	0	7	13	6	92
Totals		174	13	18	57	97	56	2526

TODD BODINE

Truck: No. 30 Toyota • **Date of birth:** 2/27/64
Hometown: Chemung, N.Y. • **Owner/Team:** Stephen Germain

Year	Rank	Starts	Wins	Poles	T5	T10	Races led	Laps led
CAREER STATISTICS								
1995	31	5	0	0	1	5	1	1
2004	27	10	2	0	4	5	3	127
2005	3	25	5	0	12	15	12	502
2006	1	25	3	1	12	16	10	287
Totals		65	10	1	29	41	26	917

CHAD CHAFFIN

Truck: No. 59 Toyota • **Date of birth:** 7/20/68
Hometown: Smyrna, Tenn. • **Owner/Team:** Jim Harris

Year	Rank	Starts	Wins	Poles	T5	T10	Races led	Laps led
CAREER STATISTICS								
2000	55	3	0	0	1	1	0	0

Year	Rank	Starts	Wins	Poles	T5	T10	Races led	Laps led
2001	60	2	0	0	1	1	0	0
2002	77	2	0	0	0	0	0	0
2003	10	25	0	2	2	9	5	115
2004	10	25	2	0	6	10	4	61
2005	26	21	0	0	1	5	5	41
2006	28	16	0	0	0	1	1	6
Totals		94	2	2	11	27	15	223

STACY COMPTON

Truck: No. 20 Ford • **Date of birth:** 5/26/67
Hometown: Grit, Va. • **Owner/Team:** Wood Brothers

CAREER STATISTICS								
Year	Rank	Starts	Wins	Poles	T5	T10	Races led	Laps led
1997	13	26	0	0	3	8	0	0
1998	7	27	2	2	9	14	7	467
1999	4	25	0	6	12	17	14	224
2001	44	4	0	1	1	4	0	0
2002	50	3	0	0	0	1	0	0
2006	62	2	0	0	0	0	0	0
Totals		87	2	9	25	44	21	691

TERRY COOK

Date of birth: 2/26/68
Hometown: Sylvania, Ohio

CAREER STATISTICS								
Year	Rank	Starts	Wins	Poles	T5	T10	Races led	Laps led
1996	60	3	0	0	0	0	0	0
1997	24	15	0	1	0	0	0	0
1998	20	27	1	1	3	6	2	42
1999	15	25	0	0	1	3	1	15
2000	14	24	0	0	1	8	5	25
2001	7	24	0	1	5	16	5	67
2002	8	22	4	2	9	17	9	490
2003	9	25	0	2	0	13	4	84
2004	16	25	0	1	2	7	4	56
2005	15	25	0	0	2	8	5	127
2006	8	25	1	0	3	12	5	65
Totals		240	6	8	26	90	40	971

MATT CRAFTON

Date of birth: 6/11/76
Hometown: Tulare, Calif.

CAREER STATISTICS								
Year	Rank	Starts	Wins	Poles	T5	T10	Races led	Laps led
2000	83	1	0	0	0	1	0	0
2001	12	24	0	0	0	11	3	29
2002	15	22	0	0	0	6	0	0
2003	11	25	0	0	0	11	2	11

Year	Rank	Starts	Wins	Poles	T5	T10	Races led	Laps led
2004	5	25	0	0	6	17	5	41
2005	9	25	0	1	2	10	3	32
2006	14	25	0	0	4	10	2	2
Totals		147	0	1	12	66	15	115

RICK CRAWFORD

Truck: No. 14 Ford • **Date of birth:** 7/26/58
Hometown: Mobile, Ala. • **Owner/Team:** Tom Mitchell

CAREER STATISTICS								
Year	Rank	Starts	Wins	Poles	T5	T10	Races led	Laps led
1997	12	26	0	0	1	10	2	24
1998	18	27	1	0	4	5	1	31
1999	14	25	0	0	3	10	4	46
2000	11	24	0	0	2	12	2	20
2001	8	24	0	0	10	16	10	201
2002	2	22	0	2	12	17	12	476
2003	7	25	1	0	10	16	8	256
2004	12	25	0	1	4	9	2	92
2005	16	24	1	2	3	11	4	106
2006	9	25	1	0	5	13	6	155
Totals		247	5	4	54	119	51	1407

ERIN CROCKER

Date of birth: 3/23/81
Hometown: Wilbraham, Mass.

CAREER STATISTICS								
Year	Rank	Starts	Wins	Poles	T5	T10	Races led	Laps led
2005	91	2	0	0	0	0	0	0
2006	25	25	0	0	0	0	0	0
Totals		27	0	0	0	0	0	0

ERIK DARNELL

Truck: No. 99 Ford • **Date of birth:** 12/2/82
Hometown: Beach Park, Ill. • **Owner/Team:** Jack Roush

CAREER STATISTICS								
Year	Rank	Starts	Wins	Poles	T5	T10	Races led	Laps led
2004	98	1	0	0	0	0	0	0
2006	12	25	0	1	4	12	3	24
Totals		26	0	1	4	12	3	24

KERRY EARNHARDT

Date of birth: 12/8/69
Hometown: Kannapolis, N.C.

CAREER STATISTICS								
Year	Rank	Starts	Wins	Poles	T5	T10	Races led	Laps led
2005	67	2	0	1	0	0	1	1

Year	Rank	Starts	Wins	Poles	T5	T10	Races led	Laps led
2006	22	25	0	0	0	0	1	5
Totals		27	0	1	0	0	2	6

WAYNE EDWARDS

Truck: No. 03 Chevrolet • **Date of birth:** 6/23/67
Hometown: Shepherdsville, Ken. • **Owner/Team:** Green Light Racing

CAREER STATISTICS								
Year	Rank	Starts	Wins	Poles	T5	T10	Races led	Laps led
2000	26	13	0	0	0	0	0	0
2001	91	2	0	0	0	0	0	0
2002	57	4	0	0	0	0	0	0
2003	39	8	0	0	0	0	0	0
2004	64	4	0	0	0	0	0	0
2005	33	10	0	0	0	1	0	0
2006	84	3	0	0	0	0	0	0
Totals		44	0	0	0	1	0	0

BRENDAN GAUGHAN

Truck: No. 77 • **Date of birth:** 7/10/75
Hometown: Las Vegas • **Owner/Team:** Michael Gaughan

CAREER STATISTICS								
Year	Rank	Starts	Wins	Poles	T5	T10	Races led	Laps led
1997	99	1	0	0	0	0	0	0
1998	75	2	0	0	0	0	0	0
1999	75	2	0	0	0	0	0	0
2000	40	5	0	0	0	0	0	0
2001	31	7	0	0	2	3	4	56
2002	11	22	2	0	5	9	4	87
2003	4	25	6	3	14	18	16	652
2005	19	23	0	0	2	7	3	17
2006	15	25	0	0	4	5	2	14
Totals		112	8	3	27	42	29	826

BOBBY HAMILTON

Date of birth: 5/29/57
Hometown: Nashville

CAREER STATISTICS								
Year	Rank	Starts	Wins	Poles	T5	T10	Races led	Laps led
1996	82	2	0	1	0	0	1	116
1997	56	2	0	0	1	2	0	0
1998	59	3	0	0	0	0	0	0
1999	36	5	0	1	1	1	2	89
2000	42	5	1	1	1	2	4	278
2001	38	5	1	0	2	3	2	258
2002	66	2	0	0	0	0	0	0
2003	6	25	2	1	10	18	13	394
2004	1	25	4	0	12	16	14	416
2005	6	25	2	1	6	12	5	126
2006	49	3	0	0	0	0	0	0
Totals		102	10	5	33	54	41	1677

JESUS HERNANDEZ

Truck: No. 46 Chevrolet • **Date of birth:** 4/1/81
Hometown: Fresno, Calif. • **Owner/Team:** Ginn Racing/Morgan-Dollar

No career NASCAR Craftsman Truck Series statistics

RON HORNADAY JR.

Truck: No. 33 Chevrolet • **Date of birth:** 6/20/58
Hometown: Palmdale, Calif. • **Owner/Team:** Kevin Harvick Inc.

CAREER STATISTICS								
Year	Rank	Starts	Wins	Poles	T5	T10	Races led	Laps led
1995	3	20	6	4	10	14	12	944
1996	1	24	4	2	18	23	14	834
1997	5	26	7	3	13	17	15	1213
1998	1	27	6	2	16	22	18	882
1999	7	25	2	0	7	16	16	943
2002	53	2	1	0	1	1	1	21
2004	85	1	0	0	0	0	0	0
2005	4	25	1	1	7	13	10	460
2006	7	25	2	1	8	12	5	313
Totals		175	29	13	80	118	91	5610

SHANE HUFFMAN

Date of birth: 12/30/73
Hometown: Hickory, N.C.

CAREER STATISTICS								
Year	Rank	Starts	Wins	Poles	T5	T10	Races led	Laps led
2006	48	4	0	0	0	0	0	0
Totals		4	0	0	0	0	0	0

BRAD KESELOWSKI

Date of birth: 2/12/84
Hometown: Rochester Hills, Mich.

CAREER STATISTICS								
Year	Rank	Starts	Wins	Poles	T5	T10	Races led	Laps led
2004	34	8	0	0	0	0	0	0
2005	21	25	0	0	0	1	5	10
2006	40	6	0	0	0	1	1	2
Totals		39	0	0	1	6	12	

CASEY KINGSLAND

Date of birth: 12/14/84
Hometown: Las Vegas

CAREER STATISTICS								
Year	Rank	Starts	Wins	Poles	T5	T10	Races led	Laps led
2005	92	1	0	0	0	0	0	0
2006	70	2	0	0	0	0	0	0
Totals		3	0	0	0	0	0	0

KRAIG KINSER

Truck: No. 46 Chevrolet • **Date of birth:** 10/8/84
Hometown: Bloomington, Ind. • **Owner/Team:** Morgan-Dollar

CAREER STATISTICS

Year	Rank	Starts	Wins	Poles	T5	T10	Races led	Laps led
2006	29	18	0	0	0	1	0	0
Totals		18	0	0	0	1	0	0

KYLE KRISILOFF

Date of birth: 3/3/86
Hometown: Indianapolis

CAREER STATISTICS

Year	Rank	Starts	Wins	Poles	T5	T10	Races led	Laps led
2006	33	12	0	0	0	0	1	16
Totals		12	0	0	0	0	1	16

TRAVIS KVAPIL

Truck: No. 6 Ford • **Date of birth:** 3/1/76
Hometown: Janesville, Wis. • **Owner/Team:** Jack Roush

CAREER STATISTICS

Year	Rank	Starts	Wins	Poles	T5	T10	Races led	Laps led
2001	4	24	1	0	11	18	9	55
2002	9	22	1	0	10	14	7	170
2003	1	25	1	0	13	22	11	49
2004	8	25	2	1	6	10	7	176
Totals		96	5	1	40	64	34	450

SCOTT LAGASSE JR.

Date of birth: 1/31/81
Hometown: St. Augustine, Fla.

CAREER STATISTICS

Year	Rank	Starts	Wins	Poles	T5	T10	Races led	Laps led
2006	37	10	0	0	0	0	0	0
Totals		10	0	0	0	0	0	0

BILL LESTER

Date of birth: 2/6/61
Hometown: Oakland

CAREER STATISTICS

Year	Rank	Starts	Wins	Poles	T5	T10	Races led	Laps led
2000	86	1	0	0	0	0	0	0
2001	59	5	0	0	0	0	0	0
2002	17	22	0	0	0	0	0	0
2003	14	25	0	1	0	1	2	17
2004	22	25	0	0	0	1	2	32

Year	Rank	Starts	Wins	Poles	T5	T10	Races led	Laps led
2005	17	25	0	2	2	4	4	38
2006	20	24	0	0	0	0	1	3
Totals		127	0	3	2	6	9	90

DAMON LUSK

Date of birth: 9/18/77
Hometown: Kennewick, Wash.

CAREER STATISTICS

Year	Rank	Starts	Wins	Poles	T5	T10	Races led	Laps led
2001	89	1	0	0	0	0	0	0
2006	41	5	0	0	0	0	0	0
Totals		6	0	0	0	0	0	0

MARK MARTIN

Date of birth: 1/9/59
Hometown: Batesville, Ark.

CAREER STATISTICS

Year	Rank	Starts	Wins	Poles	T5	T10	Races led	Laps led
1996	52	2	1	0	2	2	2	88
2005	70	1	0	0	0	1	1	1
2006	19	14	6	3	11	12	9	661
Totals		17	7	3	13	15	12	750

CHAD McCUMBEE

Truck: 08 Chevrolet • **Date of birth:** 10/15/84
Hometown: Supply, N.C. • **Owner/Team:** Bobby Dotter

CAREER STATISTICS

Year	Rank	Starts	Wins	Poles	T5	T10	Races led	Laps led
2006	17	24	0	0	0	3	5	5
Totals		24	0	0	0	3	5	5

JOHN MICKEL

Truck: No. 07 Chevrolet • **Date of birth:** 1/28/75
Hometown: Cambridge, England • **Owner/Team:** Gene Christensen

CAREER STATISTICS

Year	Rank	Starts	Wins	Poles	T5	T10	Races led	Laps led
2005	81	1	0	0	0	0	0	0
2006	43	5	0	0	0	0	1	1
Totals		6	0	0	0	0	1	1

CHASE MILLER

Truck: No. 4 Dodge • **Date of birth:** 1/28/87
Hometown: Canton, Ga. • **Owner/Team:** Bobby Hamilton

CAREER STATISTICS							
Year	Rank	Starts	Wins	Poles	T5	T10	Races led	Laps led
2006	38	8	0	0	0	1	0	0
Totals		8	0	0	0	1	0	0

Year	Rank	Starts	Wins	Poles	T5	T10	Races led	Laps led
2004	9	25	0	0	5	10	5	99
2005	22	22	1	0	2	4	3	22
2006	35	10	0	0	0	1	0	0
Totals		61	1	0	8	16	9	131

CHASE MONTGOMERY

Date of birth: 9/29/83
Hometown: Lebanon, Tenn.

CAREER STATISTICS								
Year	Rank	Starts	Wins	Poles	T5	T10	Races led	Laps led
2003	106	1	0	0	0	0	0	0
2004	21	25	0	0	0	0	0	0
2005	23	25	0	0	0	0	0	0
2006	59	2	0	0	0	0	0	0
Totals		53	0	0	0	0	0	0

TIMOTHY PETERS

Date of birth: 8/29/80
Hometown: Providence, N.C.

CAREER STATISTICS								
Year	Rank	Starts	Wins	Poles	T5	T10	Races led	Laps led
2005	28	16	0	0	0	2	1	46
2006	27	17	0	0	0	1	0	0
Totals		33	0	0	0	3	1	46

RYAN MOORE

Date of birth: 8/10/83
Hometown: Scarborough, Maine

CAREER STATISTICS								
Year	Rank	Starts	Wins	Poles	T5	T10	Races led	Laps led
2006	36	11	0	0	0	0	0	0
Totals		11	0	0	0	0	0	0

BOSTON REID

Date of birth: 12/29/82
Hometown: Logansport, Ind.

CAREER STATISTICS								
Year	Rank	Starts	Wins	Poles	T5	T10	Races led	Laps led
2006	26	20	0	0	0	0	1	3
Totals		20	0	0	0	0	1	3

TED MUSGRAVE

Truck: No. 9 Toyota • **Date of birth:** 12/18/55
Hometown: Franklin, Wis. • **Owner/Team:** Bob Germain

CAREER STATISTICS								
Year	Rank	Starts	Wins	Poles	T5	T10	Races led	Laps led
1995	66	1	0	0	1	1	0	0
1996	69	2	0	0	1	1	0	0
2001	2	24	7	2	13	18	15	810
2002	3	22	3	3	12	16	15	757
2003	3	25	3	4	14	18	18	796
2004	3	25	2	2	11	16	13	757
2005	1	25	1	1	11	15	4	185
2006	6	25	0	0	10	13	6	155
Totals		149	16	12	73	98	71	3460

ROBERT RICHARDSON

Date of birth: 4/4/82
Hometown: McKinney, Texas

CAREER STATISTICS								
Year	Rank	Starts	Wins	Poles	T5	T10	Races led	Laps led
2005	62	3	0	0	0	0	0	0
2006	30	20	0	0	0	0	0	0
Totals		23	0	0	0	0	0	0

KEN SCHRADER

Truck: No. 18 Dodge • **Date of birth:** 5/29/55
Hometown: St. Louis • **Owner/Team:** Bobby Hamilton

CAREER STATISTICS								
Year	Rank	Starts	Wins	Poles	T5	T10	Races led	Laps led
1995	29	7	1	0	3	3	1	54
1996	46	4	0	0	0	2	0	0
1997	69	2	0	0	0	1	1	48
1999	120	1	0	0	0	0	0	0
2000	35	5	0	0	1	3	1	59
2001	28	8	0	0	1	5	0	0
2002	27	8	0	0	0	3	0	0
2003	23	11	0	0	0	3	0	0
2004	28	12	0	0	1	4	0	0
2005	31	10	0	0	0	1	0	0
Totals		68	1	1	6	25	3	161

STEVE PARK

Date of birth: 8/23/67
Hometown: East Northport, N.Y.

CAREER STATISTICS								
Year	Rank	Starts	Wins	Poles	T5	T10	Races led	Laps led
1996	48	3	0	0	1	1	1	10
1997	101	1	0	0	0	0	0	0

DENNIS SETZER

Truck: No. 75 Chevrolet • **Date of birth:** 2/27/60
Hometown: Newton, N.C. • **Owner/Team:** Spears Motorsports

CAREER STATISTICS								
Year	Rank	Starts	Wins	Poles	T5	T10	Races led	Laps led
1995	28	8	0	0	1	2	1	27
1997	124	1	0	0	0	0	0	0
1998	28	13	1	0	1	5	2	31
1999	3	25	3	1	11	19	12	427
2000	7	24	1	0	8	16	4	73
2001	9	24	1	2	8	15	7	99
2002	6	22	1	0	8	14	6	142
2003	2	25	3	0	15	23	8	437
2004	2	25	2	0	8	16	8	93
2005	2	25	4	0	10	13	8	414
2006	13	25	0	0	1	11	4	83
Totals		217	16	3	71	134	60	1826

TODD SHAFER

Date of birth: 11/29/76
Hometown: Ashland, Ohio

CAREER STATISTICS								
Year	Rank	Starts	Wins	Poles	T5	T10	Races led	Laps led
2006	90	1	0	0	0	0	0	0
Totals		1	0	0	0	0	0	0

MIKE SKINNER

Truck: No. 5 Toyota • **Date of birth:** 6/28/57
Hometown: Susanville, Calif. • **Owner/Team:** Bill Davis

CAREER STATISTICS								
Year	Rank	Starts	Wins	Poles	T5	T10	Races led	Laps led
1995	1	20	8	10	17	18	13	1053
1996	3	24	8	5	17	20	18	1533
1997	44	4	0	0	2	2	2	40
1998	49	2	0	0	1	1	1	4
2003	48	4	0	0	0	0	1	3
2004	11	25	0	2	4	9	11	448
2005	5	25	2	7	9	13	15	864
2006	10	25	1	8	8	13	14	596
Totals		129	19	32	58	76	75	4541

JACK SPRAGUE

Truck: No. 60 Toyota • **Date of birth:** 8/8/64
Hometown: Spring Lake, Mich. • **Owner/Team:** Jeff Wyler

CAREER STATISTICS								
Year	Rank	Starts	Wins	Poles	T5	T10	Races led	Laps led
1995	5	20	0	1	4	15	3	55
1996	2	24	5	2	18	21	10	733
1997	1	26	3	5	16	23	13	1004
1998	2	27	5	4	16	23	13	837
1999	1	25	3	1	16	19	15	581
2000	5	24	3	0	13	15	10	492
2001	1	24	4	7	15	17	19	1386
2003	66	2	0	0	2	2	0	0
2004	7	25	1	6	8	13	10	510
2005	8	25	1	1	7	11	7	199
2006	5	25	2	2	10	14	7	307
Totals		247	27	29	125	173	107	6104

DAVID STARR

Date of birth: 10/11/67
Hometown: Houston

CAREER STATISTICS								
Year	Rank	Starts	Wins	Poles	T5	T10	Races led	Laps led
1998	43	5	0	0	0	0	1	1
1999	22	24	0	0	0	0	1	8
2000	29	13	0	0	0	0	1	6
2001	47	5	0	0	3	4	0	0
2002	5	22	1	2	8	16	8	111
2003	13	21	0	0	5	13	3	16
2004	6	25	2	1	8	16	4	78
2005	7	25	0	2	4	10	2	58
2006	4	25	1	0	6	12	3	126
Totals		165	4	5	34	71	23	404

J.C. STOUT

Truck: No. 91 Chevrolet • **Date of birth:** 9/15/83
Hometown: Castile, N.Y.• **Owner/Team:** Donald Stout

CAREER STATISTICS								
Year	Rank	Starts	Wins	Poles	T5	T10	Races led	Laps led
2005	71	2	0	0	0	0	0	0
2006	52	4	0	0	0	0	0	0
Totals		6	0	0	0	0	0	0

TAM TOPHAM

Truck: Chevrolet • **Date of birth:** 3/31/60
Hometown: Wytheville, Va. • **Owner/Team:** Tam Topham

CAREER STATISTICS								
Year	Rank	Starts	Wins	Poles	T5	T10	Races led	Laps led
2005	66	3	0	0	0	0	0	0
2006	82	1	0	0	0	0	0	0
Totals		4	0	0	0	0	0	0

TYLER WALKER

Truck: No. 36 Toyota • **Date of birth:** 7/15/79
Hometown: Los Angeles • **Owner/Team:** Bill Davis Racing

CAREER STATISTICS								
Year	Rank	Starts	Wins	Poles	T5	T10	Races led	Laps led
2003	71	3	0	0	0	0	0	0
Totals		3	0	0	0	0	0	0

>> 2006 POINTS STANDINGS <<

NASCAR Craftsman Truck Series

Rk. Driver	Points	Starts	Run at fin.	Top fin.	Times led	Laps led	Laps completed	Miles completed	Money won
1. Todd Bodine	3,666	25	25	1	22	287	4,075	4,813.94	$1,043,680
2. Johnny Benson	3,539	25	24	1	17	315	4,047	4,782.26	$770,157
3. David Reutimann	3,530	25	24	3	17	160	4,024	4,781.79	$525,531
4. David Starr	3,355	25	25	1	4	126	4,073	4,810.69	$515,985
5. Jack Sprague	3,328	25	24	1	12	307	3,974	4,603.61	$586,879
6. Ted Musgrave	3,314	25	23	2	6	155	3,889	4,584.85	$560,083
7. Ron Hornaday Jr.	3,313	25	24	1	11	313	4,025	4,743.06	$544,667
8. Terry Cook	3,265	25	25	1	5	65	4,076	4,816.43	$483,630
9. Rick Crawford	3,252	25	21	1	11	155	3,943	4,653.14	$508,602
10. Mike Skinner	3,219	25	20	1	35	596	3,739	4,334.52	$568,535
11. Mike Bliss	3,151	25	25	1	10	92	4,006	4,494.20	$439,725
12. Erik Darnell	3,136	25	23	2	3	24	3,910	4,583.02	$443,114
13. Dennis Setzer	3,129	25	23	2	5	83	3,966	4,661.80	$374,688
14. Matt Crafton	3,102	25	24	3	2	2	3,953	4,726.07	$371,253
15. Brendan Gaughan	2,984	25	23	2	3	14	3,852	4,491.02	$390,915
16. Bobby Hamilton Jr.	2,671	25	24	4	6	36	3,913	4,693.13	$342,517
17. Chad McCumbee	2,515	24	22	7	5	5	3,800	4,321.99	$282,023
18. Aric Almirola	2,471	25	22	9	0	0	3,910	4,553.22	$298,643
19. Mark Martin	2,313	14	13	1	38	661	2,009	2,438.92	$595,561
20. Bill Lester	2,252	24	20	11	1	3	3,571	4,057.41	$263,781
21. Marcos Ambrose	2,228	22	20	3	5	77	3,428	3,770.98	$272,313
22. Kerry Earnhardt	2,199	25	19	11	2	5	3,725	4,301.50	$245,259
23. Bobby East	2,186	23	20	11	0	0	3,434	3,816.33	$231,328
24. David Ragan	2,122	19	16	5	2	77	2,978	3,438.72	$237,401
25. Erin Crocker	2,113	25	20	16	0	0	3,517	4,133.05	$246,791
26. Boston Reid	1,792	20	15	14	1	3	2,938	3,279.01	$198,796
27. Timothy Peters	1,672	17	14	6	0	0	2,670	3,044.37	$181,310
28. Chad Chaffin	1,566	16	14	8	1	6	2,277	2,697.12	$160,440
29. Kyle Kinser	1,541	18	14	9	0	0	2,661	2,651.56	$167,008
30. Robert Richardson	1,514	20	14	16	0	0	2,584	3,091.53	$174,489
31. Joey Miller	1,429	15	12	5	0	0	2,345	2,634.42	$165,225
32. Kyle Busch	1,107	7	7	1	6	227	1,232	1,196.40	$166,396
33. Kyle Krisiloff	1,106	12	10	16	2	16	1,860	2,046.15	$136,416
34. Kelly Sutton	977	12	9	19	1	1	1,777	2,216.78	$115,581
35. Steve Park	971	10	9	10	0	0	1,569	1,859.97	$101,449
36. Ryan Moore	911	11	8	14	0	0	1,744	1,844.50	$95,364
37. Scott Lagasse Jr.	741	10	8	18	0	0	1,452	1,746.89	$96,180
38. Chase Miller	675	8	4	10	0	0	928	1,218.98	$75,530
39. Michel Jourdain Jr.	616	7	7	13	0	0	1,071	1,443.70	$66,505
40. Brad Keselowski	521	6	3	16	1	2	799	1,032.75	$65,690
41. Damon Lusk	470	5	4	17	0	0	623	803.84	$49,007
42. Clint Bowyer	434	3	3	1	5	195	594	560.87	$83,865
43. John Mickel	430	5	5	20	1	1	743	854.18	$43,825
44. Jon Wood	408	3	3	6	1	6	343	674.90	$38,165
45. Kevin Grubb	376	4	3	14	0	0	647	450.31	$40,272
46. A.J. Allmendinger	350	3	2	5	2	9	307	481.66	$33,230
47. Mike Wallace	327	4	1	22	1	4	396	822.88	$48,774
48. Shane Huffman	325	4	3	20	0	0	516	612.81	$32,960
49. Bobby Hamilton	315	3	3	14	0	0	342	670.86	$39,920
50. Sean Murphy	315	4	3	20	1	1	397	760.54	$44,105
51. Cameron Dodson	313	4	4	24	0	0	732	590.34	$28,735
52. J.C. Stout	301	4	3	28	0	0	646	675.63	$31,295
53. Joe Nemechek	292	3	2	6	3	37	239	466.86	$36,050
54. Peter Shepherd	273	3	2	18	0	0	465	527.04	$28,941
55. Travis Kittleson	263	3	2	16	1	0	462	480.19	$14,195
56. Justin Allgaier	252	3	2	21	0	0	367	451.00	$28,770
57. Johnny Sauter	224	2	2	12	0	0	450	331.50	$16,430
58. Johnny Chapman	201	4	3	29	0	0	475	617.00	$35,765
59. Chase Montgomery	188	2	2	19	0	0	241	463.50	$23,905

Rk. Driver	Points	Starts	Run at fin.	Top fin.	Times led	Laps led	Laps completed	Miles completed	Money won
60. Sammy Sanders	185	2	2	22	0	0	347	303.35	$13,955
61. Kevin Lepage	179	2	2	21	0	0	298	400.00	$23,005
62. Stacy Compton	173	2	2	25	0	0	206	462.00	$24,005
63. Carl Edwards	170	1	1	2	0	0	200	200.00	$31,650
64. Bobby Labonte	170	1	1	2	2	10	102	204.00	$22,075
65. Jeremy Mayfield	164	2	1	23	0	0	260	394.56	$17,149
66. Derrike Cope	161	2	1	27	0	0	220	442.96	$20,355
67. Robert Turner	152	2	2	26	0	0	414	243.83	$18,430
68. Butch Miller	152	2	1	27	0	0	394	350.42	$19,120
69. Mike Greenwell	149	2	2	26	0	0	448	273.50	$17,085
70. Casey Kingsland	149	2	2	28	0	0	276	340.50	$17,305
71. Denny Hamlin	142	1	1	8	0	0	200	105.02	$7,225
72. Kevin Hamlin	135	1	1	11	1	1	102	255.00	$17,275
73. Chris Wimmer	116	2	1	34	0	0	199	243.00	$15,483
74. Michael Waltrip	112	1	1	17	0	0	134	201.00	$12,140
75. Auggie Vidovich	106	1	1	19	0	0	250	125.00	$13,191
76. Kelly Bires	106	1	1	19	0	0	129	198.66	$8,240
77. T.J. Bell	105	1	1	21	1	1	200	211.60	$10,065
78. Justin Martz	103	1	1	20	0	0	160	200.00	$11,390
79. Justin Labonte	94	1	1	23	0	0	146	219.00	$8,165
80. Boris Jurkovic	88	1	1	25	0	0	150	187.50	$9,605
81. Tim Fedewa	76	1	0	29	0	0	131	196.50	$7,590
82. Tam Topham	76	1	1	29	0	0	196	103.10	$6,165
83. David Stremme	67	1	1	32	0	0	203	106.78	$6,965
84. Wayne Edwards	64	3	0	33	0	0	70	109.64	$30,069
85. Martin Truex Jr.	61	1	0	34	0	0	96	192.00	$9,890
86. Eric Norris	58	1	0	35	0	0	48	96.00	$10,420
87. Carl Long	58	1	0	35	0	0	78	117.00	$7,590
88. Scott Lynch	58	1	0	35	0	0	10	15.00	$7,440
89. Willie Allen	0	1	1	25	0	0	132	198.00	$10,765
90. Todd Shafer	0	1	0	36	0	0	69	47.33	$7,308

>> 2006 RACE RESULTS <<

NASCAR Craftsman Truck Series

No.	Date	Race	Track	Winner	Pole
1.	February 17	GM Flex Fuel 250	Daytona International Speedway	Mark Martin	Mark Martin
2.	February 24	Racetickets.com 200	California Speedway	Mark Martin	David Reutimann
3.	March 17	John Deere 200	Atlanta Motor Speedway	Todd Bodine	Todd Bodine
4.	April 1	Kroger 250	Martinsville Speedway	David Starr	Bobby Hamilton Jr.
5.	April 29	Missouri/Illinois Dodge Dealers Ram Tough 200	Gateway International Raceway	Todd Bodine	David Ragan
6.	May 19	Quaker Steak & Lube 200	Lowe's Motor Speedway	Kyle Busch	Mike Skinner
7.	May 27	City of Mansfield 250	Mansfield Motorsports Speedway	Ron Hornaday Jr.	Todd Bodine
8.	June 2	AAA Insurance 200	Dover International Speedway	Mark Martin	David Reutimann
9.	June 9	Sam's Town 400	Texas Motor Speedway	Todd Bodine	Mike Skinner
10.	June 17	Con-way Freight 200	Michigan International Speedway	Johnny Benson	Mike Skinner
11.	June 23	Toyota Tundra Milwaukee 200	The Milwaukee Mile	Johnny Benson	Ron Hornaday Jr.
12.	July 1	O'Reilly Auto Parts 250	Kansas Speedway	Terry Cook	Mike Skinner
13.	July 8	Built Ford Tough 225 pres. by the Greater Cincinnati Ford Dealers	Kentucky Speedway	Ron Hornaday Jr.	Marcos Ambrose
14.	July 15	O'Reilly 200	Memphis Motorsports Park	Jack Sprague	Jack Sprague
15.	August 4	Power Stroke Diesel 200 pres. by Ford and International	O'Reilly Raceway Park	Rick Crawford	David Ragan
16.	August 12	Toyota Tundra 200	Nashville Superspeedway	Johnny Benson	Erik Darnell
17.	August 23	O'Reilly 200	Bristol Motor Speedway	Mark Martin	Mark Martin
18.	September 16	New Hampshire 200	New Hampshire International Speedway	Johnny Benson	Mike Skinner
19.	September 23	Smith's Las Vegas 350	Las Vegas Motor Speedway	Mike Skinner	Mike Skinner
20.	October 7	John Deere 250	Talladega Superspeedway	Mark Martin	Mark Martin
21.	October 21	Kroger 200	Martinsville Speedway	Jack Sprague	Jack Sprague
22.	October 28	EasyCare Vehicle Services Contracts 200	Atlanta Motor Speedway	Mike Bliss	Mike Skinner
23.	November 3	Silverado 350	Texas Motor Speedway	Clint Bowyer	Clint Bowyer
24.	November 10	Casino Arizona 150	Phoenix International Raceway	Johnny Benson	Johnny Benson
25.	November 17	Ford 200	Homestead-Miami Speedway	Mark Martin	Mike Skinner

2006 CHAMPION

30 TODD BODINE

Truck: Toyota • **Truck owner:** Stephen Germain
Birth date: February 27, 1964 • **Hometown:** Chemung, N.Y.

NASCAR Craftsman Truck Series Statistics

Seasons competed: 4 (1995, 2004-2006)
Career starts: 65   **Career wins:** 10   **Career poles:** 1

2006 championship season recap: In only his second full season driving in the NASCAR Craftsman Truck Series, Bodine won the championship by finishing 127 points ahead of Johnny Benson Jr., the runner-up. It was the third-largest margin in NASCAR Craftsman Truck Series history. Bodine, who held the points lead from the season's fifth race, Gateway, until Homestead-Miami, won by focusing on consistency; his 8.4 average finish for the season was the best of all full-time NASCAR Craftsman Truck Series competitors.

2006 CHAMPIONSHIP LINESCORE

Starts	Wins	Poles	Top 5	Top 10	Races Led	Laps Led	DNF
25	3	1	12	16	10	287	0

TODD BODINE 2006 RACE BY RACE

No.	Race	Start	Finish	Points	Rank	Laps/ Completed	Money won	Status
1.	GM Flex Fuel 250	8	2	175	2	102/102	$59,100	Running
2.	racetickets.com 200	5	2	175	2	106/106	$43,250	Running
3.	John Deere 200	1	1	185	2	135/135	$59,425	Running
4.	Kroger 250	9	12	127	3	250/250	$10,515	Running
5.	Missouri/Illinois Dodge Dealers Ram Tough 200	3	1	190	1	160/160	$63,925	Running
6.	Quaker Steak & Lube 200	26	3	165	1	134/134	$24,050	Running
7.	City of Mansfield 250	1	15	123	1	250/250	$10,465	Running
8.	AAA Insurance 200	7	3	165	1	200/200	$28,050	Running
9.	Sam's Town 400	6	1	185	1	168/168	$71,600	Running
10.	Con-way Freight 200	25	4	160	1	102/102	$17,525	Running
11.	Toyota Tundra Milwaukee 200	7	20	108	1	199/200	$10,640	Running
12.	O'Reilly Auto Parts 250	35	7	151	1	167/167	$13,450	Running
13.	Built Ford Tough 225	9	10	134	1	150/150	$16,575	Running
14.	O'Reilly 200	19	15	118	1	202/202	$11,915	Running
15.	Power Stroke Diesel 200	29	7	146	1	200/200	$11,675	Running
16.	Toyota Tundra 200	21	8	147	1	151/151	$9,875	Running
17.	O'Reilly 200	11	2	170	1	200/200	$30,225	Running
18.	New Hampshire 200	7	4	160	1	200/200	$19,400	Running
19.	Smith's Las Vegas 350	8	12	127	1	146/146	$11,115	Running
20.	John Deere 250	4	4	165	1	94/94	$23,875	Running
21.	Kroger 200	7	14	121	1	200/200	$9,090	Running
22.	EasyCare Vehicle Service Contracts 200	10	25	88	1	128/130	$7,990	Running
23.	Silverado 350K	26	14	121	1	148/148	$11,315	Running
24.	Casino Arizona 150	3	4	160	1	150/150	$15,275	Running
25.	Ford 200	12	21	100	1	133/134	$13,990	Running

1 TED MUSGRAVE

Car: Dodge • **Car owner:** Jim Smith
Birth date: December 18, 1955 • **Hometown:** Franklin, Wis.

NASCAR Craftsman Truck Series Statistics

Seasons competed: 8 (1995-1996, 2001-2006)
Career starts: 149   **Career wins:** 16   **Career poles:** 12
2005 championship season recap: Musgrave won only one race, but his consistency won him the NASCAR Craftsman Truck Series title; he had only two DNFs. He became the oldest champion ever in NASCAR's three premier series at 49 years and 1 day old. The title was Musgrave's first in the series after finishing in the top three in points each of his previous four seasons. The title also was the first for owner Bill Smith, who helped to start the NASCAR Craftsman Truck Series in 1993.

4 BOBBY HAMILTON

Truck: Dodge • **Truck owner:** Debbie Hamilton
Birth date: May 29, 1957 • **Hometown:** Nashville

NASCAR Craftsman Truck Series Statistics

Seasons competed: 11 (1996-2006)
Career starts: 102   **Career wins:** 10   **Career poles:** 5
2004 championship season recap: Hamilton, at 47, became the oldest champion in series history in 2004—though the record was broken one year later by Ted Musgrave, who won the 2005 championship at age 49. Hamilton was the first driver/owner to win a NASCAR national touring series title since Alan Kulwicki in 1992. His 2004 championship also was a breakthrough for Dodge; it was the first driver's championship for the company in 10 years of NASCAR Craftsman Truck Series racing.

16 TRAVIS KVAPIL

Truck: Chevrolet • **Truck owner:** Steve Coulter
Birth date: March 1, 1976 • **Hometown:** Janesville, Wis.

NASCAR Craftsman Truck Series Statistics

Seasons competed: 4 (2001-2004)
Career starts: 96   **Career wins:** 5   **Career poles:** 1
2003 championship season recap: Kvapil, a former NASCAR Craftsman Truck Series Raybestos Rookie of the Year, came from third in the points standings entering the final race of the 2003 season to win the championship. It was the second consecutive title for XPress Motorsports, which also had won the 2002 championship with Mike Bliss. The season was an important one for Kvapil, and not just because he finished atop the points standings—he set a record for the fewest uncompleted miles and laps in a season.

16 MIKE BLISS

Truck: Chevrolet • **Truck owner:** Steve Coulter
Birth date: April 5, 1965 • **Hometown:** Milwaukie, Ore.

NASCAR Craftsman Truck Series Statistics

Seasons competed: 9 (1995-99, 2001-02, 2005-2006)
Career starts: 174   **Career wins:** 13   **Career poles:** 18
2002 championship season recap: Bliss' 2002 season began with an engine failure at Daytona, but he quickly rebounded with a string of five top five finishes. He finished the season first in points and became the fourth series champion to have competed in the inaugural NASCAR Craftsman Truck Series event, at Phoenix in 1995. His title for XPress Motorsports was the first in the NASCAR Craftsman Truck Series for an organization with no NASCAR NEXTEL Cup Series affiliation.

1997&99, 2001 CHAMPION

24 JACK SPRAGUE

Truck: Chevrolet • **Truck owner:** Rick Hendrick
Birth date: August 8, 1964 • **Hometown:** Spring Lake, Mich.

NASCAR Craftsman Truck Series Statistics

Seasons competed: 11 (1995-2001, 2003-2006)
Career starts: 247   **Career wins:** 27   **Career poles:** 30
Championship season recap: Sprague was the first (and so far, only) three-time NASCAR Craftsman Truck Series champion. He might have had more titles; Sprague has been runner-up twice, once by three points to Ron Hornaday Jr. in 1998. But Sprague also has won his share of close battles—late in the 1999 season, with Greg Biffle ahead of Sprague by more than 100 points, a technical violation erased much of Biffle's lead, and Sprague edged Biffle by only eight points to win the championship. Sprague also is capable of winning big; his 1997 championship was by a record 232 points over Rich Bickle.

2000 CHAMPION

54 GREG BIFFLE

Truck: Ford • **Truck owner:** Jack Roush
Birth date: December 23, 1965 • **Hometown:** Vancouver, Wash.

NASCAR Craftsman Truck Series Statistics

Seasons competed: 5 (1998-2001, 2004)
Career starts: 81   **Career wins:** 16   **Career poles:** 12
2000 championship season recap: The 1998 Raybestos Rookie of the Year set a season record for most victories—nine—in a season in 1999, but it wasn't enough to win the title. Biffle followed up that season in 2000 with a series-high five wins and 18 top fives. He finished outside of the top 15 in a race only once during the season and mathematically won the 2000 championship before the final race began. Also in 2000, Biffle became the first series competitor to win more than $1 million in a season.

1996 & 98 CHAMPION

16 RON HORNADAY JR.

Truck: Chevrolet • **Truck owner:** Teresa Earnhardt
Birth date: April 5, 1965 • **Hometown:** Palmdale, Calif.

NASCAR Craftsman Truck Series Statistics

Seasons competed: 9 (1995-99, 2002, 2004-2006)
Career starts: 175   **Career wins:** 29   **Career poles:** 14
Championship season recap: Hornaday, who won the pole for the first-even NASCAR Craftsman Truck Series race, cemented a prominent place in series history with two championships. He captured his first in 1996, and consistency was key; Hornaday finished in the top 10 in 23 of 24 races. His second, in 1998, came when he beat Jack Sprague by a record three points. In a dramatic finish to the season, with Sprague running in first place in the final lap of the final race, Hornaday moved from fourth place to second to edge Sprague for the title.

1995 CHAMPION

3 MIKE SKINNER

Truck: Chevrolet • **Truck owner:** Richard Childress
Birth date: June 28, 1957 • **Hometown:** Susanville, Calif.

NASCAR Craftsman Truck Series Statistics

Seasons competed: 8 (1995-98, 2003-2006)
Career Starts: 129   **Career wins:** 19   **Career poles:** 29
1995 championship season recap: Skinner won the first-ever NASCAR Craftsman Truck Series race, held at Phoenix. It was a sign of things to come. Skinner won seven more races in 1995 and ended the season 126 points ahead of Joe Ruttman to win the inaugural NASCAR Craftsman Truck Series championship. Skinner won eight races in 1996, too, but the first series champion finished third in points behind Ron Hornaday Jr. and Jack Sprague.

99 ERIK DARNELL

Truck: Ford • **Car owner:** Jack Roush
Birth date: December 2, 1982 • **Hometown:** Beach Park, Ill.

NASCAR Craftsman Truck Series Statistics

Seasons competed: 2 (2004, 2006)
Career starts: 26   **Career wins:** 0   **Career poles:** 1

2006 season recap: Darnell was one of two Raybestos Rookie of the Year winners for Roush Racing in 2006. (Roush's Danny O'Quinn won the award in the NASCAR Busch Series.) Darnell started and finished the season well—he had a sixth-place finish at Daytona and five consecutive top 10s in the season's last five races.

2006 LINESCORE

Starts	Wins	Poles	Top 5	Top 10	Races Led	Laps Led	DNF
25	0	1	4	12	3	24	2

RAYBESTOS ROOKIES OF THE YEAR

Year	Driver	Points	Rank	Races	Poles	Wins	Top 5	Top 10	Winnings	Hometown
1996	Bryan Reffner	2,961	9	24	2	0	3	9	$200,898	Wisconsin Rapids, Wis.
1997	Kenny Irwin	3,220	10	26	0	2	7	10	$349,645	Indianapolis
1998	Greg Biffle	3,276	8	27	4	0	8	12	$459,782	Vancouver, Wash.
1999	Mike Stefanik	3,074	13	25	0	0	1	9	$287,981	Coventry, R.I.
2000	Kurt Busch	3,596	2	24	4	4	13	16	$745,632	Las Vegas
2001	Travis Kvapil	3,547	4	24	0	1	11	18	$560,661	Janesville, Wis.
2002	Brendan Gaughan	2,893	11	22	0	2	5	9	$422,647	Las Vegas
2003	Carl Edwards	3,416	8	25	1	3	13	15	$608,080	Columbia, Mo.
2004	David Reutimann	2,904	14	25	2	0	4	10	$356,582	Zephyrhills, Fla.
2005	Todd Kluever	3,074	11	25	0	0	6	12	$443,641	Sun Prairie, Wis.
2006	Erik Darnell	3,136	12	25	1	0	4	12	$443,114	Beach Park, Ill.

ROOKIE RECORDS

Best finish, rookie: 1st—Kenny Irwin (2 times, 1997); Tony Raines (1997); Randy Tolsma (1997); Andy Houston (1998); Kurt Busch (4 times, 2000); Ricky Hendrick (2001); Travis Kvapil (2001); Brendan Gaughan (2 times, 2002); Carl Edwards (3 times, 2003)
Most wins by rookie: 4—Kurt Busch, 2000
Most rookie winners (season): 3—1997 (Kenny Irwin, Tony Raines, Randy Tolsma)

Quickest win by rookie: 5th start—Tony Raines, 1997
Most top five finishes by rookie: 13—Kurt Busch, 2000; Carl Edwards, 2003
Most top 10 finishes by rookie: 19—Ricky Hendrick, 2001
Most poles by rookie: 4—Greg Biffle, 1998; Kurt Busch, 2000
Most consecutive poles by rookie: 3—Greg Biffle, 1998
Most money won: $745,632—Kurt Busch, 2000
Best championship finish: 2nd—Kurt Busch, 2000

SERIES RECORDS, SEASON

Most wins: 9—Greg Biffle, 1999
Most short track wins: 7—Mike Skinner, 1996; Ron Hornaday Jr., 1997
Most road course wins: 2—Ron Hornaday Jr., 1995; Joe Ruttman, 1997
Most superspeedway wins: 6—Brendan Gaughan , 2003
Most consecutive wins: 3—Mike Skinner, 1996 (Tucson, Colorado, Topeka); Ron Hornaday Jr., 1997 (Milwaukee, Louisville, Colorado); Greg Biffle, 2000 (Texas, Kentucky, Watkins Glen); Todd Bodine, 2005 (Texas, Phoenix, Homestead)
Most poles: 10—Mike Skinner, 1995
Most poles, rookie: 4—Greg Biffle, 1998; Kurt Busch, 2000
Most top five finishes: 18—Ron Hornaday Jr., Jack Sprague, 1996; Greg Biffle, 2000
Most top 10 finishes: 23—Ron Hornaday Jr., 1996; Jack Sprague, 1997, 1998
Most laps completed: 4,939—Jay Sauter, 1998
Most miles completed: 4,816.4—Terry Cook, 2006
Fewest uncompleted laps: 1—Travis Kvapil, 2003
Fewest uncompleted miles: 0.5 miles—Travis Kvapil, 2003
Most laps led: 1,533—Mike Skinner, 1996
Most races completed: 27—Joe Ruttman, Jay Sauter, 1998
Best races completed percentage: 100 percent—Joe Ruttman, 1995; Ron Hornaday Jr., 1996; Mike Bliss, 1997; Jay Sauter, Joe Ruttman, 1998; Travis Kvapil, 2003; Bobby Hamilton, Dennis Setzer, 2004; Mike Bliss, Todd Bodine, Terry Cook, David Starr, 2006.
Most races completed/lead lap: 24—Jack Sprague, 1997, 1998; Travis Kvapil, 2003; David Reutimann, 2006
Most money won (race): $88,850—Mark Martin, Daytona, February 17, 2006

SERIES RACE RECORDS, WINS

Most wins: 29—Ron Hornaday Jr.
Most short track wins: 16—Ron Hornaday Jr.
Most road course wins: 3—Ron Hornaday Jr., Joe Ruttman
Most superspeedway wins: 14—Jack Sprague
Most wins, track: 4—Brendan Gaughan, Texas, 2002-2003
Most consecutive short track wins: 5—Ron Hornaday Jr., 1997 (Bristol, Louisville, Denver, Indianapolis, Flemington)
Most consecutive road course wins: 2—Ron Hornaday Jr., 1995 (Topeka, Sonoma)
Most consecutive superspeedway wins: 3—Mike Skinner, 1995 (Phoenix, Milwaukee, Phoenix); Todd Bodine, 2005 (Fort Worth, Phoenix, Homestead)
Most consecutive wins, track: 4—Brendan Gaughan, Texas, 2002-2003
Win from furthest back: 36th—Bobby Hamilton, Daytona, February 18, 2005
Most wins from pole: 6—Ron Hornaday Jr.
Consecutive wins from pole: 2—Rich Bickle, 1997; Portland, May 3, and Evergreen, May 10
Most winners, season: 14—1998, 2005
Most consecutive different winners, same season: 12—1998 (August 2, New Hampshire, through October 24, Phoenix)
Most races before first win: 111—Bryan Reffner (first win came at Texas, October 13, 2000)
Most races between wins: 120—Rick Crawford (Homestead, April 4, 1998, to Daytona, February 14, 2003)
Most races without win: 154—Lance Norick

POLES, SPEED

Most poles: 32—Mike Skinner
Most superspeedway poles: 21—Jack Sprague
Most road course poles: 3—Ron Fellows, Ron Hornaday Jr., Boris Said
Most short track poles: 12—Mike Skinner
Most poles, track: 5—Jack Sprague, Phoenix
Most fast qualifiers/pole winners, season: 15—1998
Most consecutive different pole winners, same season: 8—1997, 1998, 2006

Most consecutive different pole winners, continuing: 9—1995-1996
Most wins by pole winner, season: 10—2000
Fastest official lap: 187.563 mph—Joe Ruttman, Daytona, February 16, 2000
Fastest official superspeedway lap: 187.563 mph—Joe Ruttman, Daytona, February 16, 2000
Fastest official road course lap: 117.366 mph—Ron Fellows, Watkins Glen, August 24, 1997
Fastest official short track lap: 126.922 mph—Ken Schrader, Bristol, August 25, 2004

SERIES FIRSTS

First race: Phoenix, February 5, 1995
First winner: Mike Skinner
First pole winner: Ron Hornaday Jr., Phoenix, February 4, 1995
First superspeedway race: Phoenix, February 5, 1995
First superspeedway winner: Mike Skinner
First short track race: Tucson, April 8, 1995
First short track winner: Ron Hornaday Jr.
First road course race: Topeka, July 29, 1995
First road course winner: Ron Hornaday Jr.
First Chevrolet win: Mike Skinner, Phoenix, February 5, 1995
First Dodge win: Tony Raines, I-70 Speedway, May 24, 1997
First Ford win: Joe Ruttman, Bristol, June 23, 1995
First Toyota win: Travis Kvapil, Michigan, July 31, 2004
First driver to win $1 million in career: Mike Skinner, 1996
First driver to win $5 million in career: Jack Sprague, 2004
First driver to win $1 million in season: Greg Biffle, 2000

>> ALL-TIME RACE WINNERS <<

NASCAR Craftsman Truck Series

Driver	Wins	Driver	Wins	Driver	Wins
Ron Hornaday Jr.	29	Kyle Busch	4	Jon Wood	2
Jack Sprague	27	Rick Carelli	4	Clint Bowyer	1
Mike Skinner	19	Tony Raines	4	Ricky Craven	1
Greg Biffle	16	Jay Sauter	4	Ricky Hendrick	1
Ted Musgrave	16	David Starr	4	Shane Hmiel	1
Dennis Setzer	16	Mike Wallace	4	Bob Keselowski	1
Mike Bliss	13	Rich Bickle	3	Bobby Labonte	1
Joe Ruttman	13	Andy Houston	3	Terry Labonte	1
Todd Bodine	10	Dave Rezendes	3	Jason Leffler	1
Bobby Hamilton	10	Chad Chaffin	2	Jamie McMurray	1
Brendan Gaughan	8	Stacy Compton	2	Butch Miller	1
Mark Martin	7	Ron Fellows	2	Steve Park	1
Terry Cook	6	Kevin Harvick	2	Bryan Reffner	1
Carl Edwards	6	Jimmy Hensley	2	David Reutimann	1
Johnny Benson	5	Kenny Irwin	2	Boris Said	1
Rick Crawford	5	Kasey Kahne	2	Ken Schrader	1
Travis Kvapil	5	Robert Pressley	2	Jimmy Spencer	1
Scott Riggs	5	Tony Stewart	2	Brandon Whitt	1
Kurt Busch	4	Randy Tolsma	2		

>> ALL-TIME POLE WINNERS <<

NASCAR Craftsman Truck Series

Driver	Poles	Driver	Poles	Driver	Poles
Mike Skinner	32	Carl Edwards	3	Clint Bowyer	1
Jack Sprague	29	Ron Fellows	3	Kyle Busch	1
Mike Bliss	18	Brendan Gaughan	3	Tobey Butler	1
Joe Ruttman	17	Bill Lester	3	Matt Crafton	1
Ron Hornaday Jr.	13	Mark Martin	3	Erik Darnell	1
Greg Biffle	12	Jamie McMurray	3	Michael Dokken	1
Ted Musgrave	12	Dennis Setzer	3	Kerry Earnhardt	1
Jason Leffler	10	Mike Wallace	3	Tom Hubert	1
Stacy Compton	9	Johnny Benson Jr.	2	Kenny Irwin	1
Terry Cook	8	Chad Chaffin	2	Travis Kvapil	1
Rich Bickle	6	Bobby Hamilton Jr.	2	Terry Labonte	1
David Reutimann	6	Boris Said	2	Butch Miller	1
Bobby Hamilton	5	Jay Sauter	2	Steve Park	1
Bryan Reffner	5	Randy Tolsma	2	David Ragan	1
Scott Riggs	5	Brandon Whitt	2	Tony Raines	1
David Starr	5	Jon Wood	2	Dave Rezendes	1
Kurt Busch	4	Marcos Ambrose	1	Ken Schrader	1
Rick Crawford	4	Geoffrey Bodine	1	Bill Sedgwick	1
Jimmy Hensley	4	Todd Bodine	1	Jimmy Spencer	1
Andy Houston	4	Chuck Bown	1	Tim Steele	1

>> MOST STARTS <<

NASCAR Craftsman Truck Series

1. Rick Crawford	247	6. Mike Bliss	174
2. Jack Sprague	247	7. Joe Ruttman	168
3. Terry Cook	240	8. David Starr	165
4. Dennis Setzer	217	9. Lance Norick	154
5. Ron Hornaday Jr.	175	10. Matt Crafton	147

>> 2006 SEASON <<

Pos.	Driver	Points	Starts	Poles	Wins	Top 5	Top 10	Winnings
1.	Todd Bodine	3,666	25	1	3	12	16	$604,310
2.	Johnny Benson	3,539	25	1	5	13	17	$574,975
3.	David Reutimann	3,530	25	2	0	7	19	$365,855
4.	David Starr	3,355	25	0	1	6	12	$383,815
5.	Jack Sprague	3,328	25	2	2	10	14	$461,965
6.	Ted Musgrave	3,314	25	0	0	10	13	$463,175
7.	Ron Hornaday Jr.	3,313	25	1	2	8	12	$446,015
8.	Terry Cook	3,265	25	0	1	3	12	$398,920
9.	Rick Crawford	3,252	25	0	1	5	13	$441,520
10.	Mike Skinner	3,219	25	7	1	8	13	$496,630

>> RACE WINNERS 12

Mark Martin	6
Johnny Benson	5
Todd Bodine	3
Ron Hornaday Jr.	2
Jack Sprague	2
Mike Bliss	1
Clint Bowyer	1
Kyle Busch	1
Terry Cook	1
Rick Crawford	1
Mike Skinner	1
David Starr	1

>> MONEY WON LEADERS

Todd Bodine	$1,043,680
Johnny Benson	$770,157
Mark Martin	$595,561
Jack Sprague	$586,879
Mike Skinner	$568,535
Ted Musgrave	$560,083
Ron Hornaday Jr.	$544,667
David Reutimann	$525,531
David Starr	$515,985
Rick Crawford	$508,602

>> POLE WINNERS 12

Mike Skinner	8
Mark Martin	3
David Reutimann	2
Jack Sprague	2
Marcos Ambrose	1
Johnny Benson	1
Todd Bodine	1
Clint Bowyer	1
Erik Darnell	1
Bobby Hamilton Jr.	1
Ron Hornaday Jr.	1
David Ragan	1

>> 2005 SEASON <<

Pos.	Driver	Points	Starts	Poles	Wins	Top 5	Top 10	Winnings
1.	Ted Musgrave	3,535	25	1	1	11	15	$880,553
2.	Dennis Setzer	3,480	25	0	4	10	13	$780,312
3.	Todd Bodine	3,462	25	0	5	12	15	$805,908
4.	Ron Hornadary	3,369	25	1	1	7	13	$527,787
5.	Mike Skinner	3,273	25	7	2	9	13	$579,918
6.	Bobby Hamilton	3,164	25	1	2	6	12	$554,378
7.	David Starr	3,148	25	2	0	4	10	$398,163
8.	Jack Sprague	3,137	25	1	1	7	11	$459,350
9.	Matt Crafton	3,095	25	1	0	2	10	$356,699
10.	Johnny Benson	3,076	25	0	0	6	10	$399,499

>> RACE WINNERS 14

Todd Bodine	5
Dennis Setzer	4
Kyle Busch	3
Bobby Hamilton	2
Mike Skinner	2
Ricky Craven	1
Rick Crawford	1
Bobby Labonte	1
Ron Hornaday	1
Ted Musgrave	1
Steve Park	1
Jack Sprague	1
David Reutimann	1
Brandon Whitt	1

>> MONEY WON LEADERS

Ted Musgrave	$880,553
Todd Bodine	$805,908
Dennis Setzer	$780,312
Mike Skinner	$579,918
Bobby Hamilton	$554,378
Ron Hornaday	$527,787
Jack Sprague	$459,350
Todd Kluever	$443,641
David Reutimann	$423,105
Johnny Benson	$399,499

>> POLE WINNERS 13

Mike Skinner	7
David Starr	2
David Reutimann	2
Rick Crawford	2
Bill Lester	2
Brandon Whitt	2
Ted Musgrave	1
Ron Hornaday	1
Bobby Hamilton	1
Jack Sprague	1
Matt Crafton	1
Kyle Busch	1
Kerry Earnhardt	1

>> 2004 SEASON <<

Pos. Driver	Points	Starts	Poles	Wins	Top 5	Top 10	Winnings
1. Bobby Hamilton	3,624	25	0	4	12	16	$973,428
2. Dennis Setzer	3,578	25	0	2	8	16	$707,011
3. Ted Musgrave	3,554	25	2	2	11	16	$728,883
4. Carl Edwards	3,493	25	2	3	9	17	$638,905
5. Matt Crafton	3,379	25	0	0	6	17	$444,307
6. David Starr	3,298	25	1	2	8	16	$542,108
7. Jack Sprague	3,167	25	6	1	8	13	$532,741
8. Travis Kvapil	3,152	25	1	2	6	10	$511,563
9. Steve Park	3,138	25	0	0	5	10	$356,001
10. Chad Chaffin	3,122	25	0	2	6	10	$445,514

>> RACE WINNERS 13

Bobby Hamilton	4
Carl Edwards	3
Dennis Setzer	2
Ted Musgrave	2
David Starr	2
Travis Kvapil	2
Chad Chaffin	2
Todd Bodine	2
Kasey Kahne	2
Jack Sprague	1
Rick Crawford	1
Shane Hmiel	1
Jamie McMurray	1

>> MONEY WON LEADERS

Bobby Hamilton	$973,428
Ted Musgrave	$728,883
Dennis Setzer	$707,011
Carl Edwards	$638,905
David Starr	$542,108
Jack Sprague	$532,741
Travis Kvapil	$511,563
Chad Chaffin	$445,514
Matt Crafton	$444,307
Rick Crawford	$402,161

>> POLE WINNERS 11

Jack Sprague	6
Ted Musgrave	2
Carl Edwards	2
Mike Skinner	2
David Reutimann	2
David Starr	1
Travis Kvapil	1
Terry Cook	1
Ken Schrader	1
Jamie McMurray	1
Bobby Hamilton Jr.	1

>> 2003 SEASON <<

Pos. Driver	Points	Starts	Poles	Wins	Top 5	Top 10	Winnings
1. Travis Kvapil	3,837	25	0	1	13	22	$872,395
2. Dennis Setzer	3,828	25	0	3	15	23	$654,455
3. Ted Musgrave	3,819	25	4	3	14	18	$764,195
4. Brendan Gaughan	3,797	25	3	6	14	18	$771,290
5. Jon Wood	3,659	25	2	2	10	20	$545,965
6. Bobby Hamilton	3,627	25	1	2	10	18	$521,915
7. Rick Crawford	3,578	25	0	1	10	16	$505,240
8. Carl Edwards #	3,416	25	1	3	13	15	$608,080
9. Terry Cook	3,212	25	2	0	0	13	$337,160
10. Chad Chaffin	3,143	25	2	0	2	9	$333,770

Raybestos Rookie of the Year contender

>> RACE WINNERS 12

Brendan Gaughan	6
Carl Edwards	3
Ted Musgrave	3
Dennis Setzer	3
Bobby Hamilton	2
Jon Wood	2
Rick Crawford	1
Kevin Harvick	1
Travis Kvapil	1
Jason Leffler	1
Jimmy Spencer	1
Tony Stewart	1

>> MONEY WON LEADERS

Travis Kvapil	$872,395
Brendan Gaughan	$771,290
Ted Musgrave	$764,195
Dennis Setzer	$654,455
Carl Edwards	$608,080
Jon Wood	$545,965
Bobby Hamilton	$521,915
Rick Crawford	$505,240
Terry Cook	$337,160
Robert Pressley	$337,085

>> POLE WINNERS 12

Mike Skinner	7
Ted Musgrave	4
Brendan Gaughan	3
Chad Chaffin	2
Terry Cook	2
Jason Leffler	2
Jon Wood	2
Carl Edwards	1
Bobby Hamilton	1
Andy Houston	1
Bill Lester	1
Jimmy Spencer	1

>>2002 SEASON<<

Pos.	Driver	Points	Starts	Poles	Wins	Top 5	Top 10	Winnings
1.	Mike Bliss	3,359	22	4	5	13	18	$894,388
2.	Rick Crawford	3,313	22	2	0	12	17	$544,359
3.	Ted Musgrave	3,308	22	3	3	12	16	$651,797
4.	Jason Leffler	3,156	22	8	0	11	15	$525,619
5.	David Starr	3,144	22	2	1	8	16	$473,712
6.	Dennis Setzer	3,132	22	0	1	8	14	$502,040
7.	Robert Pressley	3,097	22	0	2	7	15	$495,817
8.	Terry Cook	3,070	22	2	4	9	17	$521,465
9.	Travis Kvapil	3,039	22	0	1	10	14	$414,326
10.	Coy Gibbs	3,010	22	0	0	4	14	$364,907

>>RACE WINNERS 11

Mike Bliss	5
Terry Cook	4
Ted Musgrave	3
Brendan Gaughan	2
Robert Pressley	2
Kevin Harvick	1
Ron Hornaday Jr.	1
Travis Kvapil	1
Dennis Setzer	1
David Starr	1
Tony Stewart	1

>>MONEY WON LEADERS

Mike Bliss	$894,388
Ted Musgrave	$651,797
Rick Crawford	$544,359
Jason Leffler	$525,619
Terry Cook	$521,465
Dennis Setzer	$502,040
Robert Pressley	$495,817
Brendan Gaughan	$422,647
Travis Kvapil	$414,326

>>POLE WINNERS 6

Jason Leffler	8
Mike Bliss	4
Ted Musgrave	3
Terry Cook	2
Rick Crawford	2
David Starr	2

>>2001 SEASON<<

Pos.	Driver	Points	Starts	Poles	Wins	Top 5	Top 10	Winnings
1.	Jack Sprague	3,670	24	7	4	15	17	$967,493
2.	Ted Musgrave	3,597	24	2	7	13	18	$726,406
3.	Joe Ruttman	3,570	24	4	2	10	20	$597,129
4.	Travis Kvapil #	3,547	24	0	1	11	18	$560,661
5.	Scott Riggs	3,526	24	4	5	14	16	$677,888
6.	Ricky Hendrick #	3,412	24	0	1	8	19	$442,031
7.	Terry Cook	3,327	24	1	0	5	16	$427,773
8.	Rick Crawford	3,320	24	0	0	10	16	$423,761
9.	Dennis Setzer	3,306	24	2	1	8	15	$416,492
10.	Coy Gibbs	2,875	24	0	0	2	7	$290,922

Raybestos Rookie of the Year contenders

>>RACE WINNERS 9

Ted Musgrave	7
Scott Riggs	5
Jack Sprague	4
Greg Biffle	2
Joe Ruttman	2
Bobby Hamilton	1
Travis Kvapil	1
Ricky Hendrick	1
Dennis Setzer	1

>>MONEY WON LEADERS

Bobby Hamilton	$973,428
Jack Sprague	$967,493
Ted Musgrave	$726,406
Scott Riggs	$677,888
Joe Ruttman	$597,129
Travis Kvapil	$560,661
Ricky Hendrick	$442,031
Terry Cook	$427,773
Rick Crawford	$423,761
Dennis Setzer	$416,492
Lance Norick	$303,697

>>POLE WINNERS 7

Jack Sprague	7
Scott Riggs	4
Joe Ruttman	4
Ted Musgrave	2
Dennis Setzer	2
Stacy Compton	1
Terry Cook	1

>> 2000 SEASON <<

Pos.	Driver	Points	Starts	Poles	Wins	Top 5	Top 10	Winnings
1.	Greg Biffle	3,826	24	4	5	18	18	$1,002,510
2.	Kurt Busch #	3,596	24	4	4	13	16	$745,632
3.	Andy Houston	3,566	24	1	2	13	18	$614,539
4.	Mike Wallace	3,450	24	2	2	13	16	$624,505
5.	Jack Sprague	3,316	24	0	3	13	15	$567,536
6.	Joe Ruttman	3,278	24	8	3	10	11	$578,086
7.	Dennis Setzer	3,214	24	0	1	8	16	$431,711
8.	Randy Tolsma	3,157	24	0	1	6	15	$447,892
9.	Bryan Reffner	3,153	24	2	1	3	16	$375,542
10.	Steve Grissom	3,113	24	0	0	6	11	$310,529

Raybestos Rookie of the Year contender

>> RACE WINNERS 11

Greg Biffle...5
Kurt Busch 4
Joe Ruttman 3
Jack Sprague 3
Andy Houston 2
Mike Wallace...2
Rick Carelli 1
Bobby Hamilton...1
Bryan Reffner 1
Dennis Setzer 1
Randy Tolsma 1

>> MONEY WON LEADERS

Bobby Hamilton $973,428
Greg Biffle $1,002,510
Kurt Busch $745,632
Mike Wallace $624,505
Andy Houston $614,539
Joe Ruttman $578,086
Jack Sprague..................................$567,536
Randy Tolsma $447,892
Dennis Setzer $431,711
Bryan Reffner.................................$375,542
Jimmy Hensley................................$317,936

>> POLE WINNERS 8

Joe Ruttman 8
Greg Biffle..4
Kurt Busch 4
Mike Wallace...2
Jamie McMurray 2
Bryan Reffner 2
Bobby Hamilton..1
Andy Houston 1

>> 1999 SEASON <<

Pos.	Driver	Points	Starts	Poles	Wins	Top 5	Top 10	Winnings
1.	Jack Sprague	3,747	25	1	3	16	19	$834,016
2.	Greg Biffle	3,739	25	4	9	14	19	$763,238
3.	Dennis Setzer	3,639	25	1	3	11	19	$628,835
4.	Stacy Compton	3,623	25	6	0	12	17	$481,922
5.	Jay Sauter	3,543	25	2	2	8	16	$482,118
6.	Mike Wallace	3,494	25	0	2	12	14	$478,900
7.	Ron Hornaday Jr.	3,488	25	0	2	7	16	$576,152
8.	Andy Houston	3,359	25	1	0	5	14	$312,323
9.	Mike Bliss	3,294	25	3	1	6	13	$349,284
10.	Jimmy Hensley	3,280	25	0	1	7	14	$332,170

>> RACE WINNERS 10

Greg Biffle...9
Dennis Setzer 3
Jack Sprague 3
Ron Hornaday Jr. 2
Jay Sauter...2
Mike Wallace...2
Mike Bliss 1
Rick Carelli 1
Ron Fellows 1
Jimmy Hensley 1

>> MONEY WON LEADERS

Jack Sprague..................................$834,016
Greg Biffle $763,238
Dennis Setzer $628,835
Ron Hornaday Jr. $576,152
Jay Sauter......................................$482,118
Stacy Compton................................$481,922
Mike Wallace $478,900
Terry Cook......................................$438,676
Mike Bliss $349,284
Jimmy Hensley................................$332,170

>> POLE WINNERS 12

Stacy Compton 6
Greg Biffle..4
Mike Bliss 3
Boris Said 2
Jay Sauter..2
Ron Fellows 1
Bobby Hamilton..1
Andy Houston 1
Dennis Setzer 1
Jack Sprague 1
Tim Steele 1
Randy Tolsma 1

>> 1998 SEASON <<

Pos.	Driver	Points	Starts	Poles	Wins	Top 5	Top 10	Winnings
1.	Ron Hornaday Jr.	4,072	27	2	6	16	22	$915,407
2.	Jack Sprague	4,069	27	4	5	16	23	$745,171
3.	Joe Ruttman	3,874	27	2	1	14	19	$547,933
4.	Jay Sauter	3,672	27	0	1	7	14	$457,765
5.	Tony Raines	3,596	27	1	3	9	15	$453,846
6.	Jimmy Hensley	3,570	27	0	1	9	15	$430,328
7.	Stacy Compton	3,542	27	2	2	9	14	$433,855
8.	Greg Biffle #	3,276	27	4	0	8	12	$459,782
9.	Ron Barfield	3,227	27	0	0	2	10	$268,910
10.	Mike Bliss	3,216	27	4	2	5	9	$395,844

Raybestos Rookie of the Year contender

>> RACE WINNERS 14

Ron Hornaday Jr...................................6
Jack Sprague 5
Tony Raines...3
Mike Bliss 2
Stacy Compton 2
Rick Carelli...1
Terry Cook...1
Rick Crawford 1
Jimmy Hensley 1
Andy Houston 1
Joe Ruttman 1
Boris Said 1
Jay Sauter 1
Dennis Setzer 1

>> MONEY WON LEADERS

Ron Hornaday Jr. $915,407
Jack Sprague $745,171
Joe Ruttman $547,933
Greg Biffle $459,782
Jay Sauter $457,765
Tony Raines $453,846
Stacy Compton.......................$433,855
Jimmy Hensley.......................$430,328
Mike Bliss $395,844
Andy Houston.........................$350,487

>> POLE WINNERS 15

Greg Biffle...4
Mike Bliss 4
Jack Sprague 4
Stacy Compton 2
Ron Hornaday Jr.....................................2
Joe Ruttman 2
Chuck Bown 1
Terry Cook...1
Ron Fellows 1
Andy Houston 1
Tom Hubert 1
Tony Raines...1
Boris Said 1
Randy Tolsma 1
Mike Wallace...1

>> 1997 SEASON <<

Pos.	Driver	Points	Starts	Poles	Wins	Top 5	Top 10	Winnings
1.	Jack Sprague	3,969	26	5	3	16	23	$880,835
2.	Rich Bickle	3,737	26	4	3	15	17	$485,180
3.	Joe Ruttman	3,736	26	2	5	13	17	$641,444
4.	Mike Bliss	3,611	26	6	1	11	18	$541,555
5.	Ron Hornaday Jr.	3,574	26	3	7	13	17	$604,830
6.	Jay Sauter	3,467	26	0	1	10	15	$412,264
7.	Rick Carelli	3,461	26	0	0	6	17	$331,325
8.	Jimmy Hensley	3,385	26	2	0	4	13	$312,820
9.	Chuck Bown	3,320	26	0	0	4	13	$290,921
10.	Kenny Irwin #	3,220	26	0	2	7	10	$349,645

Raybestos Rookie of the Year contender

>> RACE WINNERS 11

Ron Hornaday Jr.....................................7
Joe Ruttman 5
Rich Bickle 3
Jack Sprague 3
Kenny Irwin 2
Mike Bliss 1
Ron Fellows 1
Bob Keselowski 1
Tony Raines..1
Jay Sauter 1
Tandy Tolsma 1

>> MONEY WON LEADERS

Joe Ruttman $641,444
Ron Hornaday Jr. $604,830
Mike Bliss $541,555
Rich Bickle.............................$485,180
Jay Sauter $412,264
Kenny Irwin $349,645
Rick Carelli............................$331,325
Jimmy Hensley.......................$312,820
Butch Miller $298,225

>> POLE WINNERS 10

Mike Bliss 6
Jack Sprague 5
Rich Bickle 4
Ron Hornaday Jr.....................................3
Jimmy Hensley 2
Joe Ruttman 2
Terry Cook...1
Michael Dokken 1
Ron Fellows 1
Dave Rezendes 1

1996 SEASON

Pos.	Driver	Points	Starts	Poles	Wins	Top 5	Top 10	Winnings
1.	Ron Hornaday Jr.	3,831	24	2	4	18	23	$625,634
2.	Jack Sprague	3,778	24	2	5	18	21	$580,112
3.	Mike Skinner	3,771	24	5	8	17	20	$602,495
4.	Joe Ruttman	3,275	24	0	0	7	16	$276,013
5.	Mike Bliss	3,190	24	2	2	9	11	$345,322
6.	Dave Rezendes	3,179	24	0	3	9	13	$335,840
7.	Butch Miller	3,126	24	1	0	7	11	$258,333
8.	Jimmy Hensley	3,029	24	1	0	5	14	$228,936
9.	Bryan Reffner #	2,961	24	3	0	3	9	$200,898
10.	Rick Carelli	2,953	24	0	1	2	9	$227,575

Raybestos Rookie of the Year contender

>> RACE WINNERS 7

Mike Skinner	8
Jack Sprague	5
Ron Hornaday Jr.	4
Dave Rezendes	3
Mike Bliss	2
Rick Carelli	1
Mark Martin	1

>> MONEY WON LEADERS

Ron Hornaday Jr.	$625,634
Mike Skinner	$602,495
Jack Sprague	$580,112
Mike Bliss	$345,322
Dave Rezendes	$335,840
Joe Ruttman	$276,013
Butch Miller	$258,333
Jimmy Hensley	$228,936
Rick Carelli	$227,575
Rich Bickle	$204,169

>> POLE WINNERS 14

Mike Skinner	5
Bryan Reffner	3
Rich Bickle	2
Mike Bliss	2
Ron Hornaday Jr.	2
Jack Sprague	2
Johnny Benson	1
Geoffrey Bodine	1
Tobey Butler	1
Bobby Hamilton	1
Jimmy Hensley	1
Kenny Irwin	1
Butch Miller	1
Steve Park	1

1995 SEASON

Pos.	Driver	Points	Starts	Poles	Wins	Top 5	Top 10	Winnings
1.	Mike Skinner	3,224	20	10	8	17	18	$428,096
2.	Joe Ruttman	3,098	20	1	2	9	18	$264,798
3.	Ron Hornaday Jr.	2,986	20	4	6	10	14	$296,715
4.	Butch Miller	2,812	20	0	1	9	14	$182,633
5.	Jack Sprague	2,740	20	1	0	4	15	$116,501
6.	Rick Carelli	2,683	20	0	0	5	10	$132,013
7.	Bill Sedgwick	2,681	20	1	0	6	13	$119,918
8.	Mike Bliss	2,626	19	0	1	5	12	$144,354
9.	Scott Lagasse	2,470	20	0	0	2	7	$88,100
10.	Tobey Butler	2,358	20	0	0	3	5	$86,146

>> RACE WINNERS 7

Mike Skinner	8
Ron Hornaday Jr.	6
Joe Ruttman	2
Mike Bliss	1
Terry Labonte	1
Butch Miller	1
Ken Schrader	1

>> MONEY WON LEADERS

Jack Sprague	$834,016
Mike Skinner	$428,096
Ron Hornaday Jr.	$296,715
Joe Ruttman	$264,798
Butch Miller	$182,633
Mike Bliss	$144,354
Rick Carelli	$132,013
Bill Sedgwick	$119,918
Jack Sprague	$116,501
Dave Rezendes	$90,814
Scott Lagasse	$88,100

>> POLE WINNERS 6

Mike Skinner	10
Ron Hornaday Jr.	4
Terry Labonte	1
Joe Ruttman	1
Bill Sedgwick	1
Jack Sprague	1

NASCAR LADDER SYSTEM

It takes a special blend of talent, ambition and perseverance to rise to the top levels in NASCAR racing. But there are opportunities for drivers in many parts of the country.

THE FIRST STEP: NASCAR WHELEN ALL-AMERICAN SERIES

A network of nearly 60 racetracks across North America comprises the NASCAR Whelen All-American Series—and provides the first step. NASCAR-sanctioned short track races are held on dirt and asphalt tracks of all shapes and sizes. In this series, many drivers race as a weekend hobby on their hometown tracks, while others are looking to move up the ladder.

Greg Biffle, Clint Bowyer, Jeff Burton, Dale Earnhardt Jr., Carl Edwards, Denny Hamlin, Travis Kvapil, Bobby Labonte, Jamie McMurray, Scott Riggs and Elliott Sadler all began their careers in this series.

THE NEXT LEVEL: REGIONAL SERIES OFFER DRIVER DEVELOPMENT

For NASCAR Whelen All-American Series competitors who aspire to reach NASCAR's three national series—the NASCAR NEXTEL Cup Series, NASCAR Busch Series or NASCAR Craftsman Truck Series—there are a few career-advancing options. The regional series competes on a variety of tracks, providing valuable experience for up-and-coming drivers, while providing special events for local fans.

The NASCAR Grand National Division includes the Busch East Series and the West Series, with identical race cars that are similar to the cars used in the NASCAR Busch Series. For NASCAR Grand National Division racers, new cost-saving technology makes this division a more cost-effective driver development program.

An optional "spec" engine was introduced in 2006. It is designed to be powerful and durable, yet is made from a precisely-specified set of components that keeps engine costs down. A composite body, molded from synthetic materials, also is available as an alternative to expensive sheet metal bodies. These items help teams control costs while providing them the opportunity to advance from their hometown short tracks to the next level.

Many of today's top drivers began their careers in the NASCAR Grand National Division, including David Gilliland, Kevin Harvick, Ron Hornaday Jr., Martin Truex Jr. and others. It's a feeder system for NASCAR's three national series.

Along with the NASCAR Grand National Division, two open-wheel NASCAR Modified racing series are found on the East Coast. The NASCAR Whelen Modified Tour traces its roots to the very first NASCAR race, held in Daytona Beach, Fla., in 1949. Early NASCAR racecars were "modified," and the division evolved from there. Today, these unique racecars remain wildly popular along the eastern seaboard. The Whelen Modified Tour competes across the Northeast while the Whelen Southern Modified Tour races throughout the Southern states.

Sean Caisse's NASCAR Grand National Division car (left); Reggie Ruggiero's NASCAR Whelen Modified Tour car (below).